JM Hawthorne

MODERN REAL ESTATE FINANCING

A Transactional Approach

MODERN REAL ESTATE FINANCING

A Transactional Approach

Michael T. Madison
Professor of Law
Fordham University

Robert M. Zinman
Professor of Law
St. John's University

Little, Brown and Company
Boston   Toronto   London

Library of Congress Catalog Card No. 91-60221

ISBN 0-316-54363-2

Second Printing

MV-NY

Published simultaneously in Canada
by Little, Brown & Company (Canada) Limited

Printed in the United States of America

*To the memory of my beloved
mother, Thelma M. Madison*

— M. M.

*To Ruth and Arthur Zinman
and to Lillian and Noah Janel*

sine qua non

— R. Z.

Summary of Contents

Contents

Chapter 4

The Nature of a Mortgage and the Mortgage Market
for Income-Producing Real Estate   283

PART II

FUNDAMENTALS OF REAL ESTATE FINANCING 353

Chapter 5

Postconstruction, or "Permanent," Financing 357

Chapter 6

Construction Financing   585

PART III

SPECIAL FINANCING TECHNIQUES   665

Chapter 7

Equity Financing   667

Chapter 8

Leasehold and Leaseback Financing   711

Chapter 11

The Impact of Bankruptcy on Real Estate Transactions

PART V

CURRENT ISSUES IN REAL ESTATE FINANCING

1133

Chapter 12

Lender Liability

1135

Preface

It has been our experience that most law students are more stimulated when they see some practical value in what they are learning in the classroom. To the extent that the professor can simulate real world conditions and avoid pedantic discussions of peripheral issues (such as the doctrine of equitable mortgages, which rarely arises in a commercial real estate practice), the professor can stimulate students' intellectual curiosity to deal with the complex issues in land finance that they will confront in the real world of practice. This is why we have used a transactional approach in this casebook.

Notwithstanding the regulatory impact of public law on land investment and development, in our judgment freedom of contract still remains the dominant theme in the law of commercial real estate financing. This means that as long as the real estate project does not fail and the borrower remains solvent, general rules of law will normally apply only in the absence of an agreement to the contrary. In other words, the transactional rights and responsibilities of the borrower, the lender, and other interested parties will usually be governed by means of the written word contained in some standard form of agreement that will be tailored to meet the needs of a particular transaction. Perhaps this is because in most commercial real estate transactions the parties will be sophisticated — they will be represented by counsel and in a position to defend themselves at the bargaining table. For example, at common law the general rule of law (absent language to the contrary in the mortgage note) is that a lender does not have to accept a voluntary prepayment of the mortgage indebtedness prior to maturity. While we examine this rule in the chapter on postconstruction financing (Chapter 5), it is of equal if not greater importance for students to see what a typical prepayment privilege provision looks like and to understand the legal consequences of using one draftsmanship approach as opposed to another, so that someday the students, as counsel to borrowers or lenders, will be able not only to solve present problems but also to avoid potential problems for their clients. This is what real estate planning is all about.

In addition, the practice of real estate financing law requires an understanding of how, within a particular transaction, one step may be related to another and how, within the commercial real estate lending cycle, one transaction flows from another. For example, in Chapter 5 we explore the interrelationship between the prepayment privilege and due-on-sale provisions and raise the double whammy question whether a lender can and ought to be able to enforce both clauses simultaneously. And in Chapter 6 we examine the reason why a borrower's ability to obtain construction financing will often depend on whether the borrower is able beforehand to secure a loan commitment for the postconstruction, or "permanent," loan.

Accordingly, the aim of this casebook is to expose students to the legal issues they will confront in practice and to teach them to think as real estate lawyers do. To that end, the book attempts to follow the transactional approach wherever feasible and includes questions and planning problems designed to test the students' ability to spot issues and arrive at a logical conclusion based on principles and considerations embodied in cases, documents, articles, and other materials.

The organization of the book follows chronologically the actual lending cycle that exists in modern real estate financing. It is hoped that when the students begin to understand how one stage in the lending cycle follows from another they will perceive a natural and cohesive flow in the classroom discussion.

If the real estate borrower should become insolvent or if the project should fail, which is not infrequently the case in today's soft market, the lender may be forced to institute foreclosure proceedings or the borrower may invoke the protection of the Bankruptcy Code, in which event the law needs to be more paternalistic in order to protect the financially distressed borrower and resolve the competing claims against the real estate. In such an instance public law may supersede the language in the mortgage and other loan documents; as a consequence the private bargain between the borrower and lender becomes less relevant. This is where the methodology of the book shifts from an analytical-transactional to an analytical-doctrinal approach. Inasmuch as borrower default is presently a "hot" area of the law, we have devoted Part IV to an examination of defaults, workouts, foreclosure, and bankruptcy. Recently, borrower insolvency has become a litigation trigger for lawsuits against lenders. Accordingly, in Part V we examine the related topic of lender liability, which is currently a major issue in the law of real estate financing.

The organization of the book also reflects its transactional approach. The book consists of five parts and each part begins with an introductory overview. Part I focuses on prefinancing considerations. By exposing students to concepts that are somewhat familiar we have attempted to ease their transition into the financing materials that follow. Part II deals with the fundamentals of real estate financing, and in doing so employs a master hypothetical involving a typical real estate developer

("Dan Developer") who plans to construct an office building in the state of Fuller. In Part II the students accompany Dan chronologically as he wades his way through the commercial real estate lending cycle, first (in Chapter 5) by negotiating a loan commitment from a typical postconstruction lender ("Ace Insurance Company") and then (in Chapter 6) by obtaining his construction financing from a typical construction lender ("Fuller National Bank") on the strength of the takeout commitment from Ace. Special financing techniques are examined in Part III. For example, as explained in Chapter 7, if the supply of mortgage money is tight and the economy becomes inflationary, Dan might not seek straight mortgage financing but instead secure some form of equity financing such as a convertible mortgage or a joint venture arrangement. Or perhaps, as discussed in Chapters 7 and 8, Dan might choose a subordinated purchase money mortgage, a leasehold mortgage, or a sale and leaseback of the underlying land to reduce his initial cash outlay and possibly increase his tax deductions by separately financing the cost of the land. If the transaction is large enough, Dan may even turn to Wall Street for his financing by issuing a commercial mortgage-backed bond. This recent phenomenon, called "securitization," which someday may revolutionize the way in which real estate is financed, is examined in Chapter 13. Then, as explained in Chapter 9, once the project has been completed and is successful Dan may want to translate some of the accumulated equity in the project into tax-free cash by refinancing the Ace mortgage or by obtaining secondary financing before he sells the property or engages in a tax-deferred exchange of the property. Finally, unless Dan engages in a sale and leaseback of the land and building (or just the building), he may decide to sell the property and invest the net proceeds in other income-producing real estate, in which event the factors discussed in Chapter 3 (dealing with contracts and conveyancing) would become postfinancing rather than prefinancing considerations.

Because tax considerations play such an important role in real estate investment and financing decisions, the book attempts to integrate tax aspects of these decisions into the discussion. The need to do so is reinforced by the emerging trend among firms and corporations to demand such dual expertise from their young attorneys. There is little discussion of condominium financing and federally subsidized multi-family financing, however, on the premise that these subjects have so many special ramifications that they deserve separate treatment elsewhere.

As noted above, the book contains documentary excerpts because our aim has been to make the relevant documentation the matrix for our discussion. However, in order for the students to grasp fully the transactional nature of the materials (especially in courses that have a clinical component) they should be able to read the major documentary provisions in conjunction with one another. Therefore, we have prepared a separate Documents Manual, which includes the major documents in their entirety. Also, to make the book more "user-friendly" for professors and to ameliorate the intimidation factor for those who have not practiced in this area of the law, we have prepared a Teacher's Manual, which provides answers to the questions and planning problems. The Teacher's Manual also provides suggestions as to which materials ought to be covered considering the number of classroom hours available and the nature of each course. While this book was designed for a basic course in real estate financing or real estate transactions, it can be adapted for use in a course on mortgage law or in any number of advanced courses (e.g., real estate workouts, defaults and bankruptcy, or tax aspects of real estate transactions), seminars, and clinicals.

We would like to thank the many people who have helped us in the preparation of the book. First we are grateful for the patience and generous support of Dean John Feerick, Marilyn Alexander, and the staff of Fordham University Law School. We are particularly grateful to Carol DeVito for her competent and loyal help with the typing and production of the manuscript. We also appreciate the help received from the administration and staff of St. John's University School of Law. Our special thanks go to Robert V. Tiburzi, Jr., a former Fordham student and a member of the New York Bar, for his loyalty, dedication, and tireless efforts as a research assistant. We were fortunate to receive a high level of research support from Ronald J. Lafferty, Matthew J. Jeon, and David Blechner, all of the New York Bar, and the other law students at Fordham who gave us research assistance. We give special thanks for the valuable suggestions and comments of Professors Roger Bernhardt, Karl Holtzschue, David Schmudde, and Aaron Schrieber and for the fine editorial assistance of Jane Zanichkowsky and the rest of the staff at Little, Brown and Company.

Finally, we are indebted to the noted teacher and scholar of real estate financing Emerson G. Spies, professor emeritus of the University of Virginia School of Law, for his words of encouragement. During the early stage of this book's development he remarked: "Other authors have tried to cover the waterfront and have not approached this area from a transactional point of view. Rather, they have organized the materials around conventional subject matters such as mortgages, partnerships, related tax law, with the result that the teacher invariably is forced to select from a hodgepodge of subject matters that are often supplemented with their own materials . . ." We hope that this book does justice to the concept of a transactional approach to the law of real estate financing.

                                                        Michael T. Madison
                                                        Robert M. Zinman

May 1991

Acknowledgments

We would like to thank the following authors and copyrightholders for permission to reprint excerpts from their works.

Agar, Sale and Leasebacks, Part 2, in Proceedings, ABA Section of Real Prop., Prob. & Tr. L. 61 (Jan. 1965). Reprinted by permission.

American Council of Life Insurance, Investment Bulletin, *Survey of Mortgage Commitments on Commercial Properties,* 1065; Tables 4 (Loan Terms), 3 (Loans with Special Features), F (Amortization Provisions), G (Closed Periods) (April 10,1989). Reprinted by permission.

Asbestos Litigation Reporter, para 17,037 (May 20, 1988). Reproduced with permission of Andrews Publications.

Bell, Negotiating the Purchase Money Mortgage, 7 Real Est. Rev. 51 (Spring 1977). Reprinted by permission of Warren, Gorham & Lamont, Inc.

Bendel, A Real Estate Primer, The New York Times (Jan. 17, 1989). Copyright © 1989/90 by The New York Times Company. Reprinted by permission.

Canfield, Strategies Involving Sandwich Leases, 18 Real Est. Rev. 22 (Spring 1988). Reprinted by permission of Warren, Gorham & Lamont, Inc.

Committee on Real Estate Financing, Disposition of Rents After Mortgage Defaults, 16 Real Prop., Prob. & Tr. J. 835-838 (1981). Reprinted by permission of the American Bar Association.

Coopers & Lybrand, Real Est. Newsletter on the Tax Reform Act of 1986, app. A, Table 17 (Oct. 1986). Reprinted by permission. This table reflects the changes made by the Tax Reform Act of 1986. More current updates may be obtained from Coopers & Lybrand.

Cowan and Eastman, Debt/Equity Transactions — An Approach to Recharacterization 153. Reprinted with permission from Practicing Law Institute, *Protecting the Real Estate Lender: Workout, Bankruptcy and Financing Strategies* (1988). Order No. 4492.

Davis, The Permanent Lender's Role in the Construction Process, 3 Real Est. Rev. 70 (Spring 1973). Reprinted by permission of Warren, Gorham & Lamont, Inc.

DeWitt, Foreign Direct Investment in U.S. Real Estate, 16 Real Est.

Rev. 66 (Winter 1987). Reprinted by permission of Warren, Gorham & Lamont, Inc.

Ellwood, Appraisal for Mortgage Purposes, Encyclopedia of Real Estate Appraising (3d ed. 1978). Reprinted by permission of the Appraisal Institute.

Federal Research Press, 5 Real Est. Fin. 13 (table) (Spring 1988); 6 Real Est. Fin. 8 (table) (Spring 1989). Reprinted by permission.

Fiflis, Land Transfer Improvement: The Basic Facts and Two Hypotheses for Reform, 38 U. Colo. L. Rev. 431, 438-440. Reprinted by permission.

Forte, Environmental Liability Risk Management, 1989 Prob. & Prop. 57 (Jan./Feb.). Reprinted by permission of the author.

Freedman, Changing REITs Find Broader Interest and Acceptance, 1 Real Est. Fin. J. 72 (Winter 1986). Reprinted by permission of Warren, Gorham & Lamont, Inc.

Friedman, Contracts and Conveyances of Real Property 476. Reprinted with permission from Contracts and Conveyances of Real Property, 4th ed. by Milton Friedman (1984), © Practising Law Institute.

Fuller, Sale and Leasebacks and the *Frank Lyon* Case, 48 Geo. Wash. L. Rev. 60 (1979). Copyright © 1979 by the George Washington Law Review. Reprinted with permission.

Garfinkel, The Negotiation of Construction and Permanent Loan Commitments II, 25 Prac. Law. 37 (April 15, 1979). Copyright © 1979 by the American Law Institute. Reprinted with the permission of the Practical Lawyer.

Goldman Sachs, Yields on U.S. Treasuries, The Real Estate Report (Mar. 1990). Reprinted by permission.

Goldstein, When Does a Real Estate Broker Earn His Commission?, 27 Prac. Law. 43 (1981). Copyright © 1981 by the American Law Institute. Reprinted with the permission of the Practical Lawyer.

Gunning, The Wrap Around Mortgage — Friend or UFO?, 2 Real Est. Rev. 35 (Summer 1972). Reprinted by permission of the author.

Halper, Introducing the Ground Lease, 15 Real Est. Rev. 24 (Fall 1985). Reprinted by permission of the author and Law Journal Seminars-Press. Based on materials appearing in *Ground Leases and Land Acquisitions* by Emanuel B. Halper. Reproduced with the approval of the publisher. Published and copyrighted by Law Journal Seminars-Press, 111 Eighth Avenue, New York, New York 10011. All rights reserved.

Harris, Construction and Development Financing 3.3A (Supp. 1987). Reprinted by permission.

Harris, Legal Opinions: Real Estate Contracts, 14 Real Est. Rev. 12 (Spring 1972). Reprinted by permission.

Hayes, Depression Guru Ravi Batra: Economist or Mystic? Tune in Around 1990 to Find Out. New York Times, Aug. 30, 1987, p. 5, col. 1. Copyright © 1989/90 by The New York Times Company. Reprinted with permission.

Hershman, Lease Pitfalls and Pratfalls, address presented at N.Y. Life Insurance Co. Reprinted by permission of the author.

Holmes, The Path of the Law, 10 Harv. L. Rev. 457 (1897). Copyright © 1897 by the Harvard Law Review. Reprinted with permission.

Introductory Comment, Uniform Simplification of Land Transfer Act, 14 U.L.A. 271 (1977). Reprinted by permission of the National Conference of Commissioners on Uniform State Laws, Chicago, IL.

Johnson, Purpose and Scope of Recording Statutes, 47 Iowa L. Rev. 231 (1962). Reprinted by permission.

Joyce, Financing Real Estate Developments, 11 The Colo. Law. 2093 (Aug. 1982). Reprinted by permission of the Colorado Bar Association.

Kotlarsky, Capital Gains and Tax Policy, 41 Tax Notes 319 (1988), Reprinted by permission.

Levy, Construction Loan Decision-Making: Issues and Documents; Risks and Benefits. Chemical Bank, 1989. Reprinted by permission of the author.

Lieberman and Mallenbaum, When Borrowers Sue Lenders, 4 Real Est. Fin. 67 (Winter 1988). Reprinted by permission.

McKee, The Real Estate Tax Shelter: A Computerized Exposé, 57 Va. L. Rev. 521, 556-567 (1971). Reprinted by permission.

Madison and Dwyer, The Law of Real Estate Financing, paras. 2-2, 3.05, 3.09, 4.04, 12.01[5], Supp. No. 2 para. 1.05[2][e]. Reprinted by permission of the publisher from The Law of Real Estate Financing, © 1981 by Warren, Gorham & Lamont, Inc.

Maisel, Inflation, Leverage, Vacancies, Taxes and Returns to Office Buildings 3-10 (Mar. 1987). Reprinted by permission of Salomon Bros., Inc.

Manvel, Paying for Civilized Society 163 (1986). Reprinted by permission of Tax Analysts.

Mark, Leasehold Mortgages — Some Practical Considerations, 14 Bus. Law. 609 (1959). Reprinted by permission.

Mehr and Kilgore, Enforcement of the Real Estate Loan Commitment: Improvement of the Borrower's Remedies, 24 Wayne L. Rev. 1011 (1978). Reprinted with permission from The Wayne Law Review.

Mortgage and Real Estate Executive's Report, Mar. 1, 1985, p.5; May 15, 1987, pp.3-6; and June 1, 1989, pp.5-6. Reprinted by permission from the Mortgage and Real Estate Executive's Report. Copyright © by Warren, Gorham & Lamont, Inc. All rights reserved.

Nessen and Ragalevsky, The Changing Role of Lawyers in Real Estate Transactions, 5 Real Est. Fin. 32 (Spring 1988). Reprinted by permission from Federal Research Press.

New York Life Insurance Company, Minimum Ground Lease Requirements of Leasehold Mortgages. Reprinted by permission.

Note, Taxation of Sale and Leaseback Transactions, 32 Vand. L. Rev. 945 (1979).

Oharenko, The Battle Over the Juniors: Second Mortgage vs. Wrap Around Financing, 14 Real Est. Rev. 99 (Fall 1984). Reprinted by permission of Warren, Gorham & Lamont, Inc.

Richards, "Gradable and Tradable": The Securitization of Commercial Real Estate Mortgages, 16 Real Est. L.J. 99 (1987). Reprinted by permission of Warren, Gorham & Lamont, Inc.

Roberts, Negotiating and Drafting Workout Agreements, 3 Mod. Real Est. Trans. 1393 (1987). Copyright © 1987 by The American Law Institute-American Bar Association Committee on Continuing Professional Education. Reprinted by permission.

Roegge, Talbot, and Zinman, Real Estate Equity Investments and the Institutional Lender: Nothing Ventured, Nothing Gained, 39 Fordham L. Rev. 579 (1971). Reprinted by permission.

Rose and O'Neil, Impact of the Tax Reform Act of 1986 on Rents and Property Values, 15 J. Real Est. Tax. 145 (Winter 1988). Copyright © 1988 by Warren, Gorham & Lamont, Inc. Reprinted with permission.

Ross, Real Estate Master Limited Partnerships, 17 Real Est. Rev. 28 (Spring 1987). Reprinted by permission from Warren, Gorham & Lamont, Inc.

Ross and Klein, New Directions for Real Estate Investment Trusts, 1 Real Est. Fin. J. 67 (Winter 1986). Copyright © 1986 by Warren, Gorham & Lamont, Inc. Reprinted with permission.

Salomon Bros., Inc., Japanese Investment in U.S. Real Estate: An Update, Fig. 1 (Feb. 17, 1988). Reprinted by permission.

Salomon Bros., Inc., Real Estate Market Review 8 (table) (Jan. 1988). Reprinted by permission.

Schneider, The Elusive Definition of a Security, 14 Rev. Securities Regulation 981-991 (1981). Reprinted by permission of Standard & Poor's Corp.

Schurtz, A Decision Model for Lease Parties in Sale-Leasebacks of Real Estate, 23 Wm. & Mary L. Rev. 385, 435-438 (1982). Reprinted by permission of the author.

Schwartz, Real Estate and the Tax Reform Act of 1986, 16 Real Est. Rev. 28 (Winter 1987). Reprinted by permission of Warren, Gorham & Lamont, Inc.

Smith, Refinancing a Syndicated Property, 16 Real Est. Rev. 16 (Spring 1986). Reprinted by permission of Warren, Gorham & Lamont, Inc.

Smith and Lubell, The Permanent Mortgage Loan Commitment, 4 Real Est. Fin. 7 (Winter 1975). Reprinted by permission of Warren, Gorham & Lamont, Inc.

Smith and Lubell, Real Estate Financing: The High Credit Lease, 4 Real Est. Rev.21 (Summer 1974). Reprinted by permission of Warren, Gorham & Lamont, Inc.

Smith and Lubell, Real Estate Financing: The Streamlined Mortgage, 4 Real Est. Rev. 21 (Summer 1974). Reprinted by permission of Warren, Gorham & Lamont, Inc.

Standard & Poor's, Securitizing Commercial Real Estate, CreditWeek 13 (Feb. 24, 1986). Reprinted by permission.

Stark, Negotiating Interest Rate Exchange Agreements, 4 Real Est. Fin. 93 (Spring 1987). Reprinted by permission of Federal Research Press.

Strum, Current Trends of Institutional Financing of Real Property in the U.S., 17 Real Prop., Prob. & Tr. J. 486 (1982). Reprinted by permission of the author.

Tanzi, Fiscal Deficits and Interest Rates in the United States, 31 Intl. Monetary Fund Staff Papers 551 (1984). Reprinted by permission.

Tax Notes, Factors Affecting Federal Deficit Growth, 1970 to 1986, at 803-805 (Aug. 12, 1985). Reprinted by permission of Tax Notes.

Uri, The Participating Mortgage: Spreading the Risks and Rewards of Ownership, 5 Real Est. Fin. 37 (Spring 1988). Reprinted by permission of Federal Research Press.

Washburn, The Judicial and Legislative Response to Price Inadequacy in Mortgage Foreclosure Sales, 53 S. Cal. L. Rev. 843 (1980). Reprinted with the permission of the Southern California Law Review.

Welborn, Convertible Mortgages — Legal and Drafting Issues, 2 Mod. Real Est. Transactions 1191 (1986). Copyright © 1986 by The American Law Institute. Reprinted with the permission of the American Law Institute-American Bar Association Committee on Continuing Professional Education.

Wetterer, Introducing the Zero Coupon Real Estate Mortgage, 3 Real Est. Fin. 121 (Spring 1986). Reprinted by permission of Federal Research Press.

Wetterer, What Is Value?, 3 Real Est. Fin. 77 (Summer 1986). Reprinted by permission of Federal Research Press.

Zerbst and Cambon, Real Estate: Historical Returns and Risks, 10 J. Portfolio Mgt. 5 (Spring 1984). Reprinted with permission from Institutional Investors, Inc.

MODERN REAL ESTATE FINANCING

A Transactional Approach

PART I

INTRODUCTION TO REAL ESTATE FINANCING

The aim of this book is to have you become familiar with the legal, financial, economic, and tax issues that you will be confronting as attorneys in the practice of real estate financing law. To that end, these issues will be examined wherever possible in the context of the relevant transaction and (if available) document. As the legal advisor to "Dan Developer," a typical real estate borrower who is the main character in the book's master hypothetical, you will be accompanying him as he works his way in a chronological fashion through today's commercial real estate lending cycle. For example, in the case of new construction of some income-producing real estate such as an office building or shopping center, you will see that Dan usually will obtain his commitment for a postconstruction (or "permanent") loan before negotiating the terms and conditions of the construction financing. This fundamental real estate financing scenario is the subject of Part II.

The book employs both a transactional and a chronological approach, and therefore it will be important for you to understand how, within a particular transaction, one step leads to another and how, within the real estate lending cycle, one transaction follows from another. Accordingly, certain basic prefinancing considerations are examined in Part I. Certainly, anyone aspiring to practice real estate law as a specialty must be well-grounded in these matters in today's sophisticated interdisciplinary legal environment. Some of these prefinancing considerations should be familiar territory for you, and they should ease your transition into the book by acting as a bridge between what you learned (or didn't learn) in first-year property and what you will learn in the financing materials in Parts II and III.

Part I is comprised of four chapters. The first, The Nature of

1

Modern Real Estate Financing, attempts to explain the nature of creative real estate planning and what will be expected of real estate attorneys during the 1990s and beyond.

As you might surmise, knowledge of real estate financing is not needed until some individual or entity decides to acquire or develop a parcel of real estate; in other words, it is difficult to explain the *how* of financing without examining the *why* of investing in real estate. Therefore, Chapter 2, Real Estate as an Investment, will examine the nature of real estate as an investment, including its current status as a limited tax shelter (after the Tax Reform Act of 1986) and the important prefinancing decision of selecting the ownership entity that will be best suited for the dual purposes of securing the financing and raising the venture capital necessary to acquire and develop the real estate.

Once the ownership entity is selected, the next important prefinancing decision for Dan Developer (and the outside investors) is whether to purchase or lease the land and building or, in the case of new construction, whether to purchase or lease the land on which the new building will be situated. Likewise, after the real estate is owned for a while the owners must decide if and when to both sell the property and deliver title by means of a contract of sale and delivery of a deed. Accordingly, Chapter 3, An Overview of Contracts and Conveyancing, is in Part I on the premise that most real estate financing transactions begin and end with a contract of sale and that some students may not have covered contracts and conveyancing (or dealt with the legal consequences of choosing one draftsmanship approach over another) in the first-year course on property law. Finally, Chapter 4, The Nature of a Mortgage and the Mortgage Market for Income-Producing Real Estate, is included as a theoretical prelude to the transactional materials that follow in Parts II and III.

C h a p t e r 1

The Nature of Modern Real Estate Financing

A. THE ROLE OF THE REAL ESTATE LAWYER AS A PLANNER IN TODAY'S COMMERCIAL LENDING CYCLE

Real estate financing, in practice, is an area of the law in which the transactional rights and responsibilities of the parties are usually governed by the written word as embodied in some fairly standardized form of agreement (e.g., a loan contract or "commitment," mortgage, or ground or occupancy lease) that has been negotiated by the parties and tailored to the particular transaction. Accordingly, the materials in this book follow a transactional approach and wherever possible the legal, business, and tax issues will be examined in the context of the relevant documentation. To illustrate this approach reference will be made throughout these materials to a master hypothetical (detailed in Chapter 5B) involving a typical real estate borrower ("Dan Developer") who intends to construct an office building or shopping center. As is usually the case, Dan plans to first obtain his postconstruction (or "permanent") financing from a typical institutional lender ("Ace Insurance Company") and then to obtain his construction financing from a commercial bank ("Fuller National Bank").

It is true that the freedom of contract principle has eroded somewhat as a consequence of both the regulatory impact of public law on real estate transactions and the emerging trend toward striking down bargains that are either unconscionable or offensive to public policy.[1] So if, for

---

1. Over the past few decades the financing of income-producing real estate has become a much more complicated and interdisciplinary area of the law. This can largely be explained by the emergence of public law as a major determinant of how real estate will be owned and how land may be developed, for what uses, and to what design. For example, both the federal tax law and the securities laws must be taken into account in selecting an ownership entity. See Chapter 2B and Chapter 13A, note 3. Also, at various governmental levels, zoning and subdivision regulations, building codes, and

example, Dan Developer, in developing a shopping center, were to organize a limited partnership syndicate and without full disclosure solicit equity capital from a prospective limited partner, chances are that such ill-informed investor might be able to cancel the bargain with Dan and get its money back if Dan were to violate any of the laws governing the sale of securities to investors. Or if, in a jurisdiction such as New York, Dan should demand an exculpatory provision in a lease with one of his occupancy tenants, such bargain may be deemed void (by statute or case law) as against public policy on the rationale that the clause purporting to exempt and indemnify Dan from any and all tort liability only encourages negligence on his part.

Alternatively, suppose Dan obtains a mortgage loan from Ace Insurance Company to finance the shopping center. If Dan should default or if either Dan or Ace should become insolvent during the mortgagor-mortgagee relationship, the loan agreement between the parties may be superseded by either local or federal law. For example, if a mortgagee such as Ace Insurance Company bargains with a mortgagor-landlord such as Dan Developer for the right to collect the rents from Dan's tenants if he should default, that right may not be automatically enforceable in a "lien theory" jurisdiction where Dan as mortgagor would retain the legal right to rents and possession prior to foreclosure. Or, if Dan should file in bankruptcy, Ace's rights as a secured creditor could be affected by the provisions of the Bankruptcy Code.

Nevertheless, subject to the public law and policy constraints discussed above, in most instances involving the financing (as well as sale or leasing) of commercial real estate general rules of law apply

---

environmental law will determine whether and under what circumstances land may be acquired and developed. See Chapter 5B9. An extreme example of this phenomenon is the federal superfund law, the Comprehensive Environmental Response, Compensation, and Liability Act of 1980 (CERCLA), which imposes liability on land owners (including lenders who foreclose on and take title to mortgaged real estate) for expenses incurred to clean up property contaminated by hazardous waste even though the present owner is not at fault and the spillage had occurred before it acquired title to the land.

In addition, a recently emerging trend toward paternalism in the law has prompted attorneys for developers and lenders to readjust their common-law thinking with respect to bargains that are struck by their clients. For example, §5.6 of the Restatement (Second) of Property Law (as adopted by the American Law Institute in 1976 and construed by the accompanying comment) would render certain written provisions (in commercial as well as residential leases) unenforceable based on the doctrine of unconscionability; over the past few years disgruntled (albeit sophisticated) borrowers have begun to challenge their commercial loan agreements ("commitments") with real estate lenders invoking the so-called duty to negotiate in good faith. See Chapter 5A3, note 3. For a discussion of the impact of public law on commercial real estate transactions see generally Hershman, Introduction in M. Madison and J. Dwyer, The Law of Real Estate Financing xxxi-xxxiii (1981) (hereinafter Madison and Dwyer).

only in the absence of an agreement to the contrary. In other words, on the commercial or high-finance side of real estate, freedom of contract may no longer reign supreme — but it still reigns! Perhaps this is so because the interested parties (e.g., the developer, postconstruction and construction lenders, fee owner, ground lessee, and occupancy tenants) are usually sophisticated business professionals or entities that almost invariably are represented by legal and tax counsel and who, unlike the average consumer or investor, have the bargaining clout and business sophistication to protect themselves in their negotiations with one another and whose private bargains require less public scrutiny and paternalism on the part of local and federal authorities. So, for example, if Dan Developer, who wants to construct a shopping center, should be foolhardy enough to bargain for a high-interest long-term postconstruction loan from some lender like the Ace Insurance Company without demanding some right to prepay the mortgage loan prior to its maturity date (referred to as a "prepayment privilege"), the law will not rescue Dan from his folly if interest rates should later decline and Dan is precluded from "refinancing" (paying off the existing loan with a new one) at a lower interest rate. Another example is the so-called implied warranty of habitability. In virtually all jurisdictions that treat the warranty as superseding the written word in a lease agreement, commercial tenants are precluded from invoking the protection of the warranty because its underlying policy purpose applies only to the consumer-oriented residential transaction.

Thus one can easily see that any student of real estate finance when confronted with a particular transaction should know what general rule of law governs and should be prepared to analyze its underlying rationale or policy purpose. Perhaps even more important is to see how the rule can be superseded by mutual consent of the parties and to learn the process by which the real estate planner not only attempts to address present issues but may also anticipate legal, business, and tax problems that might befall his or her client in the future and to devise means of avoiding them by using one approach or another in the relevant documentation.

In addition, the tax aspects of real estate financing will be integrated into the discussion. For instance, as discussed in Chapter 2B, note 4c, if Dan Developer were to be organized as a limited partnership (as is frequently the case), he may be forced to use a no personal liability mortgage ("nonrecourse financing") as opposed to a personal liability mortgage ("recourse financing") to fund his land acquisition and construction costs; otherwise, the investors in the limited partnership may be precluded from deducting tax losses in excess of their actual economic investment in the partnership.

The materials in the book reflect the chronological pattern that exists in practice. In most cases involving the financing of income-producing property, the developer will first select, primarily on the basis of tax shelter considerations, which form of ownership entity is best suited for the dual purposes of raising the venture capital and securing the financing for the balance of the costs for the land and the building. See Chapter 2B, note 7. In the case of new construction, once the entity of ownership and borrowing is selected, the developer must make another important prefinancing decision: how to finance the cost of the underlying land. If the developer already owns the land or decides to purchase it the developer may simply decide to obtain a fee mortgage loan to fund the remainder of the land acquisition and construction costs. Alternatively, to reduce the initial cash outlay for the project and possibly increase the tax deductions, the developer may decide to finance the cost of the land separately by means of a subordinated purchase money mortgage from the seller (see Chapter 9B, note 5a), sever the land from the improvements and finance each component separately (see Chapter 8B1, notes 2 and 3), or lease rather than purchase the fee and obtain a leasehold mortgage to help fund the cost of constructing the leasehold improvements. See Chapter 8A.

Customarily, the first stage in the commercial real estate lending cycle is for the developer to approach some institutional lender, frequently with the aid of an intermediary such as a mortgage broker or loan correspondent, for a postconstruction loan commitment. See Chapter 5A2. Once approached, the lender must initially decide whether the loan investment is economically feasible and whether it complies with certain external constraints on its lending authority, such as the limitations imposed by local usury laws (see Chapter 5B3, note 4) and statutes that regulate its investment portfolio. See Chapter 2A, note 2. If the application for the postconstruction loan is approved, then ordinarily the developer, on the strength of the postconstruction lender's commitment, obtains a short-term interest-only construction loan from some interim lender such as a commercial bank, whose construction loan is "taken out" or, in effect, purchased by the postconstruction lender once the project is completed in accordance with the terms and conditions of the postconstruction loan commitment letter and producing rental income. See Chapter 6B. Finally, at the end of the lending cycle, when the postconstruction loan is funded the lender will receive from the borrower its promissory note for the loan indebtedness and a mortgage (or deed of trust) as security for the borrower's performance of the loan obligation. In practical terms, the real function of the note, mortgage, and other loan documents is but to implement and enforce the loan obligation as defined by the postconstruction loan commitment letter, namely, the terms and conditions of the postconstruction financing (e.g., the rate of interest, amortization period, and prepayment privilege) that were negotiated by the parties at the beginning of the lending cycle. See Chapter 5B. So, not only does the lending cycle for new income-producing property begin and end with the postconstruction loan commitment letter, but this cardinal document to a large extent also defines the business and legal parameters of the mortgagor-mortgagee relationship during the life of the mortgage loan.

A note of caution: During the recent past the financing of commercial real estate has been in a state of flux in response to fundamental changes in both the economy and in the investment practices of the various groups of institutional lenders. To some extent these changes have caused a restructuring of the customary post-World War II financing cycle faced by real estate developers. For example, during the late 1970s and early 1980s life insurance companies and other traditional postconstruction (or "permanent") lenders became disenchanted with long-term fixed-rate mortgages because of the high levels of inflation and resultant volatility in market rates of interest.[2] This prompted postconstruction lenders to demand inter alia full equity participations by entering into joint ventures with developer-borrowers or by insisting on postconstruction mortgage loans that are convertible into an equity interest. See Chapter 7A and Chapter 7B. In addition, as an alternative to forgoing substantial equity and with the decline in the availability of forward, or takeout, commitments from postconstruction lenders, some developers were able to obtain "open-end" construction financing without a backup takeout commitment and, on occasion, the same lender was willing to provide both the construction and postconstruction financing. Since then, however, inflation has subsided and interest rates have stabilized, and the real estate financing cycle has returned to its customary pattern. Therefore, the organization of the materials in this book reflects the traditional dichotomy between postconstruction and construction financing.[3]

After the project has been completed and produces a positive cash flow, and Dan Developer brings the project "on stream," he may wish to translate some of the equity into cash and assemble additional working capital by refinancing the existing loan for a larger amount and a longer term (possibly at a lower interest rate) with the same or another postconstruction lender. See Chapter 9A. Alternatively, if the prepayment penalty is steep, the interest rate on the existing loan is low, or Dan wants to attain "higher-ratio financing" (which would make the loan amount higher in relationship to the market value of the mortgaged property), he may seek a second or third mortgage from a so-called secondary lender. See Chapter 9B. In addition, if the improvements

---

2. See Strum, Long-Term Fixed Rate Mortgages, ABA Section of Real Prop., Prob. & Tr. Law, Financing Real Estate During the Inflationary 80s, at 23 (1981).

3. A second note of caution: Special financing considerations apply in the case of non-income-producing property such as the development and sale of lots in a subdivision. See Chapter 9B, note 5b.

are over-depreciated or the project is land-intensive, Dan might obtain, as an alternative to debt financing, the necessary capital by means of a sale-and-leaseback arrangement with some institutional investor. By so doing he might obtain more working capital and tax deductions than by retaining the fee ownership and either refinancing or obtaining secondary financing. See Chapter 8B.

Leaving the worst for last, if the project should start to fail (or, in the parlance of the trade, "go belly-up"), foreclosure and other remedies are available to the mortgagee, and "work-outs" and bankruptcy complications are contingencies every real estate planner must know how to handle. See discussion in Chapters 10 and 11.

Before delving into the commercial real estate lending cycle let us see what's in store for real estate attorneys in the changing legal environment of the 1990s.

Nessen and Ragalevsky, The Changing Role of Lawyers in Real Estate Transactions
5 Real Est. Fin. 32 (Spring 1988)

During the 1990s, lawyers will be called upon to create something of additional value in the real estate transactions they handle. This "value-added lawyering" will require that firms go far beyond simply responding to technical problems posed by clients. Indeed, they will be asked to come up with innovative techniques and structures that will improve clients' positions and make their products more saleable in capital markets. They will also have to help clients gain access to the capital needed for their projects.

In order to meet these client demands, law firms will have to offer more than "traditional" legal services — something progressive firms are already beginning to recognize. This rather startling, albeit welcome, development is a culmination of over thirty years of growing complexity in the real estate industry.

THE CHANGING IMAGE OF THE REAL ESTATE LAWYER

Back in the 1940s and 1950s real estate lawyers were expected to know little more than how to complete a conveyancing or traditional mortgage financing. At least to most of us who were engaged in other areas of the profession, real estate practice was something of a subprofession. In fact, many of the most prestigious law firms (especially the so-called "Wall Street" firms) either stayed away from real estate altogether or submerged it almost to the point of invisibility. Many senior members of the bar eschewed real estate as an insignificant and barely respectable backwater of legal practice. To the extent a firm engaged in real estate at all, it was done almost surreptitiously.

All of this has changed radically over the past thirty years. Even among the most "respectable" firms, real estate has become an integral part, if not the centerpiece, of their success. Real estate practitioners have been taken out of the shadows, allowed to wear three-piece suits, and even permitted to meet with their firms' most valued clients.

An Expanding and Complicated Environment

Why has this come about? Primarily because real estate has become far more complicated and conceptual than in the past. The development

TODAY'S REAL ESTATE
PLANNER

of a real estate project today involves an excruciatingly complex mix of elements. Just consider, for example, this short list of concerns a contemporary real estate lawyer must address:

- contracts for acquisition, design and construction;
- land use;
- zoning and subdivision control;
- condominium and cooperative forms of ownership;
- environmental impact;
- joint venture structures, partnerships, corporations and trusts;
- title and conveyancing matters;
- leasing, ground leases and sale-leasebacks;
- financing from conventional lenders, pension funds and foreign investors;
- federal and state tax issues;
- federal and state securities laws.

Clearly, real estate law encompasses far more than ever before.

The need to deal with all of these diverse areas has increased the function and role of the real estate lawyer in the development process. Not so many years ago, the lawyer was often the last person brought into that process — the one who was required simply to reduce to writing the business arrangement struck by the principals. Now, the lawyer generally is one of the developer's most important advisers.

All real estate professionals have felt the pains of this growing complexity. To varying degrees, environmental, land use, tax and other considerations must be appreciated by the real estate broker, banker, architect and accountant. Clients, however, do not expect these professionals to have the same breadth of knowledge in so many areas as the real estate lawyer.

An accountant, for example, is not expected to have in-depth experience in environmental or land use issues; a broker is not expected to know very much about the impact of tax and securities laws; an architect is not ordinarily going to be an expert in mortgage and equity financing. But an experienced real estate developer or property owner would not hire a real estate lawyer or law firm that did not have a considerable base of knowledge in all facets of development. The need for this wide range of experience is one reason why the real estate lawyer must be brought into a transaction as close to its inception as possible.

There are other reasons as well. Real estate remains an area of the law where legalistic formality and the rule of caveat emptor still apply with vitality and vigor. The potential pitfalls in any transaction can be staggering. The developer must not only identify and anticipate all likely contingencies connected with a project, but also must estimate intelligently the amount of time it will take to satisfy those contingencies. Failure to do so may mean forfeited deposits and squandered up-front capital.

Further, the lawyer is likely to be the only professional who will be involved with and have access to all the other professionals on the development team (e.g., engineers, bankers, accountants and investors). This, combined with the highly transactional nature of the real estate business, positions the lawyer better than any other single advisor to spot potential problems and identify genuine opportunities.

Breaking the Bonds of Tradition

Thus, it has become imperative that lawyers be involved in the actual structuring of transactions — well before legal services have traditionally been required. Indeed, a client would be foolish not to get a lawyer involved at an early stage. After all, a successful real estate developer may do two or three deals a year; a successful real estate lawyer may participate in ten times that number, albeit on a more vicarious and less intense level. Thus, both lawyers and clients have begun to recognize that the lawyer's role has grown — from that of draftsman, to advisor, to consultant.

All of this adds up to a fairly simple bottom line. The legal profession has to break the bonds of tradition. Indeed, the scope of services it is now being asked to provide would have been almost incomprehensible not more than a decade ago.

Accountants have gone through a similar experience. Long before law firms saw the need to expand their services, accountants were moving well beyond an auditing practice. Today, for example, management consulting contributes a significant, if not the most significant, portion of gross revenues for the largest accounting firms.

This trend has even extended to banks which were once deemed the bastion of conservatism. These institutions are now selling a full package of personal financial services — such as banking, insurance, tax and investment advice — to preferred clients through so-called "private banker" systems.

At long last, law firms are joining the club. They are beginning to understand the need to widen their scope if they are to meet the changing needs of their clients. There is no area in which those needs are clearer than real estate and real estate financing. In this context, obviously, we are talking about matters that go far beyond routine legal work — matters such as networking, consulting, financing advising, structuring and strategic planning. Each of these is examined briefly below.

EXTENDED SERVICES

First, a law firm usually has an impressive internal networking system which, too often, it does not make available to clients. In the case of a real estate transaction, a developer should be able to use the firm as a resource for contacts among accountants, mortgage brokers, and banking and other financial institutions.

Second, a law firm can offer general consulting services, such as developing conceptual products, that will help a client put together recurring transactions on an efficient basis. It can also help clients assess the legal and political environment surrounding issues that affect them. The truth is that lawyers already do a lot more in the way of general consulting than they think they do — generally because they give advice to clients on a broad range of issues at no charge through seminars and newsletters.

Third, a law firm can provide developers with a variety of financial services akin to those offered by investment bankers in the corporate setting. Many lawyers provide these kinds of services every day on an informal basis by introducing clients to sources of financing, including debt and equity investors. Real estate lawyers often have developed a list of contacts over the years that is the envy of most investment bankers and mortgage brokers.

Fourth, a law firm can be of inestimable value in helping clients structure basic business transactions. While some clients prefer to structure their own deals, the successful ones are smart enough to use all the cost-effective resources available to them. If clients can be shown that they will save time and money by getting the lawyer involved in a project at the planning stage and by using the lawyer as a consultant rather than simply as a draftsman, the client generally will do so.

For example, the capital resources available to finance any given transaction are far more involved and varied than they were just ten or fifteen years ago. Because of its continuous contact with the capital markets on behalf of many clients, the law firm may have a keener sense than the client as to whether a pension fund or an "offshore" lender might offer a better package than traditional mortgage sources. Moreover, the lawyer frequently has greater access to these sources than the client.

Finally, a law firm can do strategic planning for the client through specialized or "boutique" services that cannot be characterized as purely "legal" products. For example, a law firm with expertise in environmental matters can — in a consulting capacity — help the client design strategies that will eliminate, minimize or contain potential pollution liability problems.

LAW FIRM RESPONSE

The response of the legal profession to these new demands has run the gamut from refusal and reluctance to acceptance and enthusiasm. Our firm, for example, recently established a Corporate and Real Estate Finance Group consisting of lawyers specializing in taxation, health care, real estate, environmental law, securities law, banking and finance. It has become a team — a SWAT team, as someone has suggested — that can be mobilized quickly and efficiently to attack a client's problems in their broadest context.

Most clients do not cubbyhole problems as "legal problems," "accounting problems" or "banking problems." They want answers on a comprehensive level: Can we do the deal or not? Is there a better way to structure the transaction? How should the financing be put together so as to get the most money at the lowest cost? The Group's reason for being is to approach problems on this level, giving the firm an opportunity to address the clients' total needs.

Consider the following example. A corporate client needs capital. In order to raise it, the company has to make a series of decisions. First, it must decide whether to obtain the capital through the use of its general credit standing. If so, it could go to the public equity or bond markets for financing, or use its unsecured bank credit lines. Another alternative would be to finance off of its assets, such as its real estate and equipment.

If the company decides upon asset-based financing, it faces another series of decisions. It can borrow directly against its assets by obtaining mortgage debt, or it can take a more convoluted route and borrow indirectly, as would be the case with a sale and leaseback transaction. In deciding whether to take the direct or indirect approach in asset-based financing, the company is then faced with a set of considerations that will require highly sophisticated analysis. The company's law firm has an obligation to help the client make this analysis because its decision will affect the company in a number of very sensitive ways:

- It will affect the company's federal tax position.
- It will have significant impact on the company's financial statements, including the manner of reporting the transaction on its balance sheet.
- It will make a serious difference with regard to the company's cost of capital.
- It will affect the company's capacity to obtain capital in the future.

This may be territory where angels fear to tread, but lawyers must. To serve their clients properly, they have to venture forward.

Take another area where clients are in dire need of help from their lawyers — syndications. Since the 1986 Tax Reform Act, the syndication industry has been in a state of disarray. If it is to survive, it must regroup, and it should be able to look to the legal profession for a comprehensive and sophisticated level of assistance.

Law firms should be at the forefront of finding new ways to structure transactions so that they will be saleable in the retail market. Investors are no longer looking to the tax benefits first and the quality of the real estate and developer second; old-fashioned economics now govern the success or failure of real estate syndications in the capital marketplace. Persuading retail investors to accept this "economic" analysis will require new methods of putting the transactions together, including developing appropriate credit facilities to stand behind them. When it comes to devising these new methods, lawyers cannot stand back as observers. They have to actively participate by bringing together several different disciplines within the law firm — from tax and securities to finance and real estate — to come up with a structure that will meet both client requirements and investor demands.

We believe law firms will have a better chance of success if they form ongoing, inter-disciplinary groups to function on a comprehensive "oversight" level. The group's combination of diverse talents and expertise will go far to help define as well as resolve client problems, whether these involve asset-based financing for corporations or new structures for syndications. With regard to real estate and the financing of real estate projects, such a group should serve the following functions:

It should assist in determining the type of capital the client should obtain.   As discussed earlier, there are a myriad of possibilities to be explored in almost every real estate and other asset-based financing. For example, debt may be the least burdensome form of financing in terms of legal complications but the most expensive in terms of cost. Equity or participating or convertible debt may appear cheaper, but also may be far more complicated, creating additional indirect costs. Being able to determine the optimum capital structure — the most appropriate configuration of debt and equity — requires the ability to analyze and structure a transaction across legal and business lines. This means that the lawyer, to be of relevance to the client, must bring to the table legal, business and financial expertise.

It should recommend structures that meet both the needs of the client and the demands of the capital markets.   To meet this objective, the law firm's team must be constantly on top of developments in these rapidly changing markets.

It should provide the traditional legal services necessary to implement the transaction, including the negotiation and drafting of documents.   In this regard, there is no substitute for technical excellence. At the same time, there is no reason that such excellence should be sacrificed or impaired by broadening the scope of legal services.

It should assist clients in obtaining access to the capital markets.   This objective refers back to the law firm's networking capabilities. A law firm usually has an enviable source of contacts in these markets, and it should be prepared to give clients access to this network.

SUMMARY

If a law firm is to grow and prosper over the next decade, it can no longer sit back and wait for the client to come up with the ideas — or the problems. Whether in real estate or other areas, lawyers can no longer be bystanders. They must be deeply immersed in the totality of a transaction from both a legal and business point of view. Most importantly, they must be prepared to add value to a client's product — a value far beyond simply putting together a set of papers based upon a term sheet originated by the client.

Such "value-added"· lawyering in the 1990s will require that lawyers be not only legal technicians, but also innovators and conceptualizers. The ability to be both is the key factor in a successful journey from draftsman to consultant.

B.   TODAY'S CREATIVE REAL ESTATE PLANNING: THE ART OF MAKING THE SUM OF THE PARTS GREATER THAN THE WHOLE

At the turn of the century most commercial real estate and apartment buildings were constructed by and occupied or rented by a single owner who had fee simple title to both the building and the underlying land. Typically, the owner would finance its land acquisition and construction costs by obtaining an ordinary mortgage loan with a low loan-to-value ratio (so that the loan amount was small relative to the market value of the mortgaged real estate) from some institutional lender that would obtain, as security, a mortgage lien on the borrower's fee ownership of the land and building until the loan was repaid. Therefore, in those days the focus of the average real estate practitioner was on the present use and single ownership of income-producing real estate. However, by the middle of the century this all changed as real estate development began to spread its wings. By then the use of reinforced steel had transformed single-story office buildings into skyscrapers, and our entry into the automobile age had created the regional shopping mall that we know today. Spurred by the economic boom that followed World

War II, real estate developers began to demand higher ratio financing to fund the new construction that was needed to keep pace with the increasing demand for commercial and multifamily residential space. Real estate planners, always an innovative breed, responded to the challenge by devising novel methods (generically referred to as "split financing") to attain higher ratio financing for their developer-clients by splitting the fee ownership of the land into separate leasehold and reversionary interests and financing each component separately.

For example, a so-called leasehold mortgage came into vogue whereby a developer could lease (rather than purchase) the underlying fee under what is known as a ground lease (or, if the developer already owned the land, he or she could sell the land and lease it back under what is known as a sale and leaseback)[4] and obtain a mortgage to finance the cost of developing the land and constructing the leasehold improvements. By not purchasing the fee the developer obviously would forgo the benefit of realizing any appreciation in the value of the underlying land. However, since the developer's initial cash outlay would be less and yet the net rental income would usually remain about the same,[5] the developer would be able to leverage the development costs and increase the rate of return on the cash investment for itself and its investors. As security for the leasehold mortgage a lender would obtain a mortgage lien on the borrower's leasehold estate (along with the improvements to be erected thereon) rather than a lien on the fee.[6]

Later, this concept of making the sum of the real estate financing parts greater than the whole became refined on the ownership, or "equity," side of real estate. For example, while vacationing in Hawaii one William Zeckendorf, Sr. allegedly was fretting over a building in New York City that he had contracted to purchase without having the money to pay for it. Early one morning while fishing he suddenly conceived of an idea called the "Hawaiian technique." He claimed that he became so excited that he dropped his fishing rod into the ocean and ran to call his business associates in New York.

The concept consists of carving the cash flow and rental income stream from a single building or project into layers of leasehold interests known as "sandwich leases" that are situated between the owner of the ground lease and the owner of the operating position in order to expand the real estate ownership "pie" and attract the widest range of equity participants.[7] The concept is analogous to the leveraged returns

---

4. Sale and leasebacks are examined in greater detail at Chapter 8B.

5. The ground rent frequently approximates in amount the extra debt-service payments that the developer-borrower would have to pay if it were to obtain a larger fee mortgage to cover the cost of the land as well as the cost of the building.

6. Leasehold mortgages are examined in greater detail at Chapter 8A.

7. Sandwich leases are examined in greater detail at Chapter 8C.

provided to shareholders owning common stock in a corporation whose assets are acquired by means of high-ratio financing and where the shareholders are able to take advantage of the spread between corporate earnings and the fixed rates of return on corporate debt owed to bondholders and preferred stockholders.

Nowadays, it is not uncommon in large commercial developments such as office buildings for the fee title to the project to be vested in A or a subsidiary of A that had purchased the land from B and then leased it back to B under a long-term net ground lease. The improvements would then be constructed by B, whose leasehold interest might be subject to a leasehold mortgage that would be used to finance the construction, with fee title to the buildings remaining in B for the term of the ground lease. The buildings would then be subleased by B under a long-term net sandwich lease to a public or private limited partnership, then sub-subleased under a long-term net "operating lease" to a real estate management company that would actually manage and operate the buildings, and finally sub-sub-subleased to the actual occupants. The sandwich and operating leases might also be encumbered by leasehold mortgages. Hence, what is sold or mortgaged in each instance would be neither a segment of the physical real estate nor a slice of time but merely interests in the cash flow and rental income stream from the income-producing real estate.

However, if the income stream and cash flow from a single building can be fragmented, why can't the use and ownership of the building be likewise segmented? In the case of a skyscraper, why not have a leased mezzanine on the first floor for shoppers and above that leased space for office workers and above that a hotel or residential condominium for those who wish to own the air they breathe, along with several floors of leased residential space for the perennial renters? Perhaps a portion of the fee ownership of the hotel or residential condominium could be split up and sold as time-shares to those occupants who want the psychic joy of owning a piece of the fortieth floor but who can only be in town each year during the month of December. Novel? Yes. Unheard of? No. It has already been done; for example, the multi-use project in Chicago called Water Tower Place comes close to the pattern described above. This is what creative financing is all about.[8]

---

8. Another connotation of the phrase "creative real estate financing" refers to the innovative financing techniques employed by lenders to cope with inflation and volatile interest rates. The common characteristic of these financing approaches is that they involve some degree of equity (ownership) participation. Some, such as the participating mortgage, are at the debt end of the debt-equity spectrum. See Chapter 5B3. Others, such as the joint venture, represent a pure equity position; while still others, such as the convertible mortgage, variable rate mortgage, and shared appreciation mortgage, are somewhere in the middle of the debt-equity spectrum. See Chapter 5B3, note 5 and Chapter 7A.

A final example of the art of making the sum of the real estate parts greater than the whole is the recent trend toward the "securitization" of commercial real estate. As observed at Chapter 2A, real estate investments historically have tended to be less volatile, less risky, and a better hedge against inflation than other investment media such as stocks and bonds. In addition, real estate investors are afforded unique opportunities to leverage their costs of acquiring and improving real estate and to shelter their rental income from immediate taxation. See Chapter 2B. However, one disadvantage for real estate investors has been the lack of liquidity associated with their investment shares. In response to this problem the public security format is now being used in innovative ways to enhance the liquidity and marketability of both debt and equity participations in real estate. Exemplifying this trend on the equity, or ownership, side of real estate are the master limited partnership (MLP) and new kinds of equity real estate investment trusts (REITs) such as the "finite-life closed-end REIT." See Chapter 13A, note 2. On the debt side of real estate, credit-rating agencies (such as Standard & Poors) and underwriters have allowed and sponsored public offerings of commercial mortgage-backed bonds (CMBBs), enabling real estate developers to obtain their long-term fixed-rate financing from Wall Street sources on terms that are more attractive than what would otherwise be available from traditional long-term private lenders. In the opinion of some real estate experts this trend may revolutionize the way in which commercial real estate is financed in this country. See Chapter 13B.

NOTES AND QUESTIONS

Any would-be practitioner of real estate law should be aware of the major publications and other available reference materials for research on a particular point or to achieve a deeper understanding of some aspect of real estate investment or financing. In addition, the discussion in this book presents and defines many of the vocabulary terms most frequently used by real estate attorneys and other professionals. But before we start grappling with the materials that follow, let us take note of a glossary of a different variety that appeared in the *New York Times* on January 17, 1989, at A25.

A Real Estate Primer
By John Bendel

Looking for your "starter home" in the current impenetrable housing market? This glossary of recurring words and phrases interprets the real estate advertising hyperbole you're bound to encounter:

"Spacious" — average.
"Charming" — small.
"Comfortable" — very small.
"Cozy" — very, very small.
"Low maintenance" — no lawn.
"Walk to stores" — nowhere to park.
"Prestigious" — expensive.
"Bright and sunny" — venetian blinds not included.
"Townhouse" — former tenement.
"Modern" — 30 to 50 years old.
"Contemporary" — at least 20 years old.
"Sprawling ranch" — inefficient floor plan.
"Secluded setting" — far away.
"Executive neighborhood" — high taxes.
"Near houses of worship" — fanatical sect next door.
"Park-like setting" — a tree on block.
"Unaffected charm" — needs paint.
"Starter home" — dilapidated.
"Hurry! Won't last!" — impending collapse.
"And much, much more" — nothing more to mention.

Books

Nelson and Whitman, Real Estate Finance Law (2d ed. 1985): an authoritative treatise with abundant citations on the law of mortgages and real estate financing.

Madison and Dwyer, The Law of Real Estate Financing (2d ed. 1992) (forthcoming): a treatise on the law of real estate financing that follows a transactional approach and is tax-oriented.

Harris, Construction and Development Financing (1982): a practice-oriented treatise on construction and subdivision financing.

Bernhardt, California Mortgage and Deed of Trust Practice (1979): a treatise on the law of mortgages and real estate financing geared to California law.

Kratovil, Modern Mortgage Law and Practice (2d ed. 1981): a practice-oriented book with abundant examples that provides a brief overview of the law of mortgages and real estate financing.

Bruce, Real Estate Finance (2d ed. 1985): a student-oriented hornbook that provides a brief overview of the law of mortgages and real estate financing.

Other books on real estate financing and related real estate law topics include: the annual editions of Modern Real Estate Transactions, published by the American Law Institute-American Bar Association Committee on Continuing Professional Education (ALI/ABA), which are designed to keep practitioners abreast of recent developments and techniques with respect to all aspects of sophisticated real estate transactions and which use the relevant documentation as the referential point for discussion; the following publications of the Real Property, Probate and Trust Law Section of the ABA: Current Developments in Real Estate Law (annual), Financing Real Estate During the Inflationary 80s (1981), Environmental Risk in Real Estate Transactions — The Innocent Landowner Defense (1989), and Real Estate in Midcentury (1974), a selective (albeit dated) compilation of publications by the Section between 1938 and 1974; Rohan and Reskin, Condominium Law and Practice (1972); and the following publications by the Practicing Law Institute: Friedman on Leases (2d ed. 1983), Friedman, Contracts and Conveyances of Real Property (3d ed. 1975), and the Real Estate Law and Practice Course Handbook series of booklets, which deals with the multifarious aspects of real estate law practice.

Other books on the tax and securities law aspects of real estate investment include: Haft and Fass, 1988 Investment Limited Partnerships Handbook, which has an in-depth discussion of the federal securities laws in chapter 4; Madden, Taxation of Real Estate Transactions — An Overview (1987) (Tax Management Portfolio No. 480-2nd), an excellent overview with ample citations and an in-depth bibliography; Robinson, Federal Income Taxation of Real Estate (4th ed. 1984); Willis, Pennell, and Postlewaite, Partnership Taxation (1989); McKee, Nelson, and Whitman, Federal Taxation of Partnerships and Partners (1977), and the General Explanations of the various tax reform acts (referred to by tax lawyers as "blue books") prepared by the Staff of the Joint Committee on Taxation.

Journals

Real Estate Finance Journal, published quarterly by Warren Gorham & Lamont.

Real Estate Finance, published quarterly by Federal Research Press, which includes a quarterly survey of trends in commercial real estate financing and securitization.

In addition to the various law reviews, the following real estate law-related journals are recommended, in order of preference: Real Property, Probate and Trust Journal, published by the Section of Real Property, Probate and Trust Law of the ABA, which contains an annual spring survey of current developments in real estate law in each state; Real Estate Law Journal, published by Warren Gorham & Lamont, which contains regular columns on real estate tax ideas, digests of recent cases and statutes, and bibliographies of recent books and articles; Real Estate Review, published by Warren Gorham & Lamont, which is business-oriented and short on citations; and the Practical Real Estate Lawyer by ALI/ABA, which is practice-oriented and short on citations.

Recommended tax law journals include (in order of preference): the Journal of Real Estate Taxation, published by Warren Gorham & Lamont; the annual N.Y.U. Institute on Federal Taxation, which on a regular basis surveys recent developments in the tax aspects of real estate; and the general tax journals and institutes such as Tax Law Review, Journal of Taxation, and Taxes.

Newsletters

First and foremost is the Mortgage and Real Estate Executives Report, published bimonthly by Warren Gorham & Lamont, which is so well-written that it is both informative for the sophisticated reader and readily understandable by the novice. It covers the legal, business, and tax aspects of real estate investment and financing. Other recommended newsletters are those published by the American College of Real Estate Lawyers, the Crittenden Report on Real Estate Financing, and The Commercial Lease Law Insider, published by Brownstone Publishers, Inc.

Chapter 2

Real Estate as an Investment

In real estate ventures, an important prefinancing consideration is the type of ownership entity best suited for the dual purposes of raising the venture capital and securing the debt financing needed to fund the acquisition and improvement of the real estate. Selection of an ownership entity presupposes that some individual or group of individuals has decided to invest in real estate. Accordingly, let us first examine why income-producing real estate is such an attractive investment medium. Indeed, it is difficult to explain the *how* of financing without discussing the *why* of investing in real estate.

The profitability of investing in income-producing real estate as compared to other traditional investment media such as ordinary stocks and bonds[1] can be explained to a large extent by the interplay between the following factors: (1) historically, rental real estate has yielded a relatively high pretax rate of return to investors and has been a relatively good hedge against inflation; (2) real estate investors are afforded the unique opportunity to obtain high-ratio financing in order to leverage their cost of acquiring and improving real estate; and (3) unique tax shelter benefits are accorded to the owners of income-producing real estate, notwithstanding the curtailment of real estate tax shelter by the Tax Reform Act of 1986.

A. ECONOMIC REWARDS AND FINANCIAL LEVERAGE

Notwithstanding the current slump in most real estate markets, the traditional view held by most researchers and commentators in the

---

1. One of the most exciting trends in recent years has been the transformation of illiquid real estate assets and liabilities into capital market instruments that are tradeable on Wall Street — for example, commercial mortgage-backed bonds and stock in a real estate master limited partnership. Securitization on the equity and debt sides of real estate are examined in Chapter 13A and B.

literature on investments is that rates of return from direct ownership
of commercial real estate and from indirect ownership of real estate
equities,[2] as measured by various indices,[3] historically have tended to
be higher and have exhibited significantly less volatility than returns
on corporate equities. In addition, real estate returns have exhibited
low or negative correlations with stocks and bonds, making real estate
a valuable asset in constructing well-diversified portfolios.[4] Moreover,
in contrast to stocks and bonds, the nominal yields from real estate
tend to increase with both anticipated and unanticipated inflation.

Perhaps the most attractive feature of real estate is that the owner
can leverage the cost of acquiring and constructing a real estate asset.
"Leverage" refers simply to the commonsense business principle that
if an investor can borrow a portion of the equity requirement at an
interest rate lower than the anticipated rate of return from the investment, the effective rate of return is increased. Such an investment
is said to be leveraged. A simple example will introduce the excerpts
that begin on page 27.

If an investor can acquire a real estate asset that is expected to
produce an annual "cash-on-cash" rate of return of 10 percent[5] for a

2. See discussion at Chapter 13A.

3. Among the principal indices and sources of data for measuring changes in the
rental income and appreciation rates of return for income-producing real estate are: (1)
the FRC Property Index, created by the Frank Russel Company and the National
Council of Real Estate Investment Fiduciaries, which takes into account both income
and changes in appraised property values of *unleveraged* commercial properties held in
pension fund portfolios in the form of commingled real estate funds (CREFs) (CREFs
are usually selected and managed by life insurance companies who, as fiduciaries for
the pension funds, are subject to the rules and requirements imposed by the Employee
Retirement Income Security Act (ERISA)); (2) the National Association of Real Estate
Investment Trusts (NAREIT) Index, which is a market-value-weighted index of all
listed equity and mortgage REITs; (3) the Morguard Property Index (MPI), which
measures both income and appreciation changes based on performance data from approximately 200 *unleveraged* commercial Canadian properties; (4) data on CREF returns
in Real Estate Profiles, prepared by Evaluation Associates, Inc., and similar data prepared
by the Real Estate Research Corporation. See generally Zerbst and Cambon, Real Estate:
Historical Returns and Risks, 10 J. Portfolio Mgmt. 5, 6 (Spring 1984); Hoag, Toward
Indices of Real Estate Value and Return, 35 J. Fin. 569 (May 1980); Cohen, New Life
in Real Estate Stocks, 2 Real Est. Fin. 17, 18-19 (Fall 1985).

The major indices and sources of data for measuring changes in the income and
capital appreciation rates of return for corporate equities include: (1) the Standard and
Poor's 500 Total Returns Index; (2) the Salomon Brothers Broad Investment-Grade
Bond Index; (3) data prepared by Moody's Investor Service, the Board of Governors
of the Federal Reserve System, and the U.S. Bureau of Labor Statistics.

4. See Hartzell, Real Estate in the Portfolio 1, 4-5 (Salomon Brothers, Inc., Aug.
27, 1986).

5. This simplest measure of performance is calculated by dividing the money
received by the money expended in a particular year. In contrast to more sophisticated

cost of $100,000 and is able to borrow 80 percent of the acquisition cost with an 8 percent interest-only loan, the investor, by leveraging the acquisition cost, can increase the rate of return from 10 percent to 18 percent. This is because the ratio of money received to money expended increases from 10 percent ($10,000 ÷ $100,000) to 18 percent ($10,000 − $6,400 interest = $3,600 net income ÷ $20,000). Another way to explain the result is that while the investor earns a 10 percent rate of return on the one-fifth of the investment financed with the investor's own cash, the other four-fifths of the investment earns the same 10 percent but costs only 8 percent; accordingly, the cash-on-cash rate of return is increased by four times the rate spread (2 percent) or 8 percent, which increases the before-tax rate of equity return from 10 percent to 18 percent, as diagrammed below.

		Rate Spread
1/5	$20,000 All cash	- 0 -
1/5	$20,000 leveraged	- 2 -
1/5	$20,000 leveraged	- 2 -
1/5	$20,000 leveraged	- 2 -
1/5	$20,000 leveraged	- 2 -
		8% + 10% = 18%

Conversely, financial leverage can also multiply an investor's reduction in the rate of return on equity if the income from the investment should decline. Thus, in the foregoing example, if the income rate of return were only 7 percent the investor's overall rate of return would drop to 3 percent as a consequence of negative leverage.

Observe that leverage also works for the investor if the value of the underlying land appreciates owing to inflation or demand's exceeding supply. Alternatively, an increase in net rental earnings could cause an increase in the value of the building.[6] Suppose, for example, the investor purchases some land for $100,000 that is financed with an 80 percent loan-to-value ratio loan. The investor's cash or equity

---

yardsticks of profitability such as the net present value method (NPV) and the internal rate of return method (IRR), it takes into account neither federal income tax consequences nor the time value of money. These methods are discussed later in this section.

    6. See Chapter 5B1.

requirement would be $20,000, and a 5 percent increase in the value of the land during the first year (from $100,000 to $105,000) would produce an unrealized appreciation rate of 25 percent on the investor's equity investment (before taking financing charges into account) since the $100,000 (the full leveraged cost of the real estate and not merely the $20,000 equity) is the base to which the 5 percent rate applies.

In the foregoing example, the cash on cash rate of return at the end of the year was used for simplicity's sake to measure the profitability of the real estate investment. Another common measure is the free and clear rate of return, which is determined by dividing the projected net operating income (without taking into account the payment of income taxes and debt-service payments on the mortgage, if any) by the acquisition cost of the investment. Another approach, used primarily by appraisers to measure the current value of real estate (as opposed to its profitability), is the capitalization rate (or "cap rate"), which is discussed at Chapter 5B1, note 2. To the sophisticated investor, however, these methods are but crude and static measures of profitability because they fail to take into account both the tax and time-value aspects of the investment picture.[7] The investor in the example obviously knows that some day it will dispose of the real estate and receive as a residual amount its share of the net sale proceeds after the outstanding mortgage and tax liability on the gain, if any, are satisfied. Furthermore, the investor knows that, depending on the cost of capital or interest rate, a dollar of future economic benefit from the investment (during its holding period) is worth less than a dollar of benefit that is presently available, because of the time value of money: today's dollar can be invested to provide the investor with more than the dollar next year. Consequently, the investor will want to use some yardstick for profitability that is sensitive enough to take these time-value variables into account so that it can intelligently compare a particular real estate investment with other investment opportunities. In the excerpts that follow we will be examining and comparing the two principal sophisticated methods of investment analysis used by virtually all real estate professionals, the net present value (NPV) method and the internal rate of return (IRR) method, along with some other time-value-oriented measures of profitability. All of these methods, which are generically referred to as methods of "dynamic return analysis," have one thing in common: they take into account future cash flows and apply discount factors to arrive at the present value of the real estate investment in today's dollars.

7. However, as observed at Chapter 5B1, note 3, the traditional capitalization rate theory recently has been modified by many appraisers to take into account the time value of money and anticipated rates of inflation during the holding period of the real estate being valued.

Madison and Dwyer, The Law of Real Estate Financing

¶1.05[2][e] (Cum. Supp. No. 2) (1989)

[e] MEASURING THE PROFITABILITY OF A TAX SHELTER INVESTMENT [NEW]

One method of investment analysis that provides a more complete picture and provides a means of comparing investments is called the Net Present Value (NPV) method. The formula is as follows:[95.12]

NPV = (Present value of future cash flows) minus (initial investment cost plus present value of future expenditures)

In mathematical terms:

$$NPV = \left(\frac{CF_1}{1 + i} + \frac{CF_2}{(1 + i)^2} + \cdots + \frac{CF_n}{(1 + i)^n} \right) - (OI)$$

$$- \left(\frac{I_1}{1 + i} + \frac{I_2}{(1 + i)^2} + \cdots + \frac{I_n}{(1 + i)^n} \right)$$

In the above formula, CF_n is cash flow in period n, OI is the original investment, I_n is the investment period n,[95.13] and i is the assumed interest rate (cost of capital). To simplify our understanding of how NPV works, let us assume that no future expenditures are incurred. If so, the formula would read as follows:

$$NPV = \left(\frac{CF_1}{1 + i} + \frac{CF_2}{(1 + i)^2} + \cdots + \frac{CF_n}{(1 + i)^n} \right) - OI$$

For any assumed investment period and interest rate, a positive NPV indicates that the total investment "inflows" exceed the total investment "outflows"; that is, the investor ends up with more (in present dollars) than he gave up. Accordingly, a negative NPV indicates

95.12. For example, most college textbooks on finance include present-value tables indicating that if L's cost of obtaining money were 10 percent on a three-year investment, he should invest no more than 75 cents for every dollar he expects to receive three years from now, or, if L must pay 15 percent to obtain money, the present value of the future dollar would be only 65 cents.

95.13. For example, if the property were held for five years, n would be 5, CF_5 would be cash flow in Year 5, and I_5 would be the investment outlay made in Year 5.

that an investment should not be undertaken. For a simple example of the NPV computation, assume an initial investment of $15,000 and cash flows of $6,000, $7,000, and $8,000 for the first three years and an interest rate of 12 percent.

$$\left(\frac{6{,}000}{1.12} + \frac{7{,}000}{(1.12)^2} + \frac{8{,}000}{(1.12)^3} \right) - 15{,}000$$

$$= \left(\frac{6{,}000}{1.12} + \frac{7{,}000}{1.25} + \frac{8{,}000}{1.40} \right) - 15{,}000$$

$$= \quad 1671$$

If there are tax benefits available from an investment, these tax benefits must be factored into the NPV analysis. This is accomplished by treating the dollar amount of a tax saving (e.g., a deduction of $50,000 is a tax saving of $15,500 to a taxpayer with a 31 percent marginal tax rate) as part of the cash inflow in the year the tax saving is realized. Similarly, any tax expenditure must be treated as a negative cash flow. By factoring these tax aspects into the NPV equation, the investment can be analyzed from an after-tax viewpoint to support a more valid investment decision.[95.14]

The Internal Rate of Return (IRR) is the most sophisticated method of investment analysis. The IRR is the discount rate that equates the present value of cash inflows with the present value of cash outflows.[95.15] The IRR represents the exact rate of investment return that will allow an investor to receive economic benefits (discounted to present value) equivalent to the present value of his investment outlays for a given investment period. For example, a $1,000 bond that returns the initial $1,000 investment plus $100 interest exactly one year after investment would have an IRR of 10 percent. The IRR is computed by the following formula:

$$0 = \frac{CF_1}{(1+i)} + \frac{CF_2}{(1+i)^2} + \frac{CF_3}{(1+i)^3} + \cdots + \frac{CF_n}{(1+i)^n} - I$$

95.14. There are two remaining weaknesses to this analysis. First, an appropriate interest rate must be assumed. When comparing investments of differing durations, the assumptions must vary and estimations require greater accuracy. The problem of an assumed interest rate is alleviated somewhat by an analysis called the Internal Rate of Return (IRR). Second, certain assumptions must be made about expected inflows. In the real estate scenario, these assumptions include rental income, maintenance expense, real estate taxes, and ultimate sale price. This second problem is dealt with by using risk analysis, the methodology of which is beyond the scope of this book.

95.15. See generally Clettenberg & Kroncke, How to Calculate Real Estate Return on Investment, 2 Real Est. Rev. 105, 108 (Winter 1973); F. J. Weston & E. F. Brigham, Managerial Finance 291, 295 (6th ed. 1978).

The IRR is represented by i; n is the desired investment period; and CF_1, CF_2, . . . again represent net inflows and are calculated in the same manner as in the NPV analysis.[95.16] The IRR equation is solved for i by a trial-and-error method called iteration. An investor who uses computers can avoid the trial-and-error process in solving the equation or so-called iteration. For a simple example of the IRR computation, assume: (1) an initial investment of $15,000 and (2) cash flows of $6,000 in Year 1, $7,000 in Year 2, and $8,000 in Year 3. Thus:

$$0 = \frac{6,000}{(1+i)} + \frac{7,000}{(1+i)^2} + \frac{8,000}{(1+i)^3} - 15,000$$

Solve for i. First try 15 percent:

$$0 = \frac{6,000}{1.15} + \frac{7,000}{(1.15)^2} + \frac{8,000}{(1.15)^3} - 15,000$$

$$= 5,217 + 5,293 + 5,260 - 15,000$$

$$0 \neq 15,770 - 15,000$$

Therefore, 15 percent is too low; try 20 percent:

$$0 = \frac{6,000}{1.2} + \frac{7,000}{(1.2)^2} + \frac{8,000}{(1.2)^3} - 15,000$$

$$= 5,000 + 4,861 + 4,630 - 15,000$$

$$0 \neq 14,491 - 15,000$$

Since 20 percent is too high, try 18 percent:

$$0 = \frac{6,000}{1.18} + \frac{7,000}{(1.18)^2} + \frac{8,000}{(1.18)^3} - 15,000$$

$$= 5,084 + 5,027 + 4,869 - 15,000$$

$$0 = 14,980 - 15,000$$

In this example, the IRR is approximately 18 percent.

95.16. As with the NPV analysis, the IRR method includes in cash flow all net items of cash received or tax benefits as a positive amount and all net items of cash paid or tax expenditures as a negative amount. In real estate investment, the computation for CF_n (the last year of ownership) should reflect the gain or loss on sale less any outstanding mortgage debt.

The Mortgage and Real Estate Executive's Report
5-6 (June 1, 1989)

COMPARING INTERNAL RATE OF RETURN AND NET PRESENT VALUE

. . . In essence, the NPV method involves (1) determining the appropriate annual return for the particular investment based on the three elements of riskiness, inflation, and real return; and (2) using the return percentage as a discount rate to reduce projected future cash flows to present value, which is compared to the initial investment. If the NPV (present value minus initial investment) is positive, the investment should be made.

INTERNAL RATE OF RETURN

. . . First, a brief overview of IRR. An internal rate of return is the rate at which the NPV of a project's cash inflows and outflows (including the initial investment and the anticipated resale proceeds) is equal to zero. Both the IRR and NPV methods require the investor to make the same projections as to future cash flows. The difference between the two methods lies in how the annual return is arrived at:

[1] Under the NPV method, the investor arrives at the annual return by comparing the particular investment with a "standard asset" such as a basket of New York Stock Exchange stocks. This return is then used as the "discount rate" by which future cash flows are reduced to present value.

[2] Under the IRR method, by comparison, the investor does not start with any specific return. Instead, different interest rates are tested to find the one that reduces future cash flows to a present value exactly equal to the initial investment (so that the NPV is zero). The interest rates can be guessed at or a computer can be used to determine the IRR. Once the investor has determined the IRR, he can decide if it is high enough for him to proceed with the investment.

The IRR and NPV methods will usually, but not always, give the same answer as to the desirability of an investment.

CHOOSING THE MOST PROFITABLE INVESTMENT

The IRR method can tell an investor if a project is good or bad (in terms of required return), but it cannot tell which investment is best. For example, consider the [following two projects], each with a risk-adjusted discount rate of 10 percent:

	Initial Investment	Payoff (1 Year)	IRR	NPV (r = 10%)
Project A	$2,000	$2,500	25%	$273
Project B	$1,000	$1,300	30%	$182

In project A, the $2,500 payoff after one year has a present value of $2,273, using a 10 percent discount rate; the NPV thus is $273 more than the $2,000 investment, or an actual return of 10 percent plus $273.

In project B, the $1,300 payoff after one year has a present value of $1,182 using a 10 percent discount rate; the NPV thus is $182 more than the $1,000 investment, or an actual return of 10 percent plus $182.

In this example, project B has the higher IRR, but the NPV is lower. If project B were chosen on the basis of IRR, the investor would not be maximizing his wealth.

WHY NPV IS BETTER

To explain why this is so, assume an investor has $2,000 in an investment yielding a 10 percent annual return that properly reflects its riskiness. He is given the choice of investing in project A or B but not both. As the table shows, both projects (with the same riskiness as the present investment) produce a return higher than 10 percent ($273 more for project A and $182 more for project B).

If the investor were to proceed solely on the basis of the IRRs, he would choose project B, investing $1,000 for a 30 percent IRR. However, he would actually be better off investing the entire $2,000 in project A because, even though it has a lower IRR of 25 percent, it yields $91 over and above the risk-adjusted 10 percent return. In other words, if the investor puts the additional $1,000 into project A, he will increase his wealth by $91 while assuming no more risk as compared to leaving it in the present investment. Use of the IRR method will not tell him this, but the NPV method will.

Put another way, NPV analysis has a distinct advantage over IRR analysis because it will encourage investing any incremental amount in a project as long as the additional investment has a return equal to or exceeding the risk-adjusted cost of the investment.

On the other hand, a mere comparison of IRRs can be misleading. If an investor were paying an investment manager on the basis of the IRR generated, a rational manager would invest in project B, since his compensation would be higher than it would have been had he chosen project A. Nevertheless, the investor would be worse off by $91 (the NPV of the forgone incremental investment).

DIFFERENT DISCOUNT RATES

To make matters even more confusing, it may be that the discount rates (riskiness) of two investments differ. For example, the discount rate (i.e., the required risk-adjusted return from the project) for project *A* may be 10 percent while the discount rate for project *B* is 15 percent. The IRR remains unchanged because it has nothing to do with the discount rate. But now comparison between the two projects is even more difficult; the only way to distinguish between the two is to calculate the NPV using the discount rate specific to the project.

Observation: There are several other reasons why the IRR method is not as satisfactory as the NPV method in measuring return . . . lack of space prevents their being detailed here. However, the foregoing discussion should indicate the greater precision of the NPV method. In normal practice, . . . the use of NPV enables the investor to quantify in dollars the amount of gain, something IRR cannot do.

Zerbst and Cambon, Real Estate: Historical Returns and Risks
10 J. Portfolio Mgmt. 5 (Spring 1984)

What real returns can be expected from investing in real estate over the long term? What are the risks and uncertainties surrounding these return expectations? How are these returns correlated with returns expected from other asset classes in a diversified portfolio?

Numerous empirical studies have been undertaken in an attempt to provide some indication of real estate's investment performance. Unfortunately, these studies are not directly comparable because they vary in so many dimensions: property type sampled, property location, time period covered, assumptions regarding degree of leverage, taxation, rate of return, and risk measures. Despite these differences, a great deal of valuable information on real estate performance has been collected. . . .

[One] group of measures is holding period returns, which account for all cash flows during the life cycle of the investment, both from annual operations and from changes in asset value. Our analysis includes only those studies employing holding period returns. Even within the group studied, there is considerable variation in application. Some studies measured returns before tax and others after tax. Returns were calculated on total investment in some studies and on leveraged equity in others.

The specific holding period return measures used in the studies reviewed are the internal rate of return (IRR) and the average annual rate of return (geometric mean). The IRR is a "dollar weighted" return that is applicable to measurement of the return on an investment or portfolio. The average annual return, on the other hand, is a "time weighted" return that is most appropriate for evaluating investment manager performance. Both measures produce the same results when the same initial capital is invested and there are no contributions or distributions of investment capital during the time over which we are measuring the return.

COMPARISON OF REAL ESTATE TO OTHER ASSET CLASSES

In making the asset allocation decision, the investor must compare the expected performance of real estate with other asset classes. We compared the historical performance of real estate to common stocks, bonds, and Treasury bills by examining measures of return, risk, and correlation. [See Exhibit 12.] The studies covering longer holding periods, and those analyzing returns in the 1950s and 1960s, tend to show roughly comparable returns from common stocks and real estate, with a slight edge to stocks. Note, however, that real estate returns during those "early" years were based on agricultural land or single-family home indexes and, where commercial properties were studied, conservative no-growth assumptions were employed.

The studies during inflationary periods of the 1970s were characterized by vastly improved real estate data bases. All of these studies concluded that real estate outperformed common stocks as well as fixed-income investments and the rate of inflation. For example, the nominal index returns of Hoag, CREFs, and MPI[8] were 14.2%, 14.0%, and 15.6% respectively, compared to common stock returns of 3.7%, 6.5%, and 10% reported by Ibbotson and Sinquefield for the corresponding time periods.[15]

In our examination of the standard deviation of returns, real estate returns appear less volatile than common stocks and corporate bonds. The standard deviation of CREF returns for 1973-1981 was 4.7%, compared to 21.2% for common stocks and 7.8% for corporate bonds. We can explain this differential in the standard deviation of real estate versus other asset classes in part by the way in which real estate returns are calculated and the method of periodic asset valuation. The real estate studies employing IRRs ignore any intermediate asset value changes during the holding period and thus implicitly assume a constant rate of change in value. The studies using average annual returns rely

8. For definitions of CREFs and MPI see footnote 3, supra. — ED.

15. Roger G. Ibbotson and Rex A. Sinquefield, Stocks, Bonds, Bills and Inflation: The Past and the Future, The Financial Analysts Research Foundation, 1982.

Comparison of Risk and Nominal Returns on Real Estate, Stocks, Bonds, and Treasury Bills

Study	Time Period	Real Estate	Common Stocks	Bonds	Treasury Bills	CPI
Ibbotson & Fall	1947-1978					
% Return		8.1	10.3	2.9	3.5	3.7
Std. Deviation		3.5	18.0	5.5	2.1	3.2
Coef. of Variation*		0.43	1.75	1.90	0.60	
R C & P	1951-1969					
% Return		9.5	11.9	1.3	3.0	2.2
Std. Deviation		4.5	17.4	5.0	1.5	1.8
Coef. of Variation		0.47	1.46	3.85	0.50	
McMahan	1951-1978					
% Return		13.9	11.4	3.5	3.9	3.7
Std. Deviation		3.8	18.3	6.7	1.9	3.0
Coef. of Variation		0.27	1.61	1.91	0.49	
% Return	1969-1978	18.0	4.8	6.2	6.0	6.7
Std. Deviation		1.5	18.4	8.8	1.3	2.6
Coef. of Variation		0.08	3.83	1.42	0.22	
Ricks**	1951-1978					
% Return		9.0	11.4	3.5	3.9	3.7
Std. Deviation		0.9	18.3	6.7	1.9	3.0
Coef. of Variation		0.10	1.61	1.91	0.49	
% Return	1969-1978	10.1	4.8	6.2	6.0	6.7
Std. Deviation		0.5	18.4	8.8	1.3	2.6
Coef. of Variation		0.50	3.83	1.42	0.22	
Kelleher	1960-1973					
% Return		13.2	7.2	3.8	4.3	3.3
Std. Deviation		5.1	14.0	6.7	1.5	2.3
Coef. of Variation		0.39	1.54	1.76	0.35	
Brachman	1970-1979					
% Return		10.3	4.7	5.6	6.3	7.4
Std. Deviation		4.9	19.6	8.0	1.8	3.4
Coef. of Variation		0.48	4.17	1.43	0.29	
Smith — REITs	1965-1977					
% Return		9.8	4.6	4.2	5.4	5.4
Std. Deviation		22.1	18.4	8.7	1.3	2.8
Coef. of Variation		2.26	4.00	2.07	0.24	
Burns & Epley	1970-1974					
% Return		3.0	–2.3	6.7	5.9	6.6
Std. Deviation		24.2	19.3	8.4	1.8	3.8
% Return	1975-1979	37.4	14.8	5.8	6.7	8.2
Std. Deviation		29.5	16.9	9.9	2.2	3.2
% Return	1970-1979	16.0	4.7	5.6	6.3	7.4
Std. Deviation		28.5	19.6	8.0	1.9	3.4
Coef. of Variation		1.78	4.17	1.43	0.30	

* The coefficient of variation measures the relative dispersion of the returns of the various investment classes and is calculated as follows:

$$\text{Coefficient of Variation} = \frac{\text{Standard Deviation}}{\text{Return}}.$$

** Not calculated in original study, but based on stated methodology, with the exception that capitalization rates were used as the proxy for income returns.

E x h i b i t   12 (Continued)

Comparison of Risk and Nominal Returns on Real Estate, Stocks, Bonds, and Treasury Bills

Study	Time Period	Real Estate	Common Stocks	Bonds	Treasury Bills	CPI
Hoag	1973-1978					
% Return		14.2	3.7	6.4	6.2	8.1
Std. Deviation		17.2	20.8	8.0	1.0	1.2
Coef. of Variation		1.21	5.62	1.25	0.16	
CREFs	1972-1981					
% Return		14.0	6.5	3.0	7.8	8.6
Std. Deviation		4.7	21.2	7.8	3.4	3.3
Coef. of Variation		0.34	3.26	2.60	0.44	
Morguard***	1973-1981					
% Return		18.5	10.1	4.2	N/A	9.8
Std. Deviation		8.3	21.9	8.4	N/A	2.0
Coef. of Variation		0.45	2.17	2.00		

*** All figures in Canadian dollars.

Source: Pension Real Estate Services, Inc.

on periodic property appraisals to establish unit or index values. Property appraisals are more reflective of the real estate's long term asset value and, consequently, are much less volatile than prices of frequently traded securities.

There were two exceptions to the above findings. Equity REIT returns exhibit essentially the same volatility as common stocks, which is not surprising since REIT shares are traded securities.[9] . . .

A relative measure of risk among investment classes with different rates of return is the amount of variation per unit of return, or coefficient of variation. The coefficient values shown in Exhibit 12 indicate that stock returns consistently contain the greatest relative variation, followed by bonds, real estate, and finally Treasury bills. The coefficient of variation of real estate exceeds that of bonds only in the case of the REITs.

In a portfolio context, we measure the risk of an investment by its contribution to the variance of overall portfolio returns. Therefore, riskiness of real estate returns is determined not only by its own variation, but also by its correlation with returns of other assets in the portfolio. . . .

THE SIGNIFICANCE OF THE EVIDENCE

The range of real rates of return from real estate based on studies during the period 1947 to the present was −6.8% to 19.5%. Both the

9. Equity real estate investment trusts (REITs) are discussed at Chapter 13A. — ED.

high and low values in this range came from returns on REITs, but REIT returns are much more volatile than those of other real estate investment vehicles. Excluding REIT results, real returns were positive over most periods and ranged from 1% to over 18%. The variance is further explained by the length of the period analyzed. Both the high and low results are from short holding periods (less than five years). Returns tended to stabilize after five years. . . .

The comparison of real estate to other investment classes indicates that real estate returns generally equaled or exceeded those from common stocks, particularly during the 1970s. Further, real estate returns were consistently greater than those of bonds, Treasury bills, and the rate of inflation. Due to arbitrage, returns on real estate investments are closely related to returns on alternative investments.

Over the long term, risk-adjusted returns on alternative investments would be expected to equalize. Historical returns on common stocks and bonds are available over much longer time periods than real estate. From 1926 to 1981, the average real return was 5.9% on common stocks, 0.5% on corporate bonds, and 0% on Treasury bills. To the extent that true risk is comparable, real estate returns would be expected to be closer to the returns on common stocks over the long term.

The relative risk of real estate, when measured by either standard deviation of returns or the coefficient of variation, appears to be less than that for common stocks. On the other hand, statistics measuring variability of returns tend to understate the actual volatility in real estate prices. When values are set by appraisals rather than transactions, they are much more stable because the appraisals are based on the long term underlying asset value. In real estate markets, a short run decline in property values is normally reflected in a reduced level of trading activity and longer marketing periods rather than in lower prices. . . .

Nevertheless, the risk of real estate as an asset class is measured by its contribution to the variation in total portfolio returns. The studies reviewed consistently found a negative correlation between real estate and common stock returns. This relationship may be the most important result of this study. Consequently, real estate has the potential to become an important diversification element in a portfolio because of its ability to add real returns, yet not increase the total variability of a portfolio's returns. . . .

T a b l e 2-1*

Comparative Returns, 1977-1984

Year	REITs Unrealized Appreciation	REITs Income Return	REITs Total Return	Pooled Real Estate Funds Unrealized Appreciation	Pooled Income Return	Pooled Total Return	S&P 500 Stocks Unrealized Appreciation	S&P Income Return	S&P Total Return	CPI
1977	10.1%	8.0%	18.1%	3.2%	8.8%	12.0%	-8.4%	4.6%	-3.8%	6.8%
1978	-8.5	8.4	-0.1	8.0	9.6	17.6	3.4	5.3	8.7	9.0
1979	18.0	10.7	28.7	11.2	9.6	20.8	8.4	5.5	13.9	13.3
1980	10.5	9.7	20.2	8.9	9.3	18.2	26.4	5.3	31.7	12.4
1981	-0.2	9.5	9.3	7.7	9.0	16.7	-8.2	5.2	-3.0	8.9
1982	16.1	10.0	26.1	0.6	8.5	9.1	11.9	5.8	17.7	3.9
1983	15.8	9.6	25.4	5.6	8.3	13.9	21.2	5.4	26.6	3.8
1984	3.9	9.2	13.1	5.3	8.4	13.7	-0.3	4.6	4.3	4.0
Arithmetic mean	8.2%	9.4%	17.6%	6.3%	8.9%	15.2%	6.8%	5.2%	12.0%	7.8%

Note: Income returns are averages for the year; appreciation reflects fourth quarter to fourth-quarter changes.

Sources: *National Association of Real Estate Investment Trusts; Real Estate Profiles, Real Estate Associates, Evaluation Associates, Westport, Connecticut, 1985; Standard & Poor's; Board of Governors of the Federal Reserve System; U.S. Bureau of Labor Statistics; Real Estate Research Corporation.*

Reprinted with permission from "Emerging Trends in Real Estate: 1986," prepared for Equitable Real Estate Group, Inc. by Real Estate Research Corporation, Chicago, Illinois.

* Additional comparisons of real estate with common stocks and bonds include Hartzell and Shulman, Real Estate Returns and Risks: A Survey (Salomon Brothers, Inc., 1988) and Real Estate in the Portfolio (Salomon Brothers, Inc., 1986). — ED.

Maisel, Inflation, Leverage, Vacancies, Taxes, and Returns to Office Buildings
3-10 (Salomon Brothers, Inc., March 1987)

The Effect of Leverage on Yields and Discount Rates. To many individuals, a major attribute of real estate investments is the ability to fund a substantial part of an investment with other people's money (one form of leverage). In contrast, pension funds, insurance companies and other institutional investors often own property without borrowed funds.

If the debt service is fixed, leverage becomes one of the main causes for cash flows to differ from projections. The mechanism through which leverage affects yields, both in cases where inflation is correctly anticipated and in those where it is not, is important in projecting yields.

Three basic types of leverage exist:

(1)　Financial leverage (the main type considered in this paper) arises when borrowing fixes the debt service. This causes any movements in net operating income to have a magnified impact on the equity's yield. The smaller the equity, the greater the impact.

(2)　Operating leverage occurs as a result of differences between the movements of income and expenses. Since successful

F i g u r e   1

The Effect of Leverage on the Return on Equity from Operating Income

($1,000,000 Purchase Price; $100,000 Annual NOI)[a]

Leverage Ratio	Equity (000)	Return on Capital Assets (ROR)	Positive Leverage (ROR > K)		Negative Leverage (ROR < K)	
			Debt Service Constant (K)	Return on Equity	Debt Service Constant (K)	Return on Equity
0%	$1,000	10%	9%	10.0%	11%	10.0%
25	750	10	9	10.3	11	9.7
50	500	10	9	11.0	11	9.0
80	200	10	9	14.0	11	6.0
90	100	10	9	19.0	11	1.0

[a] An interest-only mortgage is assumed for this example, so the debt service constant K is equal to the mortgage interest rate m.

Figure 2

The Effect of Leverage on the Return from Appreciation and the Internal Rate of Return

($1,000,000 Purchase Price; $1,100,000 Sales Price, Five-Year Holding Period)

| Leverage Ratio | Equity | | Percentage Appreciation | | Internal Rate of Return from Operations and Appreciation |
	Down Payment (000)	Cash on Sale (000)	Total	Compounded Per Year	
0%	$1,000	$1,100	10.0%	1.9%	11.6%
25	750	850	13.3	2.5	12.4
50	500	600	20.0	3.7	14.0
80	200	300	50.0	8.4	20.6
90	100	200	100.0	14.9	30.0

projects have expenses lower than income, an equal percentage growth of both will increase the NOI and the cash flow to the equity.

(3) Tax leverage arises primarily because depreciation deductions reduce taxable income, and such savings are concentrated on the equity. To the extent that the deductions are higher than actual depreciation, the return to equity is shielded from current taxes.

When future cash flows are projected, the effect of leverage automatically enters into the estimated yields and the price of a property. Financial leverage alters yields (and perhaps the price) of a property through both the operating period cash flow and, if the sales price differs from the purchase price, through the amount received upon sale. The amount by which leverage alters yields depends on the difference between the rate of interest and amortization (the debt service constant K) and the overall return on the capital assets (ROR), on the amount of appreciation or depreciation, and on the leverage ratio.

Figure 1 illustrates that if the return on assets exceeds the debt constant, then the greater the leverage, the higher are operating returns on equity. The effects of leverage on the return on equity rise as the leverage percentage increases. On the other hand, as the last two columns show, a negative gap between the return on capital and debt service means that leverage reduces yields, again with a multiplied effect that depends on the leverage ratio.

The first five columns of Figure 2 illustrate the impacts from appreciation and depreciation. Again, the larger the leverage ratio, the greater the degree of multiplication. The final column shows the combined effects resulting from leverage through changes in both the operating cash flows and cash flows upon sale. . . .

INFLATION AND REAL ESTATE RETURNS

A major attraction of real estate investments is that, unlike bonds and common stocks, their nominal yields rise with both anticipated and unanticipated inflation. If the inflation is fully anticipated, real pretax yields will remain as projected no matter what the level of inflation. Price-corrected returns are not affected by inflation because buyers, sellers and lenders correct for the actual inflation. More important, if inflation is greater than expected, real returns will increase, thus offering protection against what would be unpleasant surprises in most portfolios. Contrariwise, if inflation falls below that anticipated at the time of purchase, real returns will fall. . . .

Real estate acts as a hedge against unexpected inflation: Nominal and real returns both increase if prices rise faster than anticipated, and both fall when the rate of inflation drops below the expected level. Moreover, while returns in both leveraged and nonleveraged situations are not affected by correctly anticipated inflation, leverage serves to multiply the returns when actual earnings differ from projected ones. The greater the degree of leverage, the higher the yields that result from unanticipated inflation.

At the time of purchase, prices are based on projected net operating income and a projected inflation rate. If actual revenues differ from projections, actual income will also differ, as will actual real yields.

Real estate is a protection against inflation to the degree that, in equilibrium, rents depend on the level of replacement cost. If demand is expanding, new construction is necessary. Vacancies check increases in effective rents and may cause them to fall. Rents below the level required to make new construction profitable halt new building. In a growing economy, vacancies will eventually disappear. Rents and selling prices will rise to levels consistent with replacement costs. Developers will not build unless they expect a profit. If lenders allow developers to "mortgage out" — that is, to make a profit from the development process irrespective of operating and sales prices — developers need not pay attention to the market vacancies. However, at some point lenders will refuse additional loans if vacancies, new rent levels and property prices lead to defaults. . . .

Acting together, leverage and unanticipated inflation were major causes of the high returns to real property in the late 1970s and of the high (incorrectly projected) expected returns of the early 1980s. . . .

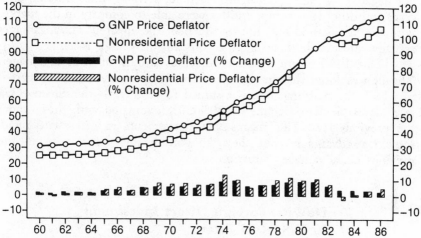

F i g u r e 5

Inflation in the General Price Level and for Nonresidential Structures 1960–85

(1982 = 100)

Source: U.S. Department of Commerce, Bureau of Economic Analysis.

INFLATION AND REPLACEMENT COSTS

Although we speak of real estate as a protection against general inflation, this holds true only to the extent that inflation and building replacement costs move in tandem. How close is this relationship? Figure 5 plots the year-to-year percentage changes in an index of general inflation and in the cost of constructing nonresidential structures. (Both are based on the gross national product [GNP] implicit price indexes, with a base in 1982 equal to 100.) We note from this figure that over the past 25 years the price index for nonresidential structures has increased at a somewhat faster pace than have prices in general. The annual average rate of construction inflation over the period was 5.8%, compared with a 5.3% gain for prices in general.

TAXES

The tax system has been of great significance to individual investors in real estate. Prior to the Tax Reform Act of 1986, high depreciation deductions, the ability to take tax advantage of nonrecourse loans, the capital gains exclusion, and the right to reduce taxable income from other sources by paper losses meant that the after-tax rate of return on heavily leveraged properties was somewhat higher than the before-tax yields. The ability to postpone taxes to a later period and then be taxed at the lower capital gains rate meant that taxes had a positive — not negative — impact on yields. Even so, pension funds, foreign concerns and other tax-exempt entities were able to compete in the market with the tax-assisted individuals. Much of the apparent tax advantages actually reflected high leverage accompanied by high risks.

[T]he Tax Reform Act of 1986 removed most of these advantages. The figures show that in the specific cases examined in this paper — in which the marginal rate is assumed to be 33% — the effective tax rate causes yields to decline by 20%-30% compared with those under the previous law. This means that investments in real estate retain some tax advantages, but they are considerably lower than in the previous tax-advantaged situation. . . .

DeWitt, Foreign Direct Investment in U.S. Real Estate
16 Real Est. Rev. 66 (Winter 1987)

Historically, the rising value of the dollar relative to other currencies made U.S. real estate investment attractive. One could invest in U.S. real estate and realize a potential economic gain, not only from the appreciation of the property but from a rising dollar-denominated investment. In recent years the dollar had achieved new heights against "hard" European currencies and the Canadian dollar. This fact had propelled many European and Canadian investors out of their national currencies and into dollar-denominated real estate. The continuing strength of the dollar has made U.S. properties more expensive, but this has been offset by a European perception that U.S. properties are bargains compared with domestic purchases.[10]

The U.S. market remained attractive to foreign investors for several reasons in addition to exchange rate considerations. For instance, despite faster rates of economic growth in countries such as Japan, West

---

10. The recent fluctuations in the value of the U.S. dollar have introduced the element of currency speculation into the U.S. real estate market. Suppose, for example, that a Japanese investor purchases some U.S. real estate for $10 million when the dollar is trading at or about 130 yen. (On November 29, 1988 the dollar closed at 212.83 yen.) If the property were to appreciate at a rate of 10 percent, a gain of $1 million or 130 million yen would be recognized. If the U.S. dollar were to rise against the yen to 150 yen, the institution would recognize an extra gain of 20 million yen, or $133,333.33. — ED.

Germany, and France, the United States has maintained its reputation for political and economic stability, good labor relations, and relatively limited government intervention in private enterprise.

Additionally, for some investors, particularly those from soft currency countries like Mexico or Argentina, a flight into dollar-denominated real estate can protect their wealth from continuing currency devaluations at home.

A recent in-depth study of foreign investment in real estate revealed that about 90 percent of the money that flowed into real estate investment in the United States during 1980 to 1984 was from six countries: Canada, the United Kingdom, the Netherlands, the Netherlands Antilles, Germany, and Japan. Exhibit 1 illustrates the foreign direct investment position in the United States and capital inflow in real estate by major country and area for 1980-1985. . . .

A LONG-RUN FORECAST

For the long term, the prospects for foreign investment in U.S. real estate appear bright. The dollar has stabilized against most major currencies and strengthened against many. The Tax Reform Act of 1986 has finally been passed, and the problems with the national debt, although serious, certainly do not outweigh other important investment considerations.

STABILITY AND YIELDS WILL ATTRACT PRIVATE INVESTORS

Foreign investors continue to believe that the U.S. real estate market is the largest and most stable national marketplace. It provides them with opportunities to diversify risk by investing in a wide variety of different types of property. In addition, although the rents in some U.S. cities seem to be lower than rents in other major cities of the world, the yields on U.S. investments are more attractive because of a lower tax burden and higher growth rates, especially in Sun Belt states.

Exhibit 2 indicates that in 1985, even though London leads the international rent list with $81.83 per square foot, U.S. cities like New York ($67.72 per square foot), Chicago ($33.53 per square foot), Los Angeles ($36.35 per square foot), and San Francisco ($42.50 per square foot) represent extremely attractive values when compared with European cities where high rents are consumed by equally high taxes. In London, taxes are 52 percent in the Center City and 33 percent in the West End. When one compares the rent per square foot after taxes, U.S. cities appear relatively attractive. Far Eastern cities are

E x h i b i t   1

Foreign Direct Investment Position in the United States 1980-1985

	All Industries						Real Estate					
	1980	1981	1982	1983	1984	1985	1980	1981	1982	1983	1984	1985
All countries	83,046ᵃ	107,590	123,590	135,313	164,583	182,951	6,120	8,889	11,397	13,946	17,761	18,557
Canada	12,162	11,870	11,435	11,115	15,286	16,678	1,158	1,770	1,882	2,106	2,844	2,580
Europe	54,688	71,945	82,767	92,481	108,211	120,906	2,254	3,675	5,035	6,638	8,255	8,821
European Communities (10)	47,107	63,731	73,540	82,217	96,555	106,004	2,119	3,450	4,651	6,224	7,714	8,238
Belgium	1,554	1,891	1,908	2,198	3,548	2,288	4	9	11	10	10	9
France	3,731	5,833	5,666	6,045	6,591	6,295	24	24	24	28	66	26
Germany	7,596	9,239	9,683	10,482	12,330	14,417	493	651	780	815	966	1,049
Italy	408	808	1,105	1,254	1,438	1,401	4	4	5	3	0	—ᵇ
Luxembourg	261	290	347	316	753	584	23	28	29	25	0	24
Netherlands	19,140	26,800	25,994	28,817	33,728	36,124	999	1,507	1,742	2,189	2,471	2,325
United Kingdom	14,105	18,471	28,386	32,512	38,387	43,766	569	1,220	2,051	3,140	4,135	4,623
Denmark, Greece, and Ireland	311	399	451	593	779	1,129	2	7	11	12	42	—ᵇ
Other Europe	7,582	8,215	9,227	10,264	11,655	14,902	135	225	384	414	541	583
Sweden	1,670	1,690	1,731	2,067	2,258	2,386	0	0	0	0	0	0
Switzerland	5,070	5,458	6,391	7,132	8,146	11,040	80	150	300	324	393	444
Other	842	1,067	1,105	1,065	1,251	1,478	56	75	84	90	148	139

Japan	4,723	7,688	9,679	11,145	16,044	19,116	264	302	394	457	744	1,054
Australia, New Zealand, and South Africa	428	685	838	945	2,152	2,702	56	55	60	61	120	117
Latin America	9,678	11,300	13,833	14,379	16,201	17,050	1,979	2,566	3,273	3,816	4,664	1,808
South and Central America	1,260	1,401	2,763	2,852	2,859	3,385	233	268	313	379	372	307
Panama	811	897	2,135	2,128	1,924	2,137	171	185	216	275	256	139
Other	449	504	628	724	935	1,248	62	83	98	103	116	108
Other Western Hemisphere	8,418	9,899	11,070	11,527	13,343	13,665	1,746	2,298	1,959	3,437	4,292	4,501
Bermuda	727	688	978	849	1,370	1,903	61	111	119	108	151	110
Netherlands Antilles	6,651	8,196	9,205	9,546	10,935	10,603	1,437	1,880	2,547	2,973	3,715	3,945
U.K. Islands, Caribbean	640	726	663	906	866	983	228	265	238	273	369	399
Other	400	289	223	225	172	177	20	43	55	83	57	47
Middle East	916	3,586	4,404	4,435	5,336	4,961	—[b]	362	542	597	709	746
Israel	324	312	428	450	525	505	—[c]	0	0	0	0	1
Other	592	3,273	3,976	3,985	4,811	4,455	—[b]	362	542	597	709	745
Other Africa, Asia, and Pacific	450	515	635	814	1,353	1,538	—[b]	160	212	271	423	430
Memorandum — OPEC	642	3,335	4,047	4,058	4,892	4,560	300	373	551	610	707	737

[a] Dollars in millions.
[b] Suppressed to avoid disclosure of data to individual companies.
[c] Less than $500,000 (±).

Source: Survey of Current Business, Oct. 1984, at 37-38, June 1985, at 32, Aug. 1985, at 52; U.S. Department of Commerce, News, June 25, 1986, at 6.

E x h i b i t   2

World Rent Levels

Cities	Rents Per Sq. Ft. 1984	Rents Per Sq. Ft. 1985	Percent Rent for Taxes 1984	Percent Rent for Taxes 1985	Rents Per Sq. Ft. After Taxes 1984	Rents Per Sq. Ft. After Taxes 1985
New York						
Midtown	$67.92	$67.72	12%	23%	$59.77	$52.14
Downtown		50.32		31		34.72
Chicago	36.67	33.53	15	25	31.17	25.15
Los Angeles	36.89	36.35	6	10	34.68	32.72
San Francisco	42.61	42.50	6	12	40.05	37.40
Amsterdam	11.88	10.94	1	15	11.76	9.30
Barcelona	8.10	9.36	5	5	7.70	8.89
Brussels	10.00	11.17	11	17	8.90	9.27
Frankfurt	18.22	16.23	1	1	18.04	16.07
Glasgow	19.99	22.11	65	73	7.00	5.97
Hong Kong	36.48	39.00	10	5	32.83	37.05
London						
City	76.16	81.83	55	52	34.27	39.29
West End	50.24	57.33	40	33	30.14	38.41
Madrid	13.38	15.20	5	5	12.71	14.44
Manchester	17.75	19.43	54	51	8.17	9.42
Melbourne	22.75	23.80	12	12	20.02	20.94
Paris	29.04	37.27	5	4	27.59	35.78
Perth	16.86	14.40	16	18	14.16	11.81
Sao Paulo	14.51	12.16	5	5	13.78	11.55
Singapore	40.58	29.53	30	19	28.41	23.92
Sydney	32.58	27.05	10	6	29.32	25.42
Tokyo	61.08	71.39	10	10	54.97	64.25

Source: N.Y. Times, May 12, 1984, at 12; R. Ellis, World Rental Levels: Offices, Nov. 1985.

exceptions to this generalization. Tokyo commercial properties, for example, command a high rent ($71.39 per square foot), but are subject to a low tax burden (10 percent).

Although U.S. rents after taxes continue to be attractive, the percentage of rent used for taxes in the United States increased considerably in 1985. A comparison of the percentage of rent used for taxes in 1984 and 1985 reveals the following: in midtown New York it rose from 12 percent to 23 percent; in Chicago, from 15 percent to 25 percent; in Los Angeles, from 6 percent to 10 percent; and in San Francisco, from 6 percent to 12 percent. The decline in after-tax rents may have contributed to the decrease in U.S. real estate acquisitions by foreigners in the United States in 1985.

For the long pull, U.S. real estate is attractive, because U.S.

Figure 2-1

Japanese Investment Flows to U.S. Real Estate, Pre-1984-88P

(Dollars in Billions)

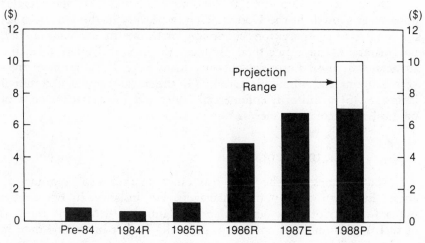

E Estimate.
P Projection.   R Revised.

Source: Salomon Brothers Inc., Japanese Investment in U.S. Real Estate: An Update
(Feb. 17, 1988).

properties have fewer restrictions on property ownership and transfer compared with overseas properties. Moreover, development controls are moderate when compared with the rigid standards of some European countries. One would expect these factors to encourage international investment in U.S. real estate. U.S. real estate continues to be a haven from the political and economic instability found in other nations and a hedge against the inflation and currency devaluations, especially in soft currency nations, currently being experienced in many parts of the world.

PENSION FUND INVESTMENTS

Recently, a number of European pension funds have been buying into the U.S. real estate market. A Dutch pension fund, the Dutch Institutional Holding Company, has recently invested in the 730-acre Grand Cypress Resort in Orlando, Fla. One reason for these investments seems to be the lower rates of growth in many European economies. This is particularly true for the United Kingdom, where low rates of growth have been endemic and the falling British pound has encouraged British pension funds to move into stronger currencies.

European pension funds are also concerned about political stability. This is especially true in Great Britain, France, and Italy where the threat of increasing public sector control of the economy has been encouraging domestic capitalists to invest abroad.[6]

Other factors important to pension fund managers include: (1) population growth in the United States, especially in the Sun Belt; (2) the long-term prospects for economic growth due to abundant energy, raw materials, and agricultural products; (3) U.S. real estate financing advantages (typical European property loans have a maximum of five-year balloons and adjustable rates);[7] (4) the advantages of a common language; (5) a uniform commercial code; and (6) a track record of political and economic success.[8]

LACK OF REGULATIONS

The openness of the U.S. real estate market also continues to attract European pension fund managers. For instance, in Europe the use and density of every acre of land is planned in detail, and the cost of such regulations and controls is generally higher in Europe than in the United States.

The openness of the U.S. marketplace to foreign investors is also reinforced by the absence of federal government restrictions. The U.S. government imposes no restrictions on the ownership of U.S. real estate by foreign persons or entities. With some minor exceptions discussed below, there are no federal restrictions on the investment of capital in the United States by nonresidents. There are no restrictions on the repatriation of earnings or the convertibility of dollars. Some *states,* however, do require that real estate within the state be owned by a domestic corporation or by a person or entity resident within the state.

Most foreign countries, on the other hand, have stringent requirements governing rules and areas of foreign direct investment, and they also impose exchange control regulations.

Most of the federal limitations on U.S. real estate investments are concerned with disclosure. The main reporting requirements are imposed by the following legislation:

- The Agricultural Foreign Investment Disclosure Act of 1978 (AFIDA) requires the registration of agricultural land held by a foreign investor.

---

6. Investment in U.S. Real Estate, Urban Land 3 (1982).
7. Id. at 9-11.
8. Friedman, The Truth About Foreign Investors in U.S. Real Estate, 11 Real Est. Rev. 13-14 (1981).

- The International Investment Survey of 1976 (ILSA) requires that each U.S. business enterprise in which a foreign person owns or controls a direct or indirect interest of 10 percent or more file a disclosure with the U.S. Department of Commerce.
- The Foreign Investment in Real Property Tax Act (FIRPTA) requires (as of January 1, 1985) that buyers of properties owned by foreign investors withhold 10 percent of the purchase price for the Internal Revenue Service.

By and large, however, with the exception of these disclosure requirements, the U.S. market for foreign direct investment remains one of the most open and least regulated in the world. The positive regulatory environment, stability, and capital appreciation of U.S. properties denominated in stable dollars continue to make the U.S. marketplace in real estate attractive to foreign investors. . . . Real estate investments should, therefore, buck the declining tide of foreign direct investment flows in the United States.

NOTES AND QUESTIONS

1. *Economic Risks and Rewards.* As of this writing, rents and prices in some overbuilt real estate markets (e.g., office buildings) are sagging because of the untimely convergence of some macroeconomic factors including a credit stringency problem caused primarily by the weakened condition of the U.S. banking industry and the adverse impact of the Tax Reform Act of 1986 on real estate tax shelter. See Chapter 4D. Over the long run, however, real estate has performed well in comparison to other investments such as stocks and bonds. Among the more prominent events affecting U.S. capital markets during the second half of the twentieth century have been the introduction of inflation into the economy and the burgeoning of real estate values. Between 1947 and 1982 a general index of total income and appreciation returns from income-producing real estate increased approximately seventeenfold, for a compounded annual rate of 8.3 percent. Even more impressive, these figures represent the total returns from *unleveraged* real estate, and since most real estate investors held leveraged real estate and obtained significant tax-shelter benefits (especially since 1981, when depreciation benefits were increased by the Economic Recovery Tax Act of 1981), their after-tax leveraged rates of return were much higher. See generally Ibbotson and Siegal, Real Estate Returns: A Comparison with Other Investments, 12 AREUEA J. 219, Table 2 at 229-230 (1984). What demographic factors might explain, in part, the histor-

ically high rate of appreciation in the value of real estate during this period?

As observed by Zerbst and Cambon, the attraction of income-producing real estate compared to alternative investments can be explained to some extent by the following economic factors: (1) historically, the rates of income and appreciation returns from real estate have been higher than for stocks and bonds, most researchers say; (2) real estate generally appears to be a less volatile and less risky portfolio investment, as reflected by its lower standard deviation of returns and lower coefficient of variation, respectively, compared to common stocks and corporate bonds; and (3) real estate is superior to stocks and bonds as a hedge against inflation (also suggested by Maisel). On relative investment performance, see generally Ibbotson and Siegel, Real Estate Returns: A Comparison with Other Investments, 12 AREUEA J. 219 (1984); Kelleher, How Real Estate Stacks up to the S&P 500, 6 Real Est. Rev. 60 (Summer 1976); Wendt and Wong, Investment Performance: Common Stocks Versus Apartment Houses, 20 J. Fin. 633 (Dec. 1965). Regarding relative risks and volatility, see generally Hartzell and Shulman, Real Estate Returns and Risks: A Survey (Salomon Brothers, 1988); Liebowitz, Total Portfolio Duration: A New Perspective on Asset Allocation (Salomon Brothers, 1986).

In addition, because of the negative correlation between real estate and common stock (income and appreciation) returns most commentators agree with Zerbst and Cambon that an investor's overall portfolio risk can be reduced by combining real estate with stocks and other portfolio assets. See, e.g., Hartzell, Real Estate in the Portfolio (Salomon Brothers, 1986). Based on your general understanding of macroeconomics, can you think of the reason for this negative correlation? Why is real estate (other than REIT shares) a less volatile portfolio asset than stocks and bonds? Why, do you think, is the portfolio risk factor higher for stocks and bonds than for real estate and Treasury bills?

Zerbst and Cambon report that between the total returns from stocks, corporate bonds, and Treasury bills and the rate of inflation, the highest positive correlation is between real estate and the rate of inflation. This suggests that real estate is a better hedge against inflation than are stocks and bonds. But why is this so? There is no easy answer. During periods of economic expansion and inflation, when the economy is reaching its full capacity, the demand for short-term credit by business borrowers, combined with the anti-inflation actions of the Federal Reserve Board, tends to tighten the supply of loanable funds and drive up the level of short-term interest rates (and eventually long-term interest rates as well). This increase in interest rates usually crowds out the leverage-minded real estate borrower, who is more sensitive to interest-rate fluctuations than other borrowers because such a large portion of a real estate owner's operating expenses consists of mortgage

F i g u r e   2-2

Real Estate, Stocks, and Inflation

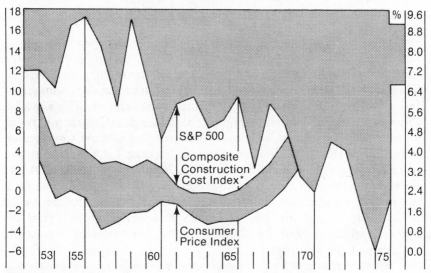

Chart prepared by   All series are 5 year compounded
The Boston Company, Inc.   annual growth rates.

*Composed of
DOECKH INDICES
ENG. NEWS-RECORD INDEX
DEPT. OF COMM. INDEX

Source: The Mortgage and Real Estate Executive's Rpt. 1 (July 1, 1977).

interest charges. Therefore, in times of inflation, when interest rates
are high, the market for existing commercial real estate should generally
decline much as a jump in mortgage rates tends to slacken sales and
prices for single-family residential real estate. But historically this has
not been the case. One of the reasons, as suggested by Maisel in the
foregoing excerpt, is the correlation between inflation and replacement
or construction costs. As noted above, during periods of inflation short-
term interest rates rise (as explained at Chapter 4D and Chapter 6A),
increasing the cost of construction financing, and the extra construction-
period interest coupled with inflationary increases in the costs of labor
and materials (as measured by the so-called Construction Cost Index
(CCI)) causes an increase in building replacement costs. For example,
as reflected by Figure 2-2, the CCI increased at a faster pace than the
Consumer Price Index (CPI) between 1952 and 1975. By contrast,
during the same period Standard & Poor's Index of 500 generally
moved contrary to changes in the rate of inflation.

After carefully reviewing the excerpt by Maisel, can you explain why the CCI/CPI relationship has helped make the ownership of existing income-producing real estate (especially well-located and well-built properties) a relatively good hedge against inflation? To answer the question you need to understand a fundamental principle concerning the valuation of income-producing real estate: namely, that the appraised market value of a piece of rental real estate will depend *directly* on how much net operating income it produces. As suggested by the excerpts on measuring profitability, and as more fully explained at Chapter 5B1, note 2, the chief method of appraisal for commercial and multifamily real estate is the "income approach," in which market value is determined by dividing the anticipated net operating rental income (NOI) by a risk-adjusted market rate of interest (or discount factor) called the "capitalization rate," or "cap rate." A simple example: assume that an office building yields one million dollars of NOI and the appraiser selects a cap rate of 10 percent. Under the income approach, the market value of the building would be $1 million divided by 10 percent, or $10 million (or "ten times earnings"), which figure the appraiser would confirm by checking recent sale prices of comparable buildings in the same area.

Another reason why real estate acts as a hedge against inflation is that rental real estate is one of the few types of assets whose value is protected by lease provisions (called "escalation clauses") that pass certain cost increases (e.g., increases in insurance premiums and local property taxes) to tenant-users. Other inflation hedges employed by owner-landlords include the use of percentage rentals and shorter lease terms. See Chapter 5C. Can you think of any other reasons that might explain why real estate has been a good hedge against inflation? Additional reasons are suggested by Maisel.

As Zerbst and Cambon point out, real estate has been, relatively speaking, a better hedge against inflation than either stocks or bonds. In the case of bonds the explanation is straightforward. During periods of inflation, when interest rates rise, the prices of existing bonds tend to fall because of their lower interest rates; conversely, when interest rates drop the prices of existing bonds tend to rise. For example, a 30-year Treasury bond issued in January 1989 at an annual rate of 10 percent obviously became more valuable in July 1989 when comparable bonds were being issued with only an 8 percent interest rate.

The explanation for the weaker performance of common stocks as an inflation hedge is not so simple. Certainly, as a matter of supply and demand, during periods of inflation, when interest rates rise, there is usually a shift in investment capital from stocks to higher-paying bonds, and the resultant softening in demand for stocks will obviously depress their market value as measured by the Dow-Jones and Standard & Poor's indices. Theoretically, however, common stock, like real estate, should in the long run be a relatively good hedge against inflation. Why? In that regard don't forget that a share of common stock is nothing more than an indirect ownership or proprietary interest in the property owned by the corporation.

The negative side of the real estate coin is its lack of liquidity as an investment. Investment shares in equity REITs have been publicly traded for a number of years (and were spared from the debacle in mortgage REITs in the early 1970s), and there is a recent trend towards securitization of real estate, on both the equity and the debt side, as exemplified by the master limited partnership (MLP) (whose investment shares are also publicly traded as "depositary receipts" on the public securities exchanges). See discussion at Chapter 13A, note 1. However, as explained at Chapter 2B, note 7di, infra, most investment shares in commercial real estate are held by limited partners, who have no access to any formal secondary market for trading or liquidating their shares, and consequently the inimitable liquidity of publicly held corporate stocks and bonds constitutes a distinct investment advantage for corporate equities compared to real estate. Can you think of any other economic reasons for investing in stocks and bonds rather than in real estate?

2. High-Ratio Financing Available for Real Estate. In the world of real estate financing, the mortgage portfolios of most institutional lenders such as life insurance companies, commercial banks, savings and loan associations, and mutual savings banks are regulated by state statutes (or by federal regulations in the case of federally chartered banks and savings associations) that specify maximum loan-to-value ratios (expressed as a percentage of appraised value) and amortization requirements depending on the nature of the real property that secures the mortgage loan. For example, the maximum loan-to-value ratio on the postconstruction ("permanent") financing of nonresidential income-producing real estate (e.g., office buildings and shopping centers) is 75 or 80 percent for life insurance companies (in most jurisdictions). See, e.g., Va. Code Ann. §38.2-1437(A)(3) (1990). It is 90 percent for federally chartered savings and loan associations and savings banks. 12 C.F.R. §545.32(d)(3). As a general rule most institutional lenders lend at or near the maximum loan-to-value ratio. See Table 5-1, at Chapter 5B1, for a tabulation of average loan-to-value ratios on multifamily and commercial mortgage loans made by U.S. life insurance companies from 1979 to the present. Can you think of an underwriting or business reason why this is so? See generally Schacht, Mortgages: Leveraging Real Estate, 38 Inst. on Fed. Taxn. §14.01 (1980); Goggans, Leverage — A Strategy for Real Estate Investments, 58 Taxes 89 (1980).

As illustrated by the example at Chapter 2A, supra, financial leverage allows a real estate borrower to increase its income and appreciation pretax rates of return. In addition, as Maisel points out, so-called operating leverage produces another benefit for the real estate investor: it enables the real estate owner to increase his equity in the investment. Simply defined, "equity" means net assets (e.g., real estate assets minus mortgage liabilities) and, as such, is a way of measuring for accounting purposes either the book value of the real estate (if the asset is reflected at cost) or its cash value (if the asset is reflected at its market value). See Chapter 9A, note 2. For example, in the example of the moderately leveraged real estate syndication in the excerpt by Madison and Dwyer at Chapter 2B, infra, the assumed rate of inflation is 4 percent for purposes of calculating the estimated revenues and expenses during the 8-year holding period of the property. Can you explain why any assumption as to a positive rate of inflation will cause an increase in each limited partner-investor's share of equity in the project? Tax leverage is discussed at Chapter 2B, note 1, infra.

Observe that the largest proportion of multifamily and commercial real estate in this country is either directly owned or indirectly owned by private investors such as partners in a privately held limited partnership or shareholders in a Subchapter S corporation. Real estate ownership entities are discussed at §2B, note 7, infra. While such private partnerships and Subchapter S corporations hold legal title to the underlying real estate assets, there is a direct pass-through of taxable income or loss, net refinancing proceeds, and net sale proceeds when the property is sold. Hence, when these pass-through ownership entities leverage their acquisition and construction costs, the investors directly benefit from such financial leverage and, based on their leveraged income and appreciation returns, are able to calculate their yield to maturity from their interests in the underlying real estate. See Table 13-1, at Chapter 13A, which diagrams the difference in tax and financial consequences of direct versus indirect ownership of income-producing real estate. By contrast, owners of publicly traded stock do not receive such pass-through benefits and their dividend-income and appreciation returns are not as directly related to the way in which the assets of the corporation are financed. The closest analogue on the real estate side (other than an ordinary Subchapter C corporation that owns real estate and whose shares are publicly traded) would be an open-ended equity REIT. See discussion at Chapter 13A.

In contrast to leverage-minded real estate developers and investors (who have a penchant for using other people's money and even dream about 100 percent financing, as discussed at Chapter 9D), stock and bond investors shy away from leveraging the cost of acquiring their ownership shares. Indeed, as explained below, only a small fraction of corporate investors buy on margin. Perhaps this is because they may be able to achieve the risk-return objectives they seek by carefully assessing the risk-return characteristics of available securities based on annual reports (and other past-performance data) and the help provided by advisory services. This kind of detailed evaluative information is not as readily available to real estate developers and private investors, whose ownership interests are not publicly regulated and traded the way most corporate securities are. So, for example, a high-risk-oriented investor who pays cash for risky securities may be tantamount to the investor who buys a less risky portfolio on margin. Is the all-cash purchaser of stock in a highly leveraged company that's been recently acquired in a hostile takeover (by means of a leveraged buyout) analogous to a real estate investor in a limited partnership who pays all cash for her indirect ownership interest in some leveraged real estate that is directly owned by the partnership? In what respect does the analogy fail?

Another major reason why investors tend to avoid buying corporate securities on margin is that regulatory constraints are imposed by the Federal Reserve Board and the New York Stock Exchange. A complex system of regulations governs the purchase of securities on credit and the use of securities as collateral. A securities broker may not extend credit to a customer for the purchase of securities in an amount exceeding 50 percent of the market value of securities in the customer's account (after excluding the value of thinly traded securities). Securities Exchange Act §7, 15 U.S.C. §78g (1982); Regulation T, 12 C.F.R. §§220.1 to 220.130 (1990). The Federal Reserve Board is also responsible for regulating the extension or maintenance of securities credit by others, and thus it regulates the extension of securities credit by banks, Regulation U, 12 C.F.R. §§221.1 to 221.123 (1989), and certain other lenders, Regulation G, 12 C.F.R. §§207.1 to 207.112 (1989). The Board also regulates the obtaining of securities credit by United States persons. See Securities Exchange Act §7(f), 15 U.S.C. §78g(f) (1982); Regulation X, 12 C.F.R. §§224.1 to 224.3 (1989). The Board's regulations do not require brokers to demand more collateral if the value of the securities in a margin account declines, but industry practice and the rules of the various self-regulatory organizations to which all brokers belong do require customers to maintain the value of collateral. For example, with limited exceptions, members of the New York Stock Exchange must require their customers to maintain an equity of at least 25 percent of the market value of the securities in their margin accounts. N.Y.S.E. Rule 431, N.Y.S.E. Guide (CCH) ¶2431; see also N.A.S.D. Rules of Fair Practice §30, N.A.S.D. Manual (CCH) ¶2180. Brokerage firms are free to require higher margins on their own, and they often do. These maintenance requirements impose a continuing and potentially substantial burden on those who trade securities on credit, for if the market value of an investor's portfolio falls he may be required to provide more collateral or liquidate. Perhaps because of the high margin requirements and the possibility of margin calls, relatively few securities investors trade on margin. For example, according to the New York Stock Exchange, over 47 million Americans owned common stocks in 1985 (many by means of mutual funds); however, there were only about 2,550,000 margin accounts held by NYSE member firms. 1988 New York Stock Exchange Fact Book 60-61, 82 (1988).

3. Measuring the Profitability of Real Estate Investments. If necessary, review the relevant excerpts above. A standard real estate calculator of the Hewlett-Packard or Texas Instruments variety can speed up the trial-and-error, or "iterative," process of finding the correct IRR discount factor.

Irma Investor has the choice of investing $100,000 in the moderately leveraged real estate syndication described in the excerpt by Madison and Dwyer, at Chapter 2B, supra, or investing the same amount in a triple-A-rated corporate bond with an annual interest rate of 11 percent. Which investment would be more profitable for Irma? Assume that the assumptions in the excerpt from Madison and Dwyer at 2B, infra, prove to be accurate, that the holding period for both investments would be 5 years, and that the real estate will appreciate at an annual rate of 5 percent. Assume that the current rate of interest (or discount factor) is 8 percent (as reflected by the current rate for 5-year Treasury bills). Determine the NPV and IRR for each alternative investment and explain why you would choose one over the other.

As suggested by the excerpts from the Mortgage and Real Estate Executives Report, experts in the area are bothered by certain perceived deficiencies in the IRR method of calculation. Do your results in the foregoing problem illustrate any of these deficiencies? Another criticism of the IRR calculation is that it assumes that the net cash benefits received during the investment period will be reinvested at the resulting IRR rate and therefore the higher the IRR, the higher the assumed reinvestment returns; thus the overall rate of return for the investment period may be overstated. Why is this an unrealistic assumption, especially in the case of a long-term investment? By contrast, the NPV method implies reinvestment at whatever discount rate is selected. To correct this deficiency, the IRR should be calculated based on an assumed reinvestment rate that can be prescribed in advance by the investment advisor or analyst. This modification of the IRR method is called the modified internal rate of return (MIRR) or the financial management rate of return (FMRR) and can be factored into the IRR calculation on most modern advanced-function calculators. See Wetterer, Comparing Investor Return — Consistency Is Crucial to Any Meaningful Comparison of Investment Options, 1 Real Est. Fin. 76, 78-79 (Fall 1984); Messner and Findlay, Real Estate Investment Analysis: IRR vs. FMRR, Real Est. Appraiser 5 (July-Aug. 1975).

Further refinement of the IRR calculation is also possible by altering assumptions as to the tax bracket of the investor-taxpayer, timing and amounts of rentals, expenses, capital expenditures, and so on; the degree of risk exposure can therefore be quantified based on varying potential scenarios so that the investor can obtain both the "downside" and "upside" picture before selecting the investment. See Russell, Appraising Real Estate Investments for Pension Funds, 2 Real Est. Acctg. and Taxn. 33, 42-44 (Winter 1988).

Proponents of the IRR method contend that it provides a clear ranking of investments according to percentage returns and is more comprehensible to the average unsophisticated investor than is the NPV method. Can you think of any other advantages? See Kusnet and Parisse, Financial Analysis of a Real Estate Investment 86-87 (1984).

Other measures of profitability include: (1) the adjusted rate of return (ARR), which attempts to equate the present value of the investment with the future value of its economic benefits; (2) the accounting return method (ARM); and (3) the payback method, all of which are described in comprehensive detail in R. Haft and P. Fass, Real Estate Syndication Tax Handbook 2-13 to 2-21 (1986-1987 ed.).

B. REAL ESTATE AS A LIMITED TAX SHELTER

The tax shelter benefits associated with the ownership of income-producing real estate provided by the Economic Recovery Tax Act of 1981,[11] as modified by the Tax Equity and Fiscal Responsibility Act of 1982[12] and the Tax Reform Act of 1984,[13] and as curtailed by the

11. Pub. L. No. 97-34, 95 Stat. 172 (1981) (codified as amended in scattered sections of 26 U.S.C.) (hereinafter ERTA). See Aronsohn, Real Estate Investment and the Economic Recovery Tax Act of 1981, 8 J. Real Est. Taxn. 291 (1981) for discussion of the legislative history and the two major precursors of ERTA: the Kemp-Roth rate reduction proposal and the so-called 10-5-3 depreciation proposal.

12. Pub. L. No. 97-248, 96 Stat. 324 (1982) (codified as amended in scattered sections of 26 U.S.C.) (hereinafter TEFRA).

13. The Tax Reform Act of 1984 (hereinafter TRA 1984) is Division A of the Deficit Reduction Act of 1984, Pub. L. No. 98-369, 98 Stat. 494 (codified as amended in scattered sections of 26 U.S.C.). TRA 1984 follows a conventional tax reform approach and does not lean in the direction of a flat-rate income tax (of the variety reflected by the Bradley-Gephardt or Kemp-Kasten proposals) or a value-added tax. For a concise explanation of the legislative history underlying ERTA, TEFRA, and TRA 1984, including a statement of prior law, reason for change, and explanation with respect to each new or amended IRC section, see the respective reports for each of the statutes entitled "General Explanation" (in the parlance of tax professionals, the "blue book") by the staff of the Joint Committee on Taxation, which are available for purchase

Tax Reform Act of 1986,[14] the Revenue Act of 1987,[15] and the Revenue Reconciliation Act of 1990,[16] further explain why real estate is such an attractive investment medium.

The examples at pages 105-115, involving both a moderately and a deeply leveraged real estate investment, are designed to illustrate: (1) how the profitability of a real estate investment depends on the interaction of two factors — financial leverage and tax shelter; and (2) how the tax shelter device has been curtailed but not eliminated by the Tax Reform Act of 1986 (1986 Act). Under current tax law, the depreciation deduction allowed by I.R.C. §167 is no longer available to convert ordinary income into long-term capital gain, and because of lower tax rates it has become worth less to the individual taxpayer. However, in most cases the depreciation deduction still shelters ordinary rental income from immediate taxation, and this deferring of tax liability until the real estate is sold is what produces a time-value benefit for the real estate investor that is not available to those who invest in corporate securities. Don't underestimate the importance of the time value of money. For example, if a taxpayer who owns depreciable real estate decides to sell it in 10 years, at an assumed interest rate (or discount factor) of 10 percent, the taxpayer would save 62.5 cents on every dollar of current tax liability that is deferred (as a consequence of the depreciation deduction) until the year of sale. This is why real estate can be fairly characterized as a limited tax shelter under current law. Perhaps some day real estate may regain its original status as a complete tax shelter if Congress decides to restore preferential tax treatment for long-term capital gain to the extent that it becomes meaningful for taxpayers.[17]

---

from the Superintendent of Documents, U.S. Government Printing Office, Washington, D.C. 20402.

14. Pub. L. No. 99-514, 100 Stat. 2085 (1986) (codified as amended in scattered sections of 26 U.S.C.) (hereinafter the 1986 Act).

15. The Revenue Act of 1987 (hereinafter the 87 Act) is the tax portion of the Omnibus Budget Reconciliation Act, Pub. L. No. 100-203, 101 Stat. 1330 (1987) (codified as amended in scattered sections of 26 U.S.C.).

16. The Revenue Reconciliation Act of 1990 (hereinafter 1990 Act) is the tax portion (Title XI) of the Omnibus Budget Reconciliation Act of 1990, Pub. L. No. 101-508, — Stat. — (1990) (codified as amended in scattered sections of 26 U.S.C.).

17. Under the 1990 Act the maximum tax rate on net long-term capital gains was fixed at 28 percent, which is only three percentage points lower than the maximum marginal rate of 31 percent on other income earned by individuals. Section 11101(c) of the 1990 Act, amending I.R.C. §1(j). A differential this small is not likely to affect economic incentives; however, this concession to proponents of a tax preference for capital gains may constitute an invitation to return to Congress within the next year or so with a bid for a still lower rate.

Crane v. Commissioner
331 U.S. 1 (1947)

MR. CHIEF JUSTICE VINSON delivered the opinion of the Court.

The question here is how a taxpayer who acquires depreciable property subject to an unassumed mortgage, holds it for a period, and finally sells it still so encumbered, must compute her taxable gain.

Petitioner was the sole beneficiary and the executrix of the will of her husband, who died January 11, 1932. He then owned an apartment building and lot subject to a mortgage,[1] which secured a principal debt of $255,000.00 and interest in default of $7,042.50. As of that date, the property was appraised for federal estate tax purposes at a value exactly equal to the total amount of this encumbrance. Shortly after her husband's death, petitioner entered into an agreement with the mortgagee whereby she was to continue to operate the property — collecting the rents, paying for necessary repairs, labor, and other operating expenses, and reserving $200.00 monthly for taxes — and was to remit the net rentals to the mortgagee. This plan was followed for nearly seven years, during which period petitioner reported the gross rentals as income, and claimed and was allowed deductions for taxes and operating expenses paid on the property, for interest paid on the mortgage, and for the physical exhaustion of the building. Meanwhile, the arrearage of interest increased to $15,857.71. On November 29, 1938, with the mortgagee threatening foreclosure, petitioner sold to a third party for $3,000.00 cash, subject to the mortgage, and paid $500.00 expenses of sale.

Petitioner reported a taxable gain of $1,250.00. Her theory was that the "property" which she had acquired in 1932 and sold in 1938 was only the equity, or the excess in the value of the apartment building and lot over the amount of the mortgage. This equity was of zero value when she acquired it. No depreciation could be taken on a zero value.[2] Neither she nor her vendee ever assumed the mortgage, so, when she sold the equity, the amount she realized on the sale was the net cash received, or $2,500.00. This sum less the zero basis constituted her gain, of which she reported half as taxable on the assumption that the entire property was a "capital asset."

The Commissioner, however, determined that petitioner realized a net taxable gain of $23,767.03. His theory was that the "property" acquired and sold was not the equity, as petitioner claimed, but rather

---

1. The record does not show whether he was personally liable for the debt.

2. This position is, of course, inconsistent with her practice in claiming such deductions in each of the years the property was held. The deductions so claimed and allowed by the Commissioner were in the total amount of $25,500.00.

the physical property itself, or the owner's rights to possess, use, and dispose of it, undiminished by the mortgage. The original basis thereof was $262,042.50, its appraised value in 1932. Of this value $55,000.00 was allocable to land and $207,042.50 to building. During the period that petitioner held the property, there was an allowable depreciation of $28,045.10 on the building, so that the adjusted basis of the building at the time of sale was $178,997.40. The amount realized on the sale was said to include not only the $2,500.00 net cash receipts, but also the principal amount of the mortgage subject to which the property was sold, both totaling $257,500.00. . . .

On the Commissioner's appeal, the Circuit Court of Appeals reversed, one judge dissenting. We granted certiorari because of the importance of the questions raised as to the proper construction of the gain and loss provisions of the Internal Revenue Code.

The 1938 Act, §111(a), defines the gain from "the sale or other disposition of property" as "the excess of the amount realized therefrom over the adjusted basis provided in section 113(b) . . . ." It proceeds, §111(b), to define "the amount realized from the sale or other disposition of property" as "the sum of any money received plus the fair market value of the property (other than money) received." Further, in §113(b), the "adjusted basis for determining the gain or loss from the sale or other disposition of property" is declared to be "the basis determined under subsection (a), adjusted . . . [(1) (B)] . . . for exhaustion, wear and tear, obsolescence, amortization . . . to the extent allowed (but not less than the amount allowable) . . . ." The basis under subsection (a) "if the property was acquired by . . . devise . . . or by the decedent's estate from the decedent," §113(a)(5), is "the fair market value of such property at the time of such acquisition."

Logically, the first step under this scheme is to determine the unadjusted basis of the property, under §113 (a)(5), and the dispute in this case is as to the construction to be given the term "property." If "property," as used in that provision, means the same thing as "equity," it would necessarily follow that the basis of petitioner's property was zero, as she contends. If, on the contrary, it means the land and building themselves, or the owner's legal rights in them, undiminished by the mortgage, the basis was $262,042.50.

We think that the reasons for favoring one of the latter constructions are of overwhelming weight. In the first place, the words of statutes — including revenue acts — should be interpreted where possible in their ordinary, everyday senses. The only relevant definitions of "property" to be found in the principal standard dictionaries are the two favored by the Commissioner, i.e., either that "property" is the physical thing which is a subject of ownership, or that it is the aggregate of the owner's rights to control and dispose of that thing. "Equity" is not given as a synonym, nor do either of the foregoing definitions suggest that it could be correctly so used. Indeed, "equity" is defined as "the value of a property . . . above the total of the liens. . . ."

A further reason why the word "property" in §113(a) should not be construed to mean "equity" is the bearing such construction would have on the allowance of deductions for depreciation and on the collateral adjustments of basis. . . .

Under these provisions, if the mortgagor's equity were the §113(a) basis, it would also be the original basis from which depreciation allowances are deducted. If it is, and if the amount of the annual allowances were to be computed on that value, as would then seem to be required, they will represent only a fraction of the cost of the corresponding physical exhaustion, and any recoupment by the mortgagor of the remainder of that cost can be effected only by the reduction of his taxable gain in the year of sale. If, however, the amount of the annual allowances were to be computed on the value of the property, and then deducted from an equity basis, we would in some instances have to accept deductions from a minus basis or deny deductions altogether. The Commissioner also argues that taking the mortgagor's equity as the §113(a) basis would require the basis to be changed with each payment on the mortgage, and that the attendant problem of repeatedly recomputing basis and annual allowances would be a tremendous accounting burden on both the Commissioner and the taxpayer. Moreover, the mortgagor would acquire control over the timing of his depreciation allowances. . . .

We conclude that the proper basis under §113(a)(5) is the value of the property, undiminished by mortgages thereon, and that the correct basis here was $262,042.50. The next step is to ascertain what adjustments are required under §113(b). As the depreciation rate was stipulated, the only question at this point is whether the Commissioner was warranted in making any depreciation adjustments whatsoever. . . .

As we have just decided that the correct basis of the property was not zero, but $262,042.50, we . . . conclude that an adjustment should be made as the Commissioner determined.

Petitioner urges to the contrary that she was not entitled to depreciation deductions, whatever the basis of the property, because the law allows them only to one who actually bears the capital loss, and here the loss was not hers but the mortgagee's. We do not see, however, that she has established her factual premise. There was no finding of the Tax Court to that effect, nor to the effect that the value of the property was ever less than the amount of the lien. . . . Whatever may be the rule as to allowing depreciation to a mortgagor on property in his possession which is subject to an unassumed mortgage and clearly worth less than the lien, we are not faced with that problem and see no reason to decide it now.

At last we come to the problem of determining the "amount

realized" on the 1938 sale. Section 111(b), it will be recalled, defines the "amount realized" from "the sale . . . of property" as "the sum of any money received plus the fair market value of the property (other than money) received," and §111(a) defines the gain on "the sale . . . of property" as the excess of the amount realized over the basis. Quite obviously, the word "property," used here with reference to a sale, must mean "property" in the same ordinary sense intended by the use of the word with reference to acquisition and depreciation in §113, both for certain of the reasons stated heretofore in discussing its meaning in §113, and also because the functional relation of the two sections requires that the word mean the same in one section that it does in the other. If the "property" to be valued on the date of acquisition is the property free of liens, the "property" to be priced on a subsequent sale must be the same thing. . . .

Starting from this point, we could not accept petitioner's contention that the $2,500.00 net cash was all she realized on the sale except on the absurdity that she sold a quarter-of-a-million dollar property for roughly one percent of its value, and took a 99 per cent loss. . . .

Petitioner concedes that if she had been personally liable on the mortgage and the purchaser had either paid or assumed it, the amount so paid or assumed would be considered a part of the "amount realized" within the meaning of §111(b). The cases so deciding have already repudiated the notion that there must be an actual receipt by the seller himself of "money" or "other property," in their narrowest senses. It was thought to be decisive that one section of the Act must be construed so as not to defeat the intention of another or to frustrate the Act as a whole, and that the taxpayer was the "beneficiary" of the payment in "as real and substantial [a sense] as if the money had been paid it and then paid over by it to its creditors."

Both these points apply to this case. The first has been mentioned already. As for the second, we think that a mortgagor, not personally liable on the debt, who sells the property subject to the mortgage and for additional consideration, realizes a benefit in the amount of the mortgage as well as the boot.[37] If a purchaser pays boot, it is immaterial as to our problem whether the mortgagor is also to receive money from the purchaser to discharge the mortgage prior to sale, or whether he is merely to transfer subject to the mortgage — it may make a difference to the purchaser and to the mortgagee, but not to the mortgagor. Or put in another way, we are no more concerned with

---

37. Obviously, if the value of the property is less than the amount of the mortgage, a mortgagor who is not personally liable cannot realize a benefit equal to the mortgage. Consequently, a different problem might be encountered where a mortgagor abandoned the property or transferred it subject to the mortgage without receiving boot. That is not this case.

whether the mortgagor is, strictly speaking, a debtor on the mortgage, then we are with whether the benefit to him is, strictly speaking, a receipt of money or property. We are rather concerned with the reality that an owner of property, mortgaged at a figure less than that at which the property will sell, must and will treat the conditions of the mortgage exactly as if they were his personal obligations. If he transfers subject to the mortgage, the benefit to him is as real and substantial as if the mortgage were discharged, or as if a personal debt in an equal amount had been assumed by another.

Therefore we conclude that the Commissioner was right in determining that petitioner realized $257,500.00 on the sale of this property. . . .

The following excerpts highlight the long and tortuous history of real estate tax reform culminating with the Tax Reform Act of 1986, as modified by the Revenue Act of 1987.

avoid the torture

McKee, The Real Estate Tax Shelter: A Computerized Exposé
57 Va. L. Rev. 521, 556-567 (1971)

THE NEED TO ELIMINATE THE REAL ESTATE TAX SHELTER

Although the real estate tax shelter resulted primarily from a mistake in drafting, its proponents attempt to justify its continued existence as an incentive to investors to invest in depreciable realty. . . .

Since it is virtually impossible to fashion a subsidy that does not provide benefits to those who would engage in a favored activity anyway, any subsidy is inherently inefficient. But because the size of a deduction-funded subsidy, such as the tax shelter, is determined by the investor's tax bracket, rather than by an assessment of the inducement actually needed to encourage investment, such a subsidy compounds inefficiency. If a deduction-funded subsidy is to be effective to encourage lower bracket investors to place their capital in depreciable realty, high bracket investors must be given a "windfall" profit.[87] Indeed, in order

---

87. One might postulate that the higher an individual's tax bracket, the higher the rate of return required to induce him to invest, since at higher tax brackets a higher before tax rate of return is necessary to equalize the after tax rate of return to investors in lower brackets. But in real estate, high bracket investors get higher *after tax* rates of return than their lower bracket counterparts — a hard notion to justify as an efficient subsidization of desired activities.

to have the same impact as the deduction-funded tax shelter incentive, a system of direct cash subsidies would have to provide a 70% bracket investor with seventy cents of immediate subsidy, while his 30% bracket counterpart would receive only thirty cents for the same activity. Thus, deduction-funded subsidies are inequitable as well as inefficient. Finally, deduction-funded subsidies have an undesirable effect on the theory and administration of tax policy. The federal income tax law is based on the theory that those who make more should contribute a greater proportion of their income in taxes than their less affluent counterparts; but deduction funded subsidies are highly regressive and are therefore irreconcilable with tax theory. Such subsidies also narrow the tax base, causing tax rates to be maintained at high levels.

These objections can be leveled against all deduction-funded tax incentives, and alone seem sufficient to call for change. But the peculiarities of real estate investments merit special attention. . . .

[T]he inequity among taxpayers in different brackets is extreme. Although deduction-funded subsidies are always worth more to high bracket investors, the subsidy, in most cases, constitutes only a moderate portion of the overall rate of return, so that differences in rates of return are not very large in an absolute sense. But a high bracket investor in depreciable realty uses the principles of leverage to apply the benefits of his larger subsidy to a small equity.[90] The subsidy thus can become the major source of the return, with the result that high bracket investors often receive twice the rate of return that their lower bracket counterparts receive. Additionally, the fairly small difference in rates of return created by most deduction-funded subsidies at least allows the lower bracket investor to participate in the subsidized activity. But in real estate the rate of return available to a high bracket investor will often be sufficient to induce his investment in times when his lower bracket counterpart is effectively excluded from the industry by high mortgage interest rates. If there are sufficient high bracket investors to meet the demand for new buildings, the real estate industry as a whole will not exert pressure to improve market conditions; and low bracket investors will continue to be excluded until external pressures in the economy force interest rates down. . . .

ARGUMENTS IN SUPPORT OF THE REAL ESTATE TAX SHELTER

The arguments which are made in support of deduction-funded tax incentives in general have been analyzed and refuted elsewhere.

---

90. Moreover, the high bracket investor is more likely to be sufficiently wealthy to be able to increase his leverage by borrowing on his personal credit.

Again, however, the peculiarities of depreciable real estate merit special attention.

THE IMPACT OF INFLATION

It can be argued that accelerated depreciation is justified to offset the impact of inflation, even though the building does not decline in dollar value. Taubman and Rasche conclude that inflation does indeed impose a negative subsidy upon investors:

> A further complication in setting tax depreciation rules involves the appropriate adjustments to make when inflation is occuring. To determine what economic income should be in this instance, it is useful to first suppose that there are no taxes. Then suppose that all prices (including rents) double. Under the circumstances described, the owner of an asset would find that its current selling price has also doubled. However, his real economic income is unchanged since all prices doubled. That is, if he sold the investment he would be unable to consume more goods and services than in the preinflation situation. Now let taxes be reintroduced. When the inflation occurs, to guarantee that a person's real after tax income remains constant the depreciation allowance must be blown up by the price increase. The tax law, however, bases depreciation on original cost, thereby imposing a negative subsidy on investors. This problem occurs for any depreciable asset as well as for financial assets, whose market valuation can be affected by inflation. While the comparative position of investors and wage earners has been answered, it is interesting to compare real estate investors with other investors.[95] . . .

But, there seems to be no reason for treating real estate owners any differently than owners of other assets. Since our tax system treats all owners of assets alike in that they are taxed somewhat unfairly because of inflation, and since introducing any discrepancy between tax depreciation and economic depreciation produces substantial distortions in tax equity, the problem of inflation should not be handled by adjusting the size of depreciation deductions.

PROTECTING THE REAL ESTATE INDUSTRY FROM INTEREST RATE FLUCTUATIONS

Since a major portion of most real estate investments is financed with borrowed funds, the cost of those funds — interest — should have a major impact on the profitability of such investments. Although the industry is sensitive to interest rate changes, this sensitivity is substan-

95. Taubman & Rasche, [The Income Tax and Real Estate Investment (presented at the Symposium on Tax Incentives of the Tax Institute of America) (1969)], at 6-7.

tially less than it would be in the absence of the tax shelter. The tax shelter renders high bracket taxpayers relatively impervious to interest rate changes, and thus immunizes a part of the investment community from the impact of interest rate changes. Since wide fluctuations in the interest rate are often created by government policy as opposed to market forces, it can be argued that the industry needs the damper provided by the tax shelter to provide insulation from interest rate fluctuations.

Even if it is assumed that the real estate industry needs protection from interest rate fluctuations, the tax shelter is not an apt method of supplying the protection. To begin with, even without the tax shelter the fact that interest is deductible substantially lessens the impact of interest rate changes on the rate of return. Moreover, the tax shelter materially lessens the impact of rate changes only on high bracket investors, who are also those primarily insulated by the interest deduction. The low bracket investor remains quite sensitive to interest rate changes, and to the extent that low bracket investors constitute a substantial source of investment funds the tax shelter does not provide the allegedly needed protection.

LOW GOVERNMENT COST

Unlike many forms of government subsidy, a substantial portion of the tax revenues lost because of unwarranted depreciation are returned to the government when the building is sold. To the extent that the tax is eventually collected, the government assumes the position of a lender. Although the loan may be extremely valuable to the investor-borrower, the cost to the government is more modest — the government's cost of raising funds to provide the interest free loan is the interest rate which it must pay to borrow these funds. It is true that much of the initial subsidy is never repaid because of incomplete recapture, but nevertheless the governmental cost of the loan element of the subsidy is less than the benefit provided to the investor to the extent of the difference between the rate of return which the investor can earn and the interest rate which the government must pay.

Of course, the essence of this lower cost of subsidization is the government's willingness to make an interest free loan without security. But rather than tie the amount of the loan to the investor's tax bracket, a direct low interest loan program would produce the same benefit at a lower cost and without the distortions inherent in deduction-funded subsidies.

ALTERNATIVE METHODS OF ELIMINATING THE REAL ESTATE TAX SHELTER

For reasons of efficiency, equity and tax policy, the tax shelter should be eliminated and another method of subsidizing the industry created, if continued subsidy is thought to be desirable. The means by which the tax shelter is eliminated, however, is quite important. It is not enough simply to eliminate accelerated depreciation, since even straight line depreciation creates a substantial tax shelter.

The surest method of eliminating the real estate tax shelter is to limit allowable tax deductions to economic depreciation. This would require that buildings be classified according to their precise economic depreciation rates. . . .

The problem with limiting tax depreciation to economic depreciation lies in the difficulty of determining the proper classification of buildings and their corresponding depreciation rates. Variations in economic depreciation rates depending upon construction techniques and geographic location are probably substantial. . . .

CONCLUSION

The real estate tax shelter is an inefficient and inequitable form of subsidy; it should be eliminated. If limiting depreciation deductions to actual economic depreciation proves too complex or politically impractical, limiting the investor's depreciable basis to the amount of his equity is a viable alternative.

Panel Discussions on General Tax Reform Before the House Ways and Means Committee
93d Cong., 1st Sess., ser. 11, pt. 4 (Tax Treatment of Real Estate) 510-520 (1973)

PREPARED STATEMENT OF ALAN J. B. ARONSOHN, NEW YORK, N.Y.

INTRODUCTION

An understanding of the size and complexities of the real estate industry is a necessary prerequisite to any discussion of the proper income tax treatment to be accorded to certain activities in the real estate field. . . .

While real estate is a major American industry, it has nevertheless operated through a diffused aggregation of small and medium-sized businesses. Unlike certain segments of the manufacturing industry, economic power in this sector is not concentrated in the hands of a relatively small number of major corporations. Consequently, the vast aggregations of capital and managerial talent which are a feature of such segments of the economy are not typical of real estate.

The fact that the real estate industry is not composed of a few large enterprises is of some significance in the determination of proper tax policy. In contrast to the continuity of businesses like the manufacture of automobiles or the production and distribution of oil, the ownership and operation of rental real estate is a relatively discretionary activity. Most private sector initial investment in rental property is entirely voluntary.

It is fair to assume, therefore, that the willingness of large numbers of comparatively small investors to continue to invest in an essentially voluntary investment market, such as real estate, will be affected more immediately by changes in the costs, risks and potential rewards of doing business than might be the case if the industry were characterized by a greater concentration of economic power and dedication to continuity of enterprise.

Other aspects of real estate are also relevant to tax policy considerations. Real estate investments are materially less liquid than investments in marketable securities, and they usually require fairly substantial long-term financial commitments. Once the investment is made, it cannot readily be moved or abandoned. This characteristic has been responsible in part for the comparative ease with which real estate has long been subject to all kinds of government control and taxation. When faced with increases in local taxes, pollution control costs and even rent controls, the owner of investment real estate does not have the same flexibility to shift his business investment as may be available, for example, to a manufacturer of diverse products capable of being produced in varying locations.

As a consequence of some of these factors, investments in real estate, in order to be competitive in the free capital market, have generally been forced to yield somewhat higher rates of return than marketable securities of comparable risk. . . .

THE DEDUCTION FOR DEPRECIATION

What is the proper concept and function of depreciation or amortization in our income tax system?

Probably no question has been so thoroughly debated and confused.

Actually, the basic purpose of such an allowance is quite simple. It is intended to account for loss of capital in determining a taxpayer's net income for tax purposes within a system which taxes net income, not gross income, on an annual basis.

It is based upon the elementary and equitable doctrine that if a taxpayer is deriving income from a wasting economic asset, an appropriate measure of his taxable net income on an annual basis is obtained by prorating the cost of the asset over its life, as an offset against the gross income from it. . . .

The Treasury's Income Tax Regulations have historically described the depreciation allowance as "that amount which should be set aside for the taxable year in accordance with a reasonably consistent plan (not necessarily at a uniform rate), so that the aggregate of the amounts set aside, plus the salvage value, will, at the end of the estimated useful life of the depreciable property, equal the cost or other basis of the property . . . The allowance shall not reflect amounts representing a mere reduction in market value."[1] This interpretation of the depreciation allowance for income tax purposes has consistently been supported by the courts.[2]

The depreciation allowance is therefore simply a capital cost recovery system. It is essentially an accounting convention. It does not correspond with an economist's definition of depreciation, which would involve continuous revaluation of the projected income stream from the asset. Under the Internal Revenue Code depreciation has nothing to do with fluctuating values.

Strenuous efforts have been made to introduce value as a factor in computing allowable depreciation for income tax purposes, for in an inflationary economy a depreciable asset cannot generally be replaced for its original cost. Spokesmen for industry have repeatedly suggested that the allowable deductions for depreciation be increased to take into account inflated capital replacement costs. However, to date taxpayers have been permitted to recover only original cost, not replacement value, via the allowable deductions for depreciation and amortization. . . .

Perhaps the easiest way to visualize the functioning of the deduction for depreciation with respect to a real estate investment is to examine a simple illustration involving the acquisition of a leasehold interest. I have deliberately chosen a leasehold interest for this purpose since, in the case of the acquisition of a leasehold estate for a fixed term of years, without any renewal options, there is no question or ambiguity concerning the life of the assets acquired.

For example, let us assume that taxpayer Able leases land under a ground lease having a fixed term, without renewal options, which

1. Treas. Reg. §1.167(a)-1(a).
2. E.g., Crane v. Commissioner, 331 U.S. 1 (1947).

provides for ground rent of $5,000 a year. Able constructs a building upon the leased land. He then agrees to sublease the property to a supermarket for a period co-terminous with that of the ground lease, and at a rental which will provide an estimated return, after payment of ground rent and other expenses, of $15,000 per annum. Let us further assume that, at a time when the ground lease and the sublease each have a remaining term of 20 years, Able sells his leasehold estate and interest in the subleased building to Mr. Baker for the sum of $100,000, reflecting a capitalization of the projected net earnings at a rate of 10% ($15,000 net rent less $5,000 (recovery of $100,000 investment over 20 years) = $10,000 cash profit each year, or 10% on $100,000).

Under existing law, assuming that the remaining life of the supermarket building is greater than the remaining term of the ground lease, purchaser Baker is required to amortize his $100,000 cost over the 20 year remaining life of the ground lease. This means in effect that $5,000 (1/20 of $100,000) of the $15,000 received by Baker each year is treated as amortization of his investment. There is nothing particularly surprising or startling in this.

To my knowledge, no one has ever seriously contended that the grant to Mr. Baker of an amortization deduction for his cost of acquiring a non-renewable leasehold constitutes a special tax shelter of any kind.

It is important to note that the deduction of $5,000 amortization per year to which Mr. Baker is entitled in the illustration which I have just given is totally independent of the value of the purchased leasehold from time to time during the 20 year period.

Of course, at the end of the 20 year period the value of Mr. Baker's interest in the property will be zero, since the leasehold will have expired. However, during the 20 year period, the value of the leasehold may vary substantially.

For example, if the supermarket sublease provides for payment of percentage rentals based on the lessee's gross sales in addition to the basic rent (the usual form of store lease), Baker, as owner of the leasehold estate, may derive a gross income from the property, after the payment of ground rent and other expenses, in excess of the $15,000 which was being realized from the property at the time he purchased the leasehold estate. . . .

The fact that the leasehold may be salable at the end of ten years, after $50,000 of the original $100,000 cost has been recovered by the taxpayer, does not mitigate against the correctness of permitting the taxpayer to deduct $5,000 per year over the first ten years of the leasehold term as capital cost recovery. . . .

Any system of income taxation which altered the present rule by providing that a taxpayer's right to recover his capital cost over the life of the asset was dependent upon the asset's value at the end of each year for which an amortization deduction was claimed would represent a radical change in existing law and would involve such monstrous problems of continuous valuation as would probably overwhelm any attempt to administer the tax laws fairly. . . .

The assumptions underlying the leasehold example which I have just given relate equally to buildings. The confusion which exists in many quarters concerning depreciation with respect to buildings is generally the consequence of the inability of anyone to predict with absolute certainty the future economic (earning power) useful life of a long-lived wasting asset, such as a building and its many components, or to establish a reasonable capital cost recovery period for long term assets. While these matters cannot be determined with exactitude, this cannot justify ignoring reality — buildings and their components do wear out, they do become economically obsolescent or non-competitive and require replacement, and our economy does require some mechanicism within the tax system to provide capital replenishment for such purposes. Although tax theoreticians often refer to depreciation as a "paper" deduction, the actual need to replace worn-out and obsolescent building components and entire buildings, often long before the expiration of the Internal Revenue Service's estimate of useful lives, is well known to experienced owners of real property. This has been particularly true in our competitive industrial society where suburban shopping centers, for example, have replaced many downtown shopping areas, and are in turn being replaced by enclosed mall regional shopping plazas, all within a relatively brief number of years. The same is true of office buildings, where tenants' requirements for air conditioning, high speed elevators and increased electrical capacities for technical equipment have forced owners of many older buildings into a choice between making substantial capital expenditures to alter, replace and modernize or suffer economic obsolescence and deteriorating earnings.

Statements of some economists to the contrary notwithstanding,[3] the depreciation deduction as applied to real estate does not represent a tax incentive or tax abuse in favor of owners of buildings, but merely allows the recovery of original capital cost over an estimated useful life. . . .

It has been suggested that recovery of the cost of depreciable improvements by means of an accelerated depreciation deduction con-

3. For those who view depreciation as a function of declining value, it is not surprising that, in an inflationary economy, a long-lived asset may not have "depreciated" at all, despite the fact that it is wearing out. As previously stated, the economists' concept of depreciation as a function of declining value may be a theoretical alternative to the capital cost recovery system embodied in the current Code, Regulations and cases but is entirely inconsistent with the accounting concept and is impossible to incorporate into a workable tax statute.

stitutes a tax loophole. In fact, accelerated depreciation for real property is perfectly sound, for several reasons. First, the earning power of a building, in relation to its economic useful life, is usually greater when it is new; as it grows older, the costs of operation increase and the operating revenues decline. As our tax accounting system is based on the concept of matching anticipated annual income with related costs, including consumption of capital, the higher depreciation allowances produced by accelerated depreciation in the early years of operation are required properly to reflect the taxable income derived from the property during such years. Second, denial of accelerated depreciation methods to real estate discriminates in the competitive market for capital. Third, denial of accelerated methods reduces effective rates of return on unrecovered investment. This requires the imposition of higher rentals, in order to produce yields competitive with other industries, resulting in higher rents to tenants and increased inflation. . . .

EFFECTS OF DEBT FINANCING

Probably the single most distorted criticism of real estate is its characterization as a so-called tax shelter, based on the fact that most real estate is purchased with substantial debt financing. The inclusion of long-term mortgages in the depreciable basis of real property, under the authority of the decision of the United States Supreme Court in Crane v. Commissioner, appears to have created a vast mythology which characterizes rental real estate as a "tax shelter" whenever the cash receipts from the property exceed the taxable income for any period. Nevertheless, it would seem clearly inequitable for the tax consequences of the ownership of an asset to be dependent upon the method of financing its purchase, or upon whether it is rental real estate, user real estate or personal property, such as machinery. . . .

To illustrate, an industrial corporation requires a new plant. It can rent the plant from a third party who will borrow two-thirds of the cost on a mortgage loan, or the corporation can build the plant itself with borrowed funds. The latter can be obtained via either a mortgage loan or from the sale of a general purpose long-term debenture. None of the proposed depreciation changes would limit the corporation's depreciation deduction to cash equity if it mortgaged the property. Even if the proposals were broadened to limit depreciation allowable on property occupied by the owner, this still would not affect an owner using proceeds derived from a debenture loan or other general borrowings to pay the cost.[18]

18. These earlier proposals to limit the depreciation deduction are discussed in note 3 infra. — ED.

I do not question that proposals of this sort are made in good faith and with the intention to cure certain real or imagined tax abuses. However, as in the case of so many apparently simple solutions to complex problems, the cure in this case would seem to be worse than the disease.

"TAX SHELTERS"

The foregoing is not intended to dispute the fact that in certain cases, the combination of substantial long-term debt financing and certain very rapid methods of accelerated depreciation may result in what may fairly be described as a "tax shelter." . . .

Professor Surrey and others have argued strenuously that such tax incentives represent indirect subsidies. In their judgment, such "subsidies" are less equitable and sensible than a direct Federal grant intended to accomplish the same goals. However, practical experience with direct Federal subsidies in the housing area has not created a high degree of confidence in the efficiency and equity of direct subsidies, nor has it shown their superiority in these respects over the indirect subsidies created by the limited number of existing tax incentives to private sector investment. In fact, our past experience with these programs would seem to indicate that until direct subsidy programs demonstrate a much higher degree of efficiency and equity than they have in the past, scrapping all private sector inducements by the elimination of tax incentives in this area would be highly imprudent. A key distinction between these two forms of incentive, which has obvious practical consequences, is that tax incentives are within the powers of Congress. They do not depend upon continuing administrative implementation for their success. (See, e.g., Robert F. Tomasson, "Freeze on Federal Housing Subsidies Affects 52 Projects in City," New York Times, January 28, 1973). . . .

CONSTRUCTION INTEREST

Among the many legislative proposals recently introduced which look toward the "reform" of the tax rules currently applicable to the real estate industry, it has been suggested that interest and real estate taxes incurred during the construction of a rental building should be capitalized in all cases, rather than permit the taxpayer to expense such items in full as incurred.

These suggestions appear to flow from a superficial analogy between interest and taxes, on the one hand, and construction wages and materials, on the other. . . .

The payment of interest and taxes is an out-of-pocket expenditure and does not involve any question as to the amounts expended. The only real question is that of the proper accounting period to which such expenditures relate.

Money paid in construction wages or for materials which go into the building obviously relate to the building and it is proper to capitalize such expenditures and write them off over the life of the asset. Similarly, the principal amount of any construction loan, which serves as the source of payment for such wages and materials becomes part of the capitalized cost. On the other hand, the interest paid on a construction loan represents simply the current charge for the use of the money borrowed and bears no relation to the building as such.

This can best be illustrated by comparing the alternatives open to a taxpayer who has the option either to (1) dispose of other income producing assets and invest the proceeds in the building or (2) to borrow the money to build it.

Under the first alternative, taxpayer has no interest deduction, but, of course, he no longer has taxable income from the investment assets which he sold to obtain the construction funds. By selling the investment assets and putting up the cash for construction, rather than borrowing it, the taxpayer, in effect, saves the interest and has reduced his taxable income by the elimination of the investment income. If the amount of investment income and interest expense are equal, the net result is that his taxable income is the same as if he had retained the investment funds, received the income therefrom, and paid interest on a loan of equal principal amount.

Under the second alternative, the taxpayer continues to receive taxable income from the retained investments. Should he not have an offsetting deduction for the current interest paid on the money borrowed, so that his taxable income is the same as in the first alternative? The proposals relating to construction interest would deny such a deduction.

This illustration demonstrates the discriminatory nature of any legislative proposals which would differentiate between taxpayers who must borrow and those more fortunate taxpayers who may or may not borrow; the latter probably will not borrow, if the tax law discriminates against borrowing. In fact, since the proposals do not apply to interest generally, but simply to interest incurred to construct buildings for rental, the proposals are not only theoretically unsound, but are radically discriminatory towards a particular segment of the economy (without apparent social purpose).

Apart from their discriminatory effect, enactment of the proposals would create substantial problems of administration and taxpayer compliance. For example, how can the Internal Revenue Service objectively determine whether borrowed funds, other than a direct construction loan, were obtained to fund construction? I suggest that the Internal Revenue Service already has more administrative problems in connection with the tracing of the source and application of borrowed funds than it can adequately handle, e.g., for purposes of the investment interest limitations (which do limit the deductibility of certain construction interest). Burdening taxpayers and the Service with the additional requirement of trying to determine when funds borrowed from one source are in fact being applied towards the construction of an apparently unrelated building or other asset would add one more straw to a back which is creaking pretty badly now.

The arguments for deductibility of real estate taxes during the construction period are similar to those with respect to interest. Real estate taxes paid with respect to a personal residence are deductible. Real estate taxes paid by a railroad or a steel company are deductible. Real estate taxes are generally paid for a current period. There seems to be no reason in logic or equity for singling out real estate taxes paid during the period of construction of rental property for unique and dissimilar treatment. Why have the proponents of such legislation not required capitalization of interest incurred by an industrial corporation which constructs its own plant, or manufactures its own machine tools? . . .

SPILLOVER LOSSES

A number of legislative proposals for "reform" in this area have included suggestions to limit tax losses incurred with respect to any building to the income derived from it. These proposals are, of course, subject to the same criticism of rank discrimination as has been leveled against the other so-called "reform" proposals which are limited and applicable only to certain types of real estate investment.

Our tax system does not generally limit losses incurred with respect to one particular investment or activity to the income to be derived from it, nor in my judgment should there be any such limit. Thus, for example, the investment interest provisions, enacted in 1969, which limit the type of income against which interest may be deducted (i) discriminate against taxpayers who do not have the required type of income to offset against the particular expenses; and (ii) particularly discriminate against taxpayers who are unfortunate enough to make poor investments which result in actual economic losses. They appear to be simple methods for eliminating alleged tax abuses. The fact is that they do so at the risk of distorting the essential nature of a tax system based upon taxing a person's total net income rather than gross income, and by creating very substantial administrative problems for taxpayers and government alike. Such provisions may stifle risk-taking and capital mobility in areas where the total economy and well-being of the nation profits from encouraging the maximum involvement of the private sector.

CONCLUSION

The real estate industry is a major factor in the American economy, upon whose success millions of Americans depend for wages, adequate housing, commercial facilities and livable cities and neighborhoods. The citizens participating in this productive industry deserve to be treated, from a tax viewpoint, with more care than that given a step-child upon whom theorists feel free to impose experimental tax programs, or a convenient (and politically relatively impotent) whipping boy whose punishment is intended to satisfy populist demands for "tax reform."

The myth that the real estate industry is in essence one vast tax shelter mechanism is based on total disregard of the illiquidity of capital invested in real estate and the resulting necessity for the use of borrowed funds to make the risk and rate of return competitive with other investments. This myth fails to consider the special credits and allowances provided other industries, which increase their liquidity and rates of return.

The facts do not substantiate a need for the imposition of drastic changes, particularly of the nature heretofore suggested, which involve very pointed discrimination against real estate investment, and which certainly imperil the flow of private capital into the industry as we know it. The end result of discouraging private capital investment in real estate will be a requirement for increased government participation in areas such as housing and revitalization of urban commercial facilities. Few would find this result attractive. . . .

Staff of the Joint Committee on Taxation, Tax Shelter Proposals and Other Tax-Motivated Transactions
4-13 (Feb. 17, 1984)

II. OVERVIEW OF TAX SHELTERS

Many of the tax-motivated transactions addressed in this pamphlet are commonly known as tax shelters. This section discusses some of the features of tax shelters. . . .

B. THE ELEMENTS OF A TAX SHELTER

Although tax-shelter investments take a variety of forms, there are several elements that are common to most tax shelters. The first of these is the "deferral" of tax liability to future years, resulting, in effect, in an interest-free loan from the Federal Government. The second element of a tax shelter is the "conversion" of ordinary income (subject to tax at a maximum rate of 50 percent for individuals) to tax-favored income (such as capital gains subject to tax at a maximum rate of 20 percent). Finally, many tax shelters permit a taxpayer to leverage his investment (i.e., to use borrowed funds to pay deductible expenditures), thereby maximizing the tax benefit of deductibility. These elements of a tax shelter are described below. . . .

C. SCOPE OF TAX SHELTER CASES

According to an industry newsletter, taxpayers invested approximately $8.4 billion in "public program" tax-advantaged investments (i.e., limited partnerships registered with the Securities and Exchange Commission) in 1983, compared to approximately $5.5 billion in 1982. The largest increases from 1982 to 1983 were in real estate investments and investments in income-producing oil and gas properties. Many of these investments represented real capital formation for the economy; however, the data are indicative of the increasing use of abusive tax shelters as well. The flourishing of tax shelters in recent years has affected the administration of the tax laws in three ways. First, the limited audit resources of the Internal Revenue Service have increasingly been diverted to focus on tax shelters. Second, the judicial process, particularly the Tax Court, has been burdened by a substantial increase in the number of pending cases. Third, the rise of the tax-shelter industry may have contributed significantly to the general deterioration in compliance by undermining taxpayer confidence in the fairness and effectiveness of the tax laws. . . .

III. ECONOMIC ANALYSIS

Limited Partnership Tax Shelters

Generally speaking, a tax shelter is any investment which results in a mismatch between deductions (or credits) and income, so that the deductions (or credits) "shelter" unrelated income from tax. For purposes of analysis it is useful to distinguish between tax shelter benefits that arise from tax incentives provided by Congress and those that result from the creative use of structural tax rules to accomplish results not intended by Congress. A so-called abusive tax shelter is structured to give the investor larger write-offs than may be warranted under current law or take advantage of uncertainties under the law. Abusive tax shelters may constitute tax evasion rather than avoidance, and sometimes involve fraudulent overvaluation of assets. . . .

Economic Effects of Tax Shelters

The proliferation of tax shelters has had an important impact on revenues and on the efficiency and equity of the income tax system. The growth of shelters feeds on itself: as the tax base is eroded, rates must be raised to maintain revenues, which in turn increases the demand for tax shelters. This vicious circle threatens the integrity and fairness of the tax system as the tax burden falls increasingly on taxpayers who do not or cannot take advantage of tax shelters. . . .

Even the tax shelters based on incentives can have important effects on tax equity. For example, the Accelerated Cost Recovery System (ACRS) increased the value of depreciation deductions on rental housing purchased after 1981. This contributed to a construction boom which has glutted the real estate market in several southwestern cities. Post-1981 investors (often limited partnerships) can afford to lower rents or sustain high vacancy rates because of the generous ACRS deductions. However, the income of pre-1981 investors in real estate who rely on the old depreciation rules may have been reduced as rents fell in response to this oversupply. Thus the effect of some tax shelters can be to transfer wealth from existing investors to new investors. In other cases, taxpayers have bid up the price of existing buildings, providing windfalls to the existing owners. . . .

Why Is Tax Shelter Marketing Increasing?

The continuing growth of tax shelters may appear surprising in view of the enactment of the Economic Recovery Tax Act of 1981, which reduced the top marginal rate from 70 percent to 50 percent, and the enactment of the Tax Equity and Fiscal Responsibility Act of 1982, which was a major effort to broaden the tax base and improve compliance. To understand why tax shelter activity has not abated, it is useful to analyze the market for tax shelters. On the demand side of the market are taxpayers with substantial taxable income confronting high marginal tax rates. On the supply side of the market are users of tax-advantaged assets, such as real property, which during certain periods generate tax deductions in excess of income. The users of tax-shelter assets have an incentive to rent them from a tax shelter partnership, rather than own them, if they cannot take full advantage of the tax deductions because (1) they lack sufficient unrelated income to shelter, or (2) they have low marginal tax rates. Also on the supply side of the market are tax shelter promoters who organize and market limited partnerships interests in tax-shelter assets. The growth of tax shelter marketing is attributable to factors increasing both the supply and demand for tax shelters. . . .

The growth of tax shelters may have had an adverse impact on the efficiency as well as the fairness of the tax system. Tax shelter activity has significantly reduced the tax base over time, which has contributed both to higher deficits and the need for higher tax rates. In addition tax shelter marketing absorbs the talents of thousands of highly skilled professionals who might otherwise be employed in activities which contribute to the growth of GNP rather than the redistribution of the tax burden. Finally, in the case of shelters based on tax incentives, there is evidence that the government has lower cost alternatives than the creation of tax shelters, such as targeted spending programs, for encouraging certain types of economic activity. Tax shelters tend to be inefficient incentive mechanisms as a result of the high organizational and management fees charged by the tax shelter promoters. Tax shelter incentives are also inefficient to the extent that they attract investors taxed at less than the top tax bracket. If investors in the 40-percent bracket are interested in a tax shelter, then the benefit passed through to the users of the assets are determined by the tax benefits of these marginal investors. In this case, however, high-income investors in the 50-percent bracket are receiving a windfall, since the value of write-offs is 25 percent larger for these upper income investors. Thus, to the extent that these windfalls and organizational fees absorb the tax benefits of an incentive-type shelter, the tax system is an inefficient mechanism for increasing desirable economic activity.

Staff of the Joint Committee on Taxation, General Explanation of the Tax Reform Act of 1986
209-214 (May 7, 1987)

PRIOR LAW

In general, no limitations were placed on the ability of a taxpayer to use deductions from a particular activity to offset income from other activities. Similarly, most tax credits could be used to offset tax attributable to income from any of the taxpayer's activities. . . .

In the absence of more broadly applicable limitations on the use of deductions and credits from one activity to reduce tax liability attributable to other activities, taxpayers with substantial sources of positive income could eliminate or sharply reduce tax liability by using deductions and credits from other activities, frequently by investing in tax shelters. Tax shelters commonly offered the opportunity to reduce or avoid tax liability with respect to salary or other positive income, by making available deductions and credits, possibly exceeding real economic costs or losses currently borne by the taxpayer, in excess or in advance of income from the shelters.

REASONS FOR CHANGE

Congress concluded that it had become increasingly clear that taxpayers were losing faith in the Federal income tax system. This loss of confidence resulted in large part from the interaction of two of the system's principal features: its high marginal rates (in 1986, 50 percent for a single individual with taxable income in excess of $88,270), and the opportunities it provided for taxpayers to offset income from one source with tax shelter deductions and credits from another.

The increasing prevalence of tax shelters — even after the highest marginal rate for individuals was reduced in 1981 from 70 percent to 50 percent — was well documented. For example, a Treasury study revealed that in 1983, out of 260,000 tax returns reporting "total positive income"[4] in excess of $250,000, 11 percent paid taxes equaling 5 percent or less of total positive income, and 21 percent paid taxes equaling 10 percent or less of total positive income. Similarly, in the case of tax returns reporting total positive income in excess of $1 million, 11 percent paid tax equaling less than 5 percent of total positive income, and 19 percent paid tax equaling less than 10 percent of total positive income.[5]

Congress determined that such patterns gave rise to a number of undesirable consequences, even aside from their effect in reducing Federal tax revenues. Extensive shelter activity contributed to public concerns that the tax system was unfair, and to the belief that tax is paid only by the naive and the unsophisticated. This, in turn, not only undermined compliance, but encouraged further expansion of the tax shelter market, in many cases diverting investment capital from productive activities to those principally or exclusively serving tax avoidance goals.

Congress concluded that the most important sources of support for the Federal income tax system were the average citizens who simply reported their income (typically consisting predominantly of items such as salaries, wages, pensions, interest, and dividends) and paid tax under the general rules. To the extent that these citizens felt that they were bearing a disproportionate burden with regard to the costs of government because of their unwillingness or inability to engage in tax-oriented investment activity, the tax system itself was threatened.

4. Total positive income was defined as the sum of salary, interest, dividends, and income from profitable businesses and investments, as reported on tax returns.

5. Other studies similarly reached the conclusion that tax shelters, by flowing through tax benefits to individuals with positive sources of income, permitted some taxpayers with sizeable economic incomes substantially to reduce their tax liabilities. See Joint Committee on Taxation, Tax Reform Proposals: Tax Shelters and Minimum Tax (JCS-34-85), August 7, 1985.

Under these circumstances, Congress determined that decisive action was needed to curb the expansion of tax sheltering and to restore to the tax system the degree of equity that was a necessary precondition to a beneficial and widely desired reduction in rates. So long as tax shelters were permitted to erode the Federal tax base, a low-rate system could provide neither sufficient revenues, nor sufficient progressivity, to satisfy the general public that tax liability bore a fair relationship to the ability to pay. In particular, a provision significantly limiting the use of tax shelter losses was viewed as unavoidable if substantial rate reductions were to be provided to high-income taxpayers without disproportionately reducing the share of total liability under the individual income tax borne by high-income taxpayers as a group. . . .

The question of what constituted a tax shelter that should be subject to limitations was viewed as closely related to the question of who Congress intends to benefit when it enacts tax preferences. For example, in providing preferential depreciation for real estate or favorable accounting rules for farming, it was not Congress's primary intent to permit outside investors to avoid tax liability with respect to their salaries by investing in limited partnership syndications. Rather, Congress intended to benefit and provide incentives to taxpayers active in the businesses to which the preferences were directed.

In some cases, the availability of tax preferences to nonparticipating investors was viewed as harmful to the industries that the preferences were intended to benefit. For example, in the case of farming, credits and favorable deductions often encouraged investments by wealthy individuals whose principal or only interest in farming was to receive an investment return, largely in the form of tax benefits to offset tax on positive sources of income. Since such investors often did not need a positive cash return from farming in order to profit from their investments, they had a substantial competitive advantage in relation to active farmers, who commonly were not in a position to use excess tax benefits to shelter unrelated income. This significantly contributed to the serious economic difficulties being experienced by many active farmers.

The availability of tax benefits to shelter positive sources of income also harmed the economy generally, by providing a non-economic return on capital for certain investments. This encouraged a flow of capital away from activities that provided a higher pre-tax economic return, thus retarding the growth of the sectors of the economy with the greatest potential for expansion.

Congress determined that, in order for tax preferences to function as intended, their benefit should be directed primarily to taxpayers with a substantial and bona fide involvement in the activities to which the preferences related. Congress also determined that it was appropriate to encourage nonparticipating investors to invest in particular activities, by permitting the use of preferences to reduce the rate of tax on income from those activities; however, such investors were viewed as not appropriately permitted to use tax benefits to shelter unrelated income.

Congress believed that there were several reasons why it was appropriate to examine the materiality of a taxpayer's participation in an activity in determining the extent to which such taxpayer should be permitted to use tax benefits from the activity. A taxpayer who materially participated in an activity was viewed as more likely than a passive investor to approach the activity with a significant nontax economic profit motive, and to form a sound judgment as to whether the activity had genuine economic significance and value. . . .

Moreover, Congress concluded that restricting the use of losses from business activities in which the taxpayer did not materially participate against other sources of positive income (such as salary and portfolio income) would address a fundamental aspect of the tax shelter problem. Instances in which the tax system applies simple rules at the expense of economic accuracy encouraged the structuring of transactions to take advantage of the situations in which such rules gave rise to undermeasurement or deferral of income. Such transactions commonly were marketed to investors who did not intend to participate in the transactions, as devices for sheltering unrelated sources of positive income (e.g., salary and portfolio income). . . .

Further, in the case of a nonparticipating investor in a business activity, Congress determined that it was appropriate to treat losses of the activity as not realized by the investor prior to disposition of his interest in the activity. The effort to measure, on an annual basis, real economic losses from passive activities gave rise to distortions, particularly due to the nontaxation of unrealized appreciation and the mismatching of tax deductions and related economic income that could occur, especially where debt financing was used heavily. Only when a taxpayer disposed of his interest in an activity was it considered possible to determine whether a loss was sustained over the entire time that he held the interest.

The distinction that Congress determined should be drawn between activities on the basis of material participation was viewed as unrelated to the question of whether, and to what extent, the taxpayer was at risk with respect to the activities.[7] In general, the fact that a taxpayer placed a particular amount at risk in an activity did not establish, prior to a disposition of the taxpayer's interest, that the amount invested, or any amount, had as yet been lost. The fact that a taxpayer was potentially

---

7. The at-risk rules of prior law, while important and useful in preventing overvaluation of assets, and in preventing the transfer of tax benefits to taxpayers with no real equity in an activity, were viewed as not addressing the adverse consequences arising specifically from such transfers to nonparticipating investors.

liable with respect to future expenses or losses of the activity likewise had no bearing on the question whether any amount had as yet been lost, or otherwise was an appropriate current deduction or credit. . . .

A further area in which the material participation standard was viewed as not wholly adequate was that of rental activities. Such activities predominantly involve the production of income from capital. . . . Rental activities generally require less ongoing management activity, in proportion to capital invested, than business activities involving the production or sale of goods and services. Thus, for example, an individual who was employed full-time as a professional could more easily provide all necessary management in his spare time with respect to a rental activity than he could with respect to another type of business activity involving the same capital investment. The extensive use of rental activities for tax shelter purposes under prior law, combined with the reduced level of personal involvement necessary to conduct such activities, made clear that the effectiveness of the basic passive loss provision could be seriously compromised if material participation were sufficient to avoid the limitations in the case of rental activities.

Congress believed that a limited measure of relief, however, was appropriate in the case of certain moderate-income investors in rental real estate, who otherwise might experience cash flow difficulties with respect to investments that in many cases were designed to provide financial security, rather than to shelter a substantial amount of other income.

Additional considerations were viewed as relevant with regard to limited partnerships. In order to maintain limited liability status, a limited partner generally is precluded from materially participating in the business activity of the partnership; in virtually all respects, a limited partner more closely resembles a shareholder in a C corporation than an active business entrepreneur. Moreover, limited partnerships commonly were used as vehicles for marketing tax benefits to investors seeking to shelter unrelated income. In light of the widespread use of limited partnership interests in syndicating tax shelters, Congress determined that losses from limited partnership interests should not be permitted, prior to a taxable disposition, to offset positive income sources such as salary.

Schwartz, Real Estate and the Tax Reform Act of 1986
16 Real Est. Rev. 28 (Winter 1987)

The long-awaited tax reform is with us, and we are learning to live with it. Hereafter we will refer to the Tax Reform Act of 1986 as the "Act" or the "1986 Act." The Act's well-publicized cornerstone

good luck

X

is, of course, rate reduction. Congress has boldly equalized rates applicable to capital gains and ordinary income, with both slated to be 28 percent.[19] The corporate maximum rate becomes 34 percent for both classes of income.

To offset the revenue loss from rate reduction, Congress placed stringent statutory limitations on the utilization of tax shelters (or any form of activity) that, in Congress's view, resulted in an unintended tax advantage. . . .

Although it touches virtually every person in the country, the Act has a particularly dampening effect on certain types of real estate activity. Rental real estate and real estate activities that previously enjoyed unrestricted benefits in the form of tax credits have been most severely hit. On the other hand, it can be argued that dealer-type activities, such as building for sale or condominium and cooperative conversion, have been significantly aided by the reduction in the tax rate applicable to the ordinary income that the developer derives from such activities. . . .

The totally new statutory provisions affecting real estate are (1) restrictions on utilization of passive losses to offset income from salaries and portfolio investments and (2) the low-income housing credit. The passive loss restriction provision undoubtedly has the most immediate and direct impact upon tax shelter syndications, and it affects syndications that were established prior to the effective date of the statute. The low-income housing credit, which is a novel and unique form of incentive, becomes the only pure tax advantage to investing in low-income housing.

Let us now go hand-in-hand through the wondrous provisions of the 1986 Act that affect real estate ownership and transactions.

THE NEW ACCELERATED COST RECOVERY SYSTEM

The Act continues the accelerated cost recovery system (ACRS) that was introduced with the Economic Recovery Tax Act of 1981.

19. The 1986 Act reduced the number of individual tax brackets from 14 to 2, 15 percent and 28 percent. However, commencing in 1988 the benefit of the 15 percent marginal tax rate was phased out for taxpayers filing joint returns with taxable incomes between $71,900 and $149,250 and for individual taxpayers reporting taxable incomes between $43,150 and $89,560; hence, these taxpayers have a marginal tax bracket of 33 percent. The 1990 Act imposes three tax brackets for individuals: 15 percent, 28 percent, and 31 percent. Section 11101(a) of the 1990 Act, amending I.R.C. §§1, 2. However, the phase-out of personal exemptions together with a limitation on itemized deductions may result in an effective maximum marginal rate that is higher than 31 percent. In addition, under the 1990 Act the phase-out of personal exemptions together with the existing phase-out of the 15 percent bracket will result in the repeal of the "bubble" tax rate of 33 percent mentioned above. — ED.

Basically, under ACRS a taxpayer's investment in depreciable property is recovered (through depreciation deductions) over an arbitrarily determined recovery period rather than over the asset's expected useful life, as was true under pre-1981 law. To the delight of the real estate community, the recovery period assigned in 1981 to all real estate was fifteen years. Moreover, the method of depreciation was the rapid 175 percent declining balance method (200 percent declining balance for low-income housing). The ACRS, as first enacted, produced an astounding first-year deduction of 12 percent of depreciable cost (13 percent for low-income housing).

At various times since 1981, Congress lengthened the real estate recovery period until it reached nineteen years (May 1985), but fifteen-year recovery was retained for low-income housing.

The 1986 Act establishes a new ACRS that applies to all tangible business property placed in service after December 31, 1986. Real estate is divided into two classes — residential rental property and nonresidential real property. The new recovery period for residential rental property is 27.5 years, and the recovery period for nonresidential realty is 31.5 years. Both classes of real estate must be depreciated by the straight-line method of depreciation.

DEFINITIONS AND REGULATIONS

Residential property.   The Act defines residential rental property as buildings or structures that earn 80 percent or more of gross rental income from dwelling units. The term "dwelling unit" does not include units in a hotel, motel, inn, or other establishment in which more than one half of the units are used for transient occupancy. . . .

Nonresidential property.   Generally, the Act defines nonresidential real property as depreciable real property that is not residential real property.

A comparison of 1981 and 1986 ACRS.   The full impact of the change becomes evident when we compare the annual deductions that were available to a taxpayer under the 1981 Act versus those of the 1986 Act. The comparative annual deductions available under the two Acts to an investment in nonresidential realty with a depreciable basis of $1 million are shown in Exhibit 1.

At the end of fifteen years, the old ACRS fully returned the taxpayer's cost, whereas the new ACRS has returned less than one half. The remainder must be recovered during the balance of the 31.5-year recovery period. Under both Acts, salvage value is not taken into account in determining depreciable basis subject to recovery.

Mid-month convention.   A mid-month convention applies to both residential rental property and nonresidential real property. The depreciation allowance for the first year that property is placed in service is based on the number of months the property was in service, and

E x h i b i t 1

**Annual Deductions Available to a $1 Million
Depreciable Basis Under 1981 and 1986 Tax Acts**

Year	1981 Act (15-Year ACRS, 175% Declining Balance)	1986 Act (31.5-Year ACRS, Straight-Line)
1	$ 120,000	$ 31,746*
2	100,000	31,746
3	90,000	31,746
4	80,000	31,746
5	70,000	31,746
6	60,000	31,746
7	60,000	31,746
8	60,000	31,746
9	60,000	31,746
10	50,000	31,746
11	50,000	31,746
12	50,000	31,746
13	50,000	31,746
14	50,000	31,746
15	50,000	31,746
Total	$1,000,000	$476,190

* Depreciation in year 1 should be reduced to reflect mid-month convention. — ED.

the property is treated as having been placed in service in the middle of its first month. Similarly, property that the taxpayer disposes of at any time during the month is treated as having been disposed of in the middle of the month. . . .

Alternative depreciation system.   The alternative depreciation system permits taxpayers to depreciate real property over a forty-year life, using only straight-line depreciation. This election to decelerate depreciation is irrevocable. To be sure, few taxpayers would voluntarily elect the alternative method. It *must,* however, be used for:

- Foreign realty;
- Realty that is financed by tax-exempt bonds; and
- Realty leased to or used by an exempt organization. (Further, the recovery period of property leased to an exempt organization cannot be less than 125 percent of the lease term.)

Leasehold improvements.   Under prior law, a tenant who made leasehold improvements could either depreciate the cost over the applicable real estate ACRS recovery period or amortize them over the remaining lease term, whichever was shorter. Under the 1986 Act, the tenant recovers the costs of his leasehold improvements according to the rules applicable to real estate generally, without regard to the lease term. In other words, the tenant depreciates the improvement over either 27.5 years or 31.5 years. He can deduct any unrecovered cost at the end of the lease term. . . .

REHABILITATION TAX CREDIT

NB JB Sullivan

Under prior law, a three-tier tax credit was available for the qualified rehabilitation of buildings:

- A 15 percent credit for the rehabilitation of nonresidential buildings at least thirty years of age;
- A 20 percent credit for the rehabilitation of nonresidential buildings at least forty years of age; and
- A 25 percent credit for the rehabilitation of certified historic structures.

The 1986 Act replaces the existing three-tier structure with a 20 percent credit for rehabilitations of certified historic structures and a 10 percent credit for rehabilitations of other buildings if they were placed in service before 1936. As under prior law, the credit for the rehabilitation of buildings that are not certified historic structures is limited to nonresidential buildings, but the credit for rehabilitation for historic buildings is available for both residential and nonresidential buildings.

The old law requirements for determining whether a rehabilitation qualifies for the credit are generally retained in the Act. Further, the Act continues the requirement that the taxpayer must recover the rehabilitation costs using straight-line depreciation. Since straight-line depreciation is the only type permitted by the 1986 Act, this requirement is restrictive only if the property qualifies under a transitional rule for old ACRS depreciation methods. Tenant rehabilitation expenditures do not qualify for the credit unless the remaining lease term, on the date the rehabilitation is completed, is at least as long as the recovery period applicable to the property (either 27.5 or 31.5 years).

EXTERNAL WALLS REQUIREMENT

The amount of demolition that can take place before the alteration becomes more than a rehabilitation has been modified. The old law provision that requires at least 75 percent of the existing external walls to be retained in place as external walls is replaced by the following dual requirement:

- At least 75 percent of the external walls must be retained in place (and 50 percent must remain external); and
- At least 75 percent of the internal structural framework of the building must be preserved.

Thus, under the 1986 law, a building that is completely gutted internally can no longer qualify for the rehabilitation credit. In the case of certified historic structures, Congress has given the Secretary of the Interior discretion to determine what is a historic rehabilitation. The Secretary need not comply with the external walls requirement.

FULL BASIS REDUCTION

The Act eliminates a limited exception in prior law that applies to certified historic rehabilitation. That exception required a depreciable basis reduction for only 50 percent of the amount of the credit. The new law requires a full basis adjustment for any rehabilitation credits. . . .

CAPITAL GAINS AND LOSSES

Since passage of the Economic Recovery Tax Act of 1981, individuals have enjoyed a deduction equal to 60 percent of their net long-term capital gains each year. This deduction has effectively limited the tax rate on capital gains to 40 percent of the ordinary income rate. Because the maximum ordinary income rate was 50 percent, the capital gain rate was capped at 20 percent. The new Act repeals the net capital gain deduction for individuals and puts a top rate on net capital gains of 28 percent, thus equalizing the rates on capital gains and ordinary income. . . .

The Act generally continues to permit taxpayers to offset capital gains against capital losses and, if capital losses exceed capital gains, permits up to $3,000 of such excess losses to be deductible against ordinary income. This is a slight modification of preexisting law. Previously, one half of the excess of long-term capital losses over long-term gains could be deducted against ordinary income. . . .

CORPORATIONS

The maximum corporate capital gain rate is increased from 28 percent to 34 percent (34 percent is also the maximum corporate ordinary income rate). The 34 percent rate applies to gain recognized by corporations after December 31, 1986.

It should be noted that the distinction between capital gains and ordinary income (and the network of statutes, regulations, and rulings that have built up around the differences between the two) has remained firmly in place, even though the rates applicable to capital gains and ordinary income are now equal. Thus, if Congress in its wisdom determines in the future that the ordinary income rate should be increased, the increase could be accomplished without increasing the long-term capital gain rate.

EXTENSION OF AT-RISK RULES TO REAL ESTATE ACTIVITIES

Pre-1986 law imposed an at-risk limitation on all losses incurred by taxpayers from business and income-producing activities. The rule was designed to prevent a taxpayer from deducting losses larger than his actual economic investment in an activity, but did not apply to losses arising from real estate holdings.

Under the at-risk rules, a taxpayer's deductible losses from an activity for any taxable year were limited to the amount the taxpayer had placed at-risk in the activity. The initial amount at risk was generally the sum of the following taxpayer contributions to the activity:

- His cash contributions to the activity;
- The adjusted basis of other property that he contributed to the activity; and
- Amounts that he borrowed for use in the activity for which he has personal liability or for which he has pledged, as security for repayment, property not used in the activity.

The total sum of at-risk investments was generally increased each year by the taxpayer's share of income, and it was decreased by the taxpayer's share of losses and withdrawals from the activity.

Real estate activities were excluded from the at-risk limitation. An investor in real estate could deduct losses up to the full acquisition cost of the property, even though a significant portion of the property was financed with nonrecourse mortgage indebtedness.

The 1986 Act now extends the at-risk limitation to real estate activities. Generally, a taxpayer's losses are limited to the amount of his at-risk investment (including *personal liability* on mortgages). But a taxpayer *cannot* deduct losses that reflect the full cost of real property if a portion of the cost is financed by nonrecourse indebtedness.

SOME DEFINITIONS

Qualified nonrecourse financing. To understand the real estate implications of the new at-risk rules, we must examine the following definitions:

- Qualified nonrecourse financing[20]
- Partnership interest
- Transferee

Qualified nonrecourse financing. The one saving exception to the at-risk rule for real estate is the qualified nonrecourse financing. The amount of a qualified nonrecourse loan may be included in the taxpayer's at-risk basis.

A qualified nonrecourse financing is a nonrecourse mortgage given by a lender who regularly makes loans. It cannot be a loan from a person related to the taxpayer (unless the loan is commercially reasonable and is made under the same terms as would be available from an unrelated person) or to any person from whom the taxpayer acquired the property. Further, it cannot be a loan from the recipient of a fee with respect to the transaction (promoter) or from a person related to such fee recipient. A loan can nevertheless be a qualified nonrecourse financing if the lender normally makes loans and is otherwise qualified, even if it is a joint venture partner in the real estate activity. A loan from a government or governmental entity or a loan guaranteed by a government or governmental entity is deemed to be a qualified nonrecourse financing.

Partnership interest. A partner's basis for his partnership interest, which determines the amount of tax losses arising out of partnership activities that he can deduct, can be increased by his share of any qualified nonrecourse financing of the partnership provided that the financing would be a qualified nonrecourse financing if he, as an individual, were the borrower.

Subsequent transferees. A transferee of the property or a transferee of a partnership interest will be permitted to treat the qualified nonrecourse financing as a qualified nonrecourse financing in the transferee's hands if the debt would otherwise be qualified with respect to the transferee. . . .

---

20. The new at-risk rules applicable to real estate are examined in detail at Chapter 2B, note 7diii, infra. — ED.

LIMITATIONS ON LOSSES AND CREDITS FROM PASSIVE ACTIVITIES

The 1986 Act provides that deductions from passive trade or business activities may not exceed income from all such passive activities; that is, generally, they may not be deducted against other income. Similarly, credits from passive activities generally are limited as offsets to the tax that is allocable to the passive activities. Suspended losses and credits are carried forward and treated as deductions and credits from passive trade or business activities in the next year. Cumulative suspended losses from an activity are allowed in full when the taxpayer disposes of his entire interest in the activity. . . .

Losses and credits from one passive activity may be applied against income for the taxable year from other passive activities or against income subsequently generated by any passive activity. Such losses and credits generally cannot be applied to shelter other (nonpassive) income, like compensation for services or portfolio income (interest, dividends, royalties, and gains from the sale of property held for investment). The passive loss limitation provision is intended to ensure that salary and portfolio interest income, or other nonpassive income, cannot be offset by tax losses from passive activities until the amount of such losses is determined upon disposition of the passive activity.

DEFINING PASSIVE INCOME

A taxpayer has passive income if the activity from which the income is derived involves the conduct of trade or business in which the taxpayer does not materially participate. A taxpayer participates materially only if he is involved in operations on a regular, continuous, and substantial basis. Even if the individual owns the trade or business directly or owns an interest in an activity like a general partnership or Subchapter S corporation, he must nevertheless be involved in operations on a regular, continuous, and substantial basis, in order to be materially participating. The Act treats income from a limited partnership interest as intrinsically passive, and losses from trade or business activities that are allocable to a limited partnership interest may not, prior to disposition, be applied against any of the taxpayer's income other than income from passive activities. The passive loss rule applies to individuals, estates, and trusts. The rule also applies to personal service corporations.

RENTAL INCOME

The Act defines most rental income as passive, *whether or not the taxpayer materially participates in the activity.* A preexisting distinction in the law between "active rental activity" and "passive rental activity" is continued. Thus, activities that involve the active rendering of substantial services like the operation of a hotel or similar transient lodging are not passive activity. Nor is activity as a dealer in real estate considered passive. But long-term rentals or leases of realty generally are considered to be passive rental activities and the losses from such rental activities are allowed against income from other passive activities, but not against other income.

ACTIVE PARTICIPATION IN RENTAL REAL ESTATE ACTIVITY

A relief provision from the absolute rule that rental activity must always be considered passive is available for taxpayers of moderate income. An individual may offset up to $25,000 of nonpassive income by using losses and credits from rental real estate activities in which the individual *actively participates*. (Note "active participation," as defined in the relief provision, differs from material participation, the term used above.) The relief provision applies only to individuals, and only if they have at least a 10 percent interest in the activity, and only if they do not have sufficient passive income for the year to use fully the losses and credits available from their rental real estate activities.

The $25,000 amount is reduced by 50 percent of the amount by which the taxpayer's adjusted gross income for the year exceeds $100,000. (It may not go below zero.) Thus, the relief is totally eliminated when the taxpayer's taxable income reaches $150,000.

The "active participation" standard in this provision is less stringent than the "material participation" requirement which distinguishes active from passive interests. The active participation requirement can be satisfied without regular continuous and substantial involvement in operations, as long as the taxpayer participates in management decisions or in arranging for others to provide services (such as repairs) in a significant and bona fide manner. Management decisions that are relevant in this context include approving new tenants, deciding on rental terms, and approving capital or repair expenditures. Thus, the relief provision is specifically targeted at a taxpayer who owns and rents out an apartment that may or may not be his part-time vacation home or a former residence, even if he hires a rental agent and others to provide services like repairs. A limited partner and the lessor under a net lease of real estate are unlikely to have the degree of involvement that active participation entails.

TREATMENT OF LOSSES AND CREDITS

Losses arising from a passive activity generally are deductible only against income from that or another passive activity. Suspended passive activity losses for the year are carried forward indefinitely, (but are not carried back) and may be used in subsequent years against passive activity income. If any passive losses are not allowed in any given year, a portion of the suspended losses is allocated to each passive activity on a pro rata basis. This allocation is necessary in order to establish the suspended losses that are allowed in full upon a disposition of an activity.

Credits arising with respect to passive activity generally are treated in the same manner as deductions. That is, credits may not be used to offset tax attributable to income other than passive income.

For example, if a taxpayer owes $50,000 of tax disregarding net passive income, and $80,000 of tax considering both net passive and other taxable income, then the amount of tax attributable to passive income is $30,000. In this case, any credits not in excess of $30,000 attributable to the taxpayer's passive activities are allowable. In the absence of net passive income for a taxable year, no tax is attributable to passive income, and passive credits generally are not allowable for the year. . . . .

INTEREST DEDUCTION LIMITATIONS

The 1986 Act has significantly expanded the categories of interest expense that are denied unlimited deductibility. . . .[21]

THE LOW-INCOME HOUSING CREDIT

The 1986 Act eliminates the three major tax incentives that previously encouraged the acquisition, development and operation of low-income housing:

- Fifteen-year accelerated cost recovery with 200 percent declining balance depreciation.
- Five-year (sixty-month) amortization of qualified expenditures to rehabilitate low-income housing.
- The full deductibility of construction period interest expense during the construction or rehabilitation of low-income housing.

These incentives have been replaced by a low-income housing credit, a level annual deduction from income that the taxpayer may

21. The expansion of the limitation on the deduction of investment interest and the additional limitations on the interest deduction imposed by the 1986 Act are examined at Chapter 5B3b, note 5. — ED.

take each year for ten years. The credit gives the owner of low-income property a tax benefit that has a present value of:

- 70 percent of the taxpayer's cost basis in qualified new buildings and rehabilitation expenditures that are not federally subsidized dwelling units; and
- 30 percent of the taxpayer's cost basis attributable to other qualifying expenditures.

Expenditures qualifying for the 30 percent present value credit consist of the cost of acquisition, certain rehabilitation expenditures incurred in connection with the acquisition of an existing building and federally subsidized new building or rehabilitation expenditures. A taxpayer's credit amount in any taxable year is computed by applying the appropriate credit percentage to the appropriate qualified basis amount in that year.

Rehabilitation expenditures are treated as a new building if:

- They are not federally subsidized;
- They were incurred during any twenty-four-month period; and
- They average $2,000 or more per low-income dwelling unit.

The overall tax benefit is achieved by the following calculations: Owners of projects that are acquired or in which construction starts prior to January 1, 1988 receive a credit of 9 percent annually (in the case of the 70 percent present value credit) and 4 percent annually (in the case of the 30 percent present value credit). For projects in which construction or acquisition occurs after 1987, the Treasury Department is directed to make monthly adjustments to the credit percentages in such manner that the credits shall have then present values of 70 percent and 30 percent of costs. For such projects, the applicable credit percentages that are to be consistently taken each year will be the credit percentages determined for the month in which construction begins. . . .

REQUIRED SET-ASIDE PERCENTAGE FOR LOW-INCOME TENANTS

In order that owners of residential rental projects qualify for the low-income credit, 20 percent or more of the aggregate residential units in all existing buildings in a project must be occupied by individuals with income of 50 percent or less of area median income, as adjusted for family size. Alternatively, 40 percent or more of the aggregate residential units in a project must be occupied by individuals with incomes of 60 percent or less of area median income, as adjusted for family size. . . .

The determination of whether a tenant qualifies for purposes of the low income set aside is made on a continuing basis, rather than only on the date the tenant initially occupies the unit. An increase in a tenant's income may, therefore, result in a unit's ceasing to qualify. Increases within certain de minimis guidelines provided in the statute are not considered.

GROSS RENT LIMITATION

The gross rent paid by families occupying units qualifying for the credit may not exceed 30 percent of the applicable qualifying income for a family of its size. Vacant units formerly occupied by low-income individuals may continue to be treated as if they were occupied by a qualified low-income individual provided the landlord makes reasonable attempts to rent the unit and no other units of comparable or smaller size in the project are rented to nonqualifying individuals.

CONTINUING COMPLIANCE REQUIREMENT

The minimum set-aside requirement must be met within twelve months of the date the building (or rehabilitation) is placed in service, and complied with continuously thereafter for a period of *fifteen years* beginning on the first day of the first taxable year in which the credit is claimed. Within ninety days of the end of the first taxable year for which the credit is claimed, and for each taxable year thereafter during the fifteen-year compliance period, the taxpayer must certify to the Internal Revenue Service that the project has continuously complied with the set-aside requirement, and he must furnish other information relating to the credit. . . .

TRANSFERABILITY

A purchaser who acquires a project during the period for which the property is eligible to receive the credit is eligible to continue to receive the credit as if the purchaser were the original owner. The old owner's credit will, however, be recaptured upon a transfer unless he posts a bond to insure continued compliance of the building for the remainder of the fifteen-year compliance period.

FEDERALLY SUBSIDIZED BUILDING

A federally subsidized building, even if it is a new building, can qualify only for the 30 percent present value credit. A federally subsidized building is:

- A building financed with tax-exempt bonds; and
- A building receiving federal interest subsidies with respect to financing.

UTILIZATION OF CREDIT

A happy note for the taxpayer who successfully wends his way through the maze of qualifying rules is that the low-income housing credit is generally not subject to the provision limiting passive loss deductions, because the credit is treated as arising from rental real estate activities in which the taxpayer actively participates. Thus, the low-income housing credit could be utilized to recoup tax liability from income generated from other sources, such as salaries and portfolio income, but not in excess of $25,000. Further, the taxpayer's depreciable basis in a project is not reduced by the amount of low-income credits claimed. . . .

Conclusion

The jury will be out for years on the issue of whether the Tax Reform Act of 1986 will do its intended job of simplifying and reducing taxes without causing a shrinkage in revenue. This writer believes that Congress has set the stage for a possible rate increase on ordinary income that can be accomplished without changing the 28 percent rate on long-term capital gains. For this reason, investors should not abandon structures that preserve capital gain income, notwithstanding today's parity of rates.

Undoubtedly, the Act has dealt a severe blow to the holding of real estate for investment and/or rental purposes. Perhaps the best that can be said for the changes is that they will force investors to make decisions on the basis of the economics rather than the tax benefits of individual real estate transactions. Dealer-type activity and the conversion of rental housing to cooperative or condominium status will probably be encouraged by the rate reductions. The benefits eliminated from low-income housing investments will undoubtedly dampen the enthusiasm of developers for this type of property. It does not seem possible that the low-income housing credit, horribly encrusted with restrictions, provisions, requirements and threats of recapture, will be a meaningful replacement for the benefits that were available in the past.

Time alone will tell whether the Act represents a historic coup that will bring glory to the Reagan Administration or will lead to a budget-threatening disaster.

As you know by now, in enacting the 1986 Act Congress changed tax history by eliminating the longstanding preferential tax treatment for long-term capital gains, thereby obliterating a major underpinning of the real estate tax shelter: the ability of the depreciation deduction under I.R.C. §167 to convert what would otherwise be ordinary rental income (previously taxed at a maximum rate of 50 percent for individuals) into long-term capital gain (previously taxed at a maximum rate of 20 percent for individuals). After the repeal of the 60 percent deduction for long-term capital gains under I.R.C. §1202, the maximum individual tax rate on such gains (which includes gain from the sale of income-producing real estate and raw land)[22] increased from 20 percent to 33 percent, and then under the 1990 Act decreased to 28 percent. The following excerpts deal with the question whether this increase in the maximum rate from 20 to 28 percent makes sense as a matter of sound tax and social policy, including the issue of whether the increased tax rate will produce an overall growth or decline in tax revenues.

Congressional Budget Office, How Capital Gains Tax Rates Affect Revenues: The Historical Evidence
xi-41 (Mar. 1988)

The Tax Reform Act of 1986 lowered marginal personal income tax rates but also eliminated many tax preferences, including the 60 percent deduction for long-term capital gains. The maximum tax rate on long-term gains was increased from 20 percent under previous law to 28 percent for the highest-income taxpayers and 33 percent for taxpayers just below the highest-income group. The reasons for eliminating the capital gains deduction were to help finance the reduction in ordinary income tax rates, to allow the top rate to be cut substantially without providing disproportionate relief to the highest-income group, and to simplify the tax system.

How much additional revenue will be obtained by increasing tax rates on capital gains is uncertain. Taxpayers can defer the payment of capital gains taxes by not realizing the gains — that is, by holding onto

---

22. Gains from the sale of income-producing real estate used in a trade or business (such as an office building or shopping center) and raw land were both eligible for long-term capital gain treatment under I.R.C. §§1231(b)(1) and 1221, respectively, provided that the seller was not a "dealer" (a taxpayer who held the real estate as inventory or sold the real estate to customers in the ordinary course of business) for tax purposes.

assets instead of selling them; they can avoid taxation of gains entirely by passing on their assets to others at death. If realizations decline by a greater percentage than the tax rate increases, revenues from capital gains taxes could fall instead of increasing.

A number of statistical studies have provided strong evidence that realizations of capital gains decline when tax rates on gains are increased. The estimated size of this response of capital gains realizations, however, differs greatly among studies. The responses estimated in some studies have been used to support a claim that the 1986 act reduced revenue from capital gains taxes when it increased the tax rates, and that lowering the maximum tax rate on long-term gains to 15 percent would increase revenue. The estimates in other research suggest an opposite conclusion. Moreover, all of these studies have used methodologies that are open to criticism.

This study provides new evidence on the relationship between realizations of long-term capital gains and tax rates on capital gains, based on statistical analysis of data for the years 1954 through 1985. The statistical results offer additional support for the view that higher tax rates do lower realizations of capital gains. As a result, increases in tax rates on capital gains produce much less revenue than they would if taxpayers' behavior were unaffected. On the other hand, simulations using the estimated behavioral responses still show a net revenue increase from the 1986 act. They also indicate that lowering the top rate on long-term capital gains to 15 percent would result in a net revenue loss.

The estimates of the behavioral response contain considerable statistical uncertainty. The proposition that a maximum tax rate of 15 percent would yield more revenue than current law rates cannot be ruled out with certainty, although the probability attached to this result is very low. Similarly, the proposition that revenue from capital gains taxes is maximized at rates far above those of current law also cannot be ruled out.

This report is concerned only with the issue of estimating revenue. Many other factors need to be considered in deciding how to tax capital gains. Arguments for lower tax rates on gains are that they promote saving and investment and channel more resources into new ventures. In addition, a preferential rate on nominal gains provides a rough adjustment for the fact that some gains reflect inflation instead of real increases in purchasing power (though one could directly eliminate the taxation of the inflationary component of gains without introducing a preferential rate). Arguments against reintroducing a differential between long-term and short-term capital gains and ordinary income by lowering the tax rate on capital gains are that the differential would add complexity to the tax system, encourage tax shelter activity, and distort choices among financial instruments and real assets.

Kotlarsky, Capital Gains and Tax Policy
41 Tax Notes 319 (1988)

I. INTRODUCTION

During most of the history of the United States tax system, capital gains have enjoyed preferential treatment. Prior to 1913, capital gains were not thought to be income and were not taxed. For a short eight-year period after the adoption of the Sixteenth Amendment, capital gains and ordinary income were taxed at the same rate. The Revenue Act of 1921 allowed net capital gain to be taxed at an alternative rate of 12.5 percent, much below the maximum rate on ordinary income. Although tax laws changed many times during the next 65 years, capital gains were always taxed at a lower effective rate. The capital gain rate preference became one of the pillars of our tax policy. It was here to stay.

Then came the tax reform movement and the unthinkable happened. In the Tax Reform Act of 1986, Congress eliminated, at least temporarily, the preferential treatment of capital gains.

Despite the repeal of the capital gains rate preference, the Tax Reform Act of 1986 did not abandon the entire notion of capital gains. Apparently expecting that the preference may be reintroduced, Congress retained the definition of capital assets and other related provisions in the new Internal Revenue Code of 1986. Not surprisingly, before the proverbial ink had dried, a capital gains rate cut was proposed. The capital gains preference debate had begun.

The debate has attracted a wide range of participants on both sides of the issue. As one may expect, Republicans generally are in favor of reducing the rate of the capital gains tax. President Reagan expressed his support for a capital gains rate cut in the State of the Union Address. No less than 12 Republican-sponsored bills to restore the capital gains tax preference have been introduced since then. Vice President Bush has committed his presidential campaign to a capital gains rate cut. A restoration of the preference was supported by the White House Conference on Small Business, the United States Chamber of Commerce, the American Council for Capital Formation, the *Wall Street Journal* and numerous economists.

The opponents of a capital gains preference are just as numerous. A capital gains rate cut is virtually unanimously opposed by the Democrats. A capital gains tax preference also is opposed by Citizens for Tax Justice, the *New York Times,* the *Washington Post,* and the *Los Angeles Times.* Articles opposing a capital gains tax preference were published in *Tax Notes,* the *Wall Street Journal,* and the *Legislative Journal.* . . .

IV. HORIZONTAL EQUITY

A capital gains preference clearly violates the principle of horizontal equity because it allows a taxpayer realizing $100 of capital gains to pay less tax than a taxpayer realizing $100 of ordinary income. It has been argued, however, that the existing tax system unfairly taxes capital gains at ordinary rates and a capital gains preference is needed to correct this unfairness. Proponents of the preference have advanced, at various times and in various forms, four types of arguments: income-bunching, general double taxation, inflation, and double taxation of "C" corporation earnings. . . .

The remaining two arguments — inflation and double taxation of "C" corporations — correctly point out that the lack of inflation adjustments and double tax on "C" corporation earnings violate the principle of horizontal equity. Unfortunately, the proposed solutions are unrelated to the problems, leading essentially to a "two wrongs make a right" approach.

The first "two wrongs" argument is that reduction in capital gains tax rates compensates for inflation. This argument is correct only in some fairly unique circumstances. In most cases, a capital gains preference will under-compensate or over-compensate the taxpayer. For instance, if a capital asset appreciates at the rate of inflation, there is no real gain, and any tax, even at reduced rates, is rather unfair and the reduced rate does not sufficiently compensate the taxpayer. On the other hand, if the asset's appreciation outpaces the rate of inflation by a wide margin, a lower tax rate will be a windfall.

A general reduction of the capital gains tax rate, applied without any consideration to the rate of inflation and the length of the holding period, does not even begin to approximate taxation of real economic income. Furthermore, if capital gains tax rates are to be reduced to compensate taxpayers for the effect of inflation, it is only sensible and logical to reduce the tax rates applicable to interest income. I believe that no supporters of capital gain tax cuts have argued for the same treatment of interest. And nobody seems to suggest that capital gains tax rates should be higher than ordinary income tax rates during periods of deflation.

The final major "two wrongs" argument is that the capital gains tax preference is needed to reduce the effect of double taxation of corporate earnings. The major and obvious flaw in this argument is that it may be applied to the stock of "C" corporations only and cannot possibly support an across the board capital gains rate cut. . . .

VII. EFFICIENCY

Tax policy is not baseball, and six strikes do not make two outs. The remaining factor may be overwhelmingly in favor of the legislation.

Therefore, it is necessary to analyze the economic effects of a capital gains preference. Two main economic efficiency arguments are that a capital gains tax cut is efficient because it resolves the "lock-in" problem and because it promotes risk taking.

A. "LOCK-IN"

The "lock-in" argument is another "two wrongs make a right" statement. However, because of its popularity and substantial lack of common sense, it deserves a detailed analysis.

The argument goes, more or less, as follows: An investor *"I"* has a relatively unproductive asset, *"A."* The fair market value of *A* is $100 and it produces after-tax cash flow of $9 per year. This return is below the market rate of return of 12 percent. In a tax-free world, *I* would sell *A* and would invest $100 at 12 percent. Unfortunately, *I* has to pay taxes. If *I* bought *A* many years ago for $20, if *I* sells *A* for $100, *I* will recognize $80 of capital gain, pay $32 in tax and will be able to invest only $68 at 12 percent. This will produce a return of $8.16 per year and *I* will be better off keeping the unproductive asset *A*. On the other hand, if the capital gains tax rate is 20 percent, *I* will pay only $16 in tax, invest $84, and his return will be $10.08 per year. In this case, *I* will sell asset *A* and *I* will not be locked into an unproductive asset; since the ownership of unproductive assets is inefficient, the efficiency of the system will be increased if the "lock-in" problem is eliminated through reduction of the capital gains tax rate.

The first response to the "lock-in" argument is that the "lock-in" is a problem brought about by the lack of taxation of interim appreciation. To remedy this problem by a capital gains tax preference is not only a second wrong to make a right, but also is a second tax giveaway — a lower rate on top of deferrals. . . .

Additionally, a capital gains tax cut is not likely to resolve the "lock-in" problem in most cases. A capital gains rate cut is not likely to unlock personal depreciable assets because such assets tend to depreciate and because the depreciation recapture is taxed at ordinary rates, a capital gains preference will not significantly reduce the effective tax rate on gain from the sale of depreciable personal assets. Therefore, a capital gains preference may be only helpful in unlocking real estate and nondepreciable assets.

Professor McDonald, however, has demonstrated that in the case of nondepreciable assets the "lock-in" problem exists unless the tax rate is reduced to zero.[40] He has proven further that a depreciable real

---

40. McDonald, Depreciability of Assets and the Taxation of Capital Gains, 32 Nat'l Tax J. 83-85 (1979). Professor McDonald's proof is only applicable to a limited

property may be completely unlocked only if the ratio of the capital gains tax rate to the ordinary income tax rate is equal to or less than the ratio of the present value of all depreciation deductions to the purchase price of the property. Routine computations indicate that within the reasonable range of the applicable discount rates, the value of depreciation deductions constitutes between 12 and 18 percent of the fair market value of real property. Therefore, to unlock real properties completely, it will be necessary to reduce the capital gains tax rate to about five percent. Theoretically, a reduction of the rate to 15 percent will not unlock many assets.

B. RISK TAKING

The remaining argument is that a capital gains tax cut will promote risk taking and that investments in risky capital assets will increase economic efficiency. I have serious reservations about both parts of the argument.

First, a reduction in the capital gains tax rate does not change investors' mentality. No matter what the tax rate on capital gains is, an investor will invest only if he believes that his potential after-tax returns justify the risk. No doubt, a capital gains tax cut will not reduce the risk of any particular investment. A risky investment can become more attractive only because a tax cut will increase the value of the investment. Unfortunately, the increase in value is likely to be accompanied by an increase in price.

For example, assume that A wants to buy an asset from B. A valued the asset and concluded that the value of the asset is $10. If B wants to sell the asset for $12, A will not be interested. If the tax rate applicable to income derived from the asset is reduced, the value of the asset will increase. Suppose after the tax reduction, the value of the asset is $15. If B does not react and sells the asset for $12, A will make a risky investment. However, B is likely to raise the price to $18 and, again, A will not invest in the asset. In this situation, it is difficult to see how a tax cut promotes risk taking.

Supporters of a capital gains preference usually point out that the capital gains tax increase in the early 1970s was followed by a virtual elimination of available venture capital. I, however, do not find this historical evidence convincing. I believe that high capital gains tax rates were responsible for virtual elimination of venture capital and IPO investments, but not because they caused the investors to stand on the sidelines. Rather, high tax rates reduced the value of new

---

set of circumstances, but I believe that the technique can successfully be generalized with similar results.

businesses and their owners, unwilling to sell their companies at bargain-basement prices, priced their wares out of the market. . . .

Second, the increase in the value of risky assets in most cases will do nothing to improve the efficiency of the United States economy. I do not see how the increased prices of speculative investments — art, gold, stamps, coins, rugs, etc. — will have any effect on economic efficiency. Similarly, I do not believe that a capital gains tax cut will have any significant effect on the use of personal residences. As was pointed out before, most personal depreciable assets do depreciate and will not benefit from any tax cut. Depreciable real estate will benefit substantially from a tax cut and it may be expected that a tax cut will encourage construction of new apartment complexes, shopping malls, and office buildings. Our previous experience clearly indicates that the untold zillions of office buildings constructed primarily for the sake of tax benefits is not such a good idea. It is difficult to see how, in the present economic environment, government subsidies to commercial real estate will improve the United States economic outlook. . . .

VIII. Conclusion

While the economic efficiency factor does support a reduction in the capital gains tax rate, I do not perceive rather unclear economic efficiency gains which may be achieved by a capital gains preference to be of major importance. Therefore, I must conclude that what weight the economic efficiency factor has is insufficient to overcome the negative influence of the other factors. In fact, I find very little good to be said about an across-the-board capital gains tax cut and do not see any justification, other than nostalgia, for the restoration of the pre-Tax Reform Act of 1986 system.

Can this conclusion be changed by a slight tinkering with the proposed tax cut? Maybe. It is possible that the conclusion will not be so negative if, for example, a capital gains tax cut is restricted to certain assets or tied to the holding period.

I do not believe, however, that such an effort is worthwhile. The existing system of capital assets taxation has numerous fundamental tax policy problems. For example, violating the principle of neutrality, it allows the recognition of gain to be deferred until the sale. In violation of principles of neutrality and horizontal equity, earnings of "C" corporations are subject to double tax. The existing system does not allow inflation adjustments, limits capital loss deductions, creates the preference of debt over equity and causes capital assets to be locked-in. In addition, it may be argued that the existing system does not raise enough revenue and does not provide sufficient start-up business and venture capital incentive.

Proposed capital gains preferences are not specifically designed to correct any of these problems. A little tinkering will not make a square peg fit a round hole. I suggest that politicians and tax professionals should abandon any quick fix solutions and dedicate time and energy to the creation of a new capital gains taxation system, free of the fatal faults of the existing one.

Rose and O'Neil, The Impact of the Tax Reform Act of 1986 on Rents and Property Values

15 J. Real Est. Taxn. 145 (Winter 1988)

ECONOMIC CONSEQUENCES OF TRA '86

Investors with negative before-tax cash flows will be hit the hardest by TRA '86, especially those who are also in high-income tax brackets. Investors with positive before-tax cash flows will experience the least amount of lost-tax savings under TRA '86. . . .

. . . Real estate investors can be expected to pass along the lost-tax savings to tenants in the form of higher rents when and wherever market conditions allow. If the economic conditions in an area will not permit rents to be adequately increased, investment property values may decline as investors seek other forms of investment. This could be more detrimental to tenants than rent increases if rental housing shortages occur. It is believed that property values will decline 8 to 12 percent in areas in which rents cannot be increased unless investors accept lower returns.

According to the National Association of Home Builders, approximately 80 percent of renters have total incomes of less than $25,000 per year and, as can be expected, pay a larger share of their income for housing than other income groups.[2] The modest income tax reductions that individuals in the lower tax brackets will receive from TRA '86 may be more than offset by higher rents.

In a study by the National Association of Realtors in 1986, the group reported during the Senate Finance Committee's debate on tax revision that lengthening the depreciation period for structures to thirty years would cause rents to increase by more than 10 percent or about $40 per month, for a typical apartment rented by a family earning less than $15,000 per year. Our analysis not only takes into consideration the depreciation changes but also includes the elimination of the capital gains tax, the passive loss limitation rule, and the lower tax rates. As a result, our estimate of the impact on rents is higher. When these additional provisions aimed at limiting real estate investment tax write-

2. Report prepared by the National Association of Home Builders, Summary Analysis of the Impacts of Tax Reform Proposals on Housing Costs and Housing Activities (Jan. 23, 1985).

offs are taken into consideration, rents may need to increase at least 17 percent in order to offset the lost after-tax cash flows as a result of TRA '86.

In essence, prior tax law was subsidizing both real estate investors and tenants. Although restricting write-offs for real estate investors may have been politically desirable, doing so may have an unintended economic impact on tenants. Rent increases in any geographic area as a result of TRA '86 will be determined by specific economic conditions in the area. Just as TRA '86 may affect each taxpayer differently, upward pressure on rents will be different in each geographic area.

Madison and Dwyer, The Law of Real Estate Financing
¶1.05[6][c] (Cum. Supp. No. 1) (1990)

EXAMPLE 1: MODERATELY LEVERAGED REAL ESTATE INVESTMENT

The following examples involving the "L-G partnership" illustrate the effects of the numerous changes made by the Tax Reform Act of 1986 that affect real estate investments. The first example (example A) illustrates the impact of prior law on a moderately leveraged investment that is being depreciated over a 19-year ACRS cost recovery period.

The second example (example B) applies all the rules of the Tax Reform Act of 1986, including straight line depreciation over a twenty-seven and one half year cost recovery period and the full implementation of the passive loss limitations under I.R.C. §469. In the absence of outside passive income, passive losses cannot be utilized as current deductions. Unused or "suspended" passive losses can be carried forward and are allowable in subsequent years against passive income and the balance of the suspended losses are allowed in full to offset gain from the sale of the real estate in 1999.

In the third example (example C), the rules under the 1986 Act are fully implemented, but passive losses are not suspended. It is assumed that outside passive income is available to absorb the passive losses. This example graphically illustrates the net effect of the passive loss limitation.

The following assumptions are made in all three examples:

1. Newly constructed apartment building costing $10,000,000; the land is ground leased.
2. Total limited partner capital contributions: $2,000,000 paid over 4 years.
3. Financing terms: 15-year "qualified" nonrecourse first mortgage for $8,000,000 at 9 percent, level monthly payments based on 30-year amortization with balloon payment in year 15.

4. Building/property placed in service on June 1, 1991 and sold on May 1, 1999.
5. Sales price: (A) $1 over mortgage balance; (B) 5 percent annual compound appreciation.
6. Inflation (for purposes of revenue and expense): 4 percent per year.
7. The general partners receive one percent interest in partnership but do not make any cash contributions.
8. The limited partners are allocated 99 percent of income or loss from operations and 99 percent of any gain or loss on sale; however, once the negative capital account balances are restored, any excess gain will be allocated 20 percent to the general partners and 80 percent to the limited partners.
9. The limited partners are individuals with maximum marginal tax brackets of 50 percent under prior law and with tax brackets of 28 percent under current law. Note, however, that under the 1990 Act the minimal marginal tax rate for individuals is 31 percent. See footnote 19, supra.

Year	Gross Revenue	Operating Expense	Net Operating Income	Interest Expense
1991	$ 950,000	$ 498,000	$ 452,000	$ 419,303
1992	1,976,000	1,035,840	940,160	714,847
1993	2,055,040	1,077,274	977,766	709,445
1994	2,137,242	1,120,365	1,016,877	703,536
1995	2,222,731	1,165,179	1,057,552	697,072
1996	2,311,641	1,211,786	1,099,854	690,002
1997	2,404,106	1,260,258	1,143,848	682,269
1998	2,500,270	1,310,668	1,189,602	673,811
1999	1,083,450	567,956	515,494	278,072
	$17,640,480	$9,247,326	$8,393,155	$5,568,357

The following changes brought about by the 1986 Act are illustrated in the chart on the next page. Note that the effects of the passive loss limitations have been segregated.

- The figures in row A clearly show that the deductions are severely diminished.
- Row B demonstrates that the taxable income prior to a sale under the 1986 Act is increased to zero from a loss of $2,478,913. But it is also important to note that the suspension of losses only creates a very small proportion of the increase in taxable income. If the losses were not suspended, the taxable loss would only be $45,325.

- Row C compares the effects of the pre- and post-1986 Act computations. If the investment were undertaken before 1986 and were sold at $1 over the mortgage balance it would generate cash and tax benefits of $562,415, or an internal rate of return of 13.6 percent, an acceptable investment. However, after 1986, the investment would not be profitable since it would generate a loss, whether or not the passive losses are available to the investors.
- Row D illustrates a sale when the property has appreciated at a rate of 5 percent per year. Under these conditions, the investment generates an acceptable return on investment under all sets of assumptions. The rate of return is diminished under the 1986 Act (from 32.9 percent to 22.2 percent IRR) but it remains an acceptable investment.

Chart Outlining Comparative Impact

			Tax Reform Act of 1986	
		Prior Law	Losses Suspended	Losses Utilized
(A)	Depreciation	$5,328,750	$2,870,581	$2,870,581
(B)	Taxable income (loss) before sale	($2,478,913)	$0	($ 45,325)
(C)	Sale at $1 over mortgage balance:			
	Taxable income (loss)	$1,737,116	$1,691,791	$1,737,116
	Cumulative cash flow and tax benefits to limited partners	$ 562,415	($ 282,184)	($ 282,184)
	Internal Rate of Return	13.6%	0.0%	0.0%
(D)	Sale at 5 percent annual appreciation:			
	Taxable income (loss)	$4,083,967	$4,038,642	$4,083,967
	Cumulative cash flow and tax benefits to limited partners	$5,256,117	$4,927,825	$4,927,825
	Internal Rate of Return	32.9%	22.2%	23.0%

This analysis demonstrates the greater role economic considerations would play in such an investment after the 1986 Act. The venture made investment sense before the 1986 Act, even if there were no appreciation in value. After the 1986 Act, however, appreciation would be critical to the success of the investment.

(handwritten, top of page)
basis Cost 10M - 5328750 = 4,671,250
sell 8M - 611145 = 7 368 855 ; ML profit is 2,277,605

Results Under Prior Law

(Example A)*

Year	L.P.† Capital Contribution	Net Operating Income	Mortgage Interest Paid	Mortgage Principal Paid	Total Mortgage Payments	Total Depreciation	Taxable Income (Loss) to L.P.	Tax Savings (Cost) to L.P.	Cash Distribution to L.P.	Cash Flow/ Tax Benefits to L.P. Net of Capital Contribution
1991	$ 500,000	$ 452,000	$ 419,303	$ 31,286	$ 450,589	$ 500,000	($ 462,630)	$ 231,315	$ 1,397	($ 267,288)
1992	500,000	940,160	714,847	57,591	772,438	880,000	(648,140)	324,070	166,045	(9,885)
1993	500,000	977,766	709,445	62,993	772,438	790,000	(516,462)	258,231	203,275	(38,494)
1994	500,000	1,016,877	703,536	68,902	772,438	720,000	(402,592)	201,296	241,995	(56,709)
1995		1,057,552	697,072	75,366	772,438	650,000	(286,625)	143,312	282,263	425,576
1996		1,099,854	690,002	82,435	772,438	590,000	(178,347)	89,173	324,142	413,316
1997		1,143,848	682,269	90,168	772,438	540,000	(77,637)	38,818	367,697	406,515
1998		1,189,602	673,811	98,627	772,438	490,000	25,534	(12,767)	412,993	400,226
1999		515,494	278,072	43,777	321,849	168,750	67,986	(33,993)	191,709	157,716
	$2,000,000	$8,393,155	$5,568,357	$611,145	$6,179,502	$5,328,750	($2,478,913)	$1,239,456	$2,191,517	$1,430,973
Sale at $1 over mortgage							$1,737,116	($ 868,558)	$ 1	$ 562,415
Sale at 5 percent annual appreciation							$4,083,967	($2,041,984)	$5,867,128	$5,256,117

(handwritten near depreciation total) = 99%

† Limited Partner

* Example A demonstrates the impact of tax shelter on a moderately leveraged and income-oriented real estate investment under prior law. Even if the property were sold in 1999 for only $1 more than the mortgage balance, the property would be an economically viable investment because upon the sale of the real estate, the net tax cost would not exceed the sum of the prior cash and tax benefits to the limited partners. If the property were to appreciate at an annual 5 percent rate, the property would be a very attractive investment. The total tax benefit would be $1,239,456 over the life of the investment and be the equivalent of receiving a comparable amount of rental income in before-tax dollars.

Results Under Tax Reform Act of 1986

Losses Suspended (Example B)*

Year	L.P. Capital Contribution	Net Operating Income	Mortgage Interest Paid	Mortgage Principal Paid	Total Mortgage Payments	Total Depreciation	Taxable Income (Loss) to L.P.	Tax Savings (Cost) to L.P.	Cash Distribution to L.P.	Cash Flow/Tax Benefits to L.P. Net of Capital Contribution
1991	$ 500,000	$ 452,000	$ 419,303	$ 31,286	$ 450,589	$ 188,763	$ 0	$ 0	$ 1,397	($ 498,603)
1992	500,000	940,160	714,847	57,591	772,438	363,636	0	0	166,045	(333,955)
1993	500,000	977,766	709,445	62,993	772,438	363,636	0	0	203,275	(296,725)
1994	500,000	1,016,877	703,536	68,902	772,438	363,636	0	0	241,995	(258,005)
1995		1,057,552	697,072	75,366	772,438	363,636	0	0	282,263	282,263
1996		1,099,854	690,002	82,435	772,438	363,636	0	0	324,142	324,142
1997		1,143,848	682,269	90,168	772,438	363,636	0	0	367,697	367,697
1998		1,189,602	673,811	98,627	772,438	363,636	0	0	412,993	412,993
1999		515,494	278,072	43,777	321,849	136,364	0	0	191,709	191,709
	$2,000,000	$8,393,155	$5,568,357	$611,145	$6,179,502	$2,870,581	$ 0	$ 0	$2,191,517	$ 191,517
Sale at $1 over mortgage							$1,691,791	($ 473,702)	1	($ 282,184)
Sale at 5 percent annual appreciation							$4,038,642	($1,130,820)	$5,867,128	$4,927,825

*Example B illustrates the full impact of the 1986 Act on the investment shown in Example A. The depreciation deductions are computed on the straight line method using a twenty-seven and one-half year useful life. The passive loss limitations of I.R.C. §469 are used to disallow the deduction of any losses against non-passive income and all such disallowed losses are suspended and carried forward until the property is sold. The result is that there are no tax savings being realized during the life of the investment. The only return on the investment is purely economic and is represented by the cash flow distributions to the limited partners. Thus, the net return on investment, $191,517, without any tax benefits, makes the same investment relatively unattractive. A sale of the property for $1 more than the mortgage balance provides a net loss from the total investment after the taxes are paid. The tax bill is reduced by the suspended losses when the property is sold, but not eliminated. If the property appreciates in value by 5 percent each year, the net after-tax profit is $4,927,825 on the $2 million original investment. An investment that generated both cash distributions and tax savings sufficient to justify the expenditure under prior law now would not be undertaken unless the investor could expect a very significant appreciation in the property.

Losses Currently Allowed

(Example C)*

Year	L.P. Capital Contribution	Net Operating Income	Mortgage Interest Paid	Mortgage Principal Paid	Total Mortgage Payments	Total Depreciation	Taxable Income (Loss) to L.P.	Tax Savings (Cost) to L.P.	Cash Distribution to L.P.	Cash Flow/Tax Benefits to L.P. Net of Capital Contribution
1991	$ 500,000	$ 452,000	$ 419,303	$ 31,286	$ 450,589	$ 188,763	($ 154,505)	$ 43,261	$ 1,397	($ 455,341)
1992	500,000	940,160	714,847	57,591	772,438	363,636	(136,940)	38,343	166,045	(295,612)
1993	500,000	977,766	709,445	62,993	772,438	363,636	(94,362)	26,421	203,275	(270,303)
1994	500,000	1,016,877	703,536	68,902	772,438	363,636	(49,792)	13,942	241,995	(244,063)
1995		1,057,552	697,072	75,366	772,438	363,636	(3,125)	875	282,263	283,138
1996		1,099,854	690,002	82,435	772,438	363,636	45,753	(12,811)	324,142	311,331
1997		1,143,848	682,269	90,168	772,438	363,636	96,963	(27,150)	367,697	340,547
1998		1,189,602	673,811	98,627	772,438	363,636	150,634	(42,177)	412,993	370,816
1999		515,494	278,072	43,777	321,849	136,364	100,048	(28,013)	191,709	163,695
	$2,000,000	$8,393,155	$5,568,357	$611,145	$6,179,502	$2,870,581	($ 45,325)	$ 12,691	$2,191,517	$ 204,208
Sale at $1 over mortgage							$1,737,116	($ 486,393)	$ 1	($ 282,184)
Sale at 5 percent annual appreciation							$4,083,967	($1,143,511)	$5,867,128	$4,927,825

* Example C highlights the total impact of the 1986 Act. The effects of the change in the depreciation schedule without implementing the passive loss rules of I.R.C. §469 are illustrated. Even though the tax benefits are realized on a yearly basis, it should be noted that with the reduced depreciation schedule and lower tax rate the tax benefits in each year are significantly smaller than those under prior law (as illustrated in Example A). If the property were sold for $1 over the mortgage balance in 1999, the investment would still result in a net loss to the investors. A profit can only be realized when the property appreciates in value over the intervening years.

EXAMPLE 2: DEEPLY LEVERAGED REAL ESTATE INVESTMENT

ASSUMPTIONS

1. Newly constructed apartment building costing $10 million; land is ground leased.
2. Total limited partner capital contributions: $1 million paid over 4 years.
3. Financing terms: 15-year "qualified" nonrecourse mortgage for $9 million at 9 percent, level monthly payments based on thirty year amortization with balloon payment in year 15.
4. Building placed in service on June 1, 1991 and sold on May 1, 1999.
5. Sales price: (A) $1 over mortgage; (B) 5 percent annual compound appreciation.
6. Inflation (for purposes of revenue and expense): 4 percent per year.
7. The general partners receive a 1 percent interest in the partnership but do not make any cash contributions.
8. The limited partners are allocated 99 percent of income and loss from operations, and 99 percent of any gain or loss on sale; however, once the negative capital account balances are restored, any excess gain will be allocated 20 percent to the general partner and 80 percent to the limited partners.
9. The limited partners are individuals with maximum marginal tax brackets of 50 percent under prior law and with tax brackets of 28 percent under current law. Note, however, that under the 1990 Act the maximum marginal rate for individuals is 31 percent. See footnote 19, supra.

Year	Gross Revenue	Operating Expense	Net Operating Income	Interest Expense
1991	$ 950,000	$ 498,000	$ 452,000	$ 471,716
1992	1,976,000	1,035,840	940,160	804,203
1993	2,055,040	1,077,274	977,766	798,125
1994	2,137,242	1,120,365	1,016,877	791,478
1995	2,222,731	1,165,179	1,057,552	784,206
1996	2,311,641	1,211,786	1,099,854	776,253
1997	2,404,106	1,260,258	1,143,848	767,553
1998	2,500,270	1,310,668	$1,189,602	758,037
1999	1,083,450	567,956	515,494	312,831
Total	$17,640,480	$9,247,326	$8,393,155	$6,264,402

Results Under Prior Law

(Example D)

Year	L.P. Capital Contribution	Net Operating Income	Mortgage Interest Paid	Mortgage Principal Paid	Total Mortgage Payments	Total Depreciation	Taxable Income (Loss) to L.P.	Tax Savings (Cost) to L.P.	Cash Distribution to L.P.	Cash Flow/ Tax Benefits to L.P. Net of Capital Contribution
1991	$ 250,000	$ 452,000	$ 471,716	$ 35,196	$ 506,912	$ 500,000	($ 514,519)	$ 257,259	$ 0	$ 7,259
1992	250,000	940,160	804,203	64,789	868,992	880,000	(736,603)	368,301	70,456	188,757
1993	250,000	977,766	798,125	70,867	868,992	790,000	(604,255)	302,126	107,686	159,814
1994	250,000	1,016,877	791,478	77,515	868,992	720,000	(489,654)	244,827	146,406	141,233
1995		1,057,552	784,206	84,786	868,992	650,000	(372,887)	186,444	186,674	373,118
1996		1,099,854	776,253	92,740	868,992	590,000	(263,734)	131,867	228,553	360,420
1997		1,143,848	767,553	101,440	868,992	540,000	(162,067)	81,034	272,107	353,141
1998		1,189,602	758,037	110,955	868,992	490,000	(57,851)	28,925	317,404	346,329
1999		515,494	312,831	49,249	362,080	168,750	33,574	(16,787)	151,880	135,093
	$1,000,000	$8,393,155	$6,264,402	$687,538	$6,951,939	$5,328,750	($3,167,997)	$1,583,998	$1,481,166	$2,065,165
Sale at $1 over mortgage							2,107,323	(1,053,662)	$ 1	$1,011,504
Sale at 5 percent annual appreciation							4,158,620	(2,079,310)	5,128,243	5,114,097

Handwritten marginal notes:

these #s are wrong

NOI – Pmt = cashflow – depr = taxable income (loss)

A   B   C   D   E   F   G   @50%

11%   3199997

Sale at $1 over mortgage = 3128753

I = NOI – E $.99

I = NOI – E

Results Under Tax Reform Act of 1986

Losses Suspended (Example E)

Year	L.P. Capital Contribution	Net Operating Income	Mortgage Interest Paid	Mortgage Principal Paid	Total Mortgage Payments	Total Depreciation	Taxable Income (Loss) to L.P.	Tax Savings (Cost) to L.P.	Cash Distribution to L.P.	Cash Flow/ Tax Benefits to L.P. Net of Capital Contribution*
1991	$ 250,000	$ 452,000	$ 471,716	$ 35,196	$ 506,912	$ 188,763	$ 0	$ 0	$ 0	($ 250,000)
1992	250,000	940,160	804,203	64,789	868,992	363,636	0	0	70,456	(179,544)
1993	250,000	977,766	798,125	70,867	868,992	363,636	0	0	107,686	(142,314)
1994	250,000	1,016,877	791,478	77,515	868,992	363,636	0	0	146,406	(103,594)
1995		1,057,552	784,206	84,786	868,992	363,636	0	0	186,674	186,674
1996		1,099,854	776,253	92,740	868,992	363,636	0	0	228,553	228,553
1997		1,143,848	767,553	101,440	868,992	363,636	0	0	272,107	272,107
1998		1,189,602	758,037	110,955	868,992	363,636	0	0	317,404	317,404
1999		515,494	312,831	49,249	362,080	136,364	0	0	151,880	151,880
	$1,000,000	$8,393,155	$6,264,402	$687,538	$6,951,939	$2,870,581	$ 0	$ 0	$1,481,166	$ 481,166
Sale at $1 over mortgage							$1,372,914	($384,416)	$ 1	$ 96,751
Sale at 5 percent annual appreciation							$3,424,211	($958,779)	$5,128,243	$4,650,630

*These numbers assume a marginal tax rate of 28 percent; observe, however, that the maximum marginal tax rate is currently 31 percent, as provided for by the Revenue Reconciliation Act of 1990. — ED.

113

Losses Currently Allowed

(Example F)

Year	L.P. Capital Contribution	Net Operating Income	Mortgage Interest Paid	Mortgage Principal Paid	Total Mortgage Payments	Total Depreciation	Taxable Income (Loss) to L.P.	Tax Savings (Cost) to L.P.	Cash Distribution to L.P.	Cash Flow/Tax Benefits to L.P. Net of Capital Contribution*
1991	$ 250,000	$ 452,000	$ 471,716	$ 35,196	$ 506,912	$ 188,763	($ 206,394)	$ 57,790	$ 0	($ 192,210)
1992	250,000	940,160	804,203	64,789	868,992	363,636	(225,403)	63,113	70,456	(116,431)
1993	250,000	977,766	798,125	70,867	868,992	363,636	(182,155)	51,003	107,686	(91,310)
1994	250,000	1,016,877	791,478	77,515	868,992	363,636	(136,854)	38,319	146,406	(65,275)
1995		1,057,552	784,206	84,786	868,992	363,636	(89,387)	25,028	186,674	211,703
1996		1,099,854	776,253	92,740	868,992	363,636	(39,634)	11,098	228,553	239,651
1997		1,143,848	767,553	101,440	868,992	363,636	12,533	(3,509)	272,107	268,598
1998		1,189,602	758,037	110,955	868,992	363,636	67,250	(18,830)	317,404	298,574
1999		515,494	312,831	49,249	362,080	136,364	65,637	(18,378)	151,880	133,502
	$1,000,000	$8,393,155	$6,264,402	$687,538	$6,951,939	$2,870,581	($ 734,409)	$ 205,635	$1,481,166	$ 686,801
Sale at $1 over mortgage							$2,107,323	($ 590,050)	$ 1	$ 96,751
Sale at 5 percent annual appreciation							$4,158,620	($1,164,414)	$5,128,243	$4,650,630

*These numbers assume a marginal tax rate of 28 percent; observe, however, that the maximum marginal tax rate is currently 31 percent, as provided for by the Revenue Reconciliation Act of 1990. — ED.

[Handwritten margin notes:]
net = cap contrb less Tax savings less cap contrb
+ 135957 = 3.6%
net income pretax
net
@28% all =
@26% all =

Comparative Impact

	Prior Law	Tax Reform Act of 1986 Losses Suspended	Tax Reform Act of 1986 Losses Utilized
Depreciation	$5,328,750	$2,870,581	$2,870,581
Taxable income (loss) before sale	($3,167,997)	$0	($ 734,409)
Sale at $1 over mortgage balance:			
Taxable income (loss)	$2,107,323	$1,372,914	$2,107,323
Cumulative cash flow and tax benefits	$1,011,504	$ 96,751	$ 96,751
Internal Rate of Return	23%	2.5%	12%
Sale at 5 percent annual appreciation:			
Taxable income	$4,158,620	$3,424,211	$4,158,620
Cumulative cash flow and tax benefits	$5,114,097	$4,650,630	$4,650,630
Internal Rate of Return	66.8%	30.8%	42%

The authors wish to acknowledge their gratitude to Professor David Schmudde of Fordham University School of Law for his assistance in the preparation of this example.

CHOICE OF ENTITY FOR REAL ESTATE OWNERSHIP

The form of ownership of real estate assets is driven by a combination of many factors including:

- Tax implications
- Personal and business liability exposures
- Liquidity of ownership interests
- Managerial control
- Compensation and benefits
- Estate planning
- Capital requirements

Tax rate changes, the passive loss limitations, the at-risk rules, and other provisions of TRA 1986 change the tax focus regarding the most appropriate entity for acquisition, operation, and disposition of real estate assets. The following table summarizes key tax factors in comparing business forms. See also note 7 on page 143.

	Partnership	S Corporation	Regular Corporation	MLP	REIT
Liability	Unlimited for general partners	Limited to amounts invested and loaned	Limited to amounts invested and loaned	Same as partnership	Limited to amounts invested
Double taxation	No	No	Yes	No	No
Pass through profits and losses	Yes	Yes	No	Yes	Profits only
Losses deductible by owners	Limited to amount at risk (generally, investment plus prorated share partnership liabilities) or basis	Limited to amount at risk (generally, only amount invested and loaned to corporation) or basis	No	Same as partnership	No
Tax rates	Business income taxed to owners at their *marginal* tax rates	Business income taxed to owners at their *marginal* tax rates	Corporate tax rates apply	Same as partnership	Taxed as corporation if 95% of taxable income is not distributed
Special allocations	Yes, if substantial economic effect	No	No	Same as partnership	No
Fiscal year	Generally, calendar year required	Generally, calendar year required	Generally, any year-end is permitted	Same as partnership	Generally, calendar year required

	May be deducted in current year if paid within first 2½ months of year-end	Generally may not be deducted until the year paid	May be deducted in current year if paid within first 2½ months of year-end	Same as partnership	Not available
Payments to owners			All permitted by law		
Tax-free fringe benefits	Limited	Most permitted		Limited and unlikely	Not available
Public offering	Yes	No	Yes	Yes	Yes
Liquidity of interests	No	No	Maybe	Yes	Yes
Accumulated earnings tax	No	No	Yes	No	No
Personal holding company tax	No	No	Yes	No	No
Limits on tax-free cash distribution	Tax-free to the extent of amount at risk	Tax-free to the extent of amount at risk	Return of cash basis if dividends exceed E&P	Same as partnership	Tax-free (to the extent of basis) if distributions exceed taxable income
2% Limitation on investment expenses applies	Yes	Yes	No	Yes	No

Source: Coopers & Lybrand, Real Estate Newsletter on the Tax Reform Act of 1986 (Oct. 1986), Appendix A.

NOTES AND QUESTIONS

1. *The Interplay Between Financial Leverage and the Depreciation Deduction.* Perhaps the simplest method of measuring the before-tax profitability of income-producing realty is to determine its annual "free and clear rate of return" by dividing its projected net annual income (before tax and finance charges) by its purchase price. In the foregoing example from Madison and Dwyer involving the L-G partnership, the free and clear rate of return is 9.4 percent, so if the limited partner-investors were to furnish the entire $10 million on their own their pretax rate of return on their equity investment would be $940,160, or 9.4 percent in the first full operational year (1992). However, if the mortgage were interest-only with a balloon payment of principal in year 15, by borrowing nine-tenths of the $10 million construction cost at a mortgage interest rate of 9 percent during the first year they could increase their before-tax rate of return on their investment from 9.4 to 13.6 percent. See Example 2 in the excerpt from Madison and Dwyer supra. Moreover, were the investors to purchase rather than lease the fee they would also receive the benefit of leveraged appreciation in land value if the land component should increase in value because of inflation or because demand exceeds supply.

Also, observe that §167 of the I.R.C. produces a constant amount of depreciation allowance for an investor regardless of what part of the cost of the project the investor furnishes and what part is financed by a mortgage. Under the so-called *Crane* Doctrine, when depreciable property is acquired for cash and a mortgage, the cost tax basis, and basis for depreciation of the property, includes the mortgage indebtedness whether or not the owner is personally liable under the mortgage. Accordingly, the same dollar amount of depreciation will increase the investor's rate of return on its equity to the extent it is able to reduce its equity and thereby leverage its acquisition costs by means of mortgage debt financing. Returning to the L-G partnership example (in Example 2), if there were a $9 million mortgage and an equity investment of only $1 million instead of an $8 million mortgage and a $2 million equity investment, then the same $363,636 of straight-line depreciation (under current law) would nearly double the amount of tax savings to the investors in the year 1992 and increase their after-tax returns from 10.2 percent to 13.4 percent. Compare Example C in Example 1 with Example F in Example 2.

2. *Amount of Tax Shelter Equals Excess of Deductible Depreciation over Nondeductible Mortgage Amortization.* Before we examine the impact of the 1986 Act on the status of real estate as a tax shelter and ask whether these changes make sense as a matter of sound tax and social policy let's first address a threshold question: why has the own-

ership of income-producing real estate commonly been regarded as a tax shelter? As suggested in the first excerpt by the staff of the Joint Committee on Taxation, the elements common to most tax shelters have been: (1) financial leverage (the use of borrowed money to fund the investment) (discussed previously); (2) deferral (the ability to postpone a taxpayer's tax liability until the later years of a venture, as when the property is sold, so that the taxpayer has the time-value benefit of holding and reinvesting funds that would otherwise be immediately payable); and (3) under prior law, the ability to convert what would be otherwise taxable as ordinary income into tax-favored long-term capital gains.

As you know, real estate investors are afforded the unique opportunity to leverage their cost of acquiring and improving real estate by means of high-ratio financing. But why has income-producing real estate been able to accomplish both deferral and (prior to the 1986 Act) conversion benefits for taxpayers who either directly own the property or indirectly own the property as investors in pass-through entities such as limited partnerships and Subchapter S corporations? The answer is quite simple if you understand how and why the depreciation deduction is able to shelter rental income from immediate taxation and produce taxable losses that (subject to the "at risk" and "passive loss" limitations imposed by the 1986 Act) can be used to shelter outside income.

On the positive side of the tax shelter coin is I.R.C. §167 — the principal underpinning for real estate tax shelter. I.R.C. §167 allows a depreciation deduction for the "exhaustion, wear and tear . . . of property used in the trade or business, or . . . held for the production of income." The notion underlying this provision is that while depreciation does not involve any cash outlay, a real estate owner computing taxable income should be allowed to take into account the fact that rental income-producing property is wearing out and becoming obsolescent. Accordingly, like the cost of making repairs and paying employees' salaries, the cost of building or purchasing the real property should be allocated over the period during which the property is producing income. See Treas. Reg. §1.167(a)-1(a).

Conversely, on the negative side of the tax shelter coin is mortgage "amortization," which simply means repayment of principal during the life of a loan. To obtain financial leverage, many if not most real estate borrowers will fund their acquisition or improvement of rental real estate by means of high-ratio and constant-payment mortgage financing. Under a constant payment arrangement, since the amount of the periodic debt-service payment on the mortgage remains constant, the portion of the payment allocable to interest starts to decline as the principal balance is repaid; therefore the remaining portion allocable to amortization correspondingly must increase over time. In contrast to depreciation, mortgage amortization does involve a cash outlay, and yet is not deductible for tax purposes. What fundamental tax principle tells you this is so? It is the excess of depreciation (which does not involve any cash outlay and yet is deductible) over mortgage amortization (which does involve a cash outlay but is not deductible) that produces tax shelter. However, in the recent past amortization has become less important in the tax shelter picture as institutional lenders have begun to make mortgage loans featuring partial or even zero amortization ("interest-only") as opposed to the more traditional fully amortized ("self-amortizing") mortgage loan. See Table 5-6 and discussion at Chapter 5B4.

To illustrate, let us take a look at the example involving the L-G partnership (see Example A in Example 1) and assume for simplicity's sake that the limited partners make all of their capital contributions (totalling $2 million) on June 1, 1991. Based on the cash flow results in the first full operational year, 1992, and assuming the apartment building is "prime" real estate (i.e., in a good location, in good physical condition, and with high-quality tenants), would you say that the partnership is an economically viable venture? The answer is a resounding yes. As observed above, the free and clear rate of return is a respectable 9.4 percent — yet paradoxically, on the tax side the venture looks like a disaster! Instead of producing taxable income, the venture under prior law would have produced a whopping tax loss of $648,140! The cash distributions to the limited partners amount to $166,045, which represents their 99 percent share of the venture's net rental income (after payment of debt service on the mortgage), which income is *ordinary* income. And yet, under prior law, not only were all these cash distributions sheltered from immediate taxation as a "tax free return of capital" (as explained in note 3, infra), but the venture also was able to produce tax losses ($648,140) that the partner-distributees could have used to offset their ordinary income from outside sources such as salaries and dividends. At marginal tax rates of 50 percent, these tax losses could have been worth as much as $324,070 to the partners. When added to their cash distributions, this would have *tripled* the rate of return on their equity investment from a cash on cash return of 8.3 percent ($166,045 cash flow ÷ $2 million equity investment) to an *after-tax* rate of return of 24.5 percent ($166,045 + tax savings of $324,070 = $490,115 ÷ $2 million equity investment = 24.5 percent). Under current law the after-tax results are less dramatic because of a reduced and slower stream of tax benefits (as explained below). Nevertheless, assuming that the partners have outside passive income to offset their current tax losses, their rate of return would also increase from a cash-on-cash return of 8.3 percent to an after-tax rate of return of 10.6 percent ($166,045 cash flow + tax savings of $38,343 = $204,388 ÷ $2 million equity investment = 10.2 percent).

How does the tax shelter phenomenon explain the paradoxical result whereby our hypothetical venture appears to be economically viable (as reflected by the cash flow results) and yet is able to produce losses on the tax side of the picture? As observed above, the amount of tax shelter equals the excess of deductible depreciation over non-deductible mortgage amortization; hence, under prior law (as in Example A), the 99 percent amount of depreciation allocated to the limited partners in 1992 ($871,200) exceeded the limited partners' share of mortgage amortization ($57,015) by $814,185, which was the amount of tax shelter (1) that could have been used to shelter the partners' share of cash flow from immediate taxation ($166,045); and (2) whose remainder ($648,140) showed up in the form of tax losses that were passed through to the partners and could have produced a tax savings for them in the amount of $324,040.

Conceptually, the easiest way to understand these tax shelter results (under prior or current law) is to think of a "tax shelter bag" comprised of excess depreciation, diagrammed as follows.

Limited Partners'
  99% Share of Depreciation: 871,200

Limited Partners'
  99% Share of Amortization: <u>57,015</u>
                            814,185

Tax Shelter Bag in 1992 (under prior law)

How to use the shelter that's in the bag? First take out $166,045 of shelter to shelter the cash flow to the partners in 1992; otherwise, their distributive shares of net operating (rental) income would have been immediately taxable as ordinary income. Whatever is left over in the tax shelter bag is what produced the partnership's tax loss in 1992 in the amount of $648,140, diagrammed as follows:

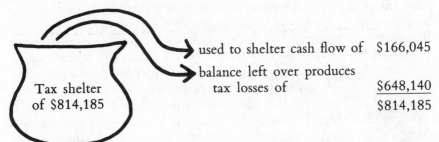

used to shelter cash flow of	$166,045
balance left over produces tax losses of	$648,140
	$814,185

Tax shelter of $814,185

Now draw a tax shelter bag for the limited partners to illustrate their tax shelter results in 1992 *under current law* (assuming that their losses are currently allowed) as in Example C. What amount of tax shelter, if any, would be produced by an owner's payment of one dollar of mortgage interest? What about a one-dollar payment by the owner of an employee's salary, or of a utility bill? Are these kinds of payments distinguishable?

Observe that under prior law the amount of the depreciation deduction and resultant shelter would decrease each year as the depreciable basis of the property declined by the amount of the accelerated depreciation taken the year before. Also, under a constant payment mortgage arrangement, the amount of shelter would decrease as the percentage of each payment allocable to nondeductible amortization increased. Returning to the L-G partnership (Example A), under prior law, in what year would the shelter have "burned out"? In other words, in what year would the crossover point have been reached at which the excess of depreciation over amortization became insufficient in amount to shelter all the cash distributions to the limited partners so the investment started to produce taxable income? Under prior law, in most cases the property would have been sold as soon as the shelter burned out. Under current law, when would the shelter burn out if the losses are suspended (as in Example B)? When would it burn out if the losses are currently allowed (as in Example C)? As you may have surmised, under current law the burnout issue has become less significant, and chances are that business rather than tax considerations will predominate in the decision by the general partners as to when the property should be sold.

To some degree the problem of disappearing shelter can be mitigated by refinancing the mortgage (substituting a new, often larger, loan for an existing one) to de-escalate the amount of nondeductible amortization, or, in the case of a burned-out shelter, by selling the overdepreciated property (e.g., under current law, residential property held for more than 27½ years) and using the net sale proceeds to fund the acquisition of some substitute property. This would start the depreciation cycle anew, since the partnership would obtain a new depreciable basis equal to the cost of the newly acquired property.

3.   Tax Shelter Is Made Anemic by the Tax Reform Act of 1986.   It is difficult to understand the significance of the complex changes wrought by the Tax Reform Act of 1986, as modified by the Revenue Act of 1987, without first understanding how income-producing real estate was treated under prior law. So let us now compare prior law with the current law and see how deferral and conversion — two mainstays of real estate tax shelter — have been affected by recent tax law changes.

To review prior law: if a taxpayer sold or exchanged real property that had been used in its trade or business and held for more than six months, the taxpayer would have been charged with an I.R.C. §1231 gain that was ordinarily taxed as long-term capital gain. By contrast, if the taxpayer received rental or other operating income from the property, or as a "dealer" sold some real property to a customer in the ordinary course of the taxpayer's trade or business, the income or gain would have ordinarily been taxed as ordinary income. See I.R.C. §§1231(b)(1)(A), 1231(b)(1)(B).

Over the years, Congress had seen fit to accord preferential tax treatment to long-term capital gain. However, in enacting the Economic Recovery Tax Act of 1981, Congress shifted its emphasis in tax policy somewhat by reducing the top marginal rate on ordinary income from 70 percent to 50 percent to encourage both the earning and the saving of after-tax income by high-bracket taxpayers. However, the preferential treatment for long-term capital gain continued. Since the taxable 40 percent portion of long-term capital gain was subject to the top 50 percent marginal rate, the effective maximum rate on long-term capital gain was reduced from 28 percent to 20 percent, whereas the top marginal rate on ordinary income was reduced from 70 percent to 50 percent.

Prior to the 1986 Act Congress also liberalized the depreciation rules to encourage capital investment in income-producing real estate by permitting both an accelerated rate for depreciation (175 percent declining balance or 200 percent in the case of low-income housing, with a switchover to straight-line in later years) and an ACRS accelerated cost recovery period (in lieu of useful life) of 15 years for low-income housing and 19 years for other real estate. However, if the owner used accelerated depreciation rather than the straight-line method, in the case of residential real estate (other than low-income housing) gain was recaptured as ordinary income under I.R.C. §1250 on the sale of the property only to the extent that the accelerated depreciation exceeded the amount that would have been allowable if the straight-line method had been used. A special recapture-phaseout rule applied to low-income housing. In the case of commercial real estate, the full amount of accelerated depreciation (and not just the excess over the straight-line amount) was recaptured as ordinary income. Accelerated depreciation was also treated as a "tax preference item" for purposes of the alternative minimum tax (AMT) under I.R.C. §55.

An example involving the L-G partnership (in Example 1) will illustrate these rules under prior law, but first, you need to know some fundamental rules dealing with how partners and partnerships are taxed under Subchapter K of the Internal Revenue Code. Under the "aggregate approach," a partnership is treated under I.R.C. §§701 and 702 as a nontaxable conduit by which items of income, gain, loss, deduction, or credit are transmitted to the partners. Conversely, with the exception of the Subchapter S corporation, the "entity approach" applies to corporate taxation: The corporation can avail itself of the depreciation deductions to offset its taxable income, but it cannot pass through its depreciation-caused losses to its stockholders. See Chapter 2B, note 7dii, infra.

Also, every dollar of depreciation deduction reduces the partnership depreciable basis in the property so that the partnership (and partners) realize an extra dollar of gain when the property is sold. I.R.C. §1016(a)(2). However, each partner's share of such extra gain would increase the adjusted basis in his or her partnership interest under I.R.C. §705(a)(1)(A) and, to the extent that I.R.C. §1250 recapture does not apply, the gain would be capital gain under I.R.C. §1231. Also, in addition to each partner's share of tax losses, every dollar of tax-free distribution would be treated as a tax-free return of capital since the distributee-partner would in effect be receiving a $1 refund of the investment cost and accordingly the partner's adjusted basis in the partnership interest would be reduced by $1.   I.R.C. §§705(a)(2), 733(1). Accordingly (unless the partnership is a "collapsible" one under I.R.C. §751), the partner would realize an extra dollar of capital gain when his or her interest is sold or liquidated. I.R.C. §§731(a)(1), 741.

Returning to the example involving the L-G partnership (in Example 1), and assuming for simplicity's sake that had the partnership used the straight-line method to deduct $526,316 each year during the 19-year cost recovery period and sold the building and other leasehold improvements (at the end of the 8th year) for its original cost at a taxable gain of $5,789,474, there would have been no recapture and the entire gain would have been treated as an I.R.C. §1231 gain and taxed at the preferential long-term capital gain rate. This means that for every dollar of excess first-year depreciation in 1992 passed through to the limited partners (total depreciation of $526,316 × 99 percent = $521,053 less a 99 percent share of amortization, $57,015 = excess depreciation of $464,038) used by them to offset the otherwise taxable cash distributions from the partnership ($166,045) and used by them as tax losses (net operating income of $940,160 less interest of $714,847 less total depreciation of $526,316 = taxable loss of $301,003 × 99 percent = limited partners' distributive share: $297,993) to offset their ordinary income from outside sources, the partners would have been taxed on an extra dollar of long-term capital gain when either the real estate or their partnership interests were sold.

Thus, not only were the limited partners allowed to use their share of excess depreciation ($464,038) to convert what would otherwise have been ordinary income (taxable at the 50 percent rate) into their share of extra long-term capital gain ($526,316 × 99 percent = $521,053, taxable at the 20 percent rate) worth $126,783 in net tax benefits for them (50 percent of $464,038 less 20 percent of $526,316 = $126,783), but they were also able to defer payment of the tax shelter benefit (in the form of the extra long-term capital gain) until May 1, 1991, when the property was sold. So, in effect, the limited partners received during 1992 a one-year interest-free loan of first-year tax benefits worth $232,019, for which they would have repaid only an extra $126,783 (or less if the property was sold for less than its original cost) in inflation-eroded dollars (at the end of the 8-year holding period); the tax payment dollars would have been worth less (because of the time value of money) than the tax benefit dollars they received in 1992. Incidentally, in the hypothetical facts given above the partners' share of the first year's depreciation deduction was $521,053, and of this amount they were able to use $464,038 for tax shelter purposes. Can you think of what happened to the $57,015 remainder?

By contrast, under the 1986 Act, as modified by the 1990 Act, while the maximum marginal tax rate for individuals was reduced from 50 percent to 31 percent, the preferential treatment for long-term capital gain was abolished for individuals; thus the limited partners in our example would no longer enjoy the tax benefit of converting ordinary income into capital gain, equal under prior law to 30 cents on the tax shelter dollar. However, in contrast to a shareholder or corporate bondholder who is currently taxed on dividend and interest income, respectively, the partners can still obtain the time value of tax deferral (equal to the interest-free use of as much as 31 cents) for every dollar of cash flow that is sheltered from immediate taxation and for every dollar of tax loss (subject to the new limitations on losses) that is used as a current deduction to offset their passive income from outside sources.

However, the *amount* of tax shelter, and consequently the opportunity for tax deferral, has been reduced by the 1986 Act, as explained in the excerpt by Schwartz, supra. This is due to a reduction in the marginal tax rates for individuals, the decrease in the amount of depreciation allowed as a deduction (caused by the repeal of accelerated depreciation and the extension of the ACRS cost recovery period), and the new limitations on losses under the so-called at-risk rules under I.R.C. §465 and the limitation on passive losses under I.R.C. §469.

The 1986 Act mandates a straight-line cost recovery period of 27½ years for all residential real estate (including low-income housing) and a period of 31½ years for commercial real estate. I.R.C. §168(c). Under current law there is no longer any recapture problem under I.R.C. §1250 because the straight-line method is now mandated.

The following chart compares depreciation under the prior ACRS recovery periods with the amounts of depreciation under the new 27½, 31½, and (optional ADS) 40-year cost recovery periods for real property with a tax basis of $10 million (such as the property owned by the L-G partnership) over an 8-year holding period and assumes that the property was placed into service in the first month of the first tax year.

Year	19-Year ACRS	19-Year ACRS S/L	27.5-Year S/L	31.5-Year S/L	40-Year S/L
1	$ 882,675	$ 504,386	$ 348,485	$ 304,233	$ 239,583
2	839,754	526,316	364,208	317,894	250,000
3	762,408	526,316	364,208	317,894	250,000
4	692,186	526,316	364,208	317,894	250,000
5	628,432	526,316	364,208	317,894	250,000
6	570,550	526,316	364,208	317,894	250,000
7	518,000	526,316	364,208	317,894	250,000
8	470,289	526,316	364,208	317,894	250,000
Total	$5,364,294	$4,188,598	$2,897,941	$2,529,491	$1,989,583
Net Present Value*	$3,739,760	$2,787,920	$1,928,729	$1,683,522	$1,324,261

* Over eight years assuming a 10 percent discount rate.

Returning to the L-G partnership (Example C), the excess of straight-line depreciation (computed over 27½ years under the new version of ACRS) in the amount of $363,636 over mortgage amortization yields a substantially lower amount of shelter in each taxable year. This explains why the shelter burns out in 1996, at which time the venture would no longer be able to generate passive losses that could be used by the limited partners to offset their passive income from outside sources.

Opponents of the *Crane* Doctrine such as Professor McKee (in the excerpt above) have long argued that a real estate investor's depreciable basis should be limited to the equity investment in the property or, alternatively, that aggregate depreciation losses should be limited to the equity amount. In addition, these tax shelter critics have taken the position that so-called artificial losses produced by depreciation should not be allowed to shelter unrelated outside income such as salaries and dividends. One example of this approach is the now-defunct proposal known as the limitation on artificial accounting losses system (LAL). For an in-depth explanation of LAL, see H.R. Rep. No. 658, 94th Cong., 2d Sess. 25 (1976). In the critics' opinion, the use of nonrecourse financing and other risk-limiting transactions to shelter outside income is tax abusive because it allows tax losses that may never be matched by economic losses and induces capital into real estate ventures that are not economically viable. Following this line of reasoning, the 1986 Act extended the general at-risk rules under I.R.C. §465 to real estate activities with an exception provided for "qualified *nonrecourse* financing," that is, generally third-party financing. This is discussed at Chapter 2B, note 7diii, infra.

By far the most onerous antishelter provision under the 1986 Act is the one whereby losses or credits arising from "passive" business activities in which the taxpayer does not "materially participate" are not allowed to offset earned income and "portfolio" income (dividends, interest, royalties, and gains on sale of investment property). The passive loss limitation under I.R.C. §469 applies to individuals as well as to estates and trusts. In the case of pass-through entities such as partnerships and Subchapter S corporations, the limitation does not apply to the ownership entity itself. However, it applies to individual partners or Subchapter S shareholders because such individuals are subject to the rule regardless of whether they own an interest directly or indirectly in the passive business activity. Closely held corporations are able to deduct rental-passive losses against active business income (or passive income) but not against portfolio (investment) income. Publicly held corporations are not subject to the passive loss limitation; however, the stringent AMT provisions of the 1986 Act might discourage real estate tax shelter investments by such corporations. All limited partnership interests and all rental activities (other than those in which substantial services are rendered to occupants, such as the operation of a hotel) are deemed passive in nature regardless of whether the taxpayer materially participates in the activity. However, losses and credits from rental or other passive activity may be applied against income from other passive activities in the same taxable year. Netting is not allowed with interest income, even interest from real estate mortgages. Also, disallowed losses and credits can be carried forward (but not back) indefinitely and will be allowable against passive activity income in subsequent years. See Staff of the Joint Committee on Taxn., General Explanation of the Tax Reform Act of 1986, at 215-222 (1987).

Accordingly, in the case of a moderately leveraged income-oriented

real estate investment, the absorption of deferred losses in the latter
years of the venture may result in an after-tax rate of return (e.g.,
internal rate of return) comparable to the result that would be obtained
without the passive loss limitation. See Example B. Assuming a sale
of the real estate at an annual appreciation rate of 5 percent, the internal
rate of return would be 32.9 percent under prior law, compared to
22.2 percent under the Act (assuming that losses are suspended). By
contrast, if the real estate investment is deeply leveraged (e.g., a two-
to-one write-off) instead of moderately leveraged (as shown in Example
2), the loan-to-value ratio is 90 percent instead of 80 percent (assuming
that cost and market value are equal), and the transaction is tax-oriented
rather than income- or appreciation-oriented, the passive loss limitation
and reduction in depreciation benefits would have a severe impact on
the limited partners' rate of return. In Example D the internal rate of
return under prior law would be 66.8 percent as opposed to a rate of
30.8 percent under the 1986 Act, assuming a sale at an annual appreciation rate of 5 percent and suspended losses. Under the 1986 Act,
suspended losses are allowed in full on a taxable disposition of the
activity. However, losses from one passive activity cannot be used to
offset gain on the sale of an interest in another passive activity.

Under a relief provision (I.R.C. §469(i)), an individual may deduct
up to $25,000 each year of passive losses that are attributable to rental
real estate activities in which the individual (or the individual's spouse,
in the case of jointly owned property) "actively participates," to offset
nonpassive income of the taxpayer. I.R.C. §469(i). The active participation test is less rigorous and requires less personal involvement than
the material participation standard; however, neither a limited partnership interest in rental real estate nor an individual interest of less
than 10 percent in the activity will qualify. The $25,000 allowance is
phased out ratably as the individual's adjusted gross income (computed
without taking passive losses into account) increases from $100,000 to
$150,000, and the exception is entirely eliminated for adjusted gross
income in excess of $150,000.

To ameliorate the impact of the new limitation on passive losses,
an individual investor should consider the following suggestions:

1. Investors subject to the passive loss limitation should consider
    retaining their interests in "burned-out" shelters (e.g., those
    currently generating taxable income in excess of cash flow) as
    a source of passive income.
2. In the case of a small individual investor involved in a large
    loss-generating rental activity (especially one whose adjusted
    gross income is too high or whose ownership interest is too
    small to qualify for the relief provision under I.R.C. §469(i)),
    the investor should consider purchasing an interest in an in-

come-oriented passive investment that will allow the investor to use existing losses (a so-called passive income generator, or PIG) such as a master limited partnership (MLP) that is not a publicly traded partnership or a Subchapter S corporation that owns some income-generating real estate. See discussion at Chapter 13A, note 1. By doing so the investor can also diversify his or her investment portfolio. I.R.C. §469(e)(1)(A) was intended to prevent an individual with portfolio assets from sheltering such portfolio income by transferring such assets into a limited partnership that generates passive losses; it does not, however, prevent an individual from selling portfolio assets such as stocks and bonds and using the net sale proceeds to fund the acquisition of a PIG that is expected to yield a comparable rate of return.

3. In the case of a proportionately large investment in a small rental real estate activity, it might be useful for the investor to consider tenancy-in-common or the general partnership format to qualify for the relief provision under I.R.C. §469(i).

4. Partnership special allocations (discussed at Chapter 2B, note 7dii, infra) may help alleviate the problem, provided that such allocations meet the substantial economic effect test imposed by I.R.C. §704(b)(2). For example, an ordinary Subchapter C corporation (which is not subject to the passive loss limitation) could be made a partner in a partnership engaged in a loss-generating rental activity and, in exchange for receiving a special allocation of passive losses (which the corporation could use to offset its active trade or business income), the corporate partner might make concessions (e.g., less cash flow) to the partners who are individual taxpayers.

For a discussion of planning suggestions see generally Madison and Dwyer ¶1.05[6][a] (1989 Cum. Supp. No. 2); Ewart and Hopkins, Reversing the Effects of the New Tax Law on Existing Real Estate Tax Shelters, 2 Real Est. Acctg. and Taxn. 5 (Spring 1987); Stoller, Tax Topics: Passive Income Generators, 4 Real Est. Fin. 63 (Fall 1987).

Finally, as explained in the excerpt by Schwartz, when the investment tax credit was repealed the three-tiered rehabilitation credit was replaced with a two-tiered credit system. For buildings originally placed into service before 1936 a 10 percent credit is available, and a 20 percent credit is allowed for certified historic structures. Prior I.R.C. §§46, 48. The 1986 Act also eliminated the special tax treatment accorded to low-income housing under ACRS and replaced it with the new 4 percent and 9 percent tax credits (explained by Schwartz). I.R.C. §§42(a) to 42(h). Also, construction-period interest and taxes (which were formerly amortized over a 10-year period) must generally be capitalized and recovered as depreciation deductions over the cost recovery period of the property under the uniform capitalization rules imposed by the 1986 Act. I.R.C. §263A, repealing I.R.C. §189.

On October 27, 1990 Congress enacted the Revenue Reconciliation Act of 1990 (see footnotes 17 and 19, supra), which is likely to have little impact on the behavior of individual taxpayers since the marginal rate for ordinary income was reduced by only 2 percentage points and the maximum rate on net long-term capital gains was fixed at 28 percent, only 3 percentage points below the maximum rate for ordinary income.

The following is a list of additional recommended readings that relate to the impact of recent tax reform on real estate as an investment: Aronsohn, The Tax Reform Act of 1986 — Some Selected Real Estate Problems and Possibilities, 14 J. Real Est. Taxn. 203 (Spring 1987); Behrens and Padgett, The Uniform Capitalization Rules' Effect on Real Estate, 2 Real Est. Acctg. and Taxn. 45 (Winter 1988); Coughlin and Boasberg, How the Tax Reform Act of 1986 Affects Real Estate, 2 Prac. Real Est. Law. 11 (Nov. 1986); Ewart and Hopkins, Reversing the Effects of the New Tax Law on Existing Real Estate Tax Shelters, 2 Real Est. Acctg. and Taxn. 5 (Spring 1987); Finks and Everidge, Tax Planning for Real Estate Entrepreneurs After Tax Reform, 1 Real Est. Acctg. and Taxn. 29 (Winter 1987); Follain, Hendershott, and Ling, The Impact of the 1986 Tax Reform Act on Real Estate, 17 Real Est. Rev. 76 (Spring 1987); Gibson, The Impact of the Tax Reform Act of 1986 on Real Estate Tax Shelters, 11 Rev. Taxn. Individuals 323 (1987); Goodman, Tax Ideas: Losses from Rental Property After the Tax Reform Act of 1986, 15 Real Est. L.J. 361 (Spring 1987); Green, Summary of the 1986 Tax Act, 1 Real Est. Acctg. and Taxn. 4 (Winter 1987); Grossman and Crnkovich, "Passive Activity" — Tax Reform's Latest Oxy Moron, 3 Real Est. Fin. J. 97 (Summer 1987); Howard, How to Handle Tax Planning for Real Estate After Tax Reform, 20 Prac. Acct. 18 (May 1987); Hopkins, Surviving in the Current Tax Environment, 4 Real Est. Acctg. and Taxn. 37 (Spring 1989); Jennings and Bolar, Passive Loss Planning for Real Estate Lessors and Developers, 4 Real Est. Acctg. and Taxn. 21 (Spring 1989); Kanter, Reaching for the Outer Limits in Tax Shelters: The Right Stuff or the Twilight Zone?, 62 Taxes 879 (Dec. 1984); McClure and Witner, How the Revenue Act of 1987 Affects Real Estate, 4 Prac. Real Est. Law. 11 (May 1988); O'Neil and Rose, Real Estate Tax Shelters Under the Tax Reform Act of 1986, 14 J. Real Est. Taxn. 115 (Winter 1987); Rier, Tax Ideas: TRA '86 — The Extent of the Disaster, 16 Real Est. L.J. 253 (Winter 1988); Stoller, Tax Topics: Passive Income Generators, 4 Real Est. Fin. 63 (Fall 1987); Thielen, Real Estate Syndications After Tax Reform, 3 Real Est. Fin. 67 (Winter 1987); Tucker and Schwinger, TRA 1986 Will Have a Pervasive Impact upon Real Estate Transactions, 66 J. Taxn. 130 (March 1987); Tyson, Impact of Proposed Tax Reform on Real Estate Tax Shelters, 2 Real Est. Fin. J. 67 (Fall 1986); Williamson, Tax-Oriented Investments, 4 Real Est. Acctg. and Taxn. 61 (Spring 1989).

For additional background on rehabilitation and new low-income housing credits see generally Bunn and Ingram, Rehabilitation Tax Credits: A Surviving Tax Shelter, 17 Real Est. Rev. 96 (Winter 1988); Callison, New Tax Credit for Low-Income Housing Provides Investment Incentive, 66 J. Taxn. 100 (Feb. 1987); Carlisle, The Credit for Low-Income Housing: Whose Shelter Is It?, 3 Real Est. Fin. 44 (Winter 1987); Goldstein and Edson, The Tax Credit for Low-Income Housing, 17 Real Est. Rev. 49 (Summer 1987); Goodman, Tax Ideas: Real Estate Tax Credits After the Tax Reform Act of 1986, 16 Real Est. L.J. 172 (Fall 1987); Goodman, Tax Ideas: New Regulations Shed Light on Low-Income Housing Credit, 17 Real Est. L.J. 153 (Fall 1988); Greer, Tax Credits: Still the Best Show in Town, 18 Real Est. Rev. 67 (Summer 1988); Higgens and Covell, Historic Rehabilitation and the Tax Reform Act of 1986, 3 Real Est. Fin. J. 144 (Summer 1987); Nowell, Historic Rehabilitations Under Today's Tax Rules, 5 Real Est. Fin. 25 (Summer 1988); Shenkman, Structuring Investments in Real Estate Rehabilitation Projects After the TRA of '86, 5 J. Taxn. Inv. 3 (1987); Tyson, Syndicating Low-Income Housing Tax Credit Projects for Capital, 4 Real Est. Fin. J. 44 (Summer 1988).

4.   *The* Crane *Doctrine.* Under the *Crane* doctrine, when property is acquired (or constructed) with cash and a mortgage, the tax basis of the property includes not only the cash or equity investment but also the mortgage indebtedness whether or not the purchaser (or developer) is personally liable under the mortgage.

Returning to the example involving the L-G partnership in Example 1 in the excerpt from Madison and Dwyer, supra, the partnership would initially obtain a tax basis in the real estate of $10 million for purposes of computing depreciation and gain or loss on the sale or exchange of the realty even if the partnership obtains "nonrecourse financing" whereby neither the partnership nor the partners would be personally liable for the $8 million mortgage indebtedness. Moreover, if the partnership were to sell the property to a purchaser who pays $2 million and assumes the $8 million mortgage (for which the purchaser would be personally liable) or to a purchaser who pays $2 million but takes subject to the mortgage so that the purchaser is not personally liable — in either instance the tax basis for the purchaser would be the full leveraged cost of $10 million for the property.

a.   What is inconsistent about the petitioner's contention in the *Crane* case that all she realized on the sale was $2,500 after depreciation of $28,045 was allowed on the building while she held the property? 331 U.S. at 4.

b.   Returning to Example 1, how much depreciation should be allowed as a deduction for the limited partners in the first full year (1992), if, as the petitioner in the *Crane* case contends, "property" (for purposes of adjusted basis under I.R.C. §1001(b)) should be defined as "only the equity, or the excess in the value of the apartment building and lost over the amount of the mortgage"? 331 U.S. at 4. Some opponents of real estate tax shelter agree and have proposed that a real estate investor's depreciable basis should not be equal to the total leveraged cost but that it should be limited to the taxpayer's equity investment in the property.

To clarify the issue, let us compare two simplified examples. Let us assume in both cases that a purchaser acquires real estate worth $50,000 and the property has a useful life of five years with zero salvage value and produces $15,000 of income each year before deduction of straight-line depreciation. In the first example, assume that the entire purchase price is paid in cash. In the second example, assume that $10,000 is paid in cash and $40,000 in the form of a five-year no-personal-liability purchase money note and mortgage. For simplicity assume there are no interest payments on the mortgage. Finally, assume that the purchaser is not required to repay the mortgage indebtedness until the last two years, so that the amortization payment is $20,000 at the beginning of the fourth and fifth years of the loan. In both cases, how big a depreciation deduction would the purchaser-taxpayer be entitled to each year if the depreciable basis were limited to the taxpayer's equity (total cash) investment in the property? Do you see any problems with this approach? See Adams, Exploring the Outer Boundaries of the Crane Doctrine: An Imaginary Supreme Court Decision, 21 Tax L. Rev. 159 (1966); McKee, The Real Estate Tax Shelter: A Computerized Exposé, 57 Va. L. Rev. 521, 565-567 (1971); Panel Discussions on General Tax Reform Before the House Ways and Means Committee, 93d Cong., 1st Sess., ser. 11, pt. 4, at 515, 571, 582 (1973) (discussion of proposals to limit depreciable basis to equity and/or limit aggregate losses to equity amount). What are some tax policy arguments in favor of and against such proposals? Suppose the investor is not personally liable on the mortgage; should this make a difference?

    c.   Under the *Crane* doctrine no distinction is made between a personal-liability mortgage ("recourse financing") and no-personal-liability mortgage ("nonrecourse" financing), as evidenced by the court's conclusion that the correct basis of the property for purposes of depreciation was not the taxpayer's zero equity interest but $262,042, the value of the property, undiminished by mortgages thereon, notwithstanding that she was not personally liable on the mortgage. 331 U.S. 1, at 11. Otherwise, as the court suggests, if the petitioner's depreciable basis was her zero equity interest, the annual depreciation allowances "will represent only a fraction of the cost of the corresponding physical exhaustion" of the property and this result would presumably ignore the accounting convention that income should be matched with related deductions such as depreciation in each tax year. Id. at 9. In addition, this equating of personal liability with the absence of that liability seems responsive to the business realities that a mortgagor without personal liability would feel essentially the same economic compulsion to have the mortgage debt paid in order to keep the growing equity in the property, that permanent lenders generally rely on the collateral value of the property and not the net assets of the borrower to secure the mortgage indebtedness, and that only a small dollar-amount percentage of deficiency judgments are ever collected by lenders against defaulting borrowers. See Prather, A Realistic Approach to Foreclosure, 14 Bus. Law. 132 (1958). Observe, however, that there are obviously limits to the *Crane* doctrine, as suggested by the following dictum of the court: "Whatever may be the rule as to allowing depreciation to a mortgagor on property in his possession which is subject to an unassumed mortgage and clearly worth less than the lien, we are not faced with that problem and see no reason to decide to now." Crane v. Commissioner, 331 U.S. 1, 12 (1947).

Returning to the hypothetical in the second paragraph of note 4b, and assuming the market value of the property remains at $50,000 (unless otherwise noted), what should be the purchaser's initial depreciable basis in the property under the following circumstances: (1) the purchaser pays zero cash in the first year and $50,000 in the form of a four-year no-personal-liability purchase money note and mortgage with amortization payments of $10,000 each year during the next three years and with a $20,000 payment in the last year; (2) the same facts as in (1) except that the property is only worth $40,000 during the five-year period; or (3) the same facts as in (1) except that the purchaser agrees to pay $60,000 and the seller is willing to accept a lump sum or "balloon" payment *at the end of* the fifth year? Compare Mayerson v. Commissioner, 47 T.C. 340 (1966), acq. Rev. Rul. 69-77, 1969-1 C.B. 59 and Bolger v. Commissioner, 59 T.C. 760 (1973) (*Crane* rule affirmed) with Estate of Franklin v. Commissioner, 64 T.C. 752 (1975), affd., 544 F.2d 1045 (9th Cir. 1976) (no part of nonrecourse indebtedness included in taxpayer's basis). To the extent that the purchase price is artificially inflated beyond its market value to increase the purchaser's depreciation deductions, the seller will be charged with more gain on the sale. Accordingly, if the tax interests of the parties are antithetical, why should the Internal Revenue Service want to challenge such a transaction?

Subsequent to the *Franklin* decision, the *Crane* doctrine has been successfully challenged where there was a price-value discrepancy, especially in sale transactions where the parties did not bargain with one another at arm's length. See Graf v. Commissioner, 80 T.C. No. 50

(1983); Flowers v. Commissioner, 80 T.C. No. 49 (1984); Odend'hal v. Commissioner, 80 T.C. 588 (1983); Siegel v. Commissioner, 78 T.C. 659 (1982); Brannen v. Commissioner, 78 T.C. 471 (1982); Lemmen v. Commissioner, 77 T.C. 1326 (1981); Hager v. Commissioner, 76 T.C. 759 (1981); Narver v. Commissioner, 75 T.C. 53 (1980), affd., 670 F.2d 855 (9th Cir. 1982); Beck v. Commissioner, 74 T.C. 1534 (1980), affd., 678 F.2d 818 (9th Cir. 1982); see generally Avent and Grimes, Inflated Purchase Money Indebtedness in Real Estate and Other Investments, 11 J. Real Est. Taxn. 99 (1984); Biuttker, Tax Shelters, Nonrecourse Debt, and the *Crane* Case, 33 Tax L. Rev. 277 (1978); Javaras, Nonrecourse Debt in Real Estate and Other Investments, 56 Taxes 801 (1981); *Crane* Case Updated, 32 Tax. L. Rev. 289 (1979); Wildman v. Commissioner, 78 T.C. 943 (1982).

    d. The Supreme Court, in Commissioner v. Tufts, 461 U.S. 300 (1983), revg. 651 F.2d 1058 (5th Cir. 1981), and affg. 70 T.C. 756 (1978), resolved a conflict that had emerged at the appellate level between the Fifth Circuit and Third Circuit over whether the amount realized (I.R.C. §1001(b)) from the taxable sale or exchange of property can exceed its fair market value when the outstanding nonrecourse indebtedness on the date of disposition exceeds the market value of the property being sold or exchanged. See footnote 37 in the *Crane* case excerpt.

    An example would be if X were to purchase the property for $100,000 with an interest-only $100,000 no-personal-liability mortgage and a zero cash investment so that on the date of sale the outstanding balance on the nonrecourse debt would still be $100,000. Finally, let us assume that the fair market value of the property being sold equals its adjusted basis of $80,000 on the date of disposition and that the purchaser buys the property with zero cash by assuming or taking the property subject to the $100,000 mortgage. The question that confronted both courts is whether in the hypothetical the amount realized on the sale should not exceed the $80,000 market value of the property, in which event X would receive a tax windfall by having $20,000 of his depreciation deductions escape any taxation when the property is sold.

    The issue is of special importance to real estate investors who leverage their acquisition and construction costs with nonrecourse financing. However, if the value of the property declines below the amount of the outstanding mortgage indebtedness, not only will the investors face a loss of cash profits on the sale and a large amount of reported gain (caused by the depreciation write-off, which reduces the original basis in the property) but they must also confront the specter of being forced to recognize "phantom" gain ($20,000 in the example) on an amount realized ($100,000 in the example) that exceeds the market value of the property ($80,000 in the example) merely because the property being sold is subject to a nonrecourse mortgage in the higher amount in respect to which the investors never have been, nor ever will be, personally liable for repayment.

After reviewing Millar v. Commissioner, 577 F.2d 212 (3d Cir. 1978), and Tufts v. Commissioner, 651 F.2d 1058 (5th Cir. 1981), do you think Justice Blackmun, in delivering the opinion of the Supreme Court, made the correct decision in siding with the Third Circuit and rejecting the Fifth Circuit's distinction between recourse and nonrecourse financing? See McGuire, Tufts at the Supreme Court, 10 J. Real Est. Taxn. 54 (1982); Newman, The Demise of Footnote 37: Commissioner v. Tufts, Tax Notes 259 (July 25, 1983); Sanders, Supreme Court, Ending Crane Controversy, Says Nonrecourse Debt Is Always Part of Sale Price, 59 J. Taxn. 2 (1983). Incidentally, the holding in the *Tufts* case has been codified as I.R.C. §7701(g).

5.   *Should Real Estate Tax Shelter Be Resuscitated?* Opponents of the real estate tax shelter frequently look askance at the forest without examining the trees. Now that we have examined how tax shelter works and have become reacquainted with the *Crane* doctrine, let us separately scrutinize each component of tax shelter and consider in the context of real estate whether and to what extent each component (as modified by the 1986 Act) makes sense as a matter of sound tax and social policy.

a.   *Should Depreciation Be Accelerated Again?* Prior to the enactment of the ERTA, Publ. L. No. 97-34, 95 Stat. 172 (1981), depreciation of income-producing realty was determined for purposes of I.R.C. §167 by estimating the property's useful life under a fact and circumstances test or by using prescribed Treasury guidelines that ranged from 40 years for apartment buildings to 60 years for warehouses. Rev. Proc. 62-21, 1962-2 C.B. 418. Subsequent guidelines (for estimating useful life) were also created under the Class Life Asset Depreciation Range System. Prior I.R.C. §167(m). Prior to the enactment of the 1986 Act, the taxpayer had the option under ACRS of using the 175 percent declining balance or straight-line method of depreciation over a 19-year cost recovery period for most real property. A 35- or 45-year extended recovery period could also be elected. As observed earlier, under current law income-producing real estate must be depreciated over a straight-line cost recovery period of either 27½, 31½, or (under ADS) 40 years.

If we assume that a building wears out and grows obsolete at a constant rate and that the depreciation deduction should relate to its historical cost, a building that costs, say, $1 million with a useful life of 40 years and zero salvage value should generate a straight-line depreciation deduction each year of $25,000. Under this method we would be accommodating the basic tax accounting convention that periodic income should be matched to its related costs, otherwise net income would be distorted. For example, permitting a taxpayer to double the straight-line amount to $50,000, under this theory, would result in understating the taxpayer's real net income in the first year (prior to mortgage payments) by $25,000. Likewise, if instead of doubling the *rate* of depreciation (from 1/40th, or 2½ percent, of cost to 1/20th, or 5 percent) we decrease the cost recovery period from 40 years to 15 years (as was the case for low-income housing prior to the 1986 Act), we would also be overstating depreciation by $41,667 (from $25,000 to $66,667) and understating income by $41,667 during the first 15 operational years and understating depreciation along with overstating income by $25,000 during the 25-year remainder of the building's useful or income-generating life.

The foregoing example presupposes that an average building wears out and becomes obsolescent at a constant rate. However, some economic studies have suggested that actual economic depreciation of office buildings and apartment buildings is minimal over the first ten years. See Taubman and Rasche, Economic and Tax Depreciation of Office Buildings, 22 Natl. Tax J. 334, 344 (1969); Taubman and Rasche, The Income Tax and Real Estate Investment (1969) (presented at the Symposium on Tax Incentives of the Tax Institute of America).

Consequently, if we define "tax shelter" as any investment that results in a mismatch between deductions and income so that the deductions "shelter" unrelated income from immediate taxation (as does the Joint Committee on Taxation in the excerpt, supra, on tax shelter proposals) then it would appear that the 1986 Act's deceleration of the rate of depreciation (from the 175 percent declining balance method to straight-line) and its elongation of the ACRS cost recovery period (from 19 years to 27½ years for residential and 31½ years for commercial real estate) makes sense from a sound tax policy standpoint.

Mr. Aronsohn (an articulate proponent of real estate tax shelter) makes the point (based on language in Treas. Reg. §1.167(a)-1(a)) that the depreciation allowance is essentially an accounting convention that has nothing to do with fluctuations in value. Instead, it provides as good a system as any to recover original capital cost over an estimated useful life and accordingly the depreciation deduction does not represent a special tax shelter benefit. In what respect does his analogy between a leasehold estate and a building fail? Suppose that, in his example involving the acquisition of a leasehold estate, Baker were allowed to amortize his $100,000 cost over a 10-year cost recovery period rather than over the 20-year remaining life of the groundlease. Could Mr. Aronsohn still maintain that operation of the amortization (or, by analogy, straight-line depreciation) deduction does not amount to a tax shelter?

If, in the previous example involving the L-G partnership (see

Example A of the excerpt from Madison and Dwyer, supra), the limited partners were receiving the benefit of a tax shelter under prior law, what are some arguments in support of the contention by tax shelter opponents that the operation of the accelerated depreciation deduction over the 19-year cost recovery period amounted to an inefficient deduction-funded subsidy or a tax shelter that unfairly favored taxpayers in the position of the limited partners over other taxpayers? What are the arguments against such a characterization? Both Professor McKee and the Joint Committee on Taxation assume that the depreciation deduction-funded subsidy is regressive and inherently unfair unless low-bracket investors are also encouraged to invest their capital in depreciable realty. Is this a sound assumption? How would you reconcile this assumption with Code provisions such as I.R.C. §103 (exempting from gross income interest on local governmental obligations) that exempt certain items from gross income in order to achieve certain congressional policy aims? Do you agree with Professor McKee's statement that the depreciation deduction and other deduction-funded subsidies are irreconcilable with a progressive tax theory?

According to the Joint Committee on Taxation, ACRS has contributed to a construction boom that has glutted the real estate market. Remember that prior to 1981 and before ACRS the tax law gave lesser depreciation benefits to buyers of existing real estate (as opposed to developers of new real estate). For example, the Tax Reform Act of 1969 had restricted the use of accelerated depreciation to newly constructed real estate (the 200 percent declining balance and sum-of-the-years digits method for new residential housing and the 150 percent declining balance for commercial real estate) and had required the use of the straight-line method for used commercial real estate. I.R.C. §§167(j)(2), 167(j)(5) (1969). Suppose ACRS were limited to *new construction* of low-income housing and other real estate with respect to which there is a current shortage. How would this affect your attitude toward ACRS? Are direct government expenditures to aid the housing industry preferable over indirect deduction-funded subsidies? Which approach would you recommend? See generally Glasser, "Gimmee Shelter" Reform of Real Estate Tax Shelters, U. Mich. J.L. Rev. 267, 277-285 (1974); Surrey, Tax Incentives as a Device for Implementing Government Policy: A Comparison with Direct Government Expenditures, 83 Harv. L. Rev. 705, 720-725 (1970).

b. Should Refinancing Proceeds Be Taxable? Returning to example 1 involving the L-G partnership, if the property were hypothetically worth $12 million shortly after being completely constructed and rented, the syndicate might "mortgage out" by refinancing at the same 80 percent loan-to-value ratio for about $9,600,000 and distribute the $1,600,000 of excess mortgage proceeds to the limited partners as a tax-free return of capital. Should the tax consequences to the limited partners be characterized as a "tax shelter"? If so, do you think that net refinancing proceeds should be subject to immediate taxation, so that in the above example the limited partners would recognize gain on the net refinancing proceeds to the extent that the amount of the gross refinancing proceeds ($9,600,000) exceeds the partnership's adjusted basis in the refinanced property? Do you see any problem with this tax result under our present system of taxation?

c. *Should Preferential Treatment Be Restored for Construction Period Interest and Taxes?* Prior to the Tax Reform Act of 1976, amounts paid for interest and taxes were generally allowable as a current deduction, except to the extent the taxpayer elected to capitalize these items as carrying charges under I.R.C. §266. Under the Tax Reform Act of 1976 taxpayers generally could capitalize and amortize construction-period taxes and interest over a 10-year period under I.R.C. §189. Returning to the example involving the L-G partnership (see Example A), if the construction-period interest and taxes had been $1,200,000 in 1990 and the apartment building was ready for rental in 1991, the $1,200,000 would have had to be capitalized, a $120,000 deduction (10 percent of the total) would have been allowed as amortization in 1990, and the $1,080,000 remainder would have been deductible at $120,000 per year for nine years beginning in 1991. Under the uniform capitalization rules imposed by the 1986 Act, construction-period interest and taxes must be capitalized and added to the cost basis of the constructed property; these expenditures are now recovered as depreciation deductions over the cost recovery period of the property. I.R.C. §263A (repealing I.R.C. §189).

Most buildings have an actual useful life of 40 to 60 years. What would be the argument for the proposition that the treatment of construction-period interest and taxes under I.R.C. §189 amounted to a tax shelter for the limited partners? What would be the counter-argument?

d. *Should Preferential Treatment Be Restored for Long-Term Capital Gains?* As of this writing, the Bush Administration is still attempting to convince the Democratic-controlled Congress to re-establish a permanent lower tax rate on capital gains, contending that it would bring the Treasury an extra $5 billion in revenues in the first year. Under the Administration's 1989 proposal, the maximum tax rate on long-term capital gains for individuals would have been reduced to 15 percent and the reduced rate would have applied to gains from the sale of stocks, bonds, and nondepreciable real estate such as raw land that is held by the taxpayer for at least three years. N.Y. Times, Feb. 9, 1989, at D1, col. 6. Meanwhile, as observed at footnote 17, supra, the Revenue Reconciliation Act of 1990 established a maximum tax rate of 28 percent on net long-term capital gains, compared to a maximum rate of 31 percent for other income earned by individuals. A differential this small is not likely to affect the behavior of individual taxpayers; however, this change under the 1990 Act may signal a willingness on the part of Congress to consider further rate reductions in the future. As pointed out in the excerpt by Kotlarsky, the 1986 Act preserved the definitional difference between ordinary income and capital gain in the event that preferential treatment is restored for long-term capital gains.

If the tax rate on capital gains were reduced, would net tax revenues increase or decrease over time? As suggested by the excerpts, this is the one issue over which there is no disagreement. All the experts seem to agree that nobody knows the answer. Certainly the increase in the maximum effective rate for individuals from 20 percent to 33 percent under the 1986 Act and to 31 percent under the 1990 Act will increase collections when a capital asset (such as raw land) or when a trade or business asset (such as rental real estate) is sold, but there is no clear-cut answer as to what extent the rate increase will discourage taxpayers from realizing gains by selling their assets. Among the complicating factors is that taxpayers have more control over when to incur capital gains than they do over most other taxes; moreover, it is difficult to isolate the impact of tax rates on realizations from other more pervasive economic factors such as the level of interest rates. The Bush Administration projected that the rate reduction in its 1989 proposal would have provided $16.1 billion in extra revenues between 1989 and 1993, while the Joint Committee on Taxation estimated that the federal budget deficit would have increased by $13.3 billion during the same period.

As suggested by the excerpts, the proponents of a tax preference for capital gains have contended that a rate reduction would: (1) promote saving and investment in our economy (where the flow of savings to finance investment has declined from 7.4 percent of national income from 1950 to 1980 to 2.8 percent during the 1980s, as reported in the N.Y. Times, July 2, 1989, at Sec. 3, col. 1); (2) help protect real gains from being eroded by inflation; and (3) promote economic efficiency. Conversely, the opponents have argued that reintroducing the differential in tax rates would: (1) encourage abusive tax shelter activity; (2) distort investment choices as to financial assets; and (3) jeopardize the fairness and progressivity of our tax system. With regard to the latter argument, the Joint Committee on Taxation has found that taxpayers with incomes over $200,000 (less than 1 percent of all taxpayers) received three-quarters of the benefit of the prior tax preference for capital gains. N.Y. Times, Feb. 16, 1989, at A34. And yet as a matter of common economic knowledge taxpayers with a high taxable income have a greater propensity to save and invest than taxpayers with a low taxable income.

After reviewing the arguments on both sides of the capital gains debate, which point of view do you favor? Why?

    e. Should Rental Real Estate Be Treated as a "Passive" Activity?

Historically, rental income or gain from the ownership and sale of income-producing real estate (such as an apartment building or shopping center) was treated as active income or gain from a trade or business (as opposed to passive-type investment income) where active services were rendered to the tenants (as opposed to "net-leased" real estate, where the tenants make their own repairs and pay their prorata share of property taxes and insurance premiums). See prior I.R.C. §163(d)(4) (relating to limitation on investment interest); I.R.C. §1231(b)(1) (relating to capital gain treatment for trade or business property). Compare I.R.C. §162 with I.R.C. §212; cf. Treas. Reg. §1.761-1(a) (relating to tax distinction between a partnership and a tenancy-in-common); prior Treas. Reg. §1.1372-4(b)(5)(vi) (relating to prior passive income test for Subchapter S corporations). Then along came the 1986 Act, which changed the course of tax history by creating new categories of income, called "portfolio" income (dividends, interest, royalties, and gains on sale of investment property); "positive" income, such as salaries and other income from services; and "passive" income, which includes income or gain from *any* rental activity *regardless of whether or not the taxpayer materially participates* in the activity (other than those in which "substantial" services are rendered, such as the operation of a hotel). I.R.C. §469(c)(2); see Staff of the Joint Committee on Taxation, General Explanation of the Tax Reform Act of 1986, at 217 (May 7, 1987). According to the Joint Committee (see the previous excerpt from the General Explanation of the 1986 Act), Congress felt that all rental activities should automatically be deemed "passive" in nature whether or not the owner actively conducted a trade or business (such as an apartment building) because "rental activities generally require less ongoing management activity, in proportion to capital invested, than business activities involving the production or sale of goods and services." Do you agree with Congress? Can you think of some service-oriented businesses that require a minimal amount of venture capital and less management effort than would be required in the case of a typical apartment building?

    In the words of one commentator, "[t]he chief and most controversial provision [in the 1986 Act] is the limitation on passive-rental losses. The restriction, when combined with the more stringent investment interest limitation, the extension of the at-risk rules (in the case of seller financing), and the more onerous application of the AMT, means that a tax shelter loss might be deferred or denied even though the loss is an economic one that is matched by income that is related in a business or economic sense. The Internal Revenue Code traditionally has made a distinction between passive investment activities and those involving an active trade or business. However, under the 1986 Act, an individual taxpayer who earns income from one business source (e.g., the construction and development of real estate) may not be able to deduct losses from a related business source (e.g., renting the newly constructed building) based on its unprecedented tax distinction between 'positive' and 'passive' business activities, even though both businesses may be economically oriented activities and the taxpayer actively participates in both, depends on both for his livelihood, and is potentially liable for losses and expenses from both activities." (See General Explanation, cited in the previous paragraph, at 249.) Madison and Dwyer ¶1.05[6][c] (Cum. Supp. No. 2) (1989) (footnotes omitted). Based on what Mr. Aronsohn had to say about prior proposals to limit so-called spillover losses, are there any other arguments you can think of against the new limitation on passive-rental losses?

And yet, as pointed out by the Joint Committee, prior to the 1986 Act rental activities had been extensively used as tax shelters. Indeed, as observed by the Joint Committee in Tax Shelter Proposals, "[o]n the supply side of the market are users of tax-advantaged assets, such as real property, which during certain periods generate tax deductions in excess of income. The users of tax-shelter assets have an incentive to rent them from a tax shelter partnership, rather than own them, if they cannot take full advantage of the tax deductions . . ."

If, as suggested above, Congress overreacted to the use of tax shelters in the area of rental real estate, what would be a compromise approach that would insulate rental real estate from tax shelter abuse and yet allow individual taxpayers to offset their losses against their business income from other outside sources without segregating income and losses into artificial categories (as does I.R.C. §469)?

f. Is Low-Income Housing Getting the Tax Attention It Deserves? Low-income housing is the sector of the real estate industry most in need of venture capital, and because of restrictions on rents and profits, subsidized low-income housing traditionally has been dependent on tax incentives such as tax-exempt bond financing (discussed at Chapter 9D, note 2) and the other tax sweeteners mentioned below. Nevertheless, the 1986 Act abolished the many existing tax incentives for the construction of low-income housing, including: (1) a current deduction for construction-period interest and taxes under prior I.R.C. §189; (2) a 5-year cost recovery period for rehabilitation expenditures under prior I.R.C. §167(k); (3) a rapid depreciation schedule including the exclusive right to use the 200-percent declining balance method of depreciation over a 15-year cost recovery period; and (4) the phaseout of depreciation recapture under prior I.R.C. §1250, with no recapture after the property had been held for 16 years and 8 months. Consequently, under the 1986 Act low-income housing is treated as ordinary residential property for purposes of depreciation and construction-period interest, and taxes must be capitalized.

To replace the tax incentives that were repealed, the 1986 Act provides under I.R.C. §42 for an annual tax credit for 10 years equal to either 4 percent (for newly constructed or rehabilitated low-income housing financed with tax-exempt bonds or otherwise subsidized) or 9 percent (for newly constructed or rehabilitated low-income housing that is financed with private funds and qualifies based on the percentage of low-income units in the project). After reviewing the excerpt by Schwartz, which explains the credit in greater detail, do you think that low-income housing has been helped or shortchanged by the 1986 Act? See also Carlisle, The Credit for Low-Income Housing: Whose Shelter Is It?, 3 Real Est. Fin. J. 44 (Winter 1987); Goodman, Tax Ideas: Real Estate Tax Credits After the Tax Reform Act of 1986, 16 Real Est. L.J. 172 (Fall 1987); Goolsby and Williams, Maximizing Low-Income Housing Tax Benefits, 18 Real Est. Rev. 79 (Winter 1989); Novogradac and Fortenbach, The Low-Income Housing Tax Credit, 16 J. Real Est. Taxn. 223 (Spring 1990).

Low-income housing is a good example of how social policy considerations can affect tax legislation. The low-income housing credits are tax-framed subsidies that obviously are designed to achieve the social policy goal of affordable housing for the poor. In "Tax Shelter Proposals" the Joint Committee on Taxation states that "in the case of shelters based on tax incentives, there is evidence that the government has lower cost alternatives than the creation of tax shelters, such as targeted spending programs, for encouraging certain types of economic activity." In the case of low-income housing the primary alternative to indirect tax deduction or credit-funded subsidies would be direct government subsidies such as public housing, which, in the opinion of Professor Surrey (who is quoted in the excerpt of Alan Aronsohn's statement before the House Ways and Means Committee), are more equitable and sensible. Tax shelter proponents such as Mr. Aronsohn strenuously disagree. After reviewing his comments, what is your position on this issue? In your judgment, is more information necessary? See Surrey, Tax Incentives as a Device for Implementing Government Policy: A Comparison with Direct Government Expenditures, 83 Harv. L. Rev. 705 (1970).

6. *The Tax Shelter Is Feeble Without Rental Income.* An allowance for depreciation is available to the owner of real estate that is being used in a trade or business or held for the production of income. I.R.C. §§167(a), 212. Thus, real estate either held for personal use or held by a "dealer" primarily for sale to customers is not subject to depreciation. Examples of "dealer" real estate include raw land held by a subdivider for resale to home builders and improved real estate (e.g., condominiums) held by a developer for sale to consumers. In both cases the real estate owner would be deprived of a depreciation deduction because the land is being held as inventory for sale to customers in the ordinary course of its business. However, while owning

the real estate the seller may be entitled to deductions for business expenses (e.g., advertising, employees' salaries) and for interest and property taxes paid or accrued during the ownership period. See Chapter 5B3, note 6 and Chapter 5B6, note 2.

Even in the case of income-producing real estate the owner's potential for tax deferral is quite limited until the project becomes operational and starts producing rental income. Prior to the completion of construction, for instance, the depreciation deduction is not available because by definition to be eligible for depreciation the property must be *in use* as a business or investment activity. This makes sense because the notion underlying the depreciation deduction is that the owner of an income-producing but wasting asset should be able to recoup the cost of the asset over some cost-recovery period, as an offset against its income. Prior to the completion of construction it would be difficult to establish and measure the depreciable cost basis of the income-producing real estate. Also, any cost incurred to obtain a mortgage loan, such as a commitment fee, is not currently deductible but must be amortized over the term of the loan. See Chapter 5B15, note 4. Finally, since organizational and startup expenditures are usually capital in nature they are not currently deductible. See generally Reichler, It's What's up Front that Counts: Tax Treatment of Front End Expenses in Real Estate Investments, 40 N.Y. Inst. on Fed. Taxn. §24.00 (1982).

7.   Selection of the Ownership Entity.[23]   Let us consider which type of ownership or organizational entity is best suited for the dual purposes of raising the venture capital and securing the debt financing needed to fund the acquisition and improvement of the real estate. See pages 115-117, supra. Selecting an ownership entity is not only a vital prefinancing consideration; such a decision is also bound to have serious spillover effects in the financing area. For example, if the choice is that of a limited partnership, the developer might feel compelled to use nonrecourse financing as opposed to recourse financing; otherwise, the limited partners could be deprived of their ability to deduct tax losses in excess of their actual economic investment in the partnership. The choice of ownership vehicle is a wide one. It includes use of the tenancy-in-common, joint venture, general partnership, limited partnership, ordinary Subchapter C corporation, Subchapter S corporation, land trust, or real estate investment trust. The limited partnership has generally been the entity most preferred by investors because it best combines the tax advantages of individual ownership with the nontax advantages of corporate ownership. However, any such determination

23. The following notes and comments are based in part on materials that appear in M. Madison and J. Dwyer, The Law of Real Estate Financing ¶¶1.02-1.06 (1981). — ED.

should always involve the careful balancing of the competing tax, financing, and legal attributes that characterize each entity. Unfortunately, this balancing process is complicated by the truism that what is otherwise suitable from a legal or financing standpoint is often intolerable from a tax perspective, and vice versa. Accordingly, in selecting the optimum alternative no fewer than three horses must be harnessed, one of which — tax — is always on the run!

a. *Tenancy-in-Common.* The tenancy-in-common is the simplest but rarest form of co-ownership. The right of partition and the requirement of unanimous consent for decision-making render this mode of operation too cumbersome except in small, closely knit groups of investors whose purpose is solely to own the property and to passively collect the rental income. In addition, on the death of one of the co-owners, title to the property may be clouded by an unsettled estate in the event of a prospective sale, since all of the co-owners are ordinarily required under state law to execute the deed of conveyance at the time of transfer. However, in contrast to the general partnership, it permits free transferability of the ownership shares.

To appreciate the tax advantages and disadvantages inherent in this form of ownership, one must first understand the conflict in the tax law between the so-called aggregate and entity approaches. In determining tax consequences, an ownership entity can be treated as an aggregate of equity participants who pool their assets and resources for some common purpose. Under this approach, the entity is treated merely as a nontaxable conduit through which tax consequences flow directly to each constituent member. By contrast, under the entity approach the organization itself is treated as an entity that is separate and distinct from its participants; accordingly, separate tax consequences accrue to both the entity and its members. For example, the entity approach applies to corporate taxation and accounts for the double taxation problem faced by shareholders other than those owning stock in a small business corporation (Subchapter S corporation) under I.R.C. §1361. By contrast, Subchapter K of the Internal Revenue Code (dealing with partnerships) sidesteps the conflict and applies whichever approach produces the most desirable result. For example, to permit flexible arrangements among partners, the Code permits partners to make special allocations of deductions and income items (the aggregate approach). I.R.C. §704(b). Yet it recognizes most partner-partnership dealings for tax purposes (the entity approach). I.R.C. §707(a). At the other end of the spectrum is the tenancy-in-common, with respect to which the aggregate approach is strictly applied.

The following are the advantages of the tenancy-in-common as compared to both partnership and corporate taxations:

i. Any election affecting the computation of taxable income may be made separately by each tenant. For example, one co-owner may capitalize carrying charges (see I.R.C. §266) or (under prior law) claim accelerated depreciation while another may elect to currently deduct or "expense" such charges or claim straight-line depreciation.

ii. No partnership return is required for a tenancy-in-common. Thus, if a tenant is audited, it is less likely that his co-owner will be audited, since there is no return filed that links them to one another.

Indeed, this advantage was reinforced by TEFRA. In order to facilitate the audit of partners, especially those engaged in tax shelter activities, TEFRA provides that the tax treatment of partnership income, loss deduction, and credit items will be audited at the partnership level in a unified partnership proceeding rather than at the individual partner level. I.R.C. §§6221 to 6233. A partnership, though required to file an information return (Form 1065), is itself a nontaxable conduit. Accordingly, each partner separately reports his distributive share of each item on his individual return (Schedule K-1). Under prior law the fragmented nature of separate audits of partners with respect to the same partnership tax items had caused inconsistent audit results, duplication of effort, and other administrative problems, prompting Congress to enact I.R.C. §§6221 to 6232. Under the current law, which applies to all partnerships (including foreign-based partnerships with direct or indirect U.S. partners) except those consisting of ten or fewer partners where no special allocation has been made under I.R.C. §704(b), a partnership is required to furnish every person who was a partner at any time during the tax year a copy of the information appearing on the partnership return, and each partner is required to treat items on this return consistently with the treatment on the partnership return as audited and determined at the partnership level. I.R.C. §6031.

In addition, under current law notice of a partnership-level audit and any resultant administrative action will generally be sent only to the so-called tax matters partner (TMP), who, unlike an ordinary partner, may have the authority to enter into a settlement agreement on behalf of the other partners and who is empowered to file a petition for review of any final partnership administrative adjustment (FPAA) within 90 days. I.R.C. §6231(a)(7). See Hesch, Operating Under the New Partnership Audit Rates, 41 Inst. Fed. Taxn. §16.01 (1983); Rosen, TEFRA's New Partnership Auditing Procedures: Was the Small Partner Left Out? 38 Tax L. Rev. 479 (1983).

The following are the disadvantages of a tenancy-in-common as compared to both partnership and corporate taxations:

— Each tenant must separately report only her proportionate part of net operating income or net gain from the sale or exchange of the property. For example, if one tenant pays a larger share of the total expenses than do the others, she is entitled to deduct only her pro rata share. The excess payment is treated as an advance to her co-owners. E.g., Estate of Webb v. Commissioner, 30 T.C. 1202 (1958), acq. 1959-2 C.B. 3.

— A corollary disadvantage lies in the fact that tenants-in-common, unlike partners and joint venturers, may not reallocate income and deduction items such as depreciation in a ratio at variance with their interest in the common-owned property.

— In the event of the death, insolvency, incompetency, or retirement of a tenant-in-common, title to his share of the realty may pass to his heir or devisee, creditor, court-appointed trustee, or assignee, as the case may be. By contrast, if property is taken in the name of a partnership, legal title in specific partnership property remains unencumbered if the remaining partners should agree to continue the partnership — subject, of course, to the rights of the former partner's legal representative or assignee to his share of the partnership profits and surplus. Unif. Part. Act §§825(2), 27(1) (1914) (hereinafter UPA).

Perhaps the most constraining disadvantage is definitional. The Treasury Regulations define the term "partnership" so broadly that it includes any "syndicate, group, pool, joint venture, or other unincorporated organization through or by means of which any business, financial operation, or venture is carried on, and which is not a corporation or a trust or estate within the meaning of the Code." Moreover, the Regulations provide that "the term 'partnership' is broader in scope than the common law meaning of partnership, and may include groups not commonly called partnerships." Treas. Reg. §1.761-1(a). This definitional problem could create serious difficulty for taxpayers if the Internal Revenue Service should later determine that what purported to be a tenancy-in-common was in reality a partnership for tax purposes.

In light of the broad tax definition of the term "partnership," and based on what you may know about commercial real estate, can you think of an example in which the co-owners of income-producing (rental) realty would be treated for tax purposes as tenants-in-common rather than as partners? See Treas. Reg. §1.761-1(a). Curiously, I.R.C. §761(a) provides that an organization, at the behest of all its members, "elect out" of partnership treatment if it is formed for "investment purposes only and not for the active conduct of a business." But why should such election be necessary if the ownership entity is passive and does not engage in substantive management activity? See Hager v. Commissioner, 76 T.C. 759 (1981) (relating to hobby losses under I.R.C. §183).

b. *Joint Venture.* A joint venture is distinguishable from the ordinary partnership in that it is generally formed to carry out a single undertaking rather than an indefinite number of transactions; it is also frequently of short duration. J. Crane and A. Bromberg, Law of Partnership §35 (1968); Jaeger, Partnership or Joint Venture?, 37 Notre

Dame Law. 138 (1961). However, in all essential aspects it is either analogized to or simply treated as a partnership under local law and is subsumed for tax purposes under the definition of a partnership. I.R.C. §7701(a)(2). As a concomitant to making a postconstruction mortgage loan commitment, life insurance companies and other diversified institutional lenders will often demand a joint venture or convertible mortgage arrangement so as to obtain the right to purchase an equity interest in the secured property either immediately or on substantial completion of the improvements. In most instances, this occurs during a period of inflation, when mortgage money is tight and interest rates are high, or when the prices of alternative investments such as stocks and bonds are falling. At such times, these lenders or their subsidiary corporations will frequently obtain a joint venture position both as a hedge against inflation and as a device to circumvent interest rate ceilings imposed by local usury laws. See discussion at Chapter 7B.

    c. General and Limited Partnerships. In contrast to the general partnership format, the limited partnership offers limited liability for the investors, who, as limited partners, can relegate unwelcome management responsibilities to the promoter-general partners, which may be desirable if unsophisticated or numerous investors are involved. The Uniform Limited Partnership Act §7 (1916) (amended 1976) (hereinafter ULPA) provides that a "limited partner shall not become liable as a general partner, unless, in addition to the exercise of his rights and powers as a limited partner, he takes part in the control of the business." Accordingly, §7 of ULPA requires that a limited partner forgo participation in the control of the business as a quid pro quo for limited liability with respect to outside creditors. See, for example, Holzman v. De Escamilla, 86 Cal. App. 2d 858, 195 P.2d 833 (Dist. Ct. App. 1948). But what constitutes partaking in control? In his excellent article "The 'Control' Test for Limited Partnerships," Alan Feld maintains that under ULPA even the reservation of the right to give advice might constitute "control," since advice could have the color of command, especially where the party reserving such a right is an investor of substantial size. 82 Harv. L. Rev. 1471, 1477 (1969). Prior case law suggests, however, that a limited partner can safely engage in a limited degree of management activity. For example, in Silvola v. Rowlett, 129 Colo. 522, 272 P.2d 287 (1954), a limited partner, as shop foreman, was occasionally allowed to discuss business matters when his advice had been solicited by the general partner. And in Grainger v. Antoyan, 48 Cal. 2d 805, 313 P.2d 848 (1957), a limited partner, as sales manager, was permitted to perform certain ministerial functions (e.g., signing checks) during a crisis period but had no authority to hire personnel, purchase inventory, or set prices. However, neither the statute nor the underlying case law defines the threshold limits to which a limited partner may go without being regarded as partaking in control. Consequently, the Revised Uniform Limited Partnership Act (hereinafter RULPA), which was adopted in 1976 by the National Conference of Commissioners on Uniform State Laws, amended §7 of the prior law to provide a "safe harbor" rule for limited partners. Section 303(b) of RULPA provides that a limited partner may engage in the following activities without being deemed to have taken part in the control of the business:

> (b) A limited partner does not participate in the control of the business . . . solely by doing one or more of the following:
>   (1) being a contractor for or an agent or employee of the limited partnership or of a general partner;
>   (2) consulting with and advising a general partner with respect to the business of the limited partnership;
>   (3) acting as surety for the limited partnership;
>   (4) approving or disapproving an amendment to the partnership agreement; or
>   (5) voting on one or more of the following matters:
>   (i) the dissolution and winding up of the limited partnership;
>   (ii) the sale, exchange, lease, mortgage, pledge, or other transfer of all or substantially all of the assets of the limited partnership other than in the ordinary course of its business;
>   (iii) the incurrence of indebtedness by the limited partnership other than in the ordinary course of its business;
>   (iv) a change in the nature of the business; or
>   (v) the removal of a general partner.
>   (c) The enumeration in subsection (b) does not mean that the possession or exercise of any other powers by a limited partner constitutes participation by him in the business of the limited partnership.

In addition, because of the difficulty in determining when the "control" line has been overstepped, §303(a) of RULPA mitigates the exposure of a limited partner by imposing liability on a limited partner only to the extent that a third party has "actual knowledge" of the limited partner's participation in control of the business, so long as the limited partner's participation is not substantially the same as that of a general partner. Why did the commissioners introduce the "is not substantially the same" test in the 1976 version of RULPA? See comment to RULPA §303, 6 U.L.A., 1990 Supp., at 308-309. By contrast, in 1985 the commissioners once again amended §7 of the prior Act by expanding the "safe harbor" list beyond what had been denominated in the 1976 version and, in addition, changed the control test spelled out in the 1976 version of §303(a) by deleting the "is not substantially the same" test and by imposing liability on a limited partner only where the third party had reasonably believed, "based upon the limited partner's conduct, that the limited partner [was] a general partner." Which of the formulations proposed by the 1976 and 1985 Acts do you favor as a matter of sound public policy?

To date, 43 states have adopted some variant of RULPA. See, e.g., Cal. Corp. Code §§15611 to 15723 (West Supp. 1990); Mass. Ann. Laws ch. 109, §§1 to 62 (Law. Co-op. 1985); N.J. Stat. Ann. §§42:2A-1 to 42:2A-72 (West Supp. 1985); Ohio Rev. Code Ann. §§1782.01 to 1782.62 (Page 1985); Va. Code Ann. §§50-73.1 to 50-77 (Supp. 1985). 6 U.L.A., 1990 Supp., at 226-227. See generally Burr, Potential Liability of Limited Partners as General Partners, 67 Mass. L. Rev. 22 (Winter 1982); Kempin, The Problem of Control in Limited Partnership Law: An Analysis and Recommendation, 22 Am. Bus. L.J. 443 (1985); Kessler, The New Uniform Limited Partnership Act: A Critique, 48 Fordham L. Rev. 159 (1979).

While §7 of ULPA mandates that management authority be relegated to the general partners, the general partners seldom retain responsibility for ordinary management decisions. For example, the syndicate will frequently delegate management control to outsiders, perhaps to a real estate concern for a prearranged fee or percentage of the profits, or sometimes to the previous owner under a sale-and-leaseback arrangement. Alternatively, the syndicate might sublease the realty on a long-term net rental basis to insiders, for example, to the syndicate promoters themselves or to their wholly owned affiliate. By agreement, however, the general partners ordinarily will retain the exclusive right to make important policy and nonmanagement decisions, such as if and when to lease, mortgage, refinance, or sell the realty.

Also, observe that §107 of RULPA (like §707(a)(1) of the Internal Revenue Code) allows a limited partner to lend money and otherwise transact business with the limited partnership. In addition, the limited partners are accorded priority over general partners as to income and recapture of capital when accounts are settled in the event the partnership is dissolved. ULPA §23.

Another advantage is the so-called continuity of enterprise of a limited partnership. While the death, insanity, or withdrawal of a general partner may dissolve a limited partnership, the continuity of the partnership will not be affected if such a contingency should occur with respect to a limited partner. See ULPA §§20, 21. By contrast, under the UPA, the death, bankruptcy, incompetency, and perhaps withdrawal of any partner in a general partnership dissolves the partnership. UPA §§31(4), 31(5), 32(1)(a); J. Crane and A. Bromberg, Law of Partnership, §§77, 78(b) (1968). However, this oft-cited advantage of the limited partnership is somewhat illusory; the case law clearly suggests that such continuity can also be effectuated by special agreement among the partners in a general partnership, without contravening the statute. See e.g., Zeibak v. Nasser, 12 Cal. 2d 1, 82 P.2d 375 (1938); Storer v. Ripley, 12 Misc. 2d 662, 178 N.Y.S.2d 7 (1958). This view has also been adopted in a number of states by statute. E.g., Cal. Corp. Code §15031(4) (West 1977 and West Cum. Supp. 1990); Tex. Rev. Civ. Stat. Ann. art. 6132b, §31(4) (Vernon 1970).

A major disadvantage of the limited partnership form is that while a limited partner's interest can automatically be transferred to her legal representative if any of these involuntary contingencies should occur, the interest is not very marketable except for the so-called master limited partnership (MLP), whose investment shares, called depositary receipts, are usually traded on Wall Street. See discussion at Chapter 13A. Consequently, a nearly insolvent estate or legal representative may be forced into a real liquidity bind. By contrast, when a partner in a general partnership or a general partner in a limited partnership dies or becomes insolvent or legally incapacitated, the interest of the affected partner is customarily liquidated under a "buy-sell" or "first refusal" provision in the partnership agreement. Under the former, the interest of such partner is either sold to the remaining partners or retired by means of a liquidating distribution from the partnership at a prearranged formula price that may later be determinative of value for federal estate tax purposes. Otherwise, the interest of the deceased or incapacitated partner might be sold to a stranger at a sacrifice price or passed on to an heir or devisee whose intrusion into the management decisionmaking process could spell disaster for the remaining partners. See §5.2(2) of the sample limited partnership agreement in the Documents Manual for an illustration of a typical buy-sell provision and §5.1.(2) of same for an illustration of a typical right-of-first-refusal provision; see generally Black, Partnership Buy-Sell Agreements, 36 Inst. Fed. Taxn. 51 (1978).

On balance, the limited partnership is the ownership vehicle most often chosen by investors who decide to use the partnership format. The general partnership form of organization is frequently employed by relatively small and intimate groups of sophisticated insiders who do not depend on outside sources for venture capital. Such individuals are willing to forgo the advantages of being limited partners (e.g., limited liability) in exchange for control over policy decisions and some liquidity for their estates in the event of their demise. This need for control is why many if not most institutional lenders will insist on the general partnership format in their joint venture arrangements with developers. See Chapter 7B.

For further study see Tax Planning for Partnership Agreements, 37 Inst. on Fed. Taxn. §§13.01 to 16.01 (1979); Banoff, Tax Distinctions Between Limited and General Partners: An Operational Approach, 35 Tax L. Rev. 1 (1979); Partnerships and Tax Shelters — Issues and Solutions, 38 Inst. on Fed. Taxn. §§9.01 to 12.01 (1980); Shelters and Partnerships, 40 Inst. on Fed. Taxn. §§14.01 to 18.01 (1982).

   d.   *Limited Partnership vs. Incorporation.*   Because the limited partnership combines the tax advantages of partnership ownership with the legal and business advantages of incorporation, it is the most popular choice for real estate investors. Both private or "closely held" and public limited partnerships became very popular during the 1950s with the latter reaching its peak in 1961 when syndicate "units" costing $39 million were sold to acquire a major New York City office building. See 1 Roulac, Syndication Landmarks 19 (PLI 1974). This upsurge in popularity came about largely because of high federal income tax rates following World War II and the 1954 Internal Revenue Code, which, to a large extent, extricated taxpayers from the imbroglio of pre-1954 Code partnership taxation. However, as a consequence of some well-publicized failures caused by careless accounting and management practices, the limited partnership lost ground to the corporate type of syndicate during the early 1960s. The bankruptcy of Louis J. Glickman in 1963 is a prime example. Yet the limited partnership form of ownership has rebounded since the late 1960s, especially with the decline in popularity of the equity real estate investment trust.

Most limited partnerships are still closely held and are not regulated by the federal securities laws because their investment shares are sold intrastate or qualify for the private offerings exemption. See Chapter 13A, note 3. However, there was an upsurge in master limited partnerships and other publicly held syndications, most of which were registered with the Securities and Exchange Commission prior to the Tax Reform Act of 1986. See Table 13-2, at Chapter 13A. Since about 1972, some of the nation's largest brokerage houses, such as Merrill, Lynch, Pierce, Fenner & Smith, Kidder Peabody and Co., and E. F. Hutton & Co. have been underwriting limited partnerships at prices the public can afford. While these public syndications had originally emphasized newly constructed residential real estate, especially federally subsidized housing, they expanded their investment portfolios to include commercial income-producing real estate. A recent development has been the entry of both thrift organizations and life insurance companies into the real estate syndication business.

i. *Legal and Financing Considerations.* Traditionally, the main incentive for selecting corporate rather than partnership ownership has been the limited tort and contract liability available to shareholder-investors, especially with regard to construction projects. In addition, corporate ownership offers investors the ability to relegate management and title-handling problems to the agents of the corporation. It also offers promoters the ability to reach a wide variety of investors in order to secure the necessary venture capital. Yet these factors have become less significant in the present era of maximum public liability insurance, nonrecourse financing, and liberalized fringe benefits for individual employers. Moreover, as noted above, limited liability, easy access to investors, and centralized management also inhere in the use of the limited partnership or trust as the ownership vehicle. Also, while the death or withdrawal of a partner causes the dissolution of a general partnership absent an agreement to the contrary, UPA §31, ULPA provides that a limited partnership shall not be dissolved by the death or withdrawal of a limited or even general partner if, in the latter case, the certificate so provides or if the remaining members agree. Compare UPA §3 with ULPA §§20, 21. In addition, a partnership, whether it be general or limited, can, like a corporation, hold title to real estate in its own name. UPA §8(3). However, two distinct advantages of the corporate form remain, especially when the mortgage money market is tight: the inimitable liquidity of publicly held corporate stock and the corporation's exemption from local usury restrictions.

In contrast to corporate shares, investment units in a public limited partnership syndicate (other than an MLP) may not be readily marketable because of self-imposed constraints of alienability legalized under ULPA. While §19 of ULPA permits a limited partner to assign freely, the assignor cannot convey to the assignee full privileges as a limited partner unless the assignor is empowered to do so under the certificate or unless the remaining members agree. For example, if the assignee does not become a "substituted limited partner," he may share in future profits but may not ask for an inspection of partnership books or seek an accounting for partnership transactions. ULPA §19(3). In addition, the articles of limited partnership customarily place restrictions on the class of persons with respect to which an interest can be assigned to achieve certain business or legal objectives. For example, the transferee often is required to be 21 years of age or older, a resident of the state in which the partnership is doing business, or subject to approval by the general partners. Moreover, except for the master limited partnership (MLP) (discussed at Chapter 13A), there is an absence of any formal secondary markets for trading shares (such as the New York Stock Exchange). While a few publicly held partnership syndicates (that are not MLPs) currently maintain an aftermarket for shares at the issue price, the cashing in of a syndicate unit is almost always made expensive and cumbersome. (Why?) Consequently, a limited partner must ordinarily invoke her own resources to sell or exchange her investment share. In this respect, her plight resembles the liquidity bind faced by shareholders in a closely held corporation.

A correlative disadvantage is that for credit purposes, the collateral value of the partnership interest is quite low. While the maximum loan-to-value ratio for high-grade common stocks is apparently about 75 percent and for AAA municipal bonds about 80 percent, it is doubtful whether any banks will value for credit purposes an investment unit in a noncorporate real estate syndicate for more than a fraction of its real worth.

In addition, whereas the corporation, as a borrowing entity, is exempt from usury restrictions in most jurisdictions, the limited partnership is not. Accordingly, if the loan is not exempt for some other reason, the syndicators might be forced to use a nominee or "straw" corporation or to otherwise circumvent local usury law restrictions. See discussion at Chapter 5B3, note 4. In today's money market, the interest rate on a mortgage would otherwise probably exceed the maximum contract rate allowable by local law. See Nosari and Lewis, How Usury Laws Affect Real Estate Development, 9 Real Est. L.J. 30 (1980). Finally, as noted at Chapter 13A, note 3, real estate securities are equally regulated in today's investment market, whether the issuer is a corporation or a partnership syndicate.

    ii.   Tax Advantages of Partnership over Incorporation.   Under the aggregate approach a partnership is treated as a nontaxable conduit by means of which items of income, gain, loss, deduction, or credit are transmitted to the partners. I.R.C. §§701, 702. Hence, the tax losses of the partnership can be passed through to the partners. By contrast, with the exception of a Subchapter S corporation, the entity approach applies to corporate taxation, under which a corporation is regarded as a tax entity that is separate and distinct from its shareholders. Consequently, the tax losses of an ordinary C corporation can be used by the corporation to offset its own income. Indeed, these losses can be carried forward or backward if the corporate taxpayer's current income is insufficient to absorb such losses. I.R.C. §1212. However, such tax losses of the ordinary corporation cannot be passed through to the investor-shareholders.

    In addition, while the corporation can avail itself of depreciation deductions to offset its own taxable income, the entity approach requires separate tax treatment for the corporation's shareholders. Under I.R.C. §316 any distribution to a shareholder is a dividend, taxable as ordinary income (at a maximum rate of 34 percent) to the extent the distribution is from the corporation's current or accumulated earnings and profits. The starting point in computing earnings and profits is the corporation's taxable income, which amount is adjusted by applying certain tax accounting rules. Treas. Reg. §1.312-6; B. Bittker and J. Eustice, Federal Income Taxation of Corporations and Shareholders ¶7.04 (1979 and Cum. Supp. 1985). Madden, Taxation of Real Estate Transactions — An Overview, Tax Management Portfolio 480-2nd A, 152-154 (Bureau of National Affairs) (1987).

    The corporation must use a relatively slow 40-year cost recovery period to determine the amount of depreciation for purposes of computing its earnings and profits (as opposed to its taxable income); therefore, the shareholders are less able to shelter their cash distributions from immediate taxation than are the distributee partners in a partnership. I.R.C. §§312(k)(3), 168(g)(2).

    Returning to the example involving the L-G partnership (see

Example C, what would be the tax results in 1992 for the investors if the syndicate were organized as a corporation rather than as a partnership? What would the tax results have been in 1998 if the corporation had no accumulated earnings and profits and decided to distribute all of its cash flow for the year to the shareholders? Suppose that when the project is worth $12 million the corporate syndicate refinances at the same 80 percent loan-to-value ratio for $9,600,000 and distributes the excess mortgage proceeds of approximately $1,600,000 to the shareholders. How would these results compare with their tax posture as partners?

For further discussion see August and Silow, S Corporation vs. Partnership for Real Estate Ventures, 1 J. Taxn. Inv. 91 (1984); Mullaney and Blau, An Analytic Comparison of Partnerships and S Corporations as Vehicles for Leveraged investments, 59 J. Taxn. 142 (1983); Neis, Changing the Form of Doing Business: Selected Topics Under Subchapters C, K, and S, 61 Taxes 870 (1983); Starr, Recent Legislative Changes Affect the Selection of the Proper Entity for Tax Purposes, 59 J. Taxn. 340 (1983).

Since the corporation is a tax entity distinct from its shareholders, the composite nature of its income or loss of income is of no direct concern to shareholders whose entitlement to a share of profits depends on the amount, not the nature, of the constituent income and deduction items. Conversely, I.R.C. §704(b) applies the aggregate theory. In their partnership agreement partners can allocate among themselves a specific share or item of partnership income or loss (such as bottom line profits or losses, depreciation, or capital gains or losses) provided that the special allocation has "substantial economic effect," that is, when the allocation "may actually affect the dollar amount of the partners' shares of the total partnership income or loss independently of tax consequences." Prior Treas. Reg. §1.704-1(b)(2). If the agreement is silent as to a partner's share of income, loss, or constituent item, or, in the alternative, if a special allocation is devoid of economic substance, the partner's share will "be determined in accordance with the partner's interest in the partnership . . . by taking into account all facts and circumstances." I.R.C. §704(b). Among the relevant factors to be taken into account, according to the legislative history, are the partner's share in profits and losses, cash flow, and the partner's right to distribution of capital on liquidation. See Staff of the Joint Committee on Taxation, 94th Cong., 2d Sess., General Explanation of the Tax Reform Act of 1976, at 96 (Comm. Print 1976).

Although example (3) in the prior regulations under Reg. §1.704-1(b)(2) does not involve real estate, it provides a simple and concise illustration of the phrase "substantial economic effect." In the example, the partners in an equal *A-B* partnership agree to invest surplus partnership funds in equal dollar amounts of municipal bonds and stock.

They agree that *A* is to receive all the tax-exempt interest income and gain or loss from the tax-exempt bonds and that *B* is to receive all the dividend income and gain or loss from the corporate stock. Even though the allocation benefits *A*, who is in a higher tax bracket than *B*, it has substantial economic effect for the partners, since the respective amounts of partnership income credited to their capital accounts will differ in dollar amount. On the other hand, if the agreement provides that *A* and *B*'s distributive shares of partnership income shall be the first $10,000 of interest and dividend income, respectively, with the balances to be divided equally, the allocation will fail, since its principal purpose is to allocate tax-exempt interest to *A*, the higher-bracket partner, and accordingly it is but a tax avoidance fiction devoid of any economic reality.

Accordingly, if in a real estate partnership there is an allocation of "bottom-line" profits or losses disproportionate to capital contributions, or the ratio for sharing profits and losses varies from year to year, or certain constituent items such as depreciation are all allocated to one partner or class of partners, these arrangements will be recognized if they reflect business and economic reality. As a general rule, this means that the special allocation must be reflected in the capital accounts of the partners, that any resulting disparity in the capital accounts must be respected at liquidation, that cash flow must be apportioned in the same manner as taxable income or loss, and that in later years there must be no subsequent adjustments in the capital accounts to offset the effects of the special allocation.

For example, based on the foregoing criteria, a special allocation was sustained in the case of Harris v. Commissioner, 61 T.C. 770 (1974). In that case a loss had been incurred on the sale of an interest in a shopping center. The entire loss was allocated to the taxpayer whose capital account was debited, and future shares of profits and losses were reduced accordingly. See also Hamilton v. United States, 687 F.2d 408 (Ct. Cl. 1982) ("flip-flop" allocation of bottom-line income and losses requiring shift in sharing ratio after payout held to be in accordance with economic reality); Lewis v. Commissioner, 65 T.C. 625 (1975). By contrast, decisions involving special allocations that failed to pass judicial muster include Holladay v. Commissioner, 72 T.C. 571 (1979), affd., 649 F.2d 1176 (5th Cir. 1981); Boynton v. Commissioner, 72 T.C. 1147 (1979), affd., 649 F.2d 1168 (5th Cir. 1981), cert. denied, 454 U.S. 1146 (1982); Magaziner v. Commissioner, 37 T.C.M. (CCH) 873 (1978); Sellers v. Commissioner, 36 T.C.M. (CCH) 305 (1977), affd. on other grounds, 592 F.2d 227 (4th Cir. 1979). Other factors that could relate to the determination of the validity of an allocation include the following: whether the partnership or a partner individually has a business purpose for the allocation; whether related items of income, gain, loss deduction, or credit from the same source are subject to the same allocation; whether the allocation was made without recognition of normal business factors and only after the amount of the specifically allocated item could reasonably be estimated; the duration of the allocation; and the overall tax consequence of the allocation. See prior Treas. Reg. §1.704-1(b)(2); Staff of the Joint Committee on Taxation, 94th Cong., 2d Sess., General Explanation of the Tax Reform Act of 1976, at 96 (Comm. Print 1976). See also current Treas. Reg. §1.704-1(b). For an excellent discussion of "flip-flop" allocations (those that shift items in favor of the general partners after the shelter "crossover" point has been reached) and other specific issues with regard to special allocations, see R. Haft and J. Fass, 1988 Tax Sheltered Investments Handbook §13.04.

Certain allocations encountered most frequently in limited partnerships are considered fairly safe by the experts. They include a special allocation to the limited partners, who provide all of the capital: (1) all the start-up losses generated by such front-end items as interest, taxes, sales tax, construction loan points, or standby fees; and (2) early depreciation losses, frequently accompanied by a provision that once the partnership "turns the corner" they shall receive all bottom-line profits until they have recouped the losses previously charged to them. This is a customary business arrangement, even absent a tax motivation. See Town & Country Plymouth, Inc. v. United States, 20 A.F.T.R.2d (P-H) 5823 (C.D. Cal. 1967); 2 A. Willis, Partnership Taxation 320 (2d ed. 1976). Alternatively, the limited investor partners might receive all the profits and cash flow until they recoup their capital contributions. At that time the general service partners would be permitted to share in the profits, cash flow, and losses of the partnership. Some planners prefer not to allocate any share of these items that is disproportionate to the service partners' capital contributions, but instead favor allocating an extra share of the residual net assets of the partnership once the partnership is liquidated and the debt claims and capital account claims of the investor partners have been satisfied. Again, such arrangements would have an economic reality independent of their tax consequences.

For additional background on special allocations, see generally W. McKee, W. Nelson, and R. Whitmire, Federal Taxation of Partnerships and Partners ¶¶10.01 to 10.07 (1977); A. Willis, J. Pennell, and P. Postlewaite, Partnership Taxation §§103, 104 (4th ed. 1989); Charyk, An Overview of the Proposed Section 704 Partnership Allocation Regulations — Implications for Real Estate Partnerships, 11 J. Real Est. Taxn. 34 (1983); Comment, Partnership Allocations and Capital Accounts: A Technical Advice Memorandum as Administrative Minefield, 35 Tax L. Rev. 441 (1980); Cowan, Substantial Economic Effect — The Outer Limits for Partnership Allocations, 39 Inst. Fed. Taxn. 23-1 (1981); Kirkland, Drafting Special Allocation Provisions Under Section 704(b) and (c)(2), 60 Taxes 203 (1982); McGuire, Special

Allocations of Partnership Gross Income, 57 Taxes 504 (1979); Peiser, Partnership Allocations in Real Estate Joint Ventures, 13 Real Est. Rev. 46 (Fall 1983); Westin, The Hazy Boundary Between Partnership Allocations and Distributions, 9 J. Real Est. Taxn. 22 (1981).

iii. Tax Pitfalls in Using the Limited Partnership. The limited partnership is generally the most appropriate ownership vehicle for real estate investors. This still holds true after the Tax Reform Act of 1986 and the Revenue Act of 1987. However, precautionary measures must be taken to ensure: (1) tax treatment of the entity as a partnership and not as an "association" taxable as a corporation; and (2) a maximum amount of adjusted (tax) basis for each limited partner's interest in the partnership, inasmuch as this amount is the ceiling for taking his share of partnership losses.

The first tax pitfall of which the real estate planner must be aware is having the limited partnership characterized as an "association" taxable as a corporation under Treas. Reg. §§301.7701-2 to 301.7701-4 (as amended on April 25, 1983). To avoid this, the proposed terms and conditions of the partnership agreement must be tested under the Regulations and careful draftsmanship must be used when the agreement is finalized. Under the Regulations, if the organization bears a close enough resemblance to a corporation it will be treated as such for tax purposes, notwithstanding its local law denomination as a partnership. The Regulations delineate six basic corporate characteristics: (1) having associates; (2) having the objective to carry on a business and divide the gain therefrom; (3) having continuity of life; (4) having centralization of management; (5) having limited liability; and (6) having free transferability of interests. Since the first two characteristics are common to both corporate and partnership organizations, an unincorporated organization will be taxed as a corporation only if it possesses more than two of the remaining four corporate attributes. See generally Larson v. Commissioner, 66 T.C. 159 (1976), acq. 1979-1 C.B. 1; Zuckman v. United States, 524 F.2d 729 (Ct. Cl. 1975).

Returning to the tax shelter example involving the L-G partnership (see Example C in Madison and Dwyer, excerpted supra), if the partnership were taxed as a corporation the tax losses ($136,940 in 1992) could not be passed through to the limited partners and only $95,470 of the net cash distributions to the limited partners, as constructive shareholders, would be sheltered from immediate taxation as ordinary income.

The second tax pitfall is the tax basis problem for limited partners caused by recourse financing and nonrecourse financing that does not qualify under I.R.C. §465(b)(6). See the excerpt by Schwartz, supra, for a definition of "qualified nonrecourse financing." As you know, corporate losses may not be deducted by shareholders except for those owning stock in a Subchapter S corporation. By contrast, the ability of partners to deduct their distributive share of partnership losses to the extent of their adjusted bases in their partnership interests has been a keystone of partnership taxation. A partner's adjusted basis in her partnership interest is ordinarily equal to the sum of cash and her adjusted basis in property contributed to the partnership. I.R.C. §§705, 722. However, if the partnership obtains qualified nonrecourse (as opposed to recourse) financing, all partners' adjusted bases in their partnership interests would also include their share of the liabilities of the partnership.

Under I.R.C. §752 the position of a general partner under the *Crane* doctrine is identical to that of someone who individually purchases an undivided interest in the property. The general partner's adjusted basis in the partnership interest for purposes of the §704(d) loss limitation not only includes the amount of cash and adjusted basis of property contributed but also the partner's share of partnership liabilities. However, a special rule has existed for the limited partner. Under Treas. Reg. §1.752-1(e) a limited partner's share of partnership liabilities for the purpose of increasing his adjusted basis shall not exceed the amount of future capital contributions he is obligated to make. However, where none of the partners have any personal liability with respect to a partnership liability, as in the case of nonrecourse financing, then all partners, including limited partners, shall be considered as sharing such liability in the same proportion as they share profits provided that the nonrecourse financing is "qualified."

Example: G is a general partner and L a limited partner in a partnership formed to acquire an apartment building costing $1 million. Each makes a cash contribution of $100,000 and the partnership obtains a mortgage in the amount of $800,000 to fund the balance of the construction costs. Under the terms of the partnership agreement they are to share profits equally, but L's liabilities are limited to the extent of his contribution. Neither the partnership nor either of the partners assumes any liability on the mortgage and the loan is obtained from a "qualified" lender who regularly makes loans and who is not related to the partnership.

Results: The basis of G and L for their partnership interest is increased from $100,000 to $500,000, since each partner's share of the partnership liability has increased by $400,000. However, had G assumed personal liability by not insisting on an exculpatory provision in the mortgage note, G's basis for her interest would have increased by $800,000, and L's basis would remain at $100,000.

Returning to our hypothetical involving the L-G partnership (see Example F in the excerpt from Madison and Dwyer, supra), if the financing were recourse in nature or did not constitute qualified nonrecourse financing, the failure to increase the bases of the limited partners could be disastrous. Since each year the limited partners' bases are being reduced by their share of losses and tax-free cash distributions, their bases would be reduced to zero by the end of 1994. I.R.C. §705(a)(2). See also Prop. Reg. §§1.465-22(b), 1.465-22(c). Thereafter, they would be precluded from deducting their shares of partnership losses and would start realizing gain on their cash distributions. I.R.C. §731(a)(1). By contrast, if the financing were qualified nonrecourse financing, the limited partners' tax bases at the end of 1994 would be a whopping $8,834,646! Can you explain the reason for this difference?

    e. *Subchapter S Corporation.* By electing to be taxed under Subchapter S of the Internal Revenue Code (§1361 et seq.), the co-owners of some income-producing real estate can avail themselves of limited liability and the other nontax advantages associated with corporate ownership along with the advantages associated with partnership taxation. As with a partnership, a Subchapter S corporation is treated as a nontaxable conduit rather than as a separate tax entity. Accordingly, under I.R.C. §1366 there is a pass-through of tax losses to the shareholders and, in contrast to an ordinary Subchapter C corporation, there is no problem of double taxation inasmuch as the earnings of the Subchapter S corporation are subject to taxation only at the shareholder level (in proportion to each shareholder's pro rata share of stock).

    However, as in the case of individual partners in a partnership, individual shareholders in a Subchapter S corporation are subject to the limitation on passive losses under I.R.C. §469 (discussed at Chapter 2B, note 3). In addition, there are definitional constraints that preclude the use of this form of entity for many real estate transactions. To qualify as a Subchapter S corporation under I.R.C. §1361, the entity must be a domestic corporation that does *not:* (1) have more than 35 shareholders; (2) have as a shareholder a person who is not an individual (except for certain trusts and estates); (3) have as a shareholder a nonresident alien; and (4) have more than one class of stock.

    Moreover, use of a Subchapter S corporation as a real estate ownership vehicle for income-producing real estate is severely limited by the onerous at-risk rule under I.R.C. §1366(d)(1). Under this rule the amount of deductible losses is limited to the shareholder's adjusted basis in the stock plus the amount of any indebtedness of the corporation *to the shareholder.* By contrast, as previously discussed, in the case of a limited partnership the ceiling amount for deducting losses is the adjusted basis of the limited partner's interest in the partnership plus the partner's share of any qualified nonrecourse indebtedness of the partnership *to outside creditors,* including mortgagees. I.R.C. §752(a) and Treas. Reg. §1.752-1(e); I.R.C. §§465(b)(6)(A), (B), and (C). In other words, while a partner is able to obtain a step-up in its adjusted basis equal to its share of mortgage liabilities, a Subchapter S shareholder cannot. Therefore, in the case of a typical leveraged real estate investment that is funded by nonrecourse financing an investor may not be able to take full advantage of its share of tax losses if the venture is organized as a Subchapter S corporation. To illustrate this point take a look at the example involving the L-G partnership (see Example F in the Madison and Dwyer excerpt, supra) and assume for simplicity's sake that the investors make all of their capital contributions (totalling $1 million) on June 1, 1991. If the venture were organized as a Subchapter S, each year the shareholders' bases in their stock would be reduced (under I.R.C. §1367) by their pro rata share of tax losses and tax-free cash distributions so that, without the step-up in basis, their ceiling amount for deducting losses would be reduced to zero and they would start realizing gain on the distributions by the end of 1994. By contrast, if the venture were organized as a limited partnership the ceiling amount, with the step-up in basis, would be $8,834,646. Consequently, the Subchapter S corporation is used primarily to hold real estate that is not expected to yield sizeable tax losses (e.g., raw land) or where the investors have a substantial equity investment (and tax basis) in the real estate or where the investors decide to incorporate their venture in order to avoid local usury restrictions (which would otherwise prevent them from obtaining mortgage financing at a market rate of interest). For additional background on Subchapter S corporations, see generally Mullaney and Blau, An Analytic Comparison of Partnerships and S Corporations as Vehicles for Leveraged Investments, 59 J. Taxn. 142 (1983); Madden, Taxation of Real Estate Transactions — An Overview, Tax Management Portfolio 480-2nd A, 154-155 (Bureau of National Affairs) (1987).

Chapter 3

An Overview of Contracts and Conveyancing

In the previous chapter we observed how a typical real estate entrepreneur such as Dan Developer needs to carefully weigh certain legal and tax considerations in deciding on an ownership entity. Once the ownership entity is selected the next question is how to acquire title to the real estate. In a sense this next prefinancing consideration may be a postfinancing consideration as well, depending on the nature of the transaction. For example, in the case of new construction Dan Developer may decide to acquire fee title to (rather than lease) the land on which the proposed improvements will be situated. If so, developers like Dan will usually obtain a regular fee mortgage loan to fund both the purchase price of the land and the costs of developing the land and constructing the building and other improvements. Alternatively, Dan might decide to finance separately his land acquisition cost by means of a subordinated purchase-money mortgage from the seller or with a land development loan from some institutional lender. These techniques are examined at Chapter 9B, notes 5a and 5b, respectively. Under either financing approach Dan will be acquiring fee title to the land underlying the improvements and therefore the legal issues and draftsmanship considerations associated with contracts of sale and conveyancing form the subject matter of this chapter.

These issues and considerations re-emerge and become more complicated if and when the tenanted building and underlying land are sold by Dan and his investors at the end of the real estate financing cycle. After translating some of the accumulated value (or "equity") in the office building project into tax-free cash by means of a second mortgage or by substituting a new, larger first mortgage loan for the existing one (a process called "refinancing"), Dan may eventually want to dispose of the property. After weighing the possibility of a sale and leaseback or a tax-free exchange Dan most likely will decide to sell the real estate and start the financing cycle anew by using the net sale proceeds to acquire or construct another piece of income-producing real estate. (These special financing techniques are examined in Part III of this book.) Prior to the Tax Reform Act of 1986 the project usually would be sold once its tax shelter potential had "burned out" (the seventh full operational year in Example A on page 108). Now in deciding when to sell, business and economic factors will predominate over tax considerations. Alternatively, instead of purchasing land and constructing improvements thereon a developer such as Dan may decide simply to purchase an existing tenanted building, in which event many of the same issues and considerations would arise.

In this chapter let us assume that Dan has decided to purchase an office building (perhaps with the aid of some intermediary such as a real estate broker) and Dan has alerted you, his legal advisor, that negotiations have already begun between himself and the prospective seller (Sam Seller). Based on current earnings (as capitalized), Sam is insisting on a sale price of $40 million. Further assume that Dan plans to expend $10 million in renovation and carrying costs for the project before he converts the office building into a 100-unit multi-use condominium complex and that he expects to sell the units at an average per-unit price of $600,000, totalling gross revenues of $60 million for a potential net profit of $10 million.

After negotiations Dan and Sam agree on a total price of $40 million subject to the following payment terms: $5 million in earnest money to be delivered when the contract for sale is executed and an additional $35 million in cash at closing. Dan expects to obtain a mortgage loan from Ace Insurance Company or some other institutional lender in the amount of $30 million at the market rate of interest for first mortgage money that will be used to fund the balance of the agreed-on purchase price. Dan now comes to you and asks you to review a contract of sale that has been submitted by Sam's attorney. Your initial reaction should be one of relief: your client had the foresight to consult with you before executing the contract. In many instances (especially in single family residential and small commercial transactions) the initial contract will be drafted by the seller, broker, banker, or title company involved in the transaction and then submitted to one or both parties for acceptance and return even though the individual who prepares the contract may have neither sufficient information (other than price and payment details) nor an adequate legal background to prepare a complete contract and protect the interests of the parties. You should be especially wary of the broker who is more concerned about "making a deal" than attending to the legal consequences of the transaction. Once a contract has been signed, renegotiation on your client's behalf can be a very frustrating and difficult undertaking and can make you feel like you are conducting a salvage operation all the way to the closing date. In any event, welcome to the law of contracts and conveyancing.

Before we begin negotiating the terms of the contract (see note 1, infra, Draftsmanship Approaches to the Contract of Sale), and examine the other materials in this chapter, let us take a brief glimpse at the theory and mechanics of land acquisition and transfer. Expressed in virtually every contract of sale is a promise by the seller to deliver title that is good and free of all legal encumbrances except those that are agreeable to the buyer ("marketable title") on or before the closing date. During the period between the date the contract is fully executed and the closing date[1] the status of the seller's title will be examined by the purchaser's attorney based on a title search conducted by a title insurance company, an abstract company, or the purchaser's attorney himself. In that regard, the title searcher will inspect copies of relevant deeds and other documents that are recorded in either the Registry of Deeds or Registry of Probate office. If, for example, one of the seller's predecessors-in-title had conveyed the same real estate to two or more grantees, the title searcher must determine whether the seller has the better, or "paramount," chain of title under the local recording statute. If not, the record defect, unless cured, may render the title unmarketable. Likewise, there may be recorded encumbrances (e.g., easements, liens, restrictive covenants, leases) that adversely affect the value of the property. If there are no exceptions to marketable title or if they can be resolved to the satisfaction of the purchaser's attorney prior to the closing date (or a reasonable time thereafter) then the title will be closed on the stipulated date, at which time the seller will convey title by means of a deed to the purchaser, who must simultaneously deliver the balance of the agreed-on purchase price. Absent language to the contrary, once the purchaser accepts the deed its rights under the contract of sale terminate and "merge" with the deed so that the purchaser's sole recourse against the seller will depend on the covenants, if any, contained in the deed from the seller. However, even if the purchaser were to bargain for the highest degree of protection obtainable by a covenantee, namely, the standard English covenants contained in a general warranty deed (e.g., covenant of seisin, covenant against encumbrances, covenant of warranty), the title protection affordable to the covenantee is limited inasmuch as these covenants are nothing more than promises to indemnify, which might be rendered worthless if the seller-covenantor becomes insolvent. Moreover, the amount of damages recoverable against the covenantor generally is limited to the amount of the original purchase price plus accrued interest. Consequently, a prudent purchaser will demand additional title protection in the form

---

1. In the case of an ordinary contract of sale this interim period between the execution of the contract and the closing date is ordinarily about two months. By contrast, in the case of an installment land contract like the one in the *Luette* case, infra, the seller agrees to finance the purchase price and therefore retains the legal title (deed) as security until all the installment payments are made; hence, in duration the contract period will resemble the term of a mortgage loan. See Chapter 9C.

of title insurance, which is backed by the considerable net worth of the parent corporation that issues the policy. In some locations purchasers may rely instead on an attorney's opinion as to the status of the title, backed only by the attorney's professional liability insurance and personal assets. Incidentally, in about 40 states attorneys' opinions can be backed by attorney guaranty funds, which are companies whose members are practicing attorneys. Holtzschue, Real Estate Transactions: Purchase and Sale of Real Property §8.02[6][b][E] (1989). Observe, however, that in contrast to the title company, which is an absolute insurer, the attorney or his insurance carrier would be liable only if the attorney were negligent in rendering an opinion.

Those students who haven't covered this subject in first-year property law might want to consult one of the standard hornbooks such as Friedman, Contracts and Conveyances of Real Property (3d ed. 1975) or American Law of Property (Casner ed. 1952) as we wade through the materials that follow. Two observations before we begin: first, any comprehensive treatment of contracts and conveyancing is beyond the scope of this book, and this chapter is intended merely to provide you with an overview of the subject; and second, those of you who are contemplating the general practice of law might be interested to know that in contrast to the law of real estate financing, the theory of land acquisition and transfer is essentially the same regardless of whether the transaction is a large one involving commercial real estate or a small one.

A.   CONTRACTS FOR SALE OF REAL ESTATE

Like the law of real estate financing, the disposition of commercial real estate is an area in which freedom of contract virtually reigns supreme. This is especially true where the sale of commercial real estate is involved, since the seller and the purchaser are likely to be sophisticated, roughly equal in bargaining power, and represented by legal counsel. In other words, the law tends to be less paternalistic in this area than in other areas such as residential landlord-tenant law. This means that in commercial transactions for the most part general rules of law apply only in the absence of an agreement to the contrary. Since the transactional rights and responsibilities of the seller and purchaser are invariably set forth in writing (as evidenced by the sample of contract of sale, infra) there is little need in this overview to examine those general property and contracts law rules that can be overridden by means of the written word. One example should suffice. Under the so-called doctrine of equitable conversion (based on the dubious maxim that "equity regards as done what ought to be done") the positions of the parties are reversed so that the purchaser becomes the real, or "equitable," owner once the contract of sale is executed.[2] This means that the risk of loss between the date on which the contract is executed and the closing date will be borne by the "real" or equitable owner, the purchaser.[3] By contrast, under a contract-theory approach a minority of jurisdictions hold that the seller should bear the risk of loss until the purchaser receives what he bargained for, namely, the legal title in the form of a deed on the closing date.[4] Finally, under §1 of the Uniform Vendor and Purchaser Risk Act, which has been adopted in some states,[5] the risk of loss is on the party in possession. But none of these rules apply should the contract of sale expressly provide otherwise, and (as illustrated by §9 of the sample contract of sale, infra) the typical contract for the sale of commercial real estate will address this issue. Consequently, in this overview the focus will be on draftmanship approaches to the contract of sale and on those legal theories that either are imposed by way of judicial gloss on the written words of the parties (e.g., treatment of earnest money deposit as penalty rather than as liquidated damages) or that relate to the essence of their legal relationship with one another (e.g., the doctrine of marketable title). The first excerpt, by way of preface, is designed to strike a cautionary note about your client's dealings with real estate brokers.

Goldstein, When Does a Real Estate Broker Earn His Commission?
27 Prac. Law. 43 (1981)

READY, ABLE, AND WILLING

For a broker to recover a fee in most jurisdictions, a writing for his hiring is not necessary, and the real estate transaction does not have to be consummated. See Note, 5 Mem. St. U.L. Rev. 59 (1975).

The expression is often heard that the broker earns his commission when he produces a ready, able, and willing customer on the terms

---

2. See generally Friedman, Contracts and Conveyances of Real Property §4.11 (3d ed. 1975) (hereinafter Friedman); Holtzschue, Real Estate Transactions: Purchase and Sale of Real Property (1989); 3 American Law of Property §11.22 (Casner ed. 1952) (hereinafter A.L.P.).

3. See, e.g., Ross v. Bumstead, 65 Ariz. 61, 173 P.2d 765 (1946).

4. See, e.g., Capital Savings & Loan Assn. v. Convey, 175 Wash. 224, 27 P.2d 136 (1933).

5. E.g., N.Y. Gen. Oblig. L. §5-1311 (McKinney 1991).

given to him by his principal. 12 C.J.S. Brokers §182 (1980). Let us examine this statement by considering it in the context of the following fact patterns.

Given the terms for a sale by the owner of a piece of land in New York City, the broker brings a proposal to the seller. The prospect, the seller, their counsel, and the broker arrange to meet for the purpose of signing a contract.

Seller's counsel employs a printed form of contract, distributed by the New York Board of Title Underwriters, which states that "the seller shall give and the purchaser shall accept such title as _____ , a Member of the New York Board of Title Underwriters, will be willing to approve and insure." The clause can, of course, be deleted; but if it remains, then rather than name a particular company, the way the matter is usually handled is to insert in the blank space the words "any title company," i.e., any one that is a member of the New York Board of Title Underwriters. However, this seller's counsel inserts the name of "X Title Company."

Buyer's counsel does not like the provision about the X Title Company and he asks seller's counsel to correct the clause so that it applies to any title company that is a member of the New York Board of Title Underwriters. But buyer's counsel resists any change, despite the arguments of buyer's counsel that the buyer should not be limited in his selection of a title company.

At this juncture, buyer's counsel tells his client:

> You know, there's something peculiar here. The insistence of seller's counsel upon the X Title Company makes me a little bit suspicious about his title. He may have had a defect — a little blemish that he is unable to remove — but somehow he has prevailed upon the X Title Company to omit it as an exception on the seller's title policy when he acquired the property. Furthermore, the insistence upon using the X Title Company may create an embarrassing situation if we try to procure financing and the proposed mortgagee uses the Y Title Company, not the X Company, for its title search.

As a consequence, the sale is never consummated.

The following day, the broker appears at the seller's office and hands him a bill for the brokerage commission. The seller says, "Evidently there is some misunderstanding. Don't you recall — you were there yesterday — that the deal broke up because of the title company problem?" "Oh," replies the broker, "so it did. But I had nothing to do with that. You said nothing in your offering that I handed to the prospect concerning the X Title Company." The broker is right. Freeman v. Creelman, 60 Cal. App. 14, 212 P.56 (1922); Tanenbaum v. Boehm, 202 N.Y. 293, 95 N.E. 708 (1911).

Compare these facts with the following. The buyer makes an offer for a residence through the broker. The seller finds the offer acceptable and arrangements are made for the parties to meet to sign a contract. At that point, before any written contract is executed, the buyer calls the broker and says: "My wife now has different feelings about the house, and we don't want it." In this case, the broker cannot recover his fee. Annot., 12 A.L.R.2d 1410, 1413 (1950).

In the first situation, the progress of the transaction to its ultimate consummation was interrupted by the interjection of an entirely new idea by seller's counsel. But in the second situation, while an understanding was reached orally, the prospect withdrew before signing a contract, so that the objective the seller sought in hiring the broker — to sell the property — was never achieved.

CONDITIONAL HIRING

The seller of the land in the first example, having had a bad experience with the broker, decides, when selling his residence, to engage a broker on the condition that a commission would be payable only if title actually closes. The broker procures a customer who makes an offer on the seller's terms. The contract is prepared by seller's counsel, based upon the seller's title papers. The contract is signed. A short while later, the buyer asks his counsel whether he could withdraw from the contract. Counsel responds, "It doesn't look as though you can. There might be objections to title, but seller's counsel showed me the seller's title policy issued when the seller acquired the property, and the contract followed that policy."

Fortunately for the buyer, the seller, when giving the title papers to his attorney to prepare the contract of sale, forgot to tell counsel that after acquiring title, he and his neighbors had made an arrangement for the construction of drainage ditches for their common use. Because the architect needed approval for the construction of the drainage ditches, he filed the necessary papers in the county clerk's office. Since the documents were recorded after the issuance of the title insurance policy to the seller on his acquisition of the property, they were not reflected in the title papers that were given to seller's counsel.

When buyer's counsel, in due course, received his title report from the title company, he discovered that the property was encumbered by a common drainage easement, for which there was no exception in the contract. The buyer refused to accept title and the closing never materialized.

Although title never closed, the broker still can recover his commission, because the seller's act made performance impossible. 3 A. Corbin, Contracts §767 (West Publishing, St. Paul, 1960). While a broker's commission can be contingent upon the consummation of the transaction, the seller cannot take advantage of conditions that he himself created to make performance impossible and thereby deprive the broker of his commission. Shear v. National Rifle Ass'n of America, 606 F.2d 1251 (D.C. Cir. 1979); Annot., 45 A.L.R.3d 1326 (1972).

On the other hand, had the brokerage agreement stated that no commission would be paid in case of a failure to close for any reason whatsoever, no commission would have been recoverable. Dixon v. Bernstein, 182 F.2d 104 (D.C. Cir. 1950); Douglas L. Elliman Co. v. Sterling Garage, Inc., 279 App. Div. 20, 107 N.Y.S.2d 308 (1951), aff'd without opinion, 304 N.Y. 846, 109 N.E.2d 715 (1952). Even in that case, if the closing did not take place because of the bad faith or fraudulent action of the seller, the broker could recover. Langfan v. Waltzer, 13 N.Y.2d 171, 194 N.E.2d 124, 244 N.Y.S.2d 305 (1963). But if the contract stated that commissions would not be paid if there was a failure to close for any reason whatsoever except willful default, if the seller released the buyer from the commitment prior to closing, there was no willful default. Warnecke v. Countrywide Realty, Inc., 29 App. Div. 2d 54, 285 N.Y.S.2d 428 (1967) aff'd without opinion, 22 N.Y.2d 823, 239 N.E.2d 656, 292 N.Y.S.2d 917 (1968).

THE PURCHASER'S LIABILITY

There is a minority view that the broker's engagement is not satisfied until title actually closes — unless failure to close is attributable to the principal — even without a specific provision to that effect in the brokerage agreement. Ellsworth Dobbs Inc. v. Johnson, 50 N.J. 528, 236 A.2d 843 (1967). See Tristram's Landing Inc. v. Wait, 367 Mass. 622, 327 N.E.2d 727 (1975). However, in order to protect the broker, if the purchaser rejects the deal capriciously and title does not close, Ellsworth suggests that the broker has an action against him for the loss of commission on the theory of an implied obligation by the purchaser to complete the transaction. For the nonapplicability of this purchaser liability in a noncommercial transaction like the purchase of a home, see Rothman Realty Corp. v. Bereck, 73 N.J. 590, 376 A.2d 902 (1977).

A purchaser, of course, can employ a broker. But the mere shuttling back and forth between purchaser and seller does not, without more, constitute the broker the employee of the purchaser. "Employment" is a word of art; it means "I hire you to do a job." A purchaser, of course, can do this: "I hire you to obtain this property, and I will pay you a commission." But the arrangement can be: "I hire you to obtain this property, but you must look to the seller for the commission." In the latter case, if the purchaser improperly cancels the deal, there is a cause of action for damages against him, based upon the commission that the broker has lost because of his act. Duross Company v. Evans,

22 App. Div. 2d 573, 257 N.Y.S.2d 674 (1965); Annot., 30 A.L.R.3d 1395 (1970).

EXCLUSIVE ARRANGEMENTS

Recently, many brokerage contracts have involved exclusive arrangements. There is a distinction between a complete exclusive arrangement, where the principal is foreclosed from competing with the broker, and an exclusive agency where such competition is not foreclosed. Annot., 88 A.L.R.2d 936 (1963). See Brown v. Miller, 45 Ill. App. 3d 970, 360 N.E.2d 585 (1977).

Real problems arise in connection with the so-called "extension" period. How are transactions concluded after the end of the exclusive period, the impetus for which originated during the period, to be treated? In Kaye v. Coughlin, 443 S.W.2d 612 (Tex. Civ. App. 1969), the owner sought to invoke the doctrine of unconscionability of section 2-302 of the Uniform Commercial Code as a defense to liability to the broker on a sale that was consummated directly with the purchaser during the extension period. The purchaser had learned of the offering during the exclusive period from the broker's advertisement. Although the broker had made no effort to bring owner and purchaser together, the court found for the broker under the terms of the brokerage agreement, ruling that the exclusive contract was not unconscionable. See generally Annot., 51 A.L.R.3d 1149 (1973).

Thus, an exclusive arrangement should define both the duration of the extension period and the stage at which the negotiations must be at the end of the exclusive period for a transaction concluded during the extension period to be eligible for a commission. For example, only a transaction that is in active negotiation at the end of the exclusive period might entitle the broker to a commission if consummated during the extension period. . . .

CONCLUSION

As in other areas of the law, the rules dealing with the relationship of principal and broker and generalizations that outline basic premises to guide the resolution of controversies arising between the parties. . . .

Form 1 — A Nonexclusive Brokerage Agreement

Gentlemen:

Relative to the matter of the sale of the premises at 1373 Broad Street, Port Washington, New York, if you procure a purchaser, your commission shall be [insert proper rate].

The commission shall be deemed earned only when, as, and if title actually closes upon terms and conditions that are in all respects satisfactory to me, in accordance with a written contract embodying those terms and conditions as well as such others, both as to form and substance, as are required by my counsel. The particulars given by me to you are subject at all times to changes by me, whether or not communicated to you. Moreover, the submission of any particulars shall in all instances be subject to any prior sale and withdrawal from the market without prior notice to you. I shall not be responsible for any inaccuracies or errors by you regarding particulars or any other information supplied by me.

Failure to close title for any reason whatsoever shall excuse me completely from any liability for the payment of any commissions. Without limiting the foregoing, I shall have the right to break off negotiations with any prospect submitted by you for any reason whatsoever at any stage of negotiations.

It is understood further that neither you nor I may claim any change or modification in the terms of this letter or any termination of the stipulations and conditions herein unless set forth in a writing signed by the party against whom the modification is claimed.

Very truly yours,

_____

Owner

Accepted for
Jisrae Associates

By _____

COMMENTS

1. In the third paragraph, the exculpation clause in the first sentence — but not in the second sentence dealing with the break-up of negotiations — may be qualified by such phrases as "except willful default," "other than conscious design to thwart earning of commission," "other than bad faith conduct," "but not unfair dealing," or similar language. . . .

3. If desired, a clause providing for arbitration by the American Arbitration Association may be added:

If any controversy shall arise between the parties with respect to any of the matters set forth in this clause [set forth in this agreement] [required by this agreement to be resolved by arbitration] and such dispute shall not be resolved by the parties within 10 days after either of the parties shall notify the other of its desire to arbitrate the dispute, then the dispute shall be settled by arbitration by the American Arbitration Association in accordance with its then prevailing rules, and judgment upon the award may be entered in any court having jurisdiction. The arbitrators shall have no power to change any of the provisions of this agreement in any respect [nor shall they have any power to make an award of reformation], and the jurisdiction of the arbitrators is hereby expressly limited accordingly. The arbitration shall be by a panel of three arbitrators, one of whom must be an attorney-at-law actively engaged in the practice of his profession for at least 10 years. Neither party shall interrupt the progress of its performance under this agreement pending the determination in the arbitration proceeding.

4.   For a clause that provides for arbitration by arbitrators chosen by the parties involved, see Goldstein, The Power of Arbitrators in Commercial Arbitration, The Practical Lawyer, Sept. 1980, p. 75.

Harris, Legal Opinion: Real Estate Contracts — Some Things to Think About
14 Real Est. Rev. 12 (Spring 1984)

It might seem that of all real estate transactions, the purchase and sale of real estate are the simplest. The buyer turns over the money and the seller gives a deed. What could be easier than that? Compared with financing, syndicating, or developing real estate, the purchase/sale transaction looks pretty fundamental.

However, it's not quite as simple as buying a bottle of milk at the grocery store, and most real estate transactions are accomplished pursuant to a written contract.[6]

WHY A CONTRACT?

Apart from strictly legal considerations, the intangible nature of interests in real estate, the fact that money is often borrowed to pay part of the purchase price and because defects in the nature of the seller's ownership are not apparent without review of public real estate (and other) records, the parties usually find it prudent and appropriate to negotiate the deal, reflect the terms in a written contract, and con-

---

6. The Statute of Frauds requires that a contract for the sale of real property must be in writing and subscribed by the party to be charged. See, e.g., N.Y. G.O.L. §5-703 (McKinney 1990). — Ed.

summate or "close" the transaction at some future time which may be as short as a few days or very much longer.

The contract sets the purchase price, states the terms, establishes a time and place for closing, specifies situations that may allow one party or the other to withdraw from the deal (e.g., because financing cannot be obtained), describes just which title exceptions will be acceptable to the buyer and which won't, and describes the parties' rights if, prior to closing, surprises occur like the building burning down or part of the property being condemned. All this is pretty basic, but it does make the transaction a little more complicated than the purchase of milk.

It also makes the real estate contract begin to sound pretty important, and it is. It is also often the most casually, quickly, and poorly drafted legally binding document. Beleaguered real estate lawyers often discover that their clients have signed such a document before the attorney has had a chance to read it, revise it, or negotiate it. When this happens, there usually isn't much the lawyer can do but try to get the deal closed.

THE PREPRINTED CONTRACT FORM

Preprinted forms of real estate contracts abound. There may be no other legal document more commonly appearing in preprinted, fill-in-the-blank form. Title companies promulgate them, stationery stores sell them, legal printers prepare them, real estate brokers distribute them. Printed forms are designed to facilitate the quick completion and execution of real estate contracts without the help of lawyers. Often the forms are filled out by nonlawyers, real estate brokers, or the parties themselves. And, this does not just happen in house transactions.

There is nothing inherently wrong with printed forms. Most real estate deals include terms that are largely stereotypical and vary little from deal to deal. The forms can ensure that all these terms get included in an acceptable way. There is no need to "reinvent the wheel" for every transaction. The intelligent use of printed forms can be a real time-saver, and the lawyer who drafts every contract from scratch probably is wasting time and, perforce, his client's money.

PITFALLS OF PRINTED FORMS

However, there are two pitfalls in the use of printed forms.

Forms can suppress thought. There is something seductive about the terms in a printed form. If they're in the form, they must be standard, must be boilerplate, must be right. Just because terms appear in print doesn't mean the parties to the deal and their lawyers shouldn't think about every term. Just because the form says that the seller pays for title insurance doesn't mean that the parties can't (in appropriate circumstances) shift this cost to the buyer.

Second, the forms inevitably allocate the risks and some of the economic obligations of a transaction in subtle ways. Let's face it, a real estate transaction is not a murder trial, but it is adversarial. In many respects, the parties' interests are inevitably and irrevocably in conflict. The problem with printed forms is that they resolve these conflicts in mysterious ways. In a state where real estate taxes are paid one year in arrears, it will usually be to the buyer's advantage to "reprorate" real estate tax when the actual bills are out in order to be protected from the almost inevitable tax increase. Yet, a form that says, "If the amount of the current general taxes is not then ascertainable, the adjustment thereof shall be on the basis of the amount of the most recent ascertainable taxes," . . . has shifted the economic risk of tax increases to the buyer.

SOME SUBTLE AND NOT SO SUBTLE PROBLEMS

Following are some of the problems that the parties to a contract should address, rather than relying on the terms in a form:

Who is the buyer?   The phrase "x-company or assignee" is often inserted in the space for the buyer's name. The ostensible reason is to permit the buyer to designate at a later date a different entity to hold title to the purchased real estate. But if this is the intent, it can and should be expressed in just those words. For the seller, contracting with x-company or assignee may permit the named buyer to assign its rights and *and* obligations to an unnamed substitute party. The seller can lose the credit of the buyer on the transaction and, worse yet, the named buyer's credit on a purchase money note and mortgage.

Who is the seller?   Some care is also in order to have the titleholder of the property be the seller. If the seller doesn't own or can't convey title, the buyer will have an action for damages, for whatever that's worth. But will a suit for a specific performance against a nonowning seller encumber the real property? Probably not.

What is the property?   Legal descriptions may not be in mind or at hand when the parties, anxious to get on with their deal, are ready to sign, but using a street address or permitting one or the other of the parties to fill in the legal description at a later date is illusory comfort. What if the address is wrong? Does it include the vacant lot next door? Does it include the driveway easement rights over adjoining land or will these terminate? . . .

"Covenants, conditions, and restrictions of record."   When the parties are getting ready to sign the contract, no one may know the covenants,

conditions, and restrictions affecting the property. The printed forms often resolve this dilemma easily (and horribly for the buyer) by saying that title will be conveyed subject to "all covenants, conditions and restrictions of record."

Resolving this can be a hard problem. If possible, the buyer should demand to know what "covenants, conditions and restrictions" he is expected to take subject to and examine these for acceptability. But even the purist will admit that this will not always be easy or possible within a short time frame. An acceptable solution for some deals and some property may be to obligate the buyer to take subject to restrictions "not violated by the present improvements and uses of the property or by purchaser's intended use of the property."

Damages I, title defects.   It doesn't happen too often, but a deal can fail if unpermitted title exceptions crop up which the seller can't have waived. When this happens, it's usually an unpleasant surprise for everybody, like the building burning down prior to closing. Yet, most contract forms treat this "default" the same as if the seller did not appear at the closing with his deed. Does the seller want to be sued for damages or specific performance due to an unexpected title defect? If not, the parties should draft around it.

Damages II, earnest money.   If the earnest money is substantial, the seller *may* be content to retain it as liquidated damages if the buyer defaults. With admirable symmetry, form contracts often provide that if the seller defaults, the earnest money is returned to the buyer. But getting his money back is cold comfort for the buyer. It is often necessary to modify the form to be sure the remedies of damages and specific performance are available to the buyer.

Damages III, broker's commission.   Contracts often provide that if the buyer defaults, the earnest money goes first to pay the broker's commission then to the seller as damages. Interestingly, these form contracts are often promulgated by brokers. Yet, if sellers could vote, how many would agree that the broker should get a commission on a defaulted transaction?

Actually, arrangements with the broker including a statement of his commission don't belong in the real estate sale contract at all, but in the seller's agreement with the broker, the listing agreement. (This is another form the attorneys often don't see until after their client has signed.) Brokers don't usually sign the real estate sale contract, so anything said there about their rights or position may not bind them. A broker can be asked to sign the sale contract solely to evidence his agreement with the provisions about the broker's rights, and if one side or the other wants to repair the damage done by the listing agreement, this may be the way to do it.

When and where is the closing?   Here is another vexing question the parties may be too fatigued to grapple with when the contract is signed so these unimportant details are left to be "mutually agreed to by the parties." Without delving too deeply into the metaphysics of contract law, the parties should be warned that generally "agreements to agree" are unenforceable and may taint the entire contract with unenforceability. Aside from this, without a definite time and place for closing, how will either party know when the other has defaulted?

If the parties have made a bad choice, they can always change it by mutual agreement as they can change any term of a contract, and it isn't even necessary to say so. It's surprising how many people fail to understand this simple fact.

CONCLUSION

It should be emphasized that the purpose of the above is not to induce everyone to run to his lawyer at the first hint of a real estate deal (laudable as that sentiment may be), but rather to get the parties to think about some of the second-order subtleties of real estate transactions at a time when such careful thought may be discouraged by the often illusory urgency to get the contract signed.

Sample Sale Agreement

THIS AGREEMENT is made this ＿＿＿＿＿＿＿＿ day of
＿＿＿＿＿＿＿ , 19 ＿＿ , between
LIMITED PARTNERSHIP, an Oklahoma limited partnership, having
a notice address at Post Office Box   ,   ,
Oklahoma (the "Seller"), and
ASSOCIATES, INC., a California corporation, having a notice address
at   , Oklahoma City,
Oklahoma (the "Buyer").

W I T N E S S E T H:

1. *Sale of Project.*   The Seller agrees to sell and the Buyer agrees to
purchase on the terms hereafter stated all of the Seller's right, title
and interest in and to the following described property (hereafter called
the "Project"):

   1.1 *Real Property.*   All of the land situated in Oklahoma County,
        Oklahoma, described at Schedule "A-1" attached as a part
        hereof, together with the buildings, improvements, fixtures
        and other items of real property located on such land.

   1.2 *Tangible Personal Property.*   All tangible personal property lo-
        cated on such real property which is owned by the Seller
        and used in the ownership, financing, operation and main-
        tenance of the aforesaid buildings, improvements and land,
        including, without limitation, all furniture, furnishings, ranges,
        refrigerators, swimming pool equipment, maintenance equip-
        ment, vehicles, signs, draperies and carpeting.

   1.3 *Intangible Personal Property.*   All intangible personal property
        owned by the Seller and used in the ownership, financing,
        operation and maintenance of the aforesaid buildings, im-
        provements and land, including, without limitation, the non-
        exclusive right to use the trade name "Washington Park
        Apartments," all contract rights, escrow accounts, insurance
        policies, deposits, instruments, documents of title, general
        intangibles and business records pertaining to said buildings,
        improvements and land, excluding only cash on hand and in
        bank accounts.

2. *Purchase Price.*   Subject to the adjustments and prorations hereafter
described, the total purchase price to be paid by the Buyer to the Seller
for the purchase of the Project is the sum of FOUR MILLION
DOLLARS ($4,000,000.00). The purchase price will be paid in the
following manner:

2.1 *Earnest Money.* The sum of Fifty Thousand Dollars ($50,000.00) in collected funds (the "Earnest Money Deposit") is herewith deposited as earnest money with the Seller to be applied against the total purchase price on the Closing Date.

2.2 *Cash at Closing.* On the Closing Date, the Buyer will pay to the Seller the further sum of Four Hundred Fifty Thousand Dollars ($450,000.00), in collected funds.

3. *Title.* Within ten (10) days after the written request of the Buyer, the Seller will provide to the Buyer a copy of the existing survey of the Project and a preliminary binder for issuance of an ALTA Form B owner's title insurance policy issued by Title Insurance Company, Mid America Tower, Oklahoma City, Oklahoma 73102 (the "Title Insurer") showing fee simple title to the Project to be in the Seller and containing the exceptions (hereafter called the "Approved Title Exceptions") described at Schedule "A-3" attached as a part hereof. The Buyer will have ten (10) days after receipt of the preliminary title binder to provide to the Seller a letter setting forth all of the Buyer's objections to the Seller's title to the Project and the Seller shall have thirty (30) days after receipt of such letter to correct the defects in title objected to by the Buyer. If the Seller is unwilling or unable to correct such defects within such thirty (30) day period, the Buyer will have the option to waive such defect or terminate this Agreement and obtain a refund of the Earnest Money Deposit. On the Closing Date, the Seller will cause to be issued to the Buyer a policy of owner's title insurance in an amount equal to the purchase price containing the Approved Title Exceptions and any other exceptions to coverage waived or approved by the Buyer.

4. *Closing.* The Buyer and the Seller agree that the purchase will be consummated as follows:

4.1 *Title Transfer.* The Seller agrees to convey title to the Project to the Buyer by general warranty deed on or before the close of business on the Closing Date and, effective on the delivery of such deed by the Seller to the Buyer, beneficial ownership and the risk of loss of the Project will pass from the Seller to the Buyer.

4.2 *Closing Date.* This transacton will close on or before _____ , 19 ____ (the "Closing Date"). The closing will take place at the offices of Hastie and Kirschner, 3000 First Oklahoma Tower, 210 West Park Avenue, Oklahoma City, Oklahoma, with the exact time and date for closing to be designated by the Seller and approved by the Buyer.

4.3 *Seller's Instruments.* At closing, the Seller will deliver or cause to be delivered to the Buyer the following items (all documents will be duly executed and acknowledged where required):

    4.3.1 *Warranty Deed.* A general warranty deed and assignment of leases in substantially the form of Schedule "A-4" attached as a part hereof executed by the Seller conveying to the Buyer marketable fee simple title to all of the Seller's right, title and interest in and to all of the real property comprising a portion of the Project, free and clear of all liens and encumbrances except the Approved Title Exceptions;

    4.3.2 *Bill of Sale.* A bill of sale and assigment in substantially the form of Schedule "A-5" attached as a part hereof conveying all of the Seller's right, title and interest in and to all of the tangible and intangible personal property comprising a portion of the Project free and clear of all liens and encumbrances except the Approved Title Exceptions;

    4.3.3 *Certificate.* The Seller's certificate in substantially the form set forth as Schedule "A-6" hereto with attached copies of a current rent roll, a listing of refundable tenant deposits, an inventory of personal property and a listing of accounts payable and contracts relating to the Project;

    4.3.4 *First Mortgagee Consent.* A consent to the sale of the Project to the Buyer executed by the holder of the first mortgage loan described at Schedule "A-3";

    4.3.5 *Insurance Policies.* Original or certified copies of all policies of insurance covering the Project and evidence of premium payment therefor;

    4.3.6 *Lien Affidavit.* An affidavit in form acceptable to the Title Insurer certifying that the Project is free from claims for mechanics', materialmen's and laborers' liens; and

    4.3.7 *Additional Documents.* Such additional documents as might be reasonably required by the Buyer to consummate the sale of the Project to the Buyer.

  4.4 *Buyer's Instruments.* At closing, the Buyer will deliver to the Seller the payment required by paragraph 2.2 and appropriate Oklahoma sales tax return and such additional documents as might be reasonably required by the Seller to consummate the sale of the Project to the Buyer.

  4.5 *Costs.* The Seller will pay the following costs: the Seller's attorney's fees, all abstracting costs, the Oklahoma mortgage registration tax applicable to the Wraparound Mortgage Documents, any brokerage commission payable as described in paragraph 11.4, and the cost of any documentary stamps to be affixed to the deed. The Buyer will pay the following costs: the Buyer's attorney's fees, the costs of recording the deed conveying title to the Project to the Buyer, all sales and transfer taxes imposed by any governmental authority and the premium expense of the policy of owner's title insurance.

5. *Project Condition.* The Seller agrees that the Buyer will be permitted for a period ending on the date ten (10) days after the date of execution of this Agreement by the Seller to inspect the Project at the Buyer's expense to determine whether the physical properties and structures are sound and in good working order and to have access to and make reasonable examination of the utility costs, real estate title, contracts, leases and accounts of the Seller insofar as the operation and maintenance of the Project is concerned. If during such ten (10) day period the Buyer determines that the condition of the Project is unsatisfactory or that repairs are required and the Seller refuses to make such repairs, the Buyer will have the option to terminate this Agreement by written notice to the Seller and the Earnest Money Deposit will be returned to the Buyer on such termination. It is understood that the Seller has made no representation as to the condition or state of repair of the Project and has made no agreement to alter, repair or improve the Project. After the expiration of such ten (10) day period, the sole obligation of the Seller will be to deliver possession of the Project to the Buyer on the Closing Date in substantially the same condition (normal wear and tear and casualty loss excepted) as existed on the date of execution of this Agreement by the Seller and the Buyer has agreed to accept possession of the Project on the Closing Date in an AS IS condition WITH ALL FAULTS.

6. *Adjustments and Prorations.* All receipts and disbursements of the Project will be prorated on the Closing Date and the purchase price will be adjusted on the following basis:

    6.1 *Project Rents.* All rents receivable from tenants of the Project earned and attributable to the period prior to the Closing Date will be paid to the Seller to the extent that such rents have been collected on or before the Closing Date; rents earned and attributable to the period beginning on the Closing Date and thereafter will be paid to the Buyer. On receipt after the Closing Date by the Buyer of rents earned by the Project prior to the Closing Date the same will be paid to the Seller; provided, that the Buyer will have no obligation to enforce collection of such rents.

    6.2 *Security Deposits.* On the Closing Date, the Seller will deliver to the Buyer an amount of money equal to all refundable security deposits theretofore paid to the Seller by tenants occupying the Project.

6.3   *Accounts Payable.* All sums due for accounts payable which were owing or incurred by the Project prior to the Closing Date will be paid by the Seller and the Seller agrees to indemnify and hold the Buyer harmless with respect thereto. The Buyer will furnish to the Seller any bills for such period received after the Closing Date for payment, and the Buyer will have no further obligation with respect thereto. All accounts payable incurred on or after the Closing Date will be paid by the Buyer and the Buyer agrees to indemnify and hold the Seller harmless with respect thereto.

6.4   *Property Taxes.* All real and personal property ad valorem taxes and installments of special assessments, if any, for the calendar years preceding the year in which the Closing Date occurs will be paid by the Seller. All real and personal property ad valorem taxes and special assessments, if any, whether payable in installments or not, for the calendar year in which the Closing Date occurs and any amount held in any impound account by any mortgage lender with respect to the Project will be prorated to the Closing Date, based on the latest available tax rate and assessed valuation.

6.5   *Utility Charges.* All utility charges will be prorated to the Closing Date and the Buyer will obtain a final billing therefor. All utility security deposits, if any, will be retained by the Seller.

6.6   *Employee Wages.* All employees' wages, including accrued vacation and fringe benefits, if any, will be prorated to the Closing Date and paid by the Seller.

6.7   *Insurance.* The Seller will assign all existing insurance policies to the Buyer and all insurance carriers will be notified of the change in title to the Project. The cost of insurance premiums and any amount held in any impound account by any mortgage lender with respect to the Project will be prorated to the Closing Date and the Buyer will reimburse the Seller for the prepaid portion thereof.

7. *Covenant to Operate.* Prior to the Closing Date the Seller agrees to maintain, repair, manage and operate the Project in a businesslike manner in accordance with the Seller's prior practices and agrees that the Seller will not dissipate the Project or remove any property therefrom.

8. *Possession.* Possession of the Project will be delivered to the Buyer on the Closing Date free from management contracts, employment agreements and parties claiming rights to possession of the Project other than as tenants in possession.

9. *Casualty Loss.*   In the event of damage to or destruction of all or any part of the Project prior to the Closing Date, it is agreed as follows:

    9.1   *Damage.*   If the amount of the casualty loss is not more than Ten Thousand Dollars ($10,000.00), this Agreement will continue, all insurance proceeds collectible by reason of such damage will be absolutely payable to the Buyer and the purchase price will be paid without reduction.

    9.2   *Destruction.*   If the amount of casualty loss is more than Ten Thousand Dollars ($10,000.00), the Buyer and the Seller will have the mutual option for ten (10) days after receipt of notice of such destruction to cancel this Agreement by service of written notice of cancellation. On the exercise of such option, this Agreement will thereupon become null and void, and the Earnest Money Deposit will be returned to the Buyer. If, in such event, neither party affirmatively exercises the option to cancel this Agreement, such option will lapse, the Buyer will be entitled to receive all insurance proceeds collectible by reason of such destruction and the purchase price will be paid without reduction.

10. *Default; Remedy.*   In the event that either party fails to perform such party's obligations hereunder (except as excused by the other's default), the party claiming default will make written demand for performance. If the Seller fails to comply with such written demand within ten (10) days after receipt thereof, the Buyer will have the option to waive such default or to terminate this Agreement; and on such termination, the Earnest Money Deposit will be returned to the Buyer. If the Buyer fails to comply with such written demand within ten (10) days after receipt thereof, the Seller will have the option to waive such default or to terminate this Agreement; and on such termination, the Seller will be entitled to retain the Earnest Money Deposit as liquidated damages arising from such default. On such return or payment of the Earnest Money Deposit, the parties will be discharged from any further obligations and liabilities hereunder.

11. *Miscellaneous.*   It is further agreed as follows:

    11.1   *Time.*   Time is of the essence of this Agreement.

    11.2   *Notice.*   All notices required hereunder will be in writing and served by certified mail, return receipt requested, postage prepaid, at the addresses shown above, until notification of a change of such addresses.

    11.3   *Survival.*   All representations and warranties of the Seller and the Buyer contained in this Agreement will terminate on and as of the Closing Date and will not survive the closing of this transaction, except for the warranties of title of the Seller expressed in documents delivered at closing, the agreement of the Buyer with respect to rents collected after the Closing Date set forth at paragraph 6.1, the agreements of the Buyer and Seller with respect to payment of accounts set forth at paragraph 6.3 and the agreement regarding brokerage fees set forth at paragraph 11.4. The provisions of paragraph 10, limiting the remedies of the Buyer and the Seller will not apply to any action brought by either party after the Closing Date to enforce any covenant or representation described in this paragraph 11.3.

11.4　*Brokerage.*　The Buyer represents to the Seller that the sale hereby contemplated was brought about by the efforts of Seller & Associates Realtors and that the Buyer has dealt with no other broker in connection with the Project. The Seller agrees to pay the brokerage commission, if any, earned by such broker as a result of the consummation of the sale of the Project to the Buyer and the Buyer agrees to hold the Seller harmless from any claim for real estate brokerage commissions asserted by any other party as a result of dealings with the Buyer. The Seller agrees to indemnify and hold the Buyer harmless from any claim for real estate brokerage commissions asserted by any party other than Seller & Associates Realtors as a result of dealings with the Seller.

11.5　*Entire Agreement.*　This instrument constitutes the entire agreement between the Buyer and the Seller and there are no agreements, understandings, warranties or representations between the Buyer and the Seller except as set forth herein. This Agreement cannot be amended except in writing executed by the Buyer and the Seller.

11.6　*Binding Effect.*　This Agreement will inure to the benefit of and bind the respective successors and permitted assigns of the parties hereto.

11.7　*Expiration.*　This Agreement has been executed by the parties on the dates set forth below their respective signatures. It is understood that the obligation of the Buyer under this Agreement will terminate on the date ten (10) days after the date of the Buyer's execution of this Agreement unless the Seller shall have duly executed and returned a copy of this Agreement to the Buyer prior to such date.

11.8　*Assignment.*　The rights of the Buyer under this Agreement cannot be assigned in whole or in part without the prior written consent of the Seller. It is understood that the Buyer contemplates such assignment and that the Seller has specifically reserved the right to approve the financial condition, management capability and all other matters concerning the proposed assignee at the Seller's sole discretion.

IN WITNESS WHEREOF, this instrument has been executed by the parties on the date first above written.

ASSOCIATES, INC.,
a California corporation

By _____

President

Date Executed: _____
(the "Buyer")

LIMITED PARTNERSHIP, an
Oklahoma limited partnership

By   Associates, Inc.,
an Oklahoma corporation,
Sole General Partner

By _____

President

Date Executed: _____
(the "Seller")

Source: Hastie, Contracts for Disposition of Commercial Properties, ALI-ABA, 1 Modern Real Estate Transactions, 371 (7th ed. 1986).

Rife v. Lybarger
49 Ohio St. 422, 31 N.E. 768 (1892)

BRADBURY, J. The plaintiff in error seeks to reverse a judgment of the circuit court of Seneca county, denying him the specific performance of the following written contract for the sale of real estate: . . .

The finding of the court was that the plaintiff had a perfect title extending back to the United States, but that the premises were incumbered by "a mortgage given by said William Rosetter and wife on the 16th day of March, 1866, to one Morris P. Skinner, then living in Fostoria, O., and recorded in the mortgage records of said Seneca county, Ohio, volume 18, p. 293, March 19, 1866, securing to said Morris P. Skinner the promissory notes of the said William Rosetter for the following sums: Two hundred dollars on the 16th day of March, 1867; two hundred and seventy-two 75-100 dollars, March 16, 1868; two hundred and ninety-nine and 47-100 dollars, March 16, 1869; and the court do find that as to the said two hundred dollar note all claim is barred by the statute of limitations. The court also find that Morris P. Skinner died at Fostoria, Seneca county, Ohio, on the —— day of April, 1876, intestate; that Jane M. Skinner was appointed and qualified as his administratrix; that his estate was settled up, and that his administratrix was discharged by the probate court of Seneca county, Ohio, on the 25th day of March, 1883; that his children were all of age at his decease; that his estate was largely solvent; that on the 27th day of April, 1887, the said widow and administratrix, Jane M. Skinner, and all the children of the said Morris P. Skinner, executed and delivered to the said plaintiff their quitclaim deed in proper form and with proper acknowledgment, releasing and quitclaiming to the said plaintiff all their interest and estate in said real estate, and for the purpose, as therein expressed, of releasing the said mortgage of the said William Rosetter and wife to said Morris P. Skinner, dated March 16, 1866, calling for $771.72, recorded volume 18, p. 293, in the mortgage records of said Seneca county, Ohio, and that the execution and delivery of such deed to the plaintiff was fully made known to the defendants before the expiration of thirty days from April 15, 1887."

The only question that arises on the record for our consideration is whether this uncanceled mortgage created an incumbrance of such character that it should defeat the plaintiff's right to a specific performance of the contract. The circuit court found as a fact that all claim arising out of the first or $200 note was barred by the statute of limitations. The same evidence that supports that finding would require a finding that an action founded directly upon the other notes was also barred by the statute, for the last one of them to fall due had been due more than 18 years when the contract was made, and more than 19 years when the trial was had. More than 21 years had elapsed from the due date of the first note to the time of the trial, but the other two notes had then been due only 19 and 20 years, respectively. The shorter period, however, was longer by 4 years than that required by the statute to bar an action directly founded upon the notes themselves. The circuit court, therefore, must have held that there was cause of action arising upon the mortgage, independent of the notes and unaffected by the bar that had attached to the latter, which was only barred by the lapse of 21 years; for upon no other hypothesis can the finding that all claim to the same represented by the first note was barred by the statute of limitations be reconciled with the finding that the statute had not attached to that part of the debt which was represented by the second and third notes. We do not care to discuss at any length the question whether an action may be maintained upon a mortgage to recover a debt, when the notes representing the debt are barred by the statute of limitations. Section 4979, Rev. St., provides that "civil actions, other than for the recovery of real property, can only be brought within the following periods, after the cause of action accrues"; and the longest period within which other than real actions can be brought is provided by section 4980, Rev. St., which permits an action "upon a specialty, or an agreement, contract, or promise in writing," to be brought within 15 years. The only actions known to our Code of Civil Procedure are "civil actions." This description, therefore, includes those proceedings that before the adoption of the Code were governed by the rules of equity, as well as those denominated "legal"; and it would seem to follow that, if the statute is not wholly disregarded, the only action that can be maintained upon a mortgage, after 15 years from the time the debt secured by it fell due, if one can be maintained at all, is one to recover the mortgaged property, conceding that such action may be maintained generally. Yet as the mortgagee, Morris P. Skinner, was dead, his estate solvent and fully settled, and his administratix formally discharged by the probate court having jurisdiction of the administration of the estate, no one could have any beneficial interest in any part of his estate, except his widow and heirs at law. These persons executed to the plaintiff a quitclaim deed of the premises, for the express purpose of releasing the lien of the mortgage thereon. Whether it would have been more formal and regular to have had the release of the lien made by his personal representative, or whether, in view of the fact that the only remedy not barred by the statute of limitations was an action to recover the mortgaged property itself upon a title which, by the death of the mortgagee, descended to his heirs at law, a release by them was equally regular, need not be determined, for, however this may be, a release executed by those having the entire beneficial interest will bind them, if not at law, at least in equity. Therefore any claim or lien that belonged to the estate of the mortgagee was released by the quitclaim deed executed by his widow and heirs at law, all of whom were of full age.

Any claim that the representatives of the mortgagee could assert having been released by the quitclaim deed, no cloud remained on the plaintiff's title, except what might arise from a possibility that the mortgagee might have assigned the notes, and that they were outstanding in the hands of the assignee. No testimony was introduced from which an assignment could be inferred. The contention at the trial does not seem to have embraced this question, but was confined almost entirely to the issue respecting the mistake in reducing the contract to writing. It is evident, however, that, if the notes were assigned, it must have been before the death of Mr. Skinner, the mortgagee, and that occurred more than 11 years before the contract was made, and more than 12 years before the trial, and during that long period the assignee in no way had made known or asserted his claim. In the absence of evidence tending to show that an assignment or transfer of the notes was in fact made, the circumstances that the mortgagee continued in life for 10 years after the mortgage notes were made; that at his death the notes were not found among his papers, and for a period of more than 10 years after his death no claim was asserted upon either the mortgage or the notes, make the inference that the debt was discharged by its payment to the mortgagee in his lifetime very strong, and against this inference no contrary presumption arises from any incident disclosed in the record. The doubt, if any can be said to exist, arises, not from any circumstance found by the court or suggested by the evidence, for no such circumstance is disclosed, but because in the nature of things an assignment or transfer was possible, and the evidence does not exclude that possibility. The title of the plaintiff was complete and perfect, and this title he could convey subject to the possibility that the mortgage debt was outstanding. To parties who really wished to complete the purchase, this would present no impediment that could not be readily overcome. The plaintiff did all in this respect that reasonably could be required of him, when he offered to leave in the hands of the defendants a sum sufficient to pay all that part of the debt which the court did not find to be barred by the statute of limitations, until the incumbrance could be formally removed; thus affording them complete protection against the claim, if ultimately one was found to exist. An objection to a title should have some merit in order to defeat the claim of the vendor to the specific performance of the contract of sale. "Captions objections to the title ought not to prevail when made by a purchaser who seeks to avoid the performance of his contract." Walsh v. Barton, 24 Ohio St., on page 40 of Judge MCILVAINE's opinion; and in Ludlow v. O'Neil, 29 Ohio St. 184, Judge WELCH employs the following language: "It will never do to say that a doubt, . . . however honestly entertained by the purchaser, will justify him in refusing to execute his contract. As I understand the rule in equity, it is only in cases where the court itself is in doubt as to the title that a specific execution will be refused on the ground that the title is not marketable." If the title is such that it ought to satisfy a man of ordinary prudence, it is sufficient. In the case under consideration the title was perfect, but was subject to a mere possibility that a claim might be asserted on an old, uncanceled mortgage, against which full indemnity was tendered. Under such circumstances the objection presents all the features of an excuse for the nonperformance of a contract no longer desirable. It is said that the vendees bought the land with a view to its subdivision into town lots, and its immediate resale, which purpose was made known to the vendor, and that, by reason of this incumbrance, they lost a sale at a considerable advance on the price they were to pay. This may be true, but the plaintiff is no more to be affected by the captious objections of possible purchasers of the vendees than by similar objections on the part of the vendees themselves. Whether the sale should be of the entire purchase as a whole, or in parcels upon its subdivision into building lots, a perfect title, free from any reasonable apprehension of this possible lien, could be made to contemplating purchasers. The case presents an aspect of some hardness, however viewed. The real-estate market at Fostoria, at the time the contract was made, and for a short time thereafter, seems to have been highly excited, and the plaintiff had reason to believe that he could sell the premises for as great or perhaps a greater price than he was to receive from the defendants; and when the uncanceled mortgage was discovered, of which he had no previous notice, he offered to rescind the contract, which proposition the vendees declined, and an opportunity to sell upon an excited, if not an inflated, market was lost to the plaintiff. The excitement soon began to subside, and within less than four weeks from the time the sale should have been completed, as the court found, the premises were only of the value of $4,000, a shrinkage of $3,000 from the contract price. If specific performance of the contract is refused, there is thrown upon the plaintiff's hands property of the value of $4,000, which he had sold for $7,000, and which, if defendant had accepted his offer to rescind, he might have sold at even a greater price. On the other hand, the defendants, by a specific performance of the contract, will be compelled to pay $7,000 for the property when it is worth only $4,000.

The contract, however, was fairly made. Moreover, it was entered into at the solicitation of the defendants, who were at the time speculating in real estate at Fostoria, and presumably more familiar with its values than the plaintiff, who resided in an adjoining county, though just how distant from Fostoria does not appear. The title of the plaintiff was perfect, and full indemnity offered against what, in all human probability, was an imaginary incumbrance. Therefore the hardship resulting from the halt in completing the sale should be attributed to the excessive particularity of the defendants. We think that upon the facts found by the court, together with such circumstances as appear from the undisputed evidence, the plaintiff is entitled to a specific performance of the contract. The decree in the circuit court, if it had been rendered in favor of the plaintiff in error, should have provided for an indemnity against any claim that might be asserted under the Rosetter mortgage, but if no claim has been yet asserted, as any claim founded on the mortgage itself has become barred, the provision for indemnity is no longer necessary. Decree accordingly.

Van Vliet & Place, Inc. v. Gaines
249 N.Y. 106, 162 N.E. 600 (1928)

O'BRIEN, J. Martha A. Gaines owned real property on the corner of Jane street and Eighth avenue, in the borough of Manhattan. In the year 1923 it was in the market, and the president of plaintiff, which is a real estate broker, approached the owner and drafted a letter, which he addressed to his corporation, and which was signed by Mrs. Gaines. In this letter she authorized plaintiff to act as her broker and named her terms of sale. No mention was made concerning any restrictive covenant on the premises. Within the stipulated time, plaintiff procured a purchaser, who was ready to buy on the terms and conditions stated in the owner's letter to the broker; but, when the time for closing arrived, a covenant embraced in a deed of the premises executed in the year 1834 and unknown both to the owner and to the broker caused the title company to refuse to insure the title or to loan money on a mortgage, and caused the prospective purchaser to refuse to take title. This covenant provides that if, at any time, the grantee, his heirs or assigns, should permit upon the premises a cemetery, slaughter house, manufactory of gunpowder, glue, varnish, vitriol, turpentine, a tannery, blacksmith shop, forge, or furnace, or any other occupation usually deemed unwholesome, noxious, or offensive, "then said premises and every part thereof shall revert to said party of the first part and their heirs. . . ."

[1-5] The possibility of reverter included in this covenant renders the title unmarketable. In view of the existence of statutes and ordinances

which prohibit the maintenance of most of the objectionable structures enumerated in the deed, the ordinary covenant against nuisances has in recent years lost much of its force. Yet, even in populous cities, a blacksmith shop or a forge has not been wholly outlawed. The expression "any other occupation usually deemed . . . offensive" has been interpreted to include many which do not amount to a nuisance. Rowland v. Miller, 139 N.Y. 93, 34 N.E. 765, 22 L.R.A. 182. The improbability that facts may some time arise to call the possibility of reverter into actual being will not create marketability in a title where it does not otherwise inhere. The contingencies are not so improbable that they can be totally disregarded. We cannot say as matter of law that they are mere theoretical possibilities. They are no more remote than the possibility that, after the adoption of the Eighteenth Amendment and the enactment of the prohibition enforcement act, a purchaser of realty would wish to open a drug store on the premises and sell liquor in accordance with the law. Isaacs v. Schmuck, 245 N.Y. 77, 156 N.E. 621, 51 A.L.R. 1454. The record does not tell us whether these residential premises are located in a zone restricted to residential use. If they are so situated, changes may occur by which the district may be relegated to a business or mixed use. The possibility of a change in the zoning ordinance cannot be said to be too remote for practical consideration. Bull v. Burton, 227 N.Y. 101, 124 N.E. 111; Isaacs v. Schmuck, supra. The penalty for a violation of this covenant goes beyond payment of money or subjection to an injunction: the title reverts to the heirs of the vendors of 1834. This is not the ordinary covenant against nuisances. It seems to be quite unusual. A prudent purchaser may not be labeled as unduly cautious when he refuses such a title. He would encounter difficulty in obtaining a loan or in conveying title. He would be under no obligation to assume risks of the drastic nature manifested by this covenant. A reasonable doubt as to the title is sufficient to authorize its rejection. Moore v. Williams, 115 N.Y. 586, 22 N.E. 233, 5 L.R.A. 654, 12 Am. St. Rep. 844. . . .

Luette v. Bank of Italy National Trust & Savings Assn.

42 F.2d 9 (9th Cir.), cert. denied, 282 U.S. 884 (1930)

KERRIGAN, District Judge.

This is an appeal from an order dismissing a third amended and supplemental bill of complaint and from the decree of dismissal entered thereon.

The complaint alleges that the plaintiffs entered into a contract in June, 1926, with the predecessor in interest of the defendant for the purchase of a certain parcel of real property. The purchase price was $6,500, $1,625 of which was paid at the time of the execution of the contract. The balance was to be paid in monthly installments, which plaintiffs paid to July, 1928; the complaint showing that such payments would continue to May, 1933, under the contract. Plaintiffs allege in effect, construing all of the allegations as to defendant's title together, that defendant has record title to the property in question, and that an adverse claim has been asserted through the filing of homestead claims upon the theory that title to the land is in the United States, the outcome of which claims is uncertain; the matter being now before the Department of the Interior on appeal. It may be fairly concluded from the description of the present state of these homestead proceedings that the decision in the first instance in the Land Office was unfavorable to the homestead right, and that the appeal is that of the claimants; in other words, that the Land Office has held that the land in question is not part of the public domain.

Plaintiffs allege that, on discovery of the existence of the homestead claims, they demanded of defendant that it exhibit its title, and offered, if and when defendant should do so, to pay the amount due under the contract, but that defendant has refused to exhibit its title and, on demand, has refused to repay to plaintiffs the sums already paid upon the contract. The prayer of the complaint is that defendant be enjoined from canceling the contract of plaintiffs and forfeiting plaintiffs' rights thereunder, and that plaintiffs be relieved from paying further installments pending the outcome of the proceedings before the Department of the Interior. Plaintiffs further pray that, in the event the court is unable to grant the relief prayed for, the contract between plaintiffs and defendant be rescinded, and that plaintiffs have judgment for the moneys already paid under the contract. In seeking to rescind, plaintiffs allege that the only thing of value received by them is the contract of sale itself, which they tender.

[1] In considering whether this complaint states a cause of action, its aspect as a bill for an injunction must be disregarded, as plaintiffs state no ground for the intervention of equity to preserve all of their rights under the contract pending the determination of defendant's title, while at the same time relieving them from the duty of performing their part of the bargain. There is no allegation that defendant is, or is likely to become, insolvent, nor any pleading of other equities to justify such relief. The question therefore is whether the complaint states grounds for rescission of the contract.

[2,3] The vendees under an executory contract here seek to rescind on account of an uncertainty as to the state of the vendor's title, at a time long prior to the date when the vendor will be required to convey title under the installment contract. The complaint shows that the plaintiffs attempted to put the vendor in default by demanding that

the title be exhibited and tendering the balance due. The rule has long been settled in California that there can be no rescission by a vendee of an executory contract of sale merely because of lack of title in the vendor prior to the date when performance is due. Joyce v. Shafer, 97 Cal. 335, 32 P. 320; Shively v. Semi-Tropic Land & Water Co., 99 Cal. 259, 33 P. 848; Brimmer v. Salisbury, 167 Cal. 522, 140 P. 30. And the vendee cannot place the vendor in default by tendering payment and demanding a deed in advance of the time and under circumstances not contemplated by the contract. Garberino v. Roberts, 109 Cal. 126, 41 P. 857; Hanson v. Fox, 155 Cal. 106, 99 P. 489, 20 L.R.A. (N.S.) 338, 132 Am. St. Rep. 72. In the present case the pleading does not show the vendor to be in default, as under the contract, assuming a defect to exist, the time within which title must be perfected does not expire until May, 1933.

In this connection an attempt is made to strengthen plaintiffs' position by averring that, in the event that the homestead claims are allowed and the whole tract in which plaintiffs' lot is situated is declared to be part of the public domain, defendant will be financially unable to procure title to the whole tract, and hence can never perform its obligation to convey title to plaintiffs. The whole tract contains over 16,000 acres. Plaintiffs' lot comprises about one-fourth of an acre. The complaint does not show that defendant would be unable, for financial or other reasons, to procure title to the one-fourth acre which it has contracted to convey to plaintiffs and with which alone plaintiffs are concerned.

[4,5] There remains to be considered the question as to whether certain allegations of fraud bring this case within the rule that, even though the vendor is not in default, the vendee may rescind an executory contract for material fraudulent misrepresentations of the vendor as to a matter of title upon which the vendee was justified in relying. Crane v. Ferrier-Brock Development Co., 164 Cal. 676, 130 P. 429; Brimmer v. Salisbury, 167 Cal. 522, 530, 140 P. 30. Plaintiffs allege that they are inexperienced in business and relied upon the defendant for fair treatment, being accustomed to put complete trust in and rely upon banks and bankers. The latter allegation is insufficient to establish a fiduciary relationship between plaintiffs and defendant, as there is no suggestion that defendant voluntarily assumed a relation of personal confidence with plaintiffs. Ruhl v. Mott, 120 Cal. 668, 53 P. 304. The parties to the contract must therefore be regarded as having dealt at arm's length. Viewing the pleading in this light and looking to the averments as to the state of the title referred to above, it appears that plaintiffs have not charged defendant with material misrepresentations, unequivocally averred to be false, upon which plaintiffs relied to their injury.

The orders appealed from are affirmed.

Maxton Builders v. Lo Galbo
68 N.Y.2d 373, 509 N.Y.S.2d 507, 502 N.E.2d 184 (1986)

Chief Judge WACHTLER.

The plaintiff contracted to sell a house to the defendants and accepted a check for the down payment. When the defendants canceled the contract and stopped payment on the check, the plaintiff sued for a breach claiming a right to the down payment — a right traditionally allowed in this State under the rule set forth in Lawrence v. Miller (86 N.Y. 131). The trial court denied plaintiff's motion for summary judgment holding that a fact question was presented as to whether recovery of the down payment would constitute a penalty under the circumstances. The Appellate Division modified and granted summary judgment to the plaintiff for the amount of the down payment.

The defendants appealed claiming there was no breach because they effectively exercised a contractual right to cancel. In the alternative, defendants urge that plaintiff's recovery should be limited to actual damages, and that we should, therefore, reexamine the rule of Lawrence v. Miller (supra), which permits a vendor on a real estate contract to retain the down payment when the purchaser willfully defaults.

I

In 1983 the defendants contracted to purchase a newly constructed house from the plaintiff for $210,000. At the contract signing on August 3, the defendants gave the plaintiff a check for $21,000 as a down payment to be held in escrow. A handwritten rider, included in the contract at the defendants' request, provided: "If real estate taxes are in excess of $3,500 based on a full assessment of house sold for $210,000.00, buyer shall have the right to cancel this contract upon written notice to the seller within three days of date and escrow funds to be returned."

The following day defendant Cynthia Lo Galbo and plaintiff's president, Scott Seeman, went to the county tax assessor's office to obtain an estimate of the taxes on the new house. The assessment was in excess of $3,500.

The defendants' attorney then called the plaintiff's counsel and informed him that the defendants had decided to exercise their option to cancel. He also sent a certified letter to the defendants' attorney informing him in writing of the defendants' decision to cancel. The letter was mailed on Friday August 5 and was received by plaintiff's attorney on August 9. Several days later plaintiff's attorney also received a bank notice that defendants had stopped payment on their check.

On September 20, 1983, the plaintiff commenced this action against the defendants to recover the amount of the down payment claiming that the defendants breached the contract when they stopped payment on the check. In their answer the defendants contended that they had properly exercised their right to cancel in accordance with the rider. On December 20, 1983, the plaintiff sold the house to another purchaser for the same amount the defendants had agreed to pay. However this sale, unlike the contract with the defendants, was arranged by a real estate broker who charged the plaintiff a fee of $12,000 for finding the new purchaser.

Both sides subsequently moved for summary judgment on the complaint, the defendants asserting their right to cancel, and the plaintiff claiming the cancellation was ineffective because it was not made in the time or manner prescribed by the contract. Relying on Lawrence v. Miller (86 N.Y. 131, supra), the plaintiff urged that the defendants had lost the right to the down payment by defaulting on the contract. Plaintiff also alleged that although it was not seeking actual damages, it had suffered real financial losses in excess of the down payment. Plaintiff contended that as a result of the defendants' breach, it had incurred additional carrying charges for mortgage, interest, taxes and insurance, as well as other losses including the $12,000 fee paid to the real estate broker for bringing about the second contract.

Special Term found that the defendants' cancellation was ineffective primarily because it had not been received by the plaintiff within the three-day period stated in the contract. However, on the damages issue the court denied the plaintiff summary judgment concluding that the "substantial amount of the deposit, namely, $12,000, coupled with the fact that plaintiff was successful in selling the subject premises to another purchaser, albeit with the incurring of certain losses, creates a question of fact as to whether plaintiff's claim to the deposit constitutes the seeking of a penalty."

The Appellate Division modified and granted summary judgment to the plaintiff for the amount of the down payment. The court agreed with Special Term that there had been a breach but stated: "Where there is a willful default by the vendee or a repudiation of the contract of purchase upon which a down payment has been made, it is settled in this State that the vendee may not recover his down payment even though the vendor resells the premises for a sum equal to or greater than the contract price." (113 A.D.2d 923, 924.)

[1] On this appeal the defendants again urge that their refusal to perform did not constitute a breach because they had reserved and adequately exercised a right to terminate. Although the plaintiff did not receive written notice of termination within three days, as the contract required, the defendants contend that this is not fatal when, as here, the contract does not provide that time is of the essence. The defendants argue that under these circumstances all that is required is reasonable notice and that this requirement was met here when the

defendants mailed the notice and gave the plaintiff's attorney actual oral notice within the three-day period. It is settled, however, that when a contract requires that written notice be given within a specified time, the notice is ineffective unless the writing is actually received within the time prescribed (see, Peabody v. Satterlee, 166 N.Y. 174; Kantrowitz v. Dairymen's League Co-op. Assn., 272 App. Div. 470, affd. 297 N.Y. 991; cf. Sy Jack Realty Co. v. Pergament Syosset Corp., 27 N.Y.2d 449). In short, the defendants bargained for and obtained a limited right to cancel which they failed to exercise within the time agreed upon. The cancellation was, therefore, ineffective and the de-fendants' refusal to perform constituted a breach (Morgan & Brother Manhattan Stor. Co. v. Balin, 39 N.Y.2d 848).

The defendants' alternative argument is that the Appellate Division erred in permitting the plaintiff to recover the entire down payment, and should instead have limited recovery to actual damages. On the basis of existing law it is clear that the defendants cannot prevail. For more than a century it has been well settled in this State that a vendee who defaults on a real estate contract without lawful excuse, cannot recover the down payment (Lawrence v. Miller, supra; Steinhardt v. Baker, 163 N.Y. 410; Cohen v. Kranz, 12 N.Y.2d 242; 32 Beechwood Corp. v. Fisher, 19 N.Y.2d 1008; Sommer v. General Bronze Corp., 21 N.Y.2d 775; Laba v. Carey, 29 N.Y.2d 302; Morgan & Brother Manhattan Stor. Co. v. Balin, 39 N.Y.2d 848, supra; Willard v. Mercer, 58 N.Y.2d 840; 62 N.Y. Jur., Vendor and Purchaser, §137). The rule, however, has been criticized as being out of harmony with the general principle that actual damages is the proper measure of recovery for a breach of contract and, it has been abandoned by several jurisdictions (Freedman v. Rector, Warden & Vestrymen, 37 Cal. 2d 16, 230 P.2d 629; Perillo, Restitution in the Second Restatement of Contracts, 81 Colum. L. Rev. 37, 50; Friedman, Contracts and Conveyances of Real Property, at 931 [4th ed.]). The defendants' argument on this appeal presents the question as to whether the long-standing rule should be retained in this State.

II

In the leading case, Lawrence v. Miller (86 N.Y.131, supra), decided by this court in 1881, we denied the assignee of the defaulting vendee recovery of a $2,000 down payment, reasoning that the vendor acquired the money rightfully, failed in no duty to the vendee, and the money would have been his but for the vendee's breach. We stated (at p 140): "To allow a recovery of this money would be to sustain an action by a party on his own breach of his own contract, which the law does not allow . . . Nor can the specious view be taken, presented by the plaintiff, that the defendant is entitled to no more than he has actually been damaged."

Much of the criticism of Lawrence v. Miller (supra) is directed at the rule on which it is based, which broadly holds that a party who defaults on a contract cannot recover the amount or value of part performance (Corbin, Right of a Defaulting Vendee to the Restitution of Installments Paid, 40 Yale L.J. 1013; 1942 Report of N.Y. Law Rev. Commn., at 179). This parent rule is applicable to contracts generally, and has been applied to a wide variety of circumstances including the sale of goods, employment contracts for a fixed term, construction contracts, and installment land sales (Corbin, op. cit.). In all of these cases the common law would deny any relief to the defaulting party even when there had been substantial, or nearly complete performance. It was these holdings especially which prompted the criticism calling for reform of the parent rule on the ground that it produced a forfeiture "and the amount of the forfeiture increases as performance proceeds, so that the penalty grows larger as the breach grows smaller." (Corbin, ibid., at 1029; also see, Act, Recommendation and Study Relating to Installment Land Contracts, 1937 Report of N.Y. Law Rev. Commn., at 343; Act and Recommendation Relating to Installment Land Contracts, 1938 Report of N.Y. Law Rev. Commn., at 47; Act, Recommendation and Study Relating to Recovery for Benefits Conferred by Party in Default Under Contract, 1942 Report of N.Y. Law Rev. Commn., at 179; Act, Recommendation and Study Relating to Right of Buyer of Goods to Restitution for Benefits Conferred Under a Contract of Sale on Which He Has Defaulted, 1952 Report of N.Y. Law Rev. Commn., at 83.)

The "modern rule" advocated by the critics permits the party in default to recover for part performance in excess of actual damages, but places the burden on him to prove the net benefit conferred (see, Perillo, op. cit., at 49-50; Corbin, op. cit., at 1023-1024; Restatement [Second] of Contracts §374; Friedman, op. cit., at 931). The rule was designed primarily to protect the party who had made a number of payments or substantial performance before default, and provides little relief to the defaulting purchaser seeking to recover a down payment or first installment. Corbin notes: "In such cases, it is unlikely that the amount retained by the vendor was greater than the injury suffered by the plaintiff's breach. Whatever the amount, the plaintiff must show that it is greater than the injury done. In most cases that injury is wholly unliquidated and difficult of accurate estimation; and in few cases does the plaintiff attempt to show how much it was." (Corbin, op. cit., at 1024-1025.)

The Restatement (Second) of Contracts adopts the "modern rule," but recognizes an exception for liquidated damages, and also for "money paid" under an understanding or "usage" that it be retained in the event of a breach (§374 comment c). The illustration involves the right of a seller on a real estate contract to retain the first installment equal to 10% of the contract price, upon the buyer's default.

In 1834 New Hampshire became the first State to reject the parent rule and permit a defaulting party to recover for part performance in a case involving a laborer who had defaulted on a one-year employment contract after working for nine and one-half months (Britton v. Turner, 6 N.H. 481). In most areas of the law the Legislature and the courts, have now adopted rules generally permitting a party in default to recover for part performance to the extent of the net benefit conferred (see, e.g., Williston, Contracts §1473; Amtorg Trading Corp. v. Miehle Print. Press & Mfg. Co., 206 F.2d 103 [summarizing New York law]; Jacob & Youngs v. Kent, 230 N.Y. 239 [permitting contractor to recover for substantial performance]; U.C.C. 2-718; Act, Recommendation and Study Relating to Recovery for Benefits Conferred by Party in Default Under Contract, 1942 Report of N.Y. Law Rev. Commn., at 179; but also see, Comment, Forfeiture: The Anomaly of the Land Sale Contract, 41 Alb. L. Rev. 71). However in cases dealing with recovery of down payments on real estate contracts, a majority of jurisdictions still follow the principle of Lawrence v. Miller (supra), especially where the down payment does not exceed 10% of the contract price (see, Modern Status of Defaulting Vendee's Right to Recover Contractual Payments Withheld by Vendor as Forfeited, Ann., 4 A.L.R.4th 993; Friedman, op. cit., at 928; 77 Am. Jur. 2d, Vendor and Purchaser, §499).

Several years ago the Law Revision Commission proposed that the Legislature of this State abrogate Lawrence v. Miller (supra), and adopt a "more equitable" rule (Act, Recommendation and Study Relating to Recovery for Benefits Conferred by Party in Default Under Contract, 1942 Report of N.Y. Law Rev. Commn., at 179, 188, 237-239). The proposed law was not adopted. It is interesting to note, however, that although the proposed reform would generally have permitted the defaulting buyer to recover the net benefit conferred, it would also have allowed the seller, in any event, to retain "twenty percent of the value of the total performance for which the buyer is obligated under the contract" (ibid., at 183).[2] A similar proposal was later made, and adopted by the Legislature, with respect to the right of a buyer to recover for part performance after defaulting on a contract for the sale of goods (Act, Recommendation and Study Relating to Right of Buyer

---

2. On this point, the report states (at p. 188): "While it may be argued that the defaulting buyer should be allowed complete restitution for the benefit conferred, the Commission recognizes the practical difficulties which would result from the adoption of such a principle. Because of the difficulty of establishing the damages in many cases or because provable injury is sometimes not included within the rules of damages, and because a rule permitting complete restitution would encourage the breaking of contracts, the seller should be allowed to retain in any event a reasonable part of the net benefit conferred."

of Goods to Restitution for Benefits Conferred Under a Contract of Sale on Which He Has Defaulted, 1952 Report of N.Y. Law Rev. Commn., at 83, 643; Personal Property Law former §145-a, now U.C.C. 2-718 [2] [permitting seller to withhold 20% of the value of the total performance up to a limit of $500]).

III

[2] We have previously noted that a court should not depart from its prior holdings "unless impelled by 'the most cogent reasons' " (Baker v. Lorillard, 4 N.Y. 257, 261). This standard is particularly apt in cases involving the legal effect of contractual relations. In fact, when contractual rights are at issue, "where it can reasonably be assumed that settled rules are necessary and necessarily relied upon, stability and adherence to precedent are generally more important than a better or even a 'correct' rule of law" (Matter of Eckart, 39 N.Y.2d 493, 500). The rule permitting a party in default to seek restitution for part performance has much to commend it in its general applications. But as applied to real estate down payments approximating 10% it does not appear to offer a better or more workable rule than the long-established "usage" in this State with respect to the seller's right to retain a down payment upon default.

In cases, as here, where the property is sold to another after the breach, the buyer's ability to recover the down payment would depend initially on whether the agreement expressly provides that the seller could retain it upon default. If it did, the provision would probably be upheld as a valid liquidated damages clause in view of the recognized difficulty of estimating actual damages and the general acceptance of the traditional 10% down payment as a reasonable amount.

If the contract itself is deemed to pose no bar, then the buyer would bear the burden of proving that the amount retained exceeded the actual damages. As the authorities note, this is a difficult burden in any case involving real estate sales, and is not likely to be met in suits on down payments or first installments where the actual damages will generally be very close to the amount of the traditional 10% retained. Thus, in most cases, a change in the law will provide a forum for the disputants to further dispute their differences, but cannot be reasonably expected to save any party from true financial loss. Indeed in the case now before us the defendants made no effort to show that the actual damages were less than the plaintiff alleged or that there was, in fact, a net benefit conferred.

Finally, real estate contracts are probably the best examples of arm's length transactions. Except in cases where there is a real risk of overreaching, there should be no need for the courts to relieve the parties of the consequences of their contract. If the parties are dissatisfied with the rule of Lawrence v. Miller (supra), the time to say so is at the bargaining table.

Accordingly, the order of the Appellate Division should be affirmed.

Judges MEYER, SIMONS, KAYE, ALEXANDER, TITONE and HANCOCK, JR., concur.

Order affirmed, with costs.

Reid v. Auxier
690 P.2d 1057 (Okla. Ct. App. 1984)

BRIGHTMIRE, Judge.

Two fundamental questions arise in this review. One, is a liquidated damages provision in a real estate sales agreement valid? Two, does the contract here prevent the sellers from pursuing any remedy provided by law? The trial court held that the liquidated damages clause in the parties' sales contract was valid and prohibited plaintiffs from obtaining more than $2,500 for buyers' refusal to close the sale.

We hold, however, that to the extent the liquidated damages agreement purports to be binding on either party it is against public policy and void. We further hold that subject contract does not otherwise prohibit plaintiffs from recovering their actual legal damages. The summary judgment in favor of plaintiffs for $2,500 is vacated as to the amount of damages awarded.

I

Facts controlling the resolution of the legal question raised are not disputed.

Plaintiffs, John and Karen Reid, owned an improved ten-acre tract of land in the City of Broken Arrow, Wagoner County, Oklahoma. On July 25, 1981, they contracted with defendants, Mike and Lee Auxier, for the sale of subject realty for $140,000. The contract provided for, among other things, an earnest money deposit of $2,500, a closing date on or before August 15, 1982, and in paragraph 3, a financing condition to the effect that the Auxiers would promptly seek and be able to obtain a conventional thirty-year loan in an amount equal to at least 70% of the purchase price at an interest rate of not more than 15% plus discount points of not more than 2.5%.

The contract was on a printed form furnished by the selling broker, defendant Merrill Lynch Realty/Detrick Company — a form "approved by the Metropolitan Tulsa Board of Realtors." The problem in this case arises out of paragraph 8 which reads:

8. Breach or Failure to Close:

Subject to the provisions of paragraph 3 [financing condition], if, after the Seller has performed Seller's obligations under this Contract, and if within five (5) days after the date specified for Closing under paragraph 7 the Buyer fails to make the payments or to perform any other obligation of the Buyer under this Contract, then all sums theretofore paid on the purchase price shall, at the option of the Seller, be retained as such or as liquidated damages for the breach of this Contract by the Buyer. The Seller and Buyer agree that such amount is a reasonable amount for liquidated damages and that it would be impractical and extremely difficult to determine actual damages. In such latter event, the Seller and Buyer agree that the undersigned Broker(s) may retain and shall be paid from such funds one-half of such retained funds, not exceeding the agreed commission for services in obtaining this Contract. If the conditions in paragraph 3 are met, or waived, the Buyer shall perform all of the obligations of Buyer hereunder, and if Seller breaches this Contract or fails to perform any of Seller's obligations hereunder, then Buyer shall be entitled either to cancel and terminate this Contract, return the abstract to Seller, and receive a refund of the earnest money or pursue any other legal remedy.

In a letter dated December 1, 1981, the Auxiers advised Merrill Lynch Realty that they had contacted four different lending institutions and were unable to obtain a loan within the contractual parameters. Consequently they said they considered the contract void and requested the broker to obtain a "written release" from the Reids and to refund the $2,500 earnest money deposit.

On May 18, 1982, Reids' attorney wrote Auxiers' lawyer saying the Reids were willing to finance 70% of the purchase price ($98,000) on a thirty-year payout at an annual rate of interest of 15% plus a point payment of 2.5%. A conforming note and mortgage were enclosed in the letter with a reminder that all contractual contingencies had been met and that therefore closing should be held May 24, 1982. The contingencies referred to included sellers' furnishing an abstract of title which had been done. It had been examined by purchasers' lawyer and the title passed without any objection.

Auxiers' lawyer found no fault with the proposed note and mortgage, but the purchasers nevertheless declined to perform.

This action was filed June 11, 1982, in which in material parts the Reids asked for $29,000 actual and $10,000 punitive damages for the Auxiers' breach of the contract and fraudulent misrepresentation of their financial ability to perform.

The Reids relisted their property November 15, 1982, and on February 5, 1983, it was sold to another party for $115,000 — $25,000 less than what the Auxiers had agreed to pay.

Both parties moved for summary judgment. These motions were

heard April 26, 1983. The court held as a matter of law that: (1) the failure of the purchasers to close on May 24, 1982, was a breach of the sales contract; (2) the liquidated damages provision (paragraph 8) "is a bargained-for, unseverable provision of the . . . contract, and Seller (Plaintiffs) [sic] is estopped to introduce evidence on the issue of actual damages; that . . . notwithstanding the provisions of Title 15 O.S. §214, Seller is limited to recovery of the earnest money deposit. . . ."

The court thereupon granted plaintiffs a summary judgment for $2,500. Plaintiffs appeal, contending the liquidated damages clause is void because they can easily prove recoverable damage.

II

For the purpose of disposing of plaintiffs' single contention, we will assume, as the parties do, that the liquidated damages clause in question is an agreement that bindingly fixes the amount of damages in the event of a breach by either party. At the same time we want to state, parenthetically, that paragraph 8 is so loosely drawn that the provisions are equivocal if not ambiguous. Though an amount is fixed, it does not appear to us that either party is required to accept the set sum — an effect that will be dealt with later.

[1,2] In order to determine whether the liquidated damages provision in question is enforceable, it is necessary to review the controlling law. It is set out in 15 O.S.1981 §§214 and 215. The first section reads:

> Every contract, by which the amount of damages to be paid, or other compensation to be made, for a breach of an obligation, is determined in anticipation thereof, is to that extent void, except as expressly provided by the next section. (footnote omitted)

Section 215 reads:

> A stipulation or condition in a contract, providing for the payment of an amount which shall be presumed to be the amount of damage sustained by a breach of such contract, shall be held valid, when, from the nature of the case, it would be impracticable or extremely difficult to fix the actual damage.

The plain language of these statutes declares that liquidated damages clauses in contracts are void unless the nature of the breach is such that it would be "impracticable or extremely difficult to fix the actual damage." This law is augmented by yet another statutory curtailment of a liquidated damages clause; that is, if the amount of liquidated damages agreed upon is such as to be in effect a penalty, it is void under the terms of 15 O.S.1981 §213, which specifies that "[p]enalties imposed by contract for any nonperformance thereof, are void." Thus it was held in Mid-Continent Life Ins. Co. v. Goforth, 193 Okla. 314, 143 P.2d 154 (1943), that where land was being sold for $12,000 and the contract provided for a $6,000 cash down payment which was to be retained by seller as liquidated damages in the event buyer failed to perform, the provision would be regarded as a penalty and therefore void.

[3] The measure of damages established by 23 O.S.1981 §28, for the breach of an agreement to buy an interest in real estate "is deemed to be the excess, if any, of the amount which would have been due to the seller under the contract over the value of the property to him." This language has been construed to mean "the difference between the actual contract price and the actual value of the land at the time of the breach." Harman v. Franks, 178 Okla. 560, 565, 63 P.2d 54, 59 (1936).

[4] The question, then, that evolves from this law may be framed this way: is it impracticable or would it be extremely difficult for the trial court to determine the difference between the contract price defendants agreed to pay and the actual or fair market value of the property at the time of the breach? We hold it would be neither impracticable nor extremely difficult and therefore the liquidated damage proviso is void.

[5] We further hold that paragraph 8, dealing as it does with the subject of remedial recourse in the event of a failure to close, is independent of the primary purpose of the contract — the sale of certain real property — and is therefore severable.

Though the defending Auxiers recognize the import of the statutory law, they say section 214 has been "drafted around" in the form contract by inclusion of a stipulation that the amount of liquidated damages is reasonable "and that it would be impractical and extremely difficult to determine actual damages." This language, defendants argue, cloaks paragraph 8 with the saving protection of section 215 and, in effect, nullifies the force and effect of section 214. The legal catalyst recommended by defendants to accomplish such neutralization of section 214 is the equitable doctrine of estoppel — that is, the court should declare that each party is estopped from asserting a position inconsistent with the stipulation.

[6] This approach, while perhaps resourceful, has a fatal flaw. It requires us to hold that contractual terms declared by law to be against public policy may be enforced in our courts if the parties so stipulate in the contract. The effect of the stipulation in question is that the parties agreed in advance of any breach that it would be impractical

or extremely difficult to determine the difference between the contract price and the fair cash value of the property at the time of the breach. This is an impermissible attempt to contravene public policy and is therefore void.

[7] The burden of establishing the section 215 exception — that it is impracticable or extremely difficult to prove actual damages — remains upon the party seeking enforcement of the fixed damage clause, and the stipulation does not shift such burden. Waggoner v. Johnston, 408 P.2d 761 (Okla. 1965).

We are not prepared to hold with defendants on their estoppel theory. If it is true, as defendants contend, that the market place will find it difficult to live with sections 214 and 215, then the solution is not judicial nullification but legislative modification.

III

There is yet another and much stronger reason why summary judgment is wrong — one which emerges from an analysis of paragraph 8 — and that is that the terms do not actually require either party to accept an agreed-to amount of liquidated damages or forbid the pursuit by either party of all available remedies afforded by law.

Paraphrased, the previously quoted paragraph 8 provides both buyer and seller optional alternatives to the acceptance of the agreed amount of liquidated damages. Should the Seller breach the contract, "Buyer shall be entitled either to cancel and terminate this Contract . . . and receive a refund of the earnest money or pursue any other legal remedy." (Emphasis added). If the Buyer fails to perform, then the Seller has the "option" of retaining the down payment "as liquidated damages for the breach of this Contract by the Buyer."

Granting sellers such an option means that sellers may opt not to accept the down payment as their full measure of damages and implies they have the same rights granted buyers — to "pursue any other legal remedy."

[8] This construction of paragraph 8 not only affords the parties a judicially favored mutuality of remedies, but averts the necessity of condemning the liquidated damages provision as being contrary to section 214, and, more importantly, permits the continued use of paragraph 8's form and substance to amicably settle breach of contract disputes in a great many situations in which neither party will want to litigate.

The summary judgment appealed is reversed as to the amount of damages awarded plaintiffs and remanded for further proceedings limited to determining the amount of legal damages sellers have sustained.

DeMier, P.J., and Stubblefield, J., concur.

Sample General Warranty Deed

Standard N.Y.B.T.U. Form
8003

THIS INDENTURE, made the   day of   , nineteen hundred and
BETWEEN

party of the first part, and

party of the second part,

WITNESSETH, that the party of the first part, in consideration of ten dollars and other valuable consideration paid by the party of the second part, does hereby grant and release unto the party of the second part, the heirs or successors and assigns of the party of the second part forever,

ALL that certain plot, piece or parcel of land, with the buildings and improvements thereon erected, situate, lying and being in the

TOGETHER with all right, title and interest, if any, of the party of the first part in and to any streets and roads abutting the above described premises to the center lines thereof; **TOGETHER** with the appurtenances and all the estate and rights of the party of the first part in and to said premises; **TO HAVE AND TO HOLD** the premises herein granted unto the party of the second part, the heirs or successors and assigns of the party of the second part forever.

AND the party of the first part, in compliance with Section 13 of the Lien Law, covenants that the party of the first part will receive the consideration for this conveyance and will hold the right to receive such consideration as a trust fund to be applied first for the purpose of paying the cost of the improvement and will apply the same first to the payment of the cost of the improvement before using any part of the total of the same for any other purpose.
AND the party of the first part covenants as follows: that said party of the first part is seized of the said premises in fee simple, and has good right to convey the same; that the party of the second part shall quietly enjoy the said premises; that the said premises are free from incumbrances, except as aforesaid; that the party

of the first part will execute or procure any further necessary assurance of the title to said premises; and that said party of the first part will forever warrant the title to said premises.

The word "party" shall be construed as if it read "parties" whenever the sense of this indenture so requires.

IN WITNESS WHEREOF, the party of the first part has duly executed this deed the day and year first above written.

IN PRESENCE OF :

STATE OF NEW YORK, COUNTY OF   ss:

On the   day of   19   , before me personally came

to me known to be the individual   described in and who executed the foreoging instrument, and acknowledged that   executed the same.

STATE OF NEW YORK, COUNTY OF   ss:

On the   day of   19   , before me personally came

to me known to be the individual   described in and who executed the foreoging instrument, and acknowledged that   executed the same.

STATE OF NEW YORK, COUNTY OF   ss:

On the   day of   19   , before me personally came

to me known, who, being by me duly sworn, did depose and say that   he resides at No.
                                        ;
that   he is the
of
                , the corporation described in and which executed the foregoing instrument; that   he knows the seal of said corporation; that the seal affixed to said instrument is such corporate seal; that it was so affixed by order of the board of directors of said corporation, and that   he signed h   name thereto by like order.

STATE OF NEW YORK, COUNTY OF   ss:

On the   day of   19   , before me personally came

the subscribing witness to the foregoing instrument, with whom I am personally acquainted, who, being by me duly sworn, did depose and say that   he resides at No.
                                        ;
that   he knows
                to be the individual described in and who executed the foregoing instrument; that   he, said subscribing witness, was present and saw
execute the same; and that   he, said witness, at the same time subscribed h   name as witness thereto.

NOTES AND QUESTIONS

1. *Draftsmanship Approaches to the Contract of Sale.* Now that the terms of payment have been agreed on (see introductory text), let us assume that on January 1 of this year your client, Dan Developer, and Sam Seller, along with his attorney, came to your law office for the purpose of negotiating the other terms of the contract. Dan and Sam would like to close the transaction on or before March 31 of this year. Let us further assume that the sample sale agreement, excerpted supra, will be the matrix for the negotiations that follow. You and Sam's attorney agree that it represents a suitable standardized form of agreement that must be tailored to the unique facts and circumstances of this particular transaction.

Just a brief reminder of what your perspective should be as Dan's representative in the negotiations. First, you should assess Dan's bargaining clout with Sam and identify the risks and rewards of the transaction before attempting to allocate them between the parties. Also, when assessing language that is proposed by the other party to the negotiations, try to think in terms of the worst-case scenario; in other words, if your client, Dan, should accept the proposed language, what rights (at common law, as modified by statute), if any, will Dan be forfeiting, and what additional responsibilities will he be assuming that someday might cause a serious legal, business, or tax problem for him? And, assuming there is relative parity in bargaining power, what alternative or compromise language might you suggest that should obviate or at least ameliorate the problem and yet be reasonably acceptable to the other side?

a. *Purchase Contingent on Financing.* As you know by now, most real estate developers and purchasers, like Dan, want to leverage their acquisition costs; consequently, commercial real estate is rarely sold on a cash basis. Therefore, it is essential that the purchaser's attorney include a contingency clause for financing the purchase price; otherwise, the purchaser might lose the earnest money deposit (as discussed infra) if the necessary financing cannot be procured from the seller or a third-party lender.

If the real estate being sold is encumbered by a mortgage that secures the owner's promise to repay the mortgage note indebtedness and the owner is personally liable for performance of the underlying obligation (see note on nonrecourse financing at Chapter 4B3, note 1), the existing mortgage might be *assumed* by the purchaser (in which event the purchaser would become personally liable on the mortgage note) or the purchaser might merely take title to the real estate *subject to* the mortgage (in which event the purchaser would not assume personal liability on the mortgage note). See Nelson and Whitman, Real Estate Finance Law §§5.1 to 5.35 (2d ed. 1985). If, however, the existing mortgage note contains a due-on-sale clause (authorizing the lender to accelerate the mortgage indebtedness if the property should be sold without its consent), the purchaser may be compelled to pay the market rate of interest on the existing mortgage or to substitute a new mortgage for the existing one by "refinancing" if the mortgagee so demands. See Chapter 5B8. If the purchaser is allowed to assume the existing mortgage debt the seller will remain secondarily liable unless it is able to obtain a release agreement from the mortgagee (a form of "novation").

In most cases the purchaser will arrange third-party financing from some institutional lender and the seller will use the sale proceeds to satisfy the existing mortgage, in which case the purchaser's attorney will insist on a mortgage contingency clause that specifies the minimum financing requirements of the purchaser; for example, "a mortgage in the amount of no less than $ _____ (to cover the financed portion of the purchase price) at an interest rate of no more than ____ %, with a fully amortized term of no less than _____ years." By contrast, the seller's attorney should resist any such open-ended contingency clause and might insist, for example, that the purchaser accept any mortgage from an institutional lender so long as the interest rate does not exceed the market rate and the loan amount covers the minimum financing needs of the purchaser. The seller's attorney should also demand that the mortgage commitment be secured within a reasonable period of time. If there is any doubt about the creditworthiness of the purchaser, the purchaser should be required to submit financials before the contract is executed; otherwise, valuable time might be wasted on a purchaser who is unable to obtain the necessary financing.

Another option is seller financing. In seller financing, the noncash portion of the purchase price is funded by means of a purchase-money mortgage from the seller. This technique is discussed at Chapter 9B, note 5.

Sometimes a contingency clause that appears innocuous on its face can cause problems for the parties. Suppose, for example, that a contract of sale is conditioned on a county's grant of a sewer allocation for the lots being sold, a contingency that is beyond the control of the parties. Can you think of any rule of law that you learned in first-year property that might render such a contract a sale unenforceable? See Dorado, Limited Partnership v. Broadneck Development Corp., 317 Md. 148, 562 A.2d 757 (1989).

   b. *Right of Inspection.* Absent language to the contrary the doctrine of caveat emptor applies. This means that unless the seller (or his agents) makes misrepresentations about the condition of the premises or fails to disclose latent defects known to him and not to the purchaser, the risk of any pre-existing defect will be borne by the purchaser. See Friedman §1.2(n). Consequently, it is essential that the purchaser have the right to inspect the property and that the parties agree on what representations and warranties, if any, will be made by the seller with respect to the condition of the premises, whether such promises by the seller will survive the closing of the transaction, and what remedies will be afforded to the purchaser in the event such promises are breached by the seller. Depending on the bargaining clout of the parties the contract may provide for an "as is" sale, in which event the onus is on the purchaser to make a thorough inspection before the contract is executed. At the other end of the spectrum would be a purchaser-oriented provision whereby the seller not only warrants in detail the condition of the premises but also agrees that the warranties shall survive the closing date. How does the language in §5 of the sample sale agreement, supra, strike a delicate balance between both of the foregoing approaches? The language in §5 presupposes, as is frequently the case, that the inspection by the purchaser will not be completed until after the contract is executed. Doesn't this language in effect provide the purchaser with nothing more than an option to purchase the property? If so, can you think of any draftsmanship approach that would protect the seller?

   c.   *Risk of Loss.*   Closely related to the inspections clause is language in the contract that addresses the question of who should bear the risk of any casualty or condemnation loss prior to the closing date. As noted above, the majority rule places the onus on the purchaser by reason of the doctrine of equitable conversion unless the parties agree otherwise. See Friedman §4.11. By contrast, the approach taken by §1 of the Uniform Vendor and Purchaser Risk Act is that, absent language to the contrary, the risk of loss should be borne by the party in possession, who not only reaps the beneficial use of the property but who normally is in a better position to protect the real estate against casualty loss and to keep the premises insured pending the closing date. The foregoing approach is sensible, and it explains why most contracts will shift the risk of loss to the seller, who in the case of an ordinary contract (as opposed to an installment land contract) will probably retain possession until the transaction closes.

   As Dan's legal advisor, what do you think of the language in §9 of the sample contract? Suppose, in the case of a partial destruction or condemnation of the premises, Sam's mortgage does not require that the insurance or condemnation award proceeds be used for restoration but instead allows the mortgagee to reduce the loan balance with the proceeds. See Chapter 5B12, notes 4 and 5. If this is the case, what alternative language might you suggest that should be reasonably acceptable to Sam's attorney? In §9 an arbitrary loss amount is used to differentiate between a partial and a total casualty loss so that Sam can extricate himself from the contract if the loss should exceed $10,000 (even though the restoration work might not substantially interfere with his intended use of the property). Can you think of a more flexible approach?

d. *Time Is of the Essence.* In most jurisdictions the times for performance of the seller's and purchaser's obligations will not be strictly enforced, and a court of equity will grant relief notwithstanding a delay in performance by either the purchaser or the seller, unless the parties stipulate that time is of the essence. See A.L.P. §11.45. Moreover, there is case law allowing the seller a reasonable time beyond the closing date to remove an encumbrance or curable defect in order to render the title marketable, absent a time-is-of-the-essence clause in the contract. See Friedman §4.8(h).

Observe that §11.1 of the sample sale agreement, supra, stipulates that time is of the essence. Moreover, in most states contracts for the sale of single-family residences usually stipulate that time is of the essence. Holtzschue, Real Estate Transactions: Purchase and Sale of Real Property §8.02[10][c] (1989). What risks does this language pose for your client? What about Sam? Can you envision any special circumstances that might prompt either Dan or Sam to assume such a risk?

e. *Assignment of the Contract.* Absent language to the contrary, a contract for the sale of real estate is assignable by the buyer without the consent of the seller. See Friedman §2.1. Can you think of any reasons why Sam might require that any assignment be subject to his approval? See §11.8 of the sample contract, supra.

f. *Allocation of Purchase Price Between Land and Building.* By way of review of the materials covered in Chapter 2B, why is such an allocation important to both parties for federal income tax purposes? Such allocation is also important in determining both transfer and sales tax liability.

g. *Other Important Provisions.* The draftsmanship approaches to default provisions and exceptions to marketable title are discussed separately below. In addition, the sale agreement should include and address treatment of: definitions and use of plain language; schedules; the legal description of the real estate and chattels; the good-faith deposit; use of escrow arrangements to permit a closing of the transaction pending the resolution of a problem; title examination and insurance; the date, place, and mechanics for closing the transaction; prorations of rents, ad valorem taxes, and insurance premiums; tenant security deposits; employees of the seller; transfer of existing insurance policies; bills of sale; brokerage liability and agreements; deeds (discussed below); notices to suppliers and creditors; and ancillary documentation. See generally Hastie, Contracts for Disposition of Commercial Properties, in ALI-ABA, 1 Modern Real Estate Transactions 373 (7th ed. 1986); Taylor, Some Agreement of Sale Basics (with Forms), 4 Prac. Real Est. Law. 69 (May 1988).

2.   *The Doctrine of Marketable Title.*   Marketable title has been defined as "one free of encumbrances and free of any right or interest in a third person which is incompatible with full enjoyment and ownership of the property." Friedman §4.1. Simply put, in the absence of language to the contrary, the purchaser by implication is entitled to receive on or before the closing date a title that is free of record defects and encumbrances (such as leases, easements, mortgages and other liens, or restrictive covenants) that might adversely affect the value of the property. The rationale for the doctrine is that a purchaser should not be compelled to accept a title that may subject the purchaser to the hazard and expense of future litigation. See, e.g., Messer-Johnson Realty Co. v. Security Savings & Loan Co., 208 Ala. 541, 94 So. 734 (1922).

In plain language, when a buyer such as Dan Developer executes a contract of sale he is bargaining for the land and not for a lawsuit. However, the requirement that the title be marketable will be governed by a standard of reasonableness: title must be "free from reasonable doubt both as to matters of law and fact, a title which a reasonable purchaser, well informed as to the facts and their legal bearings and willing and ready to perform his contract, would, in the exercise of that prudence which businessmen ordinarily bring to bear upon such transactions, be willing to accept and ought to accept." A.L.P. §11.48; see generally Friedman §4.2.

However, like most definitional standards, the foregoing "prudent person" rule is abstract and leaves certain questions unresolved. For example, when confronted with a cloud on the title or the possibility of an encumbrance, how bleak must the worst-case scenario be before the purchaser can prudently abandon the bargain? When a record defect suggests that the title may be unmarketable, to what extent can extrinsic evidence (from outside the Registry of Deeds office) be used by the seller to rebut the negative inference? What is the burden of proof on the seller where the title depends upon a question of fact? What is the burden where the title depends upon a question of law? To what extent can a record defect in the seller's chain of title be rendered obsolete because of adverse possession by the seller or one of his predecessors in title? When must the title be marketable in the case of an installment land contract, where the seller may not deliver the title for a number of years? These are but a few of the many questions that are provoked by the doctrine of marketable title.

Let us now address some of these questions in view of the case law excerpts.

a.   In the *Rife* case, while the mortgage lien on the real estate being sold had not yet been expunged and the mortgagee possibly had assigned the debt before he died, the evidence at the time of the trial suggested that the mortgagee's estate had long been settled and that the mortgagee's heirs had relinquished to the seller any interest that they may have had in the mortgage. In addition, the mortgage claim was 19 years old and the statute of limitations was about to expire in two years. Likewise, in *Van Vliet,* while the fee simple title was subject to a possibility of reverter that prohibited certain commercial uses, the real estate was residential and probably was situated in a zoning area restricted to residential use. If, as suggested above, the possibility of an adverse claim was remote in both cases, can you reconcile the contrasting conclusions as to marketability in these cases? In that regard you might want to think about the rationale for the doctrine of marketable title and also about the worst-case scenario for the purchaser in each case if the purchaser were compelled to accept title.

b.   Suppose a seller contracts to sell real estate and promises to deliver a general warranty deed to the purchaser on or before the closing date. The seller's title is defective and the purchaser refuses to accept the title and pay the purchase price. Decide if the seller will be able to obtain specific performance (or recover damages) against the purchaser under the following circumstances.

i. The seller concedes that the record title is defective but alleges (and the evidence so suggests) that the adverse possession by the seller's predecessor in title has rendered the title marketable. Compare Conklin v. Davi, 76 N.J. 468, 388 A.2d 598 (1978), with Messer-Johnson Realty Co. v. Security Savings & Loan Co., 208 Ala. 541, 94 So. 734 (1922). See Friedman §4.3. What might the seller do of his own accord to render the title marketable? See N.Y. Real Prop. Acts L. §1501 (McKinney 1990).

ii. The seller merely agrees to deliver a quitclaim deed (whereby the seller, as grantor, makes no promises to the purchaser, as grantee) and, when the title fails, the seller contends that by agreeing to accept a quitclaim deed the purchaser waived her right to marketable title. Compare Blanck v. Sadlier, 153 N.Y. 551, 47 N.E. 920 (1897), with McManus v. Blackmarr, 47 Minn. 331, 50 N.W. 230 (1891).

c.   Is the issue in *Luette whether* the title is marketable or *when* the title must be marketable? After reviewing *Luette* consider the following question.

Suppose that the owner of some real property contracts to sell the property by means of a 12-year installment land contract and shortly thereafter an adjacent property owner erects a fence on a part of the property sold to the purchaser. After promising the purchaser that he would take care of the problem, the seller takes no action to remove the encroachment. Six months thereafter the purchaser moves out and brings an action to recover the monies she had paid toward the purchase price. In a jurisdiction that follows *Luette* and holds that a cause of action in ejectment can only be maintained by someone holding the legal title to real property, could you make an argument on behalf of the purchaser that the instant facts are distinguishable from the facts in *Luette?* See Mid-State Homes, Inc. v. Brown, 47 Ala. App. 468, 256 So. 2d 894 (Ala. Civ. App. 1971).

There are several ways to address the issue of marketable title in the sale agreement. The first approach, which is seldom used in practice, is for the contract to be silent as to the nature of the title to be conveyed, in which event the purchaser would be entitled to receive marketable title, free and clear of any exceptions. This presupposes an expectation on the part of the seller's attorney that any title problems can be resolved prior to the closing date. The second approach, as reflected by the language in §§3 and 4.3.1 of the sample sale agreement, supra, would be for the seller's attorney to provide for delivery of marketable fee simple title free and clear of any exceptions that are not specified (as "Approved Title Exceptions") in the sale agreement. Under this approach the seller's attorney would designate as exceptions to marketable title those that showed up in Schedule B of the seller's standard A.L.T.A. owner's policy when the seller acquired title along with any new easements, restrictions, or other encumbrances that were created by the seller and found to be acceptable by the purchaser's attorney. Once the contract is executed the seller's attorney would then order a preliminary title report from a title insurance company. (In some localities she might procure a title abstract from an abstract company. Alternatively, the purchaser's attorney might himself search the title and render an opinion.) If any unapproved exceptions should show up that are not listed in the agreement, and they are not waived by the purchaser's attorney or cured by the seller within a stipulated period of time, then the purchaser may rescind the contract and obtain a return of his earnest money deposit. In some instances, the encumbrance may be in the nature of an unpaid mortgage or tax lien or other liquidated claim against the property, in which event the parties might agree to have a portion of the sale proceeds used (or held in escrow) to satisfy the obligation in the event the seller presently does not have the funds on hand to discharge it prior to the scheduled closing date. Frequently, as in the sample contract, the title standard is stated obliquely in the description of the deed to be delivered on the closing date.

Exemplifying this second approach is the following passage from the standard form of Purchase and Sale Agreement prepared by the Greater Boston Real Estate Board: ". . . and said deed shall convey a good and clear record and marketable title thereto, free of all encumbrances, except . . ."

The third approach is for the seller's attorney to ignore the marketability issue by merely providing for the delivery of fee simple or insurable title, free of any exceptions that are not designated as approved exceptions in the sale agreement. For example, paragraphs 5 and 6 of NYBTU Form 8041, used in New York, provides as follows:

> 5. SELLER shall give and PURCHASER shall accept such title as _____ , a member of the New York Board of Title Underwriters, will be willing to approve and insure in accordance with their standard form of title policy, subject only to the matters provided for in this contract.
> 6. "CLOSING" means . . . delivery to PURCHASER of a _____ deed in proper statutory form for recording so as to transfer full ownership (fee simple title) to the PREMISES, free of all encumbrances except as herein stated.

Another example of this third approach is the following excerpt from the standard Form A (Residential) contract sponsored by the Chicago Title Insurance Company:

> Seller shall deliver or cause to be delivered to Purchaser, not less than 5 days prior to the time of closing, a title commitment for an owner's title insurance policy issued by Chicago Title Insurance Company in the amount of the purchase price, covering title to the real estate on or after the date hereof, showing title in the intended grantor subject only to . . . The title commitment shall be conclusive evidence of good title as therein shown as to all matters insured by the policy, subject only to the exceptions as therein stated.

Of the three foregoing draftmanship approaches, which one would you favor as Dan's legal advisor? As Sam's legal advisor?

Once the standard of title is defined in the contract, additional draftmanship issues are bound to arise in connection with defining and addressing the exceptions that are stipulated in the agreement. The most straightforward and common approach is for the seller's attorney to list all known title exceptions, usually by reference where possible to a recorded instrument (e.g., "easement recorded in liber 200 at page 12"). As the attorney for the purchaser would you feel duty-bound to review such recorded documents before the contract is executed? A second approach, born out of either laziness or fear of omitting something, is for the seller's attorney to add the following at the end of the list of known exceptions: "and all covenants, easements and restrictions of record." More conciliatory attorneys, however, would add the qualification "provided such restrictions of record do not prohibit existing structures or use." As to the foregoing language, does the phrase "of record" provide sufficient protection for the seller? What about the word "prohibit"? Would you accept this phraseology on behalf of the purchaser?

If the contract should merely state that transfer of title is subject to the condition that the title be insured by a title company or that the purchaser be supplied with title insurance then the contract will be deemed to refer to a title policy without exceptions. See Friedman §3.11. Accordingly, if the contract of sale makes the transfer of title subject to a lien or other exception, any provision for title insurance should be likewise qualified. Id.

Another common exception relates to the survey of the property. Surveys are discussed at Chapter 5B15. A conservative approach on the part of the seller's attorney is to stipulate that the title is subject to "any state of facts an accurate survey may reveal" (repeating the standard exception to title insurance coverage, examined at Chapter 3B2, note 4, infra). The more usual approach is to add the qualification "except such facts as would render the title unmarketable." Does the qualification of the exception leave anything left over?

3.   *Default Remedies.*   Under standard remedies principles, both the seller and the purchaser may rescind the contract, recover damages, or obtain specific performance against one another for breach of the sale contract. See Friedman §§12.1, 12.2. However, nettlesome problems may arise. For example, suppose in the hypothetical that Dan defaults under the contract after delivering the stipulated earnest money deposit of $5 million, which has been delineated as "liquidated damages" in §10 of the sample sale agreement supra, and that Sam sends a formal notice of default to Dan and terminates the contract. If immediately thereafter Sam is able to resell the property for $41 million, however, the question arises as to whether Sam will be allowed to retain the $5 million as liquidated damages. As suggested by the holdings in the *Maxton Builders* and *Reid* cases this area of law is fraught with uncertainty, and any automatic reliance on the written words of the parties is misplaced. There are, for instance, a few jurisdictions (such as Connecticut and Utah) where the seller who treats the contract as abandoned may not retain any more of the down payment than is necessary to make the seller whole again. See Friedman §12.1(c). In addition, liquidated damages clauses have been struck down as unenforceable penalties where the actual damages were readily ascertainable or the stipulated amount was unreasonable. See, e.g., Johnson v. Carman, 572 P.2d 371 (Utah 1977); Randall v. Riel, 123 N.H. 757, 465 A.2d 505 (1983); 77 Am. Jr. 2d, Vendor and Purchaser, §500. Thus it has been held that, despite a forfeiture provision in the contract, a defaulting purchaser was entitled to at least a partial restitution where the real estate was resold by the seller for a higher price. See Morris v. Sykes, 624 P.2d 681 (Utah 1981); Freedman v. The Rector, Wardens & Vestrymen of St. Matthias Parish of Los Angeles, 37 Cal. 2d 16, 230 P.2d 629 (1951). But see Cal. Civ. Code §1677 (West 1990) (renders

liquidated damages provision enforceable in agreements for sale of nonresidential real estate where provision is separately signed or initialed and set out in bold print, and amount stipulated is less than 3 percent of the sale price).

Most jurisdictions, however, follow the rule of Lawrence v. Miller, 86 N.Y. 131 (1881), that allows the seller to retain the down payment after a resale even though the contract calls for neither liquidated damages nor forfeiture. The rule is based on the doctrine that a party cannot recover the amount or value of a mere partial performance. The rule has been applied even where the property has been resold at a higher price. See, e.g., First National Bank of Barrington, Trust No. 11-1317 v. Oldenburg, 101 Ill. App. 3d 283, 427 N.E.2d 1312 (Ill. App. Ct., 2d Dist. 1981); see also Friedman §12.1(c). This has been especially true where the party seeking recovery is the defaulting purchaser rather than the aggrieved seller. However, the enforceability results are more evenly divided, especially in cases involving installment land contracts, where the purchaser's payments totaled 10 percent or more of the purchase price. See 4 A.L.R.4th 993 (cases where real estate not resold after default); compare McNorton v. Pan American Bank of Orlando, N.A., 387 So. 2d 393 (1980), rev. denied, 392 So. 2d 1377 (Fla. 1981) with Hommerding v. Peterson, 376 N.W.2d 456 (Minn. 1985). See generally Comment, A Critique of the Penalty Limitation on Liquidated Damages, 50 S. Cal. L. Rev. 1055 (1977); Unif. Land Transactions Act §2-516 (1978). After reviewing *Maxton Builders* and *Reid,* excerpted above, can you reconcile the conflicting results in these cases based on the difference in their facts? If in *Maxton Builders* the parties had agreed to a liquidated damages clause like the one in §10 of the sample sale agreement might this have changed the results in the case?

Returning to the hypothetical, if you were Sam's legal advisor, what would you think of §10 of the sample sale agreement supra? Suppose that, when the contract is executed, the local real estate market is soft or volatile. Do you see any pitfall for Sam if this language is accepted without modification? What does the court in *Reid* suggest by way of dictum? See Coble v. Scherer, 3 Kan. App. 2d 572, 598 P.2d 561 (1979); Lyons v. Philippart, 140 Ariz. 36, 680 P.2d 172 (1983). See Unif. Land Transactions Act §2-516(c). In light of the relatively large earnest money deposit ($5 million, or 12½ percent of the purchase price), what protective language might you, as Dan's legal advisor, want to insert in §10 of the sample sale agreement? In a minority jurisdiction where liquidated damages clauses are vulnerable to attack as penalties what do you, as the attorney for the seller, think about recharacterizing the earnest money deposit as something else (such as a rental payment or consideration for an option to purchase)? See N.Y. Real Estate Law Reporter, March 1987, at 6. The doctrine of liquidated damages itself has been characterized by Corbin as nothing more than discharge by accord and satisfaction. 6 Corbin, Contracts §1319, at 310-312 (1963). See generally Dunbar, Drafting the Liquidated Damages Clause — When and How, 20 Ohio St. L.J. 221 (1959).

4. *The Doctrine of Merger.*   As noted earlier, regardless of which kind of deed is stipulated in the contract of sale, under the doctrine of merger the purchaser's acceptance of the deed discharges most of the seller's obligations under the contract including the duty to deliver marketable title. Thereafter, the purchaser's sole recourse (as grantee) against the seller (as grantor) must be based on the covenants (if any) contained in the deed. See Friedman §7.2. However, this rule (like most others) applies absent language to the contrary. Accordingly, from the perspective of the purchaser what contractual obligations and warranties of the seller should be made to survive the closing date?

5. *Deeds and Covenants for Title.*   The deed is the formal instrument of conveyance and the legal evidence of title for the purchaser. The form of deed will depend on which deed is customarily used in the particular jurisdiction, whether or not the purchaser plans to obtain additional title protection and by what means, and, finally, on the bargaining positions of the parties. At one end of the spectrum is the general warranty deed, which affords maximum protection to the grantee because it contains all of the standard "English" covenants for title, including: (1) the covenant of seisin; (2) the covenant of the right to convey; (3) the covenant against encumbrances; (4) the covenant of quiet enjoyment; (5) the covenant of warranty; and (6) the covenant for further assurances. At the other end of the title-protection spectrum is the special warranty deed, in which the grantor merely warrants that it has done or suffered nothing to encumber the property, and the quitclaim deed (or bargain and sale deed in some jurisdictions), in which the grantor makes no covenants whatsoever and simply promises to convey to the grantee whatever interest, if any, the grantor might have in the property.

For all practical purposes the covenant of quiet enjoyment and the covenant of warranty are identical. Likewise, for purposes of the discussion that follows, the covenant of seisin can be combined with the covenant of the right to convey because they both serve the same function (except for one difference, which will be explained below). The covenant for further assurances simply means what the phrase implies; namely, that the grantor promises to do whatever further acts are within its power to perfect the title of the grantee. Accordingly, in the discussion that follows, the focus will be on the three major covenants: the covenant of seisin, the covenant against encumbrances, and the covenant of warranty. With regard to each covenant we will examine its definition and how it works, its nature either as a "present" or "future" covenant, whether it "runs with the land," the pertinent statutes of limitations that apply, and the measure of damages recoverable by the covenantee against the covenantor in the event that the covenant is breached. The following diagram will be used to illustrate the rules that apply and their consequences to the seller (as grantor) and purchaser (as grantee).

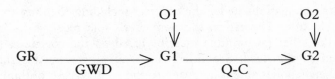

In the diagram above, GR refers to the grantor who originates the chain of title; G1 and G2 are subsequent grantees; O1 and O2 are potential adverse claimants who have better, or "paramount," title (perhaps by reason of the local recording statute) and are thus in a position to oust and evict G1 and G2, respectively; GWD refers to a general warranty deed; and Q-C refers to a quitclaim deed.

   a.   *Covenant of Seisin.*   This is created by means of the language in the sample general warranty deed supra that "the party of the first part covenants . . . that said party . . . is seized of the said premises in fee simple" or by phraseology of similar import. "Seisin" is simply the old common-law code phraseology for possession based on ownership of a fee simple or other freehold estate, so the grantor is promising at the time of conveyance (usually the closing date) that the grantor has good title and ownership of a fee simple absolute and has the right to convey it. See A.L.P. §12.127.

   At the time of conveyance the grantor *(GR)* either has good title or the grantor does not; hence the covenant is deemed to be a "present" covenant, since if it is breached it must be breached when made. See, e.g., Hilliker v. Rueger, 228 N.Y. 11, 126 N.E. 266 (1920). Like other present covenants, the covenant of seisin generally does not "run with the land." This means that while the immediate covenantee, *G1,* can avail himself of the covenant if he should be ousted by someone with better title *(O1),* remote grantees like *G2* who are evicted cannot. This is based on the formalistic rationale that a present covenant, once broken, leaves nothing left over that is assignable. However, a minority of jurisdictions adhere to the so-called English rule to the effect that a subsequent conveyance by the covenantee (e.g., from *G1* to *G2)* amounts to an assignment of a "chose in action" in favor of any remote grantee (like *G2)* who suffers damage by breach of the covenant (e.g., by *GR).* See A.L.P. §12.127; Schofield v. Iowa Homestead Co., 32 Iowa 317 (1871).

For the purpose of the statute of limitations, *G1*'s cause of action against *GR* generally does not accrue until *G1* has been evicted by *O1*. See, e.g., N.Y. Civ. Prac. L. and R. Law §206(d) (McKinney 1972). However, it is not essential in an action to recover damages that *G1* be evicted. All that's required is that *G1* prove that there has been a total or partial failure of title. Hilliker v. Rueger, 228 N.Y. 11, 126 N.E. 266 (1920). Don't forget the doctrine of adverse possession — that there is a second statute of limitations involved in *O1*'s right to eject *G1* in the event that *O1* has the better record title. Finally, the measure of damages for breach of the covenant of seisin is actual loss sustained *not exceeding purchase price plus interest*. In other words, if *G1* pays $100,000 for the real estate in 1980 and is ousted by *O1* in 1990 when the property is worth $500,000, *G1*'s maximum recovery against *GR* (assuming that *GR* is to be found and is solvent) is $100,000 plus accrued interest. This is why title insurance is so important for grantees in the position of *G1*, where coverage may be increased (by periodic endorsements) to reflect the current market value of the insured property. Otherwise owners may find themselves underinsured, especially in an inflationary economy. Indeed, as explained at Chapter 3B2, infra, in commercial transactions the purchaser will almost invariably obtain title insurance from a title company. Finally, a covenant of the right to convey is essentially the same as a covenant of seisin, except where the grantor has the right to convey but does not own the property, as when the grantor is conveying the property by means of a power of appointment in a will.

   b. Covenant Against Encumbrances. This is created by means of language in the sample general warranty deed supra that "the party of the first part covenants . . . that the said premises are free from encumbrances except as aforesaid." Like the covenant of seisin, it is a present covenant that does not run with the land except in a few jurisdictions (such as New York). Geiszler v. DeGraaf, 116 N.Y. 339 (1901). The covenant is breached when broken at the time of conveyance; however, for purposes of the statute of limitations, the cause of action accrues generally when there is an eviction. See, e.g., N.Y. Civ. Prac. L. and R. Law §206(d) (McKinney 1972). Also, the covenant is deemed to be a covenant of indemnity so that the measure of damages is the actual loss sustained by the covenantee. Don't forget that if the encumbrance involved should be a lien (e.g., mortgage, tax, or judgment lien), the lienor is also subject to a statute of limitations on his or her claim. As noted earlier, in the case of a special warranty deed the grantor merely covenants that it has done nothing to encumber the property, so that a cause of action will not lie if the property were encumbered by the grantor's predecessor-in-title. See generally A.L.P. §12.128.

   c. Covenant of Warranty. This is created by means of the language in the general warranty supra that "said party of the first part will forever warrant the title to said premises." The distinction between the covenant of seisin and the covenant against encumbrances, on the one hand, and the covenant of warranty, on the other, is that the first two relate to the status of the title when the property is conveyed and are thus broken when the covenant is made, while the last deals with the quiet enjoyment of possession and is not broken until there has been a disturbance in the future, for example, if *G1* should be evicted by *O1,* by the foreclosure of a tax lien, or by the enforcement of a restrictive covenant. Hence, the covenant of warranty is a "future" covenant that runs with the land in favor of remote grantees like *G2.* Once again the measure of damages generally is the actual loss sustained but not in excess of the purchase price plus interest.

 d.　Questions.

  i. In the *Schofield* case cited at (a) supra, a court of first impression had to decide whether the covenant of seisin should run with the land. In deciding in favor of the English rule (under which the covenant does run with the land), Justice BECK argued as follows against the majority rule ("American rule"): "When the grantee [*G1*], under the deed, has sold and received pay for the land, it would be gross injustice to permit him to recover, for he would not in that case sustain damages. But under the rule to which we are now objecting [American rule], the grantee may recover on the covenant of seisin and, if there be covenant of warranty in the deed, the subsequent grantee [*G2*] may also recover upon that contract against the first grantor [*GR*]." In your opinion, is this double-damages argument against the American rule a cogent one? If not, why not?

  ii. In the hypothetical, if, in a jurisdiction that adheres to the American rule, *G2* should be ousted by *O2* because *O2* had received an earlier conveyance from *G1* and under the local recording statute *O2*'s title is better than *G2*'s title, what remedy, if any, would *G2* have against *G1?* Would *G2* have a remedy against *GR?*

  iii. In the hypothetical, *GR* conveyed title to *G1* by means of a general warranty deed that included a covenant of warranty. Even though *G2* received a mere quitclaim deed from *G1, G1* received a general warranty deed from *GR.* Since the covenant of warranty in the deed to *G1* runs with the land it protects *G2* as well as *G1,* so why would someone in the position of *G2* ever demand (and presumably pay extra compensation for) a general warranty deed from the grantor *(G1)?* In most commercial transactions the seller (especially an institutional lender) will most likely refuse to deliver a general warranty deed to the purchaser. Can you think of any reason why this is so? See Friedman §7.1.

  iv. In the hypothetical, suppose that in a jurisdiction following the American rule *GR* sells the real estate to *G1* for $100,000 and *G1* resells the property to *G2* for $80,000. If *G2* were to be ousted by someone claiming under paramount title *(O2)*, should *G1* be able to recover from *GR?* If so, how much?

B. TITLE PROTECTION

As shown in the excerpt that follows, there are a variety of title protection methods used in this country, depending on local usage and custom and the predilections of the purchaser's attorney. In some jurisdictions abstract companies perform the title examination function of a title insurance company. However, each method or combination of methods uses the recording statute system as the basis for title examination. Moreover, in large commercial real estate transactions the parties will almost invariably utilize title insurance and the services of a title insurance company in those jurisdictions where they are available.[7]

Fiflis, Land Transfer Improvement:
The Basic Facts and Two Hypotheses
for Reform
38 U. Colo. L. Rev. 431, 438-440

RECORDING — GENERALLY

Recording acts were adopted by most of the states in the nineteenth century. The system used in the United States is probably indigenous to this country and probably originated from an act adopted by Plymouth Colony in 1640. The similarity between the 1640 act and the "modern" recording acts illustrates the lack of progress in improving this method. The 1640 act reads:

> No morgage, bargaine, sale, or graunt hearafter to bee made of any houses, lands, rents, or other hereditaments, shalbee of force against any other person except the graunter & his heires, unlesse the same bee recorded, as is hearafter expssed.

Recording is utilized in almost one hundred per cent of all transactions in registered land in every state but Louisiana.

There are four major types of practice which utilize the title

---

7. Title insurance is available in every state except Iowa. Holtzschue, Real Estate Transactions: Purchase and Sale of Real Property vii (1989).

protection of the recording acts. These might be designated the attorney opinion method, the abstractor-attorney method, the certificate method, and the title insurance method. The "title insurance method" is a broad category including several different types, some of which cut across the other three categories.

The attorney's opinion, the abstract, the certificate, and the title insurance policy are based on documents of title covering some period of time ending with the present. The period varies from place to place. In the Middle West and West, the search may start from the federal patent. In the East, where the patents are old, or, where, as in most places, there are none, the search almost never exceeds sixty years for residential real estate or one hundred years for valuable commercial real estate. Most careful examiners search a period of forty to sixty years; many examiners search for only twenty years.

Under the attorney opinion method, the attorney searches the records or causes a search to be made and then makes up an abstract and renders an opinion. This traditional method is practiced only in rural areas and in small towns today except for New England where it is used even in large urban areas.

Under the abstractor-attorney method, a professional abstractor or abstract company searches the records, makes up the abstract and an attorney then examines the abstract and gives his opinion. This is the most widely used technique, probably accounting for fifty percent of conveyancing transactions.

Under the certificate method, which is used in only a few locales, an abstractor will furnish a certificate setting forth the state of the title. Typically the abstract is kept by the abstractor and no attorney's opinion is obtained.

RECORDING — THE TITLE INSURANCE METHOD

In this category are numerous patterns resulting from the fact that the functions of examining title, providing advice, and closing the transaction, may be performed in any combination of modes between the title insurer and its agents or subcontractors, other lay agencies, or the attorneys of the parties.

Even where the buyer consults his own attorney, and that attorney closes the transaction, there are at least seven types of practices with respect to the title examination function. Examination may be by: (1) an attorney selected by the buyer without limitation of choice, (2) an attorney selected by the buyer from a wide list of approved attorneys selected by the title insurer, (3) an attorney selected by the buyer from a very limited list of approved attorneys selected by the title insurer, (4) an attorney in private practice selected by the title insurer, (5) an attorney employed by the title insurer, (6) laymen employed by the title insurer, or (7) no one, (i.e. no title examination is made and an insurance policy is issued on a casualty basis).

Under modes (4) through (7), in some areas, the title insurer also handles the closing of the transaction.

Note that under the certificate method and modes (4) through (7) an independent attorney is not utilized to give an opinion of the title. An attorney nevertheless should be retained for such matters as: drafting or examining the contract, the deed and the mortgage instruments; considering zoning, subdivision and building laws, tax effects and casualty insurance matters; checking for matters not covered by the certificate or insurance policy and for title defects arising in the interim between initial search and the closing; explaining the significance of the exceptions from, and limitations on, the title certificate or title insurance policy; advising the parties with respect to curing title defects; and checking title insurance policies for correctness. However, where an independent attorney is not retained for the title examination, the tendency is to dispense entirely with these services.

Where employees of the insurer examine the title, the records searched may be in the title insurer's title plant or they may be in the public records. Companies with a title plant may employ staffs which copy entries daily from the public records for transmittal to the company's records, or the recorder of deeds may take microfilm pictures, photostats or electrostatic pictures of all documents being recorded for the use of the company. When an application for insurance is received by a title plant company, a search of the company's own duplicate set of records is made, and a title report is issued. Under a second type of practice, the company maintains no daily take-off system, but utilizes the public records to fill individual orders, searching either from the date of its own title report on the same parcel, or if the company had not previously issued a policy on that parcel, for the conventional period. Some few small companies operate without use of the records on a casualty basis. . . .

1. The Recording Statute System

In contrast to a system of title assurance based on registration of the title itself (such as the nearly defunct Torrens System),[8] the recording

8. Under the Torrens system, ownership interests in real property are established and transferred pursuant to a governmental certification and registration process. By contrast, under the conventional deed-recording statute system the government's role is limited to providing public information about land ownership, and the validity of interests in real property is predicated primarily on the private legal system. See generally

statutes merely require that the *evidence* of title be recorded in the format of a recorded copy of the original deed; hence, under the recording statute system a grantor has the capacity to convey the same real property to two or more grantees. Returning to the hypothetical, if, for example, one of Dan's predecessors-in-title had conveyed the land underlying the office building to more than one grantee, then an adverse claimant under a different and conflicting chain of title might have paramount title to the property. Such an adverse claimant with the better record title could bring a bill to quiet title and, subject to a defense of adverse possession, have Dan ejected.

How does the recording statute system resolve these conflicts, and what is its underlying rationale? To illustrate these conflicts let us diagram the classic tripartite scenario: a common grantor *(GR)* conveys some real property, called Blackacre, by means of a general warranty deed *(GWD)* to one grantee who pays value *(G1)*, and then *GR* conveys Blackacre to a subsequent purchaser *(G2)* for value:

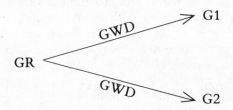

At common law the result was both clear and logical. *G1* would always prevail over *G2* because once the *GR* conveyed the entire fee simple interest to *G1, GR* would have nothing left over to convey to *G2*. Accordingly, *G2* would have no recourse but to sue *GR* based on the covenants of seisin and warranty (assuming that *GR* was still around and still solvent). The problem with this approach in today's complex land-based society is that someone in the position of *G2* would have to undertake a time-consuming and expensive investigation to ascertain whether someone like *G1* is in the picture before *G2* would safely purchase the property.

Goldner, The Torrens System of Title Registration: A New Proposal for Effective Implementation, 29 UCLA L. Rev. 661 (1982); 4 American Law of Property §§17.37 to 17.48 (Casner ed. 1952). Among the reasons why the Torrens concept has failed to take hold in the United States are its failure to eliminate the need for professional examination of title and the fact that the Torrens certificate of ownership neither identifies nor protects the certificate-holder against potential claims against the property including, for example, federal tax liens, liens for unpaid local taxes, short-term leases, and mechanics' liens for unpaid services to improve the land. Nor does the system establish the priority of claims as between lienors and other parties holding an interest in the registered property. See Shick and Plotkin, Torrens in the United States 2-9 (1978).

The approach taken by the recording statute system is a good example of the doctrine of "relativity of title"[9] that permeates the law of property in that it rejects the notion of "absolute" ownership and instead attempts to resolve the conflict between the relatively innocent parties (G1 and G2) by weighing the equities between them. In a symbolic or societal sense, G1 represents the need for someone who has paid value for land to be secure in that ownership, while G2 represents the demand of the commercial community that land transfers be expedited by empowering someone in the position of G2 to make a safe purchase of land based simply on the appearance of good title.

Johnson, Purpose and Scope of Recording Statutes
47 Iowa L. Rev. 231 (1962)

The general purpose of the land recording acts is quite clear: it is to provide a public record of transactions affecting title to land. More specific objectives are also readily discernible: (1) to enable interested persons, including public officials such as tax collectors, to ascertain apparent ownership of land; (2) to furnish admissible evidence of title for litigants in a nation where landowners did not adopt the English practice of keeping all former deeds and transferring them with the land; (3) to enable owners of equitable interests to protect such interests by giving notice to subsequent purchasers of the legal title; and (4) to modify the traditional case-law doctrine that purchasers and other transferees, no matter how bona fide, get no better title than the transferor owned. It is no doubt safe to make these generalizations about all of the land recordation statutes in force in the United States, but deeper probing renders generalization hazardous. This is especially true of item four on the above list. The first-in-time rule of priorities is quite logical, but it is of doubtful justice and is utterly incompatible with an economy in which commercial transfers of land occur frequently. But, despite widespread agreement that this doctrine should be changed, the recording acts of the various states and court decisions applying them reflect significant divergence of policy.

A basic policy question is whether emphasis should be upon penalizing those who fail to record or upon protecting those who deserve protection. Conceivably, strict adherence to the penalty approach could lead to requiring recordation as essential to the validity of a deed, even as to the grantor, in addition to the requirements of delivery

---

9. See, e.g., Corbin, Legal Analysis and Terminology, 29 Yale L.J. 163 (1919).

and writing. On the other hand, it would be consistent with the protection approach to regard unrecorded deeds void only as to those who actually examine the records and who substantially change their positions in reliance thereon. No modern recording act (excluding Torrens acts) goes to either of these extremes. Rather, the impact of both policies — penalty and protection — may be observed in the acts now in force. How these seemingly inconsistent policies have been accommodated is a major question to be considered in this review of the salient features of land recording acts.

I. Basic Types of Statutes

Recording acts typically are classified as (1) race, (2) notice, or (3) race-notice. If conveyees are allowed a specified period of time within which to record — a feature which may be added to any of the above types of acts but which is not common today — the statute is also categorized as a "period of grace" act. A recent survey placed the recording acts of only two states, Louisiana and North Carolina, in the race category generally, and those of three other states in that category as to some instruments — mortgages in Arkansas, Ohio, and Pennsylvania (except for purchase money) and oil and gas leases in Ohio. Most states have acts either of the notice or race-notice type, each type having about an equal following.

Of these types, the race statute is most consistent with the penalty principle. The North Carolina act provides: "No conveyance of land . . . shall be valid to pass any property, as against lien creditors or purchasers for a valuable consideration . . . but from the time of registration thereof . . ." Under this act, as construed, an unrecorded conveyance is void even as to a subsequent purchaser who knew of its existence, and a subsequent bona fide purchaser gains no priority over the earlier unrecorded instrument unless he records first. Thus, priority is determined by a race to the records. Of course, an unrecorded conveyance would be valid as to the grantor, his heirs, devisees, donees, and anyone else other than "lien creditors or purchasers for a valuable consideration." The North Carolina act is very similar to the Colonial prototypes. While there are many factors which may have shaped the early acts, it has been asserted that the most significant was a desire to provide a substitute for the publicity afforded by livery of seisin, which had been discarded as a mode of conveyance. In this context there would be a tendency to look upon recording acts as an additional conveyancing formality and to emphasize what was to be required of the grantor rather than what should be the qualifications of those to be protected. Subsequently, probably as a result of experience with actual cases, attention shifted to the latter and to "the view generally accepted in America today that the Recording Acts are an extension of the equitable doctrine of notice."

In some of its applications the race statute seems unfair and out of harmony with the stated objectives of recordation. But instances in which bad faith purchasers are benefited and good faith purchasers are harmed are probably infrequent, and can be almost eliminated by prompt recording. Indeed, the threat of such dire consequences may provide added incentive to prompt recordation. The best argument in favor of the race statute, however, is that it enables the title searcher to rely upon the records without the substantial risk under other types of acts that one will have constructive notice of unrecorded instruments.

A representative "notice" type act is the Iowa statute, which provides: "No instrument affecting real estate is of any validity against subsequent purchasers for a valuable consideration, without notice, unless filed in the office of the recorder of the county in which the same lies, as hereinafter provided." California's act is an example of the "race-notice" type: "Every conveyance of real property . . . is void as against any subsequent purchaser or mortgagee of the same property, or any part thereof, in good faith and for a valuable consideration, whose conveyance is first duly recorded. . . ." Both acts give priority over unrecorded instruments to subsequent purchasers only if they are without notice, and the California act also requires the bona fide purchaser to record first. The latter is an obvious compromise of the objectives of penalizing non-recordation and protecting those who are likely to rely upon the records. By withholding protection from one who has not himself obeyed the statutory mandate to record, the race-notice act may be thought to have the merit of fairness and to encourage recording to a greater extent than would the notice act. But the seeming fairness of putting beyond the pale of the act both non-recorders is quite superficial, since only one has caused harm. It is also extremely doubtful that recording is actually stimulated by acts of the race-notice type, since even in a state having a notice type statute failure to record makes those protected by the act vulnerable to subsequent claims.

II.   Groups Protected

Although not always referred to specifically in the statutes, the subsequent purchaser for a valuable consideration is the major beneficiary of the recording system. It would be a mistake, however, to assume that this category includes all purchasers, and only those purchasers, who part with value in reliance upon the records. . . .

According to one view, the recording acts benefit as purchasers those who have parted with only nominal consideration, but most courts appear to require something more substantial. The latter position is obviously sound if there is to be any real distinction between purchasers and donees.

On the other hand, one who parts with value in reliance upon the record is not necessarily protected. Some courts declare that this is the fate of one who receives notice of the unrecorded instrument after having parted with the consideration but prior to execution of the deed. The thought seems to be that such a person is not a "purchaser." Of course, the equitable doctrine of bona fide purchaser protected only those who acquired a legal title, but the recording acts are much broader and are now generally deemed to protect those who have acquired equitable interests. As a matter of policy, there would seem to be no reason for attaching significance to the execution of the deed. The time when protection is needed is the moment when consideration is given. This problem is most likely to arise when the contract provides for payment of the consideration over a period of years and the execution of a deed at or near the end of that period. It is generally recognized that one who has acquired the legal title but who has paid only a portion of the purchase price before he acquires notice is a pro tanto bona fide purchaser and, as such, entitled at least to a lien and in some cases to the legal title, subject to a lien in the adverse party. The same should be true of a purchaser who has only a contract and there is authority to that effect. Essentially the same problem is raised in a race-notice jurisdiction when notice is received after delivery of the deed but prior to its recordation. The conclusion seems sound that "after having paid the consideration and received a conveyance, the purchaser is qualified to race for priority of record unhampered by any notice that he may thereafter receive."

Other limitations on the protection accorded purchasers by the recording system may be briefly noted. Although a lessee is considered a purchaser, as a practical matter this means very little to the lessee, since he is protected only to the extent of rent paid prior to notice and must vacate the premises at the end of the period for which such rent was paid. This may result in a great hardship when the lessee has made expensive improvements or has otherwise substantially changed his position, as a lessee for a long term may well have done. A mortgagee also comes within the broad category "purchaser," but not when the mortgage is given to secure an antecedent debt, according to the majority view. Not to be overlooked is the omnipresent threat to all groups of recording act beneficiaries that they will be charged with notice of claims which they could not reasonably be expected to discover. This subject will not be explored at this point, but one example may be noted. Consider the burden imposed upon the purchaser who is paying the price in installments by holding that he gets notice of a prior unrecorded deed whenever it is recorded, which means that he must examine the records immediately before paying each installment. . . .

It is generally true that one cannot assert that an unrecorded instrument is void as to himself unless he is either a purchaser or a creditor. A few states also deem worthy of protection the plaintiff in a title suit who is unaware of unrecorded claims of persons not made parties to the litigation and who would thus not be bound by a judgment obtained by the plaintiff, provided he has filed a notice of lis pendens. . . .

III. NOTICE

Notice plays two major roles in the recording system. When an instrument is recorded, the record gives constructive notice of its existence and thus may be an important factor in any controversy in which notice is relevant, even in controversies not involving instruments required to be recorded. Even when an instrument is not recorded, notice disqualifies purchasers and creditors from gaining priority and thus, in effect, notice is a substitute for recording. Another way of stating the distinction is to say that in its first role notice aids those who record and in its second role it aids those who do not record.

The policy aspects of these two roles of notice are not identical. To allow notice to substitute for recording at all is debatable, since to do so favors one who was at fault in not recording and tends to weaken the incentive to record. It would seem to follow that notice which disqualifies purchasers and creditors should be narrowly confined. No such consideration is involved in determining what constitutes notice of a recorded instrument. The person who has recorded is not at fault and the only question is whether it would be reasonable, in view particularly of the condition of the records, to expect the party in question to have discovered the recorded instrument. In this situation, there would be no basis for a preference of either a broad or narrow scope of notice. However, the cases do not seem to reflect an awareness of this distinction. Indeed, it is arguable that the scope of notice of recorded interests has been restricted too much and that the scope of notice of unrecorded interests has been unduly expanded.

A. RECORD NOTICE

Although the statutes typically declare that the recording of an instrument shall be notice to "all persons," the courts have generally held that one is given constructive notice only of those recorded instruments which are within his "chain of title." The justification for thus rendering ineffective the recording of some instruments as to some persons is that the burden of search of the records would otherwise be unreasonable. While there is disagreement as to the proper application of the "chain of title" concept, it is clear that some limitation of this sort is needed when the only available access to the records is through inadequate official indexes, a situation all too common. But this justification for the "chain of title" limitation largely disappears in a community where easy access to information on the official records is available through unofficial abstracts and where the customary practice is to rely upon the abstracts rather than the official indexes. Unfortunately, this fact seems not to have had an appreciable impact upon shaping the "chain of title" concept. . . .

Another example of instruments appearing on the record which are deemed not to be recorded is that where the instrument is not authorized to be on the record, such being true in most states of unacknowledged instruments and instruments of a type not included in the statutory list of recordable instruments. This position has the merit of logic and is probably sound statutory construction, but it is disturbing that purchasers and creditors who could have discovered an instrument by a reasonable search of the records are not deemed to have been given constructive notice. To go further and say that purchasers and creditors may ignore such instruments even if they see them seems unsound, but there is a conflict of authority on this point.

B.   NON-RECORD NOTICE

Knowledge of the existence of an unrecorded interest is notice, but notice is broader than knowledge. The most common example is notice of facts which inquiry of the possessor would produce. Implicit here is the policy of protecting only the reasonably cautious, and it is assumed that such persons would not be content with a record search. Granting the soundness of that policy and assumption, the rub is that formulation and application of the required standard of care are likely to be uneven and in some cases too severe.

Thus, there is a conflict as to whether the duty to inquire of the possessor is created by the mere fact of possession or whether it is confined to instances where the fact of possession was known to the purchaser or was discoverable by a reasonable effort. There are also instances of imposition of an unduly severe burden of inquiry. If the purchaser knows, from the record or other sources, that the possessor is a lessee or a tenant in common, the purchaser might reasonably suppose that inquiry would be pointless, nevertheless, in many states he would be charged with notice of additional unrecorded interests of the possessor. According to one view, notice is imparted by such acts as cultivation or erection of improvements by a possessor who does not live on the land, even though such acts point to no one other than the record owner.

But if the purchaser has been abused by the possession-is-notice concept, he has also been spared undeservedly in some instances, particularly where a grantor of a recorded deed remains in possession and claims an unrecorded interest, even though here possession is inconsistent with the record and therefore inquiry-provoking. The unconvincing justification offered for this result is that the "grantor's deed is a conclusive declaration that he has reserved no rights and estops him from setting up any arrangement by which the deed is impaired." This misses the point: the one who has failed to record is always at fault; the relevant question is whether there is notice.

Knowledge of facts unrelated to possession may also raise a duty to inquire, though it appears that, in the absence of such knowledge, a stranger need not investigate the reputation of the title in the community.

Perhaps the most outrageous notice doctrine is that which denies that a purchaser who claims through a quitclaim deed is a bona fide purchaser. In the doctrine's most extreme form, the quitclaim is a bar even though it is remote and inquiry would be unproductive. In this form, the doctrine can hardly be said to be a notice doctrine at all, and justification must be sought in the notion that a quitclaim conveys only what the grantor owns and that a grantor who previously had conveyed his entire interest has nothing left to convey. If this idea is valid, one would expect to encounter it even in states having a race statute, but the Supreme Court of North Carolina has rejected it, saying that it "overlooks the registration statutes," by virtue of which " 'the grantor retains a power to defeat his earlier conveyance.' " Since this power would pass in most states to a donee, devisee, or heir, no reason is apparent why it would not also pass to a quitclaim grantee. If the only effect of the quitclaim is to excite inquiry and charge one with notice of unrecorded interests reasonably discoverable, the question is raised as to what line of inquiry is suggested by the fact that the vendor is reluctant to give more than a quitclaim or that he derives title through a quitclaim. The latter would probably be ignored by the prudent purchaser and the former would, at most, cause a vague suspicion which apparently could not be resolved. It is conceivable, but improbable, that flagrantly suspicious circumstances, though not suggestive of lines of inquiry which would lead to evidence of unrecorded interests, might so strongly indicate lack of title in the grantor that the purchaser would be denied the status of a bona fide purchaser, but the vendor's insistence on giving a quitclaim, standing alone, is hardly such a case. It is generally understood that honest vendors having some confidence in their titles are sometimes unwilling to execute any conveyance other than a quitclaim.

IV. CONCLUSION

To the extent that the recording system protects against unrecorded interests persons who have not relied upon the record and are not members of a group which typically rely upon it, the system appears to be based upon the penalty principle. Perhaps the most notable manifestation of this policy is the extension of benefits to creditors. Also consistent with the penalty principle is the withholding of benefits from those who themselves have failed to record, in the race and race-notice states. The principle of protecting the deserving certainly has had no less influence in shaping the system, as is amply demonstrated by the sweeping effect of notice in nearly all states. It may seem unfortunate that there has not been a forthright adoption of one of these conflicting policies to the exclusion of the other. A still more serious matter is the presence in the system of features which serve neither policy. Examples are decisions charging persons with notice of unrecorded interests which they could not reasonably discover; these fail to penalize the non-recorder and also fail to protect those who may have relied upon the record.

Which policy should be preferred? All would agree that the "ideal goal of the Recording Acts is to furnish in the public record office a complete history of the title of every tract of land within the jurisdiction to the intending purchaser or incumbrancer, so that he may determine therefrom whether the title is good." It may also be conceded that emphasis upon the penalty principle tends to make the records more complete. It might seem to follow that notice, as a substitute for recording, should be discarded and that it should be immaterial whether benefited groups ever consult the record. It is true, as was indicated in the first paragraph of this Article, that the recording system serves purposes other than the protection of purchasers and creditors. But what purpose, other than protection of those who rely, or are likely to rely, upon the records, is of sufficient magnitude to warrant depriving one of his land for failure to record? Unlike the Torrens system, the recording system provides no fund for compensating those whose titles are cut off.

NOTES AND QUESTIONS

1. *Purposes of the Recording Statute System.* Under the recording statute system *G1* will always prevail if the evidence of title (deed) is immediately recorded at the Registry of Deeds office. But if *G1* is slow to record and *G1*'s failure to record misleads *G2* into a purchase, then as a general rule *G2* will prevail (1) in a "notice" jurisdiction if at the time he pays value *G2* does not have record or actual notice of

G1's prior claim; and (2) in a "race-notice" jurisdiction if at the time he pays value *G2* has neither record nor actual notice of the prior claim *and G2* wins the race to the recorder's office by recording his deed ahead of *G1*. In the third major jurisdiction, a "race" jurisdiction, notice is irrelevant, and the party who records first wins. Thus, while the policy emphasis of these statutes varies from a penalty approach (that penalizes someone who is slow to record in a race jurisdiction) to one that emphasizes protecting a bona fide purchaser without notice (in a notice and race-notice jurisdiction), the fundamental policy rationale for the recording statute system is to effect a substitution of burdens — namely, *G1* must record promptly so that *G2* can be extricated from the more onerous common-law burden of making a full inquiry — so that land transactions can function more smoothly.

A few threshold observations before we begin our examination of how the recording statutes operate:

1. Don't be intimidated by the recording statutes — they appear at first glance to be more complex than they really are. It will help if you diagram the facts. However, to familiarize yourself with the mechanics of the statutes, you may want to consult one of the standard first-year hornbooks such as Cribbet, Principles of the Law of Property (Foundation Press 1989) or Boyer, Survey of the Law of Property (West 1981).

2. The key to understanding recording statute results is to comprehend the mechanics of searching title (see note 2 infra). Remember that no matter how convoluted the facts, almost all of the case law results can be explained on the basis of a title-search burden rationale.

3. Remember that the recording statutes are designed to help only *subsequent* purchasers and encumbrancers for value; thus a prior taker *(G1)* will never prevail because of the recording statutes. If the subsequent taker *(G2)* complies with *all* the requirements of the statute then it will prevail. If it does not, then the contest is thrown back to the common-law rule ("first in time first in right"), under which *G1* will automatically win the contest.

4. In a notice and race-notice jurisdiction always ask yourself who misled whom into a purchase by failing to promptly record; and in all jurisdictions, to what extent, if any, would the title examiner who works for *G2* have to expand his or her title search beyond the normal bounds of a title search examination (as explained in note 2 infra) to be able to spot the earlier conveyance from *GR* to *G1*.

5. The recording statute system is designed to protect only: (a) a bona fide purchaser or encumbrancer who pays value (e.g.,

donees are not protected); and (b) someone who claims through such a BFP or encumbrancer.

2. *The Mechanics of Searching Title.* As noted above, it is difficult to understand recording statute results without some familiarity with the mechanics of searching title. As we shall see in the note that follows, when a contest is decided in favor of G2 even though G1 records first, chances are that G1's recordation was "outside the chain of title," which simply means that the title searcher working for G2 would have to go beyond a normal title search in order to spot the recorded conveyance in favor of G1. What, then, is a normal title search? In this brief overview of conveyancing, the following simplified explanation (as diagrammed below) will have to suffice.

First, at the Registry of Deeds office are certain indices, the most important of which are the "grantor index," the "grantee index," and, in some (primarily rural) jurisdictions, the "tract index."

a. *Grantor Index.* This index is arranged alphabetically by the name of the grantor and lists all the conveyances (with volume and page number references to the applicable Deed Book) from the grantor to grantees during stipulated periods of time.

b. *Grantee Index.* This index is the converse of the grantor's index in that it is arranged alphabetically by grantee, and for designated periods of time (e.g., decennial periods) each index book lists all conveyances to a particular grantee from various grantors.

c. *Tract Index.* In some jurisdictions the title examiner *(T)* can look at a map of the county or town that has been divided into geographical units called "blocks" and, based on the lot number of a parcel within a particular block, T will be able to locate the tract index book that contains a list of all conveyances with respect to a particular parcel. In contrast to the grantor and grantee indexes, all conveyances are listed in one spot regardless of their chronological order; thus T will find conveyances that might otherwise be outside the chain of title under the grantor or grantee index.

Second, T will start the title search by going backwards in time and using the grantee index to establish all of the predecessors-in-title in a particular chain of title in order to establish the links in the chain of title. Let us assume for example that Sam Seller *(G4)* has record title as of January 1 of this year (the date on which the contract with Dan Developer is executed). The title examiner will obtain a copy of Sam's deed from Sam's predecessor-in-title *(G3)* and, if the deed does not contain a reference to the G2-G3 conveyance (by deed book volume and page number), T will start examining the grantee index under G3's name starting with the date on which G3 conveyed to G4 (e.g., 1970) and work backwards in time until T spots the conveyance to

$G3$ from $G2$ (e.g., 1960), the conveyance to $G2$ from $G1$ (e.g., 1940), and finally the conveyance to $G1$ (e.g., 1910). How far back in time must T go? If Dan $(G4)$ has a general warranty deed, the rule of thumb is for T to go back 60 years. Theoretically, if $G4$ has record title based on a mere quitclaim deed, T should go back to the original grantor. Obviously, the extent of the search under the grantee index will depend on the unique facts and circumstances of each transaction, including the extent to which record defects are cured by local law under a so-called marketable title act and the amount that the parties are willing to pay for the title search.

Suppose T cannot find any reference to the $G2$-$G3$ deed in the grantee index. T will then examine the records in the Registry of Probate next door to check whether $G3$ received his title as a legatee under $G2$'s will or as an heir of $G2$ under the local inheritance statute. But suppose $G2$'s will had been probated in another county or $G3$'s last name is not the same as $G2$'s, so T is not readily able to find any linkage between $G2$ and $G3$ in the Registry of Probate, where wills are probated and letters of administration are filed alphabetically by decendent? In such an event, T may need to go on a fishing expedition to find $G2$, the missing link in the chain of title.

The next step in the title examination is for T to go forward in time, starting with an arbitrary date (e.g., 1910) to determine, by using the grantor index, whether any of Sam's predecessors-in-title had conveyed to a stranger grantee (such as X) before conveying to the next person in Dan's direct chain of title. For example, if $G1$ had conveyed to X, who recorded his deed in 1912, before $G2$ recorded in 1940, the entire chain of Sam's title would fail and Sam's title would be rendered unmarketable, necessitating litigation on his part to clear the title. If, for example, Sam could prove adverse possession by himself or by one of his predecessors-in-title he would have to bring a bill to quiet title and obtain a new chain of title (starting with a judicial deed) in order to be able to deliver marketable title to Dan. If there is no evidence of a prior conveyance from G1, T would have to check the grantor index once again to see whether the next grantor, G2, had deeded out to someone else between the date that G2 recorded his deed, 1940, and 1960, the date of G3's recordation, and so forth, until T determines that none of the grantors in Dan's chain of title had made an earlier conveyance that was recorded. There is a saving grace for T, if any of Sam's predecessors had obtained title insurance: most title companies will provide T with a "back date letter" so that T can begin his search under the grantor index as of the last date on which a policy was issued. So, for example, if G3 had been insured as of his closing date in 1960, T could commence his search on that date without going back to 1910 in the grantor index.

3. *Record Notice.* The following benchmark cases are discussed in the hornbooks because they present the basic record-notice issues that one might confront under the recording statute system.

a. Board of Education of City of Minneapolis v. Hughes, 118 Minn. 404, 136 N.W. 1095 (1912):

1) G2 records
2) G3 records
3) G1 records

Result: In all jurisdictions G3 will prevail because G2's earlier recordation is "outside the chain of title."

Rationale: G2 was negligent in not insisting that his predecessor *(G1)* record before G2 took title. A title searcher on behalf of G3 *(T)* would not be able to spot the G1-G2 deed in the grantor index until he spots the GR-G1 deed, which had not been recorded until after G3 paid value; hence, G2 misled G3 into a purchase. Even in a race jurisdiction G2's deed would not be regarded as a valid recordation. Would the title-search problem posed by *Hughes* be cured in a jurisdiction that has adopted a tract index?

b. Morse v. Curtis, 140 Mass. 112, 2 N.E. 929 (1885); contra, Woods v. Garnet, 72 Miss. 78, 16 So. 390 (1884):

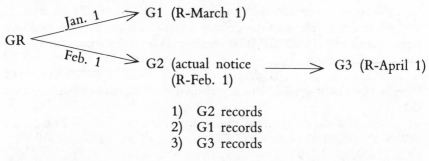

1) G2 records
2) G1 records
3) G3 records

Result: According to the majority view in Morse v. Curtis, *G3* will prevail in all jurisdictions because *G1*'s recordation is outside the chain of title.

Rationale: Once *T*, the title searcher for *G3*, spots the recorded deed to *G2* he should be able to stop his search in the grantor index under *GR*'s name; otherwise, the normal title search burden would be expanded to an oppressive degree. Why? Incidentally, in a race jurisdiction *G2* would prevail over *G1*, notwithstanding *G2*'s actual notice of the prior conveyance to *G1;* therefore, *G3* would automatically win his contest with *G1.* In other words, *G3* should only be required to race other grantees from his grantor. Would the title search-burden problem posed by Morse v. Curtis be cured in a jurisdiction that has adopted a tract index?

c.   Wheeler v. Young, 76 Conn. 44, 55 A. 670 (1903); contra, Ayer v. Philadelphia & Boston Face Brick Co., 159 Mass. 84, 34 N.E. 177 (1893):

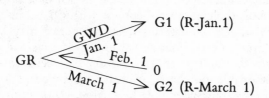

1) G1 records
2) 0 deeds to GR
3) G2 records

Result: According to the overwhelming majority view, *G2* will prevail because *G1*'s recordation is outside the chain of title.

Rationale: *G1* would argue "estoppel by deed," specifically, that even though *GR* had no title at the time of the conveyance to *G1,* the deed into *GR* "fed the estoppel" created by the covenant of seisin in *G1*'s *GWD* that would estop *GR* from denying good title to

G1. Moreover, since *GR* had immediately lost title to *G1* on Feb. 1, he had nothing left over to convey to *G2*. However, the majority view is that of *G1* and *G2, G2* would prevail; otherwise, the normal title search burden for someone searching title for *G2* would be expanded to an oppressive degree. Can you think of the reason why? Would the result change in a jurisdiction that has adopted a tract index?

   d. Buffalo Academy of the Sacred Heart v. Boehm Bros., Inc., 267 N.Y. 242, 196 N.E. 42 (1935); contra, Finley v. Glenn, 303 Pa. 131, 154 A. 299 (1931):

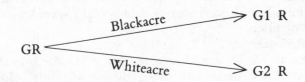

In these cases the issue is whether *G2* has record notice of restrictions in the Blackacre deed that are intended to affect the use of Whiteacre as well as Blackacre. Once again the majority view to the effect that *G2* has no record notice is based on a title-search burden rationale. Can you think of a reason? What would be the result in a jurisdiction that has adopted a tract index?

   4. *Inquiry Notice: An Insidious Doctrine.* In a jurisdiction where notice is relevant, a subsequent purchaser or encumbrancer for value *(G2)* who has neither record nor actual notice of a prior conveyance (to *G1*) may nonetheless lose the contest with *G1* because of a doctrine called inquiry notice. Under this doctrine, notice may be imputed to a purchaser (even one without actual notice) if facts and circumstances exist either on the land or at the Registry of Deeds office that would prompt a reasonable purchaser to make an investigation. Moreover, such a prospective purchaser will be charged with notice of whatever a diligent search would reveal even where no search is actually made. However, if the search discloses nothing, the purchaser can safely take title. 4 American Law of Property §17.11 (Casner ed. 1952).

   An example of inquiry notice based on information contained in the Registry of Deeds office is the holding in Guerin v. Sunburst Oil & Gas Co., 68 Mont. 365, 218 P. 949 (1923), to the effect that inquiry notice of an unrecorded instrument can be based on reference to its existence in a recorded instrument. In that case, the facts of which are diagrammed below, the grantor *(GR)* first executed a long-term lease with *G1*, then *GR* granted an option to purchase the property (subject to the lease) to *G2*, and finally, *GR* conveyed the property (without mentioning the lease) to *G3*.

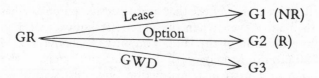

This case was decided in a notice jurisdiction where the court held that while *G1* failed to record its lease, *G3* took subject to the lease inasmuch as reference to the lease in the recorded option agreement had put *G3* on inquiry notice of *GR*'s lease with *G1*. Likewise, in some jurisdictions the mere taking of title by means of a quitclaim deed will charge the purchaser with inquiry notice. Most jurisdictions take the position that a conveyance in the form of a quitclaim deed need not imply a defect in the grantor's chain of title; hence, the grantee can qualify as a bona fide purchaser without notice. Why might a purchaser prefer a quitclaim deed over a general warranty deed? In support of the majority view, can you think of any valid reasons why anyone selling real estate might refuse to convey the property by means of a general warranty deed? Compare Moelle v. Sherwood, 148 U.S. 21 (1893), with Houston Oil Co. v. Niles, 255 S.W. 604 (Tex. Commn. App. 1923).

The more prevalent source of inquiry notice is based on possession of the land that is inconsistent with its record ownership. Suppose, for example, that (as diagrammed below) *GR* conveys the property to *G1* (who enters into possession but fails to record the deed from *GR*) and then *GR* conveys the property to *G2*, who pays value for the land, immediately records, and takes without actual or record notice of the prior conveyance to *G1*.

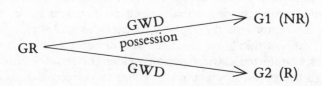

In most notice and race-notice jurisdictions that recognize inquiry notice, *G1* would have the paramount record title because *G2* would be charged with inquiry notice of *G1*'s claim to the land. See Galley v. Ward, 60 N.H. 331 (1880). However, the extent of the inquiry notice burden can vary greatly. For example, it has been held that possession by a life tenant, although consistent with record title, may constitute inquiry notice of an inconsistent fee simple claim based on an unrecorded conveyance of a remainder interest to the life tenant. Toland v. Corey, 6 Utah 392, 24 P. 190 (1890), affd., 154 U.S. 499 (1894). Conversely, there is authority to the effect that a prospective purchaser has no duty to make an inquiry even when the purchaser knows that a stranger of record is in possession of the land. Toupin v. Peabody, 162 Mass. 473, 39 N.E. 280 (1895). Moreover, to determine the extent of the inquiry-notice burden in a particular jurisdiction one must scrutinize the case law and not depend on the phraseology of the recording statute. For example, in both Utah (Toland v. Corey) and Massachusetts (Toupin v. Peabody) the respective recording statutes were of the same "notice" variety (protecting "purchasers without notice") and yet the inquiry notice results were diametrically opposite.

The inquiry notice doctrine is a questionable if not spurious feature of the recording statute system, in the opinion of many commentators. See, e.g., Philbrick, Limits of Record Search and Therefore of Notice, 93 U. Pa. L. Rev. 259-273 (1944). In the excerpt by Johnson, supra, the author criticizes case decisions "charging persons with notice of unrecorded interests which they could not reasonably discover." An example of this might be the aforementioned case of Toland v. Corey, where *G2*, as a mortgagee, in the opinion of the court, was obligated to look beyond the record to discover *G1*'s fee simple ownership even though *G1*'s possession was consistent with her record title as a life tenant. In light of the underlying rationale for the recording statute system, what's wrong with case results like Toland v. Corey that extend the doctrine of inquiry notice to its threshold limits?

5. *Questions.* Based on the foregoing, do your best to answer the following questions.

a. A typical notice-type statute is Mass. Gen. Laws Ann. ch. 183, §4, which reads as follows: "A conveyance of an estate in fee simple . . . or for life, or a lease for seven years . . . , shall not be valid as against any person, except the grantor or lessor, his heirs and devisees and persons having actual notice of it, unless it, or an office copy . . . is recorded in the registry of deeds. . . ."

Why, do you think, are the heirs and devisees of the grantor not regarded as a protected class of persons under the statute? How would you change the phraseology above in order to convert the notice-type statute into a race-notice statute? Into a race statute?

b. *O*, the owner of Blackacre, executes and delivers deeds conveying the same parcel, Blackacre, in chronological order, to three successive purchasers, *X, Y,* and *Z*. Immediately thereafter, *X* records his deed, then *Z* records, and finally *Y* records. Assume that all deeds are warranty deeds and delivered for valuable consideration. In a notice, a race-notice, and a race jurisdiction, who would prevail in a contest between *X, Y,* and *Z*?

c. Blackacre is located in a jurisdiction that has not adopted a tract index. Its owner, *O*, conveys Blackacre to *A* on July 1 and *A* records on October 1. *O* also conveys Blackacre to *B* on September 1. *B* immediately records. In that same year *B* conveys Blackacre to *C* on November 1 and *C* immediately records. Neither *B* nor *C* had actual notice of *O*'s conveyance to *A;* however, one month before *O* conveyed Blackacre to *B*, *A* had posted a few notices (signed by *A*) on Blackacre that simply read: "No Trespassing."

Assume that all deeds are warranty deeds and delivered for valuable consideration. In a notice jurisdiction, who would prevail in a contest between *A* and *C*? Who would prevail in a race jurisdiction?

d.   *O* executes and delivers to *A* a general warranty deed conveying to *A* certain land ("Blackacre") that *O* owns. *A* does not record. *A* then executes and delivers to *B* a quitclaim deed covering Blackacre. *B* immediately records. *O* then executes and delivers to *C* a general warranty deed covering Blackacre. *C* immediately records. Finally, *C* executes and delivers to *D* a general warranty deed covering Blackacre. *A* immediately records and then *D* records. Assuming that all of the foregoing grantees are purchasers for value, who, *B* or *D*, would prevail in a race-notice jurisdiction? Would the result change if Blackacre were located in a jurisdiction that has a tract index?

e.   The language of the recording statutes varies with respect to the protection afforded to judgment lienors and other subsequent creditors. Suppose, for example, that *O*, the owner of Blackacre, delivers a warranty deed for valuable consideration to *A*, who does not record. Further assume that *B* subsequently obtains a judgment against *O* and immediately dockets the judgment, which creates a lien on all of *O*'s real property (including Blackacre) in the county where the judgment is docketed. In a contest between *A* and *B*, some states (such as North Carolina) would treat *B* like any other encumbrancer and *B* would prevail. Others (such as New York) do not afford any protection to judgment lienors. Can you think of any reason for this difference in result? Compare N.C. Gen. Stat. §47-18 (Michie 1990) with N.Y. Real Property Law §291 (McKinney 1968).

6.   *Weaknesses of the Recording Statute System.*   The conveyancing literature is replete with constructive criticism of the recording statute system. Some critics advocate title registration (such as the Torrens system) as a substitute. See Fiflis, Land Transfer Improvement: The Basic Facts and Two Hypotheses for Reform, 38 U. Colo. Law Rev. 431 (1966). Most, however, recommend structural changes and other reforms that would improve the system. See Cross, Weaknesses of the Present Recording System, 47 Iowa L. Rev. 245 (1961); Payne, The Crisis in Conveyancing, 19 Mo. L. Rev. 214 (1954). For example, the use of name indices like the grantor-grantee index (as opposed to a tract index) makes it extremely difficult to locate certain title documents. In addition, while most title-transfer instruments fall within the re-

cording acts, some may not be easily recordable (e.g., executory contract to purchase, assignment of a mortgage) and certain government liens (e.g., a superlien for toxic-waste cleanups) are creatures of statutes that do not depend on recordation for their viability. Moreover, the recording statute system does not afford protection against certain contingencies and problems that may affect the status of the title, such as adverse possession, short-term leases, implied easements, marriage and divorce, and the scope of restrictive covenants. See generally McDougal and Brabner-Smith, Land Title Transfers: A Regression, 48 Yale L.J. 1125 (1939); Behringer and Altergott, Searching Title and Clearing Away What You Find, 4 Prac. Real Est. Law. 11 (Nov. 1988).

2. *Title Insurance*

Returning to the master hypothetical, let us assume that shortly after the contract is executed the parties take the next step in the land transfer cycle by arranging for a preliminary title examination to determine whether Sam Seller can convey marketable title, that is, convey title as described in the contract to Dan Developer without any additional defects, liens, or encumbrances that might adversely affect the value of the property. You and Sam's attorney will have to address any outstanding encumbrances or other exceptions to marketable title that may be revealed by the preliminary title examination.

Schedule A of the preliminary title report will indicate whether Sam is vested with fee simple title in the property, and Schedule B will indicate whether the property is encumbered by any mortgage, tax lien, judgment lien, easement, restrictive convenant, or other interest that might interfere with Dan's beneficial use of the property.

Some of the encumbrances listed in Schedule B will be anticipated inasmuch as they represent an integral part of the bargain; for example, if there were an existing first mortgage with Sam's mortgagee such mortgage would be listed as an encumbrance if Dan should assume the mortgage or take subject to it as part of the agreed-on purchase price. Others will not be objectionable to you as Dan's attorney because they will maintain or enhance the value of the property (for example, utility easements and the leases with those prime tenants whose units will not be sold when Dan converts the building into a condominium). Of course you will want to review the language of the easements or leases to which title will be subject, to determine that they contain no objectionable provisions such as rights of the utility to block access to the property or options of tenants to purchase the property.

Just before title closes, a final "rundown" check will be made by the title examiner to make sure that no intervening conveyances or encumbrances were recorded after the preliminary title report was issued.

Finally, on the date of closing or shortly thereafter, Dan will receive his title insurance policy, insuring him of fee simple title as of the closing date subject to the exclusions from coverage, the conditions and stipulations of the policy, and the approved title exceptions, all enumerated in the policy.

There is no question but that title insurance represents the principal source of protection for purchasers and mortgagees in today's commercial real estate transactions, especially in light of the limited protection afforded to grantees under covenants for title in deeds. Remember that warrantees amount to nothing more than promises to indemnify that depend on the future solvency of the grantor, while title insurance is backed by the net worth of the company that underwrites the policy (which in most cases will exceed the grantor's assets). Moreover, if the seller is a bank, insurance company, or other institutional lender it will most likely refuse to make such warranties to the purchaser. Furthermore, the alternative of obtaining an attorney's opinion of title has virtually disappeared in commercial real estate transactions because attorneys are ill-equipped to undertake the search such an opinion requires (the cost of which would in most cases be prohibitive) and because they are generally unwilling to do so unless their opinion assumes the accuracy of a title report prepared by a title company (thus affording little protection to the client).

Accordingly, in commercial real estate transactions, major reliance is placed not only on the accuracy of a title search but also on the insurance of that accuracy by a title company or companies. This section will examine whether and under what circumstances such reliance is justified.

In 1987 the national trade association for the title insurance industry, the American Land Title Association (ALTA), completed its revision of all of the standard ALTA policy forms (the first major revision since 1970), including: (1) the Owner's Policy (insuring the purchaser or other policyholder of fee simple title); (2) the Loan Policy (insuring the mortgagee, whether it be a postconstruction ("permanent")[10] or construction lender, that title is valid and the insured mortgage has lien priority; (3) the Construction Loan Policy (insuring the construction lender);[11] and (4) the Leasehold Owner's and Loan Policies (insuring the lessee and leasehold mortgage,[12] respectively).

In some states the ALTA policy forms were not readily available until recently, notably in California, where the standard forms prepared by the California Land Title Association are gradually being replaced by the 1987 ALTA forms, and in New York, where the forms are

---

10. See discussion at Chapter 5B15.
11. See discussion at Chapter 6B3, note 6.
12. See discussion at Chapter 8A1.

now being used along with the earlier policy forms prepared by the state trade association, the New York Board of Title Underwriters. In Texas these forms are not yet available because they do not meet the restrictions imposed by the state regulatory authorities.

At this juncture let us review the sample 1987 ALTA Owner's Policy. First, we will examine the insuring provisions of the Owner's Policy (and of the Loan Policy as well), which tell the insured, whether it be the owner or lender-mortgagee, what coverage is being provided. Then we will analyze what these Insuring Provisions are "subject to," namely, the standard exclusions from coverage, the specific exceptions from coverage contained in Schedule B, and the standard conditions and stipulations. For the most part the Owner's and Loan Policies contain the same exclusions, conditions, and stipulations except that extra language is included in the latter policy. In some instances depending on local law variations and the proclivities of a particular title company it may be possible on payment of an additional premium to expand the coverage of the insuring provisions by obtaining a so-called special endorsement to nullify one of the exclusions, exceptions, conditions, or stipulations. For example, as discussed at Chapter 5B9, note 6, in some states it is possible to obtain a zoning endorsement to insure against the adverse affects of local land use regulations notwithstanding the language in Exclusion 1(a) of the 1987 policy.

Policy of Title Insurance

Issued by

BLANK TITLE INSURANCE COMPANY

SUBJECT TO THE EXCLUSIONS FROM COVERAGE, THE EXCEPTIONS FROM COVERAGE CONTAINED IN SCHEDULE B AND THE CONDITIONS AND STIPULATIONS, BLANK TI-TLE INSURANCE COMPANY, a Blank corporation, herein called the Company, insures, as of Date of Policy shown in Schedule A, against loss or damage, not exceeding the Amount of Insurance stated in Schedule A, sustained or incurred by the insured by reason of:

1. Title to the estate or interest described in Schedule A being vested other than as stated therein;
2. Any defect in or lien or encumbrance on the title;
3. Unmarketability of the title;
4. Lack of a right of access to and from the land.

The Company will also pay the costs, attorneys' fees and expenses incurred in defense of the title, as insured, but only to the extent provided in the Conditions and Stipulations.
[Witness clause optional]

BLANK TITLE INSURANCE COMPANY

BY: _____
PRESIDENT

BY: _____
SECRETARY

Exclusions from Coverage

The following matters are expressly excluded from the coverage of this policy and the Company will not pay loss or damage, costs, attorneys' fees or expenses which arise by reason of:

1. (a) Any law, ordinance or governmental regulation (including but not limited to building and zoning laws, ordinances, or regulations) restricting, regulating, prohibiting or relating to (i) the occupancy, use, or enjoyment of the land; (ii) the character, dimensions or location of any improvement now or hereafter erected on the land; (iii) a separation in ownership or a change in the dimensions or area of the land or any parcel of which the land is or was a part; or (iv) environmental protection, or the effect of any violation of these laws, ordinancs or governmental regulations, except to the extent that a notice of the enforcement thereof or a notice of a defect, lien or encumbrance resulting from a violation or alleged violation affecting the land has been recorded in the public records at Date of Policy.
    (b) Any governmental police power not excluded by (a) above, except to the extent that a notice of the exercise thereof or a notice of a defect, lien or encumbrance resulting from a violation or alleged violation affecting the land has been recorded in the public records at Date of Policy.
2. Rights of eminent domain unless notice of the exercise thereof has been recorded in the public records at Date of Policy, but not excluding from coverage any taking which has occurred prior to Date of Policy which would be binding on the rights of a purchaser for value without knowledge.
3. Defects, liens, encumbrances, adverse claims or other matters:
    (a) created, suffered, assumed or agreed to by the insured claimant;
    (b) not known to the Company, not recorded in the public records at Date of Policy, but known to the insured claimant and not disclosed in writing to the Company by the insured claimant prior to the date the insured claimant became an insured under this policy;
    (c) resulting in no loss or damage to the insured claimant;
    (d) attaching or created subsequent to Date of Policy; or
    (e) resulting in loss or damage which would not have been sustained if the insured claimant had paid value for the estate or interest insured by this policy.

Schedule A

[File No.   ] Policy No.

Amount of Insurance $
[Premium $]

a.m.
Date of Policy _____ [at p.m.]

1. Name of Insured:

2. The estate or interest in land which is covered by this policy is:

3. Title to the estate or interest in the land is vested in:

[4. The land referred to in this policy is described as follows:]

If Paragraph 4 is omitted, a Schedule C, captioned the same as Paragraph 4, must be used.

Schedule B

[File No.   ] Policy No.

EXCEPTIONS FROM COVERAGE

This policy does not insure against loss or damage (and the Company will not pay costs, attorneys' fees or expenses) which arise by reason of:

1.

[POLICY MAY INCLUDE REGIONAL EXCEPTIONS IF SO

2. DESIRED BY ISSUING COMPANY]

[VARIABLE EXCEPTIONS SUCH AS TAXES, EASEMENTS,

CC & Rs, ETC.]

3.

4.

Conditions and Stipulations

1. DEFINITION OF TERMS.

The following terms when used in this policy mean:

(a) "insured": the insured named in Schedule A, and, subject to any rights or defenses the Company would have had against the named insured, those who succeed to the interest of the named insured by operation of law as distinguished from purchase including, but not limited to, heirs, distributees, devisees, survivors, personal representatives, next of kin, or corporate or fiduciary successors.

(b) "insured claimant": an insured claiming loss or damage.

(c) "knowledge" or "known": actual knowledge, not constructive knowledge or notice which may be imputed to an insured by reason of the public records as defined in this policy or any other records which impart constructive notice of matters affecting the land.

(d) "land": the land described or referred to in Schedule [A][C], and improvements affixed thereto which by law constitute real property. The term "land" does not include any property beyond the lines of the area described or referred to in Schedule [A][C], nor any right, title, interest, estate or easement in abutting streets, roads, avenues, alleys, lanes, ways or waterways, but nothing herein shall modify or limit the extent to which a right of access to and from the land is insured by this policy.

(e) "mortgage": mortgage, deed of trust, trust deed, or other security instrument.

(f) "public records": records established under state statutes at Date of Policy for the purpose of imparting constructive notice of matters relating to real property to purchasers for value and without knowledge. With respect to Section 1(a)(iv) of the Exclusions From Coverage, "public records" shall also include environmental protection liens filed in the records of the clerk of the United States district court for the district in which the land is located.

(g) "unmarketability of the title": an alleged or apparent matter affecting the title to the land, not excluded or excepted from coverage, which would entitle a purchaser of the estate or interest described in Schedule A to be released from the obligation to purchase by virtue of a contractual condition requiring the delivery of marketable title.

247

2. CONTINUATION OF INSURANCE AFTER CONVEYANCE OF TITLE.

The coverage of this policy shall continue in force as of Date of Policy in favor of an insured only so long as the insured retains an estate or interest in the land, or holds an indebtedness secured by a purchase money mortgage given by a purchaser from the insured, or only so long as the insured shall have liability by reason of covenants of warranty made by the insured in any transfer or conveyance of the estate or interest. This policy shall not continue in force in favor of any purchaser from the insured of either (i) an estate or interest in the land, or (ii) an indebtedness secured by a purchase money mortgage given to the insured.

3. NOTICE OF CLAIM TO BE GIVEN BY INSURED CLAIMANT.

The insured shall notify the Company promptly in writing (i) in case of any litigation as set forth in Section 4(a) below, (ii) in case knowledge shall come to an insured hereunder of any claim of title or interest which is adverse to the title to the estate or interest, as insured, and which might cause loss or damage for which the Company may be liable by virtue of this policy, or (iii) if title to the estate or interest, as insured, is rejected as unmarketable. If prompt notice shall not be given to the Company, then as to the insured all liability of the Company shall terminate with regard to the matter or matters for which prompt notice is required; provided, however, that failure to notify the Company shall in no case prejudice the rights of any insured under this policy unless the Company shall be prejudiced by the failure and then only to the extent of the prejudice.

4. DEFENSE AND PROSECUTION OF ACTIONS: DUTY OF INSURED CLAIMANT TO COOPERATE.

(a) Upon written request by the insured and subject to the options contained in Section 6 of these Conditions and Stipulations, the Company, at its own cost and without unreasonable delay, shall provide for the defense of an insured in litigation in which any third party asserts a claim adverse to the title or interest as insured, but only as to those stated causes of action alleging a defect, lien or encumbrance or other matter insured against by this policy. The Company shall have the right to select counsel of its choice (subject to the right of the insured to object for reasonable cause) to represent the insured as to those stated causes of action and shall not be liable for and will not pay the fees of any other counsel. The Company will not pay any fees, costs or expenses incurred by the insured in the defense of those causes of action which allege matters not insured against by this policy.

(b) The Company shall have the right, at its own cost, to institute and prosecute any action or proceeding or to do any other act which in its opinion may be necessary or desirable to establish the title to the estate or interest, as insured, or to prevent or reduce loss or damage to the insured. The Company may take any appropriate action under the terms of this policy, whether or not it shall be liable hereunder, and shall not thereby concede liability or waive any provision of this policy. If the Company shall exercise its right under this paragraph, it shall do so diligently.

(c) Whenever the Company shall have brought an action or interposed a defense as required or permitted by the provisions of this policy, the Company may pursue any litigation to final determination by a court of competent juridiction and expressly reserves the right, in its sole discretion, to appeal from any adverse judgment or order.

(d) In all cases where this policy permits or requires the Company to prosecute or provide for the defense of any action or proceeding, the insured shall secure to the Company the right to so prosecute or provide defense in the action or proceeding, and all appeals therein, and permit the Company to use, at its option, the name of the insured for this purpose. Whenever requested by the Company, the insured, at the Company's expense, shall give the Company all reasonable aid (i) in any action or proceeding, securing evidence, obtaining witnesses, prosecuting or defending the action or proceeding, or effecting settlement, and (ii) in any other lawful act which in the opinion of the Company may be necessary or desirable to establish the title to the estate or interest as insured. If the Company is prejudiced by the failure of the insured to furnish the required cooperation, the Company's obligations to the insured under the policy shall terminate, including any liability or obligation to defend, prosecute, or continue any litigation, with regard to the matter or matters requiring such cooperation.

5.   PROOF OF LOSS OR DAMAGE.

In addition to and after the notices required under Section 3 of these Conditions and Stipulations have been provided the Company, a proof of loss or Damage signed and sworn to by the insured claimant shall be furnished to the Company within 90 days after the insured claimant shall ascertain the facts giving rise to the loss or damage. The proof of loss or damage shall describe the defect in, or lien or encumbrance on the title, or other matter insured against by this policy which constitutes the basis of loss or damage and shall state, to the extent possible, the basis of calculating the amount of the loss or damage. If the Company is prejudiced by the failure of the insured claimant to provide the required proof of loss or damage, the Company's obligations to the insured under the policy shall terminate, including any liability or obligation to defend, prosecute, or continue any litigation, with regard to the matter or matters requiring such proof of loss or damage.

In addition, the insured claimant may reasonably be required to submit to examination under oath by any authorized representative of the Company and shall produce for examination, inspection and copying, at such reasonable times and places as may be designated by any authorized representative of the Company, all records, books, ledgers, checks, correspondence and memoranda, whether bearing a date before or after Date of Policy, which reasonably pertain to the loss or damage. Further, if requested by any authorized representative of the Company, the insured claimant shall grant its permission, in writing, for any authorized representative of the Company to examine, inspect and copy all records, books, ledgers, checks, correspondence and memoranda in the custody or control of a third party, which reasonably pertain to the loss or damage. All information designated as confidential by the insured claimant provided to the Company pursuant to this Section shall not be disclosed to others unless, in the reasonable judgment of the Company, it is necessary in the administration of the claim. Failure of the insured claimant to submit for examination under oath, produce other reasonably requested information or grant permission to secure reasonably necessary information from third parties as required in this paragraph shall terminate any liability of the Company under this policy as to that claim.

6.   OPTIONS TO PAY OR OTHERWISE SETTLE CLAIMS: TERMINATION OF LIABILITY.

In case of a claim under this policy, the Company shall have the following additional options:

(a)   *To Pay or Tender Payment of the Amount of Insurance.*
To pay or tender payment of the amount of insurance under this policy together with any costs, attorneys' fees and expenses incurred by the insured claimant, which were authorized by the Company, up to the time of payment or tender of payment and which the Company is obligated to pay.

Upon the exercise by the Company of this option, all liability and obligations to the insured under this policy, other than to make the payment required, shall terminate, including any liability or obligation to defend, prosecute, or continue any litigation, and the policy shall be surrendered to the Company for cancellation.

(b) *To Pay or Otherwise Settle With Parties Other than the Insured or With the Insured Claimant.*

(i) to pay or otherwise settle with other parties for or in the name of an insured claimant any claim insured against under this policy, together with any costs, attorneys' fees and expenses incurred by the insured claimant which were authorized by the Company up to the time of payment and which the Company is obligated to pay; or

(ii) to pay or otherwise settle with the insured claimant the loss or damage provided for under this policy, together with any costs, attorneys' fees and expenses incurred by the insured claimant which were authorized by the Company up to the time of payment and which the Company is obligated to pay.

Upon the exercise by the Company of either of the options provided for in paragraphs (b)(1) or (ii), the Company's obligations to the insured under this policy for the claimed loss or damage, other than the payments required to be made, shall terminate, including any liability or obligation to defend, prosecute or continue any litigation.

7. DETERMINATION, EXTENT OF LIABILITY AND COINSURANCE.

This policy is a contract of indemnity against actual monetary loss or damage sustained or incurred by the insured claimant who has suffered loss or damage by reason of matters insured against by this policy and only to the extent herein described.

(a) The liability of the Company under this policy shall not exceed the least of:

(i) the Amount of Insurance stated in Schedule A; or,

(ii) the difference between the value of the insured estate or interest as insured and the value of the insured estate or interest subject to the defect, lien or encumbrance insured against by this policy.

(b) In the event the Amount of Insurance stated in Schedule A at the Date of Policy is less than 80 percent of the value of the insured estate or interest or the full consideration paid for the land, whichever is less, or if subsequent to the Date of Policy an improvement is erected on the land which increases the value of the insured estate or interest by at least 20 percent over the Amount of Insurance stated in Schedule A, then this Policy is subject to the following:

(i) where no subsequent improvement has been made, as to any partial loss, the Company shall only pay the loss pro rata in the proportion that the amount of insurance at Date of Policy bears to the total value of the insured estate or interest at Date of Policy; or

(ii) where a subsequent improvement has been made, as to any partial loss, the Company shall only pay the loss pro rata in the proportion that 120 percent of the Amount of Insurance stated in Schedule A bears to the sum of the Amount of Insurance stated in Schedule A and the amount expended for the improvement.

The provisions of this paragraph shall not apply to costs, attorneys' fees and expenses for which the Company is liable under this policy, and shall only apply to that portion of any loss which exceeds, in the aggregate, 10 percent of the Amount of Insurance stated in Schedule A.

(c) The Company will pay only those costs, attorneys' fees and expenses incurred in accordance with Section 4 of these Conditions and Stipulations. . . .

9. LIMITATION OF LIABILITY.

(a) If the Company establishes the title, or removes the alleged defect, lien or encumbrance, or cures the lack of a right of access to or from the land, or cures the claim of unmarketability of title, all as insured, in a reasonably diligent manner by any method, including litigation and the completion of any appeals therefrom, it shall have fully performed its obligations with respect to that matter and shall not be liable for any loss or damage caused thereby.

(b) In the event of any litigation, including litigation by the Company or with the Company's consent, the Company shall have no liability for loss or damage until there has been a final determination by a court of competent jurisdiction, and disposition of all appeals therefrom, adverse to the title as insured.

(c) The Company shall not be liable for loss or damage to any insured for liability voluntarily assumed by the insured in settling any claim or suit without the prior written consent of the Company.

10. REDUCTION OF INSURANCE; REDUCTION OR TERMINATION OF LIABILITY.

All payments under this policy, except payments made for costs, attorneys' fees and expenses, shall reduce the amount of the insurance pro tanto.

11. LIABILITY NONCUMULATIVE.

It is expressly understood that the amount of insurance under this policy shall be reduced by any amount the Company may pay under any policy insuring a mortgage to which exception is taken in Schedule B or to which the insured has agreed, assumed, or taken subject, or which is hereafter executed by an insured and which is a charge or lien on the estate or interest described or referred to in Schedule A, and the amount so paid shall be deemed a payment under this policy to the insured owner. . . .

13.   SUBROGATION UPON PAYMENT OR SETTLEMENT.

(a) *The Company's Right of Subrogation.*
Whenever the Company shall have settled and paid a claim under this policy, all right of subrogation shall vest in the Company unaffected by any act of the insured claimant.

The Company shall be subrogated to and be entitled to all rights and remedies which the insured claimant would have had against any person or property in respect to the claim had this policy not been issued. If requested by the Company, the insured claimant shall transfer to the Company all rights and remedies against any person or property necessary in order to perfect this right of subrogation. The insured claimant shall permit the Company to sue, compromise or settle in the name of the insured claimant and to use the name of the insured claimant in any transaction or litigation involving these rights or remedies.

If a payment on account of a claim does not fully cover the loss of the insured claimant, the Company shall be subrogated to these rights and remedies in the proportion which the Company's payment bears to the whole amount of the loss.

If loss should result from any act of the insured claimant, as stated above, that act shall not void this policy, but the Company, in that event, shall be required to pay only that part of any losses insured against by this policy which shall exceed the amount, if any, lost to the Company by reason of the impairment by the insured claimant of the Company's right of subrogation.

(b) *The Company's Rights Against Non-insured Obligors.*
The Company's right of subrogation against non-insured obligors shall exist and shall include, without limitation, the rights of the insured to indemnities, guaranties, other policies of insurance or bonds, notwithstanding any terms or conditions contained in those instruments which provide for subrogation rights by reason of this policy. . . .

In contrast to other forms of insurance (such as life or hazard insurance), title insurance is predicated more on risk-prevention (based on prior events) than risk-assumption (based on future events). Based on a careful examination of the public records (and perhaps the insured premises as well), the title company purports to do nothing more than assure the owner or mortgagee, as the case may be, that the title is marketable and not subject to any defects, liens, or encumbrances (other than those designated as exceptions) as of the date the policy is issued. This is the date on which the title examination ceases, normally when the deed to the purchaser is recorded or, in the case of the Loan Policy, the date on which the mortgage is recorded. Therefore, the policy will not cover charges that do not accrue against the property until after the policy is issued. This makes sense; how could the title examiner be expected to discover defects or liens that don't come into existence until after the title examination is completed? But suppose the defect or lien is inchoate; that is, the charge against the property is based on *prior* public events but does not come to fruition until after the policy is issued. Should the title company be responsible? This is the question confronting the court in the following case.

Metropolitan Life Insurance Co. v. Union Trust Co.
283 N.Y. 33, 27 N.E.2d 225 (1940)

Action by the Metropolitan Life Insurance Company against the Union Trust Company of Rochester and the Abstract Title & Mortgage Corporation for breach of provisions in title insurance policies issued by defendants. From a judgment of the Appellate Division, 257 App. Div. 906, 12 N.Y.S.2d 1010, affirming a judgment for defendant title company, 168 Misc. 657, 6 N.Y.S.2d 410, on an order of the Special Term granting such defendant's motion to dismiss the complaint as to it on the merits, plaintiff appeals by permission after denial of appeal in the Appellate Division, 257 App. Div. 1044, 14 N.Y.S.2d 492.

Affirmed.

CONWAY, Judge.

Plaintiff sues for a breach of provision in each of a number of policies of title insurance issued in September, 1929. After service of answer, defendant title company had summary judgment dismissing the complaint under rule 113 of the Rules of Civil Practice.

Taking the text of the policies in provision most favorable to plaintiff, they insured against "defects in, incumbrances upon or liens or charges against the title of the mortgagors or grantors to premises described in the mortgage or trust deed" existing at or prior to the date of the policy "and not excepted under Schedule 'B.'" This form of policy was suggested by plaintiff and the assessments hereafter referred to were not excepted. It is not claimed that these assessments were statutory liens at the time of the issuance of the policies but it is contended that they were charges and incumbrances within the meaning of those terms as used in the policies. The typical complaint alleges in paragraph Twelfth that the certificate and policy of insurance of defendant title company "did not state or mention that future assessments would be made against the said real estate on account of improvements already made which when made would become prior liens" to the mortgage purchased by plaintiff and that it was defendant's duty under its contract to do so.

The assessments came into being because of local improvements such as sewers, pavements and sidewalks, which had been constructed, under applicable statutes, in suburban property in certain towns in Monroe county outside the city of Rochester. The improvements had been completed one or two years prior to the issuance of the policies and paid for through bond issues of the several towns. The bonds were to be paid by annual assessments to be levied upon the individual properties benefited. The parties in their briefs have selected chapter 549 of the Laws of 1926 as the statute principally involved. The other statutes are substantially similar.

Taking as an example the town of Brighton, the minutes of the Town Board showed that on June 9, 1928, there was considered the question of the apportionment of the cost of certain street improvements which had theretofore been made; that a proposed assessment roll, apportioning the expenses of the improvements upon the property benefited, having been prepared and submitted, was approved, and a date for the hearing of objections to the said roll was set and the Town Clerk ordered to give the notices required by law; that on June 25, 1928, the Board met for the purpose of hearing objections to said roll, and none having been made the roll and the apportionment therein made on the several lots was finally approved and adopted and the tax therein provided assessed.

Under chapter 549 of the Laws of 1926 the only power to levy assessments is found in section 11. It reads: "The town board shall thereafter in each year, and before the annual meeting for that year of the board of supervisors of the county in which such town is situated, report to said board of supervisors, the amount of such bonds, which will mature within the ensuing year; and the amount of interest payable within said ensuing year; and a statement of the lots or parcels of land liable to pay the same, and the amount chargeable to each. The board of supervisors shall levy such amounts against the property liable, and shall state the amount of the assessment in a separate column, in the annual tax roll, under the name 'street improvement'; and such assessment when collected shall be paid to the supervisor, and be by him applied in payment of the principal and interest of said bonds. The amount annually apportioned by the town board, as provided in this section, on any lot or parcel, and included in the annual tax roll by said board of supervisors, shall be a lien prior and superior to any lien or claim except the lien of an existing tax or local assessment."

The power of apportionment and assessment was conferred on the Town Board by section 9 of chapter 549 and permission granted a property owner to pay in full based upon such assessment, but there could be no levy and no lien until there was annual report by the Town Board of the amount of bonds maturing during the ensuing year, with the amount of interest payable for the same period, followed by annual apportionment by the Town Board upon the lots and parcels liable therefor and inclusion in the annual tax roll by the Board of Supervisors of the county.

It is clear that there was no lien at the time of the issuance of the policies. The question remains, Was there a charge or incumbrance? If we consider the insurance contract as analogous to a covenant against incumbrances, it is evident that in this State the word charges is used synonymously with liens and incumbrances. It has no larger meaning. In the Real Property Law (Consol. Laws, ch. 50, §253) it is provided:

> 3. *Freedom from incumbrances* — A covenant 'that the said premises are free from incumbrances,' must be construed as meaning that such premises are free, clear, discharged and unincumbered of and from all former and other gifts, grants, titles, charges, estates, judgments, taxes, assessments liens and incumbrances, of what nature or kind soever.

In Doonan v. Killilea, 222 N.Y. 399, 401, 118 N.E. 851, 852, it was said that section 253 of the Real Property Law had reference "not to inchoate assessments or other charges, but to legal liens fully matured. The covenant against incumbrances operates in præsenti and is broken the instant it is made, if an incumbrance exists; but, unless the assessment is then an actual lien, the covenant is not broken."

The case of Mayers v. Van Schaick, 268 N.Y. 320, 197 N.E. 296, is controlling here. It is stronger against plaintiff than is the instant case, since the word used there was "requirements." There Judge Loughran said: "Title insurance operates to protect a purchaser or a mortgagee against defects in or incumbrances on a title existing at the date of such insurance. It is not prospective in its operation and has no relation to liens or requirements arising thereafter. Trenton Potteries Co. v. Title Guarantee & Trust Co., 176 N.Y. 65, 72, 68 N.E. 132. . . . It follows, we think, that Lawyers Title & Guarantee Company no more agreed with plaintiff to protect him against liability for the unpaid assessment in question than it undertook to indemnify him for taxes to be levied against the premises after delivery of its certificate of title insurance." 268 N.Y. at pages 323, 324, 197 N.E. at page 297. . . .

The judgment should be affirmed with costs.

LEHMAN, C.J., and LOUGHRAN, FINCH, and RIPPEY, JJ., concur.

SEARS and LEWIS, JJ., taking no part.

Judgment affirmed.

The recent proliferation of land claims by American Indians demonstrates both the importance and the limitations of title insurance as a title protection device. Were the Indians to win their cases and divest present owners of title to their property, the insuring title companies would sustain countless losses. The title industry clearly would not have the assets to fund even a fraction of this potential liability. Perhaps this is why property owners in areas affected by these claims have seen a precipitous drop in the value of their property. The following case tells the story of how these ancient claims may be finally coming to fruition.

County of Oneida v. Oneida Indian Nation
470 U.S. 226 (1985)

JUSTICE POWELL delivered the opinion of the Court.

These cases present the question whether three Tribes of the Oneida Indians may bring a suit for damages for the occupation and use of tribal land allegedly conveyed unlawfully in 1795.

I

The Oneida Indian Nation of New York, the Oneida Indian Nation of Wisconsin, and the Oneida of the Thames Band Council (the Oneidas) instituted this suit in 1970 against the Counties of Oneida and Madison, New York. The Oneidas alleged that their ancestors conveyed 100,000 acres to the State of New York under a 1795 agreement that violated the Trade and Intercourse Act of 1793, 1 Stat. 329, and thus that the transaction was void. The Oneidas' complaint sought damages representing the fair rental value of that part of the land presently owned and occupied by the Counties of Oneida and Madison, for the period January 1, 1968, through December 31, 1969. . . .

The respondents in these cases are the direct descendants of members of the Oneida Indian Nation, one of the six nations of the Iroquois, the most powerful Indian Tribe in the Northeast at the time of the American Revolution. See B. Graymont, The Iroquois in the American Revolution (1972) (hereinafter Graymont). From time immemorial to shortly after the Revolution, the Oneidas inhabited what is now central New York State. Their aboriginal land was approximately six million acres, extending from the Pennsylvania border to the St. Lawrence River, from the shores of Lake Ontario to the western foothills of the Adirondack Mountains.

See 434 F. Supp., at 533.

Although most of the Iroquois sided with the British, the Oneidas actively supported the colonists in the Revolution. Ibid.; see also Graymont, supra. This assistance prevented the Iroquois from asserting a united effort against the colonists, and thus the Oneidas' support was of considerable aid. After the War, the United States recognized the importance of the Oneidas' role, and in the Treaty of Fort Stanwix, 7 Stat. 15 (Oct. 22, 1784), the National Government promised that the Oneidas would be secure "in the possession of the lands on which they are settled." Within a short period of time, the United States twice reaffirmed this promise, in the Treaties at Fort Harmar, 7 Stat. 33 (Jan. 9, 1789), and of Canandaigua, 7 Stat. 44 (Nov. 11, 1794).

During this period, the State of New York came under increasingly heavy pressure to open the Oneidas' land for settlement. Consequently, in 1788, the State entered into a "treaty" with the Indians, in which it purchased the vast majority of the Oneidas' land. The Oneidas retained a reservation of about 300,000 acres, an area that, the parties stipulated below, included the land involved in this suit.

In 1790, at the urging of President Washington and Secretary of War Knox, Congress passed the first Indian Trade and Nonintercourse Act, ch. 33, 1 Stat. 137. See American State Papers, 1 Indian Affairs 53 (1832); F. Prucha, American Indian Policy in the Formative Years 43-44 (1962). The Act prohibited the conveyance of Indian land except where such conveyances were entered pursuant to the treaty power of the United States. In 1793, Congress passed a stronger, more detailed version of the Act, providing that "no purchase or grant of lands, or of any title or claim thereto, from any Indians or nation or tribe of Indians, within the bounds of the United States, shall be of any validity in law or equity, unless the same be made by a treaty or convention entered into pursuant to the constitution . . . [and] in the presence, and with the approbation of the commissioner or commissioners of the United States" appointed to supervise such transactions. 1 Stat. 330, §8. Unlike the 1790 version, the new statute included criminal penalties for violation of its terms. Ibid.

Despite Congress' clear policy that no person or entity should purchase Indian land without the acquiescence of the Federal Government, in 1795 the State of New York began negotiations to buy the remainder of the Oneidas' land. When this fact came to the attention of Secretary of War Pickering, he warned Governor Clinton and later Governor Jay, that New York was required by the Nonintercourse Act to request the appointment of federal commissioners to supervise any land transaction with the Oneidas. See 434 F. Supp., at 534-535. The State ignored these warnings, and in the summer of 1795 entered into an agreement with the Oneidas whereby they conveyed virtually all of their remaining land to the State for annual cash payments. Ibid. It is this transaction that is the basis of the Oneidas' complaint in this case.

The District Court found that the 1795 conveyance did not comply with the requirements of the Nonintercourse Act. Id., at 538-541. In particular, the court stated that "[t]he only finding permitted by the record . . . is that no United States Commissioner or other official of the federal government was present at the . . . transaction." Id., at 535. The petitioners did not dispute this finding on appeal. Rather, they argued that the Oneidas did not have a federal commonlaw cause of action for this violation. Even if such an action once existed, they contended that the Nonintercourse Act pre-empted it, and that the Oneidas could not maintain a private cause of action for violations of the Act. Additionally, they maintained that any such cause of action was time-barred or nonjusticiable, that any cause of action under the 1793 Act had abated, and that the United States had ratified the conveyance. The Court of Appeals, with one judge dissenting, rejected these arguments. Petitioners renew these claims here; we also reject them and affirm the court's finding of liability.

III

At the outset, we are faced with petitioners' contention that the Oneidas have no right of action for the violation of the 1793 Act. Both the District Court and the Court of Appeals rejected this claim, finding that the Oneidas had the right to sue on two theories: first, a common-law right of action for unlawful possession; and second, an implied statutory cause of action under the Nonintercourse Act of 1793. We need not reach the latter question as we think the Indians' common-law right to sue is firmly established.

A. FEDERAL COMMON LAW

By the time of the Revolutionary War, several well-defined principles had been established governing the nature of a tribe's interest in its property and how those interests could be conveyed. It was accepted that Indian nations held "aboriginal title" to lands they had inhabited from time immemorial. See Cohen, Original Indian Title, 32 Minn. L. Rev. 28 (1947). The "doctrine of discovery" provided, however, that discovering nations held fee title to these lands, subject to the Indians' right of occupancy and use. As a consequence, no one could purchase Indian land or otherwise terminate aboriginal title without the consent of the sovereign. *Oneida I,* 414 U.S., at 667. See Clinton & Hotopp, Judicial Enforcement of the Federal Restraints on Alienation of Indian Land: The Origins of the Eastern Land Claims, 31 Me. L. Rev. 17, 19-49 (1979).

With the adoption of the Constitution, Indian relations became the exclusive province of federal law. *Oneida I,* supra, at 670 (citing Worcester v. Georgia, 6 Pet. 515, 561 (1832)). From the first Indian claims presented, this Court recognized the aboriginal rights of the Indians to their lands. The Court spoke of the "unquestioned right" of the Indians to the exclusive possession of their lands, Cherokee Nation v. Georgia, 5 Pet. 1, 17 (1831), and stated that the Indians' right of occupancy is "as sacred as the fee simple of the whites." Mitchel v. United States, 9 Pet. 711, 746 (1835). This principle has been reaffirmed consistently. . . .

Numerous decisions of this Court prior to *Oneida I* recognized at least implicitly that Indians have a federal common-law right to sue to enforce their aboriginal land rights. In Johnson v. M'Intosh, supra, the Court declared invalid two private purchases of Indian land that occurred in 1773 and 1775 without the Crown's consent. Subsequently in Marsh v. Brooks, 8 How. 223, 232 (1850), it was held: "That an action of ejectment could be maintained on an Indian right to occupancy and use, is not open to question. This is the result of the decision in Johnson v. McIntosh." More recently, the Court held that Indians have a common-law right of action for an accounting of "all rents, issues and profits" against trespassers on their land. United States v. Santa Fe Pacific R. Co., 314 U.S. 339 (1941). Finally, the Court's opinion in *Oneida I* implicitly assumed that the Oneidas could bring a common-law action to vindicate their aboriginal rights. Citing United States v. Santa Fe Pacific R. Co., supra, at 347, we noted that the Indians' right of occupancy need not be based on treaty, statute, or other formal Government action. 414 U.S., at 668-669. We stated that "absent federal statutory guidance, the governing rule of decision would be fashioned by the federal court in the mode of the common law." Id., at 674 (citing United States v. Forness, 125 F.2d 928 (CA2), cert. denied sub nom. City of Salamanca v. United States, 316 U.S. 694 (1942)).

In keeping with these well-established principles, we hold that the Oneidas can maintain this action for violation of their possessory rights based on federal common law.

B.   PRE-EMPTION

Petitioners argue that the Nonintercourse Acts pre-empted whatever right of action the Oneidas may have had at common law, relying on our decisions in Milwaukee v. Illinois, 451 U.S. 304 (1981) (*Milwaukee II*), and Middlesex County Sewerage Authority v. National Sea Clammers Assn., 453 U.S. 1 (1981). We find this view to be unpersuasive. In determining whether a federal statute pre-empts common-law causes of action, the relevant inquiry is whether the statute "[speaks] *directly* to [the] question" otherwise answered by federal common law. *Milwaukee II,* supra, at 315 (emphasis added). As we stated in *Milwaukee II,* federal common law is used as a "necessary expedient" when Congress has not "spoken to a *particular* issue." Id., at 313-314 (emphasis added). The Nonintercourse Act of 1793 does not speak directly to the question of remedies for unlawful conveyances of Indian land. . . .

IV

Having determined that the Oneidas have a cause of action under federal common law, we address the question whether there are defenses available to the counties. We conclude that none has merit.

A.   STATUTE OF LIMITATIONS

There is no federal statute of limitations governing federal common-law actions by Indians to enforce property rights. In the absence of a controlling federal limitations period, the general rule is that a state limitations period for an analogous cause of action is borrowed and applied to the federal claim, provided that the application of the state statute would not be inconsistent with underlying federal policies. See Johnson v. Railway Express Agency, Inc., 421 U.S. 454, 465 (1975). See also Occidental Life Ins. Co. v. EEOC, 432 U.S. 355, 367 (1977). We think the borrowing of a state limitations period in these cases would be inconsistent with federal policy. Indeed, on a number of occasions Congress has made this clear with respect to Indian land claims. . . .

B.   LACHES

The dissent argues that we should apply the equitable doctrine of laches to hold that the Oneidas' claim is barred. Although it is far from clear that this defense is available in suits such as this one, we do not reach this issue today. While petitioners argued at trial that the Oneidas were guilty of laches, the District Court ruled against them and they did not reassert this defense on appeal. As a result, the

Court of Appeals did not rule on this claim and we likewise decline to do so.

C. ABATEMENT

Petitioners argue that any cause of action for violation of the Nonintercourse Act of 1793 abated when the statute expired. They note that Congress specifically provided that the 1793 Act would be in force "for the term of two years, and from thence to the end of the then next session of Congress, and no longer." 1 Stat. 332, §15. They contend that the 1796 version of the Nonintercourse Act repealed the 1793 version and enacted an entirely new statute, and that under the common-law abatement doctrine in effect at the time, any cause of action for violation of the statute finally abated on the expiration of the statute. We disagree.

The pertinent provision of the 1793 Act, §8, like its predecessor, §4 of the 1790 Act, 1 Stat. 138, merely codified the principle that a sovereign act was required to extinguish aboriginal title and thus that a conveyance without the sovereign's consent was void ab initio. See supra, at 6, and n. 3. All of the subsequent versions of the Nonintercourse Act, including that now in force, 25 U.S.C. §177, contain substantially the same restraint on the alienation of Indian lands. In these circumstances, the precedents of this Court compel the conclusion that the Oneidas' cause of action has not abated. . . .

D. RATIFICATION

We are similarly unpersuaded by petitioners' contention that the United States has ratified the unlawful 1795 conveyances. Petitioners base this argument on federally approved treaties in 1798 and 1802 in which the Oneidas ceded additional land to the State of New York. There is a question whether the 1802 treaty ever became effective. Assuming it did, neither the 1798 nor the 1802 treaty qualifies as federal ratification of the 1795 conveyance. . . .

E. NONJUSTICIABILITY

The claim also is made that the issue presented by the Oneidas' action is a nonjusticiable political question. The counties contend first that Art. 1, §8, cl. 3 of the Constitution explicitly commits responsibility for Indian affairs to Congress. Moreover, they argue that Congress has given exclusive civil remedial authority to the Executive for cases such as this one, citing the Nonintercourse Acts and the 1794 Treaty of Canandaigua. Thus, they say this case falls within the political question doctrine because of "a textually demonstrable constitutional commitment of the issue to a coordinate political department." Baker v. Carr, 369 U.S. 186, 217 (1962). Additionally, the counties argue that the question is nonjusticiable because there is "an unusual need for unquestioning adherence to a political decision already made." Ibid. None of these claims is meritorious.

This Court has held specifically that Congress' plenary power in Indian affairs under Art. 1, §8, cl. 3, does not mean that litigation involving such matters necessarily entails nonjusticiable political questions. Delaware Tribal Business Committee v. Weeks, 430 U.S. 73, 83-84 (1977). Accord, United States v. Sioux Nation, 448 U.S. 371, 413 (1980). See also Baker v. Carr, supra, at 215-217. If Congress' constitutional authority over Indian affairs does not render the Oneidas' claim nonjusticiable, a fortiori, Congress' delegation of authority to the President does not do so either.

VI

The decisions of this Court emphasize "Congress' unique obligation toward the Indians." Morton v. Mancari, 417 U.S. 535, 555 (1974). The Solicitor General, in an amicus curiae brief for the United States, urged the Court to affirm the Court of Appeals. Brief for United States as Amicus Curiae 28. The Solicitor General recognized, as we do, the potential consequences of affirmance. He observed, however, that "Congress has enacted legislation to extinguish Indian title and claims related thereto in other eastern States, . . . and it could be expected to do the same in New York should the occasion arise." Id., at 29-30. See Rhode Island Indian Claims Settlement Act, 25 U.S.C. §1701 et seq; Maine Indian Claims Settlement Act, 25 U.S.C. §1721 et seq. We agree that this litigation makes abundantly clear the necessity for congressional action.

One would have thought that claims dating back for more than a century and a half would have been barred long ago. As our opinion indicates, however, neither petitioners nor we have found any applicable statute of limitations or other relevant legal basis for holding that the Oneidas' claims are barred or otherwise have been satisfied. The judgment of the Court of Appeals is affirmed with respect to the finding of liability under federal common law, and reversed with respect to the exercise of ancillary jurisdiction over the counties' cross-claim for indemnification.

NOTES AND QUESTIONS

1. *Insuring Provisions of Title Policy.* The insuring provisions of the 1987 ALTA Owner's Policy ("owner's policy") and the 1987

ALTA Loan Policy ("mortgagee's policy") protect the owner or mort-gagee, as the case may be, against loss or damage sustained or incurred by reason of: "1) Title to the estate . . . being vested other than as stated therein [in Schedule A]; 2) Any defect in or lien or encumbrance on the title; 3) Unmarketability of the title; and 4) Lack of a right to access to and from the land."

In addition to the foregoing, the mortgagee's policy insures the mortgagee, whether it be a postconstruction lender or a construction lender, against the following contingencies:

5. The invalidity or unenforceability of the lien of the insured mortgage upon the title;

6. The priority of any lien or encumbrance over the lien of the insured mortgage;

7. Lack of priority of the lien of the insured mortgage over any statutory lien for services, labor or material:

(a) arising from an improvement or work related to the land which is contracted for or commenced prior to Date of Policy; or

(b) arising from an improvement or work related to the land which is contracted for or commenced subsequent to Date of Policy and which is financed in whole or in part by proceeds of the in-debtedness secured by the insured mortgage which at Date of Policy the insured has advanced or is obligated to advance;

8. The invalidity or unenforceability of any assignment of the insured mortgage, provided the assignment is shown in Schedule A, or the failure of the assignment shown in Schedule A to vest title to the insured mortgage in the named insured assignee free and clear of all liens.

Insuring Provision 1 essentially assures the owner or mortgagee that title to the property is vested in the individual or entity described in Schedule A so that, for example, the title company would be liable if the property purchased by Dan Developer were vested in Danielle Developer or if Dan's interest turned out to be a mere life estate even though it is designated as a fee simple interest in Schedule A.

Insuring Provision 2 is a vital provision inasmuch as it protects the insured against any loss or damage sustained as a consequence of any defect, lien, or encumbrance that is not excepted under Schedule B or excluded from coverage by means of a boiler-plate exclusion, condition, or stipulation.

Insuring Provision 3 assures the owner that if it should enter into a contract of sale with a purchaser the title to the insured property (as described in Schedule A) will be "marketable" (subject to the exceptions enumerated in Schedule B), as the term is indirectly defined in Section 1(g) of the Conditions and Stipulations.

In some states such as Oregon the ALTA form of policy does not insure against unmarketability unless the insured is willing to pay an extra premium. But why is this so? Based on the definition of marketable title, discussed at Chapter 3A, note 2, supra, why would Insuring Provision 3 provide additional protection to the insured? If title were "unmarketable" because of a defect that existed as of the date of the title policy, doesn't this mean that the title must be vested otherwise than as described in Schedule A (Insuring Provision 1)? Or, in the alternative, doesn't this mean that there must be a defect in or lien or encumbrance on such title (Insuring Provision 2)?

In regard to the question posed above, consider the following hypothetical. A purchaser, Dan Developer, obtains a title insurance policy that does not contain Insuring Provision 3 from Worthier Title Company (Worthier). Five years later he contracts to sell the property to Irma Investor. Shortly before the closing, an adjoining owner claims the rear 10 feet of Dan's property based on a 12-year-old deed recorded by the previous owner that was not mentioned in Dan's title policy. Dan's contract of sale purports to convey the entire property, including the rear 10 feet in question. The title company defends on the ground that Dan acquired title by adverse possession (i.e., that Dan had occupied the 10 feet openly, continuously, notoriously, and adversely for the period of applicable statute of limitations for actions by way of ejectment); hence, the neighbor was barred from contesting Dan's title. The neighbor disputes this defense, claiming that Dan had never occupied the rear 10 feet, and the matter goes to litigation. Meanwhile, Irma, searching for a way to extricate herself from the contract, successfully maintains that the neighbor's claim constitutes a cloud on the title, rendering it unmarketable, and Irma is released from the contract. One year later the neighbor's claim is held to be invalid by the courts. Dan, however, can not find another buyer. Would Worthier Title be liable? See Hilliker v. Rueger, 228 N.Y. 11, 126 N.E. 266 (1920). Suppose Dan's policy included Insuring Provision 3 and Dan is not able to find another buyer who is willing to pay what Irma had offered. Would Worthier Title Co. be liable for Dan's loss of the bargain? (See Montemarano v. Home Title Insurance Co., 258 N.Y. 478, 180 N.E. 241 (1932).) If so, is §9 of the Conditions and Stipulations in conflict with Insuring Provision 3?

Suppose instead that the neighbor's claim is held to be a cloud on the title but that Dan nevertheless is able to convince Worthier Title Co. to insure the title against loss or damage from the alleged defect. Should Irma be compelled to take title? If not, why not? See Nebo, Inc. v. Transamerica Title Insurance Co., 21 Cal. App. 3d 222, 98 Cal. Rptr. 237 (1971).

Insuring Provision 4 provides coverage against "lack of right of access to and from the land." What does this mean? Would this provision be complied with if the only access were by helicopter? By footpath? By a road that leads to a dead end? Observe that this provision only relates to "legal" access and does not ensure the physical nature and extent of the access. The limitations of this insuring clause point out the importance of a current survey and the need for the buyer's attorney to review the survey carefully.

Insuring Provision 6 is designed to assure the mortgagee that its mortgage lien will have lien priority over any competing interest in the property as of the date on which the policy is issued. This competition for lien priority may determine whether a mortgage or other interest in the mortgaged property will survive or expire in the event of a foreclosure action. This topic is discussed at Chapter 4C. Under Insuring Provision 7(a) postconstruction lenders are protected against statutory liens (such as mechanics' liens) that are based on prior construction activities that may not accrue as liens against the property until after the building is completed and the title policy is issued. By contrast, construction lenders are afforded similar protection against mechanics' liens under Insuring Provision 7(b) that are based on future construction activities. Alternatively, to obtain coverage against mechanics' liens it may be necessary for a construction lender to obtain the 1987 ALTA Construction Loan Policy (examined at Chapter 6B3, note 6), whereby endorsements would be added to take into account local law variations.

Finally, observe that the title company will also pay all attorneys' fees and other litigation expenses regardless of whether such expenses exceed the coverage face amount of the policy.

2. Exclusions from Coverage. As observed earlier, the insuring provisions are made subject to the exclusions from coverage, the exceptions, and the conditions and stipulations in the policy. The first three exclusions are essentially the same for both the owner's and mortgagee's policies, except that the following parenthetical is added at the end of Exclusion 3(d) in the mortgagee's policy: "(except to the extent that this policy insures the priority of the lien of the insured mortgage over any statutory lien for services, labor or material)." The mortgagee's policy contains the following additional exclusions:

4. Unenforceability of the lien of the insured mortgage because of the inability or failure of the insured at Date of Policy, or the inability or failure of any subsequent owner of the indebtedness, to comply with applicable doing business laws of the state in which the land is situated.
5. Invalidity or unenforceability of the lien of the insured mortgage, or claim thereof, which arises out of the transaction evidenced by the insured mortgage and is based upon usury or any consumer credit protection or truth in lending law.
6. Any statutory lien for services, labor or materials (or the claim of priority of any statutory lien for services, labor or materials over the lien of the insured mortgage) arising from an improvement or work

related to the land which is contracted for and commenced subsequent to Date of Policy and is not financed in whole or in part by proceeds of the indebtedness secured by the insured mortgage which at Date of Policy the insured has advanced or is obligated to advance.

Finally, in May 1990 the ALTA endorsed a new exclusion for the mortgagee's policy that has not yet been adopted in most jurisdictions (including New York) pending its approval by state regulatory authorities. The new exclusion applies to "any claim which arises out of the transaction creating the interest . . . insured by this policy by reason of the operation of Federal Bankruptcy, state insolvency or similar creditor's rights laws." The impact of this exclusion on bankruptcy matters is explained at Chapter 10C5, note 8.

a. Exclusions 1 and 2 generally eliminate from coverage the effect of laws, ordinances, governmental regulations, and exercise of police power or the power of eminent domain, except to the extent that notice of the defect, lien, or encumbrance or the exercise of police power or eminent domain is recorded in the public records at the date of the policy. To understand what is meant by the phrase "public records," see definition 1(f) in the Conditions and Stipulations, which limits public records to records established under state statutes for the purpose of imparting constructive notice to bona fide purchasers. Is a county clerk's office, established by the county pursuant to a state enabling statute, a public record? Do you think the title company could successfully maintain that it is not?

Consider whether a title company would be liable in the following situations:

i. It is determined that Dan Developer's use of the property is unlawful under the zoning law.

ii. Assume that the State of Fuller has adopted an environmental cleanup statute that granted a lien to the applicable governmental agency for the cost of cleaning up hazardous waste. Further assume that Dan Developer acquired property and obtained a title policy that contained no exception in Schedule B for a hazardous waste lien. Finally, assume that Ace Insurance Company held a mortgage on the property and that it had obtained a mortgagee's policy from Worthier Title Company, which had no exception in its Schedule B for a hazardous waste lien. To what extent will the title company be liable in the following situations and, if it is not liable, on what provisions of the title policy will it be relying?

— Three years before Dan acquired the property, the state had cleaned up a spill and had obtained a lien against the property that was filed in the Office of Environmental Protection of the State of Fuller.

— Assume the same facts as above, except that the lien was

filed pursuant to the state environmental law in the Office of the County Clerk for the County of Feerick, where the property was located.

— After the mortgage had been recorded, and prior to foreclosure, the state cleaned up a spill and obtained a lien against the property that was filed pursuant to the state environmental law in the Office of the County Clerk for the County of Feerick, where the property was located.

— After the mortgage was recorded, the state cleaned up a spill and obtained a lien against the property that was not filed prior to foreclosure. On foreclosure, Ace's mortgagee policy insured Ace as fee owner as provided in the Conditions and Stipulations of the ALTA Loan Policy. In addition, Ace obtained a new title policy insuring its fee interest that did not contain an exception in Schedule B for a hazardous waste lien. One month after foreclosure, the hazardous waste lien was filed in the Office of the County Clerk for the County of Feerick, where the property was located.

The so-called Superfund statutes, which impose liens for cleanup costs, and other environmental protection legislation are discussed at Chapter 12B.

b. The third exclusion covers five different situations. Exclusions 3(a) and (e) are fairly obvious. Do you understand why the title company is justified in imposing these limitations on coverage? Based on your understanding of the recording statute system, can you think of the probable rationale for Exclusion 3(e)?

Exclusion 3(c) eliminates any liability for the insurer where the defect, lien, or encumbrance does not result in any loss or damage to the insured claimant. Moreover, Condition 7(a)(ii) of the owner's policy stipulates that the liability of the title company may not exceed the diminution in value of the insured property caused by the defect encumbrance. But how is loss or damage to the insured to be measured? Assume, for example, that Dan Developer purchases three acres of raw land at a price of $4,000 per acre and that Dan obtains an owner's policy with a face amount of $12,000. In the case of an owner's policy the amount of insurance coverage is usually the purchase price paid for the land plus the cost of any improvements on the land. Further assume that 10 years later, when the land is worth $6,000 per acre, an adverse claimant establishes superior ("paramount") title to one of the three acres (by means of a bill to quiet title) based on a record defect in Dan's chain of title. To use the phraseology of the owner's policy, what is the amount of the "loss or damage" not exceeding the amount of insurance ($12,000) "sustained or incurred" by Dan? The title company might contend that title insurance operates to protect a purchaser or a mortgagee against defects or encumbrances on the title *as of the date of the policy* and that therefore the policy is retroactive rather than prospective in its operation (as postulated by Judge Conway in the *Metropolitan Life Insurance Co.* case). If this is the case, then how can there be a loss sustained by Dan when the value of the untainted portion of his property (2 acres at $6,000 per acre) has not been reduced below its original purchase price? Even if a loss were sustained by Dan, since the policy necessarily looks to the past and not the future, the diminution in value caused by the defect arguably should be measured as of the date of the policy (at $4,000) rather than the time of its discovery (at $6,000). As counsel to Dan, what would be your counterargument in favor of the $6,000 damage amount? Compare Beaullieu v. Atlanta Title & Trust Co., 60 Ga. App. 400, 4 S.E.2d 78 (1939) with Overholtzer v. Northern Counties Title Insurance Co., 116 Cal. App. 2d 113, 253 P.2d 116 (1953). See Note, The Insured's Rights Against the Title Insurer, 6 Case W. Res. L. Rev. 49 (1954). Or, in the case of a mortgagee's title policy, suppose an insured mortgagee discovers a prior lien on the mortgaged property that was not designated as an approved exception in Schedule B. If perchance the mortgaged property were to double or triple in value after the issuance of the policy, should the mortgagee be able to recover against the title company by reason of its lack of lien priority even though the probable sale price at foreclosure would clearly exceed the sum of the two liens? If so, should the mortgagee be forestalled from any recovery until and unless it forecloses on its mortgage?

Exclusion 3(d) exculpates the title company for defects created or attaching after the date of the policy. Based on what you know of the mechanics of searching title (discussed at Chapter 3B1, note 2, supra), what is the probable rationale for this exclusion from the standpoint of a title insurer? Does it appear to strike a fair balance between the needs of the insured and the obligations of the insurer? In other words, does the title examination rationale justify the holding in *Metropolitan Life,* or does the holding in the case justify a change in the ordinary title search burden assumed by title companies? In what respect is the court's analogy to a covenant against encumbrances in a warranty deed inapposite? What is the argument for the proposition that even though the liens for street assessments in *Metropolitan Life* arose after the date of the policies (issued in September 1929), the affected properties nevertheless had at least been encumbered by the prospective assessments when they were approved by the Town Board on June 25, 1928? See Strass v. District-Realty Title Insurance Corp., 31 Md. App. 690, 358 A.2d 251 (1976); Annot., What Constitutes a Charge, Encumbrance or Lien Within Contemplation of Title Insurance Policy?, 87 A.L.R.3d 764 (1978). While the 1987 ALTA Loan Policy does not purport to cover inchoate liens of the street assessment variety, it arguably does. Can you spot the relevant language? Incidentally, a special endorsement for such assessments may be had for an extra premium in most states.

3. *Conditions and Stipulations.* The following questions and comments are designed to highlight some of the more important sections of the Conditions and Stipulations. While frequently ignored by practitioners, these "boilerplate" provisions may determine whether or under what circumstances the insured will be allowed a recovery against the title company.

a. *§1 of the Conditions and Stipulations.* Observe that "knowledge" (para. 1(c)) is defined as "actual knowledge" (as opposed to "constructive knowledge"). This is important in applying such provisions as paragraph 3(b) of the Exclusions from Coverage. Suppose, for example, that the insured party, Dan Developer, decides to purchase real estate that is apparently in the possession of someone other than the seller. In a jurisdiction that recognizes "inquiry notice" (discussed at Chapter 3B1, note 4, supra), would Dan have a claim against the title company if the party in possession, who paid value for the land but failed to record, should prevail against Dan in an action to quiet title?

Look at the definition of "land" in §1(d). Schedule A of the title policy describes the "land" covered by the policy. Would a description in Schedule A of the "land" that Dan owns in fee simple include an appurtenant easement over a neighbor's land? If not, what would you want to add to the description?

b. *Continuation of Insurance After Conveyance of Title (§2 of the Conditions and Stipulations).* Coverage continues under a title policy only as long as the insured retains an interest in the property. Suppose Dan conveys his property by means of a general warranty deed, and a defect is later discovered that predates Dan's purchase of the property and that had not been excepted in the deed description or in Schedule B of Dan's prior title policy. The purchaser then makes a claim against Dan under some covenant or warranty contained in the deed. Would Dan's prior title policy protect him? Suppose Dan sells the property and takes back a purchase money mortgage. Would his original fee policy protect him as mortgagee? If so, as of what date? Suppose that instead of selling the property to a third party Dan transfers title as a gift to his children, without warranties. If a defect should be subsequently asserted, would Dan's children be protected under his policy? With respect to a mortgagee under a loan policy, the form provides that coverage will continue to protect the insured if it should become the new owner after foreclosure or acceptance of a deed in lieu of foreclosure.

c. *Notices (§§3 and 5 of the Conditions and Stipulations).* There are two notices that an insured must provide to the title company under the terms of the conditions and stipulations. The first is prompt notice of any claim that is adverse to the title as insured. What is prompt notice? What are the consequences set forth in the policy for failure to provide such notice?

The second notice is a proof of loss statement that must be submitted within 90 days after the insured shall "ascertain the facts giving rise to the loss or damage." By contrast, the 1970 ALTA form of policy required that such proof of loss be submitted within 90 days after "such loss or damage shall have been determined." The 1987 ALTA Forms Committee disclaimed any intention on their part to change the substance of this notice requirement. Nevertheless, the subtle shift in phraseology to a less objective standard might precipitate substantial litigation in the future. Why? Compare the consequences to the insured of a failure to comply with the first and the second notice requirements. Suppose, for example, that in both instances such a failure costs the title company a mere $100 on a $1 million loss claim. Would the consequences to the insured be the same? Can you think of the ALTA's motivation for imposing the 90-day requirement with respect to the proof of loss statement? Inasmuch as a title company does not have to pay a claim unless and until it receives a notice of loss statement, why would it be to the company's advantage to impose such a requirement?

d. *Defense (§§4, 5, 6 and 9(b) of the Conditions and Stipulations).* Suppose Dan Developer purchases real estate worth $1 million and obtains title insurance coverage in the same amount. Ten years later, when the property is worth $3 million, a defect is discovered that, if substantiated, would result in a total loss for Dan. The title company agrees to defend and assigns the case to a law firm in which Dan does not have much confidence. With $2 million over the insurance amount at stake, would Dan be able to demand that the title company employ another firm? What, if anything, could Dan do if the title company rejected his demand? Observe that in the event of a dispute over litigation strategy, the title company will most likely prevail over the insured based on the language in §4(b). Suppose, for example, that Dan discovers the possibility of an adverse claim but would prefer to do nothing until his adverse possession ripens into title, whereas the title company insists on bringing an action to quiet title. Can the title company sue the adverse claimant on behalf of Dan notwithstanding Dan's objections to the lawsuit? The answer is yes, and if the title company were to lose Dan could wind up with a right to some money but be ejected from the land. Suppose that, in the worst case, the title company loses the cause of action and Dan is ejected by the adverse claimant. The title company, however, decides to appeal the decision to the highest court in the state if necessary, which may take five years or more. Must Dan wait until there is a final adjudication before obtaining either the land or his money from the title company?

e. *Subrogation (§13 of the Conditions and Stipulations).* Subrogation is the substitution of one person in the place of another with respect to a claim. When a title company pays a claim, it is subrogated to the rights and remedies of the insured claimant as against third parties resulting from the title defect. Based on this right of subrogation in favor of the title company, most sellers in a commercial transaction (especially banks and other institutional lenders) will refuse to provide the purchaser with a general warranty deed. Can you think of the reason why? See discussion at Chapter 3A, note 5, supra.

Suppose Dan Developer buys property and obtains mortgage financing from Ace Insurance Company. Pursuant to Ace's commitment, Dan pays for a title policy insuring Ace's mortgage. To save money, Dan decides not to get his own title insurance coverage. Later a defect turns up. Ace makes a claim under its policy, which the title company pays. As most mortgages do, Ace's contains covenants of title under which the borrower assures the lender that the title is as described in the mortgage. Can the title company claim to be subrogated to Ace's rights against Dan under these covenants, for the amount of its payment to Ace? Would your answer be different if the mortgage were non-recourse? How might Dan protect himself from subrogation liability?

f. Payment of Loss and the Extent of Liability (§§6 and 7 of the Conditions and Stipulations).   These are important provisions that should be reviewed thoroughly. For example, the prefatory language to §7 provides that the contract is nothing more than a contract of indemnity against monetary loss. This is an attempt by the 1987 ALTA Forms Committee to counteract post-1970 case law holding title companies liable for damages beyond what had been previously contemplated. This burgeoning of insurer liability based on tort theories, along with the doctrine of "reasonable expectancy of the insured," has made title companies more cautious about rejecting claims. See, e.g., Jarchow v. Transamerica Title Insurance Co., 48 Cal. App. 3d 917, 122 Cal. Rptr. 470 (1975) (title company held liable for inflicting emotional distress); MacBean v. St. Paul Title Insurance Corp., 169 N.J. Super. 502, 405 A.2d 405 (1979) (company held liable based on reasonable expectations of the insured); Moe v. Transamerica Title Insurance Co., 21 Cal. App. 3d 289, 98 Cal. Rptr. 547 (1971) (company held liable for punitive damages). See also discussion of lender liability in Chapter 12.

An important point to keep in mind is that the title company is never liable for more than the policy amount. Thus, if the property subject to the insurance appreciates significantly in value, the insured should consider obtaining an increase in the coverage amount for an additional premium in those areas where the title companies are willing to do so.

4. Schedules A and B.   Schedule A tells you what is being insured. It contains the date of the policy and the face amount of insurance. This is important information since, as we observed earlier, the date of the policy is the operative date for insuring the title and the amount of insurance establishes the maximum amount of the title company's liability. Schedule A furnishes the name of the insured and indicates the nature and extent of the estate covered by the policy and in whom the estate is vested as of the policy date. It describes the land and specifies the mortgages, deeds of trust, or assignments encumbering the land.

Schedule B contains the exceptions to the coverage of the policy. There are two types of exceptions: general exceptions applicable to all policies and "special exceptions" relating only to the property-specific circumstances. In the 1970 form of policy, the general exceptions were expressly enumerated in Schedule B, whereas in the 1987 policy forms they have been omitted so that they can be adapted for local use. Nevertheless, most of these earlier general exceptions are still appearing in present policies; therefore, you should become familiar with them. They read as follows:

General Exceptions:

(1) Rights or claims of parties in possession not shown by the public records.

(2) Encroachments, overlaps, boundary line disputes, and any other matters which would be disclosed by an accurate survey and inspection of the premises.

(3) Easements or claims of easements not shown by the public records.

(4) Any lien, or right to a lien, for services, labor, or material heretofore or hereafter furnished, imposed by law and not shown by the public records.

(5) Taxes or special assessments which are not shown as existing liens by the public records.

In most instances at least some of these general exceptions will require some form of reasonable modification. For example, the first exception for rights of parties in possession is apparently aimed at tenants in possession. As observed at Chapter 3B1, note 4, supra, a purchaser may be charged with inquiry notice of the rights of parties in possession even if these rights have not yet been recorded. Thus, a tenant with a life estate or an option to purchase the property may be excepted from coverage by this clause. How could this clause be modified by the title company to provide reasonable protection for a purchaser client while retaining its purpose?

The second exception addresses matters that would be disclosed by an accurate survey or inspection of the premises. This is normally not acceptable to the attorney for the insured. For example, even if the purchaser has obtained a recent survey that shows no defects, this exception would exclude liability if the survey happens to be inaccurate. Often title companies will agree to delete the printed exception and insert a specific exception for matters disclosed by the purchaser's survey. This is sometimes known as "reading in" the survey.

The third exception relieves the title company of liability for easements or claims of easements not disclosed by the public records. Sometimes the title company will delete this exception. What precaution should you, as counsel to the title company, take before agreeing to the deletion? What precaution should you, as counsel to the insured, take if the title company should refuse to delete the exception?

The fourth printed exception deals with coverage against mechanics' liens. This is discussed at Chapter 6B3, note 6.

The fifth printed exception covers liability for unpaid taxes not yet elevated to the status of an existing lien in the public records. What sort of tax or assessment is contemplated by this exception? What argument could you, as counsel to the insured, make to the title company for the deletion of this exception?

In addition to the general exceptions, Schedule B contains exceptions applicable to the unique facts and circumstances of a particular piece of property. Each exception must be reviewed carefully by the attorney for the insured. Every recorded document referred to in Schedule B must be read thoroughly. All easements should be traced on the survey. Even a simple utility easement could pose a problem if, for example, it should block access to the property or cause parking areas to be below the size mandated by local law.

1. Ad valorem taxes for 19 — and subsequent years;
2. Utility easements of record;
3. Encroachments of existing improvements onto utility easements;
4. Covenants, conditions, and restrictions filed in the Office of the Clerk of the County of Feerick, State of Fuller on November 15, 1973 in Liber 325, page 20.
5. Mortgage dated _____ , 19 — , in the principal amount of $25,000,000 made by Law Drive Associates in favor of Ace Insurance Company, recorded in the Office of the Clerk of the County of Feerick, State of Fuller, in Liber 596, page 120 on _____ , 19 — .
6. Assignment of Lessor's Interest in Leases dated _____ , 19 — , made by Law Drive Associates in favor of Ace Insurance Company and filed in the Office of the Clerk of the County of Feerick, State of Fuller, in Liber 683, page 23 on _____ , 19 — .
7. Mineral interests previously recorded or conveyed of record and all rights incident thereto.

As counsel to a purchaser such as Dan Developer what affirmative insurance might you ask for, and what documents would you want to review, before approving or rejecting the foregoing exceptions?

For a general discussion of title insurance see Taub, Rights and Remedies Under a Title Policy, 15 Real Prop. Prob. & Tr. J. 422 (1980). See R. Jordan, ALTA Forms Committee Revises Title Insurance Policies (Lawyers Title Insurance Corp. 1987) for an excellent analysis of the 1987 ALTA forms. See also Christie, The Title Insurance Industry: A Reexamination Revisited, 18 Real Est. L.J. 354 (Spring 1990); Rooney, Title Insurance: A Primer for Attorneys, 14 Real Prop. Prob. & Tr. J. 608 (Fall 1979).

5. *Indian Claims.*   The *Oneida* case illustrates the nature of land claims being made by American Indians based on the Nonintercourse Act of 1793. Notwithstanding the prohibition against purchasing land from Indians without congressional approval, New York and other states continued to contract with Indian tribes for the acquisition of land. Indeed, these purchases continued even after a specific warning as to the illegality of the treaties had been issued by President George Washington's Secretary of War, Timothy Pickering, to some well-known politicians including New York's Governor John Jay. See Comment, Oneida Indian Nation v. County of Oneida: Tribal Rights of Action and the Indian Trade and Intercourse Act, 84 Colum. L. Rev. 1869 (1984). Why, do you think, did the states ignore the statute? Like the beginnings of many marriages, the early days of the Union were marked by disputes over "turf." Perhaps Governor Jay might have looked on this law as an unwarranted intrusion of the federal government into affairs that had or should have been (in his opinion) left to the states. If so, why didn't the federal government take any action to contest these acquisitions? See Comment, Indian Land Claims Under the Nonintercourse Act, 44 Albany L. Rev. 110 (1979).

As suggested by the *Oneida* decision, doctrines of estoppel and laches and statutes of limitation do not necessarily apply. Why is this so? How could Congress resolve this problem? For additional reading on the subject see C. F. Wilkinson, American Indians, Time, and the Law (1987); V. Deloria, Jr. and C. Lytle, American Indians, American Justice (1983); and Note, The Oneida Land Claims: Equity and Eject-ment, 39 Syracuse L. Rev. 830 (1988).

3. *Closing the Transaction*

The closing date has finally arrived and, pursuant to §4 of the sample sale agreement, you and Sam's attorney will be supervising the execution and exchange of the closing documents whereby Sam will transfer the benefits and burdens of ownership to Dan in exchange for Dan's payment of the balance of the purchase price. During the negotiations the parties have modified §4 of the agreement. Both the closing expenses of the parties and the items to be delivered by Dan and Sam, as set forth in the "Closing Memorandum," should be read in conjunction with the negotiated language in §4 of the sample sale agreement supra. As you will see, the closing memorandum does nothing more than implement the terms of the contract of sale between the parties.

Friedman, Contracts and Conveyances of Real Property
746-765 (3d ed. 1975)

SECTION 11.13　PREPARATION FOR THE CLOSING

Promptly after execution of the contract of sale, the buyer's attorney arranges for examination of title. On receipt of the title report he examines the report, makes a list of any objections and sends a copy of the list to the seller's attorney. The latter then proceeds to clear the objections. Thereafter, seller's attorney prepares the deed, purchase money mortgage instruments, any other necessary closing instruments and the closing adjustments. All this — in fact, everything happening after execution of the contract of sale — is in preparation for the closing. Questions involving the examination of title, marketability of title, the deed, purchase money mortgage instruments, the medium of payment and other matters have already been considered in detail. This section will consider putting them together.

It is not essential to put all these matters together before the closing, but it is highly desirable to do so. The ordinary closing can be completed within a half hour, but it is a rare closing that is. Assuming the existence of a minimum amount of experience and competence in the attorneys for the buyer and seller, the chief reason for a failure of title to close efficiently and expeditiously is a failure on the part of either or both to prepare well. While the standing of a real estate lawyer is not customarily dependent upon his record for speed, a competent real estate lawyer will ordinarily close a title properly and without waste of time or effort, provided he obtains cooperation from the other side. It is possible that, because of some error or misinformation, even a well-prepared closing must necessarily be followed by a correction deed or a correction mortgage or a recomputation of adjustments. But there is little excuse for wrangling for hours at a closing over matters which should have been settled previously. Buyer's attorneys have been known to check insurance adjustments interminably at the closing and claim an overcharge — after covering sheet after sheet of paper with figures — only to learn that a change in coverage or rate had been overlooked. Insurance adjustments can be made in minutes by use of tables available from insurance companies.

The instruments to be delivered at the closing, such as the deed and purchase money mortgage papers, should be prepared in advance by seller's attorney. Unless these are routine, it is good practice to give copies to buyer's attorney, for checking, prior to the closing and before they are executed. For the most part, printed forms for these instruments are available and, if previously tested, they offer assurance against formal omissions or errors which may creep into typewritten papers. In a printed form of deed, for instance, there is less likelihood of error or omission in the granting and habendum clauses, the acknowledgement, or some statutory provision, such as the New York "lien clause," than if the deed is entirely typewritten. When a deed is hurriedly dictated, typewritten and checked at the closing, the lawyers, distracted by other matters, may see in the instrument what they expect to see and if a line, such as the granting clause, should be left out, the omission may easily be missed by all concerned. But the use of accepted printed forms does not dispense with the necessity of checking. The deed and purchase money mortgage will have a typewritten metes and bounds description of the premises. The mortgage papers will recite the amount of principal and time of payment of principal and interest. All these instruments must be dated. It is desirable that these and other instruments be checked by both attorneys when this can be done leisurely, without the distractions of a closing, and when errors can be corrected and differences resolved without embarrassment to anybody. Disposition of these matters in advance reduces the work necessary at the closing and makes for a smoother, more satisfactory and generally friendlier closing.

Usually, the closing instruments are executed at the closing by the principals and it is preferable that it be so done. It is certain, then, that the grantor is alive when the deed is delivered; and questions of identification and competency are thereby reduced. It may not be feasible to do this if a principal cannot be at the closing, and if the absentee is a grantor, the buyer should obtain an explanation of the absence. If the grantor's execution is more than a day or two before the closing, it is important to have proof that the grantor is alive. If execution is by an attorney-in-fact, proof should be obtained that the principal is alive and the power-of-attorney unrevoked.

The closing adjustments are necessarily detailed, though the amounts involved in many of the items may be very small in comparison with the total consideration for the conveyance. They are prepared by the seller's side from data taken from the seller's records. The computations may be made by the seller, his accountant or bookkeeper or attorney. In any event, they must be checked by his attorney in the light of the contract of sale and any relevant law. Thereafter, a statement of the figures should be sent to buyer's attorney for checking in advance of the closing. The adjustments may present an issue of fact, as the amount of fuel at the premises. And there may be a question of law with respect to the inclusion of some items. Mostly, however, the adjustments involve simple mathematics. Their preparation and checking are a chore which can be time-consuming at the closing and are more apt to be so than any other matter. Until they are agreed on, the buyer cannot obtain the cash payable to the seller in the proper amount and medium. It is a matter, then, which should be cleared in advance. The statement of adjustments should be reasonably detailed. If not, the items cannot be checked and are not much use as part of the permanent record of the closing. If the statement charges buyer with, for instance, $57.12 for insurance, this item cannot be verified. It is necessary to state the amount of insurance, the rate, the beginning and expiration of the term of policy and the length of the unexpired term as of the closing date. If the policy has been changed during the term, as by additional coverage or change in rate, this should appear. It is preferable to include the name of the insurance company and number of the policy. Rent adjustments should show the amount of rent and period covered by the adjustment, e.g., one month's rent at $100 per month, and the number of days and amount chargeable to seller or buyer. A typical statement of adjustments appears as part of the closing statement set forth in the following section. Some figures may not be available until the day of closing. If buyer is to pay for fuel on the premises on that date, a reliable estimate will not be available much in advance. If the closing is on the sixth day of the month, and rents are to be adjusted accordingly, the amount of current rents in the seller's hands will not be known before that day. Nevertheless, most computations can be determined well in advance of the closing and it is good practice to get tentative figures, i.e., those complete, in the buyer's hands and checked in advance.

Seller's attorney should prepare a check list of things to be done at the closing. These will include papers he is to deliver and receive, papers which he should inspect, and others which he must exhibit. . . . Other instruments may be necessary to clear seller's title, such as a mortgage satisfaction, an affidavit of title or an affidavit addressed to some particular question raised by an examiner of title.

The list might read:

Deliver:

1. Deed, with $ _____ in stamps affixed and cancelled.

2. Leases.
   a. Leases and rental agreements listed in contract of sale.
   b. Instruments necessary to establish validity of rents under emergency rent laws, if any.
3. Check for tenants' security deposits.
4. Insurance.
   a. Original rent insurance policy.
   b. Certificates of fire policies (originals held by mortgagee).
5. Statement of first mortgagee (showing unpaid principal and interest and rate of interest).
6. Building certificates.
   a. Certificate of occupancy.
   b. Certificate of electrical inspection.
   c. Certificate of fire underwriters.
   d. Certificate of plumbing inspection.
7. Keys to premises.
8. Bill of sale to personal property included in sale.
9. Fuel estimate (letter of reliable fuel merchant) (retain counterpart copy).

Exhibit:

Receipted bills for —
   Real estate taxes.[3]
   Water.
   Franchise taxes; (of corporate seller) or deposit with buyer or title company to insure payment; or letter of seller undertaking to pay amount ultimately fixed.[4]

Inspect:

Certificate of incorporation of buyer.[5]

---

3. If real estate taxes are payable in installments, it will be convenient for the buyer in paying future installments accruing during the current fiscal year if in possession of the tax bill. A meticulous seller may prefer to keep the receipt for his records. Delivery of a photostatic copy may be the solution.

4. The only satisfactory disposition of franchise taxes is evidence of final payment. This may be impossible if, as often occurs, the tax has not been finally fixed at the time of the closing. The insurance of a responsible title company against collection of this tax (and the same goes for estate and transfer taxes) is a common practical solution but leaves title technically unmarketable until actual payment, and may not be acceptable to a subsequent purchaser or mortgagee, particularly if a rival title company is used in the later transaction. If the seller fails to carry out an undertaking to pay franchise taxes, the removal of their lien may be a nuisance to the buyer.

5. Seller is interested in the certificate of incorporation of a corporate buyer only if the latter is to execute and deliver a purchase money mortgage to the former.

Obtain:

1. Balance of purchase price, as per closing computations.
2. Purchase money mortgage papers.
    Mortgage note.
    Mortgage.
3. Expenses re purchase money mortgage.
    Cost of recording mortgage.
    Mortgage tax.
    Legal charge for preparing mortgage papers.
4. Receipts for instruments, etc., delivered to buyer.

This list will, of course, vary with the circumstances. . . .

The buyer's attorney should prepare his own checklist. This should recite virtually the same closing instruments as those on the list of the seller's attorney. If not, there may be some misunderstanding at the closing unless the difference is resolved in advance. The preparations of the buyer's attorney are not limited to closing papers. There is other preliminary work for him to do or have done. He must inform his client of the sums necessary and see that these are brought to the closing in cash or proper checks. The insurance to be transferred at the closing should be reviewed by the buyer's insurance representatives, who may recommend changes to improve the coverage or reduce the rate. It might be advisable to obtain types of insurance which the seller does not maintain. If any seller's policies are nontransferable — his public liability insurance may not be transferable — additional policies in replacement will be necessary. In any event, as soon as the deed and keys to the premises belong to the buyer — and not a day or a week later — the buyer should be covered by binder, endorsement or new policies with all the insurance he intends to have. In view of the rule that insurance is not transferable without the consent of the insurer, the best way of handling this is by having policies or endorsements, showing the new interest, at the closing. A telephone call made at the closing to an insurance broker is a poor substitute.

When the buyer leaves the closing he should be in a position to take over administration of the property with no breach of continuity. Gas, electricity and other services must be continued. Building employees who are to be retained will expect their pay at the customary time. Tenants must be notified of the change and directed where and to whom rent will be payable. New contracts for services and utilities may be necessary. Some service contracts may be taken over from the seller. Tenants' rights, respecting services, maintenance, decorating, credit for security or advance rent, etc., must be observed. Some of this may be indicated in the leases. Others may be based on the custom at the premises. Whoever is to manage the property must be ready with all these things. If the property is large enough for the seller to employ a managing agent, there are obvious advantages in the buyer's continuing this agent. If the buyer supersedes the seller's agent with his own, it would be well for new and old agents to meet, at the closing or before, to turn over data to the new agent. If this should not be practical, because of resentment on the part of the superseded agent, it would be well for the buyer to continue the old agent temporarily and take over management of the property gradually.

Seller's attorney should have any necessary deed stamps on hand at the time of closing. A seller's practice of delivering the deed without stamps, and paying the buyer or title company closer for his cost is not recommended. There is no occasion to affix the stamps until the end of the closing. If anything should go awry, it will be a nuisance to obtain a refund for canceled but unused stamps. In this connection, it should be noted that if a formal tender of the deed should be necessary, in order to lay the basis for some claim, the deed will be in proper form for this purpose without stamps affixed and canceled.

A last minute inspection of the property should be made by the buyer or on his behalf to make sure that all personal property and fixtures included in the sale are on the premises, that no parties are in occupation other than those contemplated by the contract of sale and that the premises have sustained no damage warranting rescission or an abatement in the purchase price.[13] . . .

13. See generally Lane and Clack, Preparing for a Real Estate Closing, 4 Prac. Real Est. Law. 61 (Sept. 1988). — ED.

283-284
293 n.3
294
301-308
311-320

Chapter 4

The Nature of a Mortgage and the Mortgage Market for Income-Producing Real Estate

Zen and the Art of Mortgage Financing

This chapter examines some basic theories with respect to the nature of a mortgage and the fundamental macroeconomic variables that govern the supply and demand for mortgage credit as a prelude to the more practice-oriented discussion of modern real estate financing that follows. While the mortgagee's remedy of foreclosure is closely examined in Chapter 10B and C, reference is made to it in the intervening chapters; accordingly, a brief overview of foreclosure is presented herein. In addition, the cases and questions on the mortgage note as the underlying obligation of a mortgage should help you understand some of the practical considerations that are addressed in the discussions of postconstruction financing (Chapter 5) and construction financing (Chapter 6). For example, as a general rule a valid mortgage must be supported by an existing obligation, and yet construction financing is to a large extent based on an exception to the rule, namely, a mortgage that secures future (as opposed to present) loan advances. Whether or not the exception makes sense as a matter of legal theory is discussed at Chapter 4B2, note 2b. Another basic question that relates to the nature of a mortgage is whether the underlying indebtedness or other obligation must be enforceable against the mortgagor. The answer is generally no (see Chapter 4B3). This explains the existence of "nonrecourse" financing, a valuable technique that is commonly used in postconstruction financing for tax reasons (see Chapter 2B, note 7diii) and business reasons (see Chapter 5A and Chapter 6A1). Also, an understanding of how a mortgage competes for lien priority (discussed at Chapter 4C) is fundamental to our discussion of credit leases (Chapter 5C), leasehold mortgage financing (Chapter 8A), foreclosure by a mortgagee (Chapter 10B and C), and a host of other financing issues.

It has often been said that the mortgage is the legal cornerstone of real estate financing. And yet the borrower's promise to repay the indebtedness (as evidenced by the "note") and the mortgage instrument itself simply implement the terms and conditions of the loan contract between the lender and the borrower, the "commitment letter." So why study the law of mortgages at this juncture? Well, there are several good reasons. For students, especially those with (pardon the expression) a "left-brain" point of view (remember *Zen and the Art of Motorcycle Maintenance?*), studying the terms and conditions of modern real estate financing without understanding the function of the mortgage and nature of the obligation it secures is like knowing the parts of a motorcycle without understanding what makes it run. The mortgage is the device that makes real estate financing work!

In addition, while the question as to whether there has been a default under the note or mortgage will usually turn on language that has been negotiated beforehand in the commitment letter, the question as to what will happen in the event of a default is sometimes governed by rules of law and policy considerations that supersede the written words of the parties. In other words, the question of default will most likely be governed by freedom of contract principles but the consequences of default may not. For example, in the case of a financially distressed borrower who defaults in making payments on the mortgage note, the legal system becomes more paternalistic, and the consequences to the mortgagor, the mortgagee, and the mortgagor's other creditors will depend less on the private bargain between the borrower and the lender and more on the nature of a mortgage and the rules relating to foreclosure and bankruptcy that are examined in Chapters 10 and 11, respectively.

We will first review the history of the mortgage device and ask ourselves some commonly raised threshold questions about the function of a mortgage and the nature of its underlying obligation, namely: (1) Can a mortgage secure the performance of an act by the mortgagor other than its promise to repay some indebtedness? (2) If so, must the mortgagor's promise of performance be an underlying obligation that is supported by valid consideration and enforceable, and when must the obligation be enforceable? And (3) must the mortgagor be personally liable for the performance of such underlying obligation?

Finally, we will examine how a mortgage competes with other liens and interests in the same real estate held by parties other than the mortgagee and how a mortgagor competes with other borrowers in the short- and long-term money markets in order to obtain construction and postconstruction financing, respectively, to develop and purchase income-producing real estate such as an office building or shopping center.

A. A HISTORICAL OVERVIEW OF MORTGAGE LAW

The theory of mortgage law in American jurisprudence has largely been forged by developments in the early English common law. At common law the first property security device was the pledge. You probably know the term better by its modern-day corollary, the pawn. In a pledge transaction, the lender would lend money to the borrower and the borrower would transfer possession of the property to the lender as security for the indebtedness. When the loan was repaid, the lender would return the property. If the loan was not paid, the lender could keep the property.[1]

Early judges liked the pledge because it eased their virtual paranoia about "secret liens." Since possession was transferred to the lender, prospective creditors could not be misled into believing that the borrower owned the property.[2]

With real estate, it is impractical to transfer possession of the property to the lender except in rare situations. The borrower needs the property to run the business or as shelter for the borrower's family. How, then, could a person use real estate as security for a loan? The answer was the common-law mortgage. While it may have been impractical to transfer possession of real estate, it was nevertheless feasible to transfer fee title. Accordingly, beginning around the fourteenth century the mortgage took the form of a deed from the borrower, whom we call the "mortgagor," to the lender, whom we call the "mortgagee."[3] The differences between this common-law mortgage and

---

1. The forerunners of the modern mortgage were but variants of the pledge device and included the Glanvillian gage, the Jewish gage, and the Bractonian mortgage. See G. Osborne, Handbook on the Law of Mortgages 2-8 (2d ed. 1970) (hereinafter Osborne); Rabinowitz, The Story of Mortgage Law Retold, 94 U. Pa. L. Rev. 94 (1945); 1 G. Glenn, Mortgages (1943).

2. Recording statutes were devised to counter the early fears about "ostensible ownership" in borrowers who gave "secret liens" to lenders. As suggested in the textual material elsewhere, the courts would strike down security interests, including mortgages, as fraudulent conveyances where the borrower retained possession of the property. Should they not have been equally concerned about the lender who took possession of the collateral and therefore might appear to the lender's creditors as having ownership of the collateral? If not, why not?

3. Even though the term "mortgage" literally means "dead pledge," as Littleton once said, "the cause why it is called mortgage is, for that it is doubtful whether the feoffer will pay at the day limited . . .; and if he doth not pay, then the land . . . is *taken from him* forever, and so dead (to him. . . . And if he doth pay the money, then pledge is dead) as to the tenant, etc." (Sir Thomas Littleton, Tenures bk. III, ch. v, §332 (Wambaugh 1903) (emphasis added)). See Osborne §1.

the ordinary deed absolute were that the mortgagor was ordinarily allowed to remain in possession of the real estate during the term of the mortgage and that the mortgage conveyance was subject to a condition subsequent. If the borrower paid interest in a timely manner and otherwise performed the obligations under the note and the mortgage, including the payment of the balance of the principal indebtedness on the due date, called the "law day," the deed would become void and title would automatically revert to the mortgagor. If, however, the mortgagor defaulted in its obligations, title would vest indefeasibly in the mortgagee. What happened to all the judicial concern about ostensible ownership? This was eventually resolved by recording statutes that substituted public notice — the recording of the mortgage document — for the change in physical possession.

The results of all this could be very severe for the borrower. What if on the date the mortgage became due the mortgagor's horse suffered an accident and it was impossible to get into town to make the payment until the next day? Too late. Time was regarded as of the essence. While this may have been unfair, there was no remedy for the mortgagor at law. As you may remember, when there was a wrong, and no remedy was available at law, the person wronged could appeal to the King's chancellor (later the courts of equity) to redress the injustice. To mitigate the harsh result to the defaulting borrower, the King's chancellor would frequently permit the mortgagor to "redeem," or buy back, the mortgaged property from the mortgagee subsequent to the law day on a special showing of fraud, accident, or some other equitable ground. By the seventeenth century this "equity of redemption" was routinely recognized by equity courts.[4] Eventually the mortgagor's equity of redemption became recognized as an "equitable estate," and, like other full-fledged interests in land, it could be transferred, subdivided into lesser estates, devised, and could even be mortgaged again by the same mortgagor.

On the other side of the coin, the mortgagor's equity of redemption, if unlimited, would have produced severe consequences for any mortgagee facing the specter of a redemption by a borrower at some uncertain time in the future. The mortgagee would be inhibited from improving the real estate and would encounter significant difficulty in selling the property in order to recoup its loan investment. Consequently, mortgagees, without any remedy for this wrong at law, turned to the same chancellor or equity court for relief, asking the court to cut off, or "foreclose," the borrower's equity of redemption. Born of this plea by

---

4. See R. Turner, The Equity of Redemption 22 (1937); G. Osborne, Handbook on the Law of Mortgages 15-17 (2d ed. 1970). The notion that a seller has an equitable right to redeem property from the purchaser appears to have originated in Biblical law. See Leviticus 25:25-32.

mortgagees there developed what we now call foreclosure proceedings. On proper petition by a mortgagee, the early courts of equity responded by ordering the mortgagor to repay the outstanding indebtedness and accrued interest within a stipulated period of time. If the mortgagor failed to do so, the mortgage would stand foreclosed and the mortgagee would retain absolute fee title to the mortgaged real estate.

This common-law mortgage has essentially remained the basis of mortgage financing until the present time. There have been some important changes, however. First, in a majority of jurisdictions the mortgagee is regarded as merely obtaining a lien on the real estate to secure repayment of the indebtedness. These states are called "lien theory" states. In other jurisdictions, the "title theory" states, the original common-law view is followed, so that the mortgagee is regarded as obtaining both legal title and the right to possession of the mortgaged premises. However, in title theory states, the mortgagee's rights, as transferee of the legal title, generally have been ignored by both mortgagees and the courts except for the mortgagee's right to possession and rents to protect its security interest prior to a foreclosure sale of the property. Indeed, in the opinion of commentators these rights to possession and rents are the only important practical differences between the title and lien theory points of view.[5]

5. See Sturges and Clark, Legal Theory and Real Property Mortgages, 37 Yale L.J. 691 (1928). Professor Sturges observed that unlike their counterparts in lien theory states, mortgagees in title theory states retain the legal right to possession and rents prior to foreclosure. However, in practice few mortgagees exercise the right to possession prior to default. Otherwise, the mortgagor would be deprived of the meaningful use of the property either as residential shelter or as a source of rental income. Even after default, most mortgagees prefer to avoid entry into possession as a preforeclosure remedy because of the strict quasi-fiduciary responsibilities and potential tort-contract liabilities associated with being a mortgagee in possession. However, if in the event of a default a mortgagee should desire to obtain control over rents and profits (generally by virtue of phraseology in the mortgage or in a separate assignment-of-lease instrument), the mortgagee will generally encounter less difficulty in a title theory jurisdiction. See Chapter 10B2, note 1 and Chapter 10B4, note 1.

In other significant respects, according to Professor Sturges, courts in title theory states generally have regarded the mortgagee as but taking title for security purposes and, except as between the mortgagor and the mortgagee, the mortgagor is deemed to be the real owner for both theoretical and practical purposes.

Consider the following test of the validity of the theory propounded by Professor Sturges that, despite theoretical distinctions, in actual decisions made by courts it makes little difference whether a particular jurisdiction adheres to the lien theory or the title theory:

(a) Suppose that A, the owner of Blackacre, mortgages it to B to secure a loan. Thereafter, X procures a judgment against A and seeks to docket his judgment against Blackacre. Will he succeed in a title state even though title to Blackacre has, in theory, already passed to B?

(b) Suppose, instead, that X is a judgment creditor of B, the mortgagee in a title

Second, the format of the mortgage device has been discarded in some states, especially in the western part of the country, in favor of the so-called deed of trust format. California is a notable example. Under a deed of trust, real property owned by the borrower ("grantor" or "trustor") is conveyed to a third party "trustee" who holds the property in trust as security for the repayment of indebtedness owed to the lender ("beneficiary"). Since the real function of a deed of trust is to operate as a security device, courts have generally accorded the trustee and deed of trust beneficiary only those incidents of ownership to which a mortgagee would be entitled in such jurisdiction. For example, in a lien theory state the trustee may be said to have acquired legal title for the benefit of the lender, as beneficiary, but it is the borrower-trustor who will ordinarily be accorded the legal right to possession.[6]

Third, the methodology of foreclosure has changed. For example, "strict foreclosure," under which the lender keeps the mortgaged property on cutting off the borrower's equity of redemption, is still used in a few American jurisdictions.[7] However, because of the unfairness that can result to the borrower in the event that the value of

---

state. Can X docket his judgment against Blackacre, since B, theoretically, has title to Blackacre?

Professor Sturges, who painstakingly examined court decisions in numerous title and lien theory states, concluded that regardless of theoretical adherence to title or lien theories the court decisions in these cases were uniform. In example (a), A's judgment creditor could have execution against the property mortgaged by A, while in example (b), the mortgagee's judgment creditor could not get execution against such property. Sturges and Clark, Legal Theory and Real Property Mortgages, 37 Yale L.J. 691 (1928).

Is Professor Sturges' view still valid today, a half-century after it was expressed? Are contested claims relating to legal rights in mortgaged property today determined primarily by whether a state adheres to the title, lien, or intermediate theories, or is the factual context of the dispute of greater importance? To answer this question, one would have to undertake an exhaustive examination of current court decisions, state by state, as was done by Professor Sturges over fifty years ago. However, many contemporary authorities appear to agree with Professor Sturges. See G. Osborne, G. Nelson, and D. Whitman, Real Estate Finance Law §4.1 (1985); Kratovil, Mortgages — Problems in Possession, Rents, and Mortgagee Liability, 11 De Paul L. Rev. 1 (1961); R. Kratovil and B. Werner, Modern Mortgage Law and Practice §20.02 (2d ed. 1981).

6. In the words of one court "At common law and, in fact, in nearly every state in the United States, a deed of trust, both in legal effect and in theory, is deemed to be a mortgage with a power of sale, and differs not at all from a mortgage with a power of sale. . . ." Bank of Italy National Trust & Savings Assn. v. Bentley, 217 Cal. 644, 20 P.2d 940, cert. denied, 290 U.S. 659 (1933). See G. Osborne, Handbook on the Law of Mortgages, 663 (2d ed. 1970); see generally Note, Comparison of California Mortgages, Trust Deeds and Land Sale Contracts, 7 UCLA L. Rev. 83 (1960); Comment, Mortgages and Trust Deed, 5 S. Cal. L. Rev. 227 (1931-1932).

7. See, e.g., Conn. Gen. Stat. Ann. §§41-51 (West 1987); Vt. Stat. Ann. tit. 12, §4531 (1975).

the property exceeds the amount of the outstanding mortgage indebtedness,[8] most jurisdictions have supplanted strict foreclosure with foreclosure by public sale.

There are generally two types of public sales. One is judicial
foreclosure, whereby the property is sold pursuant to court order (see
Chapter 10C2b), and the other is foreclosure without a judicial proceeding under a power of sale contained in the mortgage or deed of
trust instrument. See Chapter 10C2c. In contrast to strict foreclosure,
both of these methods envision a sale of the encumbered property. In
addition, those parties such as the mortgagor and junior lienors who
hold interests that are subject to termination by the foreclosure sale
have a right of "equitable redemption" (as noted above) whereby they
can prevent foreclosure by paying off the amount of the delinquent
mortgage indebtedness or, in the case of a junior lienor, be subrogated
to the rights of the foreclosing mortgagee. The sale must be conducted
in a fair manner and the proceeds are first used to defray the expenses
of the proceedings, then to satisfy junior liens. The balance, if any, is
remitted to the defaulting mortgagor. If the net proceeds are insufficient
to satisfy the debt claim, in most jurisdictions the foreclosing mortgagee
has the right to obtain a deficiency judgment against the mortgagor.
See Chapter 10C3a.

The economic depression of the 1820s spawned in many jurisdictions the so-called redemption statutes, which afforded the mortgagor
the additional right to buy back or redeem the property *after foreclosure*
by paying the foreclosure sale price to the person who was the purchaser
at the foreclosure sale. This statutory protection is known as a "right
of redemption," distinguished from the judicially created "equity of
redemption" *prior* to foreclosure. The purpose of this additional right
of redemption is to protect those parties whose interests could be
extinguished at foreclosure from an unreasonably low foreclosure sale
price. See Chapter 10C3b, note 1.

Judicial foreclosure has traditionally been the more popular of the
two methods (especially in those states east of the Mississippi), perhaps
because a judicially supervised sale tends to be the best method for
resolving the conflicting claims of the interested parties and for producing the firmest and most defensible title.[9] However, judicial foreclosure is complicated, time-consuming, and expensive. Consequently,

8. Typically, lenders will advance less than the appraised value of the property in
order to protect themselves against possible diminution in the value of the property
and because of loan-to-value constraints contained in statutes regulating their investment
portfolios. However, to the extent that the value of the mortgaged real estate exceeds
the outstanding loan balance, it is more likely that the mortgagor will be able to
arrange a disposition or refinancing of the property to avoid foreclosure.

9. See G. Osborne, Handbook on the Law of Mortgages 663 (2d ed. 1970).

in many states the second method of foreclosure, whereby the fore-closure is conducted pursuant to a provision in the mortgage or deed of trust empowering the mortgagee or trustee to sell the property without direct judicial interference, is more commonly used. State statutes authorizing such sales by a mortgagee or trustee require fewer and less complicated procedural steps than does judicial foreclosure; for example, neither actual notice nor a hearing is generally required for the benefit of the mortgagor and other affected parties. In most states all that is required is notice by advertisement for a designated period of time. Consequently, this method is frequently chosen by lenders seeking to avoid the delay of judicial foreclosure and by defaulting borrowers wanting to minimize the cost of foreclosure, which, when added to the mortgage indebtedness, reduces whatever equity or surplus proceeds they may realize once the foreclosure sale is concluded.[10]

B. THE NATURE OF A MORTGAGE

1. The Mortgage as Security for Mortgagor's Performance of an Obligation

Can a mortgage secure performance of an act by the mortgagor other than the promise to repay indebtedness owed to the mortgagee? Consider the following materials.

In the Matter of Jeffrey Towers, Inc. v. Twin Towers, Inc. et al.
57 Misc. 2d 46, 291 N.Y.S.2d 41 (1968)

GAGLIARDI, J. This is a petition to compel satisfaction of a mortgage dated October 29, 1965, in return for payment of the sum of $225,000, with interest in the sum of $3,712.50, on premises consisting of approximately five acres off Central Park Avenue in Yonkers, New York. The mortgagees do not contest that this is the amount due on

---

10. This brief review of the history of mortgages paints with a very broad brush. For those who have not had the opportunity to study mortgage law previously, the following background materials may be helpful. Chaplin, The Story of Mortgage Law, 4 Harv. L. Rev. (1890); Rabinowitz, The Story of Mortgage Law Retold, 94 U. Pa. L. Rev. 94 (1945); American Law of Property §§16.1 to 16.7 (Casner ed. 1952).

the bond secured by this purchase-money mortgage which was part of the price of the sale of the land to petitioner's predecessor in title, but they do insist that they are entitled to keep the mortgage open of record to secure other promises made by the mortgagor in the mortgage agreement to benefit eight adjacent acres of land which the seller-mortgagees have retained. Those promises are (1) to install a 12-inch sewer main from Central Park Avenue across the petitioner's property to service the mortgagees' property before October 29, 1967, with provisions permitting the mortgagees to construct the sewer at the mortgagor's expense upon default and for a $20,000 surety bond to secure completion by October 29, 1973; (2) to construct a 561.18 foot "alternative driveway" from Young Avenue across petitioner's property to service the mortgagees' property by October 29, 1968, with similar right to complete the driveway at mortgagor's expense; (3) to consent to any applications for variances, changes of zone or special exception uses affecting the mortgagees' retained parcel; and (4) to complete a 292-family apartment house. . . .

The initial question is whether a mortgage can secure the performance of unliquidated engagements, such as the promise to build a road and sewer. A mortgage has been defined as "any conveyance of land intended by the parties at the time of making it to be security for the payment of money *or the doing of some prescribed act*" (Burnett v. Wright, 135 N.Y. 543, 547) (emphasis added). This definition which can be found in modern treatises . . . admits the possibility of such an unusual purpose although it does not obviate the problems which would be caused by it.

There are recorded cases of mortgages securing promises to provide support in slated installments for the mortgagee's lifetime. . . . So, too, a mortgage was employed to secure a promise to purchase all of the gasoline sold at a garage premises from the mortgagee in Blakeley v. Agency of Canadian Car & Foundry Co. (73 N.Y.S.2d 571 [Sup. Ct., N.Y. County, 1947]). There, the court refused to compel satisfaction of the mortgage even when the principal amount was paid because of the open promise to purchase gasoline for an unexpired term. In addition section 1921 of the Real Property Actions and Proceedings Law which authorizes this proceeding to compel discharge of the mortgage states that the satisfaction piece must certify "that the mortgage has been paid or *otherwise satisfied and discharged*" (emphasis added). The court concludes that in the absence of defects such as illegality, unliquidated promises in the nature of those presented in this case may be secured by a mortgage. It follows, therefore, that such promises must be fulfilled to entitle petitioner to a discharge of the mortgage. . . .

[T]he court doubts that the promise to consent to zoning applications is enforceable [sic] by the mortgage or may hinder its satisfaction.

The reason is that the promises to do work are readily translatable into money, albeit without precision. But the value of a consent to a zoning application (which might not even influence the zoning authority) is of such speculative monetary value that it cannot be enforced as a mortgage lien. It would be impossible for the court in the event of foreclosure to fix the amount of the lien and direct the disposition of proceeds of a foreclosure sale. . . .

A final consideration is petitioner's right of prepayment of the principal and interest. Under the instrument, it is clear that this right is unfettered so that petitioner by making tender of the principal and interest stops the further accrual of interest. Thus, the mortgage lien can only remain to secure the performance of the unliquidated obligations. Petitioner is entitled to have this reduction of the lien established of record. Therefore, the petition is granted to the extent that upon payment of $225,000, with interest in the sum of $3,712.50, the mortgagees must deliver an instrument in recordable form certifying that the principal and interest stated in the mortgage have been paid . . ."[11]

NOTES AND QUESTIONS

1. As noted by the court, the problem with a mortgage purporting to secure a promise that is not measurable in monetary terms is that "it would be impossible for the court in the event of foreclosure to fix the amount of the lien and direct the disposition of proceeds of a foreclosure sale . . ." Can you foresee any other problems that might arise if such a mortgage were enforceable?

2. Martha, a law student who owns unencumbered real estate worth $2,000, wishes to borrow $1,000 from her uncle for one year and agrees to give him a mortgage on the property to secure her promise. The uncle, a grocer, heads the antismoking drive being sponsored by the local cancer-prevention society. Which, if any, of the following promises are enforceable by the mortgage?

   (a) Martha's promise to stop smoking immediately in addition to her promise to repay the loan;

---

11. The judgment of the court was modified on appeal to reflect that the plaintiff was not entitled to an absolute satisfaction and discharge of the mortgage on the record until the mortgagor performed the covenant to construct a driveway and sewer main. Jeffrey Towers, Inc. v. Straus, 31 A.D.2d 319, 297 N.Y.S.2d 450 (2d Dept. 1969), affd., 26 N.Y.2d 812, 257 N.E.2d 897, 309 N.Y.S.2d 350 (1970). — ED.

(b) The uncle's promise to cancel $500 of the loan indebtedness
     if Martha stops smoking within one year;
(c) Martha's promise to purchase all her groceries from her uncle
     during the school year in addition to her promise to repay
     the loan.

3. Suppose Dan Developer purchases his property from Alice
Agricola, who owns a much larger tract and intends to continue to
use the remainder of the property to grow corn. Dan realizes that in
order to build his building he will need a variance, and Alice agrees
to consent to and support Dan's zoning application. Because the variance
is so important to Dan, he insists on obtaining security for this promise
from Alice in the form of a mortgage on Alice's remaining land. Can
a mortgage secure such a promise? Do you agree with the court's
apparent conclusion in *Jeffrey Towers* that a promise to consent to a
zoning change is not sufficiently translatable into money to be enforced
as a mortgage lien? Why, do you think, did the court not simply
subtract the value of the property without the zoning change from
the value of the property with the zoning change to determine the
value of the obligation?   *but written as a K w/a default in $ is*

Assume Ace Insurance Company has a commitment agreement
with Dan Developer under which, in consideration of an equity contribution by Ace, Dan agrees to convey the property (upon completion
of construction) to a partnership or joint venture composed of Ace and
Dan. Do you think that Dan's obligation could be secured by a mortgage
on Dan's property? If you were the official in the local mortgage
recording office charged with recording a mortgage that does not set
forth a specific indebtedness, how would you calculate the mortgage
tax (which is normally based on a percentage of the indebtedness)?
What effect would such mortgages have on Dan's ability to obtain
secondary financing or refinancing or to sell the property? What do
you think might be drafted into the note to avoid these problems?

2. The Mortgage Note as Underlying Obligation

As you might surmise, the obligation to be secured by a mortgage will
almost invariably be a note in which the mortgagor promises to repay
some indebtedness owed to the mortgagee. It is this note, and not the
mortgage, that is the legal evidence of indebtedness. Accordingly, the
note must delineate the terms of repayment, such as the loan amount,
rate of interest, amortization period, and any prepayment privilege.
Ordinarily, the mortgagee will insist that the note contain an "acceleration clause," which reserves to the mortgagee the right to declare
the entire balance of the indebtedness to be immediately due and

payable in the event of a material default by the mortgagor. These and other terms and conditions of postconstruction and construction financing will be analyzed in Chapters 5 and 6, respectively.

At this juncture, let us confine our attention to the following question relating to the nature of the underlying obligation. If the function of a mortgage is to secure any obligation that is translatable into money, does it necessarily follow that the validity of the mortgage should depend on whether or not the underlying obligation is enforceable?

Tyler v. Wright
122 Me. 558, 119 A. 583 (1923)

PER CURIAM. This is a real action to obtain possession of certain lands. The demandant claims under a mortgage given her by Charles R. Foote in his lifetime. The defendants are the heirs at law of said Foote. By way of brief statement the defendants alleged that the mortgage was not intended to secure, and did not secure, any valid legal obligation or indebtedness, and was never executed by Foote for that purpose; that there was no valid legal consideration for said mortgage; and that said mortgage was never delivered by Foote to the plaintiff. Briefly, the defendants invoke the familiar legal principle that it is essential to the validity of a mortgage, and to the right of the mortgagee to enforce it, that it should be supported by a valid consideration (27 Cyc. 1049); or, to state the principle in more quaint form, since a conveyance cannot be a mortgage unless given to secure the performance of an obligation, the existence of an obligation to be secured is an essential element, without which the mortgage instrument is but a shadow without substance (19 R. C. L. 294).

The case was tried before a jury, and at the conclusion of the testimony the presiding justice directed a verdict for the defendants. Upon plaintiff's exception to this ruling the case comes before us.

"It is a well-established and familiar rule of procedure in this state that the court may properly instruct the jury to return a verdict for either party when it is apparent that a contrary verdict would not be allowed to stand." Wellington v. Corinna, 104 Me. 252, 71 Atl. 889.

We are to examine the report, therefore, in order to test the question whether upon the same a verdict for the plaintiff could be sustained. It is the opinion of the court that such verdict could not stand, and that the presiding justice was correct in his determination, upon the law involved and the testimony given in the case, to rule as he did.

Exceptions overruled.

Potwin State Bank v. J. B. Houston & Son Lumber Co.
183 Kan. 475, 327 P.2d 1091 (1958)[12]

SCHROEDER, Justice.

This is an action brought by the appellee in the lower court to foreclose a mortgage reciting a consideration of "One Dollar ($1.00) and the further covenants, agreements and loans and advances hereinafter specified" with a specific recital that it was "intended as a mortgage to secure the payment of any sum or sums of money which may be loaned or advanced by the mortgagee, its successors or assigns, to the mortgagor at date hereof or from time to time, as the parties hereto may now or hereafter agree, with interest" — commonly called a "Dollar Mortgage."

The underlying question concerns the priority of liens where a mortgage is given to secure future advances and mechanic's lien claimants supply labor and materials for the erection and construction of a dwelling house on the mortgaged premises after the recording of the mortgage but before the making of the advances by the mortgagee. . . .

This court has recognized that mortgages are valid and enforceable according to their terms. In Union State Bank v. Chapman, 124 Kan. 315, 259 P. 681, it was held that a valid mortgage may be made to secure future advances as well as for an existing liability of a mortgagor, and, if executed in good faith, it will be regarded as a valid security. In the Chapman case the court was dealing with a "Dollar Mortgage," the form of which was substantially the same as that of the Bank's mortgage in the instant case. There money was advanced at several times for various purposes.

State Bank v. Tinker, 131 Kan. 525, at page 527, 292 P. 748, 749, also involved a "Dollar Mortgage," in form identical with the mortgage involved in this case. The court said:

> That such a mortgage may be lawfully made *and will be judicially enforced* was settled in Union State Bank v. Chapman, 124 Kan. 315, 259 P. 681, and the error based on this phase of the judgment cannot be sustained. (Emphasis added.)

12. This excerpt only addresses the threshold issue faced by the court as to whether an "open-end" mortgage given to secure future advances is enforceable. See Chapter 6B3, note 2 for discussion on the distinction between "optional" and "obligatory" advances, and when future advances will be accorded lien priority over the claims of third party creditors (such as a mechanic's lien) which attach after the recordation of the open-end mortgage but before the future advances are made by the mortgagee. — ED.

Our decisions are thus in accord with the majority rule stated in 36 Am. Jur., Mortgages, §64 pp. 720, 721, as follows:

> There is a diversity of opinion on the question of the validity of mortgages for future advances. A majority of cases on the subject support the rule that a mortgage may be valid although given to secure future advances, and the same rule has been applied to a mortgage given to secure future indorsements. Under this rule, the obligation secured need not actually be in existence at the date of the execution of the mortgage, but may legally be given to secure advances to be made to the mortgagor, or other obligations to be assumed by him, in the future, or to indemnify against future liabilities to be incurred in his behalf. Indeed, it would be a great hardship if a different rule obtained, for mortgages of this character enable parties to provide for continuous dealings, the nature or extent of which may not be known or anticipated at the time, and they avoid the expense and inconvenience of executing a new security on each new transaction. . . .

In conclusion we hold in accordance with our prior decisions that a mortgage given to secure future advances is valid and will be judicially enforced . . .

Emporia State Bank & Trust Co. v. Mounkes
214 Kan. 178, 519 P.2d 618 (1974)

FONTRON, Justice:

The Emporia State Bank and Trust Company brings this action to foreclose a real estate mortgage. The defendants, Mr. and Mrs. Mounkes, filed an answer and cross petition. The court rendered personal judgment against the defendants for $1651.51 and a judgment in rem for $5911.53. The mortgage was foreclosed as to both sums. Judgment was also entered in favor of the bank on the defendants' cross petition. Mr. and Mrs. Mounkes have appealed.

No dispute exists concerning the facts. On February 13, 1963, Mr. and Mrs. Mounkes executed their promissory note to the bank in the amount of $12,500, and secured the same by a mortgage on an Emporia property which was their homestead. The face of the note indicates that monthly payments were started April 1, 1963. When the present proceedings were commenced the indebtedness had been reduced to $1573.57.

On February 27, 1971, some eight years after the mortgage was given, Mr. Mounkes executed his personal note to the bank for $5100. We were advised on oral argument that this loan was procured by Mr. Mounkes to assist a son in starting a restaurant business. A third note in the amount of $3711 was executed by Mr. Mounkes August 6, 1971. This loan was secured by a security agreement covering a 1970 Ford car and had been paid down to some $529 by the time the present action was filed.

To complete the factual picture, Mr. and Mrs. Mounkes were adjudicated bankrupts August 25, 1971, and both were duly discharged January 19, 1972.

In its petition the bank prayed for the foreclosure of its mortgage not only as to the balance due on the original note executed by Mr. and Mrs. Mounkes in 1963, but also as to the amounts alleged to be unpaid on the two subsequent notes signed by Mr. Mounkes in 1971. The bank's contention in such regard was and is predicated on a so-called dragnet provision contained in the mortgage. It reads as follows:

> This mortgage is given to secure payment of the sum of Twelve Thousand Five Hundred & no/100 Dollars ($12,500.00) and interest thereon, according to the terms of promissory note/s this day executed and subsequently to be executed by the mortgagors to the mortgagee, and all other sums which may hereafter be owing to the mortgagee by the mortgagors or any of them, however evidenced; it being understood and agreed that the mortgagee may from time to time make loans and advances to the mortgagors or any of them and that all such loans and advances and the interest thereon will be secured by this mortgage: provided that the aggregate principal amount of the loans and advances hereunder shall at no time exceed the amount hereinbefore stated.

The trial court agreed with the bank's position so far as the $5100 note was concerned and decreed that the balance due thereon as well as the balance due on the original note be made a lien on the mortgaged property. The court further ordered the mortgage foreclosed as to both amounts, which then totaled $7563.10. In so doing, the court forebore to enter personal judgment on the $5100 note signed by Mr. Mounkes, but granted judgment in rem against the real estate for the face amount thereof, plus interest. No judgment appears to have been rendered on the third note secured by the Ford car.

We should say at this point the defendants concede that the unpaid balance of the original note is secured by their mortgage of February 13, 1963. However, they take a quite different position with respect to the subsequent note signed by Mr. Mounkes on February 27, 1971, and they rely heavily on our opinion in Stockyards National Bank v. Capitol Steel & Iron Co., 201 Kan. 429, 441 P.2d 301. Before examining that decision in depth, we pause for a look at some guiding principles.

The dragnet syndrome is not a stranger in banking circles. Indeed, it has long found legislative recognition in what is now K.S.A.1973 Supp. 9-1101(4). Moreover, we apprehend that a future advances clause in a mortgage may provide an extremely useful and practical tool in facilitating many business and commercial type operations which involve frequent or continuing advancement of funds and extension of credits. (First Nat. Bank of Guntersville v. Bain, 237 Ala. 580, 188 So. 64.) One example, among others which come readily to mind, is found in the construction or building trade where the open end or dollar mortgage serves as a convenient device in facilitating the flow of funds at minimal expense. (See Potwin State Bank v. Ward, 183 Kan. 475, 327 P.2d 1091.) Some of the advantages which accrue both to the lender and to the borrower are pointed out by Professor Blackburn in Mortgages to Secure Future Advances, 21 Mo. Law Review 209.

In the great majority of cases where the question has arisen, the courts have held that future advancements made pursuant to a dragnet or open end type of mortgage came within the contemplation of the parties and were thus secured thereby. . . .

Despite recognition by both judicial and legislative bodies that the dragnet mortgage fills a contemporary need in the complex world of business, it is not a favorite of the law and is subject to interpretation and construction. As the Iowa Supreme Court so aptly observed in First v. Byrne, 238 Iowa 712, 28 N.W.2d 509, 172 A.L.R. 1072, " 'Dragnet' clauses are not highly regarded in equity. They should be 'carefully scrutinized and strictly construed.' " (pp. 715, 716, 28 N.W.2d p. 511.) This view was mirrored in Berger v. Fuller, 180 Ark. 372, 377, 21 S.W.2d 419, 421, where the Supreme Court of Arkansas, in speaking of a mortgage having a future advancements clause, said:

> . . . Mortgages of this character have been denominated 'anaconda mortgages' and are well named thus, as by their broad and general terms they enwrap the unsuspecting debtor in the folds of indebtedness embraced and secured in the mortgage which he did not contemplate, and to extend them further than has already been done would, in our opinion, be dangerous and unwise. . . .

Where the construction of a mortgage is brought in issue the primary question for determination is what was the intention of the parties. In arriving at a decision of the matter, all the circumstances attending the execution of the mortgage and the nature of the transaction are to be considered as well as the language of the instrument itself. (Hendrickson v. Farmers' Bk. & Trust Co., 189 Ark. 423, 433, 73 S.W.2d 725.) . . .

It occurs to us that a number of circumstances bear on the intention of the parties to the mortgage now before us. It was executed in 1963 to secure an indebtedness contemporarily incurred. The record shows no additional funds advanced to the Mounkes or further financial dealings had between them and the bank for more than eight years, when Mr. Mounkes "by his lonesome" signed a note for $5100. This latter note contains no reference of any sort to the real estate mortgage jointly executed eight years before. We believe the omission is significant, especially in view of the fact that a space was provided in the note for recording the description of collateral security. In the space thus provided there was typed, presumably by the bank, the word "Sig." The record reveals from statements made by plaintiff's counsel that this means "signature" and that "Normally, you think of a signature loan as being a loan on which there was no security whatsoever." Furthermore, the record bares no evidence of any relationship between the 1963 loan to Mr. and Mrs. Mounkes and the subsequent loan to Mr. Mounkes. There is not the slightest intimation that any part of the loan to Mr. Mounkes was to be used in the repair or improvement of the Mounkes residence — indeed, such a suggestion is negated by the statement that it was to help a son get into the restaurant business. . . .

An opinion we find persuasive hails from our sister state in the far reaches of the Pacific Ocean. In Akamine & Sons v. Am. Sec. Bank, 50 Haw. 304, 440 P.2d 262, questions of priority arose between two creditors, it being contended on the part of one bank that its dragnet mortgage gave it priority as to property which had been mortgaged to a second bank at a later date. The Supreme Court of Hawaii did not look kindly on the contention thus advanced, nor did it view dragnet mortgages in general with unjaundiced eye. In the opinion it was said:

> We are prevented from holding a mortgage to secure future advances contrary to public policy by its statutory authorization and the undeniable benefits which it may engender. As a court of equity, however, we will construe such mortgages very strictly against the mortgagee. . . . Completely unrestricted enforcement of such mortgages would tend to reduce the borrower to the status of economic serf. . . .
>
> Under the ejusdem generis rule, the statute does not require us to enforce a dragnet, or anaconda, clause in a mortgage as to debts or obligations not of the same kind as the specific principal debt or obligation for which the mortgage is given. Unless the prior or subsequent advance relates to the same transaction or series of transactions, the mortgage must specifically refer to it for the advance to be secured. This court will not assist a lending institution in an attempt to captivate a borrower by inclusion in a mortgage of a broad all inclusive dragnet clause. . . . To attempt to foreclose, for example, on the mortgagor's home for debts incurred in operating a business and which debts are not specifically covered by the mortgage would be unconscionable and contrary to public policy. (pp. 312, 313, 440 P.2d p. 267.)

We are aware that the trial court, in entering judgment in rem in favor of the bank, found it was the parties' intention at the time of the execution of the mortgage that it would secure payment of any sums of money which the mortgagee might loan the mortgagors or either of them. The difficulty with that conclusion is that the record contains no supporting evidence except for the dragnet clause itself. That clause we deem to be insufficient in the face of this record. As we have heretofore said, it is necessary, when determining the intention of the parties to a mortgage, that the attending circumstances and the nature of the transaction be considered. Here there is nothing from which it may be inferred that by mortgaging their homestead the defendants contemplated it would stand as security for a loan obtained by Mr. Mounkes to start his son in business eight years later. There is a total lack of evidence to sustain a presumption the two loans were related in any sense. The evidence is, indeed, quite to the contrary and we are constrained to hold the finding of the trial court is not sustained by the record.

In summary, we hold that in the absence of clear, supportive evidence of a contrary intention a mortgage containing a dragnet type clause will not be extended to cover future advances unless the advances are of the same kind and quality or relate to the same transaction or series of transactions as the principal obligation secured or unless the document evidencing the subsequent advance refers to the mortgage as providing security therefor. The loan extended to Mr. Mounkes in 1971 does not meet these criteria. . . .

The judgment entered against the defendants for $1651.51 on the original note and decreeing foreclosure of the mortgage as to such amount is affirmed. The judgment in rem in the amount of $5911.53 is reversed. The judgment in plaintiff's favor on the defendants' cross petition is affirmed.

It is so ordered.

NOTES AND QUESTIONS

1.   The Necessity of Consideration to Support a Valid Mortgage.   In Tyler v. Wright the defendants invoked the familiar legal principle that "it is essential to the validity of a mortgage, and to the right of the mortgagee to enforce it, that it should be supported by a valid consideration." But what is meant by this principle? As you know by now, a mortgage is the transfer of an interest in land as security for the repayment of money or for the performance of some other obligation that is measurable by money. Returning to the example at Chapter 4B1, supra, suppose Martha does not borrow $1,000 from her uncle but gratuitously promises to purchase all her groceries from him during the school year; she gives him a mortgage on her property to secure the promise. Would such a promise on her part support a valid mortgage?

Based on the foregoing definition of a mortgage, couldn't it be argued that the legal mortgage itself is an executed conveyance of an interest in land and no more requires consideration than does a gift or any other executed conveyance of an interest in land? See, e.g., Perry v. Miller, 330 Mass. 261, 112 N.E.2d 805 (1953), as commented on by Updike, Mortgages, in the 1953 Annual Survey of American Law, 29 N.Y.U. L. Rev. 829, 830 (1954). Moreover, the notion that a mortgage is enforceable without consideration is supported by the general rule, noted infra, that a valid mortgage may be given to secure a preexisting debt that is no longer enforceable under a local statute of limitations. Nevertheless, numerous case law decisions and commentators take the position (followed in Tyler v. Wright) that while the mortgage itself is an executed conveyance, the obligation that the mortgage secures must be supported by adequate consideration and be enforceable. See, e.g., Morvay v. Drake, 295 Ala. 174, 325 So. 2d 165 (1976); G. Nelson and D. Whitman, Real Estate Finance Law §2.3 (2d ed. 1985) (hereinafter Nelson and Whitman). But perhaps the real issues are *when* the obligation must be enforceable, against *whom* or *what,* and for *what purpose* the mortgagor becomes obligated to the mortgagee.

2. *Exceptions to the General Rule Requiring an Enforceable Obligation.* The general black-letter rule of law is that since ". . . the mortgage is a mere security for the debt . . . it logically follows that there must be some obligation for the lien to secure. When that obligation is discharged the mortgage becomes functus officio and legally dead." Egbert v. Egbert, 235 Ind. 405, 132 N.E.2d 910, 918 (1956).

However, the general rule requiring an enforceable obligation is subject to the following qualifications:

a. The Statute of Limitations on Indebtedness. Traditionally, separate remedies have existed for the enforcement of a mortgage and the debt that it secures. In the few jurisdictions that, like California, follow the "one action rule," the mortgage debt can only be enforced by an action to foreclose. Cal. Civ. Proc. Code §§580 (West 1976), 725a, 726 (West Supp. 1987). However, in most jurisdictions, the holder of a note secured by a mortgage has the right to sue in a personal action on the debt, to foreclose on the property, or to pursue both remedies concurrently.

In the opinion of most courts a mortgage is enforceable even though the underlying indebtedness is barred by a statute of limitations. The rationale generally provided reflects a "positivist" mode of thinking: the statute of limitations extinguishes the remedy of suing on the debt but not the debt itself. Accordingly, the mortgagee can still maintain an action to foreclose its lien on the property. And in the so-called title theory states, where ab initio the mortgagee retains both title and the legal right to possession, the mortgagee may also take possession or maintain an action of ejectment against a defaulting mortgagor even though the statute of limitations on the underlying indebtedness has expired. See, e.g., Phinney v. Levine, 116 N.H. 379, 359 A.2d 636 (1976); Taylor v. Quinn, 68 Ohio App. 164, 39 N.E.2d 627 (1941); Note, The Statute of Limitations as a Defense to Foreclosure in Illinois, U. Ill. L.F. 469 (1957); Nelson and Whitman §6.11. However, in a minority of lien theory states, the barring of any remedy on the debt also precludes foreclosure or any other remedy on the mortgage. See, e.g., Allen v. Shepherd, 162 Ky. 756, 173 S.W. 135 (1915); 161 A.L.R. 882, 890 (1946); Nelson and Whitman §6.11.

    b.   Open-end Mortgages and Dragnet Clauses.   In *Potwin State Bank* the mortgagor was a home builder who obtained an open-end mortgage so that he could finance, on an ongoing basis, the construction of a number of houses on lots owned by him. Such mortgages to secure future advances are commonly used with respect to construction financing and where the borrower and lender plan to transact business with one another on a continuous basis. The advantages to such an arrangement (whereby loan funds are advanced in increments rather than in one lump sum at the beginning) are that: (a) in continuous dealings the parties to a multiple loan transaction are spared the expense and inconvenience of refinancing the original loan or executing a series of junior mortgages on each new transaction; (b) in the case of construction financing the lender is assured prior to each loan advance that the work to date has been completed on schedule in accordance with approved plans and specifications and that the loan funds are being used properly to pay off the claims of subcontractors furnishing either labor (mechanics) or materials (materialmen); (c) both parties to the loan transaction may not be able to anticipate the nature or extent of the indebtedness at the time the mortgage is executed; and (d) the borrower is spared the cost of paying interest on the future advances until he is ready to use the funds.

    In the case of construction financing, a well-drafted construction or building loan agreement will specify the amount of the initial advance and the terms and conditions under which specified amounts of future advances will be made. However, as noted above, in some loan transactions (such as the one involved in *Potwin State Bank*) it may be impossible for the parties to stipulate either the amount or the terms of the future indebtedness, in which event phraseology of the "Dollar Mortgage" variety is frequently employed. See the first paragraph in Justice Shroeder's opinion. Do you see any problems with enforcing this type of broad-based language? What about the possibility of misleading third-party creditors?

    A broad variant of this approach is the so-called dragnet or anaconda clause whereby the secured real estate purports to secure automatically all other present or future indebtedness owed to the mortgagee regardless of when it is incurred and whether or not it relates to the instant transaction. While traditionally valid under mortgage law, these clauses have increasingly become the object of judicial scrutiny, for, as one court noted: "By their broad and general terms they enwrap the unsuspecting debtor in the folds of indebtedness embraced and secured in the mortgage which he did not contemplate." Berger v. Fuller, 180 Ark. 372, 377, 21 S.W.2d 419, 421 (1929). The recently emerging trend in the case law, as reflected by the holding in *Emporia State Bank and Trust Co.*, is to construe such clauses narrowly against the mortgagee and to limit their reach to additional indebtedness only if it relates to the current business transaction. In light of this, what precautionary measures should be taken by a prudent mortgagee who wishes to secure additional indebtedness not related to the original mortgage transaction?

In Tyler v. Wright the court states that ". . . the existence of an obligation to be secured is an essential element, without which the mortgage instrument is but a shadow without substance." By contrast, in *Potwin State Bank,* which involved a mortgage for future advances, the court recites the majority rule to the effect that such an "open-end" mortgage is valid because ". . . the obligation secured need not actually be in existence at the date of the execution of the mortgage . . ." Finally, in *Emporia State Bank and Trust Co.,* the court appears to acknowledge the validity of an open-end type of mortgage but holds that such a mortgage, by use of a dragnet clause, ought never to be so construed as to secure subsequent indebtedness that does not relate to the same transaction. On the basis of sound social policy can you think of a way to reconcile these apparently conflicting judicial points of view?

For additional discussion on mortgages for future advances and dragnet clauses see Blackburn, Mortgages to Secure Future Advances, 21 Mo. L. Rev. 209 (1956); Meek, Mortgage Provisions Extending the Lien to Future Advances and Antecedent Indebtedness, 26 Ark. L. Rev. 423 (1973); Note, Refinements in Additional Advance Financing: The "Open End" Mortgage, 38 Minn. L. Rev. 507 (1954); Note, Future Advance Clauses in Tennessee — Construction and Effect, 5 Mem. St. U.L. Rev. 586 (1975); Nelson and Whitman §12.7. See also discussion at Chapter 6A.

c. After-Acquired Property Clauses. If a mortgage can secure future indebtedness, does it logically follow that present indebtedness can be secured by a mortgage lien on after-acquired property? The answer is a qualified yes. To the extent that the after-acquired property consists of subsequent improvements on the land originally mortgaged, or additional personal property that is classified as a fixture under state law and becomes part of the real estate, the mortgagee should be able to enjoy the benefit of this after-acquired property, even without an after-acquired property clause, because by their very nature the improvements and fixtures automatically become part of the mortgaged real estate under the real estate property law. 3 G. Glenn, Mortgages §14.50 (1943); Nelson and Whitman §9.3.

If the mortgage is recorded before any fixture filings are made by others under Article 9 of the Uniform Commercial Code, the mortgagee's rights will normally be superior to the rights of holders of such security interests in the fixtures. However, under certain circumstances, the mortgagee's interest may be subordinate to holders of purchase money security interests in the fixtures. See U.C.C. §9-313(4)(a).

As to additional personal property that does not qualify as a fixture, an after-acquired property clause in a mortgage, properly identifying the collateral, creates only an unperfected security interest in such personal property when the property is subsequently acquired by the mortgagor. In order to perfect this security interest it would be necessary to file a financing statement under the applicable state's version of the Uniform Commercial Code. See U.C.C. §§9-401, 9-402.

A difficult problem exists when a mortgage purports to cover separate real property that the borrower may acquire in the future. Obviously, such property cannot be described in the original mortgage, and it may not be possible to record a new mortgage in the proper indexes for such after-acquired property. In such a situation the majority rule appears to be that the after-acquired property clause will be considered, in substance, a promise by the mortgagor to subject the after-acquired property to the lien of the mortgage and that such promise creates only an equitable lien warranting specific performance when the property is later acquired. 3 G. Glenn on Mortgages §412 (1943); Cunningham and Tischler, Equitable Real Estate Mortgages, 17 Rutgers L. Rev. 679, 719 (1963) (hereinafter Cunningham); Comment, Mortgages — After-Acquired Property Clause in Mortgage Is Valid, 28 Rocky Mtn. L. Rev. 432 (1956); Uniform Land Transactions Act §3-205(b) (1975). However, in some states such as New Jersey, the clause is effective only if the subsequently acquired property bears a functional relationship to the property originally mortgaged. E.g., Williamson v. New Jersey Southern Railroad, 29 N.J. Eq. 311, 337 (1878). See Cunningham, at 718; 3 G. Glenn on Mortgages §414 (1943); Nelson and Whitman §9.3.

However, even in those states where the clause is effective the mortgagee may be confronted with certain lien priority problems. Suppose, for example, that Dan Developer obtains a postconstruction mortgage loan from the Ace Insurance Company to fund the construction of an office building and that the mortgage contains an after-acquired property clause. Further assume that the land belonging to Dan and covered by the lien of Ace Insurance Company's mortgage

("Greenacre") is surrounded by adjacent farm land ("Whiteacre") that Dan would like to acquire as a future building site. Dan plans to use some of the postconstruction loan proceeds to construct a power plant on the mortgaged land that could service the future building site as well as the existing office building on Greenacre. While the equitable lien created by the after-acquired property clause is binding between the parties Dan and Ace, it will generally be subordinate to any liens placed on it prior to Dan's acquisition of Whiteacre, including any purchase-money mortgage given by Dan to acquire the additional property. See, e.g., Associates Discount Corp. v. Gomes, 338 So. 2d 552 (Fla. App. 1976); Chase National Bank v. Sweezy, 281 N.Y.S. 487 (1931), affd., 261 N.Y. 710, 185 N.E. 803 (1933). It may also pose serious lien priority problems for Ace under the local recording statutes, as suggested by the following hypothetical facts, as diagrammed in Figure 4-1.

F i g u r e   4-1

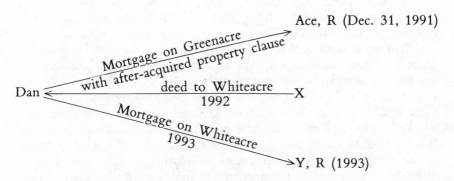

After reviewing the mechanics of searching title and the concept of record notice at Chapter 3B1, notes 2 and 3, consider the following dilemma confronting Ace: Since the after-acquired property clause in the original Ace mortgage (securing the postconstruction loan that was closed on December 31, 1991) could not and did not contain a legal description of the after-acquired property, Whiteacre, and the Ace mortgage was recorded *before* Dan acquired title to Whiteacre, the rule in the overwhelming majority of jurisdictions (based on a title-search burden rationale) is that any subsequent mortgagee or purchaser in the position of Y would not be put on record notice of Ace's security interest in Whiteacre and therefore Y would obtain a superior mortgage lien or take title to Whiteacre free and clear of Ace's interest. Otherwise, a title examiner who is searching Dan's chain of title on behalf of Y would have the onerous burden of checking in the grantor's index not only for conveyances and mortgages from each grantor (Dan's predecessors-in-title) after the grantor had acquired title, but also *prior* to the time that the grantor had acquired title (and conceivably as far back as the grantor's birth date). See Wheeler v. Young, 76 Conn. 44, 55 A. 670 (1903). Ayer v. Philadelphia & Boston Face Brick Co., 159 Mass. 84, 34 N.E. 177 (1893), is one of the few cases of record that holds to the contrary based on the so-called doctrine of estoppel by deed. This majority view would probably hold true even in a jurisdiction with a tract index, since the after-acquired property clause in Ace's mortgage makes no specific reference to Whiteacre; however, it is possible that the general reference to after-acquired property might constitute inquiry notice to subsequent takers in some jurisdictions. See, e.g., Guerin v. Sunburst Oil & Gas Co., 68 Mont. 365, 218 P. 949 (1923).

In addition, even in a jurisdiction that has adopted a tract index, the majority rule is that the after-acquired property clause in the Ace mortgage would constitute neither record nor inquiry notice to Y because the Ace mortgage relates to a different parcel of land and therefore would be outside of Y's chain of title. See Buffalo Academy of the Sacred Heart v. Boehm Brothers, 267 N.Y. 242, 196 N.E. 42 (1935). But see Guillette v. Daly Dry Wall, Inc., 367 Mass. 355, 325 N.E.2d 572 (1975).

Can you, as counsel to Ace, think of any protective language or procedure that might assure Ace of lien priority over Whiteacre as against any adverse or subsequent claimant in the position of Y? See Cunningham and Tischler, Equitable Real Estate Mortgages, 17 Rutgers L. Rev. 679, 719, n. 188. Suppose Ace and Dan know on December 31, 1991, the date on which the postconstruction loan on Greenacre is scheduled to close, that Dan plans to acquire Whiteacre, and Ace insists that the legal description in its mortgage make reference to Whiteacre as well as Greenacre even though at the time Dan has no legal or equitable title to Whiteacre. Assuming that Ace's lien on Whiteacre could somehow be recorded in a way that would show up in the present owner's (X's) chain of title and thus constitute record notice to Y, how might the present owner, X, be injured by such an unauthorized recordation? What, if any, recourse would X have against Ace or Dan? See Cawrse v. Signal Oil Co., 164 Or. 666, 103 P.2d 729 (1940).

3. Equitable Mortgage. The doctrine of equitable mortgages, which is broad-based and complicated, rarely surfaces in real estate financing because the parties to a transaction, especially where the financing of income-producing real estate is involved, are apt to be sophisticated and are almost invariably represented by legal counsel who will formalize the intentions of the parties by using forms of mortgages and other documentation that are tailored to the particular transaction.

Since a mortgage involves the transfer of an interest in land to the mortgagee, a mortgage must be in writing to comply with the Statute of Frauds. See, e.g., N.Y. Gen. Oblig. Law §5-703 (McKinney 1989). However, equitable principles may dictate that a mortgage is created and enforceable at equity even though it is neither written nor subscribed to by the mortgagor or a lawful agent. Simply put, the doctrine holds that equity will interpret what is a defective security agreement (such as a mortgage instrument that fails under the Statute of Frauds or the recording statutes) or what purports to be a nonsecurity transaction (such as a deed absolute) according to the intentions of the parties, and, as between the parties, such arrangement will be given effect as a lien or other security interest even though it does not meet the technical requirements for a legal mortgage. In addition, a lien will sometimes be imposed by an equity court purely as a remedial device to protect someone who would otherwise be treated unfairly. See generally Cunningham, at 683.

a. *Absolute Deed as Disguised Mortgage.* There have been a few cases involving unsophisticated borrowers in which at the behest of a lender a borrower delivered an absolute deed of conveyance on the oral understanding that the property would be reconveyed to the borrower once the indebtedness was repaid. Historically, the common-law mortgage was also in the form of an ordinary deed of conveyance, but with an express defeasance clause providing that the conveyance would be void on the payment of a sum of money or the performance of some other act. It is when this condition of defeasance is not appended in writing to the deed, but is claimed orally, that the problem arises. If the borrower can prove that the conveyance was merely intended as a security device, most courts will treat the deed as an "equitable mortgage" even though its real nature is not reflected by the terms of the instrument. Moreover, the clear majority rule under the case law in this country is that parol or extrinsic evidence is admissible at equity to demonstrate that a deed absolute on its face was knowingly intended as a mortgage. See Havana National Bank v. Wiemer, 32 Ill. App. 3d 578, 335 N.E.2d 506 (3d Dist. 1975); Nelson and Whitman §3.6. In a few states the party seeking reformation of the deed must prove that the defeasance clause was inadvertently or fraudulently omitted. Newton v. Clark, 174 N.C. 393, 93 S.E. 951 (1917). And in a few other states there are statutory restrictions. See, e.g., Ga. Code Ann. 44-14-32 (1982); Pa. Stat. Ann. tit. 21, §951 (Purdon 1955); N.H. Rev. Stat. Ann. §479:2 (1983). See R. Kratovil and B. Werner, Modern Mortgage Law and Practice §3.05(a)(1) (1981).

To discourage fraud by unscrupulous grantors who wish to rescind their bargains, clear and convincing evidence is generally required to establish the proposition that a deed absolute on its face is in reality a mortgage. As counsel to a borrower who claims that a deed he gave to a lender is really a mortgage, what evidence would you cite to prove your client's allegation? See Cunningham and Tischler, Disguised Real Estate Security Transactions as Mortgages in Substance, 26 Rutgers L. Rev. 1 (1972).

Sometimes a deed may be given to a third party to hold in escrow to secure payment of the debt. If the debt is not paid, the deed is to be released to the lender. In such a case, even if the deed is released, it does not give the lender good title to the property. The instrument is deemed to be a mortgage. See Hamud v. Hawthorne, 52 Cal. 2d 78, 338 P.2d 387 (1959); Pollak v. Millsap, 219 Ala. 273, 122 So. 16 (1929); Plummer v. Ilse, 41 Wash. 5, 82 P. 1009 (1905). It should be noted that a grantor who gives a deed absolute on its face instead of a mortgage runs a risk that the grantee may sell the land to a bona fide purchaser for value without notice. This BFP would then obtain an interest in the land superior to that of the borrower-grantor. If the grantor, however, remains physically in possession of the land, this may constitute inquiry notice, preventing the ultimate purchaser from acquiring BFP status. See R. Kratovil and B. Werner, Real Estate Law §223 (7th ed. 1979). Also, where the grantor delays in asserting his rights, he may be barred by the doctrine of laches. See Clontz v. Fortner, 88 Idaho 355, 399 P.2d 949 (1965); R. Kratovil and B. Werner, Modern Mortgage Law and Practice §3.05(c) (1981). See generally Fogelman, The Deed Absolute as a Mortgage in New York, 32 Fordham L. Rev. 299 (1963).

b. Negative Lien. Another type of "equitable mortgage" may arise where a borrower covenants not to transfer or encumber her land as long as certain indebtedness owed to the lender-covenantee remains unpaid. As opposed to a traditional mortgage, the negative lien, or negative pledge, arrangement can be advantageous where: (1) a traditional security interest is disallowed; (2) a lender is prohibited by its regulatory statute from lending against a junior lien; (3) it would be bothersome and expensive for a lender to use foreclosure to enforce a junior lien, especially where the debtor has other assets that could satisfy a small debt. Since such a negative covenant evinces an intention to create a security interest in the debtor's land, some courts have held that such arrangement constitutes an equitable mortgage. Compare Coast Bank v. Minderhout, 61 Cal. 2d 311, 38 Cal. Rptr. 505, 392 P.2d 265 (1964), revd. on other issues, 21 Cal. 3d 943 (1978), with Tahoe National Bank v. Phillips, 4 Cal. 3d 11, 480 P.2d 320, 92 Cal. Rptr. 704 (1971). For an excellent discussion of this financing device see Reichman, The Anti-Lien: Another Security Interest in Land, 41 U. Chi. L. Rev. 685 (1974). The negative pledge is also used extensively in corporate debenture financing. Such financing is unsecured, but the lender is protected by covenants made by the obligor that are designed to ensure that its assets will be available to satisfy the unsecured indebtedness.

    c. *Equitable Liens for Vendors and Vendees.* A purchaser of real
property who has paid the purchase price to the seller but has not
received title may have a lien thereon, especially if the vendee has
taken possession of the property in addition to payment. See Elterman
v. Hyman, 192 N.Y. 113, 84 N.E. 937 (1908); N.Y. Civ. Prac. Law
§3002(f) (Supp. 1988); Comment, The Vendee's Lien in New York:
Its Development, Applications and Status, 37 Alb. L. Rev. 470 (1973).
Similarly, a vendor of real property who has conveyed title may have
an equitable lien on the property conveyed for the unpaid balance of
the purchase price even though there is no express reservation in the
deed or elsewhere. See Boyer and Evans, The Vendor's Lien in Florida,
20 U. Miami L. Rev. 767 (1966). For the value of having an equitable
mortgage declared where the debtor is insolvent, see Application of
Ross Development Co., 102 F. Supp. 753 (E.D.N.Y. 1952). Where
the vendor inserts into the deed a reservation of a lien on the land,
this is sometimes viewed as a legal, rather than an equitable, mortgage.
See Norvell, The Vendor's Lien and Reservation of the Paramount
Legal Title — The Rights of Vendors, Vendees and Subvendees, 44
Tex. L. Rev. 22, 24 (1965). Some states have enacted legislation
recognizing such liens. See G. Osborne, Mortgages 29 (1970). While
such liens are binding as between the vendor and the vendee they are
subordinate to a federal tax lien, the claim of a trustee in bankruptcy,
and junior encumbrances that are recorded.

3. *Personal Liability of the Mortgagor*

Based on the foregoing discussion it might be argued that, regardless
of theory, the requirement that a mortgage be supported by an underlying obligation that is enforceable has been all but ignored in the
real world of real estate financing. However, on the assumption that
the general rule remains valid and requires the existence of an enforceable obligation, let us address the final question of whether the
mortgagor must be personally liable for the performance of such obligation.

Bedian v. Cohn
10 Ill. App. 2d 116, 134 N.E. 2d 532 (4th Dist. 1956)

SCHEINEMAN, Justice.
    In this suit the plaintiffs seek to hold defendant personally liable
for the balance due on the purchase price of real estate, notwithstanding

express provisions in the mortgage and note that defendants should not be liable for any deficiency.

The undisputed facts are that defendant Arnold Cohn contracted orally to purchase the property from plaintiffs, Asadour and Elizabeth Bedian, at a fixed price, to make a down payment, to pay the balance in installments, the defendant not to be liable for a deficiency in the event of foreclosure.

It is undisputed that the property is inadequate to cover the balance, but the chancellor decreed that though the plaintiffs were entitled to the property there was no personal liability on defendant.

On this appeal, it appears to be undisputed that pursuant to the oral contract, the parties met in a law office, the down payment was made, plaintiffs executed a deed to defendant, and the latter gave a mortgage and note for the balance, both of which expressly limited collection of the balance to the property pledged, and stated that the maker should not be personally liable for any deficiency. Some installments were paid.

Plaintiff contends these provisions are inconsistent, and ambiguous, and the court should hold the restriction on personal liability void. Defendant cites cases from other states that it is valid. While there is no reported decision in this state of precisely similar facts, the principle has been stated in accord with the weight of authority. Thus, in City of Joliet v. Alexander, 194 Ill. 457, 62 N.E. 861, 863, the opinion states:

> The provision for a mortgage implies a debt, since a mortgage cannot exist without a debt. The mortgage is a mere incident to a debt or obligation secured by it, and which is an essential element in a mortgage. . . . It is not essential to a debt or to a mortgage that there should be any promise of the mortgagor to pay the debt. The mortgage may be merely to secure payment, and a debt exists in many cases where there is no personal liability, and where there could be no suit at law, and no personal decree could be rendered for a deficiency. One who pawns or pledges his property, and who will lose the property if he does not pay, is indebted, although the creditor has nothing but the security of the property; and so, also, is a mortgagor who is liable to lose his property if he does not pay the money secured by the mortgage.

Again in Evans v. Holman, 244 Ill. 596, 91 N.E. 723, it was held that there must be a debt to constitute a mortgage, but there need not be any promise to pay the debt, and it is not essential that the obligation to pay be direct.

Accordingly, we hold that a mortgage and note are evidence of a debt, but an agreement therein that the collection of the debt is limited to the property pledged, without personal liability on the maker, is valid and will be enforced according to the expressed terms. . . .

We hold that where the contract of purchase contemplates that the buyer is not to be personally liable, and the documents are drawn in accordance with the agreement, the provisions therein are valid, and the seller cannot assert personal liability of the buyer. The decision of the chancellor was correct and is affirmed.

Decree affirmed.

NOTES AND QUESTIONS

1. *Recourse Versus Nonrecourse Financing.* In the case of income-producing real estate the postconstruction lender traditionally regards the improved real estate as the real security for its loan. See the introduction to Chapter 5A and Chapter 5C. In contrast to construction financing, it is the rental income stream from the mortgaged property and not the evanescent solvency of the developer-borrower that secures the obligation. Indeed, in appraising the value of the property to be mortgaged the lender will look primarily at the projected net rental income and make certain that the loan amount is low enough that the property will "pay for itself" by generating sufficient net income to cover the annual debt service payments on the mortgage. In addition, most postconstruction lenders will insist on receiving, as additional collateral, the right to receive an assignment of the high-credit leases and rents from the mortgaged real estate in the event of a material default by the borrower. See Chapter 5C and Chapter 10B4.

Accordingly, in most cases (especially when the loan amount is large) the lender will agree to accept nonrecourse financing, which means that in the event of a default and possible foreclosure the lender will only seek recourse against the property and not sue the borrower on the debt or seek a deficiency judgment against the borrower. To accomplish this objective, simple nonrecourse language such as "the borrower shall not be personally liable hereunder," or "in the event of default, mortgagee will not seek a deficiency judgment against the borrower and recourse may only be had against the property," or alternative phraseology of similar import should be inserted, as an exculpatory provision, in the mortgage note. And, if the property to be acquired is already subject to an existing mortgage, the purchaser should take the property "subject to the mortgage" and not "assume" the mortgage by means of an assumption agreement. Would such language be necessary to achieve nonrecourse financing in a jurisdiction that follows the "one action rule"? See Chapter 10C3, note 3. What about a jurisdiction that does not recognize deficiency judgments? Antideficiency judgment legislation is discussed at Chapter 10C3a.

In addition, if (as is frequently the case) the borrowing-ownership entity is a limited partnership, the investor partners may not be able to deduct their distributive share of tax losses in excess of their equity investments if the partnership engages in recourse as opposed to "qualified" nonrecourse financing to fund its cost of acquiring or constructing the mortgaged income-producing real estate. I.R.C. §465(b)(6); Treas. Reg. §1.752-1(e). See discussion at Chapter 2B, note 7diii.

2. *Tyler v. Wright and Bedian v. Cohn.*   After reviewing Tyler v. Wright, Bedian v. Cohn, and the notes in the preceding section, consider the following question. If it is axiomatic that a mortgage cannot exist without the survival of an underlying obligation, which of the two following black letter rules of law is *more* justifiable from a theoretical and practical standpoint? First is the majority rule, noted above, that a mortgage is valid and enforceable even though the underlying indebtedness is barred by the statute of limitations. Second is the well-settled rule that a mortgage is valid even though the mortgage note exculpates the mortgagor from personal liability with respect to repayment of the underlying indebtedness. See Nelson and Whitman §§2.1, 6.11.

3. *Illustrations of the General Rule.*   The general rule that a mortgage need not be supported by the personal obligation of the mortgagor is further illustrated by the following. First, there is authority to the effect that a mortgage remains valid even where the mortgagor is discharged from personal liability on the indebtedness as a consequence of bankruptcy proceedings. Second, it is clear that a mortgage to secure the promise of a third-party debtor is enforceable even where the mortgagor, himself, is under no obligation to the mortgagee. Nelson and Whitman §2.1; see Theodore v. Mozie, 230 S.C. 216, 95 S.E.2d 173 (1956).

C. THE MORTGAGE IN COMPETITION WITH OTHER REAL ESTATE INTERESTS

Let us briefly examine the nature of a mortgage in relation to other competing claims and interests in the same property. As you know, a mortgage is the transfer of an interest in land as security for the mortgagor's performance of an obligation to the mortgagee. Among the more typical claims and interests that may also encumber the mortgaged real estate are: (1) the lien of another mortgage on the same property; (2) a lease, which, as you may recall, is both the conveyance of an interest in land (leasehold estate) and a contract between the landlord-owner and tenant;[13] (3) the lien of a judgment creditor if the judgment against the owner of the land is docketed in

---

13. 2 R. Powell and P. Rohan, Real Property ¶¶478-482 (1981).

the county where the real estate is situated;[14] (4) the lien of a trustee at bankruptcy (or debtor in possession) where the owner of the real estate becomes a debtor under the Bankruptcy Code (see Chapter 10C2);[15] (5) the lien of the federal government against the owner's property (including the real estate) for unpaid income taxes;[16] (6) the lien of local government for unpaid real property taxes;[17] (7) the liens of a general contractor or subcontractors who are not paid after furnishing labor (mechanics' liens) or supplying materials (materialmen's liens) in connection with the construction of improvements on the land (see Chapter 6B3); (8) the equitable interest (under the doctrine of equitable conversion) of a purchaser of the mortgaged real estate (see Chapter 3A, note 1c and Chapter 4B2, note 3c); and (9) the interest of a holder of an easement on the land.

In the event of a default by the mortgagor, the mortgagee will most likely choose to pursue a course of action less drastic than accelerating the indebtedness and instituting an action to foreclose the mortgage. However, if the mortgagee, mortgagor, and other interested parties are confronted with foreclosure they must concern themselves with the priority of their respective claims and interests in the mortgaged property. This is true because the very purpose of foreclosure is to enable the mortgagee to be made whole again from the security as it existed at the time the mortgage was created, free and clear of any junior interests. Accordingly, when the mortgaged property is sold at foreclosure the mortgagor and the holders of junior interests, including liens and encumbrances ("junior parties"), must face the specter of having their interests extinguished and of sharing whatever surplus remains after the foreclosure sale (in order of their lien priority) after payment of the mortgage indebtedness and the expenses of the foreclosure sale. See Chapter 10C2, note 2. By contrast, the position of senior interest-holders ("senior parties") is not vulnerable to foreclosure.

1. Principles Governing Priority of Interests

How are priorities established for conflicting liens and interests in mortgaged real estate? Priority problems abound throughout the law of mortgages. For example, special rules apply to after-acquired property clauses (see Chapter 4B2, note 2c, supra); to mechanics' and materialmen's liens and the doctrine of obligatory versus optional advances (see Chapter 6B, note 2); to leasehold mortgages (see Chapter 8A); to liens on personal property under the Uniform Commercial Code; to

14. See, e.g., Pa. Stat. Ann. tit. 21, §351 (Purdon 1955).
15. Bankruptcy Code, 11 U.S.C. §544(a) (1988).
16. See I.R.C. §6321.
17. See, e.g., N.Y. Real Prop. Tax Law §902 (McKinney 1990).

purchase-money mortgages (see Chapter 9B, note 5); and to the doctrine of marshalling assets (see Chapter 9B, note 3) and other miscellaneous subject areas. However, in this brief overview let us confine our attention to general principles.

Prioritization of conflicting liens and interests in the mortgaged real estate generally follows the common-law rule "first in time, first in right," as modified by the recording statute in the jurisdiction where the mortgaged property is situated. The policy purpose of the recording statute system is to facilitate land transfers by enabling a subsequent purchaser or encumbrancer to rely on what was recorded in the registry of deeds office as a source of information with respect to the status of title and existence of any prior claims. Some recording statutes, called "race statutes," emphasize the race to the registry of deeds office; thus "first in time" means the time that the subsequent interest is "perfected" by recordation. The emphasis of these statutes is to penalize the interest-holder that fails to record its interest promptly. At the other end of the policy spectrum are "notice statutes," which emphasize protecting the subsequent purchaser or encumbrancer who takes without notice of any prior claim even if the subsequent taker is slow in recording its interest. Under these statutes "first in time" means the time that the subsequent interest is taken without notice. In the middle of the penalty-protection spectrum are "race-notice" statutes, under which a subsequent purchaser or encumbrancer is afforded protection against a prior claim only if the subsequent interest is recorded first *and* is taken without notice of the prior interest. Accordingly, "first in time" in this context means the time that the subsequent interest is taken without notice and recorded.[18]

As applied to foreclosure this means, for example, that if Dan Developer executes and delivers a mortgage to Ace Insurance Company and Ace immediately records, then, subject to certain exceptions, Ace would occupy the position of a senior party and be accorded lien priority over any interest that is created after Ace records its mortgage. In general, this means that Ace's mortgage will take priority over subsequently recorded lessees, mortgagees, buyers, judgment creditors, holders of easements, and other subsequent interests in the property.

Notable exceptions to the general rule are: (1) that a lien for unpaid local property taxes will generally be accorded priority over all other interests in the mortgaged real estate, regardless of when recorded;[19] (2) that in some jurisdictions, a mechanic's lien may take precedence over a previously recorded real estate mortgage;[20] and

18. For a discussion of recording statutes see generally American Law of Property §17 (Casner ed. 1952); see also discussion at Chapter 3B1.

19. See, e.g., N.Y. Real Prop. Tax Law §§912, 914 (McKinney 1990). Local property taxes are discussed at Chapter 5B6, note 2.

20. See R. Powell and P. Rohan, Real Property ¶¶483 to 490 (1981); see generally discussion at Chapter 6B3.

(3) that an unrecorded purchase-money mortgage may prevail over any prior judgment lien creditor (see discussion at Chapter 9B, note 5c).

While a junior party is afforded limited protection by virtue of its right of redemption and its ability to bid in at the foreclosure sale (as discussed at Chapter 9B, note 2 and Chapter 10C2c, note 4), the general rule is that the mortgagee that forecloses its mortgage can terminate all interests that are junior in lien priority to the mortgage that is being foreclosed. Returning to our hypothetical, assume that Dan Developer has fee simple title to some rental real estate ("Greenacre") that is security for a fee mortgage loan made to Dan by the Ace Insurance Company. Dan then executes a long-term lease with the Widget Corporation of America ("WCA"), which is recorded after Ace records its mortgage. Finally, Dan obtains a second mortgage loan from Fuller National Bank ("FNB"), the lien of which also covers Greenacre, as diagrammed in Figure 4-2.

F i g u r e   4-2

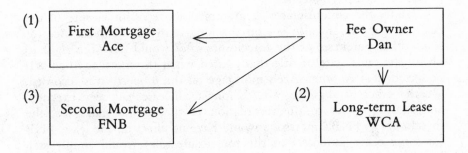

The numbers indicate the chronological order of recordation.

Suppose that the first mortgage (held by Ace) had a loan-to-value ratio of 75 percent and was in the amount of $25 million, and the second mortgage (held by FNB) amounted to $8 million. Because of Ace's lien priority over FNB, the foreclosure of Ace's mortgage could cut off FNB's mortgage. FNB could protect itself by attending the foreclosure sale and bidding an amount at least equal to the balance of Ace's mortgage, thus in effect paying off Ace's mortgage and obtaining the property free and clear of the first mortgage lien. If there were competitive bidding at the foreclosure sale, FNB might have to bid even beyond the amount of the first mortgage, up to the total of both mortgages, in order to protect itself.

Are the consequences of the first in time rule fair? Suppose, for example, that Greenacre had a value of $33 million at the time Ace and FNB made their mortgage loans. Ace's loan would then have been secured by a mortgage lien on 75 percent of the original value of the property, which would still have provided FNB with an equity cushion of $8 million as security for its loan. Further assume that when Ace forecloses its mortgage the balance of the loan has been scaled down to $22 million, which amount exactly equals the current market value of the property. Could FNB reasonably contend that Ace's lien priority should be limited to 75 percent of the $22 million loan balance, or $16.5 million in order to preserve the relative lien priorities that existed at the time the mortgages were consummated? Such an approach would compel both the senior and junior interest holder to share the burden of any loss caused by the reduced value of the property, thus enabling FNB to protect itself at the foreclosure sale by bidding in only $16.5 million instead of $22 million for the property.

Although clearly not the law, "relative priority" (as opposed to what amounts to "absolute priority") raises some interesting questions. For example, why would Ace limit its loan to 75 percent of the value of the property in the first place? When FNB made its loan, did it assume the risk that any future erosion of Dan's equity cushion might impair its security interest?

Under the circumstances diagrammed above, a foreclosure of the Ace mortgage might also cut off the long-term lease because Ace (or some other purchaser at the foreclosure sale) would have the right to obtain the same state of title that existed when the mortgage lien was perfected, that is, when Ace's mortgage on the property was recorded. On the other hand, since WCA's long-term lease had been executed and recorded prior to the recordation of the second mortgage, the foreclosure of FNB's mortgage would have no effect on the lease. FNB (or some other purchaser at the foreclosure sale) would simply step into Dan's shoes and acquire title (subject to the interests of both senior parties), Ace's mortgage, and WCA's leasehold estate.

2. Changing Priorities: Subordination and Nondisturbance Agreements

Lien priorities (or their consequences at foreclosure) can be altered by means of an agreement between the parties such as a subordination or a nondisturbance agreement.[21] Such agreements are used for various kinds of real estate financing situations. For example, a seller of land

---

21. See G. Osborne, Handbook on the Law of Mortgages 549-554 (1951) (real estate); U.C.C. §9-316 (priority subject to subordination).

who takes back a purchase-money mortgage from a buyer-developer might be required by the latter to subordinate the lien of its purchase-money mortgage to any subsequent mortgage lien held by an institutional lender. Otherwise, the developer might be required to pay off the purchase-money indebtedness before it could finance the improvement of the real estate inasmuch as most institutional lenders will require a first mortgage lien on the improved property. See Chapter 9B, note 5a.

In the context of foreclosure, subordination frequently becomes important with respect to certain mortgage loans where the security for the loan is the value attributable by the lender's appraiser to the rental obligations of specified credit, or so-called prime tenants. Examples include loan transactions involving shopping centers, office buildings with long-term tenants, warehouses and other industrial facilities, and urban renewal projects that are master-leased to a local housing authority. As discussed at Chapter 10C2a, when judicial foreclosure is employed, a junior interest cannot be terminated in most jurisdictions unless the junior party is joined as a party defendant in the foreclosure proceedings.[22] Consequently, with respect to Figure 4-2, WCA's leasehold estate would not be terminated unless Ace joins in WCA as a party-defendant. However, in some deed-of-trust jurisdictions such as California, and in a few states where the mortgage form is employed, any lease that is subsequently recorded or otherwise made subordinate to a mortgage will be automatically extinguished at foreclosure, whether or not the lessee is joined as a defendant.[23] In such a jurisdiction Ace might execute and record a subordination agreement whereby Ace would agree to subordinate its mortgage to the WCA lease. Otherwise, this valuable lease (that feeds Ace's mortgage) could be inadvertently terminated at foreclosure, and Ace or some other purchaser at the foreclosure sale could no longer rely on the rental income stream from the WCA lease to defray the expenses associated with the ownership and operation of the property.

As an alternative to subordination, a junior lease will survive foreclosure, even in a jurisdiction where such a lease is ordinarily extinguished at foreclosure, if a tenant such as WCA agrees to execute a so-called attornment agreement, whereby the lessee agrees beforehand to "attorn to," or recognize, the mortgagee or other purchaser at the foreclosure sale as the new landlord. As quid pro quo for the attornment agreement a well-advised tenant would require the mortgagee to execute

---

22. See Metropolitan Life Insurance Co. v. Childs Co., 230 N.Y. 285, 130 N.E. 295, rehg. denied, 231 N.Y. 551, 132 N.E. 885 (1921); Davis v. Boyajian, 11 Ohio Misc. 97, 40 Ohio Op. 2d 344, 229 N.E. 2d 116 (1967).

23. E.g., McDermott v. Burke, 16 Cal. 580, 590 (1860).

a nondisturbance agreement, whereby Ace agrees that if its senior mortgage is foreclosed, it will, depending on state foreclosure procedure, not cut off the lease with WCA; or, if the lease is nevertheless terminated, Ace agrees to recognize WCA as tenant under a lease containing the same terms and conditions as the previous lease.

As attorney for WCA, you would want to caution your client that a nondisturbance agreement does not afford the same protection as a subordination agreement. The nondisturbance agreement is a contract that might be disaffirmed by any trustee in bankruptcy or any conservator appointed in the event of Ace's insolvency, while a subordination agreement, once executed and recorded, is an accomplished act that is not subject to disaffirmance under §365(a) of the Bankruptcy Code. In addition, statutes regulating the investment portfolios of institutional lenders often prohibit the making of a leasehold mortgage if the underlying fee is subject to any prior lien. See Chapter 8A2. While a subordination agreement would obviate this problem, a nondisturbance agreement would not. Thus, if WCA should contemplate leasehold mortgage financing at some time in the future, it would be well-advised to insist on a subordination rather than a nondisturbance agreement. Also, much of the recent litigation pertaining to subordination agreements deals with whether such contracts are sufficiently definite and reasonable on their face to be enforceable; hence the need for careful draftsmanship by the party who is seeking enforcement.[24]

Finally, any provision in the lease agreement with a "prime" tenant that automatically subordinates the lease to *any* mortgage would be objectionable to a lender such as Ace, which holds the first mortgage on the property, since a second mortgagee that forecloses its mortgage could inadvertently or purposely terminate the WCA lease without Ace's consent.[25]

3. Direct Versus Indirect Encumbrances

An indirect encumbrance is an interest (such as a leasehold mortgage) that does not *directly* encumber the fee but merely encumbers one that does (such as a leasehold estate that constitutes the security for the leasehold mortgage). See Figure 4-3. As you read the materials dealing with leasehold mortgage financing at Chapter 8A, keep in mind the

24. See generally Lambe, Enforceability of Subordination Clauses, 19 Real Prop. Prob. & Tr. J. 631 (1984).

25. See discussion at Chapter 5C. See, e.g., Handy v. Gordon, 65 Cal. 2d 578, 422 P.2d 329, 55 Cal. Rptr. 769 (1967); Malani v. Clapp, 56 Haw. 507, 542 P.2d 1265 (1975). See generally 26 A.L.R.3d 855; Miller, Starr, and Regalia, Subordination Agreements in California, 13 UCLA L. Rev. 1298 (1966); Nelson and Whitman §12.9.

special priority rule that in the event of a foreclosure the rights of indirect interest holders, like those of a leasehold mortgagee, will depend *not* on their own lien priority but on the lien priority of the direct encumbrancers. The following figure illustrates this rule.

F i g u r e   4-3

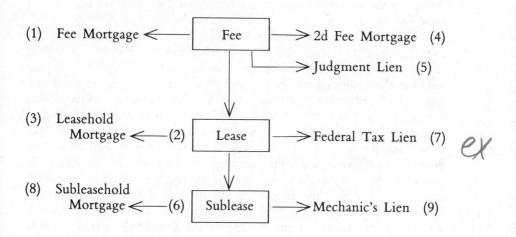

Once again the parenthetical numbers indicate the chronology of recordation and perfection of the various interests. First, the fee owner obtains a mortgage loan secured by a first mortgage lien on the fee owner's title to the land. Next, the fee owner ground leases the fee to the ground lessee, who in turn borrows money to construct a building on the land by obtaining a leasehold mortgage, the lien of which covers the leasehold estate (including the building and other leasehold improvements situated on the land). Then, the fee owner obtains a second mortgage loan; thereafter a judgment is docketed by a judgment creditor, thus creating a lien on the fee title to the land. Next, the ground lessee subleases the building to an occupancy tenant. Then the ground lessee fails to pay a tax liability that is owed to the federal government and a tax lien is filed on the leasehold estate. Finally, the subtenant obtains a subleasehold mortgage to fund the cost of renovating the building, and a subcontractor files a mechanic's lien on the subleased building.

Based on the foregoing scenario, what would happen to the federal tax lien if the second mortgagee were to foreclose its mortgage? The answer is: nothing. Even though the federal tax lien was filed after the recordation of the second mortgage, there is no direct legal relationship between these encumbrances because the federal tax lien encumbers the leasehold estate, while the second mortgage lien encumbers the fee. As for the *direct* encumbrances that encumber the fee, the ground lease is senior in lien priority to the second mortgage because it was recorded earlier; hence, the federal tax lien will survive because its viability depends on the lien priority of the interest to which it attaches rather than on its own lien priority as an indirect encumbrance. Conversely, if the second mortgage had been recorded ahead of the ground lease, foreclosure of the former could terminate the latter and indirectly terminate the federal tax lien, which depends on the ground lease for its survival.

Likewise, there is no direct legal relationship between the fee mortgage and the leasehold mortgage because the former encumbers the fee while the latter is an indirect encumbrance that merely encumbers the leasehold estate. Nevertheless, foreclosure of the fee mortgage could indirectly terminate the leasehold mortgage. Why is this so? Indeed, as observed at Chapter 8A2, this is why regulatory statutes frequently prohibit lenders from making a leasehold mortgage loan where the fee title to the underlying land is subject to a prior lien or possibility of reverter. After reviewing the discussion at Chapter 4C2, supra, can you explain why a leasehold mortgagee would be protected against a prior first mortgage lien on the fee if the first mortgagee agrees to subordinate its lien to the ground lease? Would such a subordination mean that foreclosure of the leasehold mortgage could extinguish the fee mortgage, or would its sole effect be to prevent the foreclosure of the fee mortgage from affecting the ground lease and the leasehold mortgage?

Based on the hypothetical facts in Figure 4-3, what would happen to the sublease (6) if the ground lease (2) were terminated because of a default under the lease by the ground lessee or because the fee mortgagee forecloses its mortgage (1)? Do you see why the consequences for the sublessee (6) are the same as they would be for the leasehold mortgagee (3)? Would a nondisturbance agreement from the fee mortgagee (1) in favor of the sublessee (6) protect the subleasehold mortgagee (8) in the event that the fee mortgagee were to foreclose its mortgage (1)? Similarly, could a foreclosure of the judgment lien (5) threaten the viability of the subleasehold mortgage (8)?

D. SUPPLY AND DEMAND FOR MORTGAGE CREDIT

Throughout this book reference will be made to the master hypothetical at Chapter 5B. In the hypothetical a typical real estate borrower, Dan

Developer, decides to construct an office building that he thinks will be worth at least $33⅓ million on completion and applies for a relatively long-term postconstruction loan of $25 million from the Ace Insurance Company and a short-term construction loan in the same amount from a separate lender, the Fuller National Bank. Both loans will be secured by mortgages. However, sometimes a developer will not seek a mortgage loan but instead use some alternative financing technique such as a sale and leaseback, sale and buyback, installment land contract, or perhaps a tax-free exchange. Nevertheless, projects involving rental real estate usually depend on some form of mortgage financing. Accordingly, we will briefly examine the mortgage market for income-producing real estate by learning which variables in our economy govern the supply and demand for mortgage credit. The related questions of who the major types of mortgage lenders are and how they function are discussed at Chapter 5A2. The recent trend toward the securitization of commercial real estate mortgages in the form of commercial mortgage-backed bonds (CMBBs) is examined at Chapter 13B.

As explained above, the profitability of investing in income-producing real estate, as opposed to other investment media such as stocks and bonds, can be explained to a large extent by the interplay between the financial leverage and tax benefits accorded to the real estate investor. See Chapter 2A, note 2 and 2B. Accordingly, the cost and availability of mortgage credit is of paramount concern to any leverage-minded purchaser or developer of some income-producing real estate. So, for example (returning to the hypothetical at Chapter 5B), with a loan-to-value ratio of 75 percent the debt service payments on the $25 million mortgage can represent such a large percentage of Dan Developer's operating expenses that a mere one- or two-point increase in the annual interest rate of 10 percent could reduce his investors' rate of equity return to a point at which they decide to abandon the project.

One of the few truisms in real estate is that the financing and profitability of any project are bound to depend on a number of economic factors that are unique to the particular transaction. So, for example, the terms of the postconstruction financing sought by Dan (such as the interest rate, loan-to-value ratio, and maturity date) will depend on a number of deal-specific factors such as the type of lending institution and property involved. However, as explained in the first excerpt that follows, the cost and availability of mortgage credit will also be influenced by certain macroeconomic variables such as household savings and also by the actions of the Federal Reserve Board. As a consequence, the cost and supply of mortgage money historically have tended to be countercyclical. In plain language this means that, except for a few instances of "stagflation" (such as during the 1980-1981 recession) and credit stringency (as in the recession that started in 1990) real estate borrowers seem to fare well when the economy is lagging and to fare poorly when the economy is doing well. A good example is the real estate boom that originated during the 1970-1971 and 1980-1981 recessions.[26] The first excerpt attempts to explain this paradox.

Postconstruction financing is relatively long-term, and therefore the cost of mortgage credit from a postconstruction lender ordinarily is geared to the level of long-term interest rates (such as the yields on 10-year Treasury bonds), which tend to be a function of: (1) inflationary expectations; (2) "uncertainty" over the federal budget and other future financial and political developments; and (3) the "real" or "time" value of money[27] (which most economists project to be in the 3.5 percent to 4.0 percent range over a long period). The level of short-term interest rates (such as the prime rate), which governs the cost of mortgage credit from a construction or "interim" lender (during the two- or three-year period of construction), is also influenced by the long-term factors mentioned above. For the most part, however, short-term rates are a product of Federal Reserve action to combat inflation (by constricting the money supply and thereby increasing short-term rates) or to encourage economic growth (by reducing short-term rates). But in any event, as noted in the first excerpt, real estate borrowers are so leverage-minded that demand for mortgage credit historically has been "passive" relative to supply. In other words, until recently, new construction often took place even when additional real estate space was not needed, if interest rates fell low enough. However, this did not hold true for the recession of the second half of 1990. Because of the slump in demand caused by overbuilding during the 1980s (as reflected by a national vacancy rate of about 20 percent for downtown office space in 1990) and the curtailment of real estate lending by commercial banks and insurance companies (especially in the Northeast), real estate borrowers encountered difficulties in obtaining mortgage credit at the beginning of 1991 notwithstanding a reduction in short- and long-term interest rates between September 1990 and February 1991. See Madison and Dwyer at ¶2.01[1][2][i] (Cum. Supp. no. 1) (1991).

As to the demand for new housing and rental space in office buildings, shopping centers, apartment buildings, warehouses, and hotels, real estate professionals attempt to analyze and forecast the relevant macroeconomic variables such as changes in population, employment, households, income and consumption expenditures; construction, en-

---

26. As a consequence of recent deregulation and less disintermediation within the mortgage lending industry, these countercyclical fluctuations should become less severe. See discussion at note 2, infra.

27. The time value of money is one of the most important financial principles, and yet it still appears to be an underrated topic in the curricula of most law schools. See discussion at Chapter 2A, note 3.

ergy, and maintenance costs; the opportunity costs of foregoing equity investment alternatives such as stocks and bonds; tax considerations; and political and socioeconomic factors. For example, the October 1987 collapse in stock prices and the subsequent contraction in the banking industry presaged a diminished demand for new office space in financial centers like New York City. By monitoring these macroeconomic variables, real estate developers and lenders are better able to make well-informed decisions.

Madison and Dwyer, The Law of Real Estate Financing
2-2 (1981)

¶2.01 THE STRUCTURE OF THE MORTGAGE MARKET

[1] COST AND AVAILABILITY OF MORTGAGE CREDIT

The cost and availability of mortgage credit at any moment in time depends on (1) the size of the savings inflow into the total credit stream; (2) the competition between real estate and business/government sectors indirectly in the short-term money market and directly in the long-term capital market for their fair share of credit; (3) the role that the federal government chooses to play at any given time in regulating both credit for new real estate development and the secondary residential mortgage market; and (4) the demand for credit by real estate developers, owners, and investors.

[a] Savings-Based Supply of Total Credit

Picturing the total supply of credit as a stream, the size of this stream flowing into the mortgage sector will initially depend upon the amount of net national savings, which in all its forms constitutes the ultimate financing source for real estate and all other capital formation in the economy. Accordingly, one key to understanding the availability of mortgage money in broad terms is to understand what variables affect the ebb and flow of net national saving, especially that portion generated by household saving.

Gross savings by household is the amount of after-tax disposable income left over after expenditures for current consumption needs, and net savings is the balance of gross savings remaining after expenditures for the purchase of such durables as automobiles and refrigerators. While business and government sectors contribute to the gross savings inflow, both sectors are primarily net borrowers. By far, the most important source of net savings is the consumer or household sector, which has generated between 66 and 80 percent of gross national savings in recent years.

Historically, real aggregate income and household income both rise, as does the nation's gross national product (GNP), in a growing economy. As household income increases, so will household saving, because a household's propensity to save an extra dollar of disposable income increases percentagewise as the household has more and more income left over after paying for needed goods and services. Conversely, as national income declines, as in a recession, or in a rampaging inflation, real household income and gross savings tend to fall, since households collectively must use a greater percentage of their incomes to meet current needs. Likewise, when households buy a disproportionate amount of capital goods, as when automobile sales are unusually high, their rate of net savings tends to decrease. It is primarily this net savings inflow by households that directly fuels the total credit system, and indirectly fuels the mortgage market.

However, for these funds to flow into the mortgage market, household savings deposits must be made into the financial intermediaries: commercial banks, mutual savings banks, savings and loans (S&Ls), life insurance companies, pension trusts, and real estate investment trusts (REITs). In turn, the financial intermediaries themselves must decide what portion of the investment reserves (from deposits, retained earnings and loan payments) to allocate to mortgages.

If households tend to emphasize other investments, such as savings bonds, stocks, or other securities, and if the financial intermediaries themselves also favor nonmortgage instruments to invest in, there can be a dramatic removal of funds available to make mortgage loans.

[b] Countercyclical Mortgage Credit Supply

Historically, mortgage credit and construction begin to rise as a *percentage* of GNP during economic downswings and begin to decline as the economy reaches full capacity. During an economic expansion period, the demand for short-term credit by business borrowers, combined with Federal Reserve anti-inflation monetary measures, drives up the money market rate structure faster than both savings and time-deposit rates and the long-term capital market structure, of which mortgage credit is a part. In response, both households and financial intermediaries tend to invest in these higher-yielding assets and cause an outflow of available mortgage money. This process is referred to as disintermediation.

The capital assets themselves can also cause additional disinter-mediation from the mortgage market. Traditionally, a rate spread has existed between the higher-yielding mortgage and the lower-yielding corporate and U.S. long-term bonds, since bonds tend to be more liquid and entail less administrative expenses. However, when loanable funds are in short supply and business demands intensify, corporate bond rates start to rise at a faster rate than contract yields on mortgages. Within recent times, diversified lenders, such as insurance companies and mutual savings banks, have switched a large portion of their portfolios from mortgages to bonds. However, even with record high bond yields, institutional lenders have become somewhat reluctant to invest in long-term bonds because of their fear that rampant inflation will erode the fixed yield from bonds and that falling bond prices may prevent them from liquidating their assets without incurring substantial portfolio losses.

Conversely, during a period of economic decline and impending recession, the business demand for short-term credit to finance inventories and output-producing capital goods slackens. During this time, demand for credit falls relative to household saving, which causes money market and corporate bond rates to fall faster than long-term mortgage yields. Moreover, the Federal Reserve often increases bank credit, which drives down money market interest rates even further. As short-term rates fall faster than long-term rates, a form of disintermediation-in-reverse occurs as both households and financial intermediaries reallocate investment funds into mortgages and other capital investments.

It is this countercyclicality that has led to four recent credit crunches for real estate borrowers: first in 1966, then in 1969-1970, next in 1973-1974, and finally in 1978-1979. Each occurred when the American economy was approaching full capacity and short-term interest rates began to outpace long-term rates. Conversely, the largest real estate boom in history started during the 1970-1971 recession when real GNP had dropped from 724.7 billion in 1969 to 715.9 billion by the last quarter of 1970.

[c] Demand "Passive" Relative to Supply

While the amount and cost of mortgage money flowing into the real estate sector is determined by counterfluctuations, it also depends to some extent on the collective demand for credit on the part of real estate borrowers.

In general, business borrowers enjoy a preferential claim to available funds because they tend to be such large and regular depositors. Thus, real estate borrowers fare better not when real estate demand is strong but when business demand is weak.

Real estate developers have traditionally leveraged their investments to a much greater degree than their rivals in the business sector. Often a one- or two-point increase in mortgage rates will decrease an investor's rate of equity return to a point of unprofitability. Therefore, a real estate borrower or developer remains out of the mortgage market (if he can) during high rates, since the projects he had in mind have become financially unfeasible. Therefore, levels of real estate construction activity depend more upon the availability and cost of mortgage money than upon market demand for space. . . .

The following excerpts deal with a longstanding (and two-edged) economic policy dispute that is bound to have a profound impact, not just on the real estate sector, but the entire economy as well during the 1990s and beyond. On the fiscal side of the coin is the still-raging debate among respected economists as to what if any impact the escalating federal budget deficits will have on future interest rates and the future supply of credit for real estate borrowers. On the monetary side of the debate is the dilemma that has long confronted the Federal Reserve Board (as illustrated by its meanderings during the post-1979-1980 economic recovery): whether it should ease the nation's supply of credit and lower interest rates in order to stimulate economic growth or tighten the money supply and increase interest rates in order to combat inflation and preserve the value of the dollar.

Before we examine two weightier excerpts dealing with the budget deficit problem, let's see what a more pedestrian commentator has to say. By the time you read this excerpt we should all know whether doomsday is really at hand as predicted by Dr. Batra in his book *The Great Depression of 1990.*

Hayes, Depression Guru Ravi Batra: Economist or Mystic? Tune in Around 1990 to Find Out
N.Y. Times, Aug. 30, 1987, sec. 3, p. 7, col. 1

At the Crescent Club a few weeks ago, a slightly built professor told more than 200 of Dallas's richest people that a terrible depression was looming. But there was a way out, he said: Every American family worth more than $2 million would have to accept a wealth tax averaging 5 percent of net worth.

"People in a position to pay taxes should pay them now" and erase the Federal budget deficit, Dr. Ravi Batra urged his audience. "If they do, we still have time. We still have two and a half years to go."

There were several gasps and snickers audible from the rear and, in a few minutes, some men in dark suits walked out. But most listeners, including the wealthy Hunt brothers, stayed on, some taking notes, as the professor detailed his vision of international economic chaos and doled out doomsday investment advice. . . .

His book, "The Great Depression of 1990," is No. 3 on today's New York Times best-seller list for non-fiction. His predictions in the early 1980's of low inflation, falling oil prices, a wave of mergers and a booming stock market — mocked for years — have proved close to the mark.

What will the start of a new depression look like? Dr. Batra said there will be trade deficits and Federal budget deficits through the next two years, and, probably by 1989's fourth quarter, foreign investors will lose confidence in the American economy and unleash a free-fall in the value of the dollar. He said central banks in the United States, Japan, Germany and Britain will be unable to break the fall. . . .

Investors will conclude that the rising cost of Japanese goods in the United States will dampen future exports from Japan, and rush to liquidate their holdings in the Japanese stock market. A selling panic will spread to Wall Street and other foreign markets. Within six months, the Dow will fall as much as 85 percent — as big a drop as occurred between 1929 and 1933 — to 600 or 700 from a peak of around 4,000.

Over time, he said, banks and thrift institutions will fail in alarming numbers. Millions will lose their savings, he said, if they have not stockpiled cash in their homes or safe deposit boxes or invested in gold.

Now let us see what more traditional economists have to say about what is perhaps the most important macroeconomic issue of our time for real estate borrowers: what impact, if any, fiscal deficits (such as the projected federal budget deficit of $280 billion for fiscal year 1992) will have on the level of future interest rates.

The first excerpt, by Vito Tanzi, presents the familiar "crowding out" argument in support of the orthodox view that there is a causal connection between large deficits and high interest rates.

In support of the contrary view that deficits do not necessarily affect interest rates are the two classic arguments deftly summarized below by Tanzi, namely, that if fiscal deficits tend to increase interest rates, such imbalances can be redressed either by: (1) compensating behavior on the part of the corporate and household sectors of the economy; or (2) by the fact that the demand for U.S. government bonds by domestic and foreign investors tends to be extremely (if not infinitely) elastic.

Tanzi, Fiscal Deficits and Interest Rates in the United States
31 International Monetary Fund Staff Papers 551 (1984)

Few relationships in economics have attracted as much attention as that between the U.S. fiscal deficit and U.S. interest rates. A large and growing number of theoretical and empirical papers have recently analyzed such a relationship, and financial analysts as well as politicians often refer to it. Some economists have attributed the historically high real interest rates since 1981 to the fiscal policy pursued by the United States in recent years. Others have denied the contribution of such a policy. . . .

I.   THEORETICAL CONSIDERATIONS

The fiscal deficit can increase (1) because government expenditure rises while revenue remains unchanged, (2) because tax revenue falls while government expenditure stays unchanged, or (3) because tax revenue falls while government expenditure rises. Regardless of which of these three cases is behind the increase in the fiscal deficit, government bond sales will have to increase. Other things being equal, for the government to induce people to buy a larger quantity of its bonds than previously, it must discount the bonds somewhat. Put a different way, interest rates must rise from the level that they would have reached in the absence of the deficit.

The above conclusion follows from the most fundamental law in economics — the law of demand. That law tells us that if one wants to sell more of something, one has to reduce its price. This result thus should not be controversial. Still, much controversy persists about whether fiscal deficits bring about increases in interest rates. What is the source of this controversy? Stripped to the bare essentials, the lines of criticism against the orthodox conclusion stated above are two. First, there is the assumption of spontaneous compensating behavior on the part of the private sector — in other words, of a compensating behavior *not* induced by the increase in interest rates. Second, there is the assumption that the elasticity of the supply of funds schedule for the sale of government bonds is high or even infinite. Let us discuss briefly these two lines of criticism.

COMPENSATING BEHAVIOR

Compensating behavior may be related either to the behavior of the corporate sector or to the behavior of the household sector. Suppose, for example, that as the government increases its expenditure, private investment falls. If there is a dollar per dollar trade-off between the rise in deficits and the fall in private investment, it is conceivable then that the rate of interest could remain unchanged. To a large extent this happened during World Wars I and II, when the large increase in government expenditure was met in part by tax increases, in part by an increase in household saving, and in large part by a sharp fall in private investment. Of course, the fall in private investment must not itself be caused by the increase in the rate of interest, but such decrease could be caused by changes in expectations or by direct prohibition (on the part of the government) of some productive activities.

The accommodating behavior on the part of the household sector could come in different ways. If, for example, the deficit is caused by a decrease in taxes and if this decrease in taxes is seen as temporary by the taxpayers, it is conceivable that the additional disposable income received by the taxpayers could in large part be saved and used to purchase the bonds that the government is selling. The requirement for this behavior is the permanent income hypothesis of consumption behavior. Alternatively, as argued by Barro (1974), if the household sector has perfect foresight it would realize that the public debt being created now must be repaid at some future date, so that in time taxes would have to go up. In other words, the household sector would realize that government bonds are not net wealth, so that holding more bonds would not make taxpayers richer and, thus, induce them to consume more. In such case taxpayers would presumably save the income associated with the tax cut. This so-called Ricardian equivalence hypothesis thus implicitly assumes that there are no permanent tax cuts, regardless of the declaration of the government. The hypothesis must also assume that no tax cuts are ever self-financing, as argued by Arthur Laffer and some supply-siders (see Laffer and Seymour (1979)).

If deficits are associated with tax cuts, households can go on maintaining the same level of consumption as before and still increase their rate of saving because their disposable income has increased. The increase in disposable income makes it easier for them to increase their rate of saving. If the increase in the deficit is not associated with a tax cut but with an increase in government expenditure, then the behavior Barro (1974) envisions seems far less likely. In such case households would actually have to cut their present level of consumption to behave as Barro foresees. Ratchet effects presumably would make such a cut in consumption difficult, at least in the short run. Furthermore, there is no valid reason for households, even if they had perfect foresight, not to see the increased level of spending as temporary and, thus, as not requiring a drastic change in their consumption behavior. Thus, the rate of interest would have to go up, and some investment expenditure, including the purchase of durable goods by households, would have to be crowded out by higher interest rates to accommodate the higher deficit. Even when the deficit is caused by tax reductions — the case more favorable for a behavior described by Barro — the requirements for a reaction consistent with a Ricardian equivalence hypothesis are so stringent that many economists have difficulties in accepting them. A full discussion of this aspect would require far more space than can be allocated here.

SUPPLY OF FUNDS ELASTICITY

The issue here is not whether the rate of interest must increase when the government attempts to increase its sale of bonds, but by how much. If the government faced a perfectly elastic supply of funds schedule, the rate of interest would not rise. We shall distinguish two alternative versions of this issue, a domestic one and an international one.

Domestic Supply of Funds Schedule

Several economists have called attention to the fact that the fiscal deficit, at 4-5 percent of gross national product (GNP), is still a very small fraction (say, 1 or 2 percent) of the total wealth of the United States. Therefore, a small reallocation in the portfolios of households, they argue, can absorb the additional public bonds that finance the deficit (see Phelps (1985), Rutledge (1982), and U.S. Treasury Department (1984)). Because the American capital market is quite efficient, this reallocation can be brought about by a very small increase in the interest rate. That such portfolio shifts can be accomplished through slight changes in the interest rate is a clever argument that would have great validity in a frictionless world. Unfortunately, the real world is not frictionless.

The main shortcoming of this argument is its lack of recognition of the often substantial transaction costs that an individual faces when he converts one type of asset (say, stocks, buildings, land, durables, and the like) into another (say, government bonds). Some of these costs may be commissions to be paid to brokers, real estate agents, and the like. Others may be taxes that arise from those shifts (income taxes on realized capital gains, transfer taxes, and the like). As a consequence of these costs, the supply of funds schedule that the government faces at any moment is upward sloping, and the slope increases the more the government tries to borrow. Transaction costs are obviously very small when bonds are purchased out of current net savings; the deficit may therefore have less of an effect on interest rates in countries, such as Japan, where the rate of saving is high.

International Supply of Funds Schedule

A country faces not only its domestic supply of funds but an international one as well. In a recent paper the author emphasized the international character of the capital market and pointed out that in today's world the interest rate is likely to be determined by the intersection of international supply and demand schedules (Tanzi (1985a, p. 104)):

> The U.S. demand for credit, whether originating in the public or in the business sector, can be met by the U.S. supply of credit *as well as* by the rest of the world's supply of credit. But, obviously, the U.S. demand for credit must compete against the rest of the world's demand for credit. If the U.S. demand rises because of a higher fiscal deficit at a time when the rest of the world's demand falls, interest rates need not rise. *Mutatis mutandis,* given the U.S. demand for credit, an increase in net investment or in fiscal deficits in Europe or Japan is likely to cause U.S. as well as foreign interest rates to rise.

Thus, if an increase in the fiscal deficit in the United States leads to a rise in the rate of interest, this rise will attract capital from abroad. The resultant capital inflow will moderate the rise in the rate of interest. This, many argue, is what has happened in recent years. Without the large capital inflows, interest rates in the United States would probably have increased more than they did. In this context the size of the economy is important. The U.S. economy is so large that it takes a substantial proportion of foreign savings to finance its deficit. In this case, too, the (foreign) supply of funds schedule is likely to be upward sloping. As the share of dollar-denominated bonds in the foreign portfolios increases, foreigners are likely to demand higher rates of return to keep investing in U.S. bonds (see Marris (1985)). . . .

IV.   SUMMARY AND CONCLUSIONS

This paper has addressed the ongoing controversy about whether fiscal deficits bring about higher interest rates and whether the historically high fiscal deficits that the United States has experienced in recent years have been the main factor explaining the extraordinarily high level of real interest rates. On the basis of a simple model of interest rate determination that included among the explanatory factors nonfiscal variables as well as fiscal variables, it was shown that interest rates are indeed positively influenced by fiscal deficits and (possibly) by levels of public debt. The empirical results indicated that if the U.S. fiscal deficit had been lower, interest rates would have been somewhat lower, other things being equal. On the basis of the statistical tests, it

Figure 4-4

Outlook on the Federal Budget Deficit

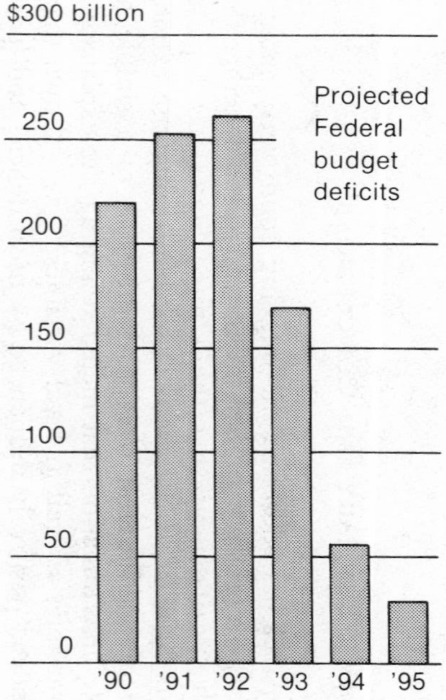

Estimated figures in billions of dollars for each fiscal year.

	1990	1991	1992	1993	1994	1995
Outlays*	1,252	1,363	1,447	1,428	1,400	1,458
Deposit insurance** (part of outlays)	58	91	107	28	–44	–29
Revenues	1,031	1,110	1,185	1,258	1,344	1,429
Deficit	220	253	262	170	56	29
Social Security trust fund surplus	58	66	74	83	98	114
Deficit excluding Social Security	278	319	336	253	154	143

*Figures assume that Congress takes further action to keep military and domestic spending below limits set in the October budget deal.

**Sale of insolvent savings and loan associations is assumed to bring in more than the Government spends on such institutions in 1994 and 1995.

Projected Federal budget deficits

$300 billion

250

200

150

100

50

0

'90   '91   '92   '93   '94   '95

Source: Congressional Budget Office (as of 12/6/90).

* In fact, the 1991 deficit turned out to be over $300 billion and on February 4, 1991 Mr. Boskin, President Bush's chief economic adviser, fearlessly projected the 1992 deficit at $280 billion. — ED.

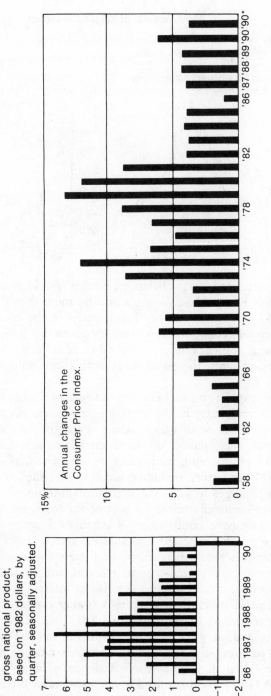

F i g u r e 4-5

Overview of Macroeconomics (cont.)

Inflation

Economic Growth

Annual rate of change in the gross national product, based on 1982 dollars, by quarter, seasonally adjusted.

Annual changes in the Consumer Price Index.

Source: Commerce Department.

Sources: Commerce Department; Labor Department.

*excluding energy prices

333

F i g u r e   4-5 (cont.)

Overview of Macroeconomics

Value of the U.S. Dollar

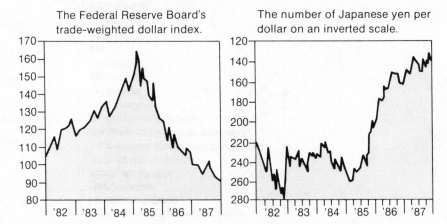

The Federal Reserve Board's trade-weighted dollar index.

The number of Japanese yen per dollar on an inverted scale.

can be estimated that a balanced budget would have reduced interest rates on one-year U.S. Treasury bills by more than 2 percentage points in 1984. A reduction in the fiscal deficit in the order of 1 percent of GNP would reduce interest rates by about 50 basis points (or half a percentage point). Thus, on the issue of whether fiscal deficits affect real interest rates, the paper sides with those who maintain that they do.

The paper also concludes, however, that a large part of the increase in real interest rates in the 1981-84 period was *not* associated with the fiscal deficit but with other factors. Potential candidates among these factors are deregulation of the financial market, mergers, changes in monetary policy, and, perhaps more important, changes in tax legislation. (Other factors, including nondomestic ones, may also have played a role.) Changes in U.S. tax legislation introduced in 1981 and 1982 may have been responsible for part of the total rise. . . . [T]hese other factors may have contributed as much as 4 percentage points of the total rise in the expected real interest rate that occurred in 1981-84. Whether this rise is permanent or temporary remains to be seen. By inducing a large capital-spending boom, the changes in tax rules are likely to have contributed to the rise in interest rates in the short run. As additional investment leads to a higher capital stock, however, the rate of return to investment must fall, thus reducing further capital spending and, as a consequence, reducing interest rates.

In addition, the sensitivity of interest rates to fiscal deficits seems to have fallen in recent years. A deficit of a given magnitude (as a share of GNP) gives rise to a lower increase in interest rates now than it did in the past. This is consistent with the hypothesis that international

F i g u r e   4-5 (cont.)

Overview of Macroeconomics

Unemployment (Jobless rate, seasonally adjusted)

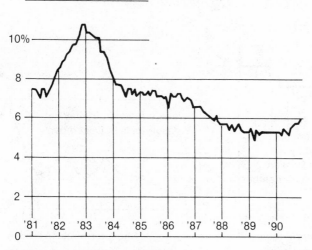

Source: Bureau of Labor Statistics.

The Trade Deficit

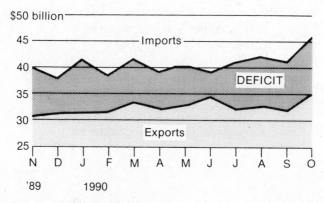

Source: Commerce Department.

Overview of Macroeconomics

Interest Rates

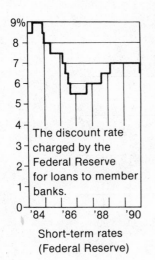

Short-term rates
(Federal Reserve)

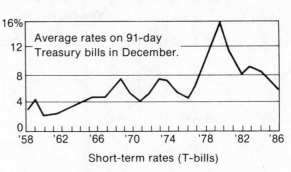

Short-term rates (T-bills)

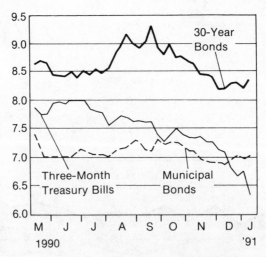

Current short- and long-term rates
(see also Table 5-1 at Chapter 5B1)

financial markets are now much better integrated than they were even a few years ago. The consequence of this development is that a rise in interest rates in one country (say, caused by a rising fiscal deficit) attracts capital from abroad. Because part of the deficit is financed by foreigners, there is less pressure on the *domestic* financial market. Therefore, interest rates rise by less than they would have risen in the past. Of course, this advantage does not come without costs, since growing reliance on foreign financing is inevitably accompanied by growing economic uncertainty and potential instability in the capital market. . . .

Perhaps a closing word of caution is necessary. Although the statistical results of the paper are relatively strong and, in the author's judgment, consistent with economic theory, they cannot be taken as proving the deficit's effect on real interest rates beyond doubt. The type of work undertaken here can never give definitive answers and is never beyond criticism. Some will undoubtedly disagree with the statistical tests. Others may point out that the relationships tested are not based on a fully specified structural model. Nevertheless, the results presented are unusually strong and, for those who believe in empirical tests, seem to indicate that fiscal deficits weigh heavily in the determination of real interest rates.

Factors Affecting Federal Deficit Growth, 1970 to 1986
Tax Notes, Aug. 12, 1985, at 803-805

As measured in the national income and product accounts (NIPA) the federal budget was essentially in balance at the beginning of calendar 1970 — one year into the Nixon presidency. Since then, without exception, the budget (in NIPA terms) has shown annual deficits, which reached $179 billion in calendar 1983 and $176 billion in 1984 and are expected — as estimated from projections in the *1986 Budget* — to equal $186 billion in calendar 1985 and $164 billion in 1986.

A highly informative study by the staff of the Commerce Department's Bureau of Economic Analysis has measured the major sources of change in the annual federal deficit during this 17-year period. . . .

Three sources of change are distinguished in accounting for deficit trends: automatic cyclical effects, automatic inflation effects, and "legislation and other factors," generally referred to simply as "legislation."

"Automatic cyclical effects," the study authors say, "reflect the automatic responsiveness of receipts and expenditures to the business cycle and are estimated by calculating what budget levels would be if the economy were operating on a hypothetical trend of GNP — middle-

Figure 4-6

Bank and S&L Failures During the 1980s

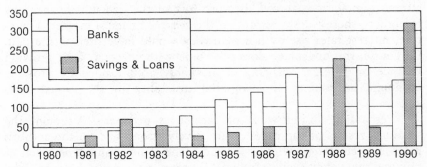

Sources: Federal Deposit Insurance Corporation; Resolution Trust Corporation.

Figure 4-7

Percentage Points of Change in the Federal Deficit Relative to GNP During Three Presidential Administration Periods, 1970 to 1986, Showing Amounts of Change Attributable to Various Factors

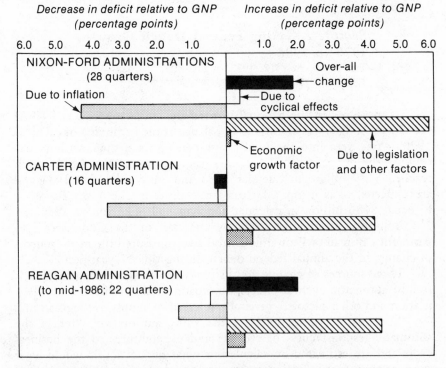

Source: Manuel, Paying for Civilized Society 163 (1986).

expansion trend GNP — rather than its actual path." Because federal receipts respond much more sharply to economic growth than do federal expenditures, this factor has tended to dampen the deficit in times of economic upturn, and to enhance the deficit when the economy turned downward or grew at a less-than-average rate.

The second source of change, automatic inflation effects, reflects "the automatic responsiveness of receipts and expenditures to price changes." Both receipts and expenditures tend to be increased by inflation (which took place throughout the 17-year period), but receipts respond more sharply than expenditures, so that this tends especially to dampen the deficit in periods of rapidly rising prices, and to be less potent in its restraining impact when prices rise but slowly.

The third source of change, "legislation and other factors," is a "residual after netting changes due to automatic cyclical effects and automatic inflation effects from total changes." . . .

When the change in the deficit-GNP relationship since the beginning of 1970 is broken down by presidential administration . . . one especially notable fact emerges. Belying the widely accepted notion that Democratic administrations are profligate and Republican administrations are comparatively frugal, it appears that during the Carter Administration the federal budget moved toward surplus — by .4 percentage point of GNP — while a marked shift toward higher deficit-to-GNP ratios is recorded both for the Nixon-Ford era and for the initial 5½ years of the Reagan presidency. . . .

Volker, Statement Before the Joint Economic Committee of the United States Congress
1987 Fed. Reserve Bull. 275 (Feb. 2, 1987)

. . . Plainly, in their particulars, many of the strains and imbalances in our economy can be traced to specific circumstances beyond the reach of broad fiscal or monetary policies. . . .

The direct effects of the trade deficit are clear enough. Burgeoning imports over several years, while exports in real terms have risen much more slowly, largely account for the overall sluggishness of manufacturing. With capacity ample, that sluggishness feeds back on spending for plant and equipment.

The effects of the budget deficit, in current circumstances, may be less obvious — after all, as many have noted, interest rates have fallen while the deficits have been so large, the huge new issues of Treasury securities have found a market, and private debt creation has been high as well. How is that possible when, to take one simple

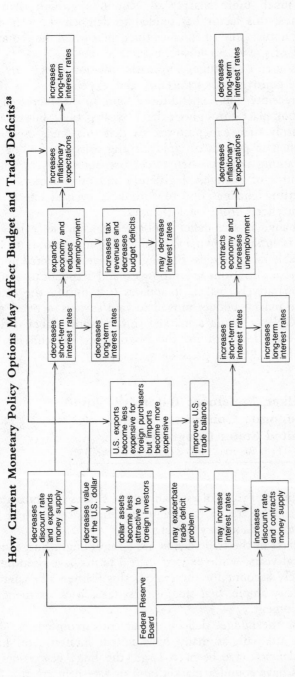

Figure 4-8

How Current Monetary Policy Options May Affect Budget and Trade Deficits[28]

[28]Ceteris paribus is a term in economics that means "all other things remain constant." While the permutations displayed on the chart above accurately portray one likely outcome of Federal Reserve action, Table 4-8 cannot hope to capture the complexities inherent in monetary policy and its effect on the macroeconomy without the assumption behind ceteris paribus.

For example, as shown in the lower half of Table 4-8, an increase in the discount rate immediately leads to an increase in both long- and short-term interest rates. Yet the same movement of the discount rate could also lead to more foreign purchasing at the United States credit window, lowering interest rates in the secondary markets. The equity markets might also be of the mind that federal action would increase demand for the dollar, and a sudden surge in stock prices could tick off a rally, buoying the economy against any interest rate increase.

The real estate developer, in taking into account prefinancing considerations, must understand the economic theories that underlie the movements in the chart above, and that such charts can only represent the most likely outcome. — ED.

benchmark, our federal deficit has averaged about two-thirds of the net savings generated by our economy over the past four years?

In effect, the answer is that we are drawing on the savings of others: in 1986, the net influx of foreign capital appears to have exceeded all the savings generated by individuals in the United States. That capital influx is the mirror image of the deficit in our current account — we cannot, at one and the same time, borrow abroad (net) to cover a domestic investment-savings imbalance *and* run a balanced current account.

In a sense we have been fortunate. We have been able to increase consumption rather rapidly, sustain overall growth, and reduce inflation and interest rates even in the face of a large federal budget deficit by calling upon other nations' savings, which they have readily provided. But the cost has been a rising trade deficit and increasing international indebtedness, strong pressures on manufacturing in the here and now, and an unsustainable pattern of economic activity for the future fraught with political as well as economic risks.

Stated simply, we are living beyond our means — individuals, businesses, and government have collectively been spending more than we produce. That might be acceptable *if* we were matching the foreign borrowing with a surge in productive investment in the United States. That has been the case at times in the distant past in the United States and in other countries more recently. But we are not making that match now — it's consumption that has been leading the economic parade.

In that context, the challenge for economic policy over the next few years is clear enough. We have to work toward better *external* and *internal* balance at the same time. The adjustments required are large. Given our extended position, the difficulties and risks are substantial. We do not want to achieve the needed external adjustments by recession, nor can we reasonably float off our debts by rekindling inflation — and I do not think it is realistic to think we have the option of trading one of those possibilities for the other.

That may sound like abstraction. I will be more specific.

One requirement is progress in reducing our trade deficit. That, on the face of it, will bring benefits to manufacturing in the United States. The potential is huge — to close our $150 billion trade deficit by increased manufacturing (and I do not see any other practical avenue) implies a 15 to 20 percent increase in industrial output over the coming years above and beyond that required to support domestic growth. While a surge of that kind would be welcome in many respects, the challenge is to achieve it without renewed inflationary pressure in that sector. That will require continuing restraint on costs, more modernization, and in time more capacity, which in turn will require both money and real resources.

By definition, as we close the current account deficit, those funds and real resources will no longer be available from abroad. So we will have to increase our own savings or reduce other demands on savings at home. The obvious candidate — again, as a practical matter, it must be the largest "contributor" — is a reduction in our federal budget deficit. And, unless productivity in the economy as a whole is to dramatically increase above the recent trend of 1 percent or so — and unhappily there is no solid evidence for that — we will not be able to close the gap in trade and meet our domestic investment needs without slowing the growth in domestic consumption well below the 4 percent pace it has averaged during the current expansion.

In concept, all those things are "doable." They provide the outline of an appropriate economic strategy. The result would be a more balanced economy, greatly enhancing the prospects for sustained growth and greater exchange rate and financial stability. . . .

NOTES AND QUESTIONS

1.   *The Real Estate Atmosphere Is Clouded by Uncertainties on the Macroeconomic Horizon, Including Looming Budget Deficits.*   As of the beginning of 1991 the rate of economic growth in the United States has plummeted, and yet the other major underpinnings of the economy — the rate of inflation, interest rates, and the level of employment — are, for the most part, in equilibrium. However, during the late 1980s the value of the U.S. dollar dropped in relation to other currencies. This lowered our trade deficit but increased inflationary expectations. In the opinion of many economists the specter of escalating federal budget deficits for the balance of the 1990s and beyond is imperiling not only the future cost and availability of mortgage credit but the overall state of the economy as well. The amount of these deficits averaged less than $10 billion a year in the 1960s, increased to $60 billion by 1980, and had grown to $80 billion by the time Ronald Reagan assumed office in 1981. Nevertheless, President Reagan, along with a complaisant Congress, managed to increase the deficit to $230 billion by 1986, at which time *interest alone* on the national debt was costing the federal government approximately $136 billion a year. While the deficit had decreased to $150 billion by fiscal year 1987, because of disagreements over how to account for the Social Security surplus and how to calculate the enormous cost of bailing out the savings and loan industry the Congressional Budget Office is projecting an increased deficit ranging between $262 billion and $336 billion for fiscal year 1992 (see Figure 4-4, supra).

a.   *Do Budget Deficits Affect Interest Rates?*   The orthodox view touted by such prominent economists as Gardner Ackley, Martin Feld-stein, Walter Heller, Paul McCracken, and Charles Schultze, all of whom once served as the chairman of the Council of Economic Advisors, has been that there is a causal connection between larger fiscal deficits and higher interest rates. Frequently economists who subscribe to this majority view argue that large deficits tend to increase long-term interest rates because of their impact on inflationary expectations and (under the theory enunciated in the excerpt by Tanzi) the federal government must increase interest rates (by lowering the price of its bonds) in order to "crowd out" other borrowers such as business and real estate borrowers. However, the leverage-minded real estate borrower is more likely to be crowded out, because of its greater sensitivity to any increase in interest rates. See Ackley, Deficits Are Dangerous — And the Reagan Administration Must Face up to This Reality, 12 Dun's Bus. Month 57 (Nov. 1983); Bianco, The Deficit Keeps Spooking Wall Street — No Matter What, Bus. Week 37 (Oct. 22, 1984); Schultze, The Deficit Still No. 1 Problem, N.Y. Times, Mar. 15, 1988, at A27. Moreover, while substantial deficits may be tolerable in a recessionary economy, according to this view, they are surely inappropriate and possibly dangerous when the economy is expanding. See Ackley, supra, at 57.

By contrast, the emerging minority view rejects the paradigm that large deficits necessarily produce high interest rates and takes the position that the relevant question is not whether a fiscal deficit increases or decreases rates but *how* these changes occur. For example, under the "spontaneous compensating behavior theory," if the budget deficit were to increase because of some tax-cutting legislation (such as the Economic Recovery Tax Act of 1981), theoretically the extra disposable income available to taxpayers could, to a large extent, be saved and used to buy the additional government bonds needed to fund the increase in the deficit. In other words, the increase in the deficit could be met in part by an increase in domestic household saving. As a consequence, the rate of interest might remain the same without major dislocations in the economy. See, e.g., Dwyer, Federal Deficits, Interest Rates and Monetary Policy, 17 J. Money, Credit, & Banking 655, 656 (Nov. 1985).

A steadily increasing number of empirical studies (most of which are imcomprehensible to a reader without a background in econometrics) have analyzed the corollation, if any, between the U.S. budget deficits and U.S. interest rates; however, so far the results have been inconclusive. Based on their research, some economists have attributed the historically high interest rates (in real dollars) since 1981 (see Figure 4-5) to the fiscal policy pursued by the United States in recent years; others have denied such a causal relationship. Compare Tanzi, supra, at 571-573 (concluding that on the basis of statistical tests interest rates were positively influenced by fiscal deficits during the 1960-1984 period) with Dwyer, supra, at 655, 656, 676-677 (suggesting that the "Ricardian equivalence hypothesis" may account for tenuousness of any historical relationship between government debt and interest rates). See also Evans, Do Large Deficits Produce High Interest Rates?, 75 Am. Economic Rev. 68, 86 (March 1985) (no positive association between deficits and interest rates proven); Kotlikoff, Economic Impact of Deficit Financing, 31 Intl. Monetary Fund Staff Papers 549, 571-580 (Sept. 1984) (concluding that after empirical analysis of "crowding out" hypothesis, changes in domestic savings caused by "economic" deficits — as opposed to deficits recorded by government accountants — can produce major changes in real interest rates, especially long-term rates). In addition, some economists have cited historical facts. For example, Evans, supra, at 68, points out that there were three periods in United States history during which the federal deficit exceeded 10 percent of the GNP, and in none of these periods did real interest rates rise appreciably. According to Evans, "In over a century of U.S. history, large deficits have never been associated with high interest rates. Even the postwar periods separately offer no support for a positive association between deficits and interest rates. . . ." Id. at 86. In addition, the two major economies with the lowest overall inflation rate during the 1980s, West Germany and Japan, have had larger deficits (as measured by a percentage of their GNP) than the United States.

   b. *To Be (For Economic Growth) Or Not To Be (So We Can Combat Inflation and Stabilize the Dollar), That Is the Question Facing the Federal Reserve Board.* To wipe out double-digit inflation in the late 1970s, the Federal Reserve Board sharply increased short-term interest rates (by raising the discount rate charged to its member banks) and constricted the nation's money supply. However, the public paid dearly for the disinflation with the deep recession and high unemployment of 1980-1982. So bad was this period that some prominent economists such as Benjamin Friedman of Harvard have been forced to defend and temper their fidelity to Keynesian principles. According to Professor Friedman, "What we are doing now is to respond to what is happening in the macroexperience of the 1980s, for the Eighties have brought disappointments. The promise of costless disinflation has not been fulfilled; the policy of relying heavily on money supply has failed. The monetarist experiment ended in October 1982, and the central bank now places little reliance on these policies." Friedman, Harvard and Keynesian Economics, 1936-1986, 89 Harv. Magazine 51 (Jan.-Feb. 1986).

   Striking the right balance in U.S. monetary policy has always been a delicate business for the seven governors of the Federal Reserve Board. However, as suggested by the foregoing remarks by Professor Friedman, the Fed appears to be more cautious than usual in dealing with the 1990s. During the late 1980s a debate took place among economists based on facts that have already become dated. Nevertheless, it illustrates the all but perennial policy dilemma confronting the Federal Reserve Board. On the one hand, some economists (perhaps a majority) were urging a more expansionary policy in order to invigorate the economic recovery that began in 1983. During the late 1980s the rate of inflation was relatively low while the GNP (as measured in real dollars) grew at an annual rate of only about 2 percent. See Figure 4-5. According to this view, the issue was not inflation but anemic economic growth and relatively high unemployment. Therefore, these experts said, real short-term interest rates (the nominal interest rate less the inflation rate) were still too high compared with comparable rates during cyclical upswings in prior years. Moreover, low short-term rates were necessary to sustain the relatively low value of the U.S. dollar in order to effect further reductions in the U.S. trade deficit (which amounted to approximately $150 billion as of the beginning of 1988). As American goods grew less expensive abroad and foreign goods more expensive, the declining value of the dollar strengthened the demand for U.S. exports overseas. At the same time, domestic demand for American products increased as the prices of foreign imports began to rise. By 1990 the trade deficit had been reduced to about $120 billion. See Figure 4-5.

Conversely, other macroeconomic experts were concerned that if the Federal Reserve Board were to substantially reduce the discount rate and expand the money supply, the dollar, along with U.S. interest rates, would drop too far too quickly in relation to foreign currencies and interest rates (e.g., those of Japan and West Germany) and thereby cause U.S. dollar assets to become less attractive to foreign investors, whose funds have helped finance the U.S. budget deficit and stabilize U.S. interest rates. Moreover, with oil prices firming, partly in response to OPEC's production accord, and with intermittent signs that the economy was gaining strength and that equilibrium in the currency exchange market was increasing the value of the dollar and dollar prices of imports, these economists worried about a new inflationary spiral and urged the Federal Reserve Board to continue its role as the country's staunchest watchdog against inflation. For quite some time the Fed was noncommital in its choice between, on the one hand, easing monetary policy in order to calm the financial markets and spur economic growth and, on the other hand, tightening the nation's money supply in order to stabilize the value of the U.S. dollar and curbing future inflation. As of this writing the economy is in the midst of a recession caused by a drop in consumer confidence (and exacerbated by the war in the Persian Gulf), a steep increase in oil prices, and the tight lending practices of commercial banks and thrift organizations. Indeed, as of the beginning of 1991, the rising number of bank failures (see Figure 4-6), caused partly by failed real estate projects, along with the new regulatory restraints imposed by FIRREA on thrift organizations and commercial banks (see note 2, infra), has so worried the banking community that even creditworthy borrowers are being denied credit. See Lohr, Banking's Real Estate Miseries, N.Y. Times, Jan. 13, 1991, sec. 3, at A1. In response to the current economic slowdown and credit crunch the Federal Reserve Board is moving haltingly in the direction of expanding the nation's money supply and lowering short-term interest rates. How fast and how far the Board moves in this direction is bound to have serious repercussions for real estate borrowers for the balance of the 1990s and beyond.

   c.   Questions.   Before addressing the following questions review the previous excerpts, and keep in mind that while historical facts soon become stale, macroeconomic principles tend to endure.

   i. Based on what you have learned so far about macroeconomic theory and on your assessment of today's economic picture (e.g., rate of real economic growth, rate of household consumption and savings, level of employment, inflationary expectations), what is your prediction as to the cost of construction financing and permanent financing in the short-term future?

   ii. On December 17, 1985, the United States Commerce Department reported a sharp (12.2 percent) drop in housing starts; bond prices immediately soared. N.Y. Times, Dec. 18, 1985, at D1. Conversely, bond prices plummeted on April 23, 1987 in response to news that the value of the U.S. dollar declined to a near-record low level. N.Y. Times, April 23, 1987, at A1. Can you explain the macroeconomic reasons for the foregoing results?

   iii. After more than six months of rising interest rates and diminished demand for long-term bonds, the stock market crashed on October 19, 1987 amidst reports that the U.S. trade deficit for August had shrunk only half as much as was expected and that the West German Central Bank had breached a currency accord with the United States by increasing its rate of interest. Immediately thereafter U.S. interest rates declined (e.g., a drop in the prime rate to 9 percent), and the Federal Reserve Board indicated that it would expand the money supply and support a further decrease in short-term interest rates. In addition, former president Reagan announced that he wanted to meet with congressional leaders to talk about deficit reduction measures. N.Y. Times, Oct. 23, 1987, at A1. Can you explain the macroeconomic reasons for the foregoing results? In what respect were the actions taken by the Federal Reserve Board and President Reagan contradictory? How do the facts in the N.Y. Times article, although dated by now, illustrate the notion that mortgage credit tends to be countercyclical? Based on today's economic conditions, would you urge the Federal Reserve Board to expand, contract, or do nothing with respect to the nation's money supply?

   iv. A standard complaint about the Reagan Administration is

that it presided over a near-doubling of gross U.S. indebtedness from $1.0 trillion to about $1.8 trillion by fiscal year 1989. However, if one measures deficit growth as a percentage of GNP, the rate of growth during the Reagan era (2.0 percent) was comparable to the rate of growth experienced during the Nixon-Ford Administrations (1.9 percent). See Figure 4-7. In any event, as noted earlier, there is a respectable minority of economists who take the position that the relevant issue is not whether or to what extent a fiscal deficit has increased or decreased but *how* these changes occur. Based on your review of the excerpt entitled "Factors Affecting Federal Deficit Growth, 1970 to 1986" and perusal of the accompanying Figure 4-5, what would be your argument for the proposition that when one considers the *sources* of deficit growth (e.g., effects of the business cycle, inflation, and legislation) the deficit increase during the Reagan Administration may have been no worse for the economy than the increases experienced during the Nixon-Ford and Carter eras?

Based on his statement (excerpted supra), what would Paul Volker's objection be, if any, to the way in which the budget deficit was *funded* during the tenure of the Reagan Administration?

v. Some experts have suggested that the most sensible way to deal with the nation's "twin towers of debt" (budget and trade deficits each amounted to about $220 and $120 billion, respectively, in 1990), or "triple towers of debt" if the cost of the savings and loan industry bailout is counted separately (as high as $500 billion over the next 40 years, according to the General Accounting Office), is for Congress to reduce federal spending to the bone and then "bite the bullet" by raising taxes. However, during the late 1980s most economists were predicting an economic slowdown or a recession. As observed at Chapter 2B, note 3, on October 27, 1990 Congress enacted the Revenue Reconciliation Act of 1990, which increases taxes by increasing the maximum marginal rate for individuals from 28 to 31 percent. Do you think this makes macroeconomic sense?

As noted above by Tanzi, real interest rates have been historically high since 1981. See Figure 4-5. What would be the theoretical argument that any increase in the income tax to fund a reduction in the U.S. budget deficit may decrease real interest rates? What would be the counterargument?

After reviewing Paul Volker's statement before the Joint Economic Committee of the Congress, do you understand the interrelationship between the U.S. trade deficit and budget deficit problems? What is Volker's advice with respect to solving the twin-deficit problem?

vi. Assume the worst-case scenario, namely that the U.S. economy slips into another severe recession that coincides with a run on the dollar. What would be the likely impact on the U.S. budget deficit, and how might real estate borrowers fare?

vii. Economists have observed that by year-end 1990, for the first time since the 1940s, deflation (falling prices) was appearing in the real estate and manufacturing sectors of the economy. In addition, in December 1990 the unemployment rate had climbed to 5.9 percent, the highest rate since October 1987. N.Y. Times, December 8, 1990, at A1 and December 25, 1990, at A1. What impact is this likely to have on long-term interest rates?

2. *Recent Deregulation of the Mortgage Lending Industry.* On the (mostly) positive side of the macroeconomic coin for real estate borrowers is the escalating trend toward the deregulation of financial institutions and the usury laws in this country. The regulatory statutes that impose qualitative and quantitative constraints on the mortgage loan portfolios of commercial banks and thrift organizations have become less restrictive, and these lending institutions have had access to new and more diversified sources of loanable funds (albeit at a somewhat higher cost) as a consequence of such deregulatory legislation as the Depository Institutions Deregulation and Monetary Control Act of 1980, Pub. L. No. 96-221, 94 Stat. 132 (1980) and the Garn-St. Germain Depository Institutions Act of 1982, Pub. L. No. 97-320, 96 Stat. 1469 (1982). For example, under prior law construction loans made by federally chartered or insured commercial banks with maturities of five years or less on commercial and industrial real estate were exempted from the regulatory constraints (e.g., maximum loan-to-value ratios, amortization requirements) otherwise applicable to real estate loans only if the bank had a firm takeout commitment from a responsible postconstruction lender. 12 U.S.C. §371(c). However, the Federal Reserve Act was amended by the Garn-St. Germain Act to remove virtually all regulatory restrictions on real estate loans made by national banks. 12 U.S.C. §371(c), as amended by Pub. L. No. 97-320 §403 (1982); 12 C.F.R. pt. 34 (Sept. 9, 1983).

While real estate borrowers may have benefitted from deregulation in the short run, many of the current problems faced by thrifts and commercial banks originated with the aforementioned legislation, which caused a major restructuring of the mortgage market. In the deregulatory environment of the 1980s, the thrift organizations (including savings and loan associations and mutual savings banks) were adversely affected by: (1) a drastic reduction in their market share of residential mortgage originations because of competition from mortgage bankers; (2) a continued deterioration in their net assets and earnings caused by a mismatch between the interest being earned by their depositors from market-rate instruments (such as money market certificates geared to six-month Treasury bills authorized by Congress in 1978) and the low-yielding long-term mortgage portfolios acquired prior to the 1979-1981 period of escalating interest rates; (3) losses on unsecured business loans and riskier real estate loans authorized by Garn-St. Germain; and (4) lax regulation by the Federal Home Loan Bank Board and conflicts of interests among thrift regulators and thrift executives, caused in part by the thrift industry's exercise of undue political influence on Congress. See generally Ordway, The Deregulation Dilemma and the Banking System, 2 Real Est. Fin. J. 91-93 (Summer 1985).

By 1987 the savings and loan industry had registered a net loss of $6 billion. The figure escalated to $11 billion in 1988 and $20 billion in 1989. By 1990 the annual number of bank and S&L failures had escalated to about 450. In response to public concern over the thrift and banking industries Congress enacted the Financial Institutions Reform, Recovery, and Enforcement Act of 1989 (FIRREA), codified as 12 U.S.C. §1813(c)(1), which transferred regulatory authority from the Federal Home Loan Bank Board to the director of a new agency, the Office of Thrift Supervision, and established a new corporation, the Resolution Trust Corporation, to manage the federal bailout program. Current estimates of the cost of the federal bailout range from a low of $89 billion (the anticipated cost of funding the bailout in today's dollars according to Nicholas Brady, Secretary of the Treasury) to as high as $500 billion (the cost of paying for the bailout, including interest payments on bond payments, interest on short-term working capital, and administrative costs, according to the General Accounting Office). Rosenbaum, A Financial Disaster with Many Culprits, The Savings Debacle, N.Y. Times, June 9, 1990, at 1, col. 1. For an excellent discussion of the new regulatory scheme for thrifts including additional capital requirements for real estate loans see Malloy, Nothing to Fear but FIRREA Itself: Revising and Reshaping the Enforcement Process of Federal Bank Regulation, 50 Ohio St. L.J. 1117 (1990). See also Madison and Dwyer ¶2.02[3][e] (Supp. no. 2) (1990); Sahling and Lavin, Will RTC Asset Dispositions Ruin the Real Estate Markets?, 20 Real Est. Rev. 15 (Summer 1990); Sussman, Can Thrifts Support FIRREA's Conservative Capital Requirements?, 20 Real Est. Rev. 22 (Summer 1990); Wood, Young, Frost, and Nichols, An Overview of FIRREA, 6 Prac. Real Est. Law. 43 (July 1990).

In addition to the regulatory statutes mentioned above, many states still limit the amount of interest that may be charged, even for business loans to sophisticated borrowers, and in some instances the maximum rate may be unrealistically low. In these cases, unless the real estate borrower is incorporated or otherwise exempt from the usury restrictions, it might be difficult if not impossible to obtain a loan from some institutional lender. The usury problem for real estate borrowers is examined at Chapter 5B3, note 4. However, over the past decade or so many states have deregulated their usury laws by lifting their usury ceilings completely or partially on most kinds of real estate loans, by expanding the exemption for corporate borrowers to include other kinds

Real Mortgage Interest Rates 1970 to 1989

Year	Long Term Mortgage Rates	Consumer Price Index (%)	Real Mortgage Interest Rates
1970	8.3	5.7	2.6
1971	7.6	4.4	3.2
1972	7.5	3.2	4.3
1973	7.8	6.2	1.6
1974	8.7	11.0	−2.3
1975	8.8	9.1	−0.3
1976	8.8	5.8	3.0
1977	8.8	6.5	2.3
1978	9.3	7.6	1.7
1979	10.5	11.4	−0.9
1980	12.3	13.5	−1.2
1981	14.2	10.3	3.9
1982	14.5	6.1	8.4
1983	12.2	3.2	9.0
1984	11.9	4.3	7.6
1985	11.1	3.6	7.5
1986	9.8	1.9	7.9
1987	8.9	3.7	5.2
1988	8.8	4.2	4.6
1989(1)	9.8	5.0	4.8

Average

1970 to 89 = 3.6%   1970 to 79 = 1.5%   1980 to 89 = 5.8%

Source: REF Financing Update, 6 Real Estate Finance 12 (Exhibit C) (Winter 1990).

of commercial entities such as limited partnerships and by enacting sunset provisions that will require state legislatures to reexamine the appropriateness of their usury laws within a designated period of time (usually two years). For an excellent survey of recent developments in usury laws see the annual surveys appearing in the Business Lawyer, published by the ABA Section of Corporation, Banking, and Business Law. The last annual survey was edited by Joseph Gelb and Seth C. Berman, and appears in vol. 44, no. 3, at 1039 (May 1989). For prior surveys see Burke, Recent Developments — The New Federal Usury Laws, 36 Bus. Law. 1237 (1981); Burke and Kaplinsky, Unraveling the New Federal Usury Law, 37 Bus. Law. 1079 (1982); Culhane and Kaplinsky, Trends Pertaining to the Usury Laws, 38 Bus. Law. 1329 (1983); Kaplinsky, ed., Recent Usury Law Developments, 39 Bus. Law. 1251 (1984); Kaplinsky, ed., Recent Usury Law Developments, 41 Bus. Law. 1039 (1986); Gelb, ed., Recent Usury Law Developments, 42 Bus. Law. 915 (1987).

On the federal side of the usury picture there have been significant deregulatory developments. For example, by federal preemption under Title V of the Depository Institutions Deregulation and Monetary Control Act of 1980, most state usury statutes no longer apply to first mortgage loans on residential real estate, which is important from our standpoint because residential real estate loans include apartment building loans for purposes of the statute. 12 U.S.C. §§1735f to 1737, 1811 (1989). For a discussion of federal preemption see Burke, Recent Developments — The New Federal Usury Law, 36 Bus. Law. 1237 (1981) and Burke and Kaplinsky, Unraveling the New Federal Usury Law, 37 Bus. Law. 1079 (1982); Culhane and Kaplinsky, Trends Pertaining to the Usury Laws, 38 Bus. Law. 1239 (1983).

3. Keeping Tabs on Supply and Demand for Mortgage Credit. A watchful eye on the seven Federal Reserve aggregates in the daily newspaper will enable you to anticipate trends in Federal Reserve monetary policy and help you make an educated guess about the cost and availability of mortgage credit in the future.

The following publications should also help you keep tabs on the supply and demand for mortgage credit: the Financial and Business Statistics Section of the Federal Reserve Bulletin issued monthly by the Federal Reserve Board, Mail Stop 138, Washington, D.C. 20551; the Federal Reserve Bulletin (especially the Financial and Business Statistics Section), which is issued monthly by the Federal Reserve Board; the annual fact books published by each lender group, including life insurance companies (Life Insurance Fact Book, by the American Council of Life Insurance, 1001 Pennsylvania Avenue N.W., Washington, D.C. 20004), thrift organizations (National Fact Book of Savings Institutions, by the National Council of Savings Institutions, 1101 Fifteenth St. N.W., Washington, D.C. 20005); and real estate investment trusts (REIT Fact Book, by National Assoc. of REITs, Inc., 1101 Seventeenth Street, Washington, D.C. 20036); various publications by Crittenden News Service, P.O. Box 1150, Novato, California 94948; various publications (including Real Estate Market Review) by Salomon Brothers Inc., One New York Plaza, NY, NY 10004; (5) The Mortgage and Real Estate Executives Report, published bi-monthly by Warren Gorham & Lamont, 210 South Street, Boston, MA 02111; and various publications (including the Real Estate Report) by Goldman Sachs, NY, NY.

353–370
376–380
387–398
400–438
445–450
454 455
412–470

477–506
508–538

PART II

FUNDAMENTALS OF REAL ESTATE FINANCING

Once the necessary venture capital is raised from outside investors and the other prefinancing considerations are resolved, the next step is customarily for the real estate borrower to decide how and where to obtain the financing to fund the balance of the cost to either purchase the income-producing real estate or, in the case of new construction, to acquire the land and construct the improvements. Although in the case of new construction it is possible to finance the cost of the underlying land separately by means of one of the special high-ratio financing techniques discussed in Part III (e.g., subordinated purchase-money mortgage, installment land contract, sale and leaseback of the land only, or some variant of component financing), in most cases a developer will obtain an ordinary fee mortgage to cover the cost of the land as well as the new improvements. This fundamental mortgage financing scenario involves three major actors: the developer-borrower, the postconstruction, "permanent," lender, and the construction lender. Postconstruction financing of new or existing real estate is the subject of Chapter 5, and construction financing is covered in Chapter 6. The financing of nonincome-producing real estate such as land held for resale by a subdivider is briefly mentioned in Chapter 6.

Throughout this casebook reference will be made to the master hypothetical at Chapter 5B, infra, to illustrate the trials and tribulations of a typical real estate developer as the developer wades its way through the commercial real estate lending cycle. In the master hypothetical, Dan Developer decides to construct an office building in the State of Fuller and applies for a postconstruction loan of $25 million from the Ace Insurance Company. Since Ace will not fund the loan unless and until the construction is completed, Dan also approaches the Fuller National Bank, which agrees to supply the construction financing (in

the same amount, $25 million) on the strength of the "takeout commitment" from Ace whereby Ace agrees to buy the loan from FNB once the project is completed.

In a practical sense it is the loan contract, or "commitment letter," between Dan and Ace, rather than the mortgage, that is the cornerstone of real estate financing. As we shall see, based on freedom of contract principles, the transactional rights and responsibilities of the parties during the postconstruction period will be governed by the negotiated language in the postconstruction commitment letter and, for the most part, prior to default, the note, mortgage, and collateral loan documents (such as the assignment of lease instrument) do nothing more than implement the terms and conditions of the commitment letter.

Moreover, in the case of most commercial real estate loans (such as those involving office buildings and shopping centers) the real security for the loan is not the value of the bricks and mortar but instead the rental obligations of specified creditworthy tenants. Therefore, Ace will demand, as a nonnegotiable condition of its commitment, the right to approve the form and content of the leases with the prime tenants (whose lease terms must coincide with the term of Ace's loan).

In addition, from the perspective of FNB, while Dan is personally liable on the mortgage note, in most cases the real security for the loan is not the ephemeral net worth of the borrower but rather the promise by Ace to supply on completion of the project the loan funds that will be used to "take out" the construction loan and make the construction lender whole again. However, even if Ace should expressly agree to purchase the construction loan from FNB (by means of a tripartite agreement between Dan, Ace, and FNB), Ace's obligation to do so will be conditioned on Dan's compliance with all the terms and conditions of Ace's takeout commitment. Accordingly, the construction loan commitment must closely track the terms of the postconstruction loan commitment letter. Therefore, the unifying theme of the materials in Part II of this book (to the extent one exists) is the postconstruction commitment letter between Dan and Ace, because of its singular impact on the financing and leasing of the mortgaged real estate.

Chapter 5

Postconstruction, or "Permanent," Financing

According to conventional wisdom, mortgage financing is the foundation of real estate development. While it is possible for some developers to fund the acquisition and improvement of real estate with their own money, few are able to do so. Even if able, still fewer would forego the tax and business advantages of financial leverage that result from using the mortgage device and other forms of real estate financing. In the case of debt financing, not many real estate borrowers have the wherewithal to borrow on an unsecured basis, that is, without furnishing collateral on which the lender alone can rely for satisfaction of its loan indebtedness. Woe to the lender who is relegated to the status of an unsecured creditor; for if the defaulting borrower were to become insolvent without security, the lender's sole remedy would be to compete with the borrower's other general creditors for recourse against the unsecured, and no doubt depleted, assets of the borrower. In most modern real estate transactions, the borrower's loan indebtedness is evidenced by a promissory note, and the borrower, as mortgagor, transfers a security interest in the real estate to the lender, as mortgagee, to secure the mortgagor's promise to repay the borrowed funds. Thus, the mortgage becomes a lien on the real estate until the indebtedness is satisfied.

Real estate is able to serve as collateral for loans far in excess of its value at the time the lender agrees or commits to make a mortgage loan. As we shall see, in the case of new improvements, while the postconstruction lender normally commits to make the loan before construction commences, it does not actually "close" the loan until the building is constructed; therefore the security for the postconstruction loan is the lender's mortgage lien on a fully completed project. However, what really secures (or "feeds") the postconstruction mortgage, even more than the land and the intrinsic ("brick and mortar") value of the building, is the projected rental income stream from the future tenants, as estimated by the lender's appraiser. This is a major reason why nonrecourse financing (whereby the borrower-developer is exculpated from personal liability) is so prevalent in the postconstruction financing of income-producing real estate.

The improvements are usually constructed with funds provided by a construction lender, whose security is merely a partially completed project consisting of the underlying land and the materials supplied and services rendered by the general contractor and subcontractors at the building site. Even though the developer-borrower is personally liable for repayment of the construction loan, there is no rental income to feed the construction mortgage, and therefore the real security for the construction loan is frequently the agreement of the postconstruction lender to supply funding on the completion of construction that will be used to "take out," or to satisfy, the construction loan. In most cases, both the postconstruction lender and the construction lender will obtain a first mortgage on the improved real estate so that in the event of a default by the mortgagor the mortgagee need not compete with other encumbrancers who might be holding a lien or other competing interest in the same real estate.

A. PREFINANCING CONSIDERATIONS

It has been said that back in the 1950s a developer could invest virtually anywhere and probably become wealthy. If this was true, it is no longer so. Today, with periodic inflation, tight mortgage money, and an oversupply in certain types of building stock, a developer must be willing to endure a tremendous amount of homework before deciding whether a proposed project is feasible and, if so, how to obtain the necessary financing and venture capital to fund the land acquisition and construction costs. The following is a summary of the more important prefinancing considerations.[1]

1. Some salient prefinancing considerations that are examined elsewhere include deciding: (1) which ownership entity should be used (see Chapter 2B, note 7); (2) whether the underlying land should be purchased or leased and, if leased, determining if leasehold financing will be available (see Chapter 8A); (3) how to obtain fee title and title protection for the purchaser (see Chapter 3A and Chapter 3B) and whether any zoning or environmental law constraints exist in connection with owning, leasing, or using the property (see Chapter 5B9); (4) whether the cost of the land should be *separately* financed by means of a subordinated purchase-money mortgage (see Chapter 9B, note 5a), an installment land contract (see Chapter 9C), sale and leaseback of the land (see Chapter 8B), or some variant of component financing (see Chapter 8B1, notes 2 and 3); (5) whether the project should be financed by means of a mortgage loan, joint venture, or some combination of debt and equity financing (see Chapter 7A and Chapter 7B); and (6) whether the cost of developing or acquiring the real estate can be super-leveraged by means of some high-ratio financing technique such as high-credit lease financing, a tax-free exchange, or tax-exempt bond financing (see Chapter 9D). For an in-depth discussion of prefinancing considerations see Hastie, Real Estate Ac-

1. Selection of the Real Estate   *John Rouse*

Before selecting the real estate to be developed, a developer will need
to commission a marketing survey reflecting consumer demand, tax
rate trends, and rent and vacancy levels for comparable properties and,
based on such information (along with efforts to pre-lease the building),
the developer will make an educated guess as to whether there will
be sufficient rental income from the project to both cover the anticipated
operating expenses (primarily interest payments on the mortgage) and
yield an after-tax rate of return that will be acceptable to the investors
in light of the probable degree of risk involved. The developer must
also conduct engineering studies at the construction site to determine
if soil conditions and other topographical features are suitable and
whether sufficient utilities exist to service the proposed site. If the
developer plans to acquire existing real estate, it will also be necessary
to examine the physical condition of the improvements, prior rent
schedules and operating expenses, the quality of the tenants, and the
lease terms and determine what rate of return can be expected based
on an estimate of future rental income and expenses (including financing
costs). For discussion on rates of return see Chapter 2A, note 3.

2. The Function of Postconstruction Financing

The search for the financing of new income-producing real estate will
normally commence with the "permanent loan commitment" from a
permanent lender such as a life insurance company, thrift organization,
or, more recently, a credit corporation or pension fund. On the strength
of the permanent commitment, the developer-borrower then seeks to
obtain short-term construction financing from an interim lender, most
often a commercial bank. Historically, the postconstruction loan was
known as the "permanent loan" because it had been used to replace
the temporary construction financing. Also, prior to the demise of the
fixed-rate "long-term" mortgage, postconstruction financing frequently
lasted as long as 25 to 30 years. Recently, with lenders reducing the
term of postconstruction loans and demanding more stringent call
options as a hedge against inflation, the phrases "permanent" and "long-
term loan" have become misnomers. For this reason, we have chosen
the phrase "postconstruction loan" to describe that type of financing
that replaces and still remains distinct from construction financing.

---

quisition and Development — The Developer's Perspective, in 1 Modern Real Estate
Transactions 503, 503-563 (7th ed. 1986).

Joyce, Financing Real Estate Developments
The Colo. Law. 2093, 2101 (Aug. 1982)

MORTGAGE LENDERS

Life insurance companies are the principal source of nonresidential permanent financing. The main source of their funds [is] insurance premiums, which are not generally thought to be as subject to interest fluctuation as voluntary withdrawal deposits. However, loan demand against policy value ultimately does affect mortgage funds availability through insurance companies. Traditionally, insurance companies loan at about 75 percent of value for moderate-length terms without prepayment flexibility. The interest rates of insurance companies are often slightly better than banks or S&Ls because money is marginally less expensive to them. The loan amounts are usually larger due to the wholesale, rather than retail nature of their operations.

Commercial banks are the principal source of shorter term construction lending when a permanent loan commitment is available. Banks obtain money principally from deposits, and federal reserve and other borrowings. Banks are immediately affected by federal credit and monetary policy, due to their use of short-term borrowings to fund bank operations. Therefore, banks tend to lend only on a short-term basis, and usually only when the real estate involved is secondary security to a permanent loan commitment or other take-out guarantee. Rates paid for bank loans tend to float over prime and have terms of three years or less, but are more flexible in loan-to-value ratios.

Traditionally, S&Ls are the mortgage lenders for residential properties, both single and multi-family. S&Ls obtain funds principally from depositor savings, mortgage payoffs and borrowings from the Federal Home Loan Bank Board. S&Ls have experienced significant problems in asset and liability management in recent years and are heavily affected by the volatility of interest rates. The recently huge disintermediation of savings from S&Ls to money market funds has had a disastrous effect on S&Ls in terms of both current income and net worth. The response to these conditions by S&Ls generally has been to shorten the terms of loans available, increase interest rates and to become considerably more aggressive in terms of equity participations.

Several other institutions, including mutual banks and real estate investment trusts, from time to time, have become significant lenders. However, the current "hope" of the developer lies in the vast reservoir of money potentially available in pension funds as a result of increasingly liberal tax treatment of such funds. If societal trends in Europe can be

seen as predictive of those in the United States, these funds may grow
even larger. Since these funds do not borrow the money they lend on
a short-term basis, they are not as subject to volatile interest rates as
are other lenders. Also, as insurance companies, pension funds are not
interested in receiving tax benefits, generally leaving them to the
developer.

a. The Commercial Lending Cycle

The commercial lending cycle begins with the commitment for
and ends with the closing of the postconstruction loan. As noted above,
once the borrowing entity is selected and the other prefinancing considerations addressed, the financing process starts when the developer
seeks to obtain a mortgage commitment from a postconstruction lender.
This is the all-important first step, because the construction loan commitment frequently will be issued only after there is a firm commitment
from a postconstruction lender.

Once the developer has the postconstruction commitment in hand,
the next step is obtaining the construction loan commitment. Often
the construction loan commitment will be accompanied by the execution
of a "buy-sell" agreement between the construction lender, the postconstruction lender, and the borrower under which the construction
lender agrees to sell and the postconstruction lender agrees to buy the
construction loan.

After the construction mortgage is recorded, the fourth stage occurs,
in which the developer complies with the predisbursement requirements
under the construction loan agreement (sometimes referred to as a
"building loan agreement"). Next, the improvements are constructed
with the construction loan funds that are periodically advanced by the
construction lender ("progress payments") in accordance with the construction loan agreement.

Finally, the construction loan is assigned to (or "taken out" by)
the postconstruction lender pursuant to the buy-sell agreement, and
the postconstruction loan is closed when the project is completed in
accordance with the terms and conditions of the postconstruction loan
commitment letter. Hence, the commercial lending cycle, as diagrammed in Figure 5-1, begins and ends with the takeout commitment
from the postconstruction lender.

The closing of the postconstruction loan does not represent the
end of the story for the developer. After the project has been constructed
and in operation for some time ("on stream," as developers call it) the
developer may seek to "mortgage out" tax-free equity to the investors

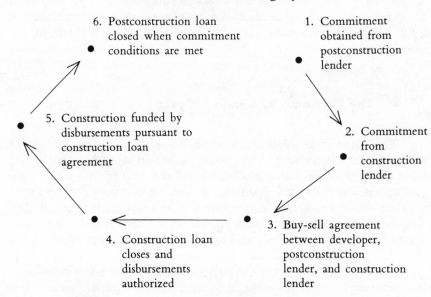

Figure 5-1

a. The Commercial Lending Cycle

6. Postconstruction loan closed when commitment conditions are met

1. Commitment obtained from postconstruction lender

5. Construction funded by disbursements pursuant to construction loan agreement

2. Commitment from construction lender

4. Construction loan closes and disbursements authorized

3. Buy-sell agreement between developer, postconstruction lender, and construction lender

b. Percentage Distribution of Mortgage Holdings by Depository Institution, by Type of Loan and Property, January 1, 1988

	Savings Banks	Savings & Loans	Commercial Banks	Life Insurance Companies
By Type of Loan				
FHA	4.3	0.7	1.5	1.1
VA	4.3	1.1	0.9	0.5
Conventional and other	84.1	87.5	72.7	97.8
Construction	7.3	10.7	24.9	0.6
TOTAL	100.0	100.0	100.0	100.0
By Type of Property				
Residential	76.4	75.2	45.4	16.7
1- to 4-family	65.7	65.4	42.5	6.2
Multifamily	10.7	9.8	2.9	10.5
Nonresidential	16.3	14.1	27.2	77.9
Farm	*	*	2.5	4.7
Construction	7.3	10.7	24.9	0.7
TOTAL	100.0	100.0	100.0	100.0

* Less than 0.05%.
Note: Construction includes land loans.

Source: National Council of Savings Institutions, 1988 Factbook of Savings Institutions, Table 18 at 24 (1988).

(see Chapter 2B, note 5b and Chapter 9A, note 1) or raise additional working capital by refinancing the existing loan for a longer term and possibly at a lower rate of interest. See Chapter 9A, notes 2 and 3. Alternatively, if the prepayment fee is steep or the interest rate on the existing loan is low, the developer may seek an ordinary secondary mortgage or perhaps "wraparound" financing. See Chapter 5B7 and Chapter 9B, note 4. If the value of the land component is relatively high or the depreciation of the improvements is relatively low, the developer might obtain more working capital and tax deductions by means of a sale and leaseback arrangement (see Chapter 8B). In the alternative, the developer may increase its financial leverage by means of a tax-free exchange, component or split financing, or some other high-ratio financing technique. See Chapter 9D.

b. Selection of the Postconstruction Lender

In selecting the postconstruction lender, the developer will have to consider which type of lending institution specializes in the kind of financing being sought. The loan preferences of the various types of postconstruction lenders are the product of each lender's historical habits, external regulation of its investment portfolio, the source and stability of its funding sources, market competition, and a host of other variables. For example, most life insurance companies have tended to prefer large projects such as office buildings, shopping centers, and apartment houses, in order to reduce their overhead-per-loan costs. Savings banks and savings and loan associations traditionally have made loans involving small- to medium-size apartment buildings. In their heyday, the less regulated and more audacious real estate investment trusts were generally more likely to be interested in land development loans and high-risk loans to develop hotels, motels, mobile home parks, and other specialty properties. These traditional distinctions, however, have become blurred in recent years, and within each group of lenders, individual institutional preferences may vary dramatically.

An experienced developer will probably have little difficulty in choosing the right lender to approach. Developers with less of a track record may choose to act through an intermediary who will place the loan with the most appropriate postconstruction lender. Such a developer may use a broker, who will undertake to find a postconstruction lender and, if successful, earn a fee geared to a percentage of the loan amount. Alternatively, the developer may look to a mortgage banker or, in the parlance of postconstruction lending institutions, a mortgage loan correspondent, who will commit to make the postconstruction loan based on an agreement from the ultimate postconstruction lender to purchase the closed loan from the correspondent. Generally, this process is used for smaller loans, because the assets of the correspondents are limited. If the correspondent handles a larger loan, it will normally wish to use the institution's money to fund the making of the loan. The loan is then closed in the name of the institution or simultaneously assigned to the institution if closed in the name of the correspondent. This procedure requires the correspondent to work very closely with counsel for the postconstruction lender so that all documentation can be approved prior to the initial closing.

When a transaction becomes very large and complex, even experienced developers will look to an intermediary in the form of a consultant, usually a prominent individual in real estate brokerage circles, who will charge a fee for placing the loan.

3. The Mortgage Loan Application: The Commitment

In large, complex transactions, the proposed borrower will apply for the loan, furnishing the lender with the information it requires, often on the lender's loan application form. The mortgage is then negotiated, and the agreement by the postconstruction lender to make the loan is documented in an individually prepared, lengthy contract called a "commitment letter."

The borrower's attorney should carefully examine the terms of the lender's normal commitment form so that the developer can determine in advance whether the essential terms are acceptable. This should certainly be done when the form of application incorporates by reference the lender's commitment terms. In that event, a commitment from the lender tracking the application might constitute a binding contract. Moreover, a developer who feels uncomfortable with a provision in the application should not count on the lender's real estate or finance committee to agree to modify or delete the objectionable terms in the form. Any objections the developer may have should be resolved during the application stage.

To simplify matters, some lenders, especially in small transactions, use a single integrated document that incorporates all the terms and conditions of both the application and commitment letter. The rule of thumb, however, is that the more complicated and the larger the transaction, the less the developer and the lender will make use of prepared forms and the more the final documents will be tailored to the particular facts and circumstances of the transaction.

Smith and Lubell, Real Estate Financing: The Permanent Mortgage Loan Commitment
4 Real Est. Rev. 7 (Winter 1975)

Mortgage loan commitments are as essential to the financing of real estate as contracts of sale are to the selling of real estate. However, while one can purchase a standard form of contract of sale at most neighborhood stationery stores, there are no standard forms of loan commitments. *Black's Law Dictionary* does not contain a definition of a mortgage loan commitment, and one will find in law reviews and journals few articles or commentaries on the legal aspects of commitments. Since we cannot today conceive of a mortgage loan which has not been initiated by a commitment, it is strange that we lack the same standardization for this important document that exists for mortgages, deeds of trust, promissory notes, deeds, and a considerable number of other instruments routinely encountered in real estate transactions.

WHAT IS A COMMITMENT?

A mortgage loan commitment is a contract between a prospective creditor and debtor under which the debtor agrees to borrow a sum of money from the creditor and the creditor agrees to lend such sum to the debtor. It customarily arises as a consequence of an application for mortgage loan financing by an owner, purchaser, or developer. The application is an offer by the prospective debtor to borrow a specified amount of money upon stated terms and conditions, and the commitment is the lender's acceptance of the offer. Both application and commitment should set forth the amount, rate of interest, maturity, and other basic terms and conditions of the proposed loan. If the terms and conditions set forth in the commitment vary materially from those set forth in the application, the commitment constitutes a counteroffer which must be accepted by the borrower before a contract arises.

THE ESSENTIAL CONDITIONS OF A COMMITMENT

Commitments are issued by savings banks for loans on single-family residences, by commercial banks and real estate investment trusts for construction loans of all kinds, and by life insurance companies for permanent financing on office, apartment, retail, and other income-producing properties. While the substance of a commitment varies considerably with the purpose and type of property, the following common elements should be contained in all commitments:

- Agreement by the lender to lend a specific amount.
- Designation of the party to whom the loan will be made (name of mortgagor or identity of borrowing entity).
- Terms of the loan including rate of interest and maturity.
- Method of repayment (e.g., constant monthly installments, interest only, etc.).
- Prepayment privilege, if any.
- Description of the security. (A legally satisfactory description, such as metes and bounds, is not essential; the description need only adequately identify the mortgaged property. If the lender requires a lien on personal property, it should be included in the description of the security.)

The above elements of the commitment reflect the essential business considerations of both lender and borrower — the heart of the loan transaction.

OTHER USUAL COMMITMENT CONDITIONS

Let us assume that a developer has applied to the ABC Life Insurance Company for a loan of $4,275,000, with interest at 8.5 percent per year and a term of twenty-seven years, to be repaid in equal monthly payments of $33,700 each, such payments to be applied first in payment of interest and the balance in reduction of principal. The security is a proposed garden apartment project containing 422 units and recreational facilities, to be constructed by the developer on a 22-acre site. The developer and ABC have negotiated a prepayment privilege effective after ten loan years with a declining penalty for prepayment. The commitment issued by ABC should incorporate all of the foregoing basic elements of the loan and should also contain the following customary conditions or requirements:

- *Documents.* All documents which evidence or secure the loan must be in form and substance satisfactory to the lender's attorney. This includes the note, the mortgage, or deed of trust, the assignment of rents and any other instruments which may be unique to the particular loan transaction. The lender cannot be arbitrary and capricious in its legal requirements. Otherwise the commitment would be a hollow instrument devoid of the substance of a contract.

- *Title insurance.* All prudent lenders insist upon title insurance in a form approved by their attorneys.
- *Survey.* Most lenders require a survey dated within a reasonable time prior to the date of closing the mortgage loan (usually thirty days). The survey should not only show the dimensions of the exterior lot lines but should also include the dimensions and location of improvements and easements, if any.
- *Hazard insurance.* Policies in amount, form, and substance satisfactory to the lender are required. Such policies must name the lender as beneficiary, as its interest may appear.
- *Fees and expenses.* Lenders invariably impose upon the borrower the cost of title insurance, survey, recording and filing fees, mortgage taxes, and attorneys' fees, if any.

VARIATIONS ON A THEME

The insertion of further conditions in the commitment is largely determined by the amount of the loan, the nature of the security, and the complexity of the transaction. In a commitment for a large and complicated loan transaction, the lender is much more likely to include additional provisions for the greater protection of its interests. In the foregoing example of a $4,275,000 loan on a garden apartment complex, there are a number of conditions that may be contained in the commitment, depending upon the lending policies of the institution making the loan. For example, a lender concerned with the ability of the mortgagor to obtain anticipated rents may require certain leasing criteria to be met as a condition precedent to the loan closing. The condition might read as follows:

> It is a condition of this loan that the annual rental from not more than 77.5% of the rooms in the development on an unfurnished basis shall be not less than $625,000 and the space rented shall be rented on a basis so that if the building were 100% rented, the annual rental would be at least $807,480. Such rooms shall be occupied by tenants on a current rent-paying basis under written leases or rental agreements having terms of not less than one year.

Where the commitment has such a *rental achievement requirement,* the lender naturally will require evidence that the leasing requirement has been accomplished before it funds the loan. The result is the additional condition "that the borrower shall deliver to the lender a rent roll certified to be correct, indicating the apartments of which said rooms comprise the total rooms relied upon to satisfy the condition."

If the loan is to be made on the security of a shopping center or office building, the credit-oriented lender will look carefully at the source of the leases and evaluate the credit of the tenants. In these transactions, the lender wants to pass upon the acceptability of the tenants, and a condition reflecting this will be inserted in the commitment.

In almost all cases where the commitment requires occupancy leases with specific tenants, the lender will insist upon being given in the commitment the right to approve or disapprove of the leases. The lender looks to the leases for the income which will repay the mortgage indebtedness. The prudent lender further reluctantly visualizes itself as a potential owner of the property in the event of the mortgagor's default. For these reasons there are many caveats which the developer, as a prospective borrower, must keep in mind when negotiating shopping center or office leases.

The commitment must also be tailored to the nature of the borrower's ownership. A leasehold loan made to the lessee of a long-term ground lease will necessarily contain conditions aimed at assuring the lender of a satisfactory mortgageable ground lease. The commitment involving a subjected (subordinated) fee and leasehold mortgage loan will contain conditions unique to that form of transaction.

THE COMMITMENT FOR NEW CONSTRUCTION

If our hypothetical $4,275,000 loan commitment on the garden apartment complex contemplated the construction of the development by the borrower, there would ordinarily be two commitments involved in the financing — a commitment for a construction loan and a commitment for a permanent loan. These two are usually obtained from different institutions. Life insurance companies are a common source of permanent mortgage loan financing and commercial banks are often a source of construction financing. Legal and regulatory restrictions imposed on each of these lenders limits their respective construction and permanent lending activities.

The permanent loan commitment is usually obtained first and forms the basis for the construction loan commitment. The construction lender, relying upon the permanent "takeout" supported by a buy-sell agreement among itself, the borrower and the permanent lender, patterns its construction loan commitment after that of the permanent lender.[1]

Conditions which are unique to new construction and are found

1. See Davis, The Permanent Lender's Role in the Construction Process, Real Estate Review 70 (Spring 1973).

in most permanent loan commitments are often incorporated verbatim into construction loan commitments. They include the following:

- *Dates of commencement and completion of construction.* In the absence of these dates, the borrower is afforded an opportunity to "shop" for the most favorable mortgage loan.
- *Requirement for approval of plans and specifications.* Obviously, the lender desires to determine, in advance, the value of the security for its loan and will prohibit material changes in the plans and specifications without its consent for the same reason.
- *Completion of construction in accordance with plans and specifications.* The lender wants to be assured that it is receiving, as security for its loan, exactly what it bargained for.
- *Compliance with law.* Evidence must be submitted that the improvements comply with applicable building and zoning laws. In addition, some lenders now insist in their commitments upon evidence of compliance with all applicable environmental protection and equal opportunity employment laws.
- *Street dedication.*   Streets necessary for access to the security must be completed, dedicated, and accepted for public use by the appropriate governmental authorities, and evidence of this must be submitted to the lender.

COMMITMENT FEES

Before seriously entertaining an application for a mortgage loan, an institutional lender must appraise the property, evaluate the borrower's integrity and financial responsibility, and also determine the economic feasibility of the real estate as security for the proposed loan. These tasks involve expenses which call for payment of an application fee by the borrower. Such fee is usually expressed as a fractional percentage of the loan and is paid simultaneously with the submission of the application. In some cases, the application fee is also regarded as the consideration paid by the borrower for the issuance of the commitment. An application fee should be distinguished from a commitment fee, which is in the nature of a security deposit to protect the lender against the uncertainties of the money market since a borrower may go elsewhere for his loan if interest rates soften. The amount of the security deposit or commitment fee constitutes a designation of the monetary damages which the lender will sustain in the event of the borrower's breach of the commitment.[2]

---

2. See Boston Road Shopping Center, Inc. v. Teachers Ins. & Annuity Ass'n of

In the ordinary mortgage loan transaction, actual damages are uncertain and difficult to ascertain because of the vagaries of the money market and the complexities of attributing a precise cost to the lender for holding funds available for the loan and for the post-commitment processing of the loan. Therefore, an arbitrary commitment fee expressed in the form of a percentage of the loan is usually employed. Although arbitrarily fixed, such fee should represent a reasonable estimate of the loss to the lender in the event of the borrower's failure to honor the commitment. Commitment fees of at least 2 percent of the face amount of the loan are most common.

Sometimes, in an effort to hedge his bet, a prospective borrower anticipating more favorable rates or terms in the future secures a "standby" commitment from a lender. Such a commitment obligates the lender to make the loan but does not obligate the borrower to take down the loan. Fees for this commitment are frequently geared to the period of time during which the commitment remains outstanding. This form of commitment usually constitutes a developer's last resort in the event he is unable to secure more favorable financing elsewhere and is generally obtained by him solely because his construction lender requires some type of firm takeout.

A Binding Contract

The commitment is the initial contract between the borrower and the lender. It defines the terms and conditions of the loan. The subsequent loan documents are to a commitment what the deed is to a contract of sale. . . . Therefore, commitments should be treated with the same regard accorded any other binding contract.

Teachers Insurance & Annuity Association of America v. Butler
626 F. Supp. 1229 (S.D.N.Y. 1986)

Opinion

Edward Weinfeld, District Judge.

Plaintiff, Teachers Insurance and Annuity Association of America ("Teachers"), is a New York nonprofit corporation which provides annuities and insurance programs to colleges, independent schools and

---

Am., 213 N.Y.S.2d 522 (1961); Regional Enterprises, Inc. v. Teachers Ins. & Annuity Ass'n of Am., 352 F.2d 768 (9th Cir. 1965).

other educational institutions, and derives income for such programs from various investments, including long-term loans on commercial real estate.

The defendant, One City Centre Associates ("OCCA"), is a California limited partnership which undertook the development and construction of a high rise office building, One City Centre, in Sacramento, California. It has three general partners, David L. Butler, James E. Kassis and James L. Grauer, also named as defendants (collectively "defendants" or "the Butler group").

In connection with the development of the building, OCCA needed temporary or construction financing for the period during which the building was under construction and upon completion "permanent financing," which would be applied to the repayment of the construction financing. Bank of America made the construction loan.

Teachers, after extended negotiations with representatives of Sonnenblick-Goldman Corp., mortgage bankers and realtors who acted as the defendants' agents, and with Butler and Kassis on behalf of OCCA, issued on September 9, 1982 a Commitment Letter which was accepted by the individual defendants on behalf of OCCA. Under the Commitment Letter, which the parties acknowledge constituted a binding agreement between them, Teachers agreed to lend and OCCA agreed to borrow $20,000,000 for a thirty-five year term at a fixed interest rate of 14.25% per annum, to be secured by a first deed of trust on the building. The Commitment Letter, among other matters, granted Teachers a contingent interest in the rental returns over the life of the loan, referred to as a "kicker." One provision precluded the defendants from prepayment of the mortgage during the first seventeen years (the "Lock-in Period") and another permitted prepayment during the remainder of the loan upon payment of a premium ("Prepayment Premium") at 6% in the eighteenth year and in reduced amounts thereafter until the expiration date of the loan. These provisions, to be discussed hereafter, are at the heart of this litigation.

In October 1982, Teachers, OCCA and Bank of America, the construction lender, executed a related agreement called a Take-Out Agreement. It provided that Teachers would "take out" (i.e., purchase) Bank of America's construction loan or repay it the sums it advanced for construction of the building and succeed to its rights.

In July 1983, Teachers' counsel sent to OCCA for review and comment the closing documents which Teachers proposed be executed by OCCA at the closing of the loan, including a California Deed of Trust and California Deed of Trust Notes, which in relevant part provided:

> In the event Holder exercises its right to accelerate the maturity date following default by Maker, any tender of payment of the amount

foreclosure is prepayment w/ penalty

necessary to satisfy the entire indebtedness secured hereby made thereafter at any time prior to a foreclosure sale, either by Maker, its successors or assigns or by anyone in behalf of Maker, shall be deemed to constitute evasion of the prepayment privilege and shall be deemed to be voluntary prepayment herein and such prepayment, to the extent permitted by law, shall include the premium required to be paid under the prepayment privilege set forth herein. If such occurrence takes place prior to the eighteenth loan year then the agreed premium due and owing one [sic] the unpaid indebtedness shall be the product of the premium otherwise due under the formula herein for prepayment during the eighteenth loan year multiplied by three.

The parties refer to this provision as the "Default Prepayment Fee Language" and to the second sentence thereof as the "Lock-In Period Default Prepayment Fee Language."

Prior to the time set for the closing on April 30, 1984, Teachers and OCCA, through their respective counsel, had resolved all disagreements with respect to the language of the closing documents except the Default Prepayment Fee Language. On April 30, 1984, Kassis and Grauer (with a power of attorney authorizing them to act for Butler) appeared at the office of the escrow agent the parties had mutually agreed upon and made certain changes in provisions unrelated to the Default Prepayment Fee Language which had been agreed upon by their respective attorneys. However, they also struck the Default Prepayment Fee Language in each Deed of Trust Note and the Deed of Trust before signing the documents. Later that day, OCCA's attorney informed plaintiff's attorney that OCCA was unwilling to accept the Teachers loan as long as the documents contained the Default Prepayment Fee Language. Teachers then drew the full amount of a $200,000 letter of credit which previously had been provided by OCCA under the Commitment Letter. Soon thereafter, Teachers commenced this diversity action.

Plaintiff seeks to recover damages upon a claim of breach of contract — that defendant failed to negotiate in good faith the dispute with respect to the Default Prepayment Fee Language and that OCCA's claimed objection thereto was no more than a pretext for its unwillingness to proceed with the transaction as a result of a dramatic decline in interest rates from the date the Commitment Letter was signed to the date of the closing; that OCCA adamantly refused to negotiate the amount of the Default Prepayment Fee and insisted upon its deletion in its entirety — in sum that its position was wholly arbitrary and in bad faith. Plaintiff seeks to recover as damages the sum of $3,991,408, the difference between 14.25%, the rate of interest set forth in the Commitment Letter and 11.89%, the prevailing rate of interest on Teachers' loans during the month after the closing, over the thirty-five year period of the loan, discounted to present value. . . .

The defendants reject plaintiff's claim, essentially upon the ground that the Commitment Letter makes no provision for a Default Prepayment Fee payable after Teachers' exercise of a right to accelerate for default during the first seventeen years of the loan. The essence of their position is that although the Commitment Letter contains a detailed provision entitled "prepayment," that provision does not mention anything about Teachers' right to an 18% default prepayment fee. Therefore, according to the defendants, it was plaintiff that breached the contract by insisting on the inclusion of a provision in the closing documents that was not in the Commitment Letter. Defendants counterclaim to recover the $400,000 commitment fee retained by plaintiff and the $25,000 appraisal and engineering inspection fee paid to plaintiff. . . .

Under New York law, a duty of fair dealing and good faith is implied in every contract. As this Court has said: "Where the parties are under a duty to perform that is definite and certain the courts will enforce a duty of good faith, including good faith negotiation, in order that a party not escape from the obligation he has contracted to perform." Here, defendants signed the Commitment Letter, an agreement they concede was binding on both parties, obligating them to borrow and plaintiff to lend $20,000,000. Obviously the Commitment Letter did not contain, and the parties understood that it did not contain, all the final and definitive terms that were to be incorporated in the closing documents. Both parties were required to negotiate in good faith with respect to the closing documents needed to consummate the transaction. Defendants breached that duty to negotiate in good faith and therefore breached the contract with Teachers. . . .

The evidence supports a finding, however, that the Butler group, almost from the time the parties obligated themselves under the Commitment Letter, communicated with various lenders and brokers to avoid taking the Teachers loan. Beginning shortly after the Commitment Letter, with its interest rate of 14.25%, was signed, interest rates started to decline and as construction went forward, continued to decline so that when the loan was ready to be closed, financing was available at approximately 12% and without a kicker. Having obtained the permanent loan commitment necessary for construction to begin, defendants took advantage of the nineteen-month period before the scheduled closing to seek a more favorable loan package from other lenders.

Defendants do not deny communicating with other lenders in an attempt to arrange for permanent financing, but they contend that their purpose was to protect themselves against their inability to meet a requirement of the Commitment Letter that the building be 50% preleased at the time of closing. Defendants point to the financial difficulties of Attorneys Office Management Inc. ("AOMI"), a tenant to whom the defendants were required to lease a fixed percentage of building space. The evidence establishes that this claim was spurious. The pre-leasing requirement clearly was for the benefit of Teachers alone; a condition which Teachers could, and ultimately did, waive. . . .

Defendants' actions during the last few months prior to the scheduled closing date conclusively establish that, as the closing drew near, the defendants deliberately intended not to proceed with this loan — at least not on the terms contained in the Commitment Letter. By contrast, Teachers not only took the steps necessary to close the loan, as it was obligated to do under the Commitment Letter, but it offered the defendants alternatives designed to reduce the likelihood of a default. . . .

Defendants said nothing about any of the provisions of the closing documents until it became apparent that their attempts to convince Teachers not to go forward with the loan or alternatively, to lower the interest rate, would not succeed. Although Butler admitted knowing sometime in February that the closing documents contained the Default Prepayment Fee Language, neither he nor Kassis ever mentioned defendants' objections to the inclusion of this provision in the closing documents in any of their conversations or communications with Teachers. In fact, the Butler group's objections to the Default Prepayment Fee Language were not raised until April 26, 1984 — only four days before the closing — in a letter sent to Teachers' counsel.

Defendants insisted that the Default Prepayment Fee Language be deleted in its entirety. They made no counteroffers with respect to the amount of any default prepayment fee nor were they willing to negotiate its terms. . . .

Here, defendants not only had an implied duty of good faith negotiation, but they expressly agreed in the Commitment Letter to abide by all matters pertaining to the due execution of documents that Teachers' attorneys found "reasonably necessary for the transaction." The Default Prepayment Fee Language included by Teachers in the closing documents was not only "reasonably necessary," it was essential to protect Teachers from a voluntary default by OCCA.

The purpose of such language is to protect a lender against a drop in market interest rates which induces the borrower to default in the early years of the loan, forcing the lender to accelerate the balance, and enabling the borrower to prepay the loan with a second loan obtained at the lower interest rate. There can be no doubt that the loan, if consummated, would have been a highly desirable one to plaintiff, with its prospect of a stream of income over a thirty-five year period at a high interest rate and additional income by way of a kicker. The Default Prepayment Fee Language was intended to implement the Lock-in provision of the loan; without it, the borrowers could circumvent the Lock-in without consequence, depriving Teachers of the benefit of its bargain. Financial lenders in the California market, to protect themselves against such practices, included in their closing documents Default Prepayment Fee clauses at fixed amounts which were not immutable but subject to negotiation. The evidence fully establishes that the inclusion of such clauses was the custom and practice in the California real estate financing market. Indeed, defendants' own expert acknowledged this was so, although he testified some loans were closed without its inclusion. . . . Teachers' inclusion of such language in the closing documents for the OCCA loan is consistent with both Teachers' practice and industry practice.

Even Teachers probably would agree that it would have been more prudent for it to have included the Default Prepayment Fee Language in the September 1982 Commitment Letter. Some lenders include it in their commitment letters and the industry trend during the past few years appears to be towards greater specificity in commitment letters, in part due to a desire to avoid litigation such as this over provisions not contained in commitment letters. But this does not undermine the Court's conclusion that the Butler group breached its duty to negotiate in good faith to close the loan. As discussed above, defendants had the closing documents in their possession for nine months and, despite repeated reminders from Teachers to review the documents, they waited until four days before the closing to object to the Default Prepayment Fee Language. Then, instead of making a counteroffer or engaging in good faith negotiations with respect to the amount of the fee or its terms, defendants arbitrarily refused to negotiate and insisted that it be deleted in its entirety. Nine months after insisting that Teachers delete the Default Prepayment Fee Language from the closing documents, defendants signed the closing documents from Aetna Life Insurance Company which provided defendants with more money at a lower interest rate and without a kicker, but which contained a Default Prepayment Fee based on a formula which potentially could result in the imposition of a fee much greater than the 18% fee in Teachers' documents.

In sum, the inescapable conclusion the Court draws from the totality of the evidence is that defendants' refusal to negotiate with respect to the Default Prepayment Fee Language was simply a last-ditch attempt to scuttle the loan agreement they had entered into nineteen months earlier. The defendants signed the permanent financing agreement with Teachers to enable themselves to obtain construction financing from Bank of America. Almost immediately thereafter, as interest rates declined, defendants sought alternative financing from other lenders. When they were unable to persuade Teachers to lower the interest rate agreed to in September 1982 and when they realized that Teachers was serious about living up to its commitments, defendants engaged in an eleventh hour comparison of the closing documents to the Commitment Letter to come up with an ostensible reason for not going forward with the loan. Defendants breached the Commitment Letter and are obligated to Teachers for its damages. . . .

NOTES AND QUESTIONS

1. Vague Language. From the lender's perspective, the application form, the commitment letter, and any form of application-commitment should contain precise language and should include all the essential terms and conditions (e.g., agreement to lend a specified amount; identity of the borrower; loan terms; method of repayment; prepayment privilege, if any; and a description of the security). Otherwise, any vague language will be construed against the lender, or the agreement may be unenforceable for want of certainty in its terms. For example, in Willowood Condominium Assn. v. HNC Realty Co., 531 F.2d 1249 (5th Cir. 1976), the loan agreement for a $4.7 million loan to develop a condominium project failed to specify how and when the "floating rate" interest would be paid, failed to fix a closing date, and was ambiguous as to the method of disbursement and repayment of principal. The court held that there was no binding contract. See also Leben v. Nassau Savings & Loan Assn., 40 A.D.2d 830, 337 N.Y.S.2d 310 (1972), affd., 34 N.Y.2d 671, 356 N.Y.S.2d 46, 312 N.E.2d 180 (1974) (vague language construed against mortgagee).

The standard form of commitment letter is usually hedged with numerous conditions to protect the lender's interests. One such condition normally provides that the "form and substance of each and every document evidencing the loan and the security therefor or incident thereto, and the title and evidence thereof must be satisfactory to Lender and its counsel." What, if any, legal problems do you see with the language of this boilerplate provision? See Draper, Tight Money and Possible Substantive Defenses to Enforcement of Future Mortgage Commitments, 50 Notre Dame Law. 603, 606-611 (1975). See also Mehr and Kilgore, Enforcement of the Real Estate Loan Commitment: Improvement of the Borrower's Remedies, 24 Wayne L. Rev. 1011, 1015 (1978).

2. Offer and Acceptance. As observed in the excerpt by Smith and Lubell, if there has been little negotiation and the lender's commitment letter tracks the application without significant change, the commitment letter would normally be construed as an acceptance by the lender of the borrower's offer, and would constitute a binding contract for a loan. Would the inclusion of language requiring the borrower's "acceptance" or "confirmation" of the commitment letter change that result? See Consolidated American Life Insurance Co. v.

Covington, 297 So. 2d 894 (Miss. 1974) and 1 A. Corbin, Corbin on Contracts §61, at 252 (1963).

    3. Duty to Negotiate in Good Faith. At common law, each party to a contract is obligated to exercise good faith and fair dealing in the performance and enforcement of the contract. Restatement (Second) of Contracts §205 (1981). Lender liability based on this duty of good faith is discussed at Chapter 12A. The precise content of these duties varies according to the particular circumstances but will typically reflect the justified expectations of the parties and community standards of decency and fairness. By way of analogy, §1-203 of the U.C.C. makes explicit the requirement of good faith in contracts governed by the Uniform Commercial Code; however, its coverage is narrower in scope than that of the common law inasmuch as good faith is defined by §1-201(19) subjectively as "honesty in fact in the conduct or transaction concerned."

    A recent trend has emerged in the case law wherein real estate borrowers and lenders have been held accountable to one another for their conduct while negotiating and closing mortgage loans based on a standard of good faith and fair dealing. With regard to the *Butler* case, keep in mind the essential interrelationship between the mortgage loan commitment and the loan documents that are executed when the loan closes, such as the note and mortgage (or deed of trust). Contrary to popular belief, the single most important document in real estate financing is the commitment for the postconstruction loan, not the mortgage, because, with few exceptions, it is the commitment letter (or application-commitment) that establishes the legal and business parameters for the postconstruction financing.

    In the *Butler* case the court assumed that the contested provision in the mortgage (deed of trust) note, the so-called default prepayment provision, was a customary ("boilerplate") provision in the California real estate financing market as opposed to an unusual or essential term that might precipitate serious negotiations between the borrower and lender during the application-commitment stage. Examples of boilerplate provisions in the loan documents include the standard affirmative covenants (e.g., the duty to make repairs, the duty to pay insurance premiums and property taxes) and negative covenants (e.g., not to cancel a credit lease or alter the mortgaged premises without the mortgagee's consent) by a mortgagor that are designed to protect and preserve the mortgagee's security interest during the term of the loan. By contrast, examples of essential and negotiable terms in the loan documents include the financial terms of the loan (e.g., fixed and contingent interest, amortization period, prepayment privilege) and the other basic terms and conditions of postconstruction financing that are examined in Chapter 5B, infra. Had the mortgage (deed of trust) note provision in the *Butler* case not been viewed as a customary provision do you think the result in the case might have been different? In *Butler* the borrower had waited until four days prior to the closing date before objecting to the default prepayment provision. Meanwhile, during the 19-month commitment period, interest rates had declined dramatically. Obviously, this fact must have influenced the court, and common sense would dictate (as a planning suggestion for both borrowers and lenders) that any objectionable language in the loan closing documents should be brought to the attention of the other party as soon as possible to render the dissatisfied party less vulnerable to a charge of bad faith, especially if market conditions are improving for the party who is objecting; and to obviate or minimize the possibility of an impasse in negotiations and possible accusations of bad faith, the parties should seriously consider "preclosing" the loan transaction by using a preclosed form of buy-sell agreement, discussed at Chapter 5B14.

    Another recent case in the Southern District of New York illustrates the scope of the duty to negotiate in good faith during the commitment and prior to the closing of the loan. In Teachers Insurance & Annuity Association of America v. Tribune Co., 670 F. Supp. 491 (S.D.N.Y. 1987), the borrower breached its obligation to negotiate in good faith by insisting that Teachers accept a condition to closing that had not been included in the commitment letter. The transaction in *Tribune* was the three-cornered sale of an office building. The owner contracted to sell the property to a third party in exchange for a long-term purchase-money note and obtained a loan commitment from Teachers secured by the note. Since the borrower wanted to keep the loan liability off its balance sheet, it required the right to pay the loan by assigning to Teachers the mortgage note, thus permitting it to use "offset accounting" to match off the loan and note in its balance sheet footnotes. Although the importance of offset accounting was apparently mentioned in precommitment discussions, there was no mention of it in the commitment letter, and only in the postcommitment negotiations, when a newly issued FASB opinion put offset accounting into question, did the borrower make its availability an absolute condition of the loan. Teachers acquiesced in other demands and offered to postpone the closing date but refused to accede to the offset accounting requirement, whereupon the borrower walked away from the deal.

    In analyzing the parties' postcommitment obligations, the court stated that the principal duty imposed by a commitment is good-faith negotiation of the details left open by the commitment letter. Making negotiations depend on the other party's acceptance of new terms unexpressed in the commitment or on terms inconsistent with the commitment agreement is unjustified and therefore in violation of the duty of good faith. As in *Butler*, the court in this case also pointed out that a significant drop in postcommitment interest rates may have motivated the borrower's breach of good faith. See also Penthouse International v. Dominion Federal Savings & Loan Assn., 855 F.2d 963 (2d Cir. 1988), cert. denied, 490 U.S. 1005 (1989), revg. in part and affg. in part 665 F. Supp. 301 (S.D.N.Y. 1987), wherein the lender's bad faith was held to have constituted an anticipatory breach of a loan commitment in which the defendant-lender had a $35 million participation share. The Second Circuit overturned a $128.7 million award for the plaintiff-borrower on the ground that the plaintiff had not been ready, willing, and able to perform at the time of the alleged breach.

B. TERMS AND CONDITIONS OF POSTCONSTRUCTION FINANCING

Real estate financing is an area of the law in which freedom of contract has traditionally reigned supreme. However, in recent years, federal law, state and local regulation, and case law have intruded somewhat on the ability of the parties to write the law that will govern their relationship. Nevertheless, subject to these intrusions, the transactional rights and responsibilities of the interested parties (e.g., the developer, the postconstruction lender, the prime occupancy tenants) are usually governed by means of the written word, embodied in some fairly standardized and well-tested agreements that are tailored by legal counsel representing each of the parties to the particular transaction.

With few exceptions, the postconstruction loan commitment will establish the legal and business terms and parameters for the postconstruction financing and, to some extent, for the construction loan also, because the postconstruction lender may refuse to take out the construction loan, notwithstanding a buy-sell agreement, unless the terms and conditions of the postconstruction loan commitment have been met. Moreover, in a sense, prior to foreclosure the mortgage or deed of trust merely implements, or "tracks," the terms of the commitment letter, since the language of the former, unless the parties agree otherwise, must be consistent with the terms and conditions of the latter document, and except for standard provisions that are customary in a particular geographical area, no essential conditions or provisions omitted from the commitment letter can be foisted on the borrower by means of retroactive language in the mortgage or deed of trust.

Essentially, the postconstruction lender's position is that it does not want to have to fund the loan if, on the closing date, the proposed security for the loan is not as it was represented on the commitment date and that, at the time of funding, the completed property must constitute a sound, safe, and legal security for the loan. Conversely, the objective of the developer and the construction lender is to make sure that the postconstruction loan will close when construction is completed and that there is no language in the commitment that would enable the postconstruction lender to reconsider its decision to fund or to impose unanticipated requirements prior to the closing date.

The discussion that follows will be devoted to a provision-by-provision analysis of a postconstruction loan commitment and correlative language, if any, in the mortgage or deed of trust. We will be examining the legal and business issues in the context of the relevant documentation. As real estate planners, our aim will be to consider the pitfalls and legal consequences of each approach in the documentation. As you look at each clause of the commitment and mortgage documents, consider the following questions:

1. What does the language in the clause mean?
2. What did the borrower or lender intend to accomplish by such language?
3. Do cases, statutes, or regulations affect the enforceability of the clause and, if so, how?
4. Does the clause accomplish its objective?

Except in the more routine transactions, no two commitments or mortgages are alike. The commitment and mortgage provisions we will be studying represent one approach used in the more complex real estate financing transactions. Although the terms of each transaction may vary, many of the legal considerations are common to all. The postconstruction loan commitment and mortgage forms in these materials are typical in the sense that they reflect most of these common concerns.

MASTER HYPOTHETICAL

In analyzing postconstruction financing, reference will be made to the book's master hypothetical problem in which Dan Developer (Dan) is a leading real estate entrepreneur with an excellent track record for developing office buildings and shopping centers. Dan acquired from Francine Farmer (Francine) the fee simple title to some land in a growing area of downtown McNiece in the County of Feerick, State of Fuller, on which he intends to construct an office building. He has already talked to several prospective tenants, each of whom has expressed interest in leasing one or more floors in the building, and he expects to have leases (or at least letters of intent) executed with a few credit ("prime") tenants (including the Widget Corporation of America) in the next month or so. Dan paid Francine $8 million for the land, and he anticipates spending approximately $25 million on the so-called soft costs (e.g., architectural and legal fees, engineer's report) and hard ("brick and mortar") costs of constructing the office building. Based on the estimated net rental income he expects to receive from the prime and secondary tenants, Dan is assuming that the fair market value of the project will just about equal its cost of $33 million. (This assumption that future market value equals cost is being made for simplicity's sake. In reality a developer would probably not undertake the project unless the anticipated market value were to exceed the projected cost.)

Dan has decided to finance the cost of the project by means of a straight fee mortgage loan from some institutional lender that specializes in postconstruction financing of commercial real estate, such as a life insurance company. He anticipates that the lender will require a first mortgage lien on the land and the completed improvements. He also expects to receive a maximum loan-to-value ratio on the loan of about 75 percent. Therefore, since the estimated market value of the project is about $33 million he anticipates receiving a loan amount of approximately $25 million, which means that he will have to fund the balance of the venture costs ($8 million) either by using his own funds or (if he is as leverage-minded as most developers) by raising the equity capital from outside investors. Under the latter alternative, the ownership entity would probably be a limited partnership in respect to which he would become the general partner and the outside investors would become the limited partners. Dan anticipates that his net rental income in the first operational year of the venture will be about $4 million (excluding debt-service payments on the mortgage and income tax payments); thus the initial free and clear rate of return from the property will be about 12 percent.

On January 1 of this year, Dan applies to the Ace Insurance Company for a postconstruction loan of $25 million at an interest rate of 10 percent per annum for a term of 15 years,[2] with a closing date scheduled for December 15 of next year. His constant monthly payment of principal and interest will be $268,651.29. He expects that construction will commence on June 15 of this year and be completed on or before the closing date, December 15 of next year. Dan has determined that construction financing will be available from the Fuller National Bank (FNB), provided that he is able to obtain a takeout commitment from some postconstruction lender.

In the discussion that follows, we may vary some of the foregoing

---

2. One of the points for negotiation between the parties is how the principal balance of the loan will be amortized. Amortization is the partial repayment of the principal balance of the note at stated times during the term of the loan. See Chapter 5B4, infra.

hypothetical facts for illustrative purposes as we address the many questions and considerations that relate to postconstruction financing.

1.   The Loan Amount as a Percentage of Appraised Value

The mortgage loan portfolios of postconstruction lenders such as life insurance companies, thrift organizations, and state-chartered commercial banks are frequently subject to both qualitative and quantitative constraints imposed by state regulatory statutes and federal agencies. For example, in most states a life insurance company is required by statute to limit the amount of any mortgage loan to a percentage of the appraised value of the mortgaged property that serves as security for the loan. While the maximum loan-to-value ratios for multifamily and commercial real estate loans vary from state to state, they are generally in the range of 75 to 80 percent.[3] However, the recent liberalization of the New York statute (which has been a prototype for regulatory statutes elsewhere) may portend a trend away from these restrictions.[4] As reflected by the loan-value data in Table 5-1, infra, life insurance companies (like other institutional lenders) tend to make loans at maximum loan-to-value ratios. Another example is federally chartered and insured thrift organizations, which ordinarily are subject to a maximum loan-to-value ratio of 90 percent for apartment building and commercial real estate loans.[5] Moreover, in the absence of such external restrictions, prudent underwriting practices dictate some form of self-imposed limitation on loan-to-value ratios, and therefore every mortgage lender will require an appraisal of the mortgaged property as a condition precedent to the issuance of a commitment letter.

In the following excerpt, Leon W. Ellwood (a former chief appraiser of the New York Life Insurance Company and widely regarded as the forerunner of modern mortgage loan appraisal theory) explains how the "income method" of appraisal operates and why it has become the primary method for valuing income-producing real estate.[6] While the article excerpt is somewhat outdated as to capitalization rates, the principles expounded by Mr. Ellwood are still widely accepted by mortgage loan appraisers in their valuation of real estate for purposes of determining maximum loan amounts.

3. See, e.g., Mass. Ann. Laws ch. 175, §63(7) (Law. Co-op. 1987) (limited to 75 percent appraised value of the real estate in most cases).

4. N.Y. Ins. Law §81(6)(a) (McKinney Supp. 1983), as amended in 1984 by N.Y. Ins. Law §§1402, 1403(a)(1), and 1405(a)(3) (McKinney Supp. 1990).

5. 12 C.F.R. §545.32(d)(3) (1990).

6. L. W. Ellwood, Appraisal for Mortgage Loan Purposes, in Encyclopedia of Real Estate Appraising 1095 (E. J. Friedman, 3d ed. 1978).

Ellwood, Appraisal for Mortgage Loan Purposes

Encyclopedia of Real Estate Appraising
1095 (E. J. Friedman, 3d ed. 1978)

GOVERNMENT REGULATION OF INSTITUTIONAL LENDERS

Loans by institutional investors are subject to Federal and state regulation. . . . If there is any serious doubt as to the appraisal, the institutional investor must defend it successfully or be found guilty of an illegal investment. The appraisal report in each case is therefore not only a means of estimating the margin of security offered for a prospective mortgage investment, but also a legal requirement for lending agencies. . . .

NATURE OF VALUE FOR MORTGAGE LOAN PURPOSES

There is no validity to an appraisal made from the viewpoint of a prospective seller. The seller's interest in property ceases upon receipt of his price. Success of any mortgage investment depends upon the future performance of the property. In this respect, both the mortgage lender and buyer have common interests. They both depend upon *future benefits of ownership.* For this reason, any appraisal for mortgage loan purposes must be based on anticipated benefits of ownership, and must be made from the standpoint of a well-informed and prudent buyer.

Thus, the value of real property as security for mortgage investment may be defined broadly as follows:

> The maximum amount in dollars that a prudent purchaser, well-informed as to the potential benefits of ownership, and buying subject property for the right to enjoy such benefits, would be justified in paying for it as of the effective date of appraisal on the following terms: cash down to the maximum available ratio of mortgage loan to purchase price, with such loan at the prevailing rate of interest, and with provision for sufficient periodic amortization to protect the margin of security against future decline in value from all causes.

INCOME APPROACH TO VALUE

The economic or Income Approach to value is generally the primary method used in appraising income-producing real estate for mortgage loan purposes. This is the only process that employs future benefits of ownership as the basis of valuation, and the only approach to value from a prudent buyer's point of view. Moreover, it is the only method in which value is geared to the ability of the property to produce income and pay all expenses, including debt service. Every mortgage investor knows that he will encounter difficulty in collection of interest and amortization whenever the security for a loan fails to earn them.

. . . The Income Approach to value usually consists of dividing net income by a selected rate of capitalization. The resulting quotient is the estimate of value. Net income (the numerator) and rate (the denominator) are judgment factors. The reliability of the result will depend on the quality of judgment exercised in selecting these critical factors. The estimate of income must be acceptable to prudent buyers, and the capitalization rate must be a composite of yields with provisions for recovery of capital that will attract mortgage and equity money to produce a price acceptable to the market place. . . .

ESTIMATING NET INCOME

Net income derived from property is a benefit of ownership; gross income, in itself, is not. For this reason, in using the Income Approach to value, the appraiser must compile a careful estimate of *average annual net income* and apply to such net income a proper capitalization rate in order to estimate value. Net income is arrived at by deducting expenses and allowances from gross income. The appraiser must itemize the costs of management, fuel, utilities, payroll, repairs, painting, taxes, insurance, vacancies, and other expenses and allowances.

SELECTION OF A CAPITALIZATION RATE

The capitalization rate in mortgage loan appraisals is made up of the following components:

1. Available ratio of mortgage money to appraised value.
2. Interest rate that will attract mortgage money at the time of appraisal.
3. Maximum full mortgage amortization term available at the time of appraisal.
4. Income projection term in years.
5. Prospective yield that will attract prudent equity money at the time of appraisal.
6. Allowances for decline or increase in market value during the income projection period.

The first three components of the capitalization rate listed above are known at the time of appraisal, and there is little or no conjecture concerning them. The limit of loan in relation to appraised value is fixed by law. The prevailing interest rates with regard to various property types in the locality are readily ascertainable. The required provision for repayment is known. For example:

Assume that:

1. The legal loan limit is 75% of appraised value.
2. The prevailing interest rate is 8½% per annum.
3. The available term for full amortization by level monthly installments is 25 years.

The required monthly installment in this case would be $8.06[1] per $1,000 of borrowed purchase capital. Multiplying $8.06 by 12 to get the annual requirement, dividing by 1,000, and taking three-fourths of the quotient, gives a capitalization factor that takes care of both yield and capital recovery with regard to three-fourths of the appraised value, to wit:

$$\frac{8.06 \times 12 \times 3}{1,000 \times 4} = .07254 \qquad \text{added to equity rate}$$

In other words, the factor .07254, combined with a factor based on the yield and provision for recovery that will attract prudent equity capital, comprises the correct capitalization rate. Equity capital, in this case, would represent one-fourth of appraised value. . . .

PROSPECTIVE YIELD TO ATTRACT EQUITY MONEY

The prospective yield that will attract equity money to real estate is measured by substitution (opportunity cost) or yields obtainable from alternate properties or forms of investment. The yield is never known until the investment is liquidated. It can then be computed on the basis of annual earnings and the proceeds of sale. If this results in a net yield greater than could have been realized by placing the same money in a non-speculative type of investment, the equity investment may be considered successful.

1. The periodic installment of interest and principal required to amortize a loan fully by the end of its term is taken from standard compound interest and annuity tables. The installment is rounded out to eliminate the complication of fractions and the final installment is decreased to balance out.

Potential benefits to the equity owner are usually two-fold: (1) net income in excess of mortgage payments during the term of ownership, and (2) proceeds of sale in excess of any unamortized mortgage balance at the end of the term of ownership. . . .

Since an investor is concerned not only with the rate of return but also with the risk involved, it is necessary to make a comparison with the alternate non-real estate forms of investment subject to less risk competing for the investment funds. Assume that the following yields are obtainable:

Prime commercial loans	7.75%
Municipal tax exempt bonds	5.05%
U.S. Bonds — taxable	6.78%
Commercial mortgages	8.50%

The highest yield obtainable above is the first mortgage rate. Since the characteristics of an equity investment include risk and non-liquidity, together with the added burden of management, an increment above that obtainable from a first mortgage must be necessary to attract the buyer to the equity position. The quality of judgment in estimating the equity yield and equity value is one of the most important phases of the appraisal. The mortgage balance can never be in jeopardy so long as there is a substantial and marketable equity above it. . . .

TESTING INCOME BY OTHER APPROACHES TO VALUE

A prudent buyer will not pay more for property than the cost of its duplication, as indicated by a Cost Approach and a comparative sale or Market Approach to value. Accordingly, in addition to employing the economic or Income Approach to value, the mortgage loan appraiser should further test the result of income analysis and capitalization by comparison with the estimate of value found by physical cost summation and comparable sales data.

If these tests indicate that an equally desirable property could be acquired for less money, the capitalization rate is too low. It should be adjusted to bring the estimates into line, despite the fact that an analysis of the rate appears to promise attractive profits. Such adjustments are rarely necessary when care and good judgment have been exercised in the Income Approach. Nevertheless, the appraisal will not be complete or convincing without cost and market comparisons to back it up.

Wetterer, What Is Value?
3 Real Est. Fin. 77 (Summer 1986)

As one "tax reform" proposal after another has been put forth over the past two years, the real estate industry has spent a great deal of time and energy analyzing how each new proposal will affect the "value" of real estate. After each proposal is announced, industry analysts make a few assumptions, crunch a few numbers and announce their conclusions:

- Industry Analyst A predicts real estate values will plummet.
- Industry Analyst B predicts real estate values will skyrocket.
- Industry Analyst C says real estate values will remain relatively stable over the short (or long) term.

These conflicting expert conclusions should give those of us in the industry pause. Do these experts mean the same thing when they talk about the "value" of real estate? How do they calculate that value? How do they determine the "impact" of a particular tax proposal on real estate values? This article will examine how properties are commonly valued in the syndication industry (*not* in the appraisal industry) and how the impact of a tax reform proposal on these values ought to be assessed.

Essentially, there are four methods commonly used by syndicators to value properties:

- Construction Cost
- Replacement Cost
- Capitalization Rates
- Discounted Cash Flow

COST AND VALUE

The construction cost method is probably the least relevant of the four methods. During periods of high inflation, this method leads to the conclusion that a newly constructed building is always worth more than an older building. This is simply inaccurate. Indeed, in a market such as today's when many areas are overbuilt and construction costs have remained relatively stable, properties are selling at prices below construction cost.

This leads to a consideration of replacement cost as a measure of value. While perhaps having slightly more validity than the construction cost method, this also suffers from the premise that cost equates to fair

T a b l e 5-1

Loan Terms for Multifamily and Commercial Loans Made by U.S. Life Insurance Companies 1979-1988

Period	No. of Loans	Amount Committed ($000)	Loan Amount ($000)	Interest Rate (By #)	Interest Rate (By $)	Averages				Maturity (Years/Months)
						Loan/ Value	Capitaliza- tion Rate	Debt Coverage Ratio	Percent Constant	
1979 1st Quarter	647	2,565,725	3,966	10.03%	10.02%	74.5%	10.2%	1.24	11.1%	20/7
2nd Quarter	786	3,399,869	4,326	10.23	10.26	74.5	10.4	1.25	11.1	21/5
3rd Quarter	742	2,974,591	4,009	10.45	10.42	73.9	10.6	1.28	11.2	22/1
4th Quarter	462	1,821,356	3,942	10.91	10.95	73.0	10.7	1.27	11.7	21/4
Year	2,637	10,761,541	4,081	10.36	10.36	74.1	10.5	1.26	11.3	21/5
1980 1st Quarter	194	1,021,201	5,264	12.32	12.10	73.6	11.8	1.26	12.8	20/8
2nd Quarter	83	634,865	7,649	13.20	12.95	73.6	12.6	1.27	13.6	17/7
3rd Quarter	214	1,531,289	7,156	12.58	12.40	74.3	12.1	1.27	13.0	18/3
4th Quarter	165	992,934	6,018	13.04	12.90	71.6	12.2	1.28	13.4	16/8
Year	656	4,180,289	6,372	12.69	12.53	73.3	12.1	1.27	13.1	18/6
1981 1st Quarter	155	692,842	4,470	13.90	13.48	72.3	12.8	1.32	14.2	14/3
2nd Quarter	144	1,206,421	8,378	14.28	13.48	69.0	13.0	1.29	14.5	17/8
3rd Quarter	107	916,068	8,561	14.47	14.34	71.4	13.1	1.28	14.7	17/3
4th Quarter	87	446,974	5,138	14.98	14.77	67.4	13.4	1.34	15.2	13/8
Year	493	3,262,305	6,617	14.32	13.90	70.3	13.0	1.30	14.6	15/10
1982 1st Quarter	135	1,098,020	8,133	15.23	14.63	66.2	12.9	1.39	15.5	14/3
2nd Quarter	137	847,589	6,187	15.23	14.74	66.4	12.8	1.36	15.3	12/2
3rd Quarter	139	750,754	5,401	14.75	14.49	64.9	12.0	1.28	15.1	10/0
4th Quarter	260	2,132,089	8,200	13.26	13.30	67.6	11.6	1.30	13.7	9/6
Year	671	4,828,452	7,196	14.36	14.04	66.5	12.2	1.33	14.7	11/1
1983 1st Quarter	285	2,009,854	7,052	12.89	12.85	69.8	11.4	1.30	13.2	8/9
2nd Quarter	334	2,723,891	8,155	12.25	12.28	70.7	11.0	1.26	12.6	10/0
3rd Quarter	328	2,894,789	8,826	12.29	12.29	69.2	10.8	1.28	12.6	9/10
4th Quarter	234	2,337,340	9,989	12.67	12.57	70.5	11.1	1.23	13.1	9/10
Year	1,118	9,965,874	88,439	12.49	12.46	70.0	11.1	1.27	12.8	9/7

1984	1st Quarter	357	3,482,348	9,754	12.59	12.55	70.3	10.8	1.26	12.8	10/0
	2nd Quarter	285	3,345,201	11,738	12.97	12.95	68.1	10.5	1.27	13.2	9/10
	3rd Quarter	142	2,131,375	15,010	13.40	12.85	72.5	11.2	1.16	13.6	9/9
	4th Quarter	354	4,009,911	11,327	12.91	12.90	70.5	10.8	1.22	13.2	9/1
	Year	1,138	12,968,835	11,396	12.88	12.81	70.1	10.8	1.24	13.1	9/8
1985	1st Quarter	528	4,405,871	8,344	12.38	12.28	70.0	10.5	1.25	12.7	8/7
	2nd Quarter	473	4,973,043	10,514	12.17	11.98	70.8	10.2	1.23	12.4	8/1
	3rd Quarter	603	5,234,854	8,681	11.42	11.40	71.5	9.9	1.24	11.7	8/3
	4th Quarter	555	6,020,011	10,847	11.25	11.20	71.5	9.8	1.25	11.5	8/1
	Year	2,159	20,633,779	9,557	11.77	11.67	71.0	10.1	1.24	12.1	8/3
1986	1st Quarter	549	5,986,204	10,904	10.39	10.25	71.6	9.5	1.28	10.9	8/10
	2nd Quarter	720	7,769,458	10,791	9.62	9.47	71.2	9.3	1.28	10.4	9/3
	3rd Quarter	423	4,713,001	11,142	9.40	9.30	71.4	9.1	1.32	10.1	9/0
	4th Quarter	443	5,595,257	12,630	9.36	9.03	70.2	9.1	1.40	10.0	8/9
	Year	2,135	24,063,920	11,271	9.72	9.53	71.1	9.3	1.32	10.3	9/0
1987	1st Quarter	394	3,998,061	10,147	9.16	8.97	72.0	9.1	1.31	9.8	8/9
	2nd Quarter	578	6,453,991	11,166	9.40	9.31	72.0	9.2	1.31	10.0	9/0
	3rd Quarter	428	4,907,178	11,465	9.80	9.76	71.6	9.2	1.27	10.2	8/1
	4th Quarter	491	5,591,966	11,389	10.11	10.00	71.7	9.4	1.26	10.5	7/5
	Year	1,891	20,951,196	11,079	9.63	9.54	71.8	9.2	1.29	10.1	8/4
1988	1st Quarter	420	5,321,804	12,671	9.60	9.47	72.4	9.0	1.28	9.9	7/9
	2nd Quarter	566	6,335,410	11,193	9.65	9.59	72.0	9.1	1.29	10.1	7/8
	3rd Quarter	410	4,715,738	11,502	9.98	9.84	71.6	9.1	1.26	10.3	7/8
	4th Quarter	404	5,697,393	14,102	10.00	9.93	71.4	9.3	1.28	10.4	8/3
	Year	1,800	22,070,345	12,261	9.79	9.70	71.9	9.1	1.28	10.2	7/10

Note: Data represent new commitments for future disbursement. Similar data for a smaller sample of companies are available beginning in 1951. Except for the dollar weighted interest rate, averages are based on number of loans for which the data were available. Rates vary in part with the changing composition of loans as to property type, location, purpose of loans, amortization, call, and prepayment provisions and are particularly affected by such loan provision.

Source: American Council of Life Insurance, Invest. Bull. No. 1065, Table A (April 10, 1989) (Data based on mortgage commitments on multifamily and commercial properties, as reported by major life insurance companies that account for two-thirds of nonfarm mortgages held by U.S. companies).

market value. Certainly that is not the case in the severely overbuilt residential markets of the Southwest, or in most downtown office markets where rents have declined in response to high vacancy rates.

For example, in the early 1980s, many syndicators liked to boast about properties they had acquired at a discount from replacement cost. Now, when they go to sell, they find that "discount" has widened — in favor of the new buyer. Rents and income drive property values, not escalating construction or replacement costs.

CAPITALIZATION RATES

Capitalization rates have been perhaps the most widely used valuation tool. Simply stated, cap rates are determined by capitalizing a property's net operating income (rents minus operating expenses exclusive of debt service and non-cash charges) at a specified rate. If a property is sold at 9% cap rate, for example, its current (or next year's) net operating income should provide the buyer with a 9% yield on the buyer's investment. . . .

The use of the capitalization rate method of valuation is an attempt to view real estate as a financial asset, and to facilitate a comparison between returns from real estate assets and other types of financial assets. Most comparable to a dividend or an interest yield, it assumes a stable income flow over the holding period of the property. Hence, it fails to account for the dynamics of most properties leased for a normal term at fair market rates. In addition, since the tax benefits are not considered (at least directly) in the cap rate process, changes in tax benefits are not reflected, unless through some ephemeral adjustment to capitalization rates in general.

DISCOUNTED CASH FLOW

Used for years in making other types of capital investment decisions, the discounted cash flow is finally becoming more popular as a tool for valuing real estate. Under this method, future net cash flows are projected, (thereby reflecting expected changes in the property's profitability) and then discounted at a specified rate to account for anticipated inflation. Further, a reinvestment rate is projected for excess cash flow and reinvestment income is considered as part of the property's total return. This method arrives at value by determining the price that might be offered by a purchaser who desires to achieve a particular rate of return.

This method is the most realistic of the four alternatives. In addition to accounting for the time value of money, it permits taxable investors to include the tax effect of non-cash charges in their analysis. It also permits the effect of debt financing to be reflected, adding value to those properties with favorable financing, and penalizing those properties with high debt costs. . . .

NOTES AND QUESTIONS

1. *Real Estate Appraisal.* It may be a gross understatement to say that appraisal of real estate is an inexact science. Indeed, one often hears the story of the attorney who saw "M.A.I." (Member, Appraisal Institute) after an appraiser's name and thought the letters stood for "Made As Instructed." In reality, appraisers may be getting a bad press. It is fairly easy to determine with reasonable accuracy the value of a three-bedroom split level home in a development with comparable sales occurring all the time. It is far more difficult to determine the value of the land underlying an office building, especially when it is being valued as if the land were vacant and unimproved. Likewise, in the master hypothetical, further difficulties would be encountered in appraising the value of a property such as Dan Developer's office building as of the date the loan commitment two or three years before the building is constructed and fully leased. Yet these are some of the questions confronting appraisers when appraising income-producing real estate. See Miller and Kates, How to Value Real Estate Subject to an Equity Participation, 2 Real Est. Rev. 89 (Spring 1972).

However, as explained in the excerpt by Wetterer, the methodology of appraisal is being refined to take into account such dynamic variables as the time value of money and fluctuations in future cash flows. Another harbinger of things to come is what is happening in the realm of securitization. As reflected by the discussion in conjunction with Figure 13-1 at Chapter 13B, the quest for securitization of real estate has prompted credit rating services such as Moody's to attempt to develop the requisite computer technology to valuate office buildings and other commercial real estate even though the rental income streams from such properties are based on a heterogeneous mix of leases that are disparate in their terms, quality, and creditworthiness.

2. *The Income Method.* As pointed out by Ellwood, the economic, or income, approach is the primary method used in appraising commercial property for postconstruction loan purposes. As discussed above, under the income method the net income from the property is divided by a capitalization rate to determine the value of the property.

Observe that in the example provided by Ellwood the capitalization (cap) rate consists of two major components: an equity yield and a mortgage yield on the debt-financed portion three-fourths of the property based on assumptions as to the loan-to-value ratio, amortization, and level of interest rates. This correlation between the levels of interest rates and cap rates is reflected by the data in Table 5-1, supra. The cap rate, then, is essentially a composite of two rates: the market, or prevailing, rate for first mortgage money combined with the rate of return on an equity investment that would attract a prudent person to purchase the property. The initial rate is then adjusted to take into account certain purchase risk factors (e.g., depreciation, decline or increase in future market value) to arrive at a final capitalization rate.

Expressed as a formula, fair market value would equal the estimated annual net income divided by the final capitalization rate. Therefore, the appraised value will decrease to the extent that the cap rate increases because of any increase in the anticipated rate of interest and risk factors (noted above) or because of any decrease in the anticipated stream of net operating income, and vice versa. For example, by using a cap rate of 10 percent, a building that produces annual net rental income of $100,000 would be valued at $1 million, or "ten times earnings." By contrast, a building that produces the same net rental income but happens to be a riskier investment (for example, a motel situated on a secondary road that has been superseded by a new highway) might be assigned a cap rate of 20 percent and be valued at only $500,000, or "five times earnings." It is not unusual for appraisers to differ both as to the anticipated stream of income that is to be capitalized and the appropriate cap rate to be applied, especially in the case of new construction where the appraisal is made before the improvements are completed. Moreover, even slight changes in these variables can dramatically change the estimated value. However, the objective of any mortgage loan appraisal based on the income approach is to apply a cap rate that is high enough to produce a correspondingly low enough appraised value and loan amount so that the projected net rental income stream from the mortgaged property will be sufficient to cover the borrower's debt service payments and his other operating expenses.

Under the income method of appraisal, if property is expected to produce an annual net income of $1 million, and this stream of income is capitalized at 15 percent, the present value of the property would be the amount that would be needed at a 15 percent return to produce $1 million per year, or $6,666,666. ($.15X = 1 million.) What would the present value be if a 10, 20, or 25 percent cap rate were applied to the $1 million stream of income, and what would those values be if the income stream were estimated at $750,000 or $1,250,000?

3. Ellwood Today.   Outlined in the excerpt by Ellwood is what is known as the classical appraisal theory, that is, the income method, as corroborated by the "cost" and "market" approaches to value. During the 1979-1982 period of stagflation, many real estate professionals discovered that the classical theory did not always work with large rental projects; the real estate failures of that era tended to expose the inaccuracy of appraisers' estimates of anticipated income and capitalization rates. As suggested in the excerpt by Wetterer, the traditional cap rate theory may be too static a method of valuation for a cyclical economy that becomes volatile unless the theory is modified to take into account the time value of money and expected rates of inflation during the property's holding period. In 1981, G. Gordon Blackadar, then vice-president of the Metropolitan Life Insurance Company, propounded a theory of "dynamic capitalization," a corollary to Ellwood's classical theories under which appraisal is accomplished with the use of what he calls "real rates of interest" that are designed to take into account the time value of money. In a vast oversimplification, the theory might be explained as modifying capitalization rates based on projected inflationary and deflationary pressures during a forward period of approximately 10 years. Mr. Blackadar's monograph is available from Metropolitan Life. See discussion on measuring the profitability of a real estate investment (based on the net present value and internal rate of return methods) at Chapter 2A, note 3.

4. Fluctuations in Appraised Value.   Assume in the master hypothetical that Ace Insurance Company is limited by regulatory statute or by its internal underwriting standards to a maximum loan amount not in excess of 75 percent of the appraised value of the mortgaged property and that Ace's appraiser anticipates that Dan Developer's net operating income from the completed building will be $4 million per year, thus producing a free and clear rate of return of 12 percent (estimated net income of $4 million ÷ estimated cost of $33 million). As observed in the excerpt by Wetterer, there is a common misconception that cost equals value. Why are these two measurements not necessarily equivalent? Based on the difference between the two, how could a leverage-minded borrower such as Dan achieve 100 percent financing with a mortgage from Ace that has a loan-to-value ratio of only 75 percent? What capitalization rate would produce the requisite value to justify the $25 million loan amount?

Under the income method of appraisal, a mortgage with a fixed rate of interest (such as the assumed 10 percent annual rate in the hypothetical) will steadily lose its investment value in an inflationary economy as the level of interest rates (and capitalization rates) increases.

Frequently with real estate syndications the prospectus or offering statement will include an assumption as to the rate of inflation for purposes of estimating the future revenues, operating expenses, and net operating income to be derived from the property being offered to real estate investors. For example, in Examples 1 and 2 in the excerpt from Madison and Dwyer at Chapter 2B, the assumed rate of inflation is 4 percent. Assuming the same cap rate, and assuming that everything else remains the same, can you think of a mathematical reason why the estimated value (in *real* dollars) of the property (and its equity) will increase over time even though its ability to produce net rental income, or "profitability," remains the same? See the excerpt by Maisel at Chapter 2A.

2.   *The Gap Financing Problem*

In the master hypothetical, the construction loan from FNB will in all likelihood be limited to the $25 million amount in Ace's postconstruction loan commitment. Therefore, if construction costs exceed $25 million, Dan will have to find alternative sources of financing to fund the gap caused by the cost overruns; or, in the alternative, he may have to do something developers normally like to avoid, namely, contributing more of their own funds to the project.

The gap financing problem for Dan may be exacerbated if Ace Insurance Company, the postconstruction lender, imposes a rent roll requirement, as is frequently done in the case of office buildings and shopping centers that are not preleased and in virtually all apartment and garden apartment project loans. This requirement may be in the form of what is known as a "platform," "floor-ceiling," or "floor-top" loan, under which part of the loan (the "floor" amount) will be funded on the closing date if Dan has obtained executed leases providing him with a rent roll equal to a specified minimum amount, with the remainder "ceiling" or "top" amount to be disbursed if and when the aggregate rent roll requirement is achieved within a stipulated period of time following the closing date. Ace may also insist on an escrow arrangement, or a "hold back" provision, under which Ace will be able to withhold a portion of the loan amount pending completion of all standard tenant work or other construction items.

Let's look at how these requirements are translated into the applicable language in Ace's commitment letter. The following excerpt briefly explains the gap financing problem; it is followed by a sample commitment letter provision for a floor-ceiling loan, under which the loan amount may increase depending on whether a certain rent roll requirement is achieved.

Garfinkel, The Negotiation of Construction and Permanent Loan Commitments (Part 2)
25 Prac. Law. 37, 41-43 (April 15, 1979)

GAP STANDBY COMMITMENTS

Standby commitments might be characterized either as gap standby commitments or full-value standby commitments. A gap standby commitment is often intended to cover the contingent portion of the permanent commitment — that amount by which the maximum sum to be advanced by the permanent lender in the event of maximum rental achievement exceeds the sum to be advanced without regard to rental achievement. The minimum sum to be paid under the most disadvantageous rental experience is referred to as "the floor" of a permanent commitment, while the spread between the minimum and maximum amount of the commitment is referred to as the "gap."

The conventional practice is for the gap to be covered by the developer's cash deposit with the construction lender. An exceptionally credit-worthy developer might be permitted to cover the gap with a personal guarantee. Other developers may supply a letter of credit from a bank or deposit securities or other collateral with the construction lender. A marginal developer with neither cash, credit, or securities to cover the gap may resort to a commitment from a standby lender to provide a second mortgage for the amount of the differential.

Dependence upon a gap standby commitment is, at best, a dangerous approach for the developer, for it may face a catastrophic exposure in the event projected rental or sales are not achieved. A knowledgeable construction lender will be leery of any standby commitment so onerous as to indicate that the standby lender does not contemplate funding the commitment or that the developer will seek to prevent the construction lender from assigning the loan to a standby lender who may immediately call the loan.

HOLDBACKS

Commitments for investment type projects often involve holdbacks of all or a portion of the loan proceeds pending satisfaction of completion, occupancy, or rental achievement requirements. On occasion, holdback requirements are absolute in nature, as when the full funding of the permanent commitment is conditioned upon meeting specific conditions. More often, a period of time after the delivery of the loan will be allowed for the satisfaction of the holdback requirements. For instance, a $5 million permanent commitment for an apartment house may call for delivery of the loan within 2 years, with the full $5 million being paid by the permanent lender only if a rent roll of $960,000 is achieved. The same commitment may provide that if at closing the rent roll is less than $960,000, only four and a half million dollars is to be disbursed, with the remaining $500,000 to be paid only if the $960,000 rent roll is achieved within one year thereafter.

Typically, a rent achievement clause is not based only upon gross rentals. The lender has to protect itself against a reduction in scheduled unit rents by a developer pressed to meet a rent achievement clause. The usual requirement, therefore, interrelates the gross rent to a specified level of rent. Often a rental achievement clause is articulated in terms both of a minimum occupancy and a minimum rent roll for actual occupancy. Permanent lenders are leery of the possibility of a rental achievement condition being satisfied with a limited number of high rent leases that provide for rents in excess of those anticipated at the time the permanent commitment was issued, since those leases may not reflect the long-term rental potential of the project.

In the case of a shopping center or a special-purpose building such as a movie theater or hotel, the disbursement by the permanent lender of the entire amount of the loan will usually depend upon the existence at settlement of fully executed leases, in form and substance acceptable to the permanent lender, with major tenants either specified by name or who satisfy specified conditions. Since the construction lender is looking to the permanent commitment as its principal payment source, it will generally not disburse funds equal in amount to the contingent portion of the permanent commitment until it is satisfied that all "accomplished rental" provisions have been met.

As with all commitment conditions, a construction lender feels most secure when the permanent lender acknowledges prior to the commencement of construction that a commitment condition has either been satisfied or waived. Thus, a construction lender will seek at the time of the construction loan closing to have the permanent lender waive a condition based on a lease that is already in existence. There is, of course, the possibility that circumstances occurring after the construction loan settlement and prior to permanent loan closing may invalidate or terminate the lease. At issue is whether the construction lender or the permanent lender should bear the risk of changed circumstances, such as the bankruptcy of a major tenant prior to the permanent loan closing or the failure of the developer to satisfy all of the conditions of a major lease. Usually it is the construction lender who assumes substantially all the risks of events prior to the permanent loan closing.

Sample Floor-Ceiling Loan Leasing Requirement

Rent Roll. The annual rental from the Real Property shall not be less than $ _____ and the space rented shall be rented on a basis so that if the building were 100% rented, the annual rental would be at least $ _____ . Such rental shall be payable by tenants in possession of their demised premises on a current, rent-paying basis, under leases for terms of not less than five years. The Borrower shall have furnished Lender with a rent roll certified to be correct, indicating the tenants, space and annual rentals relied upon to satisfy this condition.

Floor Loan. Upon completion of construction and compliance with all the terms and conditions of this Commitment except the rent roll requirements set forth in paragraph — , Lender shall disburse or acquire a reduced loan of $ _____ (herein referred to as the "Floor Loan") with the same terms as the Loan except that the monthly interest and principal payments shall be $ _____ each, beginning on _____ . Lender's obligation to disburse or acquire the Floor Loan shall expire on _____ , unless prior thereto, Lender, having the sole option to do so, extends such time in writing.

Top Loan. If only the Floor Loan has been disbursed, Lender, upon receipt of evidence on or before _____ , that the rent roll requirements of the foregoing paragraph have been achieved, will, provided the loan is not in default, increase the Floor Loan by $ _____ to $ _____ and the Loan documents shall be amended to increase total monthly payments of principal and interest to $ _____ each beginning on the first day of the month following disbursement, with interest from the day of disbursement.

NOTES AND QUESTIONS

1. *The Problem Caused by Construction Cost Overruns.* A gap financing problem frequently arises in an inflationary economy in which the costs of labor and materials are escalating and the borrower-developer is unable to obtain a firm commitment from a general contractor (or from subcontractors, if the developer is acting as his own general contractor) whereby the contractor(s) agree or "guarantee" that the overall hard costs of construction will not exceed a specified maximum amount. However, even with firm commitments from contractors it is virtually inevitable that the building design and specifications will be changed (by means of "change orders") on numerous occasions during

the construction period. Because such changes are frequently "upgrades" that are beyond the guaranteed maximum amount, an excessive number of these changes can create a gap financing problem unless the developer's contingency fund is large enough to cover these self-imposed cost overruns. To obviate this problem, the developer should solicit firm bids that are as detailed as possible, and most of the prefinancing requirements (e.g., trade payments, construction surveys, title work, an architectural rendering of plans and specifications, organization of ownership entity) should be completed before construction commences to avoid unnecessary and costly delays in the completion of construction. In addition, developers should avoid the so-called fast track method of construction whereby construction is commenced before the plans and specifications are completed. Although this method is designed to save construction time (and interest on the construction loan), it prevents the developer from obtaining bids of the "guaranteed max" variety and invites the possibility of cost overruns. Another real concern for the developer and the construction lender is the possibility that notwithstanding a fixed price contract, the general contractor might become insolvent or simply abandon the project because of cost overruns. While this contingency can be addressed by a bonding requirement, performance bonds tend to be expensive and are so fraught with exculpatory provisions that, in the opinion of some commentators and practitioners, they constitute little more than a license to sue. See, e.g., G. Nelson and D. Whitman, Real Estate Finance Law §12.2, at 836-844 (2d ed. 1985); Hart and Kane, What Every Real Estate Lawyer Should Know About Payment and Performance Bonds, 17 Real Prop., Prob. & Tr. J. 674 (1982). See generally discussion at Chapter 6B4b.

Returning to the master hypothetical, why, do you think, would a prudent construction lender (in the position of FNB) limit its loan amount to the $25 million amount specified in Ace's commitment letter? If the total cost of construction were to exceed this amount and if Dan were unable to raise extra venture capital to fund the cost overruns, he might request additional loan funds from FNB or, as a last resort, be compelled to borrow the shortfall from a so-called gap lender. In either case, the gap financing would be secured by a second, not a first, mortgage lien, and would be quite expensive for Dan. Why is this so? See discussion of gap financing at Chapter 9B, note 1; see also Cheatham, Gap Financing: An Opportunity for Venturesome Thrift Organizations, 15 Real Est. Rev. 49 (Summer 1985).

   2. The Gap Problem Caused by the Lender's Leasing Requirements. Observe the postconstruction lender's leasing requirement for a floor-ceiling loan in the foregoing excerpt from the commitment letter. Can you think of the reason why the annual rental requirement is geared to the percentage of space actually rented as of the closing date? Since the real security for the loan is the anticipated rental income stream, the lender requires that the building be completed and ready for occupancy before it closes the postconstruction loan and disburses the loan funds. In the case of a garden apartment or apartment building loan, where the leases are virtually the same (and "fungible commodities" from the lender's perspective), as opposed to a shopping center or office building loan, where specific high-credit leases secure the loan, a postconstruction lender will frequently impose a leasing requirement whereby the loan amount is two-tiered and the borrower's entitlement to the maximum or "top" loan amount is dependent on the borrower's achievement of a minimum aggregate rent-roll amount when the project is completed and the postconstruction loan is closed. If the leasing requirement is not met on or before the closing date the loan is funded for the "floor" amount and the borrower is given a few months beyond the closing date to meet the leasing requirement and obtain the additional funds.

Returning to the master hypothetical: Suppose the security for the loan is an apartment building (instead of a preleased office building). Ace commits to a floor-ceiling loan with a floor amount of $22 million and a ceiling amount of $25 million on the condition that if the rent roll requirement is not achieved by the closing date, Dan will only receive the floor amount; but Dan has three months beyond the closing date within which to achieve the rent roll requirement, in which event Dan would obtain the extra $3 million. Why, do you think, might postconstruction lenders such as Ace insist on the floor-ceiling loan format? What is the worst-case scenario for the construction lender, FNB, if in its construction loan commitment it agrees to lend Dan the full $25 million rather than the floor amount of $22 million? Can you think of any precautionary measures that Dan might take to avoid the gap financing problem? Suppose the project is being syndicated to limited partners. Can you think of any protective language that Dan should include in the limited partnership agreement? Suppose that on the closing date Dan is only entitled to the floor amount of $22 million because of a leasing gap (e.g., a shortfall of $50,000 in the monthly rentals from residential tenants or unleased commercial space in the amount of 5,000 square feet). Can you think of any interim solution that should satisfy Ace whereby Dan would be able to obtain the extra $3 million in loan funds while the project is being "leased up?"

Suppose that Ace's commitment to make the 15-year postconstruction loan of $25 million requires that a 15-year occupancy lease be executed with a major ("prime") tenant, Widget Corporation of America (WCA), whereunder WCA agrees to rent 10 percent of the leasable space in the office building at a minimum rental of $20 per square foot. Otherwise, the loan amount will be reduced to $24 million. Observe that the term of WCA's lease coincides with the self-amortizing term of Ace's proposed mortgage loan. Is this a mere coincidence? Suppose that WCA has executed a letter of intent to lease the requisite space at the requisite rental but WCA refuses to execute a lease until construction of its office space is completed in accordance with WCA's plans and specifications. As the attorney for FNB, the construction lender, what maximum construction loan commitment amount would you recommend to your client, and why?

In addition to negotiating alternative means of satisfying the rent roll requirement, Dan must also pay close attention to the language of the rent roll provision itself. See the sample provision, supra. For Dan to comply with this requirement, not only must the leases be executed, but the tenants must also be in possession and be currently paying their rents. If you were negotiating this provision on behalf of Dan, what changes might you request from Ace? See generally Madison and Dwyer 3-15 (1981).

3. The Rate of Interest

In today's creative real estate financing environment, the straight fixed-rate fee mortgage (of the variety sought by Dan Developer in the master hypothetical) is but one of the many techniques presently used to finance income-producing real estate. Real estate financing has changed dramatically since the 1960s, the decade that marked the beginning of substantial inflation in the United States, and the rampant inflation and volatility of interest rates during the era of stagflation from 1979 to 1981 prompted life insurance companies, thrift organizations, pension funds, and other traditional long-term postconstruction lenders to become increasingly disenchanted with long-term fixed-rate mortgages or deeds of trust. These developments are well-laid out in Strum, Current Trends in Institutional Financing of Real Estate in the United States, 17 Real Prop., Prob. & Tr. J. 486 (1982). Today there is a multitude of possible financing approaches, and each transaction must be carefully tailored to meet the deal-specific needs of both the lender and the borrower. This makes the task of the real estate lawyer far more interesting — and far more complex.

Most real estate financing techniques fit somewhere within a debt-equity spectrum that ranges from the traditional long-term fixed-rate mortgage to pure equity financing. See Table 5-2.

As suggested in Table 5-2, postconstruction lenders may not be content with fixed rates of return on their mortgage loan investments and may instead (or in addition, as a hedge against inflation) require a contingent rate of interest or even an ownership (equity) interest in the property. During the inflationary period of 1979-1981 some lenders

T a b l e   5-2

The Debt-Equity Spectrum

PURE DEBT FINANCING	$\longrightarrow$	PARTICIPATING MORTGAGES (borrower shares income with lender but retains ownership, tax benefits, and management control)	$\longrightarrow$	POTENTIAL EQUITY	$\longrightarrow$	PURE EQUITY FINANCING (lender shares ownership, tax benefits, and management control)
1) Fixed Rate Mortgage 2) Variable Rate Mortgage		1) Contingent Interest Mortgage 2) Shared Appreciation Mortgage		1) Convertible Mortgages		1) Joint Venture

would only make a mortgage loan in conjunction with acquiring an equity interest in the mortgaged property. Such equity-sharing arrangements usually consist of a "joint venture," whereby the lender purchases an interest in the property and creates a general or limited partnership between itself and the developer, or a convertible mortgage, whereby the lender reserves the right to convert some or all of the mortgage indebtedness into a partnership interest or, alternatively, obtains an option to purchase all or part of the mortgaged property during the term of the loan. Both the joint venture and the convertible mortgage, which together represent the equity financing extreme of the debt-equity spectrum, are discussed in Chapter 7.

At this juncture we will focus on the so-called participating mortgage whereby the lender's investment return is contingent on the income and appreciation in the value of the mortgaged property. While situated on the debt side of the debt-equity spectrum, the participating mortgage represents a kind of "debt joint venture" inasmuch as the lender is allowed to share in the profits from the venture but the borrower nevertheless retains most of the incidents of ownership including the tax benefits, control over management decisions, and most if not all of the appreciation.

The following is a typical interest payment provision from a mortgage note pursuant to a postconstruction loan commitment letter that contemplates a straight fixed-rate mortgage.

Commencing on the date of this Note, Interest shall accrue at the rate of _____ per annum on the unpaid principal balance of this Note and said Interest shall be paid in monthly installments on the first day of _____ .

Commencing on the first day of _____ and continuing on the first day of each calendar month thereafter, to and including the first day of _____ , principal and Interest at the rate of _____ per annum on the unpaid principal balance of this Note shall be paid in equal monthly Installments in the amount of _____ each, and shall be due and payable on the first day of _____ and on the first day of each and every calendar month thereafter to and including the first day of _____ .

The entire unpaid principal balance of this Note, together with all accrued and unpaid interest thereon, shall, if not sooner paid, be due and payable on the first day of _____ . Each monthly Installment, when paid, shall be applied first to Interest at the rate of _____ per annum due monthly on the unpaid principal balance of this Note and the balance of each monthly Installment shall be applied in reduction of the unpaid principal balance of this Note.

Except as otherwise expressly provided herein, Maker shall not be entitled to prepay all or any portion of the principal sum of this Note until the first day of _____ .

If a postconstruction lender is dissatisfied with a straight fixed-rate return, there is a plethora of contingent return approaches designed to make interest rates more responsive to changing market conditions. For example, it would not be unusual for such a lender to require not only a fixed rate of interest but also a so-called kicker whereby the lender would receive, as contingent interest, a percentage of the gross income (receipts) or net income (cash flow) from the property or a percentage of the gain based on appreciation in the value of the mortgaged property when it is sold or refinanced. The following is a sample contingent interest clause (excerpted from a commitment letter) that is geared to the gross income from the property, along with a typical audit provision, which provides the lender with the right to monitor the financial operation of the property to assure itself that the borrower is complying with its obligation to pay the agreed-on amount of contingent interest.

Additional Interest. In addition to payments of the fixed monthly installments as herein above provided, Borrower shall pay Lender annually, as additional interest, within thirty days after the expiration of each fiscal year of Borrower, a sum equal to 25% of the amount, if any, by which the gross income from the Property in such fiscal year shall exceed $ _____ . Additional interest for any partial fiscal year shall be pro rated. The term "gross income" as used herein shall mean the total revenue derived from the Property by Borrower as owner, from rents for the use and occupancy of space in the building, fees from parking facilities, and charges, if any, for heating, air conditioning, and utilities, without any deductions whatsoever except that (1) tax increases after the first full year in which the property shall be assessed as a completed building and (2) insurance premium increases after the first year in which the Property shall be occupied as a completed building shall be deducted from gross income before computing the additional interest.

Audit.   The mortgage documents shall contain a covenant requiring the mortgagor, without expense to us, to deliver to us (a) within 30 days after the expiration of each fiscal year of the mortgagor, a written statement signed by the mortgagor setting forth in reasonable detail the gross income for such fiscal year, (b) within 90 days after the close of such fiscal year, an annual audit of the operation of the Real Property, showing in complete detail total income received and total expenses, together with annual balance sheets and profit and loss statements, prepared and certified by a certified public accountant, and (c) such rent rolls and interim balance sheets and profit and loss statements as may be required by us. The mortgage documents shall contain further covenants by the mortgagor (i) permitting us at any time to examine the books, records and accounts of the mortgagor in so far as they relate to the Real Property, and to make copies thereof, (ii) requiring the mortgagor to exhibit such books, accounts and records to us or to any person designated by us for that purpose, and (iii) if any such audit by us or any person designated by us discloses that the actual gross income for any fiscal year exceeded that reported to us by more than 3%, that the mortgagor shall pay the cost of such audit.

Uri, The Participating Mortgage: Spreading the Risks and Rewards of Ownership
5 Real Est. Fin. 37 (Spring 1988)

The participating mortgage loan has become popular with many real estate lenders and investors as a way to finance both acquisitions and development projects. Typically, such mortgages are originated by pension fund accounts and life insurance companies — institutional investors with the sophistication and experience necessary to structure these complex transactions. . . .

GENERAL CHARACTERISTICS

In its generic form, a participating mortgage is a real estate loan with a normal coupon interest rate, and additional or contingent interest in the form of a percentage of the cash flow, refinancing proceeds, sales proceeds and, if applicable, casualty and condemnation proceeds related to a particular property. The additional or contingent interest is also known as the participation or profits interest.

A participating mortgage is a debt instrument: the loan investor is the lender, and the real estate investor is the owner/borrower. Generally, both the loan amount and the loan-to-value ratio are higher than those achievable with a conventional mortgage loan. The coupon interest rate is usually lower. The higher loan amount and lower coupon rate compensate the owner for relinquishing a percentage of its ownership rewards to the lender, and for the lender's priority of payment. Because the loan is secured debt, not equity, the lender is entitled to its return (i.e., currently due principal, coupon interest and participation interest) prior to the receipt of any proceeds by the borrower. Conversely, the lender's additional contingent interest is its compensation for providing full financing at below-market rates and thereby assuming a higher degree of risk.

The participating mortgage loan appears to be a fairly simple transaction. In practice, however, it is an inherently complex financing tool that should be pursued only by sophisticated real estate players.

The participation interest is usually calculated pursuant to an agreed-upon formula included in the loan documents. There are normally several different transactions, events or time periods that may trigger calculation and payment of the participation. For example, it may be due and paid:

- monthly based upon project cash flow;
- upon repayment of the loan;
- upon refinancing with a new and subordinate loan;
- upon sale of the property;
- upon receipt of condemnation awards or casualty insurance proceeds; and/or
- upon maturity of the loan.

The negotiations that establish the basic structure of a participating mortgage are often arduous.

A CONDUCIVE ENVIRONMENT

Participating mortgages usually gain in popularity during periods of high market interest rates, such as between 1981 and 1985 in the U.S. In such an environment, the flow of investment capital generally and real estate investment capital in particular is severely curtailed. Many lending institutions, including commercial banks, thrifts and life insurance companies, suffer disintermediation and are forced, through actions of the Federal Reserve, to tighten credit policies and thereby restrict the amount of funds available for real estate and other investments. These institutions also shift a higher proportion of their investment portfolios to higher yielding, safer, fixed-income investments such as high-grade government and corporate bonds.

More [important], it is difficult to justify the economics of a real estate project during periods of high interest rates, when the real estate developer or investor normally is faced with negative leverage. This occurs when the cost of debt expressed as a percent is greater than the ratio of the project's net operating income (i.e., gross income less vacancy and operating expenses) to its cost. In addition, interest expense, included as part of the "soft costs" of development, typically comprise 10% to 20% of the total development budget. As interest rates rise, costs can mushroom, making the project uneconomical.

Thus, a developer or investor may have difficulty finding a conventional mortgage loan without a large infusion of equity. Yet, at the same time, high financing rates reduce the return available to equity investors, thereby making equity investment more difficult to attract.

In a high interest rate environment, the lender and borrower may structure a participating loan with the coupon rate lowered to achieve a 1:1 debt coverage ratio, i.e., the project's net operating income is equal to current debt service. (As noted above, negative leverage occurs when the ratio is less than one with 100% financing.) Although the coupon rate on such a loan is lower than the market rate, the lender derives additional yield from its future profits interest. Furthermore, the lower rate permits a development cost budget that is both reasonable and financable.

While in today's market interest rates are not particularly high, other factors have stimulated interest in participating mortgages — particularly the recently enacted tax legislation. The Tax Reform Act of 1986 restricts a taxpayer's ability to use passive tax losses, such as those usually generated by real estate-oriented partnerships and Subchapter S corporations, to offset income from other sources (e.g., wages, salaries or income from "portfolio" investments). These restrictions, along with numerous other provisions targeted at the real estate industry, have reduced dramatically the popularity of real estate tax shelter investments that lack a current cash yield, and have severely curtailed the flow of equity dollars into real estate. . . .

Thus, real estate investors are increasingly attracted to the participating mortgage device. It enables them to obtain high leverage with little or no equity investment — something few lenders are generally willing to permit. By using the participating mortgage structure, however, the lender is able to create a potentially more profitable and safer transaction. In lieu of cash equity, the lender may negotiate recourse provisions and other guarantees, and/or direct any excess cash flow to principal amortization or to a sinking fund. The participating mortgage also permits institutional mortgage investors, many of whom lack the market prowess, management capabilities and entrepreneurial insight to locate and enhance the value of real estate projects on their own, to share in some of the rewards of ownership.

THE LENDER'S PERSPECTIVE

From the lender's perspective, the participating loan provides the opportunity to achieve a higher overall rate of return (generally 20% to 30%) over a five- to ten-year holding period. The participation interest also gives the lender an inflation hedge since the return from the participation interest will increase as rents and net cash flow increase.

The potential for higher returns also entails a higher degree of risk — a result of the higher loan-to-value ratio and the contingent nature of the participation interest. Usually, the lender will fund 100% of acquisition costs, or 80% to 90% of appraisal value for a development project. The higher the level of debt, the greater the risk of nonpayment and monetary loss to the lender. The risks are mitigated by the lender's due diligence on the project, the market and the borrower. The due diligence process requires a thorough review and an in-depth understanding of the project economics, the market, the lease structure and the physical condition of the property, and the experience of the owner/borrower.

The participating loan as discussed here provides the lender with additional security because it is a debt obligation secured by a recorded mortgage or deed of trust. This structure is in contrast to a joint venture investment that is considered as equity, not debt. Normally, however, the borrower will not be required to invest cash equity. While this does not by itself make the transaction precarious, it does reduce the borrower's incentive to maintain and enhance the value of the real estate. . . .

THE BORROWER'S PERSPECTIVE

From the borrower's perspective, a well-structured loan may be the most useful real estate financing tool available. The owner can obtain 100% financing with little or no equity investment, and can achieve an infinite rate of return.

The disadvantage of putting in no equity is that most likely the lender will require the owner to guarantee all or a portion of the loan. This recourse is necessary to give the owner some incentive to maintain and enhance the value of the property. The guarantee also provides a degree of protection to the lender, which advances 100% of the funds but must wait to receive the majority of its return from the property's future profits.

Another disadvantage is that a participating mortgage generally subjects the owner to numerous loan requirements that severely limit the owner's flexibility. For example, the loan documents usually place restrictions on prepayment rights, sale of the project, execution of new leases, and the use of casualty or condemnation proceeds. It may also require the lender's approval for major repairs. . . .

CURRENT CASH FLOW

In addition to the stated interest rate on the mortgage, the participating lender usually receives a portion of the project's net cash flow (see Table 1). The amount of this interest and the frequency of payment (monthly, quarterly, annually) are subject to negotiation, and there is an infinite variety of ways to calculate the amount to be paid. Federal tax regulations restrict the ability of many institutions, particularly pension plans and REITs, to receive income from an interest in a property's *net* cash flow. Under certain circumstances, these institutions may be subject to tax on income received from non-passive sources, e.g., from residual cash flow or profits that accrue to owners. To comply with these regulations, such institutions generally seek to structure their cash flow participation interest as either a percentage of the property's *gross* income (which is considered passive), or as a percentage of gross income in excess of a specified floor amount.[7] . . .

FUTURE PROPERTY PROFITS

In addition to an interest in the property's current cash flow, the lender also receives an interest in the future profits generated by a capital transaction — primarily sale or refinancing of the property or maturity of the loan. In all of these events, the most critical factor for both lender and borrower is the determination of the value of the participation interest.

Upon refinancing (or the addition of a new loan subordinate to the existing participating mortgage), the lender will receive the negotiated percentage of the proceeds of the new financing. In a typical refinancing, this will be calculated as the gross amount of the new loan, less reasonable and necessary closing costs and the balance of the participating mortgage. The loan base for future calculations of any remaining participation interest becomes the new loan amount. Most participating loans restrict the borrower's prepayment rights to prevent

7. See discussion at Chapter 13A, note 2. — Ed.

T a b l e   1

**Typical Calculation of Lender's Participation Interest
in Property Cash Flow**

Net operating income before debt service	$5,000,000.00
Debt service (based on coupon rate)	4,000,000.00
Net distributable cash flow	$1,000,000.00
Lender's participation interest (50%)	× .50
Additional interest payable to lender	$ 500,000.00

refinancing without payment of the participating interest. In the event of any addition of new debt, the lender usually will retain a profit interest subordinate to that of the new mortgagee. The subordinate interest will then be held and paid upon maturity of the original participating mortgage.

Upon a sale of the property, the lender is paid the remaining principal balance of the mortgage loan, plus its future profits interest. In negotiating the original loan documents, the lender must take care to protect its position by establishing strict guidelines to police any sales transaction. For example, the loan documents should:

- give the lender the right to approve the sale;
- preclude any sale to a buyer affiliated with the borrower;
- require that the sales price be determined pursuant to arm's-length negotiations as evidenced by a purchase contract; and
- require that the entire arrangement be a bona fide sales transaction.

These provisions will protect the lender from a bogus or dummy sale engineered by the borrower to escape payment of the participation interest.

Once the property has been sold, the lender will receive as its participation interest the negotiated percentage of the net value of the property, i.e., the contract sales price, less reasonable closing costs and the principal balance of the participating mortgage (see Table 2). In some participating loans, the borrower will get credit for any contributions to equity prior to the lender's receipt of its participation interest. . . .

Overbuilt Markets

Currently, many opportunities exist to acquire high-quality real estate in softer, overbuilt markets across the country with financing

T a b l e 2

**Typical Calculation of Lender's Participation Interest
upon Property Sale**

Gross sales price	$20,000,000.00
Closing costs	250,000.00
Participating mortgage principal balance	$16,000,000.00
Net distributable sales proceeds	$ 3,750,000.00
Lender's participation interest (50%)	× .50
Sales proceeds payable to lender	$ 1,875,000.00

provided by participating mortgages. Cities such as Dallas, Houston and Denver continue to be major centers of industry and commerce, yet now suffer from overbuilding and depressed economies. Nonetheless, these areas all have inherently good demographics and future growth potential.

Rental rates and occupancy levels in these areas have declined to near disaster levels. The combination of high vacancies and low rents, however, provides opportunities to acquire properties at deeply discounted values. Significant future gains may be realized when these markets turn around.

In many overbuilt areas, there is a considerable spread between contract rents and effective rents. A tenant who takes out a five-year lease at a contract rent of $25 per square foot, and receives two years free rent as an incentive to sign, pays an effective rent of $15 per square foot over the five-year term. As the surplus of property is absorbed and overall market conditions tighten, real estate investors should profit handsomely from the conversion of effective rents to contract rents.

For example, in certain areas of Dallas, effective rents currently range from $12 to $15 per square foot for Class A suburban office space, while contract rents range from $20 to $25 per square foot. Many such properties can be purchased at cap rates of 7.5% to 9%. At this level, a participating lender can obtain a reasonable coupon rate, as well as a significant participating interest in current income and future property appreciation — both of which should increase substantially as rent levels rise. Thus, opportunities exist for both the real estate owner and the participating lender to receive generous total returns.

NOTES AND QUESTIONS

1. *The Participating Mortgage: Risks and Rewards.* As a rule of thumb, participating arrangements between borrowers and lenders be-

T a b l e 5-3

Commitments of $100,000 and Over on Multifamily and Nonresidential Mortgages

Loans with Special Features, Year, 1988

Neanderthal

Loans with Provision For Additional Return	No. of Loans	Amount Committed ($000)	Loan Amount ($000)	Interest Rate (By #)	Interest Rate (By $)	Loan/Value	Capitalization Rate	Debt Coverage	Percent Constant	Maturity (Years/Months)	% of Total Loans By #	% of Total Loans By $
							Averages					
Income participation only	61	1,937,173	31,757	9.40%	9.35%	81.3%	9.3%	1.19	9.8%	26/8	3.4%	8.8%
Income and equity participation without equity purchase	12	328,712	27,393	9.07	8.37	78.0	8.7	1.26	9.1	14/2	0.7	1.5
Joint venture loans	7	422,890	60,413	9.86	9.87	78.1	9.5	1.25	10.0	13/9	0.4	1.9
No equity purchase	1	34,000	34,000	*	*	*	*	*	*	*	0.1	0.2
10% or less equity purchase	1	289,000	289,000	*	*	*	–	–	*	*	0.1	1.3
Over 10-25% equity purchase	1	4,100	4,100	*	*	*	*	*	*	*	0.1	**
Over 25-50% equity purchase	1	25,540	25,540	*	*	*	*	*	*	*	0.1	0.1
Over 50% equity purchase	1	43,000	43,000	*	*	*	–	–	–	*	0.1	0.2
Existing joint venture	2	27,250	13,625	*	*	*	*	*	*	*	0.1	0.1
Purchase/leaseback loans	18	205,072	11,393	9.35	9.10	77.4	8.2	1.12	9.6	14/8	1.0	0.9
Purchase/leaseback only	1	7,500	7,500	*	*	*	*	*	*	*	0.1	**
Purchase/leaseback with income participation	6	42,965	7,161	9.48	9.48	76.5	7.9	1.09	9.5	15/0	0.3	0.2
Purchase/leaseback with income and equity participation	11	154,607	14,055	9.19	8.93	78.4	8.3	1.13	9.5	14/11	0.6	0.7
TOTAL	98	2,893,847	29,529	9.38	9.30	79.9	9.0	1.19	9.6	22/0	5.4	13.1

Property Type with Additional Return Provisions											
Apartment — Conventional	27	321,467	9.35	9.33	78.1	8.5	1.09	9.6	16/10	9.3	11.5
Commercial Retail	11	324,600	9.26	8.69	80.5	8.7	1.16	9.7	16/10	3.0	7.1
Office Building	43	1,784,260	9.37	9.42	81.8	9.3	1.21	9.7	26/4	6.5	17.1
Industrial	4	34,825	9.50	9.50	74.6	9.2	1.30	9.5	15/0	1.6	2.0
Hotel and Motel	7	243,100	9.83	9.73	76.7	9.7	*	*	29/0	13.0	30.2
Multiple Property Complex	6	185,595	9.20	8.55	80.3	8.5	1.23	9.6	20/0	18.2	20.1
TOTAL	98	2,893,847	9.38	9.30	79.9	9.0	1.19	9.6	22/0	5.4	13.1
Accrual Loans Only	2	20,800	*	*	*	*	*	*	*		
Adjustable rate	106	968,035	9.63	9.54	73.5	8.9	1.22	10.2	9/7		
Variable	1	9,800	*	*	*	*	*	*	*		
Rate Review	105	958,235	9.63	9.54	73.6	8.9	1.22	10.2	9/8		

Total line includes 75 loans with non-refundable fees amounting to $7,701 thousands.
Accrual loans include 1 loan with non-refundable fees amounting to $100 thousands.
Adjustable rate includes 66 loans with non-refundable fees amounting to $6,358 thousands.

* Data not shown for a limited number of loans.
** Less than 0.05%.

Source: American Council of Life Insurance, Invest. Bull. No. 1065, Table 3 (April 10, 1989)

come more popular during periods of high interest rates, when the supply of mortgage money declines. This is what happened during the credit crunch of 1980-1982. See Table 5-1, supra. During such tight-money periods, high fixed-rate mortgages may require debt-service payments that exceed the free and clear rate of return from the property (discussed at Chapter 2A, note 3), and developers, when confronted with the specter of negative leverage, or worse, a negative cash flow, may be willing to sacrifice a share of the future increases in cash flow (or a share of refinancing or sale proceeds) by means of a participating mortgage, for the sake of obtaining an initial below-market fixed rate of interest and a correspondingly sufficient amount of cash flow at the beginning of the project. Otherwise, the project may have to be abandoned as unfeasible if there is not enough cash flow to attract outside equity investors and pay the operating expenses of the venture. Don't forget that when interest rates increase, so do capitalization rates (see Table 5-1, supra), which means lower valuations and loan amounts. Borrowers accordingly become more dependent on outside equity capital as a funding source unless the rental income from (and value of) the project increases because of some inflation hedge such as a percentage rental.

Moreover, just like a commercial tenant that agrees to pay a fixed rent plus a percentage rental (in lieu of a higher fixed rent), a developer-borrower may not mind sharing his profits and gains with the lender if gross receipts were to escalate because of inflation or if his profits should increase because the project is doing well, since the developer (like the percentage-rental tenant) knows that the converse is also true, namely, that the total (fixed plus contingent) interest (and rental) will decline if gross receipts or profits shrink because of a recession or lack of business success. In other words, such profitsharing arrangements may constitute a hedge against inflation for the lender (and landlord), but they also act as a hedge against recession for the developer (and tenant).

On the other hand, when interest rates are declining or are already relatively low (in comparison to the free and clear rate of return from the mortgaged property), developers generally prefer to pay the fixed market rate of interest rather than enter into a participation arrangement that will dilute their profits and gains from the property. To some extent this may explain why loans associated with joint ventures between developers and life insurance companies experienced a dramatic decline (from 6.2 percent of all loans made in 1983 to 1.9 percent in 1988) from 1983 to 1988 as the weighted average fixed rates of interest charged by U.S. life insurance companies on multifamily and commercial loans decreased from 12.46 percent (in 1983) to 9.70 percent (in 1988). See Table 5-1, supra, and compare American Council on Life Ins., Bull. No. 874, Table 3 (May 8, 1984) with Bull. No. 1065, Table 3 (April 10, 1989).

Paradoxically, during the same period (1983-1988) of declining interest rates and expansion in the supply of loanable funds, the percentage of participating loans (with income and/or appreciation kickers) made by life insurance companies remained about the same (11.6 percent of all loans made in 1983, compared to 10.3 percent for 1988). See Table 5-3, supra. To some extent this continued popularity can be explained by the fact that lenders have become increasingly familiar with the participating mortgage. Another part of the explanation may be the Tax Reform Act of 1986, which, among other things, decimated tax shelter benefits for income-producing real estate and eliminated the distinction in tax treatment between ordinary income and long-term capital gain. Can you think of any reason why the 1986 Act may have contributed to the "rise" of participating mortgages and "fall" of joint venturing between borrowers and lenders?

As suggested in the excerpt by Uri, any prudent postconstruction lender that makes a participating loan will attempt to prohibit the sale of the property during the original and agreed-on term of the loan. By way of analogy, a landlord who receives a percentage rental would likewise fetter the right of the tenant to assign or sublet without the landlord's consent. Do you think these restrictions are necessary to protect the interest of a lender or landlord who is receiving a contingent return based on the income from the property? Why? From the borrower's perspective, can you think of any compromise language (less stringent than a flat prohibition against the sale of the property) that would address the legitimate concerns of the lender and not render the property unmarketable during the term of the loan?

2. *Contingent Interest Based on Gross Income.* Real estate borrowers such as Dan Developer are apt to raise strenuous objections to any contingent interest clause that is geared to gross (as opposed to net) income, while postconstruction lenders such as Ace may insist on the former type of kicker in a participating mortgage. Why? In the master hypothetical, Dan might insist that the occupancy leases provide for escalations of rentals based on any increase in local property taxes, insurance premiums, operational expenses, or some cost of living index such as the Consumer Price Index. However, each such rent escalation payment will itself increase Dan's gross income and could increase the amount of the contingent interest payment payable to Ace. Observe that the gross income clause excerpted on page 402 (captioned Additional Interest) provides that rent escalations for tax and insurance premium increases will be excluded from the definition of gross income. Would Dan be justified in insisting that the definition of gross income for contingent interest purposes also exclude any other of these increases (resulting from an escalation clause) in his gross income? See Richman, Negotiating Operating Expense Provisions in Office Leases, 18 Real Est. Rev. 44 (Fall 1988).

The gross income clause excerpted above provides for contingent interest equal to 25 percent of the gross income in excess of a yet-to-be negotiated floor amount. If Ace were to propose such an onerous provision, Dan would undoubtedly make every effort to negotiate as high a floor amount as possible. At a minimum, he would insist that the floor amount be sufficient to cover his estimated operating expenses and debt service payments and that it provide a cushion for unanticipated contingencies. In addition to a floor amount, what additional limitation on contingent interest might Dan try to obtain in his negotiations with Ace?

3. *Contingent Interest Based on Net Income.* From the borrower's perspective, a contingent interest clause based on *net* income is both fairer and safer than one based on gross income, because the borrower will have to share with the lender only that portion of his income that exceeds his debt service payments and other operating expenses. From a lender's point of view, however, the net income approach has serious drawbacks that, taken together, make it the less desirable alternative. Drafting the definition of net income is itself a major undertaking. Merely providing that contingent interest equals a percentage of net income is an open invitation to litigation since the parties most probably will disagree on what items should be deducted from gross income to arrive at net income. See, e.g., Mileage Realty Co. v. Miami Parking Garage, Inc., 146 So. 2d 403 (Fla. 1962), cert. denied, 153 So. 2d 307 (1963) (involving, by way of analogy, a contingent rental based on profits in a percentage lease). A prudent lender will most probably demand a comprehensive definitional clause that starts with a broad definition of gross income and then specifies with particularity the various deductions that must be subtracted to arrive at the net income amount.

Even with an adequate definition, the lender will be concerned about how to enforce the clause and will undoubtedly insist on annual audited financial statements from an independent certified public accountant approved by it. See the sample audit provision (from a commitment letter) on p. 403. Any participating lender should be cautioned against undue reliance on such a statement as a method of ensuring compliance, because the financial statements will not reveal, for example, whether Dan is paying a market rate for cleaning services or is paying a premium to the cleaning company in exchange for obtaining such services at a discount in other buildings he owns that are not covered by the participating mortgage. In addition, the borrower's financial statements may not reveal whether the borrower is paying for services that are not being performed; packing the office staff with relatives in no-show jobs; including a personal automobile on the building's insurance policy; or charging a private jet as a building expense. What can a prudent lender do to protect against potential abuses by the borrower?

In addition, a participating mortgage based on profits rather than on gross income would render the debt financing arrangement more vulnerable to a recharacterization as equity by the Internal Revenue Service (discussed in the excerpt from Madison and Dwyer at Chapter 7A) as well as to litigation against the lender by third-party creditors and tort plaintiffs on the theory that the profitsharing arrangement is in substance a partnership between the lender and the borrower, especially if the lender were to participate in the control of the venture in order to protect its profit share. See generally Madison and Dwyer ¶3.04[3][a]; Kelley, Advantages of Participating Mortgages, 17 Real Est. Rev. 54 (Spring 1987).

4. *The Usury Constraint on the Rate of Interest.*   In biblical times, before the "time value of money" concept was understood, the word "usury" simply meant the taking of interest — any interest — for the use of borrowed funds. With few exceptions, usury in this broad sense was forbidden. Psalm 15, often called the "gentleman's psalm," seems to convey the spirit of this biblical proscription: "Lord, who shall abide in thy tabernacle? Who shall dwell on thy holy hill? . . . He that putteth not out his money to usury. . . ." It was not until the late middle ages that a distinction arose between the taking of interest, which was lawful, and the exaction of unlawful interest, which was usury.

The early revulsion concerning the receipt of interest was probably due to the fact that most borrowers were hard-pressed or poverty-stricken individuals funding their personal, family, or household needs. Accordingly, the underlying rationale for the prohibition on the taking of interest was undoubtedly protection of the necessitous borrower. Much of our modern usury legislation is still based on this rationale.

As businesses began to borrow for the purpose of making money, however, it became apparent that using or borrowing someone's money to be able to manufacture, say, widgets for sale was not much different than using or leasing someone's factory for making the widgets, or using or leasing someone's horses or trucks for transporting the widgets. It began to be understood that there was no moral or ethical reason why there should not be a charge for the use of money in this context.

While the price for factory space or transportation equipment was generally determined by the law of supply and demand, the price of money, with the early biblical injunctions in mind, was regulated by statutes known as usury laws. Many of these statutes imposed artificial limits on the price of money, a requirement that has often produced counterproductive results such as the debacle in the housing and thrift banking industry in the early 1980s. From the standpoint of real estate entrepreneurs, artificial limits on interest have contributed to the tightening of available credit, forcing them either to adopt cumbersome financing structures to avoid the application of the usury laws or to abandon otherwise sound development projects.

As explained in greater detail by Mendes Hershman in his noted article Usury and the Tight Mortgage Market, 22 Bus. Law. 333, 336-338 (1967), the common definitional elements of usury, all of which must be present for a finding against the lender, consist of the following: (1) an agreement to lend money or its equivalent or to forbear to require repayment for a period of time; (2) the borrower's obligation to repay absolutely and not contingently; (3) the exaction of a greater compensation for making the loan or agreeing to forbear than is allowed by the applicable state constitution or usury statute; and (4) an intention to violate the usury statute. As suggested by the first definitional element, the usury laws generally apply only to transactions that are structured as loans. Therefore, as observed elsewhere, one advantage of this "form over substance" approach for borrowers and lenders is that non-debt financing techniques such as the installment land contract, sale and leaseback, and tax-free exchange are generally beyond the scope of the usury laws. The second element means that there must be an absolute obligation on the part of the borrower to repay the debt and the interest payable on the debt. Can you think of the rationale for this requirement? As pointed out by Hershman, the last definitional requirement should not be construed too literally inasmuch as the lender need not actually intend to commit usury. Under case law the intent to collect the money is usually enough. 22 Bus. Law. 336.

In an attempt to address these problems, states traditionally exempted loans to corporate borrowers from usury law restrictions. In recent years, we have seen a further retrenchment of usury limitations, with states enacting exemptions for business loans and loans over a specified dollar amount. The Uniform Land Security Interest Act would remove usury restrictions entirely for commercial loans and, if the state so elects, for certain consumer loans (to "protected parties") as well. Unif. Land Sec. Int. Act §403, 74 Uniform Laws Ann. (Supp. 1989). In addition, by federal exemption, many state usury statutes no longer apply to first mortgage loans on residential real estate, which is important from our standpoint because residential real estate loans for the purposes of the statute include apartment building loans. Depository Institutions Deregulation & Monetary Control Act of 1980, 12 U.S.C. §1735f-7 (1989). For a discussion of statutory exemptions and circumvention devices (such as incorporation of the borrower and invoking choice of law principles), see generally Madison and Dwyer at ¶¶5.04, 5.05. Each year (starting with 1981, in an article by William Burke entitled Recent Developments — The New Federal Usury Laws, vol. 36, p. 1237) the journal Business Lawyer has kept lawyers advised on this trend toward liberalization by faithfully including an excellent annual survey of developments pertaining to both federal and state usury laws. The result of this deregulation has been to make usury a less serious problem in commercial lending. However, the penalties for committing usury can be onerous. For example, in Texas the borrower has the right to recover three times the amount of all interest "contracted for" in violation of the usury statutes, even if the interest has not been paid. Texas Rev. Civ. Stat. Ann. art. 5069-1.06(1) (Vernon Supp. 1989). Consequently, it is essential for lenders' attorneys to recognize what circumstances may render a loan usurious. Likewise, in order to enable their clients to obtain mortgage financing, attorneys for borrowers must understand the usury law so that they can participate in the process of structuring financing that will meet the requirements of the usury laws.

    5. *Alternative Mortgage Instruments and Inflation-Related Commercial Mortgage Devices.* As a hedge against inflation and to make loans more affordable for borrowers, depository institutions that make home mortgage loans, such as thrift organizations, commercial banks, and credit unions, have originated and popularized a variety of innovative residential mortgage devices (resembling the participating mortgage) called "alternative mortgage instruments," which can be subsumed under the "contingent return" portion of the debt-equity spectrum. See Table 5-2, supra. These new residential mortgage devices make reference to formulas that require periodic adjustments of the interest rate and principal balance and may also require some participation by the lender in the appreciation of the mortgaged real estate. While the adjustable interest rate format is commonly employed in construction financing, as of this writing alternative mortgage instruments are rarely used in postconstruction financing of commercial real estate, with the possible exception of the so-called variable rate mortgage (VRM). VRMs include different varieties of variable interest rates that are geared to some objective reference point, either domestic (e.g., U.S. Treasury bill rates) or foreign (e.g., Eurobond and the London Interbank Offered Rate rates), or simply renegotiated at regular intervals. See Table 5-3, supra. Can you think of any reason why the variable interest rate format has become popular for the postconstruction financing of residential real estate but not for the postconstruction financing of commercial real estate?

    For additional discussion of alternative mortgage instruments see Browne, The Development and Practical Application of the Adjustable Rate Mortgage Loan: The Federal Home Loan Mortgage Corporation's Adjustable Rate Mortgage Loan Purchase Program and Mortgage Loan Instruments, 47 Mo. L. Rev. 179 (1982); Hyer and Kearl, Legal Impediments to Mortgage Innovation, 6 Real Est. L.J. 211 (1978); Comment, The New Mortgages: A Functional Legal Analysis, 10 Fla.

St. U.L. Rev. 95 (1982); Note, Alternative Mortgage Instruments: Authorizing and Implementing Price Level Adjusted Mortgages, 16 U. Mich. J.L. Ref. 115 (1982).

In addition to the variable rate and renegotiable rate mortgages, which are somewhat more popular on the residential side of real estate financing, other inflation-related commercial mortgage devices that are presently being marketed by institutional lenders as alternatives to the long-term fixed mortgage include:

a. *Bullet Loans.* These are relatively short-term loans (with 3- to 10-year terms) with provisions for periodic interest rate adjustments (e.g., every 5 years) and with interest-only payments or with partial amortization based on long-term (e.g., 25- to 35-year) amortization schedules. Sometimes bullet loans are structured as long-term loans (e.g., 25-year term) with a so-called call provision permitting the lender to call in the loan after a stipulated period of time (e.g., 10 years), at which time the borrower must satisfy the outstanding loan balance by refinancing or by selling the property. Originally, these loans were designed for developers without takeout commitments whose construction loans had expired and who could not immediately obtain adequate postconstruction financing. At present, these loans are being made primarily by life insurance companies to developers who are purchasing or refinancing existing properties with strong rental schedules. See generally Ling and Peiser, Choosing Among Alternative Financing Structures, 17 Real Est. Rev. 39, 40 (Summer 1987). Sometimes they are also used by insurance companies in a process called "matched funding" whereby monies received from pension funds (in respect to which a fixed rate of return is guaranteed under a so-called guaranteed investment contract) are loaned out as bullet loans at slightly higher rates (without any prepayment privilege) to assure the lenders of a profit spread during the matching terms of the investment contracts.

b. *Mini-perms and Bowtie Loans.* The mini-permanent loan, or mini-perm, is a combined construction-permanent loan that is relatively short-term (e.g., 7 to 10 years) and converts from an interest-only construction loan to a (prenegotiated) fixed rate permanent loan once construction is completed. The principal advantage to the developer-borrower is that it has a number of years after construction is completed to negotiate a satisfactory postconstruction loan without paying a prepayment fee; moreover, based on the accumulating equity in the project the borrower can refinance for a larger loan amount when interest rates decline and be in a position to pay off the mini-perm loan amount and cash out some tax-free equity.

The "bowtie loan" is attractive to developers because, while it features a floating rate (like the variable rate mortgage), it contains a cap on interest payments, so that any interest above a stipulated ceiling amount is deferred as a balloon payment that is not payable until the loan matures. Conversely, if rates should decline, the lower interest expenses may help offset declining revenues during a recession. These loans are made primarily by commercial banks, thrift organizations, and finance companies. They are usually short-term (e.g., loan terms of 5 to 10 years), permit prepayment without a penalty, and are secured by second as well as first mortgage liens. They derive their name from the fact that their rates move up and down in irregular patterns.

   c.   *Rollover Mortgages.*   Ordinarily, the rollover mortgage has a long-term amortization schedule (e.g., 25 to 35 years), and because the term of the loan is so short (e.g., 3 to 5 years) it is customary for the lender to extend, or "roll over," the loan for another short-term period at the prevailing market rate of interest for short-term loans if the borrower has not refinanced elsewhere. For a discussion of these mort-gage devices see generally Madison and Dwyer ¶3.04[3][d] (Cum. Supp. No. 2) (1989).

   As observed in the foregoing excerpts, alternative mortgage in-struments such as the variable rate mortgage have become increasingly popular with residential borrowers as the affordability index for home-owners has decreased (because the average price of new and existing homes in the United States has been rising at a faster rate than household income). By contrast, most developers and syndicators are reluctant to commit themselves to mortgages (like the variable rate mortgage) with floating rates during the postconstruction period after the mortgaged property becomes operational. How do you account for this difference in attitude?

   6.   *Deducting Mortgage Interest.*   In general, interest is deductible by a cash-basis taxpayer in the year in which it is paid and by an accrual-basis taxpayer in the year in which it accrues. I.R.C. §§163, 446. Accordingly, like any other accrual-basis taxpayer, a real estate borrower may be able to deduct interest prior to the time of actual payment if the borrower's liability for such payment is absolute and the amount of such payment can be determined with reasonable accuracy (the "all-events" test). Treas. Reg. §1.446-1(c)(1)(ii). See, e.g., Rev. Rul. 77-135, 1977-1 C.B. 133, involving a graduated payment mortgage where unpaid interest was added to the principal balance of the loan during the beginning of the loan term and the Internal Revenue Service ruled that an accrual basis mortgagor could deduct the unpaid but accrued interest.

   Also, the interest deduction can be accelerated by refinancing an existing mortgage with a new constant payment mortgage, since the portion of the new debt service payment allocable to interest will ordinarily increase and the remainder of the constant payment attrib-utable to nondeductible amortization will decrease. Thus, for any given debt service amount the after-tax cash flow return to investors will increase but the equity buildup produced by amortization will decline. However, most investors are willing to accept this trade-off, since they regard their rate of after-tax return as their principal investment objective and in most cases will rely primarily on an increase in market value (based on inflation or higher earnings) to augment their equity in the real estate. The Internal Revenue Service, however, has announced that it will not accept the "Rule of 78s" method of interest accounting, which is a mechanical formula commonly associated with short-term consumer loans that has the effect of front-ending the portion of constant debt service payments allocable to interest rather than reflecting the effective rate of interest uniformly over the term of the loan. Rev. Rul. 83-84, 1983-1 C.B. 97; Rev. Proc. 83-40, 1983-1 C.B. 774. The position of the Service against artificial acceleration of the interest deduction has to some extent been codified in I.R.C. §461(h), as added by the TRA of 1984 §91. It provides that, with respect to expenses incurred by an accrual-basis taxpayer, the aforementioned all-events test will not be satisfied until "economic performance" has occurred. Generally, economic performance will be deemed to occur when property is provided or services are rendered to the taxpayer. However, exceptions are made for certain recurring items (that either are immaterial or better match the expense to related income) and for items in respect to which special timing rules are provided.

Also, in the case of a private loan transaction between a seller-creditor and a purchaser-borrower (discussed infra at note 6f), if the sale price were reduced in exchange for a higher rate of interest on the purchase-money indebtedness, the purchaser would be able to increase her current interest deductions rather than increase her cost basis in the property (which would merely be depreciated over the cost recovery period of the property, which could be as long as 31½ years for commercial real estate). For a discussion of planning suggestions relating to the interest deduction see generally G. Robinson, Federal Income Taxation of Real Estate ¶¶7.03, 15.03 (Cum. Supp. No. 3) (1987); R. Haft and P. Fass, 1988 Investment Limited Partnerships Handbook §§1.03, 3.07 (1988); M. Levine, Real Estate Transactions, Tax Planning and Consequences §§874 (1988); Madden, 480-2nd T.M., Taxation of Real Estate Transactions — An Overview §II.B.1 (Bureau of National Affairs) (1988); J. Morris, Real Estate Tax Planning §2.2.C (1977); Auster, The Interest Deduction for Individuals After Tax Reform, 20 Prac. Acct. 58 (June 1987); Dobensky, How to Make the Most of the Remaining Deductions for Interest Under the New Law, 15 Tax. for Law. 224 (Jan./Feb. 1987); Donovan, Interest Expenses for Real Estate, 2 Real Est. Acctg. and Taxn. 82 (Winter 1988).

Use of the basic interest deduction, however, is constrained by certain general rules and statutory limitations, which include the following:

a. Definition of Interest. A current deduction for interest paid or accrued is only allowed for any fee or charge imposed by a lender that represents compensation for the use or forbearance of money. See Deputy v. Dupont, 308 U.S. 488 (1940); Old Colony R.R. Co. v. Commissioner, 284 U.S. 552 (1932). By contrast, any loan expenses such as commitment fees, brokerage commissions, or title and appraisal fees that either represent a cost in obtaining the loan or compensation for services, are regarded as capital in nature and, if business- or investment-related, ordinarily must be capitalized and amortized on a straight-line basis over the life of the loan to which they relate.

b. Prepaid Interest. Under prior law, real estate borrowers using the cash-basis method of accounting would frequently make prepayments of interest to accelerate their interest deductions during the early years of a venture. By borrowing more than was needed and immediately repaying the excess as "prepaid interest," such borrowers were frequently able to obtain a deduction for prepaid interest without subjecting themselves to undesirable cash flow consequences. To prevent any cash-basis taxpayer from understating its taxable income, I.R.C. §461(g) now requires the taxpayer to amortize all prepayments of interest over the loan period to which the interest relates, except that "points" (based on a percentage of the loan amount) paid to obtain a home mortgage can be deducted currently. In addition, tax shelters using the cash-basis method of accounting generally may not deduct prepaid expenses (including interest) before the amount is paid and "economic performance" is rendered. I.R.C. §461(i), as added by the Tax Reform Act of 1984, §91(a). Once such prepaid interest is apportioned over the proper periods, the interest is then subject to other applicable limitations (e.g., the limitation on investment interest).

c. Construction-period Interest. As observed at Chapter 2B, note 5c, since construction-period interest relates to the production of rental income during the entire useful life of a building, it may not be deducted in its entirety when paid or accrued to offset the taxpayer's outside ordinary income during the construction period. Under prior law (I.R.C. §189), construction-period interest could be capitalized and amortized over a 10-year period. However, under the uniform capitalization rules imposed by the Tax Reform Act of 1986, construction-period interest must be capitalized and added to the cost basis of the constructed property; these expenditures are now recovered as depreciation deductions over the cost recovery period of the property. I.R.C. §263A, repealing I.R.C. §189, as added by the Tax Reform Act of 1986, §803.

d. Investment Interest. Prior to the Tax Reform Act of 1986, a taxpayer other than a corporation was able to reduce its ordinary income by deducting interest on loans used to purchase investment property provided that such interest deductions did not exceed certain statutory limits. See prior I.R.C. §163(d). Under the 1986 Act the deduction of investment interest by a noncorporate borrower is now limited to the amount of the borrower's net investment income. "Investment interest" is defined as "interest paid or accrued on indebtedness incurred or continued to purchase or to carry property held for investment"; hence, it does not include interest on a loan for the construction of property to be used in a trade or business if the taxpayer actively participates in the rental real estate activity. H.R. Rep. No. 841, 99th Cong., 2d Sess., at II-153 (1986) (hereinafter HR Report). I.R.C. §163(d)(3)(A), as added by the Tax Reform Act of 1986, §511(a). Curiously, neither the Code nor Regulations explicitly defines the distinction between an "investment" and "trade or business" activity; however, it would appear that most improved rental real estate such as an apartment building or shopping center would be "trade or business" property if active services are being rendered to the occupants and the property is not subject to a net lease. Cf. I.R.C. §§1231(b)(1)(A), 1231(b)(1)(B) (distinction between business and dealer property); I.R.C. §1221(2); Rothenberg v. Commissioner, 48 T.C. 369 (1967); Treas. Reg. §1.1372-4(b)(5)(vi). Compare I.R.C. §162(a) with I.R.C. §§212(1), 212(2). The 1986 Act expanded the definition of investment interest to include all interest incurred in an investment activity other than personal interest, qualified residence interest, and interest taken into account under the new limitations on the deduction of passive losses (imposed by I.R.C. §469). Thus, the investment interest rates now function in tandem with the passive loss rules, so that any investment interest expense that does not fit within the ambit of the definition under I.R.C. §163(d)(3)(A) would be subject to the limitations imposed by the latter. I.R.C. §163(d)(3)(B)(ii). For example, real estate held as a passive investment, such as net-leased property that was formerly considered investment property, is now excluded from the limitation on investment interest because such property is now considered a passive activity subject to the limitation on passive losses. In the jargon of real estate professionals a "net lease" is a commercial lease, commonly associated with shopping centers and retail stores, under which the tenant, rather than the landlord, is responsible for such ownership-related expenses as repairs, insurance premiums, and local property taxes. Also included as investment interest is interest paid or accrued to purchase or carry property held for the production of portfolio-type income (as defined in I.R.C. §469(e)(1)(A)) such as interest, dividends, royalties, capital gain, and rents, that does not qualify as active "trade or business" income or as passive activity income.

   The 1986 Act also changed the definition of investment income to include income from a trade or business activity in which the taxpayer does not materially participate (if the activity is not treated as a passive one under the passive loss rules). Also included is portfolio income from investment property such as royalties, interest and dividends, and net gains from the sale of such property. I.R.C. §163(d)(4)(B).

In computing net investment income (the ceiling for deducting investment interest) investment expenses (other than interest) are deducted from investment income if they are directly connected with the production of investment income. Consequently, if a taxpayer were to own both business and investment properties, it would make sense for the taxpayer to allocate as many general expense items (e.g., overhead) as possible to the former activity in order to maximize the amount of the investment income. The 1986 Act also provides that the deductibility of investment interest is subject to the rule that limits deductions for miscellaneous expenses to those in excess of two percent of the taxpayer's adjusted gross income. See HR Report at II-153.

While partnerships and Subchapter S corporations are not themselves subject to the interest limitation, their partners and shareholders must report their respective shares of net investment income on their individual returns. Moreover, interest on loans obtained by a limited partner to acquire or carry a partnership interest may also be subject to the limitation. Investment interest that is disallowed may be carried forward to succeeding taxable years as interest paid or accrued in that year. I.R.C. §163(d)(2). See generally Smith, The Investment Interest Limitation Under the Tax Reform Act of 1986, 16 Colo. Law. 36 (Jan. 1987).

   e.   Residential Interest.   Under the 1986 Act (as modified by the Revenue Act of 1987), any deduction for so-called personal interest by a noncorporate borrower will be disallowed unless it constitutes "qualified residence interest" that is paid or accrued by the taxpayer on her home acquisition or home equity indebtedness. "Personal interest" is broadly defined as all interest except: (1) interest incurred in connection with the borrower's trade or business; (2) investment interest; (3) interest that is taken into account in determining the taxpayer's income or loss from a passive activity; and (4) qualified residence interest. I.R.C. §163(h)(2). For example, personal interest would include consumer interest on a loan to purchase an automobile or a life insurance policy and credit card interest when such interest is not paid or accrued in connection with the taxpayer's trade or business.

"Qualified residence interest" is generally interest paid on indebtedness secured by the taxpayer's principal or secondary residence and is deductible to the extent that: (1) total home "acquisition indebtedness" (incurred in acquiring, constructing, or substantially improving such qualified residence) does not exceed $1 million (or $500,000 for a married taxpayer filing separately); and (2) the taxpayer's "home equity indebtedness" (qualified residence indebtedness other than acquisition indebtedness, as for example a home equity line of credit secured by a second mortgage) exceeds neither the difference between the total outstanding acquisition indebtedness and the fair market value of the residence nor the sum of $100,000 (or $50,000 for a married taxpayer filing separately). I.R.C. §§163(h)(3)(B), 163(h)(3)(C), as added by the Revenue Act of 1987, §10102. Thus, the total amount of acquisition and home equity indebtedness on a primary and secondary residence may not exceed $1,100,000 ($550,000 for a married taxpayer filing separately). However, any refinanced indebtedness is deemed to be acquisition indebtedness only to the extent that the refinanced amount does not exceed the outstanding balance of such acquisition indebtedness prior to the refinancing. I.R.C. §163(h)(3)(B)(i). Consequently, the only way to increase the ceiling for deducting interest on refinanced debt would be to increase the amount of indebtedness to fund substantial improvements to the qualified residence prior to the refinancing. The absence of restrictions on the use of loan proceeds secured by a home equity line of credit has rendered home equity financing a valuable source of funding for small real estate borrowers who might otherwise be discouraged from incurring indebtedness to purchase investment property because of the limitations imposed on the deductibility of investment interest, as discussed below. See generally Goodman, Tax Ideas: Deducting Mortgage Interest Becomes More Complicated, 16 Real Est. L.J. 344 (Spring 1988).

f. Original-Issue Discount Rules and Other Limitations on the Interest Deduction.   In the case of seller-financed deferred payment sales special rules have evolved to regulate interest deductions and interest income, since these two-party loan transactions between the seller-lender and purchaser-borrower are more vulnerable to manipulation of interest deductions and other tax-avoidance abuses than are transactions involving third-party lenders, which tend to be more arm's length in nature. Seller financing enables the purchaser to defer the purchase price over an installment period; the seller either obtains a mortgage lien on the property (by means of a purchase-money mortgage, discussed at Chapter 9B, note 5) or retains the naked legal title (deed) as security for the purchaser's promise to pay the balance of the purchase-money indebtedness (discussed at Chapter 9C). Prior to the Tax Reform Act of 1986 sellers were tempted to reduce the interest rate on the deferred payments to a below-market rate in exchange for an inflated sale price as a way of trading less ordinary income for extra capital gains. I.R.C. §483 was enacted to curb this tax-avoidance technique by imputing additional interest to installment payments where the stated interest is unreasonably low. Under Treas. Reg. §1.483-1 interest will be imputed on payments due more than six months after the date of sale (under a contract that provides for a selling price of more than $3,000 and where some or all of the payments are due more than one year after the sale) if the interest rate stipulated in the contract is less than the "safe harbor" rate (formerly 9 percent per annum simple interest). Excluded from the ambit of I.R.C. §483 are transactions to which the original-issue discount rates (discussed below) apply. Since the 1986 Act eliminated the preferential treatment for capital gains the imputed interest rules have become less significant. Also, don't forget the limitations imposed on the *Crane* doctrine, discussed at Chapter 2B, note 4, under which the IRS may disallow interest and depreciation deductions where the purchaser's cost basis in the property is so inflated by nonrecourse indebtedness that it exceeds the fair market value of the property. See Estate of Franklin v. Commissioner, 64 T.C. 752 (1975), affd., 544 F.2d 1045 (9th Cir. 1976).

The Tax Reform Act of 1984 imposed the so-called Original-Issue Discount (OID) rules, a highly complex and convoluted scheme based on a time-value-of-money approach, which are designed to constrain certain tax-avoidance techniques commonly perceived by the I.R.S. to be associated with deferred-payment sales. I.R.C. §§1271 to 1275, as added by the Tax Reform Act of 1984, §§41, 42. Specifically, the statute discourages any contrived mismatching of interest deductions and interest income by purchasers and sellers, for example, a purchase-money mortgage featuring negative amortization whereby an accrual-basis purchaser deducts interest and a cash-basis seller defers interest income by deferring the actual payment of the interest until the installment loan matures. In addition, the OID rules codify the judicial limitations on the *Crane* doctrine (discussed above) in an effort to prevent the improper manipulation of the purchase price and amount of purchase-money indebtedness to suit the tax interests of the parties. I.R.C. §1274(b)(3)(A). Also, the statute is designed to supplement the purpose of the imputed interest rules, namely, to prevent the manipulation of interest rates for tax-avoidance purposes by purchasers and sellers by imposing "test rates" that are geared to market levels of federal interest rates. The statute does not require these test rates; however, if interest rates or interest-rate schedules on deferred payment notes do not fit within certain "safe-harbor" parameters, then the OID rules will either convert part of the principal indebtedness into additional interest (if the stated interest is inadequate) or reallocate the interest over the appropriate periods of the loan term (if the interest-rate schedule is inadequate). See G. Robinson, Federal Taxation of Real Estate ¶7.12[1] (Cum. Supp. No. 3) (1987); see generally Hamilton and Comi, Time Value of Money: Section 467 Rental Agreements Under the Tax Reform Act of 1984, 63 Taxes 155 (Feb. 1985); Lipsey and Friedman, Transitional Rules for Original Issue Discount, 12 J. Real Est. Taxn. 361 (Summer 1985); McGuire, Tax Shelters: Time Value of Money Anomalies in Section 483 and Section 1232, 11 J. Real Est. Taxn. 281 (Spring 1984); Moore, Analyzing the Complex New Proposed Regs on Imputed Interest and Original Issue Discount," 65 J. Taxn. 14 (July 1986); Wiesner and Smith, Equity Participation Loans: Uncertainty Increases Under the New OID Rules, 62 J. Taxn. 330 (June 1985).

Additional limitations on the deductibility of interest include: (1)

I.R.C. §267, which generally disallows a deduction for interest payable by an accrual-basis taxpayer to certain related cash-basis individuals and controlled entities; (2) I.R.C. §265, which disallows a deduction for interest incurred to purchase or carry tax-exempt securities; (3) I.R.C. §7872 (which applies to third-party loans as well as to seller-financed debt), which imputes interest to any below-market loan that is a gift loan (where the cancellation of interest is in the nature of a gift), an employer-employee loan, a corporation-shareholder loan, or any below-market loan that has as a principal purpose the avoidance of any federal tax or where the interest arrangement has a significant effect on the tax liability of the lender or borrower. Moreover, any interest imputed under I.R.C. §7872 would simply be added to whatever discount might be imposed by the OID rules.

4. The Amortization Period

Repayment of principal during the life of a loan is known as "amortization." Most postconstruction loans are "constant payment" loans. Not many years ago, commercial real estate loans were for terms of 30 or more years and were "self-amortizing" in that the regular debt-service payments were sufficient to pay interest and repay the entire amount of the principal indebtedness by the maturity date. Such regular payments of principal and interest are called "constant" payments because the amount of each periodic debt-service payment remains the same during the life of a loan. As you can see from the amortization schedule in Table 5-4, infra, the portion of the constant payment allocable to interest will decline and the remainder allocable to amortization will increase over the life of the loan. As explained in the following excerpt by Ellwood, the rate of amortization has an important impact on capitalization rates and the rate of equity yield to investors.

Ellwood, Appraisal for Mortgage Loan Purposes
Encyclopedia of Real Estate Appraising 1095
(E. J. Friedman, 3d ed. 1978)

AMORTIZATION TERM

The amortization term may be defined as the period of time in which the loan must be repaid. This is an important factor in selecting the capitalization rate, as it represents the means by which the borrowed portion of purchase capital is actually recovered. Maximum available amortization terms are usually matters of institutional lending policy. They will vary according to type of property, physical condition, and competitive situations in the mortgage money market at the time of appraisal. No judgment or conjecture on the part of the appraiser is involved in selection of this factor; it is a matter of contrast covering a specific term of years. The appraiser should be guided by the negotiated terms of financing in selecting the amortization period.

The amortization term has a significant influence on equity yield. Mortgage payments are made from property earnings. As time goes on, every dollar of mortgage amortization which is not offset by a dollar of depreciation in the market value of the property becomes a dollar of capital gain or profit in the value of the equity. The faster the amortization, the faster this component of equity profit tends to build up. . . .

ADVANTAGE OF LEVEL, SELF-AMORTIZING LOAN

The level payment, full amortization type of mortgage loan has become almost universal in financing all types of improved property. Although the periodic payment remains at a constant level throughout the term of the contract, the interest and amortization components change. The interest charge declines and the amortization increases by a corresponding amount with each succeeding payment until nearly the whole final installment is in payment of principal. This constant increase in capital recovery, without change in the fixed periodic charge, produces capital gain for the equity at a correspondingly accelerating pace. Financing the borrowed portion of purchase capital in this way is advantageous to both mortgage and equity investor. It provides the lender with better control of the cash flow from his portfolio and a hedge against possible loss resulting from depreciation of the property. It allows the investor to stabilize the debt service over the income projection period. [Under prior law] the Federal tax advantage on capital gains as against those on annual income [made] the potential for capital gain a very important element in estimating the price obtainable in the market for investment real estate. Since this is influenced by the mortgage amortization term, provision for the available amortization term must be given proper weight in developing the capitalization rate.

Returning to the master hypothetical, Dan Developer might have preferred a long-term self-amortizing loan of 30 years instead of the 15-year term he appears to be settling for because by prolonging the repayment period and reducing amortization Dan would be able to

T a b l e 5-4

15-Year Loan with 25-year Amortization Schedule
Amortization Periods: 300 Loan Amount: $25 million
Rate: 10% Payment: $227,175.19

First Year

Payment	Principal	Interest	Balance
1	18841.86	208333.33	24,981,158.14
2	18998.87	208176.32	24,962,159.27
3	19157.20	208017.99	24,943,002.08
4	19316.84	207858.35	24,923,685.24
5	19477.81	207697.38	24,904,207.43
6	19640.13	207535.06	24,884,567.30
7	19803.79	207371.39	24,864,763.51
8	19968.83	207206.36	24,844,794.68
9	20135.23	207039.96	24,824,659.45
10	20303.03	206872.16	24,804,356.42
11	20472.22	206702.97	24,783,884.20
12	20642.82	206532.37	24,763,241.38

Tenth Year

Payment	Principal	Interest	Balance
109	46170.98	181004.21	21,674,334.54
110	46555.74	180619.45	21,627,778.81
111	46943.70	180231.49	21,580,835.11
112	47334.90	179840.29	21,533,500.21
113	47729.36	179445.84	21,485,770.85
114	48127.10	179048.09	21,437,643.75
115	48528.16	178647.03	21,389,115.60
116	48932.56	178242.63	21,340,183.04
117	49340.33	177834.86	21,290.842.70
118	49751.50	177423.69	21,241,091.20
119	50166.10	177009.09	21,190,925.11
120	50584.15	176591.04	21,140,340.96

Fifteenth Year

Payment	Principal	Interest	Balance
169	76598.57	150576.62	17,992,596.41
170	77236.89	149938.30	17,915,359.53
171	77880.53	149294.66	17,837,479.00
172	78529.53	148645.66	17,758,949.47
173	79183.94	147991.25	17,679,765.52
174	79843.81	147331.38	17,599,921.71
175	80509.18	146666.01	17,519,412.54
176	81180.09	145995.10	17,438,232.45
177	81856.59	145318.60	17,356,375.87

Fifteenth Year (cont.)

Payment	Principal	Interest	Balance
178	82538.72	144636.47	17,273,837.14
179	83226.55	143948.64	17,190,610.59
180	83920.10	143255.09	17,106,690.49

Had Dan been successful in convincing Ace to make the loan self-amortizing (with a loan term of 25 years instead of 15), the payments in the 25th year would have been as follows.

Twenty-Fifth Year

Payment	Principal	Interest	Balance
169	205641.82	21533.38	2378364.27
170	207355.48	19819.70	2171008.78
171	209083.45	18091.74	1961925.34
172	210825.81	16349.38	1751099.53
173	212582.69	14592.50	1538516.84
174	214354.21	12820.97	1324162.62
175	216140.50	11034.69	1108022.13
176	217941.67	9233.52	890080.46
177	219757.85	7417.34	670322.61
178	221589.16	5586.02	448733.44
179	223435.74	3739.45	225297.70
180	225297.70	1877.48	

lessen the amount of each debt-service payment. Also, if Dan expects interest rates to increase, he would want to "lock in" at the lower rate for the longest possible term. However, as explained earlier, lending institutions are no longer very tolerant of long-term fixed-rate mortgages. In the late 1960s, most lending institutions began to foresee the inflationary period that lay ahead and began to shorten the terms of their loans. See ABA Sec. of Real Prop., Prob. & Tr. L., Financing Real Estate During the Inflationary 80s, at 23 (B. Strum ed. 1981). For example, in the third quarter of 1982, based on loan amount, 30 percent of multifamily and commercial loans made by United States life insurance companies had terms to maturity of 30 years or more, whereas by the fourth quarter of 1988 the figure had declined to 2.7 percent. Compare American Council of Life Insurance, Investment, Bull. No. 848, Table E (Dec. 22, 1982) with Bull. No. 1065, Table E-1 (April 10, 1989). Moreover, the average term to maturity declined from 21 years, 5 months in 1979 to 7 years, 10 months in 1988. See Table 5-1. Therefore, at the current time it may be unrealistic for Dan to request a loan term in excess of 15 years. However, since the debt-service payments required to amortize a constant-payment loan in 15 years might be prohibitively expensive for Dan, he might request that the amortization schedule be recast over a period longer than the actual 15-year term of the loan, such as a 25-year period. See Table 5-4. This type of partially amortizing loan results in what is often referred to as a "balloon" payment at the end of the 15-year term, that is, the unamortized portion of the principal balance that must be paid in a lump sum at the end of the loan term.

As reflected by the data in Table 5-5, both partially amortized loans and interest-only bullet loans, without any amortization, have become increasingly popular with developers as loan terms have become shorter. For example, in the fourth quarter of 1988, 32.9 percent of loans made by life insurance companies on multifamily and commercial properties contained no provision for amortization. While these partially amortized and interest-only loans reduce the developer's debt-service payments and increase the cash flow and equity yield to the developer and investors, the developer must either refinance the property at current rates or sell the property in order to satisfy the balloon indebtedness when the loan matures. See discussion infra at note 1.

Table 5-4 contains excerpts from the 25-year amortization schedule for Dan Developer's 15-year loan from Ace Insurance Company. As you can see, an amortization schedule shows the loan amount, the interest rate, the "constant" amount that is due on each payment date, how that amount is allocated between payments of interest and payments of principal, and the principal balance after each payment. In this schedule, the constant payment is a monthly payment of $227,175.19. It is applied first to the payment of interest, the remainder is then applied to the reduction of principal. Observe how the amounts applied to interest and principal and the size of the "balloon" at the maturity date (the 180th payment, or 15 years) vary over the months. The portions of the amortization schedule set out in Table 5-4 cover the first year, the 10th year, and the 15th year of Dan's 15-year loan.

Incidentally, do not confuse the phrase "constant payment" with "annual constant." The latter refers to the annual fixed percentage of the original loan amount required to service the debt over the term of a fully or self-amortizing loan, or over the amortization period in the case of a partially amortizing loan. For example, if the loan to Dan were fully amortized over its 15-year term, this would require an annual constant of 12.89 percent that would result in a monthly debt service payment of $268,651.29. With the same 15-year loan amortized on a 25-year basis, the annual constant would decline to 10.90 percent, requiring a monthly debt service payment of only $227,175.19; however, a balloon payment in the amount of $17,106,690 would be due at the end of the term.

Table 5-5

Commitments of $100,000 and Over on Multifamily and Nonresidential Mortgages

Amortization Provisions, Fourth Quarter, 1988

Amortization Provision	No. of Loans	Amount Committed ($000)	Loan Amount ($000)	Interest Rate (By #)	Interest Rate (By $)	Loan/ Value	Averages Capitaliza- tion Rate	Debt Coverage	Percent Constant	Maturity (Years/Months)	Percentage Distribution By #	By Loan Amount
Fully amortized — uniform payments	9	205,713	22,857	10.31%	11.03%	69.6%	10.0%	1.26	11.9%	24/0	2.2%	3.6%
Fully amortized — irregular payments	12	282,350	23,529	9.27	9.22	86.2	9.3	–	–	31/1	3.0	5.0
Partially amortized — uniform payments balance at maturity over 30%	130	1,460,403	11,234	10.22	10.04	67.5	9.6	1.30	10.9	7/3	32.2	25.6
Partially amortized — irregular payments balance at maturity from 15% to 30%	3	32,700	10,900	9.71	9.68	79.3	9.1	–	–	13/4	0.7	0.6
Partially amortized — irregular payments balance at maturity over 30%	117	2,051,556	17,535	9.98	9.93	73.7	9.3	–	–	8/5	29.0	36.0
No amortization	133	1,664,671	12,516	9.85	9.82	71.8	8.9	1.26	9.8	5/10	32.9	29.2
TOTAL	404	5,697,393	14,102	10.00	9.93	71.4	9.3	1.28	10.4	8/3	100.0	100.0

Note: Averages for capitalization rate, debt coverage ratio and percent constant may represent a fewer number of loans than the total for the specified category. Averages for interest rates are based on 404 loans.

Source: American Council of Life Insurance, Invest. Bull. No. 1065, Table F (April 10, 1989).

NOTES AND QUESTIONS

1. Balloon Payments. Dan should be concerned about how he will be able to make the balloon payment in the amount of $17,106,690.49 that will become due at the end of the 15-year term of the loan. Such a large payment might be too much of a drain on the cash reserves of Dan and his investors. Consequently, Dan will probably want to refinance the loan at maturity, that is, obtain a replacement loan from Ace or some other lender. Refinancing is discussed at Chapter 9A. However, if the supply of mortgage money is tight at the time, these funds might not be readily available. Moreover, even if the substitute loan funds are available, the terms of the refinanced loan could adversely affect the profitability of the property and even put the enterprise at risk if interest rates should be significantly higher. As observed at Chapter 5B1, note 2, supra, if future interest rates were higher, this could mean higher capitalization rates and a lower loan-to-value ratio on the refinanced loan. If the rental income stream were to remain relatively stable — because of the duration of long-term lease terms, rental income does not always keep pace with capitalization rates — the application of higher capitalization rates might also result in a reduction in the appraised value of the mortgaged property, perhaps to a point where the balloon amount might exceed the maximum loan amount allowable for the new loan under local law. Don't forget that most institutional loans are subject to maximum loan-to-value ratios. If this is the case it might be incumbent on Dan to fund the shortfall with his own cash reserves (or with additional capital contributions from his investors if the ownership entity is organized as a partnership). Alternatively, prior to maturity Dan might prefer to sell the property at a net sale price that is at least equal to the balloon payment amount.

Conversely, if, as Dan hopes and anticipates, the office building project were to become viable ("on stream," in the parlance of real estate professionals), his "equity" in the project (its appraised value less the amount of the Ace indebtedness) may start to accumulate as the result of: (1) an increase in the value of the underlying land caused by inflation; and (2) an increase in the value of the building caused by higher net operating income if rent should rise because of a greater demand for rental space, management efficiency, or simply because of inflation. If market rentals increase, Dan plans to renegotiate higher rentals with his short-term "secondary" tenants as their leases expire; he also hopes to negotiate for periodic increases in rent (geared to such indices as the Consumer Price Index, the Producers Price Index, or the rental component of the All Urban Consumers Index) with his long-term "prime" rents that will take into account any increase in the rate of inflation. Based on such accumulation of equity Dan might be able to refinance for a larger loan amount that will enable him to make not only the requisite balloon payment to Ace but also to "mortgage out" the excess refinancing proceeds in the form of tax-free cash to himself and his investors. The term "equity" is defined in greater detail at Chapter 9A, footnote 2, and "mortgaging out" is explained at Chapter 2B, note 5b.

   2. Call Provisions and Partial Amortization.   In addition to abbreviating the term of the loan, some postconstruction lenders offer fixed-rate loans with relatively long terms but reserve the right to "call in" the loan prior to the original maturity date as a hedge against inflation and loss of interest income due to an increase in interest rates. For example, many partially amortized loans are structured as long-term fixed-rate loans (with 25- to 30-year amortization schedules) with perhaps a 10- to 15-year call provision. While the long-term amortization schedule makes the loan affordable to the borrower, the call provision ameliorates the lender's inflation and interest-rate risk. See generally Ling and Peiser, Choosing Among Alternative Financing Structures: The Developer's Dilemma, 17 Real Est. Rev. 39, 40 (Summer 1987).

   As a general rule, developer-borrowers are resistant to call provisions because, among other things, the financial uncertainty as to whether the mortgage will reach its full term could prove to be a problem for a prospective purchaser who wants to assume the existing mortgage (and is willing to pay the current rate, as required by a due-on-sale clause, discussed at Chapter 5B8, infra), or it could prevent the developer-owner from obtaining wraparound financing (discussed at Chapter 9B, note 4). At a minimum the developer-borrower should insist that any call provision provide adequate notice that the lender intends to exercise its privilege so that the borrower has a reasonable opportunity to refinance the loan elsewhere. Otherwise, the lender might be vulnerable to a charge of bad faith and unfair dealings. See K.M.C. Co. v. Irving Trust Co., excerpted at Chapter 12A.

   Returning to the master hypothetical, suppose Ace were to offer Dan either a 10-year interest-only loan at a fixed rate of interest (but with a call option at the end of the fifth year of the loan) or a 10-year loan at the same fixed rate, without a call option but with a requirement that the principal be repaid based on a 20-year amortization schedule. As Dan's attorney, how would you assess (in non-mathematical terms) the relative risks and rewards of these financing alternatives for Dan as a prospective owner-borrower and syndicator?

   To review, what is the impact on real estate as a tax shelter as a consequence of this trend away from long-term self-amortizing loans to short-term partially amortized loans with balloon payments? See discussion at Chapter 2B, note 2.

   The debt-coverage ratio is arrived at by dividing the net stabilized earnings from the mortgaged property by the annual amount of debt-service payments. Suppose in the master hypothetical that the assumed free and clear rate of return were 9 percent instead of 12 percent. This means that Dan would anticipate receiving an annual net rental income stream of about $3 million rather than $4 million; thus the debt-coverage ratio in the first year of the 15-year loan term would be $3 million divided by $3,223,812, or .93. What this means in plain language is that Dan may have to negotiate a lower interest rate or a longer amortization schedule to increase the debt-coverage ratio to at least 1.00 (if not higher); otherwise, Ace might not commit to make the loan because Dan would not have sufficient income (after paying his other operating expenses) to pay the debt-service on the mortgage.

5. The Prepayment Privilege

When interest rates decline, there is a tendency among borrowers to replace existing debt with new debt so that they can "refinance" at the lower rate. For example, if interest rates in the master hypothetical for the first mortgage money should decrease from 10 percent to 8 percent by the 10th year of the loan, refinancing with a new 15-year loan at the lower rate could save Dan as much as $440,172.36 in interest expenses during the first year of the new loan. In addition, a borrower such as Dan may want to refinance an existing loan with a new larger one from Ace or some other lender in order to cash out some tax-free equity in the project for the purpose of expanding or renovating the office building. Or perhaps Dan might want to use the net refinancing proceeds for another investment opportunity (assuming that he will be able to obtain an after-tax rate of return that is higher than the after-tax cost of borrowing the extra money). Finally, an inability to refinance could thwart a sale of the property to a purchaser who plans to obtain a new mortgage so that he can finance the portion of the purchase price attributable to the seller's equity in the property being sold.[8]

The chief obstacle to refinancing is the cost of the new mortgage indebtedness including origination fees, mortgage closing expenses, and especially prepayment charges imposed by the lender for the privilege of prepaying the existing indebtedness prior to the agreed-on maturity date. Under basic property law, in the absence of language to the contrary in the loan documents a lender does not have to accept a prepayment, the reason being that a lender is entitled to receive the anticipated rate of return and recapture the cost of making the loan

---

8. Refinancing is discussed in greater detail at Chapter 9A.

T a b l e 5-6

Commitments of $100,000 and Over on Multifamily and Nonresidential Mortgages

Years Closed to Prepayment for Loans Classified by Maturity, Fourth Quarter, 1988

Maturity / Years Closed to Prepayment	No. of Loans	Amount Committed ($000)	Loan Amount ($000)	Averages							Percentage Distribution	
				Interest Rate (By #)	Interest Rate (By $)	Loan/ Value	Capitaliza- tion Rate	Debt Coverage	Percent Constant	Maturity (Years/Months)	By #	By Loan Amount
Maturities of 10 years or less	356	4,284,010	12,034	10.01%	9.89%	70.7%	9.2%	1.28	10.3%	6/6	88.1%	75.2%
Not closed	108	1,969,181	18,233	9.79	9.75	70.0	9.0	1.33	10.0	5/8	26.7	34.6
Closed for 1-8 years	160	1,649,881	10,312	10.13	10.02	72.3	9.5	1.28	10.5	7/2	39.6	29.0
Closed for life	88	664,948	7,556	10.07	9.98	68.7	9.1	1.24	10.5	6/4	21.8	11.7
Maturities of 5 years or less (included above)	191	2,411,053	12,623	9.85	9.75	70.7	9.0	1.29	10.1	4/8	47.3	42.3
Maturities Over 10 Years	48	1,413,383	29,445	9.90	10.05	76.5	9.4	1.23	11.1	21/3	11.9	24.8
Not closed	4	69,645	17,411	10.34	9.96	52.2	8.9	*	12.6	15/6	1.0	1.2
Closed for 3 years	1	14,983	14,983	*	*	*	*	*	*	*	0.2	0.3
Closed for 4 years	2	29,750	14,875	*	*	*	*	*	*	*	0.5	0.5
Closed for 6 years	1	13,000	13,000	*	*	*	*	–	–	*	0.2	0.2
Closed for 7 years	5	24,660	4,932	10.23	9.68	76.4	10.0	1.24	10.9	14/10	1.2	0.4
Closed for 8 years	5	98,770	19,754	10.13	10.14	81.2	9.7	*	11.2	15/7	1.2	1.7
Closed for 9 or more years	30	1,162,575	38,753	9.71	10.05	80.3	9.3	1.24	10.9	24/9	7.4	20.4
TOTAL	404	5,697,393	14,102	10.00	9.93	71.4	9.3	1.28	10.4	8/3	100.0	100.0

*Data not shown for a limited number of loans.

Note: Averages for capitalization rate, debt coverage ratio and percent constant may represent a fewer number of loans than the total for the specified category. Averages for interest rates are based on 404 loans.

"Years Closed to Prepayment" refers to the number of years during which no prepayment is permitted.

Source: American Council of Life Insurance, Invest. Bull. No. 1065, Table G (April 10, 1989).

435

during the agreed-on term of the loan.[9] Moreover, these provisions are used by lenders in conjunction with "due-on-sale" clauses to protect themselves against fluctuations in market rates of interest. When interest rates climb above the rate on the existing mortgage, the due-on-sale clause encourages refinancing by the purchaser and prepayment by the borrower when the property is sold, thereby enabling the lender to relend the recaptured funds at the higher market rate. Conversely, when interest rates decline, the prepayment penalty discourages borrowers from refinancing at the lower market rate.[10]

This conflict in the interests of the parties usually results in a compromise. The mortgage note may provide for a "lock in" period so that no prepayment is permitted for a certain number of years after the inception of the loan. See Table 5-6. Thereafter, there is usually a prepayment charge or fee that the borrower will have to pay equal to a specified percentage of the loan amount that is being prepaid. This percentage is higher during the early years of the prepayment period and usually de-escalates as the loan approaches maturity. This prepayment charge is designed to be sufficiently onerous to make it unlikely that the loan will be prepaid unless interest rates decline substantially or unless expansion, sale, or tax considerations warrant the payment of the prepayment charge.

The following is a typical prepayment privilege provision that might appear in Ace's commitment letter.

> The Note shall provide . . . that the Borrower will have the privilege of prepaying the entire principal balance of the Loan (but not a part thereof) on the first day of any month commencing with the first day of the first month of the _____ Loan Year upon _____ days' prior written notice to Lender of Borrower's intention to so prepay and upon payment by Borrower to Lender of the principal balance due on the Note together with the accrued interest thereon and all other sums due and payable under the Note and a prepayment fee equal to _____ percent of the unpaid principal balance if prepayment is made during the _____ Loan Year, said prepayment fee declining _____ percent each succeeding Loan Year thereafter and with no prepayment fee if the Loan is paid at its normal maturity; and that if the Borrower gives notice of its intention to prepay as hereinabove provided, the entire principal balance of the Loan shall, at the option of Lender become due and payable on the date specified in the notice indicating an intention to prepay by Borrower.

To implement language in the commitment, the following standard form language might appear in the mortgage or deed of trust note:

---

9. Saunders v. Frost, 22 Mass. 259 (5 Pick. 275) (1827).

10. See Madison and Dwyer ¶3.04[5] (1981); G. Nelson and D. Whitman, Real Estate Finance Law §6.1 (2d ed. 1985).

Commencing with the first day of _____ , and on any monthly payment date thereafter, Maker shall have the right to prepay the entire unpaid principal balance hereof, but not part thereof, provided that Maker shall have given Holder at least ninety (90) days' prior irrevocable written notice by certified or registered mail, return receipt requested, of Maker's intention to make such prepayment, and that any such prepayment is accompanied by payment of all unpaid accrued interest hereunder to the date of prepayment and all other sums due and owing hereunder and under the Mortgage and by payment of a prepayment fee computed on the then outstanding principal balance of this Note as follows:

(i) _____ percent if prepayment is made between _____ and _____ ;

(ii) _____ percent if prepayment is made between _____ and _____ ;

(iii) _____ percent if prepayment is made between _____ and _____ ; and

(iv) No prepayment fee after _____ .

If Maker shall have given Holder written notice of Maker's Intention to prepay the entire unpaid principal balance hereof and shall thereafter fail to so prepay the entire unpaid principal balance hereof on the date of prepayment fixed by Maker's notice, then, at the option of Holder, the amount of applicable prepayment fee shall be added to the debt evidenced hereby and, at the option of the Holder, such failure shall constitute a default hereunder and the entire unpaid principal balance with all unpaid accrued interest thereon and all sums due and owing hereunder and under the Mortgage shall become immediately due and payable, time being of the essence.

To review: the following language is frequently added in modern mortgage or deed of trust notes. Can you think of the reason for the additional language?

Maker agrees that if an Event of Default (as defined in the Mortgage, such definition being incorporated herein by reference and made part hereof) shall occur and the maturity hereof shall be accelerated, then a tender of payment by Maker or by anyone on behalf of the Maker of the amount necessary to satisfy all sums due hereunder made at any time prior to judicial or public sale of the real and/or other property mortgaged under the Mortgage shall constitute an evasion of the payment terms hereof and shall be deemed to be a voluntary prepayment hereunder, and any such payment, to the extent permitted by law, therefore must include the fee required under the prepayment privilege, or if at that time there be no such privilege of prepayment, then such payment, to the extent permitted by law, must include a fee of _____ of the then unpaid principal balance of this Note.

The following case deals with the extent to which the imposition of a prepayment charge can be justified by the lender's economic impairment in the market characterized by increasing rates of interest.

Lazzareschi Investment Co. v. San Francisco Federal Savings & Loan Assn.
22 Cal. App. 3d 303, 99 Cal. Rptr. 417 (Ct. App. 1971)

DEVINE, Presiding Justice.

Plaintiff appeals from a summary judgment. Plaintiff, by its complaint, seeks recovery of an allegedly illegal penalty and seeks punitive damages against defendants for assertedly exacting it. From declarations presented by the parties at the motion for summary judgment, we have the following narration of facts.

On February 21, 1967, Frank A. Marshall borrowed $300,000 from defendant San Francisco Federal Savings and Loan Association, for which he executed a promissory note secured by a deed of trust on property used for commercial purposes. The second defendant is the trustee. In the note Marshall reserved the right to prepay in whole or in part at any time prior to maturity the $300,000 obligation. This privilege, however, was subject to a prepayment fee provision which provided for the following: "Privilege is reserved to make additional payments on the principal of this indebtedness at any time without penalty, except that as to any such payments made which exceed twenty percentum (20%) of the original principal amount of this loan during any successive twelve (12) month period beginning with the date of this promissory note, the undersigned agree to pay, as consideration for the acceptance of such prepayment, six (6) months advance interest on that part of the aggregate amount of all prepayments in excess of such twenty percentum (20%). The privilege of paying amounts not in excess of said twenty percentum (20%) of the original principal sum without consideration shall be noncumulative, if not exercised. The undersigned agree that such six (6) months advance interest shall be due and payable whether said prepayment is voluntary or involuntary, including any prepayment effected by the exercise of any acceleration clause provided for herein."

On November 17, 1967, plaintiff purchased the real property securing San Francisco Federal's loan from a court-appointed receiver, in the Contra Costa County divorce proceedings of Frank A. Marshall. The purchase price was $570,000. In order to consummate the purchase, plaintiff had to procure new financing. Immediately before the close of escrow, San Francisco Federal submitted a demand in the sum of $9,130.02, which constituted the prepayment fee computed in accordance with the provisions of the note. This sum was in addition to the price and other payments, including accrued interest, which plaintiff had agreed to pay for the real property. Plaintiff paid and defendants received the amount demanded, but plaintiff noted in the buyer's instructions that it did so under protest.

In his declaration, Mr. Lazzareschi, president of plaintiff corporation, avers that it was necessary for him to pay the money in order to close the escrow, "otherwise said judicial sale would have failed." Plaintiff also declares that the interest rate of defendants' loan was then 7¾%, substantially less than that which defendants could obtain by a new loan of the recovered funds; wherefore defendants actually profited from the early prepayment rather than being prejudiced thereby. On the basis of these circumstances, plaintiff alleges in its complaint that the amount of the prepayment charge bears no reasonable relationship to any damage allegedly sustained by the defendants by virtue of the prepayment. Plaintiff also alleges that the prepayment fee constitutes an unreasonable restraint on alienation. . . .

Appellant cites Freedman v. Rector, Wardens & Vestrymen, 37 Cal. 2d 16, 230 P.2d 629, for the principle that damages imposed must bear a reasonable relationship to the injury caused. But the *Freedman* case and all of those which have been based on it are concerned with breach of a contract in some manner. In the instant case, there has been no breach. The borrower had the option, clearly spelled out in the promissory note, of making one or more prepayments. He, by the action of the receiver, availed himself of the option. This is not a situation of liquidated damages. Although the word "penalty" is used, and perhaps properly so in that a charge is made which is equivalent to unearned interest, there is no penalty in the sense of retribution for breach of an agreement, nor is there provision for liquidated damages because of ascertaining what the damages for such breach may be. . . .

There are indications that an extortionate charge for prepayment would not be supported in judicial proceedings and that on one theory or another, yet undetermined, a person forced to sustain such a charge might have a remedy. . . .

For the purpose of this appeal, we shall assume that palpably exorbitant charges would be subject to defeat by judicial decision. We proceed to examine the contract, the promissory note, in the present case. It is necessary, however, to examine it not as an isolated transaction, but as a transaction existing with a multitude of others which the lender must enter in order to stay in business. . . . If interest rates increase sharply, the lender has no option to renegotiate the loan. Of course, if a prepayment is made at the borrower's choice (sometimes made for him as in this receiver's case, but chargeable to him) when interest rates have increased, the lender may gain from the repayment. But in the whole portfolio there may be many loans which will not be repaid although some of the borrowers have become well able to repay. The borrowers can use the money more advantageously. On the other hand, if interest rates decline, borrowers will be able to refinance at lower rates, and if there were not adequate charge for repayment, they could discharge the note, giving the original lender funds which could be put out only at a lower rate. In *Cherry v. Home Sav. & Loan Assn.*, 276 Cal. App. 2d 574, 579, 81 Cal. Rptr. 135, this fact of economic life was recognized in a due-on-sale case. Thus, unlike the *Freedman* type of case, the loan situation calls for attention to economic forces over a period which may be long — here, twenty years.

But even prescinding from the variables which are built into a loan which may run for as long as twenty years, we observe that there would be difficulty in deciding upon the advantage, if any, to the lender by early repayment. There is, of course, the matter of expense in all of the activities which lead to the decision to make the loan on a particular basis. Moreover, there is the matter of possible loss of time between repayment of the funds and placing them on loan anew. It would be impossible to trace the exact funds from one loan to another. The repaid monies surely would be used, but until the expiration of such time as would ordinarily be necessary to complete the new loan or loans (not identifiable), the funds, as part of the loanable resources of the lending institution, must remain in competition, as it were, with other resources of the lender and with the resources of similar institutions, awaiting settlement upon an acceptable borrower.

Here again, we do not foreclose inquiry into possible exorbitancy, but merely point out that a prepayment case does not fall into a simple calculation at any one point of time of the difference between the interest rate on the repaid loan and that which might be available to the lending institution on a new loan of about the same size made to a new borrower. . . .

In the absence of any statute or authorized regulation, and in the absence of any evidence produced by declaration of plaintiff in opposition to the motion for summary judgment or suggested by plaintiff as appellant in its briefs, we know of no means by which a court could come to the conclusion that the charge which appellant agreed to pay was exorbitant or out of line with that customarily provided in loan agreements. Indeed, plaintiff does not in its complaint or in its declaration in opposition to the motion for summary judgment, make the point that the charge exceeds that which is usual. Plaintiff's theory of excessiveness is that the charge bears no reasonable relationship to any damage sustained by virtue of the prepayment because of respondents' ability to lend the funds anew at a higher rate, a subject discussed above. . . .

The final case addresses the question whether a prepayment charge is enforceable when the prepayment is prompted by the borrower's default.

In re LHD Realty Corp.
726 F.2d 327 (7th Cir. 1984)

CUDAHY, Circuit Judge.

This appeal primarily involves a contest over a mortgage holder's right to receive a stipulated premium in exchange for accepting a borrower's repayment of a loan before maturity. The dispute is complicated somewhat by the fact that at the time of the prepayment the borrower was in a Chapter 11 bankruptcy proceeding. The bankruptcy court held that the mortgage holder was entitled to the prepayment premium, but the district court reversed. Because we believe that in the particular circumstances of this case the holder's right to a prepayment premium was not triggered, we affirm. . . .

Appellant National Life Insurance Company ("National") was the assignee of a promissory note and mortgage in the principal amount of $775,000. The note was secured by the mortgage on an office building and parking garage in Indianapolis known as the "1800 Building." Appellee LHD Realty Corporation ("LHD") is a real estate management and investment company which acquired the 1800 Building in 1972 and assumed the note and the mortgage on the building which secured the note. Repayment of the promissory note was to be made in monthly installments over a period of fifteen years. The note provided that, if the loan was paid before maturity, the holder was entitled to a prepayment premium.[1]

On June 13, 1980, LHD filed a voluntary petition under Chapter 11 of the Bankruptcy Reform Act of 1978, 11 U.S.C. §101 et seq.

---

1. The clause controlling prepayment states:

No prepayment of principal may be made during the first ten (10) loan years. After tenth (10th) loan year, the right is reserved upon sixty (60) days' prior notice in writing, to prepay on any interest payment date all or any portion of the note principal by paying a premium on the amount prepaid as follows: During the eleventh (11th) loan year at five (5%) per cent, declining one (1%) per cent per year thereafter to a minimum of par.

In the event of prepayment in full only, and in addition to the foregoing, an additional prepayment premium will be payable in an amount computed as follows: The average "additional interest" payments for the three (3) preceding years capitalized at thirty-three and one-third (33⅓%) per cent.

(the "Bankruptcy Code"), and since then has been operating its business and managing its property as a debtor in possession. Between July 1980 and April 1981, LHD made its monthly mortgage payments to National, although the payments were late each month. Since the April 1981 payment, however, LHD has not made any mortgage payments to National.

On August 26, 1981, with four monthly payments overdue, National filed in the bankruptcy court a request for relief from the automatic stay of proceedings against LHD provided by 11 U.S.C. §362. National stated in its complaint for relief that

> [i]t is obvious there is no reasonable likelihood of rehabilitating the ailing Debtor. . . . A continued delay in allowing [National] to foreclose its lien will cause obvious irreparable harm to [National] because of the lack of adequate protection.

National therefore asked the bankruptcy court to allow it "to proceed with foreclosure of its lien" or to dismiss the bankruptcy action or to convert the Chapter 11 proceeding to a Chapter 7 liquidation, whereupon the 1800 Building would be sold at public auction.

On September 10, 1981, shortly after National filed its complaint for relief from the stay, LHD filed an application with the bankruptcy court seeking authority to employ a realtor to list the 1800 Building for sale. The application was approved and LHD found a buyer. On December 8, 1981, LHD filed with the bankruptcy court a complaint to sell the 1800 Building. . . .

On December 23, 1981, National filed its response to LHD's motion for permission to sell the 1800 Building. National asked for payment in full or a lien on the proceeds until paid, with the proceeds being held in a restricted account controlled by the court.

On January 15, 1982, the bankruptcy court issued its decision permitting LHD to sell the 1800 Building. The court's order provided that proceeds from the sale were to be retained and segregated by the debtor until the allowed liens and claims were paid. . . .

II.

[1] The parties agree that prepayment premiums serve a valid purpose in compensating at least in part for the anticipated interest a lender will not receive if a loan is paid off prematurely. Among other things, a prepayment premium insures the lender against loss of his bargain if interest rates decline. Accordingly, reasonable prepayment premiums are enforceable. See generally Annot., 86 A.L.R.3d 599 (1978); Annot., 75 A.L.R.2d 1265 (1961).

[2-4] There are, however, some limitations upon the right to receive a prepayment premium. For one, the lender loses its right to a premium when it elects to accelerate the debt. Slevin Container Corp. v. Provident Federal Savings & Loan Ass'n, 98 Ill. App. 3d 646, 54 Ill. Dec. 189, 424 N.E.2d 939 (1981). This is so because acceleration, by definition, advances the maturity date of the debt so that payment thereafter is not prepayment but instead is payment made after maturity. For another, courts infer an exception when a mortgage upon the property being condemned is satisfied by a government exercising its power of eminent domain. Jala Corp. v. Berkeley Savings & Loan, 104 N.J. Super. 394, 250 A.2d 150 (1969). Finally, courts infer an exception when payment results from destruction of the mortgaged property through an insured-against casualty such as a fire. Chestnut Corp. v. Bankers Bond & Mortgage Co., 395 Pa. 153, 149 A.2d 48 (1959).

[5] We think that the case before us falls within the acceleration exception. The contract between National and LHD authorized National, "without notice, [to] declare the remainder of the debt at once due and payable." When a lender has the option to accelerate, " '[i]t is only necessary that the mortgagee show an *unmistakeable intention to exercise the option,* and this may be done by taking steps for foreclosure, filing foreclosure suit, sale pursuant to the mortgage, or advertisement of the property for sale pursuant to the terms of the mortgage.' " . . .

The point is, we think, that a lender may abandon or waive its claim to interest payable over a period of years and to what amounts to insurance against a decline in interest rates. Thus, the lender, by its acts, may establish that it prefers accelerated payment to the opportunity to earn interest over a period of years. It is not appropriate, under these circumstances, for the lender to receive a prepayment premium in lieu of the interest foregone since it has voluntarily waived the unpaid interest in the expectation of accelerated payment of the remaining principal. . . .

National argues, however, that a per se rule that acceleration precludes a claim for a prepayment provision will cause borrowers to default intentionally and to court acceleration and foreclosure in order to avoid prepayment liability. But this scenario seems implausible given the ramifications of default for a borrower's credit rating and the ability of the lender to sidestep the ploy by suing only for overdue payments as they mature, together with attorney's fees. Also, the borrower would run the risk of not being able to repay the loan in time to defeat the foreclosure sale. Should such intentional defaults become a problem, however, we believe courts could deal with the difficulty by denying the acceleration exception in appropriate cases. In any event, National does not suggest that LHD implemented such a strategy in the case before us. . . .

NOTES AND QUESTIONS

1. *Terms of Prepayment.* Observe that the loan payment terms, including the prepayment privilege, are found in the mortgage note. The obvious reason for this is that the note is the legal evidence of indebtedness and as such must contain all payment terms. Some lenders repeat the payment terms in the mortgage or deed of trust, while others will refuse to do so. Can you think of a reason why? Might their concern be attributable to the fact that the note is not recorded?

Ordinarily, as reflected by the language in the sample prepayment privilege clause, supra, the lender will attempt to discourage partial prepayments. However, a borrower with some bargaining clout should be able to negotiate (as did the plaintiff in *Lazzareschi Investment Co.*) a noncumulative right to make an annual payment not in excess of a specified percentage of the original loan amount without payment of a fee. Customarily, the prepayment fee is a percentage of the outstanding balance of the loan; therefore, when the borrower refinances, the prepayment fee will be reduced as a consequence of the earlier partial prepayments. A partial prepayment may also be made at the behest of the lender. For example, in the case of a partial fire destruction or condemnation of the premises, the mortgagee may be allowed under the terms of the mortgage to receive the insurance or condemnation award proceeds and use the funds to scale down the principal balance of the mortgage indebtedness. In the event of a partial prepayment, whether voluntary or involuntary, the monthly debt-service payments on the mortgage might remain the same unless the borrower bargains for a pro rata reduction in the payments over the original term of the loan.

Observe that the language in the sample clause requires the borrower to provide notice of its intention to prepay on a specified date and that failure to prepay in accordance with such notice constitutes a default under the terms of the mortgage note. Can you think of the reason why a prudent lender would impose such a notice requirement?

As noted above, prepayment charges traditionally have been geared to a percentage of the outstanding principal balance of the loan as of the date of prepayment. However, the recent trend among postconstruction lenders is to use a "yield equivalent" or "yield maintenance" formula to compensate them for the loss of their investment as a consequence of a prepayment. Some lenders prefer to use the yield equivalent formula to calculate the prepayment fee only if the loan indebtedness is accelerated because of an unauthorized prepayment (or other default) during the "lock-in" period at the beginning of the loan term, during which time the borrower has no privilege to prepay. The following is a typical yield-equivalent provision that is keyed to the market rate of interest at the time of prepayment.

The prepayment charge shall equal the amount of the excess, if any, which would be required over and above the principal balance of the Loan outstanding at the time of such prepayment [or default if such default occurs during the lock-in period] for the mortgagee to purchase on the date of such prepayment [or default], a United States Treasury Bond with a maturity date closest to that of the Loan providing the same investment yield the mortgagee would have received had all payments been made on the Note as therein provided.

Can you think of a business reason why the yield maintenance variety of prepayment clause is increasingly being used by lenders?

2. *The Prepayment Charge as a "Penalty."* Recall that the law abhors a penalty and that where a predetermined payment for breach of a contract does not bear a reasonable relationship to the anticipated loss, the courts may strike down the parties' determination as a "penalty." See generally 5 S. Williston, Contracts §775A (3d ed. 1961 & Supp. 1985). In *Lazzareschi* the court ruled that the litmus test for enforceability of a prepayment charge in a nondefault situation was whether the charge was "palpably exorbitant" and not whether the charge was an unreasonable "penalty." In that regard how relevant was it that the interest rate on the borrower's loan (7¾%) had been substantially less than that which the lender could have obtained by lending the prepaid funds to someone else? Prepayment charges are generally enforceable provided that they are not unconscionable, and, as reflected by the holding in *Lazzareschi*, courts are reluctant to apply a liquidated damages analysis in nondefault situations. Why? See Williams v. Fassler, 110 Cal. App. 3d 7, 167 Cal. Rptr. 545 (1980) (a 50 percent prepayment charge was deemed enforceable because it was neither exorbitant nor unconscionable); but see Gutzi Assocs. v. Switzer, 215 Cal. App. 3d 1636, 264 Cal. Rptr. 538 (1989); Northway Lanes v. Hackley Union National Bank & Trust Co., 334 F. Supp. 723 (W.D. Mich. 1971), affd., 464 F.2d 855 (6th Cir. 1972) (prepayment charge deemed to be neither unreasonable nor unconscionable); In re Skyler Ridge, 80 B.R. 500 (Bankr. C.D. Cal. 1987) (prepayment premium of the yield maintenance variety deemed an unenforceable penalty because Treasury Bond index rate differed from first mortgage rates and prepayment fee formula contained no discount for present value); see generally Stark, Enforcing Prepayment Charges: Case Law and Drafting Suggestions, 22 Real Prop., Prob. & Tr. J. 549, 550-552 (Fall 1987); Stark, Prepayment Charges in Jeopardy: The Unhappy and Uncertain Legacy of *In Re Skyler Ridge*, 24 Real Prop., Prob. & Tr. J. 191 (Summer 1989).

3. *Involuntary Prepayments.* Do you think the result in *Lazzareschi* might have been different had the borrower defaulted and the borrower's payment been precipitated by the lender's accelerating the

loan indebtedness after such default? One argument in support of enforcing a prepayment charge even though the prepayment is triggered by the borrower's unintentional default is that one of the principal purposes of the prepayment fee is to enable the lender to recoup its cost of making the loan over the agreed-on term of the loan. In addition to the position taken by the borrower in *LHD Realty Corp.,* what are some counterarguments in favor of the position frequently taken by borrowers that, absent language to the contrary in the loan documents, an involuntary prepayment prompted by default should not entitle the lender to a prepayment fee? See George H. Nutman, Inc. v. Aetna Business Credit, Inc., 115 Misc. 2d 168, 453 N.Y.S.2d 586 (1982); Stark, Enforcing Prepayment Charges, supra, at 553-558. Suppose the lender were to include language in the prepayment clause to the effect that the charge would become due "whether said prepayment is voluntary or involuntary, including any prepayment effected by the holder's exercise of the Acceleration Clause. . . ." See Pacific Trust Co. TTEE v. Fidelity Federal Savings & Loan Assn., 184 Cal. App. 3d 817, 229 Cal. Rptr. 269, 274 (1986); Golden Forest Properties v. Columbia Sav. & Loan Assn., 248 Cal. Rptr. 316 (Cal. Ct. App. 1988).

In the case of debt acceleration following a total condemnation or casualty destruction of some mortgaged premises, a postconstruction lender frequently will insist on the right to apply the condemnation award proceeds or hazard insurance proceeds towards satisfaction of the outstanding balance on the mortgage loan. See Chapter 5B12, notes 4 and 5, infra. If this be the case, do you think the lender will be able to enforce a prepayment charge if this contingency is not dealt with in the prepayment clause? See DeKalb County v. United Family Life Insurance Co., 235 Ga. 417, 219 S.E.2d 707 (1975) (involving condemnation); Chestnut Corp. v. Bankers Bond & Mortgage Co., 395 Pa. 153, 149 A.2d 48 (1959) (involving fire destruction). See also Landohio Corp. v. Northwestern Mutual Life Mortgage and Realty Investors, 431 F. Supp. 475 (N.D. Ohio 1976); Jala Corp. v. Berkeley Savings & Loan Assn., 104 N.J. Super. 394, 250 A.2d 150 (1969); Silverman v. New York, 48 A.D.2d 413, 370 N.Y.S.2d 234 (1975).

Suppose the parties do address the question and the loan documents specify that a fee is payable regardless of whether the prepayment is voluntary. Would enforcement of a prepayment charge following a total or partial condemnation or destruction be held to be unconscionable? In other words, which of the two innocent parties, the borrower or the lender, should bear the risk of fluctuations in the market rate of interest, if the loan is repaid prior to maturity because of circumstances beyond the control of either party? How relevant is it that the borrower might have restored the premises with the insurance proceeds had the lender been willing to transfer the funds to the borrower for that purpose? Certainly this issue becomes more troublesome in the case of a *partial* destruction or condemnation, when a restoration of the premises is usually feasible. These matters are negotiable, and any attempt by a lender to reserve the right to collect a fee while denying the borrower the right to restore the premises (and stay in business) should be strenuously resisted by the borrower. At a minimum, borrower's counsel should insist that the prepayment fee be waived in the event of any involuntary partial prepayment. Also, in the case of a partial prepayment where the loan balance is reduced by either insurance or condemnation award proceeds, borrower's counsel should insist that the debt service payments be proportionately reduced over the original term of the loan. See Madison and Dwyer ¶3.04[5] (1981).

4. *Intentional Default as a Strategem for Circumventing the Prepayment Charge.* Returning to the hypothetical, suppose Dan Developer walks into your law office during the tenth year of the loan with Ace Insurance Co., when the outstanding balance on the loan is approximately $22 million and the market rate of interest for first mortgage money has suddenly dropped from 10 percent to 8 percent. Assume that the loan documents provide that Dan must pay a prepayment fee amounting to 2 percent of the outstanding principal balance if the loan is discharged after the third year and before the twelfth year of the loan term. Dan wants to refinance the loan immediately, but he doesn't want to pay the prepayment fee, which would amount to $440,000. He tells you he intends to purposely default on the loan and, when Ace accelerates the unpaid mortgage indebtedness because of the default, he plans to redeem the property prior to foreclosure or have his brother-in-law purchase the property at the foreclosure sale. Dan plans to use the net refinancing proceeds to fund the redemption (or the purchase, as the case may be) and hopes to avoid paying the prepayment fee. In your opinion, will Dan's ploy work? Suppose Ace had the foresight to include the extra language that follows the prepayment clause in the sample mortgage note, supra? Do you think this draftsmanship approach will work to protect Ace? If not, what additional protective language should be added? See Teachers Insurance and Annuity Assn. v. Butler, 626 F. Supp. 1229, 1235 (dictum) (S.D.N.Y. 1986) (excerpted at Chapter 5A3, supra). Returning to the facts in *Butler,* the court in that case had assumed that the default prepayment clause at issue was a boilerplate provision as opposed to an essential financing term worthy of serious negotiation between the lender and borrower. Based on the probable purpose of the provision, can you think of a better rationale for the result in the case? If sound draftsmanship will not work, can you think of any pre-foreclosure counterstrategy that Ace could employ to protect itself? See Ominsky, Locked-In Borrowers May Have Found a Hole in the Hen Coop, ACREL Newsletter, Feb. 1987, at 3; Stark, Enforcing Prepayment

Charges: Case Law and Drafting Suggestions, 22 Real Prop., Prob. & Tr. J. 549, 557, 559-560 (Fall 1987).

5. *The Status of Prepayment Charges Under Tax and Usury Law.* In general, a prepayment fee is deductible as a current expense. Rev. Rul. 57-198, 1957-1 C.B. 94. As for usury, the general rule is that prepayment charges are not deemed to be additional interest because they depend on a contingency within the control of the borrower and relate to the termination (as opposed to the making) of a loan. See discussion at Chapter 5B3, note 4, supra. Can you envision any circumstances in which the general rule might or should not apply?

6. *Participating Mortgages.* As suggested in the excerpt by Uri (at Chapter 5B3, supra), any prudent postconstruction lender that makes a participating loan (whereby it becomes entitled to contingent interest based on the borrower's gross or net income) will probably insist on a stringent "lock-in period" or prepayment charge. Why?

6. *Payment of Taxes and Insurance: Escrows*

Assume in the master hypothetical that Dan Developer's office building will be assessed for tax purposes at $18 million and that the real property tax rate is $1.50 per $1,000 of assessed value, or $270,000 annually. Assume further that the insurance premiums for casualty coverage equal $25,000 per year. Since unpaid real estate taxes will normally result in a lien superior to a first mortgage or deed of trust, and since unpaid insurance premiums could result in no coverage when the casualty occurs, Ace Insurance Company is naturally very concerned that taxes and insurance be paid when due. As a consequence, Ace insists that Dan pay one-twelfth of the annual taxes and premiums along with each monthly payment of debt service. Ace will determine the amount of such deposits based on its estimate of what will be necessary to have sufficient funds to make the payments when due. Ace or its loan servicing agent will keep the funds in an escrow account and make the payments directly to the taxing authorities and the insurance company. Ace does not intend to pay interest to Dan on the funds it is holding in escrow, whether or not Ace receives interest or other compensation (such as using the escrow as compensating balances for loans) from the bank in which the funds are deposited.

In large postconstruction loans in which the borrower has significant bargaining clout, the requirement for escrow payments may be waived; or, in the alternative, the lender may agree to remit the interest on the escrows to the borrower. However, postconstruction loan documentation usually requires escrow payments. Below is a typical commitment escrow provision.

Escrows:

The Mortgage shall provide that the Borrower will deposit on the first day of each month such amount as in the discretion of Lender will enable Lender or a depositary satisfactory to Lender to pay at least thirty (30) days before due, all taxes, assessments, insurance premiums, and similar charges affecting the Property and further provide that no interest on such deposits shall be paid to the Borrower by Lender or the depositary.

This commitment language is implemented in the following language from a mortgage.

5. TAXES AND OTHER CHARGES. Mortgagor shall pay all real estate taxes, water and sewer rents, fines, impositions, and other similar claims and liens assessed, or which may be assessed, against the Premises or any part thereof, without any deduction, defalcation or abatement, not later than ten (10) days before the dates on which such taxes, water and sewer rents, fines, impositions, claims and liens commence to bear interest or penalties, and not later than such dates shall produce to Mortgagee receipts for the payment thereof in full and shall pay every other tax, assessment, claim, fine, imposition, lien or encumbrance which may at any time be or become a lien upon the Premises prior to, or on a parity with, the lien of this Mortgage; provided, however, that if Mortgagor shall in good faith, and by proper legal action, contest any such taxes, assessments, fines, impositions, claims, liens, encumbrances, or other charges, or the validity thereof, and shall have established on its books or by deposit of cash with Mortgagee (as Mortgagee may elect) a reserve for the payment thereof in such amount as Mortgagee may require, then Mortgagor shall not be required to pay the same, or to produce such receipts, during the maintenance of said reserve and as long as such contest operates to prevent collections, and is maintained and prosecuted with diligence, and shall not have been terminated or discontinued adversely to Mortgagor. In addition to the foregoing, Mortgagor will pay when due and will not suffer to remain outstanding, any charges for utilities, whether public or private, with respect to the Premises.

6. ESCROW FUNDS. Without limiting the effect of Paragraph 5 hereof, at the request of Mortgagee, the Mortgagor shall pay to Mortgagee monthly at the time when the monthly installment of principal, interest or principal and interest is payable, an amount equal to 1/12th of the annual premium for such fire and extended coverage insurance, other hazard insurance and such annual real estate taxes, water rents, sewer rents, special assessments, and any other tax, assessment, claim, lien or encumbrance which may at any time be or become a lien upon the Premises prior to, or on a parity with, the lien of this Mortgage to enable Mortgagee to pay same at least thirty (30) days before they

become due, and on demand from time to time shall pay to Mortgagee additional sums necessary to pay such premiums and other payments, all as estimated by Mortgagee, the amounts so paid to be security for such premiums and other payments and to be used in payment thereof. No amounts so paid shall be deemed to be trust funds but may be commingled with general funds of Mortgagee, and no interest shall be payable thereon. If, pursuant to any provision of this Mortgage, the whole amount of said principal debt remaining or any installment of interest, principal or principal and interest becomes due and payable, Mortgagee shall have the right, at its election, to apply any amounts so held against all or any part of the indebtedness secured hereby, any interest thereon or in payment of the premiums or payments for which the amounts were deposited. . . .

The *Carpenter* case deals with the question of whether payment of interest on escrow deposits is required absent language in the loan documents mandating such payment by the mortgagee.

Carpenter v. Suffolk Franklin Savings Bank
370 Mass. 314, 346 N.E.2d 892 (1976)

BRAUCHER, Justice.
The Carpenters and the Kayes (the plaintiffs) are mortgagors of real property in Boston to the defendant Suffolk Franklin Savings Bank (Suffolk Franklin). They made payments to Suffolk Franklin, as mortgagee, on account of municipal real estate taxes, and seek an accounting of investment profits realized by Suffolk Franklin on the tax payments. In Carpenter v. Suffolk Franklin Sav. Bank, 362 Mass. 770, 291 N.E.2d 609 (1973) (*Carpenter I*), we held that a cause of action was stated. On remand, a judge of the Superior Court denied the plaintiffs' motions to certify the action as a class action and, after trial without a jury on liability issues only, made findings of fact and conclusions of law adverse to the plaintiffs' claims against Suffolk Franklin. On report pursuant to Mass. R. Civ. P. 64, 365 Mass. — (1974), we hold that there was no reversible error. . . . We summarize the judge's rulings on the issue of liability; we omit his findings as to undisclosed intentions and emphasize standard terms and practices. During the depression of the 1930's banks in Massachusetts lost large sums of money in mortgage foreclosures and often found that tax liens had priority over their mortgages. The practice developed of requiring payments of estimated taxes, and it has been the policy of Suffolk Franklin, in other than exceptional circumstances, to require all mortgagors to make such tax payments to it. The practice of Suffolk Franklin was in all respects in accord with the long-standing custom and practice of the savings bank

industry in Massachusetts. The principal purpose was to provide additional security for mortgage loans, relieving the bank of the risk of a municipal tax lien superior in right to the mortgage.

The plaintiffs' mortgages were "upon the statutory condition," including the condition that the mortgagor pay all taxes when due. G.L. c. 183, §20. Each note contained the same clause requiring payment to the holder each month of one-twelfth of the annual real estate taxes as estimated by the holder. This clause was contained in a printed note form used by the bank and supplied by it to the attorney representing it at mortgage closings. The attorney was not authorized to waive the requirement; mortgage loan officers were, if there was a favorable ratio between the loan and the value of the real estate. It was the bank's policy not to notify the mortgagor that the requirement could be waived.

The bank fully disclosed the nature and extent of the requirement and practiced no fraud or concealment, and the mortgage transactions were in all respects fair and reasonable in the circumstances. The requirement of real estate tax payments did not affect the rate of interest. The plaintiffs paid the bank with monthly checks, each check including the tax payment and the instalment of principal and interest, and the bank made tax payments to the city of Boston, usually in October, equal to or greater than the plaintiffs' tax payments. Monthly statements to the plaintiffs disclosed the amount of estimated tax payment required, designated "suspense" until 1966 and "escrow" thereafter; annual statements showed the accumulated amounts and the amount paid out.

The amounts of the tax payments were commingled with the bank's other funds and were available for investment; all or some were probably invested. The probable gross yield on each mortgage was $10 to $15 a year; the benefit to the bank was reduced by administrative expenses. The bank has not paid to the plaintiffs any of the return on such investment. The bank was paying something over four per cent on deposits, and sought to realize at least one per cent more from investments; and its net margin between return on investments and interest on deposits was in the vicinity of one per cent.

Both the Carpenters and the Kayes refinanced their mortgages, borrowing further amounts. In 1969 Kaye spoke to a bank employee about paying his taxes directly to the city, but the employee refused to act favorably on the suggestion. Otherwise none of the plaintiffs sought any alternative arrangements. . . .

a. *Express trusts.* The judge concluded that there was no manifestation of intention to create a trust on the part of either the plaintiffs or the bank. The written agreements were silent as to investment of the tax payments, as to the retention of earnings, if any, and as to intention to create a trust. The judge further concluded that the agreements established contractual relationships, not trusts, that the tax payments constituted general deposits for a special purpose, creating debtor-creditor relationships, rather than special deposits creating fiduciary relationships, and that the bank had the right to treat such payments as its own.

Borrowers, it is said, have brought hundreds of suits such as this one in the past several years, basing their claims on a variety of legal theories, including antitrust, truth in lending, fraud, unjust enrichment, breach of contract and breach of trust. See Notes, 54 B.U.L. Rev. 516, 517 (1974), 47 Temp. L.Q. 352 (1974), 28 Okla. L. Rev. 213 (1975). . . . In most of the reported cases the plaintiffs have been unsuccessful. . . .

As to residential mortgages in Massachusetts, the point is now settled by G.L. c. 183, §61, effective July 1, 1975, requiring the payment of interest. The statute does not establish a trust or other fiduciary relationship, nor does it support an obligation to account for the fruits of investment, apart from the payment of interest.

In these circumstances the judge's findings are not clearly erroneous within the meaning of Mass. R. Civ. P. 52(a), and his findings support his conclusions. A municipal lien for unpaid property taxes under G.L. c. 60, §37, takes priority over a mortgagee's interest. See Gaunt v. Arzoomanian, 313 Mass. 38, 39, 46 N.E.2d 520 (1943). Under G.L. c. 167, §58, the note or mortgage may require periodic payment of taxes, and amounts collected by a bank for payment of taxes may be invested in obligations legal for the bank; if the amount of the loan exceeds seventy per cent of the value of the real estate, G.L. c. 168, §35, par. 4, requires such payments. Nothing is said in the statutes or the written agreements of the parties as to interest on the payments or fruits of the investment. The general understanding and practice in Massachusetts and elsewhere over a period of some forty years has been that the bank has the right to treat the tax payments as its own. We think that a mortgagor who claims that he has made a different arrangement must show a clear understanding to that effect. See Restatement (Second) of Trusts §12, comment e (1959); 5 A. Scott, The Law of Trusts §530 (3d Ed. 1967). No such showing was made.

b. *Resulting and constructive trusts.* The judge ruled that neither the nature of the transaction between the plaintiffs and Suffolk Franklin nor their relationship now calls for the imposition of a resulting trust. We agree, substantially for the same reasons that we uphold his finding that there was no express trust. Cf. Meskell v. Meskell, 355 Mass. 148, 150-151, 243 N.E.2d 804 (1969); Restatement (Second) of Trusts, Introductory Note to c. 12 (1959).

The judge also ruled that there was no occasion for the imposition of a constructive trust. We are not asked to set aside his finding that there was no fraud, and we have held that there was no fiduciary relationship. See Kelly v. Kelly, 358 Mass. 154, 156, 260 N.E.2d 659 (1970). No doubt the contracts between the plaintiffs and the bank were "adhesion" contracts, but we are not prepared to hold that they were unconscionable in the aspects here in issue. See Lechmere Tire & Sales Co. v. Burwick, 360 Mass. 718, 720-721, 277 N.E.2d 503 (1972). Customers who adhere to standardized contractual terms ordinarily "understand that they are assenting to the terms not read or not understood, subject to such limitations as the law may impose." See Restatement (Second) of Contracts §237, comment b (Tent. Drafts Nos. 1-7, 1973).

The enrichment of the bank may have been unjust in some sense. Apparently the Legislature thought so when it enacted G.L. c. 183, §61, inserted by St. 1973, c. 299, §1, effective July 1, 1975. But most of the unjust enrichment, if any, enriched the bank's depositors at the time. The plaintiffs do not suggest that those depositors should now disgorge their excess returns. Thus a judgment of restitution would ultimately result in a transfer of funds from present and future depositors to compensate for excess payments to past depositors. Doubtless for this reason the Legislature enacted its reform with an effective date over two years after enactment. We do not think we should go further in disrupting legitimate expectations than the Legislature was willing to go.

Moreover, the statutory reform requires that interest be paid "at least once a year at a rate and in a manner to be determined by the mortgagee." We infer that the Legislature thought the amount of the banks' unjust enrichment would be very difficult to measure by any objective standards. We are not prepared to substitute our judgment on this point for that of the Legislature. In this aspect, this case is a good illustration of the advantages of legislative law reform as compared with reform by judicial decision. There was no such unjust enrichment, we hold, as to justify the imposition of a constructive trust.

4. *Disposition.*   We hold that there was no reversible error in the judge's orders, findings and conclusions of law reported to us. The case is remanded to the Superior Court for further proceedings consistent with this opinion.

NOTES AND QUESTIONS

In recent years there has been an increasing amount of class-action litigation by borrowers designed to compel lenders to pay interest on escrow accounts. The *Carpenter* case represents the clear majority view at the present time. Do you think the result in *Carpenter* would have been different if the escrow clause in the mortgage had provided that the funds be held "in trust"? See Brooks v. Valley National Bank, 113 Ariz. 169, 548 P.2d 1166 (1976).

1. *"Adhesion" Contracts.* Note what Judge Braucher said in *Carpenter* about the "adhesion" quality of the residential mortgage documentation and its relationship to payment of interest on escrow accounts. His rejection of the adhesion argument may take on greater significance in light of his background as a teacher of commercial law and one of the primary drafters of the 1956 major revision of the Uniform Commercial Code. Nevertheless, Judge Braucher's discussion of unjust enrichment arising from the adhesion nature of the mortgage leaves some questions open. In his opinion, Judge Braucher states that, if the banks were unjustly enriched, the unjust enrichment inured to the benefit of the bank's depositors. The plaintiff, he said, was not asking that the depositors disgorge their ill-gotten gains. Does this make sense? Would the interest rate paid to depositors have been lower if the bank had paid interest on the escrow accounts? Notwithstanding the fact that *Carpenter* represents the majority view, many institutions have expressed concern that either through legislation or case law the day of no-interest escrow accounts may be coming to an end and that therefore the issue is negotiable (depending on the bargaining clout of the borrower). See Note, Lender Accountability and the Problem of Noninterest-Bearing Mortgage Escrow Accounts, 54 B.U.L. Rev. 516 (1974); Comment, Payment of Interest on Mortgage Escrow Accounts: Judicial and Legislative Developments, 23 Syracuse L. Rev. 845 (1972); Note, Restitution — Savings and Loan Associations — Recovery by Home Mortgagors of Interest on Prepayments of Taxes and Insurance Premiums Held in Escrow Accounts on the Principle of Unjust Enrichment — Derenco, Inc. v. Benjamin Franklin Savings & Loan Assn., 281 Or. 533, 577 P.2d 477 (1978), 12 Creighton L. Rev. 697 (1978); Note, Tax and Insurance Escrow Accounts in Mortgages — The Attack Presses On, 41 Mo. L. Rev. 133 (1976). What can a lender do at the drafting stage to strengthen its position against attack?

2. *Deducting Property Taxes.* Except for construction-period taxes (which must be capitalized, as explained at Chapter 2B, note 5c), a cash-basis taxpayer may deduct property taxes in the year paid, whether or not the taxes are prepaid, so long as the taxpayer is actually liable for the taxes under local law. For taxpayers on the accrual method, the taxpayer may deduct the taxes at the end of the taxable year in which the liability becomes fixed and determinable, which is generally the lien date rather than the assessment date. I.R.C. §164(a); Keil Properties, Inc. v. Commissioner, 24 T.C. 1113 (1955) acq., 1956-2 C.B. 4; Rev. Rul. 73-64, 1973-1 C.B. 70; Rev. Rul. 56-145, 1956-1 C.B. 612. But see Prop. Treas. Reg. §1.461-4(g)(6) (for taxable years

beginning in 1990 deduction would be allowed only in year of payment, not in earlier taxable year when obligation accrued); see also Rev. Rul. 71-146, 1971-1 C.B. 63. In many jurisdictions the lien date precedes the payment date by several months; this might enable the taxpayer to accelerate the deduction where the payment is made in a subsequent taxable year. Alternatively, the taxpayer may elect to deduct the property taxes ratably over the period to which they relate. So, for example, a fiscal year taxpayer could take a deduction for one-half of the 1984 taxes and one-half of the 1985 taxes even though the 1985 taxes are not payable until the end of the calendar year. I.R.C. §461(c)(1).

As observed in this section, most postconstruction lenders require that the borrower pay monthly, along with the debt-service payment, a deposit of one-twelfth of the annual property taxes and insurance premiums as estimated by the lender or its servicing agent, so that sufficient escrow funds will be on hand to pay for such charges when they become due. The cash-basis borrower is entitled to a deduction only when payment is actually made by the lender to the local tax authorities. Rev. Rul. 78-103, 1978-1 C.B. 58.

In the case of co-ownership of real estate by means of a tenancy-in-common or joint tenancy, one of the co-owners can pay the entire property tax and claim the deduction. Powell v. Commissioner, 26 T.C.M. 161 (1967). Also, when real estate is sold during any property tax year, the property taxes must be apportioned between the purchaser and seller. I.R.C. §164(d).

For a discussion of other "soft dollar deductions," including leasing fees, prepaid rent, payments for a covenant not to compete, fees paid to conduct a marketing study, loan guarantee fees, "rent-up fees," fees for a guarantee against negative cash flow, interest on deferred obligations, deductions associated with the "reservation of an income interest technique," sales taxes, and investment advisory fees, see R. Haft and P. Fass, 1988 Investment Limited Partnerships Handbook §3.15 (1988). For a discussion of planning suggestions with respect to the deduction of local property taxes under I.R.C. §164, see generally G. Robinson, Federal Income Taxation of Real Estate ¶6.03 (1979); Madden, 480-2nd T.M., Taxation of Real Estate Transactions — An Overview §II.C.4.a (1988); M. Levine, Real Estate Transactions — Tax Planning and Consequences §222 (1988 ed.).

7. The Prohibition of Junior Financing

Returning to the master hypothetical, suppose that 12 years after the project is completed it is now worth $40 million and that amortization payments have scaled down the principal balance on the Ace mortgage from $25 million to approximately $20 million, so the present market value of the ownership interest, or "equity," in the project is about $20 million. Dan would like to translate some of this accumulated equity into tax-free cash so that he can expand or renovate the office building; alternatively, Dan (and his investors) simply want these funds for their own personal use. One option would be for Dan to refinance the Ace mortgage with a larger substitute first mortgage loan in the amount of $30 million (at the same 75 percent loan-to-value ratio). After paying the balance on Ace's loan, Dan would have net refinancing proceeds of about $10 million. Alternatively, Dan could obtain a second mortgage loan from a secondary lender in the amount of $10 million that would become junior in lien priority to the Ace mortgage, provided that the first mortgage note (held by Ace) does not contain a provision prohibiting such junior financing and providing Ace with the right to call in ("accelerate") the first mortgage indebtedness if the provision is violated. Such a provision is often referred to as a "due-on-encumbrance" clause. It is closely related to the "due-on-sale" clause discussed in Chapter 5B8, infra. Both clauses have been recently subject to judicial challenge. The following is a typical due-on-encumbrance clause from a postconstruction commitment letter.

Subordinate Financing.

. . . The Mortgage shall contain a provision prohibiting, except as hereinafter provided, any financing by the Borrower in addition to the Loan without the prior written consent of Lender, which financing is secured by either a mortgage lien or other encumbrance on the Improvements or Property (or any part thereof).

A far more limited due-on-encumbrance clause is set forth in the following mortgage provision.

SUBORDINATE FINANCING. Mortgagor covenants and agrees that it will not further encumber or mortgage the Premises, or any part thereof, or any interest therein and will not execute, deliver or take back any mortgage or mortgages, unless such mortgage or mortgages (hereinafter referred to as "Subordinate Mortgage") shall contain provisions to the effect that upon foreclosure of such Subordinate Mortgage: (i) no tenants under leases of space in the Premises will be made parties defendant nor will any other action be taken with respect to such tenants which would result in the termination of their leases or tenancies without the prior written consent of Mortgagee; and (ii) the rents, income, receipts, revenues, issues and profits issuing from the Premises, or from any lease of space therein, shall not be collected, except through a Receiver appointed by a court after notice of application for such appointment has been given to Mortgagee; the money collected by the Receiver shall be first applied and used for the payment of interest and principal due and owing under this Mortgage and the indebtedness secured hereby, real estate taxes, water rates, sewer rents, assessments or other governmental charges affecting the Premises and all other maintenance and operation charges and disbursements incurred in connection with the operation and maintenance of the Premises, and if during the pendency of any such mortgage foreclosure proceeding, action is instituted for the foreclosure of this Mortgage, and an application is made by Mortgagee for an extension of such Receivership for the benefit of Mortgagee, any and all funds collected by the Receiver prior to the date of such application shall be held by such Receiver and applied solely for the benefit of the Mortgagee hereunder and the holder of such Subordinate Mortgage shall not be entitled to any part thereof, unless and until there is a surplus remaining after all of the aforesaid payments and any other necessary payments; and (iii) immediate notice of the institution of such foreclosure proceeding shall be given to Mortgagee and true copies of all papers served or entered in such foreclosure proceeding shall be served upon Mortgagee.

An executed counterpart of each Subordinate Mortgage shall be delivered to Mortgagee by Mortgagor within ten (10) days after the execution and delivery thereof by Mortgagor.

Such Subordinate Mortgage shall contain an express covenant to the effect that it is in all respects subject and subordinate to this Mortgage and that the Mortgagee thereunder will upon demand further subordinate said Mortgage to the lien and terms, covenants and conditions of this Mortgage as hereinafter extended, renewed, modified or consolidated.

A "wraparound" mortgage is a form of junior financing (discussed at Chapter 9B, note 4) whereby the face amount of the secondary financing includes the outstanding balance of the first mortgage debt and the junior lender pays the debt service on the senior indebtedness directly to the first mortgagee. The following variation of the due-on-encumbrance clause in a mortgage might be called a "due-on-wrap" clause.

WRAP AROUND FINANCING. Mortgagor agrees that should the Premises at any time be or become subject to the lien of any mortgage or deed of trust in connection with which payments on account of the indebtedness secured hereby are to be made directly or indirectly by or through the mortgagee or beneficiary thereunder, regardless of such mortgagee or beneficiary, the whole of the principal and interest and other sums hereby secured, at the option of Mortgagee, shall immediately become due and payable.

The La Sala case, excerpted below, is illustrative of the type of judicial challenge that has been mounted against the due-on-encumbrance clause.

La Sala v. American Savings & Loan Assn.
5 Cal. 3d 864, 489 P.2d 1113, 97 Cal. Rptr. 849 (1971)

TOBRINER, Justice.

Plaintiffs Frank La Sala, Grace La Sala, and Dorothy Iford brought a class action against American Savings & Loan Association, (hereinafter "American") alleging that a provision in American's form of trust deed, which permits American to accelerate if the borrower executes a junior encumbrance on the secured property, constituted an invalid restraint upon alienation. American offered to waive enforcement of that provision as to Iford and the La Salas. The superior court then held that by reason of this waiver the named plaintiffs no longer represented the class, and dismissed the action. . . . [W]e hold that, although the clause in American's trust deed is not per se an illegal restraint upon alienation, the enforcement of that clause unlawfully restrains alienation whenever the borrower's execution of a junior encumbrance does not endanger the lender's security. We therefore reverse the judgment that dismisses the present action on behalf of the class, and remand to the superior court for further proceedings as set forth in this opinion.

1. STATEMENT OF FACTS.

In this appeal we assume as correct the allegations in plaintiffs' first amended complaint, and the declarations of Dorothy Iford, Frank La Sala, and Norman McLeod filed with the superior court, and base our statement of facts upon those allegations.

American utilizes a form deed of trust which contains, on the reverse side in fine print, a clause stating: "Should Trustor sell, convey, transfer, dispose of or further encumber said property, or any part thereof, or of any interest therein, or agree to do so without the written consent of Beneficiary being first obtained, then Beneficiary shall have the right, at its option, to declare all sums secured hereby forthwith due and payable." We shall refer to this clause as a "due-on-encumbrance" provision; we thereby distinguish it from clauses which provide for acceleration only upon the sale, but not upon the encumbering, of secured property.

On August 13, 1958, plaintiff Dorothy Iford and her late husband borrowed $9,500, at 6.6 percent interest, from American, and executed a promissory note and a trust deed which included the due-on-encumbrance provision. On November 20, 1963, Frank and Grace La Sala, the other named plaintiffs, borrowed $20,700 from American at 6 percent interest; they also executed a note and a trust deed with the due-on-encumbrance clause.

On June 9, 1969, the La Salas borrowed $3,800 from Fred D. Hudkins, and executed a note and second deed of trust; Statewide Home Mortgage Co. acted as loan broker. On June 11, 1969, Iford borrowed $2,500 from Edward and June Ulrich, and also gave a note and second trust deed; Lanco Mortgage Co. acted as broker. About July 7 of 1969 both Iford and La Salas received a form letter from American notifying them of American's right to accelerate. The letter to La Salas offered to waive American's right to accelerate in return for a payment of $150 and an increase in the rate of interest on the first deed of trust from 6 to 9 percent. The letter to Iford was identical in form, but asked a waiver fee of $50 and an increase in interest to 8.75 percent.

Plaintiffs then filed the present action for declaratory relief "for themselves and all other persons similarly situated." . . .

We conclude, however, that whether the enforcement of the due-on-encumbrance clause unlawfully restrains alienation turns upon whether such enforcement is reasonably necessary to protect the lender's security — an issue which cannot be resolved merely by examination of the pleadings and declarations now before us. . . .

Defendants argue that whenever a borrower takes out a second lien, his very conduct demonstrates that he has become financially irresponsible or at least a poor credit risk. Such an assertion, however, is an overgeneralization, a proposition true of some borrowers but not of others. Moreover, American does not claim a right to accelerate merely upon learning that the borrower has encountered economic adversity. In light of these considerations we find no justification in American's arbitrary seizure of the making of a second lien, a fact not necessarily indicative of declining credit ability, as a basis for acceleration.

We recognize, however, as defendants point out, that instances may occur when the institution of a second lien does endanger the security of the first lien. In some cases the giving of a possessory security interest, e.g., a conveyance to a mortgagee in possession, would pose the same dangers of waste and depreciation as would an outright sale. In other cases, a second lien may be employed as a guise to effect a sale of the property. In still others a bona fide second loan may still leave the borrower with little or no equity in the property.

We conclude, then, in instances in which the borrower's subsequent conduct endangers the lender's security, the enforcement of the due-on-encumbrance clause may be reasonably necessary to protect the lender's interests. In many other instances, however, the clause serves no such purpose. In fact, American itself recognizes that enforcement of such a provision cannot invariably be sustained as reasonably necessary to protect the primary security. When a borrower takes out a secondary loan American itself maintains that it does not elect automatically to accelerate, but examines the circumstances of the transaction. If its security is safe, American states that it then waives its right to accelerate, as it eventually did for both La Salas and Iford.

Yet defendants claim, in essence, that the lender should retain an *absolute* discretion to determine whether the transaction calls for enforcement of the due-on-encumbrance clause. Such an uncontrolled power, however, creates too serious a potential of abuse. Even when the lender's security has not been exposed to danger, the lender, by threatening to accelerate, could compel the borrower to pay a fee or give other valuable consideration for the waiver. The Attorney General, as amicus curiae, charges that as a matter of practice American requires waiver fees whenever a borrower makes a junior encumbrance. Defendants deny this charge yet seek from us a declaration that a lender enjoys an unconditional right to enforce the due-on-encumbrance clause and, as a necessary corolary the unconditional right to obtain from a borrower whatever consideration it can exact for the waiver, however inequitable such exaction may be. . . .

The judgment of the superior court dismissing the action on behalf of the class is reversed, and the cause remanded to that court for further proceedings in accord with the views expressed in this opinion.

NOTES AND QUESTIONS

1. *The Borrower's Perspective.* Why is the right to obtain junior financing on the property so important to a borrower such as Dan Developer, who is locked into a long-term postconstruction loan?

2. *The Lender's Perspective.* The difference between the due-on-encumbrance clause in the commitment and the mortgage is illustrative of the historic ambivalence lenders have displayed toward secondary financing. In the past, most postconstruction lenders were not concerned about subsequent junior financing and some even welcomed such subordinate financing. Since foreclosure of the first mortgage could extinguish any junior lien, the junior lender was likely to cure any defaults of the borrower under the first mortgage and treat such outlays on behalf of the borrower as additional indebtedness under the second mortgage.

The junior lender will normally require a "cross default" clause in its mortgage, under which a default by the borrower on the first mortgage is automatically deemed to be a default under the second, thus enabling the junior lender, as a last resort, to seek recoupment of these additional expenditures by foreclosing its own mortgage. Thus, subordinate financing was viewed by the postconstruction lender as added assurance that its senior indebtedness would be paid.

In recent years, however, many lenders have begun to limit or prohibit junior financing, for a wide variety of reasons. For example, some lenders are concerned about the borrower's overburdening the property with financing that could cause the economic collapse of a project that would otherwise remain viable. If the borrower were to use all the income from the property for debt service, unexpected expenses could result in deferred maintenance and tenant dissatisfaction, eventually converting a good loan in the senior lender's portfolio into a problem one. Other senior lenders might be concerned that the borrower might not be receiving sufficient income from the property to keep him interested in the project. Most large borrower-developers have numerous concurrent projects that are bound to impose competing demands on their time and expertise. Senior lenders want to make sure that the borrower will feel it is worthwhile to devote the necessary attention to the project to make it a success.

Some lenders like the fact that the equity cushion is increasing behind their secured first position. Since in an economic downturn a borrower would be more reluctant to abandon the project if there is equity in the property, the equity tends to serve as additional security that the loan will be repaid. Others are wary of allowing junior financing because the junior mortgagee represents an additional party who might complicate any foreclosure or bankruptcy proceeding. For example, in most states a junior lender must be joined in as party defendant in a foreclosure action by the senior mortgagee. Also, the presence of a junior lender may prevent the senior lender from avoiding foreclosure by convincing the borrower to transfer the property voluntarily to the senior lender by means of a "deed in lieu of foreclosure." See Chapter 9B, note 3 and Chapter 10A, note 3. Also, if a junior lender is in the picture, it may interfere with the senior lender's control over any fire insurance or condemnation award proceeds or prevent changes in the first mortgage (e.g., loan amount) without its consent. In addition, if the junior lender is in bankruptcy, the senior lender may be prevented ("stayed") from foreclosing its own mortgage. See discussion at §11B1.

Finally, some lenders fear that if the property becomes subject to junior liens in respect to which the developer assumes personal liability, and the property becomes financially troubled, the developer might first seek to satisfy these junior creditors, who can sue him personally, rather than keep the first mortgage current. If you were Ace's lending officer, what position would you take if Dan Developer wanted to delete the due-on-encumbrance clause? If you would insist on retaining the clause, which of the foregoing reasons would be most significant in your determination? If you were counsel trying to achieve agreement, are there any compromise solutions you might suggest that might be reasonably acceptable to both the borrower and the senior lender?

3. *Wraparound Financing.* Wraparound financing is a form of junior financing whereby the wraparound lender agrees to advance funds in excess of first mortgage indebtedness and (by agreement of the parties) to repay the first mortgage indebtedness pursuant to its terms. However, the face amount of the wraparound loan includes or "wraps around" the existing indebtedness. Therefore, because of leverage provided by the low interest rate on the existing first mortgage, the wraparound lender can achieve an above-market yield on the funds it actually disburses and can afford to charge the borrower a below-market rate on the net amount of such loan advances. Why might a first mortgagee insist that a "due-on-wrap" clause be included in its mortgage?

4. *Federal Legislation.* The Garn-St. Germain Depository Institutions Act is examined at Chapter 5B8, note 2, infra. There was concern that this legislation could be read as invalidating due-on-encumbrance clauses. See Pub. L. No. 97-320, §341, 96 Stat. 1469, 1505-1507 (1982) (codified as amended at 12 U.S.C. §1701j-3 (1988)). Pursuant to the Act's mandate to the Federal Home Loan Bank Board, the Board promulgated regulations that restricted the Act's limitations on the exercise of due-on-encumbrance clauses to loans on the security of homes occupied or to be occupied by the borrower. 12 C.F.R. §91.5 (1984). The extent of the Act's limitations on due-on-encumbrance clauses and the effectiveness of the Federal Home Loan Bank Board's regulation are discussed at Chapter 5B8, infra.

5. *Questions.* The *La Sala* case held that a senior mortgagee can enforce a due-on-encumbrance clause only when such enforcement is reasonably necessary to protect the senior lender's security interest. What examples does the court cite? Can you think of any others?

An oft-cited danger to lenders' security is that a foreclosing junior mortgagee could terminate subordinate occupancy leases and thereby threaten the rental income stream on which the lender relies as primary security for its loan. See the discussion at Chapter 4C2. How do lenders address this problem in the mortgage provision set forth above? Do you think this approach will work?

8. The Right to Sell Mortgaged Property

Most postconstruction lenders will insist on a clause in the mortgage note providing them with the right to accelerate the first mortgage indebtedness if the mortgagor should sell the mortgaged property without first obtaining their consent. In lieu of acceleration, the lender may be willing to accept a provision that would permit a sale but require the purchaser to assume the existing mortgage at the current rate of interest or require that the seller-mortgagor pay a substantial prepayment or "pay down" of principal when the property is sold.

Developers are, of course, opposed to such a constraint, which could make it more difficult to sell the property if interest rates should rise and the purchaser is precluded from assuming the existing mortgage at the lower interest rate. Nevertheless, these provisions, often referred to as "due-on-sale" clauses, have traditionally been required by lenders when the developer's management expertise and credit reputation have been relied on in the decision to make the loan.

Today, due-on-sale clauses are being used by postconstruction lenders as a hedge against inflation on their fixed-rate loans. In the case of relatively long-term loans, most developer-owners will sell their properties before their loans mature; therefore due-on-sale clauses are being used by lenders during inflationary periods to obtain interest-rate adjustments when these properties are sold. Since postconstruction lenders (especially commercial banks and thrift organizations) typically borrow funds on a short-term basis (as reflected by their short-term liability structure) and lend money on a long-term basis, due-on-sale clauses enable these lenders to replace their long-term, low-yield loans with loans at current, higher interest rates. By doing so they can ameliorate the negative impact on their income when short-term rates rise, and they are in a better position to hold the line on rates charged to their borrowers on new loans. Like its companion, the due-on-encumbrance clause, the due-on-sale clause has been the subject of a protracted struggle in the courts between borrowers contending that these clauses constitute illegal restraints on alienation and lenders, who have regarded these clauses as vital protection against impairment of their security interests as mortgagees and their major source of economic protection against inflation and volatility in interest rates. Finally, in the aftermath of a favorable decision for lenders by the United States Supreme Court (prompted by a conflict between federal and state law), the issue was at last resolved by Congress, which enacted an all-inclusive statute, the Garn-St. Germain Act, that was designed to validate due-on-sale clauses, with very few exceptions.

The following is an example of a commitment provision requiring a due-on-sale clause in the mortgage note that would provide the lender with the right to accelerate, or call in, the loan if the borrower should sell the property.

> The Note and Mortgage shall contain clauses providing that in the event the Borrower conveys, transfers or assigns the property, or any part

thereof, or any interest therein, such transfer shall be deemed an "Event of Default" under which the whole of the principal sum remaining unpaid, together with all accrued interest thereon, may at the option of the mortgagee become immediately due and payable and may be recovered at once by foreclosure or otherwise.

The pay-down approach is illustrated by the following commitment provision.

The Note and Mortgage shall contain clauses in form, scope and substance satisfactory to Lender's Law Department, providing that in the event (i) Borrower conveys, transfers, assigns or sells the Property, or any part thereof, or interest therein, or (ii) any partner of Borrower transfers, sells or otherwise disposes of his or her interest, or any part thereof in the Partnership, then in any or all such events, Lender shall have the right, at its option, to declare an amount equal to 25% of the outstanding principal balance of the Loan to be immediately due and payable, where-upon it shall be so due and payable. Such prepayment shall be without prepayment fee and shall be applied to the reduction of the Loan in the inverse order of maturity of the required payments of principal. The Note and Mortgage shall contain such other provisions as Lender's Law Department deems necessary to monitor and enforce the provisions of this Article.

The following language was added in the master hypothetical at the behest of the borrower:

A transfer by Dan Developer of 100% of the outstanding common stock in Borrower to a trust or other entity acceptable to Lender for the benefit of the immediate family of Dan Developer shall not constitute a transfer for the purposes of this section so long as (i) Lender is furnished with evidence, satisfactory to Lender, that said trust or other entity is solely for the benefit of the immediate family of Dan Developer and that there are no other beneficiaries of said trust or other entity, and that Dan Developer shall continue to manage or control the management and operation of the Premises after such transfer. For purposes of this section, the term "immediate family" is defined solely as the wife and/or children of Dan Developer. A transfer by will or intestacy of the ownership interest of Dan Developer shall not constitute a transfer for the purposes of this section. . . .

The Garn-St. Germain Depository Institutions Act (Garn-St. Germain), enacted by Congress in 1982, contains the following provision:

Pub. L. No. 97-320, §341, 96 Stat. 1469, 1505-1507 (1982)
(codified as amended at 12 U.S.C. §1701j-3(b)(1)-(2) (1988))

DUE-ON-SALE CLAUSES

Sec. 341.(a) For the purpose of this section —

(1) the term "due-on-sale clause" means a contract provision which authorizes a lender, at its option, to declare due and payable sums secured by the lender's security instrument if all or any part of the property, or an interest therein, securing the real property loan is sold or transferred without the lender's prior written consent;

(2) the term "lender" means a person or government agency making a real property loan or any assignee or transferee, in whole or in part, of such a person or agency;

(3) the term "real property loan" means a loan, mortgage, advance, or credit sale secured by a lien on real property, the stock allocated to a dwelling unit in a cooperative housing corporation. . . .

(d) A lender may not exercise its option pursuant to a due-on-sale clause upon —

(1) the creation of a lien or other encumbrance subordinate to the lender's security instrument which does not relate to a transfer of rights of occupancy in the property. . . .

NOTES AND QUESTIONS

1. *The Debate Between Borrowers and Lenders.* The majority and traditional view prior to the enactment of the Garn-St. Germain Act had been that such clauses constituted neither direct nor unreasonable restraints on alienation. For example, after reviewing the Restatement of Property §404 (1944), the Nebraska Supreme Court, in Occidental Savings & Loan Assn. v. Venco Partnership, 206 Neb. 469, 293 N.W.2d 843 (1980), concluded that a due-on-sale clause does not itself constrain the conveyance of title but merely causes debt acceleration; accordingly, the restraint, if any, attaches to the mortgage rather than to the conveyance. In other words, the predicament confronting a borrower wishing to sell is not caused by the due-on-sale clause. Rather, it is caused by the borrower's inability to prepay the mortgage. See Baker v. Loves Park Savings and Loan Assn., 61 Ill. 2d 119, 333 N.E.2d 1 (1975) ("reasonableness" standard rejected on the notion that more certainty is necessary where land titles are involved); Mutual Real Estate Investment Trust v. Buffalo Savings Bank, 90 Misc. 2d 675, 395 N.Y.S.2d 583 (1977) (lender's refusal to consent to a sale involving a financially responsible purchaser was not, per se, an unconscionable or inequitable exercise of the lender's unrestricted right to accelerate the loan indebtedness); Volkmer, The Application of the Restraints on

Alienation Doctrine to Real Property Security Interests, 59 Iowa L. Rev. 747, 774 (1973). By contrast, prior to Garn-St. Germain other courts followed the approach enunciated in the *La Sala* case (excerpted at Chapter 5B7, supra) by striking down due-on-sale clauses except where the sale threatened the legitimate security interest of the lender. For example, in Clark v. Lachenmeier, 237 So. 2d 583 (Fla. Dist. Ct. App. 1970), a Florida appellate court refused to allow a mortgagee to foreclose based on an uncontested sale where, in the opinion of the court, no harm actually resulted to the mortgagee as a consequence of the conveyance. In Baltimore Life Insurance Co. v. Harn, 15 Ariz. App. 78, 486 P.2d 190 (Ct. App. 1971), petition denied, 108 Ariz. 192, 494 P.2d 1322 (Ct. App. 1972), an Arizona court likewise held that the lender must show that the security would be impaired by the sale. See also Dawn Investment Co. v. Superior Court, 30 Cal. 3d 695, 639 P.2d 974, 180 Cal. Rptr. 332 (1982).

In addition, prior to Garn-St. Germain, most courts had sanctioned the use of these clauses by lenders to maintain their mortgage loan portfolios at current interest levels during periods of inflation and increasing interest rates. See, e.g., Century Federal Savings & Loan Assn. v. Van Glahn, 144 N.J. Super. 48, 364 A.2d 558 (Ch. Div. 1976). Meanwhile, other courts had taken the position that lenders could not use these clauses merely to protect their economic position. For example, in Wellenkamp v. Bank of America, 21 Cal. 3d 943, 582 P.2d 970 (1978), the court observed that "lenders take into account their projections of future economic conditions in setting interest rates for long-term loans, and that when the projections prove to be inaccurate, it would be unfair to place the burden of the mistaken projections on property owners exercising their right to freely alienate property." 21 Cal. 3d, at 952-953. Also, see Patton v. First Federal Savings & Loan Assn., 118 Ariz. 473, 578 P.2d 152 (1978). See generally Annot., 61 A.L.R.4th 1070 (1988). See also Dunn and Nowinski, Enforcement of Due-on-Transfer Clauses, An Update, 16 Real Prop., Prob. & Tr. J. 291 (1981).

The principal rationale for striking down due-on-sale clauses is that they represent an unreasonable restraint on alienation. Lenders have argued that due-on-sale clauses do not constrain the borrower's right to sell the property. Rather, they claim that such clauses merely prevent the borrower from increasing profit at the expense of the lender. Consider the argument that when interest rates and land values are inflated, the sale of real property may produce a profit for the owner, for two principal reasons. First, the owner may realize a benefit from appreciation in the value of the real estate. Varying our master hypothetical somewhat, assume that Dan Developer purchases land with a completed building on it for $10 million, free and clear of any mortgage, and because of inflation in land values Dan is later able to sell the property for $15 million. He obviously has realized a profit of $5 million, or a 50 percent return on his equity investment (exclusive of transactional costs and income tax consequences). Second, Dan may benefit from the reduced value of a mortgage or deed of trust on the property caused by rising interest rates. Suppose Dan had obtained a $7.5 million mortgage loan from Ace at the current market rate of interest when he purchased the property. The purchase price, then, would have been funded by only $2.5 million of Dan's own money and $7.5 million from Ace. Under the mortgage, Ace would receive a steady stream of income. As observed at Chapter 5B1, note 2, supra, in an inflationary market characterized by rising interest rates the mortgage will be repaid with less valuable dollars. Increased interest rates will also produce higher capitalization rates, which, when applied to the steady stream of income Ace receives, will reduce the value of Ace's mortgage even as Ace's capital and overhead costs are increasing. Stated differently, no one would be willing to buy Ace's mortgage for the amount of the remaining principal balance if the interest rate on the mortgage were below the market rate. Ace could sell the mortgage only at a discount.

Conversely, Dan Developer could sell his property at a higher price because it would be subject to a mortgage at below-market rates. Let us assume that Dan could sell the property for $18 million (subject to the favorable mortgage) instead of $15 million if the mortgage were paid off. Assuming the mortgage balance is still $7.5 million, Dan's profit or equity would now be $8 million instead of $5 million, or 80 percent on the original purchase price (which represents a 320 percent return on Dan's original cash investment). From Ace's point of view, that extra $3 million profit comes out of its own pocket and the pockets of its other borrowers.

If the due-on-sale clause were enforceable, the property would sell for $15 million rather than $18 million. Of the $15 million purchase price, $7.5 million would go to Ace to pay off the mortgage, leaving Dan with $7.5 million, which would still allow him to realize a profit of $5 million, or a 200 percent rate of return on his original cash investment. Consequently, the purpose of the due-on-sale clause from Ace's standpoint is not to prevent Dan from alienating his property or realizing on the appreciation in its value but rather to prevent Dan from realizing on the depreciated value of Ace's property, namely, its mortgage loan to Dan. Can you think of the counterargument on behalf of borrowers such as Dan Developer? See discussion of the income method for valuing real estate and capitalization rates at Chapter 5B1, note 2, supra. Can you think of a compromise draftsmanship approach that would address the economic concerns of both parties? See Western Life Insurance Co. v. McPherson, Civ. A. No. 87-1389 (D. Ka., Dec. 29, 1988).

In addition, lenders such as Ace have contended that a due-on-sale clause is necessary to prevent a purchaser from assuming (without Ace's consent) an existing loan that was made partially in reliance on Dan's credit reputation and management expertise. In this regard, can you think of a limited version of a due-on-sale clause that should be reasonably acceptable to both Dan and Ace? Suppose Ace agrees to nonrecourse financing because the borrower is a limited partnership (see tax discussion at Chapter 2B, note 7(d)(iii). How would this change the negotiating positions of the parties with respect to the need for a due-on-sale clause?

2. *Garn-St. Germain.* This statute was not the first federal preemption in this area. Under the Homeowner's Loan Act of 1933, the Federal Home Loan Bank Board was empowered to issue regulations with respect to federal savings and loan associations. On May 3, 1976, the Board promulgated a regulation that authorized federal savings and loan associations to employ due-on-sale clauses in their mortgage loan documents (current version at 12 C.F.R. §545.6-11(f) (1989). In Fidelity Federal Savings & Loan Assn. v. De La Cuesta, 458 U.S. 141 (1982), the United States Supreme Court held that this regulation permitting the exercise of due-on-sale provisions by federally chartered savings and loan associations barred the application of contrary state laws or judicial decisions. In light of the disintermediation problem experienced by the thrift industry during the 1979-1981 era of inflation within the savings and loan industry, can you explain the federal government's position in support of due-on-sale clauses? See S. Rep. 97-536, 97th Cong., 2d Sess., 1982 U.S. Code Cong. & Admin. News 3056; Blocher, Due on Sale in the Secondary Mortgage Market, 31 Cath. U.L. Rev. 49 (1981); Dunn and Nowinski, Enforcement of Due on Transfer Clauses: An Update, 16 Real Prop., Prob. & Tr. J. 291 (1981); Henkel and Kilworth, Federal Preemption of State Due-on-Sale Clause Restrictions: Jurisdictional Considerations, 47 Mo. L. Rev. 225 (1982); Lockyer, *De La Cuesta:* Federal Determination of Contract and Property Rights?, 14 Pac. L.J. 1 (1982).

There are a number of exceptions contained in the statute. One of the most perplexing exclusions is subsection (d)(1), which prohibits the exercise of due-on-sale clauses where the property is encumbered by junior financing. This has been construed by many to prevent enforcement of due-on-encumbrance clauses. Do you agree that it does? See S. Rep. 97-536, 97th Cong., 2d Sess. 24-25, 1982 U.S. Code Cong. & Admin. News 3056, 3078-3079.

3. *The Pay-Down Approach.* Would Garn-St. Germain validate a clause requiring a pay-down of the note on sale? Under the language in the sample mortgage provision exerpted above, the borrower has

the right to prepay the entire remaining indebtedness in lieu of the stated amount of the pay-down. Observe that the prepayment fee does not apply to the pay-down. Does it apply to the borrower's election in that provision to prepay the full remaining balance? If so, why?

   4. The "Double Whammy" Question: Can a Lender Enforce Both a Prepayment Charge and a Due-on-Sale Clause? As a general prop- osition, when the mortgage instruments contain both a prepayment clause and a valid due-on-sale clause, a question arises as to whether the lender should be able to enforce both provisions simultaneously. Specifically, absent relevant language in the prepayment clause, if a lender elects to accelerate the indebtedness in the event of an unau- thorized sale, could the borrower contend that the lender is not entitled to a prepayment fee because the acceleration payment should not be treated as a prepayment? See the *LHD Realty Corp.* decision, excerpted supra at Chapter 5B5. Also see Slevin Container Corp. v. Provident Federal Savings & Loan Assn., 98 Ill. App. 3d 646, 424 N.E.2d 939 (1981); McCausland v. Bankers Life Insurance Co., 110 Wash. 2d 716, 757 P.2d 941, 946-947 (Wash. 1988); America Federal Savings & Loan Assn. v. Mid-America Service Corp., 329 N.W.2d 124 (S.D. 1983). If so, would express language in the prepayment clause authorizing such fee be enforceable or vulnerable to challenge as an illegal restraint on alienation? Compare Tan v. California Federal Savings & Loan Assn., 140 Cal. App. 3d 800, 189 Cal. Rptr. 775 (4th Dist. 1983) (see dictum at 810) and Pacific Trust Co. TTEE v. Fidelity Federal Savings & Loan Assn., 184 Cal. App. 3d 817, 229 Cal. Rptr. 269 (6th Dist. 1986), with Metropolitan Savings & Loan Assn. v. Nabours, 652 S.W.2d 820, 822 (Tex. Civ. App. 1983). Would such a clause be vulnerable as an unenforceable penalty? See the *Lazzareschi* decision excerpted supra at Chapter 5B5. See generally Stark, Enforcing Prepayment Charges: Case Law and Drafting Suggestions, 22 Real Prop., Prob. & Tr. J. 549, 555-559 (Fall 1987).
   Observe that in the mortgage pay-down provision, the lender is protected if the borrower should elect to transfer the beneficial own- ership of the mortgaged real estate to a member of the borrower's immediate family. As a general proposition, should a lender be able to invoke a due-on-sale clause where the borrower is a corporation or partnership in respect to which the majority share of ownership is sold to an outsider without the consent of the lender? See Fidelity Trust Co. v. BVD Assocs., 492 A.2d 180 (Conn. 1985); Standard Operations, Inc. v. Montague, 758 S.W.2d 442 (Mo. 1988). Can you think of some compromise language that would allow such a restructuring of the borrowing entity without unduly threatening the security interest of the lender?

9. Compliance with Land Use Regulations and Environmental Law

In the master hypothetical, when Ace Insurance Company enters into a loan commitment with Dan Developer it is relying on the fact that if Dan defaults on the loan, it can look to the land and building as security for Dan's obligation. However, if the building is constructed or used in contravention of local zoning ordinances, or if environmental statutes, flood plain regulations, and other legal requirements applicable to the project are not met, the security could be substantially reduced in value, if not rendered worthless. For this reason, a postconstruction lender will normally condition its commitment to fund the loan on receiving satisfactory evidence that all building codes, zoning restrictions, and other regulatory requirements have been satisfied.

Asking for assurance of compliance is the easy part. The difficult task for the lender is to determine what laws are applicable and what evidence is sufficient to give the lender reasonable assurance that the various requirements of law have been met. In this section, we will be exploring some of these difficulties.

The following is a typical commitment provision requiring proof of compliance with law.

> For the purpose of this Commitment, the construction of the Improvements shall be deemed to have been completed when ready for occupancy and fully equipped for proper operation of the facility as approved by Lender's Architect and when Certificates of Occupancy permitting space which is to be occupied to be legally occupied and all other proper certificates by Federal, state or local agencies or departments or any other governmental authorities having or claiming to have jurisdiction over the construction or occupancy, have been delivered to Lender.

In addition, the loan commitment will often require that, prior to closing, the lender receive an opinion from borrower's counsel (or occasionally from lender's counsel or a specialist in environmental protection or zoning) that applicable laws and regulations have been satisfied. Also, if available, title insurance against zoning violations may be required. As we shall see, these assurances are not always sufficiently comprehensive to allay the concerns of lender's counsel.

The above-quoted commitment provision requires the delivery of a "certificate of occupancy" (C.O.) to the lender. The C.O. is a statement by the local governing authorities that both the construction and intended use of the premises conform with local zoning laws. Lenders and borrowers often place great reliance on the fact that a C.O. has been issued. Consider whether such reliance is justified as you read the *S. B. Garage* case, which follows.

S. B. Garage Corp. v. Murdock
185 Misc. 55, 55 N.Y.S.2d 456 (Sup. Ct. 1945)

SMITH, Justice.

The petitioner and intervenor, as owner and mortgagee in interest, respectively, in a parcel of real property, bring this proceeding to review a determination made by the Board of Standards and Appeals in the City of New York whereby it revoked a certificate of occupancy, issued on June 1, 1921, for a public garage located on premises in the Borough of Brooklyn which are described variously as 287-305 McKibben Street, 69-85 White Street, and 298-302 Boerum Street. Upon this motion the respondent Board seeks an order dismissing the proceeding and confirming its revocation of the said certificate of occupancy.

The premises in question consist of a one-story building which was erected in 1921 as a garage for more than five motor vehicles. The building is located in an unrestricted use district and fronts on three adjoining city streets. The original application and plans which were filed with the Building and Fire Departments for a permit to erect the said garage indicated that it was to extend on the northerly side of McKibben Street between Bushwick Avenue and White Street for a distance of 200 feet from the northwest corner of McKibben and White Streets, with entrances and exits on McKibben Street. At the time when such application and plans were filed, and when the permit and the certificate of occupancy were thereafter issued, Public School No. 147 was (and still is) situated on the southerly side of McKibben Street between Bushwick Avenue and White Street, with an entrance and exit on McKibben Street, the distance between the two buildings at their nearest points of proximity being slightly in excess of 600 feet.

At the time when the permit and the subsequent certificate of occupancy were issued the pertinent Building Zone Resolution, Section 20, as amended June, 1919, read as follows: "No garage for more than five cars may be erected or extended and no building not now used as a garage for more than five cars may have its use changed to a garage for more than five cars on any portion of a street between two intersecting streets, in which portion there exists an exit from or an entrance to a public school; or in which portion there exists any hospital maintained as a charitable institution; and in no case within a distance of 200 feet from the nearest exit from or entrance to a public school; nor within two hundred feet of any hospital maintained as a charitable institution. This protection shall also apply to duly organized schools for children under 16 years of age, giving regular instruction at least five days a week for eight months or more each year, owned and operated by any established religious body or educational corporation. This limitation on the location of garages shall apply to unrestricted as well as business and residence districts; but in no case shall it apply to cases where applications for the erection or extension of garages or the conversion of existing buildings into garages may be pending before the Board of Appeals at the time of the adoption of this resolution." . . .

On January 6, 1941, after the continuous and uninterrupted use of the said property as a public garage for a period approximately twenty years, the Commissioner of the Department of Investigation of the City of New York, acting on behalf of the latter, brought on a proceeding to procure the revocation of the certificate of occupancy on the ground that it had been issued in contravention of the above-mentioned provision of the Zoning Resolution. His contention was sustained by the Board of Standards and Appeals. This proceeding to review that determination was then brought on.

Upon the hearing before the Board, evidence was adduced to disclose the following: In connection with the filing of the application in 1921 for the construction of the garage, there were filed certain plans for the proposed improvement including a diagram of the block plan. The area on McKibben Street, immediately opposite the site of the proposed garage, was marked "Park." Respondent contends that the plan, as submitted, gave the impression that the park extended for the entire length of McKibben Street, from White Street to Bushwick Avenue, although as matter of fact Public School No. 147 was located at the Bushwick Avenue end of the same block, the school having an entrance on the McKibben Street side. The diagram omitted that portion of McKibben Street which included the school as well as a substantial area immediately adjoining the same. The Commissioner of Investigation contends that the submission of a diagram of such character constituted misrepresentation on the part of the applicant. A specific finding upon that issue is unnecessary herein. Suffice it to say that it does not appear that the applicant was ever asked to submit any plot plan for the entire length of McKibben Street between the intersections of Bushwick Avenue and White Street.

Apparently on the strength of the above-indicated diagram the application for the permit was approved and following construction of the garage the certificate of occupancy was issued.

In my opinion, it is manifest beyond cavil that the issuance of the permit and the certificate of occupancy was in direct contravention of the above-mentioned provision of the Zoning Resolution. The provision is couched in such specific terms that it permits of not the slightest obscurity. The provision was intended to proscribe the construction of a garage on any part of a street between two common intersections, where there was on such street an entrance to or an exit from a public school. That specific proscription was in no way limited or lessened by the additional safeguard whereby a garage was not to be erected in any event within 200 feet from the nearest entrance to or exit from a public school. Clearly, the latter clause was included for the purpose of imposing a minimum distance between a garage and the nearest entrance or exit of a public school where they were not located on the same street. . . .

Necessarily, the right to a continuance of the building for garage purposes depends solely upon the question whether the permit and the certificate of occupancy, in the first instance, satisfied all legal prerequisites. "No building permit by an administrative official could condone, or afford immunity for, a violation of law." Marcus v. Village of Mamaroneck, 283 N.Y. 325, 330, 28 N.E.2d 856, 859. . . .

The doctrine of law adhered to in cases such as City of Buffalo v. Chadeayne, 134 N.Y. 163, 31 N.E. 443, is unavailing under the circumstances of the present situation. In that case the owner of a building was granted a permit to build in conformity with a resolution of the Common Council. Having acted upon such conforming permit, the owner thereby acquired a vested right therein. Here, however, the permit and the certificate of occupancy were issued, as stated by the Court of Appeals in Matter of Kaltenbach v. Board of Standards and Appeals, 274 N.Y. 34, at page 38, 8 N.E.2d 267, 268, "in disregard of the Zone Resolution, and . . . should, therefore, [be] revoked."

It is claimed by the petitioning owner that prior to its acquisition of title to the premises in 1939, its counsel ascertained that (1) a certificate of occupancy had been issued in 1921 for the building as a public garage; (2) that there were no violations of record; (3) that real estate taxes upon the premises had been received by the City of New York for eighteen years; (4) that the Fire Department of the City of New York had continuously issued gasoline and storage garage permits for the entire period since the construction of the building.

In addition thereto, it is claimed by the intervening trustee that its purchaser, prior to purchasing a mortgage interest in the premises in 1927, wrote letters to the Superintendent of Buildings and the Fire Commissioner, respectively, to obtain information as to any violations then pending, and was advised by each that none existed.

The foregoing circumstances, however, may not be seized upon as constituting a species of estoppel preclusive upon the right of the municipality to revoke the unlawfully issued certificate of occupancy. The promulgation of zoning ordinances constitutes a governmental function. See Premium Bond Corp. v. City of Long Beach, 249 App. Div. 756, 291 N.Y.S. 834. A municipality may not be held equitably estopped by the original misfeasant or malfeasant act of its officers or agents in having issued a permit contrary to the plain mandate of a zoning provision. . . .

I fully sympathize with the plight of the present owner and of the trustee representing the holders of participating shares in the consolidated bond and mortgage. In good faith they have invested their moneys in the property upon reliance on the lawful issuance of the certificate of occupancy. Unfortunately, they are unable to invoke any protective ordinance or statute such as is found in the Multiple Dwelling Law. Significantly, Section 301 thereof provides that whenever a bona fide purchaser has "relied upon such certificate, no claim that such building had not, prior to the issuance of such certificate, conformed in all respects to the provisions of this chapter shall be made against such person or against the interest of such person in a multiple dwelling to which such a certificate applies or concerning which such a statement has been issued." See also, Matter of Edwards v. Murdock, 283 N.Y. 529, 29 N.E.2d 74.

The apparent harshness of the result here reached, however, may well be alleviated by the adoption of a procedure in conformity with the suggestion offered by counsel to the respondent board in its brief upon this motion. In the concluding portion of said brief it is stated: "The Board of Standards and Appeals was justified in revoking the certificate of occupancy because the law prohibited the erection of a garage at the location in question. The only agency authorized to grant permission for such use is the Board of Standards and Appeals. An application should therefore be made to the said Board to maintain the said garage." . . .

Respondents' application for an order dismissing the proceeding and confirming the revocation of the certificate granted.

The following is the standard zoning endorsement to title policies, approved by the American Land Title Association and the California Land Title Association.

INDORSEMENT

Attached to Policy No. _____

Issued by _____

BLANK TITLE INSURANCE COMPANY

The Company hereby insures that, as of Date of Policy:

(a) According to applicable zoning ordinances and amendments thereto, the land is classified Zone _____ .

(b) The following use or uses are allowed under said classification subject to compliance with any conditions, restrictions or requirements contained in said zoning ordinances and amendments thereto, including but not limited to the securing of necessary consents or authorizations as a prerequisite to such use or uses:

There shall be no liability under this indorsement based on the invalidity of said ordinances and amendments thereto until after a final decree of a court of competent jurisdiction adjudicating such invalidity, the effect of which is to prohibit such use or uses.

Loss or damage as to the matters insured against by this indorsement shall not include loss or damage sustained or incurred by reason of the refusal of any person to purchase, lease or lend money on the estate or interest covered hereby in the land described in Schedule A.

This indorsement is made a part of the policy and is subject to all the terms and provisions thereof and of any prior indorsements thereto. Except to the extent expressly stated, it neither modifies any of the terms and provisions of the policy and prior indorsements, if any, nor does it extend the effective date of the policy and prior indorsements or increase the face amount thereof.

The following is a sample of the type of certificate Ace might require from the borrower's design architect, certifying compliance with law.

CERTIFICATE OF ARCHITECT

Reference is made to that certain proposed $25,000,000 loan from Ace Insurance Company (hereinafter referred to as "Lender") to Dan Developer (hereinafter referred to as "Borrower") concerning the real property described on Exhibit A attached hereto (hereinafter referred to as the "Property") and improvements constructed thereon (hereinafter referred to as the "Improvements.")

To induce Lender to advance the aforesaid proposed loan, I, Anne Architect, hereby certify to Lender that:

1. I am the design architect in connection with the construction of the Improvements.
2. The plans and specifications described on Exhibit B attached hereto were prepared by me and are in compliance with all applicable laws, building codes, ordinances, rules, regulations, and governmental authorities including, without limitation, environmental and zoning requirements.
3. To the best of my knowledge, after due inquiry, the Improvements constructed on the Property have been completed and are in full compliance with the plans and specifications described on Exhibit B and such Improvements as completed and their use as an office building and parking garage are in full compliance with all applicable laws, building codes, ordinances, rules, regulations and restrictions of local, state and national governmental authorities including, without limitation, environmental and zoning requirements. No zoning or subdivision approvals relating to the Property or the Improvements cover any real property or rights appurtenant thereto other than the Property.

_____

Anne Architect
Date:

_____

Recent disclosures of hazardous wastes and dumping activities, as well as the potential for future spills of hazardous materials and future disclosures of environmental hazards that must be cleaned up or removed, have caused increasing concern in both Congress and state legislatures that public health and safety and the environment may be seriously threatened. In response to this concern, Congress enacted the Comprehensive Environmental Response, Compensation, and Liability Act of 1980 (CERCLA), and in addition legislation has been enacted in some states, and is pending in many others, authorizing governmental authorities to clean up hazardous wastes and to impose a "super lien" on the real property for the cost of the cleanup. Lender liability under CERCLA is separately covered at Chapter 12B. This is the major environmental concern in real estate development today. However, as discussed below at note 6, there are additional environmental statutes and regulations that affect real estate development.

NOTES AND QUESTIONS

1. *The Certificate of Occupancy.* The *S. B. Garage* case is illustrative of the fact that a C.O. is not necessarily assurance that the construction and intended use of the improvements comply with applicable zoning and subdivision ordinances and building codes. In some jurisdictions, a C.O. means only that the holder can occupy the premises at the time it is issued, and it is subject to cancellation or revocation when zoning regulations or building codes are changed. See 82 Am. Jr. 2d, Zoning and Planning, §§237-241 (1976 & Supp. 1985). Even where a C.O. means that the improvements comply with zoning and building codes and other requirements of law, it may be subject to revocation if invalidly issued. The frightening aspect of the *S. B. Garage* case is that the revocation took place 20 years after the issuance of the certificate. In some jurisdictions ameliorative statutes have been enacted to protect good-faith purchasers. See, e.g., N.Y. Mult. Dwell. L. §§301-305 (McKinney 1974 & Supp. 1991) and N.Y. Mult. Resid. L. §§302-305 (McKinney 1974 & Supp. 1991), under which a certificate of occupancy would not be revocable against a good-faith purchaser of the multiple dwelling or a mortgagee thereof, even if the C.O. were issued invalidly. In light of the foregoing, what is the purpose of a lender's requiring the delivery of a certificate of occupancy at closing?

In the more recent Parkview Assocs. v. City of New York, 71 N.Y.2d 274, 525 N.Y.S.2d 176, 519 N.E.2d 1372 (1988), the New York Court of Appeals held that estoppel was not available to preclude New York City from requiring a developer to remove 12 stories of an almost completed building because of a violation of height restrictions, notwithstanding that the building was constructed pursuant to a building permit issued by the city and that the zoning map prepared by the city was at best ambiguous as to whether the building met the height restrictions. The court held that the developer was charged with the language of the zoning ordinance and could not rely on the building permit or the zoning map. The tone of the opinion, however, may indicate that the court did not consider the developer wholly innocent; if so, this may have had an effect on the holding.

In the case of existing improvements, can you think of any additional language in the inspection clause of the contract of sale that might be insisted on by the purchaser's attorney to protect the purchaser against a zoning problem? See Chapter 3A, note 1b.

2. *Zoning and Police Power.* A comprehensive examination of zoning law is beyond the scope of this book. The following overview is intended to illustrate the state of flux of the law and to sensitize you to the problems and concerns of lenders and developers as the law evolves.

State and local government, of course, have the duty to protect the health and safety of the public. The exercise of this "police power" includes the right to control the use, height, bulk, aesthetics, and location of real estate by means of zoning and subdivision regulations.

However, in Village of Euclid v. Ambler Realty Co., 272 U.S. 365 (1926), Justice Sutherland observed that in the zoning area "the line which . . . separates the legitimate from the illegitimate assumption of power is not capable of precise delimitation" and that a "zoning ordinance, which would be clearly valid as applied to the great cities, might be clearly invalid as applied to rural communities." Nevertheless, he held that a comprehensive zoning plan, even one that "excludes from residential districts, apartment houses, business houses, retail stores and shops" is not unconstitutional unless clearly arbitrary and unreasonable with no substantial relation to the public health, safety, morals, or general welfare. Of course, not all zoning ordinances pass such constitutional scrutiny. The courts will often weigh the extent of the invasion of property rights and economic harm caused by the regulation against the benefit that the land use restriction provides to the community as a whole. For example, in Nectow v. City of Cambridge, 277 U.S. 183 (1928), Justice Sutherland, again writing for the majority, struck down Cambridge residential zoning as it applied to a particular property where no practical use could have been made of the land for residential purposes and the residential designation of that property was not necessary for the general welfare of that part of the city.

Nevertheless, as a result of the *Euclid* decision, the so-called Euclidian model of zoning proliferated throughout the country as public planners failed to heed the following warning expressed by the trial court (whose opinion had been overruled): "[I]n the last analysis, the result to be accomplished is to classify the population and segregate them according to their income or situation in life." Ambler Realty Co. v. Village of Euclid, 279 F. 307, 316 (N.D. Ohio 1924). Eventually, the public policy assumption underlying Euclidean zoning — that homogeneity of land uses is desirable — was challenged by social critics who suggested that the system was being used as a device to promote classism and social segregation. See, e.g., Williams, Planning Law and Democratic Living, 20 Law & Contemp. Probs. 317 (1955).

Of major concern to real estate developers are those statutes that limit growth under the rubric of zoning by postponing development through moratoria or time zoning ordinances. For example, in Golden v. Planning Bd. of Ramapo, 30 N.Y.2d 359, 285 N.E.2d 291, 344 N.Y.S.2d 138, app. dismissed sub nom. Rockland County Bldrs. Assn. v. McAlevey, 409 U.S. 1003 (1972), an ordinance was approved that restricted development to areas where the village had made necessary capital improvements under an 18-year development plan, thereby providing the municipality with the authority effectively to exclude development through nonconstruction of facilities.

Given the legality of most "Euclidian" zoning ordinances, what would happen if, after Dan Developer constructs his office building and Ace Insurance Company makes its loan, the town of McNiece should enact a comprehensive zoning ordinance restricting the area in which Dan's building is located to single-family residences? Your response would probably be that Dan's use may continue as a "nonconforming" use, and in most cases you would be correct. However, zoning is not the only means by which governmental officials may block what they deem to be "undesirable" uses. For example, in Hempstead, New York, when a zoning ordinance imposed against the defendant to prevent excavation failed because it was a prior nonconforming use, the local government successfully enacted an ordinance, upheld by the Supreme Court, regulating dredging and pit excavation, and thus completely prohibited the beneficial use to which the property had been primarily put. Goldblatt v. Town of Hempstead, 369 U.S. 590 (1962). Yet there is a limit to the valid exercise of such police power. What if a zoning ordinance is consciously used to exclude or to segregate groups of people according to income levels or type of housing (for example, mobile homes or rooming houses) instead of by type of use? This sort of "exclusionary" zoning has been challenged on the ground that it precludes the construction of affordable housing and thus does not promote the general welfare.

For example, the New Jersey Supreme Court, in South Burlington City NAACP v. Township of Mount Laurel, 67 N.J. 151, 336 A.2d 713, appeal dismissed and cert. denied, 423 U.S. 808 (1975), held that "a developing municipality like Mount Laurel may [not] validly, by a system of land use regulation, make it physically and economically impossible to provide low and moderate income housing in the municipality for the various categories of persons who need and want it and thereby . . . exclude such people from living within its confines. . . ." The Court required that such a municipality by its land use regulations "make realistically possible an appropriate variety and choice of housing." See also the court's clarification of the meaning and scope of this opinion in NAACP v. Township of Mount Laurel, 92 N.J. 158, 456 A.2d 390 (1983).

In _Euclid_, the Supreme Court approved a _comprehensive_ zoning plan. Such a plan is quite different from the process known as "spot zoning," defined by Judge Fuld in Rodgers v. Tarrytown, 302 N.Y. 115, 96 N.E.2d 731 (1951), as "the process of singling out a small parcel of land for a use classification totally different from that of the surrounding area, for the benefit of the owner of such property and to the detriment of other owners." While specific hardships are sometimes ameliorated through variances granted by zoning boards that affect specific property, spot zoning generally has not been permitted. See, e.g., Citizens Assn. of Georgetown v. District of Columbia Zoning Commn., 402 A.2d 36 (D.C. App. 1979); Schneider v. Calabrese, 5 Pa. Commw. 444,

291 A.2d 326 (1972); Furtney v. Simsbury Zoning Commn., 159 Conn. 585, 271 A.2d 319 (1970), which state the general rule that a provision in a zoning plan or classification will be struck down as illegal spot zoning if it affects an individual piece of property or adjoining properties and is unrelated to the general plan for the community as a whole.

Also of concern to developers and lenders is the lack of time constraints on a determination that use of the mortgaged property may be unlawful because of spot zoning. See, for example, French v. Zoning Board, 408 Pa. 479, 184 A.2d 791 (1962), where the zoning of a parcel as an A-Commercial district was set aside as spot zoning after 28 years, when the nonconforming residential use was discontinued. Can a lender do anything to protect itself against the possibility of zoning being set aside in this way? For an extensive discussion of spot zoning see 2 A. Rathkopf and D. Rathkopf, The Law of Zoning & Planning, §§28.01 to 28.05 (4th ed. 1986) and R. Anderson, American Law of Zoning, §§5.12 to 5.22 (3d ed. 1986).

3. *Reading List on Land Use Regulation.* Salsich, Section of Real Prop., Prob. and Tr. L., Property Rights Under the Constitution: Are There Any Left? (August 9, 1987); R. Epstein, Takings: Private Property and the Power of Eminent Domain (1985); Alterman, Evaluating Linkage and Beyond: Letting the Windfall Recapture the Genie Out of the Exactions Bottle, 34 Wash. U.J. Urb. & Contemp. L. 3 (1988); Bauman, The Supreme Court, Inverse Condemnation and the Fifth Amendment: Justice Brennan Confronts the Inevitable in Land Use Controls, 15 Rutgers L.J. 15 (1983); Bosselman and Stroud, Mandatory Tithes: The Legality of Land Development Linkage, 9 Nova L.J. 381 (1985); Bozung and McRoberts, Land Use Planning and Zoning in 1987: A National Survey, 19 Urb. Law. 899 (1987); Costonis, Presumptive and Per Se Takings: A Decisional Model for the Taking Issue, 58 N.Y.U.L. Rev. 465 (1983); Delaney and Smith, Development Exactions: Winners and Losers, 17 Real Est. L.J. 195 (1989); Epstein, An Outline of Takings, 41 U. Miami L. Rev. 12 (1986); Heyman and Gilhool, The Constitutionality of Imposing Increased Community Costs on New Suburban Residents Through Subdivision Exactions, 73 Yale L.J. 1119 (1964); Michaelman, Property, Utility and Fairness: Comments on the Ethical Foundations of Just Compensation Law, 80 Harv. L. Rev. 1164 (1967); Palmer, Environmentally Based Land Use Planning & Regulations, 2 Pace Envl. L. Rev. 25 (1984); Payne, Housing Rights and Remedies: A "Legislative" History of *Mount Laurel II*, 19 Seaton Hall L. Rev. 889 (1984); Reynolds, The Reasonableness of Amortization Periods for Non-Conforming Uses — Balancing the Private Interest and the Public Welfare, 34 Wash. U.J. Urb. & Contemp. L. 99 (1988); Reynolds, Self Induced Hardship in Zoning Variances: Does a Purchaser Have No One but Himself to Blame?, 20 Urb. Law. 1 (1988); Rice, Re-Evaluating the Balance Between Zoning Regulations and Religious

and Educational Uses, 8 Pace L. Rev. 1 (1988); Salsich, Keystone
Bituminous Coal, First English and Nollan: A Framework for Accom-
modation? 34 Wash. U.J. Urb. & Contemp. L. 173 (1988); Wegner,
Moving Towards the Bargain Table: Contract Zoning, Development
Agreements and the Theoretical Foundation for Government Land Use
Seals, 65 N.C.L. Rev. 957 (1987); Comment, Searching for a Standard
for Regulation Takings Based on Investment-Backed Expectations: A
Survey of State Court Decisions in the Vested Rights and Zoning
Estoppel Areas, 36 Emory L.J. 1219 (1987); Annot., Validity and
Construction of Zoning Ordinance Requiring Developer to Devote
Specified Part of Development to Low and Moderate Income Housing,
62 A.L.R.3d 880 (1975); Symposium: Land-Use, Zoning & Linkage
Requirements Affecting the Pace of Urban Growth, 20 Urb. Law. 515
(1988); and Symposium: Exactions: A Controversial New Source for
Municipal Funds, 50 Law & Contemp. Probs. (Winter, 1987).

   4. *The Architect's Certificate.*   Notwithstanding their limited value,
certificates of occupancy are universally requested by lenders in those
jurisdictions that issue them. Whether or not a certificate of occupancy
is obtained, lenders will normally look to the architects for assurance
that the construction is in compliance with law. The design architect
is considered responsible for such compliance, and plans and specifications should be accompanied by a certificate from the design architect
to that effect. Architects are not anxious to subject themselves to personal
liability if they can avoid it. This means that the developer must be
careful in negotiating the terms of construction contracts and architectural agreements to provide for such certifications.
   Even if the design architect is willing to certify that the plans
and specifications met legal requirements when drawn, the lender will
need further assurance to the effect that the improvements were built
in accordance with such plans and that there have been no changes in
building codes or zoning ordinances (or no such changes pending) that
would affect the legality of the improvements. This is easier to request
than to receive. The design architect actually may not know if the
building was in fact constructed in accordance with the plans or whether
the law has changed since the plans were drawn. Observe that in the
certificate of the design architect excerpted above, the architect certifies
that the construction complies with plans and specifications "to the
best of our knowledge after due inquiry." This represents a compromise.
If you represented Ace Insurance Company in the master hypothetical,
would this be acceptable to you? If you represented Anne Architect,
what steps would you advise her to take to protect herself under the
certificate? Review the certificate and consider if there are areas of risk
for the lender not covered by the certificate. What is the probable
purpose of the last sentence of the certificate?
   In order to be certain that the construction is in fact in accordance

with plans and specifications, the lender will need an inspecting architect. The validity of such a certification will depend on the amount of time the architect spends at the site, and this will depend on the amount of money the architect is being paid to inspect. Even if the inspecting architect is on duty at the site full time, minor changes may still be made surreptitiously. Thus, a cautious architect will certify only that the construction *substantially* complies with the plans and specifications.

5. *Title Insurance.*   The lender will normally obtain a title policy insuring that the mortgage or deed of trust is a first lien on the premises subject only to the exceptions specifically set forth in Schedule B, as well as certain other exclusions and printed exceptions. See discussion at Chapter 3B2, note 4. Standard provisions in title policies except from their coverage violations of zoning laws. However, a title policy endorsement covering zoning is obtainable in many states at a substantially increased premium. The approved form of zoning "indorsement" of the American Land Title Association (the title industry trade association) is quoted above. Reread that language and, based on the facts in the master hypothetical, decide whether the title company would be subjected to liability pursuant to its standard zoning endorsement under the following circumstances:

   a. Unbeknownst to Ace, Dan Developer obtained his certificate of occupancy by bribing a local official. The certificate is revoked after the postconstruction loan is closed.

   b. The applicable zoning ordinance permits office buildings not in excess of 17 stories. Dan's building is 20 stories.

   c. Some years after the postconstruction loan is closed, Ace forecloses its mortgage and, as the new owner, contracts to sell the building for $40 million. The mortgage balance was $22 million at the time of foreclosure. Ace's sale falls through when a zoning defect is discovered.

   d. Ace committed to make the mortgage loan at 10 percent interest. At the closing date the market rate had risen to 12 percent. Ace refuses to close the loan because it has discovered a zoning defect. Dan then files a claim with the title company pursuant to a zoning endorsement in his fee title policy.

   e. A zoning defect is discovered, and Dan, as owner of the property, makes a claim under the zoning "indorsement" in his fee title policy. The title company does not agree with the adverse determination of the zoning board. It tells Dan that he, not the title company, must challenge the determination and that the title company will not make any payment until there is a final adjudication by the highest appellate court in the state where the property is located.

6. *Environmental Restrictions.* Environmental constraints may present even greater problems than zoning. Most real estate lawyers are ill-equipped to render opinions on this specialized area of the law, and title companies, exhibiting their traditional reluctance to enter new problem areas, maintain that it is not a proper subject for title insurance protection. As with zoning and building codes, the design architect should be responsible for preparing plans and specifications that conform to environmental law requirements. Where there is enough money involved, it might be advisable for the developer or the lender to engage an environmental "expert" as a consultant.

In response to the burgeoning number of environmental law restrictions on real estate development, many postconstruction lenders are now incorporating more specific language in their commitment letters to the effect that "the borrower must furnish copies of permits and other satisfactory evidence that the Land and the Improvements, and their use comply with all applicable environmental restrictions imposed by federal, state, and local law." A comprehensive examination of environmental law is beyond the scope of this book; however, the following examples are designed to illustrate the degree to which this body of regulatory law has had an impact on real estate development.

a. The National Environmental Policy Act of 1969, 42 U.S.C. §4321 et seq. (1990), mandates the preparation of an environmental impact statement (EIS) by the appropriate federal governmental agency with respect to any "major federal action" that would significantly affect the quality of the human environment. An example of such action was the funding of a federally subsidized $3.5 million loan for the construction of a small high-rise apartment building in an area containing no such projects. San Francisco Tomorrow v. Romney, 472 F.2d 1021 (9th Cir. 1973). In most instances, a time-consuming and expensive backup study will be required of the private land developer before the governmental agency will issue its own EIS.

b. Under the federal Clean Air Act, 42 U.S.C. §7401 et seq. (1990), all new "major sources" of air pollution require state-administered preconstruction permits and, as a consequence, shopping center and office building projects can be disapproved under the notion that parking facilities attract automobiles and thus a large parking lot may be indirectly responsible for causing air pollution. See, e.g., New York City Air Pollution Control Code, N.Y.C. Admin. Code tit. 24, §24-101 et seq. (1986 & Supp. 1988). By contrast, such projects can be disapproved under local zoning ordinances because of inadequate parking facilities.

c. Water pollution control permits are generally required under the Federal Clean Water Act, 33 U.S.C. §1251 et seq. (1990), with respect to the discharge of any pollutants into navigable waters, which may even include run-off from rainstorms. Under the Act, permits may be denied to industrial- and commercial-use facilities based on certain chemical and ecological standards.

d. In a number of states, notably California and New York, coastal zone management statutes give state agencies far more land-use control over real estate development in designated coastal areas than is exercised by local zoning authorities.

Lender liability under CERCLA is discussed separately at Chapter 12B.

10. Assignment of the Commitment

In deciding whether to commit their loanable funds, postconstruction lenders rely heavily on the reputation and expertise, or track record, of the borrower. This is why a lender is normally unwilling to permit the prospective borrower to assign the commitment to anyone else (other than the construction lender) without the lender's consent. In fact, lenders are so steadfast on this point that, in most cases, they will not even accept, by way of compromise, the qualification that such consent shall not be "unreasonably withheld."

A typical commitment provision prohibiting assignment might read as follows:

> Neither this commitment nor the Loan proceeds shall be assignable without the prior written consent of Lender, and without such consent there shall be no right to designate a payee of such Loan proceeds. Any attempt at assignment without such consent shall be void. It is understood, however, that consent will not be withheld to assignment of the commitment to a bank or other financial institution for the purpose of obtaining interim financing.

Garfinkel, The Negotiation of Construction and Permanent Loan Commitments (Part 2)
25 Prac. Law. 37, 43-44 (April 15, 1979)

TRANSFER OF PERMANENT COMMITMENT

A permanent commitment normally will be issued on the basis not only of the facility being built but also the developer who is responsible. On occasion, a permanent commitment will even stipulate that the developer must manage the project for a specified period of time, often for 5 years after the permanent loan closing. Thus, the assignment of the permanent commitment is usually prohibited and often a specified entity is required to own the project at the time of settlement on the permanent commitment.

A construction lender will be extremely circumspect as to any limitations in the permanent commitment upon the transferability of the commitment, the underlying real estate, or the owning entities, since it seeks to fund the commitment with the permanent loan even if it or its nominee takes over the project following a default by the developer. The construction lender will therefore require that the commitment be assignable to it. It will also generally require that in the event of a default, it be permitted to reassign the commitment to any party to whom the real estate is transferable. The permanent lender will generally resist any such right and, in fact, will seek to include "no adverse change" clauses and condition its obligation to close on the permanent loan upon the absence of default on the construction loan.

If the assignment clause permits an assignment to the construction lender but not a reassignment by the construction lender, then in the event the developer fails to complete construction, the construction lender will be forced to complete the project itself so as to be able to transfer its loan to the permanent lender. Its decision may be academic since, in the event of a developer default, the time required for the construction lender to exercise its remedies and complete the project will usually exceed the period within which the permanent commitment must be delivered. In most construction-phase project workouts, the developer remains involved in some manner, while the construction lender controls all expenditures and advances the funds to complete the project. As a practical matter, in default situations the construction lender often has to renegotiate the permanent commitment — if it is fortunate enough to have a prospective permanent lender who continues to be interested in the project.

NOTES AND QUESTIONS

Observe that in the sample commitment provision excerpted above the postconstruction lender agrees to permit an assignment of its commitment to an interim lender such as a construction lender. Such assignments are often permitted. Referring to the master hypothetical, if Dan should default under the terms of the construction loan and the construction lender, FNB, faces the specter of being forced to foreclose its mortgage before the construction is completed, why would FNB want to be able to take an assignment of Ace's postconstruction loan commitment to Dan? While not agreeing to such an assignment, some postconstruction lenders will agree to make a loan to the construction lender on terms similar to the postconstruction loan terms if the construction lender should become the new owner of the mortgaged property by virtue of a foreclosure of the construction loan.

11. Timely Completion of Improvements in Accordance with Approved Plans and Specifications

Obviously, the postconstruction lender will require that the improvements serving as security for the loan be of sound construction. If the building is poorly designed or if the materials and workmanship are shoddy, the real security for the loan, namely, the future rental income stream, may be impaired, the landlord's covenants in the leases to make repairs are more likely to be breached, tenants are more likely to leave (without liability if there has been a "constructive eviction"), and the mortgaged property would be rendered less marketable in the event of a foreclosure sale.

Since commitments for postconstruction loans are usually executed 18 to 36 months before the loans are funded, the lender must employ sound money management techniques to ensure that the requisite loanable funds will be available on the closing date. Therefore, the postconstruction lender will also insist that the construction commence promptly and that the building be completed within a designated period of time prior to the scheduled closing date for the loan. This also reduces the borrower's temptation to "shop around" for another loan with better terms from some other lender. For example, in the master hypothetical, Ace Insurance Company, as a condition precedent to funding the postconstruction loan, might require that: (i) the plans and specification be submitted to and approved by Ace and its architect; (ii) construction be commenced in accordance with the approved plans and specifications on or before a specified date; (iii) the building be fully completed at least 6 weeks prior to the scheduled closing date and, except where written approval is given by Ace, be built in accordance with the previously approved plans and specifications; and (iv) the transaction be closed, once the conditions of the commitment are met, on or before the scheduled closing date.

The following is typical language from a postconstruction loan commitment letter that purports to impose the foregoing requirements. As you read the provisions that follow, ask yourself whether the language accomplishes its objective.

Plans and Specifications:

Detailed plans and specifications for all Improvements must be submitted to Lender's architect (hereinafter referred to as "the Architect") and must meet with the Architect's written approval. Such plans and specifications shall include, but shall not be limited to, architectural, structural, mechanical, electrical, site, landscaping and sprinkler and other fire and safety control plans and specifications. In addition, complete curtain wall drawings and specifications must be submitted for review and approval by a curtain wall consultant to be retained by the Architect at the expense of the Borrower and such drawings and specifications must meet with such consultant's written approval. Whenever the Architect's requirements exceed the requirements of local codes, the Architect's requirements shall govern. Upon completion of the Improvements, Lender shall be furnished with a complete set of "as built" plans and specifications.

Construction and Inspections:

The construction of the Improvements (including any grading, landscaping and any other on-site or off-site work) shall be in accordance with the plans and specifications as approved in writing by the Architect. The Architect and representatives of the Architect shall have the right to inspect all such Improvements periodically during and after construction.

Completion of Construction:

The construction shall be completed within a reasonable period of time prior to the scheduled closing date, in accordance with the plans and specifications approved by the Architect, and the final construction must be approved in writing by the Architect as being in conformity with such plans and specifications. No review, approval, disapproval or acquiescence by Lender or the Architect during the course of construction or otherwise, shall constitute a waiver of any term, provision or condition of this Commitment, including, but not limited to, the requirements concerning completion of construction, nor give rise to any liability on Lender's part with respect to the matter reviewed, approved, disapproved or acquiesced in. . . .

Time of Disbursement of the Loan:

If the Loan does not close on or before the scheduled closing date, for any reason other than Lender's willful default, Lender's obligation hereunder shall cease, and Lender shall have all the rights and remedies provided for in this Commitment, unless prior thereto, Lender, having the sole option to do so, extends the Commitment by notice to Borrower in writing.

Commencement of Construction:

At Lender's option, this Commitment may be terminated unless actual construction is started within one hundred twenty days after the date of acceptance by Borrower of this commitment and is continuously and diligently pursued thereafter.

Purchase or Disbursement Date:

Notwithstanding anything to the contrary contained in this Commitment, Lender shall be under no obligation to disburse or acquire the Loan prior to the scheduled closing date of this loan. However, if at any time during the term of this Commitment and in the sole judgment of Lender, the Property has been sufficiently completed and otherwise complies with the terms of this Commitment, Lender may, in its sole discretion, by notice to Borrower, disburse or acquire the Loan within sixty days after such notice. Notwithstanding anything in this Commitment to the contrary, Lender shall have no obligation to disburse or acquire the Loan before sixty days after the completion of the Improvements, unless Lender, in its sole discretion, elects otherwise.

The following case illustrates the disagreements that might arise over the rather ambiguous phrase "completion of the improvements," as employed in the sample commitment provision.

Whalen v. Ford Motor Credit Co.
475 F. Supp. 537 (D. Md. 1979)

MEMORANDUM AND ORDER

BLAIR, District Judge.

This is an action arising out of the issuance of a loan commitment for a condominium project in Towson, Maryland. The plaintiffs are the owners, Towson Associates Limited Partnership and its general partner, Cornelius Whalen, and the general contractor for the project, Robert Whalen Co., Inc. The defendant is Ford Motor Credit Company (Ford Credit). In substance, the plaintiffs allege that Ford Credit breached its contractual obligations under the loan commitment by refusing to provide without justification the required funding when due. . . . Ford Credit has moved for summary judgment, contending that plaintiffs have no standing to bring this cause of action and that the financing commitment expired by its terms when the condition precedent that the building be completed was not satisfied. The plaintiffs have also moved for summary judgment on the ground that Ford Credit was bound to honor the commitment when the required architect's certificate of completion was issued. . . .

I. FACTUAL BACKGROUND

Towson Associates developed a condominium project in Towson, Maryland known as the "Towson Center." The project is a 28-story building containing approximately 240 units. Ford Credit issued a commitment in February 1973 to Towson Associates to lend it $9,750,000 for a period of two years after completion of the project. During this two-year period, Towson Associates planned on completing the sale of condominium units to the public. In exchange for the commitment, Towson Associates paid Ford Credit $195,000 and also obligated itself to pay a release fee of 1% upon the sale of each unit. Under the terms of the commitment, Ford Credit was required to advance the funds as long as the building was completed by the expiration date, March 1, 1975. Pursuant to an amendment to the commitment, the expiration date was extended to September 1, 1975 in consideration of an additional fee of $48,750 which was paid by Towson Associates to Ford Credit.

In May 1973, Equibank, a national banking association, issued a construction commitment to Towson Associates, also in the amount of $9,750,000, to provide funds for the construction of the project. On August 28, 1973, the construction loan closing was held. At that time, Towson Associates, with Ford Credit's approval, assigned to Equibank the Ford Credit commitment; this was done to provide Equibank with additional security for the construction loan it had made to Towson Associates. Also on August 28, 1973, Ford Credit issued a letter which has been referred to by the parties as a buy-sell agreement. Under the terms of this agreement, Ford Credit agreed to purchase from Equibank the loan in the maximum amount of $9,750,000 provided that the construction loan documents were assigned to Ford Credit and that Towson Associates complied with all the terms of the Ford Credit commitment, including completion of construction by September 1, 1975. In short, Equibank financed the construction of the project, and Ford Credit agreed to provide the financing thereafter by purchasing the loan from Equibank if certain conditions were met.

On September 2, 1975, when the parties intended to close the purchase by Ford Credit of Equibank's loan to Towson Associates, Equibank tendered to Ford Credit the documents required under the buy-sell agreement and asked Ford Credit to provide the funding in accordance with its commitment and the buy-sell agreement. Ford Credit, however, inspected the building and determined that it was incomplete. It therefore took the position that the condition precedent to funding, completion of the building, was not satisfied, and it did not advance the $9,750,000. . . .

One of the conditions of the Ford Credit commitment was that the building "shall be completed in accordance with plans and specifications." The expiration date of the commitment, as extended by amendment, was September 1, 1975. While the extent to which the building was completed has been hotly contested, the parties do agree that the building was not fully completed by that date. Ford Credit argues that the commitment required that construction of the building be 100% complete by the expiration date, and that substantial performance could not satisfy the condition precedent of completion, citing Della Ratta, Inc. v. American Better Community Developers, Inc., 38 Md. App. 119, 380 A.2d 627, 638 (1977). The court disagrees and holds that substantial completion of the building by the expiration date was sufficient to trigger the obligation to fund.

Ford Credit submits that *Della Ratta* holds that a condition precedent must be exactly fulfilled and that the doctrine of substantial performance does not apply to express conditions precedent. The Court of Special Appeals in *Della Ratta* stated:

> The substantial performance doctrine, therefore, applies to constructive conditions precedent and not to express conditions. Under certain circumstances, however, where there is such a substantial performance of a promissory duty, an express condition qualifying that obligation which has not fully been complied with may sometimes be excused. To prevent a serious forfeiture of labor and materials, the party who has thus substantially performed his obligation may still recover the contract price, less whatever amount may be necessary to compensate the defendant for failure to comply with the condition. See 6 Williston on Contracts (Third Edition), §805. As a general rule, however, an express condition must be fully performed.
>
> Under no circumstances would the substantial performance doctrine apply here. Since the contract was wholly executory, no forfeiture was involved. Full compliance, therefore, with the express condition precedent was necessary.

380 A.2d at 638. Thus, the court in this portion of its opinion makes it clear that under certain circumstances the doctrine of substantial performance does apply to conditions precedent. Even if it is assumed that completion of the building was an express condition precedent to Ford Credit's duty of performance under the commitment, the court concludes that substantial performance, not full performance, is all that is required to satisfy that condition under the circumstances of this case. Towson Associates has incurred substantial expense in its efforts to develop the project, and Ford Credit has received in exchange for its commitment over $200,000 in fees from Towson Associates. This is a quite different factual situation from that involved in *Della Ratta*. It would be quite inequitable to allow Ford Credit to retain the fees it has received and avoid its obligations under the commitment simply because the building was not 100% complete.

The court's conclusion that substantial completion is sufficient to

satisfy the condition of completion of the building is firmly supported
by the cases of St. Paul at Chase Corp. v. Manufacturers Life Insurance
Co., 262 Md. 192, 278 A.2d 12, 29-32, cert. denied, 404 U.S. 857
(1971); Selective Builders, Inc. v. Hudson City Savings Bank, 137 N.J.
Super. 500, 349 A.2d 564, 566-67 (1975); and First National State
Bank v. Commonwealth Federal Savings and Loan Association, 455 F.
Supp. 464, 468-69 (D.N.J. 1978). . . . In *First National State Bank,*
the loan commitment included a provision that "[t]he entire project
shall be constructed according to the plans and specifications." 455 F.
Supp. at 467. In rejecting the lender's argument that it was not bound
by the commitment since the building was not completed, the court
stated:

> it is clear that a mortgage lender is bound to perform once the building
> contractor has "substantially completed" construction. When the con-
> tractor has fairly met this requirement, the mortgage lender may no
> longer avoid its commitment, although he may be entitled to a set-off
> for minor defects or omissions. All that is required of the building
> contractor is a good faith compliance with all the important particulars
> of the plans and specifications. One hundred per cent completion, unless
> called for, is not necessary.

Id. at 468-69.

Ford Credit has attempted to distinguish these cases on the basis
that the loan commitment involved in each of them contained language
different from that present in the Ford Credit commitment. The court
recognizes that such differences do exist. However, the import of all
three cases is the same; the lender may not avoid his commitment
once the building has been substantially completed, unless 100% completion is expressly required by the commitment, which it was not in
the Ford Credit commitment. Ford Credit's position that full and exact
completion of a large construction project such as this one is required
as a condition precedent to its obligations under the commitment is
somewhat unreasonable. If that were the case, no borrower in circumstances such as these could rely on the commitment because of the
immense difficulties present in bringing, by a specific date, a complex
project to the state of 100% completion without a single item being
left unfinished. It is not surprising that Ford Credit has been unable
to cite any case in which a court has found that a loan commitment
contained such a requirement. For these reasons, Ford Credit's motion
for summary judgment will be denied. . . .

NOTES AND QUESTIONS

1. Since the sample commitment letter provides that the lender
has no obligation to fund if the loan does not close by a certain date

and that the lender is not required to close until the improvements are completed, what is the probable purpose of the language in the section of the sample commitment letter entitled "Commencement of Construction," which provides the lender with the right to terminate if construction does not *commence* within 120 days of the acceptance of the commitment by the borrower?

2. Observe that in the section of the sample commitment letter entitled "Time of Disbursement of the Loan" the lender is relieved of its obligation to fund the loan if the loan does not close by a certain date (unless the failure to close is caused by lender's willful default). This means that construction must be completed by that date. On what protective language do you think a borrower such as Dan Developer might reasonably insist?

3. Since postconstruction commitments will normally prohibit changes in the plans and specifications without the lender's written approval, one would think that a sophisticated developer or construction lender would not risk making any changes without such approval. In fact, this does not always happen. The following hypothetical scenario typifies the kinds of real-world conflicts over control that occur between postconstruction lenders and cost-conscious developers during the construction period. Returning to the master hypothetical, let us assume that the building is under construction when certain fire and safety problems associated with use of aluminum wiring generally are suddenly publicized. Ace's architect, however, is of the opinion that copper wire is superior to aluminum, and accordingly required that the plans and specifications provide for copper wiring. Dan ascertains that aluminum wiring is far less expensive. He discounts the adverse publicity and, without informing the construction lender or Ace, substitutes aluminum wire for copper wire. Meanwhile, interest rates have been rising, and the interest rate stipulated in Ace's commitment is now about 3 percent below the market rate. Ace's demand that the aluminum wiring be replaced with copper wiring is ignored by both Dan and the construction lender, FNB, which has continued to make its construction loan disbursements notwithstanding the dispute over Dan's use of aluminum wiring. Ace's experts confirm that copper wire is superior to the aluminum wire Dan is using but at this time are unwilling to state without equivocation that the aluminum wiring is defective or constitutes a significant safety hazard. After reviewing the analogous fact pattern in the *Whalen* decision, supra, can you think of anything that Ace can do, or might have done, to prevent the possible impairment of its security interest? In the hypothetical, why does the construction lender, FNB, appear to be less concerned about the problem than Ace?

4. Can you think of the probable reason for the language in the sample commitment stating that the lender is under no obligation to close the loan before the specified closing date?

5. While there is some case law holding that the doctrine of substantial performance is inapplicable to loan commitments (see, e.g., Johnson v. American National Insurance Co., 126 Ariz. 219, 613 P.2d 1275 (Ct. App. 1980) (borrower unable to obtain refund of commitment fee after failing to complete construction of office building in timely manner), the opinion in *Whalen* appears to represent the majority view, namely, that because of their abhorrence of forfeitures, courts may construe the "completion of construction" language as requiring only substantial compliance. If you were counsel to Ace Insurance Company, what drafting techniques might you employ to mitigate the effects of decisions like *Whalen?* The answer to this question is suggested, by way of dictum, in Selective Builders Inc. v. Hudson City Savings Bank, 137 N.J. Super. 500, 349 A.2d 564 (Ch. Div. 1975).

12. Satisfactory Hazard Insurance

A fire or other unanticipated casualty could destroy the very improvements and rental income stream that secure the postconstruction loan; therefore, lenders commonly regard the insurance requirement as one of the most important provisions in the commitment letter, as reflected by the companion provision (discussed at Chapter 5B6, supra) that mandates the periodic collection of escrows for insurance premiums as each debt-service payment is made to ensure continuous coverage of the mortgaged property. In this section we will scrutinize both the form and content of the hazard insurance coverage that postconstruction lenders require in their loan documents. We will also explore the issue of control over the hazard insurance and condemnation award proceeds in the event of a partial destruction or partial condemnation of the mortgaged premises.

Savarese v. Ohio Farmers Insurance Co.
260 N.Y. 45, 182 N.E. 665 (1932)

CRANE, J.

Does the repair of the premises by the owner after a fire prevent the mortgagee from recovering the insurance payable to him?

On the 6th day of June, 1927, the defendant Ohio Farmers' Insurance Company of Le Roy, Ohio, issued its policy of insurance whereby it insured Loretta Realty & Finance Corporation for the term of three years from the 26th day of May, 1927, to the 26th day of May, 1930, against all direct loss or damage by fire to the extent of $7,500 on the brick building No. 16 West 119th street, New York

City. The property was thereafter conveyed to Leopold Kirven, the defendant, and the change of ownership duly noted on the policy. Within the period covered by the insurance, and on the 28th day of June, 1929, a fire occurred, causing damage to the extent of $4,230.

At the time of the issuance of said policy and at the time of the fire, the plaintiffs, Pasquale Savarese and Giacomo Savarese, were the owners of a bond secured by a mortgage upon said premises for $7,500, upon which there was due at the time of the loss $6,500, with interest from April 1, 1929. The mortgage provided that the mortgagor should keep the premises insured against loss by fire for the benefit of the mortgagee. The policy referred to contained the usual standard mortgagee clause, reading as follows: "Loss or damage, if any, under this policy, shall be payable to Pasquale Savarese & Giacomo Savarese as mortgagee, as interest may appear, and this insurance, as to the interest of the mortgagee only therein, shall not be invalidated by any act or neglect of the mortgagor or owner of the within described property," etc.

The defendants Markowitz and Grey, as contractors with the owner, repaired the premises, so that by the 6th day of September, 1929, the property was restored to the condition in which it existed before the fire. As compensation for their work, the owner transferred to Markowitz and Grey his interest in the fire insurance policy, and the defendant insurance company stands ready to pay them the sum of $1,178.64, by applying, in calculation, the pro rata provisions of the policy. Judgment for this amount has been awarded to these contractor-defendants, and they have not appealed from the amount adjudged to be due. The plaintiffs, mortgagees, have appealed, claiming the full benefit of the policy of insurance and the recovery of the full amount of the loss, $4,230, unimpaired by any act of the owner in making repairs and restoring the property to its previous good condition.

The Appellate Division has taken the position, with some force of reasoning, and with some authority to support it, that the mortgagees sustained no damage, because when this action was commenced the security for their mortgage was the same building in the same state of repair as at the time the mortgage was taken. At first blush this conclusion seems quite plausible, but upon further analysis must yield to other considerations.

Under the mortgagee clause the policy issued by the defendant insured the mortgagees' interest as fully and to the same extent as if they had taken out a policy directly with the insurance company. In Eddy v. London Assurance Corp., 143 N.Y. 311, 322, 38 N.E. 307, 309, 25 L.R.A. 686, this court said: "The effect of the mortgage clause hereinbefore set forth is to make an entirely separate insurance of the mortgagee's interest, and he takes the same benefit from his insurance as if he had received a separate policy from the company, free from the conditions imposed upon the owners." . . .

The plaintiffs Savarese had an insurable interest in this building to the extent of $7,500. Independent of the owner they could have taken out a policy of insurance against loss by fire directly payable to them, and separate and distinct from any policies taken or held by the owner. "Whether the subject-matter of insurance be a ship or a building or a life, or whatever else it may be, although in popular language it may be called an insurance upon the ship or building or life, or some other thing, yet it is strictly an agreement with some person interested in the preservation of the subject-matter, to pay him a sum which shall amount to an indemnity, or a certain sum agreed upon as an indemnity, in case his interest in the subject-matter shall suffer diminution of value, from certain specified causes, or in certain specified contingencies." 1 May on Insurance (4th Ed.), §6.

Thus it has been held that recovery may be had by the mortgagee on his insurance policy, although his security under the mortgage is perfectly good and valid. Kernochan v. New York Bowery Fire Ins. Co., 17 N.Y. 428, 435. The court there said: "The loss against which the plaintiff [mortgagee] is insured, is, by the very language of the contract, 'to the property insured;' the destruction in whole or in part of the value of the property by the total or partial burning of the property. In case of such loss it is stated that it is 'to be paid within sixty days after due notice and proof thereof by the insured,' in conformity to the policy. Whether the loss by diminishing the mortgage security, endangers the collection of the debt, or the security remains ample, is not by the contract made of any importance; in either case it is insured against and the amount of it is to be paid."

A mortgagee, therefore, who has insured his interest at his own expense, with no agreement or understanding with the mortgagor, is not required to exhaust his remedy upon the mortgage before enforcing his policy; and he can maintain an action thereon, although the property undestroyed is equal in value to the amount of the mortgage debt. Excelsior Fire Ins. Co. v. Royal Ins. Co., 55 N.Y. 343, 14 Am. Rep. 271.

From these authorities we must conclude that whether the mortgagee takes out his own insurance, or whether he is insured by the mortgagor, under the usual mortgagee clause in the insurance policy, his right to recover in case of a fire is not dependent upon the sufficiency or insufficiency of the mortgage security after the fire. . . .

When we further analyze the terms of the policy and the situation of the mortgagee, reason also points to the conclusion that when a fire occurs the insurance company must pay the loss to the mortgagee in accordance with its contract with him. The mortgagor benefits by such payment as the insurance money reduces the amount of the mortgage debt. Waring v. Loder, 53 N.Y. 581. The value taken out of the property by the fire is taken off the mortgage by the payment of the insurance money, and the parties remain in the same relative position after as before the fire.

The policy gives to the insurance company certain options which are as binding upon the mortgagee as upon the mortgagor. One of them relates to repairs, and reads as follows:

> It shall be optional with this Company to take all, or any part, of the articles at the agreed or appraised value, and also to repair, rebuild, or replace the property lost or damaged with other of like kind and quality within a reasonable time, on giving notice of its intention so to do within thirty days after the receipt of the proof of loss herein required; but there can be no abandonment to this Company of any property.
>
> The amount of loss or damage for which this Company may be liable shall be payable sixty days after proof of loss, as herein provided, is received by this Company and ascertainment of the loss or damage is made either by agreement between the insured and this Company expressed in writing or by the filing with this Company of an award as herein provided.

The company did not exercise this option and made no election to repair. The loss, as ascertained, $4,230, was therefore payable, according to the terms of the policy, to the mortgagee, sixty days after proof of loss and ascertainment of damage. This is the contract which the company has made and for which it has received a premium. The act of the owner in making repairs was not for and in behalf of the company or as its agent. He contracted for and undertook the work without the consent of the company and without the knowledge or consent of the mortgagee. The time of the fire and of the loss established the rights of the parties, and in the absence of an election by the company to repair, the amount of the loss payable to the mortgagee became fixed as of that time. No act or neglect of the owner could invalidate or impair the mortgagees' rights under their separate policy of insurance as thus vested at the time the loss occurred.

If it be that the mortgagor can wipe out the benefits to the mortgagee under a policy by repairing the premises without the knowledge or against the consent of the mortgagee, how long can the owner take in deciding to make repairs? The policy places a time limit upon all the steps to be pursued after the fire, and even states that the repairs, if the company makes them, must be undertaken within a reasonable time. Under the ruling below, no such limit is placed upon the owner, for if he restores the property to its previous condition any time before action brought or tried, the mortgagee has sustained no loss. In the meantime the property may remain in its destroyed condition, with loss of income to the owner with which he might pay taxes and interest on prior incumbrances. Must the mortgagee litigate the extent and sufficiency of the repairs, or, if partially repaired, is his insurance to be reduced in proportion? We do not think that the insurance contract can thus be modified by the act of a third party to the material disadvantage of the mortgagee. Section 254 of the Real Property Law (Consol. Laws, ch. 50), subdivision 4, says that the mortgagee at his option may apply the insurance toward the payment of the mortgage or (at his election) "the same may be paid over either wholly or in part to the mortgagor . . . for the repair of said buildings . . . and if the mortgagee receive and retain insurance money for damage by fire to said premises, the lien of the mortgage shall be affected only by a reduction of the amount of said lien by the amount of such insurance money received and retained by said mortgagee." This choice given to the mortgagee to apply the insurance money either to his mortgage or to the repairs excludes a like choice in the owner-mortgagor without the mortgagee's consent. Such a right is single by nature; it cannot exist in both the mortgagor and the mortgagee, otherwise the former might decide for repairs and the other for payment, and nothing would result. No; the choice is with the mortgagee alone and in this case he asks for payment of the insurance money and does not consent that it be applied to repairs. . . .

The defendant, therefore, being liable to the mortgagee on the policy, how much is it obliged to pay? The plaintiffs claim the full amount of the fire damage, $4,230, but the policy does not obligate the insurance company to pay the full amount of the loss. The contract by the New York standard average clause provides: "This Company shall not be liable for a greater proportion of any loss or damage to the property described herein than the sum hereby insured bears to eighty per cent (80%) of the actual cash value of said property at the time such loss shall happen." This is the agreement; no more, no less. Had the building been free and clear, the owner could recover no larger amount, and the terms are not changed because the loss is made first payable to a mortgagee. The coinsurance clause (so-called) is not a warranty or a condition, but a statement of the amount to be paid in case of fire either to the owner or the mortgagee. The existence of the mortgage does not extend the liability. Hartwig v. American Ins. Co. of City of Newark, N.J., 169 App. Div. 60, 154 N.Y.S. 801; Pennsylvania Co. for Insurance on Lives and Granting Annuities v. Aachen & Munich Fire Ins. Co. (D.C.) 257 F. 189. . . .

The value of the property at the time of the loss was $22,500, of which 80 per cent is $18,000. The proportion of $7,500, the sum insured, to $18,000, is as 5 to 12. The loss being $4,230, five-twelfths of this amount is $1,762.50, which the insurance company must pay the plaintiffs.

The judgment should be reversed, and judgment directed for the plaintiffs in the sum of $1,762.50, with interest and costs in all courts.

Now that you are equipped with a more thorough understanding of the basic terminology contained in the insurance terms and provisions of a mortgage, consider the following language in the sample postconstruction loan commitment letter. Pay particular attention to the second paragraph of the insurance provision.

1. Borrower shall keep the Premises continuously insured against loss by fire, with extended coverage and against such other hazards, and in such amounts, as Lender may from time to time reasonably require (but such amount on the buildings and improvements on the Land shall in no event be less than the greater of (i) 100% of the full replacement cost of the buildings and improvements on the Land without deduction for depreciation; (ii) an amount sufficient to prevent the Lender or Borrower from becoming a co-insurer within the terms of the applicable policies; or (iii) the principal amount of the Loan. Borrower shall also maintain rent insurance on the Premises in an amount equal to no less than one year's gross rent from the buildings and improvements on the Land. The policy or policies for all such insurance shall contain replacement cost endorsements and shall be maintained in full force and effect until such time as the indebtedness hereby secured is fully repaid. All policies and any renewals thereof, including but not limited to policies for any amounts carried in excess of the aforesaid minimum and policies not specifically required by the Lender, shall be with an insurance company or companies, and in form and substance satisfactory to Lender, and shall be deposited, premiums paid, with Lender.

2. The loss, if any, shall be payable to Lender according to the terms of a standard mortgagee clause, not subject to contribution, or such other form of mortgagee or loss payment clause as shall be satisfactory to Lender. Lender shall have the right, at its election, to adjust or compromise any loss claims under such insurance and to collect and receive the proceeds thereof and to apply such proceeds, at its election, either to reduce the indebtedness secured hereby or to restore the Premises. All renewal policies shall be delivered, by Borrower, premiums paid, to Lender, at least ten days before the expiration of the expiring policies. The insurance company shall agree in the policy to provide Lender with twenty days prior written notice before any termination or cancellation becomes effective as to Lender. If Lender becomes the owner of the Premises or any part thereof by foreclosure or otherwise, such policies shall become the absolute property of Lender. In the event of damage by fire, other casualty or catastrophe, Borrower agrees forthwith thereafter to restore the Premises to their prior condition, without regard to the adequacy or availability of insurance proceeds.

3. All proceeds in the event of a condemnation or other taking shall be paid to the Mortgagee and applied towards the reduction of the principal balance of the loan indebtedness.

NOTES AND QUESTIONS

1. *Selection of Carrier.* Many states have legislation under which lenders are not permitted to select the borrower's insurance carrier or broker. Under the New York statute, violation of the provision is a misdemeanor. N.Y. Ins. Law §2502(a) (McKinney 1985). Do you see any conflict between such statutes and commitment language giving the lender the right to approve the carrier?

2. *Co-insurance.* As illustrated by the judgment in the *Savarese* decision, a co-insurance provision relieves the insurer of the obligation to pay a portion of the loss if the property is underinsured. Insurance companies use such a clause to equalize the distribution of premium costs among all policyholders by penalizing those who are underinsured. While the percentage of the value of the property that must be insured to avoid the application of the co-insurance provision will vary, it is typically 80 percent or more of the actual cash value of the property insured at the time of loss. "Actual cash value" usually refers to replacement cost less depreciation. A typical 80 percent co-insurance clause reads, in part, "This company shall not be liable for a greater proportion of any loss or damage to the insured property than the sum hereby insured bears to 80% of the actual cash value of said property at the time such loss shall happen."

Returning to the master hypothetical, assume that at the time of loss the actual cash value of Dan Developer's property was $34 million ($30 million for the building and $4 million in land value) and that Dan (without Ace's knowledge or consent) carried only $20 million in insurance under a policy with an 80 percent co-insurance clause. How much would Dan receive from the insurance company if he suffered a $4 million loss? If Dan carried $12 million in insurance, how much would he receive in the event of a $4 million loss? If Dan's mortgage contained a clause such as the sample clause excerpted above, and Ace did a proper monitoring job, would Dan ever be carrying these amounts of insurance?

3. *Loss Payable Clauses.* Essentially, there are two types of loss payable clauses: the old "open mortgage" clause and the more recent and widely prevalent "New York standard," "standard," or "union mortgage" clause. Under an open mortgage clause, the mortgagee is deemed to be a mere "appointee" of the mortgagor, who stands in the shoes of the latter and is therefore subject to any defenses the insurer might have against the mortgagor. See, e.g., Fred v. Pacific Indemnity Co., 53 Haw. 384, 397, 494 P.2d 783 (1972). By contrast, under the standard loss payable clause, the mortgagee may recover even if the loss is caused by the insured mortgagor and (as held in the *Savarese* case) even where the mortgagee's security interest was not

impaired by the loss. Certainly, the mortgagee would be protected if the mortgagor neglects to pay the insurance premiums in a timely manner. To review: What commitment and mortgage provision makes the latter occurrence unlikely?

Even under a standard mortgage clause, would an insurer be able to deny coverage to the mortgagee if the policy had been issued in reliance on misrepresentations by the mortgagor? What would be the likely counterargument raised by a mortgagee in response to such a defense pleaded by an insurer? See G. Nelson and D. Whitman, Real Estate Finance Law §4.14 (2d ed. 1985).

Under the standard mortgage clause, the insurer must be notified by the mortgagee of any change in ownership so that the insurer can reassess its risk and protect itself by cancelling the policy on notice or by increasing the premium. Suppose, in the hypothetical, that Dan defaults under the postconstruction mortgage and Ace, as the successful bidder, purchases the property for the full amount of the debt at the foreclosure sale but fails to notify the insurer about the change in ownership. In the event of a subsequent casualty loss, should the insurer be able to deny a claim made by Ace? See Shores v. Rabon, 251 N.C. 790, 112 S.E.2d 556 (1960), affd. per curiam, 253 N.C. 428, 117 S.E.2d 1 (1960). But see Consolidated Mortgage Corp. v. American Security Insurance Co., 69 Mich. App. 251, 257, 244 N.W.2d 434, 437 (1976) (disagreed with by Citizens Mortgage Corp. v. Michigan Basic Property Ins. Assn., 111 Mich. App. 393, 314 N.W.2d 635 (1981)). Should it matter if the loss occurs before the foreclosure sale or if Ace bids in less than the full amount of the outstanding mortgage indebtedness at the foreclosure sale? See Northwestern National Insurance Co. v. Mildenberger, 359 S.W.2d 380 (Mo. 1962); Smith v. General Mortgage Corp., 73 Mich. App. 720, 252 N.W.2d 551 (1977), mod., 402 Mich. 125, 261 N.W.2d 710 (1978); see generally Comment, Foreclosure, Loss, and the Proper Distribution of Insurance Proceeds Under Open and Standard Mortgage Clauses: Some Observations, 7 Val. U.L. Rev. 485 (1973).

4. *Control over Insurance Proceeds.* One of the most onerous provisions in a typical loan commitment, from the borrower's viewpoint, is the language (see the second paragraph in the sample commitment letter excerpted supra) providing the postconstruction lender with the option to apply the insurance proceeds toward reduction of the indebtedness or to the restoration of the premises. This provision, under which the mortgagee can effectively deny to the mortgagor, even in the case of a partial destruction, the use of the proceeds to restore and rebuild the premises, has been criticized as being inherently unfair to the mortgagor unless the mortgagee can demonstrate that its security interest will be impaired if the proceeds are not applied to the debt.

Do you agree? A mortgagor such as Dan Developer would argue that it had bargained for maintaining the loan for a stated period of time and that the lender, Ace, should not have the right to deprive him unilaterally of being able to continue to operate his office building by withholding the insurance proceeds. Can you think of any arguments that Ace can make as to why it should have control over the application of the funds? Would Ace's argument be any stronger if the loss occurred after Dan had already defaulted on the mortgage or the mortgage had already matured? See G. Nelson and D. Whitman, Real Estate Finance Law §4.15, at 177-78 (2d ed. 1985). If under this language Ace decides to use the insurance proceeds to reduce the mortgage indebtedness rather than for restoration, could Ace also insist that Dan restore the premises with his own funds?

Notwithstanding the predicament in which this clause places Dan, such clauses are enforceable. Indeed, as reflected by the holding in *Savarese,* even in the absence of specific language in the mortgage, most courts have taken the position that the mortgagee, under a standard mortgage clause in the insurance policy, may apply the proceeds toward reduction of the debt even where the value of the uninjured portion of the premises exceeds the balance of the indebtedness (see, e.g., English v. Fischer, 649 S.W.2d 83 (Tex. App. 1982), revd., 660 S.W.2d 521 (Tex. 1983); General G.M.C. Sales, Inc. v. Passarella, 195 N.J. Super. 614, 481 A.2d 307 (1984), affd., 101 N.J. 12, 499 A.2d 017 (1985); Kintzel v. Wheatland Mutual Insurance Assn., 203 N.W.2d 799 (Iowa, 1973)), and even, as in *Savarese,* where the mortgagor has restored the premises with his own funds. But see Schoolcraft v. Ross, 81 Cal. App. 3d 75, 146 Cal. Rptr. 57 (1978) and the New York statute (enacted after *Savarese*), which gives the mortgagor a qualified right to the insurance proceeds. N.Y. Real Prop. Law §254(4) (McKinney Supp. 1990).

Suppose that in the *Savarese* case the mortgagee-plaintiff had agreed beforehand based on language in the mortgage to apply the insurance proceeds toward restoration of the premises. Do you think this might have changed the result in the case? In *Savarese,* Justice Crane stated that "the defendant [insurance company] stands ready to pay them [the defendant-contractors who had repaired the premises] the sum of $1,178.64 by applying . . . the . . . provisions of the policy." Suppose that the insurance company by mistake had paid the contractors (as assignees of the mortgagor-owner's interest in the policy) or the mortgagor himself instead of the mortgagee (pursuant to the standard mortgage clause) and, on appeal by the plaintiff-mortgagee, was required (as in *Savarese*) to pay the proceeds to the mortgage. In the event of such double payment for the same loss, would you, as counsel to the insurance company, advise your client to seek a recovery? If so, against whom would you proceed and under what theory?

In light of the concerns expressed by Justice Crane in the *Savarese* decision (e.g., relinquishing control over the funds may force the mortgagee to "litigate the extent and sufficiency of the repairs") and the lender's anxiety with respect to mechanic's liens filed against the property if workers are not paid, what compromise language would you, as attorney for Dan Developer, suggest to Ace that should be reasonably acceptable to both parties? Another concern of Dan's is that under Ace's proposed language Ace would not be obligated to reduce or postpone subsequent amortization payments if Ace were to use the proceeds to reduce the mortgage indebtedness in the event of a partial destruction. What type of language should you, as attorney for Dan, insist on in the prepayment provision to protect Dan?

5. *Control over Condemnation Proceeds.* The economic predicament and negotiating demands of a mortgagor who wants to continue his business notwithstanding a partial fire destruction are analogous to those of a mortgagor confronted with a partial taking of the mortgaged premises. After reviewing the sample mortgage in the Documents Manual, what modifications in the condemnation clause in the sample mortgage would you request (as counsel for the borrower) to protect your client in the event of a partial taking? If counsel to the mortgagee agrees to your proposed changes with respect to the consequences of a partial taking, what additional protective provisions will it most likely require for its client by way of a compromise?

While it would appear that their interests should coincide at any condemnation proceeding, the mortgagor and mortgagee will sometimes be in conflict. For example, if the proposed condemnation award settlement amount is way below the balance of the mortgage indebtedness, the borrower may lose interest in the proceedings. If the settlement amount is sufficient to discharge the indebtedness, the mortgagee may not be willing to assume the risk of receiving a lesser amount at litigation, while the borrower may want to litigate because it has nothing to lose. Can you suggest any additional language in the sample mortgage provision that might help to ameliorate such potential conflicts of interest?

Observe that the sample provision requires the mortgagor to reimburse the mortgagee for all of its costs and expenses incurred in connection with collecting the condemnation award, even though it is possible that the mortgagor may receive nothing. Can you think of some alternative language that would be more balanced and yet be reasonably acceptable to both parties? See generally Teague, Condemnation of Mortgaged Property, 44 Tex. L. Rev. 1535 (1966).

To review: In the event of a total condemnation or destruction of the premises where the mortgagee uses the condemnation award or insurance proceeds, respectively, to pay off the outstanding indebtedness, could the mortgagee demand that the mortgagor pay a prepayment charge?

13. *Approval of the Security Documents*

From the postconstruction lender's standpoint, the mortgage, note, assignment of leases, and other documents creating the security interest in the real estate, together with the ancillary documents such as the hazard insurance policy, preliminary title report, and certificate of occupancy, are of utmost importance. It is through these documents that the lender receives assurance that its loan is a safe and legal investment and that it will be able to realize on the security in the event of the borrower's default. The postconstruction lender, therefore, will condition its obligation to fund the loan on approval by its in-house or outside legal counsel of the form and substance of all security and collateral documents. The following is typical commitment language to that effect:

> The form and substance of each and every document evidencing the Loan and the security therefore or incident thereto, and any proceedings incident thereto, and the title and evidence thereof, must be satisfactory to our Law Department.

NOTES AND QUESTIONS

The language excerpted above is very open-ended. Returning to the master hypothetical, suppose that the market rate of interest for first mortgage money escalates to 14 percent shortly before the date on which the loan is scheduled to close, and Ace would like to extricate itself from its loan commitment to Dan. If Ace were to employ the language in the approval clause to impose arbitrary and unreasonable closing requirements on Dan, what argument could you, Dan's attorney, make, based on general contract principles, to support Dan's contention that Ace's right to approve all loan documents should be governed by a standard of reasonableness?

In the master hypothetical, the best way for Dan Developer to avoid "closing shock," that is, discovering at the last moment that the documents are not satisfactory to Ace Insurance Company, is to obtain approval of the documents well in advance of the scheduled closing date. There is a tendency among busy people, and accomplished real estate lawyers certainly fit within this category, to put out the most immediate fire first and to put everything else on the back burner. In this hectic atmosphere, the bulk of documentary problems tend to be resolved close to the projected closing date. Sometimes the problem is caused by the business decision-makers, who may not have fully negotiated the terms of the loan transaction until shortly before the closing date. However, if the closing is to run smoothly and be consummated on schedule, the attorneys representing Dan and Ace must make every effort to resolve any title problems and to draft, negotiate, and approve the loan documentation before matters become in extremis. If Dan and Ace have previously transacted business with one another, Dan's attorney should already be familiar with Ace's requirements and loan-closing procedures. If this is Dan's first transaction with Ace, Dan's attorney should try to become familiar with these requirements long before the closing date.

Where there is a buy-sell agreement with the construction lender of the "pre-closed" variety (discussed at Chapter 5B14, infra), then some of these problems can be obviated inasmuch as it requires early approval by the postconstruction lender of the note and mortgage or deed of trust, as well as most of the collateral documents, such as the hazard insurance policy and the preliminary title report.

14. The Buy-Sell Agreement

The postconstruction loan commitment will frequently require that the borrower obtain a construction loan commitment by a specified date and that the construction or interim lender enter into a "buy-sell" agreement with the postconstruction lender and the borrower prior to the closing of the construction loan. The buy-sell is an agreement among the construction lender, the developer, and the postconstruction lender under which the construction lender agrees to assign or sell its loan to the postconstruction lender, and to nobody else; the postconstruction lender agrees to buy the loan from the construction lender provided the terms and conditions of its commitment are satisfied; and the borrower agrees to be bound by the arrangement. This tripartite agreement binds all the parties to one another by privity of contract and expressly provides for the remedy of specific performance in the event of a default. It also assures the postconstruction lender, especially when interest rates are declining, that the borrower will not "shop around" during the construction period for better terms and, in the vernacular of the trade, "walk" from the commitment to the postconstruction lender. The construction lender is assured that its loan will be "taken out" by the postconstruction lender when the construction is completed in conformity with the postconstruction commitment.

The buy-sell agreement can be "pre-closed," which means that the postconstruction lender approves the form of the construction loan note and mortgage (along with most of the collateral documentation such as the preliminary title report and leases) before the construction loan is closed and the buy-sell agreement is executed. Consequently, the form of the note and mortgage will either combine the terms and conditions of the construction and postconstruction loans or be amended to conform to the latter, so that the postconstruction lender can take an assignment of these instruments when the postconstruction loan is closed. By contrast, in a transaction that is not pre-closed, each lender will close "on its own paper" and the construction loan will, in effect, be refinanced when at the closing of the postconstruction loan the borrower executes a new note and mortgage in favor of the postconstruction lender. The advantages of pre-closing are: (1) the lien priority of the construction loan mortgage automatically inures to the benefit of the postconstruction lender, as assignee, who is thereby protected against intervening lienors who record their claims prior to the date on which the postconstruction loan closes; (2) as observed in Chapter 5B13, supra, the use of integrated loan documents permits the postconstruction lender to approve much of the documentation early in the lending cycle, while the parties still have time to resolve their differences; and (3) by collapsing the two loan-closing transactions into one, the borrower can avoid extra mortgage taxes, recording fees, and other closing expenses. The foregoing consequences of using a pre-closed form of buy-sell agreement are also examined at Chapter 6B5.

Typical commitment language requiring a pre-closed buy-sell agreement with integrated loan instruments might read as follows:

> Within 120 days after your acceptance of this commitment, you shall have obtained a construction loan commitment from an interim lender approved in writing by this Company, and you and the interim lender shall have executed loan documents incorporating the terms of the postconstruction loan to be made by this Company, which documents shall be in form and substance satisfactory to this Company as evidenced by our written approval. On or before such date, you and the interim lender shall have also entered into a written agreement with, and in form and substance satisfactory to this Company assuring us of the right to purchase such loan documents.

NOTES AND QUESTIONS

1. Why do postconstruction lenders insist on a provision requiring the borrower to obtain a construction loan by a certain date?

2. Absent a buy-sell agreement, do you think the construction lender would have recourse against a postconstruction lender that refuses

to purchase ("take out") the loan from the construction lender even though the borrower has satisfied the terms of the postconstruction commitment? See Goldbar Properties, Inc. v. North American Mortgage Investors, 51 N.Y.L.J. 1 (N.Y. Sup. Ct. 1979); Republic National Bank v. National Bankers Life Insurance Co., 427 S.W.2d 76 (Tex. Civ. App. 1968).

3. Notwithstanding the advantages of the "pre-closed" buy-sell procedure, circumstances may exist in which this procedure may pose a problem for one of the three parties to the buy-sell agreement. Suppose in the master hypothetical that the State of Fuller has a usury limit of 12 percent, two points higher than the amount of interest provided for under Ace's postconstruction loan, and that the construction loan provides for interest at a floating rate not to exceed 12 percent. If Ace has reason to believe that FNB, the construction lender, might have extracted certain fees from Dan that might be considered additional interest by the local courts, it would be foolhardy for Ace to take an assignment of the construction loan and thereby expose itself to a potential problem under the local usury law. Can you think of any other circumstances in which it might be advisable for one of the parties to avoid the pre-closed loan format?

4. Again returning to the hypothetical, suppose Dan were to obtain a "floor-ceiling" loan (examined at Chapter 5B2, supra) whereby Ace agrees to fund the $25 million ceiling amount if certain leasing requirements are met when the postconstruction loan is closed. Assume that Ace had executed a buy-sell agreement with FNB, the construction lender, and that FNB did not include the floor-ceiling condition in its own loan commitment. If the leasing requirement is not met and Ace refuses to fund more than the floor amount of $20 million on the date of closing, would FNB be able to compel Ace to take out the construction loan for the gap loan amount of $5 million?

PLANNING PROBLEM

The following is an excerpt from a buy-sell agreement used in a transaction between a borrower, a construction lender, and a postconstruction lender. In the agreement the construction lender is referred to as the "Temporary Lender" and the postconstruction lender as the "Permanent Lender." After reviewing the sample buy-sell agreement in the Documents Manual, and assuming that you are representing the postconstruction lender in its negotiations with the construction lender, what problems, if any, do you see in these provisions for your client? What would you propose to overcome these problems?

First: Transfer of Loan Documents

(a) The Temporary Lender agrees to accept payment of its loan and thereupon to transfer the Loan Documents to the Permanent Lender, and subject to compliance by the Borrower with all of the terms and conditions of the Commitment and of this Agreement, the Permanent Lender agrees to take from the Construction Lender, the Loan Documents and to fund to Borrower the full amount of its loan as set forth in the Commitment and to cause Borrower to pay to the Temporary Lender the full amount of the outstanding principal balance, together with all accrued interest thereon, and all other sums due to Temporary Lender under the Loan Documents. However, the amount to be loaned to Borrower by Permanent Lender shall not exceed the sum of Two Million Five Hundred Five Thousand Dollars ($2,505,000) or, if the requirement of Condition 21 of the Commitment (rent roll requirement) shall not have been fulfilled, Two Million Dollars ($2,000,000). Provided, however, that if the amount funded by the Permanent Lender shall be less than the amount owed by the Borrower to the Temporary Lender, the Temporary Lender shall not be obligated to transfer the Loan Documents to the Permanent Lender unless and until the difference between the amount to be funded by the Permanent Lender and the amount owed to the Temporary Lender shall be paid by the Borrower to the Temporary Lender. . . .

(b) The funding and payment contemplated by this paragraph will be offered to Permanent Lender by Temporary Lender prior to the expiration date of the Commitment unless Temporary Lender is prevented from doing so by clauses beyond its control; but in no event shall Temporary Lender be obligated to accept payment of its loan prior to five (5) days before expiration date of the Permanent Commitment. Temporary Lender agrees not to accept payment of its loan prior to five (5) days before the expiration date of the Commitment without Borrower's written consent thereto, unless such transfer is occasioned by an election by Permanent Lender [that] shall be accomplished as follows:

(i) In the event that Temporary Lender desires that Permanent Lender fund its loan prior to five (5) days before the expiration of the Commitment and Borrower consents thereto, Temporary Lender shall certify to Permanent Lender and Borrower the total amount due to Temporary Lender under the Loan Documents and the additional daily amount to accrue each day thereafter and Permanent Lender shall within ten (10) days of such certification designate, by written notice to Temporary Lender and Borrower, a date within twenty (20) days of such certification on which date Permanent Lender shall, subject to the provisions of this paragraph hereof, pay or cause to be paid, to Temporary Lender, all sums due to Temporary Lender under the Loan Documents as of such date.

(ii) In the event that Temporary Lender has not arranged for Permanent Lender to fund its loan prior to fifteen (15) days before the expiration date of the Commitment, Temporary Lender shall at such time certify to Temporary Lender and Borrower the total amount due to Temporary Lender under the Loan Documents and the additional daily amount to accrue each day thereafter and Permanent Lender shall, within five (5) days of such certification, designate, by written notice to Temporary Lender and Borrower, a date within five (5) days of the expiration date of the Commitment, on which date Permanent Lender shall, subject to the provisions of this paragraph, pay or cause to be paid to Temporary Lender, all sums due to Temporary Lender under the Loan Documents as of such date.

(c) In the event of any default by Borrower under the Loan Documents, Temporary Lender agrees to give written notice to Borrower and Permanent Lender of such default prior to taking any action with respect to such default and give Permanent Lender the opportunity, provided such default has not been cured by borrower, within twenty (20) days after written notice is given by Temporary Lender to Permanent Lender of any such default, to either:

(i) notify Temporary Lender in writing that Borrower's defaults as specified in such notice shall not affect Permanent Lender's agreements hereunder or affect any other of Permanent Lender's obligations to Temporary Lender hereunder and that Permanent Lender will indemnify Temporary Lender for any loss to Temporary Lender resulting from Temporary Lender's reliance on such waiver in the event Permanent Lender does not waive any subsequent default by Borrower under the Loan Documents; or

(ii) offer Temporary Lender in writing to fund its Loan on a date specified not more than ten (10) days thereafter by payment to Temporary Lender of the then outstanding balance of principal, accrued unpaid interest and all other sums due to Temporary Lender under the Loan Documents as of such date in which event Temporary Lender agrees to accept repayment of Temporary Lender's loan on said date.

15. Survey, Title Insurance, and Closing Costs

The obligation of the postconstruction lender to fund the loan will normally be conditioned on receiving an "as built" survey (showing completed buildings) and obtaining title insurance satisfactory to the lender. A survey is a map of the property that is prepared, signed, and certified by a licensed surveyor. The survey shows such items as the boundary lines (which form the matrix for the legal description in all the legal documents, including the mortgage and title insurance policy), the location of the improvements, streets, any easements or encroachments, set back lines, and other required details (as standardized by the American Congress on Surveying and Mapping).

The title insurance policy contains a legal description of the mortgaged property and insures the postconstruction lender that, as of the closing date, it has lien priority over any other interests in the mortgaged property, except for those liens and encumbrances specifically itemized in a schedule (usually Schedule B) to the policy. Therefore, if (as is usually the case) the commitment requires that the postconstruction mortgage be a first lien, the lender will condition its obligation to fund on the receipt of a title policy ensuring that there are no interests superior in lien priority to the mortgage other than those set forth in the commitment or not objected to by the lender's attorney. For a more detailed discussion of title insurance see Chapter 3B2.

The commitment will normally require that the borrower pay and reimburse the lender for all out-of-pocket costs and expenses incurred by it to close the loan and to pay any other costs that are expended by the lender to satisfy the terms and conditions of its commitment letter. Included among these closing costs are such items as attorney's fees, title charges, mortgage taxes, and recording fees.

In contrast to the application fee, the refundable "good-faith" security deposit, commonly referred to as the "commitment" or "standby" fee, is payable by the borrower not when the loan closes but when the loan commitment letter is executed by the borrower and postconstruction lender. The commitment fee is designed to compensate the lender by way of liquidated damages for its cost of holding funds available and for preparatory expenses for a particular loan if the borrower should default under the commitment letter and prevent the lender from closing its loan.

The following are commitment provisions covering the foregoing.

Plot Plan:

Within not more than thirty days from the date of this Commitment, lender shall be furnished with an accurate plot plan with line measurements showing the Land, location of adjoining streets and the distance to the nearest intersecting streets. Lender shall also be furnished with a detailed metes and bounds location description at the same time.

Survey:

Lender is to be furnished with a currently dated final metes and bounds survey of the Land, which must be satisfactory to its Law Department, showing: (a) the courses and measured distances of the exterior property lines of the Land, (b) the total square foot area of the Land, (c) the location of the improvements, the dimensions thereof at ground surface level and the distance therefrom to the facing exterior property lines of the Land, (d) the location of adjoining streets, (e) the location of easements, building setback lines and rights of way, (f) encroachments, if any, upon adjoining property by the Improvements upon the Land, and (g) the location and number of parking spaces.

Title Insurance:

Borrower at its sole cost and expense shall furnish to Lender an ALTA Revised 1987 policy or policies of mortgage title insurance (or its equivalent in form, scope and substance satisfactory to Lender's Law Department), with such co-insurance and reinsurance as Lender may require, in the full amount of the Loan, insuring, inter alia, that Lender has a first lien on the Property, free of encumbrances or other exceptions to title, other than those which are approved and accepted in writing by Lender. The issuing company or companies and the amount of title insurance issued by any company and any reinsurance and co-insurance shall be approved by Lender.

Unqualified Obligation of Borrower:

Exclusive of the Non-Refundable Application Fee required herein, and whether or not the Loan is made by Lender, Borrower will pay all costs and expenses in connection with the transactions contemplated herein, including, but not limited to: (a) the legal fees, charges and disbursements of special counsel of Lender, if any; (b) survey costs; (c) title company charges; (d) documentary stamp taxes or mortgage taxes, if any; (e) recording and filing fees for all documents which Lender's Law Department requires be recorded or filed; (f) inspection fees; (g) printing costs; (h) fees, charges and expenses of architects, engineers, soil consultant, vertical transportation consultant and curtain wall consultant for Lender; and (i) reasonable out-of-pocket traveling expenses of Lender's personnel.

Returning to the master hypothetical, assume that the building has now been completed by Dan Developer and that Figure 5-2 is the "as built" survey submitted to the Ace Insurance Company pursuant to the terms of the postconstruction loan commitment. The accompanying Description contains the legal description of the property that tracks the survey.

NOTES AND QUESTIONS

1. *The Legal Description.* The legal description of Dan Developer's property accompanying Figure 5-2 is a "metes and bounds" description, so called because the boundaries of the property are determined by following certain "courses and distances" from a point of beginning along the length and direction of each lot line until the description "closes," or gets back to the beginning point. While there are other methods of describing property, such as by "lot and block" or by reference to the Federal Survey of Public Lands, a description by metes and bounds is by far the most common in commercial transactions.

As you know, a circle is divided into 360 degrees (°). If a circle is split into four equal parts, or quadrants, each will have 90 degrees. North is 0, East is 90, South is 180, and West is 270. In a description by courses and distances, the first letter will indicate a direction, North, South, East or West, toward which the line is pointing. This will be

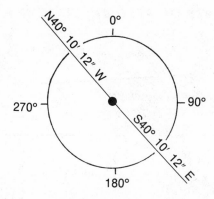

followed by the number of degrees and fractions of degrees away from that direction and facing the other direction toward which the line is pointing. Fractions of degrees are minutes (') and seconds ("). Sixty minutes equals a degree and, as you might suspect, 60 seconds equals a minute. The chart above illustrates the foregoing. The course shown is N 40° 10' 12" W. Is this course the same as S 40° 10' 12" E? Go to the description of Dan Developer's property accompanying Figure 5-2 and see if you can trace it on the survey. Notice that the Description contains three descriptions of Dan's property. The first is by metes and bounds, the second is by lot and block, and the third is by street address. If the lot and block description or the street address were the only description, would you, as Ace's attorney, be willing to accept it? If not, why not?

2. *The Survey.* Surveys are expensive, especially in large commercial transactions; therefore, where possible an existing survey should be updated rather than superseded by a new one. Since Dan Developer is obligated to pay the cost of the survey as well as the title insurance cost, he may contend that a survey or an update of one is not necessary, especially when the title insurance policy will insure that Ace has a first lien. If you were counsel to Ace, how would you answer this argument? What problems does the survey in Figure 5-2 reveal to you as attorney for Dan? For Ace? Specifically, what additional document would you demand? Assuming that the survey is correct, are there any inaccuracies in the legal description that need to be corrected? Does anything in the survey cause you to be concerned about zoning? Access?

Figure 5-2

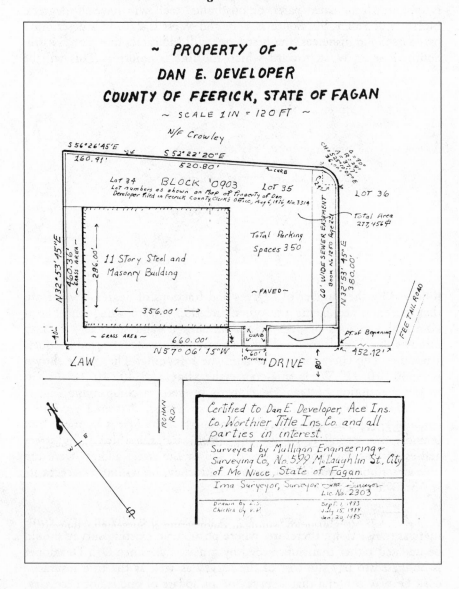

~ PROPERTY OF ~
DAN E. DEVELOPER
COUNTY OF FEERICK, STATE OF FAGAN
~ SCALE 1 IN = 120 FT ~

N/F Crowley

S 56°26'45"E   S 52°22'20"E
160.91'   520.80'   ← CURB

Lot 34   BLOCK '0903   Lot 35   LOT 36
Lot numbers as shown on Map of Property of Dan
Developer filed in Feerick County Clerk's Office, Aug 6, 1976, No. 3314

Total Area
277,456#

Total Parking
Spaces 350

11 Story Steel and
Masonry Building

296.00'

460.36'
~ GRASS AREA ~

N 32°53'45"E

~PAVED~

60' WIDE SEWER EASEMENT
Book N/250 Age 214

N 32°53'45"E
380.00'

FEE TAIL ROAD

← 356.00' →

~ GRASS AREA ~   660.00'   CURB
N 57° 06' 15"W

Pt. of Beginning

452.12'

LAW   DRIVE   80'

60'
Driveway

RICHAN RD.

Certified to Dan E. Developer, Ace Ins.
Co., Worthier Title Ins. Co. and all
parties in interest.

Surveyed by Mulligan Engineering &
Surveying Co, No. 599 McLaughlin St, City
of Mc Niece, State of Fagan.

Ima Surveyor, Surveyor Ima Surveyor
Lic. No. 2303

Drawn by I.S.   Sept. 1, 1983
Checked by V.P.   July 15, 1984
                        Jan 29, 1985

512

Description

All that certain tract, lot, piece or parcel of land being, lying and situated in the City of McNiece, County of Feerick, State of Fagan, more particularly described as follows:

BEGINNING at a point on the northerly side of Law Drive, 60 feet wide, a distance of 452.12 feet from the intersection of the northerly sideline of Law Drive, with the westerly sideline of Feetail Road, running thence the following six (6) courses and distances:

(1) North 57° 06' 15" West along Law Drive, 60 feet wide, 660 feet to a point; thence

(2) North 32° 53' 45" East, 460.36 feet to lands now or formerly of Joseph Crowley; thence

(3) South 56° 26' 45" East, 160.41 feet to an angle point in said lands; thence

(4) still along said Crowley lands, South 52° 22' 20" East 520.80 feet to a point on a curve; thence

(5) to the right in a southerly direction along the arc of said curve with a radius of 24 feet, a single angle of 90° 00' 00", a chord bearing of South 25° 10' 5" East, a chord distance of 36 feet and an arc distance of 37.70 feet; thence

(6) South 32° 53' 45" West 380 feet to the northerly line of Law Drive, 60 feet wide, the point and place of BEGINNING.

BEING Lots 34 and 35 in Block 0903 as shown on "Map of Property of Dan E. Developer in the County of Feerick, State of Fagan, surveyed by Mulligan Engineering & Surveying Company, July 1976" and filed in the Feerick County Clerk's Office on August 6, 1976, as No. 3314; and

BEING commonly known as 21 Law Drive, McNiece, Fagan, as shown on Survey made by Mulligan Engineering & Surveying Company dated September 1, 1983, and last revised January 20, 1985.

See generally ABA Real Prop., Prob. & Tr. Section, Land Surveys: A Guide for Lawyers (B. Rifkin ed. 1989); Kanner, What You Should Know About Surveys, 5 Prac. Real Est. Law. 9 (May 1989); Sutin, A Survey Requirements Checklist, 4 Prac. Real Est. Law. 45 (November 1988); Williams and Onsrud, What Every Lawyer Should Know About Land Surveys, 2 Prob. & Prop. 13 (1988).

   3.   Title Insurance.   At Chapter 3B2 we reviewed the terms of the standard title policy including insuring provisions, exclusions from coverage, conditions and stipulations, specific exemptions from coverage, co-insurance and reinsurance requirements, and differences among the forms that are available. You will recall that most postconstruction lenders will require title insurance, where available, as opposed to an attorney's opinion, and they generally prefer the form of lender's policy issued by the American Land Title Association. This form, however, is not available in some states. Why would a title policy be preferable to an attorney's opinion for most lenders?

   Postconstruction lenders will normally permit the borrower to select the title company or companies from a pre-approved list, subject to limitations on the amount of coverage the lender will accept from any one insurer. The title industry has limited assets, and lenders carefully review annual reports from each company in establishing limits on acceptable coverage. When the assets of one insurer are considered insufficient to cover the risk, the lender will require co-insurance or reinsurance with another company or companies. In this context co-insurance means the sharing of a risk between two insurers, as opposed to hazard insurance, where the risks may be shared as between the insurer and the insured.

   You should realize that title insurance in many respects is like a guaranty of the accuracy of a search of the title records. Thus, any title can be insured. The important thing is to determine what defects the search has revealed. Many weeks before the closing of a postconstruction loan, the title company should come up with a preliminary "title report," sometimes called a "title binder" or "title certificate." It is an agreement by the title company to insure the property subject to the exceptions revealed by the title search. Therefore, it is the task of both lender's and borrower's counsel to scrutinize the report very thoroughly and resolve any marketability or lien-priority problems with the title company as quickly as possible. The title report is subject to adverse claims that arise between the date of the title report and the closing.

   Returning to the master hypothetical, suppose that Dan, Ace, and FNB (the construction lender) execute a pre-closed form of buy-sell agreement on June 1 of this year, the same day that FNB records its mortgage, and that construction commences two weeks later, on June 15. Three weeks prior to the closing of the postconstruction loan (which is scheduled to close on December 31 of this year), you, as Ace's attorney, receive a copy of the preliminary title report that reveals the following encumbrances and exceptions to title in Schedule B.

a.   telephone and other utility easements recorded on May 15 of this year;

b.   mortgage to secure a gap loan of $5 million to Dan (to fund construction overruns) that was recorded by the gap lender on September 1 of this year;

c.   a long-term lease (pursuant to a leasing requirement in Ace's commitment letter) recorded on December 31 of last year; and

d.   a lien for unpaid local property taxes filed on November 1 of this year.

Which interests, if any, should be extinguished or subordinated prior to the closing date to assure Ace of a safe and legal investment? You may wish to review the discussion at Chapter 4C on how a mortgage competes for lien priority with other adverse interests in the same real property.

As attorney for Dan Developer, would you recommend that he obtain an owner's title policy in addition to paying for the cost of the mortgagee's policy? Your answer would ordinarily be yes, for several reasons. First, without an owner's policy, Dan's equity in the property will not be insured. Second, the standard mortgage or deed of trust contains a covenant of the borrower that he or she has good title to the mortgaged property, subject only to the exceptions set forth therein. If a title defect should be discovered and the title company pays the lender, under standard title policy language the title company becomes "subrogated" (steps into the shoes of) the lender and has all the lender's rights against the borrower under the covenant of title. Do you understand why Dan will not be liable to the title company if he has his own policy? Third, and the reason most likely to convince Dan, is that the cost of combining fee insurance with mortgage insurance is usually quite modest and, in some states, nominal.

Payment of closing costs by the borrower is generally nonnegotiable. Sometimes the borrower can get the lender's approval to negotiate some fees and charges directly with the supplier of the services. Borrowers are especially concerned about escalating fees of special counsel. If you were Ace Insurance Company's general counsel, what problems might you see in allowing Dan Developer to negotiate fees with your special counsel?

4. The Tax Status of Closing Charges. As observed at Chapter 5B3, note 6a, supra, under I.R.C. §163 a current deduction for interest paid or accrued is only permitted for any charge imposed by the lender that represents compensation for the use or forbearance of money. Hence, the typical closing expenses that are paid by the borrower in connection with obtaining the postconstruction loan, such as appraisal fees, title insurance premiums, recording and survey fees, brokerage commissions, and attorneys' fees, are not currently deductible as interest; they may, however, be capitalized as expenditures incurred in the carrying on of a trade or business (or in the production of investment income) and amortized over the life of the loan to which they relate. See, e.g., Anover Realty Corp. v. Commissioner, 33 T.C. 671 (1960); Rev. Rul. 70-360, 1970-2 C.B. 103. Cf. Treas. Reg. §§1.263(a)-2(a), (c), and (d). Such loan costs (as well as organization costs) may be amortized even though the mortgagor has not yet completed construction or acquisition of its income-producing property. See Blitzer v. United States, 684 F.2d 874 (Ct. Cl. 1982), which held that for purposes of deductibility under I.R.C. §162(a), a "trade or business" commences when construction of a project begins. But see McManus v. Commissioner, 54 T.C.M. 475 (1987), affd., 865 F.2d 255 (4th Cir. 1988). The language in the *Blitzer* case may also justify amortization of partnership syndication costs over the term of the partnership. See Larason, May Partnership Syndication Costs Be Written Off over a Limited Partnership's Life?, 58 J. Taxn. 336 (1983). But see McGuire, Can the Syndication Costs of a Partnership Be Amortized? An Analysis of Authorities, 59 J. Taxn. 208 (1983).

Origination fees, or points (which are geared to a percentage of the original loan amount), may be currently deducted as interest if they constitute payment for the use or forbearance of money. See, e.g., Rev. Rul. 69-188, 1969-1 C.B. 54, amplified by Rev. Rul. 69-582, 1969-2 C.B. 29; Rubnitz v. Commissioner, 67 T.C. 621 (1977). But if they are paid for services rendered by the lender they must be capitalized, as are other costs incurred to obtain the loan. However, if the parties themselves make an arm's-length allocation between a charge for services and a charge for the use of the loan funds, the Service will respect such an agreement. Rev. Rul. 69-189, 1969-1 C.B. 55. Points that constitute interest are subject to the same limitations on prepaid interest discussed supra at Chapter 5B3, note 6b. Loan "discounts" whereby the lender withholds a portion of the loan amount are treated as an interest charge for the entire loan period, and, whereas a cash-basis taxpayer may deduct a pro rata portion of the discount only when and as the principal is repaid, an accrual-basis taxpayer is allowed to amortize the discount over the life of the loan. See Lay v. Commissioner, 69 T.C. 421 (1977) (accrual-basis taxpayer); Hopkins v. Commissioner, 15 T.C. 160 (1950) (cash-basis taxpayer).

Previously, a commitment or standby fee was treated by the Service as a currently deductible business or investment expense under I.R.C. §162 or §212, respectively. Rev. Rul. 56-136, 1956-1 C.B. 92 (prior law). This made sense because such fees are paid by the borrower to compensate a prospective lender for agreeing to keep funds available pending the closing date but, absent a buy-sell agreement, the borrower may elect to forfeit the fee (especially if interest rates should decline prior to the closing date) and obtain a less expensive loan elsewhere. Nevertheless, the current position of both the Service and the Tax Court is that such fees must be capitalized and amortized over the life of the loan. Rev. Rul. 81-160, 1981-1 C.B. 312, whereby the Service revoked Rev. Rul. 56-136 by analogizing a commitment fee to the cost of an option to purchase property which, if exercised, must be added to the cost basis of the acquired property. The Ruling also suggests that if the loan commitment is not exercised, the borrower may take a loss deduction under I.R.C. §165. See Francis v. Commissioner, 36 T.C.M. 704 (1977). But see Duffy v. United States, 690 F.2d 889 (Ct. Cl. 1982), wherein the court suggested, by way of dictum, that commitment fees are currently deductible.

If the mortgaged property were to be sold prior to the maturity of the loan, or if the loan were to be prepaid, the borrower would be allowed a current deduction for the unamortized balance of any capitalized loan fees, even if the loan is prepaid solely for the purpose of obtaining a substitute loan from the same lender. S & L Building Corp. v. Commissioner, 19 B.T.A. 788 (1930), acq. X-1 C.B. 60 (1931), affd., 288 U.S. 406 (1933). See also Lay v. Commissioner, 69 T.C. 421 (1977); Baird v. Commissioner, 68 T.C. 115 (1977). See generally Malloy and Hayes, Deductibility of 'Commitment Fees': Are They for Services or for the Use of Money?, 51 J. Taxn. 278 (Nov. 1979). If an existing loan is extended or renewed, the unamortized fees (plus any new fees) must be amortized over the term of the new loan. See Great Western Power Co. v. Commissioner, 297 U.S. 543 (1936); Klyce v. Commissioner, 41 B.T.A. 194 (1940), nonacq., 1942-1 C.B. 18.

To the extent that origination and commitment fees, service charges, and other expenditures incurred to obtain the construction loan must be capitalized, prudent tax planning suggests that wherever possible these charges should be allocated to the construction loan and not to the postconstruction loan so that the borrower may be able to obtain a faster write-off over the relatively short term of the construction loan. See, e.g., Noble v. Commissioner, 79 T.C. 751 (1982); Lay v. Commissioner, 69 T.C. 421 (1977), affd., 691 F.2d 490 (3d Cir. 1982). In that regard it would be advisable, for example, to avoid a pre-closed transaction (discussed at Chapter 5B14, supra and Chapter 6B5) or a combined construction-permanent loan from the same lender so that separate loan documents would be executed by the borrower for the construction and postconstruction loans. Otherwise, the Service might contend that a unified transaction that contemplates an assignment of the construction note and mortgage to the postconstruction lender or an automatic "rollover" of the construction loan into a postconstruction loan constitutes, in substance, only one loan and that therefore the fees and charges for the construction loan should be amortized over the combined term of both loans. See Rev. Rul. 74-395, 1974-2 C.B. 45 (involving an F.N.M.A. commitment fee), mod. by Rev. Rul. 83-84, 1983-1 C.B. 97. Rev. Rul. 75-172, 1975-1 C.B. 145 (closing expenses on combined construction-permanent loan). See generally G. Robinson, Federal Income Taxation of Real Estate ¶7.02 (1979); M. Levine, Real Estate Transaction §228s (1988 ed.); Madden, 480-2nd T.M., Taxation of Real Estate Transactions — An Overview §II.B.1 (Bureau of National Affairs) (1988).

5. *Status of Closing Charges Under Usury Law.* Where the commitment fee is nonrefundable and the lender is not called on to make the loan, the prospective borrower may claim that the retention of the fee amounts to usury. The courts have generally rejected this claim on the ground that the fee does not constitute interest. See, e.g., People v. Central Federal Savings & Loan Assn., 46 N.Y.2d 41, 412 N.Y.S.2d 815, 385 N.E.2d 555 (1978); Stedman v. Georgetown Savings & Loan Assn., 595 S.W.2d 486 (Tex. 1979). As pointed out above, a commitment fee normally is not considered interest for usury purposes because it is construed as compensation for the lender's agreement to keep on hand a certain amount of loanable funds at the agreed-on interest rate until the loan is funded or as compensation for the borrower's option to take the loan at the closing date.

If a fee charged by the lender at the closing is added to the interest for the first year of the loan, a usury problem is much more likely than if the charge were prorated over the life of the loan. Do you see why? It is generally held that in determining whether interest is in excess of the legal limit, any payments received by the lender must be prorated, or "spread," over the term of the loan. See, e.g., Imperial Corp. v. Frenchman's Creek Corp., 453 F.2d 1338 (5th Cir. 1972); Sharp v. Mortgage Security Corp., 215 Cal. 287, 9 P.2d 819 (1932). But see Hoffman v. Key Federal Savings & Loan Assn., 286 Md. 28, 416 A.2d 1265 (1979), in which the court held that spreading was applicable only to points or other charges made at the inception of the loan.

Assume in the master hypothetical that Dan Developer exercises a right in the mortgage documents to prepay the loan five years after the closing date. Assume further that there were some substantial front-end charges imposed by Ace that under applicable law would be considered additional interest. The charges, however, when spread over the life of the loan would not bring the rate of return over the legal maximum. But if the charges were to be spread over just the five years before the loan was satisfied by prepayment, the usury laws would be violated. How might a court rule on the length of the permissible spreading? See Grall v. San Diego Building & Loan Assn., 127 Cal. App. 250, 15 P.2d 797 (1932).

16. *No Material Adverse Change Allowed Between Commitment and Closing*

During the interval of perhaps 18 to 36 months between the commitment date and the scheduled closing date, the postconstruction lender needs to be assured that it may terminate the commitment if there are adverse changes in the financial condition of the borrower or in certain other aspects of the transaction on which the lender relied when it decided to make the loan. Conversely, the developer wants a "bankable" commitment, that is, one that will be accepted by an interim lender as the basis for making a construction loan. The following is a typical "no material change" clause from a postconstruction loan commitment.

> At the time Lender makes the Loan, except as may otherwise be provided specifically by this Commitment, the financial condition and credit of Borrower and its major tenants, and all other features of the transaction shall be as represented to Lender without material, adverse change. No part of the Property shall have been damaged and not repaired to Lender's satisfaction nor taken in condemnation or other like proceeding, nor shall any such proceeding be pending. In the event that there has been a condemnation or other taking, Lender shall have the option to cancel this Commitment or reduce the amount of the Loan by the amount of the award received in connection with the condemnation or other taking. Neither the Borrower nor any Space Tenant under any assigned Space Lease, nor any guarantor of the Loan or any such Space Lease, shall be involved in any bankruptcy, reorganization or insolvency proceeding.

The Bankruptcy Code (11 U.S.C. §365(e) (1982)) recognizes the lender's need for protection by excepting loan commitments from its general prohibition against termination of contracts because of the insolvency or financial condition of the debtor. A similar exception to the trustee's right to assume or assign executory contracts is found in §365(c). The following is an excerpt from §365(e) of the Bankruptcy Code:

(e)(1) Notwithstanding a provision in an executory contract or unexpired lease, or in applicable law, an executory contract or unexpired lease of the debtor may not be terminated or modified, and any right or obligation under such contract or lease may not be terminated or modified, at any time after the commencement of the case solely because of a provision in such contract or lease that is conditioned on —

(A) the insolvency or financial condition of the debtor at any time before the closing of the case;

(B) the commencement of a case under this title; or

(C) the appointment of or taking possession by a trustee in a case under this title or a custodian before such commencement.

(2) Paragraph (1) of this subsection does not apply to an executory contract or unexpired lease of the debtor . . . if . . .

(B) such contact is a contract to make a loan, or extend other debt financing or financial accommodations, to or for the benefit of the debtor, or to issue a security of the debtor.

NOTES AND QUESTIONS

1. As you might expect, construction lenders who rely on take-out commitments from postconstruction lenders for repayment of their construction loans look askance at "no adverse change" provisions in postconstruction commitment letters. Indeed, some construction lenders will regard the commitment as "unbankable" unless the clause is deleted. Can you think of any alternative language that would protect both lenders and therefore should be reasonably acceptable to them as a compromise? How might a construction lender otherwise protect itself against the pitfalls of such a clause?

2. When the Bankruptcy Code was being drafted and attorneys representing lenders requested the exception for loan commitments under §365(e)(2), congressional staff members queried them as to why such an exception would be necessary inasmuch as real estate lenders often exculpate the borrower from personal liability and rely solely on the real estate for repayment of their loans. As a lender's attorney, how would you have responded to the question?

3. The "no adverse change" clause is worrisome from the borrower's perspective as well, especially if interest rates have risen since the commitment date, an event which may tempt the postconstruction lender to view this provision as an escape clause. The borrower can protect itself by making conservative estimates in the loan application as to its financial status and the financial affairs of its prime credit tenants. Can you think of any protective language that the borrower might want to include in this clause to avoid any attempt by the postconstruction lender to extricate itself from the commitment because of an adverse change in the creditworthiness of any prime tenant?

C.   CREDIT LEASES AS SECURITY

As explained in the following excerpt, the "credit leases"[11] with the major ("prime") tenants generally form the foundation of the economic viability of any commercial real estate project because it is the rental income stream from these leases (as opposed to the underlying land and physical improvements) that pays the debt-service payments on the mortgage and constitute the real security for the loan (or, in the parlance of real estate professionals, that "feeds the mortgage"). The credit leases with the prime tenants also serve as additional collateral for the loan.

This is why the postconstruction loan commitment for a commercial mortgage loan will require as a condition-precedent to funding that certain credit leases be in effect with specified tenants who are creditworthy for specified periods of time (that, for financial underwriting and security reasons, usually coincide with the term of the loan) and that the form and substance of each lease be reviewed by lender's counsel to assure the lender that the rental income stream cannot be reduced or abated by the tenants (to the extent that freedom of contract principles apply) and that the lender can tolerate the lease provisions as a would-be landlord if the lender should be forced to step into the shoes of the borrower in the event of foreclosure.

Madison and Dwyer, The Law of Real Estate Financing
¶3.05 (1981)

ANALYSIS OF SHOPPING CENTER AND OTHER CREDIT LEASES BY PERMANENT LENDER

In our hypothetical case involving a mortgage loan on a garden apartment complex, the Ace Insurance Co.'s appraisal-underwriting process involved an evaluation of the projected aggregate rental flow from the short-term occupancy leases, which are regarded as fungible by the lender. However, in the case of certain loans — those involving shopping centers, office buildings with long-term tenants, warehouses and other industrial facilities, and urban-renewal projects master-leased to a local housing authority — the security for the loan is the value attributable by the lender's appraiser to the rental obligations of specified

---

11. Don't confuse the phrase "credit lease" with "high-credit lease." High-credit, or bondable, leases are discussed at Chapter 9D, note 3.

high-credit tenants. Accordingly, in such loan transactions, the lender will want to evaluate the credit standing of each major or "prime" tenant. Also, the lender will demand, as a nonnegotiable condition of the commitment, the right to approve the form and substance of each lease, including the term, the tenants, and the rent payable, since it will expect the rental income stream from these leases to pay off the debt service on the loan. The other standard requirements in the commitment letter as to occupancy leases are that each prime lease be assigned to the lender as additional security and that the assignment be recorded and notice of the assignment served on the tenant; that the lease be in full force and effect; that there be no rental offsets or claims or defenses to enforcement; that the tenant shall have accepted its premises, confirmed commencement of its lease term, acknowledged that it is in occupancy and paying rent on current basis; and that satisfactory evidence be submitted to the lender as to all of the foregoing. Before the leases are executed and delivered, the developer's lawyer should initially familiarize himself with the lender's requirements as to leases. Lender's lawyers welcome the opportunity to work with developer's lawyers in the drafting of the leases or in advising them as to their specific requirements. Correspondence should be promptly initiated by developer's counsel while the lease negotiations are under way. Unfortunately, the developer is frequently so anxious to secure the major leases in order to assure the financing that the developer's lawyer is often faced with a "fait accompli" in the form of a completed lease. He must then try to persuade the lender's lawyers that the lease provides the necessary assurances that the rental stream will continue for the term of the loan, or must face the onerous task of cajoling the tenant to modify the lease in order to satisfy the permanent mortgagee. Occasionally, the lender's lawyers are able to persuade a major tenant to sign a side letter providing that as long as the lender has an interest in the property, the lease shall be deemed modified as required by the lender. In some instances, these leases are sufficiently long-term to liquidate the loan indebtedness by the loan maturity date. The perspicacious lender must also visualize itself as having to live with these lease provisions in the event it steps in as owner-landlord after a serious default by the mortgagor.

Consequently, when negotiating occupancy lease terms with prime tenants, the developer must be mindful of the . . . lender's requirements; these are designed to protect the rental income stream from cancellation or abatement. Otherwise, the developer or its attorney may be caught in the middle on the closing date between a permanent lender insisting upon changes in the lease and a prime tenant, with equal bargaining clout, who refuses to renegotiate a lease executed months or even years ago.

The following typifies the language in a commitment for a commercial mortgage loan whereby the postconstruction lender imposes general standards for the bulk of the occupancy leases with the minor ("secondary" tenants) but reserves the right to approve the form and substance of all the credit leases with the prime tenants (such as the Widget Corporation of America in the master hypothetical at Chapter 5B, supra) and to take a conditional assignment of these credit leases as additional collateral for the loan. By contrast, in the case of a mortgage loan on an apartment building or garden apartment complex, each lease would not be separately reviewed and approved because the same lease format would be used for all the tenants.

Space Leases

1. *General Requirements.* All Space Leases shall have a minimum term of three years. Space Leases having an original term of five or more years, or having an original term of less than five years but containing renewal options which, if exercised, would extend the total term of the lease beyond five years, shall be in form and substance satisfactory to Lender, and shall contain provisions requiring increases in annual rent, to be effective on the sixth anniversary of the lease, including renewal options, and every fifth year thereafter, in an amount equal to sixty percent of the annual increase in the United States Department of Labor, Bureau of Labor Statistics, "State of Fuller Consumer Price Index for all Urban Consumers — All Items" or such other index as may be substituted therefor (hereinafter referred to as the "Consumer Price Index" or "CPI"). All Space Leases shall be assigned to Lender as additional security for the Loan and shall be unconditionally subordinate to the Mortgage. Lender will consider granting Tenants leasing more than 15,000 Rentable Square Feet, non-disturbance agreements provided (i) the Space Lease is on the standard lease form and is otherwise satisfactory to Lender and its Law Department; (ii) the Lender's standard form of non-disturbance agreement is used; and (iii) the Borrower becomes obligated to pay reasonable processing charges with respect to each non-disturbance agreement and the fees and disbursements of any special counsel selected by Lender's Law Department.

2. *Leasing Commissions.* Any agreement to pay leasing commissions shall provide that the obligation to pay such commissions will not be enforceable against any party other than the party who entered into such agreement and will be subordinate to the Mortgage. Lender shall be furnished with evidence of the foregoing satisfactory to it and its Law Department in form and substance, and a provision incorporating the foregoing requirement in form and substance satisfactory to Lender and its Law Department shall be contained in the Mortgage.

3. *WCA Lease.* There shall be a Space Lease of at least 200,000 Rentable Square Feet in the Building to Widget Corporation of America, Inc. ("WCA Lease") at an annual rent of not less than $ _____ and with a remaining term at the Closing Date of not less than ten years. The WCA Lease shall be subordinate to the Mortgage and otherwise in form and substance be satisfactory to Lender and its Law Department, including without limitation, provisions dealing with escalation for expenses based on CPI or otherwise, and for taxes. The WCA Lease shall be in force, free from default, with the term commenced on or prior to the Closing Date. Upon approval of the form and substance of the WCA Lease, Lender shall enter into an agreement with WCA in which Lender shall agree that, in the event of a foreclosure of the Mortgage, Lender shall not disturb WCA's possession of its space in the Building provided that WCA is not then in default beyond any applicable grace period. The form and substance of said agreement shall be satisfactory to lender and its Law Department.

4. *Prohibitions in Respect of Space Leases.* No Space Lease having an original term of more than five years shall be modified, abridged or terminated, nor shall any surrender thereof be accepted, without the prior written consent of Lender. Any Space Lease having an original term of five years or less may be modified or abridged by the Borrower without the prior written consent of Lender so long as said modification or abridgement does not increase any material obligation of the landlord thereunder or decrease the rental or any other material obligation of the tenant thereunder. In addition, any Space Lease which has an original term of five years or less may be terminated by the Borrower without the prior written consent of the Lender if the tenant thereunder shall be in default.

The Borrower shall not collect rent for more than one month in advance except that Borrower may accept rent for up to three months in advance upon the execution of the Space Lease by all the parties thereto, provided that such advance rent is applied to the rents at the beginning of the term of the Space Lease, or held in trust as a security deposit for the performance of the terms of the Space Lease, with any deposit at the expiration of the term of the Space Lease to be applied to any rent then due or to be refunded to the tenant upon such expiration.

As a prelude to the Planning Problem that follows, the following excerpt of a speech made by Mendes Hershman (former vice-president and general counsel of the New York Life Insurance Company) should complete your understanding of how postconstruction lenders analyze occupancy leases. See also M. Friedman, 1 Friedman on Leases §8.3 (2d ed. 1983).

very useful

Hershman, Leases — Pitfalls and Pratfalls
Address to Business Loan Seminar, New York Life
Insurance Co., Mackinac Island, Michigan
(Sept. 26-28, 1967)

. . . This brings us to a discussion of the occupancy leases. Both the appraisal and underwriting processes for business loans involve evaluation of the fixed income flow from leases; and, in a few instances of established shopping center projects, anticipated overages. It is perhaps not too much to say that a great many loans have been made almost exclusively upon the value attributed to the obligation of high-credit tenants to pay rents under leases for terms long enough to liquidate the loan by maturity. Yet a lease, even a net lease of a high-credit tenant, is not a promissory note or bond. There are many conditions which may stop or diminish the flow of anticipated rental income: condemnation, fire damage, insolvency, breach of exclusives or radius requirements, and of many other covenants which give a tenant the right of offset against rent or right to cancel. Indeed, the lease may call for fulfillment of obligations by the landlord and therefore by the mortgagee should [it] become the landlord or give the tenant rights which for a life insurance company may actually call into question the legality of the proposed loan. In most cases, however, the question is not the legality of the loan. Most leases, particularly the leases to high-credit tenants with their massive bargaining power, present tough questions of judgment as to the adequacy of the "business-legal" components of the lease.

It is strange that the lease should still present so many imponderables for it has been with us since the Romans, plagued the kings' courts of the early Henrys when it was looked upon with suspicion as a means of avoiding the strictures of usury, and crossed the seas to the Colonies freighted with much of the technical language and many of the arbitrary rules derived from federal concepts of land tenures, concepts which hound the real property lawyer in 1967. Rents, of course, have changed from Colonial days when the annual ground rent for the entire town of Scarsdale was 5 pounds, and 20 bushels of peas was paid for Fordham.

I might note parenthetically a decision rendered in the reign of Henry V involving a restrictive covenant in a lease. The judge in that case said in his Norman [French]: "Per Dieu, si le Plaintiff fuit icy, il irra al prison tanq." ("By God, if the Plaintiff be not made [to give this up] here, to the prison tank will he go.") And restrictive covenants to this very day cause more difficulties in closing shopping center loans than any other single lease provision. What Judge Hill said in 1413, our lawyers at 51 Madison Avenue would like to say to Woolworth, Penney, Grant, and many of the other national chains in 1967.

The lawyer at the Home Office, examining the leases upon which the proposed loan is based both from an appraisal and underwriting point of view, knows the mortgage loan people expect a certain fixed rental from identified tenants for a stated period of time; that the obligations of the landlord which may become the obligations of the Company if we have to foreclose are such that the landlord can comply so as to preclude cancellation of the lease before its stated term and that the required rent not be subject to reduction, set-off or other contingency which will diminish the anticipated flow of net rent.

Parenthetically, this might also bring into play the question of tax stops and other similar provisions such as tenant's obligations to share in common expenses so as to assure a net rent upon which the appraisal is based. Particularly in office building situations, tax stops and payment by tenants of increases in maintenance expenses have become important considerations in determining the anticipated flow of income. Of course, our client, the Real Estate and Mortgage Loan Department, may be willing to accept the lease as a business risk even if there are some minimal risks of lease cancellation or rent abatement. This is part of the underwriting process. The lawyer must nevertheless bring such matters to the attention of the mortgage department because they are doing the underwriting, not the lawyer.

On the other hand, the lawyer can help to some degree in evaluating the risks. What are these risks or conditions, terms or provisions in leases which raise these business-legal questions for judgment? I will advert to some of the major pitfalls in the leases we get to review. . . .

First, the matter of subordination. In a good many states, upon foreclosure of a mortgage, all leases which are subsequent to the mortgage are automatically terminated irrespective of the parties' intentions or whether the tenant is made a party to the foreclosure.[12] In other states, and New York is an example, the mortgagee must join the tenant in the foreclosure action to terminate the lease.[13] Obviously then, in the states where there is automatic termination on foreclosure, the leases that the lender is relying on and hopes to keep must be made to prime the mortgage and as a general rule we want all credit leases in such jurisdiction prior to our mortgage. To the extent that we can, we like to retain prime rights, however, for the landlord to condemnation awards, fire insurance proceeds, and of course in respect to any option of the tenant to purchase the property. It is helpful if the mortgage instrument, in those states where leases are automatically

---

12. E.g., McDermott v. Burke, 16 Cal. 580, 590 (1860). — ED.

13. E.g., Metropolitan Life Insurance Co. v. Childs Co., 230 N.Y. 285, 296, 130 N.E. 295, 299 (1921); Davis v. Boyajian, Inc., 11 Ohio Misc. 97, 102, 229 N.E.2d 116, 119 (1967). It is well settled that a lease prior to a mortgage is unaffected by foreclosure. — ED.

terminated by foreclosure, contains a provision giving the mortgagee the right unilaterally to subordinate the mortgage to any subsequent lease.

I have seen leases which provide for subordination to all mortgages on condition that the mortgagee will agree not to disturb the tenant in the event of foreclosure. It is dangerous to accept this without the additional provision in the lease that in the event of foreclosure tenant will attorn to the purchaser at foreclosure sale. We should also see to it that if the lease is subordinated, it be subordinated only to the first mortgage so that a subsequent junior mortgagee will not have the power to cut off the lease.

If you have the opportunity to advise a developer in your state, if it is a state where there is automatic termination on the foreclosure, I suggest you tell him to try to get a provision in his leases giving him the option of subordinating the lease to a first mortgage. This will then give the mortgagee to whom he comes for financing the opportunity to control the developer's action in this respect by provision in the mortgage.

Second, the matter of covenant to pay. Many leases provide that as a condition of tenant's right to occupy the premises, rent in a specified amount be paid by the tenant, [which phraseology] does not actually [constitute a] covenant to pay. Our lawyers worry about such condition. They want tenant's express promise to pay the rent and it may indeed be important. They believe, and rightly, that the lease should expressly provide: "The tenant covenants and agrees to pay $ _____ as rent." For example, if the tenant has not covenanted to pay rent and has a right to assign the lease and assigns it, he will no longer be obligated to pay rent.[14] But with a covenant to pay in the lease, his obligation to pay would survive the assignment.

Third, the matter of default provisions — survival of liability for damages in event of default. An F. W. Woolworth lease, just by way of example, provides that if the tenant defaults in the payment of rent after 30 days' notice, the landlord may declare the lease forfeit. There is no provision giving the landlord a right to damages for this breach nor a right after termination to collect rent until he rerents or the difference between the rent he receives after rerenting and the rent reserved in the lease to Woolworth. Of course, in a case of a tenant of Woolworth's financial responsibility, there is little practical concern about this. Actually the landlord wouldn't terminate the lease but would simply sue for rent as it became due. But if it is not a lease of a high-credit tenant, we are the more likely to insist on adequate default provisions.

---

14. E.g., Fanning v. Stimson, 13 Iowa 42 (1862); Kimpton v. Walker, 9 Vt. 191 (1837); but see Samuels v. Ottinger, 169 Cal. 209, 146 P. 638 (1915). — Ed.

Fourth, the matter of continuous possession. Unless the lease specifically provides that the named tenant will continue to operate the premises for the particular use for which the premises are leased,[15] the tenant normally has a choice of discontinuing business or, if he has a right to assign or sublet,[16] then do that and discontinue his own

15. The case law has not supported specific performance actions to enforce these covenants. See, e.g., Price v. Herman, 81 N.Y.S.2d 361, 363 (1948), affd., 275 A.D. 675, 87 N.Y.S.2d 221 (1949); Security Builders v. Southwest Drug Co., 244 Miss. 877, 886, 147 So. 2d 635, 639 (1962). — ED.

16. At common law, a tenant can freely assign or sublet a leasehold estate (if it is an estate for years or periodic tenancy) without the landlord's consent in the absence of language to the contrary in the lease agreement. Friedman on Leases (2d ed. 1983) §7.2. A tenancy at will is an exception to the general rule. Id. §7.302a. However, the general rule of common law is that an absolute proscription against assignment and subletting without the landlord's consent is enforceable no matter how arbitrary and capricious the landlord's reason for withholding such consent. Id. §7.304a; Powell on Real Property (abr. ed. 1968) §246. Nevertheless, based on a policy against restraints on alienation that permeates the law of property, restrictions against assignments and subletting have been construed narrowly against landlords. For example, the qualifying language ("the consent of the landlord shall not be unreasonably withheld") has not empowered landlords to reject substitute tenants because the landlord does not like the business or business methodology of the proposed tenant, because the landlord prefers to rent other space to the prospective tenant, or because the substitute tenant plans to compete with an off-site business of the landlord. Id. §7.304c, n.172.1. Cf. Larson v. Commissioner, 66 T.C. 159 (1976), acq., 1979-1 C.B. 1, wherein the court ruled that such a restriction on the right to assign a limited partner's interest was virtually meaningless for purposes of Treas. Reg. §301.7701-2(e). Indeed, in the recent past there has emerged a strong minority rule based on the Restatement (Second) of Property to the effect that a landlord must act reasonably in deciding whether to consent to a proposed assignment or sublease "unless a freely negotiated provision in the lease gives the landlord an absolute right to withhold consent." Restatement (Second) of Property §15.2(2) (1977); see, e.g., Warmack v. Merchants National Bank, 272 Ark. 166, 612 S.W.2d 733 (1981); Fernandez v. Vazquez, 397 So. 2d 1171 (Fla. App. 1981); Funk v. Funk, 102 Idaho 521, 633 P.2d 586 (1981); Boss Barbara, Inc. v. Newbill, 97 N.M. 239, 638 P.2d 1084 (1982); Newman v. Hinky-Dinky Omaha Lincoln, 427 N.W.2d 50 (Neb. 1988); First Fed. Sav. Bank v. Key Markets, 532 N.E.2d 18 (Ind. App. 1988).

Exemplifying this trend is the decision by the California Supreme Court in Kendall v. Ernest Pestana, Inc., 40 Cal. 3d 488, 220 Cal. Rptr. 818, 709 P.2d 837 (1985). In that case, the lease simply required that any assignment be conditioned on the written consent of the landlord. The case involved a situation in which the lessor refused its consent to an assignment unless the proposed assignee agreed to an increased rental with respect to the balance of the original lease term. The court ruled that where a commercial lease provides for assignment (or subletting) only with the prior consent of the landlord, such consent may be withheld only where the landlord has a commercially reasonable objection to the assignee or the proposed use. The court rejected the majority rule by following the property theory approach taken by the Restatement to the effect that any arbitrary refusal by the landlord would constitute an illegal restraint on alienation because the landlord has the right to reject a substitute tenant for any rational protective reason (e.g., the assignee has a poor credit rating) and because the original tenant would remain secondarily liable for those lease obligations that were

operation in the premises. Inasmuch as our underwriting is predicated for the most part on the fixed minimum rent rather than overrates, the lack of a continuous operation provision will not bother us in the case of high-credit tenants. On the other hand, and this may well be true in many shopping center leases, there are leases which are made dependent on the particular high-credit tenant staying in business in the center so that unless there is a continuous operation clause in the high-credit tenant's lease and the latter goes out, a default will thereby be created in the dependent lease or leases. It is therefore incumbent on the lawyer reviewing leases for a shopping center loan to watch for the dependent leases, bring this to the attention of the mortgage department and let the latter judge the effect on its rating in the underwriting process. In a rare case a court may imply a continuous operation clause.

Fifth, the matter of tenant's rights to cure defaults. First, we should keep in mind that if tenant is given a lien for what he spends to cure the landlord's default that is not a business question but raises a strictly legal objection because creation thereby of a prior encumbrance violates our investment statutes. Second, a provision requiring landlord to pay the charges on any mortgage upon the leased premises and permitting tenant, in the event of the landlord's default, to cancel the lease — a provision contained in some national chain leases — is obviously unacceptable because tenant could then cancel for default in our own first mortgage depriving us of the security on which we relied in making the loan and at a time when the security is most needed; also, such a clause permits cancellation for defaults in junior mortgages for which there is otherwise no reason for the first mortgagee to cure such defaults.

A more common provision does not permit cancellation for landlord's default in mortgages but permits tenant to cure such defaults and recoup reimbursement out of subsequent rentals. This, too, is objectionable because such a set-off could be used to cure a junior

---

expressly undertaken by the original tenant, for example an express covenant (as opposed to an implied obligation) to pay rent. Also, the court applied a contract theory approach by emphasizing the duty of good faith and fair dealing inherent in every contract. 40 Cal. 3d at 500. However, the court in *Kendall* failed to address the question whether absolute prohibitions on transferability and clauses that allow the landlord to withhold consent in its sole discretion would be rendered vulnerable to challenge. In response to the uncertainty legislation was enacted in 1989 that expressly permits absolute prohibitions in commercial leases, but the statute does not explicitly deal with sole discretion clauses. Cal. Civil Code §§1995.010 to 1995.270. See Murray and Hamrich, Assignment and Subletting in Commercial Leases: The Impact of the New Civil Code Sections, 13 CEB Real Prop. L. Rep. 65 (Apr. 1990). See Madison and Dwyer ¶3.05[7] (1990 Cum. Supp. No. 1) for discussion of "profit-sharing" and "recapture" clauses and examination of other planning suggestions. — ED.

mortgage default and deprive us of the security of the rental to which we as first mortgagee are primarily entitled.

If the provision is applicable only to mortgages prior in lien to the lease as, for example, the Woolworth provision, we would confirm that the lease was prior to our first mortgage and require deletion of any subordination provisions in the lease. The Woolworth lease provision on tenant's right to cure defaults and how the matter was handled as between the Law Department and Real Estate and Mortgage Loan Department may be illuminating as an example of the review process at the Home Office.

The Law Department pointed out to the Real Estate and Mortgage Loan Department that Woolworth under Article 12 of its lease had the right to cure any default of the landlord in the payment of taxes, mortgage payments or other liens to which its lease may be subordinate and in the making of repairs or performing any other obligations of the landlord under the lease and to offset the cost thereof with interest at 6% against rents. The Law Department pointed out that this provision is of concern to the Company in two respects: (1) the Company's interest may be prejudiced if rents are withheld for application in payment of a second mortgage or other junior lien; and (2) that whereas our form of mortgage requires mortgagor to perform all of the landlord's covenants under the leases, the value of such a provision is largely dependent on the promptness with which the Company can learn of nonperformance by the mortgagor. We recommended, therefore, requiring an amendment of the Woolworth lease to condition the tenant's right to cure defaults upon the giving of prior notice thereof to us as first mortgagee as well as to the landlord. We pointed out that we had had at least one instance in which Woolworth had agreed to give the company notice of defaults by the landlord. The response of the Real Estate and Mortgage Loan Department to our question on this particular article of the Woolworth lease was that since Woolworth's policy is that of never accepting a subordinate position and with its concern for priming all mortgages, the Company as first mortgagee does not have any real exposure to the possibility of rents being withheld from the Woolworth premises for application in payment of a second mortgage or other junior lien but that we should try to get the notice provision as to those defaults which Woolworth might seek to cure.

In conclusion on this point of tenant's right to cure defaults, it may be well to note that any offset against rent which is permitted to a tenant in the lease should be limited to offsets arising under the lease, not from *any* indebtedness of the landlord to the tenant however incurred.

Sixth, the matter of termination for (a) "wastebasket" fires and (b) condemnation.   (a) Clauses in leases which permit termination in event of fire are completely objectionable. Some leases, like Woolworth's, provide that in the event of damage or destruction all rent abates until the landlord has restored the premises and delivered the premises to the tenant in the condition required by the tenant. This, too, is obnoxious to the lender because it makes no distinction between the "wastebasket" fire and the serious fire. So long as the fire is not ground for cancellation, the particular clause is negotiable. For example, under the Penney leases the landlord is required to keep the building of which the leased premises are a part insured for fire and extended coverage to the extent of full insurable value, [and] the landlord and Penney must be named insureds and the proceeds applied to the cost of restoration to the extent required for such purposes. It makes no provision for payment of the proceeds to a mortgagee under a standard mortgagee clause, but we are able to secure from Penney agreement to make the proceeds payable to New York Life under a standard mortgagee clause on our undertaking that the proceeds received by us shall be made available for repair and restoration upon presentation of bills and lien waivers and provided the carrier does not claim that some act of the landlord and tenant who are named insured has not voided the policies. This is satisfactory to us. So long as we control the proceeds and there is no obligation to repair beyond the amount thereof and any diminution of rent would be in proper relation to loss of space, we are satisfied to use . . . the proceeds for restoration.

(b) Provisions for condemnation while presenting similar aspects are more difficult to negotiate. Thus, if a partial taking results in a reduction of rent, the mortgagee should insist that a part of the award sufficient to offset the rent reduction be applied to the debt with only the balance available for replacing damaged improvements. National chains such as Penney generally provide in their leases an option to terminate the lease if all or any part of the premises are taken even if the part taken is inconsequential or temporary and apply this also to parking areas required under the leases; also, if the lease is not terminated, that the landlord restore the premises as required by Penney and reduce the rent proportionately on a floor space ratio; also, that the tenant share in any condemnation award to the extent of actual damage sustained by it which means, of course, a possibility of eating up most of the award. Our mortgage department has been willing to accept a condemnation clause with a highly rated tenant like Penney if Penney's right to terminate on partial condemnation is limited to a taking in excess of a reasonable percentage of floor area and parking lot area, in the latter case coupled with an obligation of the landlord to provide equivalent parking space.

In the process of underwriting, the possibility of condemnation must be thoroughly evaluated. An absolute right to cancel, no matter how slight the condemnation, is obnoxious. The right to cancel should be limited to a taking, in excess of a definite percentage of area, acceptable to the mortgage department, or if it reduces the parking area to a ratio below a rate of 1.5:1 to 2:1, or below a specified area, and provided there is a right in the landlord to preclude cancellation by substituting other parking, perhaps including double deck parking. Where the minimum rent is reduced, the minimum sales base used in computing percentage rent should be reduced pro rata and tenant should not be allowed to participate in the award except to the extent of loss to its fixtures and improvements.

Seventh, the matter of use clauses — exclusives — radius restrictions. For one very good reason shopping center leases particularly should have use clauses which specify the type of business to be conducted or the kind of merchandise to be sold on the premises. A specific use clause will minimize conflicts with exclusive clauses then or thereafter granted in other leases. Anyone who has had to review shopping center leases finds reconciling exclusives the most burdensome of all tasks. There are all too many gray areas where conflicts are or may develop and the business risks of justified lease terminations attendant thereon must be evaluated. One caveat must be kept in mind if the provision is "the tenant shall use" rather than "the premises shall be used," that on a permitted assignment or subletting there may be no restriction on the assignee or sublessee. Obviously it is better that the provision be "the premises shall be used" for such and such purposes.

Another point to be kept is that if the premises are to be used "only" for such use, the court is more likely to uphold the restriction than if such restrictive word is absent. Where a restriction is to limit tenant's sales to merchandise sold in tenant's other stores, it is best to insert "now sold" as more specific and precluding problems if the character of the tenant's operations changes. For example, many retailers want to be protected against discount houses but if a chain acquires a string of discount houses a restriction to merchandise "sold in tenant's other stores" won't prevent conversion to a discount operation in this shopping center. Our mortgage department would like to rely on the self-interest and sophistication of developers to give exclusives reluctantly and to limit their effect so as to narrow the range of merchandise and geographic area, hopefully to the existing center. Unfortunately too few developers are sophisticated and their self-interest leads them to take "name" tenants on almost any basis. Faced with the likelihood of overlapping exclusives we try at the very least to get the remedies of tenants limited to suits for injunction or damage and eliminate right to abate the rent or terminate the lease. When national chains simply won't narrow their use clause, then the landlord when giving exclusives must except the particular premises occupied by that chain from the operation of the exclusives granted to others.

The courts impose the obligation on the landlord to enforce the restriction by reasonable legal means and if he doesn't, the injured tenant may terminate the lease. They generally impose a duty of notice from the injured tenant to the landlord before finding a breach of the covenant, giving tenant a right to remove. The courts don't favor restrictions and inquire into the facts as to whether the businesses are substantially similar, that is, whether there is a substantial overlapping of products. For example, a New York court considered whether the sale of women's blouse-skirt combinations violated an exclusive for dresses and found that these are considered separate businesses in the garment industry, so held there was no violation of the exclusive; and another, i.e., New York court found that an exclusive for a restaurant was not violated by a luncheonette because of substantial dissimilarities in menu, price, and decor. Courts will also look into the percentage of total sales of each party represented by overlapping articles. For that reason it is desirable to keep away from exclusives for specified items and make the restrictions descriptive of lines of business.

One aspect of this restrictive covenant field which is particularly troublesome to the mortgage lender is the radius restriction whereby landlord agrees that neither it, nor its successors, assigns, subsidiaries, etc. will lease or permit any property within a certain radius from the shopping center, or covering the center "as it may be expanded" or with respect to land adjacent to the shopping center, to be used for the particular restricted use. In such instance the mortgagee is powerless to protect against it because the radius of the restriction goes beyond the mortgaged property and, what's more, if we foreclosed we would become bound by the restriction. Sometimes a tenant will agree that, so long as we hold the mortgage or have an interest in the premises, tenant won't exercise right to cancel or abate rent but will enforce its rights by injunction or in suit for damages. Landlords if they must take a radius restriction should try to be specific as to the area covered — not just the XYZ Shopping Center because this would include any expansion of it — and limit it to land which is covered by the mortgage all expect to get. Not only with restrictive covenants as to use but as to all other covenants — warranty of title, parking rights and ratios, payment of taxes, fire insurance, initial and continued occupancy of identified co-tenants — the landlord must be careful to limit the geographic extent of his obligation to what he owns because the mortgage lender must be satisfied that the mortgagor-landlord can comply physically and legally with the obligations under the leases which are to be mortgagee's prime security. The mortgagor-landlord is going to have to show his proposed mortgagee his capacity to comply with any lease covenant with respect to any property not owned by him in fee or not included in the lender's mortgage by reciprocal easement agreements or parking declaration or other recorded documents which will bind all subsequent interests in the property to be mortgaged by this lender.[17]

Eighth, the matter of alterations and expansions. Rights reserved in the tenant under the lease to make substantial alterations raises the question of mechanics' and materialmen's liens priming the mortgage. It is desirable to get some limitation on cost. If possible, it is useful to get bonding requirements unless, of course, the size and character of the tenant makes the possibility of unpaid mechanics liens remote.

In some chain leases, of which Penney is a good example, the tenant adds to its unconditional right to make alterations that any additional expense to which tenant is put in its alteration work by reason of requirements of state and local law will be paid by landlord. Some of the possibilities of these rights to alter and expand are enough to frighten reviewing counsel; viz., violation of other tenants' rights in service drives, maintenance of parking ratios, imposition on landlord of additional real estate taxes, insurance, heating, lighting and sewer charges, all of which are beyond landlord's control. The future expansion rights are often related to amount of gross sales which, if exceeded, impose on landlord obligations to construct a specified addition. This raises the possibility of the landlord not complying and, should we as mortgage lender take over, our legal inability to make an additional investment because it is beyond the legal ratio to appraised value and because we must go to the Superintendent of Insurance for permission to make the investment. Furthermore, in theory, since a national chain like Penney won't give up its right to assign and sublet, we may have

17. You should be aware that antitrust laws have been applied to both exclusive use and radius restrictions in shopping centers on the ground that they create illegal restraints on competition. While the courts have generally tested these restrictions against a standard of reasonableness (see, e.g., Dalmo Sales Co. v. Tysons Corner Regional Shopping Center, 308 F. Supp. 988 (D.C. Cir. 1970), affd., 429 F.2d 206 (D.C. Cir. 1970); Optivision, Inc. v. Syracuse Shopping Center Assocs., 472 F. Supp. 665 (N.D.N.Y. 1979), the FTC seems to have been moving toward the concept of "per se" violations of the antitrust laws. See, e.g., consent decrees in Tysons Corner Regional Shopping Center, 83 F.T.C. 1598 (1943); Gimbel Bros., Inc., 83 F.T.C. 1320 (1974); but see Southaven Land Co. v. Malone & Hyde, Inc., 715 F.2d 1079 (6th Cir. 1983), where a claim alleging violation of §2 of the Sherman Act, 15 U.S.C. §2, involving an exclusive use clause, was dismissed based on the evolving doctrine of antitrust "standing." The Bankruptcy Code, enacted in 1978, provides that when a trustee for a tenant assumes the lease, the trustee must, inter alia, provide "adequate assurance of future performance" under the lease. Adequate assurance of future performance is defined with respect to shopping centers in §365(b)(3) of the Bankruptcy Code as including "adequate assurance that the assumption will not substantially breach radius, location, use or exclusivity provisions in the lease." 11 U.S.C. §365(b)(3) (1982 & Supp. 1984). What effect do you think this provision has on the F.T.C. position? — ED.

Problems w/ Prime tenant?

a situation of a costly expansion and shortly thereafter the national chain with its greater sales potential assigning or subletting to a tenant without such sales potential. We have been able to negotiate with Penney an amendment as to alteration and expansion of the premises under which the tenant must get landlord's prior approval of structural changes, not to be unreasonably withheld, and give up the right to cancel if landlord doesn't undertake the expansion. If Penney nevertheless goes ahead with the expansion, tenant's right to offset the cost of the expansion is limited to percentage rentals in excess of a specified minimum rent which is reasonably satisfactory to our mortgage department.

Ninth, miscellaneous problems. There are a number of problems and pitfalls which we perhaps can treat in summary fashion not because they are not as important as those which we have treated more extensively but because we are running out of time.

   a.   Co-tenancy requirements.   It is characteristic of shopping centers to find in leases requirements for the initial occupancy by named co-tenants and sometimes continued occupancy. Where initial occupancy by named co-tenants is required, the situation is not too difficult. If the co-tenant's lease must be non-cancellable for a specified period, then we must look to see if there are exceptions arising out of default, condemnation, damage, bankruptcy, etc. and get tenant's approval of these contingencies for "cancellation." A guarantee of continued occupancy by the named co-tenant is extremely difficult to handle and presents a serious business question. At the very least the provision should be made inapplicable to temporary closings for repairs, etc. and permit landlord to substitute reasonably equivalent co-tenants within a reasonable period of time. If the co-tenant lease is not co-extensive in term with the lease in question and permits an assignment and subletting, merger and consolidation, these should be excepted from the requirement for continued occupancy by the named co-tenant.[18]

   b.   Cancellation privileges.   Some chain leases provide cancellation for any default of landlord. Any right on the part of the tenant to cancel must be carefully evaluated. A right to cancel for *any* default of the landlord must be whittled down. For example, there are covenants personal to the landlord — his own bankruptcy — default in which cannot be cured by the mortgagee and are therefore unacceptable. The mortgagee must try to make a separate agreement with the tenant that the tenant will not exercise the right to cancel until the mortgagee

---

18. A shopping center tenant obliged by a covenant to operate a first-class department store for a period of 30 years could not evade its obligation on antitrust grounds except to the extent that it would have been required to operate under the name of a bankrupt predecessor. Net Realty Holding Trust v. Franconia Properties, 544 F. Supp. 759 (E.D. Va. 1982). — Ed.

has had a reasonable time to foreclose and get into a position to cure the default.

   c. Guarantee. Where the lender is relying on a guarantee of a lease, for example, a lease to a subsidiary which is a shell corporation guaranteed by the financially strong parent, we must take great care that the guarantee will not be affected by bankruptcy, reorganization or insolvency of the tenant, its successors or assigns or the disaffirmance of the lease by a receiver or trustee of the tenant and that the guarantee will be applicable to successors and assigns of the tenant and that there will be no release of liability upon any assignment by the original tenant.

   d. Statements of landlord's operations. Provision in some chain store leases prohibits landlord from divulging the amount of tenant's sales. Penney's lease, for example, so provides, but tenant will accept a modification permitting divulging of such sales to any bona fide mortgagee in accordance with the provisions of the mortgage where, as in our mortgage, there is a requirement for periodic statements covering landlord's operations.

   e. Term of lease. Some leases provide for commencement on opening of business and ending a specified number of years thereafter, which is satisfactory if the conditions requiring commencement of business are clear and can be complied with and, in addition, as in the Penney lease, there is a right to cancel after a certain number of years on notice and payment of a certain, sometimes nominal amount. We must point this out clearly to our mortgage department which can then evaluate the effect for appraisal and underwriting considerations; also, in relation to any representation the landlord may make in other leases as to the term of this lease.

   f. Landlord's compliance with conditions as to new construction. In connection with new construction there are often numerous requirements of the landlord: physical requirements of the site, compliance with laws, with plans and specifications approved by tenant, cost of the work and its completion; compliance with which we must satisfy ourselves or secure tenant's acknowledgement of such compliance by landlord.

   g. Percentage rent. Where the rent reserved, as in some chain store leases, is set at a percentage of sales, we point this up to the mortgage department for their underwriting consideration as to adequacy. In such event, determination of sales on which the percentage is based becomes of genuine concern and, even more so, right to discontinue operations, assign or sublet. We insist that a certain definite term be set before which no right to discontinue business, assign or sublet will be approved and after such term, there shall be an appropriate alternative rent fixed in event of discontinuance and/or subletting or assignment with an option in landlord to cancel. If at all possible, where the rent is only a percentage rent, there should be an obligation on the part of the tenant to devote premises to its retail business and with all due diligence. As part of this due diligence, the mortgage lender should try to minimize the tenant's right to lease out departments to an unusual degree.

h. *Security deposit agreements.* Landlords sometimes require, particularly of tenants with medium to low credit ratios, security deposits, and these tenants may get it into their leases that if the deposit is not returned, tenant either may continue in possession without payment of rent until the deposit is recouped or will secure a prior lien on the premises till repaid. Such a lease must be subordinated to the mortgage if the tenant has acquired a lien on the premises for his deposit because the tenant's lien may be a prior encumbrance which may render the institution's mortgage illegal under investment statutes limiting investment to mortgages secured by improved and unencumbered real estate.

i. *Purchase options.* A right in the tenant to purchase must be subordinated to the mortgage even if for a price which would pay off the mortgage because even under the latter supposition it is an enlargement of the prepayment privilege and in a minority of jurisdictions gives tenant right to cut off the mortgage. A right of first refusal is not as onerous to a lender and is acceptable to many lenders. Where the option or first refusal is subject to the mortgage, the lender is unaffected except to the extent that he must guard against merger of the lease into the fee title. Options to purchase which prime the mortgage raise the question of prior encumbrance and possible illegality of the loan. I must reiterate that in this situation as in all others where the landlord's default would give tenant a right of lien against the premises, the provision is not acceptable to a mortgage lender whose lending is restricted by investment statutes which require that the mortgage not be subject to prior encumbrances.

PLANNING PROBLEM

To be a real estate lawyer handling large, complex transactions sounds glamorous. In a sense, it is. A great deal of money — perhaps hundreds of millions of dollars — is at stake. Decisions have to be made under pressure. And, most important, real estate lawyers can see the results of their labors in the form of bricks and mortar, glass and steel, literally rise before them. In the final analysis, however, the successful real estate lawyer is one who realizes that the work is not all glamour; who does his or her homework at night and on weekends; who drafts documents carefully and reads and rereads them to understand their interrelationship and how a change in one document can affect the other documents and ultimately the client's bottom line. This can sometimes be a rather tedious business, especially when it comes to a review of leases. However, only by understanding each provision in each lease and knowing how they relate to the companion provisions in that lease and other leases in the building or shopping center can the attorney determine the full extent of the risks the client is assuming.

This planning problem is designed not only as a review of some of the landlord-tenant issues affecting the developer and the postconstruction lender, but also as a training tool in developing those analytical skills a real estate lawyer must have.

The following are some clauses from an actual office building lease and an actual shopping center lease. They are based on a sample lease agreement that appears in J. Casner and B. Leach, Cases and Text on Property (3d ed. 1984) 634-655. You will see that these leases are not always drafted with precision. Assume you represent alternatively Dan Developer as the developer-landlord and Ace Insurance Company as postconstruction lender. Based on the materials you have read, examine these clauses from the standpoint of your client and be prepared to explain what legal or business problems they present and what you think can be done to avoid them.

Sections 1 and 2 of an Office Building Lease

RENTAL

1. Lessee shall pay to Lessor for the demised premises an annual rental of Fifty Thousand Dollars ($50,000), which shall be payable in equal monthly installments in advance on the first day of each month throughout the term; the aforesaid payments of rental to be made without demand at _____ Street, New York, N.Y., or such other place as Lessor may designate by notice in writing to Lessee and by checks drawn to the order of Lessor without any offset or deduction whatsoever. At or prior to the execution and delivery of this Agreement, Lessee has paid to Lessor the sum of Five Thousand Dollars ($5,000), the receipt of which is hereby acknowledged by Lessor, to be applied to the payment of the rent first coming due hereunder.

OCCUPANCY

2. Lessor does not warrant that actual occupancy shall be available to Lessee at the date fixed for the commencement of the term of this lease since the demised premises are presently rented to another tenant. In the event that such tenant shall not have removed from the demised premises on or before January 1, 1991, then Lessee shall be entitled to a prorating of rent and other charges with respect to such period as it shall not be in occupancy of the said premises following January 1, 1991. Lessor agrees, however, in the event that the present tenant vacates the said premises at any time on or before January 1, 1991 to deliver possession of the said premises to Lessee hereunder immediately thereafter, in which event Lessor shall be entitled to, and Lessee shall pay, rent and other charges on a pro rata basis for the period beginning on the

date of such delivery and ending on December 31, 1990. The term of this lease, in any event, shall begin on January 1, 1991, and terminate on December 31, 2005.

Sections 4, 5, and 12 of an Office Building Lease

REPAIRS

4. Lessee shall take good care of the demised premises and of the fixtures, and of all alterations, additions and improvements in the demised premises throughout the term hereof, and shall promptly make all repairs, alterations and changes, ordinary and extraordinary, in, to and about the said premises necessary to preserve them in good order and condition, which shall be in quality and class equal to the original work, and Lessee shall promptly pay the expense of such repair, suffer no waste or injury, and at the end of the term, deliver up the demised premises in good order and condition in all respects, damage attributable to acts of God or the elements excepted. If Lessor shall deem that Lessee has not duly and promptly made the necessary repairs, alterations and changes in this paragraph referred to, and Lessor shall give to Lessee written notification of the requirement to so do during the term of this lease, Lessee shall have a reasonable time following the giving of said notice in which to comply therewith.

INSPECTION

5. Lessor shall have the right to inspect the demised premises, at reasonable times, provided that the lessee is provided reasonable notice beforehand and such inspection does not interfere with the conduct of lessee's business.

LESSOR'S LIABILITY

12. Lessor shall be exempt from any and all liability for any damage or injury to persons or property caused by or resulting from steam, electricity, gas, water, rain, ice or snow, or any leak or flow from or into any part of said building or from any damage or injury resulting or arising from any other cause or happening whatsoever unless damage or injury be caused by or be due to the negligence of Lessor.[19]

Sections 7 and 22 of an Office Building Lease

ASSIGNMENT AND SUBLETTING

7. Lessee, its successors or assigns, shall not assign this agreement or sublet the demised premises or any part thereof without prior consent

---

19. In some jurisdictions exculpatory provisions in commercial as well as residential leases are void as against public policy. E.g., N.Y.G.O.L. §5-321 (McKinney 1989); see also Uniform Residential Landlord and Tenant Act §1.403(a)(4) (1972). Can you think of the reason why? — ED.

of landlord, which consent shall not be unreasonably withheld. In the prevent of any such assignment or subletting, Lessee shall remain liable to Lessor for the payment of rent and the performance of all other obligations of the Lessee hereunder.

NON-WAIVER

22. The failure of either party to demand strict performance of any of the terms, conditions and covenants herein shall not be deemed a waiver of any rights or remedies of such party and shall not be deemed a waiver of any subsequent default in any of the terms, conditions or covenants herein contained.

Sections 9, 19, and 21 of an Office Building Lease

DEFAULT

9. If default be made in the payment of the said rent or any part thereof, or if default be made in the performance of any of the covenants herein contained, Lessor or its representatives may re-enter the premises by force, summary proceedings or otherwise, and remove all persons therefrom without being liable to prosecution therefor, and Lessee hereby expressly waives the service of any notice in writing of intention to re-enter. In the event of re-entry by reason of such default or the removal of Lessee by summary proceedings or otherwise, Lessee shall pay at the same time as the rent becomes payable under the term hereof the sum equivalent to the rent reserved herein, and Lessor may rent the premises on behalf of Lessee, reserving the right to rent the premises for a longer period of time than fixed in the original lease without releasing lessee from any liability, applying any moneys collected, first to the expense of resuming or obtaining possession, second to restoring the premises to rentable condition, and then to the payment of the rent and all other charges due and to become due to Lessor, any surplus to be paid to Lessee, who shall remain liable for any deficiency.

19. Notwithstanding and in addition to any other rights, privileges or actions available to Lessor hereunder or at law or in equity, if Lessee shall default in the payment of rent or any part thereof, or if default be made in the performance of any of the covenants herein contained, or if Lessee shall file a petition in bankruptcy or make an assignment for the benefit of creditors, or take advantage of any insolvency act, Lessor may at its election at any time thereafter terminate this lease and the term hereof, promptly upon the giving of written notice of Lessor's intention to do so; and this lease and the term hereof shall expire and come to an end upon the giving of such notice, as if the said date were the date originally fixed in this lease for the expiration thereof.

LESSOR'S DEFAULT

21. In the case of a monetary default by Lessor, Lessor shall have a period of ten (10) days after notice thereof from Lessee to cure such monetary default. In the case of a non-monetary default, Lessor shall

commence promptly to cure such default immediately after receipt of
written notice from Lessee specifying the nature of such default and
shall complete such cure within thirty (30) days thereafter, provided that
if the nature of the non-monetary default is such that it cannot be cured
within said thirty (30) day period, Lessor shall have such additional time
as may be reasonably necessary to complete its performance so long as
Lessor has proceeded with diligence since its receipt of Lessee's notice
and is then proceeding with diligence to cure such default.

Section 13 of an Office Building Lease

SUBORDINATION TO MORTGAGES

13. This instrument shall be subject and subordinate to any mortgages
which are now on or which hereafter may be placed against said premises
to the limit of the principal sum of One Million Dollars ($1,000,000),
and upon recording, any such mortgage or mortgages not in excess of
such principal amount shall have preference and precedence and be
superior and prior in lien to this lease, irrespective of the date of recording,
and Lessee agrees to execute any instrument without cost which may
be deemed necessary or desirable to any such mortgagee to further effect
the subordination of this lease to any such mortgage or mortgages, and
a refusal to execute such instrument shall entitle Lessor, or its successors
and assigns, to cancel this lease at its option without incurring any
expense, liability or damage, and the term hereby granted is expressly
limited accordingly.

Section 18 of an Office Building Lease

CONDEMNATION

18. If all or substantially all of the demised premises shall be taken
by condemnation, the lease hereby created shall terminate upon such
taking by the acquiring authority and the rent and other charges shall
be apportioned accordingly. No part of any award, however, shall belong
to Lessee. If less than all or substantially all of the demised premises
shall be so taken, the rent for the remaining premises shall thereupon
be proportionately apportioned.

Section 20 of an Office Building Lease

ALTERATIONS

20. In the event Lessee desires to make any alterations and changes
in the demised premises, it is understood and agreed that the same shall
not be made without the prior consent of the Lessor, which shall not
be unreasonably withheld. All alterations, decorations, additions and
improvements, including paneling, partitions, railings, galleries and the
like, except movable trade or banking fixtures, shall become the property
of Lessor upon installation. It is understood and agreed that upon the
expiration or prior termination of the term of this lease Lessor may

require Lessee, at the election of Lessor and at the expense of Lessee, to restore the demised premises to the character and condition which prevailed before any said alterations or changes were made by Lessee.

Section 3 of a Shopping Center Lease

CO-TENANCY REQUIREMENT

3(a). Landlord agrees that there shall be completed and opened for business in the Shopping Center of which the demised premises are a part prior to or in conjunction with Tenant's opening, an Angel's Hardware store containing approximately forty-six thousand five hundred (46,500) square feet, or more, of ground floor space and a Lucky Discount Center store containing approximately twenty-seven thousand (27,000) square feet, or more, of ground floor space. Landlord also agrees that it shall have completed and have ready to open in the Shopping Center prior to or in conjunction with the opening of Tenant's store for business a Thrifty Drug Store containing approximately twenty thousand one hundred (20,100) square feet of ground floor space. Landlord also agrees that it shall have under construction at the time of Tenant's opening a Pic N' Save store containing approximately twenty-one thousand (21,000) square feet of ground floor space.

(b). It is understood and agreed that Tenant shall not be required to open for business nor be liable for the payment of rent unless and until the conditions contained in paragraph (a) of this Section 3 have been and continue to be fulfilled; provided, however, in the event the conditions should not be fulfilled but Tenant nevertheless opens its store for business, the conditions contained in the foregoing paragraph (a) shall be deemed satisfied and fulfilled in all respects and the lease term and Tenant's obligations hereunder shall commence as of the date Tenant opens for business.

Sections 4(a), 4(b), 4(c), 4(d), and 11 of a Shopping Center Lease

FIXED MINIMUM AND ADDITIONAL RENT

4(a). Tenant agrees to pay to Landlord an annual fixed minimum rent for the use and occupancy of the demised premises (which constitutes a portion of the Shopping Center property described in Exhibit A) during the term hereof in the sum of Fifty Thousand ($50,000) Dollars. In addition to the fixed minimum rent Tenant agrees to pay Landlord Tenant's pro rata share of costs incurred by Landlord to maintain the parking lot and other areas used in common by all the Tenants.

PERCENTAGE RENT

4(b). In addition to the minimum and additional rent hereinabove provided, Tenant shall pay to Landlord on or before the sixtieth day after the expiration of each of Tenant's fiscal years during the term of this lease, a percentage rent equal to five percent of the gross sales, as hereinafter defined, made by tenant on the demised premises during such fiscal year less the amount of fixed minimum rent received therefor by Landlord from Tenant. For the purpose of this Section 4, any fraction of a fiscal year at the commencement of such term shall be deemed a part of the first full fiscal year thereof, and any fraction of a fiscal year at the end of such term shall be deemed a part of the last full fiscal year thereof.

The term "gross sales" as used in this lease shall mean the aggregate of all moneys received by Tenant from sales of goods, wares, merchandise and services to the public made for cash or credit on the demised premises during the term thereof (including sales by Tenant's concessionaires and sublessees and including the net proceeds to Tenant from sales through vending machines) after deducting therefrom (i) all refunds, discounts and allowances made to customers by Tenant, in connection with merchandise sold or returned to Tenant, (ii) any federal excise tax on retailers' sales and (iii) any amount of any city, county, state or federal sales, luxury, excise, or other tax on such sales which is both added to the selling price (or absorbed therein) and paid to the taxing authority by Tenant, or any other impost or levy payable by Tenant and measured by the volume of Tenant's sales of any particular item or items, whether such impost or levy be denominated a "tax" or otherwise. There shall not be deducted therefrom any income, excess profits, franchise or other taxes based upon or measured by Tenant's income. The return or transfer of merchandise from one of Tenant's stores to another, or to any of Tenant's warehouses, shall not be deemed a sale, nor shall the sale of Tenant's fixtures or equipment or all or substantially all of its stock-in-trade and merchandise at a sale other than at retail.

4(c). Insurance premiums paid by Tenant pursuant to section 9(a) hereof, property taxes paid by Tenant pursuant to section 7(b) hereof, and property taxes paid by Tenant pursuant to section 4(a) hereof as a portion of Tenant's reimbursement to Landlord for common area maintenance costs, shall be credited against and deducted from additional rent payable pursuant to paragraph (b) of this Section 4.

4(d). Tenant shall keep accurate records of all sales made on the premises in accordance with good accounting practices applicable to Tenant's business, and shall furnish Landlord, as soon as possible and in any event within sixty days after the end of each fiscal year of Tenant, a verified statement showing the total gross sales on the demised premises for such fiscal year calculated as herein provided. Such annual statement shall be taken as final and correct, except that Landlord (by a certified public accountant selected by it) shall have the right after the close of each fiscal year to examine and audit Tenant's records of sales made on the demised premises during such fiscal year, upon giving Tenant written notice to that effect within six months after the expiration of such fiscal year. Such audit or examination shall not be made more often than once for any year, and shall be at the sole cost and expense of Landlord, and must be completed with all reasonable diligence. On termination of this lease by lapse of time or otherwise, Tenant shall report to Landlord as "gross sales" the unpaid balance of all credit sales, excluding only those past due more than one year and those balances which have been written off Tenant's books as uncollectible.

ASSIGNMENTS AND SUBLETTING

13. Tenant shall not assign or sublet all or any part of the premises without the prior written consent of Landlord, which consent shall not be unreasonably withheld. Every such assignment or sublease shall recite that it is and shall be subject and subordinate to the provisions of this lease, and the termination or cancellation of this lease shall constitute a termination and cancellation of every such assignment or sublease. No such assignment or subletting shall relieve Tenant of any of its obligations as Tenant hereunder.

Section 6 of a Shopping Center Lease

USE

6. Tenant shall use the demised premises for the purpose of primarily conducting thereon a sporting goods store, and for the purpose of selling other items compatible with the items offered for sale in other sporting goods stores of like character. Tenant covenants and agrees that at no time shall the premises be used for any of the following purposes: a commercial bank, savings and loan or other lending institution; a prescription pharmacy and/or a drug store for handling or selling any items of merchandise which under any law, rule, or regulation or order promulgated by a competent governmental authority, must be sold by, or in the presence of, a registered pharmacist; a hardware store, a lumber store or yard, a nursery store, a paint store, a builders' supply store, or a toy store; a variety store; a bowling alley, a skating rink or theatre; or a barber shop, beauty shop, dry cleaners or fabric store, provided that nothing contained in this paragraph shall in any way be deemed to prohibit or restrict Tenant from operating the premises or selling the products customarily sold in its other locations in this state.

Landlord agrees that none of the property described in Exhibit A, other than the demised premises, and none of the other property owned by the Landlord within a 5 mile radius of the property described in Exhibit A shall, at any time during the term of this lease, be occupied by any other sporting goods store or any store which carries sporting goods as a major line of merchandise.

A general discussion of commercial leasing is beyond the scope of this book. However, if your curiosity has been piqued by the Planning Problem the following readings are recommended: M. Friedman, Friedman on Leases (2d ed. 1983); Davidson, Leasing Commercial Real Estate: Issues and Negotiating, 18 Real Est. Rev. 69 (Spring 1988); Di Sciullo, Negotiating a Commercial Lease from the Tenant's Perspective, 18 Real Est. L.J. 27 (Summer 1989); Commercial Lease Law Insider (a newsletter published by Brownstone Publishers, Inc., N.Y., N.Y.).

D. REMEDIES FOR BREACH OF MORTGAGE LOAN COMMITMENT

With the exception of standby commitments (see the excerpt by Garfinkel), the overwhelming majority of postconstruction lenders anticipate closing and funding their loan commitments. Indeed, based on the expectation that their loans will close, life insurance companies and other institutional lenders are willing to bid for pension fund dollars to fund such loans in the form of guaranteed investment income contracts (GICs). Moreover, the real estate financing industry is a relatively small and close-knit community where reputations of borrowers and lenders depend on their willingness to respect and honor their commitments to one another; in the opinion of one commentator: ". . . a financing commitment continues to be an extremely important contractual agreement that is an integral part of the development process and, therefore, a matter worthy of the highest honor among industry participants."[20]

Nevertheless, commitment letters are breached from time to time by both borrowers and lenders, whose attorneys must be able to explain beforehand and deal thereafter with the legal consequences of default. But why do defaults occur? A large part of the answer has to do with the volatility of interest rates for first mortgage money during fluctuations in the business cycle. Don't forget that in contrast to construction financing, which is usually based on a floating rate of interest, postconstruction financing is ordinarily based on a fixed rate structure, which is negotiated beforehand when the forward loan commitment is made by the postconstruction lender even though the loan funds are not actually disbursed until two years (or more) thereafter, when the improvements are completed. Accordingly, if during this hiatus interest rates should increase, some postconstruction lenders may be tempted to find ways to extricate themselves from their previous loan commitments so that they will be able to lend the otherwise committed funds at a higher rate to some other borrower. Conversely, if interest rates should decline, a borrower such as Dan Developer would be

---

20. Under a GIC, the lender could sustain a substantial loss if a postconstruction loan backed by pension fund dollars fails to close on schedule. See Somers, A Forward Loan Should Be Equally Binding on All Parties, 1 Real Est. Fin. J. 91 (Spring 1986). The quotation is from the article by Somers, at 92.

tempted to shop around for a less expensive loan and walk away from his existing commitment with Ace Insurance Company so that he could obtain cheaper financing from some other lender.

For example, suppose Dan pays Ace both a 1-percent nonrefundable application or commitment fee and a 2-percent refundable commitment fee (sometimes referred to as a "security" or "good-faith" deposit, which might be in the nature of a liquidated damages provision), which total 3 percent of the $25 million loan amount, or $750,000. Assume for simplicity's sake that the loan is a 15-year interest-only without any amortization requirement. By way of analogy to the predicament of the borrower in the *Butler* case (excerpted at Chapter 5A3, supra) and to illustrate the worst-case interest-rate scenario for Dan, assume further that the commitment had been executed in the second quarter of 1982, when the average interest rate on commercial real estate loans made by life insurance companies was 15.23 percent and that only one year later, when the loan was about to close, the rate had dropped 300 "basis points" to a rate of 12.25 percent.[21] What this means to Dan is that the loss of the 3-percent commitment-related fee amount of $750,000 may not be a sufficient sanction to induce him to honor the commitment to Ace when the annual difference in payments on a $25 million interest-only loan at 15.23 percent and 12.25 percent would be $745,000, and the difference in total interest payments over the 15-year life of the loan would be a whopping $11,175,000! Of equal significance to Dan would be the possibility for him to increase the loan amount. Based on a debt-coverage ratio of 120 percent, a decrease of $745,000 in annual interest charges, or $62,083 in monthly debt service payments, means that, at 12.25 percent, the same monthly payments would justify a loan amount of $31,081,633, compared to a loan amount of $25 million at the higher rate of 15.23 percent. Moreover, in a mortgage market where interest rates are declining and demand is weakening relative to supply, some other postconstruction lender may be willing to reduce its front-end charges for the sake of making a "spot loan" to Dan so that it can immediately invest its loanable funds and avoid the risks of making a forward commitment to lend money in the future (as Ace is doing). Therefore, an institutional postconstruction lender such as Ace would be exposed to a significant risk of loss if the retention of the application fee and the 2-percent security deposit were its only remedy if the borrower should willfully default on its commitment to borrow the loan funds.

In addition, there are other circumstances that might cause an unintentional default by either the borrower or the lender. For example, construction cost overruns may compel the developer-borrower to aban-

---

21. See Table 5-1 at Chapter 5B1, supra.

don the project if the postconstruction lender refuses to increase the loan amount and the developer is unable to fund the shortfall by raising more equity capital or by obtaining gap financing until the postconstruction loan can be refinanced for a larger amount.[22] Or perhaps the borrower is unable to comply with any of the other major requirements imposed as a condition precedent to closing the postconstruction loan, such as obtaining free and clear title to the property,[23] securing a certificate of occupancy (or other approval from some governmental authority),[24] or completing the construction in a timely manner.[25] Likewise, an unanticipated shortfall in cash flow or other contingency might cause an unintentional default by the lender under its commitment to the borrower.

In this section we will examine the remedies available to both parties in the event of a default under the postconstruction commitment letter, including the right to damages for breach of contract and the right to specific performance. Once again, this is an area in which freedom of contract principles predominate; for example, in some jurisdictions specific performance may not be available unless the parties agree otherwise (for example, in a buy-sell agreement). Therefore, we will be closely scrutinizing the pertinent language that addresses the issue of default, especially the default provision in the postconstruction commitment letter.

1. Breach of Commitment by Borrower

As observed in the *Lincoln* decision, excerpted below, commitment-related fees serve a variety of functions. For example, the commitment will occasionally contain language providing that the borrower will deposit a sum of money as a "security deposit," "standby fee," or "good-faith deposit" for the performance of the borrower's obligations. The fee is refundable on the closing of the loan. The following is a commitment provision requiring such a deposit.

Amount and Nature of Deposit

Simultaneously with the delivery to Lender of a counterpart of this Commitment with the acceptance of Borrower endorsed thereon, Bor-

---

22. See, e.g., White Lakes Shopping Center v. Jefferson Standard Life Insurance Co., 208 Kan. 121, 490 P.2d 609 (1971), where the borrower's construction costs increased and the lender refused to modify its commitment after the third increase. See discussion of gap financing at Chapter 5B2, supra.

23. See Chapter 5B15, supra.

24. See Chapter 5B9, supra.

25. See Chapter 5B11, supra.

rower shall deposit with Lender the sum of One Million, Five Hundred
Thousand Dollars ($1,500,000.) which shall be in the form of $500,000.
in cash and the balance in the form of an irrevocable letter of credit in
the form and substance acceptable to Lender and its Law Department
(herein collectively referred to as the "Deposit"). The Deposit will be
held by Lender as security for the collection of damages Lender suffers
by reason of Borrower's failure to perform its obligations under this
Commitment, but the amount of damages that Lender shall be entitled
to collect shall not be limited to the amount of the Deposit. As used
herein, the term "damages" shall include, without limitation, loss of
interest by reason of changing interest rates or otherwise, [and] expenses
incurred by Lender including salaried time of Lender's employees in
connection with or attributable to the issuance and administration of this
Commitment.

Return of Deposit

Within five business days after the date Lender disburses or acquires
the Loan, Lender shall return the Deposit, without interest, to Borrower.

Retention of Deposit by Lender

In the event that any or all of the terms, provisions and conditions
of this Commitment are not fulfilled within the time limitations prescribed herein for any reason, other than the willful default of Lender,
and as a result thereof Lender does not disburse or acquire the Loan,
Lender may retain the Deposit to compensate Lender for time spent,
labor and services performed, loss of interest and for any other loss which
might be incurred by Lender in connection with this transaction. It is
understood that the foregoing provision for retention of the Deposit
shall not constitute an option on Borrower's part not to complete the
loan transaction herein contemplated, and that Lender reserves any and
all rights which it may have at law or in equity, including but not
limited to, specific performance.

Additional Nature of Obligations

Borrower's obligations under this Article with respect to the deposit
referred to in this Article are in addition to all obligations provided
elsewhere in this Commitment with respect to payment of fees to Lender
or to payment to any other entity, of fees, charges or expenses.

The deposit mentioned in the commitment above is refundable if
the borrower lives up to the terms of the commitment. It should not
be confused with the nonrefundable commitment fee or other charges
made by the lender at the time of commitment. Both the refundable
and the nonrefundable fees are referred to as "commitment fees," but
their objectives are quite different. The refundable deposit is designed
to keep the borrower honest, or serve as liquidated damages. In contrast,

the nonrefundable fee is usually regarded by the lender as the consideration paid by the borrower to compensate the lender for keeping sufficient loan funds on hand to disburse the loan. If the borrower has deposited fees with the lender that by the commitment's terms are nonrefundable, the courts have uniformly allowed the lender to retain them.[26] Both the refundable and nonrefundable payments are usually geared to a percentage of the loan amount, often a 1-percent application fee for each year the commitment will be outstanding and a 2-percent or greater refundable fee. The amount will often depend on the volatility of interest rates, applicable usury laws, and the bargaining power of the parties.[27]

Lincoln National Life Insurance Co. v. NCR Corp.

603 F. Supp. 1393 (N.D. Ind. 1984), affd., 772
F.2d 315 (7th Cir. 1985)

This action arises out of a "Mortgage Loan Commitment Letter" (hereinafter loan commitment letter) issued by plaintiff Lincoln as the lead lender for itself and on behalf of the other plaintiffs. The loan commitment was sought by defendant NCR through the services of a mortgage broker, United California Mortgage (hereinafter UCM), for the purposes of financing the construction of NCR's world headquarters building in Dayton, Ohio. NCR agreed to pay UCM a fee of one-half of one per cent (½ of 1%) of the principal amount of the loan for use of UCM's services. . . .

In an effort to insure that UCM could act for NCR in the transaction, plaintiff Lincoln requested and received a $50,000 good faith deposit. The plaintiffs then secured approval for the loan from their respective loan committees. Following loan committee approval, each plaintiff placed the NCR loan on its cash flow chart. These charts list investments to be funded at certain dates in the future and are used to predict future cash needs.

Assured that UCM had control of NCR's business, plaintiff Lincoln, as lead lender, drafted a loan commitment letter and circulated it among the other three plaintiffs for review. Upon receipt of the draft, Mr. Craig L. Snyder, Vice President in charge of mortgage loans of plaintiff

---

26. See, e.g., Lowe v. Massachusetts Mut. Life Ins. Co., 54 Cal. App. 3d 718, 127 Cal. Rptr. 23 (1st Dist. 1976); Goldman v. Connecticut Gen. Life Ins. Co., 251 Md. 575, 248 A.2d 154 (1968).

27. See generally Smith and Lubell, Real Estate Financing: The Permanent Mortgage Loan Commitment, 4 Real Est. Rev. 10 (Winter 1975).

Provident Mutual, suggested to Lincoln that a one per cent (1%) fee also be obtained from NCR to secure the deal. Notwithstanding this suggestion, the plaintiffs agreed to the proposed loan commitment.

By date of November 5, 1975, Charles Marcus, Administrative Manager of plaintiff Lincoln, on behalf of plaintiffs, signed the Mortgage Loan Commitment letter in Fort Wayne, Indiana and sent the same to NCR in Dayton, Ohio for signature. On November 17, 1975, Robert C. James, NCR's Director of Financial Planning and Analysis, accepted the . . . letter subject to certain proposed amendments. . . .

The amendments proposed by NCR were accepted by plaintiffs on January 20, 1976 when Charles Marcus of plaintiff Lincoln executed the acceptance. Mr. Marcus then sent a letter to Mr. James of NCR stating, "it is agreed and understood that the mortgage loan commitment as amended is now acceptable to all parties involved in the transaction." . . .

The mortgage loan commitment provided that the plaintiffs would jointly loan up to $14,000,000 (Fourteen Million Dollars) unless the total capitalized costs of the project were less than that amount. Plaintiff Lincoln agreed to loan $5,000,000 (Five Million Dollars) or 35.7%, plaintiff Provident Life $4,000,000 (Four Million Dollars) or 28.6%, plaintiff Provident Mutual $3,000,000 (Three Million Dollars) or 21.4% and plaintiff Life and Casualty $2,000,000 (Two Million Dollars) or 14.3%. The interest rate for the loan was fixed at 9⅞% for a term of twenty-five (25) years with prepayment closed for ten years and a prepayment penalty thereafter.

In the loan commitment letter, NCR "agree[d] to take the loan funds down no later than the fourth quarter of 1976." (Plaintiffs' Exhibit 1).

The loan commitment letter further required that certain conditions be met by defendant NCR. These conditions included transfer of the real estate upon which the headquarters were to be built to a subsidiary, lease of the building to NCR and assignment of the lease and mortgage to plaintiffs as security for the loan. . . .

During the first quarter of 1976, NCR noted a substantial increase in its cash balance. Because of this, questions arose regarding the need for external funding of its world headquarters building.

Partly in response to the increase of NCR's reserves, NCR's Treasurer, D. W. Russler, sent a letter to UCM regarding the mortgage loan. The letter included "an amended Letter of Authorization to either renegotiate the mortgage loan for the Headquarters Building or negotiate a reasonable penalty fee for cancelling the commitment." . . . The letter indicated that an acceptable loan would be one for $13,000,000 (Thirteen Million Dollars) at 9⅜% interest or alternatively a 1.5% penalty fee. . . .

Subsequently, on May 10, 1976, Mr. Russler of NCR sent another

letter to UCM indicating that the mortgage loan should not be consummated because (1) the interest rate was above that generally found
in the market and (2) NCR's need for such financing was no longer
evident. . . .

On May 26, 1976 plaintiff-lenders wrote NCR objecting to its
decision not to take down the loan. Mr. Russler responded on July
13, 1976 and confirmed that NCR no longer desired to fund the
building of the world headquarters by outside sources. The response
further indicated that NCR had no legal obligations to the lenders.

Following the July 21, 1976 letter from NCR, plaintiff-lenders
deleted the NCR loan from their cash flow charts.

The mortgage loan from plaintiff-lenders was never made.

Construction of NCR's world headquarters building began in 1974
and it was first put into partial use in the fall of 1976. The building
was built for the sum of $12,975,931 (Twelve Million Nine Hundred
Seventy-Five Thousand Nine Hundred Thirty-One Dollars). Had the
loan been closed, it would have been in Dayton, Ohio for that amount.

. . . Second, since the parties are in complete disagreement with
respect to whether or not the underlying transactions constituted an
enforceable contract, analysis of the nature and extent of the agreement
is necessary. Finally, consideration must be given to whether or not
damages are appropriate and, if so, to what extent. These factors will
be considered in turn. . . .

THE ENFORCEABILITY OF THE COMMITMENT

As the above recitation of facts indicates, this case revolves around
an agreement to finance construction through use of a mortgage loan.
This type of transaction is becoming ever the more popular because
"[t]he viability of virtually every major construction project depends
upon the availability of long-term financing." R. A. Groot, Specific
Performance of Contracts to Provide Permanent Financing, 60 Cornell
L. Rev. 718 (1975). "[T]he need for conditions relating to permanent
financing is obvious," Walker v. First Pennsylvania Bank N.A., 518
F. Supp. 347 (E.D. Pa. 1981), for "[i]n an economy plagued by the
twin evil of inflation and recession and the burdens which they impose
on businesses, long term lending transactions frequently break down."
Groot, supra at 718; see also In Re Four Seasons Nursing Centers, 483
F.2d 599, 601 (10th Cir. 1973). Unfortunately, this is a case in which
the transactions broke down.

Reduced to its most basic element, this case hinges upon the
interpretation given the agreement between the parties. It is plaintiffs'
position that the agreement conferred a mutuality of obligations so
that plaintiffs were committed to lend and defendant required to borrow.

Defendant suggests that the agreement only committed the plaintiffs to lend had they been called upon to do so. Taking the respective parties' positions together, the issue is obvious: was the agreement relating to the financing of the World Headquarters Building an enforceable contract? The answer, however, is not so obvious.

The difficulty in answering the question before the court stems, in part, from the fact that no other court has apparently addressed the precise issue presented in this case. Most courts which have addressed mortgage loan commitment letters have done so in two different situations. One situation arises where the lender has breached and the borrower sues for damages or specific performance, see, e.g., First National State Bank of New Jersey v. Commonwealth Federal Savings & Loan Assn., 610 F.2d 164 (3d Cir. 1980), while the other situation arises where the mortgagor or mortgage broker sues to recover a commitment fee, see, e.g., In Re Four Seasons Nursing Centers of America, 483 F.2d 599 (10th Cir. 1973). Here, as the facts make clear, it is the borrower who allegedly breached and the lenders who seek damages though no commitment fee secured the agreement. Nonetheless, the existent case law, such as it is, coupled with basic tenets of contract law suggests that the agreement between the parties as plaintiffs urge, constituted a bilateral contract instead of the unilateral contract theory advanced by defendant.

The distinction between a unilateral and a bilateral contract is a simple one:

> A unilateral contract is one in which no promisor receives a promise as consideration for his promise. A bilateral contract is one in which there are mutual promises between two parties to the contract; each party being both a promisor and a promisee.

Restatement of Contracts §12 (1932). That is, "[i]n the case of a unilateral contract, there is only one promisor; and the legal result is that he is the only party who is under an enforceable legal duty," 1A Corbin, Corbin on Contracts §21 (1963), for a unilateral contract "as its name implies is a one-sided contract while a bilateral contract confers a mutuality of obligations requiring performance on both sides." . . .

Defendant argues, as previously noted, that the commitment letter was a unilateral contract because NCR made no promises. Defendant further argues that the commitment letter was, in effect, a unilateral option contract whereby NCR's obligations would only accrue upon its compliance with certain terms expressed in the agreement. Plaintiffs, of course, are of the view that binding promises were made which ultimately culminated in the agreed to commitment letter.

Some authority can be found for both parties' positions. Courts and commentators alike have referred to mortgage loan commitments alternatively as unilateral and bilateral contracts. As stated by one commentator.

> It [a commitment letter] can be a unilateral contract: "Upon compliance with the following conditions we will loan you money," or it can be a bilateral contract: "We will lend and you will borrow . . .".

Wolf, R., The Refundable Commitment Fee, 1968 Bus. Law 1065, 1066. See also Johnson v. American Nat'l. Life Ins. Co., 126 Ariz. 219, 613 P.2d 1275 (App. 1980) (option contract); Dubin Weston v. Louis Capano & Sons, 394 F. Supp. 146 (D.C. Del. 1975) (bilateral contract). It is, however, not the least bit surprising that commitment letters have been deemed to be either a unilateral or bilateral contract for, as the above passage suggests, it is the language embodied in the instrument which controls and the parties' intention must be gleaned through application of basic tenets of contract law. It is to those basics which the court now turns. . . .

In determining the parties' intent, "[t]he strongest external sign of agreement between contracting parties is the words they use in their written contract. Thus, the sanctity of the written words of the contract is embedded in the law of contract interpretation." [Mellon Bank, N.A. v. Aetna Business Credit, 619 F.2d 1001, at 1009 (3d Cir. 1980.] And it is settled beyond question that, where one party drafts a document, in subsequent litigation, the document will be strictly construed against the drafting party and in favor of the non-drafting party. See, e.g., Williston, Williston on Contracts §621 (3 ed. 1961); First National State Bank of New Jersey v. Commonwealth Federal Savings & Loan, 610 F.2d 164, 170 (3d Cir. 1980) (ambiguity construed against drafter-lender).

Turning to the agreement between the present parties, it is clear that the finalized agreement occurred only after several exchanges between Lincoln as the lead lender and defendant NCR. Though this series of offer and counter-offers modified to a greater or lesser extent certain terms in the agreement, it did nothing to ameliorate what defendant deems to be the ultimate pitfall of the agreement: nowhere does the agreement state that the defendant is required to borrow the money. While the agreement does not, in so many words, explicitly state that "defendant is required to borrow," that requirement is, in plaintiffs' view, implicit within the context of the entire agreement. Particularly important in this regard is the paragraph relating to the date of funding, which reads:

> *Funding and Commitment Expiration Dates:* It is understood that construction of the subject building is scheduled for completion during the second half of 1976 and that NCR agrees to take the loan funds down no later than the fourth quarter of 1976. Assuming that construction is completed

according to schedule, Lenders will be prepared to fund the loan as soon as construction is completed and all of the terms and conditions of this commitment have been fulfilled and would prefer that funding of the loan take place by October 15, 1976. However, in any event, the loan must be funded by no later than December 31, 1976, since this commitment and Lenders' obligations under it shall terminate by that date unless the expiry date is extended in writing by Lenders.

(Plaintiffs' Exhibit 1) and the notation that:

THE UNDERSIGNED HAS READ, APPROVED AND ACCEPTED [subject to amendments] THE FOREGOING MORTGAGE LOAN COMMITMENT, INCLUDING THE GENERAL CONDITIONS AS OF THIS 17th DAY OF November, 1975.

> NCR CORPORATION
> /s/ D. L. McIntosh
> (Name)   (Title)
> D.L. McIntosh, Vice
> President, Finance . . .

Focusing solely upon the document and applying the rule that it is to be strictly construed against the drafter, defendant suggests that no agreement to borrow can be found. While plaintiffs contend that the phrase "NCR agreed to take the loan funds down no later than the fourth quarter of 1976" means defendant commits itself to borrow the money, defendant urges that this construction is vitiated by the remainder of that paragraph for when that phrase is read in the context of the entire paragraph, it places no obligation upon defendant but merely serves to establish an expiration date for plaintiffs' commitment to make the loan. Similarly, defendant contends that the language referring to acceptance is vague and since plaintiffs drafted the letter, no commitment to borrow should be implied.

To be sure, and as has already been ruled upon by this court in response to defendant's motion for summary judgment, the foregoing phrases are ambiguous and susceptible to more than one meaning. "Certainly there is an ambiguity in the very fact that one of defendant's officers signed the Mortgage Loan Commitment with the notation 'read, approved and accepted.'" (Memorandum of Decision and Order, Feb. 26, 1980 at p. 4). "If, as defendant contends, it regarded the document only as an offer made to it for a unilateral rather than a bilateral contract, in itself, it seems, at the least, ambiguous that defendant would so sign it." Id. At the time of entry of the ruling, the court intimated that resolution of this apparent ambiguity could only be cured through the introduction of parol evidence. . . .

As a general proposition, the parol evidence rule bars admission of extrinsic evidence to vary or contradict the terms of an unambiguous written agreement intended by the parties to be an integrated agreement. See Freeman v. Continental Gin, 381 F.2d 459 (5th Cir. 1967). Where, as here, the written agreement is ambiguous, the parol evidence rule is inapplicable and extrinsic evidence of surrounding circumstances may be admitted to explain an ambiguity. . . .

Evidence extrinsic to the commitment letter indicates that the parties sought to enter into an enforceable contract. With respect to the notation "accepted" as it appeared in the final document, several factors indicate that it obligated NCR to take down the funds.

Prior to finalization of the commitment, the question of whether NCR had an obligation to take down the loan came up in separate discussions among the plaintiffs and among the defendant and UCM. That plaintiffs, and in particular Lincoln, thought defendant was obligated to take the loan is clear. When the original draft of the commitment letter was prepared by Lincoln National and distributed to the other lenders for review, Mr. Craig Snyder of Provident Mutual made a notation which read: "Suggest at least a 1% refundable fee to anchor deal." . . .

Still another factor which indicates that the defendant viewed the commitment as a bargained-for contract was the money paid to UCM and the good faith deposit paid to Lincoln. With respect to UCM, NCR paid $70,000 under its brokerage agreement which required payment only after an acceptable commitment had been found:

> UCM is to receive a fee of ½ of 1% of the principal amount of the loan for its services in arranging a commitment as applied for herein, said fee to be due and payable upon issuance of the commitment from an institutional investor and *acceptance* thereof by NCR as provided below.

(Emphasis supplied). Likewise, the "good faith" deposit of $50,000 was paid to Lincoln which was refunded upon execution of the commitment letter. According to Mr. Alex Jokay of Lincoln, the deposit was taken to insure that the dealings through UCM were exclusive and that no other bargaining between NCR and another lender was occurring which might thwart the deal. (Trial Transcript Vol. I, pp. 53-55). The payment to UCM and the return of the deposit by Lincoln point, in the court's view, to the conclusion that the parties had agreed upon a contract which was acceptable to both sides and the binding nature of the contract made it unnecessary for Lincoln to retain the good faith deposit.

Taken together, the court is of the view that the parties bargained for, and entered into, an enforceable contract. The bargaining process consisted of offers and counter-offers in which both sides exchanged the terms and conditions which they wished to include in the contract.

The upshot of the agreement was one in which the lenders agreed to fund approximately fourteen million dollars at 9⅞% interest for a term of twenty-five years. In consideration of this promise, NCR agreed to take surveys, furnish descriptions, transfer titles, reassign mortgages and the like.

In reaching the conclusion that an enforceable contract was entered into, the court is not unmindful of the arguments advanced in opposition by defendant. Particularly worthy of note in this regard are two arguments. First, the absence of a commitment fee suggests that the parties viewed this as a unilateral contract. Second, the lenders did not specifically include language requiring the defendant to borrow though it would have been easy to do so.

With respect to the first argument, it is appealing for one reason — had a commitment fee anchored the deal, the litigation would probably not have arisen and certainly would have been less complex. However, the absence of a commitment fee is not fatal in this case and its absence has been adequately explained. The loan agreement was a financial transaction between institutional lenders and a major domestic corporation. The agreement as struck was a "triple net lease" whereby NCR's credit rating would serve as security for the lease. (Trial Transcript Vol. I, p. 48). While it could be expected that in about three percent of cases a borrower would walk away from such an obligation, (Trial Transcript Vol. I, pp. 63-4, 208) it was virtually unheard of that a borrower of NCR's corporate stature would walk away from such an obligation. Moreover, plaintiffs' assumption that the commitment letter was binding upon all parties further explains the reason behind not requiring a commitment fee. Thus there was no reason to secure the mortgage loan agreement through use of a commitment fee.

In the context of mortgage loan agreements, the reasons for commitment fees are varied. The commitment fee may be intended to constitute liquidated damages, as in *In Re Four Seasons,* supra; or it may serve as a consideration, as in Regional Enterprises, Inc. v. Teachers Insurance & Annuity Ass'n., 352 F.2d 768 (9th Cir. 1965); or it may be given as a stand-by fee as in Harding v. Pan American Life Ins. Co., 452 F. Supp. 527 (E.D. Va. 1978). Since consideration has already been found to exist in this case, and since there existed no stand-by lender, the only valid reason for a commitment fee here would have been to serve as a benchmark for liquidated damages. While such an agreed figure would have eliminated much confusion, it adds nothing to the question of whether or not a valid contract had been entered into by the parties. All such a fee would have done in this context would have been to set a price upon NCR's decision to breach the agreement. . . .

Thus far, the court has determined that the parties entered into an enforceable contract and consequently, liability is found in favor of the plaintiffs. There remains the question of damages and it is to that topic which the court now turns. . . .

In order to recover, plaintiffs have the burden of proving that they have suffered damages. . . . The damages claimed cannot be based upon conjecture nor subject to uncertainty. . . . With respect to damages for breach of contract, damages are designed to one or more interests of the non-breaching party:

> (a) His "expectation interests" which is his interest in having the benefit of his bargain by being put in as good a position as he would have been in had the contract been performed;
> (b) His "reliance interests" which is his interest in being reimbursed for loss caused by reliance on the contract by being put in as good a position as he would have been had the contract not been made; or
> (c) His "restitution interest" which is his interest in having restored to him any benefit that he has conferred on the other party.

Restatement 2nd Contracts §344.

As a corollary to the foregoing, it is absolutely clear that plaintiffs have the burden of mitigating damages. . . .

With respect to mitigation in this case, it appears altogether clear that this requirement was absolutely met by plaintiffs, for shortly after NCR raised the issue of repudiation, all of the plaintiffs removed the NCR obligation from their respective loan charts and apparently invested the allocated funds elsewhere. . . .

. . . Thus the sole type of damages which plaintiffs are seeking is that relating to their "expectation" interests. As will be seen, plaintiffs have not, in fact, established beyond speculation and conjecture that they were, in fact, so damaged.

The sum total of damages plaintiffs attribute to defendant's breach is $1,783,709 to which must be added prejudgment interest in an amount of eight per cent (8%) per annum. Though simple arithmetic is involved in the ultimate calculation, the process leading up to deriving the separate figures which form the basis for the computation is not so simple.

While the measure of damages for breach of an agreement to lend money is generally the difference between interest on the contract note and interest the non-breaching party incurred or earned in a substitute loan, . . . the substitute loan measure of damages is not feasible in this case because no particular funds were earmarked for the NCR loan. That is, the NCR loan funds were to be derived from the cash flow to plaintiffs resulting from the continued maturing of investments previously made and the availability of funds obtained from other sources. Thus, when the NCR loan funds were removed from each plaintiff's cash flow chart, the newly freed money was reinvested elsewhere, yet it is impossible to tell exactly where. Conceivably, some of the money went to other loans producing higher or lower interest and had longer or shorter yield terms.

Since it is impossible to tell exactly what happened to the NCR funds, plaintiffs argue that the measure of damages is the difference between interest on the NCR loan and a comparable loan after the breach. In this case the difference would be the 9⅞% interest agreed upon by the parties and the interest rate on a comparable loan at the lower interest rate prevailing after the breach. Using this formula, plaintiffs calculate their damage claim essentially as follows. The total amount to be funded under the agreement was $13,405,931. This amount was to be loaned at 9⅞% interest for a period of twenty-five years. Using the 8.5% prevailing rate for a comparable loan in December of 1976, the damages are calculated as the difference between the interest on the 9⅞% loan and the interest on the comparable loan with each interest amount reduced to present value as of December 1976. Graphically, the calculations are as follows:

Present value of interest at 9⅞%	$11,324,275
Less present value of interest at 8.5%	− 9,536,486
	$ 1,787,789

Thus, plaintiffs claim entitlement to damages in that amount.

As the above makes abundantly clear, plaintiffs' market damage theory rests upon several important assumptions. In making the calculations, plaintiffs presuppose, among other things, the amount of the loan, the length of time the loan would be outstanding, and the date for determining the comparative market rate with interest computed on a comparable loan as of that date. . . .

Given the foregoing options, the court would have to conclude that the July date is the correct date for assessing damages. This is so because at common law, the date for determining the market in the event of anticipatory breach of a contract is the time of repudiation. . . . While authority exists for the proposition that damages are to be computed as of the date fixed for performance (here October 1976), . . . that doctrine is wholly inapplicable in the context of this case for plaintiffs, upon learning of NCR's decision, removed that commitment from their cash flow charts in July and reinvested elsewhere as of that date.

As with plaintiffs' inclusion of the land in its damage calculation, the use of the December 1976 rate could be rectified by substituting the July figure and recalculating damages accordingly. But again, other problems exist in plaintiffs' calculation which must be taken into consideration.

Part and parcel of plaintiffs' calculation is the argument that damages should be assessed for the entire twenty-five year period. That is, prepayment should not be assumed. While some authority exists for this proposition, e.g. Pipkin v. Thomas & Hill, Inc., 298 N.C. 278, 258 S.E.2d 778, 785 (1979), it is not altogether clear that prepayment, to a greater or lesser extent, should not be factored into the calculations in this case. Arguably, prepayment could not be assumed for the first ten years because under the terms of the agreement, the loan was closed to prepayment:

> The loan will be closed to prepayment during the first ten years of the loan term. Beginning in the eleventh year, privilege will be given to prepay in part or in full the principal then outstanding upon payment of a premium of 5% based on the amount so prepaid, said premium to decline ½ of 1% each year thereafter to a minimum of 1%.

Yet, at any time in between the tenth and the twenty-fifth year, prepayment could occur. . . .

Yet before such uncertainty can be resolved against the wrongdoer, it is incumbent upon plaintiffs to prove that they have, in *fact,* been damaged. *Rauch,* supra; Alexander Hamilton Institute v. Jubelt, 89 Ohio App. 480, 102 N.E.2d 741 (1951). That fact, in the court's view, has not been proven in this case. In an effort to shed some light regarding the court's reasoning on this issue, a brief overview of plaintiffs' lending procedure, as borne out at trial, is necessary.

Plaintiffs are in the investment business. . . . These investments consisted primarily of bonds, stocks, mortgage loans and real estate. (Id.). In order to secure funding at the appropriate time, each proposed loan is placed on a cash flow chart. These cash flow projections, for the most part, are simply charts in which estimated lending dates of future investments are listed. Through the use of these charts, plaintiffs are able to predict what their cash needs will be in the future. (Transcript Vol. I, pp. 164-8). Though an item is listed on the cash flow chart, no funding is allocated for that item until shortly before the targeted funding date.

With respect to the inclusion of the NCR loan on each of plaintiffs' cash flow charts, it is altogether clear that no investments were changed as the result of that inclusion. In fact, the proposed loan to NCR was placed on each of plaintiff's cash flow charts *before* committee approval. And, the funding was removed from the charts within two months after NCR's notification that it intended not to take down the funds.

The foregoing scenario of inclusion and deletion indicates that the proposed funding for NCR was nothing more than a paper transaction. The inclusion of the NCR loan commitment on plaintiffs' charts was done to prepare for a future contingency — funding — which did not occur. Moreover, plaintiffs were aware that the loan would not be made sufficiently in advance of the targeted funding date that they had not changed any investments in preparation for funding.

So what, in fact, happened to the money which would have gone to NCR? The answer is not altogether clear. It is clear, however, that any money which would have gone to NCR was reinvested elsewhere. What those investments were, what the terms of those investments were, and what the yield of those investments were, is impossible to determine. Certainly some were below the rate to be charged NCR and had earlier maturity dates, while other investments of comparable terms in years yielded higher interest rates. (Id.). . . .

In sum, this court is of the view that plaintiffs have not established that they were in fact damaged. . . . In short, plaintiffs have wholly failed to show by a preponderance of the evidence that they lost anything as a result of defendant NCR's breach.

Conclusion

On the basis of the foregoing, the court finds that a binding, enforceable contract existed between the parties. Since NCR breached the same the court finds in favor of the plaintiffs and against the defendant. The court further finds that plaintiffs have not met their burden with respect to their claim for damages, and accordingly, no damages will be awarded. . . .

Garfinkel, The Negotiation of Construction and Permanent Loan Commitments (Part 2)
25 Prac. Law. 37, 40-41 (April 15, 1979)

The Standby Commitment

Permanent loan commitments might be roughly classified as "standby commitments" or "funding commitments." Funding commitments are issued by insurance companies and other institutional lenders that desire to acquire the loan upon the completion of construction. Standby commitments are more traditionally issued by mortgage brokers and, heretofore, by Real Estate Investment Trusts ("REITs") that do not really want the loan. For a fee, a standby lender provides the construction lender with a commitment that if alternative permanent funding is not secured by a specified date, the standby lender will acquire the loan upon the satisfaction of specific conditions precedent. The experiences of the last several years have highlighted the somewhat illusory nature of many standby commitments. As a result, at the present time many construction lenders will not advance construction funds on the basis of standby commitments.

A typical standby permanent commitment issued by a REIT in

the early 1970's might have either been due on demand immediately after the assignment of the construction loan to the standby lender or might have provided for an interest rate of perhaps five to ten points in excess of a variable prime rate of interest and be due in 3 to 5 years. It was not unusual for the REIT to charge for issuing the commitment anything from three to five points — that is, from 3 to 5 per cent of the total loan amount. Many a REIT looked upon the standby commitments that it believed it would not be called upon to fund as a good source of immediately reportable income, income that would cause its securities to be traded at high multiples and permit it to issue additional securities and thus expand its equity base. In issuing a standby commitment, it was really insuring against the unavailability of a spot commitment upon completion of construction. In light of the boom conditions existing then, those responsible for managing REITs felt that they would never be called upon to fund the commitments.

Many REITs had arranged for lines of credits with major banks, both to fund standby commitments and, if required, to refinance commercial paper. When the commercial paper no longer proved marketable and, at the same time, construction lenders sought to enforce standby commitments, the REITs exercised their rights under the standby lines of credit to borrow needed funds from the banks. In many cases, the banks had also provided credit for a fee with no expectations of actually funding the loans. In a number of instances, the REIT, mortgage company, pension trust fund, or other standby lender sought to avoid funding its standby loan commitment by raising technical defenses and, in some instances, reneging on the commitment when the project for which the standby commitment had been issued proved not be as viable as the standby lender had originally projected. . . .

NOTES AND QUESTIONS

1. *Bilateral Versus Unilateral Commitments.* The *Lincoln* decision illustrates some of the difficulties confronting an aggrieved lender that relies on a poorly drafted default provision in its commitment letter for remedial relief against a defaulting borrower. If the postconstruction lender wishes to enforce a bilateral commitment against the borrower, the commitment should expressly provide that the borrower agrees to borrow the agreed-on loan amount and to accept the loan. Otherwise, any provision that purports to compensate the lender for damages (such as a refundable commitment fee) would be rendered meaningless because there would be no default if the borrower should elect not to borrow under a unilateral commitment that constitutes merely an option to borrow. Other courts have struggled with this same issue because of

lenders' failures to clearly specify whether the loan contract was intended to be bilateral or unilateral. See, e.g., B. F. Saul Real Estate Inv. Trust v. McGovern, 683 S.W.2d 531 (Tex. App. 1984); Lowe v. Massachusetts Mutual Life Insurance Co., 54 Cal. App. 3d 718, 127 Cal. Rptr. 23 (1st Dist. 1976). If the commitment is bilateral, the lender will be entitled to recover damages if the postconstruction loan does not close because of the borrower's failure to meet the terms and conditions of the lender's commitment letter and, as the court in *Lincoln* suggests, if the lender can prove that it has suffered damages as a consequence of the borrower's default.

By contrast, if the lender agrees to lend but the borrower does not agree to borrow, the commitment would be unilateral and in the nature of an option agreement. As suggested by the facts in *Lincoln,* a sloppily drafted commitment that purports to be bilateral might be construed as a unilateral commitment. However, in the real world of real estate financing, commitments that are intended to be unilateral are almost invariably standby commitments. As observed at Chapter 6A, the risks inherent in construction lending are such that many construction lenders view the takeout commitment from the postconstruction lender as the principal source of repayment at the end of the construction period. Therefore, as explained in the excerpt by Garfinkel, if a developer is unable to obtain an ordinary postconstruction takeout commitment, it may be necessary for the developer to pay an exorbitant fee to obtain a standby commitment in order to qualify for a construction loan. Therefore, in contrast to a refundable commitment fee designed to prevent the developer from walking away from a bilateral commitment when interest rates decline, the purpose of the standby fee is to compensate the standby lender for committing to a postconstruction loan that no other lender is willing to make. In other words, the ordinary *refundable* commitment fee compensates the lender for damages if the borrower should default whereas the standby fee is *nonrefundable* compensation paid to the lender for an option to borrow if the borrower should fail to obtain a less onerous takeout loan from some other lender. In Lowe v. Massachusetts Mutual Life Insurance Co., 54 Cal. App. 3d 718, 127 Cal. Rptr. 23 (1st Dist. 1976), the borrower, relying on a liquidated damages provision in the commitment letter, contended that the so-called standby deposit should be refunded because even though the loan had failed to close, the deposit was in the nature of liquidated damages and, as such, was unenforceable as a penalty under California law. The court concluded that the loan commitment was unilateral and the lender was entitled to the fee as payment for the borrower's option. In so holding, the court pointed out that

> [i]t [the agreement] nowhere bound [the borrower] to . . . solely rely on the company as the source of funds if the project was completed. In

such event if a takeout loan on more favorable terms had been available from another lender, the developer was free to take such a loan, subject to the loss of the standby deposit.

127 Cal. Rptr. at 26. See also B. F. Saul Real Estate Investment Trust v. McGovern, 683 S.W.2d 531 (Tex. App. 1984); Goldman v. Connecticut General Life Insurance Co., 251 Md. 575, 248 A.2d 154 (1968).

In deciding whether the loan agreement between the parties was bilateral or unilateral, the court in *Lincoln* was influenced by the fact that one of the loan officers had signed the commitment with the notation "read, approved, and accepted." Why did this fact help persuade the court that the commitment was a bilateral one? In reviewing the extrinsic evidence, the court noted that another loan officer had suggested a 1-percent refundable fee "to anchor the deal" (which suggestion was never implemented) and that a "good-faith" deposit was refunded on *execution* of the commitment letter (rather than on closing of the loan). Taken together, the foregoing parol evidence helped persuade the court that the parties had intended a bilateral agreement and had bargained for mutuality in respect to their obligations to one another. Do you agree with the inference drawn by the court based on this evidence? In *Lincoln,* the borrower did not pay the lender a commitment fee. In this regard, the *Lincoln* court suggested that "had a commitment fee anchored the deal, the litigation probably would not have arisen." Why would this be so? Assuming hypothetically that the *Lincoln* court had concluded there was no mutuality in the obligations between the parties, would the payment of a refundable commitment fee by the borrower have supplied the court with a theory by which it could hold the agreement enforceable? See R. Kratovil and R. Werner, Modern Mortgage Law Practice §25.38(a) (2d ed. 1981). See also Regional Enterprises, Inc. v. Teachers Insurance & Annuity Assn., 352 F.2d 768 (9th Cir. 1965). The obvious lesson is that any lender who intends to make a bilateral commitment should require language to the effect that the borrower agrees to borrow and accept the loan. Do the facts and holding in *Lincoln* suggest any other lessons for lender's counsel?

2. *The Refundable Commitment Fee as Liquidated Damages.* Where actual damages may be difficult to ascertain, the courts will allow the parties to establish beforehand what the damages will be on default, provided they do not arrive at a predetermined amount that is plainly disproportionate to the potential loss that may be sustained by the injured party. This, as you know from contract law, is called "liquidated damages." However, if the actual damages can be ascertained with reasonable certainty or the predetermined amount is excessive, the liquidated damages clause might be struck down as an unenforceable

"penalty." See J. Calamari and J. Perillo, Contracts §14-31 (2d ed. 1977). Often the refundable commitment deposit in mortgage loan commitments is intended to serve as liquidated damages in the event of a breach by the prospective borrower.

As the *Lincoln* court suggests, in the event of a breach by the borrower the lender's damages would generally equal the difference (in present value) between the contract rate of interest and the interest the lender would be able to earn from an alternative investment at the time of the borrower's breach. However, in most loan transactions it is extremely difficult to measure the lender's actual loss of interest income and the preparatory expenses incurred for a particular loan. Unless all of the lender's remaining loanable funds are fully committed it would be expensive, time-consuming, and administratively burdensome for the lender to trace the funds earmarked for the use of the defaulting borrower. Moreover, how would you measure in monetary terms the expenses the lender would have incurred unnecessarily if the loan transaction were never consummated, such as reviewing and verifying the data in the loan application, reviewing the occupancy leases, and compensating the lender for a prospective loss of investment income while alternative investments are being sought? Consequently, courts have generally enforced liquidated damages clauses in commitment letters when the amount of damages is reasonable. See, e.g., Boston Road Shopping Center v. Teachers Insurance & Annuity Assn. of America, 13 App. Div. 2d 106, 111, 213 N.Y.S.2d 522, 528 (1961), affd., 11 N.Y.2d 83, 227 N.Y.S.2d 444, 182 N.E.2d 116 (1962); White Lakes Shopping Center v. Jefferson Standard Life Insurance Co., 208 Kan. 121, 128, 490 P.2d 609, 615 (1971).

But suppose interest rates rise and the aggrieved lender is immediately able to commit and reinvest *all* of its loanable funds at the higher rate. Do you think the defaulting borrower could argue that, since the loss of interest income would be immediately ascertainable, the lender should be precluded from receiving liquidated damages? In other words, should the validity of the liquidated damages clause be tested in light of the circumstances existing when the breach of contract occurs, rather than when the agreement is entered into? See Seidlitz v. Auerbach, 230 N.Y. 167, 129 N.E. 461 (Ct. App. 1920) (involving liquidated damages clause in commercial lease).

3. Lender's Dilemma: Liquidated Damages Versus Actual Damages. If a commitment is bilateral, the postconstruction lender should clearly specify in the default provision whether the refundable commitment fee constitutes a liquidated damages deposit or simply a security deposit (akin to the ordinary security deposit in a lease agreement) against which the lender can seek recourse for actual damages in the event of a default by the borrower that prevents the loan from being funded.

However, if interest rates were to decline precipitously after the commitment is executed (which may be the very reason for the borrower's default), the predetermined amount of liquidated damages may be insufficient to compensate the lender for its actual loss. As suggested by the hypothetical at the beginning of Section D, any significant decline will most probably cause the lender's actual damages to exceed the liquidated damages deposit, which is customarily between 1 and 3 percent of the loan amount, especially in the case of a proposed loan with a relatively long term. Conversely, if the lender were to elect to sue for its actual damages it may encounter the kinds of evidentiary and burden-of-proof problems that prevented recovery by the lender in the *Lincoln* case. Moreover, the lender that relies on actual damages may find there are none if interest rates increase during the period between the commitment date and the time of the borrower's breach. Of course, any prospective borrower capable of doing elementary arithmetic would understand why it would be silly to default in a rising interest-rate market. The default, however, may be unintentional.

Do the sample default provisions excerpted above provide for actual damages or liquidated damages? Are the two approaches mutually exclusive? Incidentally, with respect to the sample provisions, can you think of any business reason why the borrower is insisting that the damages deposit be in the form of a certificate of deposit, as opposed to cash? Certainly what the lender would really like would be both damages clauses. Do you think this might be theoretically possible based on creative draftsmanship of the default provision in the commitment letter? See Zinman, Mortgage Loan and Joint Venture Commitments: The Institutional Investor's Remedies, 18 Real Prop., Prob. & Tr. J. 750, 754-757 (Winter 1983).

Alternatively, in the case of a bilateral commitment, do you think it might be possible for a lender to collect both a commitment fee for making the loan (as would a lender who makes a unilateral loan commitment) *and* a liquidated damages deposit? See Walter E. Heller & Co. v. American Flyers Airline Corp., 459 F.2d 896 (2d Cir. 1972) (involving a commercial personal property loan).

Can you think of any reason why a lender that elects the actual damages approach might want to impose a relatively long lock-in period during which any prepayment would be prohibited? Prepayment clauses are discussed at Chapter 5B5, supra.

It has been suggested that a substantial security or good-faith deposit should preclude any additional recovery of actual damages by a lender based on the analogy to a buyer's earnest money deposit in a contract to purchase a house. "If the seller reserves the right to retain the deposit, it is often held that he can recover no additional damages." G. Nelson and D. Whitman, Real Estate Finance Law §12.3, at 852 (2d ed. 1985), citing Brewer v. Meyers, 545 S.W.2d 235 (Tex. Civ.

App. 1976) (vendors limited to retention of deposit as exclusive remedy under contract providing that vendors "shall have the right to retain" earnest money deposit "as liquidated damages"). Do you agree with this analogy? What about another analogy, namely, a security deposit in a lease? Would this latter analogy support or weaken a lender's claim for additional damages?

4. *Force Majeure.*   Returning to our master hypothetical, suppose that just before the plumbing fixtures are installed in the office building a city-wide plumbers' strike is called by the local union that delays construction and prevents Dan from obtaining a certificate of occupancy in a timely manner. As a result, Dan is not able to complete construction by the scheduled closing date. Under the terms of the sample commitment in the Documents Manual, could Ace refuse to fund the loan? If so, could Ace keep the refundable deposit? Could Dan claim "impossibility of performance" as a defense? See Hawkins v. First Federal Savings & Loan Assn., 291 Ala. 257, 280 So. 2d 93 (1973). See also discussion at Chapter 5B11, supra. If not, Dan should have insisted on protective language in the provision dealing with completion of construction or in the commitment provision dealing with defaults (discussed in this section). In light of the fact that Ace would not agree to an open-ended closing date, what type of compromise language might be reasonably acceptable to both parties?

5. *Lender's Right to Specific Performance.*   Absent relevant language in the loan documents, do you think that specific performance should be granted against either a borrower or lender who intentionally defaults under its loan commitment? In theory, a contract to lend money is not specifically enforceable by either party because there is an adequate remedy at law, namely money damages. 5 A. Corbin, Contracts §1152 (1964). The application of this doctrine to loan contracts was first enunciated in Rogers v. Challis, 54 Eng. Rep. 68 (Ch. 1859). And yet, as observed at Chapter 5D2, note 2, infra, this remedy has been generally available to an aggrieved borrower against a defaulting lender, especially where alternative financing was not available.

Conversely, there is a conspicuous lack of case law supporting specific performance against a defaulting borrower, presumably on the rationale that the aggrieved lender's money damages are readily computable. Do you agree with this underlying assumption? If not, why not? It has been suggested that a lender might argue for specific performance on the rationale that the security for a specific loan is unique (e.g., a lien on a particular parcel of real estate; the reputation, creditworthiness, and construction-management skills of a particular borrower). Also, by way of analogy to a contract of sale, this right has been extended to aggrieved purchasers on the premise that every parcel of real estate is unique. See Draper, The Broken Commitment: A Modern View of the Mortgage Lender's Remedy, 59 Cornell L. Rev. 418, 434 (1974); D. Dobbs, Remedies §12.10 (1973). In your opinion, is the analogy of a loan commitment to a contract of sale of real estate a sound one? See G. Nelson and D. Whitman, Real Estate Finance Law §12.3, at 854 (2d ed. 1985).

Another argument in support of specific performance is that no comparable investment alternatives may be available to the lender at the time of the borrower's breach. See Draper, The Broken Commitment: A Modern View of the Mortgage Lender's Remedy, 59 Cornell L. Rev. 418, 432-433 (1974). Can you think of at least one example where this may be true? In that regard don't forget our discussion of the debt-equity spectrum at Chapter 5B3, supra. Assuming this to be the case, can you think of any practical reasons why specific performance should nevertheless be denied? See G. Nelson and D. Whitman, Real Estate Finance Law §12.3, at 854 (2d ed. 1985). See generally Groat, Specific Performance of Contracts to Provide Permanent Financing, 60 Cornell L. Rev. 718 (1975) (written in response to the Draper article). Why would specific performance not be feasible if the defaulting borrower has already gone out and procured a first mortgage loan from another lender? Would equitable relief be sensible if the project is no longer a viable one? Id. at 735.

Do you think the aggrieved lender might have a stronger case if, instead of specific performance, it requests the court to enjoin the borrower from seeking a loan from any other lender? See Chicago Coliseum Club v. Dempsey, 265 Ill. App. 542 (1932). See also Zinman, Mortgage Loan and Joint Venture Commitments: The Institutional Investor's Remedies, 18 Real Prop., Prob. & Tr. J. 750 (1983).

2. Breach of Commitment by Lender

Many of the remedial considerations that we have just examined are also applicable to the enforcement rights of a borrower against a defaulting lender. However, the borrower's measure of damages is different, as explained in the *Pipkin* case.

Pipkin v. Thomas & Hill, Inc.
298 N.C. 278, 258 S.E.2d 778 (Sup. Ct. 1979)

Plaintiffs, as individuals and general partners doing business under the name of P.W.D. & W., brought this action for damages against defendant, a West Virginia corporation engaged in the mortgage banking business, to recover damages for its breach of an alleged contract to make plaintiffs a long-term loan to repay a construction loan from Central Carolina Bank (CCB). . . .

In August 1972 plaintiffs acquired property on U.S. Highway 70 and 401 just south of Raleigh for the purpose of constructing and operating a motel and restaurant. At that time they were experienced business men but inexperienced real estate developers. After extended negotiations with Ward, on 19 April 1973 plaintiffs jointly and severally filed with him, on a form furnished by defendant, an application for a "long-term permanent loan commitment from the defendant" in the amount of $1,162,500, repayable over 25 years at an interest rate of nine and one-half percent (9½%) per annum, with monthly payments of $10,156.76 for amortization of principal and interest. Plaintiffs' application was accompanied by a check for $500, the specified application fee. . . .

Again each plaintiff received a copy of the correspondence. At that time Ward and plaintiffs agreed that defendant would receive a fee of $11,625 for the loan commitment and a fee of $11,625 for closing the loan, a total of $23,250. . . .

Specifically, the question for our determination is the following:

What is the measure of damages for breach of a contract to make a loan of $1,162,500 at 9½% interest per annum, the loan to be amortized over 300 monthly installments and to be used to take out a short-term construction loan, when a substitute loan was unobtainable upon any terms at the time of the breach and, in order to forestall foreclosure, the borrowers had to refinance the construction loan by a demand note at a fluctuating rate of interest for a period of 18 months?

At trial plaintiffs sought to recover — and the judge purported to assess — their past, present and prospective damages. The case was tried upon the fiction that at the time of trial plaintiffs had obtained a permanent loan at 10½% interest, which the court found was the lowest prevailing rate of interest for a comparable long-term commercial loan as of 1 October 1974, the date of the breach. In attempting to fashion a rule which would appropriately measure plaintiffs' damages the trial judge analogized this case to those in which the borrower actually obtained another loan. On this theory, the trial court awarded plaintiffs general damages in the amount of $120,000, this amount being the difference between the interest on a 25-year loan of $1,162,500 at 10½% per annum and a similar loan at 9½%, reduced to present value *and* "discounted for the likelihood of early payment." As special damage, Judge McKinnon awarded plaintiffs $5,888.12, the total of amounts which plaintiffs reasonably expended in refinancing their construction loan with CCB to prevent foreclosure, and in their unsuccessful attempts over 18 months to secure a replacement long-term loan. The judge, however, refused to allow any recovery of the $184,619.49 in interest which plaintiffs paid CCB on the demand note during that 18-month interim.

The Court of Appeals affirmed the trial judge's award of $5,888.12 in special damages. This ruling was clearly correct, and we affirm it. As the Court of Appeals pointed out, additional title insurance and brokerage, accounting and appraisal fees "were foreseeable expenses which, but for the breach, plaintiffs would not have incurred." . . .

The Court of Appeals also ruled that the trial judge was correct in using the lowest prevailing rate of interest for a long-term commercial loan (10½%) to determine "the basic measure" of plaintiffs' damages, i.e., the difference between the interest on the loan at the contract rate during the agreed period of credit and the rate (not exceeding that permitted by law) which plaintiffs would have had to pay for the money in the market on the date of breach. Defendant argues that the use of a hypothetical loan at the lowest prevailing rate of interest for comparable long-term loans, at least in cases where an alternative lender cannot be found, is too speculative and uncertain a technique for approximating the borrower's prospective losses. However, a party seeking recovery for losses occasioned by another's breach of contract need not prove the amount of his prospective damages with absolute certainty; a reasonable showing will suffice. "Substantial damages may be recovered, though plaintiff can only give his loss proximately." . . .

In our view, plaintiffs have reasonably demonstrated that as a consequence of defendant's breach of its loan commitment they will suffer prospective losses; and we agree with the Court of Appeals that the trial court's use of the lowest prevailing rate for comparable long-term loans as a figure to be compared with the contract interest rate represents effort to provide relief from these prospective damages. We also agree that the trial judge erred in reducing the present worth of plaintiff's prospective damages ($143,282.03) to the amount of $120,000 "for the likelihood of early payment."

Although a witness for defendant opined that the average life of a commercial loan such as the one defendant was committed to make for plaintiffs was "approximately seven years," no witness attempted to fix the value of such a probability. Further, there was no evidence that plaintiffs contemplated early payment of the loan. The Court of Appeals, therefore, properly ordered this reduction stricken, and we affirm.

Finally, the Court of Appeals concluded that the trial judge erred in refusing to allow plaintiffs to recover the $184,618.49 in interest which they paid CCB on the demand notes during the 18 months elapsing between the date of defendant's breach of its contract and the date of the trial. This interest, that court said, was recoverable as special damages which defendant should have foreseen as the probable consequence of its failure to provide plaintiffs the promised long-term financing. Thus, the question remaining is whether, in order to avoid foreclosure, a disappointed borrower to whom a defaulting lender had committed long-term financing to pay off a temporary construction loan, is entitled to obtain temporary refinancing at a higher rate of interest and to recover the cost of this refinancing as special damages.

On the ground that such refinancing was an unforeseeable consequence of the breach defendant argues that the trial court properly denied plaintiffs any recovery of the interest they paid on the demand note which refinanced the temporary construction loan. In our view, this contention by a defaulting lender, fully aware of the purpose for which plaintiffs had secured its commitment, is entirely unrealistic. In 11 Williston on Contracts §1411 (3d Ed. Jaeger 1968) it is stated:

> It will frequently happen that the borrower is unable to get money elsewhere, and, if the defendant had notice of the purpose for which the money was desired, he will be liable for damages caused by the plaintiff's inability to carry out his purpose, if the performance of the promise would have enabled him to do so. . . .

Whether the loan commitment be for $4,800,000 or $1,162,500, we harbor no doubt that a committed permanent lender on a substantial building project certainly must foresee that a breach of his commitment a relatively short time before the date he has contracted to provide the money to pay off the interim construction loan will result in substantial harm to the borrower.

Defendant, in this case, being unable to find a lender willing to make the permanent loan it had committed itself to provide plaintiffs, formally notified them on 6 August 1974 — less than two months before the scheduled closing date — that it would not make the loan. At that time the same conditions which had thwarted defendant's efforts to obtain the loan also thwarted plaintiffs. In a reasonable effort to minimize their losses, while they continued their search for another permanent loan plaintiffs refinanced the construction loan to prevent foreclosure of property in which they had acquired equity of approximately $627,500. That their search during the subsequent 18 months proved futile is no reason to deny them compensation for the resulting damages they sustained during that period.

However, our conclusion that plaintiffs should recover as foreseeable damages their losses arising from the interest payments on the demand notes does not necessarily entail an award for the full amount of interest actually paid to CCB. On the contrary, we hold that the Court of Appeals erred insofar as it awarded plaintiffs both the full amount of interest actually paid CCB from the date of the breach until the date of trial *and* the present value of the difference between the interest on $1,162,500 amortized over 25 years from the date of the trial at the hypothetical rate of 10½% per year and the contract rate of 9½%.

In Bridgkort Racquet Club v. University Bank, 85 Wis. 2d 706, 271 N.W.2d 165 (1978), plaintiffs contracted with defendant University Bank for a loan of $250,000 at 10¼% to be amortized over a 15-year period. The loan closing, which was scheduled for 13 January 1976, involved both the short-term construction lender, and long-term financiers. The short-term loan was closed on 13 January, but on 23 January 1976 plaintiffs discovered that the defendant University Bank had breached its contract and would not make its long-term loan. After extensive attempts to obtain financing at a comparable rate, the plaintiffs obtained financing at 11% for the same 15-year period. The Wisconsin court recognized the plaintiff's damages as the difference between the cost of obtaining substitute money at an increased rate of interest and the interest rate specified in the contract. In the case at bar, plaintiffs contracted with defendant to have the use of $1,162,500 from 1 October 1974 until 1 October 1999. To award plaintiffs the entire amount of interest paid to CCB from the time of the breach until the time of the trial ($184,619.49), with no deduction for interest at the contract rate of 9½%, would give plaintiffs the use of $1,162,500 interest-free for that 18 months period. When defendant failed to make the agreed loan on 1 October 1974 it became liable to plaintiffs *at that time* for the increased cost of obtaining the use of the money "during the agreed period of credit," that is, 25 years from 1 October 1974.

We are of the opinion that the Wisconsin Court in *Bridgkort Racquet Club,* supra, was correct in determining the plaintiffs' damages to be the differential between the cost of obtaining new financing and the interest payments specified in the contract. Based on this principle, plaintiffs' recovery of interest payments made to CCB during this 18-month period must be reduced by the amount of interest which would have been payable to defendant at the contract rate of 9½%. . . .

This cause is returned to the Court of Appeals for remand to the Superior Court of Wake County with instructions that, after hearing such additional evidence as may be necessary to make the calculations required to determine the amounts defined in subsections (b) and (c) below, that court shall enter judgment that plaintiff recover of defendant as damages the sum of the amounts specified in subsections (a), (b), and (c) as follows:

(a) $5,888.12 expended for additional title insurance, brokerage, accounting, and appraisal fees necessitated by defendant's breach;

(b) $184,619.49, less the amount of interest plaintiffs contracted to pay defendant from 1 October 1974 until 31 March 1976;

(c) the present value of the amount determined by subtracting the interest payments which were to have been made by plaintiffs pursuant to the contract from 1 April 1976 until 1 October 1999, from the interest payable during the same period on a loan of $1,162,500, amortized over 300 months from 1 October 1974 bearing an interest rate of 10½% per annum. . . .

For the reasons stated and specified above, the decision of the Court of Appeals is affirmed in part, and reversed in part.

Mehr and Kilgore, Enforcement of the Real Estate Loan Commitment: Improvement of the Borrower's Remedies
24 Wayne L. Rev. 1011, 1025-1030 (1978)

IV.   APPLICATION OF THE TRADITIONAL EQUITY RULES

The traditional rule in equity has been that a contract to loan money will not be specifically enforced. Because equity requires an inadequate remedy at law as a prerequisite to relief, specific performance will be refused unless the borrower can demonstrate that the subject matter of the contract is unique, or that exceptional circumstances justify equitable relief. Since money is considered as a commodity, there is a strong presumption against the uniqueness of the loan commitment, and the availability of substitute performance ordinarily is assumed. Further, reliance alone is insufficient to support a claim for equitable relief, and the scope of the "exceptional circumstances" doctrine is too unclear for consistent application by the courts. Consequently, the borrower's recovery for the interest rate differential and the reasonably foreseeable costs and expenses of obtaining substitute performance has been presumed to constitute an adequate remedy at law.

This inadequacy doctrine is largely derived from the historical English division of law and chancery. Since the chancery courts were established primarily to mitigate the harsh application of common law in the law courts, the applicant in chancery had to first demonstrate that his remedy at law was "inadequate." Because the politically powerful law courts were jealous of their authority, the inadequacy requirement became solidly entrenched as a jurisdictional limitation on the power of the chancellors. Thus, the policy considerations behind the inadequacy rule are largely jurisdictional, based upon the function of the equity courts in English jurisprudence. Although the merger of law and equity has rendered these considerations anachronistic, American courts continue to apply the rule without fully evaluating the continuing validity of its underlying policy considerations.

American courts, however, do not consistently apply the inadequacy rule. Several courts have found an inadequate remedy at law when the borrower was unable to obtain alternate financing, although these courts have not clearly explained what constitutes an inadequate remedy at law. However, at least four rationales may be advanced in support of the borrower's claim that the legal claim is inadequate when refinancing is unavailable: (1) the loan commitment is unique, because it is the only one available, (2) the loan commitment is unique, because the borrower will forfeit his interest in the land upon the construction lender's foreclosure, and the law presumes all land to be unique, (3) the lack of alternative financing is an "exceptional circumstance," since the law cannot fully compensate the borrower for his consequential losses following the construction lender's foreclosure, and (4) justifiable detrimental reliance is an "exceptional circumstance" when refinancing is unavailable. Although a number of borrowers have argued these theories successfully when alternate financing was unavailable, (1), (2) and (4) have not yet been established as independent and sufficient reasons for granting specific enforcement absent actual injury not compensable at law. Thus, the primary thrust of these decisions falls under (3) in that the borrower has an actual injury which is not compensable through damages.

These theories, however, are fundamentally at odds with the traditional inadequacy rule. Under the traditional rule, the availability of damages was ipso facto an adequate remedy at law. Under this theory of "legal" adequacy, the court's inquiry was directed primarily at the availability of damages, rather than the sufficiency of such damages. Therefore, equitable relief would be granted only if the injury was not measurable in damages. On the other hand, if the term "adequate" is used as it is commonly understood, the court must determine whether damages would as fully and completely compensate the borrower for all his injury as would specific enforcement. This is essentially the inquiry under (3). Although it could be argued that this construction would obviate the need for the adequacy rule since the court would then have the discretionary power to choose the more appropriate remedy, the developer has continued to bear the burden of proving an inadequate remedy at law. However, the courts have shifted their focus from that of availability to the sufficiency of damages as the test of adequacy in cases where the borrower has not been able to refinance.

When, however, it is demonstrated that the borrower can refinance, specific performance is conceptually difficult because the most expedient means of obtaining relief appears to be substantially within the borrower's control. Consequently, the availability of damages to compensate for the increased cost of alternate financing will preclude a claim for specific performance when the borrower is able to refinance even though the borrower's remaining noncompensable injuries such as lost profits and detrimental effect on credit standing may be substantial. Although these injuries are significant, the courts continue to apply the traditional rule rigorously in cases where the borrower can refinance, and will not compare the actual sufficiency of the damage remedy with that of specific performance.

NOTES AND QUESTIONS

1. Foreseeable Damages. In Pipkin v. Thomas & Hill the court, citing the rules in Hadley v. Baxendale and §343 of the Restatement of Contracts, held that the injured borrower could recover all of the foreseeable damages proximately caused by the defendant lender's breach of the loan commitment, including not only the discounted present cash value of the difference in interest rates and other costs of obtaining alternative financing but also the borrower's consequential damages if they are "measurable and [of] reasonable certainty, i.e., they must be more than speculative." If after a breach by a lender the injured borrower is unable to obtain alternative financing, should the borrower be able to recover, by way of consequential damages, the value of the loss of business (as measured by lost profits) caused by the lender's default and resulting foreclosure by the construction lender? Compare W-V Enterprises, Inc. v. Federal Savings & Loan Insurance Corp., 234 Kan. 354, 673 P.2d 1112 (1983), with Coastland Corp. v. Third National Mortgage Co., 611 F.2d 969 (4th Cir. 1979). See also First Mississippi Bank v. Latch, 433 So. 2d 946 (Miss. 1983); Mehr and Kilgore, Enforcement of the Real Estate Loan Commitment: Improvement of the Borrower's Remedies, 24 Wayne L. Rev. 1011, 1032-1033 (1978). What about more remote damages, such as mental distress? See Westesen v. Olathe State Bank, 78 Colo. 217, 240 P. 689 (1925).

Observe that in *Pipkin* the Supreme Court of North Carolina declared that the lower court (the Court of Appeals) had given the plaintiffs the use of the $1,162,500 loan amount interest-free for the 18-month period between the date of the defendant's breach, October 1, 1974, and the date of the trial, April 1, 1976, by not subtracting the present value of the difference in interest rates (between the hypothetical 10½ percent rate and the contract rate of 9½ percent on the $1,162,500 loan amount amortized over the 25-year loan period) from the $184,619 interest paid to the construction lender during the 18-month period. Otherwise, in the opinion of the court, the plaintiff-borrower would be made more than fully whole again and be unjustly enriched at the expense of the defendant-lender. Could an argument be made on behalf of the defendant-lender that the plaintiff-borrower had been unjustly enriched based on the fact that the court had used a hypothetical rate of 10½ percent and had failed to take into account the possibility of a prepayment (assuming there was no lock-in period prohibiting any prepayment) during the balance of the 25-year term of the loan?

Also observe that in *Pipkin* the borrower was allowed to recover consequential damages of $5,888.12 expended for the additional expenses it had incurred (such as brokerage and appraisal fees) in its search for alternative takeout financing. Had the plaintiff-borrower paid the defendant the agreed-on commitment fees in the amount of $23,250 (out of the construction loan proceeds), do you think the court would have allowed the borrower to recover the $23,500 amount as additional damages? If not, why not? See Rubin v. Pioneer Federal Savings & Loan, 214 Neb. 364, 334 N.W.2d 424 (1983).

2. Borrower's Right to Specific Performance. While as of this writing there does not appear to be any case law supporting specific performance as a remedy for an aggrieved lender, there is ample case law authority supporting this remedy for the borrower (as cited in the foregoing excerpt by Mehr and Kilgore). As explained by one leading commentator, many of these case law results can be explained by the fact that the defaulting lender had already closed the loan and recorded its mortgage when it stopped making disbursements on a construction loan. Therefore, since the project had not been completed, the borrower was precluded from refinancing its construction loan with a takeout loan from a postconstruction lender. Moreover, alternative financing from another construction lender would be impractical inasmuch as the existing mortgage would render the title unmarketable and prevent a substitute lender from obtaining a first mortgage lien until the prior construction loan indebtedness is discharged. G. Nelson and D. Whitman, Real Estate Finance Law §12.3, at 857 (2d ed. 1985).

But suppose the project is already completed and the borrower is unable to refinance its construction loan because the postconstruction lender, without justification, refuses to honor its takeout commitment, and the borrower searches for but cannot find alternative financing. Under these circumstances, should a borrower be entitled to specific performance, or should the borrower's remedy be confined to consequential damages based on an estimate of what the borrower might have paid for reasonable alternative financing? In the above excerpt, Mehr and Kilgore point out two reasons why a loan commitment is unique. Can you think of any other reasons, when the breaching lender is an established and reputable one? See Madison and Dwyer ¶3.06, at 3-60. Why, do you think, are courts more apt to grant specific performance to a borrower who has not obtained alternative financing than to one who has? See, e.g., Selective Builders, Inc. v. Hudson City Savings Bank, 137 N.J. Super. 500, 349 A.2d 564 (1975). Mehr and Kilgore believe that to make such a distinction is "questionable." They assert that "the difference between a borrower who refinances and a borrower who does not is merely one of degree. The fact that the consequences are more severe in the one case does not justify a denial of relief where the consequences are less severe, if the injuries in either case merit relief and are not fully compensable in damages." Enforcement of the Real Estate Loan Commitment, at 1034. What are the "consequences" Mehr and Kilgore are talking about? By contrast, other commentators are of the opinion that specific performance should not be granted where the borrower has refinanced its construction loan with another postconstruction lender. See Groot, Specific Performance of Contracts to Provide Permanent Financing, 60 Cornell L. Rev. 718, 736-739 (1975). In your opinion, which position is more correct? If you think that specific performance should generally be available, would your opinion change with respect to a borrower who has insisted on a liquidated damages clause in the commitment letter to protect itself? See D. Dobbs, Remedies §12.5, at 825 (1973). Can you think of any reason why a poorly drafted commitment that is lacking in details could jeopardize the borrower's right, if any, to specific performance?

For a discussion of specific performance of postconstruction loan commitments see generally G. Nelson and D. Whitman, Real Estate Financing Law §12.3 (2d ed. 1985); Brannon, Enforceability of Mortgage Loan Commitments, 18 Real Prop., Prob. & Tr. J. 724, 738-749 (Winter 1983); Draper, The Broken Commitment: A Modern View of the Mortgage Lender's Remedy, 59 Cornell L. Rev. 418, 421-439 (1974); Groot, Specific Performance of Contracts to Provide Permanent Financing, 60 Cornell L. Rev. 718, 737-742 (1975); Linzer, On the Amorality of Contract Remedies — Efficiency, Equity and the Second Restatement, 81 Col. L. Rev. 111, 126 (1981); Wildman, Breach of Mortgage Commitments — An Update, Real Prop. News of the St. B. of Calif. 1 (Summer 1981).

Is the borrower the only possible plaintiff where a lender has breached the commitment? See Silverdale Hotel Assocs. v. Lomas & Nettleton Co., 36 Wash. App. 762, 677 P.2d 773 (1984), where a general contractor recovered damages from a defaulting construction lender.

3.   Additional Readings on Remedies for Breach of Mortgage Loan Commitment.   For further discussion on the subject of breach of a mortgage loan commitment see generally Brannon, Enforceability of Mortgage Loan Commitments, 18 Real Prop., Prob. & Tr. J. 724 (1983); Draper, The Broken Commitment: A Modern View of the Mortgage Lender's Remedy, 59 Cornell L. Rev. 418 (1974); Groot, Specific Performance of Contracts to Provide Permanent Financing, 60 Cornell L. Rev. 718 (1975); Mehr and Kilgore, Enforcement of the Real Estate Loan Commitment: Improvement of the Borrower's Remedies, 24 Wayne L. Rev. 1011 (1978); Wolf, The Refundable Commitment Fee, 23 Bus. Law. 1065 (1968); Zinman, Mortgage Loan and Joint Venture Commitments: The Institutional Investor's Remedies, 18 Real Prop., Prob. & Tr. J. 750 (Winter 1983); Annot., 82 A.L.R.3d 1116 (1978).

E. CLOSING THE POSTCONSTRUCTION LOAN

Closings of major loan transactions tend to be problematic no matter how much foresight is exercised by the attorneys for the borrower, the postconstruction lender, and the construction lender. Therefore, it is advisable to obtain early approval of the leases, surveys, preliminary title report, and loan documentation (by means of a preclosed transaction, or otherwise). However, it is absolutely imperative that the attorneys for the principal parties, the borrower and the postconstruction lender, secure the necessary approvals and documents and do their homework prior to the scheduled closing date so that they will be free to deal with the closing problems that will inevitably arise.

The following excerpt describes the parties at the closing and their agenda and gives a checklist of the documentation required at the closing.

Madison and Dwyer, The Law of Real Estate Financing
¶3.09 (1981)

¶3.09 CLOSING THE PERMANENT LOAN

[1] PARTIES AT CLOSING

The primary concern of the attorney representing the developer is to orchestrate a permanent loan closing as smoothly and efficiently as possible. In many cases, the developer is paying a higher rate of interest on the construction loan and can save a substantial amount of funds by closing quickly on the permanent loan. From the outset, upon issuance of the permanent commitment, he should be aware of the various parties involved in the permanent loan closing and develop a working relationship with them. Many times, a permanent closing will be helped along by the title company which often acts as escrow agent for the permanent lender, by counsel for the construction lender (who is interested in seeing that the loan funds supplied by the construction lender are repaid as quickly as possible), and last but not least, by counsel for the permanent lender.

Many permanent lenders will use their in-house staff of attorneys to close the loan. Some will rely completely on special and local counsel, and others, in effect, will use their in-house corporate attorneys together with special and local counsel selected by the permanent lender. There are advantages and disadvantages to each of three methods employed by the permanent lender. In the case where the permanent lender is using its in-house staff of attorneys only, the borrower does not have to pay the out-of-pocket legal fees incurred by the permanent lender. Just as important, the in-house attorney is very experienced in the loan closing procedures. Generally, special counsel can be helpful when an unusual question or problem arises with regard to local law. However, many of these attorneys have long represented the interests of the permanent lender and are just as familiar with the closing requirements and procedures involved with the closing as would be an in-house attorney for the permanent lender. The obvious disadvantage in using special counsel is that the legal fees must be paid for by the developer. More importantly, since there is one more person who must be satisfied that the closing requirements have been met and the funding is in proper order, there is the possibility of a loan closing being unduly dragged out, creating expense and ill will on the part of all. One adage that should faithfully be kept is that the developer's attorney should not wait until the last minute and hope that the permanent loan will close itself. Even when started well in advance, permanent loan closings tend to be postponed and extended.

In most permanent loan closings, there is a division of responsibility required by the permanent lender's counsel. Usually, it is the responsibility of the permanent lender's counsel to prepare the loan documents, although in some cases the permanent lender will require that the title company prepare the documents; accordingly, the developer's attorney should be friendly, but as persistent as possible and make certain that the permanent loan documents are prepared several months in advance. This will give the attorney and his client an opportunity to review the documents and request changes where necessary and appropriate.

[2] DOCUMENTATION AT CLOSING

The next division of work encompasses certain loan closing documents, such as the certified inventory statement, tenants' acceptance letters, architect's certificate, and estoppel certificates prepared by the permanent lender's counsel. These documents, together with the assignment of leases and notices of assignment, must be executed at or near the time of closing by third parties unrelated to the developer.

Many times, a tenant will take weeks before executing such an acceptance letter. It would be embarrassing for the attorney representing the developer to tell his client that the closing cannot take place until the architect, who drafted the plans and specifications, returns from a three-month vacation in the Amazon, and executes the architect's certificate. Before the occupancy leases (and in the case of a leasehold mortgage, the ground lease, as well) are executed, the developer's attorney should obtain early approval from the permanent lender so that the lender, prime tenants, and ground lessor will be able to work out their differences and avoid any delay in the closing of the permanent loan. Another area which he must coordinate carefully are those closing documents to be prepared by third parties — the hazard insurance policy, the title policy, and the survey. It is appropriate and beneficial for the developer's attorney to send a copy of that part of the permanent commitment pertaining to the requirements for title insurance, hazard insurance, and survey to the respective parties so that they can become completely familiar with what is required of them by the permanent lender. With regard to the title company, the developer's attorney should make certain that months in advance a title binder is sent to the permanent lender so that the permanent lender may review it and, where necessary, require endorsements to make certain that there will be no surprises or problems with the final title insurance policy to be issued at the closing. By using a pre-closed form of buy-sell agreement, the developer's attorney will be able to obtain early approval of the note and mortgage (or deed of trust) and most of the collateral documentation, such as the hazard insurance policy and the preliminary title report.

Sometimes there may be a breakdown in communications between the real estate department and the office of the general counsel of the permanent lender because many permanent lenders require the real estate department to review and make a final inspection of the property within two weeks before closing. Other permanent lenders require their in-house appraiser to inspect the property also. The developer's attorney should make certain that these arrangements have been made by the permanent lender so as not to hold up the closing. The last divisional category are documents to be prepared by the attorney for the developer, for example, the attorney's opinion letter. He should make certain that drafts of these closing requirements are prepared and submitted to the permanent lender's counsel for its review well in advance of the closing date.

Where the permanent lender is purchasing the construction lender's documents by assignment, the permanent lender will require, in addition to the foregoing documents and the assignment of the loan documents, an acknowledgment from the construction lender that the loan is current and not in default, as well as an estoppel certificate from the borrower.

Finally, three or four days before the settlement date, counsel for the permanent lender will frequently submit a closing disbursement instruction letter to the title company or some other outside closing agent.

[3]   CHECKLIST FOR CLOSING PERMANENT LOAN

- The mortgagor should review the note, security instrument, lease assignments, and guaranty (all prepared by the lender) prior to closing. Do this early, because review of these documents may require some time.
- Obtain the title insurance binder and boundary survey, making sure the title company supplies photocopies of any easements, covenants, or restrictions of record. The lender will need these to prepare the security instrument and to assess the effects of any encumbrance or exceptions.
- Request, at least 45 days before closing, the building location survey, which also should depict the location of all easements. The lender also may want a certification that the engineer is covered by errors and omissions (E&O) insurance.
- Gather the fully executed leases for review by the lender early. Use and occupancy clauses, renewal options, percentage rents, common areas contributions, etc., may require modifications which take time to discuss, negotiate, and put into effect. Check to see if any corporate parent guarantees are required and that appropriate corporate resolutions are appended to each lease.
- The lender will require forms from the tenants indicating their legal acceptance of the premises and establishing the lease and rent commencement dates. These must be obtained when construction is completed.
- A final inspection of the property must be made and a certificate of completion furnished to the lender. A letter must be obtained from the appraiser indicating that the project meets the conditions of his original appraisal. The appraiser may also need leasing data if he conditioned the value estimate on anticipated rents.
- If some portion of construction is delayed, you may have to prepare and execute an escrow agreement so that funds may be held in escrow until all work is completed.
- A satisfactory hazard insurance policy, with the first annual premium paid, must be obtained and delivered to the permanent lender. The loan commitment must be checked to determine the minimum insurance company rating acceptable to the lender.
- Obtain copies of occupancy permits issued by the local authority

when construction is completed. Also, it is advisable to obtain letters from the utility companies confirming that service is available and acknowledging payment by the mortgagor of applicable initial charges.

- Prepare and execute any joint-use documents that may be required if the project was built in stages, with an earlier phase financed by a different lender.
- Take steps to dedicate roads or other land to the state, if such action is required. This type of situation is time-consuming, and you must allow for any delays.
- Obtain the required evidence from the appropriate state commission that the mortgagor is authorized to do business in the state and that its charter is current.
- File environmental impact statements if they are required. Find out if pertinent obligations assumed by the developer have been met.
- Check to see if other miscellaneous documents are required for your specific closing. Examples might include a common-wall agreement, keyman insurance, off-site easements, or, if the lender wants his security instrument subordinated to certain leases, a subordination agreement.[345]

PLANNING PROBLEM

PART I.

The Closing Agenda. The closing agenda contemplated by the sample commitment provision excerpted in the Documents Manual raises the following questions:

a. As attorney for Ace, how would you ascertain that construction has been completed as provided in paragraph (a)? See Chapter 5B11, supra.

b. Would paragraph (b) be just as effective if it simply required that the title company insure that the lien is a first lien on the property unencumbered by any prior interests? See Chapter 5B15, note 3, supra.

c. If you were attorney for Dan Developer, how would you determine if the requirements of paragraph (c) have been met?

d. Regarding the requirements of paragraph (d), suppose the final certificate of occupancy is not available at closing. Does this mean that the closing must be delayed? Is there any way Ace can close and

---

345. See Waldron, Conscientious Effort Needed for Timely Closings on Income Loans, 36 The Mortgage Banker 15, 16, 18 (1976).

still protect itself? Why does Ace require both the temporary and final certificates of occupancy? Wouldn't Ace be fully protected if it only required final certificates prior to closing its loan? See Chapter 5B9, supra.

e. Often by statute, local real estate taxes become a lien on the property as of the beginning of the tax year or at some other time in advance of the date on which the taxes become due and payable. Because of the time value of money, most taxpayers refuse to pay their taxes until they actually become due and payable even if the taxes are alien on their property. However, assume that at the time of closing there are such taxes constituting a lien on the property that are not yet due and payable. Paragraph (e) recognizes and appears to permit this. However, is it permitted by paragraph (b)? How do you think the courts would resolve this seeming inconsistency? What should Dan's attorney have done in the drafting stage to avoid this problem?

f. With regard to paragraph (j), why is Ace concerned that the zoning or subdivision approval not extend to property other than the property covered by the mortgage? See Chapter 5B9, supra.

g. With respect to paragraph (l), if leases have been executed prior to the commitment, it may be difficult, or at least expensive, for Dan to get the tenant to subordinate or issue the certificates when needed. What could Dan have done to obviate this problem?

h. The opinion of Dan's counsel is required to cover only certain of the paragraphs in the mini-agenda. Why have some been left out? If you were Dan's counsel, would you ask that anything else be deleted?

PART II.

Returning to the master hypothetical at Chapter 5B, supra, suppose that on January 1 of this year Dan Developer executes a postconstruction loan commitment (following the same standard form as the one in the Documents Manual) with Ace Insurance Company (a life insurance company chartered in the state of Fuller) for a 15-year first mortgage loan in the amount of $25 million with a fixed interest rate of 10 percent per annum and contingent interest each year equal to 2 percent of Dan's net income. Ace's commitment also requires that prior to the scheduled closing date, December 31 of next year, a 15-year net lease be executed with the Widget Corporation of America (WCA), which lease will be identical in form and content to the sample office building lease at Chapter 5C, supra, except that there will be no reference to mortgage(s) dollar amounts in clause 13. Finally, Ace's commitment provides: (1) that on or before the scheduled closing date, 80 percent of the leasable space in the office building must be pre-leased (on the basis of executed leases or letters of intent from prospective tenants) at a minimum average rental of $20 per square foot or the loan amount will be reduced to $22 million; (2) that Dan execute prior to the closing date an assignment of the WCA lease that must contain the same terms as the sample assignment; and (3) that at the closing, WCA must execute a "Tenant's Acceptance Letter" and that a mortgagor's estoppel affidavit, attorney's certification, and architect's certificate must all be executed and submitted to Ace's closing agent.

On the strength of Ace's commitment, Dan immediately thereafter negotiates a commitment from Fuller National Bank (FNB) for a construction loan in the amount of $25 million, and on June 1 of this year, all three parties, Dan, Ace, and FNB, execute a preclosed form of buy-sell agreement under which Ace agrees to take an assignment of the construction loan note and mortgage (instead of having Dan execute a new note and mortgage in favor of Ace) on the scheduled closing date, provided that all the terms and conditions of its commitment letter are met. FNB records its construction mortgage on December 15 of this year, and Ace closes its postconstruction loan on December 31 of next year.

The foregoing loan transaction takes place in the common-law jurisdiction of Fuller, which has the following statutes: (1) a regulatory statute that mandates that real estate loans made by life insurance companies chartered in the State of Fuller must be first mortgage loans with a loan-to-value ratio of no more than 75 percent; (2) a usury statute that provides for a maximum contract rate of interest on real estate loans of 10 percent; and (3) a statute authorizing any person entitled to the legal possession of leased premises to dispossess or have ousted, by means of a summary proceeding, any occupant not so entitled to possession (otherwise, any ouster must be accomplished by means of the more expensive and time-consuming common-law action of ejectment).

Question 1: Based on the foregoing assumptions, decide if any of the following would prevent you (as counsel to Ace) from agreeing to close Ace's loan on schedule: (a) an intervening lienor, a judgment creditor of Dan, files a lien on the property two months prior to the scheduled closing date; (b) you discover that Dan is planning to sell the mortgaged real estate as soon as the Ace loan is closed, without Ace's permission; (c) while the estimated market value of the office building project (based on a capitalization of earnings test) is $34 million, the construction and land costs were only $25 million, which means that Dan would end up with 100 percent financing; or (d) any other reason you can think of as Ace's counsel.

Question 2: As attorney for Ace, what objections, if any, do you have to the following language in the proposed occupancy lease between

Dan and WCA that will be assigned to Ace as additional collateral? (Except for the following, the language in the lease is identical to the sample office building lease excerpted at Chapter 5C, supra.)

> The rent shall be $20,000 per month. . . . In the event of any material default by Lessee, this lease shall automatically terminate on 10 days' notice by Lessor, and Lessor may rent the premises on behalf of Lessee, who shall remain liable for damages with respect to the balance of the original lease term. . . .

Question 3: As attorney representing the construction lender, FNB, what maximum construction loan commitment amount would you recommend to your client, and why?

Question 4: If Dan were to execute an assignment of the WCA lease in favor of Ace, which *one* of the following would most definitely empower Ace to start collecting rentals from WCA as a pre-foreclosure remedy: (a) Dan negotiates a higher rental from WCA without the consent of Ace; (b) Dan refuses to make repairs of damage caused by the elements (as required under the lease); (c) Dan, with his own cash, purchases materials and fully pays workers to complete construction of additional office space (without violating local law or changing the use or character of the mortgaged premises, but without the consent of Ace)?

Question 5: Briefly explain what Ace's remedies are, if any, and against whom, in the event of the following occurrences, which take place one year after the postconstruction loan closes:

a. Dan obtains a wraparound mortgage from a different lender in the amount of $2 million;

b. Dan neglects to make repairs that WCA claims are necessary to correct a recently discovered latent structural defect, and WCA cancels its lease with Dan;

c. Ace discovers that Dan's certificate of occupancy for the office building is invalid because it was based on misrepresentations made by Dan's general contractor, and it will cost $1 million to make the necessary changes mandated by the local building code. Dan refuses to comply, and the city attorney has just obtained an injunction that prohibits any occupancy of the building until the violations are corrected.

Chapter 6

Construction Financing

A. THE ROLE OF CONSTRUCTION FINANCING IN THE COMMERCIAL LENDING CYCLE

The traditional dichotomy between postconstruction and construction financing can be explained by the fact that commercial banks, which do most of the construction lending, obtain their loanable funds chiefly from short-term demand and time deposits that are vulnerable to the vagaries of seasonal fluctuations and swings in the business cycle. These banks prefer to engage in short-term construction financing because of their need to maintain liquidity to meet sudden drains on their cash reserves. Also, some commercial banks and mortgage companies prefer to maintain a brisk turnover in their real estate loan portfolios so that, as "loan correspondents" for postconstruction lenders, they can earn origination fees and annual servicing charges on the construction loans that are sold and assigned to the postconstruction lender. Moreover, since the short-term interest rates charged by banks and other construction lenders are usually geared to a daily floating prime or dealer commercial paper rate, commercial banks find that as construction lenders they are in a better position than postconstruction lenders to protect themselves against inflation and shifting market conditions. By contrast, the funding sources of postconstruction lenders, such as life insurance and credit corporations, traditionally tend to be of a more stable and permanent nature, which enables them to concentrate more easily on longer-term lending.[1]

1. Institutions such as life insurance companies are not unaffected by market conditions. While high short-term interest rates during the 1979-1981 era of stagflation and resultant disintermediation caused savings and loan associations, mutual savings and loan associations, and mutual savings banks to curtail their postconstruction lending activities, many insurance companies also found themselves in a liquidity bind as lower rates on repayments of existing mortgages reduced their available reserves for loanable funds. In addition, many companies, especially those specializing in large policies with

Another reason for the dichotomy in real estate lending is that until recently construction loans made by national commercial banks with maturities of five years or less on commercial and industrial property were exempted from the regulatory constraints (e.g., maximum loan-to-value ratios, amortization requirements) otherwise applicable to real estate loans if the bank had a firm takeout commitment from a responsible postconstruction lender. However, the Federal Reserve Act was amended by the Garn-St. Germain Depository Institutions Act of 1982 to remove such regulatory restrictions on real estate loans made by national banks.[2] This was done by regulations promulgated by the Comptroller of the Currency that became effective on September 9, 1983.[3]

Over time, construction lenders have developed the unique expertise to monitor the construction activities of a developer or contractor to deal with such complex problems as mechanics' and materialmens' liens, cost overruns, and construction delays caused by shortages of labor and materials. As a result, construction lending has become a highly specialized area of real estate financing.

These distinctions between construction and postconstruction lending have affected the way these two groups of lenders view a real estate transaction. The basic objective of the construction lender is to make sure that the improvements are completed for the amount of the construction loan plus the borrower's equity investment in accordance with the terms and conditions specified in the postconstruction lender's takeout commitment. The construction lender does not have to deal with the long-term, "down the road" problems facing the postconstruction lender and will not normally concern itself with them. Since World War II the commitment from the postconstruction lender has traditionally been the condition precedent to construction lending in most real estate transactions.

Conversely, while the postconstruction lender is relieved of dealing with risks that arise during the construction period, it commits to make its loan some 18 to 36 months before closing and must anticipate any contingencies that might render the loan investment unsound during this time and during the life of the loan (such as market downturns that make a completed project unrentable). This necessitates a thorough study of the economic viability of the project; the lender's goal in

---

sophisticated policyholders, experienced an upsurge in policy loans at artificially low interest rates to policyholders who invested their borrowed funds at higher market rates. This further constricted these insurance companies' supply of loanable funds for postconstruction financing. See generally Strum, The Roles of Life Insurance Companies and Pension Funds in Financing Real Estate in the 80s, in Financing Real Estate During the Inflationary 80's, at 1 (B. Strum ed. 1981).

2. 12 U.S.C. §371 (1990).

3. 12 C.F.R. §§34.1 to 34.3 (1990).

negotiating the commitment is to make sure that, at the time of funding, the property constitutes sound and legal security for the loan.

Thus, the postconstruction lender must insert in its commitment certain conditions that the property must meet at the time of funding. For example, the lender will require that the improvements be completed within the prescribed time limits in a "good, substantial and workmanlike manner," fully equipped with "first class" equipment[4] and built in accordance with the approved plans and specifications; that the property be paid for and be free of mechanics' liens; that title to the property be good, marketable, and unencumbered by liens prior to the mortgage or deed of trust other than those specifically authorized; and that the property and improvements be in full compliance with all applicable laws and regulations for which all required governmental permits have been properly issued.

These requirements will not ensure that the project will be an economic success. This is a risk that the postconstruction lender assumes, based on its evaluation of the economic realities of the transaction. To mitigate that risk, lenders often ask for commitment provisions that require, inter alia, the achievement of certain leasing conditions and the absence of any material adverse change in the financial condition of the borrower or certain key tenants.

Recently, the distinctions between construction and postconstruction lenders have broken down somewhat. Some postconstruction lenders have been investing in real estate equity as a joint venture partner of the developer and supplying their own postconstruction financing to the joint venture.[5] In such instances, they often participate in, or actually make, the construction loan themselves. As postconstruction lenders gain experience in construction financing, we may see them gradually become more involved in the construction aspects of real estate development.[6]

---

4. You will find terms such as "first class" in many real estate documents. What does "first class" mean? What if the lender thinks the equipment is second class and the borrower thinks it is first class? See discussion at Chapter 5B11; compare Bettancourt v. Gilroy Theatre Co., 120 Cal. App. 2d 364, 261 P.2d 351 (1953) (contract to build a "first class" theater held sufficiently definite) with Hart v. Georgia R.R. Co., 101 Ga. 188, 28 S.E. 637 (1897) (contract to build a "first class hotel" held too indefinite). The lesson to be learned is that when you draft such documents, avoid the use of vague terms and wherever possible employ definitional language that is geared to some objective standard.

5. See Chapter 7B for a discussion of joint ventures and other equity-type real estate investments. To better understand what prompted this shift from debt to equity financing, see Joint Ventures: The Boon that's Reshaping the Industry, 50 Housing, Aug. 1980, at 46; Lenders Ask for a Better Piece of Upside Potential, 74 Buildings, Sept. 1980, at 54; Lenders Seek New Financing Alternatives, 41 Mortgage Banker, Mar. 1980, at 36; and Lenders Rush into Ownership, Bus. Week, Apr. 13, 1981, at 158.

6. For example, in the fourth quarter of 1988, United States life insurance companies

Conversely, as explained in the excerpt below by Harris, during the tight money period of the early 1980s some construction lenders realized that postconstruction loan commitments might not be obtainable before commencement of construction and that, if they were to remain in the construction lending business, they would have to commit without a takeout from a postconstruction lender. While construction lenders hoped that postconstruction financing would be obtained prior to the completion of construction, these "open-ended" construction commitments compelled construction lenders to address some of the same problems that postconstruction lenders have been grappling with over the years.

Over the past decade, as the economy has normalized, the traditional post-World War II dichotomy between construction and postconstruction lending has become more pronounced; nevertheless, as we shall see in the materials that follow, the risks and considerations associated with construction financing — whether the loan is made by a traditional construction lender or by a postconstruction lender — remain very distinct from those that were examined in the previous chapter.

Davis, The Permanent Lender's Role in the Construction Process
3 Real Est. Rev. 70 (Spring 1973)

Lurking in the background in any discussion of construction lending is the specter of the *permanent lender*. Writing as one who represents a permanent lender, my own inclination is to state that the permanent lender is the key man in any new real estate venture. At the very least, certainly, the permanent lender is a vital factor in a new real estate venture. It is his money that is relied upon to finance the project even though it will not be disbursed until after completion of construction. Without a permanent commitment most construction lenders will not make a construction loan.

Nevertheless, once the permanent commitment is issued, the other parties feel free to criticize the permanent lender for seeking various

---

issued commitments for multifamily and commercial real estate loans totaling $5.7 billion. Of this amount, 31.6 percent represented takeout commitments to repay construction loans and provide postconstruction financing, while only 3.1 percent represented commitments for both the construction and the postconstruction financing. The remaining 65 percent of the loan funds represented commitments for loans to refinance or purchase new or existing real estate. American Council of Life Insurance, Investment Bull. No. 1065, Table H (April 10, 1989).

rights to approve, for refusing to waive commitment requirements, and for declining to take a backseat during construction. . . .

Why should the permanent lender be interested in construction matters? He concerns himself with construction primarily because he wishes to be sure that the building to be constructed is the one on which he has committed himself to make a loan. It too often occurs that the final structure is not the one envisioned by the permanent lender at the time of making the commitment.

Second, he is concerned with construction because he will have a security interest in the building for as long as he holds the mortgage . . . (and in this age of "kickers," he may have an immediate equity interest as well). If the building is improperly constructed, the permanent lender's security can be severely impaired since in most instances, he looks first to the improvements and to the income therefrom for security, and only to a lesser extent, to the borrower. Needless to say, a potential owner is interested in the building he may someday own. . . .

Having discussed the relevance of construction matters to the permanent lender, let us now consider the relationship between the construction lender and the permanent lender. Basically, their interests are substantially similar:

- To have the building completed as provided for in their commitments and in accordance with the approved plans and specifications. (It is a good idea to have the two lenders use the same engineer or architect; this will reduce the likelihood of disputes over the adequacy of the plans.)
- To have their funds invested pursuant to their commitments.
- To have the construction loan paid upon completion of construction.
- To have the permanent lender then hold the loan with the long-term security he contemplated when making his commitment.

Notwithstanding these basic objectives, differences between the two lenders may occur. . . .

During the early stages of discussion, before he closes his construction loan, the construction lender will want approvals from the permanent lender on as many closing conditions of the permanent commitment as possible. He will ask for approval of title, survey, leases, appraisal, plans and specifications, and the operating agreement.

The permanent lender can review the state of title at this early date and set forth those exceptions or areas which disturb him. At the time of the construction loan closing, however, he can neither know nor approve the state of title for purposes of the permanent closing.

Any approvals he gives, therefore, must reserve his right to reexamine title for the permanent closing.

The permanent lender can also approve the survey at this stage, okaying the location of the premises and its relation to roads, intersections, and so forth. But he must reserve the right to see a final survey showing the improvements as built to determine if they accord with the commitment he contemplated. To avoid confusion, any approvals the permanent lender gives to plans and specifications should be by detailed plan number, date, and revision number.

The permanent lender may approve leases and any operating agreements if they are in existence at the time of the construction loan closing, but this is unlikely.

The items which the permanent lender cannot approve in advance can cause great concern to a construction lender. But by the nature of things, certain matters are not in existence at the time of the construction loan closing; and so the risk of the permanent lender not giving final approval to them must remain with the construction lender. Such items include the final survey, an independent engineer's report, any estoppel certificates that the permanent lender may want from tenants and from adjoining department stores (in the case of a shopping center), the final title search, and executed leases. . . .

GAP MORTGAGES

Further problems can develop in the relationship between the construction lender and the permanent lender when "floor loans" are made. This is particularly true of office buildings. Very often in an office building loan, the permanent lender agrees to buy the loan from the construction lender when the building shell is complete; but he will advance no additional loan funds to the borrower at that time. This is the floor loan. "Completion" is defined in such a situation as *not* including installation of the tenant partitions or similar work. When the tenants' work is fully complete and the premises occupied, the balance of the loan is funded. For the borrower, this means that additional money must be raised after the first disbursement of permanent loan funds in order to fully complete the structure, and since borrowers are loathe to invest their own funds, they will seek to finance this gap. Usually, this financing is sought from the construction lender who must, with respect to the gap financing, resort to a second mortgage for security. Since some permanent lenders do not want junior financing on their projects, a gap loan might require the permanent lender to waive any prohibitions against second mortgaging. If the construction lender has advanced more money on its construction loan than the floor amount for which the permanent lender committed, that excess would have to be deemed the advance made under the gap second mortgage. Because of technical difficulties with respect to this, most permanent lenders will restrict the construction lender in the buy-sell agreement from advancing more than the floor loan. . . .

The following excerpt by Gerald M. Levy, the managing director of Chemical Bank, one of the nation's leading construction lenders, discusses the factors and considerations that must be evaluated and reviewed by the construction lender before committing itself to making a construction loan.

Levy, Construction Loan Decision-Making: Issues and Documents; Risks and Benefits
(In-house memorandum for Chemical Bank, New York, New York) (1989)

Various participants in the banking and real estate fields have voiced strong and seemingly divergent views which alternatively support the priority of credit or real estate factors in the underwriting and administration of construction loans. A person's opinion in these matters often predictably coincides with the individual's professional background; bankers supporting the notion of credit predominance and real estate experts emphasizing "dirt kicking" and property fundamentals. This is not an astonishing correlation of experience and opinion; it is common for people to give greatest weight to those matters with which they are most experienced and knowledgeable and, thus, with which they feel most comfortable.

In the writer's opinion there is not a necessary conflict between these two views and this conclusion should be clear when the respective positions are further explored.

Commercial banks are the main source of construction funds in the United States. Such institutions also provide loans to a diverse range of businesses and individuals for many other purposes. Credit analysis and loan underwriting closely tied to credit considerations are mainstream activities of account officers in every lending sector of a commercial bank. In the examination of manufacturing, wholesaling, retailing, service or contracting enterprises, analysts can utilize a number of fairly meaningful financial ratios segmented by industry and size of company. Much useful information about typical current ratios, quick ratios, turnover ratios, returns on equity and similar financial measurements can be derived from such sources as the *Annual Statement Studies* of Robert Morris Associates, industry and trade associations, business periodicals, business school research studies and from the bank's files on similar firms. The lender usually obtains audited statements for such enterprises. In the case of publicly held companies, the U.S. Securities and Exchange Commission (SEC) provides further reporting regulations and enforcement procedures which encourage the presentation of reliable financial information.

A commercial bank's typical real estate customers, whether entrepreneurial individuals or fairly complex corporate entities, vary greatly in profile from the typical commercial and industrial borrowers previously cited. Usually, no one real estate product is manufactured in large volume by a single business enterprise. Real estate assets are unique and even properties of the same type and similar size may exhibit significant economic variation when one property is compared to another. Except for a traditionally high debt-equity relationship and minimal liquidity, there is scant evidence of industry-wide norms in financial ratios. The bulk of most customers' assets are concentrated in a number of equity positions in real estate which may have been evaluated in financial statements in a less than satisfactory manner with possibly inflated values. Frequently, real estate firms do not go to the trouble and expense of obtaining professionally prepared financial reports. Most real estate organizations are not publicly held; accordingly, they are not subject to SEC reporting requirements. Even with their bankers, some customers are very secretive about their financial affairs and future business plans.

Accounting and financial skills are important in determining the financial condition of a real estate customer. Yet, a banker may be a virtuoso in analyzing business enterprises which are more in the mainstream of credit granting activities and still prove to be woefully inadequate in gauging a real estate borrower's current financial condition and prospects. The analysis of a real estate client cannot provide meaningful conclusions without an informed and experienced approach to the investigation and analysis of the cash flows derived from individual real estate assets; the economic results of specific properties are only summarized in possibly oblique or confusing fashion in the balance sheet, income statement and other financial reports.

By the nature of the risks inherent in the construction process the account officer and the credit committee must be satisfied that the construction loan under consideration is to be made to an experienced and financially responsible borrower who is likely to comply with the terms of loan documents. At almost all stages of a construction loan, the collateral is not a completed and occupied property but an asset which is in the process of being created. If work on the project stops for any one or more of an almost endless number of reasons, a bank is in the unenviable position of deciding whether or not to "work with" the present developer. If the financial institution decides to undertake the foreclosure of the ownership position it must endure all the inherent delays and defenses built into the legal process; meanwhile, an incomplete project is exposed to possible weather damage, structural deterioration, vandalism and the escalation of construction costs. In addition, the construction of competitive developments may be continuing; consequently, market demand which the now troubled project was relying on could be preempted. All these adverse effects remind us of the need to deal with a strong, responsible and creditworthy borrower.

In prior years some construction lenders considered an extensive real estate analysis of a proposed project to be redundant; instead they placed great reliance on and "found value" in the "takeout" commitment of a permanent lender who would be expected to fund upon completion of the project with the proceeds utilized to repay the construction lender. Numerous real estate disasters illustrate that permanent loan commitments are not iron clad; some issuers may resort to narrow technical grounds, real or imagined, to avoid funding. Consequently, most experienced construction lenders have concluded that they should not finance the development of a project unless property and market fundamentals are persuasive; then, if a permanent commitment is not funded or another loan is not available in timely fashion, the construction lender will still have productive collateral. Due diligence concerning the economics of a project is even more important at the present time because many construction loans are funded "open ended," i.e., with no permanent loan takeout commitment in place.

Either a "pure credit" or a "pure real estate" approach to a construction lending decision is without significant meaning because credit and real estate factors are so entwined. Generally, it is not wise to lend construction funds to a customer of marginal creditworthiness even though he has a feasible real estate project proposal; similarly, it is not prudent to provide funds to a "strong" borrower for the construction of a poorly conceived and economically questionable project. Both the borrower and the real estate concept should be sound.

Stark, Negotiating Interest Rate Exchange Agreements
4 Real Est. Fin. 93 (Spring 1987)

Although interest rate exchange agreements ("swap agreements") are a relatively new financing technique, an estimated $100 billion in interest rate swaps were arranged in 1985. This article attempts to explain briefly what a swap agreement is, what purposes it serves, and what major issues arise in drafting the agreement.

What Is a Swap Agreement?

A swap agreement is an agreement between two parties to exchange interest payments for a set fictional amount of money (the "notional amount") over a set period. Swap agreements can be arranged in a variety of forms. In the most typical swap agreement, one party agrees to pay another party a fixed rate on a notional amount for a specific period and, in return, receives from the other party a floating rate on the same notional amount for the same period.

Swap agreements are often used either a) to hedge against fluctuations in interest rates . . . or b) to convert a floating-rate obligation into a fixed-rate obligation (see Example 2). In either case, the fixed rate contained in the swap agreement will be based upon current interest rates and a forecast of future interest rates over the period of the agreement.

E x a m p l e   2

Using a Swap Agreement to Hedge a Floating Rate Loan

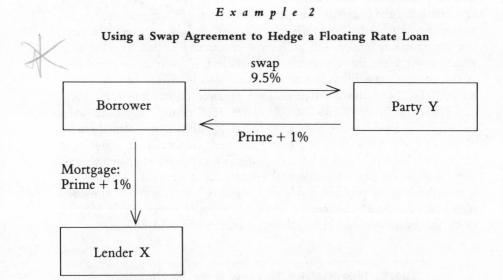

Borrower takes out a variable-rate mortgage loan with Lender X, agreeing to pay interest at 1% over prime. In order to lock in a fixed rate in this otherwise floating-rate loan, Borrower also enters into a swap agreement with Party Y, under which Borrower agrees to pay Y a fixed rate of 9.5% on a notional amount (the principal amount of the mortgage loan) for a set period (the term of the mortgage loan). In return, Party Y agrees to pay Borrower a floating rate of prime +1% on the same notional amount for the same period.

Regardless of whether the prime rate rises or falls, Borrower has fixed his net interest cost at 9.5%.

Who Uses Swap Agreements?

Many real estate developers have entered into swap agreements in order to convert floating-rate construction loans into fixed-rate obligations. The swap agreement can be drafted to match anticipated draws against the construction loan. As the developer draws down the loan to fund construction, the notional amount of the swap agreement increases; as completed units are sold and the loan is repaid, the notional amount decreases. . . .

Since most swap agreements refer to or completely incorporate the Code of Standard Wording, Assumptions and Provisions for Swaps, 1985 edition ("the Code"), it is essential for attorneys who may be involved in negotiating swap agreements to become familiar with the definitions and provisions contained in the Code. Moreover, to a great extent, the Code sets forth a "menu" of choices with respect to various key aspects of swap agreements, and attorneys should become familiar with the options available.

The Issue of Early Termination

One key issue in the drafting of a swap agreement is the determination of damages in the event the agreement is terminated early. This is the most complicated aspect of drafting swap agreements and, since no reported decision has dealt with this area, it is also the most uncertain. Therefore, attorneys should pay a great deal of attention to this issue as the agreement is being drafted.

The Code provides that in cases of early termination, "reference market-makers" will provide a "market quotation" to the party requesting such a determination. Reference market-makers are defined in the Code as individuals chosen by a party to quote the amount they would charge, if anything, to assume the interest obligations of the defaulting party under the swap agreement. The "agreement value" (the amount paid by one party to the other as a result of early termination) is based upon market quotations made by the reference market-makers.

For example, suppose a floating-rate payor defaults and interest rates have generally increased since the time the swap agreement was signed. A reference market-maker would charge a fee to step into the shoes of that floating-rate payor, since the rate he would be receiving from the fixed-rate payor would be relatively low as compared to the higher interest rates currently available. Conversely, if interest rates have generally declined during the term of the swap agreement, a reference market-maker would not charge a fee to the floating-rate payor since he would be receiving a relatively high fixed rate compared to the lower interest rates currently available. The same principles would apply in the event of a default by the fixed-rate payor. . . .

OTHER ISSUES

A second key issue with respect to the drafting of swap agreements relates to the fact that such agreements are viewed as credit arrangements. . . .

In analyzing these provisions, attorneys should bear in mind the realistic risk exposure of the parties (e.g., the net payments one party likely will be required to pay to the other party over the term of the agreement). For example, although the notional amount of a five-year swap agreement might be $30 million, the net payments that one party will make to the other party would be only $3 million (assuming a constant 2% spread between the two interest rates). It is this $3 million figure and not $30 million that should be considered the realistic credit risk of the parties. . . .

Harris, Construction and Development Financing

¶3.3A (Cum. Supp. No. 1) (1987)

¶3.3A   "OPEN ENDED" CONSTRUCTION LOAN [NEW]

The virtual unavailability of takeout commitments during recent periods has obviously not deterred all building or construction financing. Some construction lenders, particularly banks, have been willing to make construction loans and on completion of construction hold the loan for a period of up to ten years. After construction, these loans carry a fixed or fluctuating rate of interest and may or may not require principal repayment during the loan term. The parties' expectation (and hope) is that at some point prior to the end of the loan term economic changes will again make takeout loans readily available or that given time the project will prove successful enough to attract a buyer or conventional takeout lender.

One estimate, made in mid-1982, suggested that 20 to 30 billion dollars worth of open ended construction loans were outstanding.

The open ended construction loan presents its own set of underwriting problems. The factors of developer ability and independent financial strength take on greater significance. The underwriter should look for safety factors which will add security to the credit if the parties' optimistic expectations are not realized. Is the project readily salable? Is the developer-borrower predisposed to a sale if necessary to pay the loan? Does the borrower have strong financial partners or other tangible and liquid assets to which resort could be had to pay the loan or support the project? . . .

[T]he traditional method of financing a new office building by a construction loan secured by a permanent loan takeout commitment has given way to new techniques reflecting today's volatile interest-rate environment. . . . [O]ne of these new approaches is a split-time financing process in which construction and permanent financing are obtained at separate periods during the development process. . . . [T]he split-time (or two-stage) financing process involves securing an open-end construction loan (i.e., one without a permanent takeout), con-structing the building, and then obtaining a permanent loan (or selling the property) when the building is completed and substantially leased. Open-end construction loans . . . have long been a feature of the financing process but are more prevalent today than in earlier periods. Since the construction lender lacks the protection of a permanent takeout, these loans are typically reserved for financially strong devel-opers, for projects that are substantially preleased, or projects with substantial equity supplied by the developer.

A special feature of many open-end construction loans . . . is an option for the developer to convert it into a "mini-permanent" loan of three to five years' duration. The mini-perm, like the construction loan, carries a floating interest rate (e.g., two points over the prime rate or over certificate of deposit rates). In order to minimize cash flow problems for borrowers, many lenders permit them to pay interest at a fixed rate and accrue any additional interest over the fixed rate. The accrual amount typically is limited to 10 percent of the initial loan balance. . . .

[T]he second stage of the split-time financing process involves obtaining the permanent loan either at the completion of construction or at the maturity of the mini-perm loan. In today's market, a popular choice for the permanent mortgage is the bullet loan. This is an intermediate-term (three- to ten-year) fixed rate loan with a balloon payment at maturity. Bullet loans typically represent pension fund money that life insurance companies contract to purchase (borrow) for a certain period of time at a specified interest rate, commonly called guaranteed income contracts (GICs). The life insurance company uses its real estate expertise to lend this money at a higher rate, thus earning income from the spread and any upfront fees. Since the life insurance company is guaranteeing a specified rate to the pension fund, the bullet loan is "locked" (no prepayment for most or all of the loan term), unless the borrower agrees to compensate the lender for any loss in interest that may occur by reinvesting the funds at a lower rate. Bullet loan terms have recently lengthened to ten and fifteen years, although five to eight-year term loans remain most prevalent. As with most loans today, bullet loan rates tend to increase as the loan term and/or period until funding increases. Ten- to fifteen-year bullet loans carry an interest rate premium of 25-100 basis points over shorter maturities.

NOTES AND QUESTIONS

1. *The Risks and Rewards of Construction and Postconstruction Lending Compared.* As observed at Chapter 5B, there are certain conditions that the postconstruction lender would like to insert in its commitment. These include: (a) completion of the improvements in accordance with plans and specifications approved by the postconstruction lender; (b) compliance with applicable laws and regulations and obtaining of necessary permits; (c) having a title unencumbered by liens superior to the postconstruction mortgage; (d) leases in effect with certain major ("prime") tenants; and (e) no material, adverse change in the financial condition of the borrower. Do you think that any of these clauses might trouble a prospective construction lender and render a takeout commitment from a postconstruction lender "unbankable"? (A "bankable" commitment from a postconstruction lender is one that also meets the normal requirements of a construction lender.) If so, why?

In what respects do the goals of a construction lender and postconstruction lender resemble one another? In what respects are they different? Based on what you have learned about postconstruction financing, what planning suggestions would you offer to a construction lender who wishes to minimize the risks that: (1) notwithstanding a buy-sell agreement, the postconstruction lender might refuse to take out the construction loan because it does not approve the form and content of a lease with a major "prime" tenant; or (2) a gap financing problem might arise because of construction cost overruns or because of the borrower's failure to comply with a rent roll requirement contained in the postconstruction commitment letter in which event the construction lender might find itself relegated to the status of an unpaid junior lienor with respect to a portion of its loan indebtedness. See Chapter 5B2 and Chapter 5B14.

Investment returns differ qualitatively and quantitatively for construction and postconstruction lenders. For example, the rate of return is usually higher on construction loans and, in contrast to a typical fixed-rate postconstruction loan, the loan requires no amortization and the interest rate is generally a variable rate or "floating" rate geared to a certain number of percentage points over a particular bank's prime

F i g u r e 6-1

**Yields on US Treasuries:
10-Year vs. 2-Year**

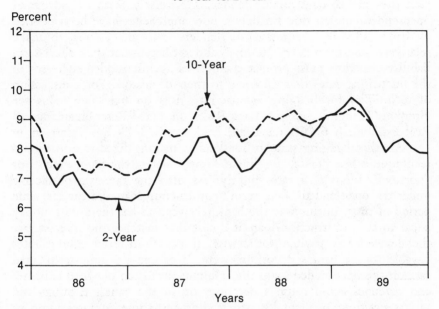

Source: Goldman Sachs, The Real Estate Report 7 (March 1990).

rate. Incidentally, while floating rates became commonplace for construction financing long before the variable rate mortgage was introduced into residential financing, as of this writing the variable rate format is still not popular in commercial postconstruction financing transactions. In addition, unlike many postconstruction loans in which the borrower is often exculpated from personal liability for the repayment of the debt and the lender only has recourse against the real estate, personal liability on the note is almost always required in construction financing. Why have these distinctions emerged?

Turning to the other side of the equation, how would you assess the relative risks involved in both kinds of lending? In what respects is a construction loan riskier than a postconstruction loan? In what respects is it safer?

2. Hedging Interest Rates with Swap Agreements and Match Funding. Construction loan interest rates are normally floating rates that fluctuate at some level above the "prime" rate. The prime rate is the rate that banks charge from time to time to their more favored customers. Floating rates are favored by commercial banks because they can be adjusted to take into account what they will be paying to their demand depositors during the periods of their construction loans. As observed in the excerpt by Stark, real estate borrowers sometimes use swap agreements as hedges against fluctuations in the floating interest rates they pay to construction lenders. Conversely, with the advent of open-ended construction financing, new approaches have been devised by banks and other construction lenders who are willing to make relatively long-term fixed-rate loans and yet because of their short-term liability structure must protect themselves against sudden increases in the fluctuating rates that they pay to their depositors. For a discussion of techniques for hedging against rate risks on fixed-rate loans see Hubsher, Hedging Interest Rate Risks on Fixed-Rate Financings, 3 Real Est. Fin. J. 6 (Winter 1988).

Another hedging strategy for lenders making fixed-rate loans is a technique called "match funding." Simply stated, the bank "buys" or "borrows" funds at a rate slightly less than the rate it will receive under the open-ended "long-term" construction loan and for the same period of time. In this way the bank receives and has the use of money equal to the construction loan at a cost that matches the interest rate the developer is paying. Otherwise, if the short-term interest rates payable to the bank's depositors were to exceed the long-term fixed rate on the open-ended loan, the resultant mismatch between expenses and revenues could cause a deterioration in the bank's earnings and profits position. Incidentally, when short-term interest rates jump so sharply that they exceed rates on long-term Treasury securities (as happened in December 1989), this phenomenon (called an "inverted yield curve") suggests to economists that the economy is abnormal and may be weakening. See Figure 6-1, supra. Why is this so? Returning to the master hypothetical at Chapter 5B, suppose that Dan Developer is not able to negotiate a postconstruction commitment from Ace Insurance Company. Further assume that Fuller National Bank nevertheless agrees to make an open-ended construction loan for a period of seven years. The interest rate will be two points (2 percent) above prime until completion of construction and then will become a fixed rate that will increase at designated intervals thereafter during the balance of the loan term. Incidentally, why would Fuller insist that the interest rate increase as the term of the loan approaches maturity?

If Dan's loan is sizeable or if Dan is a favored customer, Fuller might also permit Dan to select one of several interest rate options that would be applicable to various periods of time during the term of the loan. Dan's options might include the prime rate, the so-called LIBOR (London Interbank Offering Rate), the commercial paper rate, or the certificate of deposit rate. On Dan's selection of a particular rate, Fuller would "buy" money at that rate. Alternatively, if Fuller were to maintain a significant position in each of these interest-rate markets it would not have to allocate specific funds for Dan's loan because its "purchase" of funds would only require a bookkeeping entry on its part. Fuller would then charge Dan a premium over and above the rate it must pay to procure the match funding. For an interesting analysis of match funding as it applies to construction lending see Greenberger, Construction (Interim) Financing Without a Take-Out and with the Borrower Having Periodic Choice of Various Interest Rates in Legal and Underwriting Risks in Real Estate Financing, Practicing Law Institute, Real Estate Law and Practice Course Handbook, Ser. No. 219, 521-538 (1982).

B. TERMS AND CONDITIONS OF CONSTRUCTION FINANCING

Joyce, Financing Real Estate Developments
The Colo. Law. 2093 (Aug. 1982)

CONSTRUCTION LOAN:

Commercial banks, as the principal source of construction loans, have developed significant expertise in the monitoring and servicing of such loans, and do so as a matter of course on both their own account and for other lenders' accounts. This is particularly true when a combined construction/permanent loan is being made by a long-term lender. The servicing bank receives a fee for its services which may vary widely and is unrelated to interest rates on the loan. Because these fees may be quite substantial, it is important that the effective cost of the various loans, including interest and fees, be computed in total by the developer and that all fees be detailed in the loan documents.

Construction loans can be made on an open-end basis, but most commercial banks are limited by state regulations which frown on this practice. The experience of the REITs in 1974 would seem to bear out the general wisdom of this view. In this situation, a "win" by the developer could work against him. Even if construction financing is available, the developer must determine if he should really begin a project without permanent financing.

As previously discussed, a central focus of the construction lender is to insure the availability of a permanent loan commitment prior to making the construction loan. In order to insure that the permanent loan commitment is fulfilled, the construction lender requires the developer, in the loan agreement and associated security documents, to comply with all requirements of the permanent loan commitment. The "preclosed" form of the buy-sell agreement normally enables the construction lender to obtain the permanent lender's concurrence to the security documents and the note prior to disbursal of the construction loan proceeds. The permanent lender should also agree in advance to the form of ancillary documents, such as insurance binders, title commitments, lease forms, plans and specifications and any other matters upon which the permanent loan is conditioned.

In addition to rate, date of maturity and fees, the developer must use great care in determining the actual amount of the loan. From the construction lender's perspective, the face amount of the loan is limited by the permanent commitment, which is predicated on a preconstruction cost and income projection. The developer must have contingency funds available in the construction loan to deal with construction overruns and unexpected conditions encountered during construction, such as bad soil or construction strikes. To the extent a lender agrees to allow the developer to "mortgage out," he may be able to pay off short-term obligations associated with his general operations. Few lenders will be so accommodating, but it is certainly worth the effort to ask for this on projects with strong projected cash flow.

The construction loan application, when separate from the permanent loan application, becomes the basis of the contract between the construction lender and the developer. In addition to the items noted above as requirements for a permanent loan application, the developer will be asked to provide a variety of specific information, including the following:

1) The nature and exact identification of the ownership group;
2) The specific location of the project;
3) The site plan and plans and specifications for construction;
4) Pro forma operating statements for the project; and
5) The proposed tenants or marketing studies which support the projected income stream.

Any unusual circumstances, such as the presence of secondary financing, governmental guarantees or subsidies, and any financing risks associated with the project should be disclosed during the application process.

The construction lender often requires that construction financing be in the form of a recourse loan or that the construction loan be guaranteed by the developer. The developer will resist this requirement, but without clearly identifiable collateral other than the proposed project, the lender is unlikely to change it. Lenders make such requirements because of the possibility that if a default occurs prior to completion, its foreclosure of the deed of trust may not be sufficient to secure the entire amount of the loan. The developer may console himself that his guarantee is contingent, but it is a guarantee and binding nevertheless.

The amortization of the entire debt, including interest and principal of a development project is anticipated to come from income related to operation of the project. Because the project has little if any income prior to project completion, there is normally no reduction in principal during the construction loan period. Rather, the construction loan includes an amount sufficient to pay interest on a monthly basis and the permanent loan will ultimately include payoff of both the principal and accrued interest charges on the construction loan. If for no other reason, this feature of development loans makes it important to the construction lender that he rigorously underwrite the loan and seek additional collateral. The inclusion of the soft costs in the construction loan make it a virtual certainty that a foreclosure, in the event of a default during the construction period, will yield the lender less than the amount of the loan outstanding at the time.

In this matter, the developer may believe that, since the construction loan contains amounts sufficient for debt amortization and the developer has obtained a permanent loan commitment, the lender has no risk of default. This viewpoint, of course, seeks to minimize the possibility of strikes, cost overruns, the death of the developer or other unplanned catastrophic events. A creative developer can use third-party guarantees, such as performance bonds and life insurance policies, in an effort to avoid providing security in additional collateral or personal guarantees. However, except with FHA-insured projects in which the entire amount of the disbursed construction loan is insured, the developer's ability to avoid personal guarantees is limited.

After the construction lender reviews the developer's application, he responds in the form of a commitment letter. The commitment letter represents a counteroffer to the developer and, upon acceptance by the developer, constitutes a binding contract between the two. That commitment includes provisions related to the following matters:

1. The principal amount and form of the promissory note to be executed; and the interest to be paid, along with terms of repayment, prepayment and any provisions for early call.

2. The specific provisions made for disbursements, along with the exact documentation which must be presented to the lender prior to authorization of disbursements.

3. Identification of the specific forms of collateral, including guarantees, promissory notes, assignment of rents and leases, letters of credit and cash escrows.

4. The specific nature of the first deed of trust, along with the exact interest to be provided to the construction lender.

5. The specific personal guaranty if it is contemplated by the lender.

6. The specific construction schedule, including commencement and completion dates, as well as a projected progress schedule.

7. Any required preleasing arrangements and minimum terms and sample forms of such leases, along with the form of collateral assignment of the lease to the lender.

8. Identification of the general contractor, along with major sub-contractors, and any performance or payment bonds which must be provided to bond the various contractors' work. Bonds are not always required but should be anticipated in larger projects.

9. The specific requirements for insurance, including type and amount of coverage, terms of payment, terms of cancellation and beneficiaries. Insurance coverage normally includes builder's risk, public liability and property damage and workers' compensation insurance.

10. Specified deadlines for the delivery and approval of the plans and specifications for the project, along with appropriate engineering reports.

11. Requirements for surveys, including an initial survey, a construction survey indicating the limits of the construction contract and a post-construction survey showing improvements as built.

12. Identification of all expenses, including fees to be paid to the lender, title insurance, attorneys' fees and closing costs. Also, an allocation of those expenses between the lender and developer, along with some limits on the actual amounts to be expended, although some will not be exactly determinable at this stage. To the extent these costs can be limited, an attempt will be made to do so.

13. General conditions related to legal opinions, resolutions of corporations authorizing borrowing and any other organizational authorities required by the lender.

14. Provisions for cost certification of all expenditures, along with an audit by an identified certified public accountant.

15. Variety of certifications required related to zoning and other government approval processes, including a determination of the availability of waste water, utility and water services, water, compliance with traffic and zoning regulations and the issuance of building permits.

16. Mechanic's lien protection and specific provisions with respect to the lender's individual protection against such liens. . . .

Since the construction loan commitment forms the basis of the contractual arrangement between the developer and the lender, it is absolutely crucial that details of this arrangement be explored in great depth prior to payment of the commitment fee and acceptance of the commitment. There may be many interactions of the commitment prior to acceptance by the lender and borrower to form the loan commitment contract.

1. Loan Amount, Interest Rate, and Other Payment Terms

In the master hypothetical at Chapter 5B an assumption was made that the fair market value of the project will equal its land and building cost of $33 million and thus Dan would finance the project with the $25 million postconstruction loan from Ace and with equity funds in the amount of $8 million. In reality, most developers will not engage in such an undertaking unless they believe that the value of the project will exceed its costs. So let us assume that the projected cost of the building is only $23 million so that in effect Dan would be obtaining more than 100 percent financing of his construction costs by means of the $25 million loan from Ace. Let us further assume that the "hard costs" of constructing the building will amount to $20 million and that the "soft costs" will amount to $3 million. In the parlance of real estate the hard costs are the actual or physical costs of labor and materials, including fees paid to the construction manager and the profit return to the general contractor, and the soft costs are the intangible costs of construction, including the fees paid by Dan to attorneys, architects, appraisers, engineers, brokers, and consultants; the costs of advertising, builder's risk, insurance, and bond premiums; mortgage recording taxes and other construction loan closing expenses; and possibly construction loan interest payments as well.

Assuming that Dan's net worth and outside income are minimal and that FNB's management team is dominated by what Gerald Levy (in the excerpt at Chapter 6A) refers to as real estate experts who emphasize "property fundamentals" rather than "credit predominance," what would be the maximum construction loan amount that Dan might expect from FNB? Would it be the full $23 million cost of construction, or merely the $20 million amount of the hard costs? What would Dan's argument be in favor of a $25 million loan amount, which would allow Dan to make a profit on the construction loan (or "mortgage out") in the amount of $2 million?

In that regard FNB may retain the services of outside consultants and take other precautionary measures to make certain that Dan's cost estimates are realistic and not exaggerated. Can you think of what these other measures might entail? Specifically, FNB will be watchful about any attempt by Dan to keep his loan funds ahead of his actual costs by overestimating costs (called "front end loading") during the early phases of construction. Conversely, FNB wants to be assured that Dan has not underestimated the costs of construction for the purpose of convincing FNB that the project is feasible.

Finally, assume that the postconstruction commitment from Ace provides for a floor-ceiling loan and, in the opinion of FNB, prudence dictates that it should limit its loan commitment to the floor amount.

Would this protective measure necessarily be in FNB's best interest if Dan should need the ceiling amount to complete the construction? How might FNB and Dan protect themselves against this contingency? See discussion at Chapter 5B2.

As observed above, while postconstruction loans ordinarily bear a fixed rate of interest, most construction loans have a floating, or variable, rate geared to a percentage above the bank's prime rate. The margin above prime usually depends on several factors including market conditions, the front-end fees charged to the borrower, and the depository relationship between the bank and the borrower. Incidentally, real estate borrowers tend to be less liquid than other business borrowers. Can you think of the reason why? In rare situations a construction lender might countenance a fixed rate, for example, where it also provides postconstruction financing for the project or engages in an equity-sharing arrangement with the borrower.

Incidentally, thrift organizations that make construction loans are more inclined to make fixed-rate construction loans than are commercial banks. Can you think of the reason why?

While the interest payments might be drawn from the proceeds of the loan during the construction period, the principal amount ordinarily is not amortized but is repayable in full from the postconstruction takeout proceeds. Why? Also, in contrast to most postconstruction loans, a typical construction loan is recourse as opposed to nonrecourse, which means that the borrower will be personally liable for repayment. Why the difference in approach? To review, if the borrowing entity should be a limited partnership are there any adverse tax consequences to the limited partners if the general partner is not personally liable for repayment of the construction loan? How significant is this problem during the construction period as opposed to the postconstruction period? See Chapter 2B, note 7(d)(iii).

If the construction note is negotiable, and the note is assigned to the postconstruction lender when the permanent loan is closed, the permanent lender can qualify for "holder-in-due-course" status under the Uniform Commercial Code if it meets the value, good-faith, and notice requirements of the Code. U.C.C §3-104(2). In such event, the postconstruction lender would take the construction note free from all "personal defenses," such as lack or failure of consideration (for example, when the borrower claims that the construction lender failed to make the loan or that the loan has been paid). The note is usually drafted so that all parties who are secondarily liable — prior endorsers, guarantors — waive those formal U.C.C. requirements (such as presentment or notice of protest) that must be met before suit can be brought against them. Also, if a construction note is assigned to a lender or some other assignee, the construction lender will customarily absolve itself from any secondary liability by endorsing the note "without recourse." See generally G. Nelson and D. Whitman, Real Estate Finance Law §§5.29-5.33 (2d ed. 1985).

2. Conformity with the Postconstruction Commitment

As suggested in the foregoing excerpt by Joyce, in most cases the construction lender's real security for the repayment of its loan is the takeout commitment from some postconstruction lender rather than the lien of the construction loan mortgage on the partially completed improvements or the ephemeral net worth of the borrower. Therefore, a prudent construction lender will insist that the terms and conditions of its commitment letter closely track the requirements of the postconstruction commitment. Accordingly, most construction loan commitments will contain language to this effect, which might read as follows:

Section 5.08. Compliance with Postconstruction Loan Commitment.

Borrower will observe and comply with all of the terms, provisions, conditions, covenants and agreements on its part to be performed, observed and complied with to obtain the loan under the Postconstruction Loan Commitment, and Borrower will not amend the Postconstruction Loan Commitment or suffer or permit any conditions to exist which would permit a termination of the obligations to provide the loan pursuant to the Postconstruction Loan Commitment.

Returning to the master hypothetical, what protection will the above-quoted clause afford FNB if Dan Developer were to breach its provisions and violate the terms of the postconstruction commitment with Ace Insurance Company? Suppose Dan's default leads to an abrogation of the postconstruction loan commitment. Dan would clearly be in default under the construction loan agreement, and FNB would not be required to fund. However, if FNB has already disbursed a substantial portion of the construction loan, neither foreclosure on half-completed buildings nor an action against Dan for damages would provide FNB with a viable remedy. Indeed, the real importance of this clause is its delineation of conditions in Ace's commitment letter that should be fulfilled by Dan *prior* to any loan advances made by FNB.

Rather than rely on hollow legal remedies for Dan's possible breach of the compliance clause, FNB must determine in advance that it is feasible for Dan to comply with the terms of the postconstruction commitment and also monitor the loan transaction during the construction period to ensure such compliance. For example, the terms of the postconstruction commitment may impose certain leasing requirements. See Chapter 5B2 and Chapter 5C. Failure to execute the required leases may release Ace from its commitment entirely. Or, Dan's failure to attain a rent roll requirement might allow Ace to provide only a floor loan amount rather than the full ceiling loan amount. In either instance, sufficient funds may not be available to take out the entire amount of FNB's loan. The construction loan agreement should therefore require that these conditions be met before FNB closes its loan and becomes obliged to make disbursements. Likewise, there may be other terms and conditions in Ace's commitment letter that could be satisfied prior to the closing of the construction loan, such as Ace's approval of the preliminary plans and specifications and the status of Dan's fee simple title to the underlying land. To review: can you think of any others? See Chapter 5B.

Suppose FNB executes a buy-sell agreement with Ace. Would this cure the compliance problem and assure FNB that its loan will be taken out by Ace once the construction period is over? If not, what form of buy-sell agreement could be used to at least ameliorate the concerns of FNB? See Chapter 5B14.

3. Priority over Mechanics' Liens

The construction lender normally requires a first lien on the land and improvements to secure the construction advances. Often the developer has acquired the land with borrowed funds and may have received a development loan to finance the installation of sewers, the laying out of streets, and other site development costs. Typically, these loans are secured by mortgage liens that must either be satisfied or subordinated prior to construction. In most cases, land and development costs are considered to be part of the cost of the improvements and, therefore, these mortgages can be satisfied out of the first construction loan draw. However, when the competing lien is that of a mechanic or materialman, more complex problems arise that are not as easily resolved.

In recognition of the principle that mechanics and materialmen add value to the property and in furtherance of the public policy of encouraging rehabilitation and new construction, states have enacted mechanics' lien statutes providing mechanics and materialmen with liens that often are accorded special lien priority over existing mortgages on the property. These statutes vary widely from state to state. In some states a mortgage will take priority over subsequently filed mechanics' liens.[7] In others, the lien priority accorded to a mortgage is confined to disbursements made prior to the filing of any mechanics' liens.[8] In

7. E.g., Fla. Stat. Ann. §713.73 (1989); N.J. Stat. Ann. §2A:44-87 (1990); Pa. Stat. Ann. tit. 42, §8141 (1989).

8. E.g., N.Y. Lien Law §13 (McKinney 1990); Mass. Gen. Laws Ann. ch. 254, §7 (West Cum. Supp. 1990).

still others, the mechanic's lien will relate back to the commencement of construction.[9] And in some states mechanics' liens have priority as to the improvements but not as to the land.[10] In many states properly drawn lien waivers are effective against the mechanics and materialmen who give them.[11]

One of the greatest challenges facing the construction lender, as distinguished from the postconstruction lender, is to protect the priority of its disbursements against the rights of the mechanics and materialmen during the course of construction.

Language from a typical construction loan agreement dealing with prior liens might read as follows:

Section 5.09 — Liens

The Project shall be kept free and clear of liens and encumbrances (unless the same are bonded or insured over by the title insurance company in a manner satisfactory to Lender) of every nature or description (whether for taxes or assessments, for charges of labor, materials, supplies or service, or any other thing) other than Permitted Exceptions. . . .

Section 5.12 — Mechanics and Materialmen

Borrower will furnish to Lender upon request, at any time and from time to time, affidavits listing all materialmen, laborers, subcontractors and any other party who might or could claim statutory or common law liens and are furnishing or have furnished materials or labor to the Project or any portion thereof, together with affidavits, or other evidence satisfactory to Lender showing that such parties have been paid all amounts then due for labor and materials furnished to the project. In addition, Borrower will notify Lender immediately and in writing, if Borrower receives any notice, written or oral, from any laborer, subcontractor or materialman to the effect that said laborer, subcontractor or materialman has not been paid when due for any labor or materials furnished in connection with the construction of the Improvements. Borrower will also furnish to Lender, at any time and from time to time upon demand by Lender, Lien waivers bearing a then current date, on Lender's standard form, from Contractor and such subcontractors or materialmen as Lender may designate.

9. E.g., Cal. Civil Code §§3134, 3137 (Deering 1991); Ill. Ann. Stat. ch. 82, §16 (1989).

10. E.g., Ark. Stat. Ann. §18-44-101 (Michie 1990); Tex. Prop. Code §53.123 (1989); Va. Code Ann. §43-21 (1990).

11. E.g., Mich. Comp. Laws Ann. §570.1119 (1990).

National Bank of Washington v. Equity Investors
81 Wash. 2d 886, 506 P.2d 20 (1973)

HALE, Chief Justice

. . . Columbia Wood Products, Inc., furnished lumber for the apartment house project, commencing deliveries to the site May 26, 1969, and continuing to about August 5, 1969. As earlier noted, it received partial payment, but when construction came to a halt there was still due and unpaid the sum of $119,672 for material sold, delivered and utilized in the nearly completed buildings. The trial court awarded Columbia Wood Products, Inc., a judgment of $119,672.26 on this unpaid bill, with 12 percent accrued interest from September 5, 1969, in the amount of $28,721.34, and statutory costs. The court decreed, however, that Columbia Wood Products' judgment lien be subordinate and junior to the lien of National Bank of Washington's deed of trust to the extent of all advances made by that bank on its loan for the construction of the apartment house complex. Columbia Wood Products appeals that part of the judgment and decree which rendered its materialman's lien inferior and junior to the bank's total secured loan advanced for the construction.

Columbia Wood Products' lien was declared inferior to the entire amount of the bank's advances on a theory that the National Bank of Washington possessed a prior and superior deed of trust lien in effect before and continuing during the delivery of the lumber. According to the bank's theory, its priority was established as of about May 9, 1969, when Transamerica filed the trust deed of Equity Investors, a limited partnership, naming the National Bank of Washington as beneficiary, securing a promissory note in the amount of $1,850,000 — all in accordance with a construction loan agreement of May 7, 1969, between the National Bank of Washington as lender and Equity Investors as borrower. As work on the project progressed, the bank advanced the funds. . . .

Columbia Wood Products began deliveries of lumber to the project on May 26, 1969, and continued supplying material until August 5, 1969, but with the last delivery there was, as earlier noted, still due and unpaid on the lumber bill some $119,672. Its claim of a lien superior in part to that of the National Bank of Washington is based on the contention that the advances made by the bank under the construction loan agreement as the work progressed were optional advances and could not have been legally enforced against the bank. . . .

We think that Columbia Wood Products' contention is sound and that for the purpose of determining lien priorities the advances were in law optional. In the construction loan agreement, the bank made such explicit reservations for the disbursement of the loan as, in our judgment, render the advances of $1,750,000 optional and not obligatory at law. Although such reservation of discretionary authority appears to be a sound banking practice and designed to protect the financial interests of the party to the project which would wind up with the greater sum of money in it, these protective reservations operated, in law, we think, to subordinate the bank's lien for undelivered advances to those of the materialmen and workmen whose work, services and materials went into the project to enhance the bank's security. It has, we realize, long been the rule in this jurisdiction that a mortgage to secure future advances takes priority over mechanics' and materialmen's liens accruing after recordation of the mortgage (Home Savings & Loan Ass'n v. Burton, 20 Wash. 688, 56 P. 940 (1899)), but there is a well-established corollary to the rule that, if under the contract the advances are optional and not obligatory, then the lien priority for the advances is determined as of the time the advances are actually made.

What made the advances optional in law rather than obligatory? The very terms of the construction loan agreement gave the bank discretion as to which of the subcontractor materialmen would be paid from the advances. The construction loan agreement contained a promise to lend Equity Investors the $1,750,000 "upon the terms and conditions set forth below." This agreement provided that, after deducting all fees, charges and expenses agreed to by the borrower, the remaining proceeds of the loan would be credited to the borrower's construction loan account in the lending bank. Thus, the advances were not to be delivered over to the borrower but would remain on deposit in the lending bank as the contract stated to "finance the construction of apartment buildings on property described in the Deed of Trust."

The construction loan agreement specified that, prior to the first advance of construction funds, the bank was to be supplied with a current appraisal satisfactory to it; that all loan funds must be used for payment of material and labor; and that the loan proceeds were to be assigned by the borrower to the bank for that purpose. The borrower, according to this agreement, had to retain an architect satisfactory to the bank, and this approved architect had to supply the bank with periodic progress of construction reports, and before each advance of loaned money certify that satisfactory progress had been made and in the future would be made in keeping with the remainder of the unexpended loan.

The construction loan agreement left the loan moneys largely under the control and dominion of the bank, *"to be advanced at such times and in such amounts as the Lender shall determine."* It provided, too, that *"No advance shall be due unless, in the judgment of the Lender"* all work for which the advance had been made had been done in a good and workmanlike manner, and unless the construction be approved by the architect. The lender, at his option, could advance and pay the loan installments before they became due, if he deemed it advisable to do so — but all such advances were to be treated as a performance of the agreement and not a modification of it. Also, according to the construction loan agreement, the lender was not obligated to disburse more than 90 percent of the loan until the construction was completed and the property free of liens and claims of all kinds except the lender's lien.

There were other provisions in the construction loan agreement, giving control over the funds to the bank, including:

> If the construction of said building be at any time discontinued or not carried on with sufficient dispatch in the judgment of the Lender to protect the building from depredation or the weather, said Lender may purchase materials and employ workmen to protect the building so that the same will not suffer from depredation or the weather, or to complete said building, so that it may be used for the purposes for which it was designed under the said plans and specifications.

Accordingly, the disbursements of funds by the bank under an agreement placing discretionary controls in the lender over the disbursement of the loan funds with an additional reservation that the loan is "to be advanced at such times and in such amounts as the Lender shall determine," we think left so wide an area of discretion in the bank as to render the amounts to be advanced and the intervals of their advancing optional rather than compulsory as a matter of law. Had the borrowers sought a decree to overcome these reservations and to compel the advances, or to override the bank's discretionary power to advance or withhold the loan funds, they would have met with nearly insuperable obstacles at law. So broad and yet so specific were the bank's discretionary powers under the contract as to the times and amounts of the advances, a court could not properly override such discretion without abrogating the contract.

Although in a given case there may be difficulty in ascertaining from the circumstances and the language of the mortgage and loan papers covering the whole agreement whether the advances are to be regarded as optional or mandatory, we think that the contractual reservations giving the lender the broad discretion of deciding when and in what amounts, *or if at all,* he must advance the money render the advances optional rather than obligatory where the purpose is to decide construction lien priorities arising after the initial filing for record of the lender's security documents. As a means of protecting its security, the lender retained broad discretionary powers to determine under what circumstances it would advance the money, to withhold the advances any time that it believed its security in jeopardy or doubted the sufficiency or quality of the construction work or felt that an impending insolvency on the borrower's part would threaten the completion of the project or repayment of the loan. There was no hard and fast commitment to deliver the loan money over to the borrower at a given and stated time, nor to advance the money at more or less fixed intervals and in stated amounts. The lender, in reserving such broad protective discretion, thereby rendered the advances optional rather than obligatory for the purpose of determining the priority of liens.

Thus, we are adhering to what we perceive to be the weight of authority embodied in the rule that, where the advances of promised loan moneys are, under an agreement to lend money, largely optional, that is, where the time and the amount of the moneys to be advanced are largely discretionary in the lender, the legal effect of such provisions is to bring the transaction under the rule for optional advances rather than the rule governing mandatory advances for the purpose of determining lien priorities. Optional advances under a construction loan agreement attach when the advances are actually made. Any liens attaching prior to an optional advance would thus be superior to it, and attaching afterwards, junior to it. . . .

A contrary rule on that point would allow a lender, having power to allocate the loan moneys in such a way as to insure that those whose work, materials and efforts serve to enhance the value of the security, to sit idly by and watch his security grow, while at the same time potentially leaving the materialmen, subcontractors and workmen in the position of doing their work and supplying materials for little or nothing. The rule here contended for by lender would lead to an inevitable unjust enrichment, enabling the lender to withhold or apply the loan money as he saw fit; all the while knowing that putative lien claimants were furnishing valuable materials and doing valuable work to the enhancement of his security. The bank here had the option of withholding its advances on the loan from the borrower, and the right to apply the money to the account of Columbia Wood Products in payment of the lumber that company was delivering to the construction project. . . .

Accordingly, the judgment and decree of the trial court on the claim of Columbia Wood Products, Inc. is reversed.

Irwin Concrete, Inc. v. Sun Coast Properties
33 Wash. App. 190, 653 P.2d 1331 (1982)

Chaves [the subcontractor] contends that his lien was not foreclosed by the trustee sale because it was senior to that of Continental [the construction lender]. He argues that the loan agreement between Continental and Olympic [the developer] made advances optional with Continental; thus, he claims, to the extent of monies advanced after he started work, his lien claim was senior, citing National Bank of Washington v. Equity Investors, 81 Wash. 2d 886, 506 P.2d 20 (1973). We disagree. . . .

Unlike *Equity Investors,* the contract between Continental and Olympic did not allow Continental to disburse funds based on its own criteria. Subsection (2)(c) of the contract stated:

> The remaining $80,000 shall be disbursed after said lease to a national retail grocery chain has been secured and approved by Continental, for the purpose of site developments, plans for which shall be approved by Continental, and disbursements for which shall be made monthly against actual development costs, based on cost verification as site preparation progresses. Disbursements hereunder shall be subject to approval of Continental.

Disbursements were subject to Continental's approval. However, Continental was not free to advance or retain the money as it saw fit. The quoted language specifies the conditions under which Continental could approve or disapprove of disbursements: "disbursements for which shall be made monthly against actual development costs, based on cost verification as site preparation progresses." Continental's control over disbursements was limited to verifying each advance requested for the cost of work completed on the land. If the amount requested of Continental was verified, Continental had no option, but was required to disburse the money. Continental was obligated to loan $350,000 to Olympic. The only control Continental had over future advances was the ability to see that Olympic spent the loan money for improvements to the land. That control did not render the future advances optional.

Because Continental's advances were mandatory, its deed of trust securing the future advances was perfected on June 9, 1972, the date of filing. Chaves' mechanic's lien arose on June 16, 1972, the date he commenced work, and consequently was junior to the deed of trust. . . .

The case excerpt below discusses the application of the equitable lien theory in a jurisdiction that has also enacted a "stop notice" statute.

Swinerton & Walberg Co. v. Union Bank
25 Cal. App. 3d 259, 101 Cal. Rptr. 665 (1972)

FLEMING, Associate Justice.
Union Bank (Bank) appeals a portion of a judgment imposing an

equitable lien in favor of Swinerton & Walberg Co. (Swinerton) on funds held by Bank in a construction loan disbursement account.

FACTS

In February 1964 James and Audrey Casey (Casey) contracted with Swinerton, a building contractor, for the construction of a 78-unit apartment building on Casey's property in Redondo Beach at a price of $785,000. To finance construction and related expenses Casey in March 1964 borrowed $892,000 from Bank, signing a promissory note secured in part by a trust deed on the property.

Casey and Bank entered into a building loan agreement pursuant to which the $892,000 loan was deposited with Bank in a construction loan disbursement account. At Bank's request Casey deposited an additional $37,700 in the account to make a total of $929,700. $186,000 was to be disbursed for purposes other than construction, and $3,700 was to be held in the account for unforeseen expenses. The balance of $740,000 was to be disbursed as construction progressed to Swinerton (who was named in the agreement as the contractor) but $74,000 of that amount would be withheld until a title insurance company on completion of construction guaranteed that no mechanics' liens were outstanding against the property. The building loan agreement provided that if Casey should default on any obligation to Bank, the latter could apply funds in the construction loan disbursement account against Casey's obligation, and it recited "that nothing contained in this agreement shall be construed to vest in any contractor . . . any interest in or claim upon the funds so set aside in this agreement." As contractor, Swinerton signed a declaration in the building loan agreement that it accepted the agreements, conditions, and provisions of the loan agreement, and that these would control inconsistent provisions in its building contract with Casey.

Construction began in March 1964 and was completed in January 1965. Casey ordered extras amounting to $5,000, thereby raising the contract price to $790,000. During the construction period Bank disbursed $666,000 to Swinerton.

In March 1965 Casey defaulted on obligations to both Swinerton and Bank, and Swinerton recorded a mechanics' lien for $150,932.93 against Casey's property. On 16 September 1965 Swinerton offered to release its mechanics' lien, the only lien outstanding, if Bank would disburse the withheld amount of $74,000 on deposit in the construction loan account. Bank refused. In November 1966 Bank foreclosed its trust deed on the Casey property, buying in the property on the foreclosure sale for $810,000 and thereby wiping out Swinerton's mechanics' lien, a result Swinerton did not challenge.

Bank never sought to press its claim under the building loan agreement to apply undisbursed construction funds to Casey's defaulted obligation to Bank, and $104,472.68 remains undisbursed in the construction loan account. Swinerton instituted the present action against Casey and Bank for breach of contract and for imposition of an equitable lien against funds on deposit in the construction loan account.

TRIAL COURT'S DETERMINATION

The trial court found: Swinerton was induced to construct the apartment building by Casey and Bank; Swinerton was induced to rely on, and did rely on, the construction loan disbursement fund for payment; Swinerton, in signing the building loan agreement, did not intend to give up its rights to an equitable lien against undisbursed construction funds; Swinerton completed the construction called for by its contract in a workmanlike manner, and the reasonable value of construction exceeded $740,000; Bank had no reason to refuse to disburse $74,000 to Swinerton after Swinerton offered to release its mechanics' lien on 16 September 1965.

The trial court concluded that Casey was indebted to Swinerton for $124,000 [$790,000 contract price, less $666,000 construction loan disbursement]; Swinerton had no contractual rights against Bank; Swinerton was entitled to $74,000 plus interest from 16 September 1965 from Bank; and Swinerton's recovery against Bank was to be credited against Casey's debt to Swinerton.

Bank contents (1) as a general contractor Swinerton could not assert an equitable lien upon construction funds, (2) Swinerton waived any claim he might have had to an equitable lien, and (3) pre-judgment interest was improperly imposed on the equitable lien.

EQUITABLE LIEN

Bank argues that a general contractor may not assert an equitable lien, and it insists that this conclusion is compelled by Gordon Building Corp v. Gibraltar Savings & Loan Assoc., 247 Cal. App. 2d 1, 4, 10, 55 Cal. Rptr. 884. We disagree. In Gordon a general contractor, sued by a subcontractor for money due for labor and materials, cross-complained against a lender, in part to impose an equitable lien on construction loan proceeds held by the lender on the construction project on which the contractor had worked. The lender's demurrer was sustained without leave to amend, and judgment of dismissal was affirmed on appeal, because two allegations essential to the imposition of an equitable lien were missing from the general contractor's cross-complaint against the lender: an allegation that the general contractor directly supplied labor or materials to the construction project, and an allegation that the general contractor justifiably relied on the construction loan proceeds. Since the general contractor had made "several futile attempts to allege sufficient facts" to state a cause of action, the demurrer was properly sustained without leave to amend.

Gordon does state: "It would be a novel theory that the general contractor should accede to the benefit of loan proceeds heretofore considered to constitute a trust for the payment of liens and claims established by subcontractors and materialmen. Indeed, the demonstrated attitude of the law has been to implement the existing statutory scheme protecting subcontractors by methods calculated to forestall the misapplication or diversion of construction funds by the entrepreneurs of the project, including owner, builder, and the general contractor. . . ." (247 Cal. App. 2d at p. 9, 55 Cal. Rptr. at p. 888.) That language, however, was used to support the court's conclusion that under the circumstances of the case the general contractor's complaint did not state a cause of action based on a *third-party beneficiary theory,* i.e., a contract theory of recovery. Since recovery in the present case is not grounded on contract but rather on equitable considerations arising out of estoppel and unjust enrichment, its disposition is not controlled by the foregoing language from *Gordon.* Significantly, the latter case did not declare that a general contractor, entirely unrelated to the owner and builder, could never assert an equitable lien against construction loan proceeds.

Bank next argues that all cases in which equitable liens have been upheld involve subcontractors and not general contractors, and from this it concludes that a general contractor can never become entitled to an equitable lien against construction loan funds. Yet the fact that all other cases recognizing equitable liens have involved subcontractors, even if true, does not by itself preclude imposition of an equitable lien against construction loan funds on behalf of a general contractor. The lender of construction funds stands in the same approximate relationship to a subcontractor as it does to a general contractor who is wholly independent from the borrower. In both instances the position of the lender is that summarized in the following language: "Where the lender has received the benefit of the claimant's performance, and therefore a more valuable security for its note, it is not justified in withholding or appropriating to any other use money originally intended to be used to pay for such performance and relied upon by the claimant in rendering its performance." (Miller v. Mountain View Sav. & Loan Assoc., 238 Cal. App. 2d 644, 661, 48 Cal. Rptr. 278, 290, paraphrasing the court's statement in Pacific Ready Cut Homes v. Title I & T Co., 216 Cal. 447, 452, 14 P.2d 510.) Here, Swinerton performed its work and completed the construction of the apartment building (work whose reasonable value exceeded $740,000) but received only $666,000. Bank obtained the benefit of that performance by foreclosing on its trust deed and selling the apartment building for $810,000. It is equally clear that Swinerton was induced by the creation of the building construction loan fund to supply work, labor, and materials for the project and that in rendering its performance it relied on the fund for payment. Indeed, since Bank had acquired a first lien on the property to protect its construction loan, Swinerton could look to little else for security. The only contractual obstacle to Swinerton's right to the undisbursed construction loan fund was the existence of its own mechanics' lien against the property, a lien which on 16 September 1965 it offered to release if Bank would disburse $74,000 from the remaining construction loan funds. Bank refused the offer. Under these circumstances — full performance by the contractor and reliance by the contractor on the fund for payment — we think Swinerton became entitled to the $74,000 withheld in the construction loan disbursement account for payment of construction costs.

There are no statutory impediments to this conclusion, for the events with which we are concerned took place in 1964 and 1965. A 1967 addition to former Code of Civil Procedure section 1190.1, subdivision (n) (now Civil Code section 3264) provides:

> The rights of all persons furnishing labor, services, equipment, or materials for any work of improvement, with respect to any fund for payment of construction costs, are governed exclusively by this article, and no such person may assert any legal or equitable right with respect to such fund, other than a right created by direct written contract between such person and the person holding the fund, except pursuant to the provisions of this article.

Bank argues that this provision shows legislative opposition to the imposition of equitable liens against construction funds. We do not read such a broad meaning into that section (see Lefcoe and Schaffer, Construction Lending and the Equitable Lien, 40 So. Cal. Law Rev. 439, 459, fn. 4), but in any event that section does not apply retrospectively. The legislature specifically provided that the addition to former Code of Civil Procedure section 1190.1, subdivision (n) (now Civil Code section 3264), "shall not apply to any work of improvement commenced prior to [8 November 1967]." (Stats. 1967, ch. 789, §4.)

Finally, Bank argues that the equitable lien was designed to aid only those who are entitled to a stop notice but fail to properly perfect it, that general contractors are not entitled to stop notices (former Code Civ. Proc., §1190.1(h), now Civ. Code, §3159), and that because a general contractor's equitable rights should not exceed his legal rights, a general contractor is not entitled to an equitable lien. Bank's major premise is incorrect: The equitable lien is wholly independent of the statutory mechanics' lien and stop notice remedies (Goulden and Dent, More on Mechanics' Liens, Stop Notices, and the Like, 54 Cal. Law Rev. 179, 190; see Smith v. Anglo-California Trust Co., 205 Cal. 496, 502, 271 P. 898), and therefore does not depend on the availability to the claimant of the statutory stop notice remedy.

We conclude that in 1965 a general contractor could claim an equitable lien on construction loan proceeds, and that in this case the general contractor became entitled to such a lien. . . .

The judgment is affirmed.

In light of the problems faced by the construction lender in attempting to establish that construction advances are "obligatory" and the public policy (at least in some quarters) in favor of encouraging construction and responsible growth, it is no wonder that in some states legislation has been enacted to provide a form of limited protection to the construction lender for "optional" future advances. Many such statutes protect the lender for such future advances only when the funds are used for improvements to the real estate. Others, such as the Florida statute and the Uniform Simplification of Land Transfers Act, both excerpted below, are much broader in scope.

In Article 5 of the Uniform Simplification of Land Transfers Act (USLTA), the National Conference of Commissioners on Uniform State Laws drafted a uniform mechanics' lien statute based on what they considered the best of the emerging state legislation. In the excerpt from their introductory comment to Article 5, the Commissioners discuss the thrust of state legislation and the major issues dealt with in USLTA.

Fla. Rev. Stat. §697.04

(West 1990)

697.04. *Future advances may be secured*

(1)(a) Hereafter, any mortgage or other instrument given for the purpose of creating a lien on real property may, and when so expressed therein shall, secure not only existing indebtedness, but also such future advances, whether such advances are obligatory or to be made at the option of the lender, or otherwise, as are made within twenty years (20) from the date thereof, to the same extent as if such future advances were made on the date of the execution of such mortgage or other instrument, although there may be no advance made at the time of the execution of such mortgage or other instrument and although there may be no indebtedness outstanding at the time any advance is made. Such lien, as to third persons without actual notice thereof, shall be valid as to all such indebtedness and future advances from the time the mortgage or other instrument is filed for record as provided by law.

(b) The total amount of indebtedness that may be so secured may decrease or increase from time to time, but the total unpaid balance so secured at any one time shall not exceed a maximum principal amount which must be specified in such mortgage or other instrument, plus interest thereon; except that the mortgagor or his successor in title is authorized to file for record a notice limiting the maximum principal amount that may be so secured to an amount not less than the amount actually advanced at the time of such filing, provided a copy of such filing is also sent by certified mail to the mortgagee and in the case of an open-end or revolving credit agreement, the mortgagor surrenders to the mortgagee all credit cards, checks, or other devices used to obtain further advances at the time of filing the notice which notice shall be recorded and shall be effective from the date of filing. Notwithstanding the foregoing, any increase in the principal balance as a result of negative amortization or deferred interest shall be secured by the mortgage; and any disbursements made for the payment of taxes, levies, or insurance on the property covered by the lien, and any advances or disbursements made under a construction loan agreement referred to in a mortgage to enable completion of the contemplated improvement, with interest on such advances or disbursements, are secured by the mortgage or other instrument even though the mortgage or other instrument does not provide for future advances, or the advances or disbursements cause the total indebtedness to exceed the face amount stated in the instrument. . . .

Introductory Comment to Article 5 of the Uniform Simplification of Land Transfer Act
14 U.L.A. 271 (1977)

All states presently have mechanics' lien laws. Those laws present an extraordinarily varied approach, in substance, and in language, to the issues involved in mechanics' lien legislation. In fact, variation among the states may be greater in this area than in any other statutory area. In [an era] of national lenders and suppliers and of many multistate builders, the variation among the states as to mechanics' lien matters may be as great a hindrance to an efficient real estate market as are variations in state real estate security interest (mortgage) law. Furthermore, the present priority, and owner liability rules present difficult problems for contractors, owners, lenders, and courts and add substantial expense and risk to many real estate transactions. Therefore, it is appropriate to the purposes of a simplification of land transfers act that a uniform mechanics' act be proposed. . . .

While there is great diversity in mechanics' lien laws, they deal with common issues, and tend to fall into a limited number of patterns on each of the major issues involved. These major issues are listed below and will be considered in this introductory note: (1) who may secure a construction lien; (2) is the owner protected in making payments to the prime contractor if, at the time he pays, he has no notice of a construction lien claimant below the prime; and (3) from what time does the mechanics' lien take priority over third party purchasers or levying creditors who deal with the real estate.

WHO MAY SECURE A LIEN?

Mechanics' lien statutes give liens against the real estate being improved to persons who supply services (including labor) and materials for the improvement. In about half the states, any person who supplies services or materials is allowed a lien, no matter how far removed he is from the owner. Other states limit those who can secure a lien to two tiers (prime contractor, subcontractor), three tiers (prime contractor, subcontractor, sub-subcontractor) or four tiers. A few others allow a lien to two tiers plus all materialmen and laborers, and one gives a lien to all who contract with licensed contractors. . . .

PRIORITY OVER THIRD PARTIES

Most mechanics' lien laws date the lien claimant's priority over third parties from the time of "commencement" or "visible commencement" (hereafter both statements of the rule are referred to by the use of the word commencement) of the improvement, provided that the claimant records his lien within a limited period of time after he completes his work on the project. A commencement priority rule makes it difficult for persons who deal with real estate to determine whether it may be subject to subsequently asserted lien claims since a record title examination will not provide the necessary information. That priority rule, in effect, gives the lien claimant a secret lien. The secret lien is of limited duration since all statutes require the claimant to record a notice of lien within a fairly short period of time (2 to 18 or so months after completion) if he is to realize on the lien. Nevertheless, the title difficulties created are substantial. A commencement priority rule also creates particular difficulties for construction lenders. Such lenders usually record their mortgage at about the time the work is beginning, and, with some regularity, a construction lender discovers that work had commenced prior to the time he recorded so that he is junior to the construction lien claimant. . . .

A number of states, in response to the problems created by the commencement priority rule, have fixed other mechanics' lien priority dates. A few states date mechanics' lien priority from the time of recording the individual claimant's lien. This system protects the integrity of the real estate records, but prevents a contractor or materialman who furnishes services or materials late in the construction from getting priority equal with that of those who furnish services or materials early.

Illinois makes the time the owner and a prime contractor enter into the improvement contract the priority date for that prime and claimants who claim through him. A few states date all claimants' priority from the time the prime contract or a notice thereof is recorded in the real estate records. That system, also, protects the integrity of the public records, but gives claimants under different primes different priorities in cases in which the owner uses more than one prime contractor on an improvement project.

This Act adopts a notice recording device, first developed in Florida, under which the owner, prior to the beginning of work on an improvement, records a "notice of commencement" which puts third parties on notice that construction liens may be claimed against the real estate. If a lien claimant records his lien during the effective period of a notice of commencement, his priority date is the date the notice of commencement was recorded. . . .

Is the Owner Protected in Making Payments to the Prime Contractor, If, at the Time He Pays, He Has No Notice of a Mechanic's Lien Claimant?

In many states, under present law, an owner cannot with safety pay the prime contractor even though no claimant claiming through the prime contractor has made a demand that he be paid directly by the owner. In those states, the owner takes the risk that the prime contractor or others in the contracting chain will not apply payments received by them to the payment of suppliers of services and materials who will have a lien on the improvement. Possible owner double liability leads, in those states, to elaborate lien waiver or direct disbursement techniques where knowledgeable parties are involved. In other states, the owner is protected so long as he pays in good faith before any demand is made upon him for payment by a potential lien claimant. . . .

The following excerpts from Article 5 of USLTA indicate how the Commissioners felt the last of the three questions should be answered. These excerpts, of course, merely focus on one aspect of a rather complex statutory scheme. A full reading of Article 5 will probably convince you that the drafters may have been optimistic in their selection of a title for this Act.[12]

Uniform Simplification of Land Transfer Act §§5-102, 5-201, 5-204, 5-209, 5-301, 5-207
14 U.L.A. 282-321 (1977)

SECTION 5-102.

In this Article, unless the context otherwise requires:

(1) "Claimant" means a person having a right to a lien under this Article upon real estate and includes his successor in interest. . . .

(5) "Notice of commencement" means the notice specified in Section 5-301 whether recorded by an owner or by a claimant.

SECTION 5-201.

(a) A person who furnishes services or materials pursuant to a real estate improvement contract has a construction lien, only to the extent provided in this Article, to secure the payment of his contract price. . . .

SECTION 5-204.

(a) A lien for furnishing materials arises only if:

(1) they are supplied with the intent, shown by the contract of sale, the delivery order, delivery to the site by the claimant or at his direction, or by other evidence, that they be used in the course of construction of, or incorporated into, the improvement in connection with which the lien arises, and

(2) they are either

(i) incorporated in the improvement or consumed as normal wastage in construction operations;

(ii) specially fabricated for incorporation in the improvements and not readily resaleable in the ordinary course of the fabricator's business even though not actually incorporated in the improvement;

(iii) used for the construction or for the operation of machinery or equipment used in the course of construction and not remaining

---

12. See Pedowitz, Uniform Simplification of Land Transfers Act — A Commentary, 13 Real Prop., Prob. & Tr. J. 696 (1978).

in the improvement, subject to diminution by the salvage value of those materials; or

(iv) tools, appliances, or machinery used on the particular improvement, but a lien for supplying tools, appliances, or machinery used on the improvement is limited as provided by subsection (c).

(b) The delivery of materials to the site of the improvement, whether or not by the claimant, creates a presumption that they were used in the course of construction or were incorporated into the improvement. . . .

SECTION 5-209.

(a) Except as provided in this section, a construction lien has priority over adverse claims against the real estate as if the construction-lien claimant were a purchaser for value without knowledge who had recorded (Section 3-202) at the time his lien attached.

(b) Except as provided in subsection (c), a construction lien has priority over subsequent advances made under a prior recorded security interest if the subsequent advances are made with knowledge that the lien has attached.

(c) Notwithstanding knowledge that the construction lien has attached, or the advance exceeds the maximum amount stated in the recorded security agreement and whether or not the advance is made pursuant to a commitment,[13] a subsequent advance made under a security agreement recorded before the construction lien attached has priority over the lien if:

(1) the subsequent advance is made under a construction security agreement[14] and is made in payment of the price of the agreed improvements,

(2) the subsequent advance is made or incurred for the reasonable protection of the security interest in the real estate, such as payment for real property taxes, hazard insurance premiums, or maintenance charges imposed under a condominium declaration or other covenant, or

(3) the subsequent advance was applied to the payment of any lien or encumbrance which was prior to the construction lien.

(d) To the extent that a subsequent security interest is given to

13. Under §1-201(14) of USLTA an advance is made "pursuant to commitment" if "the obligor has bound himself to make it, whether or not a default or other event not within his control has relieved or may relieve him from his obligation." — ED.

14. Under §1-201 of USLTA a "construction security agreement" is one that identifies itself as such and "that secures an obligation which the debtor incurred for the purpose of making an improvement of the real estate in which the security interest is given . . .". — ED.

secure funds used to pay a debt secured by a security interest having priority over a construction lien under this section, the subsequent security interest is also prior to the construction lien.

(e) Even though notice of commencement has been recorded, a buyer who is a protected party takes free of all construction liens that are not of record at the time his title document is recorded or, if he is a lessee for one year or less, at the beginning of the lease term.

SECTION 5-301.

(a) A notice of commencement must be signed by the contracting owner, be denominated "notice of commencement," and state:

(1) the real estate being or intended to be improved or directly benefited, with a description thereof sufficient for identification;

(2) the name and address of the contracting owner, his interest in the real estate, and the name and address of the fee simple title holder, if other than the contracting owner; and

(3) that if, after the notice of commencement is recorded, a lien is recorded as to an improvement covered by the notice of commencement, the lien has priority from the time the notice of commencement is recorded.

(b) The notice of commencement may state its duration, but if a duration is stated of less than 6 months from the time of recording, the duration of the notice is 6 months. If no duration is stated, the duration of the notice is one year after the recording. . . .

(d) A contracting owner may extend the duration of a notice of commencement by recording before the lapse thereof a continuation statement signed by him which refers to the record location and date of recording of the notice of commencement and states the date to which the notice of commencement's duration is extended. . . .

SECTION 5-207.

(a) A claimant's lien does not attach and may not be enforced unless, after entering into the contract under which the lien arises and not later than 90 days after his final furnishing of services or materials, he has recorded a lien (Section 5-303).

(b) If a lien is recorded while a notice of commencement is effective as to the improvement in connection with which the lien arises, the lien attaches as of the time the notice is recorded (Section 5-301), *even though visible commencement occurred before the notice is recorded* [emphasis supplied]. A notice of commencement is not effective until recording and, after recording, is effective until its lapse. A notice of commencement lapses at the earlier of its expiration (Section 5-301(b)) or the date it is terminated by a notice of termination (Section 5-302).

(c) If a lien is recorded while there is no recorded notice of commencement covering the improvement in connection with which the lien arises, the lien attaches at the earlier of visible commencement of the improvement or the recording of the lien. But, if visible commencement has occurred before or within 30 days after the lapse of the last notice of commencement covering the improvement:

(1) the lien attaches at the time the lien is recorded if the lien is recorded within 30 days after lapse of the last effective notice of commencement; or

(2) the lien relates back to and attaches 31 days after the termination date if the lien is recorded more than 30 days after lapse of the last effective notice of commencement. . . .

(d) If new construction is the principal improvement involved and the materials, excavation, preparation of an existing structure, or other preparation are readily visible on a reasonable inspection of the real estate, "visible commencement" occurs when:

(1) materials are delivered to the real estate to which the lien attaches preparatory to construction;

(2) excavation on the real estate to which the lien attaches is begun; or

(3) preparation of an existing structure to receive the new construction, or other preparation of the real estate to which the lien attaches, is begun.

(e) In all cases not covered by subsection (d) the time visible commencement occurs is to be determined by the circumstances of the case.

Is the owner protected in making payments to the prime contractor, if, at the time he pays, he has no notice of a mechanics' lien claimant?

The Introductory Comment offers the following explanation of the approach taken by the Act:

This Act offers the states two alternatives which continue the two existing patterns. [One places the risk on the owner that the prime contractor will apply payments received to the payment of the subs. The other protects the owner who has paid in good faith. — ED.] Under the first alternative an owner's real estate is subject to the liens of claimants below the prime contractor only to the extent that the owner has not paid the prime contractor at the time he is notified by the claimant of the prospective lien claim. Under the second alternative, a claimant below the prime contractor can assure himself of a lien against the owner for his full contract price by notifying the owner within 20 days after the claimant first furnishes services or materials. If the claimant so notifies the owner the owner cannot defend that he has already paid the prime contractor at the time he received the notice. The 20 day notice requirement, patterned after the California lien law, however, does give the owner substantial protection against double payment.

NOTES AND QUESTIONS

1. Commencement of Construction. As observed above, many if not most states (called "priority states") provide that mechanics' liens relate back to the date of the commencement of construction. See Nelson and Whitman, Real Estate Finance Law §12.4, at 864 (2d ed. 1985). But when does the construction commence? Would the date relate back to the completion of the first engineering study or the drafting of the architect's plans and specifications? Probably not. How about delivery of materials to the site? The arrival of the bulldozers? The fencing of the property? The digging of the first ceremonial shovelful of dirt? The general rule is that construction commences when the work begun is of a nature that is conspicuous and substantial enough to make it reasonably apparent that improvements are intended to be constructed at the site. See Annot., 1 A.L.R.3d 822 (1965).

As counsel to a construction lender, what precautionary measures might you suggest to establish the fact that the construction did not commence prior to the recordation of your client's mortgage?

2. "Obligatory" Versus "Optional" Advances. As observed above, states provide various special priorities for holders of mechanics' liens over mortgagees and other holders of prior interests in the real estate. In most states the special lien priority accorded to mechanics' liens does not change the general priority rule under the recording statutes of first in time, first in right. See Chapter 4C1. Instead, priority is established by moving the date of the mechanic's lien back to a date before the actual filing of the lien, such as the date of the commencement of construction. Once the date of the mechanic's lien is determined, it will then take priority over interests in the real estate that are recorded subsequent to that date. Now let us look at the other side of the coin. When does the construction mortgage create a security interest in the real estate against which the mechanic's lien will be tested? Is it when the mortgage is recorded? For all advances made in the future? Or is a separate interest in the real estate created with each new advance?

As explained in Chapter 5, except for a floor-ceiling loan, a typical postconstruction loan is closed and funded in its entirety if and when the project is completed in accordance with the terms and conditions of the commitment letter. By contrast, as explained in greater detail at Chapter 6B5, infra, a prudent construction lender will insist on a progress payment procedure detailed in the construction loan agreement whereby loan advances are periodically made to the borrower (or directly to the general contractor) prior to each stage of the project so that the lender will be continuously assured that the improvements are being constructed in accordance with the plans and specifications (as approved beforehand by both the postconstruction and the construction lenders), that the bills for labor and materials are being paid as they become due so that neither mechanics' nor materialmens' liens are pending, and that the loan is "in balance," meaning that there are sufficient undisbursed loan and equity funds on hand to fund the balance of the projected construction costs.

The foregoing overview explains why construction loan mortgages are structured as mortgages to secure future loan advances rather than as mortgages to secure present advances. Such mortgages can either designate beforehand a specified maximum loan amount (frequently the amount of the takeout loan) that will be disbursed incrementally as the project advances, or the mortgage may merely identify the amount of the initial advance and specify that the mortgage will secure future advances as well. By way of illustration, the construction loan agreements at issue in both the *Equity Investors* and *Irwin Concrete* cases expressly stated the loan amounts to be advanced, whereas the loan agreement in the *Potwin State Bank* case (excerpted at Chapter 4B2) involved an "open-end Dollar mortgage," which merely designated beforehand the initial amount ("one dollar") to be advanced. *Equity Investors* and *Irwin Concrete* involved loans to fund income-producing real estate, whereas *Potwin State Bank* involved a loan to construct a single-family residence.

Can you explain why the courts in these cases either ruled or assumed that the mortgages to secure *future* advances were enforceable notwithstanding the general rule that a valid mortgage requires an underlying obligation that is *presently* enforceable? See discussion at Chapter 4B2, note 2b. Of the construction loan mortgage that identifies a specified loan amount and one that merely designates the amount of the initial advance, the former format is far more prevalent in the case of income-producing real estate. Why? In that regard, think about the facts in the master hypothetical and what Ace's response might be if FNB were to insist on the "Dollar mortgage" format. What reaction might FNB expect from either Dan or his general contractor?

Let us assume that FNB agrees in its loan commitment to advance to Dan a maximum loan amount of $25 million subject to the terms and conditions of its construction loan agreement. Let us further assume the facts as diagrammed in Figure 6-2 and that the State of Fuller has a statute under which all mechanics' liens (when filed) automatically date back to the date on which construction commences. Under these facts, who will have lien priority as to Advances 1 and 2 made by FNB, FNB or the mechanic (M1)? As suggested in the cases excerpted above, the answer turns on the question whether the loan advances were obligatory or optional. Based on the equitable doctrine of relation back and the operation of the recording statutes, the lien priority of an obligatory advance dates back to the time at which the original

F i g u r e 6-2

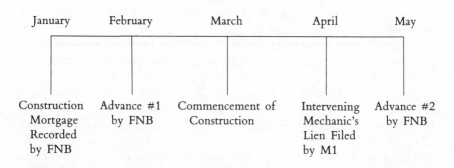

January	February	March	April	May
Construction Mortgage Recorded by FNB	Advance #1 by FNB	Commencement of Construction	Intervening Mechanic's Lien Filed by M1	Advance #2 by FNB

mortgage was created and recorded. See Nelson and Whitman §12.7, at 886. Therefore, in the hypothetical, if FNB had been obliged to make both advances (as reflected by the language in its mortgage and construction loan agreement) then both advances would date back to January and be superior in lien priority to the mechanic's lien filed by M1 that under the priority rule would date back to March.

By contrast, if a loan advance under a mortgage to secure future advances is optional and the mortgagee has notice of a subsequent lienor when the advance is made, then the optional advance is not predated and included within the original mortgage lien. Therefore, in the hypothetical, FNB's lien priority as to Advance 2 would be defeated if the advance had been optional and if FNB had notice of the intervening lien at the time the advance was made. Suppose Advance 1 had been optional but by mutual agreement the construction loan agreement had been modified on March 15 so that FNB became obliged to make Advance 2. Should Advance 2 retain its usual priority as an obligatory advance?

As stated above, if Advance 2 had been optional FNB would have lost its lien priority to M1 only if FNB had made the advance after obtaining notice of the intervening lien. But what kind of notice is required? In most jurisdictions the mortgagee must obtain actual notice of a subsequent security interest before its subsequent advance loses priority so that constructive notice will not suffice. See Nelson and Whitman §12.7, at 893. This means that FNB's lien priority as to Advance 2 will not be defeated even though the advance was optional and FNB had record notice of M1's lien before the advance was made. Can you think of the probable rationale for this result?

The doctrine of relation back has been questioned by some commentators. Why should obligatory advances be included within the prior lien of the original mortgage when optional advances are not? What does notice to the mortgagee have to do with the issue whether advances should relate back to the original mortgage? See Nelson and Whitman §12.7, at 886-887. Perhaps the notion is based on policy considerations. For example, if a mortgagee such as FNB should obligate itself to make future advances and puts itself on record as doing so (by recording its construction mortgage) then contractors and other potential third-party creditors (who might also have access to a copy of the construction loan agreement) are put on notice of the mortgagee's intentions and prior claim. By contrast, it would be inequitable to apply the equitable doctrine of relation back to impair the rights of intervening lienors when a mortgagee such as FNB can quit making optional advances at any time.

One problem with the doctrine of obligatory versus optional advances is the dilemma confronting a construction lender. As Chief Justice Hale conceded in the *Equity Investors* case, sound banking practice dictates that a cautious construction lender retain a considerable measure of control over its loan advances in order to protect its financial interests, which is the very purpose of the construction loan agreement. Indeed, as of this writing there is almost $8 billion in construction loans on the books of the 477 insolvent thrift organizations, the disposition of which will be a vexing problem for the Resolution Trust Corporation, the new federal regulatory agency created by the Financial Institutions Reform, Recovery, and Enforcement Act of 1989, 12 U.S.C. §1441a(b) (1990). And the evidence to date suggests that sloppy lending practices and poor supervision of loans in the deregulatory climate of the 1980s were significant contributory factors. See Sahling and Lavin, Will RTC Asset Dispositions Ruin the Real Estate Markets?, 20 Real Est. Rev. 15, 17 (Summer 1990); Rosenbaum, A Financial Disaster with Many Culprits, N.Y. Times, June 9, 1990, at A1, col. 2; Gerth, A Blend of Tragedy and Farce, N.Y. Times, July 3, 1990, at D1, col. 2. See discussion at Chapter 4D, note 2. And yet if a cautious lender were to overstep the ill-defined threshold limit on what is reasonable control it might lose its lien priority as to future advances and, as discussed at Chapter 6B6, infra, subject itself to third-party tort liability.

Can you think of any additional reasons in favor or against the doctrine of optional versus obligatory advances? See Kratovil and Werner, Mortgage for Construction and the Lien Priorities Problem — The "Unobligatory" Advance, 41 Tenn. L. Rev. 311 (1974); Skipworth, Should Construction Lenders Lose Out on Voluntary Advances If a Loan Turns Sour? 5 Real Est. L.J. 221 (1977).

In the *Equity Investors* case, Chief Justice Hale found that the language of the construction loan agreement made such explicit reservations for the disbursement of the loan as to render the advances optional. What provisions were looked to by Chief Justice Hale in reaching his conclusion? Do you agree with him? If so, which of those provisions, do you think, were determinative? A review of Chapter

5D1 and 5D2 may help you to put your answer in perspective. If construction lenders eliminated the offending provisions, what would the effect be, if any, on the viability of construction financing? Does the language of the contract in *Irwin Concrete* suggest how construction lenders can protect themselves without falling into the optional advance trap? After reviewing the language of the sample Construction Loan Agreement in the Documents Manual, can you identify any provisions that might render the loan advances optional?

An especially thorny dilemma may confront the construction lender who waives defaults and works with the developer to avoid foreclosure. For example, assume the construction loan agreement provides that the building must be built in accordance with the plans and specifications as approved by Ace and that FNB need not fund if Dan Developer is in default. The plans and specifications call for the marble slabs that form the "curtain wall" (the outside, non-supporting wall of the building) to be attached with stainless steel clips. With costs rising, Dan uses clips made of a less expensive alloy. Ace's architects spot the change, and Ace notifies both Dan and FNB that it considers the substitution dangerous and a violation of the postconstruction commitment. By virtue of a "cross-default" provision in the construction loan agreement, a breach of the postconstruction commitment is a breach under the construction loan agreement. FNB, Ace, and Dan consult experts, who state that if the substitute clips are anodized to reduce the possibility of corrosion the slabs will be safe but still less desirable than stainless steel clips. Dan agrees to anodize the offending clips. Ace and FNB agree to go along with this and waive the default (the failure to comply with plans and specifications). See J. I. Kislak Mortgage Corp. v. William Matthews, Builder, Inc., 287 A.2d 686, affd., 303 A.2d 648 (Del. 1973). If *Kislak* were the law of the State of Fuller, would this have made the advances optional from that point onward? Why? See House of Carpets v. Mortgage Investment Co., 85 N.M. 560, 514 P.2d 611 (1973). How should the construction loan agreement provision have been worded to avoid this problem?

3. *Stop Notice.* Stop Notice statutes enacted in a handful of jurisdictions generally give the mechanic who might otherwise have an unenforceable claim the right to enforce that claim against the undisbursed construction loan proceeds. See, e.g., Alaska Stat. §34.35.062 (1990); R. I. Gen. Laws §34-27.1-1 (1990). The mechanic accomplishes this by filing a notice under the statute, which has the effect of stopping future construction and bringing the entire project to a halt pending what may turn out to be extensive litigation to determine if the undisbursed construction funds will be available for the completion of the project.

If FNB carelessly disburses funds without requiring the assurances it is entitled to under the construction loan agreement, does the unpaid subcontractor have any grounds to argue that, because of FNB's negligence, the disbursed funds should be considered as though they had not been disbursed, leaving the subcontractor free to enforce a claim against FNB under the stop notice statute for an amount in excess of the funds actually undisbursed? In this regard see Cal. Civ. Code §3264 (1991).

Do you see any constitutional problem in the subcontractor's exercising its rights under the stop notice statute and bringing the construction to a halt without a hearing? See the discussion at Chapter 10C4 on due process as it relates to power-of-sale foreclosures of mortgages or deeds of trust and Comment, California's Private Stop Notice Law: Due Process Requirements, 25 Hastings L.J. 1043 (1974). See generally Moss, The Stop Notice Remedy in California — Updated, 47 L.A. Bar Bull. 299 (1972); Ilyin, Stop Notice! — Construction Loan Officer's Nightmare, 16 Hastings L.J. 187 (1964); Comment, Mechanics' Liens: The "Stop Notice" Comes to Washington, 49 Wash. L. Rev. 685 (1974).

4. *Equitable Liens.* In *Swinerton* the court discusses various theories underlying the doctrine of equitable liens — third-party beneficiary, estoppel, and unjust enrichment as the other. Which was successfully employed in *Swinerton?* Would any of the other theories have passed muster? The court applied the equitable lien doctrine notwithstanding the fact that there was a stop notice statute in California. If the passage of a mechanic's lien law doesn't prevent the application of the equitable lien, should not the passage of a stop notice statute do so? How did the court deal with this in *Swinerton?* See generally Lefcoe and Schaffer, Construction Lending and the Equitable Lien, 40 S. Cal. L. Rev. 439 (1967); Annot., 5 A.L.R.3d 848 (1990).

5. *Statutory Protection for the Construction Lender.* The Florida statute on future advances excerpted above provides, inter alia, that the owner-mortgagor may file a notice limiting the maximum number of advances that may take priority as of the date of the original mortgage recording to those advances already made at the time of the filing. What is the probable purpose of this provision, and when would it be used?

About half of the states limit those who may obtain a "construction lien" to the first two, three, or four tiers below the owner. Under §5-201(a) of USLTA, it would seem that *any* person furnishing materials or services under a "real estate improvement contract" (this term is defined in USLTA §5-107 as an agreement to perform services or furnish materials "for the purpose of producing a change in the physical condition of land or of a structure"), no matter how far removed from the owner, may acquire a construction lien.

Suppose Dan Developer's construction contract with the prime contractor calls for water pipes to be made of an alloy permitted by the local building code. Thereafter, but before the pipes are installed, the applicable building code is modified to require copper piping in certain areas. The prime contractor orders the required copper pipes from a subcontractor, who supplies the pipes. The sub doesn't get paid. Is the sub entitled to a construction lien on Dan's real estate under USLTA? See §5-201, comment 1, 14 U.L.A. 282-283 (1977). Suppose the prime contractor installed sheet rock in Dan's building that had been obtained previously in large quantities and stored in the prime contractor's warehouse for use in future construction as and when contracted for. If not paid, is the supplier of the sheet rock entitled to a lien on Dan's real estate under USLTA?

Consider the following broadbrush formulation of the construction lien priority rules under USLTA. A mechanic's or materialman's lien ("construction lien") is perfected by a recordation of the lien, which becomes effective as of the time a valid "notice of commencement" is filed by the owner or a lien claimant (e.g., a subcontractor) even though the visible commencement of construction occurred before the notice is recorded. (USLTA §§5-207, 5-301.) If such notice was not filed, the mechanic's lien attaches when the commencement of construction became visible or when the lien was filed, whichever came first. (USLTA §5-207(c).) The mechanic's lien will be junior in lien priority to a future advance made under a previously recorded construction mortgage ("construction security agreement") regardless of whether the advance was obligatory or optional, even where the mortgagee had notice of the intervening mechanic's lien before the advance was made and even where the advance happened to exceed the maximum loan amount stipulated in the recorded mortgage, provided that:

1. the advance was made "in payment of the price of the agreed [on] improvements";
2. the advance was made to preserve the mortgagee's security interest in the property; or
3. the advance was used toward the payment of any lien or encumbrance that was junior in lien priority to the mechanic's lien (USLTA §5.209(c)).

Returning to the facts in the hypothetical as diagrammed in Figure 6-2, assume that the state of Fuller has not adopted Article 5 of USLTA and follows the traditional priority rule to the effect that all mechanics' liens relate back to the date on which the construction becomes visible. Unbeknownst to FNB, excavation of the land by M1 and other visible preliminary site work began in December of the previous year, even though the actual "brick and mortar" construction of the improvements did not actually begin until March. FNB recorded its mortgage in January and made its first loan advance in February, and M1 recorded its mechanic's lien in April. In May, FNB made its second loan advance even though it had actual notice of M1's lien at the time the second advance was made. Finally, in August, FNB discovers that Dan used the second loan advance to pay his gambling debts. The project collapses; FNB commences a foreclosure action and attempts to extinguish M1's lien on the assumption that both its loan advances are superior in lien priority to the mechanic's lien filed by M1.

Who has lien priority as to Advance 1, FNB or M1? As to Advance 2? Would these lien priority results change with respect to either Advance 1 or Advance 2 if Fuller had adopted Article 5 of USLTA and FNB had insisted that the owner, Dan Developer, record a notice of commencement in January when it recorded its construction loan mortgage? See §5-301, comment 1, 14 U.L.A. 318-319 (1977).

A notice of commencement, if filed by Dan, not only protects FNB against contractors but also serves to put the contractor on notice that it will be subordinate to the construction financing. Also, the notice of commencement can be filed by a contractor or other lien claimant. Thus, if no notice of commencement had been filed and no mortgage recorded at the time of its contract with Dan Developer, the contractor could file a notice of commencement at that time, thereby ensuring that any construction lien it later records will date from the time of its notice and be prior to any subsequent mortgage. See USLTA §5-301, comment 1, 14 U.L.A. 318-319 (1977).

In your opinion, do the priority concepts adopted by USLTA provide a rational way to balance the interests of the construction lender and mechanic's lien claimants? Do they do justice to the purpose underlying Article 5 as enunciated in the Introductory Comment excerpted above?

Since we are dealing with commercial real estate financing, we have not touched on the concept of the "protected party" that is a part of both ULTA and USLTA. A protected party is a consumer who occupies or will occupy all or a part of the real estate involved in a purchase or covered by a security interest (mortgage or deed of trust). See USLTA §5-105. The concept is that the same rules that should apply to normal business relationships should not apply to consumers. For example, in §5-209(e), a protected party takes free of a construction lien not recorded at the time of recording of the protected party's deed even though a notice of commencement has been recorded prior to the recording of the deed.

6. *Title Insurance Protection for the Construction Lender.* The risks of construction lending can be ameliorated by title insurance from title companies with sufficient assets. However, as suggested by the excerpts that follow and the general discussion of title insurance at Chapter 3B2, the scope of the coverage is somewhat limited.

Most construction loan agreements require the following type of coverage:

> Section 4.04.   Prior to the first Advance under this Agreement, Borrower shall deliver or cause to be delivered to Lender a 1987 ALTA revised loan policy or policies of title insurance issued by a company or companies approved in writing by Lender and Post-Construction Lender, issued to Lender (and a commitment or commitments to issue a substantially similar policy or policies to the Post-Construction Lender upon substantial completion of the Project in form and content approved by Lender and Post-Construction Lender) in the face amount of the Note, as of the date of the first Advance hereunder, insuring that the Mortgage is a first lien on the Land and the Improvements as constructed (including, without limitation, specific insurance against filed and unfiled mechanic's and materialmen's liens), subject to no encumbrances or any other matters except those set forth in the Permitted Encumbrances or approved in writing by Lender and Post-Construction Lender. As a condition to each advance hereunder, such insurance shall be extended by endorsement to cover such advance. The title policy or policies shall contain such endorsements and shall be issued with such co-insurance and re-insurance as Lender may request.

Observe that the above-quoted clause requires the use of the 1987 policy forms of the ALTA, the American Land Title Association, the industry's trade organization. The ALTA has a Forms Committee whose major function is to prepare model title forms and endorsements. Insuring Provision 7 of the ALTA 1970 Loan Policy insures the lender against loss by reason of "any statutory lien for labor or materials which now has gained or hereafter may gain priority over the lien of the insured mortgage." This form was designed primarily for the benefit of postconstruction lenders but has been issued to construction lenders as well. This language in Insuring Provision 7 has been reformulated for the 1987 version of the ALTA Loan Policy, but it is intended to offer essentially the same broad coverage offered by the earlier version and can clearly be used for both kinds of lenders. See R. Jordan, ALTA Forms Committee Revises Title Insurance Policies 2 (Lawyer's Title Insurance Corp. 1987). During the recession of the mid-1970s, a major shake-out occurred in the title insurance industry that was attributable in part to heavy losses caused by payments to construction lenders based on their coverage against mechanics' liens. As a result, the Forms Committee prepared a Construction Loan Policy in 1975, revised in

1976 and 1987, that scales down the degree of risk assumption for the title companies.

The Construction Loan Policy starts by excluding from coverage any lien "imposed by law for services, labor or material, heretofore or hereafter furnished except . . . [if] recorded in the public records at Date of Policy." The form then limits this exclusion by offering four alternative endorsements, each designed to provide coverage for the priority of construction loans against mechanics' liens, so that the title company can select the particular endorsement that is consistent with the laws of the jurisdiction where a policy is being written. Excerpts from these four endorsements read as follows.

Endorsement A

The Company hereby insures against loss or damage by reason of . . . any lien imposed by law for services, labor or material, for that portion of the cost thereof the payment for which the insured has disbursed funds, and which services, labor or material were furnished prior to _____ , 19 _____ for an improvement on the land.
This endorsement does not insure against loss or damage by reason of any failure by the insured to comply with or to enforce any of the provisions of law known to the insured or of any agreement to which the insured is a party which relates to the disbursement of the proceeds of the loan secured by the insured mortgage.

Endorsement B

The Company hereby insures against loss or damage by reason of . . . any lien imposed by law for services, labor or material heretofore or hereafter furnished for that portion of the proceeds of the loan secured by said mortgage now or hereafter disbursed in compliance with a legal obligation to disburse contained in a written agreement which must exist at the date of this endorsement.
[Second paragraph the same as Endorsement A]

Endorsement C

The Company hereby insures against loss or damage by reason of . . . any lien imposed by law for services, labor or material heretofore or hereafter furnished for that portion of the proceeds of the loan secured by said mortgage now or hereafter disbursed prior to the filing of any assertion of any such lien or right thereto in the public records or thereafter disbursed with the written consent of the Company.
[Second paragraph the same as Endorsement A]

Endorsement D

The Company hereby insures against loss or damage by reason of . . . any lien imposed by law for services, labor or material heretofore or hereafter furnished.
[Second paragraph the same as Endorsement A]

By contrast, Insuring Provision 7(b) of the 1987 ALTA Loan Policy insures the construction lender against lack of lien priority over any statutory lien for services, labor, or material arising from:

> an improvement or work related to the land which is contracted for or commenced subsequent to Date of Policy and which is financed in whole or in part by proceeds of the indebtedness secured by the insured mortgage which at Date of Policy the insured has advanced or is obligated to advance; . . .

This coverage is subject to Exclusions 3 and 6, which read as follows.

3. Defects, liens, encumbrances, adverse claims or other matters:
    (a) created, suffered, assumed or agreed to by the insured claimant;
    (b) not known to the Company, not recorded in the public records at Date of Policy, but known to the insured claimant and not disclosed in writing to the Company by the insured claimant prior to the date the insured claimant became an insured under this policy;
    (c) resulting in no loss or damage to the insured claimant;
    (d) attaching or created subsequent to Date of Policy (except to the extent that this policy insures the priority of the lien of the insured mortgage over any statutory lien for services, labor or material); or
    (e) resulting in loss or damage which would not have been sustained if the insured claimant had paid value for the insured mortgage. . . .
6. Any statutory lien for services, labor or materials (or the claim of priority of any statutory lien for services, labor or materials over the lien of the insured mortgage) arising from an improvement or work related to the land which is contracted for and commenced subsequent to Date of Policy and is not financed in whole or in part by proceeds of the indebtedness secured by the insured mortgage which at Date of Policy the insured has advanced or is obligated to advance.

Returning to the master hypothetical, as counsel to the Worthier Title Company (in the State of Fuller), which priority would you say rules for mechanics' liens? What factual circumstances would prompt you to issue Endorsement A? Endorsement B? Endorsement C? Endorsement D?

As counsel to FNB, the construction lender, would you be opposed in principle to the approach towards mechanics' liens taken by the ALTA Construction Loan Policy form? Specifically, would you be concerned about the language in paragraph 2 of each of the endorsements? Does this paragraph mean that if there were a failure to comply with a provision of law prior to the date of the policy the title company could avoid liability? Shouldn't matters occurring prior to the date of the policy be part of the title company's responsibility, subject to the normal exclusion for defects not known to the title company or shown by the public records but known to the insured claimant? If FNB should fail to declare a default immediately because of Dan Developer's failure to comply with one or more of the provisions of the construction loan agreement, could FNB lose its title protection even though it has complied with all the requirements imposed by local law?

As counsel to FNB, how would you compare the approach taken by the 1987 Loan Policy with that of the 1987 Construction Loan Policy? Would you favor the former format? If so, explain why.

In Bankers Trust Co. v. Transamerica Title Insurance Co., 594 F.2d 231 (1979), the construction lender obtained a title (loan) insurance policy insuring against, inter alia, mechanics' liens. The policy contained the standard exclusion 3(a) (excerpted above), excluding from coverage "defects, liens, encumbrances, adverse claims or other matters" that are "created, suffered, assumed or agreed to by the insured claimant." The title company agreed to disburse the loan funds pursuant to the lender's commitment based on a percentage of the project's completion. Construction was halted after 13 disbursements, and the lender declared the loan out of balance and in default. Note that a loan is deemed to be "in balance" when the amount is sufficient to complete the project (whether from the loan itself or together with cash equity paid in by the developer.) Mechanics' liens were filed against the property, and the lender made a claim on its title policy. The Tenth Circuit affirmed the District Court's decision granting summary judgment dismissing the lender's complaint against the title company. The court determined that the mechanics' liens were created or permitted by the lender and therefore fell within the 3(a) exclusion from coverage because the lender had knowingly made a loan that was below the lender's estimated actual cost to complete the construction.

On similar facts, in Brown v. St. Paul Title Insurance Corp., 634 F.2d 1103 (1980), the Eighth Circuit, reversing the lower court, held the lender had "created" or "suffered" mechanics' liens within the 3(a) exclusion by failing to provide adequate funds to pay for work completed prior to developer's default on the loan. "While [the insured] admittedly was under no obligation to continue the project after default, it seems clear that the parties contemplated the insured would provide adequate funds to pay for work completed prior to the default." In a Sixth Circuit case, American Savings & Loan Assn. v. Lawyers' Title Insurance Corp., 793 F.2d 780 (1986), a title company refused to pay to the construction lender the dollar amounts of prior mechanics' liens, and the appellate court held in favor of the lender on the ground that the lender had not suffered or assumed the risk of future mechanics' liens by not financing the entire cost of construction. How did the Sixth Circuit Court of Appeals distinguish the *Brown* and *Bankers Trust* cases? Do you agree with the Sixth Circuit's reasoning?

7. *Additional Protection for the Construction Lender: Bonding and Lien Waivers.* Two additional protective devices for the construction lender are labor and materials payment bonds from a surety company and lien waivers from the contractors and subcontractors.

A labor and materials payment bond will bind the bonding company, as surety, to pay the charges of subcontractors and suppliers if the general contractor fails to make these payments. The purpose is to prevent mechanics' or materialmen's liens from being filed against the property. In addition, a separate performance bond may be issued (generally both are issued for a single premium) under which the surety company agrees that if the contractor defaults the surety company will step in and complete the project in accordance with the construction contract. As you might imagine, the more the bond is needed, the less available and the more expensive it will be, and a requirement for such bonding in a lender's proposed commitment will almost certainly be resisted by the prospective borrower. Perhaps because of this, the bonding approach has not been widely used in the real estate construction industry. Bonding is not only used for protection against mechanics' liens; it is also a device used by lenders to assure themselves that the project will be completed. See Chapter 6B4b, infra.

Waivers of liens by contractors and subcontractors are used extensively with dramatic differences in effect, depending on which jurisdiction's law applies. Generally, a waiver prior to each disbursement by a contractor, subcontractor, or materialman of a lien for work already performed will be enforceable. See Nelson and Whitman §12.4, at 867. The logistics of this can be complicated. The general contractor will provide a sworn list of subcontractors and materialmen prior to each disbursement. The contractor, subcontractors, and materialmen will then execute waivers indicating that they have been fully paid for work thus far performed. Armed with the waivers, the construction lender will then make the disbursement.

It would be much easier if the waiver would cover not only work performed or materials supplied up to the date of the waiver but also all work or materials to be performed or furnished in the future. Then only one waiver would need to be obtained from the contractor and each subcontractor or materialman. However, prospective waivers are void as against public policy in many jurisdictions, and in some of the jurisdictions where such waivers are valid they are construed rather strictly by the courts. See, e.g., Boise Cascade Corp. v. Stephens, 572 P.2d 1380 (Utah 1977).

In some states a provision in a construction contract (or in a separate agreement between the contractor and the developer that waives any rights to liens on the property) is valid against subcontractors or materialmen if the contract is executed and recorded before performance by any subcontractor or materialman. In other states, it may be valid only against the contractor and those subcontractors or materialmen who have specifically agreed to be bound thereby. See Nelson and Whitman §12.4, at 866-867. Obviously, lien waivers can be a very cumbersome form of protection in many jurisdictions, but they may, in many cases, be the best protection available to the lender.

If you represented FNB in its construction loan on Dan Developer's property, and it was decided to require both a payment and a performance bond, what would you ask for to make sure that FNB would be able to get the benefit of these bonds on default by Dan Developer? For a general discussion of the rights of the developer and lender vis-a-vis the bonding company, see Comment, Mechanics' Liens and Surety Bonds in the Building Trades, 68 Yale L.J. 138 (1958).

Section 3262 of the California Civil Code provides: "Neither the owner nor original contractor by any term of their contract, or otherwise, shall waive, affect, or impair the claims and liens of other persons whether with or without notice except by their written consent, and any term of the contract to that effect shall be null and void." Assume that Dan Developer's building will be built in California and that you represent the construction lender. Realizing that under §3262 the general contractor cannot waive liens for the subcontractors, your commitment requires that prior to each disbursement a waiver must be obtained from each subcontractor to the effect that the subcontractor has been fully paid to that date.

After construction is completed, a plumbing subcontractor asserts a mechanics' lien and brings suit, claiming that while the waiver signed by the plumber acknowledged full payment, only about half that amount had actually been disbursed to the plumber. The plumber claims that no lien rights were impaired by the signed waiver because the contract provision requiring waivers violated Civil Code §3262. Appalled, you argue that the statute merely prohibits the general contractor and Dan from attempting by agreement to waive other people's rights, but nothing in the statute prohibits a subcontractor from executing its own lien waiver. Who wins? See Bentz Plumbing & Heating v. Favaloro, 128 Cal. App. 3d 145, 180 Cal. Rptr. 223 (3d Dist. 1982). If the plumber wins, how can you protect your client against mechanics' liens? Suppose you advise that each disbursement be in the form of joint checks to pay for each subcontractor's work. Will the subcontractors' endorsement on the check pass muster under §3262 barring the sub from later claiming that payment in full had not been received?

4. Assurance of Completion

To review: the construction lender's real security for its loan is usually the commitment issued by a postconstruction lender, which will "take out," or pay off, the construction loan. The one condition to the postconstruction lender's obligation to fund the postconstruction loan common to all postconstruction loan commitments is that the building must be completed in accordance with the approved plans and specifications.

Thus, assurance of completion in accordance with the approved plans and specifications is key to the construction lender's hope for a take out of its loan. Returning to our hypothetical situation, what steps would be necessary or appropriate for FNB to take to help assure itself that Ace will have no excuse for extricating itself from the postconstruction loan commitment? See Chapter 6B2, supra. In this section we will consider two major protective devices.

a. Lender's Approval of Contractors' Building Contract and Architects

If the construction lender contemplates that the construction contract will be approved (and, with it, the contractor) prior to the execution of the construction loan agreement, the construction loan agreement would then contain a clause similar to the following.

> Both Borrower and Contractor are in full compliance with their respective obligations under the Construction Contract [defined in the agreement to mean the contract identified by date that had been reviewed by the construction lender]. The work to be performed by Contractor [defined to indicate a specific contractor who is identified by name and address] under the Construction Contract is the work called for by the Plans and Specifications [meaning the specific plans and specifications approved by the construction lender]. All work on the Project shall conform to the Plans and Specifications and shall be free of all defects. The Construction Contract shall not be amended without the prior written consent of Lender.

Similarly, the construction lender may require that the architect's contract be reviewed and approved before the construction loan agreement is executed. If so, the construction loan agreement would provide as follows.

> Both Borrower and Borrower's Architect [meaning a specific architect identified by name and address] are in full compliance with their respective obligations under the Architect's Contract [meaning a specific contract entered into on a specific date between the Borrower and the Borrower's Architect]. Borrower shall from time to time upon request by Lender cause Borrower's Architect to provide Lender with reports relative to the status of construction of the Improvements. The Architect's Contract shall not be amended without the prior written consent of Lender.

Just to make certain that nothing slips through, each disbursement pursuant to the construction loan agreement is conditioned on the approval by Lender of, inter alia, "all closing papers, Loan Documents and other matters."

Finally, the construction lender will require its approval of the construction contract between the owner-borrower and the general contractor (if the owner does not act as its own contractor). Such an agreement may be structured as: (1) a "fixed-price" contract whereby, after competitive bidding, the contractor chosen by the owner agrees to construct the improvements for a firm price; (2) a "cost-plus" contract whereby the contractor is paid for actual costs plus a fee based on a percentage of the costs; (3) a "fast-track construction" contract whereby construction commences before the plans and specifications are finalized; or (4) a "design-build" contract whereby the contractor both designs and constructs the improvements.

By way of review, why would a cautious construction lender discourage use of the fast-track format? See Chapter 5B2, note 1. Can you think of any protective strategies that a contractor might employ to protect itself against cost overruns in the case of a fixed-price contract? Can you think of any protective language that a prudent owner should insist on in the case of a cost-plus contract? Which sort of contract is most likely to be favored by the construction lender? See Symposium, Construction Management and Design-Build/Fast Track Construction, 46 L. & Contemp. Prob. 1 (Winter 1983); Goldenhersh, Essentials of Building Contracts, 13 Colo. Law. 1 (Jan. 1984).

b. Bonds; Guarantees; Letters of Credit; Insurance; Disbursement Programs

In this section we will discuss some miscellaneous devices designed to assure that the project will be completed. Perhaps the most widely known of these devices is the surety bond, under which, for a fee, the surety company purports to guarantee against unpaid claims of mechanics and materialmen and guarantee that the project will be completed on time for the contract price. A "payment bond" is one that guarantees payment of the bills of suppliers of labor and materials and is designed to reduce significantly the risk of mechanics' liens. A "performance bond" guarantees that the contractor will perform the terms and conditions of the construction contract, including completing the project for the amount set forth in the contract. Both bonds are necessary and, in the past, surety companies issued a combined form of payment and performance bond. Today, it is more likely that separate bonds will be issued, but for a single combined premium. One typical construction loan agreement contained the following provision requiring bonding.

Borrower shall obtain payment and performance bonds, in form and substance satisfactory to Lender, naming Lender as an obligee, covering the Construction Contract and such contractors and subcontractors as Lender shall have requested, true and complete copies of which, together with all amendments, supplements and modifications thereto, will have been delivered to Lender, and shall be in full force and effect, free from default, unmodified and enforceable strictly in accordance with their respective terms. Borrower will obtain such additional payment and performance bonds with respect to contracts and subcontracts for work for the Project as Lender may, from time to time, request, and will timely deliver true and complete copies thereof to Lender, in form and substance satisfactory to Lender. All such bonds shall be recorded if the recording of such bonds serves to preclude the filing of any liens.

Another area of protection is a guarantee of performance from the general contractor directly to the construction lender. The lender agrees to disburse construction advances by means of a check made payable jointly to the contractor and the borrower, thus insuring the contractor against diversion of the funds, and the contractor agrees that on default by the borrower and on demand by the lender the contractor will complete construction for the then-remaining undisbursed portion of the construction funds without personal liability by the lender under the contract.

In some cases, it is possible for the borrower to obtain a letter of credit from a bank covering part or all of the construction obligation. If it is to serve its purpose the letter of credit must be irrevocable and unconditional, with the bank obligated to pay on the tender of the sight draft. Obviously, one would have to be (or be willing to become) an important customer of the bank in order to obtain such a letter, especially if the sums involved are large, and even then it will be issued only on depositing collateral with the bank (often in the form of a certificate of deposit) equal to a substantial percentage of the letter of credit.

Even when all parties are doing their best to comply with the terms of the construction contract, casualties may occur that are beyond the control of the parties, for example, fire, windstorm, or explosion. These risks can be covered by a standard builder's "all risk" insurance policy protecting the developer, the contractor, and the lender. The "all" in "all risk" may be somewhat misleading, however. Most policies will exclude coverage for riots attending a strike, earthquake, flood, design and workmanship errors, and the like.

In the early 1970s several title companies initiated what became known as construction disbursement programs, under which the title company or its subsidiary would issue insurance guaranteeing completion of the project in accordance with the construction contract. The theory was that the title company would then supervise the disbursements and monitor construction, thus minimizing the risks normally faced by issuers of performance bonds.[15] Many of the title companies have since discontinued the program, and thus it is of only limited availability today.

At first glance the concept of bonding would appear to be an ideal completion assurance device. However, bonds are costly and often not available to contractors who do not have substantial financial strength. Secondly, where available, the bonds are usually subject to numerous defenses to payment, for example, (1) the liability of the surety may be limited to the construction described in the original construction contract for an amount of coverage geared to the original contract price, so that the surety would not be liable for design or construction changes (which are virtually inevitable); (2) losses are generally not covered if caused by matters outside the construction contract (e.g., the contract provides for a 15 percent holdback, but the loan agreement provides for only a 10 percent holdback and the developer has squandered the extra 5 percent of the construction funds) or for losses occasioned by violations of the construction contract (e.g., the developer makes payments in advance of dates specified in the construction contract); (3) where the bond covers a subcontractor, rather than the general contractor, the surety may argue that the failure to perform arose from the failure of the other subcontractors, not the bonded subcontractor; and (4) based on the so-called Los Angeles clause in some surety bonds, the surety may claim that its liability is conditional on the performance by other parties to the agreement. For example, where the project cost is $1 million, $800,000 to be supplied by the construction loan and $200,000 by the developer, the surety may claim its performance under the bond is conditioned on the developer, or, on default by the developer, the construction lender supplying the $200,000. Or, where parts of the project are being constructed by others not covered by the surety bond, the surety company may claim that the performance of the contractor was hampered or frustrated by the breach by other contractors. Or, the surety may claim that the contractor was prevented from performing because the developer delayed in approving change orders or making payments to subcontractors.

Indeed, because these bonds tend to be expensive and riddled with exculpatory provisions it has been suggested that their real importance to lenders such as FNB is the knowledge that the contractor was solvent enough to obtain the bond. See generally Hart and Kane, What Every Real Estate Lawyer Should Know About Payment and Performance Bonds, 17 Real Prop., Prob. & Tr. J. 674 (1982).

Note the last sentence of the sample bonding provision from a construction loan commitment letter. What is the probable purpose of

15. See Dwyer, New Protection for Construction Lenders, 3 Real Est. Rev. 76 (1973).

this language? How would you revise the language to better achieve this purpose?

The final protective device to assure completion of the project we will discuss is the so-called holdback requirement to "keep the loan in balance" (of the sort described in the *Equity Investors* case, excerpted at Chapter 6B3, supra). This requirement is examined in the excerpt from The Law of Real Estate Financing in the next section of this chapter.

Be aware that the various devices we have discussed for assuring completion are only as effective as the corporation, surety, bank, or other entity providing the assurance. Obviously, a contractor's guarantee is not very helpful if the contractor is virtually insolvent. Not so obvious, but just as troublesome, is the fact that some surety companies, title companies, and even banks, while completely solvent, may not be in a position to assume the significant risks associated with major real estate development construction contracts. For example, Mr. Gerald Levy, in the excerpt at Chapter 6A, supra, suggests that the surety be checked for a minimum "A" rating by A. M. Best's Key Rating Guide and that bonds not be accepted in an amount in excess of 10 percent of the surety's capital and surplus.

In representing a client relying on one of these completion assurance devices, you should recommend a thorough study not only of the financial condition of the assuring party but also of the ability of the assuring party to perform its functions under the agreement. One of the reasons title companies have been phasing out their construction disbursement programs has been the fact that they were losing money on these programs.

5. Closing the Construction Loan and Disbursement of Funds Under the Construction Loan Agreement

As discussed in the introduction to this section, the construction loan agreement is the operative document in construction financing, setting forth the rights of the parties and how and when the funds will be disbursed.

Generally, prior to each disbursement the lender will require proof that construction has commenced to the point contemplated by the agreement and that all conditions precedent to the disbursement have been complied with. See the Loan Agreement in the Documents Manual.

The sample Loan Agreement also deals with items that arise during the course of construction: inspections, defects, accounting, change orders, payment of bills, application of the loan proceeds, and the like. It also covers definitions, rights of the lender on default by the borrower, insurance, and other (largely boilerplate) provisions. Change orders are particularly sensitive, because they can lead to cost overruns. The lender will normally require that its approval be obtained for most change orders. The following excerpt explains how properly drafted construction loan agreements (or building loan agreements) can guide the construction lender's loan servicing department or loan administrator, in collaboration with the developer's architect and the title company, from the time the construction loan is closed to the day on which the construction loan will be taken out by the permanent lender.

Madison and Dwyer, The Law of Real Estate Financing
¶4.04 (1981)

[1] FUNCTION OF BUILDING LOAN AGREEMENT

The building loan agreement, unique to construction financing, identifies all of the collateral and supportive documents such as construction contracts, cost breakdowns, and payment and performance bonds. It stipulates the conditions for when and how construction is to commence, continue, and be completed. While the basic mortgage instrument secures the construction loan indebtedness and sets forth the terms and conditions of default, the building loan agreement is concerned with the day-to-day turmoil and activity encountered during the construction period. It attempts the formidable task of giving the lender control over construction, without unduly impeding its progress.

During construction and prior to any default, the building loan agreement is the operative document. Hence, counsel for lenders and developers should spend as much time reviewing and drafting this important document as they do the mortgage and note. The building loan agreement should be drafted so that it conforms to the method of construction disbursements employed by the lender, as modified by changes requested by the developer based on the characteristics of the particular project. Unfortunately, some lenders utilize methods of disbursements which, while satisfactory, are nonetheless incompatible with their standard form of building loan agreement that may have been copied from another lender's form, notwithstanding differences in their methods of disbursement.

[2] BORROWER'S INITIAL REPRESENTATIONS AND WARRANTIES

Most building loan agreements contain a warranty by the borrower-developer to the lender that the latter's loan advances will at all times be accorded lien priority over any intervening liens. However, such lien priority may depend on circumstances beyond the developer's control. For example, if under the building loan agreement the lender's discretionary authority to make loan advances is not geared to some objective criteria, such optional advances may in some states be junior in lien priority to any intervening mechanics' liens. Accordingly, reliance on this warranty by the construction lender is misplaced if it fails to utilize title insurance or some other protective device against mechanics' liens. Also, under this warranty the lender is not obligated to continue making disbursements if it cannot be assured of a first and prior lien for its loan advances, and in the so-called priority states the lender will require the developer to warrant that no work has commenced upon the land prior to the recording of the construction loan mortgage.

In addition, the developer will be required to warrant that it will commence, continue, and complete construction within stipulated time limits and in a first-class workmanlike manner, in accordance with the approved plans and specifications and in conformity with private and local law restrictions. Most lenders apply general "rule of thumb" criteria in deciding when a project should be completed (e.g., garden apartments: twelve to fourteen months; shopping centers: twelve to fourteen months); however, failure to complete construction within the stipulated period of time is a material default.[173] Indeed, during the 1973-1974 real estate shake-out, delays in construction and cost overruns were, along with monetary defaults, the most common grounds for foreclosure by construction lenders. Accordingly, in his negotiations with the construction and permanent lenders, the developer's attorney should demand realistic time limits and attempt to procure the so-called "Act of God" clause, a clause that allows for extensions in the event of strikes or other causes of delay beyond the control of the developer. However, the construction lender should resist any attempt to have this protective language inserted in its building loan agreement unless the permanent lender agrees to incorporate the same in its takeout commitment.

[3] PREDISBURSEMENT REQUIREMENTS

As each phase of construction is completed, the lender's loan administrator advances loan funds to pay for the finished work. However, he must make certain that the work conforms to the plans and specifications, that it is being done on schedule and free of mechanics'

---

173. E.g., Metropolitan Life Ins. Co. v. Hall, 10 N.Y.S. 196, 198, (1890); Emigrant Ind. Sav. Bank v. Willow Builders, 290 N.Y. 133, 145, 48 N.E.2d 293, 299 (1943).

liens, and that sufficient undisbursed loan proceeds remain to fund the remaining costs of construction. If these objectives are not met, the basic conditions of the takeout commitment will not be satisfied, and the construction lender will not be able to assign its loan to the permanent lender once the construction is completed. Although the methods employed by lenders for making disbursements vary, the following are typical of predisbursement requirements that must be met prior to each new loan advance in which the developer is not acting as the general contractor.

First, upon notification that construction has progressed to the next planned stage, the developer, after receiving the contractor's requisition for payment, will submit its formal request for payment to the construction lender. As an alternative to the "stage of completion" method of payment, the developer will request his "draws" on a monthly basis, after finishing a designated percentage of the total work to be completed under the contract. The lender will require that the request for payment be accompanied by an affidavit of the contractor that identifies all the subcontractors, indicates the nature and dollar amounts of labor and materials furnished by them to the date of the affidavit, and contains recitals by the contractor and subcontractors (partial lien waivers) to the effect that they waive their lien rights for work and materials for which they have received payments. The loan administrator or his draw inspector will then examine the dollar amounts recited in both the affidavit and lien waivers along with copies of receipted work and purchase orders. Any discrepancies are investigated to make certain that loan funds have not been improperly diverted from the subcontractors by the developer or general contractor, and the loan administrator will check the billings and lien waivers to make certain that the payments are up-to-date and in conformity with the payment schedules in the building loan agreement.

Second, prior to each loan advance, the developer's architect will inspect the work progress on the site and will match the payment request with the work completed to make certain that neither the general contractor nor the subcontractors receive payment for work that has not been done. He will also certify that the work was performed in a timely first-class manner in accordance with the previously approved plans and specifications. Many, if not most, lenders will also employ, at the developer's expense, their own draw inspectors, (licensed engineers or architects specializing in this area), to further certify these matters if the lender believes that such corroboration is necessary.

Third, after receiving the partial lien waivers, the title company will continue its search to the date of the proposed advance and will issue an endorsement to the title policy or "bring to date a letter" certifying that no liens or encumbrances have been filed against the project since the previous advance. In compliance with the lender's commitment, the building loan agreement may also require the developer to furnish a "date-down" survey to insure that the improvements are being constructed within the lot or easement lines. The title company then certifies that there are no encroachments or violations of "set back" line restrictions.

As a general rule, lenders will require between a 5 and 15 percent holdback or retainage of construction loan funds, which amount is released along with the final loan advance upon completion of the project. So, for example, a 10 percent holdback means that for each 90 cents of construction loan proceeds, the lender expects to receive performance of at least one dollar of value. However, some lenders are willing to decrease the retainage by one-half upon completion of 50 percent of the project. Many developers are also successful in having the retainage released upon completion of construction within a specific construction code instead of having to wait for completion of the entire project. In the event the developer is unable to impose holdbacks of like amounts on the contractor and subcontractors, it will be forced to fund the difference out of its own funds. In addition, prior to each loan advance, the construction lender may require that the reserves available for the completion of the improvements, whether in the form of undisbursed loan funds or the developer's equity, be sufficient to complete construction. The developer's architect is sometimes required to certify that this requirement has been met. Frequently, this predisbursement requirement will be waived by lenders, especially when the project being financed is relatively small, since such cost audits tend to be expensive and time-consuming. However, if at any time the lender discovers that these reserves have been depleted because of cost overruns, it will require the developer to deposit sufficient equity funds, which when added to the remaining balance of undisbursed loan funds, will cover the remaining cost of construction. However, in the event the lender concludes that there are sufficient funds to complete the project, and the developer objects to such a conclusion, a possible compromise would be for the parties to agree to a binding cost audit to be performed by an independent party, during which time disbursements and construction would continue. To protect the lender, the developer would be required to deposit by means of a letter of credit, cash, or a certificate of deposit, a sum sufficient to cover any deficiency amount revealed by such audit. This objective approach could also benefit the lender in the event there is a default based on a cost overrun; the existence and amount of said cost overrun would for purposes of litigation be predicated on the opinion of an independent third party.

Also, most lenders resist making any disbursements for stored materials in light of the dangers posed by possible thefts or damage caused by the elements. However, there are several avenues open for compromise, depending on the strength and the experience of the developer. For example, the lender and the developer can fix a maximum monthly dollar amount for stored materials, or can perhaps arrange a time schedule for incorporating stored materials into the project. In the event the lender does agree to fund stored on-site materials, a special endorsement to the builder's risk insurance policy for fire, damage, and theft of the stored material should be procured from the casualty company since some policies exclude such materials from coverage. Where the materials will not be stored at the project site and the lender is still willing to pay for such materials, it should insist that the materials be stored in a bonded warehouse and should carefully perfect its lien on the materials under the Uniform Commercial Code.

In addition, the building loan agreement frequently will contain a statement specifying that any request for an advance by the developer constitutes an affirmation that all of the representations and warranties made at the time the agreement was executed remain true and correct, unless the developer says otherwise. The developer must thus be very careful to review these representations at the time of each advance.

Finally, some developers, after having executed the building loan agreement, fail to take down construction advances and instead shop around for short-term credit that may be extended to them on more favorable terms on the security of the building loan agreement. To avoid this practice, construction lenders sometimes insert a clause in the loan agreement requiring the developer to pay interest on the amount of loan proceeds to which he would have been entitled on the basis of the completed construction, whether or not the loan advance is actually made, or else must provide that such a failure to take down loan funds constitutes a default.

[4] PAYMENT OF LOAN ADVANCES

When the construction loan administrator has received the report of the developer's architect, and perhaps its own inspector's affidavit as well as the updated file report, it will make the next loan advance and credit the funds to the account of either the developer (to whom the funds belong) or the general contractor, as the developer directs. As discussed earlier, loan advances can in some states be made to the title company that acts as the disbursing agent of the lender.

Frequently, the construction lender will reserve the right to make disbursement checks jointly payable to the developer and the contractor, or to the contractor and the subcontractors, or even the right to make payments directly to each subcontractor. The lender's purpose in obtaining control over the payment of disbursements is to protect itself against forged lien waivers and to forestall the improper diversion of construction loan funds from the subcontractors by either the developer or the general contractor. However, if the construction lender makes payments directly to the subcontractors, it may unwittingly become liable to the Internal Revenue Service and to the subcontractors for any unpaid or unwithheld FICA taxes.

In addition, there is case law suggesting that when a lender steps into the shoes of another party in the project, the lender must assume all of the responsibilities of that party to others and, protect the interests of the party whose prerogatives it has preempted. For example, in M.S.M. Corp. v. Knutson Co. the construction lender, bypassing the developer, made loan advances directly to the contractor and was held liable, as a fiduciary, to the developer for loan funds diverted by the lender to satisfy an unrelated debt owed to it by the contractor, even though the developer owed the contractor an amount far in excess of the diverted amounts. In so holding, the Minnesota court stated that:

> When a mortgagee undertakes to disburse funds for a mortgagor under a construction contract, a fiduciary relationship arises. Under such circumstances, the mortgagee has the duty not only to apply all of the proceeds to the use of the mortgagor without diverting them for unrelated obligations incurred by contractors or subcontractors, but also to account for all of the sums, expended on behalf of the mortgagor and to furnish adequate proof of the sums paid and the purpose of the disbursement.[185]

Likewise, in Fulmer Building Supplies, Inc. v. Martin[186] a construction lender, to protect its loan funds, bypassed the developer and made loan payments directly to the contractor even though the subcontractors, as holders of mechanics' liens, were first entitled to payment. After the contractor failed to pay the subcontractors, the subcontractors sued the lender for the amount of the diverted funds and the lender defended on the ground that the South Carolina statute automatically confers lien priority for all construction loan advances. The court, holding in favor of the subcontractors, stated:

> When the mortgagee assumed absolute control of the disbursement of the proceeds of the construction loan, it occupied the same position as the owner with respect to the duties and obligations imposed by statute as to the payment of the remaining funds after the perfection of the mechanic's lien.

---

185. 283 Minn. 527, 529, 167 N.W.2d 66, 68 (1969) (per curiam). Implicit in the court's decision is the analogy to a mortgagee in possession who must account to the mortgagor for the rentals and other income earned from the property.
186. 251 S.C. 353, 360, 162 S.E.2d 541, 544 (1968).

[5]   COST OVERRUNS AND OTHER CHANGES DURING CONSTRUCTION PERIOD

Both the construction and permanent lenders' determination of the loan amount and value of the security is based in part on a careful examination of the plans and specifications submitted by the developer's architect. Therefore, the construction lender will require its approval of any change order that provides for extra work or materials, or alters the plans and specifications in a manner that could result in additional costs or in a significant change in the improvements. Ordinarily, these change orders must be approved by the architect and the lender's draw inspector or supervising engineer, and then examined for adherence to proper construction standards and existing building codes. A prudent construction lender should also require the consent of the bonding company. Any significant changes should also be approved by the permanent lender inasmuch as such approval is required under the terms of its takeout commitment. In addition, if the lender consents to any such change order, it may require the developer to deposit additional equity funds to cover any extras or cost overruns. During the 1973-1974 real estate shake-out, if construction lenders had more carefully monitored their disbursements under this language in the building loan agreement, many of the cost overruns by defaulting developers would have been prevented.

If, however, a change order produces a cost overrun on a particular item, the developer may be able to avoid an additional cash outlay if the construction lender is willing to reallocate funds from other items listed in the cost breakdown or (if the developer is not the contractor) in the construction contract so that the net change will not result in additional dollar requirements beyond those committed by the construction lender. The building loan agreement will list by code categories loan funds earmarked to pay both hard construction costs ("construction funds") and soft nonconstruction costs such as construction period interest, hazard insurance premiums and architect's fees ("non-construction funds"). Most construction lenders treat construction loan interest as a fundable soft cost during the construction period and will disburse loan funds to the developer so that it can remit these amounts back to the lender as interest payments. However, a prudent construction lender should demand the right to discontinue such disbursements for soft costs such as construction period interest and should reserve the right to reallocate such funds toward the payment of hard construction cost overruns. Otherwise, if the developer is not required to fund the interest payments with nonloan sources, a loan headed for default could be artificially kept alive and further jeopardize the lender's ability to recoup its loan investment. Moreover, unless the building loan agreement specifies that the obligation of the developer to make interest payments is not predicated upon the disbursement of these funds by the lender, the developer could argue that such failure to fund under the interest code would force them into default and would thus constitute a breach of contract by the lender.

Throughout construction of the project, tempers on occasion flare, disputes arise, and developers in their off-moments sometimes want to fire their once-favorite architect or contractor, or even give up on the project and convey it to a third party. However, during construction, lenders usually take a very dim view of any proposed changes other than those that relate to the actual completion of construction. The lender naturally prefers that the architect who drafted the plans and specifications supervise the construction on behalf of the developer, since someone who has a first-hand familiarity with the plans and specifications is always in a better position to have them implemented. Moreover, any contractor who is thrown off the job-site during a dispute may hold up construction by filing a lien on the project or by not relinquishing the building permits. Consequently, the lender will insist upon a high degree of control if any of the foregoing types of changes are proposed by the developer.

[6] THE FINAL LOAN ADVANCE

Prior to the final loan advance, the construction loan administrator will require the following: (1) a final lien waiver from the contractor and subcontractors covering all labor and materials furnished or to be furnished so that no liens may be claimed for follow-up repairs or for the replacement of defective materials that may become necessary in the future; (2) a certificate of substantial completion executed by the developer's architect and, in some cases, by the lender's draw inspector or supervising engineer as well, along with certificates of occupancy indicating that the construction and use of the improvements comply with all zoning and other local law regulations; (3) all the necessary approvals required by state and federal regulatory agencies; and (4) where there is a permanent takeout, a letter from the permanent lender stating that the improvements have been properly constructed and that its takeout commitment is still in force and effect. Where the project is a shopping center, the lender should also condition its final advance on acceptance of the premises by the major tenants. . . .

PLANNING PROBLEM

In light of the discussion at Chapter 6A, note 1 and Chapter 6B, supra, examine the sample construction loan agreement in the Student

Manual and, as counsel to the construction lender Fuller National Bank, advise your client as to whether the provisions therein provide adequate protection against the possibility of mechanics' liens, a failure on Dan Developer's part to complete construction, and the other major risks associated with construction financing.

6. The Construction Lender's Liability to Third Parties

When things go wrong, parties who thereby suffer financial loss are apt to look around for someone to sue. And when things go wrong in construction, it is normally the construction lender who has the deep pocket. The irony is that the more the construction lender injects itself into the business of the construction in order to assure itself that the construction will be done properly in accordance with the postconstruction lender's takeout commitment, the greater the construction lender's exposure to potential liability when problems arise. It is not surprising, then, that numerous attempts have been made to seek compensation from the construction lender on a variety of legal theories. One of the most famous of these cases is the *Connor* case, which dealt with the potential liability of a lender who had the right to approve plans and specifications and inspect the construction.

Connor v. Great Western Savings & Loan Assn.

69 Cal. 2d 850, 73 Cal. Rptr. 369, 447 P.2d 609 (1968)

TRAYNOR, Chief Justice.

These consolidated appeals are from a judgment of nonsuit in favor of defendant Great Western Savings and Loan Association in two actions consolidated for trial.

Plaintiffs in each action purchased single-family homes in a residential tract development known as Weathersfield, located on tracts 1158, 1159, and 1160 in Ventura County. Thereafter their homes suffered serious damage from cracking caused by ill-designed foundations that could not withstand the expansion and contraction of adobe soil. Plaintiffs accordingly sought rescission or damages from the various parties involved in the tract development. . . .

There was abundant evidence that defendant Conejo Valley Development Company, which built and sold the homes, negligently

H/ Bank liable in negligence for forseeable harm to persons not in privity (buyers) for failure to exercise reas. power of control to prevent construct. of defect homes

constructed them without regard to soil conditions prevalent at the site. . . .

In addition to seeking damages from Conejo, plaintiffs sought to hold Great Western liable, either on the ground that its participation in the tract development brought it into a joint venture or a joint enterprise with Conejo, which served to make it vicariously liable, or on the ground that it breached an independent duty of care to plaintiffs. . . .

Great Western agreed to make the necessary construction loans to Conejo only after assuring itself that the homes could be successfully built and sold. During the negotiations on the terms of the contemplated construction loans to Conejo and the long-term loans to be offered to the buyers of homes in the proposed development, Great Western investigated Goldberg's financial condition and learned that it was weak. Moreover, Great Western received, without comment or inquiry, an August 1959 financial statement from Conejo that set forth capital of $325,000, of which $320,000 was accounted for as estimated profits from the sales of homes when the sales transactions, then in escrow, were completed. Such an entry was far outside the bounds of generally accepted accounting principles. The estimated profits, representing 64/65 of the total purported capital, were not only hypothetical, but were hypothesized on the basis of houses that had not yet been constructed.

Great Western delved no deeper into the proposed foundations of the houses than into the conjectural bases of Conejo's capital. It did require Conejo to submit plans and specifications for the various models of homes to be built, cost breakdowns, a list of proposed subcontractors and the type of work each was to perform, and a schedule of proposed prices. Conejo, which at no time employed an architect, purchased plans and specifications from a Mr. L. C. Majors that he had prepared for other developments, and submitted them to Great Western.

Great Western departed from its normal procedure of reviewing and approving plans and specifications before making a commitment to provide construction funds. It did not examine the foundation plans and did not make any recommendations as to the design or construction of the houses. It was preoccupied with selling prices and sales. It suggested increases in Goldberg's proposed selling prices, which he accepted. It also refused any formal commitment of funds to Conejo until a specified number of houses were pre-sold, namely, sold before they were constructed. . . .

When Conejo sold the lots, its sales agents informed the buyers that Great Western was willing to make long-terms secured by first trust deeds to approved persons, and obtained credit information for later submission to Great Western. This procedure was dictated by the right of first refusal that Conejo agreed to give Great Western to obtain the construction loans. If an approved buyer wished to obtain a long-term loan elsewhere, Great Western had 10 days to meet the terms of the proposed financing; if it met the terms and the loan was not placed with Great Western, Goldberg, Brown, and South Gate were required to pay Great Western the fees and interest obtained by the other lender in connection with the loan. Most of the buyers of homes in the Weathersfield tract applied to Great Western for loans. They obtained approximately 80 percent of the purchase price in the form of 24-year loans from Great Western at 6.6 percent interest secured by first trust deeds. Great Western charged Conejo a 1 percent fee for loans made to qualified buyers, and a 1½ percent fee for loans made to Conejo on behalf of buyers who, in Great Western's opinion, were poor risks.

By September, the specified number of houses had been reserved by buyers, and Great Western accordingly made approximately $3,000,000 in construction loans to Conejo. Conejo agreed to pay Great Western a 5 percent construction loan fee and 6.6 percent interest on the construction loans as disbursed for six months and thereafter on the entire amount. . . .

A subcontractor employed by Conejo began grading the property before Great Western made a final commitment to provide construction loan funds, and while Great Western still nominally owned the land. During the course of construction, Great Western's inspectors visited the property weekly to verify that the pre-packaged plans were being followed and that money was disbursed only for work completed. Under the loan agreement, if construction work did not conform to plans and specifications, Great Western had the right to withhold disbursement of funds until the work was satisfactorily performed; failure to correct a nonconformity within 15 days constituted a default. Representatives of Great Western remained in constant communication with the developers of the Weathersfield tract until all the houses were completed and sold in mid-1960.

The evidence establishes without conflict that there was no express agreement either written or oral creating a joint venture or joint enterprise relationship between Great Western and Conejo or Goldberg. Without exception the testimony of the principal witnesses discloses specific disclaimers of all intention that any such relationship should exist, and the written documents provided only for typical option and purchase agreements and loan and security terms.

A joint venture exists when there is "an agreement between the parties under which they have a community of interest, that is, a joint interest, in a common business undertaking, and understanding as to the sharing of profits and losses, and a right of joint control." . . . Although the evidence establishes that Great Western and Conejo combined their property, skill, and knowledge to carry out the tract development, that each shared in the control of the development, that each anticipated receiving substantial profits therefrom, and that they cooperated with each other in the development, there is no evidence of a community or joint interest in the undertaking. Great Western participated as a buyer and seller of land and lender of funds, and Conejo participated as a builder and seller of homes. Although the profits of each were dependent on the overall success of the development, neither was to share in the profits or the losses that the other might realize or suffer. Although each received substantial payments as seller, lender, or borrower, neither had an interest in the payments received by the other. Under these circumstances, no joint venture existed. . . .

Even though Great Western is not vicariously liable as a joint venturer for the negligence of Conejo, there remains the question of its liability for its own negligence. Great Western voluntarily undertook business relationships with South Gate and Conejo to develop the Weathersfield tract and to develop a market for the tract houses in which prospective buyers would be directed to Great Western for their financing. In undertaking these relationships, Great Western became much more than a lender content to lend money at interest on the security of real property. It became an active participant in a home construction enterprise. It had the right to exercise extensive control of the enterprise. Its financing, which made the enterprise possible, took on ramifications beyond the domain of the usual money lender. It received not only interest on its construction loans, but also substantial fees for making them, a 20 percent capital gain for "warehousing" the land, and protection from loss of profits in the event individual home buyers sought permanent financing elsewhere.

Since the value of the security for the construction loans and thereafter the security for the permanent financing loans depended on the construction of sound homes, Great Western was clearly under a duty of care to its shareholders to exercise its powers of control over the enterprise to prevent the construction of defective homes. Judged by the standards governing nonsuits, it negligently failed to discharge that duty. It knew or should have known that the developers were inexperienced, undercapitalized, and operating on a dangerously thin capitalization. It therefore knew or should have known that damage from attempts to cut corners in construction was a risk reasonably to be foreseen. (See Lefcoe & Dobson, Savings Associations as Land Developers (1966) 75 Yale L.J. 1271, 1293.) It knew or should have known of the expansive soil problems, and yet it failed to require soil tests, to examine foundation plans, to recommend changes in the pre-packaged plans and specifications, or to recommend changes in the foundations during construction. It made no attempt to discover gross structural defects that it could have discovered by reasonable inspection and that it would have required Conejo to remedy. It relied for protection solely upon building inspectors with whom it had had no experience to enforce a building code with the provisions of which it was ignorant. The crucial question remains whether Great Western also owed a duty to the home buyers in the Weathersfield tract and was therefore also negligent toward them."

The fact that Great Western was not in privity of contract with any of the plaintiffs except as a lender does not absolve it of liability for its own negligence in creating an unreasonable risk of harm to them. . . . The basic tests for determining the existence of such a duty are clearly set forth in Biakanja v. Irving, supra, 49 Cal. 2d 647, 650, 320 P.2d 16, 19, as follows: "The determination whether in a specific case the defendant will be held liable to a third person not in privity is a matter of policy and involves the balancing of various factors, among which are [1] the extent to which the transaction was intended to affect the plaintiff, [2] the foreseeability of harm to him, [3] the degree of certainty that the plaintiff suffered injury, [4] the closeness of the connection between the defendant's conduct and the injury suffered, [5] the moral blame attached to the defendant's conduct, and [6] the policy of preventing future harm."

In the light of the foregoing tests Great Western was clearly under a duty to the buyers of the homes to exercise reasonable care to protect them from damages caused by major structural defects. . . .

Great Western contends that lending institutions have relied on an assumption of nonliability and hence that a rule imposing liability should operate prospectively only. In the past, judicial decisions have been limited to prospective operation when they overruled earlier decisions upon which parties had reasonably relied and when considerations of fairness and public policy precluded retroactive effect. . . . Conceivably such a limitation might also be justified when there appeared to be a general consensus that there would be no extension of liability. Such is not the case here. At least since MacPherson v. Buick Motor Co. (1916) 217 N.Y. 382, 111 N.E. 1050, there has been a steady expansion of liability for harm caused by the failure of defendants to exercise reasonable care to protect others from reasonably foreseeable risks. (See generally Prosser, The Law of Torts (3d ed. 1964), ch. 19.) By the time of the decision in Sabella v. Wisler (1963), 59 Cal. 2d 21, 27 Cal. Rptr. 689, 377 P.2d 889, such liability had been imposed on a builder who negligently constructed a seriously defective home. . . . Those in the business of financing tract builders could therefore reasonably foresee the possibility that they might be under a duty to exercise their power over tract developments to protect home buyers from seriously defective construction. Moreover, since the value of their own security depends on the construction of sound homes, they have always been under a duty to their shareholders to exercise reasonable care to prevent the construction of defective homes. Given that traditional duty of care, a lending institution should have been farsighted enough to make such provisions for potential liability as would enable it to withstand the effects of a decision of normal retrospective effect.

Great Western contends finally that the negligence of Conejo in constructing the homes and the negligence of the county building inspectors in approving the construction were superseding causes that insulate it from liability. Conejo's negligence could not be a superseding cause, for the risk that it might occur was the primary hazard that gave rise to Great Western's duty. . . . The negligence of the building inspectors, confined as it was to inspection, could not serve to diminish, let alone spirit away, the negligence of the lender. Great Western's duty to plaintiffs was to exercise reasonable care to protect them from seriously defective construction whether caused by defective plans, defective inspection, or both, and its argument that there was a superseding cause of the harm "is answered by the settled rule that two separate acts of negligence may be the concurring proximate causes of an injury. . . .

[J]udgment is reversed.

PETERS, TOBRINER and SULLIVAN, JJ., concur.

MOSK, Justice (dissenting).

I dissent. . . .

At the threshold, it would be helpful to review some elementary economic factors and relationships that appear to be involved in this proceeding.

The function of the entrepreneur in a free market is to discern what goods or services are in apparent demand and to gather and arrange the factors of production in order to supply to the consumer, at a profit, the goods and services desired. In so doing, the entrepreneur undertakes a number of risks. The demand may be less than he calculated; the costs of production may be greater. He is not only in danger of losing his own capital investment but he incurs obligations to the suppliers of land, materials, labor and capital, and he stands liable under now-accepted principles of law for harm and loss caused by defects in his products to those persons injured thereby.

The entrepreneur undertakes these calculated risks in the hope of an ultimate substantial monetary reward resulting from the return over and above his costs, which include not only land, materials and labor but the charges incurred in obtaining capital. Indeed, "profit" has been commonly understood to be the return above expenses to innovators or entrepreneurs as the reward for their innovation and enterprise. (People ex rel. Farnum v. San Francisco Savings Union (1887), 72 Cal. 199, 202-203, 13 P. 498.) The upper limit of the entrepreneur's profit is determined by his success in the market, and this results from his skill in assessing the demand for his product and his minimizing losses through skillful production.

CONEJO VALLEY DEVELOPMENT COMPANY AND
ASSOCIATED PARTIES WERE ENTREPRENEURS.

The role of the supplier of capital is entirely different. The lender, as a supplier of capital, is to receive by contract a fixed return or price for his investment. He owns no right to participate in the profits of the enterprise no matter how great they may be. On the other hand, he is insulated from the risk of loss of capital and interest in return for making his money available, other than the risk of nonpayment of the contract obligations. Indeed, it is elementary that the owner of money lends it to an entrepreneur and receives only a fixed return, rather than obtaining the gain from using the money himself as an entrepreneur, on the condition that he be relieved of risk. The basic, underlying risk in mortgage lending is that the lender might not get back what is owed to him in principal and interest.

It seems abundantly clear, both legally and logically, that if the lender has no opportunity to share in the profits or gains beyond the fixed return for his supplying of capital, i.e., if he has no chance of reaping the entrepreneur's reward and exercises no control over the entrepreneur's business, elementary fairness requires that he should not be subjected to the entrepreneur's risks.

GREAT WESTERN SAVINGS AND LOAN
ASSOCIATION WAS A LENDER, A SUPPLIER
OF CAPITAL.

Great Western's position, as indicated above, was no different from that of any other lender: it had no contractual or statutory right to conduct the operations of the builder-borrower. Even if it were to be established that Great Western was negligent in its duty to its own shareholders by extending loans to a builder of dubious competence, this did not set in motion the subsequent relationship of the builder to the third parties, and the builder's superseding negligence insulates Great Western from liability for whatever negligence resulted from merely lending money. "If the accident would have happened anyway, whether defendant was negligent or not, then his negligence was not a cause in fact, and of course cannot be the legal or responsible cause." (2 Witkin, Summary of Cal. Law (1960) Torts, §284, p. 1484.) . . .

BURKE, Justice (dissenting). . . .

Cal. Civ. Code

**§3434. LIABILITY OF LENDER FINANCING
DESIGN, MANUFACTURE,
CONSTRUCTION, REPAIR,
MODIFICATION OR IMPROVEMENT OF
REAL OR PERSONAL PROPERTY**

A lender who makes a loan of money, the proceeds of which are used or may be used by the borrower to finance the design, manufacture, construction, repair, modification or improvement of real or personal property for sale or lease to others, shall not be held liable to third persons for any loss or damage occasioned by any defect in the real or personal property so designed, manufactured, constructed, repaired, modified or improved or for any loss or damage resulting from the failure of the borrower to use due care in the design, manufacture, construction, repair, modification or improvement of such real or personal property, unless such loss or damage is a result of an act of the lender outside the scope of the activities of a lender of money or unless the lender has been a party to misrepresentations with respect to such real or personal property.

NOTES AND QUESTIONS

1. *Theories of Liability. Connor* dealt with potential liability of the construction lender for negligence. Under what other legal theories could the action have been brought? See Ferguson, Lender's Liability for Construction Defects, 11 Real Est. L.J. 310 (1983). Other interesting articles in this area include: Pfeiler, Construction Lending and Products Liability, 25 Bus. Law. 1309 (1970); Pfeiler, Lender's Liability in Tract Financing, Legal Bull. 85 (March 1969); Comment, Lenders Who Voluntarily Assume a Right of Control over Developers May Be Liable to Home Buyers for Damages that Could Have Been Prevented by a Reasonable Exercise of Control, 6 Houston L. Rev. 580 (1969); Comment, Torts — Lender Liability for Defects in Home Construction, 73 Dick. L. Rev. 730 (1969); and Comment, The Expanding Scope of Enterprise Liability, 69 Colum. L. Rev. 1084 (1969).

Most cases dealing with lender's liability are concerned with liability for construction defects, but if it is determined that a lender is liable for construction defects, could not the same theories be applied to make the lender liable for other things as well? For example, if the construction lender carelessly misjudges the ability of the borrower to complete the project with the construction loan plus contemplated equity or postconstruction advances, has the lender, an expert in construction financing, breached some duty owed to the borrower, prospective tenants, or contract vendees? In Kinner v. World Saving & Loan Assn., 57 Cal. App. 3d 724, 129 Cal. Rptr. 400 (2d Dist. 1976), the borrower made such an argument, claiming that once the lender agreed to make a construction loan it had the obligation to the borrower to lend funds sufficient to complete the proposed construction project. The court rejected this argument, but the borrower had the hurdle of having to argue that California Civil Code §3434 was applicable only to physical defects, an argument the court did not accept.

It is fairly clear that currently the *Connor* case and extensions of the doctrine to other areas have not received much support. However, a future case involving substantial recklessness or covert complicity by a construction lender could lead to decisions that might arouse what is now a sleeping dog. If the *Connor* doctrine should ever be resuscitated, would you, as counsel to a construction lender, caution your client against using broad-based language of the sort contained in the construction loan agreement at issue in *Equity Investors,* excerpted at Chapter 6B3, supra? If so, why?

In *Connor,* Judge Mosk in his dissent seemed to rely heavily on the fact that Great Western did not participate in the profit from the enterprise. Why should this matter? Do you think Judge Mosk would have dissented if Great Western had been granted the right to interest based on gross income? Net income?

2. *Self-exculpation.* Observe that the sample construction loan agreement in the Documents Manual provides that, with respect to inspections by the construction lender "[t]he right of inspection is solely for the benefit of Lender. Borrower acknowledges and confirms that neither Lender nor its representatives, employees or agents shall be deemed in any way responsible for any matters related to design or construction of the Project. This section shall not be deemed to impose upon Lender any obligation to undertake such inspections or any liability for failure to detect or failure to act with respect to any defect which was or might have been disclosed by such inspections." How effective do you think such a clause is in avoiding *Connor*-type liability? If it is not effective, why is it used?

Section 3434 of the California Civil Code purports to overrule *Connor.* Does it?

3. *"Drafting Around" Liability.* See the discussion of Fulmer Building Supplies v. Martin, 251 S.C. 353, 162 S.E.2d 541 (1968), in the excerpt by Madison and Dwyer at Chapter 6B5, supra. In M.S.M. Corp. v. Knutson Co., 283 Minn. 527, 167 N.W.2d 66 (1969), the

court went even further and found the construction lender accountable to the borrower for the proper disbursement of funds. In that case, the lender diverted some of the construction funds to pay a collateral debt owed by the contractor to the lender.

In holding against the lender, the court in a per curiam decision held that "when a mortgagee undertakes to disburse funds for a mortgagor under a construction contract, a fiduciary relationship arises." The construction lender, according to the court, had a duty not only to refrain from diverting funds to "unrelated obligations" but also "to account for all the sums expended on behalf of the mortgagor and to furnish adequate proof of the amount paid and the purpose of the disbursement." Do you think the latter requirement may impose too heavy a burden on construction lenders? Suppose you represent the construction lender. Is there any language you can insert in the construction loan agreement that would mitigate the effects of the *M.S.M.* decision? Would that type of language help in the *Fulmer* situation? If not, what if anything could be done to reduce the lender's risk without sacrificing control?

4. *Liability of the Postconstruction Lender.* Certainly the construction lender is the lender that plays the greater role in the construction process and therefore is more susceptible to liability when the roof (literally) falls in. Does this mean that if you were to represent Ace Insurance Company, the postconstruction lender in our hypothetical, you do not have to worry about liability to third parties for construction and other defects? Didn't you carefully condition Ace's obligations on prior approval by Ace and its architects of the plans and specifications? Didn't you provide for inspection by Ace's inspecting architect to see that the building is completed in accordance with the approved plans and specifications? Did Ace know, or should Ace have known, that the building wouldn't withstand a small earthquake, that defective wiring was being installed, that the windows would fall out? What was Ace's duty, if any, to third parties? Are Ace's responsibilities any different than the construction lender's?

PART III

SPECIAL FINANCING TECHNIQUES

In Part II we observed how a typical real estate developer is able to fund the construction or purchase of income-producing real estate by obtaining an ordinary fee mortgage on the land and improvements. This background will aid you in understanding the creative financing techniques (along with their legal underpinnings) that can make real estate financing so challenging.

So far we have been examining the use of straightforward fee mortgage financing. Sometimes, however, a developer such as Dan may choose to fund the cost of the land and improvements in some other way. For example, as explained in Chapter 7, when the supply of mortgage money is tight Dan might decide not to seek straight debt financing but instead to use some form of equity financing such as a convertible mortgage or joint venture agreement. This will enable Dan to secure more favorable loan terms than would be available under an ordinary mortgage arrangement, but Dan must be willing to share his ownership and control over the property with some institutional lender such as Ace Insurance Company. Or perhaps Dan and his investors will elect to use a subordinated purchase-money mortgage or some form of leasehold mortgage or "split" financing (e.g., sale-and-leaseback of land only plus a leasehold mortgage) to separately finance the cost or use of the land in order to reduce their initial cash outlay and increase their rate of return on their cash investment in the project. See Chapter 9B, note 5a, Chapter 8A, and Chapter 8B1, note 2.

At this juncture, we have finally arrived at the end of the real estate lending cycle: the project has been completed. Assuming that the project is successful (or "on stream," as they say) and is now worth $40 million and that the amortization payments have scaled down the principal balance on the Ace mortgage from $25 million to $20 million,

Dan and his investors may decide to translate some of their accumulated equity (equal to the $20 million of net value) in the project into tax-free cash by means of a second mortgage (e.g., a wraparound mortgage) or simply by substituting a new, larger first mortgage for the existing one held by Ace (and thereby "refinancing" the Ace mortgage). These topics are covered at Chapter 9A and Chapter 9B, respectively.

Prior to the Tax Reform Act of 1986, the project ordinarily would be sold once its tax shelter potential had "burned out" (the seventh full year in Example 1 in the excerpt by Madison and Dwyer at Chapter 2B). Now, in deciding when to sell, business and economic factors will predominate over tax considerations. After briefly weighing the feasibility of a tax-free exchange (discussed at Chapter 9D, note 1) Dan most likely will decide to sell the real estate and possibly start the financing cycle anew by using the net sale proceeds to construct or purchase another piece of income-producing real estate. In such event the matters examined in Chapter 3 dealing with contracts and conveyancing would become a postfinancing consideration rather than a prefinancing one. Alternatively, Dan and his investors could keep the real estate but use a sale-and-leaseback of the land and improvements as a way of cashing out their equity and depreciating the land underlying the building under the guise of making leaseback-rental payments. See Chapter 8B.

In addition to the foregoing, at Chapter 9D we will be examining some additional high-ratio financing techniques, such as tax-exempt bond financing, high-credit lease financing, and zero coupon mortgage financing. Many of these special real estate financing techniques are designed to achieve 100 percent (or more) financing for Dan and his investors, and for developers " 'tis such stuff that dreams are made of."

Chapter 7

Equity Financing

It was not very long ago that a real estate developer such as Dan Developer could approach a postconstruction lender such as Ace Insurance Company and obtain a fixed-rate self-amortizing mortgage loan on improved real estate with a loan term as long as 30 or 35 years. However, as explained in the excerpt by Brian Strum at Chapter 7A, infra, because of unanticipated fluctuations in the business cycle and the resultant volatility in interest rates over the past two decades, postconstruction lenders have become cautious about making long-term loan commitments. During the 1979-1981 period of double-digit inflation and interest rates, postconstruction lenders were saddled with mortgage portfolios comprised of long-term loans with below-market interest rates. While their operating expenses were escalating because of inflation, the loans were being repaid in cheaper dollars and were not being prepaid (by refinancings), so the funds were not becoming available to the lenders for reinvestment at market rates.

In particular, thrift organizations were caught in an earnings squeeze between depositors demanding market rates of return on their deposits and borrowers paying below-market rates on their loans. In the case of life insurance companies, group and pension fund customers demanded market returns on their investments while policyholders were able to borrow on their policies at artificially low rates and reinvest those funds at market rates.

As a consequence, postconstruction lenders vowed "never again" to relive this painful experience and began to fashion debt investment vehicles that would be more responsive to changing market conditions and provide safer hedges against inflation. Loan terms were shortened and rates were raised. But concern with possible future surges in inflation and the natural limits on the willingness and ability of borrowers to pay increased interest rates caused insurance companies, as well as other postconstruction lenders, to develop a number of "creative financing" devices designed to yield returns more consistent with changing market conditions.

Some of these were loans indexed to actual inflation or geared to the value or economic performance of the property financed by the

667

loan. With the development of creative financing investments such as shared appreciation mortgages and the increased use of contingent interest provisions based on rental streams and sales or profits, lenders began to move from the debt end toward the equity end of the debt-equity spectrum illustrated in Table 5-2 at Chapter 5B3. While conventional postconstruction financing required the lender to consider the soundness and stability of the project being financed in order to feel comfortable that the loan would be repaid, the new loan structures involved the lender much more deeply and intimately with the kinds of risks and rewards experienced by an equity owner. The etiology of these equity aspects to mortgage lending is discussed in the excerpt by Strum. In this section we will focus on financing arrangements whereby the lender potentially or initially assumes the position of a true equity owner of the real estate being financed.

While the shift toward the equity end of the debt-equity spectrum was motivated in large part by a desire of lenders to hedge against the effects of inflation and interest rate increases, when inflation and interest rate increases eased it became apparent that these new financing devices had effected a fundamental change in attitudes that would have a profound impact on current and future financing practices. As a result, financing has moved light years away from the diet of long-term fixed-rate loans so prevalent a few decades ago into an era of flexibility that permits the structuring of real estate investment vehicles to meet a wide range of business and legal objectives. However, the path to the formation of such vehicles is beset by novel and complex legal concerns for both lender-investor and debtor-developer that will be addressed in this chapter.[1]

A.   CONVERTIBLE MORTGAGES

In the master hypothetical problem at Chapter 5B, Dan Developer expects to obtain a $25 million postconstruction loan from Ace Insurance Company. Assume, however, that economic analysts are forecasting rampant inflation and an upsurge in long-term interest rates. Further assume that both Ace and Dan are concerned that at current market rental rates the property in question will not be able to generate sufficient rental income, at least in the early years, to cover the projected debt-service payments on the mortgage. Consequently, Dan offers Ace a

1. See generally Wiggin, How Financing Works, 11 Real Est. Rev. 22 (Summer 1981).

partnership interest in the venture in exchange for a below-market interest rate on the loan. While Ace might believe that such an equity-sharing arrangement would be an effective hedge against inflation, it is hesitant to assume the risks associated with the construction and start-up phases of the project. As an alternative to such a "joint venture," Ace might propose that in exchange for a below-market rate of interest it be given an option to convert the unamortized mortgage balance at the end of ten years to a 50 percent equity interest in the property. If Dan were to agree then Dan would be obtaining what is known as a "convertible mortgage."

A recent example of a convertible mortgage is a long-term loan in the amount of $815 million obtained by Sears, Roebuck & Company in November 1989 that was secured by a first mortgage lien on its 110-story headquarters tower in Chicago. According to Wall Street analysts, the annual interest rate was fixed at about 6 percent (as compared to the then-prevailing rate of about 9 percent for large blue-chip corporate borrowers) and in exchange for the below-market rate the lending group (headed by a subsidiary of Prudential Insurance Company of America) received an option to purchase the Sears Tower at the end of the 15-year loan term. Sears will receive a share in any appreciation in the value of the building, and because of interest deductions it expects to reduce its annual after-tax cost of borrowing the money to less than 5 percent during the term of the loan.[2] Incidentally, this kind of mortgage investment has recently become popular with Japanese investors (especially insurance companies). See the excerpt by DeWitt at Chapter 2A.

In its simplest form, the convertible mortgage is a hybrid financing device that combines a debt feature (in the form of a traditional postconstruction loan to the borrower at a below-market rate) with an equity feature (in the form of a lender's option to purchase all or a portion of the mortgaged property at some future time). The excerpt by Welborn summarizes the advantages and pitfalls of such an arrangement from the perspectives of both parties to the transaction.

Strum, Current Trends of Institutional Financing of Real Estate in the United States
17 Real Prop., Prob. & Tr. J. 486 (1982)

Traditionally, developers of real estate have viewed their efforts as being creative of value so that the costs and expenses incurred in

2. N.Y. Times, Nov. 16, 1989, at D1, col. 4.

development are seen as less than the value of the improvement created. For many years this creation of value and the ability to garner income from the product has justified the developers' efforts in the construction and development of real estate.

The developers were given a larger impetus to construct real estate when institutions having substantial cash available began to look to real estate for secure investments. In the main, the funds institutions placed with real estate developers were funds previously invested in the bond market and, therefore, the form of the investment resembled the bond. It was a long-term, fixed-rate mortgage which yielded to the investor a safe return on its money while risking an amount which was less than the full value of the security. The developer welcomed this influx of capital and in most cases was able to borrow a sufficient sum to cover the entire cost of construction and then leverage off the interest rate because his expected return was invariably higher than the customary low interest rate on the loan. During this period, the long-term lease to high credit tenants was preferred by the institutions as making the investment in real estate more secure. The only equity investments of this type were sale-leasebacks where the institution provided 100 percent of the value and received as rent a sum which would return their investment, plus what the mortgage rate would be, with a premium for the extra risk of total financing and assuming the equity position over a normal period of twenty-five years. It was not unusual in these cases to see the rent decrease after the twenty-five year period, when the investment was fully recouped.

Beginning in the 1950s the United States, along with the rest of the world, began to experience creeping inflation and, in order to protect investments in terms of real dollars, institutions resorted to the device of raising the interest rate. Since the real price of money in the United States over the last fifty years has remained within the 3 percent to 4 percent range, interest rates were raised so that the real rate would be preserved in that range. For example, the average contract rate on mortgages from 1950 to 1959 was 5.2 percent, but if we were to assume a twenty-five year amortization schedule with a complete payoff in ten years and all payments were adjusted for inflation, a real return of 3.51 percent was realized. . . .

In the 1960s, inflation increased to the point where interest rates were beginning to climb close to the usury law limit. The institutions, bent on protecting their real rate of interest, pressured state legislatures by withholding funds from the market so that usury laws were amended to permit the financing of real estate at higher rates, without fear of violating the usury laws. In this manner many institutions merely continued to raise their interest rates in order to maintain the same rate of return in the face of inflation. Even so, full protection was not achieved; the average contract rate for the 1960s was 6.58 percent, but the real rate, after adjustment for inflation and assuming a ten year full payoff, was only 2.15 percent. Other institutions coupled a raise in interest rates with what was called a "kicker" — i.e., a contingent interest based upon a percentage of the gross income derived from the property. Others looked at the appreciation in value of the real estate and focused on obtaining an equity interest by forming partnerships with the developer. The developers were thus able to finance their construction completely and at the same time obtain a financial partner which could be counted on for more capital when it was needed even though they had to relinquish a portion of their ownership of the property. Investments in equity interests in real estate also gave the institutions tax advantages. For example, the after-tax return of a 10 percent bond was less than the after-tax return of a real estate investment whose before-tax return was projected to be 10 percent. Therefore, institutions were satisfied with yields over the holding period of the investment which amounted to less than the interest on a straight mortgage or bond investment.

The providers of the long-term mortgages were the life insurance companies since they were able, because of their long-term fixed obligations, to make investments geared to produce income that would be sufficient to meet their obligations. The life companies had these assets because of the sale of great amounts, during the last hundred years, of whole life insurance which paid a relatively small dividend on the amount of premium paid by the insured and built up large cash reserves. The terms of the policies fixed the obligations and the companies could actuarially determine the amount of return their investments had to produce to meet their obligations.

During the 1970s, two economic factors came into play which dramatically changed the institutional real estate investment climate in the United States. First the rate of inflation increased to double-digit numbers. This prompted more life insurance companies to switch from traditional mortgage investments to equity investments in real estate. Many pension funds had previously realized that the bond market was not an inflation protective vehicle and had turned to the stock market on the theory that the stock market would provide more inflation protection. Finding this to be a false assumption in the late 1960s, they then turned to real estate. Meanwhile, since life insurance companies had been acting as money managers for pension funds over the prior twenty years, they were able to respond to this need by establishing real estate investment vehicles for pension funds. . . .

. . . Developers, who used to hold on to their ownership positions, have been forced to become manufacturers, builders and sellers. They have lost the tax advantages of ownership, but have reaped large amounts of immediate cash from the sale of existing properties because heavy competition for these equity investments has driven prices extremely high. Interest rates in the capital market have continued to remain on a very high plateau, thus curbing the ability of developers to construct new real estate projects without having to surrender their ownership positions. . . .

Let us examine the players and their motivations to ascertain what type of investment vehicle is emerging in the current market. Although the developer wants to retain ownership, enjoy the tax benefits of ownership, manage the property and share in its appreciation in value, it is impossible to do so because of the high cost of construction financing. . . .

Resulting from the melding of these needs of this new investor and the modern developer, we see a new trend emerging in real estate financing in the United States — the convertible mortgage. The U.S. real estate investment community has not progressed to the point, as the United Kingdom has, where the real estate financing is total equity financing. Perhaps the tax incentives in the United States are such that this halfway step of a debt-equity relationship is the one which will comply with all of the needs of the respective parties. Or, perhaps it is indeed a halfway step and in the future full equity ownership will be the answer. In any event, let us examine the convertible mortgage.

The convertible mortgage is essentially a mortgage which converts to an ownership position at some point in time. . . .

Madison and Dwyer, The Law of Real Estate Financing
¶12.01[5] (Cum. Supp. No. 2) (1989)

TAX DISTINCTION BETWEEN DEBT AND EQUITY

As a hedge against inflation and volatile interest rates, lenders have and will continue to devise innovative methods and financing techniques to replace the long-term fixed-rate mortgage as the principal mode of real estate financing. The common characteristic of these various methods and combinations of methods that have been created in order to cope with inflation is equity participation. Some, like the equity kicker, are at the debt end of debt-equity spectrum; others, like the joint venture arrangement, represent a pure equity position; while still others, like the convertible mortgage and equity appreciation mortgage, are somewhere in the middle. Under a convertible mortgage, the lender has the right to convert some or all of the loan indebtedness into a partnership (equity) interest or the right to purchase part or all of the secured property.

When there is a substantial equity participation, one important issue is whether the relationship between the lender and borrower will be regarded for tax purposes as a debtor-creditor relationship or as an equity (partnership) relationship. As noted elsewhere, if the lender's investment is indebtedness, the interest paid by the borrower is deductible and the interest received by the lender is income, except when interest paid by state or local governments meets the criteria under I.R.C. §103. Moreover, if the lender is solely a creditor, the borrower can include the full amount of the loan indebtedness, whether recourse or nonrecourse, in its tax basis for purposes of computing depreciation. On the other hand, if the loan transaction is characterized by the Service as a partnership, the so-called borrower must share such tax benefits as depreciation with any lender who is constructively deemed to be a partner. Also, payments to the lender-partner by the borrower that are contingent upon net or gross income (equity kickers) will not be deductible and will be taxed as distributions from the partnership if the loan is made to the partnership in its capacity as a partner.[33.8] . . . Moreover, if the transaction is a loan transaction with an interest add-on feature geared to refinancing or sale of the property, the borrower will receive ordinary deductions equal to the interest paid, which is beneficial especially in the case of a sale, which, unlike refinancing, is a taxable event.

Another significant issue involving any borrower that is a corporation, especially in the case of a convertible mortgage, is whether the loan transaction will be reclassified as equity under I.R.C. §385.[33.10]

[a] TAX TREATMENT OF LENDER AS PARTNER OR CREDITOR

Whether the relationship between the lender and borrower is a debtor-creditor or partnership relationship depends upon the intentions of the parties as reflected by the particular facts and circumstances of the transaction. However, the following criteria are relevant in distinguishing a debtor-creditor relationship from that of a partnership relationship:

(1) Is there any characterization of intent in the documentation? However, this factor is far from conclusive.
(2) How are profits and losses shared and what are the respective contributions of capital and services by the parties?

33.8. See I.R.C. §§707(a) and 707(c); Pratt v. Comm'r, 505 F.2d 1023 (5th Cir. 1977); Rev. Rul. 81-300, 1981-2 C.B. 143; Rev. Rul. 81-301, 1981-2 C.B. 144.

33.10. The Service has formally withdrawn the Proposed Regulations (effective 7/1/83) and final Regulations (effective 8/5/83) under I.R.C. §385. See T.D. 7920, filed 11/2/83.

(3) Who controls the final disposition of the property and other important policy decisions?

(4) If there is an option to purchase, does the option price fluctuate, is the borrower forced to share profits as well, and who bears the risk of appreciation or depreciation in the value of the property?

(5) Does the transaction have independent economic significance, or is tax avoidance the motivating reason for the transaction?

(6) In the case of nonrecourse financing, is the loan-to-value ratio reasonably low?

(7) Are the traditional indicia of indebtedness (e.g., fixed maturity date) employed by the parties? . . .

Welborn, Convertible Mortgages: Legal and Drafting Issues

ALI-ABA, 2 Modern Real Estate
Transactions 1191 (7th ed. 1986)

A. GENESIS AND ADVANTAGES OF CONVERTIBLE MORTGAGE FINANCING

In response to the relatively unstable financial markets of the 1970's and 1980's and an environment of high inflation and interest rates, changing roles of pension funds and insurance companies, and deregulation of financial institutions generally, a number of so-called creative financing arrangements have appeared. These arrangements have been generated in response to market demand and have been aimed at enabling lenders to increase their portfolio yield on a long-term basis beyond that on traditional fixed interest rate instruments. The new products, which include shared appreciation mortgages, sale-leaseback instruments, and even joint ventures, typically combine elements of traditional mortgage financing with equity investment positions. One of the new financing techniques is the convertible mortgage.

The convertible mortgage is actually a combination of two rather straight-forward instruments: an ordinary long-term debt instrument together with a separate option agreement giving the lender the right to purchase the encumbered property at a specified time or during a stated period. The mortgage is considered "convertible" because the option is typically exercised and the purchase price paid by relieving the borrower of its debt obligations, or "converting" the debt to equity.

The convertible mortgage appears to have developed largely in response to market demands of borrowers/sellers for financing which provides below market rates in relation to traditional financing instruments. The borrower/seller may also be lured by the prospect of obtaining 100% financing without the need for equity infusion or secondary debt. The convertible mortgage also may provide some reasonable expectation of a built-in buyer, which reduces both long-term risk and prospective transaction costs. And the lender/buyer may retain the borrower/seller as its property manager and/or leasing agent after option exercise.

From the lender's standpoint, the economics of the transaction should also be favorable in that the convertible mortgage will achieve a minimum yield on the debt with an opportunity to evaluate a possible equity investment in the property over a relatively lengthy period of time. This approach may be particularly advantageous for institutions that are not familiar with a particular market or, perhaps, uncertain as to the timing of availability of investment capital. The overall yield to the lender would be expected to be higher than a traditional fixed rate permanent loan but the lender is also guaranteed a minimum rate of return.

Depending on the period for exercise of the option, the lender may have significant flexibility in determining when to structure the investment as debt or equity. The convertible mortgage also permits the lender to obtain management experienced in the development, leasing and operation of the property, which management may continue after exercise of the option. Flexibility is also enhanced by virtue of the availability of assignment of either or both of the instruments.

From a tax standpoint, the borrower would retain full tax benefits until exercise of the option and thus could benefit from a significant amount of the property's depreciation value. The borrower/seller may also be able to avoid ordinary income treatment of any gain from the sale based on the longer capital gain holding period or the avoidance of dealer status by the staggering of sales. Of course, with changes in the tax laws relating to lengthening of cost recovery/depreciation periods and the removal of capital gain benefits, some of these advantages would be reduced.

B. STRUCTURING THE CONVERTIBLE MORTGAGE: DOCUMENTATION AND DRAFTING

Because of the relative newness of the convertible mortgage, a number of interesting legal and drafting issues relating to it remain unresolved.

1. *Loan Documentation and Terms.* The loan documentation will typically include a standard promissory note, mortgage or deed of trust, specific assignment of leases and rents, subordination agreements or

other instruments relating to tenant leases, and other collateral assignments. Since the loan will typically be made as an initial "take-out" of the construction loan, tenant improvements may not have been installed and a punchlist of completion items may exist. As a result, holdbacks for tenant improvements and leasing commissions and/or punchlist items may be appropriate and thus a loan agreement and/or escrow agreement providing for further disbursements may also be necessary.

While the interest rate on the loan may initially be set at a below-market rate, it may be appropriate to include provisions for increase in the interest rate after the expiration of the option period or at another stated date in the future. Initial provisions for interest only payments may be phased out over the loan term; the debt may amortize after the period for option exercise. Another feature which lenders may choose to include in the convertible mortgage loan is an option to call the loan as of a certain date or during a specified period. Interest rate increases could also occur in the event that a scheduled leasing requirement is not met or other covenants are not satisfied.

2. *Option Documentation and Consideration.* In order to avoid possible problems with the violation of the doctrine against clogging the equity of redemption (as discussed below), it is critical to separately document the option and support it by separate consideration. Although the courts generally will not look behind the agreement to determine the adequacy of consideration for a grant of option, in the case of a convertible mortgage it seems more important to justify the separateness and adequacy of consideration for the option. (The option consideration may, of course, be advanced as part of the loan amount.) Separate documentation of the mortgage and option is necessary not only to avoid the availability of certain legal defenses but also to assure that the option is not terminated if and when a foreclosure occurs if the lender/buyer is outbid at the foreclosure sale. Recording of the option prior to the mortgage would, therefore, also be necessary.

Option terms vary significantly, but typically extend for a period of 10 to 15 years. Some convertible mortgages provide that the lender may exercise the option at any time; others only permit exercise to occur during specified periods (e.g., for the 3 month period at the beginning of the fifth, eighth, eleventh, etc., years). While the option price is typically fixed at the outset, which is particularly important for the lender/buyer in times of high appreciation, the lender/buyer should also consider providing for a variable purchase price that would include "earnout" provisions based on leasing and/or net income achievement levels. This is particularly important in relation to loan "holdbacks" that may never be fully funded. The option price may also be determined based on the fair market value of the property at the time of option exercise, although this is obviously detrimental to the lender/buyer unless the fair market value is used as a "cap" on the purchase price.

The option may be structured as an option to purchase a partial interest in the property or as an option to purchase an interest in a partnership owner. The increased difficulty in enforcing an option to purchase a partnership as opposed to a property interest may dictate protective efforts such as formation of the partnership at the outset of the transaction, with the option to purchase an additional interest upon "conversion." Alternatively, the transaction could be structured as an option to purchase a tenancy-in-common interest under a tenancy-in-common agreement which would have the same terms in all material respects as a partnership agreement. The tenancy-in-common may also increase the likelihood of obtaining specific performance.

If an option to purchase a partnership interest is granted, it is advisable to agree on the new form of partnership agreement at the time the option is granted. Formation of a partnership at the outset of the transaction may also avoid, depending on the property's location, certain transfer taxes or reassessments. The lender/buyer should, however, consider possible exposure to past liabilities of the owner partnership. (Note that the now fairly standard nonimputation title insurance endorsement is not so readily available when the insured buys into an existing partnership.) An option to purchase a partnership interest should also be recorded.

C. PRESERVING ENFORCEABILITY: LEGAL ISSUES OF THE CONVERTIBLE MORTGAGE

1. *Clogging of the Equity of Redemption.* The legal restriction against "clogging the equity of redemption" is a principle developed by the English common law courts in response to the perceived harsh result of a borrower losing its entire property interest in foreclosure if it fails to make a final payment on a mortgage loan, even if much of the principal has already been repaid. The resulting "equity of redemption" differs from a statutory right of redemption in that the latter normally permits the borrower to buy back or "redeem" his property after foreclosure is concluded. The equity of redemption instead arises by application of equitable principles as a ban on the foreclosure remedy.

Typically, the conclusion in the English courts that a particular device "clogged" the equity of redemption resulted from the court's finding that there had been oppression by the lender in the transaction. Thus, the principle was not usually applied unless there had been unfair or oppressive behavior on the part of the mortgagee. American courts applying the principle have considered not only the issue of whether the mortgagor may release his equity of redemption to the mortgagee, but whether the transaction may in fact be considered a "disguised mortgage." The cases do not typically discuss the issue in terms of the doctrine of clogging the equity of redemption and have often been decided on the basis of the parties' intent.

Unfortunately, the American courts have applied the "clogging" rule without any apparent regard for the fairness of the particular transaction or whether it arose in a commercial context in which the parties were sophisticated or had relatively equal bargaining power. Some courts have taken the position that an option to purchase property granted concurrently with a mortgage on the same property would in itself operate to clog the equity of redemption. See, e.g., Humble Oil and Refining Co. v. Doerr, 123 N.J. Super. 530, 303 A.2d 898 (1973); MacArthur v. N. Palm Beach Utilities, 202 So. 2d 181 (Fla. Sup. Ct. 1967); Hopping v. Baldridge, 130 Okla. 226, 266 P.2d 469 (1928); Coursey v. Fairchild, 436 P.2d 35 (Okla. 1967); Gavin v. Johnson, 131 Conn. 489, 41 A.2d 113 (1945). (See extensive discussion in Preble and Cartwright, "Convertible and Shared Appreciation Loans: Unclogging the Equity of Redemption," in 20 Real Prop. Prob. and Trust Journ., Number 3, page 821, Fall 1985.)

Application of the clogging principle should leave the mortgage intact and invalidate the option, which would, of course, seriously diminish the lender's expected return. However, because the principal purpose of the rule appears to be the avoidance of unconscionable advantage by the lender, absent unconscionability or unfairness by virtue of the lender/buyer's significant bargaining advantage, a commercial transaction that is not extremely one-sided should be upheld. Of course, if mortgage terms are far out of the ordinary or circumstances later prove that the lender/buyer has made a very favorable economic deal (even though the option price may have been fair when originally negotiated), the courts may lean toward a conclusion of unfairness.

To reduce the likelihood of a finding that the transaction violates the clogging rule, it is advisable not only to clarify the separateness of the loan and option transactions by separate documentation, but to assure that the option is not employed as a remedy for the lender/buyer in case of default under the mortgage. As a result, cross-default provisions should probably not be included in the documentation, although similar events or circumstances could both be deemed a default under the mortgage and trigger the ability of the lender/buyer to exercise the purchase option. If the courts are suspicious that the lender/buyer has used the convertible mortgage as a means to avoid usury problems or foreclosure proceedings, or as a forfeiture, the option transaction is less likely to be upheld.

It is most important to document that the parties actually intended an eventual acquisition by the lender/buyer of the property. In this regard, it is wise to obtain a certificate from the borrower/seller that confirms not only the fairness of the transaction but also waives any rights to challenge the validity or enforceability of the option agreement. . . . On the other hand, the parties should not go so far as to imply that the option must be exercised so as not to create an unanticipated burden for the lender/buyer or create consequences of immediate ownership.

Absent judicial or statutory validation, the clogging rule may thus be applied in a commercial context. In 1984, the California legislature expressly validated convertible mortgages in transactions in which the real property is other than 1-4 unit residential. Cal. Civil Code Section 2906. Section 2906 also confirms that the option will have priority as of its recording date and will be effective according to its terms if the right to exercise the option is not dependent on a default under the security instrument. Similarly, the General Obligations Law of the State of New York was amended on June 11, 1985, to validate convertible mortgages (i) granted or exercised after June 11, 1985; (ii) in which the mortgage loan amount is over $2.5 million; and (iii) in which exercise of the option is not tied to a mortgage default.

Assurances as to validity of the option in relation to the clogging rule may also be obtained by opinions of counsel (which may also help establish the good faith of the lender/buyer) and by specific title insurance endorsements that insure over the application of the rule. Title insurance protection should include both a loan policy for the mortgage or deed of trust and an owner's policy for the option to purchase. The option policy should describe the option by reference to the recorded memorandum of option agreement and will insure the validity of the option, the status of title to the property as of the date of the option, and the subordinate nature of the mortgage lien. The amount of owner's policy coverage may be stated as the expected difference between the option price and the fair market value of the property or the consideration paid for the option.

2. *Bankruptcy.* Bankruptcy of the borrower/seller would present a major problem to the lender/buyer in that the option could be disaffirmed as an executory contract. Because there is essentially no defense to such a rejection of the contract, it is critical for the lender/buyer to consider the practical effects of the term of the option and the financial wherewithal of its borrower/seller (and constituent partners, if applicable). The possibility of creating financial defaults on the part of the borrower/seller in advance of bankruptcy that could trigger exercise of the option (for example, permitting exercise of the option if the borrower's net worth falls below a certain dollar amount), have been disapproved under the bankruptcy laws.

3. *Usury.* It is quite probable that the value of the option will be treated as additional interest under the loan since the option may be considered partial consideration for the loan. However, in making

the usury determination, the option consideration usually could be spread over the loan or option term and should be calculated according to its present discounted value. See Traders Credit Corp. v. Thyle, 116 Cal. App. 252, 2 P.2d 568 (1931). A valid argument could also be made that the determinative value of the option should be its value when received without regard to future events.

4. *Exposure to Owner's Liabilities.* Because the convertible mortgage instruments may provide the lender/buyer with some significant control over operation and management of the property prior to exercise of the option, the lender/buyer could become liable for environmental cleanup costs, for defects of the property, or for personal injuries as if it were an owner. Cases such as the 1968 landmark case of Connor v. Great Western Sav. & Loan Ass'n, 69 Cal. 2d 850, 447 P.2d 609 (1968) have indicated that when a lender takes an interest in the profits of the property, it may become liable to parties that have proper claims against the developer. In seeking to codify *Connor,* the California legislature has indicated, however, that the lender does not become liable for failure of the borrower to use due care in improvement of the property encumbered by the lender's mortgage unless the loss or damage is a result of an act of the lender "outside the scope of the activities of the lender of money" or unless the lender has been a party to misrepresentations. Cal. Civ. Code Sec. 3434. . . . [See Chapter 6B6. — ED.]

5. *Unconscionability.* A 1977 addition to the Uniform Commercial Code pertaining to the concept of unconscionability in a general contract law situation supports the proposition that a transaction with an oppressive result may be invalidated even absent any particular inequality in the bargaining process. UCC Section 2-302. California has taken an even broader approach to this rule in Civil Code Section 1670.5. Of particular concern in this context is the possibility that oppression may be determined at the time of enforcement of the contract in terms of whether the results would be harsh for the borrower. Again, a retrospective application may be particularly unfair to the lender/buyer in the convertible mortgage context if the rate of return could be said to be unconscionable because [it is] far in excess of the ordinary fixed return on the mortgage. See also Uniform Land Transactions Act Section 1-311.

These principles are also in line with the increasing amount of authority in the area of the implied obligation of good faith and fair dealing, both in a lending and in a general commercial context such as leasing. See, e.g., Kendall v. Ernest Pestana, Inc., 40 Cal. 3d 488, 220 Cal. Rptr. 818 (1985); Baypoint Mortgage Corp. v. Crest Premium Real Estate Invs. Retirement Trust, 168 Cal. App. 3d 818, 214 Cal. Rptr. 531 (1985). For this reason also, it may be useful to obtain a certificate in the form described above in an attempt to verify the factual background and general fairness of the transaction.

6. *Income Taxation Issues.* Characterization of the transaction as either an immediate partnership or sale could also have serious federal income tax consequences in terms of a recharacterization of the lender's interest as equity versus debt. See, Farley Realty Corp. v. Comm'r, 279 F.2d 201 (2d Cir. 1960), aff'g 18 T.C.M. 422 (1959), indicating that a factor of substantial weight in the determination is whether the advanced funds are subject to the risks of the enterprise.[3] Other factors that should be considered are the effect of the original-issue discount rules and the discharge-of-indebtedness rules, the details of which are beyond the scope of this discussion.

7. *Foreclosure Issues.* If the transaction is recharacterized as equity rather than debt, the lender/buyer may also have difficulty in foreclosing on the debt even if it decides not to exercise the option. . . .

D. PROTECTION OF INVESTMENT VALUE: DRAFTING CONSIDERATIONS

In drafting option documents, particular consideration should be given to providing the lender/buyer with sufficient control over the property to protect its investment without putting the parties in danger of having the transaction recharacterized as a partnership or an immediate sale. Such operating controls would not, of course, replace a full due diligence investigation preceding the making of the loan, which should satisfy the lender/buyer that, at least as of the date the option is granted, the property's value is expected to support the lender/buyer's loan and the option price.

The borrower may have particularly little incentive to properly

---

3. There are additional tax pitfalls associated with exercising the option to convert debt into equity for both of the parties. From the developer's perspective, if the property is substantially appreciated and his adjusted basis low, a taxable sale on the conversion date might be burdensome since the developer would be incurring a tax liability without receiving any corresponding cash to pay for the liability. If the debt is not cancelled but simply transferred to the partnership in exchange for a partnership interest, would this generate cancellation of indebtedness income? Probably not, since the transfer arguably is a tax-free contribution to the partnership under I.R.C. §721. From the lender's perspective, suppose the value of the equity interest on the date of conversion should exceed the amount of the cancelled debt. Does this mean that it has received taxable gain? See Rev. Rul. 72-265, 1972-1 C.B. 222. Another pitfall is that under the Tax Reform Act of 1986 convertible debt does not constitute "qualified nonrecourse financing" under I.R.C. §465(b)(6)(B) for purposes of providing limited partners with a step-up in their at-risk (bases) amounts, which they might need to deduct losses and shelter their cash distributions, especially if the partnership is a leveraged one. See discussion at Chapter 2B, note 7diii. See generally Steuben, The Convertible, Participating Mortgage: Federal Income Tax Considerations, 54 U. Colo. L. Rev. 237 (1983). — ED.

operate and maintain the property if the loan amount is the same as the option price. This problem may in part be solved by using an "earnout" purchase price which takes into account factors relating to the proper operation and maintenance of the property such as net operating income (in turn permitting capital investments to be deducted on some amortized basis) or leaseup standards according to established rent guidelines.

In general, the lender/buyer will seek extensive covenants from the borrower/seller relating to the ownership, operation and maintenance of the property. These controls are typically provided in the option agreement rather than the loan agreement in hopes of avoiding issues of lender liability. The covenants should be independent of the mortgage obligations and should specifically provide an independent remedy to sue for damages in the event of breach. Another possible remedy is an offset against or reduction of the purchase price. Operating controls may also include a separate management agreement which will give the borrower/seller extra incentive to continue proper operation and maintenance of the property. . . .

The following excerpts from the conversion provisions of a loan agreement illustrate how the convertible mortgage might be documented. For reasons discussed below, the conversion language is often situated in an option agreement distinct from the note and mortgage agreement.

§5.1. *Right to Purchase Equity Interest.* During the three month period beginning after ten (10) years from the date hereof, Lender shall have the right, upon six months prior written notice to Borrower, to convert its interest in the Loan and under the Mortgage and this Agreement into a 50 percent equity interest in the mortgaged property by purchasing such interest at such time. The purchase price for such equity interest shall be the unpaid principal amount of the Loan, which Lender shall pay by endorsing the Note and assigning the mortgage and its rights under this Agreement to the borrower, who immediately thereafter shall cause the Note to be marked cancelled and cancel and satisfy the Mortgage by duly recorded instrument.

§5.4. *Additional Right to Purchase.* In addition to Lender's right to convert to an equity interest, Lender shall have the right, upon thirty days prior written notice to Borrower, to convert to an equity interest with the same stated rights and preferences as provided in this Article 5, in the event of a Permitted Sale, a Permitted Refinancing of the premises or upon the occurrence of an Event of Default under this Agreement or under the Note or Mortgage.

§5.5. *Management of the Premises.* [Herein follow provisions setting forth specific requirements with respect to repair, alteration, maintenance, and management (including rights to approve leases of space in the building) during the period prior to the exercise of the right to convert.]

Krelinger v. New Patagonia Meat & Cold Storage Co.
[1914 H.L.] A.C. 25, 109 L.T.R. (n.s.) 802

Appeal from an order of the Court of Appeal affirming an order of Swinfen Eady, J. . . .

VISCOUNT HALDANE L.C. My Lords, the appellants are a firm of merchants and woolbrokers. The respondents carry on the business of preserving and canning meat and of boiling down the carcases of sheep and other animals. In the course of this business they have at their disposal a large number of sheepskins. It appears that in the summer of 1910 the respondents were desirous of borrowing 10,000*l.*, and requested the appellants to advance that sum. The appellants, who were desirous of obtaining an option to purchase for a term of five years all the sheepskins at the respondents' disposal, agreed to lend the money in consideration of being given such an option. The negotiations which followed resulted in an agreement dated August 24, 1910. Under this agreement the appellants were to lend the respondents the sum of 10,000*l.* repayable on demand with interest at 6 per cent. If, however, among other conditions to be observed, the interest was duly paid, the appellants were not to demand repayment till September 30, 1915, but the respondents were to be at liberty to pay off the loan earlier. To secure the loan the respondents by the agreement charged their undertaking and all their property, both present and future, with the payment of the principal sum and interest. . . .

By clause 8 of the agreement the respondents were not for five years from the date of the agreement (i.e., till August 24, 1915) to sell sheepskins to any one excepting the appellants, so long as the latter were willing to buy at a price equal to the best price (c.i.f. London) offered by any one else, and the respondents were to pay to the appellants a commission of 1 per cent. on the sale price of all sheepskins sold by the respondents to any one else. . . .

LORD MERSEY. My Lords, I agree, and I desire to add only a few words. The transaction out of which this dispute arises is sufficiently described in the judgment of the Lord Chancellor. Though embodied in one document it is an agreement made up of two parts. The first part consists of a promise by the appellants, who are merchants, to lend to the respondents, who are a trading company, money at interest on the security of a floating charge over the company's undertaking; the second part consists of an agreement by the company to give to the lenders the option of purchasing for a time their periodical production of sheepskins. The whole transaction is of a most ordinary commercial kind. . . .

I have nothing to say about the [clogging] doctrine itself. It seems to me to be like an unruly dog, which, if not securely chained to its own kennel, is prone to wander into places where it ought not to be. Its introduction into the present case would give effect to no equity and would defeat justice.

LORD PARKER OF WADDINGTON. My Lords, a legal mortgage has generally taken the form of a conveyance with a proviso for reconveyance on the payment of money by a specified date. But a conveyance in this form is by no means necessarily a mortgage. In order to determine whether it is or is not a mortgage, equity has always looked to the real intention of the parties, to be gathered not only from the terms of the particular instrument but from all the circumstances of the transaction, and has always admitted parol evidence in cases where the real intention was in doubt. Only if according to the real intention of the parties the property was to be held as a pledge or security for the payment of the money, and as such to be restored to the mortgagor when the money was paid, was the conveyance considered to be a mortgage. . . .

Taking the simple case of a mortgage by way of conveyance with a proviso for reconveyance on payment of a sum of money upon a specified date, two events might happen. The mortgagor might pay the money on the specified date, in which case equity would specifically perform the contract for reconveyance. On the other hand, the mortgagor might fail to pay the money on the date specified for that purpose. In this case the property conveyed became at law an absolute interest in the mortgagee. Equity, however, did not treat time as of the essence of the transaction, and hence on failure to exercise what may be called the contractual right to redeem there arose an equity to redeem, notwithstanding the specified date had passed. Till this date had passed there was no equity to redeem, and a bill either to redeem or foreclose would have been demurrable. The equity to redeem, which arises on failure to exercise the contractual right of redemption, must be carefully distinguished from the equitable estate, which, from the first, remains in the mortgagor, and is sometimes referred to as an equity of redemption.

Now if, as was not infrequently the case, such a legal mortgage as above described contained a further stipulation that if default were made in payment of the money secured on the date specified the mortgagor should not exercise his equitable right to redeem, or should only exercise it as to part of the mortgaged property, or on payment of some additional sum or performance of some additional condition, such stipulation was always regarded in equity as a penal clause against which relief would be given. This is the principle underlying the rule against fetters or clogs on the equity of redemption. The rule may be stated thus: The equity which arises on failure to exercise the contractual right cannot be fettered or clogged by any stipulation contained in the mortgage or entered into as part of the mortgage transaction. . . .

There is another point of view from which a clog or fetter on the equitable right to redeem may be properly regarded. The nature of the equitable right is so well known that, upon a mortgage in the usual form to secure a money payment on a certain day, it must be taken to be a term of the real bargain between the parties that the property should remain redeemable in equity after failure to exercise the contractual right. Any fetter or clog imposed by the instrument of mortgage on this equitable right may be properly regarded as a repugnant condition and as such invalid. There are, however, repugnant conditions which cannot be regarded as mere penalties intended to deter the exercise of the equitable right which arises when the time for the exercise of the contractual right has gone by, but which are repugnant to the contractual right itself. A condition to the effect that if the contractual right is not exercised by the time specified the mortgagee shall have an option of purchasing the mortgaged property may properly be regarded as a penal clause. It is repugnant only to the equity and not to the contractual right. But a condition that the mortgagee is to have such an option for a period which begins before the time for the exercise of the equitable right has arrived, or which reserves to the mortgagee any interest in the property after the exercise of the contractual right, is inconsistent not only with the equity but with the contractual right itself, and might, I think, be held invalid for repugnancy even in a Court of law.

This consideration affords a possible and reasonable explanation of the rule referred to in some of the authorities, to the effect that a mortgagee cannot as a term of the mortgage enter into a contract to purchase, or stipulate for an option to purchase, any part of or interest in the mortgaged premises. Suppose the following simple case, namely, a conveyance by way of mortgage with a proviso for reconveyance if the mortgagor pay to the mortgagee 500*l.* and interest at the end of six months, and then a further stipulation that the mortgagee should have an option of purchasing the property for another six months. If the mortgagor pays the moneys secured by the specified date the mortgagee comes under a contractual liability to reconvey, and if he does reconvey he reconveys his whole interest in the mortgaged property, thus destroying his option. The option, therefore, is inconsistent with and repugnant to the proviso for reconveyance, which embodies the terms of the contractual right to redeem. It may, therefore, be rejected. It is also inconsistent with and repugnant to the equity of redemption, which arises on failure to exercise the contractual right to redeem. It is, therefore, though not strictly a penalty, sometimes referred to as a clog on this equity. . . . In the case of mortgages without such an express proviso there might, it is true, be a like inconsistency or repugnancy, but only if the real intention of the parties was that the property should be held as security for the moneys charged thereon and restored intact to the mortgagor as soon as these moneys were paid, but, as in the last-mentioned case, it is always possible that this was not the true intention, and unless it be the true intention the transaction is not really a mortgage under the rule, but something more complex. . . .

I have pointed out that in mortgages in common form an option to purchase is inconsistent with and repugnant to the proviso for reconveyance on payment of the money secured. But is there any such repugnancy or inconsistency in the following case? *A.* agrees to give *B.* an option for one year to purchase a property for 10,000*l.* In consideration of such option *B.* agrees to lend, and does lend, *A.* 1000*l.* to be charged on the property without interest, and be repayable at the expiration or earlier exercise of the option. I cannot myself see that there is any inconsistency or repugnancy between the provisions of this perfectly simple and straightforward transaction. It would have been very different if *A.* had conveyed the property to *B.* with a proviso that on payment of the 1000*l.* there should be a reconveyance, and the deed had then provided for the year's option. Here the option would be inconsistent with, and would in fact have been destroyed by, the reconveyance.

My Lords, I desire, in connection with what I have just said, to add a few words on the maxims in which attempts have been made to sum up the equitable principles applicable to mortgage transactions. I refer to the maxims, "Once a mortgage, always a mortgage," or, "A mortgage cannot be made irredeemable." Such maxims, however convenient, afford little assistance where the Court has to deal with a new or doubtful case. They obviously beg the question, always of great importance, whether the particular transaction which the Court has to consider is, in fact, a mortgage or not, and if they be acted on without a careful consideration of the equitable considerations on which they are based, can only, like Bacon's idols of the market place, lead to misconception and error. . . .

My Lords, I now come to the particular class of mortgages to which I have already referred, that is to say, mortgages to secure borrowed money. For the whole period during which the Court of Chancery was formulating and laying down its equitable doctrines in relation to mortgages there existed statutes strictly limiting the rate of interest which could be legally charged for borrowed money. If a mortgagee stipulated for some advantage beyond repayment of his principal with interest, equity considered that he was acting contrary to the spirit of these statutes, and held the stipulation bad on this ground. There thus arose the rule so often referred to in the reported decisions, that in a mortgage to secure borrowed money the mortgagee

could not contract for any such advantage. There was said to be an
equity to redeem on payment of principal, interest, and costs, whatever
might have been the bargain between the parties, and any stipulation
by the mortgagee for a further or, as it was sometimes called, a collateral
advantage came to be spoken of as a clog or fetter on this equity. It
is of the greatest importance to observe that this equity is not the
equity to redeem with which I have hitherto been dealing. It is an
equity which arises ab initio, and not only on failure to exercise the
contractual right to redeem. It can be asserted before as well as after
such failure. It has nothing to do with time not being of the essence
of a contract, or with relief from penalties or with repugnant conditions.
It is not a right to redeem on the contractual terms, but a right to
redeem notwithstanding the contractual terms, a right which depended
on the existence of the statutes against usury and the public policy
thought to be involved in those statutes. Unfortunately, in some of
the authorities this right is spoken of as a right incidental to mortgages
generally, and not confined to mortgages to secure borrowed money.
This is quite explicable when it is remembered that a loan is perhaps
the most frequent occasion for a mortgage. But it is, I think, none
the less erroneous. I can find no instance of the rule which precludes
a mortgagee from stipulating for a collateral advantage having been
applied to a mortgage other than a mortgage to secure borrowed money,
and there is the authority of Lord Eldon in Chambers v. Goldwin (1)
for saying that this rule was based on the usury laws. The right
(notwithstanding the terms of the bargain) to redeem on payment of
principal, interest, and costs is a mere corollary to this rule, and falls
with it. It is to be observed that stipulations for a collateral advantage
may be classified under two heads — first, those the performance of
which is made a term of the contractual right to redeem, and, secondly,
those the performance of which is not made a term of such contractual
right. In the former case in settling the terms on which redemption
was allowed the Court of Chancery entirely ignored such stipulations.
In the latter case, so far as redemption was concerned, the stipulations
were immaterial, but it is said that in both cases the Court of Chancery
would have restrained an action at law for damages for their breach.
This is possible, though I can find no instance of its having been done,
but clearly on a bill for an injunction to restrain an action at law the
plaintiff would have to shew some equity entitling him to be relieved
from his contract, and such equity could, I think, have been based
only on the usury laws, or the public policy which gave rise to them.

The last of the usury laws was repealed in 1854, and thenceforward
there was, in my opinion, no intelligible reason why mortgages to
secure loans should be on any different footing from other mortgages.
In particular, there was no reason why the old rule against a mortgagee

being able to stipulate for a collateral advantage should be maintained in any form or with any modification. . . . In every case in which a stipulation by a mortgagee for a collateral advantage has, since the repeal of the usury laws, been held invalid, the stipulation has been open to objection, either (1.) because it was unconscionable, or (2.) because it was in the nature of a penal clause clogging the equity arising on failure to exercise a contractual right to redeem, or (3.) because it was in the nature of a condition repugnant as well to the contractual as to the equitable right. . . .

In the present case it is clear from the evidence, if not from the agreement of August 24, 1910, itself, that the nature of the transaction was as follows: The defendant company wanted to borrow 10,000*l.*, and the plaintiffs desired to obtain an option of purchase over any sheepskins the defendants might have for sale during a period of five years. The plaintiffs agreed to lend the money in consideration of obtaining this option, and the defendant company agreed to give the option in consideration of obtaining the loan. The loan was to carry interest at 6 per cent. per annum, and was not to be called in by the plaintiffs for a specified period. The defendant company, however, might pay it off at any time. It was to be secured by a floating charge over the defendant company's undertaking. The option was to continue for five years, whether the loan was paid off or otherwise, and if the plaintiffs did not exercise their option as to any of the defendant company's skins, a commission on the sale of such skins was in certain events payable to the plaintiffs.

I doubt whether, even before the repeal of the usury laws, this perfectly fair and businesslike transaction would have been considered a mortgage within any equitable rule or maxim relating to mortgages. The only possible way of deciding whether a transaction is a mortgage within any such rule or maxim is by reference to the intention of the parties. It never was intended by the parties that if the defendant company exercised their right to pay off the loan they should get rid of the option. The option was not in the nature of a penalty, nor was it nor could it ever become inconsistent with or repugnant to any other part of the real bargain within any such rule or maxim. The same is true of the commission payable on the sale of skins as to which the option was not exercised. Under these circumstances it seems to me that the bargain must stand and that the plaintiffs are entitled to the relief they claim.

Order of the Court of Appeal reversed, and declare that the appellants are entitled to an injunction in the terms of the notice of motion with liberty to apply to the Chancery Division to dispose of the action. The respondents to pay the costs in the Court of Appeal and of the appeal to this House.

Lords' Journals, November 20, 1913.

Humble Oil & Refining Co. v. Doerr
123 N.J. Super. 530, 303 A.2d 898 (1973)

ACKERMAN, J.S.C.

The ancient doctrine that a mortgagor equity of redemption may not be "clogged" has rarely been involved in litigation in this state. This case involves a novel application of the doctrine and, so far as research by counsel and the court has disclosed, there are no precedents directly in point. The specific point involved is whether the doctrine, which bars a mortgagee from clogging the mortgagor's equity of redemption and prohibits him from taking an option to purchase the property from the mortgagor as a part of the original mortgage transaction, also bars the mortgagor's guarantor from taking such option. In the circumstances of this case it is the conclusion of the court that it does. . . .

Defendant Josephine Venice Rokita Doerr (hereinafter referred to as "Josephine") is the owner of a piece of real property located on the northeast corner of Boulevard and Michigan Avenue in Kenilworth. The parties agree that it is now one of the choice locations for a gasoline service station in Union County. The property was acquired in about 1944 by Pat Venice, Josephine's first husband. He intended to erect a service station thereon but died in 1947 without having carried his plans into effect, and Josephine succeeded to the sole ownership of the premises as well as to other parcels of real estate in Kenilworth. . . .

In 1953 Josephine remarried. Her second husband, Victor W. Rokita (hereinafter "Victor"), took over the management of the service station. In 1958 he took steps to add three bays to the garage in order to expand the facilities for performing automotive repair work. He went to the Union County Trust Company, which already held the mortgage on the premises, to arrange for additional financing, and that bank apparently agreed to advance approximately $20,000 secured by a first mortgage on the land and building. These plans came to the attention of plaintiff Humble Oil & Refining Company (then Esso Standard Oil Company and hereinafter referred to as "Humble"), whose products were sold at the station. John Alden, the Humble representative who serviced Victor's account, approached Victor and told him that Humble could get him better terms — $35,000, rather than $20,000, at a lesser interest rate and for a longer term. Alden discussed the matter and negotiated first with Victor alone and then with both Victor and Josephine. These favorable terms were to be obtained by leasing the station to Humble at a rental equal to the amount to be paid each month by Victor and Josephine on the new mortgage, which would be granted by The National State Bank, Elizabeth, N. J., and by having Victor and Josephine assign the Humble rental payments to the bank as additional security. Humble would then lease back to them at the same rental and they would continue to operate the service station. . . .

As the result of the negotiations it was agreed that the financing arranged by Humble would be accepted, and a lease was entered into between Victor and Josephine, as lessors, and Humble, as lessee, under date of September 5, 1958, for a 15-year term commencing on September 1, 1959 (approximately one year later) and ending on September 1, 1974, at a rental to be paid by Humble of $272.30 a month, the exact amount required to be paid each month to The National State Bank by Victor and Josephine under the contemplated mortgage. This lease, entitled "Lease to Company," was written on a printed Humble form bearing the legend "Lessor Built S.S.," which was drafted by Humble for use as the standard lease form to be utilized in instances where Humble leased premises with stations already built thereon or being constructed thereon by owner-lessors. The provisions of this form were obviously designed to be fully protective of Humble's interest as lessee.

The provision of the lease which is directly involved here is that which granted a purchase option to Humble. The option provision recites that the lessors, "in consideration of this lease," grant to Humble the option to purchase the property for the sum of $150,000 "at any time" during the term of the lease. The price is to be paid on transfer of good and marketable title by the lessors by warranty deed free and clear of all encumbrances, and requires that title should be closed and deed delivered on the 30th day after the exercise of the option, unless extended by mutual agreement.

On May 29, 1959 Victor and Josephine entered into a $35,000 construction mortgage with The National State Bank and formally assigned their interest in the Humble lease to the bank. Thereafter the additional three bays were apparently constructed and on January 12, 1960, the 15-year permanent mortgage loan for $35,000 was entered into. . . .

By letter dated October 7, 1968, approximately ten years after the original lease was signed and 8½ years after the 15-year term of the lease commenced to run under its terms as modified, Humble wrote to Josephine and Victor exercising the option to buy the premises, free and clear of all encumbrances, for $150,000. Humble re-exercised its option by letter dated March 3, 1969. When Josephine replied through her attorneys that the option had no legal validity, Humble started this action.

Humble sues for specific performance and, in the alternative, for damages. It claims that the value of the property in 1969 at the time of final exercise of the option was $240,000. Josephine filed an answer denying that she was even aware of the option prior to receipt of Humble's first letter exercising it in October 1968. In addition, she charged that the option was granted because of mutual mistake or mistake on her part induced because of inequitable conduct on the part of Humble, and that she was caused to sign the lease because of Humble's fraud and inequitable conduct in that she, a person of limited education and without business experience, and without legal representation or independent advice, was induced to sign the complicated lease and mortgage papers which she did not understand. . . .

As is apparent from the above recitation, at no time in her pleadings did Josephine spell out in so many words that the option was invalid because it constituted an impermissible clog on her equity of redemption. Nor was such theory specifically mentioned in her contentions contained in the pretrial order or in the trial briefs submitted in advance of trial. It was first advanced at the end of the case after the court had referred counsel to the decision in Barr v. Granahan, 255 Wis. 192, 38 N.W.2d 705, 10 A.L.R.2d 227 (Sup. Ct. 1949). . . . The factual allegations and contentions in her answer and the pretrial order, and the evidence adduced in support thereof, warrant relief on any legal theory that accommodates them, including the clogging doctrine, and Humble's objection is obviously without merit. . . .

I have concluded that Humble was not guilty of fraudulent misrepresentations or concealment and that Josephine is not entitled to relief under normal rules because of mistake. . . .

Nor is she entitled to relief, setting aside for the moment the fact that the option was given in connection with a mortgage loan, because the option price was inadequate in the light of the value of the property at the time it was given, or because of an increase in the value of the premises during the years since the granting of the option. . . .

It is also well settled that, in the normal case, an option to purchase at a named price cannot be voided merely because of subsequent enhancement of the value of the property. . . .

It is evident, therefore, that if it were not for the fact that the option was given in connection with a mortgage loan, Josephine would not be entitled to relief. Because it was so connected however, the option is void and unenforcible. It is a clog on Josephine's equity of redemption.

For centuries it has been the rule that a mortgagor's equity of redemption cannot be clogged and that he cannot, as a part of the original mortgage transaction, cut off or surrender his right to redeem. Any agreement which does so is void and unenforcible as against public policy. . . .

As a part of the doctrine it is well settled that an option to buy the property for a fixed sum cannot be taken contemporaneously by the mortgagee. . . .

The basic policy behind the doctrine has remained vital and unchanged over the years. As stated by our Court of Chancery in 1832 in Youle v. Richards, 1 N.J. Eq. 534, 538, "There would have been, without it, a door open for the imposition of every kind of restraint on the equity of redemption, and thereby the borrower, through necessity, would have been driven to embrace any terms, however unequal or cruel; which would have tended greatly to the furtherance of usury, and the conversion of the equitable jurisdiction of the court into an engine of fraud and oppression." . . .

So strong is the policy behind the rule that it is applied to hold such options absolutely void and unenforcible regardless of whether there is actual oppression in the specific case. . . . Where the option is a part of the original loan transaction it is therefore absolutely void.

Moreover, it is also the law that although a mortgagor can at a later date, after the original mortgage transaction, surrender his equity of redemption to the mortgagee and enter into an option or agreement to sell, it must be a fair bargain for an independent and adequate consideration. From the earliest days courts of equity have carefully scrutinized such arrangements. This rule is universally applied, in New Jersey and elsewhere, and it applies both to mortgages of real property and pledges of personal property. Normally the burden is imposed upon the mortgagee to prove fairness. The general rule is stated in 55 Am. Jur. 2d Mortgages §1220 at 1001:

> However any contract by which the mortgagor sells or conveys his interest to the mortgagee is viewed suspiciously and is carefully scrutinized in a court of equity. The sale and conveyance of the equity of redemption to the mortgagee must be fair, frank, honest, and without fraud, undue influence, oppression, or unconscionable advantage of the mortgagor's poverty, distress, or fears of the position of the mortgagee. . . .

The above rules, one of which applies to options taken as a part of original mortgage transactions and the other which applies to options taken at a subsequent time, are both clearly indicative of the jealousy with which courts guard mortgagors. Normally they are applied to conventional mortgagees. Here Humble was not a conventional mortgagee since it did not lend its own funds to the Rokitas. The question, then, is to what extent do the above rules apply to the option in Humble's hands?

First, it is my conclusion on the facts of this case that the anti-clogging rule applies fully to Humble and that the option is absolutely void in its hands, regardless of actual fairness or oppression, just as it would be in the hands of any regular mortgagee. . . . It is clear that equity looks to substance rather than to form, and that a guarantor or surety who takes property or an interest therein as security for his guaranty is a mortgagee thereof in equity. . . . The option was therefore a clog on the Rokitas' right to redeem from Humble as an equitable mortgagee.

Moreover, Humble had the option under the lease, in the event of a mortgage default by the Rokitas and an acceleration by the bank, to step into the bank's shoes as regular mortgagee.

In addition, . . . [i]t was Humble, not the Rokitas, which had a prior relationship with the bank and brought it into this transaction. Humble was therefore not simply an isolated guarantor, and the option was an integral part of the overall mortgage transaction in which Humble was a direct participant. Unico v. Owen, 50 N.J. 101, 112-113, 122-123, 232 A.2d 405 (1967).

Furthermore, it is clear that Humble was the dominant party in the transaction. Humble volunteered its participation and it was Humble's power and position which caused the loan transaction to come into being. It dictated the terms of the loan and offered them to the Rokitas on a "take it or leave it" basis. Its standard printed forms were used. It, rather than the bank, insisted upon the option. It was therefore the party which was in the position to "exact severe terms" and "concessions" from the Rokitas as debtors. See cases cited in Point III, supra.

Finally, it is clear that this was strictly a loan transaction. Regardless of Humble's business motives for entering into it, cf. Esso Petroleum Co., Ltd. v. Harpers Garage (Stoweport) Ltd., [1968] A.C. 269, the Rokitas were bargaining for a loan and nothing more. Humble never owned a prior interest in the property and was not a joint venturer with the Rokitas in the development of the station. The lease was what is known in the trade as a "two-party" lease rather than a "three-party" lease. It was created solely as a security device in connection with a mortgage loan and it was never intended that Humble should actually enter into possession of the property, or run the business, or invest any of its own funds in the premises. There was therefore no special reason or justification for demanding an option here — it was simply a price demanded by Humble for lending credit which permitted the loan transaction to come into being.

In these circumstances all the policy reasons behind the anti-clogging rule, applicable to mortgagees in general, apply to Humble here with full vigor. Since this is so, the option is void without necessity of inquiry as to whether or not it was unfair or oppressive. . . .

Under the alternate rule, if applied here, therefore, the option is unenforceable because close scrutiny shows that the transaction is unfair, inequitable and oppressive. See Barr v. Granahan, supra; see Williams, "Clogging the Equity of Redemption," 40 W. Va. L.Q. 31 (1933) and authorities cited above. . . .

Although the result in this case is arrived at by application of ancient rules relating to mortgages, it may be noted that these rules are in harmony with modern decisions which deal with somewhat similar problems and apply the same underlying considerations of public policy. Indeed, these ancient rules provide precedents from which the modern decisions flow. . . .

Cal. Civ. Code §2906 (1991)

Section 2906.   Secured party: Option to acquire interest in real property collateral; Priority; Validity. An option granted to a secured party by a debtor to acquire an interest in real property collateral takes priority as of its recording and is effective according to its terms if the right to exercise the option is not dependent upon the occurrence of a default with respect to the security agreement and, where the real property which is the subject of the option is other than residential real property containing four or fewer units, shall not be deemed invalid or ineffective on the basis that the secured party has impaired the debtor's equity of redemption in violation of common law or Section 2889. [Section 2889 invalidates "contracts for forfeiture of property subject to a lien, in satisfaction of the obligation secured thereby, and all contracts in restraint of the right of redemption from a lien."] This section shall not be construed to make valid or effective an otherwise unlawful option nor shall any inference be drawn from this section as to the validity or application of common law with respect to residential real property containing four or fewer units.

N.Y. Gen. Oblig. L. §5-334 (1990)

SECTION 5-334.   OPTION OR RIGHT TO
                 ACQUIRE INTEREST IN
                 PROPERTY.

1. An option or right to acquire an equity or other ownership interest in property or in a partnership, corporation, trust or other entity that owns property shall not be unenforceable because the owner of such interest grants such option or right to the holder of a mortgage which is a lien on such property or to the holder of a security interest in such property, simultaneously with or in connection with any loan or forbearance of money secured by such mortgage or security interest, if (a) the power to exercise such option or right is not dependent upon

[handwritten annotations: "The problem! com law prohibit clogging the right of redempt. Forbade lender options to acquire equity"]

the occurrence of a default with respect to such loan, forbearance, mortgage or security interest, and (b) such loan or forbearance is for the principal sum of two million five hundred thousand dollars or more when the option or right is granted. Loans or forbearances aggregating two million five hundred thousand dollars or more which are to be made or advanced to any one borrower in one or more installments pursuant to a written agreement by one or more lenders shall be deemed a single loan or forbearance for the total amount which the lender or lenders have agreed to make or advance pursuant to such agreement.

2. This section shall not be construed to limit, impair or otherwise affect the power of the holder of any option or right to acquire an equity or other ownership interest in property or in a partnership, corporation, trust or other entity that owns property, if such option or right is or would be enforceable without reference to this section.

3. This section shall apply to all options or rights which are exercised on or after the effective date of this section, notwithstanding the date when such options or rights were granted.

Uniform Land Security Interest Act §211

Section 211. Secured Party's Equity in Collateral.

[handwritten: "At A5 = s"]

Notwithstanding a rule denominated "fettering," clogging the equity of redemption," or "claiming a collateral advantage" or a rule of similar import:

(1) a secured party may, without adversely affecting its security interest, acquire from a debtor [other than a protected party] any direct or indirect present or future ownership interest in the collateral, including rights to any income, proceeds or increase in value derived from the collateral; and

(2) an option granted by a debtor [other than a protected party] to a secured party to acquire an interest in the collateral takes priority as of the date of its recording and is effective according to its terms if the right to exercise the option is not dependent upon the occurrence of a default under the security agreement.

[handwritten: "to allow lender equity"]

The following is the unconscionability provision from the now-defunct Uniform Land Transactions Act (§1-311) that was incorporated into the Uniform Common Interest Ownership Act.

[handwritten: "positions or options to acquire"]

[handwritten: "if not allowed for homeowners"]

Uniform Common Interest Ownership Act
§1-112, 7 U.L.A. 261 (1984)

§1-112. Unconscionable Agreement or Term of Contract

(a) The court, upon finding as a matter of law that a contract or contract clause was unconscionable at the time the contract was made, may refuse to enforce the contract, enforce the remainder of the contract without the unconscionable clause, or limit the application of any unconscionable clause in order to avoid an unconscionable result.

(b) Whenever it is claimed, or appears to the court, that a contract or any contract clause is or may be unconscionable, the parties, in order to aid the court in making the determination, must be afforded a reasonable opportunity to present evidence as to:

(1) the commercial setting of the negotiations;

(2) whether a party has knowingly taken advantage of the inability of the other party reasonably to protect his interests by reason of physical or mental infirmity, illiteracy, inability to understand the language of the agreement, or similar factors;

(3) the effect and purpose of the contract or clause; and

(4) if a sale, any gross disparity, at the time of contracting, between the amount charged for the property and the value of that property measured by the price at which similar property was readily obtainable in similar transactions. A disparity between the contract price and the value of the property measured by the price at which similar property was readily obtainable in similar transactions does not, of itself, render the contract unconscionable.

NOTES AND QUESTIONS

1. *Humble and* Krelinger. How would you distinguish the holdings in *Humble* and *Krelinger*? Are any of the following relevant? In *Krelinger,* the mortgagee had an option to purchase sheepskins from the borrowers at the highest market price, whereas in *Humble* the borrower would be compelled to sell real estate for an option price of $150,000; in *Krelinger* the transaction was structured as a loan made by the optionee, whereas in *Humble* the optionee was merely a lessee with an option to purchase; and in *Humble* the court assumed that the borrower was bargaining for a loan "and nothing more," whereas in *Krelinger,* as Lord Parker suggests, the parties may not have intended a mere mortgage but "something more complex" (a separate transaction)?

2. *Lord Parker's Two Rules: A Lender May Neither Clog the Equity of Redemption Nor Obtain a Collateral Advantage.* The court

in *Krelinger* was faced with the very broad formulation of the anti-clogging rule expressed in Jennings v. Ward, as, "a man shall not have interest for his money and a collateral advantage besides for the loan of it." Since a collateral advantage can be valued and the value considered as additional interest, is the *Jennings* formulation self-contradictory?

Lord Parker narrowed the application of the rule by analyzing the particular nature of mortgages that originally gave rise to it. He recognized that if a borrower failed to pay the debt secured by a mortgage (the mortgage being a conveyance to the mortgagee with a proviso for reconveyance to the mortgagor on payment of the obligation on a specified date), the mortgagee would, at law, hold an absolute interest in the property. Equity, however, he pointed out, did not treat time as of the essence and permitted the mortgagor to redeem even though the date of payment had passed. This equitable right derived from the nature of the mortgage as security, and any proviso in the mortgage that fettered reconveyance would be "repugnant" because it would contradict either the express contractual provision for reconveyance when the debt is paid on the due date or the "provision" for reconveyance after that time implied in equity. He thus stated the rule as follows: "The equity which arises on failure to exercise the contractual right cannot be fettered or clogged by any stipulation contained in the mortgage or entered into as part of the mortgage transaction."

As for the *Jennings* formulation, Lord Parker noted that the rule precluding a mortgagee from stipulating for a collateral advantage had never been applied to a mortgage other than one to secure *borrowed money* and cited authority that the prohibition on a collateral advantage had been based on the usury laws, which at the time had been repealed in England. Did Lord Parker, then, recognize two separate rules, first, the anti-clogging rule arising out of the nature of a mortgage, which would prevent the mortgagee from obtaining any right that would fetter the mortgagor's right to redeem in equity following default, and second, the anti-collateral advantage rule arising out of the laws against usury, which would prevent the mortgagee, whose mortgage secures borrowed funds, from obtaining any contractual advantage the value of which, when added to the interest, would exceed the allowed rate? Lord Parker concluded that the loan transaction was valid because the mortgagee's additional rights were outside the anti-clogging rule and not in violation of the anti-collateral advantage rule (usury laws having been repealed).

Assuming that Lord Parker did recognize two rules and that such a bifurcation is correct, how would he make the determination as to which rule applies when the circumstances are not as clear as they are in *Krelinger* or in the hypothetical he poses in his opinion? Would it be based on whether the parties intended a "mere mortgage" or "something more complex"? In *Humble*, wasn't the court looking to the intention of the parties when it concluded that the borrower was "bargaining for a loan and nothing more"? If so, what is the basic intent (or ultimate motive) of the borrower in a convertible mortgage transaction? Does this differ from the intent (or motive) of the lender?

Since the convertible mortgage contains both mortgage and option features, how can the agreement be drafted to make it less likely that it will be rendered unenforceable under the anti-clogging rule? Consider the advantages, disadvantages, and relative effectiveness of the following provisions in a convertible mortgage agreement designed to avoid anti-clogging problems: (i) separate consideration given for the option; (ii) separate documentation of the option; (iii) explicit documentation of the parties' intent in the mortgage agreement; (iv) a statement that the mortgagor is sophisticated, represented by counsel, and intends to engage in a sale-purchase transaction; (v) provision for termination of the option by the mortgagor on payment of a share of the property's fair market value to the mortgagee; (vi) limitation of the option to a partial, rather than a complete, interest in the property; (vii) designation of a third party as optionee; or (viii) waiver of the right to challenge the option's validity. What language in §5.4 of the loan agreement excerpted above would cause concern for counsel to the lender?

   3. More Case Law on the Anti-clogging Rule.   One of the principal American cases considering the anti-clogging rule in a commercial setting is MacArthur v. North Palm Beach Utilities, 202 So. 2d 181 (Fla. 1967), which reversed a lower court's holding that an option to purchase was an invalid fettering of the borrower-purchaser's right of equitable redemption. The plaintiff seller and defendant had entered into a sales contract for a large tract of land. The contract included a "utility agreement" under which the seller was to provide financing to the buyer for construction of a sewer system on the purchased property, which loan would be secured by the sewer system's land and equipment. The agreement also contained an option in favor of the seller for the purchase of the system. The court held that there was no clog on the equity of redemption since the land was encumbered by the option at the time the borrower-purchaser acquired it. The mortgage covered property subject to the option, and on repayment of the loan the borrower got its property back with the same state of title that existed when the mortgage was entered into. The *Humble* court distinguishes the facts in that case from *MacArthur*, noting that in *MacArthur* the mortgaged property was originally owned by the lender, who retained a purchase option from the time of sale. Does this mean that the lender and borrower in a convertible mortgage transaction can avoid the application of the anti-clogging rule by executing and recording the option prior to the execution and recordation of the mortgage? If not, what do you think the court would look to distinguish that situation from *MacArthur*?

In Smith v. Smith, 82 N.H. 399, 135 A. 25 (1926), a son lent his father money for the purchase of a house that secured the loan. The loan agreement gave the son a right of first refusal in the event of the sale of the property or option to purchase the property in the event of his father's death, at a price equal to the difference between the loan amount and the original purchase price. The court found the option to be "entirely independent of the mortgage" since the option did not relate to payment of the loan but only to sale of the property or the father's death. The judge stated that a collateral advantage would be held invalid only if it was found to "annul or restrict the right of the mortgagor to redeem the land from the lien of the mortgage." During his lifetime, the father was free to repay the loan and have his property free and clear of the option. Was this approach different from Lord Parker's in *Krelinger*?

The anti-clogging rule was applied to invalidate a purchase option in Hopping v. Baldridge, 130 Okla. 226, 266 P. 469 (1928). In this case the court found a clog on the equity of redemption where borrowers who were "hard pressed for money" granted an option to purchase a half interest in the oil and mining rights in the mortgaged property "at the same time and as part of the same transaction" as the loan. In Coursey v. Fairchild, 436 P.2d 35 (Okla. 1967), a borrower deeded to its mortgagee mineral rights in a portion of the mortgaged property for a term of 25 years. The deed was executed 11 days after the note and mortgage were signed but was part of the agreement to extend the mortgage debt. When the note was repaid after one year, the lenders refused to reconvey the mineral deed. The court held that retention of the deed was an impermissible restraint on the borrower's right to redeem. "Upon discharge of the debt . . . the mortgagor is entitled, by force of law, to have . . . his entire estate restored to that extent he would have had if the mortgage transaction had never taken place." 436 P.2d at 38. The court, in view of an Oklahoma statute forbidding clogging, would not consider the intent of the parties but only the form and substance of the agreement. Notwithstanding the language of the decision, wasn't a conclusion as to the intent of the parties a necessary element in the court's determination that the loan and the option to purchase mineral rights were part of the same mortgage transaction and not two separate transactions?

4. *Public Policy and Legislative Solutions.* As the cases discussed above indicate, a major element of the anti-clogging rule as applied by the courts has been to protect the hard-pressed borrower from losing his mortgaged property to a lender through the terms of a harsh or overreaching agreement. However, when the common-law rule is for-

mulated in terms of the form and not the substance of the agreement and ignores the parties' intent, its application can result in invalidating otherwise legitimate, fully negotiated business transactions between fully informed, sophisticated parties who need no public policy protection. It may be that the policy purposes that underlie the rule can be better served by applying other theories to test the enforceability of such options, such as unconscionability (see Chapter 7A, note 5, infra) and usury (see Chapter 5B3, note 4). How did the *Doerr* court deal with the public policy issue?

The New York and California statutes exempt certain classes of secured transactions from the anti-clogging rule and permit them to be governed by freedom of contract. What transactions are not exempted, and why? Note the New York dollar limitation. In New York, loans over $250,000 are not subject to usury limitations other than the 25 percent criminal usury statute, and those over $2.5 million are not subject to any usury restriction. (N.Y. Gen. Oblig. L. §5-501(6) (McKinney 1989)). If Lord Parker was correct in assuming that the anti-clogging rule is separate from the anti-collateral advantage rule, does the dollar limitation in the New York statute make sense? If certain transactions are specifically exempted from the anti-clogging rule, is it correct to infer that transactions not so exempted are subject to the rule? How does each statute handle such implication? Both the excerpted state laws and the uniform act do not permit exemption in any case where the option is conditioned on default. What policy purpose is served by this provision? If under a loan agreement default is just one of the events triggering an option to convert (as in the loan agreement excerpted above) but in fact is not the basis for the actual exercise of the option, would the existence of the default language nevertheless remove the option from the protection of these statutes?

For additional background on the clogging issue see Cooper-Hill and Slama, The Convertible Mortgage: Can It Be Separated from the Clogging Rule? 27 S. Tex. L. Rev. 407 (1986); Kane, The Mortgagee's Option to Purchase Mortgaged Property, in Financing Real Estate During the Inflationary 80s (B. Strum, ed.) (1981); Licht, The Clog on the Equity of Redemption and Its Effect on Modern Real Estate Finance, 60 St. John's L. Rev. 452 (1986); Maller, Financing Ideas, Unclogging the Equity of Redemption, 14 Real Est. L.J. 161 (1985); Preble and Cartwright, Convertible and Shared Appreciation Loans: Unclogging the Equity of Redemption, 20 Real Prop., Prob. & Tr. J. 821 (1985); Siegman and Linquanti, The Convertible Participating Mortgage: Planning Opportunities and Legal Pitfalls in Structuring the Transaction, 54 U. Colo. L. Rev. 295 (1983); and Comment, The Shared Appreciation Mortgage: A Clog on the Equity of Redemption? 15 J. Marshall L. Rev. 131 (1982).

5. *The Doctrine of Unconscionability.* Courts of equity traditionally have invoked principles akin to what we now call the doctrine of unconscionability to strike down transactions involving severe overreaching or unfair advantage obtained by one party over another of unequal bargaining power or ability. The two principal cases excerpted above reflect the fact that equity will not sanction an oppressive result.

In *Krelinger* Lord Parker stated that the court would put aside a "collateral advantage" to a mortgagee if it were "unfair and unconscionable." *Doerr* offers an alternative holding in favor of the borrowers based on the ground that the transaction was "unconscionable and oppressive." Point III of that opinion traces the policy behind the rule against clogging the equity of redemption to protection of the borrower from the superior bargaining power of the lender. Similarly, counsel for the mortgagee in *Krelinger* argued that "the doctrine [against clogging] was originally designed to prevent the conversion of a mortgage into a purchase, and to guard against the oppression of necessitous landowners by mortgagees." Neither case, however, limited the property-based anti-clogging theory to unconscionable situations. Unconscionability was viewed as a separate and independent theory.

Lenders in modern real estate transactions have two reasons to be mindful of the doctrine of unconscionability. First, while the doctrine originated in the courts of equity and was applied to deny equitable remedies such as specific performance, it recently has acquired statutory recognition and is now applicable to cases at law. The Uniform Commercial Code was amended in 1977 to include §2-302, which deals explicitly with unconscionability in sales contracts. Moreover, the doctrine has been applied to transactions outside the Code. Indeed, this section was essentially adopted by the former Uniform Land Transactions Act in 1985 as §1-311, and as §1-112 of the Uniform Common Interest Ownership Act (as excerpted above). For additional background on the doctrine of unconscionability see Berger, Hard Leases Make Bad Law, 74 Colum. L. Rev. 791 (1974); Burton, Breach of Contract and the Common Law Duty to Perform in Good Faith, 94 Harv. L. Rev. 369 (1980); Eisenberg, The Bargain Principle and Its Limits, 95 Harv. L. Rev. 741 (1982); Ellinghaus, In Defense of Unconscionability, 78 Yale L.J. 757 (1969), and Leff, Unconscionability and the Code — The Emperor's New Clause, 115 U. Pa. L. Rev. 485 (1967).

6. *Questions.* To some extent the recent popularity of the convertible mortgage can be explained by the Tax Reform Act of 1986. Can you think of the reason why? Based on what you know of the nature of a convertible mortgage, why, do you think, is it such a popular financing format for foreign investors who are interested in obtaining some form of debt or equity interest in U.S. real estate?

Returning to our master hypothetical, suppose that in ten years the unamortized loan balance on Ace's loan has been reduced from $25 million to $20 million, while the value of the net assets, or equity, in the project has increased to $60 million. If Ace were to cancel the loan indebtedness of $20 million in exchange for a 50 percent equity share, worth $30 million, pursuant to §5.1 of the convertible loan agreement, could Dan Developer successfully argue that:

1. by exercising its option to convert debt into equity, Ace would be clogging Dan's right of equitable redemption and therefore the conversion privilege would be void as against public policy;
2. Dan should be allowed all the depreciation deductions on the building prior to the date on which Ace exercised its option if pursuant to a provision (such as §5.5 of the convertible loan agreement, excerpted above) Ace has participated in the day-to-day management of the project since the loan was made. Assume that if on the date the loan was made the property had been worth $40 million instead of $33 million (see Rev. Rul. 72-350, 1972-2 C.B. 394);
3. the present value of the option should be treated as additional interest in the year of conversion for local usury law purposes; or
4. the windfall to Ace as a consequence of converting debt in the amount of $20 million to equity worth $30 million would be unconscionable and as such should not be enforceable?

If Ace should participate in the management and control of the project prior to conversion pursuant to a provision (such as §5.5 of the convertible loan agreement, excerpted above), could Dan's third-party creditors or his trustee in bankruptcy successfully maintain that Ace should be treated constructively as Dan's partner and, as such, be held liable for the debts and torts of the venture?

B. JOINT VENTURES

A real estate joint venture usually takes the form of a partnership, either general or limited, between a developer and an institution or pension fund, for the operation, management, or development of commercial real estate. For example, in our master hypothetical, Dan Developer may find it difficult in times of tight money or adverse economic conditions to obtain sufficient long-term postconstruction financing. In addition, Dan may not be able to raise the necessary equity capital to cover the shortfall between the amount of the post-construction loan and the cost of the project. To meet this problem Dan may propose a package of investments to Ace Insurance Company referred to collectively as a "real estate joint venture." Under this package, Ace would purchase an interest in the equity as a partner in a joint venture owning the property and make a postconstruction loan to the proposed joint venture.

The real estate joint venture actually antedated the convertible mortgage by almost 15 years, having emerged in the late 1960s from what, at the time, were turbulent market conditions. It represented a virtual revolution in institutional investment strategies. The development of joint ventures is described in the following excerpt.

Roegge, Talbot, and Zinman, Real Estate Equity Investments and the Institutional Lender: Nothing Ventured, Nothing Gained
39 Fordham L. Rev. 579, 579-588 (1971)

I. THE INSTITUTIONAL LENDER AS A REAL ESTATE ENTREPRENEUR

In recent years there has been much talk about the activity of institutional investors in what are loosely called "joint ventures" in real estate. These investments may include single buildings or large developments located throughout the country. While in the past institutional investors traditionally restricted their real estate investments to fixed return mortgages and sale leasebacks, with changing economic conditions their philosophy also changed, resulting in the joint venture phenomenon. Some of the problems accompanying this change are the subject of this article.

A. "REVOLUTION" IN INSTITUTIONAL THINKING

The most important institutional lenders making long term mortgage loans traditionally have been life insurance companies, savings and loan associations, mutual savings banks, and banks as trustees for pension trusts. Commercial banks, which formerly were primarily interested in construction lending, have recently stepped up their long term mortgage lending, while insurance companies have also become active in the construction-lending field.

Life insurance companies constitute the largest element in long term commercial mortgage lending, with broad investment powers (though subject to regulation), and may be considered typical institutional investors. Their development as real estate entrepreneurs may represent the greatest change in attitude and approach to real estate investment by institutional lenders. In three states which are generally considered prominent in the area of life insurance — Massachusetts, New York and New Jersey — first mortgage loans became a permitted form of investment in 1818, 1848, and 1852, respectively. Somewhat later, investment (or perhaps it should be termed speculation) in real estate with or without statutory authority, became popular. In 1870, one of the most prominent New York insurance companies invested eighty percent of its assets in its home office building. In 1905, the Armstrong Committee, considering abuses by life insurance companies, reported:

> [T]he testimony taken by the committee discloses flagrant abuses in connection with investments in real estate. Under the guise of procuring suitable accommodation for the transaction of business excessive amounts have been expended in the acquisition of land and buildings not necessary in any proper sense for the uses of the corporation, which yield a poor return upon the amount expended. . . . *No further purchase of property should be permitted under subdivisions 1 and 2 of section 20 of the Insurance Law or under section 14 of the General Corporation Law without the consent of the Superintendent of Insurance upon his finding that the acquisition is necessary.* Section 13 of the General Corporation Law, providing that the Supreme Court might authorize purchases of real property in lieu of similar property disposed of, should be rendered inapplicable to insurance corporations.

This report led directly to the passage of section 100 of the New York Insurance Law of 1909, which was the precursor of the present provision of section 81(7). This section required that the Superintendent of Insurance approve any real estate acquisition other than through foreclosure or other satisfaction of debt. Under the terms of the statute, even ownership of foreclosed properties was expected to be terminated within five years, and extensions from the Insurance Department were not automatically granted. In 1922, the Insurance Law was amended to permit the acquisition of certain housing without the Superintendent's approval.

In 1946, the New York Insurance Law was changed by adding paragraph (h) to section 81(7), to permit investment in real estate for the production of income. The law also permitted improvement or development pursuant to an existing program to make the property income-producing. Significantly, properties acquired by foreclosure or deed in lieu thereof and held under subsection 7(c) could be transferred to paragraph (h), and no longer had to be disposed of within five years from the date of acquisition.

About the same time, other states — most notably New Jersey in

1945, and Massachusetts in 1947 — were adopting similar legislation. Finally, in 1963 the new Michigan constitution and resulting legislation authorized acquisition of real estate for investment, and in 1967, Texas permitted limited ownership. Consequently, ownership by life insurers of real estate for investment is permitted, in some form, in every state. From time to time various state statutes have been liberalized as to amount and other limitations.

While the legislative history of subsection 7(h) in New York shows an intent to permit insurance company investors to acquire and profit from equity acquisitions, most acquisitions under this subsection were "sale-leasebacks," under which the institution purchased real estate and leased it back to the tenant for a fixed net rent, often with the privilege of renewing at a lower rent. Presumably this renewal at a lower rent reflected the fact that the insurer, through fixed net rent during the initial term, would recover its initial investment plus a return approximately equal to or slightly above the prevailing rate of interest on first mortgages. The slightly higher rate of return reflected the fact that the purchase price of the property acquired in the sale-leaseback arrangement usually would exceed the limitations of two-thirds or three-fourths of the value of the real property which investment statutes frequently imposed upon mortgage lending, and that rent recovery, unlike foreclosure deficiency judgments, was limited . . . in the event of the tenant's bankruptcy and . . . reorganization. Despite the higher rate of return, the result of these early equity acquisitions with a fixed return, coupled with frequently inserted limited repurchase options or rejectable offer provisions, was to give the insurer little more economically than it had in conventional mortgage investing.

However, some insurers still had various buildings acquired through foreclosure, and in some cases such properties, after transfer to paragraph (h), were managed by managing agents and became highly profitable. Through efficient operation, higher rents, and perhaps modernization, these properties produced yields far in excess of those obtainable through mortgage lending. In some cases, subsequent sales of such properties also produced substantial capital gains. These properties — and also office building properties built and partially occupied by insurers, who leased to other tenants — proved that equity ownership could be highly profitable to institutional investors.

The number of foreclosed properties suitable for retention was strictly limited, however, and insurance companies were not always the best planners, developers, builders and promoters. Those normally engaged in these activities could be hired for a fee, but perhaps could not be expected to work with the same zest shown in developing properties in which they had a financial interest. In the late forties, the fifties and the early sixties, builders and developers did not view insurance companies as fellow equity participants in the many buildings they were constructing. Hopefully, the insurance company mortgage or purchase price in a sale-leaseback would cover all costs. If not, private sources of funds — generally from high tax bracket individuals investing as limited partners — would fill the gap. This situation prevailed well into the sixties.

Beginning about 1966, however, external factors produced a revolution in real estate development. The most significant of the factors were inflation, high interest rates, tight money, and falling common stock prices.

1. Inflation

While life insurers classically paid claims in fixed dollars, factors such as expenses and dividends caused them to seek protection against inflation not offered by fixed return mortgage loans or sale-leasebacks. Contingent interest or percentage rent were answers, but not total ones. Contingent interest, which is additional interest often based on the income of the property, faced limitations imposed by usury statutes, and by its very nature yielded nothing after maturity of the loan. Percentage rent, which is additional rent also based on such income, offered better possibilities. Many developers, however, did not wish to engage in a sale-leaseback, which involved a sale of the building and loss of income tax benefits. Similarly, institutional investors did not wish to buy only the land, since they would receive no tax benefits from ownership of a nondepreciable asset.

2. High Interest Rates

While in the late sixties interest rates increased to their greatest heights since the Civil War, some state usury statutes were not amended at the same speed at which national interest rates were increasing. Thus, in many jurisdictions mortgage loans, with or without contingent interest, ceased to constitute attractive investments for institutions. On the other hand, where usury laws permitted above average rates, fixed rate mortgage loans generally were non-prepayable for many years and thus constituted a serious burden on developers.

3. Tight Money

The "credit crunch" of 1966 and the general credit situation in 1969-1970 helped produce the so-called "revolution" in institutional thinking. Insurers obtained less money from mortgage prepayments and paid more out in policy loans, and banks and savings and loan associations were subject to a lack of growth in assets or actual disintermediation. Consequently, they limited the number of mortgage loans made and carefully scrutinized each mortgage, unwilling to lend as freely as in the past. Even where financing was available, the gap between the loan amount and the amount of money needed by the builder increased.

4. Falling Common Stock Prices

As this gap increased, the availability of funds from secondary sources (often wealthy individuals seeking tax shelters) was affected by a decline in common stock prices. With the Dow Jones industrial average falling from 989.12 on December 16, 1968 to 627.46 on May 26, 1970, many prospective investors could no longer borrow on their stock and, in any case, were not interested in acquiring additional tax losses.

The situation was ripe for change, and change came. Financial institutions, first slowly and perhaps nervously and then in ever greater volume, acquired true equity interests in office buildings, office parks, apartment house developments, industrial parks and other income-producing real estate. Some took their equity interests as bonuses for making loans. However, unless the loan exceeded the permitted percentage of value, either by too generous an appraisal or through the use of a "basket" or "leeway" statute, this did not solve the basic problem which led to the "revolution," i.e., the builder's shortage of funds. Even with an oversized loan, and without considering the problem of usury, his fixed charges would probably be too high. Therefore, more insurers entering the field bought an equity interest at a fair price based upon the value not when the project would be an established success, but reflecting the possibilities, the risks, and the potential at the time of agreement — usually before construction commenced. The equity interest acquired was usually substantial — typically fifty percent.

Some insurance companies apparently went further, giving up mortgage lending and investing their real estate funds only in equity interests. They, of course, obtained the highest leverage. Such investments, however, were possible only where someone else would make the mortgage loan without an equity investment. Opportunities of this nature were limited, since many institutions were not enthusiastic about making mortgage loans to give leverage to a competitor. Thus developers, at least in very large transactions, tended to seek large life insurers as both mortgage lenders and purchasers of equity interests, and the large life insurers sought large developments where they could invest not only in a mortgage loan, but also in a substantial interest in the equity.

B. EFFECT OF THE "REVOLUTION"

The partial shift of institutional funds from fixed return mortgage loans to equity investments did not constitute the entire "revolution." Changes resulting from this shift also comprised a large part of it.

As many life insurers began to acquire common stocks, institutional investment philosophy also changed. Safety properly remained essential, but the emphasis on what constituted safety shifted. The servant who buried his talent had kept it safe, but he was rebuked by his master. A life insurance loan officer investing throughout 1969 and 1970 in seven percent fixed return mortgage loans would not be praised. While safety lay in part in avoiding or reducing the effect of inflation, it became recognized that for large institutional investors safety should be measured by the whole, not as to each part. For instance, one loan officer might invest $100,000,000 in seven percent "ultra safe" ten year mortgage loans which, ignoring repayment and reinvestment of interest and amortization, would result in $170,000,000 in assets in ten years. On the other hand, another loan officer might put $90,000,000 of his $100,000,000 in slightly less safe eight percent ten year mortgages, and $10,000,000 in related equity interests of far greater risk. Assume that one $5,000,000 mortgage goes into default and shows no return above principal, and that the $10,000,000 equity interests show returns varying from partial loss of principal to a return of forty percent, but an overall return of twenty percent per annum for the ten year period. Again ignoring repayment and reinvestment of interest and amortization, his $90,000,000 will have grown to $158,000,000 and his $10,000,000 to $30,000,000 for a total of $188,000,000. He may have had to think harder, negotiate harder, and worry more, but who is to call his performance "less safe" or call him the less deserving servant?

Furthermore, insurers as equity investors obtained a better understanding of the developer's problems and his philosophy. One of his needs is speed, and this need alone has accelerated the change toward more prompt decisions and servicing which already was underway in many insurance companies. Coupled with the shift to common stock investments, this has effected a change in the attitude of some insurance company investment officers. Together with the development of new products such as real estate investment trusts, variable annuities and separate accounts, it has led to a new image for insurance companies. Insurers will probably never be the same.

If the insurer has changed, so has the developer. Traditionally somewhat of a rugged individualist who took the institutional investor's money but tried to hold the institution at arm's length, the developer dealt with limited partners who either knew and trusted him or else were unsophisticated in the area. In any event, they were not bothersome to him. The huge institution, however, had different approaches and different philosophies. Its officers wanted to know how much architects and contractors were being paid, and perhaps share in the writing of architectural and construction contracts. They were expense conscious, organization conscious, and conflict conscious. They were interested in the status of the developer's key subordinates. They imposed limits on, or wanted to know the reasons for, transactions with related corporations or persons. All this was perhaps initially galling to him, but he learned that he had a partner with far more to contribute than mere money. It had a wealth of experience in real estate matters, acquired through many decades of good and bad times. It also made available staffs of accounting, architectural, economic and legal experts, and knowledge of the entire country, its customs, possibilities, and economic data. The developer has profited through such relationships, and he, too, will never be the same.

Society has benefited and changed from this increased efficiency. As developers established relationships with large institutions, giving them a steadier source of equity funds, greater stability and counter cyclical influences emerged.

Perhaps most important, as the large life insurance companies began to invest in real estate equities and common stock, holders of life insurance policies and annuities could effortlessly benefit from balanced investment programs designed to produce safety and yield, while reducing the effect of inflation. This was previously possible only for the rich, who had diversified investment capabilities.

Today some of the external factors that produced the so-called revolution in real estate development are no longer present. Interest rates are beginning to decline; money is less tight; and common stock prices are rising. Nevertheless, real estate equity investments by institutional lenders have continued. Inflation is still with us; institutional thinking appears to have changed irrevocably; and developers, having learned to live with and having been benefited by institutional lenders as equity partners, continue to seek institutional funds for joint ventures in real estate.

NOTES AND QUESTIONS

While both convertible mortgages and participating mortgages have become permanent fixtures on the real estate financing scene, equity participations structured as joint ventures between developers and institutional lenders (such as life insurance companies) have waned since the early 1980s, primarily because of a conflict in investment philosophy between lenders (who, at the risk of overgeneralizing, want to share in the rewards but are conservative about risk-taking) and developers (who are aggressive risk-takers but abhor loss of management control). This downward trend is reflected by a dramatic decline in joint-venture-related loans made by U.S. life insurance companies from 6.2 percent of all loans made in 1983 to a comparable figure of 1.9 percent in 1988. Compare American Council on Life Insurance, Bull. No. 874, Table 3 (May 8, 1984) with Bull. No. 1065, Table 3 (April 10, 1989). Meanwhile, from 1980 to 1987 insurance companies exhibited a growing penchant for full direct ownership of income-producing real estate, as reflected by a doubling in the amount of their real estate holdings from $15 billion to $34 billion. American Council of Life Insurance, 1988 Life Insurance Fact Book, at 88. To some extent the declining popularity in joint venturing between borrowers and lenders (as opposed to the continued popularity of equity-sharing arrangements fashioned as participating mortgages) can be explained by the Tax Reform Act of 1986. Can you think of the reason why?

The overwhelming majority of full equity participations structured as joint ventures between developers and institutional lenders have been organized as either limited or general partnerships. The legal and tax aspects of these ownership entities are examined at Chapter 2B, note 7d.

The following are additional recommended joint venture readings: Barton and Morrison, Equity Participation Arrangements Between Institutional Lenders and Real Estate Developers, 12 St. Mary's L.J. 929 (1981); Kaster and Nellis, eds., Realty Joint Ventures 1987, Working In and Working Out, Practicing Law Institute Course Handbook No. 299 (1987); Keyles, The Demise of the Long-Term Fixed Rate Mortgage: Legal Implications of Alternative Investment Techniques, 1981 American Council of Life Insurance Legal Section Proc. 265; Londergan, Joint Ventures in Real Estate Investments: What Are They and Why Are They?, Proc., Legal Section, American Life Insurance Assn. 101 (1973); Nason, Engaging in Real Estate Equity Investments with Another Party — Use of the Joint Venture Vehicle, 21 Proc., Association of Life Insurance Counsel 1 (1979); Nellis and Hastie, Real Estate Joint Ventures in the 80's, in Financing Real Estate During the Inflationary 80's, at 210 (Strum, ed. 1981).

Chapter 8

Leasehold and Leaseback Financing

A. LEASEHOLD VERSUS FEE MORTGAGE FINANCING

In addition to selecting the optimum ownership entity (see Chapter 2B, note 7) the developer of new improved real estate must make another important prefinancing decision: whether to purchase or lease the underlying land on which the newly constructed improvements will be situated. If the decision is made to purchase the land, the developer can obtain a regular fee mortgage loan to cover both the purchase price of the land and the cost of developing and improving the land. Sometimes the developer will finance land costs separately with a subordinated purchase-money mortgage (see Chapter 9B, note 5a) from the seller-fee owner or with a land development loan from some institutional lender (see Chapter 9B, note 5b). Alternatively, the developer may decide merely to (1) lease the underlying fee from the fee owner under what is known as a ground lease (or, if the developer owns the land, sell the land and lease it back from the new owner) and (2) obtain a so-called leasehold mortgage to fund the costs of both developing the land and constructing the improvements.

In the case of an ordinary fee mortgage, the lender's security for its loan is a mortgage lien not just on the mortgagor's fee title to the improvements but on his fee ownership of the land as well. In other words, a mortgage on the fee affords the lender the security of the entire estate in the land. In addition, the legal and tax status of the mortgagor with respect to the land is that of a fee owner rather than that of a ground lessee.

By contrast, in the case of a leasehold mortgage, whether the developer ground-leases the fee or engages in a sale and leaseback of land that he already owns, the security for the loan is merely the mortgagor's defeasible leasehold, or possessory estate, plus the improvements erected thereon. The leasehold mortgagee, therefore, is the lessee once removed, whereas the fee mortgagee is the fee owner once removed. In addition, the legal and tax status of the leasehold mortgagor is that of a lessee rather than that of a fee owner.

In the case of existing improvements the developer might ground-lease both the land and the building. Suppose, however, the developer ground-leases the land and purchases the building. Or, suppose the owner sells the land but only ground-leases the building to the developer. Further assume that the purchaser-developer obtains a so-called leasehold mortgage to either finance the cost of the building or, in the latter case, to fund the purchase price of the land. For the sake of accuracy, in the first instance the mortgagee would obtain a leasehold mortgage on the developer's leasehold estate and a fee mortgage on its fee title to the building. In the second instance the mortgagee would obtain a fee mortgage on the land and a leasehold mortgage on the building. Finally, if the owner engages in a sale and leaseback of the land and building and the purchaser-lessor obtains mortgage financing, the mortgagee will obtain a fee mortgage on the land and improvements. However, if the seller retains fee simple title to the building under the terms of the leaseback agreement, the mortgagee will only obtain a fee mortgage on the land.

Accordingly, any choice between leasehold and fee mortgage financing means that both lender and developer should take into account the legal, tax, and business considerations discussed at Chapter 8A1, infra. However, as we shall see at Chapter 8A4, infra, if the fee owner can be persuaded to subject his fee interest to the lien of the leasehold mortgage, such a "streamlined" mortgage arrangement can produce "the best of both worlds" for the parties by combining the tax advantages of leasehold financing with the nontax advantages of fee mortgage financing.

The following brief overview will introduce our examination of leasehold financing.

Halper, Introducing the Ground Lease
15 Real Est. Rev. 24 (Fall 1985)

INTRODUCING THE GROUND LEASE

Ground leases are strange documents, and negotiating them is not a game for amateurs. Botched ground leases have impeded development of many parcels of land for long periods. Weed fields and garbage dumps that could have supported apartment houses and office buildings have remained weed fields and garbage dumps for decades because of inept legal work.

The idea of separating the ownership of land from the right to exploit the potential of the land has venerable roots. Arrangements that were the ancestors of ground leasing were important in England at the time of the Norman conquest. Similar practices were used in many other agricultural societies. When farming was society's main industry, the groups that wielded power usually did so by retaining control over the land.

In our society, land ownership does not necessarily confer power. But, land ownership continues to give people the feeling of power. Some people buy land for no other reason than the thrill of ownership. People who inherit land may refuse to sell it because of a desire to keep it in the family. Even governmental bodies and lawyers are convinced that land is special. Land and its improvements are still called "*real* property," as if a watch, a trademark, a diamond, an automobile, or a hamburger were not "real."

Our system of real property taxation encourages land speculation and continuous ownership by people who have neither the inclination nor the resources to exploit their holdings. Local governments tax real property on the basis of its "assessed valuation." They usually assess land gently, and place the preponderant tax burden on improvements. As a result, owners of unused land do not face the pressures of stiff real estate tax bills.

From time to time, authors of popular "success" books or financial writers advise their readers to buy land because "no new land is being manufactured." Sometimes these authors attract disciples who rush to buy land that nobody needs for the time being and that, normally, nobody wants.

TO LEASE OR NOT TO LEASE

When a parcel of land is about to be developed, under normal circumstances, one party owns the land and another party wants to develop it.

The most obvious but not always the most appropriate solution is for the developer to purchase the land from the landowner. The sale may not take place because the owner refuses to sell. Here are the most obvious reasons why an owner might prefer not to sell:

- He may have emotional ties to the property.
- He may wish to avoid a capital gains tax.
- He may have an unshakable faith in the potential income he could derive from the land in the future.
- He may want his children or grandchildren to have the opportunity to own buildings to be constructed by others.

There are also many reasons why a developer may prefer not to buy:

- The developer who doesn't buy doesn't pay a purchase price. Thus he reduces his front-end investment.
- Tax deductions for depreciation apply only to buildings. If the investor doesn't allocate cash to land purchase, the ratio of depreciation deductions to invested cash is greater than if part of the cash is spent for land.
- The return of the developer's cash investment is usually higher.
- For tax and other reasons, the annual cost of ground rent may be an easier burden to bear than the annual cost of principal and interest needed to discharge the loan that finances the land purchase.

ELEMENTS OF THE LEASE NEGOTIATION

Once a landowner and developer agree to negotiate a lease, they must proceed cautiously and professionally. If a landowner negotiates lease provisions carelessly, he may lose his land entirely or at least face years of little or no rental income. A developer who does a thoughtless job of negotiating a ground lease might find himself in the midst of construction and unable to make arrangements for permanent financing because one or more clauses in the ground lease offend the lender. He may spend months trying to sublet space and find that the prospective occupants are unwilling to execute subleases because of defects in the ground lease.

Ground leases come in all sizes and varieties, just like suits. If you have a big behind and narrow shoulders, or if you have a weight lifter's chest and narrow hips, you need a good tailor. Similarly, every ground lease draftsman must tailor his product to the specific transaction.

Here is a list of only a few of the circumstances that may affect the formats of ground leases. The land might be urban, suburban, or rural. If urban, the land might be in a blighted area, in a "100 percent" location, or in a medium-grade location. If suburban, it might be in a developed or partially developed area. The land might be vacant or improved. If improved, the parties might contemplate demolishing the existing structures, improving them, or leaving them alone. The owner of a building might be selling the underlying land in an effort to raise money. The land might be an unused part of a shopping center and leased with appurtenant parking rights. There might be no land at all, and the subject transaction might concern air rights to the premises. The intended use might be development, recreation, agriculture, mining, or transportation.

Each of these circumstances suggests a different tension in the landlord-tenant relationship, and the negotiators must be prepared to adjust their favorite clauses to fit the needs of the parties.

"Subordinated" and "Unsubordinated" Ground Leases

Perhaps the most important argument that differentiates one ground lease from another is whether the ground lease is going to be "subordinated" or "unsubordinated."

Subordinated ground leases are ground leases under which the landowner agrees to execute one or more mortgages of his land to secure loans made to the developer by third parties. The guts of the relationship is that the developer borrows the money he needs to construct the buildings on the land, but part of the security he offers for the loan is the land — an asset belonging to the landowner. A lending institution is usually just as happy with a mortgage executed by a landowner *and* a developer-tenant as it would have been if the developer had purchased the land and were the sole party to execute the mortgage.

An unsubordinated ground lease, of course, does not require the landlord to execute mortgages to secure the developer-tenant's loans. However, the developer with an unsubordinated ground lease may have a difficult time obtaining a loan.

Pleasing the Institutional Investor

Whether the lease is subordinated or unsubordinated, the developer must be able to please an institutional investor that is looking for adequate security for its loan or other investment in the project. If the ground lease is subordinated, the institutional investor will probably be satisfied. But if the landowner executes the mortgage and the developer defaults on the debt secured by the mortgage, the landowner will lose his land to the institution.

On the other hand, note what happens when the developer-borrower, who is also the tenant under an unsubordinated ground lease, defaults with respect to its obligations to the institution. If the debt is secured only by the developer's leasehold estate, the institution can levy on the leasehold estate only. As a practical matter, this means that the institution becomes the tenant under the ground lease.

Institutional investors are aware that a security interest in a leasehold estate may not be worth anything at the critical moment when the developer is in trouble. At the time a developer fails to meet his obligations to repay an institutional mortgage loan, it is likely that he is also in default under the ground lease. If that is so, the landowner may be in a position to cancel the lease before the institutional lender has a chance to preserve its only security for the debt, the leasehold estate, by curing the default.

A landowner who cancels a ground lease sees himself as a lottery winner. He may become the owner of all the buildings and other improvements that the developer constructed with the institution's funds.

So the subordinated ground lease puts the landowner at risk, and the unsubordinated lease puts the lender at risk. The real artistry is to organize an unsubordinated ground lease so that a prospective mortgage lender or other institutional lender will be convinced that the borrower-tenant's leasehold estate will be adequate security for the mortgage debt despite the landowner's potential right to eliminate the security as a result of a default under the lease by the tenant.

1. Legal, Tax, and Business Considerations

From a business perspective, the most significant advantage of leasehold mortgage financing should be obvious. Since the developer is not purchasing the land (or is selling the fee title to land already owned), the initial cash outlay will be less. Therefore, the developer can maximize the cash available for working capital at the outset of the venture when it is most needed.

There is a correlative disadvantage, of course. The developer does not own the land on the expiration of the ground lease, loses the benefit of any interim appreciation in the value of the land, and must abandon any leasehold improvements to the fee owner-ground lessor at the end of the lease term. Usually the lease provides for an option to renew, and the lease term including renewals is for a period equal to or exceeding the useful life of the building, so that the ground lessee will receive the full benefit of the improvements during their useful life. Moreover, although the lease may contain one or more options for the ground lessee to purchase the fee or to have a right of first refusal, the ground lessee is still likely to forgo the increase in land value because business, legal, or tax considerations frequently dictate that the option price be geared to the current market value of the land. See Chapter 8B2, note 1, infra. In many cases, the amount of rent payable under the ground lease ("ground rent") approximates the additional debt service the developer would have paid had he decided to purchase the land and obtain a larger fee mortgage to fund the purchase price of the land as well as the cost of developing the land and constructing the planned improvements.

Accordingly, since the developer's initial cash outlay will be less and yet net rental income from the occupancy-subtenants will frequently remain about the same whether or not the developer purchases the fee, the developer may be able to use leasehold financing as a way to leverage investment costs and thereby increase the rate of return on the equity capital invested by the developer and his investors. See Table 8-1. This enhanced leveraging ability may be especially important to a particular developer in an inflationary economy when the cost of land is high and the mortgage money market is tight. Indeed, leasehold financing may be necessary to develop a particular parcel of land because some owners of prime land, particularly in urban areas, may refuse to sell their land because the anticipated rate of appreciation in the value of the land is so high. In other instances, the owner may not have the legal capacity to transfer title (as, for example, a trustee who is prohibited from doing so under the terms of the trust). The owner also may be constrained by some compelling tax consideration (as, for example, a fee owner with a low basis in the property who might obtain a higher after-tax rate of return by leasing the real estate than by selling and reinvesting the after-gain tax proceeds).

Returning to the master hypothetical at Chapter 5B and assuming that Ace Insurance Company is willing to make either a leasehold mortgage or a fee mortgage loan to Dan at the same loan-to-value ratio of 75 percent, what would be the difference in Dan's initial cash outlay should Dan obtain the former rather than the latter to fund the cost of the proposed project?

From a legal perspective, the principal consideration with respect to leasehold mortgage financing as opposed to fee mortgage financing is that the mortgagor's interest in the leasehold improvements and the continued existence of the leasehold estate is dependent upon compliance with the terms of the ground lease. Consequently, in the absence of a "streamlined mortgage" arrangement (discussed at Chapter 8A4, infra), the security of the leasehold mortgagee is but a defeasible estate that is subject to termination under circumstances where the mortgagee may not be able to cure all potential defaults by its mortgagor. Moreover, such extinguishment could occur regardless of what terms are included in the leasehold mortgage since the leasehold mortgagee is, in effect, an outside party to the lease agreement. Accordingly, as discussed at Chapter 8A3, infra, the leasehold mortgagee will require that the ground lease be drafted so as to incorporate those protective provisions that will place it in a position to control all contingencies that could terminate the leasehold estate and wipe out its security interest. Be that as it may, the lender will frequently be more restrictive in regard to the terms of the loan (e.g., higher rate of interest higher debt-coverage ratio, or lower loan-to-value ratio) with respect to ordinary leasehold financing because of the inherent risk of taking a security interest that is defeasible.

From a tax perspective, it may be advantageous for the developer to lease rather than purchase the fee, especially when the purchase price of the land is high relative to the other costs of the project. If the developer leases the land, the rent payable under the ground lease is deductible in its entirety for income tax purposes. By contrast, if the developer purchases the fee, such land ownership would not provide any depreciation deduction[1] since land is not a depreciable asset. Consequently, since the payment of mortgage interest is deductible but the repayment of principal is not, if the land is leased rather than purchased, the developer, as ground lessee, will be able to depreciate his cost of using the land in the guise of ground rent since part of the deductible ground rent really represents the extra nondeductible amortization he would have paid on the larger fee mortgage had he purchased the underlying fee.

In addition, the ground lessee-developer will still be entitled to the depreciation deductions on the leasehold improvements since he would be entitled to recoup his capital investment in the improvements.[2] Even though the fee owner has vested legal title to the improvements, the ground lessee will still be entitled to the depreciation or amortization deduction since it retains the beneficial enjoyment of the premises and bears the economic exhaustion burden of its capital investment in the property.[3] However, in the case of existing improvements where the owner engages in a sale and leaseback, the owner may insist on a leaseback of the land only and retain title to the building so that it can retain the right to take depreciation on the building, which in some instances may generate more tax deductions than the owner would receive as a lessee of the building.

The Internal Revenue Code used to provide a complicated set of tests for determining the period over which leasehold improvements can be depreciated or amortized if the lease contained a renewal option.[4] However, under current law, for improvements made after 1986 the ground lessee must recover the cost of the leasehold improvements over the applicable cost recovery period whether it be 27½ years (for

---

1. Ownership of the land would provide a limited tax deduction for payment of local property taxes; however, frequently local taxes attributable to the land are passed through and payable by the ground lessee under the terms of the ground lease.

2. Treas. Reg. §1.162-11(b)(2). If the estimated useful life of the improvements is longer than the remaining term of the lease, the cost of the leasehold improvements can be amortized over the remaining lease term. Treas. Reg. §1.167(a)-4.

3. See Helvering v. F. & R. Lazarus & Co., 308 U.S. 252, 254 (1939) (involving a sale and leaseback); Rev. Rul. 62-178, 1962-2 C.B. 91.

4. Under prior law I.R.C. §178 essentially provided that where the remaining initial term was less than 60 percent of the leasehold improvement's useful life at completion, the lease term would include renewal periods for the purpose of depreciation or amortization.

residential property) or 31½ years (for commercial property), regardless of the lease term.

As observed at Chapter 3B2, both a ground lessee and a leasehold mortgagee can obtain title insurance protection by obtaining an ALTA Leasehold Owner's Policy or Leasehold Loan Policy, respectively. The former policy, which first became available in 1975, insures the ground lessee's right to possession under the ground lease (including any renewal period). However, coverage under the policy is conditioned on the lessee's compliance with the terms of the ground lease, and the insured is not protected against breaches of a contractual nature by the ground lessor such as the latter's breach of a covenant to make tenant's alterations.

For articles discussing whether to lease or to purchase, see generally Torkildson, The Economic Recovery Tax Act: Safe Harbor Rule for Leases, 47 J. Air, L. and Commerce 565, 571-585 (1982) (advantages and disadvantages to lessor and lessee of leases); Callahan, The Lease Versus Purchase Decision in the Public Sector, 34 Nat. Tax J. 235 (1980) (lease versus purchase factors for a governmental entity); Shenkman, Ground Leases: Tax Planning Ideas for a Real Estate Financing Tool, 2 Real Est. Fin. J. 10 (Summer 1986).

The foregoing considerations can be illustrated by the following hypothetical case (see Table 8-1). Dan Developer plans to construct a shopping center on land that can be purchased for $1 million or ground leased at an initial rental of $70,300.[5] The cost of developing the land and constructing the improvements is $3 million, and the projected net rental income from the occupancy tenants (under subleases with initial 5-year terms) is $490,000 per annum. Based on a capitalization rate of 11.1 percent, the appraised value of the real estate is $4.4 million.[6] If Dan purchases the land, he can obtain a 30-year constant payment fee mortgage in the amount of $3 million (69 percent of the $4.4 million appraised value) with a 14 percent rate of interest, a 14.22

---

5. For a discussion of capitalization rate and mortgage loan appraisal see Chapter 5B1. The authors would like to thank G. Gordon Blackader, Vice-President for Real Estate Investments at Metropolitan Life Insurance Company for his assistance in the preparation of this example, which is based on assumptions as to capitalization rate and financing terms that are consistent with the dynamic Capitalization Technique. On the assumption that the value of the land is $1,100,000 (land cost to ground lessor of $1 million plus entrepreneurial factor of 10 percent) and the capitalization rate is 6.39 percent, the initial ground rent would be $70,300. This amount would be periodically adjusted based on regular reappraisals of land value.

6. The approximate value of the project would be $4,400,000 under a cost approach ($1 million land cost plus $3 million construction cost plus entrepreneurial factor of 10 percent) and an income approach ($490,000 net income ÷ 11.1 percent capitalization rate).

T a b l e 8-1

The following shows the approximate cash flow and tax results in the first operational year under each alternative:

Cash Flow	Dan Buys	Dan Leases
Cash needed over mortgage amount	$1,000,000	$700,000
Anticipated net income (gross rents less operating expenses)	490,000	490,000
Less: Mortgage debt service	426,600	327,100
Leasehold rent	NA	70,300
Cash flow	$ 63,400	$ 92,600
Return on cash investment	6.34%	13.2%

percent constant, and a 10-year call option. The annual debt service on the mortgage would be $426,600,[7] and the ratio of net income to debt service would be 115 percent.[8] By contrast, if Dan were to lease the land he would obtain an ordinary leasehold mortgage loan in the amount of $2.3 million[9] based on a leasehold value of $3.3 million.[10] The annual debt service on the mortgage would be $327,100, and the other financing terms would remain approximately the same; however, the ratio of net income to debt service would be more conservative: 128 percent (compared to 115 percent).

7. Debt service equals the loan amount ($3 million) × debt constant (14.22 percent) = $426,600.

8. Traditionally the debt coverage factor (ratio of net income to debt service) exceeds 125 percent; here the factor is 115 percent on the assumption that there will be periodic increases in rental income from the subtenant. The debt constant is 14.22 percent and the approximate loan amount equals (Net income ÷ 1.15 percent) ÷ .1422 = ($490,000 ÷ 1.15) ÷ .1422 = $2,996,400, or approximately $3 million.

9. The $2,300,000 loan amount assumes that the ground lessor has not subjected his fee interest to the lien of the leasehold mortgage (the "streamlined mortgage" discussed at Chapter 8A4), and the $3,300,000 appraised value assumes that the ground rent is a fair market rental so that the leasehold estate, without taking the improvements into account, is itself of minimal value.

10. The approximate value of the leasehold improvements would be $3,300,000 under a cost approach ($3 million construction cost plus entrepreneurial factor of 10 percent) and an income approach ($490,000 net income − $70,300 ground rent = $419,700 leasehold income ÷ 12.8 percent capitalization rate).

very interesting

T a b l e 8-1 *(cont.)*

Taxable Income	Dan Buys	Dan Leases
Anticipated net income (gross rents less operating expenses)	$ 490,000	$490,000
Less: Mortgage interest (at 14%)	419,560	321,660
Leasehold rent	NA	70,300
Depreciation (31.5-year ACRS period[11])	$ 95,238	$ 95,238
Total	514,798	487,198
Taxable income	(24,798)	2,802
Tax-free cash return (cash flow less taxable income)	$ 63,400	$ 89,798

The following shows the approximate cash flow and tax results in the *eleventh* operational year under each alternative:

Cash Flow	Dan Buys	Dan Leases
Cash needed over mortgage amount	$1,000,000	$700,000
Anticipated net income (gross rents less operating expenses)[12]	860,100	860,100
Less: Mortgage debt service	426,600	327,100
Leasehold rent	NA	151,200
Cash flow	$ 433,500	$381,800
Nominal return on cash investment	43.3%	54.5%
Real return on cash investment[13]	19.2%	24.1%

Taxable Income	Dan Buys	Dan Leases
Anticipated net income (gross rents less operating expenses)	860,100	860,100
Less: Mortgage interest (at 14%)	398,280	305,220
Leasehold rent	NA	151,200
Depreciation	95,238	95,238
Total	493,518	551,658
Taxable income	366,582	308,442
Tax-free cash return (cash flow less taxable income)	66,918	73,358

11. See discussion at Chapter 2B, note 3.

12. Under the fee alternative the example presupposes an inflation factor of 108.50 percent per year and an annual building depreciation factor of 97.50 percent. Accordingly, the projected net income in the eleventh year (prior to payment of debt service) would equal $490,000 × $(1.085)^{10}$ × $(.975)^{10}$ = $860,100. Under the leasing alternative an additional assumption obtains, namely, that the ground rent increases at an average annual rate by the above-mentioned inflation factor and decreases by a land obsolescence factor of 99.50 percent. Accordingly, in the eleventh year the projected net leasehold income after ground rent and prior to debt service payment would equal $860,100 less [$70,300 × $(1.085)^{10}$ × $(.995)^{10}$], or net income of $860,100 less ground rent of $151,200 = $708,900.

13. Under the fee alternative the nominal cash-on-cash return would be $433,500 ÷ 1,000,000, or 43.3 percent, and the real return adjusted by an annual inflation factor of 108.50 percent would be 43.3 percent ÷ $(1.085)^{10}$, or 19.2 percent.

Under the leasing alternative, the nominal cash-on-cash return would be $381,800 ÷ 700,000, or 54.5 percent, and the real return would be 54.5 percent ÷ $(1.085)^{10}$, or 24.1 percent.

2. Regulatory Law Considerations

Traditionally, the principal source of leasehold financing has been insurance companies, whose mortgage investments are subject to tighter regulatory constraints than are the investment portfolios of other institutional lenders. An earlier version of the New York statute (N.Y. Ins. Laws §81.6(a) (McKinney Supp. 1983)) has been followed as a prototype for the Massachusetts statute excerpted below and for many state regulatory statutes elsewhere,[14] and while a few state statutes specify lower loan-to-value ratios for leasehold as opposed to fee mortgage loans,[15] the Massachusetts statute makes no such distinction. The following excerpt from the Massachusetts statute typifies the kinds of regulatory constraints that are ordinarily imposed on leasehold mortgage loans.

Mass. Ann. Laws ch. 175, §63(7)
(Law. Co-op. 1991)

The capital of any domestic company, other than life, and three fourths of the reserve of any domestic stock or mutual life company, shall be invested only as follows: — . . .

7. In loans upon improved and unencumbered real property in any state of the United States or in the District of Columbia or Puerto Rico, and upon leasehold estates in improved unencumbered real property where twenty-one years or more of the term is unexpired and where unencumbered except by rentals accruing therefrom to the owner of the fee, and where the mortgagee is entitled to be subrogated to all the rights under the leasehold. No loan on such real property or such leasehold estate shall exceed seventy-five per cent of the fair market value thereof at the time of making such loan, . . . Real property and leasehold estates shall not be deemed to be encumbered within the meaning of this paragraph by reason of the existence of instruments reserving mineral, oil or timber rights, rights of way, parking rights, sewer rights, or rights in walls, nor by reason of an option to purchase, nor by reason of any liens for taxes or assessments not delinquent, nor by reason of building restrictions or other restrictive covenants, nor by the reason that it is subject to lease under which

14. E.g., Mass. Ann. Laws ch. 175, §63(7) (Law. Co-op. 1991); Va. Code Ann. §§38.2-1434, 38.2-1437 (1990).

15. E.g., Va. Code Ann. §38.2-1437 (1990), which imposes an 80 percent maximum loan-to-value ratio for fee mortgage loans and a 75 percent maximum for leasehold mortgage loans.

rents or profits are reserved to the owner; provided, that the security for such loan is a first lien upon such real property and that there is no condition or right of re-entry or forfeiture under which such lien can be cut off, subordinated or otherwise disturbed. No mortgage loan upon a leasehold shall be made or acquired by a company pursuant to this paragraph unless the terms thereof shall provide for such payments of principal, whatever the period of the loan, so that at no time during the term of the loan shall the aggregate payments of principal theretofore required to be made under the terms of the loan be less than would be necessary for a loan payable completely by the end of four-fifths of the period of the leasehold which is unexpired at the time the loan is made, and payments of interest only may be made for a period not to exceed five years, provided, that payments applicable first to interest and then to principal are made during each year thereafter. . . .

NOTES AND QUESTIONS

1. Returning to the example at Chapter 8A1, supra, as real estate counsel and tax planner for Dan Developer, briefly explain to your client the business and tax advantages and disadvantages, both short- and long-term, of leasehold as opposed to fee mortgage financing. Assuming that Dan is in a 31 percent tax bracket and has sufficient outside ordinary income to absorb any tax losses, what would be his after-tax return on his equity investment in the first and eleventh years under each mode of financing?

2. Can you think of any reason why the ratio of net income to debt service is higher in the case of ordinary leasehold mortgage financing?

3. Suppose an insurance company chartered in Massachusetts desires to make a leasehold mortgage loan. Why does the regulatory statute (excerpted above) require that the underlying property (fee) not be subject to any prior lien? Can you think of any reason why the statute mandates an unexpired leasehold term of not less than 21 years? Why does the statute require that the leasehold mortgagee be subrogated to all the rights of the ground lessor under the ground lease? In light of the foregoing restriction against a short lease term, how do you explain the fact that the statute prohibits a long mortgage amortization schedule?

Statutes in some other jurisdictions are more restrictive about encumbrances than the Massachusetts statute. For example, to be mort-gageable in Virginia a leasehold estate must be unencumbered rather than merely superior to any mortgage on the underlying fee. See Va. Code Ann. §38.2-1434(2) (1990). Do you see any problems with this approach? See discussion at Chapter 3A, note 2.

4. After reviewing the discussion at Chapter 4C3, consider the

following hypothetical facts, diagrammed below. In January of this year, a fee owner (Francine Farmer) ground leases some land (Blackacre) to a developer (Dan Developer). The ground lease is immediately recorded by Dan. In June Dan obtains a leasehold mortgage from a postconstruction lender (Ace Insurance Company, chartered in the state of Massachusetts) to fund the construction of a shopping center situated in Massachusetts. Ace immediately records its mortgage.

In July Ace's mortgage loan officer discovers that (unbeknownst to Ace) in February Francine had obtained a fee mortgage loan on Blackacre from M1 and that the mortgage was recorded in February. The loan officer is worried that Ace's loan, made in June, may be illegal under the Massachusetts regulatory statute. As counsel to Ace, what will you tell the loan officer?

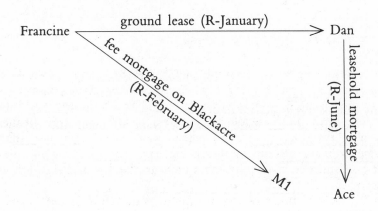

3.   Leasehold Mortgage that Does Not Encumber the Fee: Lender's Requirements

In the case of ordinary leasehold financing in which the lien of the leasehold mortgage does not cover the underlying fee, the security for the loan is merely the mortgagor's defeasible leasehold estate (which is basically the right of possession of the land and leasehold improvements for a stated term on the condition that the mortgagor, as ground lessee, pays the ground rent and otherwise complies with the terms of the ground lease). Thus, in addition to the ordinary concerns of a lender, the leasehold mortgagee must place itself in a position to control to the maximum extent possible any contingency that could terminate the mortgagor's leasehold estate and the mortgagee's security interest. Accordingly, since special language in the leasehold mortgage would be of no avail in the event the ground lease is terminated and the mortgagee is but a third party to the lease, the leasehold mortgagee will require language in the ground lease (1) affording to it all the rights that the mortgagor has as ground lessee; (2) providing to it notice of any default with a reasonable opportunity to cure; and (3) requiring its prior written approval to any modification or cancellation of the lease, as well as other safeguards that will protect it against the obliteration or impairment of its security interest as leasehold mortgagee.

Mark, Leasehold Mortgages: Some Practical Considerations
14 Bus. Law. 609 (1959)

Although real estate financing through the medium of leasehold mortgages is far from a recent innovation, it has taken on an increasingly important role in the post-war building boom and in many metropolitan areas it has become an almost standard method for providing funds for the construction of large commercial and residential structures. The leasehold mortgage, when based on a properly drawn lease, can in many cases act as a catalyst in bringing together the conflicting interests of a property owner who does not want to incur the expense of constructing an adequate improvement on his land but desires an adequate return, an operator who sees an opportunity to improve the same property but does not want buy it, and a lending institution seeking a safe investment for a large sum of money with a minimum of servicing expense. . . .

It is readily apparent that a leasehold mortgage loan, being based on an estate subject to defeasance, presents problems which do not exist where a mortgage is based on a fee estate. Since the security behind a leasehold loan is the leasehold estate, and since the leasehold estate is created by the lease, the place to deal with these problems is the lease itself. If the lease does not contain adequate protection for the leasehold mortgagee, no amount of tinkering with special mortgage provisions can be of any avail, since no mortgage can in any way impose or alter the estate on which it creates a lien. The purpose of this paper is to discuss some of the basic problems inherent in leasehold financing and to suggest solutions which it is hoped will be found useful and practical.

1. PREPARATION OF THE LEASE

Rare indeed is the lease which counsel for a leasehold mortgagee would approve unless it has been drawn with the basic requirements of such a lender in mind. Some years ago the writer had the privilege of reviewing for a lender a long term lease on a New York City property. Lessor and Lessee had been represented by brilliant counsel, learned in the law and skilled in the use of the English language. From the point of view of draftsmanship, and as a protection for the rights of their respective clients, the lease was a masterpiece, but it was completely devoid of any provisions which would make it acceptable to a leasehold mortgagee. Since the lease had not been drawn with leasehold mortgage financing in mind, it took almost a year to revise it in such a way as to afford to a leasehold lender the protection to which it was entitled. Such a vast expenditure of time (and the borrower's money) could have been avoided had the proper protective provisions been inserted in the first place. It is therefore apparent that where there is even a reasonable chance that a leasehold estate may be mortgaged at some time in the future, it is well to insert in the lease provisions for protection of prospective mortgagees. A fortiori, in a case where it is known that a project will be financed by a leasehold mortgage, participation by the lender's counsel in the preparation of the lease will be in the best interest of all concerned.

2. Length of Initial Term

Some statutes authorizing investment in leasehold mortgages provide that the term of the lease shall be for not less than a given number of years, including enforceable options of renewal. Such a statutory provision raises two questions.

The first is what is meant by "an enforceable option of renewal" or more accurately, in whose hands is the option of renewal enforceable. . . .

The second question concerning the length of the term is of equal importance. This relates to the possible bankruptcy of a Lessor who has granted a lease containing an option to renew. Under Section 70 (b) of the Bankruptcy Act a trustee in bankruptcy is authorized to reject executory contracts of the bankrupt "including unexpired leases of real property." The section further provides that "unless a lease of such property shall expressly otherwise provide, a rejection of such lease or of any covenant therein by the trustee of the lessor shall not deprive the lessee of his estate." It is thus clear that at least during the initial term of a lease, the leasehold estate would be unaffected by a rejection of the lease by the trustee of a bankrupt Lessor, unless the lease provided otherwise. It has been held, however, that the trustee of a bankrupt Lessor may reject an option of renewal. Coy v. Title Guarantee & Trust Co., 198 F. 275 (D.C. Ore. 1912) Thus, if the entire term of a leasehold mortgage exceeded the initial term of the lease, and the mortgagee relied on an option of renewal to extend the term so as to expire not earlier than the maturity of the mortgage, the mortgagee would be at the mercy of the trustee of a bankrupt Lessor, and this would be so whether or not the lease granted to the mortgagee the right to exercise the option of renewal as attorney-in-fact for the Lessee.

It is quite possible to argue that part of the Lessee's estate is the right of renewal and that therefore the rejection of the renewal option by the trustee of a bankrupt Lessor would not be effective. Indeed there is authority to the effect that upon the exercise of a renewal option there is an extension of the original term of the lease as an original demise for the original and renewal terms. Orr v. Doubleday, Page & Co., 223 N.Y. 334 (1918); Erickson v. Boothe, 79 Cal. App. 2d 266 (1947); Ackerman v. Loforese, 111 Conn. 700 (1930). However, as mentioned in Orr v. Doubleday, Page & Co., there is a considerable body of authority to the contrary. The contrary view is stated in the *Orr* case at page 340 as follows:

> This conclusion is not in accord with the view of a considerable and weighty body of judicial opinion, which is, that the interest of a lessee exercising the privilege of renewal is purely equitable. That view rests upon a distinction made between a privilege or covenant of a renewal and a privilege or covenant of an extension. It holds that the former is a right to the grant of an estate, the latter a present demise operative immediately upon the exercise of the privilege. (Sutherland v. Goodnow, 108 Ill. 528; Leavitt v. Maykel, 203 Mass. 506; Quinn v. Valiquette, 80 Vt. 434; Fergen v. Lyons, 162 Wis. 131; Luthey v. Joyce, 132 Minn. 451; Grant v. Collins, 157 Ky. 36; Miller v. Albany Lodge, 168 Ky. 755; Steen v. Scheel, 46 Neb. 252.[16]

In view of the division of authority on this subject, it would not appear safe to assume that a trustee of a bankrupt Lessor did not have the power to reject a renewal option in a lease.

The practical protection against a rejection of an option of renewal by the trustee of a bankrupt Lessor is to exclude terms available under renewal options when fixing the term of the lease for the purposes of the mortgage. Under no circumstances should the initial term of the lease expire prior to the maturity of the mortgage, and in states where the mortgage is required to mature prior to the expiration of the lease term, the initial term should be long enough so that in computing the maximum permitted maturity of the mortgage, reliance need not be

16. More recent cases upholding this distinction are: Weller v. Dalzell, 375 P.2d 467, 471 (Wyo. 1962); Sunac Petroleum Corp. v. Parkes, 416 S.W.2d 798, 802 (Tex. 1967); and Dubinsky Realty v. Vactec, Inc., 637 S.W.2d 190, 192 (Mo. App. 1982). — ED.

placed on renewal options to make certain that the term of the lease will expire sufficiently long after the maturity of the mortgage.

Of course, where a renewal option can be exercised at any time during the initial term, a mortgagee would be protected by requiring that the renewal option be exercised at the time of the closing of the loan.

3. ASSIGNABILITY OF THE LESSEE'S ESTATE

One of the most cherished possessions of any Lessor, the right to control the identity of his Lessee through control of the right to assign the Lessee's estate, becomes a casualty in a properly drawn lease securing a leasehold mortgage. A prime condition precedent to the acceptability of a lease for mortgage purposes is the unrestricted right of the Lessee to transfer the leasehold estate by assignment, without any need for the consent of the Lessor, and indeed, a lease is not acceptable for such purposes unless it so provides.

This matter of assignability has two aspects. The first relates to the question whether a covenant against assignment is violated by the making of a mortgage on the lease, or by the sale of the lease following the foreclosure of a mortgage thereon. . . .

The other aspect of the problem of assignability is of equal, if not greater, importance and relates to the ability of a mortgagee to realize on its security following the acquisition of the lease either by foreclosure or assignment in lieu thereof or following the obtaining of a new lease from the Lessor under the circumstances discussed in Part 4 of this paper. As a fee mortgagee is free to sell an acquired fee without restriction of any kind, so a leasehold mortgagee must be in a position to dispose of the leasehold estate without let or hindrance. It follows that a leasehold mortgagee cannot aloow itself to be put in the position of being required to seek the Lessor's permission in order to liquidate its security. Accordingly, a lease acceptable to a leasehold lender must provide absolute and unrestricted assignability of the Lessee's estate, free and clear of any control of the Lessor.

In dealing with this problem, Lessors sometimes suggest that their consent will not be required for any mortgage, or for any assignment to the mortgagee or to the immediate assignee of the mortgagee. Although at first blush this might appear adequate, a second look quickly reveals the flaw in the suggestion. A lease with such a provision is unmarketable as a practical matter, for the purchaser who buys the lease from the mortgagee could not thereafter dispose of it without the Lessor's consent, and therefore in the exercise of prudent judgment would decline to purchase from the mortgagee in the first place.

Another Lessor's suggestion to be avoided is an offer of a covenant by the Lessor not unreasonably to withhold its consent to an assignment of the lease. Although a covenant not unreasonably to withhold consent is in most states not without meaning, there are many bases on which a lessor may rely in withholding consent without being unreasonable, such as a poor credit rating of the assignee, the poor reputation of the assignee or a provable inability of the assignee to maintain or manage the property. Furthermore, to determine whether the Lessor is reasonable or unreasonable in withholding consent is readily capable of being the subject of litigation. Such litigation would either take the form of an action for a declaratory judgment or a summary proceeding based upon assignment without consent in which the defense is raised that consent was unreasonably withheld. The possible necessity of any such litigation, plus the possibility that it might be unsuccessful from the Lessee's point of view, would in all probability make a lease containing such a covenant entirely unacceptable to a prospective lender. Such a covenant should therefore be excluded from the lease.

It is not uncommon for a lease to provide the Lessee's estate may be assigned provided the assignee assumes the obligations of the lease, or that the acceptance of an assignment constitutes an assumption of the Lessee's obligations thereunder. Such a provision is not unacceptable to a leasehold mortgage if it is further provided that following an assignment of the lease, the assignor is relieved of all obligations under the lease except those which accrued during the period when the assignor was the Lessee under the lease. In this connection the lease should specifically provide that the leasehold mortgagee shall not be liable for the Lessee's obligations under the lease until it becomes the owner of the lease either by foreclosure or assignment in lieu thereof, or has acquired a new lease as discussed in Part 4 of this paper.

To conclude on the question of assignability, the lease should provide for complete and unrestricted assignability of the lease without the necessity for consent of the Lessor of any kind.

4. NOTICE OF DEFAULT AND NEW LEASE

As stated in the earlier portion of this paper, a basic distinction between a fee mortgage and a leasehold mortgage is that the latter is based on an estate subject to defeasance, whereas the former is not. It is therefore of paramount importance that the lease protect the leasehold mortgagee against the consequences of those events which may give to the Lessor the right to terminate the Lessee's estate. Of all the problems faced in dealing with leasehold mortgages it can be accurately said that this is the most crucial. Unless a lease provides adequate protection against defeasance of the Lessee's estate it is wholly inadequate as security for a leasehold mortgage.

Except through the operation of the power of eminent domain there is no way that the Lessee's estate can be terminated without a default on the part of the Lessee in the performance of its obligations under the lease. All properly drawn leases provide that before a Lessor can terminate a Lessee's estate because of a default, notice of default must be given to the Lessee, who then has an opportunity to cure the default within a specified time or at least to commence to cure the default. Unless, however, a leasehold mortgagee has notice that a default has been called on the Lessee, the failure of the Lessee to cure the default and the consequent termination of the Lessee's estate could occur before the leasehold mortgagee was even aware of the existence of the default. It is therefore necessary for the essential protection of the mortgagee, that the mortgagee also receive from the Lessor a notice of any Lessee's default. A lease properly drawn from the mortgagee's point of view will provide that no notice of default given by a Lessor to a Lessee shall be valid for any purpose unless simultaneously with the notice to the Lessee similar notice is given to the mortgagee.

Vital as notice of default undoubtedly is to the mortgagee, it is of little use unless the mortgagee is in a position to cure the default. The lease should therefore provide that the mortgagee is given time in which to cure the default for the account of the Lessee, and that when the mortgagee has performed the obligation, the non-performance of which was the subject of the notice of default, the default shall be deemed cured. This last provision is desirable to forestall an allegation by the Lessor that although action to cure the default was taken, it was not taken by the Lessee who therefore remains in default. Appropriate covenants in the mortgage would provide that all expenses incurred by the mortgagee in curing the Lessee's defaults would be added to the mortgage debt and be secured by the lien of the mortgage.

The right of a leasehold mortgagee to receive notice of default and to cure the default is adequate to protect the leasehold mortgagee against defaults which can be cured by the payment of money or the performance of work, such as repairs, alterations, construction and the like. It is not adequate to protect against defaults which cannot be cured by the payment of money or the performance of work. Many leases provide that the Lessee shall be deemed to be in default if the Lessee becomes a bankrupt, or confesses an inability to pay its debts, or if a receiver is appointed for the Lessee or if any one of a number of similar events shall occur. Against the destruction of the Lessee's estate following such a default the leasehold mortgagee is not protected by a provision for receipt of notice of default and a right to cure, since such a default cannot be cured by payment of money or performance of work or any other act of the mortgagee. It is the view of some counsel for lending institutions that a lease is unacceptable for mortgage lending purposes if it is subject to termination for defaults of the character above mentioned. On the other hand it seems unreasonable to preclude a Lessor from terminating a lease with a bankrupt Lessee and becoming thereby involved in the bankruptcy proceeding through no fault of the Lessor. It has been suggested that one solution to the problem of uncurable defaults is to be found in a lease provision to the effect that despite the bankruptcy of the Lessee the lease cannot be terminated as long as the rent is paid and the other terms of the lease are complied with. Such a provision is acceptable from the point of view of the leasehold mortgagee, as it restores the protection afforded by notice of default and the right to cure. It would appear to be somewhat less satisfactory to the Lessor as it would not free the Lessor from participation in the bankruptcy proceeding.

A generally used device for protecting a leasehold mortgagee against these uncurable defaults is a provision that upon the termination of the Lessee's estate following such a default, the Lessor will enter into a new lease in which the mortgagee or its nominee shall be the lessee. Such a new lease would be for the unexpired portion of the initial or renewal term as the case might be, and would be on the same terms and conditions, including rentals and renewals, as the original lease. Under the operation of such a provision, the mortgagee would be in the same position as if it had foreclosed its mortgage or had acquired the lease by assignment in lieu of foreclosure. Assuming the lease contained appropriate provisions for assignability discussed in Part 3 above, it would be able to realize on the security to the same extent as it could following a mortgage default. It would seem that such a provision would provide adequate protection for the mortgagee and at the same time would be more satisfactory to the Lessor. Obviously, either method of dealing with uncurable defaults is a matter of indifference to the Lessee.

5.   SUBORDINATION TO FEE MORTGAGES

Some statutes authorizing leasehold mortgage investments specifically require that the fee estate be not subject to prior liens. Others require that the leasehold estate shall be unencumbered. However, regardless of statutory provisions, it would appear clear that prudence on the part of the leasehold mortgagee requires either that the fee estate be unencumbered or that any encumbrances thereon be subordinated to the estate created by the lease.

It is certainly arguable that a fee mortgage is not an encumbrance on a leasehold estate, even where the lease is subordinated to the lien of the fee mortgage. However, regardless of the technical validity of this argument, the fact remains that where a fee mortgage is prior in lien to the leasehold estate, the latter can be cut off by a foreclosure of the former, and no provision of the lease or the leasehold mortgage can protect the leasehold mortgagee from the complete destruction of its security under such circumstances.

It is therefore of prime importance that the lease should in fact be prior to any fee mortgage on the premises at the time of the making of the lease or thereafter placed upon the premises. It is good practice for the lease to provide for such superiority in haec verba, thus giving notice to all subsequent encumbrancers and lienors. In this connection it seems superfluous to state that in all cases involving leasehold mortgages the lease should be recorded in the appropriate recording office.

Many leases are submitted which contain provisions directly to the contrary of the foregoing. They provide for the complete subordination of the lease to any and all fee mortgages now or hereafter placed against the premises. Such leases are wholly unacceptable from the point of view of the leasehold mortgagee for the reasons stated above.

A variation of the complete subordination to fee mortgages discussed in the immediately preceding paragraph is the so-called "nondisturbance clause," pursuant to which a fee mortgagee agrees that so long as the Lessee is not in default under the lease the Lessee's possession will not be disturbed in the event of a foreclosure of the fee mortgage. . . .

In conclusion, regardless of statutory requirements, prudence requires that a lease securing a leasehold mortgage be superior in all respects to all fee mortgages placed upon the premises at any time, and to all other title conditions pursuant to which the leasehold estate could be cut off in any way, by reverter, reversion, termination of a life estate or otherwise.

6. INSURANCE

Except for the question of disposition of condemnation awards, there is probably no subject more discussed in the negotiation of a lease than the question of disposition of hazard insurance proceeds. However, the basic needs of the leasehold mortgagee are simple. It wants to be a named insured on the hazard insurance policies pursuant to a standard mortgagee clause, to have all losses payable to it and to have the option to apply the insurance proceeds on the mortgage debt or to the restoration of the premises. However, insistence on having all these rights will undoubtedly result in a collapse of the proposed transaction, as parts of such provisions are entirely unacceptable to the Lessor and the Lessee. Both Lessor and Lessee desire to make certain that the proceeds of insurance are available for the restoration of the premises and can be readily obtained as the work of restoration progresses. The possibility that the insurance proceeds would be applied on the mortgage debt would be wholly unacceptable to the Lessor and in all probability, only slightly less unacceptable to the Lessee.

From the point of view of the leasehold mortgagee, adequate protection is afforded under lease provisions requiring that the mortgagee be insured under a standard mortgagee clause, with loss payable to the mortgagee so long as the mortgage is held by a lending institution, otherwise to an insurance trustee such as a bank or trust company, the loss proceeds to be paid out as the work of restoration progresses upon production of appropriate architects' certificates, with such provisions for hold-backs before final disbursement as the parties might agree upon. The lease should also provide that the mortgagee has the right to participate in the adjustment of losses.

7. CONDEMNATION

Another fruitful source of protracted negotiation is the subject of the taking of all or a part of the demised premises as a result of the exercise of eminent domain. Here we deal with three situations: a total taking, a partial taking and a use taking.

The last mentioned, a taking of the use of the premises without vesting of title in the condemning authority, ordinarily would present no problem to a leasehold mortgagee. Presumably the condemnor would pay the condemnation award in installments similar to rent, the debt service would be met from these payments and the mortgagee would be unaffected.

On the other hand, a leasehold mortgagee will be vitally interested in being protected against a total or partial taking which vests title in the condemnor. In the case of a total taking, or a partial taking which leaves the premises so damaged that it cannot be restored, a proper lease will provide that the leasehold mortgagee is the first to be paid out of that portion of the award which represents the value of the improvements erected on the premises. Such a provision is adequate in a situation where the Lessee has constructed the improvement, as is often the case, but it is somewhat less than realistic when the lease relates to an existing building owned in fee by the Lessor. In such a case that portion of the award representing the value of the Lessee's estate should be made available for payment of the leasehold mortgage and provision should be made for methods of determining the value of the Lessee's estate in the event that the award is silent on this subject.

Where a lease is not terminated by a partial taking, it is apparent that all parties (except perhaps the leasehold mortgagee) will wish to have the condemnation proceeds applied to the restoration of the premises. Lease provisions for this purpose resemble those discussed above relating to the use of proceeds of hazard insurance under analogous circumstances.

To assure the mortgagee of proper protection in the condemnation proceedings, the lease should provide that the leasehold mortgagee is expressly authorized to participate in the condemnation proceeding.

8. SUB-LEASES

Except in the unusual circumstance of a Lessee being itself the sole occupant of the demised premises and paying the debt service as an expense of its business, the funds for payment of principal and interest on the leasehold mortgage will be derived from rentals paid by sub-tenants occupying space in the demised premises pursuant to sub-leases in which the Lessee is the landlord. The leasehold mortgagee, as would a fee mortgagee in an analogous situation, will insist upon the sub-tenant's being of good credit rating and in all respects suitable occupants of the property. It will also insist that all subleases be approved by the mortgagee as to rent, term and the provisions of the lease.

Since the source of funds for the liquidation of its investment will be rentals under the sub-lease, the mortgagee will wish to be certain that the covenants of the sub-lease will not be changed, that the term of the sub-lease will not be reduced, that there will be no prepayment of rent nor a surrender of the sub-lease without the consent of the leasehold mortgagee. Some counsel for lenders are of the opinion that protection against these contingencies is obtained by the assignment to the leasehold mortgagee of the Lessee's interest as landlord under the sublease. It is the opinion of the writer, however, that unless following such an assignment the sub-rentals are paid directly to the mortgagee prior to default, the assignment is not effective to protect the mortgagee against sub-lease modifications and similar transactions between the Lessee and its sub-tenants. . . .

It is the opinion of the writer that in order to protect a leasehold mortgagee against the modification of sub-leases without the lender's consent, the ground lease should contain a covenant to the effect that all sub-leases will specifically provide that they cannot, without the consent of the leasehold mortgagee, be modified so as to reduce the rent, change renewal privileges, shorten the term or provide for pre-payment of rent, and that any such modification without the consent of the mortgagee shall be void as against the mortgagee. It is believed that such a provision will go far to assure the mortgagee that when it takes over the property following default, it will find in effect the same sub-leases on which it relied in making the loan in the first place.

Another problem in connection with sub-leases relates to attornment by sub-tenants in the event of a termination of the ground lease for a non-curable default and the issuance to the lender of a new lease under the circumstance discussed in Part 4 above. Since the estate created by the sub-lease stems from the leasehold estate of the Lessee under the ground lease, it is apparent that following a termination of the ground lease the estates created by sub-leases would be cut off, and the obligations of the sub-tenants to stay in possession and pay rent would cease. In order that the leasehold mortgagee may be protected against a loss of rental income after it has signed its new lease, the ground lease should contain a covenant requiring that all sub-leases must contain an agreement by the sub-tenant to attorn to the leasehold mortgagee if it becomes the holder of a new ground lease. Proper protection for the sub-tenants would be provided by a reciprocal clause to the effect that the leasehold mortgagee would accept the attornment and recognize the continued existence of the sub-lease.

9. MISCELLANEOUS

(A) ESTOPPEL CERTIFICATES

From time to time, and especially at the closing of a leasehold mortgage loan, it will be important to obtain from the Lessor a statement that the lease is in full force and effect and that the Lessee is not in default thereunder. Since there is no way in which a Lessor can be compelled to deliver such a statement, it is good practice to include in the lease a covenant that upon request the Lessor will deliver a certificate stating, if such be the fact, that the Lessee is not in default and that the lease is in full force and effect. Counsel for the Lessor may be unwilling to go this far, but any reasonable Lessor should be at least willing to certify, if such be the fact, that it knows of no default and that no notice of default has been served.

(B) FORMS OF MORTGAGE

Unlike the fee mortgage, which is susceptible of being the subject of a standard printed form, the leasehold mortgage is generally a hand-tailored job, designed specifically for the transaction at hand and closely correlated to the provisions of the lease to which it applies. In New York there is a statutory form of leasehold mortgage (New York Real Property Law Section 273). It is, however, next to useless except for emergency or ad hoc situations in which the form of the mortgage is not important.

(C) LEGAL EXPENSE

Lenders who are in the habit of quoting from a fee schedule of counsel's charges for fee mortgage loans will be well advised not to use the schedule in connection with leasehold loans. Since each leasehold mortgage is a special case, far more time is taken by counsel in drawing the loan papers and consequently counsel's charges for leasehold loans will be substantially higher than charges for fee mortgage loans of comparable amounts.

(D) FEE MORTGAGE COVENANTS

In addition to the concepts discussed above, many standard fee mortgage provisions are applicable to leasehold mortgages, such as covenants against waste, demolition without consent, compliance with orders of governmental authorities, payment of taxes, etc. It is apparent that except for the facts that the leasehold mortgage creates a lien on a defeasible estate, basic mortgage practices common to fee mortgages have equal relevance in leasehold situations and should be followed.

New York Life Insurance Co., Outline of Minimum Ground Lease Requirements of Leasehold Mortgagee
(internal memorandum) (1968)

The ground lease should contain appropriate express provisions that cover the following matters:

(1) The lessee should be granted express authority, without any requirement of the consent or approval of the lessor,

(a) To mortgage the leasehold interest;

(b) To assign the lease and the leasehold estate created thereby, including, but not limited to, an assignment in lieu of foreclosure, to a leasehold mortgagee; and

(c) To sublet the leased premises.

(2) The leasehold mortgagee shall not become personally liable for the obligations of the lease unless and until it becomes the owner of the leasehold estate by foreclosure, assignment in lieu of foreclosure, or otherwise, and thereafter shall remain liable for such obligations only so long as the leasehold mortgagee remains the owner of the leasehold estate.

(3) If the leasehold mortgagee should become the owner of the leasehold estate, it may assign the lease without any requirement of the lessor's consent, and any purchase money mortgage delivered in

connection with any such assignment shall be entitled to the benefit of all of the provisions of the lease with respect to a leasehold mortgage.

(4) The default provisions of the lease must be approved by this company and its special counsel as providing adequate protection to the leasehold mortgagee against the possibility of the loss of its investment through a termination of the lease by reason of the default of the lessee. In general, the lease should provide:

(a) A copy of each notice of default, which the lessor may serve upon the lessee, shall also be served by registered mail upon the leasehold mortgagee;

(b) In the event that the lessee shall fail to cure the default within the time proscribed by the lease, further notice to that effect shall likewise be given to the leasehold mortgagee by registered mail. The latter shall be allowed such additional time as may be required within which either to cure the default or to institute and complete foreclosure proceedings, or otherwise acquire title to the leasehold interest. Also, so long as the leasehold mortgagee shall be engaged either in curing the default or in proceeding to foreclose the mortgage, no such default shall operate, or permit the lessor, to terminate the lease;

(c) Bankruptcy and other insolvency defaults should be applicable only with respect to the lessee, the then owner of the leasehold estate, and neither the bankruptcy nor the insolvency of the lessee shall operate, or permit the lessor, to terminate the lease so long as all rent and other payments required to be paid by the lessee continue to be paid in accordance with the terms of the lease;

(d) If, for any reason, the lease should be terminated, the leasehold mortgagee shall be entitled to receive a new lease upon the same terms (except for any special requirements, such as a requirement for the construction of a new building, which has already been fulfilled by the lessee) and having the same relative priority as the original lease, provided the leasehold mortgagee agrees to take prompt steps to cure all defaults of the original lessee other than insolvency defaults and such other defaults, if any, as are not susceptible of being cured by the leasehold mortgagee;

(e) The leasehold mortgagee should be granted the right to cure any default on the part of the lessee, as well as the further right to enter upon the premises and to do all things necessary to that end.

(5) The leasehold mortgagee should be expressly authorized to exercise any renewal option granted to the lessee. If the lessee fails, within the time limit, to exercise any option of renewal, the leasehold

mortgagee must be notified by registered mail in order that the latter, if it so chooses, may exercise the option, either on its own behalf or on behalf of the lessee.

(6) Appropriate permission should be granted to the lessee to include the interest of the leasehold mortgagee in all fire and other hazard insurance policies, pursuant to a standard mortgagee clause or endorsement and to deposit the originals or copies of all such policies with the leasehold mortgagee.

(7) Hazard insurance proceeds and any condemnation awards required by the lease to be applied to the restoration of the premises shall be held by the leasehold mortgagee, or by an institutional investor or bank or trust company satisfactory to the lessor, the lessee and the leasehold mortgagee, for application in accordance with the provisions of the lease (to the extent not inconsistent with the requirement of the lease and the provisions of the leasehold mortgage).

(Note: Rent insurance proceeds, if any, may be required to be applied first to payment of any unpaid obligations owing under the lease and thereafter to the payment of any unpaid obligations owing under the leasehold mortgage, with any remaining balance to go to the lessee.)

(8) The condemnation provisions of the lease must be approved by local counsel as providing adequate protection to the investment of the leasehold mortgagee. Unless local counsel in a particular jurisdiction should advise otherwise, the condemnation provision may state that the lessor shall receive all awards made with respect to the land (or portion thereof) taken, plus any consequential damage to any portion of the land not taken. The lessee shall also receive the balance of any such awards, with an additional provision to the effect that if the court shall not find such values, the parties receiving any portion of the total award shall hold the same in trust pending determination of the respective interests of the parties by agreement or arbitration. Unless local counsel is of the opinion that the provisions of the lease are otherwise adequate to protect the interests of the leasehold mortgagee, the lease should expressly provide that title to all improvements shall be vested in the lessee throughout the period of the lease.

(9) There shall be no merger of the lease, nor of the leasehold estate created thereby, with the fee estate in the premises, by reason of the fact that the lease, or the leasehold estate created thereby, or any interest in either thereof, may be held directly or indirectly by or for the account of any person who shall own the fee estate in the premises or any portion therein, and no such merger shall occur unless and until all persons at the time having any interest in the fee estate and all persons having any interest in the lease or the

leasehold estate, including the leasehold mortgagee, shall join in a written instrument effecting such merger.

NOTES AND QUESTIONS

1. Questions. Observe that some regulatory statutes mandate an unexpired leasehold term of not less than a specified number of years *including enforceable options of renewal.* The excerpt by Mark questions the meaning of "an enforceable option of renewal." More specifically, the author wonders in whose hands the option of renewal should be enforceable. From the perspective of a leasehold mortgagee, is it sufficient that the option be enforceable by the mortgagor-lessee? If not, what protective language should be included in either the leasehold mortgage or the ground lease to assure the mortgagee that its loan will constitute both a legal and a safe investment? See 2 R. Powell, Law of Real Property §242[3] (1982).

Mark points out that a trustee in bankruptcy may have the authority to reject an option of renewal granted by a bankrupt lessor. Under the Bankruptcy Code a lessee is afforded some protection if the trustee of the bankrupt lessor should reject the ground lease. Under §365(h) of the Code, the lessee may remain in possession for the balance of the lease term (including any renewal or extension period that does not require the lessor's consent) and may offset against its future rental obligation any damages suffered by it as the result of nonperformance by the lessor of any of its obligations under the lease. Not only is the ground lessee (as tenant under the principal lease) protected, but this provision would also effectively protect the subtenants in the event the ground lessee should be a debtor under the Bankruptcy Code. Why?

Mark also appears to suggest that a covenant against assignment in the ground lease may be violated by the making of a leasehold mortgage. Based on what you have learned about the nature of a mortgage under a title approach versus a lien theory approach (discussed at Chapter 4A), on what basis, if any, could such a contention be made by a ground lessor seeking to enforce the restriction?

As noted at Chapter 5C, a fee mortgagee will sometimes require in its postconstruction loan commitment that all occupancy or space leases be unconditionally subordinate to the fee mortgage. So why, in the case of a leasehold mortgage, would a ground lease providing for the subordination of the lease to any fee mortgage be wholly unacceptable to the leasehold mortgagee? If the leasehold estate must be prior in lien to any fee mortgage, why can't the problem be solved by simply providing in haec verba for such superiority in the ground lease? From the perspective of the leasehold mortgagee, why can't a nondisturbance agreement wholly solve the subordination problem in the event the ground lease is recorded after the fee mortgage? Supposing it can't, can you think of any alternative solutions that are not mentioned by Mark?

From the viewpoint of the leasehold mortgagee, the biggest risk to its defeasible security interest is that it may not be able to cure a material nonmonetary default under the ground lease (e.g., the violation of a use or radius restriction, receivership or assignment for the benefit of creditors, violation of local law, or abandonment of the premises by the ground lessee). As protection, the leasehold mortgagee will therefore demand the right to enter into a new ground lease with the fee owner on the same terms and conditions that were contained in the original lease and for the unexpired portion of the initial or renewal term, as the case may be. In 1980 the American Bar Association Real Property, Probate and Trust Law Section issued a report on model leasehold encumbrance provisions that espoused a "new lease" provision that would provide a leasehold mortgagee with the absolute right to step into the shoes of the defaulting ground lessee-mortgagor. Based on what you learned in your first-year property course and the discussion so far, can you think of any potential problems for the leasehold mortgagee that are not addressed by the "new lease" concept? See Levitan, Leasehold Mortgage Financing: Reliance on the "New Lease" Provision, 15 Real Prop., Prob. & Tr. J. 413 (1980); Thomas, The Mortgaging of Long Term Leases, 39 Dicta 363, 366-372. See also Berger-Tilles Leasing Corp. v. York Assocs., 53 Misc. 2d 290, 279 N.Y.S.2d 62 (1967), revd., 28 App. Div. 2d 1132 (2d Dept. 1967), affd., 22 N.Y.2d 837 (1968).

You are real estate counsel to a life insurance company that is planning to make a leasehold mortgage that will not encumber the fee. Based on the Outline of Minimum Groundlease Requirements of Leasehold Mortgagee as clarified and explained by the Mark article, what additional precautionary language, deletions, and other changes would you demand of the ground lessor and ground lessee to protect the interests of your client? What other requirements would you impose as a condition precedent to the making of the loan? If you represented a sublessee in the same transaction, what protective measures would you insist on, and from whom?

2. *Ground Rent Escalation Clauses.* Since the initial term of the ground lease is apt to be long, the fee owner-ground lessee will often require as a hedge against inflation a periodic increase in the rent (geared to an inflation index such as the Consumer Price Index) or a percentage rental (geared to the net or gross subrental). Perhaps the most common type of rental adjustment clause is one that is based on periodic revaluations of the property during the leasehold term. From the perspective of the leasehold mortgagee, the latter type of provision

is objectionable because any change in the base ground rent without regard for the ability of the property to generate sufficient income to pay the rent and debt service may increase the risk of default by the mortgagor while the leasehold mortgage is being amortized. However, a percentage rental clause geared to the net income from subtenants (as opposed to one based on gross income or cash flow) will be tolerated by most lenders because such a provision provides the borrower with a hedge against declining profits but does not increase the risk of default under the leasehold mortgage. A typical clause might read as follows:

> The base rent is to be adjusted on the fourth anniversary of the execution date of this lease and at the end of four-year increments thereafter, so that the base rent shall be equal to 8 percent of the fair market value of the land subject to the leasehold estate. Said fair market value is to be determined by an MAI appraiser satisfactory to Lessor and Lessee. All costs and expenses of such appraisals are to be borne by Lessor.

Do you see any problems with the foregoing language from the perspective of the lessee, the lessor, or the leasehold mortgagee?

3. *Multiple Encumbrances.* Ordinarily an entire development — be it a shopping center, apartment building, or office building — will be constructed on a single ground-leased parcel with the improvements financed by a single lender. On some occasions, however, the ground lessee may wish to develop the parcel on a piecemeal basis and may find it necessary to finance the improvements with several lenders, each of whom will demand lien priority with respect to a particular portion of the tract and perhaps the borrower's interest in a particular high-credit sublease with an occupancy tenant. Also, if the tract is to be developed by sections or to become a part of a single integrated development plan where the adjacent parcels are under other ownership, a number of complex problems (involving subordination, nondisturbance of subtenants, joinder by the ground lessor in cross-easement agreements, and so on) must be resolved before the project becomes viable. For a complete examination of these problems and recommended solutions see ABA Section of Real Property, Probate and Trust Law Committee on Leases, Ground Leases and Their Financing, 4 Real Prop., Prob. & Tr. J. 437, 462-465 (1969).

4. *Additional Readings.* For additional background with respect to leasehold mortgages on an unencumbered fee see Anderson, Mortgagee Looks at the Ground Lease, 10 Fla. L. Rev. 1 (1957); Gunning, A Primer for Mortgageable Ground Lease, The Mortgage Banker 36 (1967); Halper, People and Property: The Anatomy of a Ground Lease,

3 Real Est. Rev. 9 (1973); Halper, Mortgageability of Unsubordinated Ground Leases, 16 Real Est. Rev. 48 (Spring 1986); Hyde, Leasehold Mortgages, XII Proc. Assn. Life Ins. Counsel 659 (1955); Kelly, Some Aspects of Leasehold Financing, 33 Notre Dame Law. 34 (1957); 2 R. Powell, Law of Real Property §242[3] (1982); Smith and Lubell, Real Estate Financing: Mortgaging the Leasehold, 7 Real Est. Rev. 13 (1977); Underberg, Ground Leasing Makes Dollars and Sense for Developers, 1 Real Est. Rev. 38 (1971).

4. Leasehold Mortgage Encumbering the Fee: The Streamlined Mortgage

One imaginative real estate financing technique is the so-called streamlined mortgage, whereby the fee owner agrees to subject (or "subordinate") her fee interest to the lien of the leasehold mortgage by joining in the mortgage. Since the security for the loan would be the fee itself and not just the mortgagor's defeasible leasehold estate, the lender would be able to take into account the value of the land for appraisal purposes. Accordingly, since the developer could anticipate larger financing, he might be in a position to construct more extensive improvements on the leased land and pay a higher ground rent to the fee owner, who would also receive greater security for the rent obligation under the ground lease.

Returning to the example at Chapter 8A1, supra, if Dan is able to convince the ground lessor to subject his fee ownership to the lien of the mortgage, Dan might be able to (1) substantially reduce his cash requirement by obtaining a loan close to the $3 million fee mortgage amount and (2) still retain the tax advantages of ordinary leasehold mortgage financing. Moreover, it is customary for the lender to both absolve the fee owner of personal liability with respect to the obligations of the mortgage and to minimize the fee owner's risk of forfeiting her interest in the land by affording her the opportunity to cure a default by the developer-lessee under the mortgage. Therefore, a streamlined mortgage that has characteristics of both a fee and a leasehold mortgage can create advantages over ordinary leasehold financing for all of the concerned parties. However, as the following excerpt suggests, all that glitters is not gold!

Smith and Lubell, Real Estate Financing: The Streamlined Mortgage
4 Real Est. Rev. 21 (Summer 1974)

THE STREAMLINED MORTGAGE

Techniques of financing real estate are limited only by the imagination of the developer and his attorney and the legal restrictions imposed on the institutional lender. The "streamlined mortgage" (a term we have coined merely for purposes of identification) is a current result of this alchemy.

All too frequently, this form of financing is erroneously referred to as a subordinated fee loan. Although it has characteristics of both a fee mortgage and leasehold mortgage, it is truly neither. A mortgage on the fee affords the lender the security of the whole pie since the entire estate stands behind the loan. The mortgagee under a leasehold mortgage, on the other hand, has only the security of a piece of the pie — the leasehold estate as evidenced by the ground lease. You might say that the fee mortgagee is the fee owner once removed, while the leasehold mortgagee is the lessee once removed.

But when, in the latter case, the landowner-ground lessor voluntarily subjects his fee to the leasehold mortgage, a streamlined mortgage results. The property owner actually joins in the mortgage, thereby telling the lender that "in the event you foreclose, you have the security of my ownership of the land."

The streamlined mortgage is widely employed as a financing vehicle for several reasons. The high cost of land and the tight money market both encourage developers to consider a leasehold plus a leasehold mortgage as a means of maintaining leverage. And since some owners of prime properties, particularly in urban areas, wish to hold their land either as a hedge against inflation or to avoid paying high capital gains taxes on a sale, a long-term ground lease may be the only viable path to development.

ADVANTAGES OF THE STREAMLINED MORTGAGE

It is an evident advantage for the developer to lease instead of purchase land. His initial capital requirements are less and the full yearly rental payments for the land are deductible. If the developer had purchased the land outright and mortgaged the fee estate, only mortgage interest would be deductible. When the land is leased, part of the rental payments are the equivalent of repayment of principal which the developer would not have been able to deduct if he had purchased the land and mortgaged the fee.

The streamlined mortgage enables the lender to value the property at a higher amount than in the case of a pure leasehold mortgage, since value can be attributed to the land as well as to the improvements. This means the developer can get a larger loan than would be possible if his leasehold estate were the only security.

Lenders, too, prefer the streamlined mortgage. Many feel trepidation about the security of a straight leasehold loan. The bankruptcy of the Penn Central Railroad raised fears that the unexpired portion of a ground lease may be construed as an "executory contract." Since a trustee in bankruptcy for the fee owner may reject an executory contract if it is detrimental to the bankrupt estate, lenders are concerned that the security for a leasehold loan could be extinguished. Until the courts decide whether a trustee in bankruptcy may reject a ground lease, lenders may be wary of straight leasehold financing.

Moreover, it is patent that a loan supported by the whole pie (the fee estate), instead of a piece of the pie (the leasehold), allows the lender greater latitude in granting indulgence upon default before resorting to foreclosure.

STRUCTURING THE GROUND LEASE TO MEET LENDER REQUIREMENTS

The ground lease is frequently an extensive document. If it has not been negotiated with the lender's requirements in mind, leasehold financing may be unavailable. Since the requirements for a streamlined mortgage are considerably less detailed, the probability of rejection of a loan application on technical grounds is reduced. In addition, any shortcomings of the ground lease can be rectified in the streamlined mortgage documents themselves, which the owner is obliged to execute in order to subject his fee to the mortgage. . . .

Lease Provisions for the Streamlined Mortgage

Where the fee owner voluntarily subjects his fee to the developer-lessee's mortgage, the requirements of the lender are considerably less stringent.

- The term of the ground lease must be at least equal to the term of the mortgage.
- The ground lease should expressly provide that the fee owner will join in the execution of the mortgage and subject his fee estate to the lender's lien.
- Although not universally required by lenders, the ground lease should be made subordinate or inferior to the mortgage lien,

so that the leasehold estate is eliminated upon foreclosure and the lender is provided with a fee simple estate. Unless the lender is satisfied that the ground lease will be eliminated upon foreclosure, it will require removal or modification of the lease provisions it finds objectionable from a legal or underwriting point of view. The developer will then have to renegotiate the ground lease, which may prove costly in terms of increased rent or other concessions to the owner.

- The ground lease should stipulate that subleases with space tenants provide for "attornment" in the event of foreclosure or any other termination of the ground lease; that is, sublessees will recognize the fee owner and his successor, the mortgagee, as the landlord and rent will continue to be paid accordingly. The reason for this requirement is illustrated in the following example of a streamlined loan on a shopping center.

Joe Developer has negotiated a forty-year ground lease with land-owner Frank Farmer. The lease contains elements satisfactory to Dollar Life Insurance Company, which agrees to lend Developer $4 million on the security of a shopping center development. Farmer agrees to join in the mortgage and subject his fee to Dollar Life's mortgage, and the ground lease has been subordinated to the lien on the fee. Subleases with a department store, supermarket, and eighteen satellite stores have been executed by Developer.

If Dollar Life forecloses its mortgage and the inferior ground lease is extinguished, the subleases which flow from this ground lease will also be wiped out. Unless the ground lease requires attornment and the space tenants agree to attorn, Dollar Life will lose the source of income to repay its loan.

To make sure subjection of the fee to the lessee's mortgage will be accomplished without difficulty, the ground lease must require the fee owner to execute the mortgage documents submitted to him. Since no state law, to the writers' knowledge, requires the fee owner to execute the promissory note to effectually subject his land to the mortgage, he need sign only the mortgage (or deed of trust) instrument itself.

Since the mortgage documents may be executed two or three years after the ground lease is signed, the lessee must be certain that the landowner's heirs and assigns are required to fulfill his obligations. In one actual situation, the ground lease was signed in 1968, the property was developed and completed as a shopping center in 1972, and the mortgage was submitted for signature of the fee owner upon completion. Unfortunately, he had died leaving heirs in Georgia, Florida, and Hawaii, all of whom were required to join in the execution of the mortgage.

HOW TO CONVINCE THE LANDOWNER TO GO ALONG

While the fee owner is entitled to compensation by way of above-market ground rent for agreeing to subject his fee to the lien of a mortgage, he may still be reluctant to consent to a streamlined mortgage because he runs the risk of losing his property in the event the lessee defaults. (The fee owner may also object to the limitations against his mortgaging the fee.) But the developer has some good arguments to meet these objections:

- If the owner developed the land himself, he would have to put up the land as security in order to get financing.
- Should the developer-lessee default, the landowner can cure the default and step into the developer's shoes. To assure the owner of this opportunity, he is entitled, by the terms of the mortgage, to prior notice of default from the mortgagee.
- The developer can obtain greater financing to permit a more extensive improvement and create greater security for the rent obligation under the ground lease.
- Since the developer can anticipate a larger loan, he may be in a position to pay a higher land rent.
- The owner will not be personally liable for payment of the loan or for any other obligation of the mortgage.

to permit
greater
skimming

CONCLUSION

The streamlined mortgage benefits all concerned. It offers the developer an opportunity for a larger loan with a smaller equity investment. The lender is afforded better security than in pure leasehold mortgage financing. The negotiation and documentation of the loan is simplified, and both developer and landowner are given greater flexibility in structuring a loan which will accommodate their respective interests.

NOTES AND QUESTIONS

1. *Subordination of the Ground Lease and Attornment by Subtenants.* Since the security for a streamlined mortgage is a lien on the fee as well as the leasehold estate, the lender's requirements as a leasehold mortgagee with respect to the ground lease are considerably less stringent than those discussed at Chapter 8A3, supra. However, as discussed in the foregoing excerpt by Smith and Lubell, the lender will often require that the ground lease be subordinate, or inferior, to its lien on the fee by insisting that the lease be recorded after the mortgage or

by having the ground lessee execute a subordination agreement. The objective of the requirement is to extinguish the inferior ground lease in the event that the lender forecloses its lien on the fee. In addition, the lender will frequently require that the occupancy subtenants agree (in the subleases or by separate instrument) to "attorn," or to recognize, the new fee owner — be it the mortgagee or the purchaser at the foreclosure sale — as the landlord and the party to whom the future rents will be paid.

The following is a brief example and diagram outlining the configuration of the relationship between the parties created by these requirements, as shown in Figure 8-1.

Dan Developer has negotiated a 40-year ground lease with Frank Fee Owner, a farmer, so that Dan can construct a shopping center complex on the leased land. The terms of the lease are approved by the Lender Insurance Co., which then agrees to lend Dan $3 million on the security of Dan's leasehold estate and improvements thereon. Frank agrees to join in the mortgage and to subject his fee ownership to the lien of Lender's mortgage, and the ground lease is subordinated to the mortgage. Subleases have been executed by Dan with a supermarket as prime tenant and with a number of secondary tenants who will operate satellite stores in the shopping center. All these space leases have been approved by Lender. Frank and Dan have *conditionally* assigned

F i g u r e   8-1

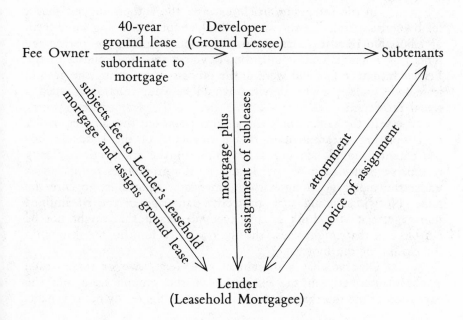

their interests in the ground lease and subleases, respectively, to Lender as additional security for the loan, and all the subtenants have executed attornment agreements with Lender.

2. *Questions.*

a. Based on what you have learned about postconstruction financing, what is Lender's purpose for demanding conditional lease assignments from both Fee Owner and Developer?

b. We already know that if the underlying fee is subject to a prior mortgage Lender will usually demand that the prior mortgage be satisfied or subordinated to the lien of its leasehold mortgage; otherwise, a foreclosure of the senior mortgage-encumbrance might extinguish Dan's leasehold estate and Lender's security for the loan to Dan.

When Fee Owner subjects his fee interest to the lien of Lender's leasehold mortgage, Lender in effect winds up with two simultaneous mortgages: one a leasehold mortgage with a lien on Dan's leasehold estate and the other in reality a fee mortgage with a lien on Fee Owner's fee. Assuming hypothetically that the initial annual ground rent is $100,000 and the total subrental is $400,000, can you think of any reason why Lender would demand that the ground lease be made subordinate to the lien of its leasehold mortgage? For general background see Chapter 4C3.

c. What is the rationale for Lender's requirement that the subtenants execute attornment agreements in favor of itself and its successors-in-interest?

d. In the foregoing article excerpt, the authors suggest that a fee owner, as ground lessor, should think about demanding some form of adjustable rent (e.g., equity participation in profits or percentage rental) as a hedge against inflation. If you were legal counsel to the Lender Insurance Co. and were in the process of reviewing the ground lease for Lender's approval, what would be your reaction to such a rental provision?

e. In the same article the authors point out that any fee owner contemplating streamlined mortgage financing of the leasehold improvements should demand a provision in the mortgage requiring reasonable notice to it of any default by the ground lessee-mortgagor under the mortgage along with an adequate opportunity to cure the same. Notwithstanding such protective language in the streamlined mortgage, can you think of any type of default that might not be curable and that might cause the fee owner to lose his fee through a foreclosure of the mortgage?

f. Observe that a substantial time (e.g., two or three years) might elapse between the execution of the ground lease and the execution of the mortgage documents. Suppose the fee owner covenants in the ground lease to subject his fee interest to the lien of the leasehold mortgage but subsequently refuses to join in either the note or the mortgage. Assuming that the agreement to encumber the fee is not unenforceable for want of certainty in its terms, what would be the arguments for and against granting specific performance of the promise? Do you see any analogy to the case for specific performance of a mortgage loan commitment? See discussion at Chapter 5D. What about specific performance of a subordination agreement by a seller who subsequently refuses to subordinate her purchase money mortgage to a construction or postconstruction loan on the property? See discussion of purchase money mortgages at Chapter 9B, note 5a. As a matter of legal theory and sound social policy, which case is the stronger? The weaker? See Grout, Specific Performance of Contracts to Provide Permanent Financing, 60 Cornell L. Rev. 718, 736-742 (1975); Mehr and Kilgore, Enforcement of the Real Estate Loan Commitment: Improvement of the Borrower Remedies, 24 Wayne L. Rev. 1011 (1978); Note, Subordination of Purchase Money Security, 52 Calif. L. Rev. 157, 166-168 (1964). For a general discussion of the streamlined mortgage see ABA Section of Real Property, Probate & Trust Law Committee on Leases, Ground Leases and Their Financing, 4 Real Prop., Prob. & Tr. J. 437, 440-453 (Fall 1969); Halper, Planning and Construction Clauses in a Subordinated Ground Lease, 17 Real Est. L.J. 48 (Summer 1988).

B. SALE-AND-LEASEBACK FINANCING

As the term implies, a sale and leaseback of real estate typically involves the sale of either undeveloped land or land together with existing improvements by a land developer or business concern to an institutional investor that simultaneously leases back the property to the previous owner for an extended period of time under a net-lease arrangement. As noted earlier, if a developer-borrower utilizes leasehold as opposed to mortgage financing, it can reduce its cash outlay and leverage its acquisition costs and also obtain a rental deduction for its ground rent payment in lieu of the extra nondeductible amortization that would be payable on the larger fee mortgage were it to purchase the underlying fee. Likewise, since land itself is not a depreciable asset, sale-and-leaseback financing affords a developer-borrower the opportunity to maximize its liquidity and cash reserves while being able to depreciate the land that is being used in the guise of rental payments.

In the case of new construction, the developer can use either fee or leasehold mortgage financing along with equity capital to fund the cost of the land and overlying improvements. Alternatively, the developer may be able to finance its land and construction costs by means of a sale-and-leaseback transaction with a sale price covering the costs of the land and if applicable the proposed improvements. This technique is frequently employed by business concerns such as retail stores that require substantial amounts of working capital to fund both inventory and operating expenses. For example, a company that wishes to build or expand its existing plant or store facilities can engage in a sale-and-leaseback transaction to fund its construction costs without sacrificing working capital for fixed assets. Similarly, by selling the proposed facility for cash and leasing it back, a company can fund the cost of construction in the event it is unable to obtain the initial construction financing from an institutional lender. For this kind of business, this technique offers the additional advantage of piecemeal financing, whereby the sale and leaseback of existing units can be timed to coincide with the construction of new units on an as-needed basis, as opposed to debt financing, wherein the proceeds are received in one lump-sum payment. Another option would be to use some variation on the sale-and-leaseback theme or even a combination of sale-leaseback and mortgage debt financing, which real estate professionals generically refer to as "split," or "component," financing. For example, a builder or business concern that already owns the land might lease the land to a separate but controlled corporation or outside entity, thereby splitting the ownership of the real estate into distinct fee and leasehold interests so that it can increase the amount of the overall financing by mortgaging each component separately. Another example of high-ratio financing, or "superleverage," that can theoretically be achieved by means of split financing is the so-called sale-buyback. Under a sale-buyback agreement, the land and projected improvements are sold prior to the commencement of construction for a sale price that covers the costs of both, and the developer simultaneously repurchases the improved real estate under a long-term installment contract. See discussion at Chapter 8B1, note 3, infra.

In the case of existing improvements, the real estate owner may likewise choose between debt financing and sale-and-leaseback financing (or some combination thereof) for the purpose of assembling additional working capital. Under the former alternative, the owner-borrower might seek to obtain a wraparound mortgage or some other variant of secondary financing (see Chapter 9B, note 4) or, in the alternative, attempt to refinance the existing mortgage indebtedness (see Chapter 9A). Frequently, if the ownership entity is a corporation it will be able to translate its equity in the real estate into cash by issuing its own debentures or by engaging in some other form of straight-debt financing. By contrast, the owner may wish to raise additional working capital by means of a sale and leaseback of either the land alone or of both the land and existing improvements.

In the case of either straight-debt or fee mortgage financing, the borrower will retain legal ownership of both the land and the building; whereas in the case of sale-and-leaseback financing (as well as leasehold mortgage financing), the legal and tax status of the borrower would be that of a lessee with respect to the land, the improvements, or both. Accordingly, any such selection between debt or sale-and-leaseback financing should always involve a careful balancing of the competing legal and tax considerations that are examined in the discussion that follows.

1. Comparison with Mortgage and Straight-Debt Financing

Agar, Sale and Lease-Backs
18 ABA Section on Tax. (pt. 2) 61, 62 (1965)

The subject is billed as "Sale and Lease-back." *A* sells to *B* and *B* leases back to *A*. This transaction has certain financial and tax consequences which are of interest and which are the real subjects of this talk. Many of these consequences are shared by all leasing transactions. Some are found in all sales. However, the parties are most conscious of them and they are best emphasized in a certain type of deal — i.e.:

> Any transaction in which a lease is made according to a pre-existing agreement between the lessee and the lessor upon acquisition of title by the lessor or the lessor's completion of a structure.

Although some deals falling within this category are not strictly sales and lease-backs, because the lessor does not acquire title from the lessee, I have included them in considering examples of the type of transactions to which we want to direct our attention. We shall compare this type of financing with the conventional mortgage method.

Here are some examples of typical deals:

> A corporation wishing to convert fixed assets into working capital and to secure the maximum amount of cash, sells land, together with an existing building, to an investor pursuant to an agreement for an immediate lease-back of the property at a rent which will provide the investor with a fair return and amortize the investment over the initial

term of the lease. A typical initial term would be 25 to 30 years (based on the depreciable life of the building),[17] which would call for a rental of around 7% of the investment to provide amortization within the initial term, assuming a 5½% income return to the investor. Such a lease might typically provide for a renewal term or terms at the tenant's option for 20 to 40 years at a rent (based on land value alone) of 30 to 40% of the rent called for during the initial term. (Note that I have said that the rent should "amortize the investment" over the initial term of the lease. This is the commonly accepted method of stating the formula but it is not strictly accurate. The rent payable for the land should be purely interest at the market rate. No amortization factor is needed because the land does not depreciate and the lessor ends up owning it. However, due to the inflationary trend and the expectation that land values in developed areas will increase, the rent for the land may be equal percentage-wise to the rent for the building although it includes no amortization component. In other words, it may be just as high as if it did contain an amortization component. Suppose for example that fair interest would be 5½% and that the sale price of the land is $3,000,000. Suppose further that the predicted value of the land at the end of the lease is $5,000,000, the land rental would then be computed as 5½% of the mean, or $4,000,000. 5½% of $4,000,000 is $220,000, which is 7⅓% of $3,000,000, the sale price of the land.)

A corporation owning a suitable site for a new plant makes an agreement with an investor which provides that upon completion by the corporation of the new plant in accordance with agreed plans and specifications, the corporation will sell the land and building to the investor for an agreed price, which may be subject to adjustment on the basis of the actual cost of the building, and that the investor will simultaneously lease the land and building back to the corporation.

A land owner constructs a building in accordance with an agreement between himself and the investor and the prospective lessee. The contract binds the investor to purchase the land and building upon completion and requires the investor and the prospective lessee to enter into a lease.

A land owner agrees with a prospective tenant to construct a building according to the tenant's specifications and the parties agree to enter into a lease upon completion.

All of the above examples relate to lease-backs of land and building. A very important and significantly different type of transaction is the ground lease sale and lease-back. In this situation title to the building, whether erected before or after the sale, is retained by the lessee who can thus take . . . depreciation on the building and deduct the full rent paid for the land. Such a ground lease may have a high market value and must, therefore, be carefully drawn so as to be mortgageable and thus saleable. . . .

---

17. See discussion of current depreciation rules at Chapter 2B, note 3. — ED.

Note, Taxation of Sale and Leaseback Transactions — A General Review

32 Vand. L. Rev. 945, 948-951 (1979)

The basic sale and leaseback transaction . . . is composed of several simple components — a sale for valuable consideration, a lease for a term of years, and various options to renew or repurchase. The possible combinations of these components, however, provide a flexible yet complex tool for financing or business expansion. The consideration paid by the purchaser is generally the fair market value of the property, but may be a lesser amount when other aspects of the sale or the leaseback favor the seller. Rental payments may be set at the fair rental value of the property, but are often set at a rate that will amortize the purchaser's investment over the lease's primary term at a specified rate of return.[20] This procedure provides the purchaser with a safe, guaranteed return on his investment. Repurchase and renewal options can also add flexibility to a sale and leaseback transaction. The renewal option assures the seller of continued use of property needed in his trade or business even though he has relinquished title. In addition, the original lease may state rentals for the renewal periods, enabling the seller-lessee to ascertain its maximum future costs of land and buildings. If the rental payments during the primary term of the lease fully amortize the purchaser's investment, many purchaser-lessors will accept reduced rent for the renewal periods. The repurchase option provides the seller with a means of reacquiring the property if necessary due to future business developments. The option may allow repurchase at any time during the lease, only at specified times, or only at the expiration of the lease. The option price may be stated, determined by appraisal, or tied to the remaining lease payments required to amortize the purchaser's investment.

In addition to the variations mentioned above, a sale and leaseback may be structured as a multiple party transaction to provide additional flexibility. For example, the seller or purchaser may be a syndicate, joint venture, or group of individuals or corporations. The purchaser may also arrange for one or more third party lending institutions to finance the purchase, using the acquired property and the lease as collateral and repaying the loan from the lease payments. These additional possibilities make the real estate sale and leaseback an extremely flexible and useful business tool.

---

20. This type of rental payment schedule closely resembles a mortgage payment schedule that provides for repayment of principal and interest in installments at a specified interest rate.

C.   FINANCIAL CONSIDERATIONS

Sale and leaseback transactions may be utilized for a variety of business and financial purposes. A principal use is to provide the seller-lessee with immediate cash to meet increased working capital needs.[22] The sale and leaseback generally provides cash equal to 100 percent of the fair market value of the property sold, while conventional financing techniques normally yield only 75-80 percent of the fair market value of the property securing the loan. In essence, the seller-lessee uses the sale and leaseback transaction to transform fixed assets into working capital while retaining possession and use of the property. As a side effect, this technique can provide a better balance sheet position for the seller-lessee, which enables it to obtain a greater amount of conventional financing in the future. The seller-lessee obtains this better balance sheet position by increasing current assets with the proceeds of the sale and thereby increasing its current ratio, an important determinant of credit standing.[23]

Many companies have found the sale and leaseback transaction a useful means for financing expansion of facilities or obtaining funds for construction. This technique has been especially prevalent in the retail sales industry. Many businesses in this industry must make a significant investment in their physical plant, and simultaneously require large amounts of working capital for inventory and operating expenses. If the business is growing rapidly, the working capital requirements often become so great that the business finds needed expansion of its physical plant impossible to finance. These businesses often expand or build new stores and then enter into sale and leaseback transactions to convert fixed assets into working capital.[25]

Another use of the sale and leaseback transaction is to obtain financing in a tight money market. When credit is tight and conventional financing is difficult to obtain, investors may be willing to enter into a sale and leaseback transaction as a substitute for a loan because ownership of property provides a hedge against inflation for the investor

22. See, e.g., Sun Oil Co. v. Commissioner, 562 F.2d 258 (3d Cir. 1977), cert. denied, 436 U.S. 944 (1978).

23. The current ratio is the ratio of current assets to current liabilities. Lending institutions view this ratio as an indicator of a debtor's ability to service immediate obligations under short-term loans. When fixed assets are sold the cash received increases current assets without a corresponding increase in current liabilities, thus increasing the current ratio and providing the debtor with a better credit standing for short-term borrowing.

25. This technique is also used by contractors to acquire funds for independent construction. The contractor first purchases a construction site with his own funds and then enters into a sale and leaseback transaction to obtain financing necessary to construct a building on the site.

and also eliminates legal problems connected with foreclosure and collection of debt if the seller is unable to meet his obligations.[27]

In addition to the advantages listed above, a seller-lessee may be able to use a sale and leaseback transaction to circumvent loan restrictions or state and federal regulations. Although loan agreements often contain provisions limiting additional borrowing and requiring the debtor to meet certain ratio tests,[28] leaseback agreements seldom have similar provisions. Moreover, the parties often can structure the sale and leaseback transaction so that it does not breach provisions of prior loan agreements that conventional financing techniques would violate. Also, several state and federal regulations relating to the ownership of property by certain organizations do not apply to leaseholds under a sale and leaseback transaction.[30]

The purchaser-lessor in a sale and leaseback may also obtain certain financial advantages from the transaction. The rate of return is generally higher on a sale and leaseback than on a loan secured by the same property. The investor in a sale and leaseback procures this higher return because he takes additional risks by investing 100 percent of the fair market value of the property, rather than the lower percentage generally securing a loan. In addition, by entering a sale and leaseback transaction rather than a conventional loan, he foregoes any rights he would have as a creditor under a mortgage loan.[32] . . . Another significant advantage to the purchaser-lessor is that the ownership of property provides a hedge against inflation since any appreciation in value will accrue to the owner.[33] Finally, since most leasebacks are "net leases,"[34] the purchaser has a relatively management-free investment with a built-in tenant and a guaranteed return.

27. Since the lessor owns legal title to the property, he need not go through foreclosure proceedings to take possession of the property. Further, the property will not be tied up in any bankruptcy proceedings that may ensue if the lessee becomes insolvent.

28. These ratio tests include the current ratio, debt-equity ratio, and quick asset ratio. These ratios are indicators of the debtor's continued ability to service its debt.

30. For example, the Federal Reserve System places limits on the amount a banking institution can invest in its banking premises. Banks can circumvent these limits by a sale and leaseback transaction. See Frank Lyon Co. v. United States, 435 U.S. 561 (1978).

32. These rights include the ability to force a debtor into bankruptcy, to obtain preferred status in bankruptcy, to sue upon the debt for execution or garnishment, and to participate in a bankruptcy distribution to the full extent of the creditor's investment.

33. This hedge against inflation may be limited or eliminated if the lease contains a repurchase option that sets the option price at anything other than the fair market value of the property at the time the option is exercised. Any other type of repurchase option is likely to allow the lessee to enjoy partially or fully the benefits of any appreciation.

34. A net lease is an arrangement under which the lessee pays all taxes, assessments,

Fuller, Sale and Leasebacks and
the *Frank Lyon* Case
48 Geo. Wash. L. Rev. 60, 60-63 (Nov. 1979)

Typical sale and leaseback transactions may be illustrated by two examples. In the first example, Seller, who owns the land and building used in his business, sells this real estate to Buyer. At the same time the parties enter into a lease contract for a long term — perhaps forty or fifty years. The rental is fixed at an amount that will give Buyer an acceptable return on his investment. Frequently, the lease gives the lessee one or more renewal options.

In the second example, a new building is constructed on land already owned by the business or land to be acquired for the purpose. The land is sold to Buyer under a contract that provides not only for a subsequent long-term lease, but also obligates Seller to construct the planned new building on the property. . . .

In either of the above transactions, the buyer typically finances his acquisition by borrowing most of the purchase price from an institutional lender. The buyer's role is that of a passive investor: not only is most of his investment made with borrowed money, but his obligations under the lease are almost non-existent. As a rule, the lessee pays real estate taxes, insurance and repair costs, and assumes the risk of casualty or condemnation. Thus the lessee bears all the operating expenses and all the burdens he would bear as owner, and the buyer/lessor enjoys his return free and clear of any costs.

Tax considerations aside, the sale and leaseback arrangement offers significant inducements to the parties. For the investor (the buyer), the return can be higher than that paid on competitive securities such as mortgages and corporate bonds. Usury laws and regulations surrounding mortgage lending do not apply to rentals and the leases under which they are paid.[3] The investment is well protected because the investor owns the property and can depend on the successful operations of a well-chosen lessee to continue to provide funds to pay the rent. Finally, the buyer can reasonably expect that the value of the property will rise over the years because real estate values in the United States have generally risen with inflation. Thus, when the lease expires, even if the useful life of the improvements has ended, the land and buildings

---

maintenance, and other expenses related to the property. The lessor thus receives his rent payments free of any expenses related to the property.

3. E.g., Cal. Const. art. XV, §1 (1980); Cal. Civ. Code §1915 (West 1972); Act of Aug. 19, 1963 §1, Ill. Ann. Stat. ch. 73, §737.15A (Smith-Hurd Supp. 1979); N.Y. Ins. Law §81(6) (McKinney Supp. 1979).

should have substantial value. In many cases, the fair market value of the property after forty or fifty years of use will still greatly exceed the original price.

The seller/lessee may also obtain significant non-tax advantages from the sale and leaseback. First, a large sum of cash is realized at once.[4] The sale of the property produces the full market value, but a loan secured by a mortgage on the same property would obtain only a portion of the value. . . . Moreover, until 1976, the Financial Accounting Standards Board did not usually require that a long-term leasehold be capitalized or that the rental obligation be carried as a liability.[5] Aside from accounting considerations, many companies may be operating under existing legal obligations (incurred, perhaps, incident to the issuance of senior securities) that severely restrict any new indebtedness. A sale and leaseback may permit such a company to obtain needed funds without renegotiating such agreements.

The tax advantages offered by the sale and leaseback transaction are also attractive. The lessee can claim all his rent payments as business expense deductible from ordinary income.[7] Any gain realized on the sale of the property will ordinarily qualify for long-term capital gain treatment under section 1231 of the Internal Revenue Code.[8]

The advantages of the sale and leaseback become apparent when the seller/lessee is compared with the owner of business property who mortgages the property to obtain a loan. Under the mortgage arrangement, the part of the owner's payments on the mortgage that represents interest is deductible, but amounts representing repayment of principal are not. The borrowing owner will also be able to take deductions for depreciation, to the extent that depreciation is allowable. The deduction,

---

4. Or, if the transaction is for the construction or acquisition of a new property, the cash will not be retained, but a major obligation will be avoided.

5. Financial Accounting Standards Board, Accounting for Leases (Opinion No. 13), reprinted in Financial Accounting Standards Board, Financial Accounting Standards, 854-55 (1979). For the earlier position see Accounting Principles Board, Reporting of Leases in Financial Statements of Lessees (Opinion No. 5), reprinted in Financial Accounting Standards Board, Financial Accounting Standards 135 (1979). Under the more restrictive current standard it is still possible that a given long-term lease incurred in a sale and leaseback transaction may not have to be carried as an asset and liability. Financial Accounting Standards Board, Accounting for Leases (Opinion No. 13), reprinted in Financial Accounting Standards Board, supra, at 854. [These opinions have been superseded by Statements of Financial Accounting Standards Nos. 13, 16, and 98, which are examined at note 4, infra. — Ed.]

7. I.R.C. §162(a).

8. Id. §1231(a). The gain will qualify as a long-term capital gain only so long as the property is used in a trade or business. Id. See also I.R.C. §1202. [Under current law preferential treatment is no longer accorded to long-term capital gain. See discussion at Chapter 2B, note 3. — Ed.]

however, may be limited by several factors: first, the basis for depreciation is historical cost, not market value;[9] second, the original basis already may have been reduced by depreciation deductions;[10] and third, any amount of basis allocable to land in no event may be subject to depreciation.[11] These limitations contrast with the allowance of all the rent paid by the lessee under sale and leaseback. Under the sale and leaseback, the rental payments are based on the full market value of the property and include amounts that, in a purchase financed by mortgage, would be allocable to amortization of principal and to the value of the non-depreciable land.[12] The tax advantage to the lessee is roughly comparable to those an owner would enjoy if he were allowed to deduct his repayment of principal and to depreciate his land.

The tax advantages of the sale and leaseback to the buyer are no less attractive. If the buyer has leveraged his investment with a substantial proportion of indebtedness, as is common, the interest payable on the debt is deductible.[13] In addition, having retained ownership of the property, the buyer/lessor is entitled to take depreciation on the leased property (other than land).[14] The rental payments represent income to the buyer, but the combined deductions for interest and depreciation often greatly exceed the rent income, thus offsetting other income of the investor. The overall effect of this combination is that the rental income is enjoyed as a kind of tax-free cash flow while the other income, freed from income tax by the surplus deductions, adds to the after-tax yield obtained by the investment. The sale and leaseback thus offers the investor a real estate tax shelter with a high degree of investment security.

Because the sale and leaseback is often a financing arrangement for a new business property, another . . . advantage is possible. The party putting up the money — whether the buyer himself or an institutional lender — may not be willing to invest the entire value of the property in the transaction. If, for example, a new building is to be erected on newly-acquired land at a total cost of $5,000,000, the buyer may only be willing to pay $4,000,000 for the purchase. The seller would then have to absorb $1,000,000. This is a trading matter and presumably could be negotiated with appropriate reductions in the rent. . . .

9. Id. §167(g). See also I.R.C. §§1011-1012.
10. Id. §1016(a).
11. Treas. Reg. §1.67(a)-2 (1960).
12. Such amounts would not, of course, be deductible. See id.
13. I.R.C. §163(a). But see id. §163(d) (limitation on the deduction of investment interest for taxpayers other than corporations).
14. Id. §167. Depreciation, however, is predicated on a capital investment in the property by the taxpayer, not bare legal title.

NOTES AND QUESTIONS

1. *Questions.* Returning to the illustration at Chapter 8A1, supra, suppose Dan had purchased the underlying fee for $1 million and had deducted straight-line depreciation in the amount of $95,238 per annum (over the 31.5-year period); now, after 10 years, based on a projected net income of $860,000 and an assumed capitalization rate of 11.1 percent, the shopping center has an appraised value of approximately $7,750,000 and a remaining useful life of 20 years. The outstanding principal balance on the fee mortgage has been reduced from $3 million to about $2,873,000 over the 10-year period. Dan would like to translate his equity (in the amount of $4,877,000) into cash so he can invest in other shopping center developments.

Dan has the option of refinancing with Ace Insurance Company for a new mortgage loan amount of about $5,800,000 (at a loan-to-value ratio of 75 percent). However, he would have to pay an origination fee and prepayment penalty totaling $800,000, so his net refinancing proceeds would amount to $5 million. While most mortgage loans are constant-payment loans (see Chapter 5B4), assume for simplicity's sake that the new mortgage is repayable in the amount of $290,000 per annum for 20 years plus annual interest at 10 percent on the outstanding principal balance, so that the total debt-service payment in the first loan year would be $870,000. Alternatively, Dan could sell the real estate for its full market value of $7,750,000 with a 20-year leaseback at an annual rental of $426,250 (enabling the purchaser to recoup his investment over the 20-year term and receive a 10 percent income return but ignoring the time value of money) and with an option to purchase at a price that would relate to the market value of the real estate on the expiration of the 20-year leaseback period.

In terms as non-mathematical as possible, explain what factors are relevant in deciding which mode of assembling working capital would be best for Dan in the short run and in the long run. Make any necessary assumptions.

The foregoing example assumes that both purchaser and lender, respectively, would receive sufficient rent or debt-service payments over the initial 20-year term of the leaseback or mortgage to both amortize its investment and receive a market (10 percent) rate of income return. Why should this be so? In contrast to a mortgage lender, a purchaser in a sale-and-leaseback transaction receives ownership of both the land and the building. Why should the purchaser be able to demand as high a rate of return on its investment?

2. *Split Financing: Sale and Leaseback Plus Leasehold Mortgage.* A developer who owns the land can sever the fee from the leasehold improvements by selling the land for its market value to an institutional

investor who would then ground lease the land back to the developer. Either the investor or another lender would make a leasehold mortgage loan to fund the construction costs of the improvements. As security for the loan the lender would obtain a leasehold mortgage on the land and a fee mortgage on the building that will be owned by the developer. As a hedge against inflation, the investor, as ground lessor, would get a specified ground rent plus a percentage rental or some other equity kicker. In this manner, the developer theoretically might be able to obtain 100 percent financing (or more) of the land cost, whereas had it obtained conventional mortgage financing the loan-to-value ratio would be about 75 percent for both the land and the improvements. See Table 5-1 at Chapter 5B1. For example, suppose a developer wants to construct a shopping center costing $4 million on land he owns worth $2 million. Assuming the loan appraisal value of both the land and the improvements is $6 million, a regular 75 percent fee mortgage loan from an insurance company or other permanent lender would yield a loan amount of $4.5 million. By contrast, if he engages in a sale-and-leaseback of the land and obtains a leasehold mortgage (with the same 75 percent loan-to-value ratio), he would end up with pretax proceeds of $5 million (the $2 million land value plus 75 percent of the $4 million building value).

Moreover, if the investor who purchases the land is willing to subject its fee interest to the lien of the leasehold mortgage in exchange for a higher ground rental or some other consideration, the developer could attain even greater leverage. The loan amount under such a "streamlined" leasehold mortgage on an encumbered fee might include 75 percent of the appraised value of the land plus the improvements. Therefore, in our example, this would theoretically yield a startling pretax total of $6.5 million for the developer — the $2 million land sale proceeds plus a loan amount equal to 75 percent of the $6 million land-plus-building value. Of course, this presupposes that the sublease, or "occupancy," rentals will be sufficient in amount to enable the developer to pay the extra ground rent necessary to induce the investor to pay the full value of the land ($2 million), notwithstanding the condition that the investor-ground lessor subject the fee to the lien of the leasehold mortgage. Alternatively, the mortgagee might accept a "partial subordination," whereby the fee owner receives an unencumbered fee on condition that it waive its right to the ground rent in the event that (1) the developer defaults and (2) the income from the property is insufficient to meet the debt-service payments on the leasehold mortgage. See Madison and Dwyer §8.09[2]; Weil, Land Leasebacks Move up Fast as Financing Techniques, 1 Real Est. Rev. 65 (Winter 1972); Katz, Alternative Real Estate Financing — The Sale Leaseback, 45 J. Kan. Bar Assn. 195, 195-196 (1976); Mandell, Tax Aspects of Sales and Leasebacks as Practical Devices for Transfer and Operation of Real Property, 18 N.Y.U. Inst. 17, 18 (1960).

3. *Split Financing: Purchase and Installment Sale-Buyback.* A high-ratio technique that is one step beyond the installment land contract is the so-called sale-buyback. Under such an arrangement, both the land and the projected improvements are sold to an institutional lender or other investor (such as an insurance company) at a stated price — usually between 80 and 90 percent of economic value and equal to 100 percent of the developer's land and audited construction costs. The developer simultaneously repurchases the real estate under a long-term installment contract. Since the developer is the "real" owner, with equitable title, and since it assumes both the benefits and burdens of ownership during the installment period, it can retain, by mutual agreement, the right to take the depreciation deductions. Under an installment sale contract, depreciation is allowed to a purchaser that has equitable title (despite the fact that it does not have legal title) where it has the obligation to maintain the property and bear the risk of loss. See, e.g., J. I. Morgan, Inc., 30 T.C. 881 (1958), revd. on other grounds, 272 F.2d 936 (9th Cir. 1959).

During the contract period, which is usually "closed" (no pre-payment of purchase price is allowed) for a longer-than-normal period of about 15 years, the investor not only recoups its capital at a modest rate of interest but — in exchange for granting what amounts to a 100 percent mortgage loan — also receives an equity kicker in the form of a contingent payment geared to a percentage of the developer's net income (after subtracting the installment payments). The amortization period is usually 10 years longer than it would be for a mortgage loan. The developer can thus maintain a reasonable overall constant payment and can shelter its rental income stream from taxation with deductions for depreciation, property taxes, and contract interest. The advantage to the investor is that it retains the benefit of a high-yield, inflation-hedged investment for a longer-than-normal "lock-in" period; the investor can invest more money, albeit at a higher risk, than would be possible for straight mortgage financing. Moreover, even though the term of the contract of sale is usually about 10 years longer than it would be if made on a mortgage basis, the installment contract payments are geared to liquidate the installment over the normal mortgage period at somewhat below the current mortgage rate. Thus, for example, if the fixed contract payment is at the rate of 8½ percent of the purchase price and the contract term is 35 years 7 months, the investor can write off its investment at a 7¼ percent yield in 26 years 7 months and continue to receive an additioal 9 years of contract payments, which, of course, would raise its average yield very sub-stantially. See Hershman, Usury and the "New Look" in Real Estate Financing, 4 Real Prop., Prob. & Tr. J. 315, 321-323 (1969).

4. *The Effect of Sale and Leaseback on the Balance Sheet of the Borrower.* As noted in the Vanderbilt Law Review excerpt, a nontax

advantage of the sale and leaseback is that the obligation of the seller-lessee, in contrast to that of a mortgagor, might not necessarily be reflected as a liability on the borrower's balance sheet. Also, the seller's borrowing ratios would improve because it would be replacing fixed assets (land, building, or both) with a current asset in the form of cash or a note that may be factored.

However, the accounting rules of the Financial Accounting Standards Board in its Statement of Financial Accounting Standards (SFAS) No. 13 (Nov. 1976) require that the conventional sale and leaseback of land and buildings be shown as a debt obligation if: (1) the leaseback term (including bargain renewals and economically compelled renewals) extends for 75 percent or more of the estimated useful life of the improvements or (2) the present value (at the commencement of the lease term) of the future base rental payments equals 90 percent or more of the fair market value of the property. The underlying assumption for respecting the transaction as a true sale and leaseback is that the seller-lessee has transferred substantially all of the benefits and risks of ownership to the purchaser-lessor. Financial Accounting Standards Board, SFAS No. 13, Accounting for Leases §§60, 72. Therefore, the seller would like to have the sale recognized for accounting purposes and have the real estate asset (and any related liabilities) removed from its balance sheet and yet be able to use the so-called full accrual method to reflect the entire profit in the year of sale. SFAS No. 66 provides that recognition of all or part of the profit for accounting purposes must be postponed if at the time of sale (1) the profit is not determinable (e.g., the collectibility of the selling price is not reasonably assured) or (2) the earnings process is not virtually completed.

Because SFAS No. 66 imposes more stringent profit recognition standards than does SFAS No. 13, new guidelines under SFAS No. 98 were promulgated to resolve the conflict. In order to recognize a gain or loss from a sale and remove the real estate asset and related debt from the seller's balance sheet, the seller-lessee must: (1) show that the purchaser-lessor will assume all of the normal risks and rewards of ownership, as reflected by the terms of the sale agreement; (2) demonstrate that it is actively using the property in its trade or business in consideration of the payment of rent under a "normal leaseback" (rental) arrangement; and (3) show that there is no "continuing involvement" by the seller in the property (for example, the providing of nonrecourse financing to the purchaser for any portion of the purchase price, participation with the purchaser in any net refinancing proceeds, or the incurring of any obligation to repurchase the property. See generally Lieberman and Kosoffsky, Sale-leaseback Accounting: The Rules Have Changed, 4 Real Est. Acctg. and Taxn. 26 (Spring 1989); The Mortgage and Real Estate Executive's Report, June 15, 1989, at 1, 2.

Based on accounting principles, can you think of any reason why a leaseback, in contrast to a mortgage or other debt financing, should not be reflected as a fixed liability on the balance sheet of the seller-lessee? Under what circumstances should the leasehold be reflected as an asset?

5. *Usury.* Another nontax advantage of sale-and-leaseback financing over debt financing is that the former, like the installment land contract financing device, is, in form, a sale and not a loan; accordingly, as a general rule local usury restrictions on lending would not apply. See Chapter 5B3, note 4.

6. *Additional Reading.* For a general discussion of sale and leasebacks see Burstein, Distinguishing True Leases from Conditional Sales and Financing Arrangements, 63 Taxes 395 (June 1985); Carey, Corporate Financing Through the Sale and Lease-Back of Property: Business, Tax and Policy Considerations, 62 Harv. L. Rev. 1 (1948); Clark, Changing Considerations in Sale and Leaseback Transactions, 42 Taxes 725 (1964); Egan, Sale-Leasebacks: Protecting the Institutional Investor Against New Risks, 6 Real Est. L.J. 199 (1978); Fuller, Sale and Leaseback Transactions of Real Property — A Proposal, 30 Tax Law. 701 (1977); Kaster, Tax Criteria for Structuring Sale-Leasebacks, 9 Real Est. Rev. 39 (1979); Mandell, Tax Aspects of Sales and Leasebacks as Practical Devices for Transfer and Operation of Real Property, 18 N.Y.U. Inst. Fed. Tax. 17 (1960); Marcus, Real Estate Purchase-Leasebacks as Secured Loans, 2 Real Est. L.J. 664 (1974); Rubenstein and London, Sales and Leasebacks: Some Valuation Problems, 37 Tax Law. 481 (Spring 1984); Sabaitis, IRS Attacks and Judicial Response Result in Uncertain Policy Regarding Sale-Leasebacks, 1 Real Est. Fin. J. 33 (Spring 1986); Steele, Sham in Substance: The Tax Court's Emerging Standard for Testing Sale-Leasebacks, 14 J. Real Est. Taxn. 3 (Fall 1986); Strum, Sale-Leasebacks: Protection for Accelerated Depreciation Deduction and Clear Title, 7 Real Prop., Prob. & Tr. J. 785 (1972); and Wilson, Sales and Leasebacks, 16 S. Calif. Tax Inst. 149 (1964).

2. Tax Pitfalls of Using Sale-and-Leaseback Financing

Notwithstanding the financial and tax advantages of using the sale-and-leaseback transaction, certain tax pitfalls are associated with the use of this technique. Because the sale and leaseback is frequently nothing more than a financing arrangement, and since the courts have uniformly held that substance controls over form, the I.R.S. has on occasion been successful in characterizing the transaction as a disguised mortgage loan, especially when the sale price was lower than the market value of the real estate and the seller was allowed to repurchase the property for a nominal price — since such facts indicated that the seller never intended to divest itself of ownership and that the purchaser was not the true owner because it was deprived of any meaningful benefit from appreciation in the value of the land. In addition, if the leaseback rental payments are disproportionately high or if they de-escalate over time, a rental deduction could be denied — in the former case on the theory that the seller-lessee is engaging in a disguised purchase of the real estate and in the latter on the ground that the rental payment is a prepayment that should be spread out evenly over the entire leaseback period. Also, some courts have disallowed a loss deduction to the seller-lessee under I.R.C. §1031 by taking the position that a sale and leaseback for a term of 30 or more years automatically constitutes a like-kind exchange of property. Like-kind exchanges are examined at Chapter 9D, note 1.

As you read the cases and materials that follow, keep in mind this question: In the case of an ordinary sale and leaseback between unrelated parties dealing with one another at arm's length, should the transaction be treated for tax purposes as a true sale followed by a leaseback, or as something else (such as a mortgage loan)? In other words, is the typical sale and leaseback an economic fact or a tax fiction — or is such a question oversimplified inasmuch as any such determination should be made on a case-by-case basis?

Frank Lyon Co. v. United States
435 U.S. 561 (1978)

MR. JUSTICE BLACKMUN delivered the opinion of the Court: This case concerns the federal income tax consequences of a sale-and-leaseback in which petitioner Frank Lyon Company (Lyon) took title to a building under construction by Worthen Bank & Trust Company (Worthen) of Little Rock, Ark., and simultaneously leased the building back to Worthen for long-term use as its headquarters and principal banking facility. . . .

. . . Worthen in 1965 was an Arkansas-chartered bank and a member of the Federal Reserve System. Frank Lyon was Lyon's majority shareholder and board chairman; he also served on Worthen's board. Worthen at that time began to plan the construction of a multistory bank and office building to replace its existing facility in Little Rock. About the same time Worthen's competitor, Union National Bank of

Little Rock, also began to plan a new bank and office building. Adjacent sites on Capitol Avenue, separated only by Spring Street, were acquired by the two banks. It became a matter of competition, for both banking business and tenants, and prestige as to which bank would start and complete its building first.

Worthen initially hoped to finance, to build, and to own the proposed facility at a total cost of $9 million for the site, building, and adjoining parking deck. This was to be accomplished by selling $4 million in debentures and using the proceeds in the acquisition of the capital stock of a wholly owned real estate subsidiary. . . . Worthen's plan, however, had to be abandoned for two significant reasons: [First,] as a bank chartered under Arkansas law, Worthen legally could not pay more interest on any debentures it might issue than that then specified by Arkansas law. But the proposed obligations would not be marketable at that rate. [Second,] applicable statutes or regulations of the Arkansas State Bank Department and the Federal Reserve System required Worthen, as a state bank subject to their supervision, to obtain prior permission for the investment in banking premises. . . . Worthen, accordingly, was advised by staff employees of the Federal Reserve System that they would not recommend approval of the plan by the System's Board of Governors.

Worthen therefore was forced to seek an alternative solution that would provide it with the use of the building, satisfy the state and federal regulators, and attract the necessary capital. In September 1967 it proposed a sale-and-leaseback arrangement. The State Bank Department and the Federal Reserve System approved this approach, but the Department required that Worthen possess an option to purchase the leased property at the end of the 15th year of the lease at a set price, and the federal regulator required that the building be owned by an independent third party.

Detailed negotiations ensued with investors that had indicated interest, . . .

Worthen then obtained a commitment from New York Life Insurance Company to provide $7,140,000 in permanent mortgage financing on the building, conditioned upon its approval of the title-holder. At this point Lyon entered the negotiations and it, too, made a proposal. . . .

. . . Worthen selected Lyon as the investor. After further negotiations, . . . Lyon in November 1967 was approved as an acceptable borrower by First National City Bank for the construction financing, and by New York Life, as the permanent lender. In April 1968 the approvals of the state and federal regulators were received.

In the meantime, on September 15, before Lyon was selected, Worthen itself began construction.

B. In May 1968 Worthen, Lyon, City Bank, and New York

Life executed complementary and interlocking agreements under which the building was sold by Worthen to Lyon as it was constructed, and Worthen leased the completed building back from Lyon.

　　1. Agreements between Worthen and Lyon. Worthen and Lyon executed a ground lease, a sales agreement, and a building lease.

　　Under the ground lease dated May 1, 1968, App. 366, Worthen leased the site to Lyon for 76 years and 7 months through November 30, 2044. The first 19 months were the estimated construction period. The ground rents payable by Lyon to Worthen were $50 for the first 26 years and 7 months and thereafter in quarterly payments:

12/1/94 through 11/30/99	(5 years) —	$100,000 annually
12/1/99 through 11/30/04	(5 years) —	$150,000 annually
12/1/04 through 11/30/09	(5 years) —	$200,000 annually
12/1/09 through 11/30/34	(25 years) —	$250,000 annually
12/1/34 through 11/30/44	(10 years) —	$ 10,000 annually

　　Under the sales agreement dated May 19, 1968, id., at 508, Worthen agreed to sell the building to Lyon, and Lyon agreed to buy it, piece by piece as it was constructed, for a total price not to exceed $7,640,000, in reimbursements to Worthen for its expenditures for the construction of the building.

　　Under the building lease dated May 1, 1968, id., at 376, Lyon leased the building back to Worthen for a primary term of 25 years from December 1, 1969, with options in Worthen to extend the lease for eight additional 5-year terms, a total of 65 years. During the period between the expiration of the building lease (at the latest, November 30, 2034, if fully extended) and the end of the ground lease on November 30, 2044, full ownership, use, and control of the building were Lyon's, unless, of course, the building had been repurchased by Worthen. Id., at 369. Worthen was not obligated to pay rent under the building lease until completion of the building. . . . The total rent for that building over the 25-year primary term of the lease thus was $14,989,767.24. That rent equaled the principal and interest payments that would amortize the $7,140,000 New York Life mortgage loan over the same period. . . .

　　The building lease was a "net lease," under which Worthen was responsible for all expenses usually associated with the maintenance of an office building, including repairs, taxes, utility charges, and insurance, and was to keep the premises in good condition, excluding, however, reasonable wear and tear.

　　Finally, under the lease, Worthen had the option to repurchase the building at the following times and prices:

11/30/80   (after 11 years) — $6,325,169.85
11/30/84   (after 15 years) — $5,432,607.32
11/30/89   (after 20 years) — $4,187,328.04
11/30/94   (after 25 years) — $2,145,935.00

These repurchase option prices were the sum of the unpaid balance of the New York Life mortgage, Lyon's $500,000 investment, and 6% interest compounded on that investment.

2. Construction financing agreement.   By agreement dated May 14, 1968, id., at 462, City Bank agreed to lend Lyon $7,000,000 for the construction of the building. This loan was secured by a mortgage on the building and the parking deck, executed by Worthen as well as by Lyon, and an assignment by Lyon of its interests in the building lease and in the ground lease.

3. Permanent financing agreement.   By Note Purchase Agreement dated May 1, 1968, id., at 443, New York Life agreed to purchase Lyon's $7,140,000 6¾% 25-year secured note to be issued upon completion of the building. Under this agreement Lyon warranted that it would lease the building to Worthen for a noncancelable term of at least 25 years under a net lease at a rent at least equal to the mortgage payments on the note. Lyon agreed to make quarterly payments of principal and interest equal to the rentals payable by Worthen during the corresponding primary term of the lease. Id., at 523. The security for the note were a first deed of trust and Lyon's assignment of its interests, in the building lease and in the ground lease. Id., at 527, 571. Worthen joined in the deed of trust as the owner of the fee and the parking deck.

In December 1969 the building was completed and Worthen took possession. At that time Lyon received the permanent loan from New York Life, and it discharged the interim loan from City Bank. The actual cost of constructing the office building and parking complex (excluding the cost of the land) exceeded $10,000,000.

C. Lyon filed its federal income tax returns on the accrual and calendar year basis. On its 1969 return, Lyon accrued rent from Worthen for December. It asserted as deductions one month's interest to New York Life; one month's depreciation on the building; interest on the construction loan from City Bank; and sums for legal and other expenses incurred in connection with the transaction.

On audit of Lyon's 1969 return, the Commissioner of Internal Revenue determined that Lyon was "not the owner for tax purposes of any portion of the Worthen Building," and ruled that "the income and expenses related to this building are not allowable . . . for Federal income tax purposes." App. 304-305, 299. He also added $2,298.15 to Lyon's 1969 income as "accrued interest income." . . . In other words, the Commissioner determined that the sale-and-leaseback arrangement was a financing transaction in which Lyon loaned Worthen $500,000 and acted as a conduit for the transmission of principal interest from Worthen to New York Life. . . .

Lyon paid the assessment and filed a timely claim for its refund. The claim was denied, and this suit, to recover the amount so paid, was instituted in the United States District Court for the Eastern District of Arkansas within the time allowed by 26 U.S.C. §6532(a)(1). . . .

The United States Court of Appeals for the Eighth Circuit reversed, [76-2 USTC ¶9589] 536 F.2d 746 (1976). It held that the Commissioner correctly determined that Lyon was not the true owner of the building and therefore was not entitled to the claimed deductions. It likened ownership for tax purposes to a "bundle of sticks" and undertook its own evaluation of the facts. It concluded, in agreement with the Government's contention, that Lyon "totes an empty bundle" of ownership sticks. Id., at 751. It stressed the following: (a) The lease agreements circumscribed Lyon's right to profit from its investment in the building by giving Worthen the option to purchase for an amount equal to Lyon's $500,000 equity plus 6% compound interest and the assumption of the unpaid balance of the New York Life mortgage. (b) The option prices did not take into account possible appreciation of the value of the building or inflation. (c) Any award realized as a result of destruction or condemnation of the building in excess of the mortgage balance and the $500,000 would be paid to Worthen and not Lyon. (d) The building rental payments during the primary term were exactly equal to the mortgage payments. (e) Worthen retained control over the ultimate disposition of the building through its various options to repurchase and to renew the lease plus its ownership of the site. (f) Worthen enjoyed all benefits and bore all burdens incident to the operation and ownership of the building so that, in the Court of Appeals' view, the only economic advantages accruing to Lyon, in the event it were considered to be the true owner of the property, were income tax savings of approximately $1.5 million during the first 11 years of the arrangement. Id., at 752-753. The court concluded, id., at 753, that the transaction was "closely akin" to that in Helvering v. Lazarus & Co. [39-2 USTC ¶9793], 308 U.S. 252 (1939). "In sum, the benefits, risks, and burdens which [Lyon] has incurred with respect to the Worthen building are simply too insubstantial to establish a claim to the status of owner for tax purposes. . . . The vice of the present lease is that all of [its] features have been employed in the same transaction with the cumulative effect of depriving [Lyon] of any significant ownership interest." 536 F.2d, at 754.

We granted certiorari, 429 U.S. 1089 (1977), because of an indicated conflict with American Realty Trust v. United States [74-2 USTC ¶9528], 498 F.2d 1194 (CA-4 1974).

II. This Court, almost 50 years ago, observed that "taxation is not so much concerned with the refinements of title as it is with actual command over the property taxed — the actual benefit for which the tax is paid." Corliss v. Bowers [2 USTC ¶525], 281 U.S. 376, 378 (1930). In a number of cases, the Court has refused to permit the transfer of formal legal title to shift the incidence of taxation attributable to ownership of property where the transferor continues to retain significant control over the property transferred. E.g., Commissioner v. Sunnen [48-1 USTC ¶9230], 333 U.S. 591 (1948); Helvering v. Clifford [40-1 USTC ¶9265], 309 U.S. 331 (1940). In applying this doctrine of substance over form, the Court has looked to the objective economic realities of a transaction rather than to the particular form the parties employed. The Court has never regarded "the simple expedient of drawing up papers," Commissioner v. Tower [46-1 USTC ¶9189], 327 U.S. 280, 291 (1946), as controlling for tax purposes when the objective economic realities are to the contrary. . . . Nor is the parties' desire to achieve a particular tax result necessarily relevant. Commissioner v. Duberstein [60-2 USTC ¶9515], 363 U.S. 278, 286 (1960).

In the light of these general and established principles, the Government takes the position that the Worthen-Lyon transaction in its entirety should be regarded as a sham. The agreement as a whole, it is said, was only an elaborate financing scheme designed to provide economic benefits to Worthen and a guaranteed return to Lyon. The latter was but a conduit used to forward the mortgage payments, made under the guise of rent paid by Worthen to Lyon, on to New York Life as mortgagee. This, the Government claims, is the true substance of the transaction as viewed under the microscope of the tax laws. Although the arrangement was cast in sale-and-leaseback form, in substance it was only a financing transaction, and the terms of the repurchase options and lease renewals so indicate. It is said that Worthen could reacquire the building simply by satisfying the mortgage debt and paying Lyon its $500,000 advance plus interest, regardless of the fair market value of the building at the time; similarly, when the mortgage was paid off, Worthen could extend the lease at drastically reduced bargain rentals that likewise bore no relation to fair rental value but were simply calculated to pay Lyon its $500,000 plus interest over the extended term. Lyon's return on the arrangement in no event could exceed 6% compound interest (although the Government conceded it might well be less, Tr. of Oral Arg. 32). Furthermore, the favorable option and lease renewal terms made it highly unlikely that Worthen would abandon the building after it in effect had "paid off" the mortgage. The Government implies that the arrangement was one of convenience which, if accepted on its face, would enable Worthen to deduct its payments to Lyon as rent and would allow Lyon to claim a deduction for depreciation, based on the cost of construction ultimately borne by Worthen, which Lyon could offset against other income, and to deduct mortgage interest that roughly would offset the inclusion of Worthen's rental payments in Lyon's income. If, however, the Government argues, the arrangement was only a financing transaction under which Worthen was the owner of the building, Worthen's payments would be deductible only to the extent that they represented mortgage interest, and Worthen would be entitled to claim depreciation; Lyon would not be entitled to deductions for either mortgage interest or depreciation and it would not have to include Worthen's "rent" payments in its income because its function with respect to those payments was that of a conduit between Worthen and New York Life. . . .

The *Lazarus* case, we feel, is to be distinguished from the present one and is not controlling here. Its transaction was one involving only two (and not multiple) parties, the taxpayer-department store and the trustee-bank. The Court looked closely at the substance of the agreement between those two parties and rightly concluded that depreciation was deductible by the taxpayer despite the nomenclature of the instrument of conveyance and the leaseback. See also Sun Oil Co. v. Commissioner [77-2 USTC ¶9641], 562 F.2d 258 (CA-3 1977), a two-party case with the added feature that the second party was a tax-exempt pension trust).

The present case, in contrast, involves three parties, Worthen, Lyon, and the finance agency. The usual simple two-party arrangement was legally unavailable to Worthen. Independent investors were interested in participating in the alternative available to Worthen, and Lyon itself (also independent from Worthen) won the privilege. Despite Frank Lyon's presence on Worthen's board of directors, the transaction, as it ultimately developed, was not a familial one arranged by Worthen, but one compelled by the realities of the restrictions imposed upon the bank. Had Lyon not appeared, another interested investor would have been selected. The ultimate solution would have been essentially the same. Thus, the presence of the third party, in our view, significantly distinguishes this case from Lazarus and removes the latter as controlling authority. . . .

There is no simple device available to peel away the form of this transaction and to reveal its substance. The effects of the transaction on all the parties were obviously different from those that would have resulted had Worthen been able simply to make a mortgage agreement with New York Life and to receive a $500,000 loan from Lyon. Then Lazarus would apply. Here, however, and most significantly, it was Lyon alone, and not Worthen, who was liable on the notes, first to City Bank, and then to New York Life. Despite the facts that Worthen had agreed to pay rent and that this rent equaled the amounts due from Lyon to New York Life, should anything go awry in the later years of the lease, Lyon was primarily liable. No matter how the transaction could have been devised otherwise, it remains a fact that as the agreements were placed in final form, the obligation on the notes fell squarely on Lyon. Lyon, an ongoing enterprise, exposed its very business well-being to this real and substantial risk.

The effect of this liability on Lyon is not just the abstract possibility that something will go wrong and that Worthen will not be able to make its payments. Lyon has disclosed this liability on its balance sheet for all the world to see. Its financial position was affected substantially by the presence of this long-term debt, despite the offsetting presence of the building as an asset. To the extent that Lyon has used its capital in this transaction, it is less able to obtain financing for other business needs. . . .

Other factors also reveal that the transaction cannot be viewed as anything more than a mortgage agreement between Worthen and New York Life and a loan from Lyon to Worthen. There is no legal obligation between Lyon and Worthen representing the $500,000 "loan" extended under the Government's theory. And the assumed 6% return on this putative loan — required by the audit to be recognized in the taxable year in question — will be realized only when and if Worthen exercises its options.

The Court of Appeals acknowledged that the rents alone, due after the primary term of the lease and after the mortgage has been paid, do not provide the simple 6% return which, the Government urges, Lyon is guaranteed, 536 F.2d, at 752. Thus, if Worthen chooses not to exercise its options, Lyon is gambling that the rental value of the building during the last 10 years of the ground lease, during which the ground rent is minimal, will be sufficient to recoup its investment before it must negotiate again with Worthen regarding the ground lease. There are simply too many contingencies, including variations in the value of real estate, in the cost of money, and in the capital structure of Worthen, to permit the conclusion that the parties intended to enter into the transaction as structured in the audit and according to which the Government now urges they be taxed.

It is not inappropriate to note that the Government is likely to lose little revenue, if any, as a result of the shape given the transaction by the parties. No deduction was created that is not either matched by an item of income or that would not have been available to one of the parties if the transaction had been arranged differently. While it is true that Worthen paid Lyon less to induce it to enter into the transaction because Lyon anticipated the benefit of the depreciation deductions it would have as the owner of the building, those deductions would have been equally available to Worthen had it retained title to

the building. The Government so concedes. Tr. of Oral Arg. 22-23.
The fact that favorable tax consequences were taken into account by
Lyon on entering into the transaction is no reason for disallowing those
consequences. We cannot ignore the reality that the tax laws affect
the shape of nearly every business transaction. See Commissioner v.
Brown [65-1 USTC ¶9375], 380 U.S. 563, 579-580 (1965) (HARLAN,
J., concurring). Lyon is not a corporation with no purpose other than
to hold title to the bank building. It was not created by Worthen or
even financed to any degree by Worthen. . . .

As is clear from the facts, none of the parties to this sale-and-
leaseback was the owner of the building in any simple sense. But it
is equally clear that the facts focus upon Lyon as the one whose capital
was committed to the building and as the party, therefore, that was
entitled to claim depreciation for the consumption of that capital. The
Government has based its contention that Worthen should be treated
as the owner on the assumption that throughout the term of the lease
Worthen was acquiring an equity in the property. In order to establish
the presence of that growing equity, however, the Government is
forced to speculate that one of the options will be exercised and that,
if it is not, this is only because the rentals for the extended term are
a bargain. We cannot indulge in such speculation in view of the District
Court's clear finding to the contrary. We therefore conclude that it is
Lyon's capital that is invested in the building according to the agreement
of the parties, and it is Lyon that is entitled to depreciation deductions,
under §167 of the 1954 Code, 26 U.S.C. §167. Cf. United States v.
Chicago B. & Q. R. Co. [73-1 USTC ¶9478], 412 U.S. 401 (1973).

IV. We recognize that the Government's position, and that taken
by the Court of Appeals, is not without superficial appeal. One, indeed,
may theorize that Frank Lyon's presence on the Worthen board of
directors; Lyon's departure from its principal corporate activity into
this unusual venture; the parallel between the payments under the
building lease and the amounts due from Lyon on the New York Life
mortgage; the provisions relating to condemnation or destruction of
the property; the nature and presence of the several options available
to Worthen; and the tax benefits, such as the use of double declining
balance depreciation, that accrue to Lyon during the initial years of
the arrangement, form the basis of an argument that Worthen should
be regarded as the owner of the building and as the recipient of nothing
more from Lyon than a $500,000 loan.

We, however, as did the District Court, find this theorizing
incompatible with the substance and economic realities of the transaction: the competitive situation as it existed between Worthen and
Union National Bank in 1965 and the years immediately following;
Worthen's undercapitalization; Worthen's consequent inability, as a
matter of legal restraint, to carry its building plans into effect by a

conventional mortgage and other borrowing; the additional barriers imposed by the state and federal regulators; the suggestion, forthcoming from the state regulator, that Worthen possess an option to purchase; the requirement, from the federal regulator, that the building be owned by an independent third party; the presence of several finance organizations seriously interested in participating in the transaction and in the resolution of Worthen's problem; the submission of formal proposals by several of those organizations; the bargaining process and period that ensued; the competitiveness of the bidding; the bona fide character of the negotiations; the three-party aspect of the transaction; Lyon's substantiality and its independence from Worthen; the fact that diversification was Lyon's principal motivation; Lyon's being liable alone on the successive notes to City Bank and New York Life; the reasonableness, as the District Court found, of the rentals and of the option prices; the substantiality of the purchase prices; Lyon's not being engaged generally in the business of financing; the presence of all building depreciation risks on Lyon; the risk, borne by Lyon, that Worthen might default or fail, as other banks have failed; the facts that Worthen could "walk away" from the relationship at the end of the 25-year primary term, and probably would do so if the option price were more than the then-current worth of the building to Worthen; the inescapable fact that if the building lease were not extended, Lyon would be the full owner of the building, free to do with it as it chose; Lyon's liability for the substantial ground rent if Worthen decides not to exercise any of its options to extend; the absence of any understanding between Lyon and Worthen that Worthen would exercise any of the purchase options; the nonfamily and nonprivate nature of the entire transaction; and the absence of any differential in tax rates and of special tax circumstances for one of the parties — all convince us that Lyon has far the better of the case. . . .

In short, we hold that where, as here, there is a genuine multiple-party transaction with economic substance which is compelled or encouraged by business or regulatory realities, is imbued with tax-independent considerations, and is not shaped solely by tax-avoidance features that have meaningless labels attached, the Government should honor the allocation of rights and duties effectuated by the parties. Expressed another way, so long as the lessor retains significant and genuine attributes of the traditional lessor status, the form of the transaction adopted by the parties governs for tax purposes. What those attributes are in any particular case will necessarily depend upon its facts. It suffices to say that, as here, a sale-and-leaseback, in and of itself, does not necessarily operate to deny a taxpayer's claim for deductions.

The judgment of the Court of Appeals, accordingly, is reversed.
It is so ordered. . . .

DISSENTING OPINION

MR. JUSTICE STEVENS, dissenting: In my judgment the controlling issue in this case is the economic relationship between Worthen and petitioner, and matters such as the number of parties, their reasons for structuring the transaction in a particular way, and the tax benefits which may result, are largely irrelevant. The question whether a leasehold has been created should be answered by examining the character and value of the purported lessor's reversionary estate.

For a 25-year period Worthen has the power to acquire full ownership of the bank building by simply repaying the amounts, plus interest, advanced by the New York Life Insurance Company and petitioner. During that period, the economic relationship among the parties parallels exactly the normal relationship between an owner and two lenders, one secured by a first mortgage and the other by a second mortgage. If Worthen repays both loans, it will have unencumbered ownership of the property. What the character of this relationship suggests is confirmed by the economic value that the parties themselves have placed on the reversionary interest.

All rental payments made during the original 25-year term are credited against the option repurchase price, which is exactly equal to the unamortized cost of the financing. The value of the repurchase option is thus limited to the cost of the financing, and Worthen's power to exercise the option is cost-free. Conversely, petitioner, the nominal owner of the reversionary estate, is not entitled to receive *any* value for the surrender of its supposed rights of ownership. Nor does it have any power to control Worthen's exercise of the option.

"It is fundamental that 'depreciation is not predicated upon ownership of property *but rather upon an investment in property.*' No such investment exists when payments of the purchase price in accordance with the design of the parties yield no equity to the purchaser." Estate of Franklin v. Commissioner [76-2 USTC ¶9773], 544 F.2d 1045, 1049 (CA-9, 1976) (citations omitted; emphasis in original). Here, the petitioner has, in effect, been guaranteed that it will receive its original $500,000 plus accrued interest. But that is all. It incurs neither the risk of depreciation, nor the benefit of possible appreciation. Under the terms of the sale-leaseback, it will stand in no better or worse position after the 11th year of the lease — when Worthen can first exercise its option to repurchase — whether the property has appreciated or depreciated. And this remains true throughout the rest of the 25-year period.

Petitioner has assumed only two significant risks. First, like any other lender, it assumed the risk of Worthen's insolvency. Second, it assumed the risk that Worthen might *not* exercise its option to purchase at or before the end of the original 25-year term. If Worthen should exercise that right *not* to repay, perhaps it would *then* be appropriate to characterize petitioner as the owner and Worthen as the lessee. But speculation as to what might happen in 25 years cannot justify the *present* characterization of petitioner as the owner of the building. Until Worthen has made a commitment either to exercise or not to exercise its option, I think the Government is correct in its view that petitioner is not the owner of the building for tax purposes. At present, since Worthen has the unrestricted right to control the residual value of the property for a price which does not exceed the cost of its unamortized financing, I would hold, as a matter of law, that it is the owner.

I therefore respectfully dissent.

Century Electric Co. v. Commissioner
192 F.2d 155 (8th Cir. 1951), cert. denied, 342
U.S. (1952)

RIDDICK, Circuit Judge.

The petitioner, Century Electric Company, is a corporation engaged principally in the manufacture and sale of electric motors and generators in St. Louis, Missouri. It is not a dealer in real estate. As of December 1, 1943, petitioner transferred a foundry building owned and used by it in its manufacturing business and the land on which the foundry is situated to William Jewell College and claimed a deductible loss on the transaction in its tax return for . . . 1943. The Commissioner of Internal Revenue denied the loss. The Commissioner was affirmed by the Tax Court and this petition for review followed. . . .

The assessed value of petitioner's foundry building and land upon which it is located for 1943 was $205,780. There was evidence that in St. Louis real property is assessed at its actual value. There was also evidence introduced by petitioner before the Tax Court that the market value for unconditional sale of the foundry building, land, and appurtenances was not in excess of $250,000.

As of December 1, 1943, the adjusted cost basis for the foundry building, land, and appurtenances transferred to William Jewell College was $531,710.97. The building was a specially designed foundry situated in a highly desirable industrial location. It is undisputed in the evidence that the foundry property is necessary to the operation of petitioner's profitable business and that petitioner never at any time considered a sale of the foundry property on terms which would deprive petitioner of its use in its business.

Petitioner's explanation of the transaction with the William Jewell College is that in the spring of 1943 a vice-president of the Mercantile bank where petitioner deposited its money and transacted the most of its banking business suggested to petitioner the advisability of selling some of its real estate holdings for the purpose of improving the ratio of its current assets to current liabilities by the receipt of cash on the sale and the possible realization of a loss deductible for tax purposes. Petitioner's operating business was to be protected by an immediate long-term lease of the real property sold.

Petitioner's board of directors rejected this proposition as unsound. But in July 1943, when a vice-president of the Mercantile bank suggested to petitioner's treasurer that it would be a good idea for petitioner to pay off all its bank loans merely to show that it was able to do so, petitioner interpreted this advice as a call of its bank loans. Acting on this interpretation, petitioner borrowed from the First National Bank in St. Louis on the security of tax anticipation notes held by it, funds with which it discharged all its bank loans. Immediately thereafter it re-established its lines of bank credit and began consideration of a sale of the foundry property and contemporaneous lease from the purchaser.

On September 2, 1943, petitioner's board of directors adopted a resolution that the executive committee of the board study the situation "and present, if possible, a plan covering the sale and rental back by Century Electric Company of the foundry property." The decision to enter into the transaction described was communicated to the Mercantile bank, but petitioner never publicly offered or advertised its foundry property for sale. The Tax Court found that petitioner "was concerned with getting a friendly landlord to lease the property back to it, as there was never any intention on the part of petitioner to discontinue its foundry operations." Several offers to purchase the foundry property at prices ranging from $110,000 to $150,000 were received and rejected by petitioner.

At a special meeting of the board of directors of petitioner on December 9, 1943, the president of petitioner reported that the officers of petitioner had entered into negotiations for the sale of the foundry property to William Jewell College for the price of $150,000 with the agreement of said college; "that in addition thereto said Trustees of William Jewell College further have agreed to execute a lease of the property so purchased to Century Electric Company for the same time and on substantially the same terms and conditions which were authorized to be accepted by the special meeting of shareholders of this corporation, held on the 24th day of November, 1943." The stockholders at the November meeting had authorized the sale of the foundry property at not less than $150,000 cash, conditioned upon the purchaser executing its lease of the property sold for a term of not less than 25 and not more than 95 years. The Board by resolution approved the proposed transaction with the William Jewell College, but on condition that "this corporation will acquire from Trustees of William Jewell College, a Missouri Corporation, an Indenture of Lease . . . for a term of not less than twenty-five years and for not more than ninety-five years." The resolution set out in detail the terms of the lease from the college to petitioner, approved the form of the deed from the petitioner to the college, authorized the president and secretary of petitioner to execute the lease after its execution by the trustees of the college, and directed "that the president and secretary of this corporation be authorized to deliver said Warranty Deed to said purchaser upon receiving from said purchaser $150,000 in cash, and upon receiving from said purchaser duplicate executed Indenture of Lease on the forms exhibited to this Board." The resolution provided that the deed and lease should be dated December 1, 1943, and effective as of that date.

The deed and the lease were executed and delivered as provided by the resolution of petitioner's board of directors. Neither instrument referred to the other. The deed was in form a general warranty deed, reciting only the consideration of $150,000 in cash. The lease recited among others the respective covenants of the parties as to its term, its termination by either the lessor or lessee, and as to the rents reserved.

As of December 31, 1942, the ratio of petitioner's current assets to its current liabilities was 1.74. The $150,000 in cash received by petitioner on the transaction increased the ratio of current assets to current liabilities from 1.74 to 1.80. The loss deduction which petitioner claims on the transaction and its consequent tax savings would if allowed have increased the ratio approximately twice as much as the receipt of the $150,000.

The questions presented are:

1. Whether the transaction stated was for tax purposes a sale of the foundry property within the meaning of section 112 of the Internal Revenue Code, 26 U.S.C.A. §112, on which petitioner realized in 1943 a deductible loss of $381,710.97 determined under section 111 of the code (the adjusted basis of the foundry property of $531,710.97 less $150,000) as petitioner contends; or, as the Tax Court held, an exchange of property held for productive use in a trade or business for property of a like kind to be held for productive use in trade or business in which no gain or loss is recognized under sections 112(b) (1) and 112(e), and Regulation 111, section 29.112(b) (1)-1. . . .

On the first question the Tax Court reached the right result. The answer to the question is not to be found by a resort to the dictionary for the meaning of the words "sales" and "exchanges" in other contexts, but in the purpose and policy of the revenue act as expressed in section 112. . . . In this section Congress was not defining the words "sales" and "exchanges." It was concerned with the administrative problem involved in the computation of gain or loss in transactions of the character with which the section deals. Subsections 112(b) (1) and 112(e) indicate the controlling policy and purpose of the section, that is, the non-recognition of gain or loss in transactions where neither is readily measured in terms of money, where in theory the taxpayer may have realized gain or loss but where in fact his economic situation is the same after as it was before the transaction. . . . For tax purposes the question is whether the transaction falls within the category just defined. If it does, it is for tax purposes an exchange and not a sale. . . . Under subsection 112(e) no loss is recognized on an exchange of property held for productive use in trade or business for like property to be held for the same use, although other property or money is also received by the taxpayer. Compare this subsection with subsection 112(c) (1) where in the same circumstances gain is recognized but only to the extent of the other property or money received in the transaction. The comparison clearly indicates that in the computation of gain or loss on a transfer of property held for productive use in trade or business for property of a like kind to be held for the same use, the market value of the properties of like kind involved in the transfer does not enter into the equation.

[4] The transaction here involved may not be separated into its component parts for tax purposes. Tax consequences must depend on what actually was intended and accomplished rather than on the separate steps taken to reach the desired end. The end of the transaction between the petitioner and the college was that intended by the petitioner at its beginning, namely, the transfer of the fee in the foundry property for the 95-year lease on the same property and $150,000.

[5] It is undisputed that the foundry property before the transaction was held by petitioner for productive use in petitioner's business. After the transaction the same property was held by the petitioner for the same use in the same business. Both before and after the transaction the property was necessary to the continued operation of petitioner's business. The only change wrought by the transaction was in the estate or interest of petitioner in the foundry property. In Regulations 111, section 29.112(b) (1)-1, the Treasury has interpreted the words "like kind" as used in subsection 112(b) (1). Under the Treasury interpretation a lease with 30 years or more to run and real estate are properties of "like kind." With the controlling purpose of the applicable section of the revenue code in mind, we can not say that the words "like kind" are so definite and certain that interpretation is neither required nor permitted. The regulation, in force for many years, has survived successive reenactments of the internal revenue acts and has thus acquired the force of law. . . .

Jordan Marsh Co. v. Commissioner
269 F.2d 453 (2d Cir. 1959)

HINCKS, Circuit Judge.

This is a petition to review an order of the Tax Court, which upheld the Commissioner's deficiency assessment of $2,101,823.39 in income and excess profits tax against the petitioner, Jordan Marsh Company. There is no dispute as to the facts, which were stipulated before the Tax Court and which are set forth in substance below.

The transactions giving rise to the dispute were conveyances by the petitioner in 1944 of the fee of two parcels of property in the city of Boston where the petitioner, then as now, operated a department store. In return for its conveyances the petitioner received $2,300,000 in cash which, concededly, represented the fair market value of the properties. The conveyances were unconditional, without provision of any option to repurchase. At the same time, the petitioner received back from the vendees leases of the same properties for terms of 30 years and 3 days, with options to renew for another 30 years if the petitioner-lessee should erect new buildings thereon. The vendees were in no way connected with the petitioner. The rentals to be paid under the leases concededly were full and normal rentals so that the leasehold interests which devolved upon the petitioner were of no capital value.

In its return for 1944, the petitioner, claiming the transaction was a sale under §112(a), Internal Revenue Code of 1939, sought to deduct from income the difference between the adjusted basis of the property and the cash received. The Commissioner disallowed the deduction, taking the position that the transaction represented an exchange of property for other property of like kind. Under Section 112(b)(1) such exchanges are not occasions for the recognition of gain or loss; and even the receipt of cash or other property in the exchange of the properties of like kind is not enough to permit the taxpayer to recognize loss. Section 112(e). Thus the Commissioner viewed the transaction, in substance, as an exchange of a fee interest for a long term lease, justifying his position by Treasury Regulation 111, §29.112(b)(1)-1, which provides that a leasehold of more than 30 years is the equivalent of a fee interest. Accordingly the Commissioner made the deficiency assessment stated above. The Tax Court upheld the Commissioner's determination. Since the return was filed in New York, the case comes here for review. 26 U.S.C.A. §7482.

Upon this appeal, we must decide whether the transaction in question here was a sale or an exchange of property for other property of like kind within the meaning of §§112(b) and 112(e) of the Internal Revenue Code cited above. If we should find that it is an exchange, we would then have to decide whether the Commissioner's regulation, declaring that a leasehold of property of 30 years or more is property "of like kind" to the fee in the same property, is a reasonable gloss to put upon the words of the statute. The judge in the Tax Court felt that Century Electric Co. v. Commissioner of Internal Rev., 8 Cir., 192 F.2d 155, certiorari denied 342 U.S. 954, 72 S. Ct. 625, 96 L. Ed. 708, affirming 15 T.C. 581, was dispositive of both questions. In the view which we take of the first question, we do not have to pass upon the second question. For we hold that the transaction here was a sale and not an exchange. . . .

The Tax Court apparently thought it of controlling importance that the transaction in question involved no change in the petitioner's possession of the premises: it felt that the decision in Century Electric Co. v. Commissioner of Internal Rev., supra, controlled the situation here. We think, however, that the case was distinguishable on the facts. For notwithstanding the lengthy findings made with meticulous care by the Tax Court in that case, 15 T.C. 581, there was no finding that the cash received by the taxpayer was the full equivalent of the value of the fee which the taxpayer had conveyed to the vendee-lessor, and no finding that the lease back called for a rent which was fully equal to the rental value of the premises. Indeed, in its opinion the Court of Appeals pointed to evidence that the fee which the taxpayer had "exchanged" may have had a value substantially in excess of the cash received. And in the Century Electric case, the findings showed, at page 585, that the taxpayer-lessee, unlike the taxpayer here, was not required to pay "general state, city and school taxes" because its lessor was an educational institution which under its charter was exempt from such taxes. Thus the leasehold interest in Century Electric on this account may well have had a premium value. In the absence of findings as to the values of the properties allegedly "exchanged," necessarily there could be no finding of a loss. And without proof of a loss, of course, the taxpayer could not prevail. Indeed, in the Tax Court six of the judges expressly based their concurrences on that limited ground. 15 T.C. 596. . . .

Rev. Rul. 60-43

1960-1 C.B. 687

The Internal Revenue Service will not follow the decision in Jordan Marsh Company v. Commissioner, 269 Fed. (2d) 453.

The United States Court of Appeals for the Second Circuit, in reversing the Tax Court, held that a transaction whereby the taxpayer in 1944 conveyed the fee of parcels of property used for its department store to a stranger for cash, equivalent to their fair market value, must be treated as a separate sale, even though, simultaneously, the property was leased back to the taxpayer for the same use at a fair and normal rental for a term of 30 years plus three days, with an option to renew for a similar term if the taxpayer as "lessee" should erect new buildings on the property.

The Court of Appeals maintained that Century Electric Co. v. Commissioner, 192 Fed. (2d) 155, certiorari denied 342 U.S. 954, relied upon by the Government, was distinguishable on its facts.

It is the position of the Service that a sale and leaseback under the circumstances here present constitute, in substance, a single integrated transaction under which there is an "exchange" of property of like kind with cash as boot.

City Investing Co. v. Commissioner
38 T.C. 1 (1962), nonacq., 1963-1 C.B. 5

RAUM, Judge: On November 9, 1950, Thirty purportedly conveyed a fee simple interest in the land at 30 and 38-40 Broad Street in New York City to Connecticut General Life Insurance Company for a cash consideration of $4 million. On the same day Connecticut leased back the same land to Thirty for an original term of 21 years for an annual rental of $180,000. The true nature of these two transactions, which the parties agree were closely linked in form as well as in substance, is the issue to be decided.

Respondent has determined that Thirty's formal sale and immediate leaseback of the land did not constitute a bona fide sale and separate leasing for tax purposes, but rather that it was an exchange of "property . . . for property of a like kind" plus boot (cash in the amount of $4 million) pursuant to sections 112(b) (1) and 112(e) of the 1939 Code with the result that the loss which Thirty claimed as a consequence of the purported sale was not deductible under the statute. Petitioner's primary position is that there was a genuine sale of the land, not an exchange of property interests. As proof that the transaction constituted a true sale, petitioner has presented evidence that the fair market value of the subject land at the time of the transfer was not in excess of the $4 million which Connecticut paid to Thirty. However, if we should hold that there was an exchange and not a sale for tax purposes, petitioner makes the secondary argument that such exchange was not of property of "like kind" as required for nonrecognition of the loss under the statute.

After careful consideration of all the evidence, we agree with petitioner that there was a bona fide sale of the land by Thirty. Cf. Standard Envelope Mfg. Co., 15 T.C. 41; May Department Stores Co., 16 T.C. 547. Therefore, we do not pass upon the question whether the exchange of the particular leasehold interest here involved for an interest in fee in the same land could be considered an exchange of "like" properties. Cf. sec. 29.112(b) (1)-1, Regs. 111; Century Electric Co., 15 T.C. 581, affirmed 192 F.2d 155 (C.A. 8), certiorari denied 342 U.S. 954.

The record shows that the transfer in question was made pursuant to Thirty's adopted policy of liquidating its property holdings in Lower Manhattan. It is this factor which in the main sets the instant case apart from prior sale and leaseback transactions considered by this Court. In particular it makes the present case distinguishable from both Century Electric Co., supra, upon which respondent chiefly relies, and Jordan Marsh Company v. Commissioner, 269 F.2d 453 (C.A. 2), reversing a Memorandum Opinion of this Court, which petitioner argues is controlling. We conclude, therefore, that it is not necessary for purposes of decision in the present case to decide whether the decision of the Court of Appeals for the Second Circuit in Jordan Marsh is inconsistent with the result in the earlier Century Electric Co. case. Cf. Rev. Rul. 60-43, 1960-1 C.B. 687.

There is no dispute that Thirty had adopted a policy of liquidating its property interests in Lower Manhattan prior to the transaction here involved. It was stipulated that Thirty sold its interest in six Lower Manhattan properties, in addition to the subject property, between November 9, 1950, and June 5, 1952. After the latter date, Thirty no longer owned nor thereafter acquired any property in Lower Manhattan. In disposing of its interest in the property at 30 and 38-40 Broad Street, Thirty decided to sell its interest in the land and its interest in the improvements thereon separately. An officer of Thirty testified that this was done not only because the officers of Thirty believed that they could thereby obtain a higher overall price for the whole property, but also because they wanted to register a tax loss on the land to offset profits on other sales by the corporation. As a result only the land was transferred to Connecticut on November 9, 1950. Although it appears that Thirty had not yet negotiated the sale of the improvements on the land together with the leasehold interest that it obtained back from Connecticut, it is apparent that at the time of the sale to Connecticut Thirty intended also to liquidate these remaining interests in the property. The record reveals that it did in fact sell these interests in the 30 and 38-40 Broad Street property to an unrelated corporation, Thirty Associates, within 2 years, on June 5, 1952.

In these circumstances we think that the transfer of the land alone on November 9, 1950, was a bona fide sale. Thirty conveyed its fee interest in the property without reserving any right of repurchase. We have made a finding that the fair market value of the land on the date of transfer was not in excess of the $4 million which Connecticut paid to Thirty. In addition, we have made a finding that a fair annual net rental for this land on November 9, 1950, was not in excess of the $180,000 which Thirty agreed to pay Connecticut. Thus, it does not appear that the leaseback arrangement which Thirty and Connecticut signed as a part of the total transaction had any separate value which can properly be viewed as a portion of the consideration paid or exchanged.

The fact that Thirty was willing to sell the land in question only with some kind of leaseback arrangement included does not of itself detract from the reality of the sale. Nor does the fact that tax considerations in part motivated the particular transaction. Both of these factors were also present in *Standard Envelope Mfg. Co.,* supra, and *May Department Stores Co.,* supra, where it was held that bona fide sales had taken place. In those cases, as here, the sale was the result of extended arm's-length negotiation, the price paid was at least equal to the property's then fair market value, and the only interest retained by the seller was that of lessee for a definite term. While those cases did not involve a segregated sale of only land apart from the improvements thereon, we think that the presence of this factor in the instant case should not change the result. Since, as already noted, the conveyance here involved was made pursuant to a policy of liquidating Thirty's property holdings in the immediate area, in many respects the instant case presents an even stronger set of facts in support of the reality of the sale.

After November 9, 1950, we think that Thirty's rights as lessee of the land at 30 and 38-40 Broad Street were in no sense a "continuation of the old investment [in the land] still unliquidated." Commissioner v. P. G. Lake, Inc., 356 U.S. 260, 268; sec. 29.112 (a)-1, Regs. 111. We are satisfied that Thirty yielded substantial economic and property rights by transferring its ownership in fee to Connecticut and that it succeeded for purposes of this transaction in liquidating its invested capital in the land. As such there was a true sale, and petitioner is entitled under the statute to recognize the loss that was thereby sustained.

Decision will be entered for the petitioner.

Schurtz, A Decision Model for Lease Parties in Sale-Leasebacks of Real Estate
23 Wm. and Mary L. Rev. 385, 435-438 (1982)

This Article has set out a basic framework for judges and planners in analyzing the complex area of sale-leaseback transactions. The decision model presented is based on sale-leaseback cases involving recourse and nonrecourse financing. The steps in the model can be summarized as follows:

STEP I: FINANCIAL INSTITUTIONS AS PARTIES TO THE TRANSACTION

1. Is the buyer-lessor a financial institution?

If no, the analysis should continue (Step I, part 2).

If yes, but the financial institution is purchasing the property for its own investment purposes, go to Step II.

If yes, and the financial institution is not purchasing the property for its own investment purposes, a financing arrangement exists. Whether the bank seeks the property as an investment is determined by the intent and conduct of the parties.

2. Is a financial institution an indirect party to the sale-leaseback transaction — i.e., neither lessor nor lessee?

If no, the courts should proceed to Step II.

If yes, does the buyer-lessor merely serve as a conduit for the payment of the loan from the seller-lessee to the financial institution? This is determined by examining the personal liability of the buyer-lessor on the loan, whether the loan was guaranteed by the seller-lessee, whether the buyer-lessor is undercapitalized, whether the loan payments coincide with the rent payments, whether the term of the loan coincides with the term of the lease, and whether the financial institution views the seller-lessee as the true debtor. If the court answers these questions affirmatively, the court should conclude that there is a financing arrangement. If it is not clear that the buyer-lessor is a mere conduit, the analysis should continue.

STEP II: IS THERE A CONDUIT ARRANGEMENT EVEN THOUGH NO FINANCIAL INSTITUTION IS INVOLVED?

The same factors discussed in part 2 of Step I should be considered. If a conduit relationship exists, there is a financing device. If no such relationship exists, the analysis should continue.

STEP III: WILL THE PROPERTY REVERT AUTOMATICALLY TO THE SELLER-LESSEE BY THE END OF THE LEASE TERM?

If yes, there is a financing arrangement.

If no, the analysis must continue.

Step IV: Is There a Bargain Purchase Price or Economic Compulsion to Exercise the Option?

If economic compulsion to exercise the option exists, the court should find a financing transaction. Economic compulsion exists when the repurchase option is a bargain purchase option or when there is a valid business reason at the time of the initial sale-leaseback transaction which compels the exercise of the option. No compulsion exists if some other reason, such as the financial condition of the lessee, indicates that the option will not be exercised.

If there is no economic compulsion the analysis should continue.

Step V: Is the Term of the Lease Plus Renewals Greater than or Equal to the Useful Life of the Property?

If yes, there is a financing device.
If no, the analysis should proceed.

Step VI: Rate of Return Similarities

1. Are there no rate of return similarities?
If the buyer-lessor is not entitled to a definite risk-free return, no financing arrangement exists. There may be a valid sale-leaseback, partnership, or joint venture arrangement, so the analysis should continue.

2. Are there clear rate of return similarities?
If no, the analysis should continue.
If yes, there is a financing arrangement.

Step VII: Value Disparities

1. Is the sales price too high or too low in relation to the fair market value of the property or the cash flow from the property?
If nonrecourse financing is involved, courts should determine whether the sales price is greater than the fair market value of the property or whether the value of the interest purchased is less than the amount paid for that interest. If either of these circumstances exist, the court should find an invalid sale-leaseback arrangement. If recourse financing is involved, the analysis should continue.

2. Are the rental payments reflective of fair market value?

If the rents are unreasonably low or unreasonably high, this is indicative but not determinative of a financing arrangement. If the payments are not clearly unreasonable, the analysis should continue.

STEP VIII: BENEFITS AND BURDENS: DOES THE EQUITY INTEREST LIE WITH THE SELLER-LESSEE?

If yes, there is a financing device.

If no, a valid sale-leaseback arrangement probably exists but the analysis should continue.

STEP IX: PURPOSE FOR ENTERING INTO THE TRANSACTION

If the actual purpose, as determined by the intent and conduct of the parties, indicates that the transaction was entered into to avoid tax, the sale-leaseback should not be recognized.

NOTES AND QUESTIONS

1. *Treatment of Sale and Leaseback as Disguised Loan.* The Internal Revenue Service has employed a "recharacterization theory" to attack loss and rental deductions by the seller-lessee and depreciation by the purchaser-lessor where the repurchase option in the sale-and-leaseback agreement stipulates a substantially below-market price or otherwise lacks the substantive appearance of a sale, on the rationale that the seller never intended to permanently divest itself of ownership and that the transaction was in reality a disguised loan. See, e.g. Fuller, Sale and Leasebacks and the *Frank Lyon* Case, 48 Geo. Wash. L. Rev. 60, 63-67 (1979); Schurtz, A Decision Model for Lease Parties in Sale-Leasebacks of Real Estate, 23 Wm. and Mary L. Rev. 385, 392-394 (1982); Note, Taxation of Sale and Leaseback Transactions — A General Review, 32 Vand. L. Rev. 945, 968-982 (1979). However, offsetting the foregoing disadvantages is the fact that any gain on the purported "sale" would not be recognized. Moreover, the seller-lessee would be entitled to deduct depreciation as the real owner of the property, and it would also be entitled to deduct that portion of the so-called rental payments that constitutes constructive "interest" on the constructive loan.

Frank Lyon Co. v. United States is the most recent Supreme Court

statement on the proper characterization of sale-and-leaseback transactions for tax purposes. The Court's opinion, however, does little to
clarify the law in this area, and its precedential value is limited by the
uniqueness of its facts. Nevertheless, the general approach taken by
the Supreme Court offers some guidance for the tax planner.

   a.   *Traditional Analysis Under Pre-Frank Lyon Co. Case ,Law.*
While judicial analysis prior to *Frank Lyon Co.* has been somewhat
inconsistent, the earlier court decisions addressed the issue of whether
a sale and leaseback was in reality a disguised mortgage loan by focusing
on whether the seller-lessee had divested itself of both the benefits and
burdens of ownership. A closely related subjective test also emerged,
namely, whether the seller truly *intended* a sale in the common-law
sense by relinquishing control over the real estate except for its right
to possession during the leaseback period. In that regard, a seller's
option to repurchase the property at a below-market price was most
determinative. In addition, an unduly low rental during the leaseback
period could reflect a disguised loan under such a benefit-burden theory.
Another important factor was the business purposes that prompted the
parties to select the sale-leaseback device. For example, in Helvering
v. F. & R. Lazarus & Co., 308 U.S. 252 (1939), the Supreme Court
restructured a two-party sale-and-leaseback transaction as a "loan secured
by the property involved." In that case, the taxpayer was a department
store that transferred title to its buildings to a trustee for the benefit
of the holders of land-trust certificates. Simultaneously, the trustee
leased the properties back to the taxpayer for 99 years. The Internal
Revenue Service disallowed the taxpayer's claim for depreciation deductions on the theory that only the holder of the legal title was
entitled to such deductions. The Supreme Court, in an opinion written
by Justice Black, held that the taxpayer was entitled to depreciation
because, as owner of the equitable title, it bore the burden of exhaustion
of the asset, and held that the transaction was in substance a loan. The
Court was influenced by these facts: (1) the sale price to the trustee
was substantially less than the net value of the property; (2) the leaseback
rentals were geared to repayment of the purchase price and were
substantially below the fair market rental of the premises; (3) the option
to repurchase stipulated a below-market price so that the seller would
enjoy the appreciation in the value of the real estate; and (4) the parties
apparently had intended a mere loan and not a true economic sale of
the real estate. In Sun Oil Co. v. Commissioner, 562 F.2d 258 (3d
Cir. 1977), cert. denied, 436 U.S. 944 (1978), the Third Circuit
concluded that a sale-leaseback between an oil company and an unrelated
tax-exempt trust was in reality a mortgage and not a sale in light of
the following benefits enjoyed and burdens borne by the seller-lessee:
(1) the net leaseback rental was geared to amortization of the purchase
price and dropped sharply after a 25-year primary lease term expired,

notwithstanding likely appreciation in the value of the property; (2) the "rejectable" option to repurchase the property was in fact nonrejectable; and (3) the "fair appraisal value" option price was geared to the unamortized principal advanced by the purchaser-lessor (rather than to the fair market value of the real estate) so that the purchaser-lessor would be precluded from enjoying the appreciation in the value of the property. In another Third Circuit decision (decided prior to the *Frank Lyon Co.* case) involving a sale-and-leaseback between unrelated parties, Leeds & Lippincott Co. v. United States, 276 F.2d 927 (3d Cir. 1960), the court denied a loss to the seller-lessee where the leaseback rental was to be applied to the repurchase price and approximated the amounts received from the purchaser-lessor. Also, in Frenzel v. Commissioner, 22 T.C.M. 1391 (CCH) 276 (1963), the Tax Court disallowed rent deductions on a leaseback where the taxpayer had an option to repurchase the property for 10 percent of its purchase price at the end of the leaseback period and where the renewal rents were very low. However, in American Realty Trust v. United States, 498 F.2d 1194 (4th Cir. 1974), the Fourth Circuit sustained as not clearly erroneous a jury verdict that the sale-and-leaseback transaction was a bona fide sale and not a disguised loan. Even though the net leaseback rental was reduced by 50 percent of any reduction in the annual mortgage payments and the seller-lessee was entitled to 50 percent of any refinancing proceeds, the court refused to hold as a matter of law that the transaction was a loan inasmuch as there was evidence that (1) the parties had intended a sale; (2) the repurchase price was "fair" and not unduly low; and (3) the lessee decided to exercise his purchase option because of the sudden availability of "wraparound" financing and not because he was under economic compulsion to do so.

   b.   *Frank Lyon Co. v. United States.*   In deciding that the Worthen-Lyon transaction was a genuine transaction with economic substance rather than a sham shaped by tax-avoidance considerations, Justice Blackmun first acknowledged that the doctrine of substance over form should apply in characterizing any such transaction. Since the facts in *Frank Lyon Co.* are so convoluted, Figure 8-2 with its factual summary may be useful.

   Applying the traditional analysis (discussed above) to the facts in *Frank Lyon Co.,* do you agree with the conclusion reached by the Court of Appeals that the benefits enjoyed and burdens borne by Lyon were more like those of a nonrecourse creditor than those of a prospective owner when Lyon advanced the $500,000 to Worthen and obtained a $7 million recourse loan from New York Life in connection with the alleged purchase of the bank building from Worthen? In writing the majority opinion for the Supreme Court, Justice Blackmun regarded as most significant whether the borrowing from New York Life was done by Lyon or by Worthen. In that regard, he emphasizes the fact

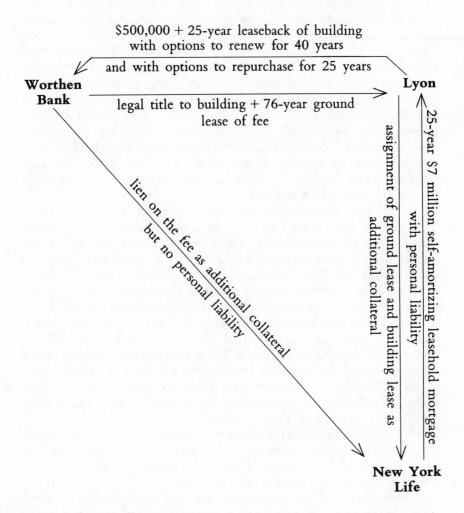

F i g u r e 8-2

During the 25-year initial term of the building lease, the rent equalled the debt-service payments that would amortize the New York Life mortgage, and the rent during the optional 40-year extension period was calculated to repay Lyon his $500,000 advance plus 6 percent compound interest.

During the 25-year primary term, Worthen could repurchase the building on specific dates at an amount equal to the sum of the mortgage balance and the $500,000 advance (plus interest).

During the first 26 years of the ground lease the rent was nominal; thereafter, it increased by increments of $50,000 during each subsequent 5-year period, and it decreased to only $10,000 per annum during the last 10 years of the 76-year term.

that Lyon alone was *personally* liable for repayment of both the construction and the permanent mortgage loans. In deciding whether Lyon assumed the risk of a purchaser or of a creditor, as a matter of economic substance would it have made any difference to the parties (including New York Life) if Lyon had simply guaranteed repayment to New York Life of its $7 million nonrecourse mortgage loan to Worthen and made a $500,000 nonrecourse second mortgage loan to Worthen, instead of Lyon's advancing to Worthen $500,000 of its own funds and then obtaining a $7 million recourse loan from New York Life? In both cases, wouldn't the risk of Worthen's insolvency and nonpayment fall squarely on the shoulders of Lyon? Even though Lyon alone was personally liable for repayment of the loan from New York Life, what about the fact that Worthen had subjected its fee interest to the lien of the leasehold mortgage?

What facts suggest that the benefits enjoyed and burdens borne by Worthen were more like those of a seller-lessee? In that regard, consider the following closely related question. Notwithstanding the district court's determination that the leaseback rentals and repurchase option prices had been "reasonable," what inferences could be drawn as to whether Worthen intended to retain irrevocable control (beyond mere possession) over the building from the manner in which the following payments had been computed: (1) both the rental payments and option prices during the initial 25-year leaseback period; (2) the rental payments during the next 40 years (assuming that Worthen opted to extend the leaseback period); and (3) the lack of any rental obligation during the next 10 years (after the 65-year building lease expired and before the ground lease terminated), during which Lyon was free to rent the building at a fair market rental?

The debate between the majority opinion and Justice Stevens, in his dissenting opinion, centered on whether Worthen would be economically compelled to exercise one of its repurchase options during the primary 25-year term of the building lease. The government's recharacterization of the transaction as a loan assumed that Worthen would exercise one of these options to repurchase the building and, if it did not, it would only be because Worthen could remain in possession for the extended term at a bargain rental. Citing the district court's factual finding to the contrary, Justice Blackmun refused to engage in such speculation and concluded that Lyon's capital had been at risk. In support of this conclusion, he pointed out that if Worthen chose not to repurchase the building but opted instead to extend the building lease at the reduced rental, Lyon might not be able to obtain a sufficient rental from a new tenant of the building during the last ten years of the ground lease to recoup its investment capital. By contrast, Justice Stevens regarded as irrelevant the question whether Worthen would exercise the option to repurchase; in his judgment, the determining factor was its *power* to do so. That Worthen could repurchase the building for an amount exactly equal to the balance of the sums advanced by New York Life and Lyon meant that Lyon's chance to benefit or be harmed from any fluctuation in the value of the building was subject to the complete control of Worthen, and therefore Lyon had at risk none of the equity on which tax ownership and the depreciation deduction are predicated. Moreover, if Worthen chose not to repurchase but to extend the building lease, Lyon had no opportunity to benefit because the bargain rentals ignored the fair market rental of the building; accordingly, Lyon's position resembled that of a lender since its only real risk was that its "debtor," Worthen, might become insolvent. In your judgment, which point of view makes more sense, that of Justice Blackmun or that of Justice Stevens? In concluding that Lyon's payments as a purchaser failed to yield the equity investment on which the depreciation deduction is predicated, Justice Stevens cites Estate of Franklin v. Commissioner, discussed at Chapter 2B, note 4. In what respect does the analogy fail?

In its abbreviated holding, the Supreme Court takes the position that a sale-and-leaseback transaction should be respected by the Internal Revenue Service where "there is a genuine multi-party transaction with economic substance which is compelled or encouraged by business or regulatory realities . . . and not shaped solely by tax avoidance features." Based on the discussion at Chapter 8B1, supra, and the fact that the purchaser in a large sale-and-leaseback transaction is most likely to finance its acquisition cost by means of a loan from a third-party lender, how difficult would it be for a taxpayer such as Lyon to meet the Court's definition in the case of an ordinary sale-and-leaseback transaction? As a matter of economic substance, should it make any difference whether two or three parties are involved in the transaction? For example, in *Frank Lyon Co.,* would the economic situation of the parties have changed had Lyon financed the cost of the building by making a nonrecourse loan to Worthen with its own funds instead of obtaining a recourse loan from New York Life? Finally, which method of judicial analysis do you favor, the "totality of the transaction" approach employed by Justice Blackmun or the traditional pre-*Frank Lyon Co.* point of view (applied by the court of appeals), which focuses on the benefits and burdens of property ownership and the intentions of the parties?

For analysis of the *Frank Lyon Co.* decision, see Del Cotto, Sale and Leaseback: A Hollow Sound When Tapped?, 37 Tax L. Rev. 1, 37-48 (1981); Fuller, Sales and Leasebacks and the *Frank Lyon* Case, 48 Geo. Wash. L. Rev. 60, 73-82 (1979); Kaster, Tax Criteria for Structuring Sale-Leasebacks, 9 Real Est. Rev. 39 (Fall 1979); Solomon and Fones, Sale-Leasebacks and the Shelter-Oriented Investor: An Analysis of *Frank Lyon Co.* and *Est. of Franklin,* 56 Taxes 618, 624-628 (Oct. 1978); Weinstein and Silvers, The Sale and Leaseback Transaction

After *Frank Lyon Company,* 24 N.Y.L. Sch. L. Rev. 337 (1978); Zarrow and Gordon, Supreme Court's Sale-Leaseback Decision in *Lyon* Lists Multiple Criteria, 49 J. Taxn. (1978); Note, Taxation — Interest and Depreciation Are Deductible by the Purchaser-Lessor in a Sale and Leaseback of Real Estate When the Transaction Is Formed for Bona Fide Business Purposes: Frank Lyon Co. v. United States, 435 U.S. 561 (1978), 28 Cath. U.L. Rev. 394, 404-410 (1979); Note, Taxation of Sale and Leaseback Transactions — A General Review, 32 Vand. L. Rev. 945, 975-982 (1979).

In *Frank Lyon Co.,* the Supreme Court cited 27 factors it considered relevant to its decision. To what extent does this approach have precendential value, informing the tax planner what criteria will govern the viability of a sale-and-leaseback transaction? More specifically, in your judgment can a cautious tax planner safely assume that a personal liability note obligation to a third-party lender and a valid business purpose form a sufficient matrix to support recognition of a sale-and-leaseback transaction even where the seller-lessee bears the major burdens and enjoys the major benefits of ownership in the property? See Note, Taxation — Interest and Depreciation Are Deductible by the Purchaser-Lessor in a Sale and Leaseback of Real Estate When the Transaction Is Formed for Bona Fide Business Purposes: Frank Lyon Co. v. United States, 435 U.S. 561 (1978), 28 Cath. U.L. Rev. 394, 409-410; Fuller, Sales and Leasebacks and the *Frank Lyon* Case, 48 Geo. Wash. L. Rev. 60, 77-82; Note, Taxation of Sale and Leaseback Transactions — A General Review, 32 Vand. L. Rev. 945, 976-979 (1979).

  *c.   Post-*Frank Lyon Co. *Case Law.*   The case law after *Frank Lyon Co.* generally has followed the *Frank Lyon Co.* definition of a bona fide sale and leaseback, that is, a genuine multiple-party transaction based on economic substance and business realities rather than one that is shaped primarily by tax avoidance features. However, the recent case law has continued to scrutinize the seller's retention of control over the real estate and examines how the benefits and burdens of ownership have been allocated between the parties.

For example, in Belz Investment Co. v. Commissioner, 72 T.C. 1209 (1979), acq., 1980-1 C.B. 1, affd., 661 F.2d 76 (1981), the Tax Court held that a sale and leaseback of a motel for an initial 20-year term was not in substance a "secured lending arrangement." Even though the seller-lessee was granted an option to repurchase after 10 years for no more than the original sale price, the option price was arguably reasonable in relation to the fair market value of the property, and the purchaser-lessor alone was obligated to pay the ground rent and the mortgage on the property. In Schaefer v. Commissioner, 41 T.C.M. 100 (1980), the Tax Court denied both rental and depreciation deductions where the buyer-lessor, a friend of the seller, received an annual guaranteed rental equal to the principal payments on an installment note taken out by the seller-lessee (with respect to which the seller remained liable), the buyer was safeguarded against any downside risks by reason of a "put" option allowing him to resell the property at any time for the original purchase price, and the seller was allowed to sublet and operate the hotel exactly as before the sale. In the opinion of the court, the buyer had not assumed the risks and burdens of hotel ownership and was motivated only by tax shelter considerations. In a series of sale-and-leaseback cases involving nonrecourse financing, including Hilton v. Commissioner, 74 T.C. 305 (1980), affd., 671 F.2d 316 (9th Cir. 1982), cert. denied, 459 U.S. 907 (1982), and Narver v. Commissioner, 75 T.C. 53 (1980), affd., 670 F.2d 855 (9th Cir. 1982), in which the nonrecourse indebtedness had exceeded the market value of the real estate, the Tax Court denied depreciation and interest deductions to the purchasers because the court failed to find a genuine multiple-party concern for nontax considerations, as required under *Frank Lyon Co.* In addition, the court applied the "abandonment test," enunciated in Estate of Franklin v. Commissioner (see discussion at Chapter 2B, note 4) in holding that in both cases the buyer-lessors would not have found it imprudent to abandon the properties. However, in Dunlap v. Commissioner, 74 T.C. 1377 (1980), revd. on other grounds, 670 F.2d 785 (8th Cir. 1982), the Tax Court found a valid sale and leaseback (as opposed to a two-party financing arrangement of the *Lazarus* variety) notwithstanding that the leaseback rental was geared to debt service payments on a mortgage with respect to which the purchaser-lessor had not assumed personal liability. As in *Frank Lyon Co.,* the transaction had a legitimate business purpose, and it was not certain that the seller would repurchase the property; in addition, based on the purchase price, the court assumed that the purchasers would not have abandoned their equity in the property.

For other cases applying *Frank Lyon Co.,* see Professional Services v. Commissioner, 79 T.C. 888 (1982) (superseded in part by statute) (sale and leaseback held invalid because there was no change in economic ownership or use of the property after the purported arm's-length transaction); Rice's Toyota World v. Commissioner, 81 T.C. 184 (1983), affd. in part and revd. in part, 752 F.2d 89 (4th Cir. 1985) (involving sale and leaseback of IBM computer; the court found that purchaser-lessor was not in a position to realize any economic value or equity, and therefore his motive was merely one of tax avoidance). But see James v. Commissioner, 899 F.2d 905 (10th Cir. 1990); Casebeer v. Commissioner, 909 F.2d 1360 (9th Cir. 1990).

For a discussion of the *Hilton, Narver,* and *Schaefer* cases see Rosenberg and Weinstein, Applying the Tax Court's Nontax Benefit Test for Multiple-Party Sale-Leasebacks, 54 J. Taxn. 366 (1981); for a discussion of *Hilton,* see Note, Sale and Leasebacks as a Tax Shelter: Hilton v. Commissioner, 1981 Utah L. Rev. 843.

2. *Prepayment and Reallocation of the Leaseback Rental.* As noted earlier, an unduly low rental during the leaseback period could render a sale and leaseback vulnerable to recharacterization as a disguised loan. In addition, a below-market sale price accompanied by the seller's receipt of a leaseback with a proportionately reduced rental may prompt the Commissioner to contend that the purchaser in effect received prepaid rent equal to the excess of the fair market value of the property over the bargain price paid by the purchaser. This tax pitfall is best illustrated by the companion cases decided by the Tax Court, Alstores Realty Corp. v. Commissioner, 46 T.C. 363 (1966), and Steinway and Sons v. Commissioner, 46 T.C. 375 (1966), acq., 1967-1 C.B. 1. See also Rev. Rul. 66-209, 1966-2 C.B. 299, involving a long-term leaseback. In the transaction at issue, Steinway sold its warehouse to Alstores for $1 million on the condition that Steinway could remain in possession for two and one-half years until its new plant was ready. Under the arrangement that was finally negotiated, Steinway conveyed fee title to Alstores for $750,000 and, by separate agreement, Steinway received a two-and-one-half-year leaseback under which (1) Steinway could remain in possession without payment of rent; (2) Steinway would be reimbursed for any interruption of its possession caused by casualty or condemnation; and (3) Alstores agreed to supply all utilities so that the leaseback would not be a net lease.

Alstores maintained that since it had not received any cash rental payments the transaction was not a sale and leaseback; in substance, Steinway had merely sold a remainder interest in the real estate for $750,000 and reserved a possessory term. Under a risk and benefit burden analysis, the Tax Court upheld the Commissioner by holding that an ownership interest in the fee had initially passed to Alstores and thus the transaction was a genuine sale and leaseback in substance as well as in form. Accordingly, Alstores was deemed to have purchased the real estate for its market value and to have acquired a cost basis of $1 million. In consideration of the leaseback, Alstores received $250,000 in prepaid rent from Steinway; thus Steinway realized $1 million from the sale but received a net cash payment of only $750,000. Steinway, therefore, had purchased the leasehold estate for $250,000 and could amortize the payment over the two and one-half years of the lease. The following are diagrams of the transaction as viewed by Alstores and the Tax Court.

If there is an option to renew the leaseback at an unduly low rental, the Commissioner may urge that a portion of the rental paid

Alstores' View of the Transaction

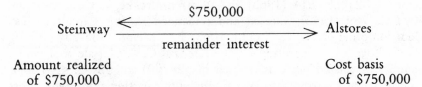

$750,000

Steinway $\longleftarrow$ —————————————————————————— $\longrightarrow$ Alstores

remainder interest

Amount realized   Cost basis
of $750,000   of $750,000

The Tax Court's View of the Transaction

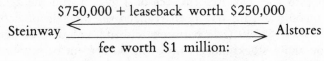

$750,000 + leaseback worth $250,000

Steinway $\longleftarrow$ —————————————————————— $\longrightarrow$ Alstores

fee worth $1 million:

Amount realized   (1)   3/4 fee worth $750,000   Cost basis
of $1 million   (2)   1/4 fee worth $250,000   of $1 million

during the original leaseback term be deferred to the renewal term as a prepaid expense. Otherwise, the lessee's taxable income arguably would be understated during the original term and overstated during the renewal period. See Treas. Reg. §1.461-1(a)(2). Main & McKinney Building Co. v. Commissioner, 113 F.2d 81 (5th Cir. 1940), cert. denied, 311 U.S. 688 (1940) (involving a straight lease transaction); cf. Shelby Salesbook Co. v. United States, 104 F. Supp. 237 (N.D. Ohio 1952), and Alstores Realty Corp. v. Commissioner, 46 T.C. 363 (1966) (part of $1 million purchase price treated as prepaid rental income to taxpayer-purchaser where seller received $750,000 plus a two-and-a-half-year rent-free leaseback). Or, if the rental for the original leaseback term is an esclating or de-escalating one, the Commissioner may argue, on the same rationale, for amortization of the entire rental payment evenly over the entire leaseback period. In either event, a portion of the rental expenses would be disallowed as a current deduction and instead would be capitalized. Finally, if the sale and leaseback is between related parties, the Commissioner may attempt to denominate the lessee's payments as something other than a rent deduction. For example, an excessive rental payment to a related individual may be treated as a nondeductible gift or personal expense. See Coe Laboratories v. Commissioner, 34 T.C. 549 (1960). Or, an excessive rental paid to a shareholder-lessor by a corporate lessee may be treated as a constructive dividend. See, e.g., J. J. Kirk, Inc. v. Commissioner, 34 T.C. 130 (1960), affd., 289 F.2d 935 (6th Cir. 1961). The Commissioner might also: (1) reallocate any excessive rental paid as additional income to the lessee (see I.R.C. §482 and the Treasury Regulations thereunder); (2) challenge the "ordinary and necessary" character of the rental expense and disallow a deduction under I.R.C. §162 or §212 (see I.

L. Van Zendt v. Commissioner, 341 F.2d 440 (5th Cir. 1965), cert. denied, 382 U.S. 814 (1965) and Warren Brekke v. Commissioner, 40 T.C. 789 (1963), vacated and remanded by 9th Circuit to Tax Court on other issues, 25 T.C.M. 1063, T.C. Memo 1966-208 (1966)); (3) disallow loss recognition on the sale, I.R.C. §267 (sale to a family member or related party as defined in §267(b)) and I.R.C. §707(b)(1) (sale between a partnership and a controlling partner who owns more than a 50 percent interest, or sale between two controlled partnerships); or (4) prior to the Tax Reform Act of 1986, charge the seller with ordinary income if gain had been realized on the sale of depreciable property, I.R.C. §1239 (sale between husband and wife or between a corporation and a stockholder who owns 80 percent or more of stock) and I.R.C. §707(b)(2) (sale between a partnership and a controlling partner who owns more than 80 percent partnership interest, or sale between two controlled partnerships).

    3. Treatment as Disguised Purchase.   Finally, if the sale and lease-back involves a tax-exempt purchaser-lessor, the parties may be tempted to trade a high leaseback rental for a low repurchase price. This would enable the seller-lessee to obtain a higher rental deduction without disadvantaging the owner-lessor, tax- or cash-wise. However, the Commissioner might argue that the transaction in substance amounted merely to a disguised installation repurchase of the property and accordingly disallow the rental payments as nondeductible installment payments. See Starr v. Commissioner, 274 F.2d 294 (9th Cir. 1959). Sale-and-leaseback transactions also run the risk of recharacterization in bankruptcy proceedings. See Liona Corp. v. PCH Assocs. (excerpted at Chapter 11C1). See generally Homburger and Andre, Real Estate Sale and Leaseback Transactions and the Risk of Recharacterization in Bankruptcy Proceedings, 24 Real Prop., Prob. & Tr. J. 95 (Spring 1989).

    4. Loss Disallowance.   I.R.C. §1031(a) mandates nonrecognition of gain or loss if property held for productive use in a trade or business is *exchanged* solely for property of a like kind. In addition, if a taxpayer receives in exchange some property not equivalent to the exchanged property, it must recognize its gain (but not loss) to the extent of the cash or fair market value of the tainted property ("boot") received. Since a leasehold of 30 years or more is regarded as like kind, or equivalent to property held in fee, Treas. Reg. §1.103(a)-1(a), an individual or syndicate that holds property worth less than its depreciated cost (adjusted basis) would want to avoid an "exchange" of the property if a leaseback of 30 years or more is received by the seller. Otherwise, an ordinary loss could not be recognized under I.R.C. §1231. See, e.g., Capri, Inc. v. Commissioner, 65 T.C. 162 (1975) (the loss on a sale of hotel assets was held deductible because the sale-and-leaseback transaction was substantial but the term of the leaseback was less than 30 years and there was no provision for renewal).

But when is there an "exchange" as opposed to a sale of a fee interest in property when the previous owner receives as consideration not only a long-term leaseback but boot as well? In the case of an exchange, the entire loss (or gain less boot) would go unrecognized, and in the case of a sale, the entire loss would be recognized regardless of whether boot was received by the seller. Unfortunately, neither the Code nor regulations define the term "exchange" with particularity; one must therefore resort to the case authorities.

   a. *Century Electric Co. v. Commissioner.* The ostensible rationale for the decision disallowing the loss was that since the taxpayer held the same property for the same use in the same business both before and after the transaction, the taxpayer's economic situation remained the same and therefore no sale took place. But under this standard, when would the economic situation of the taxpayer in a sale and leaseback ever change? What is the real issue in the case? Can you think of a better rationale for explaining the court's decision that an exchange, and not a sale, took place, based on the fact that the taxpayer gave up property worth as much as $250,000 and yet received only $150,000 in cash along with a long-term leaseback of a proportionately reduced rental?

   b. *Jordan Marsh Co. v. Commissioner and City Investing Co. v. Commissioner.* How would you reconcile the conflicting results in the *Century Electric* and *Jordan Marsh* decisions? In *City Investing Co.,* Justice Raum waffles on the sale versus exchange issue by stating that "it is not necessary . . . to decide whether the decision of the Court of Appeals for the Second Circuit in *Jordan Marsh* is inconsistent with the result in the earlier *Century Electric Co.* case" since the taxpayer in the instant case, unlike the cases cited, had transferred his property pursuant to an "adopted policy of liquidating its property holdings." In what respect does the statement by Justice Raum ignore the real issue in both of these cases? See Leslie Co. v. Commissioner, 64 T.C. 247, affd., 539 F.2d 943 (3d Cir. 1976). In what respect are the facts in *Leslie Co.* distinguishable from the facts in *Jordan Marsh?* Should a cautious tax planner rely on being able to obtain a loss deduction in a sale-and-leaseback transaction that is comparable to the one in the *Leslie Co.* decision? See Fuller, Sale and Leasebacks and the *Frank Lyon* Case, 48 Geo. Wash. U.L. Rev. 60, 70 (1979); Morris, Sale-Leaseback Transactions of Real Property — A Proposal, 30 Tax Law. 701, 706 (1977); Comment, Tax Law — Sale and Leaseback Transactions — Loss on Sale Portion of Sale and Leaseback Transactions Deductible by Seller-Lessee — Leslie Co. v. Commissioner, 52 N.Y.U. L. Rev. 672, 678 (1977).

5. *Sale and Leasebacks by Tax-Exempt Entities.* By way of review, the tax posture of an investor is quite different depending on
whether the investor engages in a loan or a sale-and-leaseback transaction. As a lender, the investor would be taxed on interest income,
but repayment of principal is nontaxable since it represents a return of
the lender's capital. By contrast, as a purchaser-lessor, the investor may
deduct depreciation, but the entire amount of the payments received
would be taxable as ordinary rental income. Therefore, if the amount
of net rental income substantially exceeds the allowable depreciation,
the investor is more likely to be a tax-exempt organization such as a
college. If, however, the leaseback is not a net lease, the leaseback
rental is a percentage rental, or if the purchaser's acquisition cost is
debt-financed, the rental income to such tax-exempt entity might be
taxable as "unrelated business income" under I.R.C. §§511, 512, and
514.

Under I.R.C. §§48 and 168, as amended by the Tax Reform Act
of 1984, certain perceived abusive sale and leasebacks by tax-exempt
entities have been curtailed, notably the past practice of tax-exempt
entities of selling real estate so that the purchaser-lessor can receive a
pass-through of depreciation deductions and investment tax credits in
exchange for a reduced rental to the seller-lessee. The end result of
such an arrangement under prior law was that the tax-exempt entity
would indirectly obtain the advantage of income tax deductions and
credits (in the guise of a reduced rental) even though it would have
no correlative liability to pay tax on the income from such property.
See generally Note, Sale-Leaseback Transactions by Tax-Exempt Entities
and the Need for Congressional Guidelines, 12 Fordham Urb. L.J. 349
(1984).

6. *Tax Planning.* The following measures can be taken to help
assure tax treatment as a sale:

1. if possible, replace the repurchase option with a series of long
    renewal periods, or "water down" the option by making the
    purchase optional for both the owner-lessor and the seller-
    lessor;
2. gear the option price to a figure that is reasonable in relation
    to the probable fair market value of the property at the date
    of its exercise;
3. avoid using a "net" leaseback or placing the risk of casualty
    loss on the seller-lessee;
4. sell to an institutional lender only if it has other sale and
    leasebacks in its investment portfolio; and
5. avoid any two-party arrangement between related taxpayers

and, if possible, use an outside lender where other financing is involved.

Notwithstanding the nonacquiescence of the Revenue Service to the results in both *Jordan Marsh* and *City Investing,* the rationale for these results ("fair market approach") is so compelling as to suggest that a taxpayer will be reasonably assured of obtaining nonrecognition treatment of gain (except to the extent boot is received) (1) by arranging for a 30-or-more-year leaseback and (2) by limiting the amount of cash or other boot received to an amount significantly below the fair market value of the transferred property — perhaps the ratio of cash to fair market value should not exceed 3:5, the ratio present in the *Century Electric* case. Conversely, if the taxpayer wants to avoid I.R.C. §1031 so that a loss will be recognized, the amount of cash received should be close to the fair market of the transferred property, and likewise the leaseback rental should not be appreciably less than the fair market rental at the time the lease agreement is executed. See Leslie Co. v. Commissioner, 64 T.C. 247, nonacq., 1978-2 C.B. 3, affd., 539 F.2d 943 (3d Cir. 1976), wherein the "fair market approach" was followed by the Tax Court and the Third Circuit. Cf. Missouri Pacific R.R. v. United States, 497 F.2d 1386 (Ct. Cl. 1974) (sale-leaseback characterized as like kind exchange despite the fact that seller received cash payment equal to fair market value of the property and the leaseback rental was at fair market value). See discussion of Frank Lyon Co. v. United States at Chapter 8B2, note 1b, supra.

For discussion of tax planning considerations see generally Blanton and Ipsen, How to Preserve the Significant Tax Benefits Available from a Sale and Leaseback Transaction, 10 Tax for Law. 324 (1982); Kaster, Tax Criteria for Structuring Sale-Leasebacks, 9 Real Est. Rev. 39 (Fall 1979); Maller, Structuring a Sale-Leaseback Transaction, 15 Real Est. L.J. 291 (Spring 1987).

7.   *Using Leaseback Flexibility as a Financing Tool (A Planning Problem).*   Illustrative of the foregoing tax rules and problems and the flexibility of sale and leaseback as a financing tool in comparison to debt financing is the following hypothetical situation.[18] The Realty Corporation (Realty) owns unencumbered land and a building of equal value that together are worth $1 million. The original cost was $500,000 ($320,000 allocable to land and $180,000 to the building), and now the combined adjusted basis is $400,000. Realty desires to raise $1 million of working capital. Assume that Realty is using an ACRS cost

18. The underlying concept for this example is based on a question that appears in Axelrod, Berger, and Johnstone, Land Transfer and Finance, 1048-1049 (2d ed. 1984).

recovery period of 31.5 years and that it can raise $1 million under any of the following alternatives.

   a. Debt Financing. Obtain $1 million by floating a bond issue (secured by the net assets of Realty as security) or by means of a constant-amortization payment mortgage loan, repayable in the principal amount of $66,666 per annum for 15 years plus annual interest at 8 percent on the outstanding principal balance. A $1 million mortgage loan amount is being used for comparison purposes even though such 100 percent loan-to-value ratio is unrealistic absent unusual circumstances (e.g., high-credit lease financing).

   b. Sale and Leaseback 1. Sell the realty to Lender Insurance Co. (Lender) for $1 million with a 15-year leaseback at an annual rental of $116,666 with an option to renew based on 10 percent of the appraised value of the land.

   c. Sale and Leaseback 2. Sell the realty to Lender for $1 million with a 30-year leaseback at an annual rental of $83,333 with an option to repurchase based on 100 percent of the appraised value of the land. Note that in both alternative b and alternative c Lender will receive a discounted 5½ percent rate of annual return over and above its recoupment of purchase price, which is somewhat less than what a mortgage lender or bondholder would demand.

   d. Combined Sale and Leaseback and Debt Financing. Sell the realty to Lender for $300,000 with a 30-year leaseback at an annual rental of $25,000. On the basis of the value of the leaseback, assume for comparison purposes that Realty can then borrow $700,000 secured by a 30-year constant amortization mortgage, repayable at $23,333 per annum plus annual interest of 8 percent on the outstanding principal balance. Observe that even though the market value of the real estate exceeds the sale price by $700,000, this does not mean that the transaction will be treated as a disguised loan of $300,000 by Lender

T a b l e   8-2

Ownership	Cash Outflow	Depreciation	RESULTS: Interest	Rent	Total Tax Deductions	Capital Gain at 34% corporate tax rate
(a) 15 years Realty	$146,666 ⋁	$ 5,714K	$80,000 ⋁	—	$ 85,714 ⋁	$ 0
(b) 15 years Lender	116,666K	—	—	$116,666K	116,666K	34% of 600,000 = 204,000
(c) 30 years Lender	83,888K	—	—	83,333K	83,333K	34% of 600,000 = 204,000
(d) 30 years Lender	104,333 ⋁	13,333K*	56,000 ⋁	25,000K	94,333 ⋁	34% of 300,000 = 102,000

* Under I.R.C. §1031(d) Realty would receive a substituted basis in the leaseback of $400,000 (plus $300,000 recognized gain less $300,000 cash boot) = $400,000 amortized over 30 years = $13,333 per annum.

to Realty. In general, courts have not scrutinized the reasonableness of the sale price. For example, in *Frank Lyon Co.* the cost of the building ($10 million) exceeded its sale price ($7,640,000); likewise, in Frito-Lay, Inc. v. United States 209 F. Supp. 886 (N.D. Ga. 1962), the market value of the real estate exceeded by a large margin the sale price, which was based on the estimated cost of construction. However, the Service might argue that Lender is really buying the realty for $1 million and receiving $700,000 from Realty as prepaid rental income. This would mean that Lender would acquire a $1 million cost basis in the realty and that Realty could amortize the $700,000 prepaid rental over the 30-year leaseback period. See Alstores Realty Corp. v. Commissioner, 46 T.C. 363, at 374 (1966); Steinway & Sons v. Commissioner, 46 T.C. 375, at 379 (1966), acq., 1967-1 C.B. 1.

i. Based on the foregoing case analysis, do you think the Internal Revenue Service could successfully apply its recharacterization theory to any of the above financing options?

ii. Based on the information in Table 8-2, determine how the business and tax results of using debt financing (alternative (a)) would compare in the short run and long run with use of (1) sale-and-leaseback financing (alternatives (b) and (c)) and (2) a combination of sale and leaseback with debt financing (alternative (d)).

8. *The Nature of Ordinary Sale and Leaseback.* At this juncture we know that certain pitfalls in sale-and-leaseback financing exist; for example, if the seller-lessee has the option to repurchase the property for a watered-down price and is charged an unduly low rental during the leaseback, the Service will most likely recharacterize the transaction as a disguised mortgage loan. In other words, we know when a transaction that purports to be a sale and leaseback may not be treated as one, but do we really know what the *ordinary* sale and leaseback is or how it *ought* to be treated for federal tax purposes? To find out, let us conclude our examination of this highly useful (yet curious) financing and tax planning device by considering the following question, which has nettled tax planners and commentators for years: In an arm's-length transaction involving unrelated parties, does the ordinary sale and leaseback reflect a genuine sale of a fee interest that is merely induced by tax considerations or, as a matter of substance over form, is it nothing more than a disguised mortgage loan (or something else) structured as a sale with a leaseback to the seller so that the parties can achieve certain tax advantages that would not otherwise be available? Put simply, the question is whether the ordinary sale and leaseback should be treated as an economic fact or as a tax fiction, and how such determination ought to be made.

In answering this question certain assumptions must be made. Let us briefly review the discussion of the ordinary sale and leaseback in the article and note excerpts at Chapter 8B2, supra. As suggested by

Agar and Fuller, in a typical transaction (1) the initial sale price is often geared to the financing or working capital needs of the seller rather than to the fair market value of the real estate being sold (see alternative (d) in note 7); (2) as in *Frank Lyon Co.,* neither the leaseback rental nor the option to repurchase is predicated on the fair market value of the real estate but instead each is calculated to provide a fair income return to the purchaser and allow the purchaser to amortize and recoup its investment over the leaseback period; (3) the estimated useful life of the improvements will not exceed the leaseback period and the leaseback itself is a net lease whereby the purchaser's role is that of a passive investor and, by contrast, the seller-lessee agrees to pay property taxes, insurance, and maintenance expenses and to assume the risk of casualty and condemnation; (4) the seller-lessee's choice of sale and leaseback financing (as opposed to mortgage or straight debt financing) is dictated by valid business reasons (e.g., high-ratio financing, avoidance of usury restrictions) beyond the need merely to retain possession of the premises during the leaseback period; and (5) the purchaser-lessor typically funds its acquisition costs by means of a nonrecourse mortgage loan from a third-party institutional lender such as a life insurance company.

Finally, in our hypothetical involving an ordinary sale and lease-back, although the leaseback rentals and option prices are not geared to fair market value, let us assume (as in *Frank Lyon Co.*) that they are *reasonable* in relation to the fair market value of the real estate and that the nonrecourse indebtedness incurred by the purchaser does not exceed the market value of the real estate. Otherwise, past precedent would compel us to treat the transaction as a sham for federal income tax purposes. See discussions at Chapter 8B2, notes 1-3, supra and Chapter 2B, note 4, respectively.

     a.   Based on the foregoing assumptions, decide as a matter of substance over form which of the following theories best describes the true tax nature of an ordinary sale and leaseback.

     i. A genuine sale followed by a leaseback, in which event the seller-lessee would be entitled to a rental deduction and the purchaser to the benefit of the depreciation. Exemplifying this traditional point of view is Weinstein and Silvers, The Sale and Leaseback After *Frank Lyon Company,* 24 N.Y.L. Sch. L. Rev. 337, 340 (1978).

     ii. A disguised mortgage loan resulting in opposite tax consequences for the parties, namely, the ostensible seller would be treated merely as a borrower so that it would retain a depreciation deduction, but any ostensible rental payments would be treated as payment of interest and loan principal during the leaseback period, and the ostensible purchaser, as lender, would treat any rentals it receives for the possessory term as nothing more than interest and amortization of its loan advanced in the guise of a purchase payment.

iii. The sale of a mere remainder interest with the reservation of a possessory term by the seller-lessee, in which event the tax consequences would be the same as in (ii) during the leaseback period, except that the seller would realize gain or loss on the sale of the remainder interest and the purchaser would obtain a cost basis in the remainder interest that could be depreciated once the leaseback period is over. If you recall, this was the position taken by the taxpayers in the *Alstores-Steinway* litigation discussed at Chapter 8B2, note 2, supra. Consider a risk-benefit theory of ownership in conjunction with the step transaction doctrine. (Professor Del Cotto is the chief proponent of this theory, as you will see in his well-reasoned article Sale and Leasebacks: A Hollow Sound When Tapped?, 37 Tax L. Rev. 1, 23-50 (1981)).

iv. The transfer of naked legal title to the purchaser by the seller, who, as the real owner under a risk-benefit theory, retains the beneficial ownership of the property (in which event the tax consequences would be the same as in alternative (ii)). See discussion of Helvering v. F. & R. Lazarus & Co. at Chapter 8B2, note 1, supra.

v. In the case of a leaseback of 30 years or more, the exchange of a fee for a leaseback rather than the sale of a fee, regardless of whether the leaseback has independent economic significance (in which event the tax consequences would be essentially the same as in alternative (i), except that the ostensible seller would not obtain the benefit of any loss deduction). Compare *Century Electric* with *Jordan Marsh;* see discussion of these cases at Chapter 8B2, note 4, supra.

b. With regard to the question posed above, does it really make any difference whether we recharacterize the ordinary sale and leaseback as a disguised mortgage loan if, as Justice Blackmun points out in *Frank Lyon Co.,* excerpted supra, "It is not inappropriate to note that the Government is likely to lose little revenue, if any, as the result of the shape given the transaction by the parties. No deduction was created that is not either matched by an item of income or that would not have been available to one of the parties if the transaction had been arranged differently"?

c. In determining the true tax nature of the ordinary sale and leaseback, maybe it is overly simplistic to apply one recharacterization theory or another. Perhaps what is needed is a decision model (like the one by Schurtz, at Chapter 8B2, supra) that applies a totality-of-transaction approach by weighing all the important variables. While such an approach provides less certainty for tax planners, it may become necessary, since the typical modern sale and leaseback tends to be a highly complex transaction (as exemplified by the facts in *Frank Lyon Co.*) involving facts that are not readily subject to generalization. To test your understanding of this alternative mode of analysis, make a decision as to whether the typical modern sale and leaseback could be recharacterized as a disguised mortgage loan by applying the criteria outlined by Schurtz to the facts in the hypothetical. Another example of this method of analysis is to be found in Note, Taxation of Sale and Leaseback Transactions — A General Review, 32 Vand. L. Rev. 945, 980-983 (1979).

C.   LEASE LAYERING: THE "SANDWICH LEASE"

So far in this chapter we have examined a number of creative real estate financing techniques that are predicated on the concepts that a leasehold estate can be severed from the fee ownership of the land and that a building can be severed from the underlying land so that each component can be separately financed in order to expand the total real estate financing pie.

This art of making the sum of the real estate parts greater than the whole can also be applied on the equity, or ownership, side of real estate. The best example is a lease layering technique whereby the fee simple ownership is carved into both a leasehold estate (the "prime lease") and an income, or operating, sublease position. Since the prime lease would be situated between the fee ownership and the operating position it is called a "sandwich lease." Frequently the fee ownership is carved into a number of sandwich leases wherein each leaseholder is entitled to a fixed rate of return. The lessee last in line, who owns the operating position, would lease space to the occupancy tenants and be entitled to any residual cash flow. By layering the fee simple ownership in this manner, it is possible to both leverage the income, or operating, position and attract the widest range of participants to the real estate investment.

The following hypothetical is based on an example that was recited by Mr. Zeckendorf to the Bull & Bear Club at Harvard Law School sometime in 1957 to illustrate his use of the Hawaiian technique. Suppose that Zeckendorf (Z) owns an office building project that is presently worth $10 million and yielding a market net rental of $1 million each year, so that Z is currently earning a 10 percent rate of return on his $10 million equity investment. But suppose Z wants to cash out most of his equity in the building so that he can reinvest the net sale proceeds elsewhere. Z might consider an ordinary sale-and-leaseback transaction whereby he would sell the building to investor A (A) in exchange for $9 million in cash plus a long-term net leaseback of the building at an annual fixed rental to A of, let's say, $900,000 so that A, as Z's landlord, would receive a 10 percent rate on its $9 million equity investment. Should the annual net operating income from the building (to which Z would be entitled as lessee) increase by $100,000 from $1 million to $1,100,000, then Z, who would only be obligated to pay A a fixed amount of rent, would increase his own rate of equity return from 11 percent ($1,100,000 ÷ $10 million equity investment) to 20 percent ($1,100,000 net income less $900,000 payment to A = $200,000 ÷ $1 million equity investment). Moreover, Z would have $9 million in cash (less his transactional costs) left over to reinvest in other properties. Conversely, if the annual net income from the building were to decrease by $100,000 to $900,000, then Z's rate of equity return would decrease from 9 percent ($900,000 net income ÷ $10 million equity investment) to 0 percent ($900,000 net income less $900,000 payment to A = 0 ÷ $1 million equity investment) if he engaged in the sale-and-leaseback transaction with A.

Alternatively, if Z were even more of a poker player he could further leverage his operating position by not only engaging in a sale and leaseback with A but also *simultaneously* assigning his lease with A to investor B *(B)* in exchange for cash of $500,000 plus a long-term net sub-leaseback at an annual fixed rental from Z to B of, let's say, $50,000 (and Z would pay B the $900,000 B owes to A); thus B, as Z's landlord on the sublease, would, like A, receive a 10 percent rate on its $500,000 equity investment. For simplicity's sake the example presupposes that B would demand the same 10 percent rate of return as would A; however, in actuality B would probably demand a somewhat higher rate of equity return (e.g., 12 percent) to compensate B for the higher risk associated with subordinating B's income stream to A's. Once again, if Z's projection is correct and the annual net operating income from the building (to which Z would be entitled as sublessee) were to increase by $100,000 (to $1,100,000), then Z could take advantage of the $150,000 spread between the fixed rental obligations to A and B totaling $950,000 and the increased net income from the building of $1,100,000 to increase his rate of return from 20 percent to 30 percent ($1,100,000 net income less $900,000 payable to A less ($50,000) payable to B = $150,000 ÷ $500,000 equity investment). In addition, Z would have $9,500,000 in cash (less his transactional costs) left over to reinvest in other properties. However, should annual net income from the building decrease by $100,000 to $900,000, then Z's rate of equity return would be reduced to negative 10 percent ($900,000 net income less $900,000 payable to A less $50,000 payable to B = ($50,000) ÷ $500,000 equity investment).

Finally, if Z were a gargantuan gambler he might not only engage in sale and leasebacks with A and B but also *simultaneously* assign his sublease with B to investor C *(C)* in exchange for $500,000 plus a long-term net sub-sub-leaseback of an annual fixed rental from Z to C of, let's say, $50,000 (and Z would pay C the $950,000 C owes to B) so that C, as Z's landlord on the sub-sub-lease, would, like A and

B, receive a 10 percent rate on its $500,000 equity investment. Once again, if *Z*'s projection is correct and the annual net income from the building were to increase by *something* (let's say one dollar, from $1 million to $1,000,001), the entire amount over and above the fixed payments to *A, B,* and *C* ($1) would go to *Z,* providing him theoretically with an infinite rate of return on his zero equity investment. What would happen if the net income from the building were to decrease by one dollar? You figure that one out!

The following are a schematic rendition of the foregoing transactions and a chart summarizing the results:

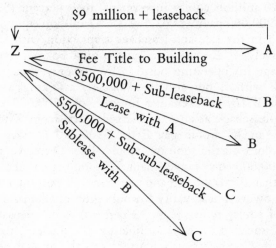

Price	Z's investment	Net income from building	Rent/Return to purchaser	Z's equity return	$100,000 increase in net income	Cash available to Z for reinvestment
——	$10 million	$1 million	——	10%	11%	0
Sale to A for $9 million + leaseback	$1 million	$1 million	$900,000/10%	10%	20%	$9 million
Sale to B for $500,000+ sub-leaseback	$500,000	$1 million	$50,000/10%	10%	30%	$9.5 million
Sale to C for $500,000 sub-sub-leaseback	0	$1 million	$50,000/10%	0	∞	$10 million

Now that we've examined the theoretical underpinnings of the Hawaiian technique using the somewhat simplified hypothetical presented by Mr. Zeckendorf, let us take a look at some more sophisticated real-world strategies that are currently employed to slice up a real estate investment in a way that will attract the widest range of participants and expand the real estate investment pie so that the sum of the parts may exceed the original whole.

Canfield, Strategies Involving Sandwich Leases
18 Real Est. Rev. 22 (Spring 1988)

The income property game is now usually played by four players: owner/developer, buyer/investor, lender, and tenant. The introduction of a fifth player can (1) improve liquidity, (2) reduce risk, and (3) enhance capital productivity. In the process, the game becomes simpler to play because the risk of uncertainty is distributed to yet another principal. At the same time, however, it becomes more complex because the possibility of coalitions among players is increased exponentially. Statistically, the chance of finding a bargain resulting from another player's need is likewise greatly increased by the expanded field of participants.

THE SANDWICH LEASE

The fifth player is a combination capital investor and property manager who deals in so-called sandwich leases. The sandwich lease is commonly thought of as a contract that can produce profit for the sandwich lessor in only one way: on the spread between the rent he pays to the owner and the higher rent that he may collect from subtenants. In a reversal, however, the sandwich lessee-lessor may also be paid by the owner under circumstances in which the owner wishes to limit for a time the depressing effect of income deficiency in his property value. Owners may find sandwich leases to be wise options, particularly during the rent-up of new property in a soft market for tenants.

THE OWNER PAYS THE LESSEE: AN EXAMPLE

Five years ago, a developer had 70,000 square feet of class A office space worth $9.8 million if it were fully leased, but the building had a 40 percent vacancy. The owner accepted a $7.35 million offer for the property, but the buyer could not find a lender willing to finance the high-vacancy property. Enter the fifth player. A pension fund took a five-year lease on the unoccupied space at $518,000 annual rent in exchange for an equity share of $2.185 million based on the subsequent prompt sale of the property at $9.6 million. The pension fund did not plan to occupy the space but to sublease it. The pension fund hired the owner/developer to sublease the space, and agreed to give the developer 60 percent of the sublease rental income. (The tenants had to be approved by the new owner.)

It took two years to find a single tenant to take the balance of the building space under sublease. The sublease rental was $532,000 annually for three years, to be bumped up to the market rate rent thereafter. At the time the property was sold, the present value of the pension fund's interest in the sublease income was $437,000, and the developer's interest was $657,000.

The developer got a far better deal than he would have gotten from the $7.35 million sale. He received $7.415 million ($9.6 million minus $2.185 million) as the result of the sale plus $657,000 for his interest in the sublease, effectively selling for $722,000 more than that for which he had originally bargained. The buyer and the buyer's lender got good cash flow from day one and wound up with excellent tenants. Furthermore, the tenant who came in under the sublease got a 10 percent rent break for three years, and finally, the pension fund did extraordinarily well. It got to use $2.185 million at a cost of about 6 percent, plus $212,800 per year, 40 percent of rental income, for three years.

THE ANALYTICAL BASES OF THE SANDWICH LEASE GAME

Understanding the problem that the sandwich lease solves is easy. Either a new building has not rented up fast enough, or an older property is filled with tenants enjoying leases that call for below-market rents. The values of these properties are depressed because the properties' income is substandard. Buyers, particularly institutional investors, are usually willing to pay no more than a price based on capitalization of existing income using the market capitalization rate, or they may attempt to acquire these properties at a substantial discount from replacement cost. As demonstrated below, this buyer's formula causes a property with a 30 percent vacancy rate to be priced at about half of its price if the property were 100 percent leased.

THE APPRAISER'S SOLUTION TO THE VACANCY PROBLEM

In a strong market environment, the appraiser's valuation is the proper valuation for a property with a curable rent deficiency. The appraiser capitalizes pro forma net income to arrive at the property's value as a fully rented property and discounts the rent's shortfall to determine "true value" for the property. This rent-shortfall discount is the present value of the rent deficiency for the period that elapses before the property achieves 100 percent occupancy at full market rent, the property's "ultimate value."

The reason that buyers balk at accepting the appraiser's solution is that the true value solution may be determined with certainty only retroactively. The time that it will take to lease up a new property to full occupancy at market rate rents can only be estimated. For new construction, is a prudent estimate for lease-up one, two, three, or more times the current rental space absorption cycle? In an existing building, the time period necessary to correct below-market-rate rents is equally as difficult to estimate, but the need for accurate valuation of a less than fully rented property becomes less crucial if there is a sandwich lease that eliminates the possibility of a buyer's loss resulting from a wrong estimate of the time period necessary to correct rent shortfall.

ENTER THE SPECULATOR

Any seller of a property that has a rent deficiency prefers the appraiser's ideal solution to a buyer's valuation that is based on capitalization of existing net income or, perhaps worse, on some discount from replacement cost. The catch is that buyers will not buy at the true market value until income has actually been established. Indeed, investors welcome maximum cash flow. Buyers usually prefer to wait and pay full price for maximum cash flow rather than purchase a property with an income deficiency even if that property is available at a discount. Buyers first prefer to avoid the uncertainty of rent shortfall. Furthermore, the property with high income affords better leverage of equity, and when investors buy real estate for appreciation, their goal

E x h i b i t   1

Calculation of Value of Hypothetical Property at Various Vacancy Rates

Vacancy	Computation		Net Income	Value
20%	$(\$15 - 5) - (0.20)\,(\$15)$	$=$	$7.00 per sq. ft.	$70 per sq. ft.
50%	$(\$15 - 5) - (0.50)\,(\$15)$	$=$	$2.50 per sq. ft.	$25 per sq. ft.

is enhanced by leverage. Therefore, when a quality tenant is found to eliminate an existing rent deficiency, both seller and potential buyer have reason to celebrate. By involving a speculator, full tenancy can be simulated in a manner that will satisfy the most prudent buyer.

CALCULATING THE SANDWICH-LEASE NUMBERS

If a seller can find a fifth player, a speculator with an impeccable credit standing, to lease all the remaining vacant space in a property at market rent for a normal lease period, how much incentive shall he pay to that fifth player? The numbers vary with the length of the normal lease period, its relation to prevailing rental space absorption, and the amount of vacant space involved.

The analysis is relatively simple, as can be shown by an example. Assume an office property in a market in which gross rent is $15 per sq. ft. Operating expenses are $5 per sq. ft. resulting in $10-per-sq.-ft. net income. At a capitalization rate of 10 percent, the property is worth $100 per sq. ft.

Using the 10 percent capitalization rate, the owner can undertake the buyer's calculation of how the property's value changes as the vacancy rate changes. Exhibit 1 calculates new values for this property when the vacancy rate is 20 percent and when it is 50 percent. As Exhibit 1 shows, a vacancy rate of 20 percent reduces both gross and net incomes by $3 per sq. ft.; a vacancy of 50 percent reduces the quantities by $7.50 per sq. ft.

How much should the owner pay to restore the property to its fully rented $100-per-sq.-ft. value? If the analysis disregards the time value of money and if it assumes that the owner has 100 percent equity in the property, the owner is better off if he pays any amount less than $30 per sq. ft. in the case of the property with a 20 percent vacancy. If the vacancy is 50 percent, the owner is better off as long as he pays less than $75 per sq. ft. The cost of buying the "phantom" tenant is, however, related to the potential sandwich lease speculator's

E x h i b i t   2

Cost of "Lease-up" by Fifth-Player Option

(Upfront Payment to Cover Rent Shortfall)

Lease Term (Yrs.)	20% Vacancy	50% Vacancy
1	$ 3 per sq. ft.	$ 7.50 per sq. ft.
2	$ 6 per sq. ft.	$15 per sq. ft.
4	$12 per sq. ft.	$30 per sq. ft.
6	$18 per sq. ft.	$45 per sq. ft.

expectations for finding tenant occupants. Exhibit 2 calculates these costs. For simplicity, the computations are not discounted for the time value of money.

The amount the owner is willing to pay is affected by the percentage of his equity. Assume that the owner's equity is in the range of 20 percent to 40 percent of the true value of $100 per sq. ft., and debt service is about 12 percent of the principal debt, or $7 per sq. ft. to $10 per sq. ft. The sandwich-lease arrangement makes sense when the value of the sandwich-lease option (amount A below) exceeds the value of the outcome when the property is just held, and the vacancy is not cured (amount B below).

$$A = Equity - Payment\ to\ Fifth\ Player + Share\ in\ Sublease\ Income$$

$$B = Equity - Opportunity\ Loss - Debt\ Service + Income$$

These calculations are undertaken in the following hypothetical example. A property worth $100 per sq. ft. fully occupied is valued at $55 per sq. ft. because of a 30 percent vacancy by applying the prevailing capitalization rate to existing income. The lower value is below current replacement cost and $65 per sq. ft. debt. Therefore, the owner spends $12 per sq. ft. to lease up for a three-year period, bringing the appraised market value to $100 per sq. ft., and he sells the property for that price. Later, the vacant 30 percent of the property is subleased returning $3 per sq. ft. to the seller. Because of the sublease, the owner/seller's net cost for utilizing the fifth-player approach is only $9 per sq. ft. When the seller reinvests the remainder of the $35-per-sq.-ft. equity recovered by the sale after the lease-up expense, he earns $18 per sq. ft. during the same three-year period. Consequently, the decision to utilize a fifth-player approach is a wise one. This is what the calculations look like:

$$A = \$35 - 12 + 3 = \$26\ recovered$$

$$B = \$35 - 18 - 22\ (say) + 20 = \$15\ recovered$$

In this case, the opportunity loss (the $18 per sq. ft. that the owner might have earned for reinvesting sales proceeds) is the determining factor because the cost of holding was only $2 ($20 income *minus* $22 debt service) during the three-year period.

It should be noted that the comparison, as given, is valid as a relative indicator (a kind of go/no-go gauge) to assist the decision of whether to lease up. It can be misleading if inferences are taken beyond this comparison, which is presented this way to emphasize the often overlooked opportunity loss.

ELEMENTS THAT AFFECT THE SANDWICH-LEASE NEGOTIATION

The success of the sandwich-lease approach is based on an anomaly of real estate that the tenant, lender, and owner each place a different value on the marginal rent dollar. This is what enables the owner/seller to buy a fifth-player sandwich lease. The numbers used above suggest that an annual rent dollar for five years may be bought for $5 or less. Yet that marginal rent dollar brings $10 from a buyer, and $7 to $8 from a lender.

When a fifth player sells an owner the service of providing a sandwich lease, the parties must decide how to handle the subleasing proceeds. If the prospect of finding tenants during the term of the sandwich lease is poor, the speculator wants most, if not all, of the money up front. In that case, the owner should ask for a major share of the subleasing proceeds. On the other hand, if tenant prospects are good, the fifth player, as a speculator, might risk some money for the opportunity to sublease at a profit in return for the bulk of the sublease proceeds. The reverse payment from property owner to speculator/tenant can take the form of income, a loan, or a share in equity, depending on how the deal is structured. Tax planning can mitigate the tax bite and prevent taxes from interfering with the intended business purpose of the sandwich lease, which is to restore property value.

OWNER/DEVELOPER CONSIDERATIONS

History has shown that anyone who has owned real estate long enough has been vindicated by appreciation no matter what the initial cost. However, sometimes owners must sell. The goal then becomes how to get the most value, which usually translates into the quickest deal at the highest price. Delaying any sale for the last dollar in price can be counterproductive. It is usually more important to get equity out and onto the next project, particularly when the opportunity loss for reinvestment is compounded by a negative cost of possession. The fifth-player sandwich lease enables the owner to sell immediately even in a poor tenant market. The owner/developer can become liquid in any stage of the tenant market cycle if he is willing to pay out a portion of the value gained.

The one thing an owner/developer cannot do is boost the value of the property above its fair market value by falsely inflating the sandwich-lease rent. Fair market value can exceed the income valuation in an "auction" market in which buyers' expectations for environmental improvement cause them to overpay for current income because of perceived future benefits (usually the hope for unbridled appreciation). The environmental growth cycle is, however, a longer cycle than the tenant absorption rate cycle, and buyers and lenders and their respective appraisers scrutinize leases carefully, comparing incomes from both sandwich leases and tenant occupant leases to market and thus recognize false inflation of rental income.

VARIOUS FIFTH-PLAYER OPTIONS

Whether selling or refinancing, the owner may elect to become the fifth player himself either by selling and leasing back with a master lease to guarantee rent or by providing a trust fund to cover a specific rent deficiency. For instance, a seller could agree to place a sum in escrow to make up for any rent deficiency up to 60 percent the first year after sale, 40 percent the year thereafter, and 20 percent in the third year after the sale. Another variation of the fifth-player option is the following. In a high-vacancy market, the owner fills the building by leasing at 60 percent of the normal market rent. When the building is filled, the owner obtains a sandwich lessor to subsidize the rent and bring the property's net income up to par for permanent financing or a selloff. The seller has accelerated the rent-up period and is able to sell as soon as possible. The technique is an especially effective tool for quick rent-up of single-tenanted properties.

An owner/seller may decide to use the fifth-player option instead of an earnout sale. An earnout sale is one in which the buyer agrees to pay only for existing income. The buyer capitalizes existing income for the initial payment. As each new tenant is added to the roll, the net rent is calculated and capitalized to establish the amount of the additional payment. The buyer thus maintains his target rate of return regardless of the state of rent-up, but the seller has to wait for his capital payout, getting less than replacement cost until the property is near full rental.

This sale could be constructed using the appraiser's solution to arrive at selling price and treating the buyer as a fifth player. The price for the property as if fully rented at market rents is discounted by the projected rent shortfall to arrive at the price paid at settlement. The buyer then pays the seller a percentage of rent received from new tenants during a period equivalent to that used to compute the rent-shortfall discount. The buyer receives the rent-shortfall discount on the purchase price, and the seller gets a reasonable selling price, plus the follow-on income from new tenants for a specific period. The concept is easy to comprehend for players who know the game.

Buyer/Investor Perspectives

Institutional investors look for current income plus long-term growth. After purchase, institutional concerns focus on security. In selecting income property for acquisition, the institutional buyer focuses on current income. The fact that quality tenants have selected a particular property, and are willing to pay the going rate to be there, confirms the institutional buyer's long-term expectation of security. Tenant occupancy is thus more important than just cash flow. The seller must not merely persuade the buyer that the phantom tenancy is no sham but that the property is a good one for long-term investment.

The involvement of a quality fifth player (either by the seller or the buyer) can satisfy this need two ways. First, it can lend stature to the project. The buyer should be able to draw the inference that the fifth player would not be involved with a project that was not completely sound and if there were not every expectation that the project would rent up to quality tenants before the sandwich lease expired. Second, the degree of risk that the fifth player agrees to accept in the sandwich-lease contract measures his confidence in the property. The sandwich lease may plainly demonstrate his belief that the rent deficiency problem is a short-term concern that will be quickly resolved.

Buyers using their own money are more concerned with relative bargain value, the test for which is: Could a buyer resell his purchase at a profit if he wanted to? Obviously, a buyer who buys a property with rent deficiency, pays a price equal to the capitalization of existing income, and subsequently eliminates the income deficiency by utilizing a fifth-player lease-up can resell that property at a quick profit. There is, however, still another reason for the sharp buyer to utilize a fifth-player option, and that is for leverage. The degree of leverage that a buyer may achieve as the result of a sandwich lease could significantly outweigh the cost of involving the fifth player. In that case, the buyer should arrange and pay for the fifth-player option. Such a maneuver might even be necessary to make a deal possible for the buyer with limited capital. It is quite conceivable that the mortgage obtainable on fully leased property could exceed the combined cost of fifth-player lease-up plus the acquisition price for depressed property. Consequently, the entire cost of the purchase could be mortgaged out.

Lenders and Sandwich Leases

Commercial mortgages seldom reach maturity. Consequently, lenders pay little attention to long-term appreciation. The lenders' focus is a "now focus" centered on the ability to pay and on underlying collateral (liquidation values). As lenders well know, however, collateral does not make debt service payments, people do. The presence of a highly rated institution as a sandwich lessee should certainly satisfy a lender's concern about ability to pay. Consequently, mortgage money should come easily to qualified buyers of properties with sandwich leases signed by creditworthy lessees. Of course, the lenders will expect that the subtenants will also be of good creditworthiness, and they may hedge their commitments with stipulations to that effect.

In workout situations, with the lender in possession or about to take possession through foreclosure, one lending institution might bail out another by stepping into the fifth-player role. Time is the enemy in workout situations, and fifth-player involvement buys time — time to cure problems. When property market value can be restored before problems are solved, unwarranted pressure is removed, and an atmosphere for sound decisions is created. In addition, with the added option of restoring property value through a lease to a fifth player, it is inevitable that accountants will find better ways to soften the harsh effect of reporting the event, which should please the regulated financial institution holding the note.

THE TENANT-IN-PLACE AND THE FIFTH PLAYER

For the tenant-in-place enjoying a lease with rent well below market rates, leasehold equity represents a potential source of inexpensive capital. By stepping into the role of fifth player, the tenant can receive a lump-sum payment from the owner in return for paying higher rent, and the cost of the money that the tenant receives could well be below the cost of funds from other sources. Understanding the value that a tenant represents to an owner invites the tenant to play the role of fifth player in extracting upfront concessions in exchange for paying full-market-rate rent. The owner would have a property that is worth more and can be readily sold. For a large tenant, the owner might well refinance just for the arbitrage profit to be made on the spread between the cost of mortgage funds and the negotiated rate for "lending" to the tenant. This application of the fifth-player solution is termed "lease-up."

Tenants searching for space would do well to seek out fifth-player subleases before direct leases on the theory that the fifth player has more to give out and is much more disposed to do so. Just putting on the fifth player's hat can be enlightening to the tenant entering lease negotiations.

THE MANY ROLES OF THE FIFTH PLAYER

As has been illustrated, the fifth player can be a second role of any of the other players in the game. The new perspective that the player achieves by assuming the role is benefit enough for just trying it, not to mention the possibility of profiting in both roles. Nevertheless, there is even more to be gained when the fifth player is a separate party.

The role of the fifth player is potentially quite lucrative. If the fifth player lacks the credit necessary to sign a lease, the funds due to the fifth player up front can be set aside in escrow, or be delivered to a trustee, to provide assurance that the rent will be paid. Under this circumstance, the fifth player must look for profit in the subleases. For that matter, the fifth player could be two parties, one, the seller of the annuity contract guaranteeing rent payments and the other, a leasing broker.

When the fifth player has triple-A credit, the other players are disposed to accept the promise of rent payment as sufficient security. Then the fifth player receives low-cost funds upfront as well as profits from future subtenants. This brings competition to the tryouts for fifth-player position, and the competition for sandwich-lease deals keeps the addition of the fifth player from eroding the benefits to the other players.

SUMMARY

The prevailing method of income property valuation for investors is capitalization of income. Replacement cost valuations are used in distress situations, and comparable sales valuations predominate in an auction market gone through the roof in which prices are running away. In a normal investment market, a property's value is depressed by income deficiency, and properties are bought and sold at compromise prices based on attempts to predict the amount of income shortfall that will be experienced before the condition is cured. The fifth-player option offers a method for correcting the income deficiency instantaneously at a price that relates to the true value of the property. For a price, the fifth player eliminates rent deficiency. That price is the present value of the income shortfall. The shortfall may be deliberately over-estimated when the fifth player is involved, inflating the fifth player's original price; however, the agreement should call for a refund from the fifth player when the estimated shortfall turns out to be less than anticipated.

The funds that an owner needs to engage the fifth player are readily obtainable through sale or refinancing because when rent deficiency is corrected, value is restored. Capitalization of the new net income yields the highest possible value for the property. It is the "fungible connection," the exchange of a small piece of equity for near-term income that in turn results in a larger immediate gain in property value, that permits the fifth player to provide a viable solution.

Any player in the game can take the position of fifth player, and all participants benefit by planning and structuring deals around the fifth-player option, whether or not the fifth player is actually brought into the transaction. Indeed, a property need not be sold to see the fifth-player solution work to advantage. A refinancing after a sandwich lease provides rewarding immediate gains in value, and although the near-term benefit is achieved at the expense of equity given up to debt capital, there is additional leverage to be gained in the process, and notably, the mortgage proceeds do not all go to the cost of leaseup. In the end, that leverage gained, plus the portion of mortgage proceeds taken in hand by the owner, tip the balance scale of savvy deal making to fifth-player resolution.

Because real estate gets its value from use, vacant property leased to a phantom tenant is better than no tenant at all — especially when the cost of arranging such a lease is not unreasonable and when a rebate is possible in the event that one pays more than necessary. A major criticism of real estate has long been that it operates in an inefficient market. That criticism can now be quieted, at least in one important respect, by the introduction of the fifth player to the income property game.

or use lessee as 5th player by giving free front rent

Chapter 9

Refinancing, Secondary Financing, and High-Ratio Financing

The current slump in real estate along with the shake-out periods of 1974-1975 and 1979-1981 have made institutional lenders wiser and warier about underwriting commercial real estate loans. Gone are the days when real estate developers could rely on self-serving appraisals and maximum loan-to-value ratios on demand.[1] In addition, the Tax Reform Act of 1986 decimated real estate as a tax shelter and so investors have become correspondingly more cash-flow-oriented and increasingly concerned about cash-on-cash rates of return and the ability to translate some of their equity into cash before the project is sold or liquidated. As a consequence, in today's real estate market many projects could not be developed, marketed to investors, or even sold, without the extra funds and higher yields available by means of certain high-ratio leasehold and debt-financing techniques. In Chapter 8 we observed how real estate developers are able to leverage their acquisition costs and thereby increase the rates of return to their investors by means of leasehold mortgage financing and split financing techniques such as the sale and leaseback of land plus a leasehold mortgage on the improvements. We also examined sale-and-leaseback financing as a means of translating accumulated equity into cash. See Chapter 8B1.

The aim of this chapter is to analyze debt-financing techniques (such as refinancing and secondary financing) used to cash out the accumulated equity in a real estate project. In addition, we will be examining certain high-ratio financing techniques that enable developers and purchasers to leverage their cost of acquiring and constructing

---

1. For example, the average loan-to-value ratio on commercial mortgage loan commitments made by life insurance companies declined from 74.1 percent in 1979 to 66.5 percent in 1982 and was in the 70-71 percent range from 1983 to 1987. American Council of Life Insurance, Investment Bull. No. 1034, Table A, at 4-6 (June 21, 1988). Mortgage loan appraisal and loan-to-value ratios are discussed at Chapter 5B1.

income-producing real estate. These techniques run the gamut from well-established ones such as the subordinated purchase-money mortgage (used in new construction to leverage the cost of the underlying land) to more exotic financing devices such as the wraparound mortgage (frequently used to expedite the sale of existing real estate) and the zero-coupon mortgage (used for the financing of both new and existing real estate). Some involve junior, or "secondary," financing techniques such as the ordinary second mortgage, the subordinated purchase-money mortgage, and the wraparound mortgage, while others, such as refinancing, involve only first-mortgage financing. Some are tax-oriented, such as the tax-free exchange and tax-exempt bond financing, while others, such as high-credit lease financing, are not. Most are debt-financing techniques but two: the installment land contract and the tax-deferred ("tax-free") exchange. All of these devices, however, have one thing in common; they are designed to make extra funds or financing available when needed, and some of these techniques theoretically can be used to achieve 100 percent or more financing.

A.   REFINANCING

Returning to the master hypothetical at Chapter 5B, let us assume that Dan Developer was able to obtain a first mortgage loan from Ace in the amount of $25 million and secure (possibly from outside investors) whatever venture capital was needed to fund both the construction of the office building and the cost of the underlying land. Further assume that the land and building, which together cost $33 million, are now worth $40 million and that amortization payments have scaled down the principal balance on the Ace mortgage from $25 million to $20 million, and thus the current market value of the ownership interest, or "equity," in the project[2] held by Dan is approximately $20 million.

---

2. "Equity" simply means net assets (assets minus liabilities) and as such is a way to measure, in accounting terms, either the book value of an ownership interest (if the assets are reflected at cost, or, in the case of an income-producing asset such as a building, at cost less accumulated depreciation) or the cash value of an ownership interest (if the assets are valued at market value, for example, the value of a building based on a capitalization of current earnings). See Chapter 5B1, wherein the income approach to appraisal is briefly examined. If the ownership entity is a partnership or corporation the net worth of the entity is reflected by the proprietary accounts of the partners, called "capital accounts" (discussed at Chapter 2B, note 7d), or shareholders (capital stock plus retained earnings), respectively. Another way to define the concept would be to regard "equity" in mortgage terms as the value of the mortgagor's equity of redemption.

At this juncture the project appears to be economically viable, and Dan Developer wants to translate some of the accumulated equity into tax-free cash. The funds could be used by Dan as extra working capital to expand or renovate the office building or for another investment opportunity.

Equity in a real estate project can accumulate as the result of debt-service payments on the mortgage, inasmuch as the portion of the payments allocable to amortization reduces the principal balance of the mortgage indebtedness; for example, in the master hypothetical the loan amount at the end of the tenth year would be paid down to $21,140,340 (because of amortization payments as reflected in Table 5-4) and, correspondingly, the amount of equity would increase by $3,859,660. Equity can also accumulate through inflation, which increases the value of the underlying land, or by means of an increase in the value of the building caused by higher net operating income[3] when rents rise because of management efficiency (especially in the case of active real estate such as hotels and parking garages), greater demand for rental space, or simply because of inflation.[4]

In the previous chapter we observed how the accumulated equity in a project can be cashed out by means of a sale and leaseback, which ordinarily is a taxable event. In this chapter we will examine two debt-financing techniques that can be used by owners to translate their equity into cash without taxation: refinancing and secondary financing. "Refinancing" simply means the substitution of a new loan for an existing one, for example, obtaining a new first mortgage loan in order to discharge an existing one that is more expensive. Returning to our hypothetical and assuming the same 75 percent loan-to-value ratio, Dan could refinance by obtaining a new first mortgage loan of $30 million, of which amount $20 million would be used to satisfy the existing mortgage and the balance of $10 million could be cashed out by Dan as net refinancing proceeds. As a rule of thumb, real estate owners

---

3. Determination of value under the so-called income method of appraisal is based on applying a capitalization rate (as determined by interest rates and by the degree of risk associated with the project) to a projected stream of net operating income; for example, a cap rate of 10 percent applied to annual income of $100,000 ($100,000 ÷ by 10 percent) would produce a market value of $1 million based on ten times earnings. The higher the risk factor the higher the cap rate. This means that if the rate were increased from 10 percent to 20 percent, a prudent purchaser or lender would respectively purchase or loan money based on a return of capital within five years as opposed to 10 years. See discussion at Chapter 5B1.

4. For example, in the hypothetical appearing in the excerpt from Madison and Dwyer at Chapter 2B, assuming everything else remains the same, in 1992 the revenue figure ($1,976,000) is greater than the expense figure ($1,035,840); hence, by applying the same assumed 4 percent rate of inflation to both figures, the net operating income would increase by $37,606 and, at a cap rate of 10 percent, because of inflation the value of the building would increase by $376,060.

prefer refinancing to secondary financing when interest rates decline or remain the same because secondary financing is generally more expensive. Moreover, secondary financing may be prohibited without the consent of the first mortgagee if the first mortgage note should contain a due-on-encumbrance clause.[5]

However, the converse may be true if first mortgage interest rates escalate. Moreover, pending a future or further decline in interest rates Dan may want to use a short-term interest-only second mortgage loan as a temporary expedient until he can refinance at a lower first mortgage rate. Moreover, secondary financing may be more feasible than refinancing where the existing first mortgage contains an onerous prepayment charge. Indeed, during the lock-in period, when no prepayment is allowed, the refinancing option might be precluded altogether.

In addition to translating equity into working capital, a refinancing may be undertaken for other reasons such as increasing the project's cash flow and net operating income (by reducing interest expenses with a new, cheaper mortgage or by reducing debt-service payments with an extended loan term) and resuscitating the real property as a tax shelter by using a new mortgage cycle in order to reduce amortization payments. Remember, it is the excess of depreciation over mortgage amortization that produces tax shelter.[6]

Smith, Refinancing a Syndicated Property
16 Real Est. Rev. 16 (Spring 1986)

Refinancing — the substitution of one mortgage for another — is one of real estate's most neglected topics, perhaps because people assume that analyzing a refinancing is simple. Actually, it is anything but. Many factors affect the attractiveness of a proposed refinancing. Without a clear understanding of *why* the partnership is refinancing, the partnership might decide unwisely.

Refinancing proceeds must first be divided into two elements: net proceeds and the cost of obtaining capital. The transaction costs or costs of obtaining capital may include (1) application fees and legal costs to prepare and review new documents and (2) up-front points to the new lender.

5. See Chapter 5B7.
6. See Chapter 2B, note 2.

REASONS TO REFINANCE

Conceptually, there are four basic uses of net proceeds:

1. To lower the cost of existing debt;
2. To provide necessary or desirable operating capital;
3. To take out cash flow and equity buildup; and
4. To reschedule obligations and thus improve the health of the entity.

A refinancing should be analyzed by allocating the net proceeds among these four uses and weighing the benefits of each use against the cost.

LOWERING THE COST OF EXISTING DEBT

Lowering the cost of the current debt is the refinancing reason most readers probably think of first. If the existing mortgage carries a rate higher than borrowing rates now available in the marketplace, a refinancing is indicated. Can it ever be wrong to refinance for this purpose?

Yes it can. Although it may carry a lower rate, the new mortgage amount will be higher than the old mortgage — if only by the amount of transaction costs. These costs vary but are always significant. Usually (but not always), the new mortgage will have a lower constant debt service payment, so there will be some annual savings resulting from the lower interest rate. In exchange, the partnership will have increased the principal amount of its debt, and thus it will have reduced the property's net residual value.

The soundness of a refinancing to reduce existing debt cost depends on holding the new mortgage long enough to make the cumulative debt service saving during that holding period exceed the decreased residual value. Any refinancing, therefore, involves the concept of a *payback period*. The partnership must be certain that it will not sell or refinance the property before the payback period expires. When the new mortgage has a rate that is subject to future adjustment, the payback period should be shorter than the period for which the rate is fixed.

Mortgages are usually held for surprisingly short periods. The median home mortgage, for instance, is prepaid after about seven years. The typical income-producing rental property changes ownership (and, therefore, its financing) roughly every ten years.

The partnership must satisfy itself that not only is the refinancing better than the current mortgage, but that the refinancing is as good as or better than mortgages that might otherwise become available during the payback period.

As a rule of thumb, a refinancing that requires a payback period of more than five years is unwise. Too many things can happen in five years.

PROVIDING NECESSARY OR DESIRABLE CAPITAL TO THE PROPERTY

Developers forced to operate properties with too little operating capital inevitably make decisions that help short-run cash flow but hurt long-run value. Time and again, such shortsightedness proves painfully costly.

A property that needs capital for physical improvements can raise it from only two sources: (1) additional contributions from the partners or (2) refinancing to liquidate equity buildup and make it available for reinvestment in the property.

In order to examine the implications of using the proceeds of a refinancing for physical improvements, the partnership must consider both benefits and costs.

Financial impact of improvements. Most well-designed capital improvement programs generate more net operating income (NOI) than the increased debt service required to pay for them. Recarpet vacant apartments, for example, and they are much more easily rented. Repaint and replace appliances, and the apartment's rent may be raised. An analyst must be careful, however, to count only that portion of anticipated increase in NOI *that results from the improvements* and to exclude NOI increases attributable to external factors (inflation or improved local economy).

Alternative capital sources. If there was no refinancing, would the repairs go undone? If another funding source is available (e.g., a contribution from the partners), then the question is no longer one of improvements. Instead, the issue would be how to choose among the alternative sources of capital. . . .

CASH DISTRIBUTIONS TO THE PARTNERS

If the refinancing will produce excess distributable cash, the partners must compare the refinancing costs to the after-tax benefits. Because the proceeds are matched by an increase in partnership indebtedness, a distribution of refinancing proceeds is tax-free. Partners should compare the after-tax rate at which they can reinvest the distribution to the after-tax borrowing cost of the money. . . .

RESCHEDULING CURRENT INDEBTEDNESS

The last reason to refinance is the simplest. If the current mortgage is in default, or if it will shortly balloon, the partnership *must* refinance or face the loss of its property and all the associated equity buildup. Here, the question is not *whether* to refinance, but *how*. . . .

NOTES AND QUESTIONS

1. Refinancing to Cash Out Equity and Provide Working Capital. Returning to the previous hypothetical, Dan Developer could translate the accumulated equity in the office building (amounting to $20 million) into cash while continuing to operate the project by means of a sale and leaseback instead of refinancing the Ace mortgage or obtaining a second mortgage on the property. What factors might prompt Dan to favor the sale and leaseback over the debt financing option? See Chapter 8B1.

Dan may decide to refinance the Ace mortgage so that he can reinvest the net refinancing proceeds elsewhere. This presupposes that Dan will be able to obtain an after-tax rate of return that is higher than the after-tax cost of borrowing the extra money. However, any such decision will be influenced by the time value of money; and no refinancing proposal can be fully evaluated without taking into account some discounted cash-flow analysis such as a determination of present value (NPV) or internal rate of return (IRR). See discussion at Chapter 2A, note 3. Indeed, a slight change in refinancing terms (e.g., brokerage commission, kicker geared to gross income, a fraction of a percentage point change in stated interest) caused by a concession or demand on a particular bargaining point could mean a difference of several thousand dollars over the term of the new mortgage loan because of the time value of money. See, e.g., Hayes, Making the Right Refinancing Choices, 8 Real Est. Rev. 92 (Summer 1978). Under such a time-value analysis the real estate owner must identify and evaluate the timing of the cash inflows and outflows associated with the contemplated refinancing arrangement, including the following:

1. the net proceeds from the new loan (gross proceeds less the repayment of the existing loan, transactional expenses, and tax impact);
2. the difference in the annual loan payments;
3. the difference in the annual tax savings from the interest payments; and
4. the difference in the loan balances and prepayment fees.

For example, let us assume that Dan's office building project is now worth $40 million and, after holding the property for five years, Dan (who has a marginal tax rate of 28 percent) decides to refinance

Table 9-1

Net Proceeds from Refinancing

Gross proceeds from new loan	$ 30,000,000
After-tax cost of loan origination fee ("points") on new loan [$300,000 − (300,000 × .72)] / 5	(256,800)
Repayment of old loan	(20,000,000)
After-tax cost of prepayment fee on old loan ($20 million × .02 × .72)[a]	(288,000)
Net proceeds from refinancing	$ 9,455,200

Table 9-2

Annual Difference in Tax Savings

(1) Year[b]	(2) Annual interest payment, new loan	(3) Annual interest payment, old loan	(4) Difference in interest payment (2) − (3)	(5) Tax rate	(6) Increase in tax savings (4) × (5)
1	$3,594,142	$1,967,049	$1,627,093	.28%	$455,586
2	3,580,335	1,837,112	1,743,223	.28%	488,102
3	3,564,777	1,693,569	1,871,208	.28%	523,938
4	3,547,246	1,534,995	2,012,251	.28%	563,430
5	3,527,492	1,359,817	2,167,675	.28%	606,949

Table 9-3

Summary of Cash Inflows and Outflows

(1) Year	(2) Net refinancing proceeds	(3) Difference in loan payments	(4) Difference in tax savings from interest	(5) After-tax Difference in prepayment penalties[a]	(6) Difference in loan balances	(7) Net cash flow (sum of (2) thru (6))
0	+$9,455,200	0	0	0	0	$ 9,455,200
1	0	−$479,190	+$455,586	0	0	−$ 23,604
2	0	−$479,190	+$488,102	0	0	−$ 8,912
3	0	−$479,190	+$523,938	0	0	+$ 44,748
4	0	−$479,190	+$563,430	0	0	+$ 84,240
5	0	−$479,190	+$606,949	−$421,905	−$16,654,794	−$16,948,940

[a] For income tax purposes, a prepayment penalty is deductible in the year of payment. Hence, the after-tax cost is calculated by multiplying the amount of the item by (1 − tax rate). By contrast, the origination fee ("points") must be amortized over the 5-year life of the new loan; however, the tax savings amount is minimal and thus was ignored in the example.

[b] Observe that year one is the sixth year of the holding period, year two is the seventh year, etc.

in order to obtain funds for another investment opportunity. Ace (or some other lender) is willing to make a new loan (based on a 75 percent loan-to-value ratio) of $30 million at 12 percent interest, amortized monthly over 30 years. Origination fees on the new loan would amount to 1 percent, or $300,000, and the commitment for the new loan requires a prepayment fee amounting to 2 percent of the outstanding principal balance if the loan is discharged after the third year and before the tenth year of its term. As indicated in the master hypothetical at Chapter 5B, the cost of constructing the office building and acquiring the underlying land was funded by a first mortgage loan with Ace of $25 million at 10 percent interest, amortized monthly over 15 years, with a 2 percent prepayment fee. At present the outstanding balance on the existing loan (at the end of the fifth loan year) is approximately $20 million; at the end of ten years it will be $12,644,171. Dan plans to sell the property five years after the mortgage is refinanced and to use the sale proceeds to satisfy the unpaid balance on the new mortgage and its prepayment fee. See Tables 9-1, 9-2, and 9-3.

Now take out your calculators and determine by trial and error the interest rate that equates the present value of the net cash outflows in years 1 to 5 (as reflected in column (7) of Table 9-3) to the net refinancing proceeds. (The computational procedures are shown in Chapter 2A, note 3.) This number, whatever it is, is the "internal rate of return." From the perspective of a real estate owner seeking to raise capital for alternative investment opportunities, the IRR is a sophisticated yardstick that takes into account the time value of cash inflows (e.g., net refinancing proceeds) and cash outflows (e.g., extra loan payments on the new mortgage) along with the federal income tax consequences (extra interest deductions on the new mortgage) associated with the proposed refinancing. Thus Dan can precisely measure the effective cost of raising the necessary capital by means of a refinancing and weigh this against the cost of other sources of capital (such as a second mortgage loan) and against the anticipated yields from alternative investments in the same degree-of-risk category. Obviously, Dan need not reinvest the net proceeds. He may prefer to use the funds to renovate or expand the property. Moreover, refinancing at a later date may be more advantageous inasmuch as his costs and opportunities will change over time. From the perspective of the lender the IRR represents the effective yield from a proposed loan, and the impact on the yield from kickers geared to net or gross income can be readily taken into account by simply adjusting the interest income stream for the applicable time period involved. See generally Dillon and Stambaugh, Refinancing Mortgages, 158 J. Acct. 107 (July 1984); Friedman, When Homeowners Should Refinance, 11 Real Est. Rev. 24 (Spring 1981); Hayes, Making the Refinancing Choice, 8 Real Est. Rev. 92

(Summer 1978); Valachi, Refinancing a Personal Residence, 11 Real Est. Rev. 73 (Winter 1982).

   2. Refinancing to Reduce the Cost of Existing First Mortgage Indebtedness.   The same discounted cash flow analysis is commonly used by real estate professionals to evaluate a refinancing choice when the purpose of the proposed refinancing is to reduce the amount of the debt-service payments on the first mortgage loan (comprised of interest and amortization) and thereby increase the amount of cash flow from the property when the interest rate on the new mortgage is lower than that on the existing one or when the term of the new mortgage exceeds the remaining term on the existing mortgage. As a rule of thumb, the decision to refinance the same loan amount at a lower interest rate or for a longer term makes sense when the transactional costs of refinancing (including loan origination fees, prepayment penalties, and closing expenses on the new mortgage) will be more than offset by reduced monthly debt-service payments during the term of the new loan before the property is resold. Therefore, the key determinant is whether the interest rate differential is large enough or the holding period on the new mortgage (the "payback period") is long enough to justify the costs of the refinancing transaction. Or, in time-value terms, the net present value of the savings must exceed the amount of the front-end transactional costs. See Chapter 2B, note 3. If the borrower pays for transaction costs out of its own pocket it stops earning interest on the cash expended; consequently, the lost income must be regarded as an additional cost of the refinancing transaction. Alternatively, if the borrower funds the transactional costs by increasing the amount of the new mortgage indebtedness, the amount of the future savings in debt-service payments will decrease, but they still must be sufficient in amount to offset the increase in loan indebtedness that will be due when the property is sold.
   A simplified technique based on the net present value (NPV) approach (discussed at chapter 2A, note 3) enables homeowners to incorporate the time value of money into the decision-making process. As illustrated by the following example, the NPV calculation balances the costs of refinancing against the benefits based on the transactional costs, the interest rate differential between the original and the new loan, the varying terms of the original and new loans, and the age of the original loan. These costs and benefits are compared in equivalent dollars of purchasing power, and by using the NPV approach the homeowner can measure how long it will take for the benefits of refinancing (the lower monthly debt-service payments) to offset or precisely equal the costs of refinancing, or, in time value terms, how long it will take for the NPV to equal zero. In the example that follows, for the refinancing to be worthwhile, the property owner must

Example

Assumptions:

- Original loan $50,000, 30 years, 15%
- Refinancing at end of 5th year at 13%, 30-year term
- New loan value of $49,360 (original loan balance at end of 5th year)
- $2,500 costs to refinance
- Discount rate equals rate of new loan

Calculations:

- Original loan payment = $7,587 yearly
- New loan payment = $6,522 yearly
- Yearly payment differential = $1,034
- Loan balance differentials (original-new):

End-of-year	Difference
6	$49,165 - 49,217 = -52$
7	$48,935 - 49,054 = -199$
8	$48,675 - 48,866 = -191$
9	$48,370 - 48,654 = -284$

NPV (end year 6) =
$$.885 \,(1,034 - 52) - 2,500 = -1,631$$
NPV (end year 7) =
$$.885 \,(1,034) + .7831 \,(1,034 - 119) - 2,500 = -868$$

NPV (end year 8) =
$$.885 \,(1,034) + .7831 \,(1,034) +$$
$$.6931 \,(1,034 - 191) - 2,500 = -191$$

NPV (end year 9) =
$$.6931 \,(1,034) + .6133 \,(1,034 - 284) - 2,500 = +401$$

Years until NPV = 0: $3 + (191/540) = 3.35$

continue to own the residence for 3.35 years in order to offset the costs of refinancing with the differentials in monthly payments. If the new loan is held for a longer period than is required for the NPV of the various cash flows to reach zero (e.g., more than 3.35 years), the homeowner will experience positive NPV amounts and start to profit from the decision to refinance.

The simplified assumptions underlying the example are as follows:

1. The original loan amount was $50,000 at an annual interest rate of 15 perent with a self-amortizing (full amortization) term of 30 years;
2. The costs of refinancing would amount to $2,500.

3.   The new loan also has a self-amortizing term of 30 years;
4.   The discount rate in the net present value calculation is the interest rate of the new mortgage loan.

The example appears in Jacobs and Tyson, It May Not Pay to Refinance an Old Loan, 16 Real Est. Rev. 84, 85–87 (Fall 1986); see also Rupple, Shilling, and Cirmans, Does It Pay to Refinance an FRM with an ARM?," 15 Real Est. Rev. 79 (Fall 1985).

While the foregoing discounted cash-flow analysis might be appropriate for homeowners, it is too simplistic for refinancing decisions involving large commercial real estate loans in that it fails to take into account the federal income tax consequences of decreasing the interest payments during the holding period and the extra interest that might be earned if the amount of the transactional costs were invested elsewhere. However, it does take into account the principal balances of the two loans. In that regard the age of the original loan at refinancing has a direct effect on the time period that the property must be held before a refinancing becomes plausible. By way of review, why is this so in the case of a constant payment mortgage where each payment is allocable to variable amounts of interest and amortization? See Chapter 5B4; Jacobs and Tyson, at 85–87. See generally Hayes, Making the Right Refinancing Choice, 8 Real Est. Rev. 92 (Summer 1978); Valachi, Refinancing a Personal Residence, 11 Real Est. Rev. 73 (Winter 1982).

   3.   Refinancing at a Lower Interest Rate Increases the Value of the Real Estate.   One of the truisms of real estate investing is that, assuming everything else remains the same, a decline in interest rates will increase the value of real estate. As you know by now, real estate investors are leverage-minded; therefore, mortgage debt-service payments typically represent a large percentage of a project's annual operating expenses and cash flow requirements. Therefore, even a modest decline in the mortgage rate of interest can cause a significant increase in net operating income and thereby enhance the market value of the project (as measured by a capitalization of the increased earnings). See discussion at Chapter 5B1, note 2. Returning to the master hypothetical, let us assume that the office building project costing $33 million yields an annual free and clear return of 15 percent (instead of 12 percent), or $5 million net rent (instead of $4 million) (after all expenses other than income taxes and mortgage payments) and that Dan obtains the same loan terms from Ace except that the interest rate on the $25 million mortgage (amortized over 15 years) is 8 percent rather than 10 percent. His constant monthly payment of principal and interest would be $192,954 instead of $227,175, and therefore as a consequence of the 2 percent rate reduction his annual pretax net income would increase from $2,273,900 to $2,684,552. After applying a capitalization rate of 7 percent, the market value of the project would increase from $32,484,285

($2,273,900 ÷ 7 percent) to $38,350,743 ($2,684,552 ÷ 7 percent), an increase in market value of $5,866,458.

4. Circumventing Prepayment Charges On Refinancing. Recall that if a borrower were to default on the mortgage or collateral loan documents the lender could exercise its pre-foreclosure remedies including entering into possession or collecting rents pursuant to an assignment of leases and rents. In addition, the lender might be willing to reschedule the debt-service payments on the defaulted loan pursuant to some "workout" arrangement if the borrower is unable to pay current expenses. See Chapter 10A, 10B2, and 10B4. If all else fails the lender would most probably accelerate the loan indebtedness proceedings, in which event the borrower could exercise its equitable right of redemption by tendering the unpaid balance and thus terminate the loan and mortgage lien. See Chapter 4A and Chapter 10B1. In such event, would a lender who accelerates the mortgage debt be able to collect a prepayment fee out of the net foreclosure sale proceeds or add the charge to the amount needed to redeem the mortgage when such prepayment was caused by the borrower's inability to make debt-service payments on the mortgage, notwithstanding the borrower's good-faith attempt to do so? There is case authority holding that, absent language to the contrary, when the lender accelerates because of default no prepayment fee is payable because "acceleration, by definition, advances the maturity date of the debt so that payment thereafter is not prepayment but instead is payment made after maturity." In re LHD Realty Corp., 726 F.2d 327 (7th Cir. 1984). Other courts have likewise ruled that the prepayment charge should not apply when the lender decides to accelerate the mortgage indebtedness after default because such prepayment is precipitated by the election of the lender and not by the voluntary act of the borrower. See Kilpatrick v. Germania Life Insurance Co., 183 N.Y. 163, 75 N.E. 1124 (1905) (improper for mortgagee to include prepayment fee in amount needed by borrower for redemption); George H. Nutman, Inc. v. Aetna Business Credit, 115 Misc. 2d 168, 453 N.Y.S.2d 586 (1982) (lender precluded from collecting fee after parties had agreed to settle foreclosure litigation and defaulting borrower was about to sell property). However, if the agreed-on prepayment clause in the existing mortgage (which is usually negotiated at the commitment stage) is broadly phrased so that the charge applies to any and all prepayments including those triggered by debt acceleration and regardless of whether the prepayment is voluntary or not, the prevailing view among commentators is that freedom-of-contract principles should prevail; thus the fee amount should be included as part of the unpaid mortgage indebtedness. See G. Nelson and D. Whitman, Real Estate Finance Law §6.3 (2d ed. 1985); see also M. Madison and J. Dwyer, The Law of Real Estate Financing ¶3104[5] (1981). To date there are at least two case decisions in accord with this view. Pacific Trust Co. TTEE v. Fidelity Federal Savings and Loan Assn., 184 Cal. App. 3d 817, 229 Cal. Rptr. 269 (6th Dist. 1986); Golden Forest Props. v. Columbia Savings & Loan Assn., 248 Cal. Rptr. 316 (Cal. App. 1988).

Suppose, however, that a borrower who wishes to refinance is discouraged by a steep prepayment charge or barred from refinancing during the initial lock-in period, when no prepayments are allowed. See Chapter 5B5. It might be possible for the borrower to circumvent the prepayment charge and lock-in restriction by intentionally defaulting on the loan, thereby compelling the lender to accelerate. Having arranged more favorable financing, the borrower could then redeem the property prior to foreclosure by paying the accelerated mortgage indebtedness (which would not include the prepayment charge), or the borrower or its affiliate could purchase the property at the foreclosure sale, as the case may be. The court in *In re LHD Realty Corp.* suggested by way of dictum that such a ploy was implausible because it would adversely affect the borrower's credit rating and because the lender might be able to avoid acceleration by electing to sue merely for the overdue payments as they mature. 726 F.2d, at 331. Suppose, however, that the prepayment fee is substantial (an initial percentage of 5 percent or more is not atypical for commercial real estate loans) and that the loan is nonrecourse, so the borrower could not be sued for each installment as it becomes due. In your opinion, should this stratagem work for a borrower who intentionally defaults? If not, why not? Compare G. Nelson and D. Whitman §6.3. with Sanders, Commercial Prepayment Fees: A New Legal Frontier, 60 Fla. Bar J. 69(2) (June 1986). To protect themselves, lenders have been including phraseology in their prepayment clauses to the effect that on any default that results in debt acceleration, a tender of payment prior to a foreclosure sale shall constitute a willful evasion of the prepayment terms and be deemed a voluntary prepayment with regard to which the charge shall apply. See Madison and Dwyer, supra, at ¶3.04[5]. However, it's uncertain whether this draftsmanship approach will work. Teachers Insurance and Annuity Assn. v. Butler, 626 F. Supp. 1229, 1235 (dictum) (S.D.N.Y. 1986). If not, can you think of any strategy that lenders might employ to protect themselves? See Ominsky, Locked-In Borrowers May Have Found a Hole in the Hen Coop, ACREL Newsletter 3 (Feb. 1987); Stark, Enforcing Prepayment Charges: Case Law and Drafting Suggestions, 22 Real Prop., Prob. & Tr. J. 549, 557, 559-560 (Fall 1987).

5. *Tax Aspects of Refinancing.* A fundamental principle of our system of taxation is that although income is taxable, cash flow is not; hence, the act of borrowing money is not a taxable event. Although the borrower receives money, it has a reciprocal obligation to repay the same; therefore the borrower receives no economic benefit and its net assets remain the same. Thus net refinancing proceeds are not

subject to taxation even if the owner of real estate "mortgages out," that is, obtains loan proceeds in excess of its tax basis in the mortgaged property. See Woodsam Assocs. v. Commissioner, 16 T.C. 649 (1951), affd., 198 F.2d 357 (2d Cir. 1952). However, while a prepayment charge is deductible as a current expense (Rev. Rul. 57-198, 1957-1 C.B. 94), loan origination fees, or "points," and commitment fees generally must be amortized over the life of the loan regardless of whether the borrower is a cash-basis or accrual-basis taxpayer. Rev. Rul. 81-160, 1981-1 C.B. 312; Rev. Rul. 81-161, 1981-1 C.B. 313. C.f. Rev. Rul. 87-22, 1987-1 C.B. 146 (since a refinanced mortgage does not finance either the purchase or improvement of a house, I.R.C. §461(g)(2) does not apply; thus points must likewise be amortized over the life of the new home mortgage). See generally Banoff, Tax Aspects of Real Estate Refinancing and Debt Restructuring: The Best and Worst of Times, 64 Taxes 926 (December 1986).

Another tax sweetener associated with refinancing is that in the case of income-producing real estate with respect to which the tax shelter benefits are waning a refinancing by means of a constant payment mortgage may resuscitate the tax shelter for the owner of the property. Can you think of the reason why? See Chapter 2B, note 2.

B.   SECONDARY FINANCING

Like refinancing, secondary financing is used both to translate equity into tax-free cash and to leverage the cost of acquiring real estate. However, in contrast to refinancing, a second mortgage (or other subsequent mortgage) supplements rather than replaces a first mortgage; hence, the former is (or becomes) junior in lien priority to the latter. In real estate jargon secondary, or junior, debt financing, consisting of ordinary second mortgages, wraparound mortgages, gap loans, purchase-money mortgages, and other types of junior mortgages, is the "grease" that makes a project operate or sell more easily because it provides the extra funds that may be needed by a real estate owner or purchaser.

Returning to our master hypothetical, suppose that Dan Developer owns an office building project now worth $40 million that is encumbered by a first mortgage loan held by Ace Insurance Company that has been scaled down to $20 million. Suppose further that Dan wants to translate one-half of the accumulated equity ($10 million) into cash for the purpose of renovating the property. As observed at Chapter 9A, supra, secondary financing is usually unattractive when interest rates decline below the first mortgage rate because a developer could simply refinance the existing mortgage at the lower market rate and pay any necessary prepayment charges. However, if first mortgage interest rates were to escalate and the first mortgage note held by Ace does not contain a due-on-encumbrance clause, it might be less expensive, on the whole, for Dan to pay a higher rate of interest on a small amount of new second mortgage money than to refinance the existing first mortgage at the increased rate for first mortgage money. If Dan favors secondary financing he can obtain either a conventional second mortgage or a special type of second mortgage called a "wraparound mortgage." A wraparound mortgage is most feasible when the interest rate on the first mortgage is substantially below the current market rate for first mortgage money. A conventional second mortgage loan tends to be expensive and relatively short-term in nature and may require interest charges and debt-service payments that Dan may not be able or willing to pay. By contrast, a wraparound mortgage may enable Dan to reduce his overall interest expenses and debt-service payments because the interest rate for wraparound financing ordinarily would be lower than what Dan would be charged for either refinancing or for conventional secondary financing. In addition, the term of a wraparound mortgage generally coincides with the remaining term of the existing first mortgage and is therefore longer than the term of an ordinary second mortgage.

An "additional-funds" wraparound mortgage is a second mortgage whereby the wraparound lender makes a cash advance to the borrower, and also, by prior arrangement between the parties, agrees to make debt-service payments on the underlying first mortgage that would otherwise be made by the borrower. The face amount of the wraparound indebtedness is overstated so that the lien of the wraparound mortgage not only covers the funds actually disbursed but also "wraps around" the unpaid balance on the existing first mortgage loan. Since the wraparound mortgage interest rate is always higher than the rate on the first mortgage, the wraparound lender is able to take advantage of the interest rate spread as to the unpaid balance on the first mortgage and thereby increase the effective rate of interest it earns on the additional funds that are actually disbursed. This leveraged yield is what enables the wraparound lender to charge less than the market rate of interest for a first mortgage loan or a conventional second mortgage loan.

To illustrate the concept let us return to our hypothetical and assume that five years after the office building project is completed and the Ace loan is closed Dan wants to cash out his equity, assuming that:

1. for simplicity's sake, all of the debt-financing alternatives discussed below are non-amortizing interest-only loans that are repayable in single lump-sum ("balloon") payments at the end of their respective terms;

2.   at a loan-to-value ratio of 75 percent, the net financing proceeds would amount to no more than $10 million (75 percent of $40 million market value less outstanding first mortgage debt of $20 million);

3.   the current market rates of interest for first and second mortgage loans are 15 percent and 18 percent, respectively;

4.   the existing first mortgage loan with Ace, which has been scaled down to $20 million for simplicity's sake, provides for an annual interest rate of 12 percent (rather than 10 percent); the current loan also requires a prepayment fee of 2 percent and has a remaining term of 10 years; and

5.   a wraparound lender offers to advance Dan $10 million, to be secured by a wraparound mortgage in the face amount of $30 million ($10 million of new money plus the $20 million balance on the Ace mortgage) with an annual interest-only rate of 14 percent, repayable in one lump sum at the end of 10 years, when the Ace mortgage reaches maturity.

If Dan were to refinance the Ace mortgage with a new $30 million 10-year first mortgage loan at the market rate of 15 percent, he would receive net refinancing proceeds of $9,600,000 (75 percent of $40 million market value less outstanding debt of $20 million less prepayment fee of $400,000) and be required to make annual interest-only payments of $4,500,000 ($30 million principal balance × 15 percent rate of interest) for the balance of the 10-year term. By contrast, wraparound financing for the same term would be available at the lower rate of 14 percent; in that case Dan's annual interest payment would be reduced to $4,200,000 ($30 million principal balance × 14 percent rate of interest). Moreover, under wraparound financing the Ace mortgage would remain intact, so no prepayment fee would be required. By charging Dan a rate of 14 percent on the $30 million face amount, the wraparound lender would take advantage of the two-point spread (as to the first mortgage loan balance of $20 million) between what it would pay Ace each year at the 12 percent rate ($2,400,000) and what it would receive from Dan at the 14 percent rate ($2,800,000) and use the excess amount ($400,000) to increase its effective yield on the monies advanced ($10 million) from 14 percent to 18 percent ($400,000 excess plus $1,400,000 interest received on the new money = $1,800,000, divided by the $10 million of new money).[7] The extra leveraged yield of 4 percent is what enables the

7. To calculate the yield to the wraparound lender take the sum of the excess interest earned on the balance of the first mortgage indebtedness (what the wraparound lender receives less what it pays as interest on the underlying debt) and the interest earned at the wraparound rate on the monies actually disbursed and then divide this sum by the disbursement amount. In the case of partially or fully amortizing loans the

wraparound lender to charge Dan less than the prevailing rate for first mortgage money and also be compensated for the additional risk associated with taking a junior lien position and possibly assuming Dan's obligations to Ace. As explained in the excerpt from Oharenko, infra, it is possible that if Dan were to obtain a conventional second mortgage loan his interest expenses would be comparable to what he would pay for wraparound financing. In our example, the annual interest payment on a second mortgage loan in the amount of $10 million at the market rate of 18 percent ($1,800,000), when combined with the first mortgage interest payment of $2,400,000, would cost him $4,200,000, the same annual interest payment that would be required on the wraparound mortgage loan. However, as explained in the excerpt by Gunning infra, wraparound financing is usually less expensive than conventional secondary financing (during the term of the first mortgage) because of the lower contract rate and the absence of the other financing costs (such as extra points and other front-end fees) that typify the latter kind of financing. Of greatest significance, however, is that institutional lenders usually require that mortgage loans be self- or partially amortized, and since a conventional second mortgage would most likely be for a shorter term (e.g., five years or less) the resultant increase in debt-service payments might render secondary financing too burdensome for Dan. Consequently, in most cases wraparound financing will be more attractive provided Dan and the wraparound lender can resolve the special legal obstacles (e.g., usury restrictions, lien priority, mortgage tax, and title insurance problems) posed by wraparound financing.

In addition to translating equity into cash, wraparound financing can be tailored to the cash needs of the borrower. Suppose for example that the existing first mortgage loan requires heavy debt-service payments yet the borrower is reluctant to refinance the mortgage because it has a low interest rate and market rates are escalating. The borrower can use wraparound financing at a below-market rate to reduce its debt service payments by deferring amortization (e.g., interest-only wraparound loan with ballooning principal), by deferring interest, or by extending the term of the wraparound loan beyond the original maturity date. By reducing the annual constant (percentage of loan amount required to service the debt), the borrower can obtain greater comfort in its ability to operate the property with a cash flow and equity yield satisfactory to its investors before it eventually sells or refinances the property.

---

yield will change after the first period to reflect the variations in amortization between the wraparound mortgage and the underlying mortgage. In such event you should consult a wraparound yield table to calculate the exact yield. See, e.g., Yield Table for Wrap-Around Mortgages (Financial Publishing Co., 1973).

In addition to converting equity into tax-free capital, developers and purchasers use junior mortgages to leverage their costs of improving and acquiring real estate. For example, returning to the master hypothetical at Chapter 5B, Dan plans to construct an office building (at a cost of $25 million) and to purchase the underlying fee from Francine Farmer, an investor in raw land (for a price of $8 million) and to finance these costs by means of an ordinary first mortgage loan on the fee from Ace Insurance Company in the amount of $25 million. This presupposes that when the project is completed the land and improvements will be worth $33 million and that the fee mortgage loan is being made at a loan-to-value ratio of 75 percent. Since the total cost of the land and improvements is $33 million, Dan must raise equity capital in the amount of $8 million to fund the balance of the venture costs. As explained at Chapter 8A, it may be possible for Dan to leverage his cost of making use of the land by obtaining an ordinary leasehold mortgage loan that does not encumber the fee. For example, if Dan were to ground lease the underlying land from Francine Farmer (instead of purchasing it) and obtain a leasehold mortgage loan at the same loan-to-value ratio of 75 percent, he would have to raise venture capital of only $6,250,000 to fund the remaining cost of constructing the improvements. Alternatively, however, Dan may be able to use a form of secondary financing called the subordinated purchase money mortgage to separately finance the cost of acquiring the land. By this method Dan would be able to reduce his cash outlay to only $800,000, and, in contrast to leasehold mortgage financing, he would not have to forfeit fee simple title to the underlying land. A purchase money mortgage is a mortgage taken back by a seller to secure the purchaser's promise to pay the remainder of the purchase price or a mortgage obtained by a third-party lender to secure purchase funds advanced to the purchaser. Like the installment land contract, which is examined at Chapter 9C, infra, the purchase money mortgage has traditionally been associated with high-ratio seller financing, wherein the purchaser of some real estate such as raw land is only able to borrow or raise part of the purchase price from outside sources and the seller agrees to accept a small down payment and allow the purchaser to pay the balance of the purchase price in installments over a designated period of time. In contrast to an installment land contract, however, the installment indebtedness is immediately secured by a purchase money mortgage lien on the land so that the purchaser obtains the legal title to the property without waiting until the indebtedness is fully repaid.

To illustrate, let us return to our hypothetical. Suppose the fee owner, Francine Farmer, agrees to separately finance Dan's purchase of the underlying land by taking back a purchase money mortgage at a high loan-to-value ratio — say, 90 percent. In order for Dan to later obtain his development financing Francine must also agree to subordinate her purchase money mortgage to the liens of any subsequently recorded construction or postconstruction mortgages to be held by institutional lenders such as the Fuller National Bank and the Ace Insurance Company. In that event Dan could reduce his net cash outlay to only $800,000 because, as the new fee owner, he could include the underlying land once as security for Ace's first mortgage loan on the land and the completed improvements and again as collateral for Francine's second mortgage loan on the fee. Hence, the total $33 million cost of the project would be supported by cumulative financing in the amount of $32.2 million ($25 million from Ace plus $7,200,000 from Francine).[8]

Gunning, The Wraparound Mortgage . . . Friend or U.F.O.?
2 Real Est. Rev. 35, 36-48 (Summer 1972)

UTILIZATION

This unusual financing arrangement takes various forms, shaped primarily by the purpose it is to serve. Before examining these variations in detail, we might first consider the particular circumstances when each can best be utilized.

THE BORROWER'S OBJECTIVES

A borrower will have a real incentive to consider WA financing in the following situations:

(1) When additional financing is desired but the present mortgage holder is unwilling or unreasonable in his demands, and the mortgage permits no prepayment, or prepayment only with an exorbitant penalty; at the same time, conventional secondary financing is too costly in rate and too heavy in debt service.

(2) When the existing first mortgage rate is very low and terms are otherwise quite favorable, but the borrower desires additional financing which the first mortgagee will not advance at a favorable rate. Conventional secondary financing would not meet these requirements.

(3) When the existing first mortgage is satisfactory in amount but

---

8. This presupposes sufficient rental income to cover the debt-service payments on both mortgages. As suggested in the excerpt by Oharenko, second mortgagees such as Francine frequently tolerate low (e.g., 100 percent) debt coverage ratios and sometimes are willing to defer some or all of the interest or amortization in order to decrease the amount of debt service on the second mortgage. Such deferral produces an increasing principal balance over time, which must be repaid in the form of a balloon payment when the property is sold or refinanced.

borrower desires to obtain debt-service relief to improve his return on equity.

(4) When a commitment for permanent financing is inadequate, although the lender has agreed to lend its statutory maximum, so that additional financing is required but conventional secondary financing would be too expensive and burdensome.

In situations (1) and (2) described above, WA financing is available in the form which herein we call the "additional-funds WA mortgage." Another WA financing form is likewise available for situation (3), to be known as the "extended-term WA mortgage." Situation (4) is remedied with a financing form we call the "simultaneous WA mortgage." All these forms will be described in detail. . . .

THE LENDER'S OBJECTIVES

The WA lender's motivation in each of these situations is quite simple and consistent: He expects to obtain the best possible effective yield, with the least amount of cash investment, yet to have the widest coverage (geographic and property type) with his limited available investment funds.

THE WA FORM GENERALLY

The WA mortgage is a second mortgage subordinate in all cases to an existing first mortgage which remains outstanding and unsatisfied. It differs from the conventional second mortgage in that the face amount overstates the actual indebtedness, and also in that it incorporates a special agreement between the parties for payment of the debt service on the first mortgage. The loan is otherwise evidenced and secured by the usual form of promissory note and second mortgage.

The face amount of the mortgage is the sum of the outstanding balance under the first mortgage plus the amount of additional funds, if any, to be disbursed by the WA mortgagee, with an annual debt service computed on this face amount. The WA mortgage interest rate is always higher than the interest rate on the first mortgage. This contract rate inevitably is equal to, or slightly less than, the then market rate for conventional first mortgage loans. The WA mortgage is, therefore, generally effective only in a high-interest period, and is seldom used in a declining interest rate market. The WA loan term and amortization, relative to the maturity of the first mortgage, will vary according to the purpose of the financing.

It is immediately obvious that, if the *contract* rate is computed on the sum of the first mortgage and any new money advanced, a much higher *effective* rate of interest on the new money will result. This provides the leverage incentive for the WA lender.

Its most distinctive feature, however, is the agreement by the WA lender, upon receipt of debt service on the WA mortgage, to deduct therefrom and remit directly to the first mortgagee the required debt service on the first mortgage. In the extended-term type, there may be a deficit in such debt service which is made up by the WA lender, who then remits the full debt service on the first mortgage. The borrower in all cases expressly agrees not to make any further payments to the first mortgagee on account of the first mortgage.

In some documents the exuberance of the parties has produced language tantamount to an assumption of the first mortgage by the WA lender. The legal effect of assumption, however, is almost always dispelled by conditioning this obligation upon *actual* receipt of the debt service on the WA mortgage. If the WA lender does not receive the debt service on the WA mortgage, there is no obligation to remit the debt service on the first mortgage. Failure to pay debt service on a WA mortgage, of course, constitutes a default under that mortgage.

The WA mortgage will otherwise contain covenants by the borrower identical with those in the first mortgage, including the escrow of taxes and insurance premiums which, upon receipt by the WA lender, will be remitted to the first mortgagee. Of course, the first mortgage cannot contain covenants personal to the borrower and covenants that cannot be cured or complied with by the WA mortgagee.

The WA borrower further agrees to comply with all nonmoney covenants in the first mortgage and, as in any other second mortgage, a default in the first mortgage constitutes a default in the WA mortgage.

The borrower will notify the first mortgagee that the payments of debt service, as well as any prepayment or payment after acceleration, are to be received from the WA lender, on behalf of the borrower. He also authorizes the first mortgagee to accept such payments and where possible, directs the due delivery to the WA lender of all notices, of default or otherwise, required to be given by the lender under the first mortgage.

Highly desirable, from the WA lender's viewpoint, is an agreement, where obtainable, by the first mortgagee to give the WA lender notice of and opportunity to cure all defaults on the part of the borrower under the first mortgage.

A first mortgagee might consider the possibility of cure by the WA lender to be additional security for his loan. On the other hand, the opposite reaction may result where the WA financing has the effect of locking in a first mortgagee to an unsatisfactory low-interest loan for which he would rather receive prepayment.

As an added measure of security, it is also desirable that the first mortgage, in fact, be prepayable, even with penalty. In a distress situation, the WA lender's inevitable remedy is to satisfy the prior lien as quickly as possible and regardless of the penalty. As to any such prepayment penalty, the WA lender might consider taking a deposit or a separate and personal undertaking of payment by the borrower. This separate arrangement is recommended, since the amount of the penalty is not included in the mathematics of the WA transaction.

In the additional-funds WA mortgage and the simultaneous WA mortgage, the face amount in excess of the first mortgage balance is disbursed at the time of closing. This is the only actual advance of funds made by the WA lender unless there is a balloon in the first mortgage, and except also in a distress situation where advances are made to cure defaults of the borrower, including possibly the payoff of the first mortgage. The payments remitted monthly on the first mortgage are not actually additional disbursements by the WA lender, since he simply remits all or part of the debt service received from the borrower. For this purpose, he merely acts as a conduit for the payment of the debt service to the first mortgagee.

As a matter of fact, there are two account ledgers maintained for the WA mortgage. One ledger conforms with the regular amortization schedule for a loan in the face amount of the WA mortgage, with interest at the contract rate and for the stated maturity. This particular accounting has no basis in reality and is used simply in the mathematical process. The second ledger is the true picture of the indebtedness and records the actual investment of the WA lender in the property. This latter figure we shall hereinafter call the "net investment." This net investment, at any point in time, is simply the difference in amount between the unamortized balance of the WA mortgage and the unamortized balance of the first mortgage, using in each case their regular amortization schedules.

In the case of the additional-funds and simultaneous WA mortgages, the net investment will consist of the loan proceeds actually advanced out-of-pocket by the WA lender, plus that part of the interest thereon which is earned but not currently paid (i.e., deferred) until the first mortgage has been satisfied or the WA mortgage prepaid. The total interest earned, for any period, on the net investment is equal to the contract interest on the unamortized face amount of the WA mortgage less the interest payable on the first mortgage.

The same amount is obtained by adding contract interest on the net investment plus interest at the differential in rates (between the two mortgages) on the balance outstanding under the first mortgage.

The extent to which earned interest is deferred is determined by the difference in debt service between the WA mortgage and the first mortgage. If the difference in debt service is less than the amount of interest earned, then such excess of earned interest is deferred. The difference in debt service which is retained by the WA lender is the only way in which he receives a return *currently* on his advance, while the first mortgage remains outstanding. The interest earned but deferred will thereafter be recouped either upon prepayment of the net investment or during the payout (according to the amortization schedule) of the WA mortgage following the payoff of the first mortgage.

All of this complicated mathematics is illustrated quite simply in the charts accompanying this article.

In the additional-funds and extended-term WA mortgages, the net investment of the lender generally increases until the first mortgage is paid off; thereafter it commences to amortize. However, in the simultaneous WA mortgage, the net investment of the WA lender is amortizing during the term of the first mortgage. This occurs because the differential in debt service between the WA mortgage and the first mortgage exceeds the amount of earned interest and the excess represents amortization of the net investment.

The form and effect of the WA financing is, however, far better illustrated with the use of specific cases. An example of each type follows.

SPECIFIC FORMS OF WA MORTGAGES

The circumstances of the borrower will influence his financing requirements and in turn will fashion the form of WA mortgage to be used.

A. ADDITIONAL-FUNDS WA MORTGAGE

A developer finds himself in either situation (1)[1] or (2)[2] previously described, and seeks additional financing of $85,000. There is an existing first mortgage in the original principal sum of $100,000, with interest at 6 percent, a constant of 8.6 percent requiring an annual debt service of $8,600, and with full payout in twenty years. After ten years there remains an outstanding balance of $64,500. The existing lender refuses to refinance but WA financing is available as follows: A loan of $85,500 to be secured by a WA mortgage in the amount of $150,000 (i.e.,

---

1. Situation (1): Present mortgage holder is unwilling or unreasonable in his demands; mortgage permits no repayment or permits prepayment only with exorbitant penalty; and conventional secondary financing is too costly in rate and too heavy in debt service.

2. Situation (2): Existing first mortgage rate is low and terms are otherwise favorable, but borrower desires additional financing that is economical.

$85,500 of new money plus the $64,500 balance on the first mortgage), with interest at 7 percent, a constant of 9.3 percent, and fully repayable in twenty years one month, with an annual debt service of $13,950.

The following chart shows the application of the debt service on the two mortgages, according to their respective amortization schedules, during the first year and the amount of interest earned, the amount of interest deferred, and the effective rate of interest on the amount advanced.

Application D/S First Year

	1st Mtge.	WA Mtge.	Differential
Interest	$3,870	$10,500	$6,630
			(Interest earned)
Principal	4,730	3,450	1,280
D/S	$8,600	$13,950	$5,350
Interest Earned	$6,630		
D/S Retained	$5,350		
Interest Earned but not retained (i.e., deferred)	$1,280		

Effective Rate of $\dfrac{\$6,630}{\$85,500}$ = **7¾% or equal to**
Interest Earned   1% × $64,500 + 7% × $85,500

This chart also illustrates the mechanics of the agreement by the WA lender to remit, directly to the first mortgagee, the debt service on the first mortgage. The amount retained, $5,350, is less than the interest earned so that a part of earned interest, $1,280, has been deferred and added to the WA lender's original advance and represents his net investment. The effect of this interest deferral and the resulting increase in net investment is confirmed in [the following chart].

Status at End of First Year

Balance of WA mortgage (owned by mortgagor)	$146,550
Balance of 1st mortgage (owned by WA mortgagee)	– 59,770
"Net investment" WA mortgagee	**$ 86,780**
Original advance	– 85,500
Deferred interest added to WA mortgagee's original investment	$ 1,280

. . . Of considerable concern to any lender is the effective rate of any such transaction over the life of the mortgage, and this is computed in the next chart, . . . which shows also the total interest earned in the same period.

Total Interest Earned Life of WA Mortgage

Annual D/S WA mortgage	$ 13,950
Term	× 20
Total D/S	$279,000
Total D/S 1st mortgage	− 86,000
D/S differential retained	193,000
Amortization original advance	− 85,500
Total net interest earned on $85,500	$107,500

Effective Yield 7.24%

The overall effective rate is less than the effective rate during the first year, and has been reducing all during the term. This follows from the fact that earned interest is the amount of differential interest computed on two differently amortizing balances. This reducing effective rate is the reason a WA lender will permit prepayment in the later years.

Is all the devious exertion worthwhile compared to simple and straightforward conventional secondary financing? Yes, the WA financing is almost always less expensive (during the term of the first mortgage) than conventional secondary financing because of the lower contract rate, the longer term, and the absence of any other financing costs so typical of the latter.

Comparison With Conventional 2nd Mortgage

A. Same Contract Rate

D/S 1st mortgage	$ 8,600.00
D/S 2nd mortgage	7,951.50
Total D/S	16,551.50
D/S WA mortgage	13,950.00
Advantage	$ 2,601.50

After Maturity 1st Mortgage

D/S 2nd mortgage	$ 7,951.50
D/S WA mortgage	13,950.00
Disadvantage	$ 5,998.50

B. Same Effective Rate

D/S 1st mortgage	$ 8,600.00
D/S 2nd mortgage	8,430.30
Total D/S	17,030.30
D/S WA mortgage	13,950.00
Advantage	$ 3,080.30

After Maturity 1st Mortgage

D/S 2nd mortgage	$ 8,430.30
D/S WA mortgage	13,950.00
Disadvantage	$ 5,519.70

To illustrate this premise in the best possible light, assume a secondary mortgage financing in the same amount of new money, $85,500, at the same contract rate of interest, and with identical term, thus requiring an annual debt service of $7,951.50. Assume also that alternate secondary financing, in the desired amount, is likewise available but for a contract rate equal to the effective rate, 7.75 percent, which the WA lender is to receive, for the same term and with debt service at $8,430.30. The advantages of the WA financing over both second mortgages are shown in the [foregoing] chart, . . . but will prevail only during the term of the first mortgage.

The distinction is even more marked when we consider the fact that conventional secondary financing is not likely to be available on the favorable terms that are used in the example. A conventional second mortgage would generally be at a higher rate and for a shorter term than in the example, thereby increasing required debt service.

B.   EXTENDED-TERM WA MORTGAGE

In this case, the intrepid developer suffers with situation (3)[3] and seeks relief as to debt service in order to improve his return on equity.

Assume, then, the same existing first mortgage in the original amount of $100,000, at 6 percent interest for twenty years, requiring a constant of 8.6 percent, and a resulting annual debt service of $8,600. After five years, this loan has been reduced to $87,000, but at this point in time this same debt service now represents a constant drain of 9.88 percent on the indebtedness.

Additional financing in the form of a WA mortgage is obtained in the same amount, $87,000, as the balance under the first mortgage, with contract interest at 7 percent, repayable over twenty years, for a constant of 9.31 percent and an annual debt service of $8,099.70. The borrower has succeeded, therefore, in reducing the amount of debt service he pays, but in turn this necessitates monthly advances by the WA mortgagee to make up the deficit in the debt service to be remitted to the first mortgagee.

The application of debt service, according to the amortization schedules for both mortgages, is shown in the following chart . . . as well as the resulting interest accrual to the WA lender. Without neglecting the fact that the first monthly payment of debt service represented an effective rate of infinity (since there had been no disbursement), also note the astronomical effective rate during the first year. . . .

---

3. Situation (3): Existing first mortgage is satisfactory in amount, but borrower desires to obtain debt-service relief in order to improve his return on equity.

Application of D/S First Year

	1st Mortgage	WA Mortgage	Differential
Interest	$5,220.00	$6,090.00	$ 870.00 (Total interest earned & deferred)
Principal	3,380.00	2,009.70	1,370.30
D/S	$8,600.00	$8,099.70	−$ 500.30 (Annual deficit D/S added by WA Mortgagee)

$$\text{Effective Rate of Interest Earned } \frac{870}{(\frac{1}{2})\ 500.30} = 346\%$$

PREPAYMENT

The right to prepay the first mortgage at any time will be denied to the borrower, and his right to prepay the WA mortgage will be strictly limited. Such restrictions are obviously necessary since the desired effective rate contemplates the continuation to maturity of the first mortgage in order that the differential in interest rate (leveraging) can be enjoyed for the longest possible period. For a like reason, prepayment of the WA mortgage is postponed to the later years — probably ten to fifteen years. A more exact statement is impossible to make, however, since the prepayment provision is always subject to negotiation. The terms of the first mortgage may also materially affect the WA mortgage prepayment provision.

The borrower may also desire a prepayment provision in order to revert to the lower service of the first mortgage. Consequently, the call privilege in the WA mortgage is strenuously negotiated. The penalty payable may very well recognize the loss to lender of the effective rate to maturity.

The WA borrower is, therefore, presented with two alternative amounts necessary to prepay the mortgage:

(1) He can prepay in an amount equal to the unamortized balance of the WA mortgage, according to the amortization schedule, plus penalty, but with an obligation on the part of the WA lender to remit the unamortized balance, if any, on the first mortgage. This presumes the first mortgage, if outstanding, is then prepayable and that a satisfactory arrangement has been made concerning payment of the prepayment penalty (if any) on the first mortgage.

(2) He can also prepay in an amount equal to the net investment plus agreed penalty. This privilege not only has the virtue of simplicity but it also permits the continuation of the first mortgage, if still outstanding.

DEFAULTS AND FORECLOSURE

There cannot be a default in the first mortgage alone, since a default in the first mortgage is automatically a default in the WA mortgage. It is also unlikely there would be a default in the WA mortgage alone, as where a foolhardy borrower attempts to pay the first mortgage and not the WA mortgage. In such a situation, the WA lender would then have the option of foreclosing the WA mortgage either with or without paying off the first mortgage.

The most likely distress situation, however, would involve simultaneous defaults in both mortgages. The nature of the default will shape the WA lender's decision to cure the default or to prepay the first mortgage. Either remedy raises questions as to the priority of the lien securing such advances, and these will be discussed below. The inevitable remedy is the payoff of the first mortgage, which thereby increases the net investment of the WA lender to an amount equal to the then unamortized balance of the WA mortgage (according to the amortization schedule), followed by the foreclosure of the WA mortgage.

A basic prerequisite of the WA lender's remedy is the right to pay off the first mortgage, before or after acceleration, with the complementary obligation on the first mortgagee to accept the tender of such payment.

Although this investment is exhilarating, nonetheless its success must still be grounded upon careful and prudent underwriting. The glitter of this financing jewel is also tarnished to some extent by a number of business and legal imperfections.

PROBLEMS IN THE WA MORTGAGE

The imperfections to which we refer are certain disabilities both familiar and unfamiliar.

VULNERABILITY OF A SECOND MORTGAGE

The lien of the WA mortgage is subordinate to the existing first mortgage, and therefore suffers from many of the infirmities of any inferior lien, the most serious of which is the likelihood of extinction upon a foreclosure of the first mortgage. A number of the usual deficiencies of second mortgages have, however, been eliminated in the WA mortgage because of the notice and cure rights, the prepayment privilege and the other concessions made by the first mortgagee. Others do remain, such as possible incurable defaults and the mandatory application of all of the condemnation award and fire insurance proceeds to reduction of the first mortgage. Any proposed financing must, therefore, be subject to close underwriting scrutiny because of the inherent priority defect. The WA mortgage may, however, also enjoy a security advantage over the conventional second mortgage to the extent that advances made to cure defaults in the first mortgage, under certain circumstances, will have a priority over intervening liens. This subject of priorities is discussed below.

Because it is a second mortgage, the WA mortgage is subject to all statutory requirements for secondary financing which prevail in an increasing number of jurisdictions. The regulation and licensing of secondary lenders is also increasing, and all such legal requirements must be carefully reviewed. . . .

CONCLUSION

There will be no need to hang lanterns tonight in the Old North Church steeple. There is no insidious invasion, and the emergence of this financing intruder is peaceful and welcome. The fears resulting from its proliferation can now be dispelled. Careful examination of its intentions reveals them to be friendly and honorable.

This investment implement has been devised solely to aid deserving borrowers and altruistic lenders in reaching a happy and satisfactory compact. As with any strong stimulant, however, the danger of over-dosage does exist and accordingly it should be kept out of the reach of the neophyte. If due care is exercised in a review of the potential problems herein discussed and all necessary legal precautions are taken, the effect can be salutary.

Oharenko, The Battle of the Juniors: Second Mortgage vs. Wraparound Financing
14 Real Est. Rev. 99 (Fall 1984)

CHARACTERISTICS OF SECOND MORTGAGES

The second mortgage is the most popular junior debt vehicle and one that is easy to understand. Second mortgages may be structured in many formats. They may assume all the forms that first mortgage instruments assume, including fixed rate, variable, participating, and convertible structures. No matter what its structure, however, a second mortgage is secured by a lien that is subordinate to a first mortgage lien.

Comparing the Benefits and Risks of Wraparound and Second Mortgages

	Second Mortgage	Wraparound Mortgage
Borrower Benefits:		
• Favorable existing financing remains undisturbed.	X	X
• Amortization period typically can be arranged to coincide with existing mortgage.	X	X
• During periods of low interest rates, high-rate existing mortgages that are not prepayable can be supplemented with junior mortgage financing, resulting in a lower overall cost of funds.	X	
• During periods of high interest rates, existing mortgages with low rates can be wrapped by a junior mortgage, resulting in a lower overall cost of funds (wraparound).		X
• Greater tax savings result when the new junior mortgage payments begin. A larger portion of interest payments and the depreciation basis of the property is increased by the amount of new money advanced toward funding additional capital improvements.	X	X
• Available for situations where the lender of the existing mortgage refuses prepayments or assesses heavy loan payment penalties for prepayment.	X	X
• Additional debt may be raised when the first mortgage lender has reached its maximum lending limit.	X	X
Borrower Risks:		
• Lenders prefer to issue shorter maturities for junior mortgages than for first mortgages.	X	X
• Higher rates than first mortgages.	X	X
• Many lenders require personal guarantees.	X	X
• When interest rates decrease, combined second and first mortgage rates and terms may be less favorable than refinancing the original first mortgage.	X	X
Lender Benefits:		
• Higher, more attractive yields than with first mortgage financing.	X	X
• Immediate funding opportunities for existing-property financing.	X	X
• New money blended with a below-market, existing mortgage makes possible more creative underwriting than do other mortgage formats.		X

E x h i b i t   2   (cont.)

	Second Mortgage	Wraparound Mortgage
Lender Benefits:		
• The wrap lender's position may be more secure than that of a conventional second mortgage lender because total mortgage payments are forwarded directly to the wrap lender. Should any default occur on the first mortgage, the wrap lender is immediately alerted and may take appropriate action.		X
• Many lenders lack understanding of junior mortgages. Consequently, institutions that offer these financing vehicles have a competitive edge.	X	X
Lender Risks:		
• The secondary lien position.	X	X
• Higher loan-to-value and debt service payments increase default probability.	X	X
• Since first mortgage payments, real estate tax, and insurance escrows may be controlled by first mortgage holder, there may be delay in finding out about default.	X	
• Complicated structuring procedures require competent legal and underwriting personnel.		X

The standard parameters of second mortgages differ from those of first mortgages. Standard yields, terms, debt coverage ratios, prepayment terms, and fees are different. We summarize some of these differences below:

Rates and yields.   Coupon rates of second mortgages are 200 to 300 basis points higher than those of comparable first mortgages. Second mortgages on higher-risk properties may carry coupon rates as high as 600 basis points or more higher than those of first mortgages. Yields are also 200 to 300 basis points above those of comparable first mortgages, and yields on high-risk properties rise proportionately. Variable, graduated, and floating rate structures are available.

Terms.   Although terms range from one to fifteen years, most second mortgages are written for terms of five years or less. Terms are usually less than or equal to the remaining term of existing financing.

Amortization.   Amortization is variable — ten to thirty-five years, depending on existing financing terms and the effective age of the property. Typically, loans for terms of five years or less are interest only loans.

Debt coverage ratios.   Ratios are lower than for comparable first mortgages. Required net income is usually 110 percent to 120 percent of total annual debt service payments. However, it may drop as low as 100 percent of total annual debt service with creative financing.

Loan-to-value ratios.   Loan-to-value ratios are higher than those required for comparable first mortgages. Usually *total* debt is limited to 65 to 75 percent of appraised value based, but creative financing may raise the total debt ratio to 75 to 90 percent of appraised value.

Prepayment penalties.   Many second mortgages permit no prepayment. Some short-term mortgages specify a 5 percent penalty that declines at the rate of 1 percent per year. Others specify a yield recapture formula based on the spread between the current rate (or index) and the stated rate along with the remaining term of the loan.

Funding period.   Second mortgages are usually available with prompt funding, usually thirty to 120 days.

Financing Fees.   Financing fees average 2-3 percent of new money for larger deals (say $2 million or more) and 4-10 percent of new money for smaller deals.

Property types.   Second mortgages are available for most categories of existing property.

Guarantees.   Most second mortgages require personal guarantees for smaller loans and for management-intensive real estate like hotels, nursing homes, and recreational properties. . . .

THE WRAPAROUND VS. THE STRAIGHT SECOND MORTGAGE

Is it wiser to negotiate a straight second mortgage or a wraparound? Second and wraparound mortgages have many features in common and selecting the most advantageous form is often difficult. Exhibit 2 summarizes the benefits and risks associated with each format from both the borrower's and lender's perspective. The exhibit indicates that benefits and risks are about evenly distributed between the two formats. The choice between a second and wraparound mortgage depends upon existing financing terms and current mortgage market conditions. If the existing mortgage has a reasonably long term and features a below-market rate, the borrower would be inclined to choose a wraparound mortgage. On the other hand, if rates in the current mortgage market are lower than those of the existing first mortgage and the borrower is unable to prepay the existing loan, the borrower is probably best off with a second mortgage.

The Mortgage and Real Estate Executive's Report
5 (Mar. 1, 1985)

CASE STUDY OF A WRAP LOAN

Here is an example of a wraparound loan transaction recently arranged by James J. Houlihan, of Houlihan-Parnes, New York City realtors and mortgage specialists. An investor purchased a shopping center in Florida for a total price of $3.1 million, all cash above an existing first mortgage of $1.372 million carrying a 10 percent interest rate and a 1998 maturity. The constant payment on the existing mortgage was $15,500 monthly, or 13.55 percent annual constant. The mortgage was not callable upon sale and the purchaser was obviously reluctant to give up the advantages of a 10 percent loan with 14 years remaining, when current mortgage rates were about 14 percent. At the same time, he was not willing to put up cash of $1.728 million to make up the balance of the price.

WRAP LOAN SOLVES PROBLEM

A solution was found by creating a new wraparound mortgage in the amount of $2.44 million at 12.75 percent interest (approximately 1.25 percent lower than the market rate) for a term of seven years. The constant payment on the wrap loan is 13.05 percent, based on a 30-year payout (i.e., the wrap is a balloon loan). The borrower paid an origination fee of $21,400, or 2 percent of the new money of $1.068 million provided by the new lender.

BENEFITS TO PURCHASER

The purchaser, by using the wrap loan:

- Reduces his cash requirement from $1.728 million to $681,000 (including the origination fee), a decline of 60 percent;
- Increases his monthly debt service from $15,454 to $26,535, an increase of $11,081 (a much smaller increase than that under a new first mortgage at 14 percent); and
- Increases the monthly deduction to $14,488 (more than the increase in debt service because the amortization factor under the wrap loan is lower than under the existing first mortgage).

BENEFITS TO THE NEW LENDER

The wrap lender advances $1.068 million (the difference between $2.44 million face value of the wrap mortgage and $1.372 million existing first mortgage).

The payment spread to the wrap lender is $11,081 per month (the difference between the debt service on the existing mortgage of $15,454 and the new debt service of $26,535). This represents a constant of 12.3 percent. However, over its seven-year life, the loan yields approximately 15.5 percent annually, slightly above the current yield on first mortgages.

The new lender also earns a 2 percent origination fee. . . .

Bell, Negotiating the Purchase-Money Mortgage
7 Real Est. Rev. 51 (Spring 1977)

. . . The purchase-money mortgage must establish a delicate balance. It must restrict the purchaser-mortgagor sufficiently to protect the mortgagee against the deterioration of security or loss of investment. However, it must not be so restrictive as to interfere with the mortgagor's intended use of the property or with his ability to deal adequately with changes in the economic or physical conditions of the property. However, too often neither the buyer nor the seller anticipates his future needs adequately, nor does he fully appreciate the economic or legal effects of the arrangement he is negotiating.

The discussion which follows examines some of the aspects of purchase-money financing (particularly subordinated purchase-money debt) and explores the options by means of which the purchaser-mortgagor and seller-mortgagee can expect to improve their respective positions. . . .

PURCHASE-MONEY MORTGAGE AS A SUBORDINATE LIEN

The purchase-money mortgagee is free to waive his priority over subsequent interests in any manner or subject to any conditions he deems appropriate. Once established, however, the conditions of any subordination will generally be strictly construed against the mortgagee. In practice, purchase-money mortgages frequently are subordinated to future debt because the purchase mortgage is intended to fill a "gap" between the buyer's desired financing and that which he anticipates he will be able to obtain from an institutional lender. Just as often, purchase-money mortgages come into existence as subordinated debt (i.e., second mortgages) because the existing financing on the property which the buyer wants to retain is not sufficient, together with his maximum cash equity, to equal the purchase price.

In analyzing the potential risks inherent in assuming a subordinated position, the seller-mortgagee should consider his own financial position after the sale is consummated since his ability to avail himself of certain key rights in the mortgage (most notably, the right to cure monetary defaults under the senior debt so as to keep the junior mortgage alive) may become a function of his own financial capabilities.

From the point of view of the buyer, the seller often is a ready and willing source of financing. However, the buyer should bear in mind that when the purchase-money mortgage is intended to become subordinated to a new mortgage to be obtained subsequently by the buyer (either for development of the property or merely the refinancing of existing senior debt), the buyer is negotiating the terms of the seller's subordination not only for the buyer himself, but also for the benefit of any future senior lender against the property. Therefore, when the seller asks for conditions or restrictions on the subordination of the seller's debt, the buyer must take care that any such restrictions or conditions do not impose burdensome affirmative obligations on the senior mortgagee or increase its basic risk.

Notes for seller's counsel

THE SELLER'S CONDITIONS TO SUBORDINATION OF THE PURCHASE-MONEY MORTGAGE

The seller's conditions to the subordination of the purchase-money mortgage fall into two general categories. First are those that may be referred to as *economic conditions;* second are those conditions which tend to be more *technical or legal* in nature. Economic conditions reflect the seller's business judgments as to the economic viability of an investment in a subordinated mortgage position. Technical or legal conditions are procedural in nature and are expected to keep the economic risk within intended limits.

ECONOMIC CONDITIONS TO SUBORDINATION

Among those conditions which might be deemed to be economic in nature are the following:

Institutional lender. An agreement by the seller to subordinate to senior debt to be arranged at some time in the future should be conditioned upon the senior lender being "a bank, insurance company or other similar institutional lender." Generally, an institutional lender will be more sympathetic to the position of the subordinated mortgagee than the private lender; the institutional lender not only is better able to temporarily withstand the financial effects of a default on its mortgage, but often has less of a desire to become the owner of the property.

Debt service. A major element entering into the valuation of real property is the amount of the annual "free and clear" cash flow generated. "Free and clear" generally means the balance after deducting both interest and amortization payments on all mortgages. Therefore, the higher the debt service on the mortgages or (from the point of view of the subordinated mortgagee) on the senior debt, the less the coverage or "cushion" which will be available to the subordinated mortgagee in terms of the owner's remaining equity in the property.

The buyer-mortgagor would be ill advised to accept an absolute limit on the interest rate which he may pay on the senior debt (particularly if it is to be a construction loan which generally has a floating rate and also in view of the possibility that the senior debt will have a variable rate clause). It may be more practical for the seller-mortgagee, in his effort to limit the total debt service payable on the senior debt, to focus on the amortization rate and leave the matter of interest rate to the protection afforded by a requirement that the lender be a financial institution. Further limitations on interest such as "market interest rate" or "prevailing rate" can cause difficulties if bank counsel is unwilling to accept the risk that the rate being charged meets such criteria.

Moratoriums. As the mortgagor makes payments of principal on the senior debt, he is increasing his equity in the property and the security of the subordinated lender. Many times, a senior lender which is comfortable with its security is willing to grant a moratorium (or reduction) in payments of principal. At the other extreme, when a property becomes distressed, a moratorium (or reduction) may be granted as an incentive to the owner to continue to operate the property. The seller-mortgagee, to protect *his* position, should seek a covenant in the purchase mortgage that all amortization payments be made according to the original terms of the senior mortgagee. This will give the subordinated mortgagee the option to decide whether such a moratorium or reduction is in his own best interest.

Proceeds of refinancing. When the seller-mortgagee is taking a position subordinate to *existing* financing, a major issue becomes the disposition of the proceeds of any future refinancing that generates cash in excess of the mortgage debt. A corollary issue is the division of proceeds if the buyer-mortgagor resells the property. In essence, the question becomes one of whether buyer or purchase-money mortgagee should have the right to withdraw his equity first, or whether such withdrawal should be in some agreed-to ratio. If there is to be a division of the excess proceeds, the buyer-mortgagor is likely to ask that he be given a credit for any capital improvements made by him prior to the sale or refinancing. As a matter of drafting the refinancing clause, it should be made clear whether the "excess" in question is over the outstanding senior debt at the time of the purchase, or at the time of the refinancing.

Release clauses. When the property is to be developed in stages and the entire parcel is subject to the seller's mortgage, the buyer generally will need to obtain the release of completed sections in order to effect a sale or permanent financing. The design of such release clauses will depend upon the nature of the project. However, certain general suggestions may be made:

- The buyer should at the appropriate time be given the right, independent of his right to obtain the release of specific parcels, to obtain a release for the installation of public utilities and the dedication of roads.
- Releases should be described in terms of an existing survey or subdivision map.
- Release prices should be related to the value of the property being released and to the effect of such release upon the value of the remaining property.
- Released parcels should be contiguous and should be located in a manner which will not destroy the marketability of the remaining acreage.
- The granting of the release should be conditioned upon the buyer not being in default under the terms of the purchase-money financing *or* under the terms of any other financing or agreements affecting the property.

Subordination to construction loan. The matter of designating the terms and conditions for subordination of the purchase-money financing to a construction loan depends upon the nature of the project to be built and the general facts and circumstances. Although an in-depth analysis of this subject is beyond the general scope of this article, certain observations may be made:

First, the seller-mortgagee should require that certain minimum rights be given to him to review and approve plans for project development and leasing of the completed facility. All agreements with architects, engineers, prospective tenants, or other agreements, permits, documents, and drawings affecting the development or use of the premises should be made assignable by their terms and be assigned (subject to the right of a prior institutional lender to such assignments) to the seller-mortgagee as additional security for his mortgage. This will put the seller-mortgagee in a position where he can either complete development or offer a more salable package in the event of the buyer-mortgagor's default.

Second, although it may not be practical to limit the senior lender as to interest rate or absolute amount of loan, consideration should be given to restricting the use of the proceeds of the senior mortgage to the physical development of the property and related costs such as interest, real estate taxes, and the like. However, any such provision must be broad enough so that the senior lender does not feel that his position will be jeopardized if an advance is made on account of an item not specifically enumerated.

Third, from the buyer-mortgagor's viewpoint, it is generally advisable to insert a requirement in the purchase-money mortgage to require the mortgagee to execute such further documents as may be necessary or appropriate to carry out the terms and intentions of the parties.

LEGAL AND TECHNICAL CONDITIONS TO SUBORDINATION

Conditions which are more procedural in nature and serve as further security to the buyer-mortgagor include the following:

Notice of default. One of the most important protections to be obtained by the seller-mortgagee is the covenant to give him notice of any default under the terms of the senior debt *and* the opportunity to cure such default. Such notice (at least as to matters relating to a monetary default such as nonpayment of interest on senior debt, real estate taxes, insurance premiums, etc.) can take the form of a notice either from the mortgagor or (preferably) from the senior mortgagee in sufficient time to permit the subordinate mortgagee to cure the default. Alternatively, the mortgage can impose an affirmative obligation on the mortgagor to deliver to the subordinate mortgagee proof of payment of all monetary obligations prior to the expiration of any applicable grace period. . . .

It is extremely difficult to impose any affirmative obligation on an institutional lender which becomes a condition precedent to a right to foreclose — for example, the obligation to give notice of default and an opportunity to cure to the junior mortgagee. But it is not unreasonable for the mortgagee to require the mortgagor to provide proof of payment (as described above) and to use his best efforts to require the senior lender to give notice of default and opportunity to cure at least those defaults which the senior lender intends to use as a basis for immediate foreclosure.

Of course, any provisions in the junior mortgagee permitting payments to be made by the seller-mortgagee should provide that the mortgage will be increased by the amount of such payments.

Protection of the property. When the cost of operating real estate escalated so dramatically during the 1974-1975 period, many owners simply abandoned their properties and left it to the mortgagees to decide what to do. Basic obligations such as the provision of heat to tenants were ignored. Typically, the mortgage in such cases would contain a clause permitting the mortgagee to increase the mortgage debt upon the lender's payment of real estate taxes and insurance. However, no provision was made for expenditures for fuel, electricity, repairs, and the like.

Obviously, it is just as important to the preservation of the junior mortgagee's position to keep a property operating as it is to maintain the senior debt in position. Therefore, the mortgage should provide for an increase in the debt if the mortgagee should make such payments.

Prepayment. The mortgagor generally has no right to prepay a mortgage unless the right is specifically set out in the instrument. To maintain flexibility for the future, the buyer-mortgagor should seek the right to prepay the purchase-money mortgage "in whole or in part at any time, and from time to time." However, from the seller's viewpoint, requiring a penalty upon prepayment is not unreasonable since he has invested an "overhead" in the form of legal and other front-end fees which he normally would recoup only after the entire life of the mortgage.

Right to financial information. It has become almost standard operating procedure of institutional mortgagees to require the submission by the mortgagor of periodic operating information. This is particularly important to the subordinate mortgagee whose anticipation of repayment may depend almost entirely on the economic growth of the property and the potential for refinancing senior debt in an amount sufficient to pay off or significantly amortize the purchase money debt. The seller-mortgagee should require that such operating statements be personally guaranteed as to accuracy by the purchaser of the property and any successor in interest to the purchaser.

If the junior mortgagee anticipates that payment of the purchase-money debt will depend upon refinancing the senior debt, he should reserve the right to negotiate for such financing on behalf of the mortgagor and to use the financial data in such negotiations. The right of the seller to seek refinancing and the obligation of the mortgagor to accept the same should be carefully spelled out in order to prevent the seller from interfering with the legitimate efforts of the mortgagor himself to obtain refinancing and to permit the mortgagor to reject what he deems to be unfavorable financing arranged by the seller. Absent such a provision, it is arguable that the seller would be liable for interfering with the mortgagor's ownership rights in the property.

INTEGRATING THE TERMS OF SENIOR AND SUBORDINATE DEBT

In the process of negotiating the terms of subordinated purchase-money debt, the parties must keep in mind the provisions of existing senior debt and try to anticipate the requirements of any senior debt which may be created in the future so that the separate mortgage instruments do not conflict or contradict each other.

Real estate tax escrows. Unpaid real estate taxes generally have a priority over all mortgages, whether created before or after the tax liability arises. In order to prevent a significant liability (e.g., a quarter- or half-year of unpaid taxes) from accruing before it becomes actionable, a mortgage will generally require a monthly escrow of real estate taxes. If the senior financing has not been arranged at the time of the sale, the escrowing of real estate tax payments with the seller-mortgagee should be subordinated to the right of the senior mortgage to require such escrows.

Defaults and grace periods. Events of default under both the junior and senior mortgages generally will parallel one another. However, the junior mortgagee should seek to have the grace periods (during which no default can be declared) be shorter in his mortgage than in the senior lien. In this way, the junior lender is in a position to declare a default — and immediately take steps to remedy it — before a default occurs under the senior mortgage. When the senior mortgage is to be arranged in the future, the seller-mortgagee can dictate the allowable grace periods by conditioning his subordination upon the senior mortgage containing specified grace periods prior to the existence of a default.

Insurance. The use of proceeds that may be paid in the future under casualty insurance policies should be treated similarly in all mortgages and in a manner compatible with leases which may affect the premises. The key issue is whether the insurance proceeds are to reduce the mortgage balance or may be used to reconstruct the premises. Whatever the decision, the treatment should be the same in all mortgages. (A distinction in this connection frequently is made between a total destruction and a partial destruction.) Similarly, the landlord's obligation to rebuild under a lease should be tied into the disposition of insurance proceeds under the terms of the mortgage.

Events of default. Any event which is an event of default under any senior mortgage should be an automatic event of default under the purchase-money mortgage permitting acceleration of the unpaid balance of the purchase-money mortgage. . . .

Sample Junior Mortgage Provisions

SELECTED JUNIOR MORTGAGE PROVISIONS — DEFAULT UNDER PRIOR MORTGAGE

Prior Mortgages. The Mortagor agrees that in the event a default occurs under the terms of any mortgage (a "Prior Mortgage") covering the Mortgaged Premises which is now or might hereafter become superior in lien to the lien of this Mortgage, or in performance under the indebtedness secured by any such Prior Mortgage, the holder of this Mortgage may, at its option, proceed to cure such default by the payment of all or any part of the indebtedness secured by such Prior Mortgage and the holder hereof will be subrogated to the lien of such Prior Mortgage to the extent of such payment or, at the option of the Mortgagee, such default under said Prior Mortgage will be deemed to be a default hereunder and will entitle the Mortgagee to exercise any or all of the rights provided herein. The Mortgagor hereby waives notice of the exercise of such option. In the event the holder of any Prior Mortgage requires the Mortgagee to subordinate the lien of this Mortgage to a Prior Mortgage executed by the Mortgagor subsequent to the recording of this Mortgage, the Mortgagee may from time to time and at any time release the lien of this Mortgage of record and subsequently rerecord the same without thereby in any way affecting the rights and obligations of the Mortgagee and the Mortgagor hereunder, and without affecting the priority of the lien of this Mortgage except as to the Prior Mortgage and instruments recorded prior to the original recording of this Mortgage.

Agreement to Subordinate. The Mortgagee, by the acceptance of this Mortgage, agrees to subordinate the lien hereby created to the lien of construction and long term first mortgage loans to be obtained by the Mortgagor covering the Mortgaged Premises. It is understood that such subordination of the mortgage lien hereby created will be effected by the Mortgagee within ten (10) days after each written request therefor by the Mortgagor and that the Mortgagee will execute such documents as might be reasonably required by the Mortgagor or the holder of such construction or long term mortgage to effect such subordination.

Subrogation. To the extent funds are advanced under the Note hereby secured for the purpose of paying the indebtedness secured by any mortgage lien having priority over the lien of this Mortgage, the Mortgagee will be subrogated to any and all rights, superior titles, liens and equities owned or claimed by the holder of such prior mortgage. Except with respect to the priority of any mortgage to which the Mortgagee is subrogated pursuant to the provisions hereof, the terms and provisions of this Mortgage will govern the rights and remedies of the Mortgagee and will supersede the rights and remedies provided under any mortgage to which the Mortgagee is subrogated.

Additional Collateral; Insecurity.   The Mortgagor agrees that the Mortgagee may from time to time call for additional security of such kind and value as might be determined to be satisfactory by the Mortgagee, and on the failure of the Mortgagor to comply with such request, or if in the judgment of the Mortgagee the security for payment of the indebtedness hereby secured has depreciated in value to the extent that such indebtedness is not regarded as adequately secured by the Mortgagee, then, at the option of the Mortgagee, the indebtedness hereby secured will become immediately due and payable.

Sample Subordination Agreement

SUBORDINATION AGREEMENT

THIS AGREEMENT is made this ____ day of _____ , 19 ____ , by LAND HOLDER and HAND HOLDER, husband and wife (the "Sellers"), in favor of INTERIM BANK, N.A., a national banking association ("IB").

WITNESSETH:

WHEREAS, the Sellers have recorded at Book _____ , Page ____ , of the records of Oklahoma County, Oklahoma, a certain Mortgage (the "Seller Mortgage") securing payment of the sum of $ _____ executed by Homestead Development Corporation, an Oklahoma corporation ("Homestead"), as mortgagor, and covering the real property described at Schedule "1" attached as a part hereof (the "Land");

WHEREAS, Homestead has mortgaged the Land to IB pursuant to a certain Mortgage and Security Agreement (the "IB Mortgage") securing payment of the sum of $ _____ recorded in Book _____ at Page ____ , of the records of Oklahoma County, Oklahoma; and

WHEREAS, IB has requested that the Sellers subordinate the lien of the Seller Mortgage to the lien of the IB Mortgage by means of this Agreement.

NOW, THEREFORE, in consideration of Ten Dollars ($10.00) and other good and valuable consideration, the receipt of which is hereby acknowledged, it is agreed as follows:

1. The Sellers hereby agree and covenant with IB and IB's successors and assigns that the lien granted by the Seller Mortgage will be in all respects subordinate, junior and inferior to the IB Mortgage.

2. Except for the agreements herein contained, the Seller Mortgage will continue in full force and effect.

IN WITNESS WHEREOF, the undersigned have executed this instrument as of the date first above written.

LAND HOLDER

HAND HOLDER

NOTES AND QUESTIONS

1. Rationale and Risks of Secondary Financing. When interest rates are rising, secondary financing can be used to reduce the overall interest expenses of a borrower. This can be cheaper than refinancing the existing first mortgage. Returning to our hypothetical, suppose for example that the office building project is now worth $40 million and that interest rates are escalating. Dan Developer decides to cash out equity in the amount of $10 million by means of a five-year conventional second mortgage loan from the Fuller Finance Company ("FFC"). Wraparound financing is not available, and it will be less expensive, on the whole, for Dan to pay the 18 percent rate on the new second mortgage money and the 12 percent rate on the $20 million balance of the Ace mortgage (for a cumulative interest-only payment of $4,200,000 each year) than for Dan to refinance the Ace mortgage with a new long-term first mortgage in the amount of $30 million at the higher rate of 15 percent, which would require an annual interest-only payment of $4,500,000.

In addition, secondary financing can be used to reduce the portion of the borrower's debt-service payments allocable to amortization and thereby increase the cash flow and the borrower's yield on its equity investment. For simplicity's sake, the above hypothetical presupposes interest-only financing; in reality first mortgage loans by institutional lenders are usually fully or partially amortized. For example, during the third quarter of 1990, about 83 percent of the mortgage commitments on multifamily and commercial properties reported by life insurance companies to the American Council of Life Insurance required some form of amortization. Moreover, of the loans reported, those with long-term maturities (e.g., 28-32 years) all required full amortization. American Council of Life Insurance, Invest. Bull. No. 1126, at Table 6 (Dec. 31, 1990). By contrast, most second mortgage loans are short-term (e.g., five years or less) and interest-only (or with amortization based on a long-term schedule of perhaps 25 to 30 years), with a balloon payment required at the end of the term. Therefore, total debt-service payments on the existing first mortgage and new second mortgage may be less than for a refinanced first mortgage because the interest rate on the existing mortgage is relatively low or because of deferred amortization (or even negative amortization, whereby interest is accrued but not paid) during the term of the second mortgage.

By way of review, can you think of any other reasons why a borrower would prefer secondary financing to refinancing? See Chapter 5B5 and Chapter 9A, supra.

In addition, secondary financing tends to be more creative than first mortgage financing, as reflected by its higher loan-to-value ratios, lower debt-coverage ratios, and more liberal prepayment clauses. As a consequence of this flexibility in loan terms, developers occasionally will use a second mortgage as interim financing on the expectation that the existing mortgage can be refinanced at a lower rate in the future when first mortgage rates decline. The extra interest expended on the second mortgage during the interim can be more than offset by the interest saved on a refinanced long-term mortgage. Likewise, junior mortgages are sometimes used to resolve a gap financing problem. For example, suppose a permanent loan is insufficient in amount to take out a construction loan because the construction lender decides to fund some unanticipated cost overruns or because it elects to fund the ceiling (maximum) amount of a platform loan even though the borrower has failed to comply with a rent roll requirement that is specified in the permanent lender's takeout commitment. If the developer is unable to finance the shortfall with its own equity capital and the construction lender is unwilling to relegate itself to the status of a junior lienor with respect to the gap amount, in order to forestall a default the developer might be compelled to repay the extra construction loan indebtedness with a second mortgage ("bridge") loan from a gap lender, which bridge loan would be satisfied when the property is sold or refinanced for a larger loan amount. See Chapter 5B2, Madison and Dwyer at ¶3.04[2].

According to conventional wisdom a second mortgage tends to be a riskier loan investment; it justifies a higher rate of interest than a first mortgage because the second mortgagee's security interest extends only to the value of the secured property in excess of the first mortgage lien. Can you think of any reason why a second mortgage may be a safer investment than a first mortgage loan? By deferring amortization or even interest payments creative secondary financing (including wraparound financing) can reduce debt-service payments and sharply increase the cash flow rate of return to an equity investor. However, to increase the yield what additional risk must be assumed by the owner-borrower?

   2.   Special Protections Demanded by Junior Mortgagees.   Returning to the hypothetical, if Dan Developer were to obtain a second mortgage loan in the amount of $10 million, on the advice of counsel, the secondary lender, FFC, would require the same protective provisions that are customarily contained in a first mortgage and the same closing documentation (including a title policy ensuring the validity of the second mortgage lien, final survey, copies of leases, and estoppel certificates from tenants). Counsel for FFC will also review the existing first mortgage loan documentation to make certain that Ace has not proscribed any secondary financing (by means of a due-on-encumbrance clause) or included any onerous provision such as predicating its consent to secondary financing on the willingness of the junior mortgagee to assign all of its rights and claims to insurance or condemnation proceeds to Ace for its use as the senior mortgagee.

   In addition, because its status as a junior lienor makes it vulnerable to a foreclosure of the senior mortgage, FFC will attempt to have the following covenants included in the loan documents:

1.   The second mortgagee will be notified of any default under the senior mortgage and be given a reasonable opportunity to cure such default; and any payment made by the second mortgagee on behalf of the mortgagor will be added to the second mortgage indebtedness.
2.   Any default under the first mortgage shall automatically be deemed a default under the second mortgage.
3.   There shall be no material change in the terms and conditions (nor any extension or renewal) of the first mortgage or of any leases without the prior written consent of the second mortgagee.

   Can you think of the reasons for the foregoing covenants? In what respects are they designed to protect the second mortgagee against any impairment of its security interest?

   What about the position of the senior mortgagee? As a prerequisite to permitting junior financing a postconstruction lender such as Ace will sometimes require that any subsequent mortgage be junior in lien priority (or become so by means of a subordination agreement) to any and all leases on the property. Why would a senior mortgagee impose such a requirement? See Chapter 5B7 and 5C. Can you think of any other precautionary measures that might be required by Ace? See Madison and Dwyer ¶7.05[2].

    3.   Statutory and Common-law Protections Afforded to Junior Mortgagees.

        a.   Appointment of a Receiver and the Right to Possession Prior to Foreclosure.   If a borrower defaults under a first mortgage it is likely to be in default under the second mortgage as well, either because it is insolvent or because of a cross-default provision in the second mortgage. When a borrower is in default under both mortgages a conflict may develop between the senior and junior mortgagees over the priorities of their respective claims to the rents and profits from the mortgaged property. While the rules are not clear as to claims based on mortgage clauses that purport to assign or pledge the rents and profits, the law is settled that a junior mortgagee who first obtains a court-appointed receiver or takes over possession will prevail over a senior mortgagee as to rents and profits collected prior to the intervention of the senior mortgagee. Otherwise, a junior mortgagee who acts promptly to prevent the property from being "milked" by the mortgagor-landlord would not be rewarded for its diligence. Moreover, but for the action of the junior mortgagee these rents would be captured by the mortgagor. As for the choice of having the right to possession and having the property managed by a court-appointed receiver, most mortgagees would prefer the latter as a preforeclosure remedy in order to avoid the stringent accounting duties and potential contract-tort liability associated with becoming a mortgagee in possession. G. Nelson and D. Whitman, Real Estate Finance Law §4.43 (2d ed. 1985); see also Tefft, Receivers and Leases Subordinate to the Mortgage, 2 U. Chi. L. Rev. 33 (1934). See discussion of preforeclosure remedies at Chapter 10B.

        b.   Rights of a Junior Mortgagee at Foreclosure.   You will recall that the principle objective of an action to foreclose is to enable the foreclosing mortgagee to become whole again by realizing on its security to the maximum extent possible. To that end the mortgagee is allowed to join in as a defendant not only the mortgagor but also any junior party whose interest might adversely affect the value of the property. As a consequence of such joinder (or public notice, in the case of foreclosure by power of sale) the mortgagee is able to extinguish the defendant's equitable right of redemption (right to prevent foreclosure by paying off the mortgage debt after default and prior to foreclosure sale) so that the property can be sold free and clear of any such adverse interest and the purchaser at the foreclosure sale can receive the same title that existed when the mortgage was executed by the mortgagee. See Chapter 4A and Chapter 10C2, notes 1 and 2; see generally Osborne, Mortgages §§321, 323 (2d ed. 1970) (hereinafter Osborne).

    Returning to the hypothetical, suppose Dan Developer defaults under the first mortgage when the outstanding balance on the first mortgage (with Ace) is $15 million and the balance on the second mortgage (with FFC) is $5 million. In the event that Ace accelerates the unpaid indebtedness and goes to foreclosure, the risk to the junior mortgagee, FFC, is that it will be joined in as a party defendant by Ace and that a forced sale of the property will attract few if any bidders besides the mortgagees themselves and that the net foreclosure sale proceeds may not be sufficient to satisfy both the junior and the senior indebtedness. Thus a net sale price at foreclosure of, let's say, $18 million would produce an economic loss of $2 million for FFC unless it is able to recoup some or all of the deficiency by exercising any one of the following rights accorded to a junior mortgagee at foreclosure:

i. *The Right to Deficiency Judgment.*   If Dan defaults under both mortgages and both mortgagees foreclose against Dan, FFC theoretically could recoup its mortgage investment by obtaining a personal judgment against Dan for the deficiency amount, provided that the second mortgage note does not exculpate Dan from personal liability and that the action takes place in a jurisdiction that does not have an antideficiency statute. The distinction between recourse and nonrecourse financing is discussed at Chapter 2B, note 7diii and Chapter 4B3, note 1, and deficiency judgments are examined at Chapter 10C3a. Obviously, however, defaulting borrowers tend to be insolvent and, in reality, only a nominal dollar-amount percentage of deficiency judgments are ever realized by lenders against defaulting borrowers. See, e.g., Prather, A Realistic Approach to Foreclosure, 14 Bus. Law. 132 (1958).

ii. *The Right to Redeem the Mortgage of Any Senior Mortgagee.*   If FFC anticipates that the current action to foreclose by the senior mortgagee, Ace, will produce net sale proceeds of less than $20 million because of adverse market conditions, FFC can prevent an untimely foreclosure sale by exercising its equitable right of redemption, that is, by paying to Ace the $15 million amount of its outstanding indebtedness. By doing so FFC would become subrogated to the rights of Ace against Dan and the other junior interest-holders and, in effect, become the holder of both the first and the second mortgage so that it could delay the foreclosure sale until market conditions improve. Or perhaps FFC feels that the sale value of the property might increase if it were managed by a court-appointed receiver pending completion of the foreclosure proceedings. See Chapter 10B3; see generally Osborne §304.

After a foreclosure by the senior mortgagee and subsequent extinction of the junior mortgagee's lien, the rights of the junior mortgagee reattach if the mortgagor subsequently redeems the property. See, e.g., Martin v. Raleigh State Bank, 146 Miss. 1, 111 So. 448 (1927). Certain states, however, do not allow the junior mortgagee's lien to reattach if the former mortgagor reacquires the property by purchase after the statutory redemption period. See, e.g., Zandri v. Tendler, 123 Conn. 117, 193 A. 598 (1937).

iii. *The Right to Purchase at the Foreclosure Sale.*   Alternatively,

FFC might believe that a purchase will be necessary to obtain the requisite control to salvage the situation. For example, if the property is beset by chronic management and leasing problems, or if the foreclosure sale attracts few if any outside bidders, FFC might want to bid up to the second mortgage amount ($20 million) and become the new owner on the expectation that with proper management and marketing efforts it might become whole again by reselling the property for no less than $20 million. See Chapter 10C2, notes 4 and 5; see generally Osborne §328.

iv. The Rights of Omitted Junior Parties. It is a well-known axiom with respect to judicial foreclosure that when a junior lienor (such as a junior mortgagee) is not named as party defendant, its lien will survive and the purchaser will take subject to it. Otherwise, the junior lienor would be deprived unfairly of the opportunity to bid for the property itself or to maximize the sale price (and its ability to recoup its investment) by stirring up other bidders. Therefore, the omitted junior lienor may still either foreclose its lien or redeem any senior mortgage, and the purchaser at the foreclosure sale in turn may eliminate the junior lien by paying it off, by re-foreclosing the senior mortgage, or, in some states, by using the strict foreclosure method against the junior lienor. See generally Nelson and Whitman §7.15 (2d ed. 1985).

v. The Right of Statutory Redemption. In some states, in order to protect junior parties from an artificially low sale price when a senior mortgage is foreclosed, junior interest-holders (such as junior mortgagees) are provided with a statutory right of redemption. For a specified period of time after the mortgagor's redemption period has elapsed, the junior lienors have the right (in order of their respective lien priorities) to redeem the title to the property from the purchaser at the foreclosure sale by paying the foreclosure sale price plus the lien of any lienor who has previously redeemed the property. See Nelson and Whitman at §8.7.

c. The Doctrine of Marshaling of Assets. Simply put, where a senior mortgage is secured by more than one parcel of land and a junior mortgage is secured by only one, under the equitable doctrine of marshaling of assets, a court may require the senior mortgagee to satisfy its claim in a manner that affords the junior claimant maximum protection. For example, assume that mortgagor owns land parcel 1 (worth $20,000) and land parcel 2 (worth $10,000) and that mortgagor obtains a mortgage from the senior mortgagee for $20,000 that is secured by both land parcels. Later, the mortgagor borrows $10,000 from a junior mortgagee, which amount is secured only by land parcel 1. Both mortgages are properly recorded and the senior and junior mortgagee have actual notice of one another. If the mortgagor defaults on both loans, the senior mortgagee can be compelled at equity to first satisfy its indebtedness out of land parcel 2 before resorting to land parcel 1. See generally Osborne at §286.

4. Wraparound Mortgages.

a. Compared to a Conventional Second Mortgage. Under which, if any, of the following circumstances would a real estate borrower most likely prefer wraparound financing to a conventional second mortgage as a way of assembling additional working capital or of reducing his overall debt service payments?

1. Interest rates for first mortgage money are rapidly declining, but the borrower cannot refinance its existing first mortgage because the lock-in period (during which any prepayment is prohibited) on the first mortgage has not expired.
2. The existing first mortgage has a favorable rate of interest, and the borrower needs additional funds to renovate the mortgaged property, which it plans to sell or refinance within two years.
3. Interest rates for first mortgage money are rapidly increasing, and to satisfy the investors (who are demanding a higher yield on their equity) the borrower wants to decrease the overall debt-service payments and thereby increase the cash flow from the property over the remaining 15 years of the existing mortgage term.

b. Purchase Money Wraparound Financing. In the case of seller financing of existing real estate, the seller will frequently take back a purchase money wraparound mortgage (PMWAM) if the purchaser is able to assume (or take subject to) a first mortgage that has a below-market rate of interest, inasmuch as the existing mortgage does not contain a standard due-on-sale clause. Sellers use this type of financing as a way of inducing a purchaser to buy the property (1) by deferring the purchase price while enabling the seller to retain the favorable spread in interest rates (between the wraparound note and the existing first mortgage note) if the purchaser is unwilling to pay a higher price because of the favorable terms of the existing mortgage; (2) by providing the purchaser with debt-service payments tailored to its cash flow needs during the remaining term of a long-term first mortgage; and (3) by reducing the cash requirement of the purchaser who is unable to pay the balance of the purchase price (over and above the amount of the existing mortgage) while permitting the seller to take advantage of the favorable spread in the interest rates. See generally Galowitz, How to Use Wraparound Financing, 5 Real Est. L.J. 107 (Fall 1976). Occasionally, a PMWAM is used to circumvent a due-on-sale clause featured in an existing mortgage with a below-market rate of interest where the clause prohibits any buyer from assuming the mortgage or taking the property subject to the mortgage (as opposed to a sale of the property by the seller) without the lender's consent. Do you think that this circumvention device will work? See Chapter 5B8.

For example, returning to the hypothetical at the beginning of Chapter 9B, supra, if Dan were to sell the property for its market value of $40 million subject to the Ace mortgage in the amount of $20 million, and the purchaser could only afford to pay down money of $4 million, Dan could take back an interest-only PMWAM in the amount of $36 million at an interest rate of 14 percent and use the two percentage-point differential between the wraparound rate and the 12 percent rate on the Ace mortgage to increase his effective yield on the net wraparound loan amount advanced to cover the $16 million balance of the purchase price due at closing from 14 percent to 16.5 percent each year during the balance of the 10-year term.

After reviewing the Mortgage and Real Estate Executive's Report excerpt, "Case Study of a Wrap Loan," supra, consider the following questions.

i. Observe that at the end of seven years, the amortization payments on the underlying first mortgage will have scaled down the loan balance to about $886,000, while the balance on the wrap loan will be $2,358,000, thereby creating a spread of about $1,472,000. Note that this spread is larger than the $1,068,000 originally advanced by the wrap lender. Can you discern how this difference in loan balances was created? What risk does this spread pose for the wrap lender?

ii. In New York City, where cooperatives coexist with condominiums, the PMWAM technique has been popularized by those developers who convert apartment buildings into cooperatives where the existing loan on the building has a below-market rate of interest at the time of conversion.

c. Risks and Protections Afforded to a Wraparound Mortgagee and the Senior Lender.

i. After reviewing the hypothetical and excerpts in Chapter 9B, supra, how would you assess the underwriting (business) risks to a wraparound lender compared to the risks borne by a conventional secondary mortgagee (such as FFC, in note 1) with respect to the hypothetical loan advance to Dan in the amount of $10 million? In that regard bear in mind, as Gunning suggests, that in the case of an "additional-funds" wraparound mortgage (as opposed to a PMWAM) the wraparound lender almost invariably will condition its obligation to make first mortgage debt-service payments on the actual receipt of the payments from the wraparound mortgagor. But suppose the wraparound lender were to actually and formally assume the first mortgage debt. Do you think that such an assumption would be enforceable against the wraparound lender? See Comment, The Wrap-Around Mortgage: A Critical Inquiry, 21 UCLA L. Rev. 1529 (1974); Nelson and Whitman, Real Estate Finance Law §5.16 (2d ed. 1985). To protect the wraparound lender, what special borrower covenants should be included in the wraparound note and mortgage? Why is such protective language necessary? Likewise, what concessions or privileges will be requested of the senior mortgagee? Why are such protections necessary for the wraparound lender? See Madison and Dwyer, The Law of Real Estate Financing ¶7.04[3][a] (1981).

ii. Returning to the hypothetical, suppose Dan were to approach Ace, the holder of the underlying mortgage, about his desire to obtain wraparound financing from the wraparound lender. What do you think Ace's reaction might be? Most senior lenders would be disturbed by the prospect of having their first mortgage indebtedness "wrapped around," and consequently they attempt to prohibit or restrict such junior financing by means of language in a so-called due-on-wrap clause. Such a clause is excerpted at Chapter 5B7. Why is this so? Can you think of any reasons why Ace might resist? If Dan wanted to obtain either an additional-funds wraparound loan or a PMWAM, what language would you, as Dan's attorney, look for in the Ace loan documentation that might prohibit such financing?

   d.   *Pitfalls and Precautions.*

   i.   *The Usury Problem.*   By far the most serious problem in connection with wraparound financing is the risk that the loan may be deemed usurious, in which event the lender could be seriously penalized. See general discussion of usury at Chapter 5B3, note 4. Indeed, this is why wraparound financing originated in Canada, where real estate loans are not fettered with usury restrictions. The real usury question in a wraparound transaction is, which rate of interest is more relevant, the face amount that the borrower *pays* on the entire wraparound indebtedness or the effective yield that the lender *receives* on the funds that are actually advanced to the borrower? For example, returning to the hypothetical at the beginning of Chapter 9B and assuming that the maximum rate of interest allowed by local law is 16 percent, it might be argued that the loan to Dan Developer from the wraparound lender is usurious because such lender is effectively receiving an annual rate of 18 percent on the $10 million amount of loan funds actually disbursed. Conversely, the argument could be made that usury is not a problem because Dan is paying a face rate of only 14 percent, as specified in the wraparound note, and even though he only receives $10 million in cash he nevertheless is making full use of the entire wraparound loan amount of $30 million.

   In your judgment, which argument makes more sense? Don't forget that if a lender receives something of value (such as an equity kicker) in addition to the stated rate of interest the additional compensation for the use of borrowed funds is generally treated as interest for purposes of a usury determination regardless of whether the additional compensation is arranged by means of a separate legal transaction. Also, it might be useful to compare the wraparound transaction to one in which Dan raises the additional $10 million working capital simply by obtaining an ordinary second mortgage loan. Compare Hool v. Rydholm, 467 So. 2d 1038 (Fla. Dist. Ct. App. 1985), with Mindlin v. Davis, 74 So. 2d 789 (Fla. 1954). See generally Galowitz, How to Use Wraparound Financing, 5 Real Est. L.J. 107, 124-125 (1976); Tanner, Usury Implications of Alternative Mortgage Instruments: The Uncertainty in Calculating Permissible Returns, 1986 B.Y.U. L. Rev. 1105, 1114-1116; Note, Wrap-Around Financing: A Technique for Skirting the Usury Laws?, 1972 Duke L.J. 785; Hershman, Usury and the "New Look" in Real Estate Financing, 4 Real Prop., Prob. & Tr. J. 315 (1969); Comment, The Wrap-Around Deed of Trust: An Answer to the Allegation of Usury, 10 Pac. L.J. 923 (1979).

   ii. The Problem of Deducting Interest.   Another pitfall — in this case, for the unwary borrower — is that it may not be able to deduct the interest component of the wraparound debt-service payments that are being used by the wraparound lender to pay off amortization on the underlying mortgage, on the rationale that the wraparound lender is merely acting as the agent, or conduit, of the borrower for making the debt-service payments on the first mortgage. Compare Rev. Rul. 75-99, 1975-1 C.B. 197 (involving an additional-funds wraparound mortgage wherein only the interest received on the additional funds was deemed to be interest income for the purpose of qualifying the wraparound lender as a real estate investment trust under I.R.C. §856(c)). Accordingly, returning to the example in the first chart in the excerpt by Gunning, supra, under this view, that portion of the earned interest in the first year ($1,280) used to defray the principal due under the first mortgage would not become deductible by the borrower (nor be charged as interest income to the wrap lender) until the wrap mortgage is paid in full (when the mortgaged property is sold or refinanced). The deductibility of mortgage interest is discussed in general at Chapter 5B3, note 6.

   iii. Other Concerns.   In addition to the foregoing pitfalls and the troublesome issues raised in the excerpt by Gunning (e.g., interest on interest, prepayment rights, title insurance, mortgage tax, full disbursement statutes), the following questions must also be addressed by any borrower or lender contemplating wraparound financing.

   1.   Notwithstanding the protective provisions suggested by Gunning (e.g., notice of default under the first mortgage and opportunity to cure), if the underlying mortgage is foreclosed there is a question as to what amount the wraparound mort-

gagee may bid in at the foreclosure sale without being required
to pay cash.

2. By definition, any wraparound mortgage will require subsequent advances by the wraparound lender. Suppose a new lien
on the property were to arise after the wrap lender records
its mortgage and makes its first payment to the senior mortgagee but before the wrap lender makes its next payment on
the underlying mortgage. Will the second advance by the
wrap lender have lien priority over the intervening lien?

3. Who should control the use of any casualty insurance proceeds
or condemnation award in the event of a partial destruction
or taking, the wraparound lender or the senior mortgagee? If
the senior mortgagee applies such proceeds to reduce the
principal balance of the underlying indebtedness so that the
net wraparound debt-service payments are increased, who should
bear the cost of restoration, the wraparound lender or the
wraparound borrower?

4. Suppose either the wraparound borrower or the wraparound
lender were to become bankrupt. What impact will this have
on their mutual obligations and on the rights of the senior
mortgagee?

These and other issues are thoughtfully examined by Galowitz in
his article How to Use Wraparound Financing, 5 Real Est. L.J. 107,
123-137 (1976). See also Saft, The Risks Facing the Borrower in
Wraparound Financing, 2 Real Est. Fin. J. 20 (Winter 1987).

5. *Purchase Money Mortgage Financing.*

*a. Separate Land Financing by Means of a Subordinated Purchase
Money Mortgage.* As observed in the introduction to Chapter 9B, developers frequently use purchase money mortgage financing (along with
the installment land contract, discussed at Chapter 9C, infra) to leverage
their cost of developing a new income-producing project. By separately
financing the cost of the underlying land by means of a high-ratio
subordinated purchase money mortgage from the seller of the land, a
developer can reduce its need for venture capital and in most cases
increase the cash-on-cash rate of return to its equity investors. Returning
to the master hypothetical at Chapter 5B, if Dan were to obtain a
straight fee mortgage in the amount of $25 million, he would need
to raise venture capital of $8.3 million to cover the remaining cost of
acquiring the land (costing $8 million) and constructing the improve-
ments (costing $25.3 million). Alternatively, if he were to obtain an
ordinary leasehold mortgage loan (wherein the land owner, Francine,
does not subject her fee interest to the lien of the leasehold mortgage),
Dan's requisite cash outlay would be reduced to $6,325,000. If Francine's

fee interest were encumbered by the lien of the leasehold mortgage under a "streamlined mortgage" arrangement, Dan's initial cash requirement could theoretically be reduced to zero because the streamlined mortgage amount (75 percent of the $33.3 million value of land and building) would just about match the $25.3 million cost of constructing the building. See discussion of streamlined mortgages at Chapter 8A4. But suppose Francine does not want to ground lease the fee or take the risk of subjecting it to Ace's mortgage lien, or that Dan wants to obtain the inherent benefits of land ownership (such as future appreciation in the value of the land)? Dan might be able to convince Francine to take back a purchase money mortgage at a high loan-to-value ratio, for example, 90 percent, in which event Dan would obtain ownership of the underlying land and also be able to reduce his initial cash outlay to $1,133,333 (the total cost of $33.3 million less 90 percent financing of the land ($7,200,000) less the fee mortgage amount of $25 million). This presupposes that Francine would be willing to subordinate the lien of her purchase money mortgage to the liens of future mortgages that Dan anticipates he will obtain from a construction lender such as Fuller National Bank and a postconstruction lender such as the Ace Insurance Company, both of whom will demand a first mortgage lien on the property.

But why would Francine be willing to assume the risk of a secondary lien position, especially on a purchase money mortgage with such a high loan-to-value ratio? Francine might be persuaded by the fact that her security interest will be enhanced by the value of the proposed improvements. After all, as Dan would explain to Francine, a second mortgage on an office building project worth $33.3 million is better security than a first mortgage on land worth only $8 million. Moreover, Dan might not be willing or able to improve the land without the additional financing. Also, in exchange for the subordination agreement Dan might be willing to pay Francine a purchase price that exceeds the market value of the land (subject to the tax constraints on nonrecourse seller financing imposed by the *Crane* doctrine and the new at-risk rules imposed by the Tax Reform Act of 1986). See discussion at Chapter 2B, note 4 and I.R.C. §465(b)(6), as added by the Tax Reform Act of 1986, also examined at Chapter 2B, note 7diii.

Let us assume that Francine agrees to subordinate. After reviewing the excerpt by Bell, supra, do you think that the sample "Agreement to Subordinate" is adequate and enforceable by the parties? What additional language might you, as Francine's attorney, require to be added to the subordination agreement (when Dan obtains his commitments from FNB and Ace) to protect the interests of your client? What additional language might Ace's attorney require? See McNamara, Subordination Agreements as Viewed by Sellers, Purchasers, Construction Lenders, and Title Companies, 12 Real Est. L.J. 347 (Spring 1984);

Korngold, Construction Loan Advances and the Subordinated Purchase Money Mortgagee: An Appraisal, A Suggested Approach, and the ULTA Perspective, 50 Fordham L. Rev. 313 (1981); Miller, Starr, and Regalia, Subordination Agreements in California, 13 UCLA L. Rev. 1298 (1966). How does Francine's risk as a subordinated purchase money mortgagee compare to the risk assumed by a fee owner who subjects his fee interest to the lien of a leasehold mortgage? See discussion of streamlined mortgages at Chapter 8A4.

In addition to new construction, purchase-money mortgage financing is also frequently used by sellers of existing real estate to induce a purchase when the purchaser assumes or takes the property subject to an existing mortgage that is attractive or where the purchaser is unable to pay in cash the balance of the purchase price. Likewise, even if the purchaser were to refinance the existing mortgage by obtaining its own mortgage from a third-party lender it might need additional seller financing to consummate the transaction.

    b. Subdivision Financing. So far the focal point of our discussion has been the financing of income-producing real estate. By contrast, land development financing includes land acquisition and development loans made to developers of subdivisions who acquire raw land at wholesale prices primarily for the purpose of building roads, installing power, and otherwise developing the land into finished lots for resale at retail prices to home builders (both professionals and individuals) and land speculators. In addition, the term "land development financing" encompasses loans made to developers of multi-unit residential developments such as condominiums and townhouse projects where the community facilities, called common areas, are owned or managed by some form of unit owners' association.

What distinguishes land development financing from the financing of income-producing real estate is the disparate natures of the security for each type of loan and the differing regulatory environment for both kinds of developments. In contrast to an ordinary construction lender, who relies beforehand on a single takeout commitment to become whole again once the construction period is over, the ultimate source for repayment of the land development loan is the borrower's legal ability to fractionalize the collateral into separate ownership interests and to sell these interests (in the form of lots or residential units) at a predetermined minimum price. This means that during the development phase of the project the market demand for the real estate might slacken or the process of development could be curtailed or even halted.

Because of the frequently speculative nature of land development, institutional lenders will normally lend only at low loan-to-value ratios, typically 50 to 75 percent. Moreover, at the present time most institutional lenders refuse to make land acquisition loans. Therefore, loans to acquire raw land are usually financed by means of high-ratio seller financing. A land development loan will usually be secured by a first mortgage on the property. This means that if a land developer has acquired the raw land by means of a high-ratio purchase money mortgage or installment land contract, the purchase money mortgage must be subordinated to the development loan or the installment obligation must be repaid before the institutional lender will permit the developer to make its first draw on the land development loan.

In the case of a development loan, additional collateral such as cash or securities or the personal guarantee of the borrowers may be sought as well. Further security may be given by assigning to the lender the promissory notes of lot purchasers or their installment land contracts in accordance with Article 9 of the U.C.C. As additional protection, in the event of the borrower's default the lender should receive an assignment of the contracts of the various parties in the development work and have a security interest in their work products; this would enable the lender to step in and complete the project if necessary. In this regard, the lender may require that it be designated as an obligee in the case of a performance bond.

In order to facilitate the sale and conveyance of individual lots, it is often desirable in the case of both land acquisition and land development loans that a mechanism be established for the release of individual lots from the lender's blanket mortgage covering the entire tract. For example, suppose an investor buys some raw land that he plans to subdivide into lots for resale to lot buyers. If the purchase is financed by means of a purchase money mortgage from the seller, the purchaser should insist on a partial-release-of-lien clause in the mortgage so that clear and unencumbered title to specific portions of the land may be acquired as the land acquisition loan is repaid. Otherwise, the purchaser would not be able to convey marketable title to any of the lots until the entire purchase money indebtedness is repaid. If the purchase price were, let's say, $200,000 the purchaser might arrange with the seller (1) to acquire clear title to 20 percent of the land when the principal balance on the mortgage note is scaled down (by 25 percent) to $150,000; (2) to acquire clear title to an additional 20 percent of the land when the balance is reduced (by 50 percent) to $100,000; and (3) to obtain clear title on all the land when the final payment is made. Under such an arrangement the purchaser would be able to resell the land and deliver clear title to buyers of individual lots and yet the seller-mortgagee would be protected because if at any time the purchaser-mortgagor defaulted the value of the unreleased land would probably be higher than the outstanding loan balance at the time of default as a consequence of the 5-percentage-point spread between the scale-down and the release-of-lien percentage rates. The following fragment of a partial release clause was the subject of litigation in Lambert v. Jones, 540 S.W.2d 256, 257 (Tenn. Ct. App. 1976):

[T]he privilege is reserved and given so that the parties of the first part, their heirs, or assigns, may at any time subsequent to January 1, 1973, and from time to time, obtain a release or releases from the lien of this deed of trust of part or parts of the aforedescribed real property upon payment to the owner and holder of the indebtedness secured hereby, either by way of obligatory payments or by way of prepayments, of the sum of $1,500.00 per acre to be released; provided further, however, that each released tract subsequent to the first tract released shall be contiguous to a tract previously released; provided further, however, that all accrued interest upon any principal sum paid pursuant to this release clause shall be paid at the time of such payment; and provided further, however, that the release payments shall apply upon the next maturing note or notes secured hereby.

Can you identify potential problems with this clause? If the tract is non-homogenous, which portion would the developer seek to have released first? Would this put the lender at an unconscionable disadvantage? As an adjunct to seeing that the loan-to-value ratio is maintained, the lender will want to be sure that the unreleased lots are not cut off from access to roads and utilities and that the size and shape of the remaining mortgaged portions are saleable. Generally, courts view release clauses as covenants running with the land so that, absent language to the contrary, they may be enforced by purchasers from the mortgagor, even where the mortgagor is in default under its obligations to the mortgagee. This comports with the primary purpose of the release clause. See generally Annot., Mortgage — Partial Release Provisions, 41 A.L.R.3d 7 (1972).

In contrast to the development of commercial real estate, the sale of residential lots and units to consumers raises important public policy concerns that have prompted protective legislation such as the Interstate Land Sales Full Disclosure Act, 15 U.S.C. §1701 et seq. (ILSFDA). Enacted in 1968 with the intention of curbing perceived abuses and providing remedies to consumers in the retail sale and leasing of building lots, the ILSFDA is in essence a disclosure and antifraud statute analogous to those regulating the sale of securities. The federal statute regulates all covered transactions except when substantially equivalent state laws have been certified by the Department of Housing and Urban Development (HUD). It generally targets high-volume sales of residential lots in large subdivisions to out-of-state purchasers; thus, for example, sales of lots with contracts for building construction to be completed within two years, sales of commercial or industrial lots, and sales to building contractors are exempt from its application. For additional background on land acquisition financing see Martin, Land Investments in Today's Market: An Overview of Factors that Influence the Success of Raw Land Investments, 4 Real Est. Fin. 49, 53-54 (Winter 1988). An excellent discussion of all aspects of land development financing can be found in R. Harris, Construction and Development Financing 1-2 to 2-31 (1982).

 c. Special Lien Priority.   A purchase money mortgagee generally has lien priority over any claim against the purchaser attaching to the property. This priority is not limited to the seller, but may extend to a third person who advances the buyer the money for the purchase as long as the money is lent solely for this purpose. See, e.g., Sarmiento v. Stockton, Whatley, Davin & Co., 399 So. 2d 1057 (Fla. Dist. Ct. App. 1981); Hand Trading Co. v. Daniels, 126 Ga. App. 342, 190 S.E.2d 560 (1972); Commerce Savings, Lincoln, Inc. v. Robinson, 213 Neb. 596, 331 N.W.2d 495 (1983). The purchase money mortgage will also prevail over claims for dower, community property, or homestead. See, e.g., Stow v. Tift, 15 Johns. 458, 8 Am. Dec. 266 (N.Y. 1818); Kreen v. Halin, 6 Idaho 621, 59 P. 14 (1899); Associates Discount Corp. v. Gomes, 338 So. 2d 552 (Fla. Dist. Ct. App. 1976). In some jurisdictions the lien priority is based on a statute. See, e.g., Cal. Civ. Code §2898 (West Supp. 1974). See generally Note, Priority of Purchase Money Mortgages, 29 Va. L. Rev. 491 (1943).

The legal rationale for the special lien priority accorded to purchase money mortgages is based on the notion that the title, once conveyed to the grantee, automatically shoots out of the grantee and into the purchase money mortgagee so fleetingly that no other interest has time to fasten itself to it; hence, the grantor-mortgagor is deemed to be nothing more than a conduit for the mortgagee. G. Nelson and D. Whitman, Real Estate Finance Law §9.1 (2d ed. 1985). Does this theory of transitory seisin make sense in a jurisdiction such as New York, which subscribes to the lien (as opposed to the title) theory with respect to the nature of a mortgage? If not, what *policy* rationale best explains why such favoritism is bestowed on purchase money mortgages? See G. Nelson and D. Whitman at §9.1.

On a precautionary note, observe that the lien priority accorded to a purchase money mortgage can be defeated if the mortgagee does not comply with the requirements of the recording statute in the jurisdiction where the property is located. For example, while a purchase money mortgagee who does not record his mortgage will nevertheless prevail over any prior judgment lien creditor under the special priority rules applicable to purchase money mortgages, a subsequent purchaser or mortgagee who takes or encumbers the property without record or actual notice of the purchase money mortgage will prevail in a notice jurisdiction and in a race-notice jurisdiction. In a pure race jurisdiction (where notice is irrelevant) all that is required is that the subsequent purchaser or mortgagee record before the purchase money mortgagee records. See Nelson and Whitman at §9.2.

 d. No Right to Deficiency Judgment.   As explained elsewhere (at Chapter 4B3, note 1 and Chapter 10C3a), in the event of foreclosure where the net sale proceeds are insufficient to satisfy the underlying debt, if recourse financing was used the mortgagee may obtain a deficiency judgment against the mortgagor in a jurisdiction that does not have antideficiency legislation. However, several states, such as California (Cal. Civ. Proc. Code §580b (Deering 1991)), Arizona (Ariz. Rev. Stat. Ann. §33-729(A) (1989)), North Carolina (N.C. Gen. Stat. §45-21.38 (Michie 1990)), Montana (Mont. Code Ann. §71-1-232 (1990)), Oregon (Ore. Rev. Stat. 88.070 (1989)), and South Dakota (S.D. Codified Laws Ann. §44-8-20 (1990)) do not permit deficiency judgments for purchase money mortgagees. Can you think of any legal or policy rationales for this rule? See G. Nelson and D. Whitman §8.3.

      e.   The Availability of the Installment Method for Reporting Gain from the Sale of Seller-financed Real Estate.   One tax advantage associated with the use of purchase money mortgage and installment land contract financing where the seller is scheduled to receive at least one payment in a taxable year subsequent to the year of sale is that the seller is allowed to use the "installment method" for reporting income under I.R.C. §453 (unless it elects otherwise) by reporting as gain, each year, only that portion of each installment "payment" that corresponds to the ratio of "gross profit" on the sale to the "contract price." The balance of the payment is treated as a nontaxable return of capital (basis). "Payment" means the cash or other property actually received in the year of payment; it includes the amount of the existing mortgage ("qualified indebtedness") assumed or taken subject to by the purchaser *only* to the extent that it exceeds the seller's adjusted basis in the property being sold. Temp. Reg. §15A.453-1(b)(3)(i). "Gross profit" means the total gain to be realized on the sale, or the selling price (as reduced by commissions and other selling expenses) less the seller's adjusted basis in the real estate being sold. I.R.C. §453(c); Temp. Reg. §15A.453-1(b)(2)(v). The "contract price" is the selling price as reduced by that portion of the qualified indebtedness that, after an adjustment to reflect commissions and other selling expenses, does not exceed the seller's adjusted basis in the property. Temp. Reg. §15A.453-1(b)(2)(iii).

      The following illustration appears in Madison and Dwyer, The Law of Real Estate Financing at §9.04[3].

> *Example.*   Seller transfers title to Blackacre worth $100,000, which is encumbered with a $40,000 mortgage and which has an adjusted basis in the seller's hands of $80,000 to the purchaser on January 1, 1989 in exchange for $10,000 in cash at the closing and a $50,000 purchase-money mortgage from the purchaser. The mortgage is payable in annual installments of $5,000, bears an annual interest rate of 10 percent, and provides that the first installment will become due and payable on June 1, 1989. Commissions and selling expenses amount to $2,000. The results are as follows:

Gross profit on sale:

Selling price		$100,000
Less:		
Adjusted basis	$80,000	
Selling expenses	2,000	82,000
		$ 18,000

Contract price:

Selling price	$100,000
Less existing mortgage	40,000
	$ 60,000

Payments received in year of sale:

Cash at closing	$ 10,000
Installment received 6/1/89	5,000
	$ 15,000

Gain reportable in year of sale:

$$\frac{\$18,000 \text{ (gross profit)} \times \$15,000 \text{ (payments in year of sale)}}{\$60,000 \text{ (contract price)}} = \$4,500$$

Accordingly, $4,500 is reported as taxable gain in the year of sale (1989) and 18/60, or 30 percent, of each of the $5,000 installments received in 1990 through 1999 ($1,500) will be reported as gain, and the balance ($3,500) will be treated as a nontaxable return of the seller's basis in the property. Over the remaining nine-year installment period, the sum of the gain to be reported (9 × $1,500 = 13,500) plus the gain reported in 1989 ($4,500) will equal the total gross profit or gain to be realized on the sale ($18,000).

Prior to the Tax Reform Act of 1986, if the seller was a "dealer" for tax purposes (one who held real estate as inventory or primarily for resale to customers in the ordinary course of his trade or business), the gain from the sale would have been taxed as ordinary income rather than as long-term capital gain. Therefore, by spreading the income over the installment period it was possible for a dealer (such as a subdivider-developer of raw land) to reduce his overall tax bracket and tax liability from the sale. Moreover, under prior law, if the real estate being sold was either a capital asset held for investment or was used in the seller's trade or business and held for more than six months, a noncorporate taxpayer might have been able to reduce his tax liability from the sale by spreading the long-term capital gain over the installment period. This is because the nonexcluded portion of the gain (40 percent) was subject to progressive ordinary income rates and the excluded portion (60 percent) was treated as "preference" income subject to the 21 percent alternative minimum tax. I.R.C. §§1221, 1231(b)(1), 1202 (prior law), and 55(b)(1).

However, the 1986 Act (as amended by the Revenue Reconciliation Act of 1990) reduced the maximum tax on ordinary income and gain from 50 percent to 31 percent (as well as the number of tax brackets), and the Revenue Act of 1987 disallowed installment treatment for dealers, so that under current law only sellers of investment or business real estate qualify for use of the installment method for reporting their gain from the sale of real estate. While qualified sellers (like Francine Farmer, who is an investor, or Dan Developer, who takes back a PMWAM, in the hypothetical) can no longer avail themselves of the same tax rate reduction benefits that were available under prior law, the installment method still provides such sellers with the ability to receive a time-value-of-money benefit by deferring their tax liability over the payment period of their purchase money mortgages or installment land contracts. See discussion at Chapter 2A, note 3.

It is worth noting that the Revenue Act of 1987 repealed the onerous "proportionate disallowance rule" (former I.R.C. §453C had required annual income recognition by a seller during the installment period based on the seller's total indebtedness from *all* her assets) but introduced a new rule (based on a time value rationale) that requires an interest charge on the deferred gain if deferred payments from all dispositions during the taxable year exceed $5 million. I.R.C. §453A(c), as added by the Revenue Act of 1987, as amended by the Technical and Miscellaneous Revenue Act of 1988. Also, special restrictions apply with respect to the use of escrow arrangements and third-party guarantees, the pledging of installment obligations as security for a loan, sales to related parties, and the sale or other disposition of installment obligations. See Madison and Dwyer ¶¶9.04[2][c], 9.04[4]. In addition, because of the new passive loss rules imposed under I.R.C. §469 and the original issue discount rules under I.R.C. §1274, the blend of interest and principal payments on an installment sale must be carefully scrutinized. In the case of an installment sale, the interest component of the debt-service payments from the purchase money mortgagor is currently treated as portfolio income (regardless of whether the interest income flows from a pass-through entity such as a limited partnership or Subchapter S corporation or is received directly by an individual taxpayer) for purposes of the limitation on passive losses. Staff of the Joint Committee on Taxation, 99th Cong., 2d Sess., General Explanation of the Tax Reform Act of 1986, at 232-233 (1987). See discussion at Chapter 2B, note 3. Also, any egregious inflation of the sale price and debt amount in exchange for a below-market rate of interest is vulnerable to challenge under I.R.C. §1274; however, the limitations imposed by the *Crane* doctrine (discussed at Chapter 2B, note 4), the elimination of preferential treatment for capital gains, and the reduction of depreciation benefits under the 1986 Act have discouraged sellers from engaging in such tax abuse. See Holthouse and Ritchie, Installment Sales Update, 15 J. Real Est. Taxn. 341, 349-352 (Summer 1988); see also Aronsohn, The Tax Reform Act of 1986 — Some Selected Real Estate Problems and Possibilities, 14 J. Real Est. Taxn. 203, 213-215 (Spring 1987).

An interesting issue has arisen in connection with the use of the installment method by sellers who take back a purchase money wraparound mortgage (such as Dan Developer in the hypothetical) or a wraparound installment obligation under a land contract when the underlying debt exceeds the seller's adjusted basis in the property. Based on the tax definition of payment and contract price, if the mortgage or installment obligation that is being assumed or taken subject to by the buyer exceeds the seller's basis in the property, such excess (determined after an adjustment to reflect selling expenses) is deemed to be an additional payment in the year of sale and added to the contract price; accordingly, extra gain might be recognized by the seller. Temp. Reg. §15A.453-1(b)(3)(i). Returning to our example, if the seller's adjusted basis were $28,000 instead of $80,000 the deemed payment in the year of sale would be $25,000 ($15,000 plus $10,000 excess of mortgage amount over basis plus selling expenses) instead of $15,000, and extra gain would be recognized on the additional payment amount in the year of sale. This is why wraparound financing has been recommended by tax advisors to avoid an acceleration of gain when the underlying debt exceeds the seller's basis in the property being sold. This presupposes that if the economic reality of a wraparound transaction is respected, there would be no assumption of liability in excess of basis inasmuch as the seller remains liable and continues to service the underlying debt, the purchaser does not formally assume liability on the existing mortgage, and (if the transaction is structured as an installment land contract rather than a PMWAM), title to the property does not pass until the purchaser makes the final payment. Likewise, under this rationale the contract price should not be reduced by the amount of the underlying debt since the full sale price is paid to the wraparound mortgagee, unlike an ordinary purchase money mortgage transaction, where the purchaser who assumes or takes subject to an existing mortgage pays a portion of the sale price directly to the seller's mortgagee. See Stonecrest Corp. v. Commissioner, 24 T.C. 659 (1955), nonacq., 1956-1 C.B. 6; Hunt v. Commissioner, 80 T.C. 1126 (1983). Returning to our example and assuming that the seller takes back a PMWAM for the same $40,000 amount of the existing mortgage, the contract price would be $100,000 instead of $60,000 and the gross profit ratio would be reduced from 30 percent ($18,000 ÷ $60,000) to 18 percent ($18,000 ÷ $100,000) so that the gain recognized in the year of sale would be reduced from $4,500 to $2,700.

In 1981 the Treasury Department promulgated temporary regulations that provide that in the case of a wraparound transaction the underlying indebtedness is deemed to be assumed or taken subject to by the purchaser, resulting in a larger deemed payment in the year of sale to the extent that the existing mortgage exceeds the seller's basis ($25,000 instead of $15,000 in the above example). In addition, the contract price would be reduced by the underlying debt, resulting in a higher gross profit ratio (30 percent instead of 18 percent in the above example). Temp. Reg. §15A.453-1(b)(3)(ii). However, in Professional Equities, Inc. v. Commissioner, 89 T.C. 165 (1987), acq., 1988-2 C.B. 1, the position taken by the 1981 Temporary Regulations with respect to wraparound transactions was rejected by the Tax Court as inconsistent with the economic reality of wraparound financing and outside the scope of I.R.C. §453. In the *Professional Equities* decision, involving a seller-dealer who sold parcels by means of installment land contracts (whereby the seller had retained legal title and remained obligated on the underlying debt until all payments were made by the buyer on the wraparound obligation), the court ruled that the taxpayer-seller was not required to reduce the total contract price by the amount of the underlying debt as required by the Temporary Regulations. See also Webb v. Commissioner, T.C. Mem. 1987-451, 54 T.C.M. 443 (1987).

Frequently the underlying debt in a PMWAM transaction is nonrecourse and, in contrast to an installment land contract, the purchaser immediately receives title. Under these circumstances how persuasive is the contention by the wraparound seller (raised by the successful taxpayer in *Professional Equities*) that the property has not been taken subject to the existing mortgage? See Holthouse and Ritchie, Installment Sales Update, 15 J. Real Est. Taxn. 341, 352-357 (Summer 1988); see generally Dickens and Orbach, Installment Reporting: Wraparound Mortgages After the IRS's Temporary Regulations and *Hunt,* 12 J. Real Est. Taxn. 137 (Winter 1985); Fowler and Wyndelts, Installment Sales: Wraparound Mortgage Regulation Invalidated by the Tax Court, 15 J. Real Est. Taxn. 203 (Spring 1988); Kennedy, Wraparound Mortgages Considered in the Context of the Commissioner's Temporary Installment Sales Regulations, 65 Taxes 530 (Aug. 1987).

As you may recall, under the *Crane* doctrine (discussed at Chapter 2B, note 4) no distinction is made between recourse and nonrecourse financing on the rationale that "the owner of property, mortgaged at a figure less than that at which the property will sell, must and will treat the conditions of the mortgage exactly as if they were his personal obligations." 331 U.S., at 14. See Chapter 2B, note 4. In light of the rationale for the *Crane* doctrine, what would be the argument in support of the position taken by the Temporary Regulations (and against the taxpayers' views in *Stonecrest Corp.* and *Professional Equities*) that a wraparound purchaser should be deemed to have assumed or taken subject to the underlying mortgage for tax purposes even though the purchaser has equitable (but not legal) title until the final payment is made, the purchaser under local law does not formally assume or acquire the property subject to the underlying mortgage, and the seller agrees with the buyer to remain responsible for making payments on the underlying debt?

C. THE INSTALLMENT LAND CONTRACT

1. *Introduction*

The installment land contract is commonly employed as an alternative to the purchase money mortgage to effect seller financing of real estate. Under this type of conveyancing, also known as the "contract for deed," "bond for deed," "long-term land contract," or "land sale contract," the purchaser typically takes possession of the property on execution of the contract, while the seller retains legal title in the property, which title is conveyed by deed only after the purchaser has completed a schedule of payments specified by the sales contract. In contrast to a purchase money mortgage, the seller does not take back a mortgage from the purchaser to secure the purchase-money indebtedness; instead the seller retains the naked legal title to secure the purchaser's promise to pay the balance of the purchase price over an agreed-on installment period. The series of installment payments may take any number of forms, including interest-only followed by a balloon payment or mixed interest and principal payments amortized over a long or short period of time. Frequently employed by vendors of moderately priced tract housing or undeveloped lots in subdivisions, the installment land contract is also used in sales of small commercial businesses and agricultural property.

The absence of a third-party lender in installment land contract transactions makes this device attractive to both buyers and sellers, for a number of reasons. It enables vendors to finance sales that, on account of either the purchaser's credit rating or the unacceptability of the property as security, would not qualify for third-party financing. Vendors also are able to reap the benefits of the finance charges they receive on the purchase price.[9] They may also derive tax benefits from reporting

9. In general, installment payment contracts and their attendant "finance charges" fall outside the reach of state usury statutes inasmuch as they do not involve the loan or forbearance of money and thus are said to constitute merely a "time-price differential," that is, the cost of the privilege of paying for goods over time. See, e.g., Peterson v.

their profits under the installment method of reporting income, as discussed at Chapter 9B, note 5e, supra. Without the necessity (and protection to the purchaser) of appraisals, engineering inspections, title searches, credit reports, and legal representation, installment contract sales can be closed quickly and inexpensively on execution of the contract and receipt of a much smaller down payment than is usually required by institutional mortgagees.

It should be obvious that each of the advantages of the installment land contract just recited is as readily available when the sale is structured as a purchase money mortgage. Differences between the two devices do, however, lead many vendors to favor the former. That legal title is not conveyed until the end of the contract term is an arrangement that makes possible, for example, the sale of residential building lots held in a "subdivision trust" under which the vendor may not convey title to individual lots until the trustee receives payment for them. The principal feature of installment land contracts that distinguishes them from their first cousin, the purchase money mortgage, is, however, their provision, in the event of the purchaser's default, for forfeiture of the property to the vendor and vendor's retention of all payments made as liquidated damages. By including in their contracts forfeiture clauses of this kind, vendors seek to circumvent the often cumbersome, protracted, and costly foreclosure procedures that apply to, and protect, defaulting mortgagors. If the forfeiture remedy can be successfully exploited by vendors, their willingness (despite the minimal cushion of a small down payment) to sell to purchasers whom other lenders would never consider assisting on any terms perhaps becomes more understandable. Yet, as the following materials suggest, the chances of vendors' being able to enforce forfeiture clauses as written, if litigated, have diminished substantially in recent years.

For a state-by-state survey of the legal treatment of installment land contracts see B. Dunaway, The Law of Distressed Real Estate, Appendix 10A (1988). Detailed discussions of this topic may be found in G. Nelson and D. Whitman, Installment Land Contracts — The

---

Wells Fargo Bank, 556 F. Supp. 1100 (Cal. Dist. Ct. App. 1981); DeSimon v. Ogden Assocs., 88 A.D.2d 472, 454 N.Y.S.2d 721 (N.Y. App. Div. 1982); Rotello v. International Harvester Co., 624 S.W.2d 249 (Tex. Ct. App. 1981). Cf. Bishop v. Linkway Stores, 280 Ark. 106, 655 S.W.2d 426 (1983); Midland Guardian Co. v. Thacker, 280 S.C. 563, 314 S.E.2d 26 (S.C. Ct. App. 1984); and Credit Alliance Corp. v. Timmco Equipment, 457 So. 2d 1102 (Fla. Dist. Ct. App. 1984), rev. denied, 464 So. 2d 556 (1985), on appeal after remand, 507 So. 2d 657 (Fla. Dist. Ct. App. 1987), rev. denied, 518 So. 2d 1274, which suggest that usury statutes may apply if the vendor has sold its interest under the contract for cash to a financing institution and has thereby sought to circumvent the application of usury laws. Some states have made installment land contract "finance charges" expressly subject to usury limitations. See, e.g., Md. Real Prop. Code Ann. §10-103(b)(8) (Michie 1989).

National Scene Revisited, 1985 B.Y.U. L. Rev. 1, reprinted in Real Estate Finance Law (2d ed. 1985); 7 Powell, Law of Real Property, Chap. 84D (1987).

The following hypothetical transaction illustrates the use of the installment land contract method of financing. Francine Farmer, owner of a large truck farm, Beanacre, just west of Miami, decides to retire to Key West. She has owned and operated Beanacre for nearly 50 years, and its value has appreciated greatly — but it would appreciate astronomically if it could be parcelled out into quarter-acre homesites sold individually. Francine, however, doesn't have the know-how to do the retail selling herself. Sam Subdivider does, but he hasn't got the cash to commit to buying Beanacre outright. Francine, therefore, gives Sam 90 percent financing on Beanacre under a purchase money mortgage and gets a good price with profits she can prorate for tax purposes over the life of the loan. To meet the debt service on his note with Francine, Sam needs to move his homesites quickly. He sets up a promotional operation in a rental hotel conference room on Miami Beach. There, dazzled by Sam's brilliant presentation of the development-community-to-be El Flamingo (Beanacre redivivus), Harry Homeowner writes Sam a check and signs the contract that appears on page 886.

NOTES AND QUESTIONS

1. Regulations (24 C.F.R. §1715.2 (1990)) promulgated under the Interstate Land Sales Full Disclosure Act, 15 U.S.C.A. §1701-1720 (Law. Co-op. 1990), give homesite buyers like Harry a seven-day option to revoke their agreement (perhaps to sober up from the complimentary cocktails served by the Sams of the real estate world). Suppose that Harry wants you, his lawyer, to shed the clear light of day on the contract he signed the night before. What reservations do you have? Consider the following.

a. How impressed are you by the provision that the warranty deed is to be delivered at Sam's expense?

b. When may Harry get free and clear title to his parcel? Read Conditions 3(a) and 4 together. If he prepays the full contract price, does he get title then? Does he get anything then? Would Francine Farmer be likely to permit prepayment and a release-of-lien arrangement in her mortgage with Sam? See discussion at Chapter 9B, note 5c, supra.

c. "We pay taxes." So proclaims Condition 5. But it would be passing strange, wouldn't it, were Harry to pay taxes on property of which Sam had possession and legal title? Isn't this just what is contemplated by Condition 3(b)(1), however?

PURCHASER (S)

	MISS / MR. / MRS. / TITLE

LAST   FIRST   MIDDLE INIT.

	MISS / MR. / MRS. / TITLE

LAST   FIRST   MIDDLE INIT.

ADDRESS _____

_____ AREA CODE _____ /TELEPHONE _____

CITY _____ STATE _____ ZIP OR COUNTRY _____

DESCRIPTION OF PROPERTY:

	UNIT / ADDITION / SECTION

LOT(S) _____ BLOCK _____ ,
(Name of Subdivision)

_____ , according to the plat of record in _____ COUNTY, FLORIDA.

PAYMENT TERMS

1. Total Cash Purchase Price .... $_____
2. Cash Downpayment .... $_____
3. Unpaid Balance of Cash Price
   (Amount Financed) .... $_____
4. FINANCE CHARGE .... $_____
5. Total of Payments .... $_____
6. Total Deferred Payment Price .... $_____

MONTHLY PAYMENTS

7. Standard Monthly Payment $_____
   Due and payable by mail or in person,
   on the 10th of each month.
8. Standard Number of Payments _____
9. Final Payment Amount $_____
10. ANNUAL PERCENTAGE RATE (Interest) _____%
11. All payments (cash, checks or money orders) must be
    made in United States currency.

HOMESITE DEVELOPMENT YEAR _____ **NEXT PAYMENT DUE** _____ **10, 19**____

There are no default or delinquency charges in the event of late payment, however, interest will continue to accrue on the unpaid balance during any default or delinquency period.

Seller retains a security interest (as defined in the Federal Reserve Board's Regulation Z) in the above real estate, in that seller retains title and possession thereto until completion of payments, in accordance with the terms of this Agreement.

ACKNOWLEDGMENT
The undersigned Purchaser(s) certifies that:
(a) I am of legal age.
(b) I have read this Agreement including the Conditions of Purchase on the reverse side and no additional representations have been made to induce me to purchase the property described.
(c) I have received and have had an opportunity to examine the Supplement to this Agreement containing a statement required by Federal law regarding my right to cancel this transaction within three (3) business days.
(d) I UNDERSTAND I HAVE THE OPTION TO REVOKE THIS CONTRACT IF I HAVE NOT RECEIVED A PROPERTY REPORT PREPARED PURSUANT TO THE RULES AND REGULATIONS OF THE U.S. DEPARTMENT OF HOUSING AND URBAN DEVELOPMENT, IN ADVANCE OF, OR AT THE TIME OF SIGNING THIS CONTRACT; I UNDERSTAND I HAVE THE FURTHER RIGHT TO REVOKE THIS CONTRACT WITHIN 48 HOURS AFTER I HAVE SIGNED IT IF I DID NOT RECEIVE SAID PROPERTY REPORT AT LEAST 48 HOURS BEFORE SIGNING THE CONTRACT. I HEREBY ACKNOWLEDGE AND AFFIRM BY MY SIGNATURE HEREON THAT I RECEIVED SUCH PROPERTY REPORT (WHICH IS ALSO THE REPORT REQUIRED UNDER FLORIDA LAW), TOGETHER WITH ANY PROPERTY REPORT OR OTHER APPROPRIATE DOCUMENT REQUIRED BY THE LAW OF _____, IN ADVANCE OF SIGNING THIS CONTRACT AND I HAVE READ AND UNDERSTAND SUCH REPORT(S).
(e) I agree to purchase the described property in accordance with the terms of this Agreement, the Supplement and any duly executed Rider thereto.

_____ SEAL
Purchaser's signature

_____ SEAL
Purchaser's signature

I have received the Initial Payment and witnessed the above signatures.

_____

☐ Cash   ☐ Check

Accepted at Miami, Florida by

_____

By: _____
Authorized Employee Signature

Witness: _____

Witness: _____

STATE OF FLORIDA   SS:
COUNTY OF DADE

I HEREBY CERTIFY that on this day, before me, a Notary Public authorized to take acknowledgments, personally appeared the person indicated as Authorized Employee above, whom I know to be the Agent of _____ in the foregoing Purchase Agreement, and acknowledged before me that he executed such contract in the name of and on behalf of _____; that as such Agent he is duly authorized by _____ to do so, and that such Purchase Agreement is the act and deed of _____.

WITNESS my hand and seal in the County and State named above,

this date _____

_____
Notary Public, State of Florida at Large

- You have the privilege of transferring your equity in this property to a home or other available property of equal or higher value in one of our Florida communities. (See Item 6 below.)

- We do not repurchase property after expiration of the cancellation periods provided by law or refund any portion of payments except as provided in Item 7 below.

- Without extra charge to you:
  - We will pay all real estate taxes on your property until we have deeded your property to you or this Agreement is recorded. (See Item 5 below.)
  - We will pave your street not later than the end of the Homesite Development Year. (See Item 2 below.)
  - We will issue you a Warranty Deed and title insurance policy. (See Item 3 below.)

CONDITIONS OF PURCHASE
PLEASE READ CAREFULLY

1. BASIC AGREEMENT

We agree to sell to you (the purchaser or purchasers named on the face page) the residential property described in this purchase agreement. This agreement also states the price and describes the other terms of this purchase. You agree to buy this property from us and to make Standard Monthly Payments in the amount shown on the face of this agreement on or before the tenth day of each month. The unpaid balance at any time will bear interest at the rate specified on the front of the Agreement (ANNUAL PERCENTAGE RATE).

2. PAVING OF YOUR STREET

This property is currently undeveloped. We agree to complete the paving of streets adjacent to your property, in accordance with the plat filed in the public records of the county in which your property is located, before the end of the Homesite Development Year.

3. YOUR WARRANTY DEED

(a) We will deliver to you at our expense a properly executed Warranty Deed if you have fully paid for this property by making all of your Standard Monthly Payments without prepayment.

(b) The Warranty Deed will convey good marketable and insurable title to you, free and clear of all encumbrances except for the following: (1) the lien for taxes for the year in which we convey the property; (2) oil, gas and mineral reservations of record, if any; (3) zoning and regulatory ordinances, restrictions and easements commonly found in Florida communities of high standards; (4) restrictions and limitations affecting the use of the property which are common to the subdivision and which now or hereafter may become of public record; and (5) easements for drainage, canal maintenance and public utilities.

(c) After this Warranty Deed is recorded, we will at our expense have issued to you a standard owner's title policy from a member firm of the American Land Title Association.

(d) Use and possession of this property will be retained by us until you have paid us the purchase price in full and until we have delivered the Warranty Deed.

4. YOUR RIGHT TO PREPAY

You have the right to prepay the outstanding balance under this agreement in whole or in part at any time without penalty. Prepayment does not, however, accelerate our obligation (a) to deliver the Warranty Deed and title insurance policy to you before the Homesite Development Date or (b) to complete paving of the streets adjacent to your property before the end of the Homesite Development Year. However, if you do prepay, we will thereupon issue you a certificate of payment in full.

5. WE PAY TAXES

We will pay all real property taxes on this property while this Agreement is in force or until you record this Agreement or until we deliver you a Warranty Deed conveying title to the property to you, whichever first occurs.

6. YOUR TRANSFER PRIVILEGE

If your payments are current, we guarantee you the privilege to transfer your equity (the portion of your payments on this property applied towards principal) at any time before you have paid your outstanding balance in full. This transfer may be toward either:

(a) The purchase of available property of equal or higher price in this or any other of our Florida communities; or

(b) The purchase of a standard home built by us in an available housing area.

If you have equities in more than one homesite, you may transfer them only to a like number of other homesites or homes.

7. YOUR RIGHTS IF WE FAIL TO PERFORM

If we fail to meet any of our obligations under this Agreement, you may elect either of the following exclusive remedies, at your option.

(a) You may exchange this property for other property of similar value in this or any other of our communities and in a similarly desirable location, or

(b) We will refund all payments made by you under this Agreement

If you elect either of these remedies, both you and we will be released from any further obligations under this Agreement. There are no other privileges of cancellation or refund except as stated above.

8. NO PERSONAL LIABILITY ON DEFAULT

You have no personal liability to make any payment under this Agreement. However, if you fail to make any payment, you will be in default and we may terminate this agreement.

Before any such termination becomes effective, you will have a grace period within which to bring your account to a current status. This grace period shall be for the period of 60 days if 10% or less of the principal amount of the purchase price has been paid, 90 days if more than 10% and less than 25% of the principal amount of the purchase price has been paid, 120 days if more than 25% but less than 50% of the principal amount of the purchase price has been paid, and 150 days if 50% or more of the principal amount of the purchase price has been paid.

If you bring your account to a current status by paying all past due principal and interest within the applicable grace period, you will no longer be considered in default. If you do not bring your account to a current status within the applicable grace period, we may terminate this Agreement without futher notice.

9. TERMINATION

If we terminate this Agreement, we will retain all monies you have paid under this Agreement, including principal and interest, as liquidated damages because we have taken this property off the real estate market, we have turned away other prospective purchasers and we have incurred or will be incurring selling, administrative and development expenses in connection with this property. Upon termination, any and all rights you may have had in this property shall immediately terminate and we may return this property to our inventory and resell it free and clear of any claims, liens or encumbrances arising out of this Agreement.

If this Agreement is terminated, our recorded affidavit attesting to your default and the termination, shall be conclusive proof of such default and termination for all purposes, and you irrevocably authorize us to thus attest and record such affidavit as though it were your own act and deed.

10. EFFECTIVE DATE

This Agreement is effective and binding on us when you have signed it and when we have signed it at our Home Office. We may accept or reject this Agreement without explanation, and if we reject it, we will return the deposit to you and both parties shall be released from any obligation hereunder.

11. ASSIGNMENT OF THIS AGREEMENT

You may assign this Agreement with our written consent upon payment of a transfer fee.

12. NOTICES

Notices under this Agreement must be in writing and addressed to the last known address of the respective party, except as to the voidance and revocation right as provided in paragraph (d) under "Acknowledgment" section on the face page.

13. FLORIDA CONTRACT

The parties agree that this Agreement shall be construed and interpreted in accordance with the laws of the State of Florida.

887

d.   Harry must pay taxes if he records the contract. (The "Acknowledgement," when signed by *Sam*'s agent before a notary, makes the contract recordable under Fla. Stat. §695.03 (1989).) This looks like a penalty for recording. Why would Sam do this to Harry? Would keeping Harry's interest off the record make it easier for Sam to resell the property if Harry defaults and forfeits? Is this the purpose of the second sentence of Condition 9? Remember, not being in possession, Harry does not give constructive notice of his interest in the property. Under most state recording statutes, this would mean a purchaser from Sam would take free of Harry's unrecorded interest. Similarly, a subsequent mortgagee would have lien priority over Harry. See generally discussion at Chapter 3B, notes 3 and 4. Also note that in Florida, where the purchaser under a recorded installment land contract is not given the right of possession, the tax assessment must be made in the name of the vendor. 42 Op. Atty. Gen. 073-131 (1973). Some of the perils to purchasers described herein have been mitigated by legislation in some jurisdictions. In Maryland, for example, installment land contracts must be recorded, and the vendor is not permitted to mortgage the subject property in an amount exceeding the unpaid balance of the purchase price. Md. Real Prop. Code Ann. §§10-103(d) and 10-104 (Michie 1989).

Observe that Harry would not be entitled to the use and possession of the land even if he were to prepay the balance of the purchase price. Under Condition 4 such a prepayment would not accelerate Sam's obligation to deliver a deed, and under Condition 3(d) use and possession of the parcel will be retained by Sam until he delivers a deed to Harry. This looks like a disguised penalty for prepayment. Why would Sam want to discourage a prepayment by Harry?

e.   In the typical third-party mortgage transaction, the lender does not finance the purchase price until the title has been searched — and usually examined on the day of the sale. Under the installment land contract device, title may not pass until principal and interest payments have been made for a number of years. What safeguards might you devise to protect Harry in this regard while maintaining the essential financial structure of the contract? What do you think of the rather open-ended qualifications to "marketable title" found in the contract?

f.   The contract period for this kind of sale can run for as long as ten years — or more. What if Harry's mind or fortunes change down the line? How flexible are the assignment and transfer "privileges" granted under the contract? The restriction on assignment probably would not curtail Harry's ability to mortgage or sell any equity he builds up under the contract. Courts construe these restrictions narrowly.

The boldface highlight in the contract speaks of "value." Condition 6 says "price." Explain the difference to Harry.

   g. Does the fact that Sam's performance under the contract is due only in the "homesite development year" trouble you? See Luette v. Bank of Italy Natl. Trust & Savings Assn., 42 F.2d 9 (9th Cir. 1930), cert. denied, 282 U.S. 884 (excerpted at Chapter 3A). If Sam breaches, what possible remedies are precluded to Harry under Condition 7? Would the refunding of all payments made under the contract make Harry whole? If he had been making payments for ten years, would a time value issue affect your answer, particularly in view of the fact that during this period Harry has not enjoyed the use of the property? What might cause Sam to default? What might entice him to default?

   h. Explain to Harry the meaning of Conditions 8 and 9. Why, do you suppose, is there a graduated grace period? A comparable scheme is mandated by legislation for Arizona installment land contracts. Ariz. Rev. Stat. Ann. §33-741 (1989).

   i. Many of the questions you would have as Harry's attorney would be answered in a "statement of record" as required under the Interstate Land Sales Full Disclosure Act (ILSFDA) to be filed with the Secretary of Housing and Urban Development and provided to purchasers. In general, the ILSFDA covers only retail sales of undeveloped lots in large subdivisions and is similar to the full disclosure provisions and philosophy of the Securities Act of 1933. A reading of the regulations issued under ILSFDA will give you an idea of some of the perceived abuses in the subdivision industry the Act was designed to curb. See 24 C.F.R. §1710, Appendix (1990). Nearly a dozen states have similar laws modeled after the Uniform Land Sales Practices Act. 7A U.L.A. 669 (1985).

2. Enforceability of Forfeiture Provisions and Recharacterization as a Mortgage

Assume in the preceding hypothetical that instead of a vacant lot Sam Subdivider sells Harry Homeowner a tract house in 1973 under an installment land contract for a purchase price of $15,000, payable at 5 percent over 15 years with interest and principal payments of $118.62 per month, and that there is a fixed grace period of 30 days instead of the graduated periods in the sample contract. For eight years Harry punctually makes his payments. He has also landscaped his lot and built a garage on it. Property values in his neighborhood are beginning to skyrocket; the fair market value of Harry's house has grown to $44,000. In year nine, Harry, alas, takes ill and is out of work and misses a month's payment. Thirty-one days after his last payment, Sam tells Harry he is exercising his termination rights under Articles 8 and 9 of the sample installment land contract, which, as Sam points out, Harry had agreed to and signed. Forfeiture under Harry's uncured default gives Sam the house, worth $44,000, and retention of about $12,000 in payments ($7,000 principal and $5,000 interest) Harry has made over the past eight and one-half years. Had Harry fully performed under the contract, Sam would have received about $21,000. Harry's misfortune enriches Sam by $35,000 (a total of $56,000 received and retained on default less $21,000 expected from full performance under the contract). If you feel Sam's enrichment is unjust, note that on just these facts the trial court in Bean v. Walker, which follows, granted summary judgment in favor of the seller in an ejectment action against the defaulting purchaser. A deal is, after all, a deal.[10]

In practice, however, most courts are unwilling to strictly follow the letter of such "deals." In refusing to enforce the forfeiture provision, the appellate court in Bean v. Walker characterized the contract sale as, in effect, a mortgage by invoking equitable principles that courts have used to alleviate the harsh consequences of forfeiture to defaulting purchasers. Looney v. FmHA (excerpted infra) likewise treats the contract as a mortgage. The equities among the parties in that case, however, were arguably less compelling, and in reaching its decision the court engaged in some rather result-oriented legal and financial maneuvering. The third case, Heikkila v. Carver (excerpted infra), while deciding against the purchasers, presents a number of arguments grounded on contract law that are typically summoned to avoid or mitigate forfeiture. The judicial as well as the legislative treatment of forfeiture is discussed in the notes. The rationales set forth by the courts have been far from consistent or predictable and, together with the results of adjudication, vary widely among jurisdictions. Installment land contracts represent an area of law that is still very much in a state of flux and that has been beset by conflicting policy and financial considerations.

---

10. A notorious illustration of a vendor's insistence on strict compliance with contact terms in order to precipitate a forfeiture can be seen in the "hog house" case. There, the purchaser in possession allegedly breached the sales contract requirement of maintaining the property by having failed to replace half a dozen small window panes in an abandoned hog house. Forfeiture for this default was claimed by the vendor after $284,000 had been paid on the $300,000 contract. The court held for the purchaser. Lett v. Grummer, 300 N.W.2d 147 (Iowa 1981).

Bean v. Walker
95 A.D.2d 70, 464 N.Y.S.2d 895 (N.Y. App. Div.,
4th Dept., 1983)

DOERR, J.

Presented for our resolution is the question of the relative rights between a vendor and a defaulting vendee under a land purchase contract. Special Term, in granting summary judgment in favor of plaintiffs, effectively held that the defaulting vendee has no rights. We cannot agree.

The facts may be briefly stated. In January, 1973 plaintiffs agreed to sell and defendants agreed to buy a single-family home in Syracuse for the sum of $15,000.[1] The contract provided that this sum would be paid over a 15-year period at 5% interest, in monthly installments of $118.62. The sellers retained legal title to the property, which they agreed to convey upon payment in full according to the terms of the contract. The purchasers were entitled to possession of the property, and all taxes, assessments and water rates, and insurance became the obligation of the purchasers. The contract also provided that in the event purchasers defaulted in making payment and failed to cure the default within 30 days, the sellers could elect to call the remaining balance immediately due or elect to declare the contract terminated and repossess the premises. If the latter alternative was chosen, then a forfeiture clause came into play whereby the seller could retain all the money paid under the contract as "liquidated" damages and "the same shall be in no event considered a penalty but rather the payment of rent."

Defendants went into possession of the premises in January, 1973 and in the ensuing years claim to have made substantial improvements on the property. They made the required payments under the contract until August, 1981 when they defaulted following an injury sustained by defendant Carl Walker. During the years while they occupied the premises as contract purchasers defendant paid to plaintiff $12,099.24, of which $7,114.75 was applied to principal. Thus, at the time of their default, defendants had paid almost one half of the purchase price called for under the agreement. After the required 30-day period to cure the default,[2] plaintiffs commenced this action sounding in ejectment seeking a judgment "[t]hat they be adjudged the owner in fee" of the property and granting them possession thereof. The court granted summary judgment to plaintiffs.

---

1. The house now has an alleged market value of $44,000.
2. Defendant's offer to bring the payments up to date and pay a higher interest rate on the balance due were unavailing.

If the only substantive law to be applied to this case was that of contracts, the result reached would be correct. However, under the facts presented herein the law with regard to the transfer of real property must also be considered. The reconciliation of what might appear to be conflicting concepts is not insurmountable.

While there are few New York cases which directly address the circumstances herein presented, certain general principles may be observed. "It is well settled that the owner of the real estate from the time of the execution of a valid contract for its sale is to be treated as the owner of the purchase money and the purchaser of the land is to be treated as the equitable owner thereof. The purchase money becomes personal property" (New York Cent. & Hudson Riv. R.R. Co. v. Cottle, 187 App. Div. 131, 144, affd. 229 N.Y. 514). Thus, notwithstanding the words of the contract and implications which may arise therefrom, the law of property declares that, upon the execution of a contract for sale of land, the vendee acquires equitable title. . . . The vendor holds the legal title in trust for the vendee and has an equitable lien for the payment of the purchase price. . . . The vendee in possession, for all practical purposes, is the owner of the property with all the rights of an owner subject only to the terms of the contract. The vendor may enforce his lien by foreclosure or an action at law for the purchase price of the property — the remedies are concurrent. . . .

The conclusion to be reached, of course, is that upon the execution of a contract an interest in real property comes into existence by operation of law, superseding the terms of the contract. An analogous result occurs in New York if an owner purports to convey title to real property as security for a loan; the conveyance is deemed to create a lien rather than an outright conveyance, even though the deed was recorded . . . and "one who has taken a deed absolute in form as security for an obligation, in order to foreclose the debtor's right to redeem, must institute a foreclosure, and is entitled to have the premises sold in the usual way" (14 Carmody-Wait 2d, §92:2, p. 612).

Cases from other jurisdictions are more instructive. In Skendzel v. Marshall (261 Ind. 226 [addressing itself to a land sale contract]), the court observed that while legal title does not vest in the vendee until the contract terms are satisfied, he does acquire a vested equitable title at the time the contract is consummated. When the parties enter into the contract all incidents of ownership accrue to the vendee who assumes the risk of loss and is the recipient of all appreciation of value. The status of the parties becomes like that of mortgagor-mortgagee.[3]

---

3. New York recognizes the similarity between mortgages and contracts for sale by noting that the latter "shall be deemed to be mortgages" for purposes of paying the mortgage recording tax (Tax Law, §250).

Viewed otherwise would be to elevate form over substance (Skendzel v. Marshall, supra, p. 234). The doctrine that equity deems as done that which ought to be done is an appropriate concept which we should apply to the present case. . . .

Because the common-law mortgagor possessed equitable title, the legal owner (the mortgagee) could not recover the premises summarily, but first had to extinguish the equitable owner's equity of redemption. Thus evolved the equitable remedy of mortgage foreclosure, which is now governed by statute (RPAPL 1301 et seq.). In our view, the vendees herein occupy the same position as the mortgagor at common law; both have an equitable title only, while another person has legal title. We perceive no reason why the instant vendees should be treated any differently than the mortgagor at common law. Thus the contract vendors may not summarily dispossess the vendees of their equitable ownership without first bringing an action to foreclose the vendees' equity of redemption. This view reflects the modern trend in other jurisdictions (see Skendzel v. Marshall) . . .

The key to the resolution of the rights of the parties lies in whether the vendee under a land sale contract has acquired an interest in the property of such a nature that it must be extinguished before the vendor may resume possession. We hold that such an interest exists since the vendee acquires equitable title and the vendor merely holds the legal title in trust for the vendee, subject to the vendor's equitable lien for the payment of the purchase price in accordance with the terms of the contract. The vendor may not enforce his rights by the simple expedient of an action in ejectment but must instead proceed to foreclose the vendee's equitable title or bring an action at law for the purchase price, neither of which remedies plaintiffs have sought.

The effect of the judgment granted below is that plaintiffs will have their property with improvements made over the years by defendants, along with over $7,000 in principal payments on a purchase price of $15,000, and over $4,000 in interest. The basic inequity of such a result requires no further comment. . . .[4]. If a forfeiture would result in the inequitable disposition of property and an exorbitant monetary loss, equity can and should intervene (Thomas v. Klein, 99 Idaho 105, 107, supra; Ellis v. Butterfield, 98 Idaho 644, 648).

The interest of the parties here can only be determined by a sale of the property after foreclosure proceedings with provisions for dis-

---

4. Some jurisdictions refuse to enforce the forfeiture provision of a land contract if the proportion of the purchase price paid is so substantial that the amount forfeited would be an invalid "penalty" (see, e.g., Hook v. Bomar, 320 F2d 536 [applying Fla. law]; Rothenberg v. Follman, 19 Mich. App. 383; Morris v. Sykes, 624 P2d 681 [Utah]; Johnson v. Carman, 572 P2d 371 [Utah]; Behrendt v. Abraham, 64 Cal. 2d 182; Land Dev. v. Padgett, 369 P2d 888 [Alaska]).

posing of the surplus or for a deficiency judgment. In arguing against this result, plaintiffs stress that in New York a defaulting purchaser may not recover money paid pursuant to an executory contract (Lawrence v. Miller, 86 N.Y. 131). Although we have no quarrel with this general rule of law . . . we observe that this rule has generally been applied to cases involving down payments . . . or to cases wherein the vendee was not in possession. . . .

By our holding today we do not suggest that forfeiture would be an inappropriate result in all instances involving a breach of a land contract. If the vendee abandons the property and absconds, logic compels that the forfeiture provisions of the contract may be enforced. Similarly, where the vendee has paid a minimal sum on the contract and upon default seeks to retain possession of the property while the vendor is paying taxes, insurance and other upkeep to preserve the property, equity will not intervene to help the vendee (Skendzel v. Marshall, supra, pp. 240, 241). Such is not the case before us.

Accordingly, the judgment should be reversed, the motion should be denied and the matter remitted to Supreme Court for further proceedings in accordance with this opinion. . . .

Ohio Rev. Code Ann. §5313.07
(Baldwin 1991)

WHEN FORECLOSURE REQUIRED; QUIET TITLE ACTION AND CANCELLATION NOT PROHIBITED.

If the vendee of a land installment contract has paid in accordance with the terms of the contract for a period of five years or more from the date of the first payment or has paid toward the purchase price a total sum equal to or in excess of twenty per cent thereof, the vendor may recover possession of his property only by use of a proceeding for foreclosure and judicial sale of the foreclosed property as provided in section 2323.07 of the Revised Code. Such action may be commenced after expiration of the period of time prescribed by sections 5313.05 and 5313.06 of the Revised Code. In such an action, as between the vendor and vendee, the vendor shall be entitled to proceeds of the sale up to and including the unpaid balance due on the land installment contract.

Chapter 5313. of the Revised Code does not prevent the vendor or vendee of a land installment contract from commencing a quiet title action to establish the validity of his claim to the property conveyed under a land installment contract nor from bringing an action for unpaid installments.

Chapter 5313. of the Revised Code does not prevent the vendor and vendee from cancelling their interest in a land installment contract under section 5301.331 [5301.33.1] of the Revised Code.

Looney v. Farmers Home Administration
794 F.2d 310 (7th Cir. 1986)

CUDAHY, Circuit Judge.

Lowry and Helen McCord ("the McCords" or the "buyers") arranged to purchase the property of John and Esther Looney ("the Looneys" or the "appellees") in Rush County, Indiana. When the McCords fell into financial troubles, they secured an emergency loan through the Farmers Home Administration (the "FmHA" or the "government"). In exchange, the FmHA received a second mortgage on the property. Later, after paying $123,280 to the Looneys, the McCords defaulted. The Looneys filed suit in the District Court for the Southern District of Indiana seeking forfeiture under the forfeiture clause in the buyers' contract. The FmHA filed a counterclaim asking instead for foreclosure, the usual remedy in cases of default. The court granted forfeiture, concluding that the buyers had paid too small an amount toward the contract principal to justify foreclosure. In light of the totality of circumstances surrounding the transactions at issue, we believe that foreclosure was the more appropriate remedy and therefore reverse.

On October 7, 1976, the Looneys and the McCords entered into a conditional land sales contract to convey 260 acres of property to the McCords for $250,000. The contract specified that this sum was to be amortized over a 20-year period at an annual interest rate of seven percent. The McCords were to make annual payments of $23,280 on November 15 of each year until the purchase price and all accrued interest was paid. They also agreed to pay real estate taxes, insurance and maintenance costs for the property.

Four years after agreeing to these terms, the McCords received an economic emergency loan for $183,800 from the FmHA under the 1978 version of the Emergency Agricultural Credit Adjustment Act, 7 U.S.C. note prec. §1961. In return for the loan, the McCords executed a promissory note for the amount of the loan plus 11% annual interest. As security for the note, the McCords granted the FmHA a mortgage on the land subject to the land sales contract. The Looneys were aware of and consented to this mortgage.

The McCords subsequently defaulted on their payment obligations to the Looneys. At the time of their default, the McCords had paid $123,280 to the Looneys but still owed $249,360.12 on the contract price. In 1983, the Looneys brought suit against the McCords and the FmHA seeking ejectment and forfeiture of the contract. Both the Looneys and the McCords moved for summary judgment and the court granted the Looneys' motion. On June 5, 1984, the government sought leave to file a counter-claim seeking foreclosure of its mortgage. The court allowed the government to file. The government then moved for summary judgment. Together with its motion, the government included two affidavits stating that the property had appreciated in value to $455,000.

The district court denied the government's motion for foreclosure. It held that the traditional presumption under Indiana law in favor of foreclosure did not apply because the McCords had made only minimal payments on the contract and had not paid their fall taxes or insurance installments. Because $249,360.12 was still owed on an initial base price of $250,000, the court found the McCords' equity in the property to be $639.88, only .26% of the principal. The court therefore found forfeiture appropriate, awarded the FmHA $639.88 and extinguished the FmHA's mortgage.

The FmHA appeals. It contends that foreclosure was the appropriate remedy because it would have protected all parties' interests. In receiving forfeiture, the government argues, the Looneys got a windfall. They kept the $123,280 that the buyers had paid over 7½ years and got back property which the government's two uncontested affidavits stated had appreciated substantially. Moreover, the government states, the court miscalculated the McCords' payments on the contract and equity in the property and thus greatly undervalued what the government could justly recover. The court's theory, in effect, left the government's mortgage unsecured for much of the contract period.

In response, the Looneys note that the government had the opportunity to cure the buyers' default but did not. If the government really believed the property to have appreciated, appellees argue, it would have protected its interest by paying up the full amount of the annual installments and expenses. Since the government did not do this, it accepted the consequences. The Looneys also contend that the government cannot challenge the court's valuation of the McCords' equity because it never disputed or even responded to appellees' requests for admission which stated that the McCords' equity in the property was only $9,394.30 at the time the McCords secured their emergency loan.

I.

Under Indiana law a conditional land sales contract is considered in the nature of a secured transaction, "the provisions of which are subject to all proper and just remedies at law and in equity." Skendzel v. Marshall, 261 Ind. 226, 241, 301 N.E.2d 641, 650 (1973) (italics omitted), cert. denied, 415 U.S. 921, 94 S. Ct. 1421, 39 L. Ed. 2d 476 (1974). Recognizing the common maxim that "equity abhors forfeitures," the *Skendzel* court concluded that "judicial foreclosure of a land sales contract is in consonance with the notions of equity developed in American jurisprudence." 261 Ind. at 240, 301 N.E.2d at 650. Foreclosure generally protects the rights of all parties to a contract. Upon judicial sale the proceeds are first applied to the balance of the contract principal and interest owed the seller. Then, any junior lienholders take their share. Any surplus goes to the buyer.

Skendzel recognized, however, two instances where forfeiture was the appropriate remedy:

> In the case of an abandoning, absconding vendee, forfeiture is a logical and equitable remedy. Forfeiture would also be appropriate where the vendee has paid a minimal amount on the contract at the time of default and seeks to retain possession while the vendor is paying taxes, insurance, and other upkeep in order to preserve the premises.

261 Ind. at 240-41, 301 N.E.2d at 650.

While the Looneys' counsel contended at oral argument that the McCords were abandoning and absconding vendees, the district court did not rely on this first *Skendzel* exception in finding forfeiture appropriate. The court in McLendon v. Safe Realty Corp., 401 N.E.2d 80, 83 (1980) described the circumstances under which this exception applied:

> [F]or there to be an abandonment of a conditional land sales contract one must actually and intentionally relinquish possession of the land and act in a manner which is unequivocally inconsistent with the existence of a contract. . . .
> Furthermore *Skendzel* spoke of an "abandoning, *absconding* vendee." The word "abscond" means to hide, conceal, or absent oneself clandestinely with the intent to avoid legal process.

No evidence in the record demonstrates that the McCords intended to relinquish all title to the property or avoid legal process.

If forfeiture is justified, then, it is only because the second *Skendzel* exception is met. This requires that the vendee have paid only a minimum amount on the contract at the time of default. In this case, the district court concluded that "this is patently a situation contemplated by the court in *Skendzel* in which forfeiture is the logical and equitable remedy." However, the buyers in *Skendzel* had in fact paid more than a minimum amount on the contract and the court cited no examples of what would "patently" constitute a "minimum amount." Rather, later Indiana cases have interpreted *Skendzel* as requiring a case by case analysis that examines the "totality of circumstances surrounding the contract and its performance." Johnson v. Rutoskey, 472 N.E.2d 620, 626 (Ind. App. 1984).

Here, while $123,280 was paid to the Looneys, the court considered all but $639.88 to be interest rather than a part of the contract price. The court equated contract price with what was paid to reduce principal and implicitly determined that all the interest owed had to be paid before principal would in any degree be reduced.

But nothing in Indiana law compels the district court's construction of payment on the contract. On the contrary, several Indiana courts have considered and given weight to both payments to reduce principal and those to reduce interest in determining whether buyer falls within the second *Skendzel* exception. See Morris v. Weigle, 270 Ind. 121, 122, 383 N.E.2d 341, 342 (1978) ("At the time the Weigles repossessed the land, Morris had paid a total of $24,722,97 on the contract; of that amount $16,922.97 was principal and $7,800 was interest"); Oles v. Plummer, 444 N.E.2d 879, 882 (Ind. App. 1983) (looking at both payments made to reduce principal and payments to reduce interest to determine that 30.55% of the contract price had been paid and was not minimal); Fisel v. Yoder, 162 Ind. App. 565, 572, 320 N.E.2d 783, 788 ("the Yoders had paid a substantial portion of the contract price. At the time of trial, they had made a $10,000 downpayment, one $1,400 claim payment . . . and two interest payments.") Here, the contract contemplates the payment of interest. If interest payments are included in the calculus, the McCords paid almost 33% toward the contract price rather than .26% as the court determined.

It is true that certain cases have looked solely at the reduction of principal to determine payment on the contract. But many of these cases have not had to include interest payments in their calculi because the interest paid was enough to justify foreclosure rather than forfeiture. See Bartlett v. Wise, 169 Ind. App. 125, 348 N.E.2d 652, 654 (1976) ("she had paid one-third of the principal amount due on the contract — certainly more than a 'minimal amount' "); Tidd v. Stauffer, 159 Ind. App. 570, 308 N.E.2d 415 (1974).

Even when no principal is paid, a buyer's stake in the property may be sufficient to justify foreclosure. As the court stated in McLendon v. Safe Realty Corp., 401 N.E.2d at 83:

> We cannot say McLendon had paid a "minimal amount" on the contract at the time of default, giving him little if any equity in the property. The trial court found McLendon had no equity in the real estate as the principal owed under the contract and the accumulated real estate taxes exceeded the original contract price. However, "equity" in

this context is the amount or value of the property above the liens and charges against it.

Here, two uncontested affidavits indicate the property to be worth over $200,000 more than the McCords owe the Looneys. With the evidence of appreciation, the court was incorrect to conclusively value the McCords' equity at only $639.88.

When the second *Skendzel* exception has been invoked it has frequently been because the vendee is contributing to a decline in the value of the security. As the court said in Johnson v. Rutoskey, 472 N.E.2d 620, 626, "the second *Skendzel* exception will be met only where the purchaser has paid a minimum amount *and* the vendor's security interest in the property has been endangered" (emphasis in original). Thus in Goff v. Graham, 159 Ind. App. 324, 337, 306 N.E.2d 758, 766 (1974), forfeiture was proper because not only had the vendees only made a down payment on the property but "[e]vidence indicated that the purchaser had committed waste and deliberately neglected the properties." There is no allegation or evidence of waste in this case.

Even the Looneys admit that the buyers "had paid substantial monies pursuant to the terms of the contract." The Looneys received $123,280 and the McCords paid the necessary real estate taxes, insurance premiums and upkeep expenses for over six years. The Looneys make no showing that foreclosure would not satisfy their interest and the court below made no such determination. While foreclosure would appear to satisfy all parties' needs, forfeiture leaves the FmHA with a $639.88 recovery on a $183,800 loan. In view of the "totality of circumstances" this result seems inequitable and unnecessary. The judgment of the district court is therefore REVERSED and REMANDED for further proceedings not inconsistent with this opinion.

Heikkila v. Carver
378 N.W.2d 214 (S.D. 1985)

FOSHEIM, Chief Justice.

This is an appeal by Russell and Norma Carver from a judgment decreeing the Carvers in default on a contract for deed. We affirm.

On January 2, 1979, Howard and Reino Heikkila sold their 5,920 acre Harding County ranch to Carvers on contract for deed. The contract fixed the purchase price at $592,000.00 allocating in part $394,900.00 for real estate, $75,000.00 for the house located on the property, and $50,000.00 for 10% of the Heikkilas' mineral interests. The contract reserved to the Heikkilas an undivided 90% interest, including future interests, in "all minerals of whatsoever nature," including the right to "prospect for, mine and/or drill for said minerals."

Under the terms of the contract, payment was to be made by the assumption of a $12,908.70 debt on a state land contract, a downpayment of $159,091.31 and annual installments of principal and interest in the amount of $41,202.00 beginning on January 3, 1980, and thereafter on the third day of January each year for nineteen years. The rate of interest stipulated in the contract was 7½%; however, upon default in making any payment, interest would accrue at a rate of 11% until the default was cured.

The contract also contained a default clause, which reads:

> In the event the Buyers default in the performance of any of the terms, covenants, conditions or obligations imposed upon them by this agreement, the Parties agree that the Sellers shall have the option to declare all deferred balances immediately due and payable, subject to the following conditions.
>
> If the Buyers fail to timely pay or breach any of the covenants or conditions or obligations imposed upon them then the Sellers shall give the Buyers sixty (60) days notice of such default during which time the Buyers may make such payment or correct the breach of any term, covenant, or conditions or obligations imposed upon them, making the contract current, but if such action is not taken by the Buyers during this sixty (60) day term, then the Sellers shall have the right to retake possession of the property described in Part III(A) and Part III(B) hereof, together with the duty on the part of the Buyers to assign back to the Sellers or their heirs or successors in interest all of their rights in the Contract for Sale with the State of South Dakota as set forth in Paragraph III or if the Contracts have been fully performed and patents been issued from the State of South Dakota to the Buyers then they shall execute deeds back to the Sellers.
>
> In such event, the Sellers and the Buyers may, and do, agree that it would be impractical or extremely difficult to fix actual damages in case of Buyers' default, and that all payments which have been made on and under the terms and conditions of this agreement by Buyers, or on their behalf by any other person shall be deemed liquidated damages, and is a reasonable estimate of damages and that Sellers shall retain said sum or sums as their sole right to damages for Buyers' default. All parties agree that in the event of any such default and the Buyers cause the reassignment of the Contracts for Sale from the State of South Dakota or a deed back on such property as hereinbefore set forth, then the remedies shall be limited to the retaking of the land under such foreclosure or other proceedings, however if the Buyers fail to reassign their interest in such Contracts for Deed or execute deeds back on said land, then such remedies shall not be exclusive and the Sellers may proceed under all of the terms of this contract and under such remedies as may be provided for under the laws of the State of South Dakota.

Carvers were delinquent in making their 1982 and 1983 payments. On each occasion, however, they tendered payment within the sixty-day grace period provided for in the contract.

In 1984, Carvers again failed to make their January 3 installment payment. On January 18, 1984, Heikkilas notified Carvers by mail of their intention to foreclose if payment was not made within the sixty-day grace period. Carvers, however, did not tender payment, and on March 23, 1984, Heikkilas brought suit for strict foreclosure of the contract.

At the time of default, Carvers had made payments on the contract to Heikkilas totaling $195,002.32 in principal and $124,343.15 in interest.

Following a trial, judgment was entered in favor of Heikkilas, granting them strict foreclosure of the contract. The trial court further ordered that Carvers could redeem the ranch property upon payment to Heikkilas within ninety days following entry of judgment of the total balance due and owing on the contract, including interest, in the amount of $448,901.52.

Carvers raise four issues on appeal, which we address in the order presented.

I. LIQUIDATED DAMAGES

Carvers first contend that the default clause in the contract for deed is an unenforceable penalty.

Whether a forfeiture provision in a contract is an enforceable liquidated damage provision or an unenforceable penalty is a question of law for the trial court to determine "based upon a consideration of the instrument as a whole, the situation of the parties, the subject matter of the contract, the circumstances surrounding its execution, and other factors." Prentice v. Classen, 355 N.W.2d 352-55 (S.D. 1984) (citing Walter Motor Truck Co. v. State, etc., 292 N.W.2d 321, 323-24 (S.D. 1980)). We have held that ordinarily such a provision will be upheld if (1) at the time the contract was made the damages in the event of breach were incapable or very difficult of accurate estimation, (2) there was a reasonable endeavor by the parties to fix compensation, and (3) the amount stipulated bears a reasonable relation to probable damages and is not disproportionate to any damages reasonably to be anticipated. Prentice v. Classen, supra; Walter Motor Truck Co. v. State, etc., supra.

The burden of establishing that the liquidated damage provision is an unlawful penalty rests with the party against whom enforcement is sought. Prentice v. Classen, supra.

Here, the trial court found that both Carvers and Heikkilas had retained competent legal counsel experienced in farm and ranch real estate sales; that at the time the contract was executed, damages in the event of default by Carvers were incapable or very difficult of accurate estimation, including the length of redemption period a court might set, the risk of overgrazing or other waste before or during the redemption period, other possible damage to the property, unknown future market value of the property, projected rental value of the ranch, and the potential loss of royalty income should the buyer interfere with mineral development. The court also found that the parties had used reasonable efforts in trying to estimate damages but were unable to do so, and that the default provision itself was the best evidence of the parties' efforts and intentions at the time of sale.

In addition, the record discloses that Russell Carver, who was experienced in real estate transactions of this nature, reviewed the contract for deed with his attorney prior to signing it. Indeed, Carvers' attorney testified that it was his practice to review real estate agreements with his clients on a "paragraph by paragraph" basis. Carvers also negotiated several changes in the contract, including an extension of the grace period in the default clause from thirty to sixty days. There is no evidence in the record of overreaching or unfairness on the part of Heikkilas or their attorney. In short, the record supports the finding that the parties bargained at arms-length over the contract for deed, including the default clause.

Based upon these considerations, we cannot say that the trial court clearly erred in finding that the parties were unable at the time the contract was made to determine prospectively what damages might arise in the event of breach by the vendee.

Nevertheless, a court may decline to enforce a forfeiture clause if the defaulting vendee establishes by clear evidence that a substantial disparity exists between the payments made on the contract, together with the improvements made to the property, and the loss of rents and other detriment suffered by the vendors due to the loss of use and possession of the property. Prentice v. Classen, supra. See SDCL 21-50-2.

The trial court found that at the time of default, Carvers had paid approximately one-third of the contract price and "had received and continue[d] to receive the benefits of the use of the land together with 10% of the mineral royalties." In contrast, the trial court determined that Heikkilas had sustained damages in excess of $500,000.00 as a result of Carvers' breach as well as Heikkilas' lost use and possession of the land. This finding was predicated on the testimony of Reino Heikkila which was offered in support of the following exhibit prepared by Heikkilas:

Heikkila Damages, Expenses, and Costs as Result of Sale and Breach of Contract

1.	Loss of rental value of the ranch for five and one half years ($36,000.00 per year)	$198,000.00
2.	Loss of natural gas royalties (10% sold to Carver)	50,000.00
3.	Loss of timber sales	14,000.00
4.	Real estate commission fees	22,000.00
5.	Abstract and attorney's fees for sale	2,006.00
6.	Loss of sale of gravel	10,683.00
7.	Loss of payment offered by Jerry McCutchin for surface damages	28,500.00
8.	Attorney's fees, taxes and costs for arbitration dispute and contract foreclosure (estimated) (LaFleur — $2,474.00)	10,474.00
9.	Expense for car, gasoline, miles and meals for travel to Rapid City and Deadwood concerning arbitration and contract foreclosure through July 17, 1984, and July 31, 1984	975.00
10.	Loss of development of oil wells by Inland Oil	_____
11.	Loss of resale value of the ranch due to change in market conditions and reduction of average price per acre of $100.00 to $80.00 ($5,920.00 × 20)	118,400.00
12.	Loss of wages from McCutchin for inspection of wells on the property for the last five and one half years (15 wells × $125.00 per = $1,875.00 per month × 66 months = $123,750.00)	123,750.00
13.	Mental anguish and inconvenience concerning surface damage claims and breach of the contract.	10,000.00
	TOTAL	$588,788.00

We conclude, upon a careful examination of the record, that several of Heikkilas' damage claims should have been disregarded by the trial court on the ground that they were either too speculative or simply unfounded, including: (2) lost natural gas royalties; (3) lost timber sales; (6) lost gravel sales; (7) lost payment for surface damages; (9) travel expenses; (12) lost wages; (13) mental anguish and inconvenience. Notwithstanding that the aforementioned items should have been disallowed by the trial court, there is still no clear evidence in the record of a substantial disparity between the relative detriment sustained by the parties.

Accordingly, we conclude that the trial court did not err in holding as a matter of law that the default clause in the contract for deed was not a penalty pursuant to SDCL 53-9-5.

II. Reinstatement of the Contract

Carvers next contend that the trial court should have reinstated the contract under its equitable powers.

Carvers first tendered their 1984 installment payment to Heikkilas on March 29, 1984, six days after Heikkilas commenced this action to foreclose on the contract. The sixty-day grace period had expired on March 18, 1984.

Carvers claim they withheld payment pending a response to their formal demand of Heikkilas, made by letter on March 5, 1984, to pay or arbitrate damages allegedly caused to the ranch property by ongoing mineral development. Carvers' March 5 demand was made pursuant to an arbitration clause in the contract that specified that "[s]ellers, heirs, etc., and/or mineral lessee shall pay the amount of the physical damage, to be determined by arbitration in the event of disagreement, to the real property or improvements caused by Sellers' said operations." The trial court, however, declined to reinstate the contract, finding that:

Defendants never officially requested arbitration of a mineral related damage claim until after their default; that, notwithstanding Defendants' default under the Contract, Plaintiffs have agreed to arbitrate any such claims, and such claims are the subject of a separate arbitration hearing; that Plaintiffs' failure to submit to arbitration before formal demand for same does not amount to either a legal or equitable defense for non-payment of the purchase price under the facts; that any damages assessed by arbitration against the Plaintiffs are irrelevant to this foreclosure action and any such damages, if any, will be paid separately by the Plaintiffs to the Defendants as a result of a subsequent arbitration hearing.

We agree with the trial court. Carvers' March 5 demand for arbitration did not empower them to unilaterally suspend their obligation to perform within the terms of the contract.

The parties had expressly agreed that time was of the essence in the performance of this contract. Moreover, Carvers were on notice of Heikkilas' intention to insist upon strict compliance with the terms of the contract. When Carvers were delinquent in making their 1982 and 1983 payments, Heikkilas, as in 1984, gave notice of default with intention to foreclose if payment was not made within the sixty-day grace period.

Most courts agree that time may be expressly made of the essence of the contract, and where this is done it is binding on the parties not only at law but in equity as well. A court of equity is not at liberty to disregard the contract of the parties in this respect where deliberately made and clearly expressed, for equity follows the law and will neither make a new contract for the parties nor violate that into which they have freely and advisedly entered. Therefore, as regards the vendor's right to enforce the contract, the time for the delivery of the deed may be made of the essence of the contract, and the time for the payment of the purchase money, if expressly made of the essence of the contract, is so recognized in a court of equity, and compliance therewith may be made essential to the right of the purchaser to compel the vendor to convey, and where such is the case a court of equity will not, as a general rule, interfere to relieve the purchaser from the consequences of his default.

Jesz v. Geigle, 319 N.W.2d 481, 483 (N.D. 1982) (quoting 77 Am. Jur. 2d, Vendor and Purchaser §73 (1975)).

III.   RESTITUTION

Carvers maintain that even if foreclosure is warranted, the trial court erred in not allowing restitution to the extent that improvements and payments made exceed the damages suffered by Heikkilas.

Carvers, however, did not present this claim to the trial court. Where the trial court has determined that enforcement of the liquidated damage provision would not be unconscionable, the defaulting vendee bears the burden of proving that the vendor would be unjustly enriched by retention of all payments made on the contract. Vines v. Orchard Hills, Inc., 181 Conn. 501, 510-12, 435 A.2d 1022, 1028 (1980); Clark & Richards, "Installment Land Contracts in South Dakota — Part II," 7 S.D.L. Rev. 44, 63 (1962). See generally, Prentice v. Classen, supra. In *Vines,* supra, the Connecticut Supreme Court stated:

The purchaser's right to recover in restitution requires the purchaser to establish that the seller has been unjustly enriched. The purchaser must show more than that the contract has come to an end and that the seller retains moneys paid pursuant to the contract. To prove unjust enrichment, in the ordinary case, the purchaser, because he is the party in breach, must prove that the damages suffered by his seller are less than the moneys received from the purchaser. It may not be easy for the purchaser to prove the extent of the seller's damages, it may even be strategically advantageous for the seller to come forward with relevant evidence of the losses he has incurred and may expect to incur on account of the buyer's breach. Nonetheless, only if the breaching party satisfies his burden of proof that the innocent party has sustained a net gain may a

claim for unjust enrichment be sustained. Dobbs, Remedies §12.14 (1973);
1 Palmer, Restitution §5.4 (1978).

Id., 435 A.2d at 1027-1028.

The trial court may order restitution to the defaulting vendee by
virtue of its powers to equitably adjust the rights of the party in a
foreclosure action. See SDCL 21-50-2. This does not, however, relieve
the vendee of his burden of proving that he is so entitled. It is only
on appeal that the Carvers raise the claim that they are entitled to
restitution. We have repeatedly said that an issue may not be raised
for the first time on appeal.

Carvers failed to claim a right to restitution below and presented
no evidence to the trial court from which such determination could
be made. We note that Carvers did present evidence to the trial court
of improvements made to the property totaling approximately $79,000.00
of which approximately $16,000.00 was insurance proceeds which was
left over after Carvers had built a home on the ranch property to
replace the one that had burned down shortly after they had taken
possession of the property. This evidence, however, was not offered
by Carvers pursuant to a claim for restitution. Rather, this evidence
was received by the trial court in considering the relative equities of
the party so as to determine whether the enforcement of the default
clause would be unconscionable under the circumstances.

Thus, we cannot hold that the trial court erred in not awarding
restitution inasmuch as restitution was not requested at trial nor was
sufficient evidence presented to the court from which it could, upon
its own accord, award restitution. . . .

HENDERSON, Justice (dissenting).

I respectfully dissent as the equities do not justify enforcement of
a forfeiture provision. An old maxim of equity proclaims "Equity abhors
a forfeiture." I dare say this case, precedentially, so far as contracts for
deed and agriculture are concerned, is one of the most important cases
in this Court's history.

In addition to the $319,345.47 buyers paid sellers, buyers improved
the ranch property by at least $80,000 consisting of improving cropland,
improving the timber stand, constructing four new wells, improving
outbuildings and corrals, and furnishing the included item of extensive
labor. These improvements are not essentially in dispute. Therefore,
in five years the buyers poured and contributed approximately $400,000
into this ranch. Buyers tendered delayed installment, including principal
and interest in full, just 11 days late! Under the decision of the trial
court, now affirmed by this Court, the buyers lose everything, the
sellers keep the $400,000, and sellers are reinvested with the entire
ranch — much improved. This is too hardball for me to swallow in
an equitable action. It is an unconscionable foreclosure. . . .

I fully appreciate that what is reasonable to one's viewpoint — is unreasonable to another. One of the first things we learn in law school is that reasonable men differ. To me, it is unreasonable to refuse a full payment when it is 11 days late and to then sue for and demand forthwith one-half million dollars; then, if the half million dollars is not paid, to cause the offering party to lose a $400,000 equity. . . .

Although paragraph XVIII of the Contract for Deed stated that time was of the essence, a party who neglects to enforce such a provision at default and later accepts performance, shall not be allowed upon subsequent default to enforce such a provision without notifying the other party of his intent to enforce it. . . .

There are different colors and hues in flowers; there are different degrees of sin; there are different degrees of breach of contract. Some breaches of contract are indeed most serious and substantial and some are not. There are often subtle gradations. However, the 11-day full, but late, tender is not such a serious and substantial breach that it deserves a total elimination of all equity in this ranch of the buyers. I perceive this forfeiture as being unconscionable. If the same penalty applies to all breaches, that is, total forfeiture, it is inversely proportional to the degree of breach. For, in some cases the facts demonstrate on contracts for deeds, that there has been a rather long and faithful performance. It is our duty on the highest Court of this state to equate and evaluate various decisions in the trial courts of this state. The judiciary, although indeed it must protect the buyers, must likewise protect the sellers from unfair consequences. Predictability must flow with equity begotten. It strikes me that an inconsistency in the fair administration of justice doth here lie. . . .

NOTES AND QUESTIONS

1.   No one questions the fact that the remedy of judicial foreclosure protects the rights of defaulting mortgagors both procedurally (by requiring notice, supervision of the sale, and judicial process) and substantively (through redemption rights and the distribution of surplus sale proceeds). The parties in *Bean* did not, however, enter a mortgage agreement — yet this is essentially what the court rewrites for them. In explaining its recharacterization of the transaction as a mortgage, the court braids together two distinct equitable concepts of real property law.

First, the court applies the doctrine of equitable conversion, which is based on the dubious maxim that "equity regards as done what ought to be done." This doctrine has been applied in the context of contracts for sale of realty to shift the risk of loss to the purchaser as the "real" or "equitable" owner in the event that the property is damaged or destroyed during the contract period prior to the transfer of legal title. As explained at Chapter 3A, this application of the doctrine has been rejected in a number of jurisdictions on the contract theory rationale that the seller should bear the risk of loss until the purchaser receives what it bargained for, namely, the legal title in the form of a deed on the closing date. See, e.g., Capital Savings & Loan Assn. v. Convey, 175 Wash. 224, 27 P.2d 136 (1933). In those jurisdictions that recognize this application of the doctrine of equitable conversion the results can be unfair to a purchaser who has not yet entered into possession when the loss occurs. See, e.g., Ross v. Bumstead, 65 Ariz. 61, 173 P.2d 765 (1946). This is why a number of states have enacted statutes that follow the approach taken by §1 of the Uniform Vendor and Purchaser Risk Act, whereby the burden of loss is imposed on the party in possession, whether it be the seller or the purchaser, on the notion that such party should bear the burdens as well as the benefits of possession and is in a better position to protect the property against a casualty loss. See, e.g., N.Y. Gen. Oblig. L. §5-1311 (McKinney 1991). The court also draws an analogy between the installment land contract and the concept of an equitable mortgage. As explained at Chapter 4B2, note 3a, the latter is predicated on the notion that a deed that is absolute on its face will be deemed to be a mortgage if this is what the parties actually intended. In your opinion, do the foregoing analogies support the court's contention that once an installment land contract is executed the "status of the parties becomes like that of mortgagor-mortgagee"?

The second strand of the court's reasoning stresses the legal and functional similarities between the installment land contract and the mortgage device. The installment vendor, like a common-law mortgagee, retains the legal title, while the installment vendee, like a common-law mortgagor, owns the equitable title. But if the vendee has equitable title does it necessarily follow that its interest can be extinguished only by foreclosure and that the vendor must waive the forfeiture remedy it bargained for in the contract? A less formalistic rationale for recharacterization is simply that the installment land contract is functionally analogous to a purchase money mortgage. As the courts in both *Bean* and *Skendzel* point out, the vendor's (mortgagee's) retention of legal title is for the purpose of securing the vendee's (mortgagor's) payments under the contract (loan). By analogy, as observed at Chapter 8B2, note 1, a sale and leaseback functionally resembles a mortgage loan and yet (as the Supreme Court in *Frank Lyon Co.* suggested) the form of the transaction will be respected if the sale and leaseback is a genuine transaction based on economic substance and business reality. Can you think of any substantive reasons (other than remedial ones) why the parties would prefer the installment land contract to the purchase money mortgage format? Are the nontax reasons for recharacterizing an installment land contract more compelling than the tax reasons for recharacterizing a sale and leaseback? Or is this question a matter of comparing apples and oranges?

2. Skendzel v. Marshall, 261 Ind. 226, 301 N.E.2d 641 (1973), cert. denied, 415 U.S. 921 (1974), is the seminal modern case characterizing the installment land contract as a mortgage. Similar decisions have occurred in other jurisdictions. See, e.g., Woods v. Monticello Dev. Co., 656 P.2d 1324 (Colo. Ct. App. 1982); Sebastian v. Floyd, 585 S.W.2d 381 (Ky. 1979); Hoffman v. Semet, 316 So. 2d 649 (Fla. Dist. Ct. App. 1975) (interpreting the definition of mortgages in Fla. Stat. §697.01). Cf. Miller v. Anderson, 394 N.W.2d 279 (Minn. Ct. App. 1986); Angus Hunt Ranch, Inc. v. REB, Inc., 577 P.2d 645 (Wyo. 1978).

3. The presence of a provision that triggers foreclosure protections when the purchaser's interest, as measured by time or money, reaches a certain level has been termed the "convertibility" approach. Does this approach create a reasonable balance between the interests of purchasers in their equity in the property and those of vendors in having a quick and inexpensive means of freeing their inventory from defaulting vendees? See Note, Installment Land Contracts: The Illinois Experience and the Difficulties of Incremental Judicial Reform, 1986 U. Ill. L. Rev. 91. What is the rationale for including the time over which payments are made as a factor to be considered when invoking foreclosure protection? Consider the sensitivities voiced by the court in Potter v. Oster, 426 N.W.2d 148 (Iowa 1988):

> Most importantly, the fair market value of the homestead at the time of forfeiture is an incorrect measure of the benefit Potters lost. It fails to account for the special value Potters placed on the property's location and residential features that uniquely suited their family. For precisely this reason, remedies at law are presumed inadequate for breach of a real estate contract.
>
> From Oster's perspective, Potters actually benefited from the forfeiture because their purchase, in light of subsequent events, proved to be unprofitable. But the record convinces us that profit measured by Wall Street standards was of little consequence to Potters. This was the Potters' home, the place their first son was born, the place Charles Potter testified "was worth everything we ever gave for it, because we planned on living there the rest of our lives."

4. In reviewing the sample installment land contract as counsel for Sam Subdivider you may well pause over the irony of its forfeiture and choice-of-law clauses. Indeed, it has been said that "the only remedy available for vendors holding agreements for deed is foreclosure pursuant to Florida law. Cancellation of the agreement for deed is only a form drafter's dream." D. Simmons, The Agreement for Deed as a

Creative Financing Technique, 55 Fla. Bar J. 395, 396 (1981). That an intimidated or unsophisticated purchaser may simply accept the terms of the contract as dictated by the vendor and not seek protection available under the law may not, however, be so dreamlike and may in part explain the continued popularity of such contracts containing forfeiture clauses. The forfeiture clause continues to remain a stock feature of contracts published in real estate form books.

5. In *Looney,* the Seventh Circuit's determination of whether forfeiture or foreclosure was the appropriate remedy for the purchasers' default hinged on its parsing of the phrase concerning payment of a "minimal amount on the contract," used in the leading Indiana case of Skendzel v. Marshall: if the purchasers had made more than "minimal" payments, foreclosure would be required; if not, the court could enforce forfeiture. The sellers wanted to construe the phrase to mean the purchaser's "net equity," that is, principal paid less current and accrued interest. The FmHA, on the other hand, held a position as second mortgagee. Forfeiture under an installment land contract will extinguish the claims of junior mortgagees, although prior to forfeiture the juniors in most jurisdictions have the right to notice and to cure defaults on the contract (an option, however, not pursued by the FmHA). It argued, therefore, that payments made on the contract should be considered in the aggregate without regard to whether they satisfied principal or interest. In *Skendzel,* the contract called for principal payments only, without interest. There, each payment "on the contract" counted, in its full amount, toward the buyer's equity in the property. The situation becomes considerably more complicated where, as in *Looney,* the contract called for payments of both principal and interest. In evaluating the reasoning applied in the *Looney* opinion, consider the following points.

a. Although the Court of Appeals does not provide details of the calculations behind the District Court's conclusion that the buyer's "equity" in the property was $640, we may assume that to arrive at that figure the lower court must have regarded the equity represented by that part of payments in prior years apportioned to principal to have been "wiped out" by accrued unpaid interest. Thus, if the McCords had made the first five years' $23,280 annual payments, totaling $116,400, assuming simple interest, $33,241 of this amount would have been credited toward reduction of principal. If they failed to make payments in years 6 and 7, accrued interest due, compounded annually, would have amounted to $32,505 at the end of year 7, leaving them with "net equity" of about $735, arguably a de minimis forfeiture. On the other hand, if their equity "vested," as it were, at the end of year 5, when their paid-up principal was over $33,000, one could argue their right to foreclosure should have been unaffected by any subsequent accrual of debt. This appears to have been the approach taken in the

McLendon case cited in *Looney*. There the buyer had paid $7,276 on a purchase price of $10,000, but also owed the seller $3,669 in back taxes and $4,266 on another debt. If *Skendzel* stands for the proposition that buyers with substantial "equity" should be able to avoid forfeiture and receive the benefits of foreclosure, is it more in keeping with that decision to equate equity with "net equity" or with principal in fact paid? If "net equity" is low or nil, would foreclosure rights matter to the buyer or its junior mortgagees unless the value of the property had significantly appreciated?

b.   Surely the court in *Looney* is mistaken when it writes that the contract "envisioned a combined payment of interest and principal of $372,640." It can only be said that the contract envisioned either payments totaling $162,960 at the end of 7 years plus 13 more annual payments of $23,280 each, or a total of $465,600 at the end of 20 years. The 33 percent the court finds the buyers to have paid "toward the contract price" was calculated according to the following formula:

$$\frac{\text{amount paid}}{\text{amount paid} + \text{balance of principal due}}$$

What does this formula represent? What legal significance should it have? The formula does not distinguish among three situations under which the resulting proportion might possibly be "substantial": (1) payments under a high interest rate, with no payment of principal; (2) payments over a long period of time under a moderate interest rate, with no payment of principal; or (3) substantial payments of principal, regardless of interest rate. Only the third instance would have any relation to what is usually meant by a purchaser's or mortgagor's "equity." Had the McCords made interest-only payments for seven years, the formula would yield 32.8 percent $(122,500 \div (122,500 + 250,000))$. As it stands, without reference to the contract's allocation of payments between interest and principal the formula can serve only as a gauge of how the payments made measured up to the purchase price. Does this provide a rational basis for avoiding forfeiture? If a contract calling for payments of interest only could be considered equivalent to a lease, should the purchaser under such a contract be given foreclosure rights? Would your answer be different if the contract had included a balloon payment of principal, the contract thus being analogous to a lease with an option to buy?

c.   An alternative reason for the court's decision is found in its statement that "[w]ith the evidence of appreciation, the [lower] court was incorrect to conclusively value the McCords' equity at only $639.88." But remember, the question before the court was whether forfeiture or foreclosure was the appropriate remedy for the buyer's default. To suggest that the buyer's equity included the appreciated value of the property is to assume what had to be decided, namely, whether the buyers were the owners. Under this approach, had the property declined in value the property would have been forfeited. However, under the formula in (b) above, depreciation or appreciation is irrelevant, and the seller would be compelled to foreclose only against the buyer who had made payments that were "substantial" in relation to the purchase price.

The court was anxious to see the government repaid for its (improvident) loan and to prevent the Looneys from receiving a "windfall." The pie had grown, so why not give everyone a piece? If the property had been sold for $455,000, without allocation of costs or accrued interest, the proceeds would have been distributed as follows:

Looneys:	249,360
FmHA:	183,800
McCords:	21,840

Ignoring the interest on the FmHA loan and assuming that the rental value of the property equaled the contractual 7 percent interest rate, we can make a rough analysis of the parties' financial position after foreclosure.

Looneys:

contract payments	123,280
principal on foreclosure	249,360
total received	372,640
property value	(250,000)
7 years' rental value	(122,500)
net gain	140

FmHA:

loan principal on foreclosure	183,380
total received	183,380
loan principal paid out	(183,380)
net gain	0

McCords:

loan principal received	183,380
7 years' rental value	122,500
"equity" on foreclosure	21,840
total received	327,720
contract payments	(123,280)
net gain	204,440

In whose camp, then, did the windfall fall? The FmHA's, in that it held a fully secured loan when it had no justification for thinking it was secured at all? Wasn't the 11 percent rate it charged on the loan the price, or risk premium, the borrower was expected to pay for an unsecured loan? Did the McCords receive a windfall in having received the benefits of the property's appreciation without exposure to the risk of its decline in value? In effect the McCords paid seven years' rent and obtained all of the property's increase in value for those years. Do you think the court would have been as solicitous of foreclosure had the FmHA loan not been made?

d.   A concurring opinion in *Skendzel* addressed the inequities foreclosure might visit on the vendor whose contract expectations would be upset thereby and suggested that if the contract is rewritten as a note and mortgage the rewriting should be complete and include "[t]erms customarily included in such notes and mortgages but frequently omitted from contracts [such as] provisions for increased interest during periods of default, provision for the acceleration of the due date of the entire unpaid principal and interest upon a default continuing beyond a reasonable grace period, [and] provisions for attorneys' fees and other expenses incidental to foreclosure." 301 N.E.2d 641, 651. How would this suggestion affect a court's decision to replace forfeiture with foreclosure?

6.   By characterizing the installment sale transaction as a mortgage, the *Bean* and *Looney* courts provided defaulting purchasers protections afforded under foreclosure procedures. In *Heikkila* the purchaser-appellants invoked, albeit unsuccessfully, a number of arguments based on contract law that are frequently raised to defeat the harsh consequences of forfeiture to purchasers. Note that these arguments accomplish the same ends of purchaser protection as does foreclosure, namely, the opportunity for redemption, or payment to the purchaser of excess sale proceeds above the amount due the seller and junior lenders. Legislation in various jurisdictions that similarly affects the parties' contractual rights is also mentioned in the following notes.

a.   *Liquidated Damages as an Unenforceable Penalty.*   The forfeiture provision in installment land contracts is very commonly contained in a liquidated damages clause (such as the one in *Bean*) that recites that in the event of the buyer's uncured default the seller shall have the right to repossess the property and retain all payments made as liquidated damages compensating for the buyer's use, rental, and occupancy of the property. The use of such clauses in the context of earnest money deposits under a contract of sale is discussed at Chapter 3A, note 3. In that context, the purchaser usually does not enter into possession and make a single deposit in the amount of a fixed percentage of the purchase price, with closing contemplated in the near future. This is readily distinguishable, however, from the long series of payments made on an installment land contract, which calls for complete performance years later. Thus, with an installment land contract the buyer's use of the property during the installment period makes the calculation of actual damages a difficult task, while at the same time it is likely that the more remote the breach the greater will be the amount forfeited by the purchaser.

Liquidated damages clauses must frequently run a judicial gamut flanked by the maxims "equity abhors a forfeiture" and "equity will not enforce a penalty." These rules in equity are based on the notion that if a liquidated damages clause is merely security for performance on the contract or an in terrorem device (i.e., a penalty designed to deter nonperformance by means of threatened punishment), then once there is a breach courts should ignore the clause and directly determine whether an award of actual damages would adequately compensate the nonbreaching party. For example, if a mortgage given on a loan of money calls for forfeiture of the mortgaged property on the borrower's default, equity would regard enforcement of that default clause as unreasonable if the borrower tendered the lender payment of principal and interest as damages, since such tender is no less than the lender expected from the borrower's full performance. See 2 Pomeroy's Equity Jurisprudence, §§433-460 (S. Symons ed. 1941). However, where actual damages cannot be measured with certainty this reasoning is inapplicable, and courts will not then use their estimate of damages to replace that of the contracting parties, provided that formation of the liquidated damages portion of the contract meets basic standards of reasonableness and fairness. Since the standard liquidated damages clause in an installment land contract calls for complete forfeiture by the purchaser regardless of whether its default is on the first payment or on the last, isn't such a clause unreasonable on its face? Would a clause be more reasonable if it were drafted to restrict forfeiture as liquidated damages to when an amount less than a certain percentage of the purchase price had been paid? See Note, Default Clauses in the Contract for Deed: An Invitation to Litigation?, 28 S.D. L. Rev. 467 (1983).

A number of states have enacted legislation limiting the enforceability of liquidated damages clauses. *Heikkila* refers to the South Dakota statute on the subject.

S.D. Codified Laws Ann. §53-9-5 (Michie 1990)

Contracts fixing damages void, exception. Every contract in which amount of damage or compensation for breach of an obligation is determined in anticipation thereof is void to that extent except the parties may agree therein upon an amount presumed to be the damage for breach in cases where it would be impracticable or extremely difficult to fix actual damage.

This statute accords with the notion that liquidated damages are appropriate only when actual damages cannot be practicably calculated.

Yet, perhaps in accordance with South Dakota's statutory provision giving courts the power to "equitably adjust" the remedies awarded in strict foreclosures of installment land contracts, the *Heikkila* court goes on to make a rough determination of actual damages and applies to the contract a conscionability test, namely, whether "substantial disparity exists between the payments made on the contract, together with the improvements made to the property, and the loss of rents and other detriment suffered by the vendors due to the loss of use and possession of the property." Comparable tests are used in many jurisdictions that decline to enforce liquidated damages clauses if they would lead to results that would "shock the conscience." See, e.g., Jenkins v. Wise, 58 Haw. 592, 574 P.2d 1337 (1978); Clampitt v. A.M.R. Corp., 109 Idaho 145, 706 P.2d 34 (1985); Soffe v. Ridd, 659 P.2d 1082 (Utah 1983). How well do you think the *Heikkila* court estimated actual damages in that case? Subtracting claimed losses disallowed by the court, the Heikkilas' alleged losses would total $350,880, consisting principally of lost rental and resale value. The fairness of enforcement, then, depends very much on the validity of the amounts submitted for these two kinds of losses. Do tenants ordinarily have to pay for a decline in the land's market value during their tenancy? Do owners of land ordinarily have to pay rent to their vendors? With respect to these apparent contradictions, see the discussion on restitution infra. Is a deficiency judgment in favor of the vendor inconsistent with the enforcement of a forfeiture provision as liquidated damages? See Germany v. Nelson, 677 S.W.2d 386 (Mo. App. 1984) (enforcement of forfeiture as liquidated damages bars damages claim for rental value of buyers' post-default occupancy of property). Cf. Meyer v. Hansen, 373 N.W.2d 392 (N.D. 1985) (liquidated damages clause does not include loss due to unreasonable and unusual use of property, therefore enforcement of forfeiture does not preclude claim for waste).

    b.   Reinstatement of the Contract.   Occasionally, in exercise of their equitable powers courts will refuse to enforce forfeiture clauses in installment land contracts and order that the contract be reinstated, provided the purchaser tenders delinquent payments due plus interest. See, e.g., Call v. Timber Lakes Corp., 567 P.2d 1108 (Utah 1977); Wu v. Good, 720 P.2d 1005 (Colo. Ct. App. 1986); Barkis v. Scott, 34 Cal. 2d 116, 208 P.2d 367 (1949). Cf. Bartley v. Karas, 150 Cal. App. 3d 336, 197 Cal. Rptr. 749 (Cal. Ct. App. 1983) (right to reinstate under Cal. Civ. Code §3275 not available to willfully defaulting buyers). Absent arrearages statutes, defaulting mortgagors are not afforded this kind of protection but rather must tender the entire balance due on the debt if they are to retain their property. Thus, contract purchasers may receive more favorable treatment than mortgagors.

    The right to reinstate the contract may also be provided for by statute. Arizona Rev. Stat. Ann. §33-472(D) (1989), for example, allows for different time periods in which the purchaser may cure default, depending on how much of the purchase price has been paid (e.g., 30 days when less than 20 percent of the purchase price has been paid, 60 days when between 20 and 30 percent of the purchase price has been paid, and so on). See also Iowa Code Ann. §656.2(1)(c) (1989) (30 days to cure); Minn. Stat. §559.21(subd. 2a) (1990) (60 days for installment land contracts executed after July 31, 1985); N.D. Cent. Code §32-18-04 (1975) (6 months if less than one-third purchase price paid, one year if more than one-third); Ohio Rev. Code Ann. §5313.05 (Baldwin 1991) (30 days from date of default).

Grace periods may also be contained in the contract itself. More typically, however, contracts contain acceleration clauses that effectively bar reinstatement by requiring the purchaser to tender on default the full balance of principal due. Some states have addressed this issue by enacting laws that permit a purchaser to cure by making only those payments that would be due without the acceleration clause. Mich. Comp. Laws §600.5726 (1990); Wash. Rev. Code Ann. §61.30.090 (Supp. 1990). In some instances, courts achieve the same result by finding a waiver of the default that would have triggered the acceleration. See Phair v. Walker, 48 Or. App. 641, 617 P.2d 616 (1980). In jurisdictions where vendors cannot enforce forfeiture clauses but must foreclose, it may be advisable for them to include express acceleration provisions in their contracts. One court, for example, rejected a seller's argument that acceleration could be implied from the forfeiture-on-default provisions of the contract and held that the seller could at most receive a judgment of foreclosure in the amount of principal and interest past due plus costs. The balance would survive as a lien on the property sold at foreclosure and would be payable in installments pursuant to the contract. Adkinson v. Nyberg, 344 So. 2d 614 (Fla. App. 1977). See also Rickel v. Energy Systems Holdings, 114 Idaho 585, 759 P.2d 876 (1988) (in absence of acceleration clause, 120-day period granted in which vendees are permitted to cure by tendering delinquent payments).

    c. Restitution. Where forfeiture is ultimately enforced, courts have become increasingly willing to mitigate its effects by awarding purchasers restitution in the amount of the forfeited property and payments that exceeded the seller's losses. This is a marked departure from traditional contract law, which denied restitution to the party at fault. A comprehensive discussion of this change in law can be found in Vines v. Orchard Hills, Inc., cited in *Heikkila.* See also G. Palmer, The Law of Restitution, Chap. 5 (1978 and Supp. 1988). In general, it may be said that "[a] claim in restitution, although legal in form, is equitable in nature, and permits a trial court to balance the equities; to take into account a variety of competing principles to determine whether the defendant has been unjustly enriched." Vines v. Orchard Hills, Inc., 181 Conn. 501, 435 A.2d 1022, 1026 (1980). Among the equities commonly weighed by the courts are the willfulness of the defaulting purchaser's breach and, as with the question of the enforceability of liquidated damages clauses, the degree to which the vendee's payments exceed the vendor's damages. The critical issue in determining restitution awards is, then, a matter of measuring what the purchaser has given up in forfeiture and what the buyer has lost by the breach; this necessarily involves thorny problems defining the parties' property interests and the valuation of those interests.

Suppose V and P enter into an installment contract for property with a purchase price of $135,000 and terms of $25,000 down and $845 monthly until the balance is paid. After 10 months, P defaults. By that time the fair market value of the property has declined to $90,000; its rental value has been $1,687.50 per month. If P forfeited the property and payments and V's damages were calculated as the rental value of the property during P's occupancy, P would be entitled to $16,575 in restitution — the amount P's payments exceed rental value. Were this the exclusive measure of damages, wouldn't the contract, in effect, be a lease with an option to buy, since the buyer could simply default when the property value dropped below the purchase price and thereafter be liable only for rental value? What result if V's damages were based on a benefit-of-the-bargain theory? Honey v. Henry's Franchise Leasing Corp., 64 Cal. 2d 801, 52 Cal. Rptr. 18, 415 P.2d 833 (1966). Should V's damages include both the rental value of the property *and* the decline in its market value? In this hypothetical, which is taken from the fact pattern in *Honey,* not only is V's property worth $45,000 less than the contract price, but V lost its use, worth $16,875, for ten months as well. Consider the reasoning in the following decision that requires the vendor to choose between two remedies based on mutually exclusive legal theories. In Kudokas v. Balkus, 26 Cal. App. 3d 744, 103 Cal. Rptr. 318 (Cal. Ct. App. 1972), an action brought by the vendor against defaulting vendees to recover and quiet title to a motel, the trial court sustained the vendor's claim and, on a benefit-of-the-bargain theory, awarded the vendees restitution in the amount by which their payments plus the depreciated value of the motel exceeded the sum of the contract price and the vendor's consequential damages. The vendors argued that the restitution award should be reduced by the rental value of the motel for the period the defendant buyers were in possession. The trial court agreed and granted a limited new trial to recalculate the vendor's damages to include rental value. The vendees appealed.

In seeking to justify the limited new trial order, plaintiff makes a number of unacceptable arguments. She compares herself to a rescinding vendor, who is entitled to recover the property's use value during the entire period of the vendee's possession. Plaintiff does not occupy that position. When the vendee breaches the contract, the vendor has an election to rescind or enforce the contract. Rescission would require plaintiff to restore or offer to restore all the money and credits she has received under the contract. She has not done so. . . .

In this action she sought forfeiture of the vendee's rights, a quiet title decree and retention of the vendee's payments. Such an action is one to enforce rather than rescind the contract. . . .

Contrary to plaintiff's contention, the benefit-of-bargain rule does not give defendants free occupancy during the two years they had possession under the contract. At this point plaintiff overlooks the fact that during these two years defendants took the risk — and relieved plaintiff of the risk — of a decline in capital value. In selecting a remedy for breach of the contract, the vendor has a choice between rescission and enforcement. Conceivably, rescission and restoration of the vendee's payments would put the vendor in a position to recover use value. Here the vendor chose not to rescind. Here the vendor seeks to quiet title "on condition that he refund the excess, if any, of the payments received over the amount necessary to give him the benefit of his bargain." . . .

This lawsuit manifests an election to treat the property as though it had been sold, not rented. In arguing for rental value in addition or as an alternative to "benefit of the bargain," plaintiff would treat the property as though it had not been sold. The trial court erred in ordering a new trial on the theory that the plaintiff-vendor was entitled to rental value during the period of the defendant-vendees' possession under the contract.

Does the argument based on legal theory in *Kudokas* dispel the intuitive inclination to award the vendor in our hypothetical both rental value and declined market value measures of damages? Forfeiture may be viewed as a component of the vendor's remedy based on contract rescission or, alternatively, contract termination. See E. Freyfogle, Installment Land Contracts, in 7 Powell, Law of Real Property ¶938.22[2] (1987). The object of recission is to return the parties to their positions before the contract was made, so forfeiture represents the return of the property to the vendor, while the purchaser receives the return of its payments as restitution. The purchaser must also "return" to the vendor the use it had of the property; this is accomplished by offsetting from the amount of restitution the rental value of the property. On the other hand, where the vendor pursues a contract termination remedy, it is entitled to an award of the benefit of its bargain, namely, the contract price. In this case, the property and payments are forfeited as credits toward the contract price, and the purchaser receives as restitution the amount by which they exceed the contract price plus consequential damages. Rent is not includable in a benefit-of-the-bargain-based award, since the contract contemplates the purchaser's receiving ownership of the property. Does this mean that if the value of the property forfeited equals the purchase price the defaulting purchaser should receive all of its payments as restitution, thereby receiving use of the property at no cost? The answer to this question depends on the contract's provision for installment payments and interest. Compensation for use of the property will have been made to the extent the purchaser has lost and the vendor has gained the use of funds paid out in installments. Similarly, when the contract calls for interest on the deferred principal, the vendor receives what in effect is a major incident of ownership of the purchase price at the same time the purchaser in possession receives incidents of ownership of the property. Thus, a simplistic formulation that calculates restitution as the amount by which the seller's payments exceed the difference between the contract price and market value of the returned property may be erroneous if the contract calls for interest payments. Such a formula credits the vendee with interest rather than including it as part of the bargain due the vendor. For a discussion of this issue in terms of the time value of money see Nelson and Whitman, Installment Land Contracts — The National Scene Revisited, B.Y.U. L. Rev. 1, 24 n.80 (1985).

If the vendor has not bargained for interest then it has in effect agreed to the purchaser's "free" use of the property, and courts should not make up for this by assessing the purchaser rent when they calculate a benefit-of-the-bargain remedy. Under what theory would restitution to the purchaser include interest on the down payment and payments of principal? This question was addressed in Dow v. Noble, 380 N.W.2d 359 (S.D. 1986), where the purchaser had paid $125,000 down. The vendor was awarded rental value of the property, but the purchaser was not credited with interest on his payments of principal. *Dow* typifies the inconsistent manner in which the courts have applied the rescission and contract termination theories of forfeiture.

When the forfeited property has appreciated in value, on account of either market changes or improvements made by the purchaser, under a benefit-of-the-bargain theory it is clear that the purchaser is entitled to restitution of this increase. Conversely, when the property's value has declined and principal payments fall short of making up this loss, the vendor is entitled to a deficiency judgment, unless, of course, forfeiture is being enforced as liquidated damages. Where the contract is rescinded, purchaser-made improvements or waste would also result in restitution or deficiency adjustments. How should the risks (rewards) of market-induced declines (increases) in value be allocated in rescission? Is it inconsistent to charge the purchaser with both rent and depreciation? Would the vendor's decision to terminate rather than rescind obviate this problem?

The concept of restitution has been incorporated in many state statutes that regulate forfeiture under installment land contracts. Pennsylvania's installment land contract law, for example, provides that payments of up to 25 percent of the purchase price together with forfeiture of the property may comprise enforceable liquidated damages for default, but that the purchaser is entitled to restitution for any payments above the 25 percent mark that exceed the seller's actual damages. Pursuant to the federal Interstate Land Sales Full Disclosure Act, 24 C.F.R. 1715.4(a)(3) (1990), similar rights vest in the purchaser who has paid at least 15 percent of the purchase price.

    d. Redemption.   The remedy granted the vendors in *Heikkila* was that of "strict foreclosure," a special kind of foreclosure action infrequently encountered except in installment land contract cases. See Chapter 10C2. In strict foreclosure, the court gives the defaulting purchaser a certain time within which it may redeem its property by paying the balance of the purchase price plus interest accrued and costs. Absent such payment title vests in the vendor free of any equitable interest in the purchaser. Unlike judicial foreclosure (or foreclosure by sale), which calls for a sale of the mortgaged property, this remedy does not mandate a sale and therefore does not afford the purchaser any right to the excess of property value over the debt owed or the opportunity to redeem during a statutory period following the sale. See Vanneman, Strict Foreclosure on Land Contracts, 14 Minn. L. Rev. 342 (1930). Courts on occasion will also exercise their equitable powers to allow defaulting vendees a period in which they are permitted to redeem their property. The decision is discretionary, and courts will weigh a number of factors including the amount of the vendee's equity, the length of the default period, the willfulness of the default, improvements made on the property by the vendee, and the vendee's care in maintaining the property. See, e.g., Grombone v. Krekel, 754 P.2d 777 (Colo. Ct. App. 1988).

    e. Waiver.   Forbearance on the part of a sympathetic seller — or one who is reaping high finance charges and doesn't want to kill the goose that lays the golden eggs — toward a purchaser who makes tardy payments may later frustrate attempts to enforce forfeiture. As the dissent in *Heikkila* suggests, acceptance of late payments may constitute a waiver by the seller of the condition that time be of the essence of the contract. Courts appear willing (and sometimes eager) to invoke this theory to protect purchasers from the harsh consequences of forfeiture. The rationale behind waiver is that by permitting late payments without protest, the vendor has lulled the purchaser into believing that tardiness will not constitute a default. If such notion is the justification for the doctrine of waiver, should it apply, as the dissent argues it should, to a case like *Heikkila,* where the payment deadline was set by court order rather than by the contract or the vendor?

    The dissent acknowledges that the vendor may revive the "time is of the essence" provision that had been waived by providing the purchaser with notice that he will require strict compliance with it in the future. A vendor's acceleration notice will not be deemed sufficient to reinstate a time-is-of-the-essence condition; effective notice must be express and unequivocal. See Aden v. Alwardt, 76 Ill. App. 3d 54, 394 N.E.2d 716 (Ill. App. Ct. 1979).

f. Specific Performance.   While defaulting mortgagors enjoy an absolute right of redemption, installment land contract vendees generally can obtain the functional equivalent of such a right, in the form of specific performance, only as an equitable remedy that may be granted subject to the court's discretion. Defaulting purchasers may counterclaim for specific performance when vendors seek to enforce contract provisions for forfeiture. In deciding whether to grant such relief, courts weigh the equities based on mitigating circumstances such as the waiver by the vendor of the requirement of timely payment, absence of notice, improvements made by the purchaser, and the purchaser's substantial equity in the property. See Annot., Specific Performance of Land Contract Notwithstanding Failure of Vendee to Make Required Payments on Time, 55 A.L.R.3d 10 (1974). California decisional law, however, permits even wilfully defaulting vendees to obtain specific performance, thus giving such vendees rights that are on a par with those of mortgagors. Petersen v. Hartell, 40 Cal. 3d 102, 219 Cal. Rptr. 170, 707 P.2d 232 (1985).

D.   SPECIAL TYPES OF HIGH-RATIO FINANCING

Certain high-ratio financing techniques based primarily on tax inducements have evolved as alternatives to ordinary mortgage-debt financing. They include: (a) certain types of industrial development bond (IDB) financing whereby some municipality or municipal agency acts as a conduit to qualify interest received by a mortgage lender for tax-free treatment under I.R.C. §103 so that the developer-borrower can reduce its interest costs on new construction. However, use of this financing technique was curtailed by the Tax Reform Acts of 1984 and 1986 (see infra this section); (b) sale-and-leaseback financing and component financing, whereby the landowner can sell the real estate without losing possession and depreciate the cost of land in the guise of a rental deduction (see Chapter 8B); (c) a tax-free exchange of real estate, whereby the owner can defer taxation on an exchange of real estate under I.R.C. §1031 in order to leverage the cost of acquiring the new real estate; (d) so-called high-credit lease financing; and (e) so-called zero-coupon bond financing.

Smith and Lubell, Real Estate Financing: The High-Credit Lease
4 Real Est. Rev. 21 (Summer 1974)

THE HIGH-CREDIT LEASE

There are very few forms of financing which offer the developer an opportunity for 100 percent mortgage financing. But in the limited area of high-credit lease financing, optimum leverage is the rule, rather than the exception. As consideration for maximum financing, the developer must frequently be prepared to accept a modest return on investment and perhaps sacrifice an inflationary hedge.

Life insurance companies are the major source of high-credit lease financing. Restrictions imposed by regulatory authorities on the investments these lenders may make determine which leases are acceptable for high-credit financing. The developer of an office, industrial, or retail property may be able to obtain 100 percent long-term mortgage financing for his project if three conditions apply:

- The entire property is leased to a single corporate tenant, or the single tenant's obligations under the lease are guaranteed by a corporation.
- The corporate tenant or corporate guarantor has a good balance sheet and a proven track record of earnings.
- The lease, in form and substance, is what is generally called a "financing" lease.

WHAT IS 100 PERCENT FINANCING?

With 100 percent financing, the lender looks primarily at the credit of the corporate tenant and only secondarily at the real estate for repayment of the loan. If the credit of the corporate tenant is acceptable and the lease meets the requirements of the lender, the loan may be in an amount equal to either the appraised value of the property or the hard-cash costs of the property to the developer, whichever is less.

Hard-cash costs are basically the costs of land acquisition and construction of the improvements. The so-called soft-cash costs attributable to the developer's time and expertise will not be recognized in determining the amount of the loan.

WHY A SINGLE TENANT?

Before a lender will furnish 100 percent financing, he must be satisfied that the net rental income from the property will be sufficient to pay interest on the loan and to amortize it in full by maturity. This requirement can most readily be fulfilled by a single net lease of the entire property, provided the tenant's credit standing is such that the lender will regard it as absolutely reliable for payment of rent and for all expenses relating to the property over the entire term of the loan. Some lenders . . . are subject to a statutory requirement that the tenant have a minimum record of earnings over a designated period of time.

In rare instances, the developer may be able to obtain approximately 90 percent financing where the property is leased to a number of tenants on either a net or a gross lease basis. However, in these times of galloping inflation, lenders are reluctant to rely on gross leases. Even where gross leases contain escalation clauses providing for additional rent to cover increases in real estate taxes and operating expenses, they may not be adequate security against skyrocketing costs. Moreover, developers frequently experience substantial difficulties in negotiating adequate "financing" leases in a multiple-occupancy situation.

WHY A CORPORATE TENANT?

The lender's greatest concern with high-credit lease financing is assurance of net rental payments throughout the life of the loan in an amount sufficient to cover debt service. With a high financial rating and permanent corporate existence, a corporation as tenant affords greater assurance of such payment than does an individual or partnership. The latter two are subject to the vagaries of death or incompetency. They are also more prone to make improvident personal investments which may result in bankruptcy or insolvency.

PROVISIONS OF THE FINANCING LEASE

Leases that obligate the tenant to pay all or substantially all of the real estate taxes, operating expenses, and other obligations arising out of the ownership and occupancy of the demised premises have been variously characterized as "net" leases, "net, net" leases, "net, net, net" leases, "absolutely net" leases, and "financing" leases. The writers do not assume an ability to define with any degree of competency the differences between the first four of these, if any differences exist at all. However, there is no doubt in our minds as to what constitutes a financing lease. Since lending on the security of a financing lease is primarily a credit transaction, such leases have also been called "bond" or "bond-type" leases.

Rental Obligations

A financing lease is a net lease pursuant to which the tenant is obligated to pay a fixed basic rent, as well as all real estate taxes and all other expenses of any nature whatsoever arising out of the ownership and operation of the premises. The basic rent must be at least sufficient to pay interest and principal on the loan to the developer, and the tenant's obligation to pay such rent must be absolute and unconditional. In many cases, the amount of each monthly payment of rent is the same as the amount of the monthly payment on account of interest and principal required by the loan documents. For this reason, many financing leases are negotiated with the term, amount, and interest rate of a particular loan in mind.

In the instances where all of the rental is used to cover principal and interest on the mortgage, the developer receives no cash flow from the property. The landlord-developer's only inducements to obtain high-credit lease financing in these cases are the tax benefits derived from ownership. The tenant, of course, pays all real estate taxes and operating expenses. Obviously, the risks to the developer would then be minimal if the tenant is a Fortune-500 corporation or its equivalent.

The lender, who is relying upon the credit of the tenant in making the loan, must have absolute assurances that the tenant's obligation to pay rent is unconditional. If for any reason whatsoever the rent obligation is not met, the lender must be assured that the loan will be repaid in full. Consequently, the lease cannot permit the tenant any rent abatement or offset, even under any of the following conditions:

- The landlord defaults or violates a term or condition of the lease.
- There is a constructive eviction of the tenant.
- There is a violation of a zoning ordinance.
- Building violations are imposed against the property.
- The landlord's title to the property is jeopardized or even fails.
- There is a temporary taking for governmental use (i.e., temporary rerouting of highway) or occupancy.

Casualty Loss

The provisions of the lease relating to damage by fire or other casualty merit special consideration. In the event the premises are damaged or destroyed by fire or other casualty, the tenant must be obligated to repair or restore, irrespective of the availability or sufficiency of insurance proceeds. There can be no abatement or reduction of rent for the period during which the premises cannot be occupied. Otherwise, the lender would be deprived of the source of repayment of its loan. The tenant can protect itself against this exposure with rent or occupancy insurance.

In view of the tenant's unconditional obligation to restore, there is no objection to letting it retain insurance proceeds above the amount necessary for restoration. The possibility of there being any such excess is, of course, remote.

Condemnation Clause

The negotiation of a condemnation clause which will be acceptable to the lender is often difficult. As a general proposition, the tenant's obligation to pay rent may be reduced only to the extent of the condemnation award received by the lender. Even though the entire premises are taken by eminent domain (or taken to such an extent as to render them unsuitable for the tenant's use), the tenant must remain obligated for the rental or a reduced rental, unless the condemnation award is sufficient to pay the debt in full.

The lease may provide, however, that the tenant can terminate by paying the lender an amount sufficient to make up the difference between the condemnation award and the outstanding mortgage debt. And in a partial taking, since the tenant is unconditionally obligated to pay rent, it is only fair to provide that the tenant may apply the entire award against the costs of restoring the untaken portion of the property.

ASSIGNMENT OF THE LEASE

To avoid any problems that might arise if the landlord became bankrupt or insolvent, the lender will require that the financing lease be assigned to him as collateral security for the loan. He will usually also require that the tenant pay the rent directly to the lender. However, since direct rental payments to the lender impose the burden of accounting to the landlord whenever a payment exceeds the periodic installments of interest and principal on the loan, a lender may occasionally permit the landlord to collect the rents.

CONCLUSION

In order to structure acceptable documents for high-credit lease financing, all parties to the arrangement (lender, tenant, and landlord-borrower) should understand the lease's basic underlying concepts. Since the lender looks to the tenant's unconditional obligation to pay rent for repayment of the loan, the lease and its assignment to the lender constitute the real security behind the loan. The property itself and the borrower's obligations under the note and the mortgage become of somewhat lesser importance. High-credit lease financing is possible only if the tenant recognizes and accepts the proposition that the loan is a credit transaction. It is up to the developer to bring the tenant to such recognition and acceptance.

Wetterer, Introducing the Zero Coupon Real Estate Mortgage
3 Real Est. Fin. 121 (Spring 1986)

In the increasingly competitive syndications market, sponsors continue their efforts to develop innovative programs to meet specific investment needs. One new concept is the "zero coupon real estate mortgage," patterned after the zero coupon Treasury securities introduced not long ago on the general capital market. Instead of paying current principal and/or interest to the investor, zero coupon mortgages accrue all interest and principal and require a balloon payment of all defined amounts at a future date.

WHY NOW?

There are a number of reasons why zero coupon mortgage programs are being offered now. The primary impetus can be found in recent tax law changes involving original issue discount (OID). Prior to 1984, purchase money mortgages played a major role in the financing of syndicated properties. Seller financing via deferred interest mortgages provided the accrual basis borrower/limited partners with large current interest deductions, while enabling the cash basis seller to defer taxes on the interest until such time as cash was actually received. But the 1984 Tax Reform Act ended this sheltering arrangement by bringing purchase money notes under the expanded OID rules, thus requiring sellers to report accrued interest as income. This left sellers with a tax liability, but no cash to pay the taxes due. Not surprisingly, sellers were no longer interested in seller financing.

Zero coupon bond mortgages have emerged as one alternative. The deferred interest/OID problem is resolved because zero coupon programs are marketed toward (and suitable only for) tax-exempt investors — institutions, IRAs and other retirement plans. The OID that must be recognized provides a current interest deduction to the taxable borrower, while placing no unfunded tax bite on the tax-exempt noteholders.

A second reason why zero coupon mortgages are becoming popular is that current property yields are simply inadequate to support significant amounts of current payment debt. While overbuilding has led to some softening of office building prices in many geographic areas, overall property prices remain quite high, as do real rates of interest (nominal rate less inflation). Zero coupon mortgages are seen by some sponsors as a way to finance acquisitions without placing impossible debt burdens on property cash flow.

A final reason for the current interest in zero coupon mortgages can be traced to investor uncertainty over future interest rates. By investing in a zero coupon mortgage today, investors can "lock in" a known, relatively high, reinvestment rate, i.e., the deferred interest compounds at the stated rate throughout the term of the mortgage. If the investor put money into a traditional mortgage (or equity) program, current cash distributions could be reinvested, but at an unknown (and potentially lower) rate of interest.

APPROPRIATE PROJECTS

Not every type of project or acquisition is suitable for zero coupon mortgage financing. Whether or not this technique makes sense — for either the lender/investors or the borrower — depends upon the specific characteristics of the property involved. For example, projects in the development stage are generally well-suited to zero coupon financing. Because not even interest payments are due currently, developers can avoid a drain on cash flow while in the development and lease-up stages. The lack of debt service also makes it easier to negotiate favorable take-out financing.

Zero coupon mortgages also make sense for new owners of commercial "rent-roll" projects. These are seasoned properties, currently leased at below-market rates, that are set to be released in the near future at substantially higher rents. The purchase price for such properties is usually based on the anticipated new rent levels, less some appropriate discount. At existing rent levels, however, the property cannot support a corresponding level of current payment debt. A zero coupon mortgage can provide the necessary financing while maintaining property cash flow. It also provides an alternative to raising additional equity in order to service traditional debt.

If zero coupon financing is to be successful on any type of property, it is essential that the *projected* cash flow of the leased-up (or roll-leased) property be adequate to service both current payment debt and the zero coupon debt. The use of zero coupon financing does not eliminate the risks of over-financing or poor property performance.

INVESTOR CONSIDERATIONS

In considering a zero coupon mortgage program, investors need to take a hard look at the specific characteristics of the investment being offered. Some specific points to investigate:

Rate of Return: This is the essential question, and the answer will depend on many variables. What is the stated compound interest rate on the mortgage investments? If the rate is variable, the investor should assess the quality and volatility of the index used as the basis for rate adjustments. What is the specific maturity date of the mortgage? Programs with open-ended or variable maturity dates should be avoided. Is the overall, projected rate of return adequate? Does it appear that property cash flow will be adequate by itself to fund the deferred obligation over the entire anticipated holding period? Investors should be especially wary of programs that anticipate repaying the entire amount of accrued principal and interest from property sale proceeds. Are investors entitled to any participation in cash flow or sales proceeds beyond the stated compound interest rate?

Investment Policy: What credit position will the program take (first, second, junior, wrap)? What loan to value ratio will be required? Will "value" be appraised value or economic value? Will loans be made to independent borrowers or affiliates of the sponsor? In my mind, the latter presents an unjustifiable conflict of interest.

Property Types: What property types will be considered for investment? Where? Will adequate diversification exist even if the program is funded at only a minimum level?

Sponsor Experience and Track Record: The reputation and prior performance of the sponsor is particularly important in zero coupon programs. With no principal distributions required and all interest accrued over the entire life of the program, the level of investor risk does not diminish over time, but rather increases. And, as with other non-tax-oriented programs, investor return is totally dependent on strong property management as reflected in cash flow and appreciation.

CONCLUSION

The use of zero coupon mortgages is an innovative technique useful in financing specific types of property where conventional mortgages are unavailable or unfeasible. For limited partner/investors, these mortgages can provide attractive rates of return without the bother and uncertainty of reinvesting current cash distributions. A program structured to provide additional participation in property appreciation can also be an inflation hedge.

Investors should be aware, however, that the potential for abuse is great in this type of program. With all principal and interest accrued, the investor's return comes from the balloon payment due ten or twelve years in the future. Unless the properties financed by the program have sufficient cash flow to support *both* the zero coupon mortgage and conventional financing, the investor's ultimate return is highly or entirely dependent on property appreciation.

This is unacceptable from the investor's point of view. Overbuilding, low inflation or simply poor property management may keep property appreciation below expected levels — and below the level necessary to repay investors all accrued amounts. Or, it may be impossible to sell the property for all cash at the mortgage maturity date. The need to take back a purchase money note could leave the seller with insufficient cash to completely service the zero coupon obligation.

For developers and syndicators, zero coupon mortgages may seem an attractive alternative to variable-rate, current payment debt. Investors, however, should view such investments as inherently high-risk. They certainly entail significantly greater risk than their counterpart/models — the zero coupon Treasuries. After all, if the federal government needs more cash to repay its obligations, it can always just print a few more dollars. . .

The Mortgage and Real Estate Executive's Report
3-6 (May 15, 1987)

SPECIAL REPORT: UNDERSTANDING TAX-FREE EXCHANGES

The major tax deferral technique left unchanged by the Tax Reform Act of 1986 (TRA '86) is the tax-free exchange of real estate. Indeed, such exchanges take on added luster with the elimination of the long-term capital gains rate. Gain on investment and business property is now subject to a 28 percent rate (and, for high-income taxpayers, can reach 33 percent beginning in 1988), significantly above the former 20 percent maximum. So it seems likely that the exchange technique will come into much greater use than ever before.

The lack of popularity of exchanging in the past stemmed from several causes. Setting up a successful exchange often takes much more patience and hard work than arranging a straight purchase and sale. In addition, many brokers and investors simply have not understood the potentials of exchanging. In fact, the real estate exchange can be a highly versatile tool both for achieving tax savings and for financing real estate. As far as the difficulty of arranging exchanges is concerned, a thorough understanding of the tax law requirements shows that exchanging can often be accomplished almost as easily as a simple purchase and sale (although the multiparty exchange does call for some intricate footwork by the parties).

Tax-free exchanges are of two types: (1) exchanges of investment and business property; or (2) exchanges of residential property (one-family homes, condominiums, or cooperatives). The discussion that follows is limited to investment and business property.

ADVANTAGES OF EXCHANGING

The key advantage of a tax-free exchange (pursuant to I.R.C. §1031) is that gain realized by one or both of the exchangers need not be recognized (i.e., tax need not be paid on the gain) at the time of sale. Instead, the tax is postponed until a future taxable disposition of the newly acquired property. Thus, a series of exchanges can defer tax indefinitely and possibly permanently (if the property ultimately acquires a stepped-up basis in the estate of the exchanger). The advantage of this tax postponement is obvious. The investor can reinvest his full capital (including appreciation) in new properties without any diminution because of tax payments. Uncle Sam, in effect, extends an interest-free loan to the investor who thus can obtain a degree of leverage over and above that obtained from standard mortgage financing.

In addition to this tax advantage, an exchange (even if it is not tax-free) can be used as a financing technique, since it permits the substitution of real estate for cash or a third-party debt obligation. The real estate exchange has a psychological advantage as well. Since a price is arrived at by matching real estate values, inflated values on both sides give the parties the satisfaction of getting their price.

The two essential requirements for a tax-free exchange relate to (1) the purpose for which the new and old properties will be held by the exchanger and (2) the need for the properties to be of "like kind."

USE OF THE PROPERTIES

An exchange can be tax-free only if the property transferred by the exchanger and the property received by him are held for productive use in a business or for investment. A personal residence may not be exchanged (although it may be eligible for tax-free treatment under another section of the tax law). Also, dealer property (that held primarily for sale) may not be exchanged tax-free.

Note that an exchange qualifies for tax-free treatment as long as the properties fall into either of the eligible classes. Thus, property held for use in a trade or business may be exchanged for investment property, and vice versa.

Observation: In order for property *not* to be classified as dealer property, the exchanger must show an intent to hold it for some period of time. No fixed period is required (e.g., the six months formerly needed for long-term capital gain treatment); instead, the exchanger must show an intent to hold the property for gradual appreciation rather than quick resale.

LIKE-KIND REQUIREMENT

The concept of "like kind" refers to the nature or character of the real estate rather than to its grade or quality. The extent to which property is improved relates only to its grade or quality. So, raw land may be exchanged for an apartment building, provided the properties have been or will be held as investments or in a business. The Treasury regulations provide that a leasehold interest having a remaining term of at least 30 years is of like kind with a fee interest in real property. (By implication, leasehold interests of shorter terms may not be exchanged tax-free with fee interest.)

Observation: The two requirements for a tax-free exchange apply to each party independently of the other. So one party may qualify for a tax-free exchange even though the other does not.

RECEIPT OF BOOT

Rarely do two properties have the same market value and equity value. So one party must receive cash or assume a mortgage in order to balance the equities. This does not preclude tax-free treatment; however, to the extent one party receives cash or is relieved of an existing mortgage, he must recognize gain.

Example: A (not a dealer) exchanges real estate held for investment purchased many years ago for $5,000 (and that is now worth $8,000) for other real estate (to be held for productive use in business) having a fair market value of $6,000, plus $2,000 in cash. The gain realized by A on the property he is exchanging is $3,000 ($8,000 less $5,000). But the gain is *recognized* only to the extent of the $2,000 cash received.

It is also important to know A's basis for the property he acquired in the exchange, since the basis will determine gain or loss on any subsequent disposition of the acquired property. A's basis for the new property remains at $5,000 — the basis of the old property ($5,000), less the amount of the boot received ($2,000), increased by the amount of gain recognized on the exchange ($2,000).

BASIS OF PROPERTY RECEIVED

A tax-free exchange merely defers tax on gain; it does not eliminate it. Deferral is achieved by having the new property take over the cost basis of the old property so when the new property is sold, both the old and new gain will be recognized and taxed.

However, if the exchanger has paid boot (cash or the assumption of a mortgage), the amount is added to the old basis, since the exchanger must then recognize gain to the extent of the boot. Similarly, if the exchanger receives cash or is relieved of a mortgage obligation, his basis will be reduced by the amounts involved and increased by the recognized gain. (See above example.)

BOOSTING DEPRECIATION DEDUCTIONS

In a tax-free exchange, the basis for depreciation deductions, as well as for ultimate gain or loss, is the carryover basis of the property given up in the exchange. This is one of the disadvantages of the tax-free exchange, but it is less important now, with recovery periods stretched to 31.5 or 27.5 years.

As under prior law, however, two techniques remain for increasing the depreciation deduction following a tax-free exchange. These involve changing the land-building ratio and exchanging for property with a larger mortgage so that the basis for depreciation is increased.

LAND-BUILDING ALLOCATION RATIO

Whenever an investor thinks about depreciating his real estate for tax purposes, his first step is to allocate his cost between the land and the improvements. Naturally, he will want to allocate as much as possible to the depreciable buildings and as little as possible to the nondepreciable land. But the allocation must be made within the context of economic realities. If the property is later exchanged, the investor must carry over his old cost (reduced by depreciation deductions taken during his period of ownership). But he is *not* bound by the land-building ratio. Consequently, if the new property has the same or a more favorable ratio, the depreciation deductions during the first few years may actually be higher than previously even though the exchange is tax-free.

Example: An investor acquires improved property for $100,000. Of this amount, $20,000 is allocated to the land and $80,000 to the building. Over the years he claims $53,000 in depreciation deductions on the building so that its tax basis is reduced to $27,000. His land and building now have an aggregate basis of $47,000 ($20,000 land cost plus $27,000 adjusted building cost).

Assume the market value of the property is $200,000. Our investor now finds a like-kind property worth $200,000 and makes a tax-free exchange. He carries over his $47,000 basis to the new property. Assume that an appraisal establishes that 80 percent of the value of the new property is allocable to the building and 20 percent to the land (the same as for the old property). Thus, 80 percent of the carryover basis of $47,000 ($37,600) is the new basis for depreciation deductions, whereas had the investor retained the original property, he would have had only $27,000 remaining in the building's basis for depreciation purposes. (See Rev. Rul. 68-36, 1968-1 C.B. 357.)

LEVERAGING PROPERTY WITH A HIGHER BASIS

When one values properties for exchange, only *equities* count, not market value. In the previous example, the investor owned property free and clear with a market value of $200,000. In that example, he swapped it for another property, free of debt, with a market value of $200,000. But he might as easily have swapped it for a property with a market value of $300,000 but subject to an existing mortgage of $100,000. The equities would remain equal, but the investor would step up his tax basis from $47,000 (the remaining cost basis in the original property) to $147,000 (his original cost basis plus the amount of new debt of $100,000). If 80 percent is allocated to the depreciable improvements, his new basis for depreciation is $117,600 (as compared to the depreciable basis of the original building of $27,000).

HOW AN EXCHANGE CAN FACILITATE PROPERTY TRANSFERS

In addition to its potential for tax saving, an exchange can be useful as a financial device, or as an additional inducement to a property transfer.

Cash-poor buyer. When a prospective buyer does not have enough cash and cannot get a mortgage, the seller's usual alternatives are to pass up the offer or extend a large purchase money mortgage. The latter, however, subjects him to substantially the same financial risks that may have been the very reason why he wanted to sell in the first place. An exchange means he can take other property of the buyer in lieu of taking back a mortgage; it also may increase the likelihood that the seller will get his asking price. That the seller also has no tax on his gain also is appealing (assuming, of course, that the exchange qualifies for tax-free treatment).

Long-term appreciation. A tax-free exchange has appeal for the real estate investor who wants to swap income-producing property for real estate (e.g., raw land) with potential for long-term appreciation. That his depreciation deductions now are low and will not be increased after the exchange makes no difference to him since (if he is seeking raw land) his new investment is nondepreciable. If such an investor exchanges his income-producing property for several parcels of raw land near some area that has good growth potential, he will have put the full amount of his capital (undiminished by taxes) to work in another investment.

Exchange for more financeable property. An investor may be able to make a tax-free exchange for property that is capable of supporting a mortgage with a higher loan-to-value ratio. For example, property that justifies a mortgage not exceeding 60 percent of its value might be exchanged for property on which a lender will extend an 80 percent mortgage. In that case, the exchange will release cash for other uses equal to 20 percent of the value of the property. Or, an investor may hold real estate subject to a mortgage that bars prepayment or permits it only for a stiff penalty. If the investor requires cash, he might consider a tax-free exchange for similar property capable of being refinanced.

Exchange for more salable property.   An investor needing cash may be able to exchange difficult-to-sell property for property that can be disposed of for cash more easily. As already noted, when there is an intent to resell the acquired property immediately, the tax-free exchange rules do not apply. The investor seeking to cash out would have an immediate taxable gain on the exchange. However, since the basis of the property acquired by him in the exchange is increased by the amount of recognized gain, the aggregate gain on the exchange and the sale will equal the same taxable gain that would have resulted had the original property been sold.

MULTIPARTY EXCHANGES

An apparent problem with tax-free exchanges is the difficulty in matching two parties who want each other's property. However, the problem can be solved by having three or even more participants in the exchange. Although this makes the process more complicated, it vastly widens the market for possible exchanges.

Consider the situation where A has property he wants to exchange. B wants to buy A's property but has no suitable exchange property. B's broker locates C who has property for sale that A would like to own. Three possible transactions can take place among the parties:

- A can sell to B for cash and then buy C's property.
- B can buy C's property and then exchange it for A's property.
- A can exchange properties with C and C can then sell A's former property to B.

The first situation clearly is a traditional purchase and sale and no exchange occurs. However, both the second and third situations can qualify as tax-free exchanges provided the various steps are carried out in the right order. The key dangers to avoid are to have A pay cash to either B or C and to have either B or C in the position of acting as A's agent. However, it is possible to tie the various transactions together through contract provisions so that an "all or nothing" situation is set up.

Example: Perhaps the earliest case to approve a three-party exchange was *Alderson,* 317 F.2d 790 (9th Cir. 1963). Alderson entered into a contract to sell his farm in California to Alloy Company for cash. Before title passed, Alderson found a farm in Salinas that he wanted. Alderson and Alloy amended their contract to require Alloy to buy the Salinas property and then swap it for Alderson's farm. Alderson would pay the difference to Alloy in cash. The transaction was completed in this manner, and the Ninth Circuit approved tax-free treatment after the Tax Court had agreed with the IRS that no tax-free exchange had occurred.

The key point of the decision was that Section 1031 did not bar Alloy from acquiring the Salinas property for the *sole purpose* of using it in a tax-free exchange to get the Alderson farm — as long as Alloy in fact acquired the property before it was transferred to Alderson.

DEFERRED EXCHANGES

Suppose *A* agrees to exchange his property for a specified property (or type of property) to be acquired by *B* within a fixed period of time. If *B* does not acquire the property, either the contract is canceled or *B* may have an option to pay the price in cash. Prior to 1984, court rulings held that such nonsimultaneous or deferred exchanges qualified as tax-free exchanges assuming the other conditions of the tax law were met. Then Congress in the Deficit Reduction Act of 1984 (DRA) imposed short time limits within which the exchange property must be designated. (Congress felt that permitting exchanges within longer periods would provide unintended benefits to property owners and would create administrative problems.)

Under the DRA, property does not qualify as like-kind property if either of two specified time limits is transgressed. The first time limit under Section 1031(a)(3) of the Code requires that the property to be received by the taxpayer must be *identified* as such on or before the forty-fifth day after the date on which the taxpayer transfers his property. The second time limit requires the property to be *received* not later than the earlier of 180 days after the taxpayer transfers his property, or the due date, with extensions, of the taxpayer's return for the year in which he transfers his property.

According to the conference committee report on the DRA, the 45-day identification requirement can be met by designating the property to be received in the contract between or among the parties. Moreover, the designation requirement will be met if the contract specifies a limited number of properties that may be transferred, and the particular property transferred will be determined by contingencies beyond the parties' control.

COMBINING OPTION WITH TAX-FREE EXCHANGE

There appears to be a way to bypass the time limits on a deferred exchange by using an option. Assume that *A,* the property owner, is willing to give *B* an option to acquire *A*'s property either by exchange or cash purchase. The IRS has ruled (prior to the DRA) that if and when the option is exercised, a tax-free exchange may take place (except that the price of the option is boot to the property owner and so he must recognize gain to that extent). (Rev. Rul. 84-121, 1984-2 C.B. 168.) It seems clear that the time limits on deferred exchanges do not begin until the option is exercised.

Observation: Use of an option, of course, gives the optionee the power to decide whether to go through with the acquisition or not. He would be bound to complete the acquisition under a contract that required him either to find suitable exchange property or to pay cash.

TAX-FREE EXCHANGES AND PASSIVE LOSSES

The new passive activity rules of TRA '86 may affect a tax-free exchange if (1) the exchange property was used in a passive activity (i.e., a rental activity or a trade or business in which the owner did not materially participate); and (2) the owner has unused passive losses from the property at the time of the exchange.

Since an exchange is not the type of disposition that permits passive losses to be used against outside income, the losses continue in a suspended state until the investor receives passive income that can be offset by the losses or until the entire gain on the exchange property is recognized (at which point the suspended losses can offset outside income).

CORPORATE TAX-FREE EXCHANGES AFTER
TRA '86

A tax-free exchange by a corporation permits nonrecognition of gain in calculating regular tax liability, just as for an individual or partnership. However, a special rule now applies for the corporate alternative minimum tax (AMT) that could reduce or even eliminate the tax benefits of an exchange. In the years 1987 through 1990, a corporation must include in its AMT income half the amount by which its book income (that reported on its financial statements) exceeds its taxable income. Thus, all or part of the unrecognized gain on an exchange will in fact be recognized for purposes of the AMT.

Biggs v. Commissioner   *3rd party ok*
69 T.C. 905 (1978), affd., 632 F.2d 1171 (5th Cir. 1980)

Some of the facts have been stipulated, and those facts are so found.

The petitioner, Franklin B. Biggs, maintained his legal residence in Florida at the time he filed his petition in this case. He filed his Federal income tax return for 1969 with the District Director of Internal Revenue, Wilmington, Del.

On, and for some years before, October 23, 1968, the petitioner owned in fee simple two parcels of land located in St. Martin's Neck, Worcester County, Md. (the Maryland property). Sometime before October 23, 1968, the Maryland property was listed for sale with a realtor. The realtor informed Mr. Biggs that he had a client, Shepard G. Powell, who was interested in acquiring the property.

On October 23, 1968, Mr. Biggs and Mr. Powell met and discussed the possible acquisition of the Maryland property by Mr. Powell. At the outset of the discussion, Mr. Biggs informed Mr. Powell that as part of the consideration for the transfer of the Maryland property to Mr. Powell or his assigns, Mr. Biggs insisted that he receive real property of like kind. It was understood that Mr. Biggs would locate the property to be received in exchange, and Mr. Powell agreed to cooperate in the arrangements for an exchange, as long as it was not harmful to him.

On October 25, 1968, Mr. Biggs and Mr. Powell executed a written memorandum of intent with respect to the sale of the Maryland property to Mr. Powell. Such memorandum provided in relevant part:

Memorandum of Intent

I.   PURCHASE PRICE: $90,000 *NET* to SELLERS.
    c. $25,000.00 down payment at signing of contract, . . .
    d. $75,000.00 additional payment at time of settlement, which shall be within ninety (90) days after contract signing, making total cash payments of $100,000.00.
II.   MORTGAGE:
    a.   Balance of $800,000.00 secured by a first mortgage on Real Estate to SELLERS at a 4% interest rate; 10 year term. . . .

The memorandum of intent contained no reference to any proposed exchange of properties.

Sometime between October 20 and October 24, 1968, Mr. Biggs consulted his attorney, W. Edgar Porter, concerning the proposed transfer of the Maryland property to Mr. Powell. Subsequently, Mr. Porter reviewed the memorandum of intent which had been executed by the parties; he advised Mr. Biggs that such memorandum was not in accordance with the proposed transaction as it had been described by Mr. Biggs, in that there was no reference to a proposed exchange of properties. Mr. Porter also advised Mr. Powell by telephone that the memorandum of intent did not comport with Mr. Porter's understanding of the proposed transaction. Mr. Powell agreed to have his attorney work out the terms of a written exchange agreement with Mr. Porter.

After his conversation with Mr. Powell, Mr. Porter advised Mr. Biggs that he could begin looking for suitable property to be received in exchange for the Maryland property. To this end, Mr. Biggs advised John Thatcher, a Maryland realtor, of his desire to locate real property which was of substantial value and which was similar in nature to the Maryland property. Subsequently, Mr. Biggs was contacted by Johna H. Davis, a real estate broker, who had in his inventory four parcels of land situated in Accomack County, Va., collectively known as Myrtle Grove Farm (the Virginia property), which appeared to satisfy Mr. Biggs' specifications. After viewing the Virginia property, Mr. Biggs instructed Mr. Davis to draft contracts of sale.

Mr. Porter reviewed the proposed contracts prior to their execution and advised Mr. Davis that they should be drawn so as to indicate that Mr. Biggs was acting as an agent for a syndicate; before their execution by Mr. Biggs, the contracts were modified to describe the purchaser as "Franklin B. Biggs, (acting as agent for syndicate)." On October 29 and 30, 1968, the four land sales contracts were executed; the terms of such contracts were as follows:

Paid on execution of contract	$ 13,900.00
Balance due at settlement	115,655.14
Indebtedness created or assumed	142,544.86
Total — gross sales price	272,100.00

At the time such contracts were signed, Mr. Biggs paid $13,900 to the sellers of the Virginia property.

Mr. Powell was either unable or unwilling to take title to the Virginia property. Mr. Biggs therefore arranged to have title transferred to Shore Title Co., Inc. (Shore), a Maryland corporation owned and controlled by Mr. Porter and his family. However, it was not until December 26, 1968, that the board of directors of Shore authorized it to take title to the Virginia property.

On January 9, 1969, prior to the transfer of the Virginia property to Shore, Mr. Biggs and Shore executed an agreement with respect to the Virginia property, which provided in relevant part:

> 1. At any time hereafter that either party hereto requests the other party to do so, Shore Title Co., Inc. will and hereby agrees to convey

unto the said Franklin B. Biggs, or his nominee, all of the above mentioned property, for exactly the same price said Shore Title Co., Inc. has paid for it, plus any and all costs, expenses, advances or payments which Shore Title Co., Inc. has paid or will be bound in the future to pay, over and above said purchase price to Shore Title Co., Inc., in order for Shore Title Co., Inc. to acquire or hold title to said property; and it [is] further agreed that at that time, i.e. — when Shore Title Co., Inc. conveys said property under this paragraph and its provisions, the said Franklin B. Biggs, or his nominee will simultaneously release or cause Shore Title Co., Inc. to be released from any and all obligations which the latter has created, assumed or become bound upon in its acquisition and holding of title to said property.

2. All costs of acquiring or holding title to said property by both the said Shore Title Co., Inc. and Franklin B. Biggs, or his nominee shall be paid by the said Franklin B. Biggs, or his nominee at the time of transfer of title under paragraph numbered 1 hereof.

On or about January 9, 1969, the contracts for the sale of the Virginia property were closed; pursuant to a direction by Mr. Biggs, the sellers delivered warranty deeds evidencing legal title to the property to Shore. The $115,655.14 balance due at settlement was advanced to Shore by Mr. Biggs; by a bond secured by a deed of trust on the property, Shore agreed to repay the same amount to Mr. Biggs. Shore also assumed liabilities of $142,544.86 which were secured by deeds of trust in favor of the sellers and another mortgagee. On January 13, 1969, Mr. Biggs paid a finder's fee of $3,026 to Mr. Thatcher; Mr. Biggs also paid all of the closing costs incident to Shore's acquisition of the Virginia property.

On February 26, 1969, Shore, as vendor, entered into an agreement of sale with Mr. Powell or his assigns, vendee, for the sale and purchase of the Virginia property. The agreement provided for the payment of the purchase price as follows:

Upon execution of the agreement	$ 100.00
Vendee assumed and convenanted to pay the following promissory notes, all secured by deeds of trust on the Virginia property:	
To Shore Savings & Loan Association	58,469.86
To those from whom Shore acquired the Virginia property	84,075.00
To Franklin B. Biggs	115,655.14
Balance due at settlement	13,900.00
Total purchase price	272,200.00

On February 27, 1969, Mr. Biggs, as seller, and Mr. Powell or assigns, as purchaser, entered into a contract of sale for the Maryland property. The terms of such contract were as follows:

Cash, upon execution	$ 25,000
Cash, at settlement	75,000
First mortgage note receivable from Mr. Powell	800,000
Total	900,000

Such contract further provided:

> Sellers and Purchaser acknowledge the existence of a Contract of Sale dated February 26th, 1969, between Shore Title Co., Inc., Vendor-Seller, and Shepard G. Powell or Assigns, Vendee-Purchaser, copy of which is attached hereto and made a part hereof, whereby that Vendor has contracted to sell and that Vendee has agreed to buy from that Vendor at and for the purchase price of Two Hundred Seventy Two Thousand Two Hundred Dollars ($272,200.00) . . . [the Virginia property]. *As a further consideration for the making of this Contract of Sale . . . for the sale and purchase . . . of . . . [the Maryland property] the said Shepard G. Powell or Assigns, for the sum of One Hundred Dollars ($100.00) in cash, in hand paid, receipt whereof is hereby acknowledged, does hereby bargain, sell, set over and transfer unto said Franklin B. Biggs all of the right, title and interest of the said Shepard G. Powell or Assigns in and to said Virginia property and said Contract of Sale relating thereto, upon condition that the said Franklin B. Biggs assumes and covenants to pay (which he hereby does) all of the obligations assumed by the said Shepard G. Powell under the aforesaid Contract of Sale between him and Shore Title Co., Inc., and said Franklin B. Biggs hereby agrees to hold Shepard G. Powell or Assigns harmless from any liability under any and all of said obligations on said Virginia property,* and the said Shepard G. Powell and said Franklin B. Biggs do hereby jointly and separately agree to execute and deliver any and all necessary papers to effect delivery of title to said Virginia property to said Franklin B. Biggs and to relieve said Shepard G. Powell from any and all obligations assumed by him thereon. [Emphasis supplied.]

Also on February 27, 1969, Mr. Powell and his wife assigned their contractual right to acquire the Maryland property to Samuel Lessans and Maurice Lessans. By an agreement of sale and assignment, dated May 22, 1969, the Lessans sold and assigned their rights to acquire the Maryland property to Ocean View Corp. (Ocean View), a Maryland corporation, for $1,300,000. Of the total purchase price, $150,000 was to be paid into escrow at the time such contract was signed; an $800,000 note (executed by Ocean View in favor of Mr. Biggs) was to be given to Mr. Biggs at settlement; a $250,000 note (executed by Ocean View in favor of the Lessans) was to be given to the Lessans at settlement; and a $100,000 note (executed by Ocean View in favor of the realtors) was to be given to the realtors at settlement.

Ocean View was incorporated on May 21, 1969. At the first meeting of the board of directors, held May 22, 1969, the directors authorized the corporation to execute all documents necessary to consummate the contract of sale assigned by the Lessans to Ocean View. The minutes of such first meeting reveal that it was:

> FURTHER RESOLVED: That the proper officers of this Corporation are hereby authorized and empowered to quit claim any of the Corporation's interest in the tract of land located in the State of Virginia referred to in the said contract of sale;

However, neither the Lessans nor Ocean View had any option, contract, or obligation to purchase the Virginia property, or any other interest in such property.

On May 24, 1969, Shore executed a deed conveying all its right, title, and interest in the Virginia property to Mr. Biggs as grantee. Mr. Powell and his wife, the Lessans, and Ocean View joined in executing the deed as grantors. The deed provided that:

> the said Shore Title Co., Inc., a Maryland corporation, executes this deed to the Grantee herein for the purpose of conveying the . . . Virginia property hereinafter described by good and marketable title, subject to the assumption by the Grantee herein of the obligations hereinafter referred to, *and all of the other Grantors herein join in the execution of this deed for the purpose of releasing and quit-claiming any interest in and to the property described herein and for the purpose of thereby requesting Shore Title Co., Inc. to convey said property to the Grantee herein in the manner herein set out;* [Emphasis supplied.]

Ocean View signed the deed upon the advice of its attorney, who, although he believed that Ocean View had no interest in the Virginia property, did not object because Ocean View was signing only a quitclaim deed involving no warranties. By the same deed, Mr. Biggs agreed to assume and pay the notes in favor of the mortgage and the owners from whom Shore had acquired the Virginia property, in the total amount of $142,544.86. On May 29, 1969, Mr. Biggs executed a deed of release in favor of Shore, evidencing payment in full of the bond dated January 10, 1969, in the amount of $115,655.14.

On May 26, 1969, Mr. Biggs and his wife, Mr. Powell and his wife, and the Lessans executed a deed conveying title to the Maryland property to Ocean View. Contemporaneously, Ocean View executed a purchase money obligation secured by a mortgage, in the face amount of $800,000, in favor of Mr. Biggs. Also on May 26, 1969, all of the contracts were closed; Ocean View received the deed to the Maryland property; and Mr. Biggs received the deed to the Virginia property.

On his 1969 Federal income tax return, Mr. Biggs reported his gain from the sale of the Maryland property as follows:

Selling price of Maryland property	$900,000.00	100.00 %
Exchange — Virginia property	ª298,380.75	33.15 %
Boot	601,619.25	66.85 %
Selling price Maryland property	900,000.00	
Basis — date of exchange	186,312.80	
Gain	713,687.20	
Not recognized — exchange (sec. 1031 I.R.C.) — 33.15%	236,587.31	
Taxable gain	477,099.89	53.011%

ª Such figure included finders' fees and legal costs incident to the acquisition of the Virginia property.

Mr. Biggs elected to report the sale under the installment sales provisions of section 453. In his notice of deficiency, the Commissioner determined that there was not an exchange of like kind properties within the meaning of section 1031; accordingly, the gain to be recognized was increased to $713,687.20, the difference between the gross sales price of the Maryland property and its adjusted basis.

OPINION

Section 1031(a) provides that no gain or loss shall be recognized if property held for productive use in a trade or business or for investment is exchanged solely for property of a like kind. If money or other property not of a like kind — or "boot" — is also received in an exchange, gain is recognized to the extent of the boot. Sec. 1031(b). The purpose of section 1031 (and its predecessors) was to defer recognition of gain or loss on transactions in which, although in theory the taxpayer may have realized a gain or loss, his economic situation is in substance the same after, as it was before, the transaction. Stated otherwise, if the taxpayer's money continues to be invested in the same kind of property, gain or loss should not be recognized. H. Rept. 704, 73d Cong., 2d Sess. (1934), 1939-1 C.B. (Part 2) 554, 564; Jordan Marsh Co. v. Commissioner, 269 F.2d 453, 455-456 (2d Cir. 1959), revg. a Memorandum Opinion of this Court; cf. Century Electric Co. v. Commissioner, 192 F.2d 155, 159 (8th Cir. 1951), affg. 15 T.C. 581 (1950), cert. denied 342 U.S. 954 (1952).

The transaction involved in the case before us is a variant of the so-called "three-corner" exchange. In such a transaction, the taxpayer desires to exchange, rather than to sell, his property. However, the potential buyer of the taxpayer's property owns no property the taxpayer wishes to receive in exchange. Therefore, the buyer purchases other suitable property from a third party and then exchanges it for the property held by the taxpayer.

In numerous cases, this type of transaction has been held to constitute an exchange within the meaning of section 1031. E.g., Alderson v. Commissioner, 317 F.2d 790 (9th Cir. 1963), revg. 38 T.C. 215 (1962); W. D. Haden Co. v. Commissioner, 165 F.2d 588 (5th Cir. 1948), affg. on this issue a Memorandum Opinion of this Court; Coupe v. Commissioner, 52 T.C. 394 (1969); J. H. Baird Publishing Co. v. Commissioner, 39 T.C. 608 (1962); Mercantile Trust Co. of Baltimore et al., Trustees v. Commissioner, 32 B.T.A. 82 (1935). In so holding, the courts have permitted taxpayers great latitude in structuring transactions. Thus, it is immaterial that the exchange was motivated by a wish to reduce taxes. Mercantile Trust Co. of Baltimore et al., Trustees v. Commissioner, supra at 87. The taxpayer can locate suitable property to be received in exchange and can enter into negotiations for the acquisition of such property. Coastal Terminals, Inc. v. United States, 320 F.2d 333, 338 (4th Cir. 1963); Alderson v. Commissioner, 317 F.2d at 793; Coupe v. Commissioner, 52 T.C. at 397-398. Moreover, the taxpayer can oversee improvements on the land to be acquired (J. H. Baird Publishing Co. v. Commissioner, 39 T.C. at 611) and can even advance money toward the purchase price of the property to be acquired by exchange (124 Front Street, Inc. v. Commissioner, 65 T.C. 6, 15-18 (1975)). Provided the final result is an exchange of property for other property of a like kind, the transaction will qualify under section 1031.

Despite the liberal treatment previously accorded taxpayers by the courts, the Commissioner asks us to hold that the petitioner's transfer of the Maryland property and receipt of the Virginia property did not constitute an exchange within the meaning of section 1031. The Commissioner argues that there was no contractual interdependence between the transfer of the Maryland property and the receipt of the Virginia property. He asks us to view what transpired as two separate transactions: a sale for cash of the Maryland property, and a separate and unrelated purchase of the Virginia property. The Commissioner stresses the form in which the transaction was cast. He asserts that the fact that the petitioner advanced funds to be used by Shore in its acquisition of the Virginia property, coupled with the fact that Mr. Powell, the Lessans, and Ocean View never acquired legal title to the Virginia property from Shore, preclude a finding that the transaction constituted an exchange.

The starting point of our analysis is the well established principle that the substance of a transaction, rather than the form in which it is cast, ordinarily determines its tax consequences. E.g., Smith v. Commissioner, 537 F.2d 972, 975 (8th Cir. 1976), affg. a Memorandum Opinion of this Court; J. H. Baird Publishing Co. v. Commissioner, 39 T.C. at 615-616. If, in substance, what occurred was a sale of the petitioner's Maryland property for cash, and a separate and unrelated purchase of the Virginia property, then the Commissioner's determination must be sustained. On the other hand, if the petitioner's transfer of the Maryland property and receipt of the Virginia property were interdependent parts of an overall plan, the result of which was an exchange of like kind properties, the transaction comes within the ambit of section 1031. Bell Lines, Inc. v. United States, 480 F.2d 710, 713-714 (4th Cir. 1973); Crenshaw v. United States, 450 F.2d 472, 475-476 (5th Cir. 1971), cert. denied 408 U.S. 923 (1972); Redwing Carriers, Inc. v. Tomlinson, 399 F.2d 652, 658 (5th Cir. 1968); Century Electric Co. v. Commissioner, 192 F.2d at 159. Having carefully reviewed the evidence in the case before us, we are convinced that the transfer of the Maryland property and receipt of the Virginia property were part of an integrated plan intended to effectuate an exchange of like kind properties, the substantive result of which was an exchange within the meaning of section 1031.

At the outset, it is clear that the parties intended and agreed that there would be an exchange of properties. From the beginning of the negotiations between the petitioner and Mr. Powell, the petitioner insisted that as part of the consideration for the transfer of his Maryland property, he receive like kind property in exchange. Alderson v. Commissioner, 317 F.2d at 792-793. Mr. Powell orally agreed to an exchange of properties, and Mr. Porter, after confirming that such an agreement in fact existed, advised the petitioner that he could begin looking for suitable property to be received in exchange. The petitioner located the Virginia property and negotiated for the sale of such property. Coastal Terminals, Inc. v. United States, 320 F.2d at 338; Alderson v. Commissioner, supra. . . . Mr. Powell, at that time, was either unable or unwilling to enter into the contract to purchase the Virginia property or to take title to it. Accordingly, the petitioner made the contract of sale to him "acting as agent for syndicate" and thereafter arranged to have the title transferred to Shore. Coupe v. Commissioner, 52 T.C. at 407. Mr. Powell subsequently contracted to purchase the Virginia property from Shore. The February 27, 1969, contract of sale between the petitioner and Mr. Powell was a written formalization of their prior agreement to exchange properties: the petitioner agreed to convey his Maryland property to Mr. Powell, and as part of the consideration for the Maryland property, Mr. Powell assigned his right to purchase the Virginia property to the petitioner. The exchange agreement was consummated at the May 26, 1969, closing, at which time the petitioner conveyed title to the Maryland property to Mr. Powell's assignees and received title to the Virginia property.

This Court previously had occasion to consider a markedly similar transaction in the case of Coupe v. Commissioner, supra. *Coupe* dealt with a transaction involving four parties: (1) The taxpayer, who wished to exchange properties; (2) a prospective purchaser of the taxpayer's property, who did not own the property the taxpayer wished to receive in exchange; (3) a prospective seller of the property the taxpayer wished to receive in exchange; and (4) a fourth party. The taxpayer transferred his property to the fourth party, who sold it to the prospective purchaser for cash. With such cash, the fourth party purchased the property the taxpayer wished to receive in exchange and transferred it to the taxpayer. The Court held that the transaction constituted an exchange within the meaning of section 1031. 52 T.C. at 406. In *Coupe,* as in the case before us, the prospective purchaser of the taxpayer's property was either unable or unwilling to obtain title to the exchange property. 52 T.C. at 407. However, that factor was not determinative; the Court found that the statute requires only that, as the end result of an agreement, property is received as consideration for property transferred by the taxpayer. 52 T.C. at 409. Accordingly, there is no merit in the Commissioner's argument that the transaction before us cannot qualify under section 1031 because Mr. Powell, the Lessans, and Ocean View never received legal title to the Virginia property. See also W. D. Haden Co. v. Commissioner, 165 F.2d at 590; but see Carlton v. United States, 385 F.2d 238, 242-243 (5th Cir. 1967).

Moreover, the fact that the petitioner advanced funds to Shore to enable it to purchase the Virginia property is not fatal to his case. Similar arguments were advanced in the case of 124 Front Street, Inc. v. Commissioner, supra. In that case, the taxpayer owned an option to acquire property that Firemen's wished to own. Firemen's agreed to advance funds to the taxpayer so that it could exercise its option and then sell or exchange the option property with Firemen's. The Court rejected the Commissioner's argument that the taxpayer had sold its option to Firemen's. Instead, the Court held that the transaction represented a valid exchange of properties under section 1031. 65 T.C. at 15. The Court further held that the funds advanced by Firemen's to the taxpayer represented a loan, and not boot received by the taxpayer on the exchange. 65 T.C. at 18.

In the case before us, the petitioner helped to finance Shore's acquisition of the Virginia property: he paid an earnest money deposit of $13,900 at the time the contracts of sale were signed and subsequently advanced $115,655.14 to Shore to enable it to close the contracts, for a total of $129,555.14. Although the petitioner received $900,000 when the exchange agreement was closed ($100,000 in cash and an $800,000 promissory note), $129,555.14 of such amount in fact represented repayment of loans previously made by the petitioner to Shore. Cf. 124 Front Street, Inc. v. Commissioner, supra. In addition, the Virginia property which the petitioner received was subject to mortgages in the total amount of $142,544.86, which the petitioner assumed; thus, part of the cash he received at the closing was to reimburse him for the assumption of such mortgages. In substance, the petitioner exchanged his Maryland property for the Virginia property and $627,900 in cash or its equivalent.

We recognize that there are factual differences between the case before us and other cases dealing with three- and four-party exchanges. For example, in Coupe v. Commissioner, supra, the Court found as a fact that the fourth party was acting as the agent of the purchaser of the taxpayer's property, rather than as the taxpayer's agent. 52 T.C. at 406-407. We have made no such finding with respect to Shore's role here. Moreover, in *Coupe,* because of the form in which the transaction was cast, the taxpayer never handled the cash used to acquire the exchange property. 52 T.C. at 409. However, in substance, the transaction in the case before us is not materially different from that in Coupe v. Commissioner.

In *Coupe,* although the Court found that the fourth party was not the agent of the taxpayer, the fourth party undertook, at the request of the taxpayer, to arrange, for the benefit of the taxpayer, an exchange of property that would qualify under section 1031. In the case before us, Shore assumed a similar role. In contracting to purchase the Virginia property, the petitioner made clear that he was acting, not for himself, but on behalf of Mr. Powell. When it developed that Mr. Powell was unable or unwilling to take title to the Virginia property, Shore accepted title to facilitate an exchange. Thus, in both *Coupe* and the case before us, the fourth party was used to facilitate an exchange, and the taxpayer never acquired legal title to the property before the exchange.

Nor do the financial arrangements in the case before us differ significantly. If Shore had borrowed money from another person to finance its acquisition of the Virginia property, and if at the closing Ocean View had paid Shore the funds to pay off such loan and discharge the mortgages, the petitioner would have received, at the closing, the Virginia property and $627,900 in cash. Certainly such a transaction would qualify as a section 1031 exchange under the rule of *Coupe.* In the case before us, although the formal structure of the transaction is different, the net result is the same. To reach a different result in the case before us, merely because the transaction was not so artfully arranged, would be to exalt form over substance.

Such an emphasis on the form in which the transaction is cast has been the object of criticism among commentators and has led an appellate court to observe that the cases in this area are " 'hopelessly conflicting.' " Bell Lines, Inc. v. United States, 480 F.2d at 714. Moreover, undue reliance on the form of these transactions frustrates the legislative purpose, that is, to defer recognition of gain or loss in instances in which the taxpayer continues his investment in property of a like kind. Undue reliance on form also produces capricious results; in cases which are not substantively different, courts are led to reach differing results. On the other hand, if we focus instead on the substance of the transactions, taking into consideration all steps which are part of an integrated plan, we reach results which are consonant with the legislative purpose and which treat all taxpayers evenhandedly. Traditionally, the courts have been guided by substance, not form, in deciding tax controversies (e.g., Commissioner v. Court Holding Co., 324 U.S. 331 (1945); Gregory v. Helvering, 293 U.S. 465 (1935); Weiss v. Stearn, 265 U.S. 242 (1924)), and such principle must be applied in deciding the case before us.

The Commissioner argued that under the rule enunciated in Golsen v. Commissioner, 54 T.C. 742, 757 (1970), affd. on another issue 445 F.2d 985 (10th Cir. 1971), cert. denied 404 U.S. 940 (1971), we are bound to follow the decision of the Court of Appeals for the Fifth Circuit in Carlton v. United States, 385 F.2d 238 (1967). In *Carlton,* the taxpayers, who had given an option on their ranch property, negotiated to acquire other ranch property which they wished to receive in a tax-free exchange. The optionee contracted to buy the other property but never acquired title to such property. Instead, the optionee paid cash for the taxpayers' property and assigned to the taxpayers its contractual right to acquire the other property. Two days later, the taxpayers purchased the other property, using the money previously received from the optionee to close the transaction. The court found that the transaction constituted a sale by the taxpayers and a purchase of other property. 385 F.2d at 242. The court distinguished an earlier decision, W. D. Haden Co. v. Commissioner, supra, pointing out that the money received by the taxpayers was not earmarked to be used in purchasing the exchange property; thus, the taxpayers had unrestricted use of the money received. 385 F.2d at 243.

Clearly, the court in *Carlton* was troubled by the harshness of the result it reached. 385 F.2d at 243. In a subsequent case, Redwing Carriers, Inc. v. Tomlinson, 399 F.2d 652 (5th Cir. 1968), the court distinguished *Carlton.* In *Redwing,* there was a sale of old property and an acquisition of new property; but, since the court found that the sale and acquisition were interdependent, it treated them as merely steps in a single transaction, which constituted an exchange under section 1031. The court distinguished *Carlton* on the basis that in *Carlton* there was no similar finding of interdependence of steps in the purported exchange. 399 F.2d at 659.

The facts in the case before us are significantly different from those in *Carlton.* In *Carlton,* the taxpayers conveyed their property for cash and 2 days later reinvested the proceeds; here, the transfer of the Maryland property and receipt of the Virginia property occurred simultaneously. Moreover, the petitioner already had committed funds to the purchase of the Virginia property; thus his use of the cash received was not unfettered or unrestricted, as was found in *Carlton.* Here, we have found that the events were merely steps designed to effect an exchange, and under these circumstances, we are satisfied that our decision is not inconsistent with the holdings of the Fifth Circuit in *Carlton* and *Redwing*. Cf. Kent v. Commissioner, 61 T.C. 133, 137-138 (1973).

NOTES AND QUESTIONS

1. *Tax-Free Exchanges.*
    a. *Rationales for Tax Deferral Treatment.* In Biggs v. Commissioner, 69 T.C. 905 (1978), affd., 632 F.2d 1171 (5th Cir. 1980), involving a "three-corner" exchange, the Tax Court states (at 913) that "[t]he purpose of §1031 . . . was to defer recognition of gain or loss on transactions in which, although in theory the taxpayer may have realized a gain or loss, his economic situation is in substance the same after, as it was before, the transaction. Stated otherwise, if the taxpayer's money continues to be invested in the same kind of property, gain or loss should not be recognized. H. Rept. No. 704, 73d Cong., 2d Sess. (1934), 1939-1 C.B. (Part 2) 554, 564 . . ."

Other rationales have been suggested. Based on pure administrative necessity, it has been suggested that no attempt should be made to measure and tax any gain or loss in the value of real estate held for investment or use in a trade or business until a sale occurs and a free-market cash valuation of the property can be made. To rule otherwise would require a subjective valuation of all property at periodic intervals that would impose an intolerable administrative burden on the Internal Revenue Service.

It has also been argued that the upgrading of income-producing property (by substituting new assets for ones that have deteriorated or become obsolete) should not be discouraged by taxation in an inflationary economy when any taxation of gain (caused in large measure by inflation) may decimate the taxpayer's liquidity and discourage him from obtaining more efficient replacement assets that are likely to produce more taxable income and more revenues for the Treasury Department.

Based on the foregoing policy rationales, how would you justify the following tax result in part (i) below? In parts (ii) and (iii) below, whose position do you favor, the Tax Court or the Internal Revenue Service?

     i. If *A* were to sell Blackacre for cash and immediately thereafter use the after-tax proceeds (along with its other funds) to purchase Whiteacre, the transaction would be immediately taxable, whereas an exchange of Blackacre for Whiteacre would be regarded as a tax-free exchange.

     ii. If *A* were to exchange its interest as a general or limited partner in the *A* partnership (whose underlying asset is Blackacre) for a comparable interest in the *B* partnership (whose underlying asset is Whiteacre), tax-deferral treatment would have been afforded to *A* by the Tax Court prior to the Tax Reform Act of 1984. See, e.g., Gulfstream Land and Development Corp. v. Commissioner, 71 T.C. 587 (1979); Estate of Meyer v. Commissioner, 58 T.C. 311 (1972), affd., 503 F.2d 556 (9th Cir. 1974), nonacq., 1975-2 C.B. 3 (the interests of general partners held to be exchangeable where the underlying assets of both partnerships are substantially similar in nature, but held that an exchange of a general for a limited partnership interest would not satisfy the like-kind requirement); see also Long v. Commissioner, 77 T.C. 1045 (1981); Pappas v. Commissioner, 78 T.C. 1078 (1982). By contrast, the Service had consistently ruled that an exchange of equity interests was precluded by the exclusionary language in former I.R.C. §1031(a) (prior to amendment by the Tax Reform Act of 1984). Rev. Rul. 78-135, 1978-1 C.B. 256.

Congress rejected the position held by the Tax Court and sided with the Service by denying tax-deferral treatment with respect to any exchange of interests in *different* partnerships. I.R.C. §1031(a)(2)(D), as added by §77(a) of the Tax Reform Act of 1984. Do you think Congress made the correct decision? If so, do you think tax-deferral treatment should also be denied to a general partner who converts his interest to that of a limited partner in the *same* partnership if his ratio for sharing profits and losses and his capital interest remain the same? See Rev. Rul. 84-52, 1984-1 C.B. 157.

iii. Treas. Reg. §1.1031(a)-1(c) deems a 30-year-or-more leaseback equivalent to a fee interest in real estate. Suppose an owner of some real estate worth $10 million (with an adjusted basis of $12 million) conveys a fee simple interest and, as part of the sale-and-leaseback transaction, receives from the purchaser both $10 million in cash and a 30-year leaseback worth zero (as reflected by the fair market leaseback rental). Under I.R.C. §1031(a) has there been an "exchange" (as opposed to a sale) so that the seller-lessee should be denied recognition of his loss in the amount of $2 million? Compare Rev. Rul. 60-43, 1960-1 C.B. 687, and Century Electric Co. v. Commissioner, 192 F.2d 155 (8th Cir. 1951), cert. denied, 342 U.S. 954 (1952) with City Investing Co. v. Commissioner, 38 T.C. 1 (1962), nonacq., 1963-1 C.B. 5 and Jordan Marsh v. Commissioner, 269 F.2d 453 (2d Cir. 1959). See discussion at Chapter 8B2, note 4.

b.   Definitional Issues.   Internal Revenue Code §1031(a)(1) provides that "No gain or loss shall be recognized on the exchange of property held for productive use in a trade or business or for investment if such property is exchanged solely for property of like kind which is to be held either for productive use in a trade or business or for investment." The first requirement is that there be an exchange. An exchange, like a sale of property, is generally a taxable transaction unless the Code provides otherwise. Simply put, a sale occurs when the owner receives cash or something that is cash-equivalent (such as a purchase money mortgage note), and an exchange takes place when the owner receives other property. See, e.g., Rev. Rul. 61-119, 1961-1 C.B. 395; Wheeler v. Commissioner, 58 T.C. 459 (1972); Carlton v. United States, 385 F.2d 238 (5th Cir. 1967). As noted above, this definitional distinction is important for purposes of determining whether a loss can be disallowed under I.R.C. §1031(a)(1) when the owner of some real estate transfers fee title to the property and receives from the new owner a leaseback with a term of 30 years or more.

The second requirement, that both properties in the exchange be "held for productive use in a trade or business or for investment," has been broadly construed so that business real estate can be exchanged for investment real estate or vice versa. Treas. Reg. §1.1031(a)-1(a). While neither the Code nor the Treasury Regulations explicitly define the difference between business real estate and investment real estate, the traditional view is that the former refers to income-producing real estate where active services are being rendered (e.g., a shopping center without net leases) and the latter refers to real estate that is being held as a passive investment (e.g., net-leased rental real estate or raw land held by a taxpayer who is not a "dealer"). Compare I.R.C. §162(a) with §§212(1) and 212(2); see also Treas. Reg. §1.761-1(a); IRC §163(d). However, the phrase "*use* in a trade or business or for investment" disqualifies dealer real estate (held as inventory or primarily for sale to customers in the ordinary course of business) and residential property held for personal use from tax deferral treatment under I.R.C. §1031. Moreover, I.R.C. §1031(a)(2)(A) expressly excludes any exchange of property held primarily for sale.

The third requirement is that the properties in the exchange be of "like kind"; in that regard Treas. Reg. §1.103(a)-1(b) and 1.103(c) provide as follows:

> . . . the words "like kind" have reference to the nature and character of the property and not to its grade or quality. . . . The fact that any real estate involved is improved or unimproved is not material, for that fact relates only to the grade or quality of the property and not to its kind or class. . . . No gain or loss is recognized if . . . a taxpayer who is not a dealer in real estate exchanges city real estate for a ranch or farm, . . . or exchanges improved real estate for unimproved real estate.

Does this language in the Regulations make sense? Isn't it possible for the grade or quality of the real estate to affect its nature and quality? Suppose for example that a building is exchanged for some unimproved raw land. In light of the rationales for nonrecognition treatment under I.R.C. §1031 (discussed in note (a), supra), do you think that such an exchange should qualify for tax deferral treatment? Compare Davis v. United States, 411 F. Supp. 964 (D.C. Haw. 1976), affd., 589 F.2d 446 (9th Cir. 1979); Rev. Rul. 78-72, 1978-1 C.B. 258; and Rev. Rul. 67-255, 1967-2 C.B. 270, with Burkhard Investment Co. v. United States, 100 F.2d 642 (9th Cir. 1938). What about an exchange of a farm for rental real estate in a city? See Braley v. Commissioner, 14 B.T.A. 1153 (1929), acq. VII-2 C.B. 6. What about an exchange of domestic real estate for foreign real estate? See Rev. Rul. 68-363, 1968-2 C.B. 336.

The fourth requirement is that the properties be exchanged *solely* for one another. However, as explained in the excerpt from the Mortgage and Real Estate Executive's Report, properties involved in an exchange rarely have the same market and equity values. Therefore, if one party to the exchange must receive cash or assume (or take subject to) a mortgage to balance the equities, the transaction will still qualify for tax deferral treatment, but gain will be recognized to the extent that the party receives "boot" in the form of cash or relief from an existing mortgage.

   c.   Three-Corner Exchanges.   As explained in the excerpt from the Mortgage and Real Estate Executive's Report and the *Biggs* case, certain multiparty exchanges (colloquially referred to as "three-corner exchanges") are allowed under I.R.C. §1031. However, Congress prohibited the use of open-ended three-corner exchanges that was permitted under Starker v. United States, 602 F.2d 1341 (9th Cir. 1979) by overruling *Starker* and requiring the transferor to designate the property to be received and complete the transaction within 180 days after the transfer of the exchanged property. I.R.C. §1031(a)(3), as added by §77(a) of the Tax Reform Act of 1984. See generally Goodman, How the New *Starker* Case Has Revolutionized Exchanges, 10 Real Est. Rev. 78 (Summer 1980); Sommers, Deferred Like-Kind Exchanges After *Starker,* 68 J. Taxn. 92 (1988).

   Simply put, a three-corner exchange makes sense where *A,* the owner of some real estate ("Blackacre"), desires to acquire some like-kind real estate ("Greenacre") from another owner, *B,* by means of a tax-free exchange, but *B* insists on receiving cash. While *A* might be able to sell Blackacre for cash, his net after-tax proceeds may not be sufficient to cover the purchase price demanded by *B;* or *A* might believe that the tax cost of a sale and purchase is too onerous (for example, *A*'s adjusted basis in Blackacre might be very low, so a sale of Blackacre would trigger a large amount of taxable gain). Under such circumstances, if *A* finds someone else who is interested in paying cash for Blackacre (someone named *"C"*) then, at *A*'s behest, *C* could buy Greenacre from *B* for cash and then *C* would exchange Greenacre for Blackacre so that *A* could obtain tax deferral treatment. Such a transaction is reflected by the following diagram.

$$A \xrightarrow{\text{Blackacre}} C \xrightarrow{\text{Cash}} B$$
$$\xleftarrow{\text{Greenacre}} \xleftarrow{\text{Greenacre}}$$

Alternatively, *A* could first exchange properties with *B,* who, as diagrammed below, would then sell Blackacre to *C* for cash.

$$A \xrightarrow{\text{Blackacre}} B \xrightarrow{\text{Blackacre}} C$$
$$\xleftarrow{\text{Greenacre}} \xleftarrow{\text{Cash}}$$

As explained in the *Biggs* decision, such a transaction will work (even when *B*'s ownership of Blackacre or *C*'s ownership of Greenacre is transitory) so long as the intermediary, *C*, uses her own funds and not the funds of *A* and does not otherwise act as a *formal* agent of *A*. See also Madison and Dwyer ¶8.02[4].

In your judgment, should the following hypothetical transaction involving "like-kind" real estate qualify for tax deferral treatment under I.R.C. §1031? If not, why not?

A, who owns Blackacre, desires to receive replacement property in an exchange, and *C* is interested in buying Blackacre for cash. Under their exchange agreement *A* transfers title in Blackacre to *C* for $100,000, which funds are to be controlled and used by *C* until *A* designates the replacement property (Whiteacre), at which time the funds would be used by *C* to purchase Whiteacre or paid to *A* if Whiteacre is not available. Six months later, at the behest of *A, C* acquires Whiteacre from *B* for $100,000 and transfers title in Whiteacre to *A.*

d. Rewards and Risks. As explained in the excerpt from the Mortgage and Real Estate Executive's Report, in addition to tax deferral treatment exchanges of real estate under I.R.C. §1031 can also be used to: (1) boost property owner's depreciation deductions by altering the transferor's land-building ratio for tax purposes, by receiving property with a larger existing mortgage so that the depreciable basis in the substitute property can be increased, or by acquiring substitute property with improvements that have a shorter useful life; (2) expedite a transfer of real estate where the purchaser is short on cash and the seller is wary of the risks associated with purchase money mortgage financing; or (3) exchange real estate for substitute property that has more potential for long-term appreciation, can support a higher debt-financing loan-to-value ratio, or is more marketable.

On the negative side of the coin is the potential tax problem caused by the interaction between I.R.C. §1031 and the new limitations on passive loss imposed by I.R.C. §469. See discussion at Chapter 2B, note 3. Don't forget that I.R.C. §1031 is mandatory, not optional. With that in mind, can you think of any situation in which a property owner would want to avoid an exchange of her real estate for like-kind property?

After reviewing Chapter 2B notes 3 and 5d, can you explain why the tax-free exchange has experienced an upsurge in popularity since the Tax Reform Act of 1986? See Goolsby and Williams, A Reevaluation of the Benefits of Like-Kind Exchanges, 19 Real Est. Rev. 40 (Summer 1989).

Notwithstanding an attempt by the Treasury Department to tighten the definition of like-kind properties and to codify minimum holding periods for the properties, Congress decided to merely deny like-kind status to foreign property and restrict exchanges between related parties. I.R.C. §1031(f), as amended by the Omnibus Budget Reconciliation Act of 1989.

For planning suggestions and pitfalls see generally Barrett and Kolbe, The Benefits of Tax-Deferred Exchanges Are Often Illusory, 17 Real Est. Rev. 56 (Winter 1988); Blackstone, Achieving Leverage Through Multiparty Exchanges, 3 Real Est. Fin. J. 85 (Winter 1988); Carlin and Novack, Tax-Free Exchanges Attract New Interest, 4 Real Est. Fin. 68 (Spring 1987); Levine and Glichlich, Tax-Free Real Estate Transactions: New Developments Involving Like-Kind Exchanges, 14 J. Real Est. Taxn. 172 (Winter 1987); Maller, Financing Ideas: Structuring Like-Kind Exchanges of Real Estate, 14 Real Est. L.J. 83 (Summer 1985); Plutchok, Let's Make a Deal: How to Swap Real Estate Tax-Free, 1 Real Est. Fin. 16 (Fall 1985); Sanders and Roady, New Real Estate Rules for Exempt Financing, Related Party Transactions, Exchanges, 62 J. Taxn. 66 (Feb. 1985); Sitnick, Like-Kind Exchanges: New Rules and Planning Considerations, 7 Real Est. Fin. 66 (Spring 1990); Wasserman, Mr. Mogul's Perpetual Search for Tax Deferral: Techniques for Section 1031 Like-Kind Exchanges — Part 3, 5 Real Est. Acctg. and Taxn. 26 (Summer 1990).

2. *Tax-Exempt Bond Financing.*   The tax-exempt mortgage is essentially an industrial development bond (IDB) structured as a tripartite mortgage loan. An IDB is a debt obligation issued in the name of a state or local government to finance the acquisition, construction, or rehabilitation of property to be leased or sold to a private developer. Advisory Commission on Intergovernmental Relations, Industrial Development Bond Financing 37 (Report A-18, 1963). By recent count, 48 states (all except California and Idaho) permit IDB financing in some form. Generally, the mortgage loan is made to a state or municipal issuer that places its bond with the lender and simultaneously engages

in either a net lease (with an option to purchase) or an installment sale of the mortgaged real estate with the developer. The payments required under the lease or sale contract (as the case may be) are usually an amount sufficient to cover interest and amortization of the bonds. In the case of new construction, when the issuer is a commercial bank the developer may be able to obtain both the permanent and the construction financing from the same bank. This is known as "one-stop financing." In reality, as diagrammed below, the developer is the real obligor on the loan; when the transaction is finalized, the mortgage lender has a first lien on the property and receives its debt-service payments directly from the developer under the lease or contract that is assigned to the lender as additional collateral for the loan. See Madison and Dwyer ¶8.06.

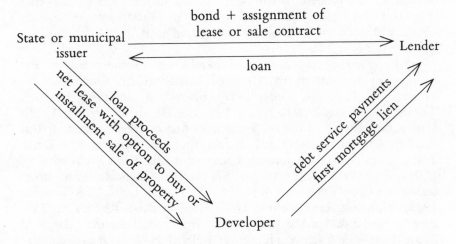

The purpose of the governmental issuer's role as a conduit is to qualify the mortgage interest for tax-free treatment. Generally, interest paid on state and local obligations is exempt from federal income taxes pursuant to I.R.C. §103(a). In a recent decision, the Supreme Court ruled that the federal government does have the constitutional right to tax interest on state and municipal bonds. The benchmark ruling upheld denial of the federal tax exemption for interest on coupon bonds with maturities of one year or more under the Tax Equity and Fiscal Responsibility Act of 1982. In so ruling the Court rejected arguments that states and municipalities have the constitutional right to issue tax-free bonds under the Tenth Amendment and the so-called doctrine of intergovernmental tax immunity. South Carolina v. Baker, 485 U.S. 505 (1988). However, to date there has been no impact on the marketing of tax-free bonds, and Congress has not evinced any intent to repeal I.R.C. §103. When interest is tax-exempt the lender frequently will reduce the interest rate by two to four percent below the market rate for conventional loans. Note, State and Local Industrial Location Incentives — A Well Stocked Candy Store, 5 J. Corp. L. 517, 536 n.150 (1980) (hereinafter Location Incentives). The resultant reduction in debt service requirements is passed on to the developer in the guise of lower rental or installment payments, hence lower financing costs. Moreover, external constraints on the loan-to-value ratios of mortgage loans made by federally chartered commercial banks, a major source of tax-exempt financing, were removed by the Garn-St. Germain Depository Institutions Act of 1982. 12 U.S.C. §371(c), as amended by Pub. L. No. 97-320 §403 (1982). See Chapter 4D, note 2. In addition, internal constraints on loan-to-value ratios may be less stringent as well. Postconstruction lenders traditionally use the "income approach" in valuating real estate for the purpose of complying with self-imposed constraints on their maximum loan-to-value ratios. The income approach involves capitalizing the projected earnings from the secured real estate. See discussion at Chapter 5B1, note 2. Since the capitalization rate is theoretically related in part to the interest rate on the loan, the lower rate of interest enables the lender to use a lower capitalization rate. Consequently, the loan amount for a tax-exempt mortgage is frequently larger than it is for an ordinary mortgage loan. See Madison and Dwyer ¶8.06.

In addition to reduced financing costs and greater leverage, the tax-exempt bond offers other significant economic advantages for the developer. First, for tax and accounting purposes, under either the net lease or installment sale arrangement the developer's expenditure of capital to acquire or construct the property entitles it to a reasonable allowance for depreciation under I.R.C. §167. Second, tax-exempt IDBs are generally exempt from registration under the Securities Act of 1933, while corporate bonds generally are not. Therefore, if the developer were to finance the project by issuing its own bonds, it would have to go through the expensive and time-consuming registration process. Finally, the developer may be relieved of paying state and local property taxes inasmuch as legal title to the property is held by the tax-exempt governmental issuer until the installment sale is consummated or the option to purchase is exercised. See Location Incentives at 537. Many states, however, require the developer to make additional property tax payments in an amount equal to what the tax liability would be if the project were taxable. See Mumford, The Past, Present and Future of Industrial Development Bonds, 2 Urb. Law. 147 (1969).

The types of projects that qualify for tax-exempt bond financing vary from state to state depending on how broadly the definition of "industrial development facility" is construed in a particular state's enabling statute. While some states permit financing of retail facilities such as shopping centers (see, e.g., N.Y. Gen. Mun. Law §§854(4), 858, 864, McKinney 1986 and Supp. 1991), others confine tax-exempt financing to manufacturing and industrial facilities. To comply with state constitutional requirements these enabling statutes explicitly or impliedly require that the project serve some (albeit remote) public purpose, and some states (such as Virginia) provide for a litigation mechanism (called a validation suit) to determine whether an intended bond issuance will comply with the statute. Va. Code Ann. §15.1-214 (1973). In addition, these enabling statutes were designed to conform to the requirements that have been periodically imposed by I.R.C. §103. For example, under the "small issue exemption" that existed under prior law, maximum ceilings on capital expenditures within a particular locality had been established in the amounts of $1 million and $10 million for small and large projects, respectively. See former I.R.C. §103(b)(6)(D) prior to the Tax Reform Act of 1986. See Madison and Dwyer ¶8.06.

In response to a spate of adverse publicity caused by the abusive use of tax-exempt bond financing to fund projects that were either economically unviable or, as in the case of fast-food franchises and discount stores, beyond the congressional intent for the program, Congress has since 1982 progressively curtailed the use of such financing for private development so that under current law tax-exempt financing remains a viable financing alternative only for private developers of low- and moderate-income multifamily housing and certain quasi-public facilities such as airports, docks and wharves, and waste treatment and disposal facilities. Briefly, the Tax Equity and Fiscal Responsibility Act of 1982 (Pub. L. No. 97-34, 96 Stat. 324) imposed more stringent

Table 9-4

Privately Developed Facilities that Qualify for Tax-Exempt Bond Financing

Facilities No Longer Qualified	Currently Qualified Facilities
Sports facilities	Hazardous waste-treatment facilities
Convention or trade-show facilities	Redevelopment projects
Parking facilities	Airports, docks and wharves (other
Air and water pollution control facilities	than lodging, retail and office facilities)
Industrial parks	Mass commuting facilities
Hydroelectric-generating facilities	Multifamily residential rental property
	Sewage and solid waste disposal facilities
	Facilities for the furnishing of water (including irrigation)
	Facilities for the local furnishing of electric energy or gas
	District heating and cooling facilities

rules with respect to "private-purpose" IDBs, such as the reduction of depreciation benefits, the imposition of additional reporting and local-law approval requirements, and the repeal of the small issue exemption and tightened the definitional and duration requirements for IDBs used to finance projects for low- and moderate-income families. Former I.R.C. §§103(b), (f), (k), and (*l*), as amended by TEFRA §§214 to 221. Next, the Tax Reform Act of 1984 temporarily extended the small issue exemption but imposed additional restrictions including a prohibition against the use of tax-exempt financing to fund the acquisition of raw land, certain luxury items, or existing facilities; an annual ceiling on the amount of "private activity" bonds that each state could issue; and a requirement that ACRS straight-line depreciation be used for all IDB-financed property except for qualified residential rental projects. Former I.R.C. §§103(b), (n), and (o), as amended or added by the TRA of 1984 §§621, 627, and 628.

To make IDB financing even more restrictive the Tax Reform Act of 1986 repealed the use of such financing for "private activities" unless: (1) the amount of the issue fits within new state volume limitations (I.R.C. §146, as added by the Tax Reform Act of 1986 (1986 Act) §1301(b)); (2) with few exceptions, the average maturity of the private activity bond does not exceed 120 percent of the average reasonably anticipated economic life of the financed facilities (I.R.C. §147, as added by the 1986 Act §1301(b)); (3) the IDB qualifies as an exempt facility bond, that is, a qualified mortgage-revenue bond used to make below-market loans to middle- and low-income first-time home buyers, a qualified veteran's mortgage bond, a qualified small issue bond to fund manufacturing facilities (which exemption is due to expire on December 31, 1991, pursuant to I.R.C. §144(a)(12)), a qualified student loan bond, a qualified redevelopment bond, or a qualified bond issued on behalf of a tax-exempt organization such as a private university or nonprofit hospital (I.R.C. §141(d), as added by the 1986 Act §§1301(b), 7703); and (4) at least 95 percent of the net bond proceeds are used for the quasi-public purpose for which the bonds were issued (I.R.C. §§141(a) to 141(c)), as added by the 1986 Act §1301(b).

Of the foregoing categories, the exempt facility bond is the most significant for private real estate developers, who may still be eligible for tax-exempt financing provided that at least 95 percent of the net bond proceeds are used for the development of facilities described in Table 9-4. I.R.C. §142, as added by the 1986 Act §1301(b). However, in the case of multifamily residential projects for low- and moderate-income families, any private developer must satisfy one of the following occupancy requirements (on a continuous annual basis): (1) 20 percent of the residential units must be occupied by tenants having incomes of 50 percent or less of the median income for the area (low-income tenants); or (2) 40 percent of the residential units must be occupied by tenants having incomes of 60 percent or less of the median income for the area (moderate-income tenants). I.R.C. §142(d), as added by the 1986 Act §1301(b). However, these broadened definitional requirements, in conjunction with the curtailment of other tax benefits for low-income housing (discussed at Chapter 2B), make it unlikely that the low-income housing market will rebound from its current slump in the near future unless direct governmental subsidies are increased to compensate developers for their loss of rental and tax benefits. Unfortunately, low-income housing is the one sector of the real estate market most in need of venture capital and yet it was more adversely affected by the Tax Reform Act of 1986 than any other. See generally Bailkin and Merlino, Private Initiatives on Industrial Revenue Bonds, 3 Real Est. Fin. J. 9 (Fall 1987); Bates, Changes Made in Tax-Exempt Bond Area by 1986 Act Usher in New Era in Public Finance, 66 J. Taxn. 72 (Feb. 1987); Joslin, Haynes, and Diskin, Multifamily Housing Bonds: A Primer, 18 Real Est. Rev. 57 (Summer 1988); Sullivan, Financing Multi-Family Housing with Tax-Exempt Revenue Bonds: The New Rules, 4 Real Est. Fin. 30 (Spring 1987); Williams, Financing Shopping Centers, 5 Real Est. Rev. 67 (Winter 1976).

3. *High-Credit Lease Financing.* After reviewing the excerpt by Smith and Lubell, how would you distinguish a "financing" or "bondable" lease from an ordinary high-credit lease with a prime tenant (discussed at Chapter 5C) with respect to which a postconstruction lender would demand an assignment (discussed at Chapter 10B4), as additional security? By way of analogy to the definition of like-kind property for purposes of I.R.C. §1031, is the difference merely one of "grade or quality," or does the difference relate to the "nature and character" of both kinds of leases? Consider how both kinds of leases are viewed by lenders such as Ace for mortgage loan appraisal purposes.

4. *Zero Coupon Bond Financing.* After reviewing the excerpt by Wetterer, how would you compare the risks and rewards for a zero coupon mortgagee to those of: (a) a seller of land (discussed at Chapter 9B, note 5a, supra) who takes back a high-ratio subordinated purchase money mortgage so that the purchaser can obtain his construction and permanent financing of improvements to be situated on the land; (b) a wraparound (or other secondary) lender who is willing to defer the payment of accrued interest in exchange for a balloon payment at the end of the loan term; and (c) a postconstruction lender who favors equity financing over straight debt-financing and who makes a "con-

vertible mortgage" to a developer of income-producing real estate (discussed at Chapter 7A).

In the case of a zero coupon mortgage, naturally the zero coupon mortgagee is concerned about the future performance of the mortgaged property; therefore it may be tempted to insist on a voice in future management to assure recoupment of its loan investment based on consistent appreciation in the value of the mortgaged property. Do you see any risk of potential liability or a recharacterization of the transaction for tax purposes if a zero coupon mortgagee were to insist on such participation in management control? See Madison and Dwyer ¶8.10. See generally Lynford, The Master Limited Partnership and Zero Coupon Debt, 4 Real Est. Fin. 27 (Summer 1987) (examines the issuance of zero coupon debt in connection with the initial public offerings of MLP units); Platner, Investor Note Financing: New Investment Opportunity Combines Advantages of Zero Coupon, Real Estate, 2 Real Est. Fin. J. 93 (Fall 1986).

5. *Loan Participation.*   A loan participation is a loan-sharing arrangement whereby the lender who originates the loan, the so-called lead lender, sells portions of the loan to other participating lenders pursuant to a loan participation agreement, either on the basis of parity or with priority provisions as to the debt-service payments and any foreclosure proceeds. Such an arrangement may be used by an institutional lender to satisfy the high-ratio financing needs of a valuable borrower that otherwise might not be met because of the lead lender's lack of loanable funds or because the loan amount exceeds some limitation on the loan amount to a single borrower that may be imposed by some regulatory statute.

Since the note, mortgage, and collateral loan documents are held by the lead lender (who is designated as the mortgagee of record) and the participation agreement is not recorded, the participating lenders would be vulnerable as unsecured creditors if an unscrupulous lead lender were to pledge, assign, or accept prepayment of the notes without satisfying their claims. Not only do the participating lenders lack the legal ability to seek recourse against the mortgaged property for satisfaction of their claims, but they must also rely on the integrity of the lead lender for protection if the mortgaged property were to go to foreclosure or if the borrower should become bankrupt. For a discussion of these and other legal issues see generally Ledwidge, Loan Participations Among Commercial Banks, 51 Tenn. L. Rev. 519 (1984); Simpson, Loan Participations: Pitfalls for Participants, 31 Bus. L. Rev. 1977 (1976); Tempsett, Interbank Relations in Loan Participation Agreements: From Structure to Workouts, 101 Banking L.J. 31 (1984). See also G. Nelson and D. Whitman, Real Estate Finance Law §5.35 (2d ed. 1985); Madison and Dwyer ¶11.01.

PLANNING PROBLEM

Let us return one last time in this chapter to the master hypothetical at Chapter 5B. Just to refresh your memory, Dan Developer wants to construct an office building and expects to have a few major leases with prime tenants executed in the next month or so. The construction cost of the building will be approximately $25 million and, based on a capitalization of estimated rents, the market value of the building should equal its cost. The underlying land is owned by Francine Farmer, who is willing to sell her fee interest for $8 million in cash, or for $8,600,000 if Dan wants to separately finance the land by means of a high-ratio (90 percent) subordinated purchase money mortgage. Alternatively, Francine would be willing to lease the land to Dan by means of a 60-year net ground lease at an annual ground rent equal to the fair-market rental of the land ($860,000 for the first year) plus annual adjustments for inflation; after 10 years Dan would have an option to purchase the land for its current market value. Dan has learned that Ace Insurance Company is willing to make either a fee or a leasehold postconstruction loan at a 75 percent loan-to-value ratio for a self-amortizing term of 15 years and that, in exchange for extra ground rent, Francine may be willing to subject her fee interest to the lien of any mortgage made by Ace. Dan has also determined that construction financing will be available from Fuller National Bank, provided that Dan is able to obtain a takeout commitment from Ace.

Part A: Dan comes to your law office and tells you that he is having trouble raising his venture capital. He wants to know which of the following financing techniques is best suited to provide the most financial leverage and thus reduce his initial cash outlay as much as possible. Briefly explain, and make assumptions where necessary.

   a. a straight fee mortgage from Ace covering the land and building;
   b. a leasehold mortgage from Ace on "an unencumbered fee";
   c. the same as (b) except that Francine agrees to subject her fee interest to the lien of Ace's mortgage;
   d. high-credit lease financing;
   e. tax-exempt bond financing;
   f. a subordinated purchase money mortgage on the land from Francine followed by a straight fee mortgage from Ace covering the land and building; or
   g. a zero coupon mortgage.

Part B: Twenty-seven years after the project is completed and financed by means of a straight fee mortgage from Ace (that was extended for another self-amortizing 15-year term) that will mature in three years, Dan comes to your law office after hearing that you are about to retire and wishes you well. He also tells you that the office building has a remaining economic useful life of 30 years or more, that the mortgage with Ace contains an onerous prepayment charge (equal to 5 percent of the *original* loan balance), and that the current market rate of interest for first mortgage money is three percentage points below the fixed rate he has been paying on the Ace mortgage. He wants you to *briefly* explain to him (in terms as non-mathematical as possible and by making assumptions where necessary) which of the following is probably the best way for Dan to cash out his equity in the project:

    a. a tax-free exchange under I.R.C. §1031;
    b. a wraparound mortgage;
    c. refinancing the existing mortgage with Ace;
    d. a conventional second mortgage;
    e. a sale and leaseback; or
    f. any other method that comes to mind.

Incidentally, Dan is more interested (because of his age) in short-term rewards (and short-term tax consequences) than what might happen in the long run.

PART IV

BORROWER DEFAULT

As long as the real estate project remains economically viable and the borrower remains solvent the transactional rights and responsibilities of the borrower and lender are governed primarily by the negotiated terms and conditions of the postconstruction loan commitment as implemented by the language in the note and mortgage (or deed of trust in some jurisdictions). While the regulatory impact of public law has eroded the freedom of contract principle somewhat, the law of the written word remains a dominant theme in commercial real estate financing. Perhaps the notion is that extrinsic judge-made and statutory law ought not to be paternalistic because in most cases the parties will be sophisticated, ably represented by counsel, and in a position to defend themselves at the bargaining table.

However, if the borrower were to become insolvent or if the project were to go "belly up," then the focal point of the documentation and the attitude of legal authorities are likely to change. While the principal grounds for borrower default are negotiated beforehand in the postconstruction loan commitment letter, it is the note, mortgage, and assignment-of-lease instruments that become the operative documents in the event of a default by the borrower inasmuch as they identify the grounds for default and spell out both the consequences of default to the borrower and the remedies available to the aggrieved lender as mortgagee. At this juncture, if the lender were to institute a foreclosure action or the borrower were to invoke the protection of the bankruptcy law, public law may intervene and supersede the language in the mortgage and other loan documents if necessary to protect the financially distressed borrower (as mortgagor) and resolve the competing claims against the real estate and the other depleted assets of the borrower. The impact of bankruptcy on real estate transactions is examined in Chapter 11. In the event of foreclosure or bankruptcy, the private bargain between the borrower and lender becomes less

963

relevant and the post-default rights and responsibilities of the parties are likely to be governed by extrinsic law based on public policy considerations.

As background for the materials that follow, it is suggested that you carefully review the basic rules of how the mortgage competes with other liens and interests in the mortgaged property discussed at Chapter 4C.

In Chapter 12 we will examine an area of law, lender liability, that has recently emerged on the real estate financing scene as a consequence of the burgeoning number of lawsuits and legal theories (such as breach of the implied duty of good faith) that are being used against lenders. With increasing frequency borrowers have been successful in suing unwary lenders for acting unfairly or in bad faith during the postdefault period of the loan.

C h a p t e r   10

Defaults, Workouts, and Foreclosure

A. WORKING OUT DEFAULTS BY AGREEMENT

Returning to the master hypothetical at Chapter 5B, assuming that Dan Developer should default, the worst-case scenario for the construction lender, Fuller National Bank, or the postconstruction lender, Ace Insurance Company, would be having to institute foreclosure proceedings. Even though Dan is personally liable for repayment of the construction loan, chances are he is insolvent and his assets have been depleted. Moreover, in the real world deficiency judgments against distressed borrowers are virtually worthless. Indeed, according to a comprehensive (albeit dated) study only a small dollar-amount of deficiency judgments are ever realized by lenders against defaulting borrowers,[1] and most foreclosing lenders dread the time-consuming delays, legal expenses, and attendant publicity. In the overwhelming majority of foreclosure sales the only bidder is the foreclosing mortgagee. Moreover, even if outside bidders are present at Dan's foreclosure sale the construction lender, FNB, knows full well that a half-completed office building or shopping center will not bring much at foreclosure, and unless FNB is able to complete the project itself and assign its loan to Ace pursuant to a buy-sell agreement, FNB will probably not be able to realize on its security and recoup its investment capital.

   Likewise, if Dan should default after the project is completed and the postconstruction loan is closed, the postconstruction lender, Ace, would be reluctant to foreclose for these same reasons. In addition, since the loan is nonrecourse (which is customarily the case for postconstruction financing, as explained at Chapters 2B, note 7diii, 4B3, note 1, and 5A2a), recourse may be had only against the property. Therefore, in most cases every effort is made by the lender and the

---

1. See Prather, A Realistic Approach to Foreclosure, 14 Bus. Law. 132 (1958).

borrower to improve the economic viability of the project and to restructure the loan transaction by means of a workout agreement between the parties that might include: (1) short-term loan forbearances or renewals; (2) modification of interest rates; (3) recasting of amortization payments; (4) infusion of outside venture capital or financing; or (5) sale of the loan at a discount to a third party. Sometimes the workout arrangement may include use of one or more of the pre-foreclosure remedies available to it, including entry into possession (Chapter 10B2, infra); taking an assignment of the rents and leases (Chapter 10B4, infra); and the appointment of a court-appointed receiver (Chapter 10B3, infra).

Timing is critical in workout arrangements. In most cases, if the developer-borrower is willing to admit to cash flow or management problems soon after they develop, a workout agreement can be arranged. However, as pointed out by Roberts in the following excerpt, not every property can be saved (especially where a projected rental market turns soft) and therefore the lender must be perspicacious about minimizing its risks if as a last resort the property goes to foreclosure.

Roberts, Negotiating and Drafting the Workout Agreement
3 Modern Real Estate Transactions 1393
(ALI-ABA 1987)

1. QUESTIONS RAISED BY DEFAULT

Before determining which course to pursue, a lender and its counsel must make appropriate inquiries. What are the net worth and liquidity of the borrower and any guarantors? Can they be expected to economically sustain the project if they retain ownership? Is the value of the mortgaged property sufficient to justify an increased loan or, if a deed in lieu of foreclosure is considered, a reduction or release of liability? Is the property one the lender willingly would own and can easily resell? Are leasing, income, and operating expense information available? What is the physical condition of the building? Is it a conforming use, and was a certificate of occupancy validly issued?

A construction lender must determine the percentage of completion of work, what contractors and suppliers remain unpaid, the quality of work to date and its conformance with plans and specifications and with the requirements of the long-term or end loan lender. Most important, it must determine the need for remedial work and the estimated cost to complete the project.

Further questions must be asked. Can the borrower do a better job than the lender in completing, marketing, or managing the property?

Does the borrower have any special benefits, such as a franchise agreement, spot zoning, development rights, or permits that are not readily transferable to the lender? Is the borrower uniquely equipped to deal with a sensitive local problem? What might be the impact of a foreclosure on a marketing program for a property such as a condominium or a land sales project? What federal or state regulatory problems might foreclosure of the property entail? In the event of a litigated foreclosure, what defenses, colorable or otherwise, might the borrower raise? How long might resolution of such issues take? How expensive might foreclosure be in terms of project deterioration, legal costs, and lost opportunity cost for invested funds?

What rights of third parties need be considered? Are there subordinate liens which eventually must be foreclosed? Will necessary consents to a negotiated workout be forthcoming from guarantors, bonding companies, or franchisors? How substantial are the borrower's debts to others? How hard are such creditors pressing? Is an insolvency proceeding imminent?

If the lender plans to take title and invest additional funds, will those funds be at risk if creditors attack the transfer as voidable under state or federal insolvency laws? Would the lender be safer waiting to negotiate a private sale with the court after the borrower has filed in bankruptcy? Does the lender have other investments with the borrower? Will the commencement of a foreclosure on this property trigger a bankruptcy?

Defaults can take various forms. The most frequent is failure to pay debt service when due. Whatever the nature of a default, and however communicated or ascertained, counsel should advise against sending any notice of default until the situation has been properly evaluated. In order to enhance the prospects for a successful workout, it is desirable to preserve the trust of the borrower, without which acceptance of new concepts may be achieved only by threats of enforcement. . . .

2.   A RESTRUCTURING WORKOUT

Where a default is to be worked out by restructuring, it is probable that the lender is satisfied with the borrower's honesty and competence as well as the economic bona fides of the project and that other creditors have agreed to cooperate. Also, possibly, the lender may not wish to own or operate the type of property involved, or the borrower may have some colorable or better defense to enforcement of the loan.

For a lender, the objectives in documenting a restructured loan depend upon the seriousness of the default, whether lender or borrower is providing additional funds, whether the borrower is remaining fully liable, whether additional security will be provided, and whether there is a reasonable expectation of consummating a successful workout.

It is a cardinal rule that any loan modification agreement, even a letter agreement effecting a minor change to a loan which is in good standing, contain an estoppel clause, to the effect that the borrower has no claim, offset or defense against the lender or with respect to the collateral. Such a provision should be included in all workout agreements. It is desirable for a workout agreement to contain an acknowledgment by the borrower that a default has occurred, and that in consideration of entering into the new agreement such default is being waived. This will provide an appropriate perspective from which a court later may determine the rights and obligations of the parties under the restructured loan arrangement. . . .

Where, based upon receiving additional collateral, a loan will be increased to provide operating capital for a period which the parties deem sufficient to market or otherwise successfully deal with the property, such collateral will be contemporaneously received only for the increased loan amount and will be subject to attack as a preference insofar as it may provide additional security for the original loan amount. It is desirable, therefore, for the operating capital to be sufficient to assure continued operations for at least the ninety-day preference period (assuming the lender is not an insider), after which the new collateral should effectively secure the entire loan. A nonbankruptcy pitfall to avoid when making operating capital available to a distressed borrower is to be sure either that such funds will not be used for payroll, or, if they are, that federal withholding taxes are paid. In most situations, the only safe way to assure this is to have the lender make the tax payments. Failure to withhold payroll taxes may subject the lender to liability to the IRS, irrespective of any claim which the lender may have against the borrower.[12]

A frequently negotiated aspect of a workout agreement is the federal income tax effects upon the borrower and any proposed new investor. Borrowers seek to avoid partnership termination, recapture of accelerated depreciation and investment tax credits, and satisfaction of debt income. Accrual basis partnerships may wish to continue to deduct interest which is not being paid.

Partnership termination, depreciation, and investment tax credit recapture, as well as satisfaction of debt income, can be avoided only by forestalling or delaying a foreclosure or other transfer of the property, a circumstance which motivates distressed borrowers to pursue dilatory tactics as long as possible. With proper structuring, new partnership

---

12. 26 U.S.C.A. §3505 (1982); Fidelity Bank, N.A. v. United States, 616 F.2d 1181 (10th Cir. 1980).

investors usually can be brought in without adverse tax consequences to benefits previously received by original partners.

In situations where the lender recognizes that the default is a product of the economy, the market, or other factors which the borrower cannot control, a loan workout may be negotiated providing for debt service to be paid only with available cash flow from operation of the property. Such "cash flow" workouts involve negotiation of a number of issues and terms which can materially affect the manner in which the property is operated and net operating funds calculated.

Forbearance agreements normally waive defaults with respect to past events, and they permit acceleration of maturity only if additional, defined defaults arise. Where appropriate, the lender may request that the waiver of prior defaults be conditioned upon no further default occurring, upon which the rights of the parties again may be governed by the original documents. When a new partner is investing with the initial borrower based upon an expectation of a minimum guaranteed period in which to operate the property and receive tax benefits, the new partner will negotiate to eliminate any future uncontrolled event of default which might shorten the agreed forbearance period. If the new partner is providing funds which will make the project viable, such investor will bargain more effectively than the borrower, and the lender will be more receptive to minimizing possible future events of default. Negotiations to obtain additional investment by a new party should be conducted by the borrower, rather than the lender, and the documents should state that the lender has made no representation or commitment with respect to the project not expressly set forth in the agreement.

Where debt is totally or partially nonrecourse, and the borrower will continue to operate the property and handle funds, the definition of nonrecourse in the original loan documents may be modified to permit the lender to sue the borrower or its general partner for a personal judgment in the event funds are misappropriated or certain other covenants of the loan agreement are not performed. If the original documents did not so provide, the workout agreement or collateral documents should subordinate repayment by the borrower of debt to any project-related party.

Where the lender is accepting a cash-flow debt service or below market rate of interest to accommodate a workout, it may bargain for the right to share in future benefits from the operation, refinancing or sale of the property. The manner in which such interest is to be received, and decisions with respect to operation, refinancing or sale of the property require careful consideration. Among other things, the lender must protect against any right to prepay the loan after the project has been turned around but before such benefits have been realized. Rights to participate in profits erode a pure borrower-lender relationship and may complicate enforcement of the workout agreement, should this later become necessary.

Projects which are benefited by state or federal housing programs or by nonassignable tax benefits entail additional workout problems. It could be highly detrimental to a project were a rent or mortgage supplement to be lost because of a foreclosure or other change in ownership. Certain federal and state agencies are sympathetic to these problems, but it is necessary to reach agreement with them before the workout can be structured.

In situations where there are other participating lenders, there may be need to review and modify the participation agreement in areas such as control of the investment after default, waiver of claims by participants, sharing of setoffs, sharing of costs of enforcement, selection of counsel, and possibly perfection of participants' interests in the loan or the underlying mortgage investment.

The workout agreement will contain provisions with respect to conditions to closing, representations and warranties, title insurance, perhaps cross-default or cross-collateralization with other outstanding credits, covenants respecting management, sales, financial statements, leasing, payment of expenses, and waiver of any alleged defenses. Representations with respect to the net worth, liquidity, and ultimate solvency of nonlending parties to a workout, coupled with accountants' financial statements and legal opinions, where available, add important layers of protection. Appraisals substantiating values of assets are desirable. Closing of the restructuring workout agreement should include title insurance for any new security instrument, or at least a continuation search, including tax lien, bankruptcy, and judgment dockets; opinion of borrower's counsel; and estoppel statements from available third parties.

3.   A DEED-IN-LIEU WORKOUT

When the holder of a defaulted mortgage is not comfortable with prospects for repayment if the property is left under continued ownership by the borrower, the relevant issue becomes whether an adversarial foreclosure proceeding must ensue or whether a friendly course can be followed.

A.   BENEFITS

Several benefits may be realized through utilization of a negotiated deed in lieu of foreclosure. Perhaps the most attractive one for a lender is speed in gaining control and use of the property. If necessary, a deed could be prepared and recorded in a day, while a litigated foreclosure may take more than a year and possibly face outstanding redemption rights thereafter. Foreclosure of a mortgage has adverse connotations for the property and the borrower, but a deed in lieu is merely a conveyance, and the property transfer can be characterized positively. Title may be taken in a designee of the lender, so that the public may assume the borrower merely sold the property. After the transfer, the borrower may continue in a management or consulting capacity for a period of time. The problem of creating an adverse image for the project and the borrower can thus be minimized. The borrower should prefer a private relinquishment of its interest in the property.

Of equal importance, the borrower and staff will cooperate and assist the new owner in taking over. They will aid in the delivery of leases, elevator wiring diagrams, utility deposits, payroll and employee benefit information, and data necessary to pursue real estate tax reduction proceedings based on prior years' operating expenses and tax payments.

There are advantages to a deed in lieu of foreclosure should the borrower subsequently file in bankruptcy. Once title and possession have passed to the lender, the property no longer is subject to automatic bankruptcy court jurisdiction or to a stay of foreclosure. Although a deed in lieu of foreclosure conveys title subject to mechanics' liens and other encumbrances, in many jurisdictions the deed may provide for nonmerger, and the mortgage thus may be preserved as a means of dealing with subordinate interests.[29]

B. NEGOTIATIONS

Once it makes the decision to take title through a deed in lieu of foreclosure, the lender must negotiate the terms of the transfer with the borrower, who may wish to bargain for certain benefits. A borrower usually seeks a reduction of or release from liability. In order to preserve reputation in the industry, the borrower may ask the lender to assume all or a portion of the trade payables. In seeking personal consideration, the borrower may bargain for a residual interest in the property or a right of first refusal to purchase the property at a later date. Not infrequently, a borrower will disagree with a lender's conclusion that a change in ownership and management is necessary. Although acknowledging default under the loan, the borrower may be seeking time in which to sell or refinance the property or to bring in a new money partner. Consequently, the borrower may offer a deed to be held in escrow for a period of time in order to induce the lender to forebear.

Apart from the usual give and take of negotiations, a number of potentially serious legal problems are inherent in such requests. These problems lie in the areas of title and insolvency.

29. See 55 Am. Jur. 2d, Mortgages §§1256-1263 (1971).

C. TITLE PROBLEMS

The borrower's offer of a deed held in escrow for a period of time while working things out may confer no benefit on the lender, at least in jurisdictions where the doctrine of clogging the equity of redemption holds sway. The procedural and substantive protections of foreclosure proceedings which evolved during the Yearbook era in England's Court of Chancery to protect a borrower's equity may not easily be contracted away. The deed offered to the lender in escrow may be deemed no more than an equitable mortgage, which the lender already holds, and the period in which such deed may be challenged as an avoidable preference will not commence until it is recorded.

Granting the borrower a residual interest in the property, in whatever form, may in time subject the lender to claims by the borrower that the property was not properly managed, leased, or sold, or that construction was performed improperly or too expensively, and such an interest may adversely affect the lender's title. One company refused to insure title on resale by the lender of property on which the original • borrower (which had given the lender a deed in lieu) had been granted an option to repurchase which long since had lapsed. The title company considered the option to be a mortgage and required that a quitclaim deed be obtained from the original borrower. This was done, but at a price.

Release of the borrower from liability on the original note may constitute a satisfaction of the mortgage debt and thus an extinguishment of the mortgage. A lender wishing to keep the mortgage alive in order to maintain priority over subordinate encumbrances should not permit that to happen. A covenant not to sue the borrower for a deficiency judgment is a substitute that preserves the mortgage. Mere release of liability or satisfaction of antecedent debt may not, in certain jurisdictions, constitute "valuable consideration."[32] Consequently, a lender which records its deed in lieu may not receive the benefits of recording acts, and the deed to the lender may be subordinate to prior unrecorded interests.

D. INSOLVENCY PROBLEMS

Significant obstacles to a lender accepting a deed in lieu of foreclosure may arise under federal and state insolvency laws. Although granting the borrower a residual interest in the property may facilitate negotiations for a deed in lieu of foreclosure, such interest may, in the event of an ensuing bankruptcy, subject the property to bankruptcy court jurisdiction. If a deed in lieu can be successfully attacked as

---

32. Powell on Real Property, ¶444 at 585-589 (1981).

preferential or as a fraudulent conveyance, and voided, the benefits for which the lender has bargained may be lost.[34] Meanwhile, if the lender has released the borrower from liability for a deficiency judgment, it has relinquished a consideration that it might have been able to use at a later date to persuade the bankruptcy court to grant leave to foreclose.

The lender's agreement not to sue a borrower on a note is consideration to the borrower. However, when a mortgage lender releases a guarantor from liability in order to induce a borrower to give it a deed in lieu of foreclosure, that may constitute a voidable preference. The theory that is suggested by logic, but not yet confirmed by the courts, is that because of the guarantor's right of subrogation to the lender's rights against the borrower, the guarantor is a creditor of the borrower. The deed, therefore, may be a voidable transfer for the benefit of creditors within the contemplation of Section 547 of the Bankruptcy Code.

Depending upon the circumstances and upon whether a deed in lieu of foreclosure is attacked as a preference or as a fraudulent conveyance, a lender may be reduced to a claim as an unsecured creditor when it attempts to recover any new consideration given for the deed. It may even lose its original secured interest in the property, particularly if it is found not to have acted in good faith. The problems that may arise if the transfer effected by a deed in lieu is subsequently voided are particularly troublesome if the property is in the course of construction, which the lender must complete. . . .

E. THE "FRIENDLY FORECLOSURE"

A far less desirable alternative that is used with some frequency is the so-called friendly foreclosure. In return for the same types of consideration that may be given to induce a borrower to grant a deed in lieu, cooperation is obtained in not resisting foreclosure. This technique has advantages when mechanics' liens exist and foreclosure is necessary to extinguish them. However, while there is no case that has so ruled, the risk exists that a negotiated and compensated agreement not to resist a foreclosure, together with the transfer of title resulting

---

34. This also may constitute a risk for a purchaser from a lender which has taken a deed in lieu from its mortgagor. Code Section 550(b) permits a subsequent good-faith transferee for fair value to retain the asset. Section 550(d) permits any good-faith transferee to have a lien for the value of improvements made prior to the avoidance. No statutory provision is made for a preferred transferee to have a lien for new consideration given (Section 547). Such provision is made for a good-faith transferee subject to avoidance powers as a fraudulent conveyance (Section 548(c)). Lack of good faith may affect the foregoing benefits.

therefrom, may be deemed a voidable transfer under the Bankruptcy Code or state law. . . .

F. RECOMMENDED STRUCTURE

. . . There are several advantages to having the borrower convey title to the lender's subsidiary rather than directly to the lender. Lenders may be able to originate or hold mortgage loans outside their home states without being required to qualify to do business locally, but an entity which owns property, particularly one that may have to undertake active development, may find it necessary to qualify and be subject to taxation, service of process, and other local burdens. Use of a subsidiary or designee entity that is locally qualified relieves the lender of these requirements. The use of a separate corporation also can insulate the lender from the liabilities of ownership. An owner whose name does not contain the word "bank" is better able to avoid the deep pocket problems of effectively negotiating terms with contractors.

The requirement of fairness of consideration given for a deed in lieu of foreclosure presents the transferee with several problems. The contract or memorandum of sale should recite, as appropriate, that the mortgage loan is in default, that the borrower has been unable to sell or refinance the property, and, accordingly, does not consider the value of the property to exceed the amount of the mortgage. It is desirable to have a current appraisal of the property showing the consideration given to be adequate. The contract also may recite the fact that taxes are unpaid and trade payables are due. In the case of a construction mortgage loan, the contract may include recitals about the uncertain cost of completion. However, while the contract description of the distress nature of the property should support the adequacy of the consideration given, it must stop short of an admission of insolvency, which could facilitate a subsequent bankruptcy avoidance attack on the transfer.

If it is the case, the memorandum or contract should contain a representation that the borrower is solvent, and the lender should attempt to obtain a recent confirming financial statement.

In any deed in lieu of foreclosure, it is prudent to pay some cash consideration to the borrower, at least the amount of title, recording, and transfer charges that the lender may in any event be required to fund. This not only strengthens the lender's position if a subsequent insolvency proceeding is instituted, but also assures valuable consideration for the purpose of qualifying for the benefits of various recording statutes. If the lender contemplates further improvement of the property, such as the completion of construction, the lender should consider assuming all or certain of the obligations of the borrower to pay for such work, so that funds expended by the lender may be deemed part of the consideration paid to the borrower for the transfer. In the event of a subsequent attack on the transfer under insolvency laws, the lender can then argue that the cost of such improvements was fresh consideration.

The lender has several approaches available to protect itself against the possibility of having to claim as an unsecured creditor for the consideration it gives to obtain a deed in lieu of foreclosure, in the event the transaction is voided.

It may have all or part of the consideration held in escrow for at least a year, to be made available to the borrower if title is not challenged. The agreement not to sue the borrower on the debt may be conditioned upon no party successfully challenging the title received by the deed in lieu. The lender may give as partial consideration a purchase-money note to be paid on a deferred and subordinate basis out of the profits of the property, after the lender has received repayment of its investment, capital improvements, interest, and fees. This note also may be held in escrow. An agreement may specify that upon disposition of the property by the lender, any proceeds in excess of the lender's investment are to be used first to pay any then remaining unpaid creditors of the borrower. Such a note should contain strong language that it is solely an unsecured debt obligation; gives the lender or its subsidiary no obligation to develop or market the property; and expires under stated conditions, such as disposition of the property at a loss. Although it may create other problems, such a note may be an effective deterrent to an attack upon the transfer by creditors, and it should be considered in sensitive situations. . . .

NOTES AND QUESTIONS

1. *Risk of Default.* According to conventional wisdom construction loans are riskier than postconstruction loans and defaults are more likely to occur during the construction period. Therefore, construction lenders should be well-prepared for defaults and informed concerning the use of workout arrangements. In the words of one commentator: "While it is true that a real estate project can fall into trouble at any time during its lifetime, the most exposed period is typically during construction. . . . From a real estate lawyer's standpoint, a serious construction loan default is usually the toughest and most troubling for both the borrower and the lender to overcome." Seneker and Wetmore, Structuring a Real Estate Loan Workout Agreement with Peripheral Vision of Possible Bankruptcy, in Real Estate Bankruptcies and Workouts 242 (ABA Sec. on Real Prop., Prob. & Tr. L. 1983). As to the respective risk factors (other than risk of default) while the postconstruction loan is secured by an existing rental income stream,

the construction loan is for a shorter term, is recourse rather than nonrecourse, and is usually backed by a takeout commitment from some postconstruction lender. How would you assess the relative investment risks assumed by construction and postconstruction lenders? See Chapter 6A, note 1.

As to the risk of default, the conventional wisdom may be correct in that many unique risks and problems may occur during the construction period, such as cost overruns, work stoppages, abandonment of the job, insolvency on the part of the general contractor or a major subcontractor, and mechanics' and materialmens' liens (as explained at Chapter 6B). These factors make defaults more probable for construction loans and, because of the number of parties involved in the event of a default, these multifarious problems are difficult to resolve by voluntary agreement. However, notwithstanding these risks, construction loan defaults are frequently the result of the lender's failure to monitor properly the periodic loan disbursement or the amount of equity capital on hand to keep the loan amount "in balance" with the projected costs of the project in accordance with the protective terms and conditions of the building loan agreement. What safeguards can the construction lender employ to ameliorate the above-mentioned risks? See Chapter 6B. Does a buy-sell agreement with the postconstruction lender protect the construction lender in the event of a default during the construction period? See Chapter 5B14. In what respect does the "assignment" provision in the postconstruction commitment provide protection for the construction lender in the event of a default by the borrower? See Chapter 5B10. See generally R. Harris, Construction and Development Financing ¶6.6, 6.7 (1982); Roberts, Workouts of Construction Mortgage Loans, in 3 Modern Real Estate Transactions 1373 (ALI/ABA 1987).

The conventional wisdom regarding risk of default under a postconstruction loan does not take into account certain trends that have emerged over the last two decades. For example, just a few years ago (prior to the current shakeout in the real estate industry) preleasing requirements in postconstruction commitment letters were not as rigorous as they once had been; lenders frequently agreed to take out the construction loan once the building was completed in accordance with the approved plans and specifications even in the absence of a rental income stream sufficient to cover the projected debt service payments in order to accommodate a developer who was "building on spec." See discussion at Chapter 5B2. How would you assess the risk of default under a standby commitment as opposed to an ordinary takeout commitment? See the excerpt by Garfinkel at Chapter 5D1. In addition to imposing a stringent preleasing requirement, can you think of any other protective devices that might be employed by a postconstruction lender to ameliorate the risk of a default (especially in today's market) during the postconstruction period?

2.   *Personal Dynamics and the Impetus for Workouts.*   Assume that Charles Credulous, a young "fast track" business school graduate, was Ace's loan officer on the transaction described in the master hypothetical at Chapter 5B. Dan was the first major developer Charles had negotiated with one-on-one, and this was Charles' first big deal. He wanted the negotiations to be successful, and they were. When he presented the transaction to Ace's Real Estate Investment Committee, Charles wasn't free of all doubts about whether the tenants Dan said were interested would actually sign leases, but as the questions were being asked by the committee he became more and more forceful in assuring them of the economic soundness of the project. (Many institutions appoint a group of experienced real estate investment officers to a committee formed to review and approve or disapprove all proposed investments, each such officer acting as a devil's advocate, poking holes in, and making the loan officer defend, the transaction.)

Now Dan is in default and comes to see Charles, bringing with him his real estate lawyer and, for emphasis, his bankruptcy lawyer. How could he have so miscalculated, Charles asks himself. Surely Dan must be right that this is a temporary difficulty and if he only had more time, it would all turn around. Charles recommends and approves forbearance. Charles meets with Dan to consult on how the project should be run. He even gets Ace to pay for some repairs and improvements. An informal workout is underway. What problems do you see developing for Ace? What arguments do you think Dan might make when Ace finally decides the situation is hopeless and commences foreclosure? Assume you work for a consulting firm called in by Ace after the Dan Developer fiasco. Would you recommend a restructuring of Ace's Real Estate Investment Department with respect to the handling of troubled properties, and if so, what would you recommend?

3.   *Deeds in Lieu of Foreclosure.*   Where a negotiated restructuring is not feasible, Paul Roberts in the material excerpted above, appears on balance to advocate a negotiated deed in lieu of foreclosure rather than an adversarial foreclosure. See also Roberts, Deeds in Lieu of Foreclosure, 8 Real Est. Rev. 4 (1979). One thing that must be understood about a deed in lieu of foreclosure is that it is *in lieu of* foreclosure. It is a consensual conveyance and therefore subject to the risks inherent in any conveyance, especially one by a grantor in financial difficulties. Assume in the master hypothetical that one year after the Ace mortgage is recorded Dan Developer has a cash flow problem. He borrows money from Friendly Bank and gives Friendly a second mortgage on the property. Dan also enters into a lease with Widget Corporation of America at a below-market rental. Later Dan defaults under the Ace mortgage and offers Ace a deed in lieu of foreclosure. If Ace were to agree, how would Ace's title to the property differ from what it would have received had it been the successful bidder at

a foreclosure sale? See Chapter 4C. As attorney for Ace, why would you require a title report before agreeing to a deed in lieu of foreclosure and require title insurance as a condition to accepting the deed?

Roberts points out that deeds in lieu of foreclosure expose the lender to the risk of allegations of fraudulent transfer and unlawful preference. Fraudulent transfers and unlawful preferences are discussed, especially in connection with the *Durrett* problem, at Chapter 10C5, infra. Fraudulent transfer provisions (11 U.S.C. §548 (1988), hereinafter cited as the Bankruptcy Code), inter alia, regard as a constructive fraud any transfers made while the transferor is insolvent within a year before bankruptcy for a consideration not reasonably equivalent to what the property being transferred is worth. It has been argued (not always successfully) that a public foreclosure sale is designed to provide a state-sanctioned method for determining value and that the price obtained at a noncollusive foreclosure sale should, therefore, be deemed to be reasonably equivalent, under the circumstances, to the value of the property. Do you see why, in a deed in lieu situation, this argument might not be available?

In general, the unlawful preference provision of the Bankruptcy Code (§547) was designed to prevent a debtor from transferring property to satisfy prior (antecedent) debts shortly before bankruptcy when the debtor's assets were insufficient to pay all creditors. Could it be argued that in a deed-in-lieu arrangement the transfer is for satisfaction of the mortgage and therefore is for contemporaneous consideration and not made on account of an antecedent debt? See Bankruptcy Code §547(c)(1)(A); compare In re Rodman, 792 F.2d 125 (10th Cir. 1986), with In re Nucorp Energy, 80 Bankr. 517 (Bankr. S.D. Cal. 1987). What about the clogging of the equity of redemption mentioned in Part C of the Roberts excerpt? Review the discussion of clogging at Chapter 7A and ask yourself whether the anti-clogging rule would be applicable to a deed-in-lieu-of-foreclosure arrangement. If so, would the anti-anti-clogging statutes eliminate the problem?

Roberts suggests that it may be advisable for the acquiring mortgagee not to satisfy the mortgage and to provide in the deed against a merger of the title with the mortgage (provided this is allowed under local law). Thus, if the deed were to be set aside, the property would still be encumbered by the mortgage. How would such preservation of the mortgage affect the fraudulent transfer, preference, and clogging issues?

4. *Forgiveness of Debt: Tax Consequences.* Workouts involving transfers of property inevitably are affected by tax consequences. Sometimes the tax consequences can adversely affect the viability of an otherwise well-conceived solution to a default problem. See generally Wichmann, The Adverse Tax Consequences of Real Estate Loan De-

fault, 17 Real Est. Rev. 92 (1988). For example, when a mortgagee accepts a deed in lieu of foreclosure, all or part of the debt is extinguished. Under I.R.C. §61(a)(12), the debt forgiveness constitutes cancellation of indebtedness income to the borrower in the year of forgiveness. However, under the Revenue Act of 1987, the borrower is no longer permitted to choose between treating the forgiven debt as current income or reducing the depreciable basis in the mortgaged property by an amount equal to the forgiven debt. Under current law the borrower must recognize the debt cancellation as current income unless the forgiveness under certain circumstances is the result of a bankruptcy proceeding or occurs at a time when the borrower is insolvent. I.R.C. §108(e)(5)(B)(ii). Therefore, if the tax consequences of a foreclosure or deed-in-lieu-of-foreclosure arrangement are too onerous, the borrower might prefer to file under Chapter 11 of the Bankruptcy Code.

Suppose a third party were to agree to purchase the troubled real estate from a solvent borrower in consideration of the lender's cancellation of a portion of the mortgage indebtedness. Under current law, the purchaser would have to recognize income rather than reduce its tax basis in the acquired property. One way to circumvent this would be to have the lender first foreclose against the property and then sell the property to the third-party purchaser by means of a purchase money mortgage at a reduced loan amount.

If the default involves a purchase money mortgage, the debt forgiveness is still treated as a reduction of the borrower's purchase price (and tax basis in the property) rather than as current income to the borrower. I.R.C. §108(e)(5). See generally Kelfer and Rocchi, Federal Income Tax Considerations in Real Estate Foreclosures and Workouts, in Real Estate Bankruptcies and Workouts 277 (ABA 1983).

5. *Recommended Reading.* A. Kuklin and P. Roberts, eds., Real Estate Bankruptcies and Workouts, ABA Sec. of Real Prop., Prob. and Tr. L. (1983). Included in this excellent book are the following: Johnson, Accounting for Troubles: Debt Restructuring of Real Estate Projects, at 329 (note the Deed in Lieu of Foreclosure Agreement, Exhibit I, at 364; Form of Workout Agreement, Exhibit J, at 371; and Deed in Lieu of Foreclosure Closing Checklist, Exhibit K, at 416); Kane and Barrett, Real Estate Workouts — Dealing with Third Parties, at 225; Kuklin, The ABC's of Workouts, at 205; Seneker and Wetmore, Structuring a Real Estate Loan Workout Agreement with Peripheral Vision of Possible Bankruptcy, at 241; and Roberts, Negotiating and Drafting the Workout Agreement (excerpted above), at 339. Other books include Kaster and Nellis, Realty Ventures, Working In and Working Out, PLI Course Handbooks 298 and 299 (1987); and Zinman, Chairman, Boom, Bust and Bankruptcy: Financing, Unfinancing and

Refinancing of Troubled Real Estate, ABA Sec. of Real Prop., Prob. and Tr. L. (1987). Articles include Lifton, Real Estate in Trouble: Lender's Remedies Need an Overhaul, 31 Bus. Law. 1927 (1976); Martin, Workouts, Takeovers and the Interstate Land Sales Act, 6 Real Est. Rev. 37 (Winter 1977); Meislin, Extension Agreements and the Rights of Junior Mortgagees, 42 Va. L. Rev. 939 (1956); Roberts, Deeds in Lieu of Foreclosure, 8 Real Est. Rev. 37 (Winter 1979); Roberts, Working out the Construction Mortgage Loan, 5 Real Est. L. Rev. 50 (Summer 1975); Rosenberg, Inter-Corporate Guaranties and the Law of Fraudulent Conveyances: Lender Beware, 125 U. Pa. L. Rev. 235 (1976).

B. RIGHTS AND DUTIES OF THE PARTIES PRIOR TO FORECLOSURE

1. *The Mortgagee's Right to Accelerate the Indebtedness*

Just about every mortgage or deed of trust note will contain the following debt-acceleration clause: "Upon any default the holder of this note, if it so elects, notice of election being expressly waived, may declare that the remaining unpaid indebtedness with accrued interest shall at once become due and payable," or phraseology of similar import. This right to accelerate the indebtedness is almost invariably exercised by the mortgagee as a prelude to foreclosure. What is a commonsense reason why this should be so? In any event, this is a boilerplate provision that is strictly enforceable and that should not be taken lightly by either party, as the following case illustrates.

Jacobson v. McClanahan
43 Wash. 2d 751, 264 P.2d 253 (1953)

MALLERY, Justice.

On May 21, 1951, the defendants McClanahan gave plaintiffs a promissory note for $13,500, payable in monthly installments of $300 on the twenty-first day of every month thereafter until paid. The note was secured by a chattel mortgage on the "Streamline Tavern" in the city of Seattle.

The note provided, inter alia:

In case of default in the payment of any installment or any interest which may be due hereon, the aggregate amount of this note remaining unpaid and every installment thereof shall *without notice or demand* at once become due and collectible, at the option of the holder of this note. (Italics ours.)

The mortgage contained an acceleration clause similar to that quoted above, and further provided:

. . . if the mortgagee deems itself insecure, thereupon the mortgagee may, without notice, declare the whole sum of both principal and interest due and payable, . . .

The installment due June 21, 1951, was timely paid. The installment due July 21, 1951, was accepted by plaintiffs on August 13, 1951. In August, 1951, defendants McClanahan disposed of the tavern business to defendants Siegel. One Kaczor negotiated the transaction between plaintiffs and defendants McClanahan, and the transaction between defendants McClanahan and defendants Siegel. Kaczor procured the consent of plaintiffs to the transfer of the business and the assumption of the obligation of the McClanahans' note and mortgage by defendants Siegel. He made two copies of the instrument of assumption of the note and mortgage. On the copy given to plaintiffs, defendants Siegel were to pay the August, 1951, installment on August 21, 1951. The copy of the assumption agreement retained by Kaczor, upon which defendants Siegel relied in good faith, provided that the next payment on the note and mortgage would fall due on September 21, 1951. Kaczor was not the agent of plaintiffs, and had no authority to alter the Siegels' copy of the assumption-contract.

Defendants Siegel took possession of the business on or about August 14, 1951. The August installment was paid by defendants Siegel on September 17, 1951. The September installment was not paid on September 21, 1951, and, while still delinquent, plaintiffs gave notice, on October 5, 1951, of their election to accelerate maturity of the note and mortgage upon the grounds (1) that there was a default in payment under the terms of the note and mortgage, and (2) that they deemed themselves insecure. The notice stated that they would accept no further installments.

On October 23, 1951, defendants Siegel tendered the overdue September 21, 1951, installment, and attempted, on October 29, 1951, to pay all the installments in arrears, and thereafter tendered them in court.

Plaintiffs refused the installment tenders, and commenced this action for a decree accelerating the note, and, in default of payment of the judgment, for the foreclosure of their mortgage.

The plaintiffs gave notice of their *election* to accelerate the payments provided for in the instruments. It was not a notice of their *intention* to do so after a period of grace during which the defendants could bring their installment payments up to date.

The trial court felt that plaintiffs having accepted late payments of installments, should have given notice of their intention, rather than their election, to accelerate the payments, and, accordingly, entered judgment for defendants. The plaintiffs appeal.

Equity abhors forfeitures and penalties, but an acceleration of payments on a mortgage is not a forfeiture or a penalty. In Seattle Title Trust Co. v. Beggs, 146 Wash. 435, 263 P. 598, 599, this court said:

> . . . Counsel invoke the general rule that forfeitures are not favored in law, and that the courts will, if possible, construe a contract so as to avoid forfeiture or rights thereunder; arguing that this default provision is, in effect, a forfeiture provision, and should accordingly be strictly construed in favor of appellant. We do not think it is in any sense a forfeiture or penalty provision. In the text of 19 R.C.L. 493, we read:
>
> > The proposition is accepted without dispute that a stipulation in a mortgage providing that the whole debt secured thereby shall become due and payable upon failure of the mortgagor to pay the interest annually or to comply with any other condition of the mortgage is a legal, valid, and enforceable stipulation, and is not in the nature of a penalty or forfeiture.
>
> This view of accelerating provisions, such as are here in question, is well supported by the decisions. . . .

See, also, Graf v. Hope Building Corporation, 254 N.Y. 1, 171 N.E. 884, 70 A.L.R. 984, and Walsh on Mortgages, 292, §71.

The instruments in question provided that appellants had a right to acceleration (1) if they deemed themselves insecure, and (2) for default in the payments.

(1) The trial court found

> That prior to plaintiffs' election to accelerate, they subjectively deemed themselves insecure; that they were in good faith in so believing, having heard adverse accounts of falling patronage and having investigated said accounts by looking into the tavern from the street on several occasions, and having checked with the brewery distributor and thereby having determined that there had been a sharp decline in Keggage; that plaintiffs' Exhibit 8 is a true record of the tavern's purchases of draft beer for the months indicated; that although plaintiffs, from their investigation, had probable cause to believe that they were insecure, they were not at anytime in fact insecure prior to their election to accelerate.

We hold that appellants must have reasonable cause to deem themselves insecure, but that they need not be insecure in fact. Skookum

Lumber Co. v. Sacajawea Lumber & Shingle Co., 107 Wash. 356, 181 P. 914, 187 P. 410; Hines v. Pacific Car Co., 110 Wash. 75, 188 P. 29; Rosenthal v. Moses, 144 Wash. 346, 258 P. 7; 125 A.L.R. 318.

The trial court found there had been a default in payment, but that it was due to a mistake of respondents Siegel in relying, in good faith, upon the unauthorized statement of Kaczor. No fault is imputable to the appellants in the matter. In such a situation, the weight of authority with which this state now aligns itself, is that a mistake of the mortgagor will not excuse compliance with the terms of the mortgage. It is only when the default is attributable to the unconscionable or inequitable conduct of the mortgagee that he cannot avail himself of the benefits of the acceleration clause. Graf v. Hope Building Corporation, supra, 254 N.Y. 1, 171 N.E. 884, 70 A.L.R. 993; Glorsky v. Wexler, 142 N.J. Eq. 55, 59 A. 2d 233; Comellas v. Varicon Corporation, Sup., 81 N.Y.S.2d 449.

The judgment is reversed.

NOTES AND QUESTIONS

1. Enforceability of Debt Acceleration Clauses. In light of the straightforward security-impairment rationale for the decision in Jacobson v. McClanahan, can you think of any non-debt-service-related defaults that would justify debt acceleration on the part of the mortgagee? See First National Bank v. Blum, 141 Ga. App. 485, 233 S.E.2d 835 (1977); Strong v. Merchants Mutual Ins. Co., 2 Mass. App. 142, 309 N.E.2d 510 (1974); Kaminski v. London Pub., Inc., 123 N.J. Super. 112, 301 A.2d 769 (1973); United States v. Angel, 362 F. Supp. 445 (E.D. Pa. 1973). As you may recall from first-year property, a rent acceleration clause whereby the landlord has the right to terminate and re-enter the demised premises while accelerating the entire rental obligation with respect to the balance of the original lease term is generally regarded to be an unenforceable penalty. See, e.g., Ricker v. Rombough, 120 Cal. App. 2d Supp. 912, 261 P.2d 328 (Cal. 1953). How do you reconcile this proposition with the universal view that a debt acceleration clause is enforceable because it simply reflects the contractual determination by the parties as to when the debt is payable? Saunders v. Stradley, 25 Md. App. 85, 333 A.2d 604 (1975); Verna v. O'Brien, 78 Misc. 2d 288, 356 N.Y.S.2d 929 (1974).

2. When the Courts Will Afford Relief to the Mortgagor. The holding in Jacobson v. McClanahan reflects the harsh common-law view that no relief will be afforded to a defaulting mortgagor against debt acceleration even where a default occurs by reason of accident or because of the mortgagor's negligence or mistake. However, some equity courts have refused to enforce such clauses where the result would be unjust or unconscionable. See Kreiss Potassium Phosphate Co. v. Knight, 98 Fla. 1004, 124 So. 751 (1929) (mortgagee had consistently accepted late payments in exchange for an exorbitant rate of interest and the value of the improved security exceeded twelve times the amount of the outstanding indebtedness); Bisno v. Sax, 175 Cal. App. 2d 714, 346 P.2d 814 (2d Dist. 1959) (a one-day delay in making a debt service payment); Middlemist v. Mosier, 151 Colo. 113, 377 P.2d 110 (1962) (acceleration was denied because it was based on inadvertent failure to correctly endorse check for single monthly payment). See generally Rosenthal, The Role of Courts of Equity in Preventing Acceleration Predicated Upon a Mortgagor's Inadvertent Default, 22 Syracuse L. Rev. 897 (1971). In addition, an increasing number of states have enacted amelioratory legislation. See G. Nelson and D. Whitman, Real Estate Finance Law §7.7 (2d ed. 1985).

Debt acceleration clauses are almost invariably "optional" because the mortgagee may wish to pursue a less drastic remedial course of action. Absent language to the contrary providing for a grace period, no formal notice is required of the mortgagee to activate a debt acceleration clause. However, the mortgagee must perform some other act evidencing its intention to invoke the clause. This may be done by taking steps to institute foreclosure, as, in the case of a power-of-sale foreclosure, the advertisement of property for sale pursuant to the terms of the mortgage. 2 L. Jones, Jones on Mortgages (1928). Otherwise, if the mortgagee fails to take such action before the defaulting mortgagor tenders what is due, the mortgagee will lose its right to accelerate for that particular default. See, e.g., Comer v. Hargrave, 93 N.M. 170, 598 P.2d 213 (1979); Ogden v. Gibralter Savings Assn., 640 S.W.2d 232 (Tex. 1982). Review Chapter 10A, supra. In light of the foregoing discussion, what planning suggestions would you make to a mortgagee-client? To a mortgagor-client?

2. Mortgagee's Right to Possession

In the world of real estate financing, most institutional mortgagees prefer to pursue a remedial course of action less drastic than foreclosure because such actions (especially judicial foreclosures) tend to be complex, time-consuming, and expensive. Moreover, because commercial borrowers are generally sophisticated enough to know what the value of their property is, they will normally sell the property if there is substantial equity above the mortgage amount rather than let the property go to foreclosure. Thus foreclosure of a commercial real estate mortgage usually occurs when the value of the property is less than the mortgage balance, and generally lenders are concerned that they will be unable to recoup more than a fraction of their loan investments.

Where a workout is not feasible, however, lenders must rely on the foreclosure remedy. With the borrower unable or unwilling under the circumstances to maintain the property, the mortgagee is anxious during the often time-consuming foreclosure process to obtain control of the property to stop deterioration and possible vandalism. To this end the mortgage document normally gives the mortgagee the right to take possession of the property as a "mortgagee in possession" prior to foreclosure.

New York & Suburban Federal Savings & Loan Assn. v. Sanderman
162 N.J. Super. 216, 392 A.2d 635 (Ch. 1978)

DWYER, J.S.C.

New York and Suburban Federal Savings and Loan Association (Association) commenced an action to foreclose a first mortgage it held against the lands and buildings which were formerly the Convalescent Hospital of the City of Newark. . . .

On September 22, 1975 a partnership consisting of Philip Tatz, Bernard Bergman et al., conveyed the subject premises to Richard Sanderman and Louis Cesarano for $901,479.10. The deed recited that it was subject to a $301,479.10 mortgage in favor of Association and that a $600,000 purchase money second mortgage in favor of the grantors was the balance of the consideration. On that same date the grantors executed the last of the documents with Association which established the amount of its first mortgage as $301,479.10.

Thereafter, Bernard Bergman assigned his interest in the second mortgage to the Franklin National Bank as part of the collateral for a loan. In connection with the liquidation of that bank the Federal Deposit Insurance Corporation (FDIC) succeeded to the bank's interest in the second mortgage. It initially contested the validity of the first mortgage and a number of items for which Association claimed a right to be reimbursed for preserving the property as a mortgagee in possession. After a hearing all issues but one were resolved — that is, Association's claim to be reimbursed the sum of $45,360 for the cost of maintaining a guard on the premises 24 hours a day at a cost of $120 a day from February 5, 1977 to February 17, 1978. . . .

In connection with the foreclosure of mortgages on real property in certain of the central cities, there have been requests for reimbursement of expenses, such as boarding up the windows and doors to

protect the property against vandalism between the date of entry of
the judgment of foreclosure and the time of sale. . . .

FDIC urges that the expense was unnecessary because the license
to operate the nursing home had been revoked, the structures could
not be economically used, and to salvage the land value the structures
will have to be torn down; hence there was no need for guard service.
Its counsel points out that the officers of the Association who testified
at the hearing admitted that when the Association received an appraisal
report from an outside appraiser pointing these facts out, the Association
immediately suspended the guard service. To allow this sum as part
of the amount to be raised will shift the cost to the junior lienholders
in this case and in others to a mortgagor seeking to redeem; therefore,
the FDIC urges that the sum be disallowed.

Association urges that under the decisions in Zanzonico v. Zanzonico, 2 N.J. 309, 66 A.2d 530 (1949), cert. den. 338 U.S. 868, 70
S. Ct. 143, 94 L. Ed. 532 (1949); Newark v. Sue Corp., 124 N.J.
Super. 5, 7-8, 304 A.2d 567 (App. Div. 1973), a mortgagee in possession
has a duty to protect against vandalism or be held liable for loss or
destruction of the property. It points to the following statement in
Zanzonico:

> A mortgagee who goes into possession of the mortgaged lands
> assumes a grave responsibility for the management and preservation of
> the property. It is notorious that in Newark untenanted property is apt
> to be wrecked by vandals. When the tenants in the six-family house
> vacated the premises on the order of the public authorities [Tenement
> House Commission — ed.], complainant could have surrendered the house
> to Antonio's devisee Michael, or he could have made the necessary repairs
> and alterations and charged the cost against future rents. But he did
> neither; he allowed the house to remain empty and took inadequate
> means to protect it. He is liable for the resulting damage. . . . [at 316,
> 66 A.2d at 533]

A mortgagee who goes into possession is under a duty to maintain
and preserve the property. The standard by which the discharge of
that duty should be judged is that of a provident owner. Essex Cleaning
Contractors, Inc. v. Amato, 127 N.J. Super. 364, 366, 317 A.2d 411
(App. Div. 1974), certif. den. 65 N.J. 575, 325 A.2d 709 (1974);
Cunningham and Tischler, op. cit., §195 at 40. However, until the
mortgagee has foreclosed he is not the owner and must act with due
regard to the interests of the junior encumbrancers and the holder of
the equity of redemption. Shaeffer v. Chambers, 6 N.J. Eq. 548 (Ch.
1847); cf. Taylor v. Morris, 1 N.J. Super. 410, 61 A.2d 758 (Ch. Div.
1948).

It is suggested in 4 American Law of Property, §16.100 at 190,
that there is a limit on the duty of the mortgagee in possession:

He must, therefore, conserve its value by making repairs, and this duty is recognized on the one hand by charging him for any loss that flows from his failure to act and, on the other hand, by allowing him credit for expenditures in carrying it out. There are, however, limitations on this. One is that he is not bound to dig into his own pocket and so need not expend more than the rents and profits he receives. Another is that he does not have to make good or prevent the depreciation caused by ordinary wear and tear — "the silent effect of waste and decay from time." Indeed, in casting upon him this duty of affirmative conduct the standard for its invocation is "willful default," "gross negligence," or "recklessness and improvidence," a rather low standard of responsibility whose [sic] mildness is explained by the fact that the mortgagor, the owner, also should look after the upkeep of his own property. . . .

Whether this suggestion is a correct statement of the law of New Jersey in all circumstances is not necessary to decide. However, the suggestion that the extent of the duty of the mortgagee in possession is influenced by the amount of rents received or receivable does accord with the holding in *Zanzonico,* supra.

Judge Bigelow, who wrote the language quoted by the Supreme Court in *Zanzonico,* supra, in essence gave the mortgagee an option either to take possession, expending funds and collecting the expenditures from future rents, or not take possession but proceed quickly to foreclosure and sale of the real property. Under the first alternative the mortgagee, like a provident owner, would have to weigh the probability of collecting rents against the cost of repairs, taxes, insurance and the mortgagor redeeming the property. Under the second the mortgagee could proceed to foreclosure quickly and rely upon the right to collect any deficiency from the mortgagor. In no circumstance was the mortgagee to take possession and then allow the real property to be dissipated before foreclosure. In other words, the mortgagee was under a duty to evaluate what to do in the same manner as a provident owner would do. . . .

FDIC employed its appraiser before June 1, 1977, the date of his rather extensive report. FDIC made a copy of it available to Association at least by October 1977. There is a suggestion that a copy was made available earlier, but there is insufficient evidence to so find. Association received a letter report from its own appraiser dated February 10, 1978. It reached the same conclusions as the FDIC report. All concur that the building will have to be demolished.

The court is not concerned with the question of how well Association monitored the mortgage or the activities on the premises such as the revocation of the license. The court is concerned with the action of Association after it went into possession and the inquiry which it then made.

There is no evidence that it inquired of the State Department of

Health as to the circumstances, if any, under which the premises could be operated as a nursing home, or as to what could be done with the premises. It basically inquired whether the structure was weather tight and structurally sound.

Although tax assessment practices in Newark have been the subject of litigation in recent years, there is no evidence that it considered that the land was assessed at almost three times the value of the structure and for an aggregate amount $50,000 below the amount of its first mortgage.

The court finds that this is not a situation where Association acted in good faith on a temporary basis in order to secure time to find out what a provident owner should do. The court concludes that a provident owner would have rather promptly gathered the data on tax assessments, licensing condition, structural condition, zoning, neighborhood conditions and the probability of generating any income from the property while in possession, as well as various means to appropriately preserve the property. Based on the record the court concludes all this data could have been available within a week or ten days if the effort had been made to get it. The court finds that this was not done.

The court also finds that a mortgagee in possession, acting as a provident owner, would give notice at least to a holder of a junior encumbrance in the amount held by FDIC before incurring a per diem expense of $120 for which it would seek reimbursement.

The court concludes that Association did not act as a provident owner and denies the application for reimbursement for guard service. Since there is no evidence of any expenditure for boarding the premises up or installing a fire or burglar alarm even since the guard service was terminated, the court does not make any determination in respect to such matters.

NOTES AND QUESTIONS

1. *The Title Theory Versus the Lien Theory.* As you will recall, some states still adhere to the early common-law theory of mortgage law, the title theory, under which the mortgagee is regarded as holding the legal title and legal right to possession until the mortgage is discharged or foreclosed. By contrast, lien theory states view the mortgage as a mere security interest that should and does not deprive the owner of the legal incidents of ownership. As a practical matter, the lien theory has predominated inasmuch as the mortgagee in both jurisdictions is generally recognized and treated merely as holding a security interest in the mortgaged premises. See discussion át Chapter 4A. However, the one area where this disparity in theory can produce different legal consequences is where the mortgagee has the right to

possession and rents, as preforeclosure remedies, in the event of a material default by the mortgagor under the loan documents.

In a title theory jurisdiction the mortgagee, in the absence of an agreement to the contrary, has the legal right to possession before or after a default by the mortgagor. However, as suggested by the *Sanderman* decision, any mortgagee-in-possession has a quasi-fiduciary duty to manage the property in a prudent and productive manner. In addition, since all net rents and profits must be applied toward the mortgage indebtedness, the mortgagee is strictly accountable to the mortgagor for such income when the mortgage indebtedness is finally paid or otherwise satisfied. See G. Osborne, Mortgages §165 (1970). By contrast, in lien theory states, the mortgagor, absent language to the contrary, is entitled as a matter of legal right to possession and rents even after his or her default. In the opinion of commentators, this distinction is the most important (if not the singular) practical difference between the title and the lien theory points of view. See R. Kratovil and R. Werner, Modern Mortgage Law and Practice §20.02 (2d ed. 1981).

In your opinion, which doctrine makes more *practical* sense in a postdefault situation? In the absence of any applicable provision in the relevant documentation, what are some policy arguments and counterarguments for allowing the mortgagee to have possession and the right to rents after a default by the mortgagor? See generally American Law of Property §16.95 (Casner ed. 1952).

After reviewing the discussion at Chapter 4A, consider the following: If a mortgagee were to enter into possession with the consent of a defaulting mortgagor in a lien theory jurisdiction, any existing leases that are not in default could not be affected regardless of whether they were junior or senior to the mortgage, except that the rents would be collected by the mortgagee and not the mortgagor. In a title theory state, a mortgagee in possession could not terminate such a lease if it were senior, notwithstanding the mortgagor's default because, the interest of the mortgagee extends only to the interest of the mortgagor at the time the mortgage was created, namely, title in the property that was subject to the prior lease. However, if the lease were junior to the mortgage, the mortgagee in possession who has not entered into a nondisturbance agreement with the tenant could terminate the lease on taking possession in at least some title theory jurisdictions. Why?

The Uniform Land Security Interest Act would change this result by providing in §505(f) that without court approval given to prevent deterioration of the property, the creditor in possession may not disturb existing leases until foreclosure even if they are subordinate. The drafters comment that "this is existing law in lien theory states but may change the rule in many title or intermediate theory states." (Under the so-called intermediate theory, the mortgagee has title but does not have a right to possession until the borrower is in default.) The ULSIA approach is based on the theory that if the mortgagee were able to terminate leases prior to foreclosure, it could negatively affect the mortgagor's equity of redemption.

2. *Liability of a Mortgagee in Possession.*   Although most mortgage agreements provide that the mortgagee may enter into possession on default by the borrower, most mortgagees are hesitant to take that step. Two reasons are the potential liability to the borrower and third parties, and the inability to recoup expenses out of the income from the property. The *Sanderman* case illustrates the fact that each expenditure the mortgagee makes with respect to the property is subject to review by the court. In that case the mortgagee was unable to recover the expense of 24-hour guard service. Suppose the mortgagee had decided against guard service. What claims might then be made against the mortgagee for failure to exercise due diligence to protect the property and third parties? For example, if vandals started a fire that burned a neighboring house or injured pedestrians or firefighters, might there be an action for failure to protect against these casualties? There may be other liabilities under other statutes, for example, the mortgagee in possession may be liable as an operator under CERCLA for hazardous wastes spilled by the borrower. See Chapter 12B.

Recognizing these problems, the Uniform Land Security Interest Act provides that a mortgagee in possession must manage the property as would a prudent person, but that if the mortgagee "by contract delegates the managerial functions to a person in the business of managing real estate of the kind involved who is financially responsible, not related to the creditor, and prudently selected, the creditor satisfies the creditor's obligation to act prudently, and is not responsible to the debtor or other persons for the omissions and commissions of the management agent." ULSIA §505(c). Would this language have protected the mortgagee's claim for the cost of guard service in *Sanderman*? Would the mortgagee have been able to recover the cost of the managing agent under the reasoning of that case? Does ULSIA protect the mortgagee against liability under federal statutes for hazardous waste under CERCLA?

3. *Mortgagee's Right to Appointment of a Receiver*

Given the potential liabilities of a mortgagee in possession, many lenders prefer to have a third-party receiver appointed by the court to take possession of and manage the mortgaged property. Thus the mortgagee hopes to prevent the defaulting borrower from "milking" the property of potential rental income and otherwise to preserve the security interest pending completion of the foreclosure proceedings. However, since receivers are not always appointed by the courts because of their expertise in managing real estate, these expectations are not always realized.

In title theory jurisdictions the principal impediment to the appointment of a receiver has been the notion among equity courts that, in contrast to lien theory states, the mortgagee already has an adequate remedy at law, namely, title and the right to possession. In both title theory and lien theory states, however, the mortgagee will generally be successful if it can demonstrate that the mortgaged property is, or will be, inadequate security without the rents and profits relative to the amount of the outstanding mortgage indebtedness.[2] In practice, institutional lenders almost invariably include in their mortgage form a "receivership" clause under which in an action to foreclose, the mortgagee, on the mortgagor's default, is entitled, without notice, to the appointment of a receiver without proving the inadequacy of the security. While these clauses are not controlling (especially where the security is clearly adequate)[3] they tend to influence courts, and in some jurisdictions such clauses are automatically enforceable.[4]

Once appointed, a receiver in a title theory jurisdiction may have the right to terminate leases that are junior to the mortgage being foreclosed and that are not protected by a nondisturbance agreement pending the completion of the foreclosure proceedings. So, for example, if the contract rental is less than market, the receiver would have the option of disavowing the existing lease and charging the junior tenant who remains in possession with the higher market rental. But suppose the tenant who is paying an above-market rental desires to extricate itself from the lease agreement. The better and prevailing view is that the junior tenant, at the option of the receiver, is bound to the lease because the receiver's action is that of the court, not the mortgagee, and thus the title of the mortgagor and its privity of estate with the junior tenant is not extinguished until the foreclosure sale. See G. Nelson and D. Whitman, Real Estate Finance Law §4.39 (2d ed. 1985).

4.   Assignment of Leases and Rents

As observed above, the prime leases with the high-credit tenants form the foundation of any major commercial real estate enterprise. As you will recall, both the loan amount and the underwriting of the postcon-

2. 2 G. Glenn, Glenn on Mortgages §173 (1943).

3. E.g., Aetna Life Ins. Co. v. Broecker, 166 Ind. 576, 77 N.E. 1092 (1906); 2 G. Glenn, Glenn on Mortgages §175.1 (1943). But see Turner v. Superior Court, 72 Cal. App. 3d 804, 140 Cal. Rptr. 475 (5th Dist. 1977); G. Nelson and D. Whitman, Real Estate Finance Law §4.38, at 208 (2d ed. 1985).

4. E.g., N.Y. Real Prop. Law §254(10) (McKinney 1990).

struction loan depend on the appraised value of the property based on a capitalization of the anticipated net rental income from the subject property. Moreover, the primary security for the loan is the projected rental income stream from the tenants, not the land and improvements or the net assets of the borrower (as reflected by the tolerant attitude of postconstruction lenders toward nonrecourse financing). This is why mortgages and deeds of trust almost invariably contain language (usually in the so-called granting clause) to the effect that the lien of the mortgage shall cover the mortgaged property (as legally described) "together with all the rents, issues, and profits thereof." In addition, to assure itself that the rents will be available if necessary to defray the debt-service payments due under the mortgage, the postconstruction lender will normally include a conditional assignment-of-the-rents clause in the body of the mortgage itself. A popular form of such assignment language contained in the New York Board of Title Underwriters mortgage form (which figured prominently in the *Ganbaum* case, excerpted below) reads in part as follows:

> 13. [T]he mortgagor hereby assigns to the mortgagee the rents, issues and profits of the premises as further security for the payment of said indebtedness, and the mortgagor grants to the mortgagee the right to enter upon and take possession of the premises for the purpose of collecting the same and to let the premises or any part thereof, and to apply the rents, issues and profits, after payment of all necessary charges and expenses, on account of said indebtedness. . . . The mortgagee hereby waives the right to enter upon and to take possession of said premises for the purpose of collecting said rents, issues and profits, and the mortgagor shall be entitled to collect and receive said rents, issues and profits, until default under any of the covenants, conditions or agreements contained in this mortgage, and agrees to use such rents, issues and profits in payment of principal and interest becoming due on this mortgage and in payment of taxes, assessments, sewer rents, water rents and carrying charges becoming due against said premises. . . . Mortgagor will not, without the written consent of Mortgagee, receive or collect rent from any tenant of said premises or any part thereof for a period of more than one month in advance . . .

In addition, in the case of a commercial real estate project (such as an office building or shopping center), where the lender's appraisal-underwriting process (and thus the security for its loan) is based on the long-term rental obligations of certain high-credit tenants, the postconstruction lender will frequently require a separate assignment instrument to cover these specified leases. This document is referred to as an "Assignment of Lessor's Interest in Leases" to avoid the implication that the mortgagee is assuming the lessor's duties under the lease. Nevertheless, some assignment instruments also include the following exculpatory language:

The Mortgagee shall not be obligated to perform or discharge, nor does it hereby undertake to perform or discharge, any obligation, duty or liability under the Lease, by reason of this assignment, and Mortgagor shall and does hereby agree to indemnify the Mortgagee against and hold it harmless from any and all liability, loss or damage which it may or might incur under the Lease or under or by reason of this assignment and of and from any and all claims and demands whatsoever which may be asserted against it by reason of any alleged obligation or undertaking on its part to perform or discharge any of the terms, covenants or agreements contained in the Lease. . . .

Although some assignments of rents are conditional on the default by the borrower under the mortgage and are generally considered assignments for security only, some, such as the mortgage language quoted above, are unconditional, with the lender waiving only the right to collect the rents until default. The effect of language providing for an unconditional assignment is discussed in the *Ganbaum* case, excerpted below.

In addition, most assignments include estoppel and "anti-milking" language similar to the following:

Owner represents that Owner now is the absolute owner of said Lease, with full right and title to assign the same and the rents, income, and profits due or to become due thereunder; that said Lease is valid, in full force and effect, and has not been modified or amended except as stated herein; that there is no outstanding assignment or pledge thereof or of the rents, income, and profits due or to become due thereunder; that there are no existing defaults under the provisions thereof on the part of either party; that the lessee has no defense, setoff or counterclaim against Owner; that the lessee is in possession and paying rent and other charges under the Lease and as provided therein; and that no rents, income or profits payable thereunder have been or will hereafter be anticipated, discounted, released, waived, compromised, or otherwise discharged except as may be expressly permitted by said Lease. Owner covenants not to cancel, abridge, surrender, or terminate said Lease or change, alter, or modify the same, either to reduce the amount of said rents, income, and profits payable thereunder, or otherwise change, alter, abridge or modify said Lease, or make any subsequent assignment of said Lease, or consent to subordination of the interest of the lessee in said Lease without the prior written consent of Mortgagee. Any attempt at cancellation, surrender, termination, change, alteration, modification, assignment, or subordination of the Lease without the written consent of Mortgagee shall be null and void.

Normally, when the postconstruction loan is closed the assignment instrument is recorded along with the mortgage, and notice of the assignments is sent (by certified mail) to the tenants mentioned in the assignment instrument. If any of the credit leases are junior in lien priority to the mortgage, the lender may also require as a condition to closing that the tenants will have executed attornment agreements (whereby each tenant agrees that in the event of any default and foreclosure it will recognize (or "attorn to") the mortgagee as its new landlord), especially in jurisdictions such as California where junior leases are automatically extinguished at foreclosure. See Chapter 4C2.

ABA Committee on Real Estate Financing, Disposition of Rents After Mortgage Default
16 Real Prop., Prob. & Tr. J. 835, 835-838
(Winter 1981)

In commercial mortgage financing rent is the thing. More so as personal liability is traded away or modified for some other goody. The bright, inflating future of the investment, 'tis said, renders recourse to the borrower less than important. Not only are the rents there but the dollars are fully dressed on a net basis and tightly escalated. Yet the defaults of the mid-seventies demonstrated rather painfully that it took much time, effort, and expense to reach those rents.

Of course, reaching rents after a default is only one approach in a sea of remedies. The waters include foreclosure, long and short, suing on a note or for an installment only, taking a deed in lieu of foreclosure, procuring a current mortgagee in possession agreement, or simply doing nothing in the face of a possible write-off. Satisfaction of a mortgage in the last mentioned situation might be preferable to acquiring the real estate and then trying to abandon it.

In exercising rights under an assignment of rents (sometimes styled an assignment of lessor's rights in leases), the lender knows that the taking of the rents deprives the borrower of funds needed to run the property. Tenants will not pay rent for very long if essential services are not provided. Nor is it likely that the borrower will provide those services if the lender has deprived the borrower of the income. Therefore, the assignment of rents remedy, absent a receiver or valid possession, is only a short-term remedy which strengthens the position of the lender in working out a viable solution to the default problem. It is not an end in itself. After tenants are notified to pay the rent to the lender, the borrower is likely to respond by notifying the tenants to continue paying their rents to him. The result is that the tenant becomes confused and pays rent to no one. This confusion could be used to encourage a judge to appoint a receiver to avoid the conflict and end the confusion.

The lender often moves speedily, even though the law may not be clearly on his side. A good offense is said to be the best defense. The tactic gives the lender cash, puts him in a bargaining position with the owner, sort of like the set off right of a bank. And maybe the effort will force a second mortgagee to get its foreclosure underway, meanwhile curing your defaults. But horrors if the second mortgagee somehow gets its own receiver in that action or by any other means. . . .

The mortgage, specifically and in the mind of the drafter, beautifully provides for an express, present assignment. The document might even recite that the mortgagor collects the rents in trust with the obvious implication that a breach of that fiduciary obligation could put the borrower in jail. Not only is there a separate covenant on assignment, but rents are made part of the "Together With" language which covers real-world things like easements and minerals. Finally there is a separate assignment running perhaps several pages, with a notice to the tenants by certified mail or however. Such assignments spawned in the depression of the thirties. Before that, mortgages usually did not provide for amortization, and renewals occurred frequently, like every three years. A set of securities then might include a dozen extension agreements, none recorded, at least in New York. The purpose of the assignment was to prevent the owner from conspiring with tenants to cancel valuable leases in return for a fee pocketed by the owner. The purpose expanded to overcome a milking of the property and to prevent third parties from reaching the rents, especially junior lienors. Then, too, the mortgagee hoped to get the rents and control a diversion of security deposits, casualty insurance proceeds, prepaid items, failure to pay taxes, and possible owner abandonment.

Immediate resort to the rents may not always be urgent if under nonjudicial sale in some states you can quickly get title. You might decide to move speedily to a foreclosure minus the rents to avoid a "can of worms" in the landlord-tenant situation. Conceivably, rent collection might be expensive and troublesome, particularly for a far away lender, if a local agent of its choosing doesn't measure up to the expected standard. Finally, a current certifiable list of tenants and their obligations may not be available for the simple reason that the lender has not been minding the store.

Not much has been written on assignment of rents. Nor is there an abundance of cases. Concern is sometimes expressed about a lender taking subject to future leases under earlier assignments unknown to it. Approximate warranties and representations afford a measure of comfort against that result. There is at times worry about the possible applicability of Article 9 of the Uniform Commercial Code. The careful draftsman will cover all bases to assure whatever compliance is needed. . . .

Generally speaking, a mortgagee is not automatically entitled to rents after default. Its right in most states is dependent upon taking actual or constructive possession of the property by means of foreclosure, the appointment of a receiver or some similar proceeding. . . .

Factors which bear on the legal state of things are numerous, such as the wording of the statute; the public policy of the state with respect to a mortgagor waiving or releasing rights to rents during redemption; the solvency of the mortgagor; the adequacy or inadequacy of the security for the debt; the nature of the property involved; the relative priority of the lease and the mortgage; the type of foreclosure to be pursued and the need for a receiver. One can find diametrically opposed views in so far as the circumstances under which, and particularly the period within which, an assignment of rents may be enforced by a mortgagee.

When collection of rents is coupled with possession, there is more clearly an assumption of the rights, duties, and responsibilities and liabilities of an owner of real property, including the right to collect rents, issues, and profits and applying the same to the cost of operating the property, paying taxes, and reducing the debt. The mortgagee must account for and may be chargeable with those rents which could have been obtained in the exercise of reasonable care and due diligence. If the mortgagee in possession takes occupancy and uses the property, it will probably be charged with the reasonable rental value. The lender has a duty here to maintain and make necessary and reasonable repairs from the rents, but it cannot use rents to improve. That would seriously impair the right of redemption. Absolutely necessary improvements are permitted. The mortgagee in possession may employ those who are reasonably necessary to manage, but it isn't compensated for its own supervisory services. A mortgagee in possession is generally responsible in tort for injury to person or property as a result of its own negligence or failure to perform other duties imposed upon owners of real property and the mortgagee can insure the property out of the rents. If a mortgagee is not an officer of the court while in possession, it would not be entitled to judicial guidance regarding its conduct. In that situation the lender must often make decisions which may be subject to an after-the-fact challenge by the borrower and others when it accounts. Certainly in a complex leasing situation like a shopping center, the file, documents, and the total operation need to be carefully reviewed before any action is taken.

[Attached to the article is a 52-page survey of current law on the disposition of rents after mortgage default in 19 states, along with a bibliography of reference materials for each state, at 16 Real Prop., Prob. & Tr. J. 841-893 (Winter 1981). — ED.]

Ganbaum v. Rockwood Realty Corp.
62 Misc. 2d 391, 308 N.Y.S.2d 436 (1970)

SPIEGEL, J.

The . . . cause of action is . . . for damages in the amount of $31,180.64, allegedly sustained by plaintiffs-mortgagees due to the failure of defendant Levine, for the period of approximately two years prior to the commencement of this action, to apply the rents upon the subject real property to the payment of real estate taxes, sewer and water rents, other charges, and interest and principal on the first mortgage and plaintiff's second mortgage, and for rent which Levine collected from the tenants thereof for more than a period of one month in advance.

The second mortgage, subject to which defendant Levine acquired title to the subject real property, contains the following clause [Here the court quotes the language of the assignment of rents clause 13 excerpted above]:

Defendant Levine contends that the . . . cause of action cannot be maintained as the "assignment of rents" clause in the mortgage does not become effective until foreclosure or until the appointment of a receiver.

The courts of this State and the Federal courts, applying the law of this State, have held that "an assignment of rents" clause in a mortgage is not self-executing, but becomes effective only upon foreclosure or upon the appointment of a receiver of the rents of the mortgaged property. . . . Plaintiffs contend, however, that the law of these cited cases is inapplicable to the case at bar, as in each of the cited cases the "assignment of rents" clause was conditional upon default of the conditions of the mortgage, whereas in the case at bar, in paragraph 13 of the mortgage there is stated an unconditional assignment in praesenti. Accordingly, plaintiffs allege defendant Levine, who became owner of record of the subject realty subject to plaintiffs' second mortgage, is bound by the assignment of rents clause therein and is personally liable for her failure, prior to foreclosure, to apply the rents for the purposes stated in that clause. To this extent plaintiffs . . . contend they were damaged thereby, and further [that] by her collection of rents for more than a period of one month in advance she violated that clause of the mortgage. . . . Research by this Court discloses a case with dictum in favor of plaintiffs' contention.

The Federal court [in Empire State Collateral Co. v. Bay Realty Corp., 232 F. Supp. 330 (E.D.N.Y. 1964)], applying the law of New York, held that the "assignment of rents" clauses in the mortgages therein sued upon were by their terms conditional upon default of the mortgagor and were not operative until the mortgagees took affirmative action to enforce them. However, the court declared (at p. 335): "It is only when a clause in a mortgage constitutes an absolute and unqualified assignment of rents, to operate in praesenti, and is clearly intended as such by the parties, that an assignment of rents clause operates as such, without more. . . ."

However, we do not herein agree with the foregoing reasoning of the learned United States District Court. . . . It is the law of New York that a mortgage gives the mortgagee only a lien upon the mortgaged premises. The common law doctrine that the mortgagee held title thereto or any incidents thereof has long ago been abolished. . . . In accordance with this policy, it has been held that in New York, a deed conveying real property, absolute on its face, when the transaction is intended by the parties to be a mortgage, not only is treated as a mortgage, but is held in law to be a mortgage and not a conveyance. . . . Defendant Levine during the period relevant to the . . . cause of action, held title to the mortgaged realty. . . . Certainly the title of defendant Levine included, for the period in issue, the rights to the rents upon the realty and the right to apply the rents as she saw fit. As a mortgage cannot convey title to the mortgagee, the assignment of rents clause in paragraph 13 in the mortgage herein sued upon cannot convey ipso facto to the mortgagee the right to the rents, which is an incident of title. Therefore, though defendant Levine is bound by the terms of plaintiffs' second mortgage, subject to which she acquired title to the subject premises, she is not liable to plaintiffs for the rents collected by her prior to foreclosure nor for the use made of them.

NOTES AND QUESTIONS

1. Enforceability of Assignment Clauses. The enforceability of these clauses depends on their format and on local law considerations. There are three major formats.

a. The simplest and least enforceable is a mere pledge of rents and profits. According to one court in a leading decision, "There is a marked difference between a pledge and an assignment. Ordinarily, a pledge is considered as a bailment, and delivery of possession, actual or constructive, is essential, but transfer of title is not. On the other hand, by assignment, title is transferred, although possession need not be." Accordingly, it was held that rents pledged to a mortgagee were not accessible because the mortgagee had not entered into possession. Nor had a receiver been appointed. Paramount Building & Loan Assn.

v. Sacks, 107 N.J. Eq. 328, 152 A. 457, 458 (1930). See generally G. Nelson and D. Whitman, Real Estate Finance Law §4.35 (2d ed. 1985); Note, An Historical Analysis of Assignment of Rents in New York, 6 Brooklyn L. Rev. 25, 52 (1936); Note, Power of First Mortgagee to Secure Rents Without Foreclosing, 43 Yale L.J. 107 (1933).

  b. The second format is an absolute and unconditional in praesenti assignment of the rents and profits that would be recorded when the postconstruction loan closes and provide that, in the absence of any default, the mortgagee will remit to the mortgagor any surplus rental remaining after the debt-service payment is made. While this approach obviates the taking of affirmative action by the mortgagee to activate the lease assignment, protects the mortgagee against the rental claims of intervening lienors, and prevents the cancellation or modifications of the leases without its consent, this form of assignment is seldom used because of the mortgagor's objection to loss of control over the income from its property prior to default. Such absolute assignments are mainly associated with high-credit lease financing (examined at Chapter 9D, note 3) where, in exchange for 100 percent or more financing, the lender will demand complete control over a high-credit noncancellable net lease that constitutes the real security for the loan. See Madison and Dwyer ¶3.08[4][i]; Note, The Mortgagee's Right to Rents After Default, 50 Yale L.J. 1424, 1425 (1941).

  c. The third and most prevalent approach is one in which the mortgagor makes an in praesenti assignment of its right, title, and interest in the leases to the mortgagee as additional security for the mortgage loan. The mortgagor does retain a present license to collect the rents and enforce the lease provisions as the lessor so long as there is no default under the note, mortgage, or assignment instrument. The enforceability of such a provision will depend to some extent on whether the local jurisdiction subscribes to a lien or a title theory of mortgage law. In many title theory and a few lien theory states it has been held that an assignment of leases and rents for additional security is self-activating on default, pursuant to the terms of the assignment, as soon as the mortgagee serves notice on the tenants (e.g., Randel v. Jersey Mortgage Investment Co., 306 Pa. 1, 7, 158 A. 865, 866 (1932); Bevins v. Peoples Bank & Trust Co., 671 P.2d 875 (Alaska 1983)), while other courts, mainly in lien theory jurisdictions such as New York (where *Ganbaum* was decided), hold that such clauses and instruments only create security interests and therefore further affirmative action is required of the mortgagee (such as commencing foreclosure, taking possession, or having a receiver appointed) before it can collect the rents. See, e.g., Bornstein v. Somerson, 341 So. 2d 1043 (Fla. App. 1977), cert. denied, 348 So. 2d 944 (Fla. 1977) (lien theory); Taylor v. Brennan, 621 S.W.2d 592 (Tex. 1981) (lien theory); Levin v. Carney, 161 Ohio St. 513, 120 N.E.2d 92 (1954) (title theory). But see In re

Ventura Louise Properties, 490 F.2d 1141 (9th Cir. 1974) (lien theory holding specific assignment absolute). See generally Kratovil, Mortgages — Problems in Possession, Rents, and Mortgagee Liability, 11 DePaul L. Rev. 1, 11 (1961); Randolph, When Should Bankruptcy Courts Recognize Lenders' Rents Interests?, 23 U.C. Davis L.R. 833 (1990); Note, Assignment of Rents Clauses Under California Law and in Bankruptcy: Strategy for the Secured Creditor, 31 Hastings L.J. 1433 (1980); Notes, 35 Colum. L. Rev. 1248 (1935).

Perhaps the court in *Ganbaum* is correct in concluding that even an in praesenti assignment of rents and leases is nothing more than an assignment for security purposes in a lien theory jurisdiction such as New York and therefore it cannot convey ipso facto the right to rents, which is an incident of title. Does it necessarily follow (as a matter of contract theory) that a mortgagor should not be liable in damages for breach of a promise contained in the mortgage?

2. *The "Anti-milking" Function of Assignment Clauses.* The "anti-milking" language of the mortgage clause and the sample assignment-of-lease clause excerpted above originated in the Depression era, when owners facing the specter of insolvency and foreclosure would sometimes out of desperation accept large lump-sum prepayments of rent in exchange for terminating or reducing the future rental obligations of the tenants and then abscond with the money. Review the restrictions in the assignment clause and observe how they are designed to prevent this. Observe also that immediately prior to the closing of the postconstruction loan, the lender will require that each prime tenant (whose lease has been assigned to the mortgagee) must receive a copy and notice of the recorded assignment by certified mail so that the tenant will be apprised in advance that the owner-landlord may not terminate or modify the lease without the lender's consent and that in the event of a default by the landlord-mortgagor the tenant will be required to pay the rent to the mortgagee.

3. *What Is the Lessor's Interest?* When a tenant assigns its leasehold estate, it is clear that what is being assigned is the tenant's right to possession for the duration of the lease term subject to terms and the provisions of the lease. However, when an owner assigns its interest as lessor under a lease, the consequences are not quite so clear. For example, is the owner's reversionary interest being temporarily assigned to the mortgagee? If so, are the burdens as well as the benefits of being a landlord transferred? Returning to the master hypothetical, if Ace Insurance Company were to take an assignment of Dan's interest in the lease with the Widget Corporation of America, would Ace be responsible for performing all of the landlord's covenants in the lease agreement (for example, Dan's promise to construct additional space

and make alterations to suit WCA) once it achieves a certain level of net operating income? Is there any language in the assignment clauses quoted above that addresses this issue?

4. *Assignment of Rents Compared to Entry into Possession.* From a mortgagee's perspective, taking an assignment of the rents is usually preferable to taking possession inasmuch as the mortgagee is able to avoid the onerous fiduciary and accountability standards associated with being a mortgagee-in-possession. Moreover, under the former preforeclosure remedy the mortgagor is allowed to retain management control and may be sufficiently motivated (with foreclosure imminent) to straighten out its financial and management problems and turn the project around before it is too late.

C. THE RIGHTS AND DUTIES OF PARTIES AT FORECLOSURE

1. Balancing the Interests of Borrower and Lender

As discussed at Chapter 4B1, a mortgage represents an interest in or lien on real estate that secures payment or performance of an obligation. Originally the mortgage took the form of a deed from the borrower to the lender, subject to a condition subsequent that if the borrower paid the amount owed on the bond or note when due, the title would revest in the borrower. Until the due date, the borrower was often allowed to remain in possession of the property. If the borrower failed to pay the debt when due, regardless of excuse, the condition subsequent failed and title vested indefeasibly in the lender in fee simple absolute.

Because of the hardships that resulted from this procedure, the equity courts stepped in and permitted the defaulting borrower to "redeem" (buy back) the property from the lender by paying the balance of the mortgage notwithstanding that the documents had vested title indefeasibly in the lender. This "equity of redemption" now resulted in hardship for the lender, however, by impeding its ability to dispose of or renovate the property. Accordingly, lenders were allowed to petition equity courts to "foreclose," or cut off, a borrower's equity of redemption. This is how the process called foreclosure originated. These historical developments are discussed in greater detail at Chapter 4A.

This early clash between the rights of the borrower and those of the lender continued throughout the history of foreclosure law. Under the original method of foreclosure, called "strict foreclosure," the court simply issued a decree foreclosing, or cutting off, the mortgagor's equity of redemption if the debtor did not pay the debt within the grace period specified by the court. Returning to the master hypothetical, suppose Dan Developer defaults on his loan with Ace Insurance Company when the principal balance on the loan is approximately $15 million. Under this procedure, Ace, on foreclosure of its mortgage, would effectively acquire Dan Developer's property for the $15 million balance of the mortgage. Assume that on foreclosure the value of the property is $20 million. Strict foreclosure would mean a $5 million windfall for Ace at the expense of Dan and Dan's creditors.

As a practical matter, it is unlikely in this type of commercial situation that Dan would let the property go to foreclosure if he had substantial equity in it; he would sell the property and keep the equity. Nevertheless, because of the possibility of such an inequitable settlement, most jurisdictions abandoned strict foreclosure in favor of a public sale of the property. In some states, however, a form of strict foreclosure is still possible, or even customary, with protections for the borrower built in by the courts and the legislatures.[5]

Another problem for borrowers was that, since there was usually a dearth of competitive bidding at foreclosure sales, lenders were able to bid nominal amounts and obtain large deficiency judgments, that is, judgments for the difference between the purchase price and the amount of the debt. To counter this, other protections were built into the process: restrictions on deficiency judgments (e.g., judgment available only to the extent the lender proved the value of the collateral was less than the debt); confirmation of the foreclosure sale by the court; the setting of upset prices below which the property would not be sold; and the statutory "rights of redemption," under which the borrower could repurchase the property for the foreclosure sale price over a period of time following the sale.

The theory of mortgage law has also changed from the early days of the common law, when a mortgage was deemed to be a conveyance subject to a condition subsequent. As explained at Chapter 4A, in most

---

5. See, e.g., Conn. Gen. Stat. Ann. §49-14 to 49-31 (Supp. 1989); 12 Vt. Stat. Ann. §4523 et seq. (1989); and Vt. R. Civ. P. Rule 80.1 (1988). On the constitutionality of strict foreclosure see Dieffenbach v. Attorney General of Vt., 604 F.2d 187 (2d Cir. 1979). With respect to the limited application of strict foreclosure in Illinois see Prather, Foreclosure of the Security Interest, U. Ill. L.F. 420 (1957), and Brodkey, Current Changes in Illinois Real Property Law, 10 DePaul L. Rev. 567 (1961). Some courts in states not providing for strict foreclosure have been known to grant it on petition of the mortgagee in special circumstances, such as to correct a good-faith failure to join certain necessary parties in a judicial foreclosure. See G. Nelson and D. Whitman, Real Estate Finance Law §7.9 (2d lawyer's ed. 1985); Note, 88 U. Pa. L. Rev. 994 (1940); and Note, 25 Va. L. Rev. 947 (1939).

lien theory states the mortgagee is regarded as obtaining nothing more than a security interest in the mortgaged property. In title theory states, while the mortgagee is regarded as obtaining both the legal title and the concomitant right to possession, these rights have been virtually ignored by both mortgagees and the courts except for the mortgagee's right to rents and possession as a preforeclosure remedy. In some states the format of the mortgage has also changed. In a deed of trust jurisdiction such as California, real property owned by the borrower ("grantor" or "trustor") is conveyed to a third party (the "trustee"), who holds the property in trust for the benefit of the lender ("beneficiary"). In the event of a default by the borrower the trustee is mandated by the terms of the trust to sell the property by means of a nonjudicial public sale for the benefit of the lender-beneficiary.

Notwithstanding the evolution of the foreclosure process and the changes in the form of mortgages, the process of balancing the rights of borrowers and lenders is not over. Today there are new attacks on foreclosure — under the Constitution, fraudulent conveyance law, and the Bankruptcy Code — the effect of which on the viability of the mortgage process is not completely clear as of this writing. In this section we will discuss modern foreclosure practices in the United States, the protections built into law to effect rough justice between borrower and lender, and the current attacks on the foreclosure process. To illustrate these effects, from time to time we will make reference to the master hypothetical at Chapter 5B. Chapter 11 will examine attacks on the mortgagee's ability to realize on the collateral in reorganizations under the Bankruptcy Code.

2. *Methods of Foreclosure*

The most prevalent method of foreclosure in the United States is foreclosure by judicial sale. It is the only procedure permitted in some states and the method most generally used in over one-half of the states. Significantly, it appears to be permitted in all states, so that even in a power-of-sale jurisdiction, when there is a dispute as to priorities or validity of liens, the mortgagee may choose a judicial foreclosure to produce a result similar to a "quiet title" action and feel somewhat more comfortable that the title obtained at foreclosure will not be subject to attack. Judicial foreclosure, however, is complex, expensive, and time-consuming. In some jurisdictions, it is not unusual for the process to go on for years, during which time costs (which are added to the debt for foreclosure purposes) eat away at whatever equity the borrower may have in the property. The following are some of the steps that normally have to be taken after commencing a judicial foreclosure.

1. The lender must have a title search made to determine who has an interest in the property. Junior interests must be joined as parties defendant or they will not be cut off by the foreclosure.
2. The lender must file a lis pendens notice to prevent bona fide purchasers and others from acquiring an interest in the property during the foreclosure proceedings.
3. The lender must next serve the summons and complaint on the necessary parties to the action — those whose interests are to be affected by the foreclosure. With our hypothetical FNB and WCA, this will not be difficult. When there are numerous tenants, as well as others whose interest may not be as clearly demonstrated, the endeavor becomes more complex.
4. A hearing will be held, perhaps before a master in chancery who will prepare and submit a report to the judge regarding the status of the debt, the debtors, and the security, following which there will be a court judgment that a sale will be held and setting forth its terms.
5. The sale is advertised to the general public pursuant to statutory requirements.
6. A court official conducts a sale. The lender will attend and will be prepared to bid to protect its interest. Determining how much to bid is a complex process that involves tax and other considerations, as will be discussed in note 4 below.
7. After the sale, a report of sale is made to the court (in many states confirmation by the court is also required) and a determination is made as to the borrower's and the borrower's other creditors' rights to any surplus.
8. The lender may petition for a deficiency judgment decree if the borrower (or anyone else) is personally liable on the note and if such a judgment is permitted and practical in the applicable jurisdiction.
9. In states that have enacted legislation giving the borrower a right of redemption after foreclosure, there is a waiting period. The foreclosure purchaser cannot possess the property until that period has expired.

The purchaser at the foreclosure sale receives the title the borrower had when the mortgage was recorded, that is, title free of all junior liens and interests in the property (provided the holders of the junior liens or interests have been joined in the foreclosure action) and subject to all senior liens and interests.

Normally, in a power-of-sale foreclosure junior interests are automatically cut off; in a judicial foreclosure only those interest-holders that are made a party defendant can be affected by the proceeding.

This gives the mortgagee the option of keeping junior interests that are beneficial (e.g., leases to good tenants with rents at market or above). The foreclosure does not normally affect senior interests, so they are not usually joined in the action.

Metropolitan Life Ins. Co. v. Childs Co.
230 N.Y. 285, 130 N.E. 295 (1921)

ANDREWS, J. The Beard Building on Liberty street, New York, was conveyed to Mr. and Miss Robinson subject to a mortgage, duly recorded, held by the Metropolitan Life Insurance Company. On May 1, 1902, they leased a portion of these premises to the Childs Unique Dairy Company which later became the defendant. This lease was to run for twenty-one years at an annual rental of $8,000. Under it the defendant went into possession. On December 8, 1913, the Metropolitan Life Insurance Company began an action to foreclose its mortgage. The Childs Company was made a defendant and the complaint demanded that its rights under the lease be ended. Evidently the plaintiff in this action was about to apply for the appointment of a receiver. To avoid the trouble and expense of this proceeding the owners agreed to adopt "another method" to secure to it the same result. They, therefore, on December seventeenth assigned to it all rents accruing after January, 1914, with full power to enforce their payment by summary proceedings or otherwise, and to pay from the rents so collected the expenses necessary for running the building. Should the foreclosure action be discontinued the agreement ended. What was practically accomplished was to make the plaintiff receiver of the rents, with much of the same powers as would have been possessed by a receiver appointed by the court. As we construe the instrument in question, it did not obtain an absolute title to such rents as it might collect. It held them in trust to satisfy any deficiency that might arise on the foreclosure sale. Any surplus necessarily would be returned to the Robinsons. The latter were still owners of the property. The Childs Company was still their tenant.

Notice of the agreement was given to the Childs Company and it paid the rent to the insurance company for January, February, March and April. On April 24, 1914, a judgment of foreclosure and sale in the usual form was obtained and on May first was served on the Childs Company. It provided that the premises be sold and that the latter company "be forever barred and foreclosed of all right, title, interest and equity of redemption in the said premises so sold." On May fifth, acting "in good faith and reasonable reliance upon said judgment," the Childs Company sold its fixtures, quit and vacated the premises and moved elsewhere. On May sixteenth the plaintiff in the foreclosure action made a motion to discontinue the action against the Childs Company, and to cancel the lis pendens and vacate the judgment as against it. This motion was opposed and was denied at Special Term, but it was granted by the Appellate Division in October, 1914. It is not claimed that this order was made without jurisdiction. On March 19, 1915, the sale occurred. The property was bought by the Metropolitan Life Insurance Company and a referee's deed was given to it, subject, however, to the defendant's lease. On December thirty-first the purchaser conveyed the premises to 406 West Thirty-first Street Corporation again subject to the same lease and on the same day assigned this lease itself to the same corporation. Under these circumstances the insurance company seeks to recover rent from May 1, 1914, to December 31, 1915.

As a general rule a tenant is liable under his contract of lease until he is evicted. Neither the beginning of an action to foreclose a mortgage superior to his lease in which he is made a defendant, nor the entry of a judgment of foreclosure and sale constitute such an eviction. The sale may never occur. The amount due may be paid by the obligors. The plaintiff may repent. Until the sale actually takes place the tenant remains liable to his landlord on his contract. (Whalin v. White, 25 N.Y. 462; Mitchell v. Bartlett, 51 N.Y. 447; Mason v. Lenderoth, 88 App. Div. 38.) If, on the contrary, he is not a party to the action his rights are not affected. There is never an eviction. Until the sale he must pay his landlord. Afterwards, the purchaser. . . .

It may well be that no privity of contract or estate exists between him and the purchaser (Sprague Nat. Bank v. Erie R. R. Co., 22 App. Div. 526), and that such a relationship is ordinarily essential to the accrual of rent. Yet we think that such a sale as was here made was a grant of the reversion within the meaning of section 223. It was a grant of what interest the mortgagor had in the property at the time the mortgage was given, less the leased estate — the grant of what was left after the leased estate was subtracted. It is precisely the same so far as the estate granted was concerned as if the lease had been prior to the mortgage. It was so held in Commonwealth Mortgage Co. v. De Waltoff (135 App. Div. 33). With that conclusion we agree.

In view of these rules there can be no question but that the Robinsons or their assignee would have been entitled to recover rent from the defendant from May 1, 1914, to March 19, 1915 (the date of the sale), and that thereafter the purchaser might recover unless facts exist which require a different result. Here such facts can arise only because of the assignment of rent by the Robinsons to the mortgagee and because, although not a party at the time of the sale, the Childs Company had been a defendant until after the entry of judgment.

It is said that the plaintiff in the foreclosure action had an election of remedies. . . .

We fail to find any basis for this claim. The doctrine of the election of remedies is a harsh rule which is not to be extended. (Friederichsen v. Renard, 247 U.S. 207.) It is only applicable "when a choice is exercised between remedies which proceed upon irreconcilable claims of right" (American Woolen Company v. Samuelsohn, 226 N.Y. 61); "where there is, by law, or by contract, a choice between two remedies" (Henry v. Herrington, 193 N.Y. 218). . . .

The Metropolitan Life Insurance Company might or might not make the defendant a party. The option was in its hands. But the power either to sue or not to sue is not the possession of inconsistent remedies. There is but one remedy which may or may not be enforced. The decision to act or not to act is not an election. If it were, serious results would follow. Such an election once made is made forever. And it is made, not merely when the rights of the parties are fixed by judgment, but when the action is begun, based upon one theory inconsistent with and destructive of the other. (Terry v. Munger, 121 N.Y. 161; Matter of Garver, 176 N.Y. 386.) If an election has been made here, therefore, it was by the commencement of the action, not by the entry of judgment. May a foreclosure action not be discontinued as to one defendant? May a defendant omitted not be subsequently made a party? May a purchaser not foreclose against a lien junior to the mortgage? (Moulton v. Cornish, 138 N.Y. 133.)

If not election, however, it is said the principle of estoppel may be applied. . . . The claim is that as assignee of the rents and as mortgagee it tells the tenants that it intends to enforce its superior rights. It formally asserts its intention by entering judgment. The tenant is given notice that if the foreclosure action proceeds to sale he will be evicted. Normally a sale follows judgment. Believing that it will in this case the tenant abandons possession. Can an estoppel be based on this state of facts?

An estoppel rests upon the word or deed of one party upon which another rightfully relies and so relying changes his position to his injury. When this occurs it would be inequitable to permit the first to enforce what would have been his rights under other circumstances. Doubtless should a landlord, before the end of his term, request a tenant to vacate his premises and should the tenant comply (Bedford v. Terhune, 30 N.Y. 453), or should he directly or indirectly command that this be done, and should the tenant obey (Cornwell v. Sanford, 222 N.Y. 248), the landlord might no longer enforce the lease because he would be estopped if for no other reason. So would be a tenant, if the landlord acted on the faith of appearances. But the action or the judgment is far from equivalent to such a request or command.

It is not argued that the beginning of the action has any bearing on this question, or that the tenant might then have vacated the premises. Certainly the Childs Company did not so construe its rights. For four months it continued to pay rent to the mortgagee. But reliance is placed upon the entry of judgment and its service on the tenant. By that judgment the plaintiff announced, as we have seen, that when the sale occurred the tenant would be evicted. The latter might take the plaintiff at its word and immediately vacate. It is difficult to see any justification for this claim for the months before the sale. If the landlord requests or orders the tenant, rightfully, to leave on the first of October may he leave on the first of July and refuse to pay rent thereafter? But is the doctrine of estoppel applicable to the situation arising after the sale?

Giving the widest meaning to any representation, any request, any order contained in the judgment we find no more than this. "When and if a sale in foreclosure occurs you must vacate the premises." Until such a sale there was no eviction. Whether it would or would not occur, or when, no one knew. That question was open. Probably a sale, yes. That the mortgagee then intended to sell, yes. Yet all knew this intention was subject to be defeated by the action of the mort- gagor — by the action of other tenants — by the action of the defendant itself. The plaintiff might discontinue the action. Could the defendant complain? Could it complain if the sale was postponed from time to time? About the judgment there was no finality. It did not state what would necessarily occur. It was not intended as a representation to the defendant. It could not in fact be so understood. It constituted no irrevocable act upon which the defendant might rely. At most it was a threat that upon certain contingencies the plaintiff would in the future exercise its legal rights and evict the defendant. And long before the time to act arrived this threat was withdrawn by the discontinuance of the action against the Childs Company. . . .

The judgment of the Appellate Division should be reversed and that of the Trial Term affirmed, with costs in this court and in the Appellate Division.

McLAUGHLIN, J. (dissenting). I am of the opinion that the plaintiff in the foreclosure action is equitably estopped from asserting that the defendant be held to its lease. After the foreclosure action had been brought, judgment entered canceling defendant's lease, and copy of the judgment and notice of entry served on its attorney, defendant was justified in assuming its lease was to be cut off and moving out of the premises.

The defendant conducted a business upon the premises. It was necessary to find another place, fit it up and remove to it, which it did at considerable expense. It was not required to remain in the premises, awaiting the sale and writ of assistance, and after it had been put upon the street, attempt to find another place in which to transact its business. It thereby changed its position to its injury, in reliance on the acts of the insurance company in the foreclosure action. The insurance company accomplished its purpose of obtaining possession of the premises, unincumbered with the lease. . . .

A majority of states authorize the other principal mode of foreclosure, the power-of-sale foreclosure. A right to foreclose by means of a sale that is not judicially supervised is usually authorized by and subject to the restrictions contained in the state foreclosure statute. There is usually a public sale of the property preceded by advertising notice. The sale is typically supervised by a trustee under a deed of trust or by the mortgagee under a power-of-sale provision contained in a mortgage.

A power-of-sale foreclosure is usually less expensive, speedier, and less complicated than a judicial foreclosure. The borrower, however, is afforded less protection, and the purchaser at the foreclosure sale is apt to receive a title that is not as firm as would be produced at a judicial foreclosure sale. This is because the proceedings are nonadversarial and lack the finality of a judicial foreclosure decree. The following are excerpts from California's statutory notice requirements for certain power-of-sale foreclosures.

Cal. Civ. Code Ann. §2924f
(Deering Supp. 1991)

---

§2924f. Sale or resale of property; notice; contents; posting and publication

(a) As used in this section and Sections 2924g and 2924h "property" means real property or a leasehold estate therein.

(b) Except as provided in subdivision (c), before any sale of property can be made under the power of sale contained in any deed of trust or mortgage, or any resale resulting from a rescission for a failure of consideration pursuant to subdivision (c) of Section 2924h, notice of the sale thereof shall be given by posting a written notice of the time of sale and of the street address and the specific place at the street address where the sale will be held, and describing the property to be sold, at least 20 days before the date of sale in one public place in the city where the property is to be sold, if the property is to be sold in a city, or, if not, then in one public place in the judicial district in which the property is to be sold, and publishing a copy thereof once a week for the same period, in a newspaper of general circulation published in the city in which the property or some part thereof is situated, if any part thereof is situated in a city, if not, then in a newspaper of general circulation published in the judicial district in which the property or some part thereof is situated, or in case no newspaper of general circulation is published in the city or judicial district, as the case may be, in a newspaper of general circulation published in the county in which the property or some part thereof is situated, or in case no newspaper of general circulation is published in the city or judicial district or county, as the case may be, in a newspaper of general circulation published in the county in this state that (1) is contiguous to the county in which the property or some part thereof is situated and (2) has, by comparison with all similarly contiguous counties, the highest population based upon total county population as determined by the most recent federal decennial census published by the Bureau of the Census. A copy of the notice of sale shall also be posted in a conspicuous place on the property to be sold at least 20 days before the date of sale, where possible and where not restricted for any reason. If the property is a single-family residence the posting shall be on a door of the residence, but, if not possible or restricted, then the notice shall be posted in a conspicuous place on the property; however, if access is denied because a common entrance to the property is restricted by a guard gate or similar impediment, the property may be posted at that guard gate or similar impediment to any development community. Additionally, the notice of sale shall be recorded with the county recorder of the county in which the property or some part thereof is situated at least 14 days prior to the date of sale. . . .

(c)(1) This subdivision applies only to deeds of trust or mortgages which contain a power of sale and which are secured by real property containing a single-family, owner-occupied residence, where the obligation secured by the deed of trust or mortgage is contained in a contract for goods or services subject to the provisions of the Unruh Act (Chapter 1 (commencing with Section 1801) of Title 2 of Part 4 of Division 3).

(2) Except as otherwise expressly set forth in this subdivision, all other provisions of law relating to the exercise of a power of sale shall govern the exercise of a power of sale contained in a deed of trust or mortgage described in paragraph (1).

(3) If any default of the obligation secured by a deed of trust or mortgage described in paragraph (1) has not been cured within 30 days after the recordation of the notice of default, the trustee or mortgagee shall mail to the trustor or mortgagor, at his or her last known address, a copy of the following statement:

YOU ARE IN DEFAULT UNDER A

(Deed of trust or mortgage)

DATED _____ . UNLESS YOU TAKE ACTION TO PRO-
TECT YOUR PROPERTY, IT MAY BE SOLD AT A PUBLIC
SALE. IF YOU NEED AN EXPLANATION OF THE NATURE
OF THE PROCEEDING AGAINST YOU, YOU SHOULD CON-
TACT A LAWYER.

(4) All sales of real property pursuant to a power of sale contained
in any deed of trust or mortgage described in paragraph (1) shall
be held in the county where the residence is located and shall be
made to the person making the highest offer. The trustee may receive
offers during the 10-day period immediately prior to the date of
sale and if any offer is accepted in writing by both the trustor or
mortgagor and the beneficiary or mortgagee prior to the time set
for sale, the sale shall be postponed to a date certain and, prior to
which the property may be conveyed by the trustor to the person
making the offer according to its terms. The offer is revocable until
accepted. The performance of the offer following acceptance, according to its terms by a conveyance of the property to the offeror
shall operate to terminate any further proceeding under the notice
of sale and it shall be deemed revoked.

(5) In addition to the trustee fee pursuant to Section 2924c,
the trustee or mortgagee pursuant to a deed of trust or mortgage
subject to this subdivision shall be entitled to charge an additional
fee of fifty dollars ($50).

(6) This subdivision applies only to property on which notices
of default were filed on or after the effective date of this subdivision.

NOTES AND QUESTIONS

1. *Judicial Foreclosure: Junior Interests.* Assume that you represent
Ace Insurance Company as foreclosing mortgagee in our master hypothetical. Which of the interest-holders (listed below) shown in the
title search you ordered would you join as a party defendant? What
considerations should be weighed in making the decision? Before answering, review the lien priority rules discussed in Chapter 4C.

The title report reveals (i) a mortgage held by Fuller National
Bank, executed and recorded after recordation of Ace's mortgage; (ii)
a mechanics' lien recorded subsequent to the mortgage but that claims
to relate back to the commencement of work two days before the
recording of Ace's mortgage; (iii) a lease to Widget Corporation of
America executed after recordation of the mortgage, together with a

subordination agreement between WCA and Ace; (iv) a lease to Sans Argent, Inc., executed subsequent to the perfection of Ace's mortgage; (v) a lease to American Telephone and Telegraph Company, executed after perfection of Ace's mortgage, the term of which will end in eleven years, covering three full floors, at a below-market rental rate; (vi) a deed executed and recorded after Ace's mortgage was recorded, conveying to Sam Speculator an undivided one-half interest in the property; and (vii) a judgment in favor of Paula Plaintiff obtained prior to the recording of Ace's mortgage and docketed in the county where the property is located after the recording of Ace's mortgage.

In judicial foreclosures a junior interest-holder must be joined as a party defendant to be cut off by a foreclosure of a senior interest. You may have heard the terms "necessary party" and "proper party" used in the consideration of who must be joined as a party defendant in a foreclosure proceeding. The meaning of these terms is somewhat obscure. Generally, a "necessary party" is one that must be joined in order to give the purchaser at the foreclosure sale essentially the same title as the borrower had on recording of the mortgage. (Would Fuller National Bank be a necessary party?) Don't be confused by the word "necessary." While failure to join a necessary party will give the mortgagee or purchaser title subject to the rights of the nonjoined junior party (see Chapter 4C), it will not invalidate the foreclosure.

A "proper party," on the other hand, is one whose interest need not be cut off to give the mortgagee or purchaser at the foreclosure sale the borrower's state of title at mortgage recording. The term refers to a party that might conveniently be joined for specific purposes and will be bound by the proceedings but not subject to being cut off by them. For example, it might be appropriate for a prior interest-holder to be joined for the purpose of definitively establishing the amount of the senior lien to which the purchaser at the foreclosure sale will take subject.

From the mortgagee's point of view, the key issue is not whether a party is labeled necessary or proper but whether the mortgagee intends that the foreclosure affect or impair the party's rights. If the foreclosure is so intended, the party must be joined for that purpose. Failure to do so not only leaves the party unaffected by the foreclosure, but breeds a host of messy consequences. See discussion at Chapter 9B, note 3biv. Determining who is to join in a foreclosure action is often time-consuming and expensive, but it's necessary to avoid the grief that an omission can cause. If you were attorney for a foreclosing mortgagee, what steps would you take to avoid missing a junior interest?

Assume in the master hypothetical that Ace holds a first mortgage and Fuller National Bank holds a second. In the foreclosure, Ace omits to join Fuller as a party defendant. As a result of this omission, the foreclosure would be ineffective as to Fuller, and the purchaser at the foreclosure sale would take title subject to Fuller's mortgage. If you represented Ace, and Ace were the successful bidder at the foreclosure sale, after overcoming your initial embarrassment at not joining Fuller (and thoroughly reviewing your professional liability policy) you might begin to think of what steps you would recommend that Ace take.

For obvious reasons, you probably would not want to recommend that Ace pay off the second mortgage, either in whole (if it had been accelerated or if prepayment were possible) or periodically as it became due. How about re-foreclosure? Are there any disadvantages? Would you have to go through a full judicial foreclosure or could you use one of the other methods we have been discussing? Courts often recognize that a first mortgage can be revived for the purpose of foreclosing against the second. The concept is that since the original foreclosure did not affect the junior interest, as to that interest it is as though the first foreclosure hadn't taken place. See Vanderkemp v. Shelton, 11 Paige 28 (N.Y. 1844), and Note, 88 U. Pa. L. Rev. 994 (1940). If this is so, what opportunities might this afford Ace? See G. Nelson and D. Whitman, Real Estate Finance Law §7.15 (2d lawyer's ed. 1985).

It should be noted that, notwithstanding the problems it can create, the joinder requirement provides the lender with a unique opportunity. Since failure to join a party means that the party is unaffected by the foreclosure, the mortgagee can pick and choose which of the junior interests it wishes to cut off and which it wishes to leave unaffected. You can readily see why many tenants and virtually all leasehold mortgagees will insist, as a condition to signing the lease or making the loan, that a prior mortgagee subordinate or agree it will not disturb the tenant on any foreclosure of the mortgage. If this is unfamiliar to you, review Chapter 4C.

2. When Is the Junior Interest Cut Off? In Metropolitan Life Ins. Co. v. Childs Co., the mortgagee joined the junior lessee as a party defendant. A foreclosure judgment was obtained and served on the lessee providing for a sale that would forever bar all interest of the lessee in the premises. The lessee vacated the premises and moved elsewhere. Thereafter (but before the sale) the mortgagee changed its mind and successfully moved to discontinue the action against the lessee and vacate the judgment against it. This meant that the foreclosure would not cut off the lease and the lessee would remain liable for rent. The lessee argued that the mortgagee either should be held to have elected its remedy against the lessee or be estopped from holding the tenant liable under the lease. What did the New York Court of Appeals majority hold? Do you agree? What do you think of Judge McLaughlin's dissenting argument that the majority would force a junior tenant to wait until it was "put upon the street" before obtaining other premises?

If you agree with the dissent, how would you deal with the lessee's rights if the judgment were vacated not because the foreclosing lender changed its mind but because the borrower sold the property and paid off the mortgage, or cured the defaults and got the mortgage reinstated prior to the foreclosure sale? In Judge McLaughlin's view, is the issuance of the judgment the determinative date, or might the mortgagee be estopped from discontinuing the action against the lessee any time the lessee acted to the lessee's detriment after being made a defendant? Would Judge McLaughlin allow a receiver or mortgagee in possession of the premises to evict the tenant prior to the sale? Recall that if a junior party such as a junior lessee or junior mortgagee is joined in as a defendant by the foreclosing mortgagee, the junior party can obtain some protection by exercising where applicable its right of equitable and statutory redemption, its right to maintain an action for a deficiency judgment, and its right to bid in as a purchaser at the foreclosure sale. See discussion at Chapter 9B, note 3b.

3. *Power-of-Sale Legislation.* Assume that Goria Swansong, an aging screen actress, owns a house on Sunset Strip in Beverly Hills, California and 30 acres of undeveloped land in the hills overlooking Malibu. There is a deed of trust on her home securing a loan from Star Savings Bank and one on the 30 acres securing a loan from Pepperdine National Bank. Ms. Swansong has not had a starring role for 25 years, and in fact has not acted in any role for the last 10 years, but she has not changed her lifestyle. Now she has just about run out of cash and is in default on both her deeds of trust. Star and Pepperdine begin foreclosure under power-of-sale provisions in their deeds of trust. Notices meeting the statutory requirements are posted at the courthouses in Beverly Hills and Malibu, recorded in the appropriate offices, and published among the legal advertisements in the *Beverly Hills Bugle* and the *Malibu Gazette* for the times required by statute. In addition, Pepperdine posts a notice on a tree on the 30 acres along Gulch River Trail, a small country road that abuts the property. Star does not post a notice on the door of Ms. Swansong's home, or any other place on her property, but does mail the statement to her as provided by subsection (c) of the excerpted statute.

Ms. Swansong does not visit her 30 acres in the 20 days prior to the sale, during which time the notice was posted. She reads the *Los Angeles Times* and *Variety* but not the *Beverly Hills Bugle* or the *Malibu Gazette.* She has never been in the recording office and has not been in the courthouse since her last divorce 15 years ago. Unaware of the sales, she does not attend either of them. At the sale of her home, Barry Broker, who does read legal notices, bids $800,000 (the mortgage balance) to become the successful bidder. In better times the house was worth $1.5 million, but there has been somewhat of a downturn in the real estate market, and Star, concerned that values would continue to fall and fearful of a large portfolio of foreclosed properties, was happy to get its money back — it ceased bidding when the price equaled the mortgage balance. At the sale of the 30 acres, there was no competitive bidding and Pepperdine acquired the property for the mortgage balance of $250,000.

On learning of the sales, Ms. Swansong engages you as her counsel. Based on those portions of the California power-of-sale legislation excerpted above, are there any arguments you can raise to overturn the sales? Will your arguments be successful? (We will come back to the question of successful foreclosure sale bids of less than the property value later, when we examine borrower protection, constitutionality, and fraudulent transfer issues.)

4. *Bidding.* Returning to the master hypothetical, assume that Ace Insurance Company is foreclosing on its mortgage on Dan Developer's building. The mortgage balance is $15 million, but Ace's in-house appraisers, perhaps motivated by a desire to show that their appraisals in making the mortgage loan were not far off the mark, appraise the property at $18 million. See discussion at Chapter 5B7. Dan, having known that the property was in trouble for some time, has been trying to sell it and thus realize some equity, but has been unsuccessful in finding any purchasers willing to pay a price in excess of the mortgage balance. He has decided to let the property go to foreclosure. Prior to foreclosure, a title search reveals a second mortgage held by Fuller National Bank (FNB) for $10 million and a real estate tax lien filed after both mortgages were recorded that by state statute takes priority over prior mortgages, in the amount of $1 million.

If there is competitive bidding at the sale, how much will Ace have to bid to protect its investment? What should its maximum bid be? How much will FNB have to bid to protect its interest? If its appraisers feel the property is worth $16 million, should FNB bid at all? See discussion at Chapter 9B, note 3biii.

5. *Circular Priorities.* Assume in the situation discussed in note 4 that the title search reveals a federal tax lien of $2 million instead of the FNB mortgage. Notice of the federal tax lien was filed after the Ace mortgage was recorded but before the real estate tax lien was filed. Under I.R.C. §6323, a federal tax lien will not take priority over mortgages recorded before the federal tax lien is filed. At the foreclosure sale, the property is purchased by a third-party bidder for $16 million. How do you think the proceeds should be distributed, given the facts that the real estate tax lien is prior to the Ace mortgage but subordinate to the federal tax lien and that the federal tax lien is subordinate to the Ace mortgage? You are encountering what is known as a "circular

priority" problem. What logical approach can you take to try to resolve it?

6. *Additional Reading.* Accomazzo, Avoiding Sister State Antideficiency Laws, 14 Colo. Law. 775 (1985); Breidenbach, Right of a Trustee to Bid at Foreclosure Sale, 21 Marq. L. Rev. 61 (1937); Bruce, Mortgage Law Reform Under the Uniform Land Transactions Act, 1976 Wis. L. Rev. 899; Crocker, Beneficiary's Underbid — A Neglected Tool, 44 L.A.B. Bull. 295 (1969); Fairchild, Foreclosure Methods and Costs: A Reevaluation, 7 Brooklyn L. Rev. 1 (1937); Kuklin, The Uniform Land Transactions Act: Article 3, 11 Real Prop., Prob. & Tr. J. 12 (1976); Lieshout, Confirmation of the Sheriff's Sale: The Final Word on Foreclosures, 9 Milwaukee Law. 16 (1985); Madway, A Mortgage Foreclosure Primer, 8 Clearinghouse Rev. 146 (1974); Madway and Pearlman, Mortgage Forms and Foreclosure Practices: Time for Reform, 9 Real Prop., Prob. & Tr. J. 560 (1974); Pedowitz, Mortgage Foreclosure Under the Uniform Land Transactions Act (As Amended), 6 Real Est. L.J. 179 (1978); Tefft, The Myth of Strict Foreclosure, 4 U. Chi. L. Rev. 575 (1937); Turner, The English Mortgage of Land as a Security, 20 Va. L. Rev. 729 (1934); Washburn, The Judicial and Legislative Response to Price Inadequacy in Mortgage Foreclosure Sales, 53 S. Cal. L. Rev. 843 (1980); Wechsler, Through the Looking Glass: Foreclosure by Sale as De Facto Strict Foreclosure — An Empirical Study of Mortgage Foreclosure and Subsequent Resale, 70 Cornell L. Rev. 850 (1985); and Note, Mortgage Foreclosures: The Lingering Effect of the Common Law of Separation of Legal and Equitable Remedies, 52 Chi-Kent L. Rev. 121 (1975).

3. Protection of the Borrower

As discussed earlier, the history of mortgages has seen the courts and legislatures constantly working to balance the rights of borrowers and lenders and keep the procedure as fair as possible to both sides. In modern times the changes have been largely designed to protect the borrower as perceptions of unfairness have developed and economic conditions have warranted. These developing rules, generally in the form of limitations on the ability of the lender to implement the terms of its agreement with the borrower, are studied in great detail in a thorough article by Professor Washburn, The Judicial and Legislative Response to Price Inadequacy in Mortgage Foreclosure Sales,[6] a part of which is excerpted below.

6. 53 S. Cal. L. Rev. 843 (1980).

a. Anti-deficiency Judgment Legislation

If real property subject to a mortgage is sold in foreclosure and brings less than the amount of the debt, the borrower is liable under the note for the deficiency. The lender's action to recover the deficiency may result in what is known as a deficiency judgment.

Imagine the onerous consequences that might arise from a deficiency judgment. Returning to the master hypothetical, assume that Ace's mortgage has a balance of $15 million and is in default. The value of the property is only $12 million, so Dan, having no equity, lets the property go to foreclosure. At the sale there are no bidders other than Ace. (This is because Ace would match any competitive bid at least up to the value of the property and probably up to the mortgage balance, which means that any third-party bidder would have to bid in excess of the value of the property to be successful.) Ace bids $100 and acquires the property. If Dan were liable on the note, Ace could theoretically obtain a personal judgment against Dan in the amount of $14,999,900. Fortunately, this scenario is unlikely, at least in a commercial setting, because deficiency judgments are extremely rare as a consequence of workout agreements between the parties, nonrecourse financing, practical considerations, and legislative restrictions.

Recall that postconstruction financing of commercial real estate is usually nonrecourse. This means that in the event of foreclosure the lender agrees to seek recourse only against the property and not against the personal assets of the borrower. Accordingly, the lender would be precluded from seeking a deficiency judgment in those jurisdictions that recognize them or from suing the borrower personally on the note. Exculpatory language is usually included in the mortgage note signed by the borrower (or by a general partner on behalf of a limited partnership). A principal reason why lenders don't object to nonrecourse financing is that in most loan transactions, especially large ones, it is the rental income stream and not the solvency of the borrower that really protects the lender and feeds the mortgage. See discussion at Chapter 4B2, note 1 and Chapter 5A2. In addition, if the borrower is a limited partnership, the limited partners may be precluded from maximizing their tax shelter benefits unless the syndicate obtains qualified nonrecourse financing. See discussion at Chapter 2B, note 7diii.

In the field of home mortgage financing, where personal liability is normal, institutional lenders seldom seek deficiency judgments because of severe limitations on deficiency judgments imposed by statute and the fact that institutions do not relish the publicity they would receive if they took away their borrowers' homes and then attached their salaries to recover a deficiency. In the following excerpt Professor

Washburn discusses the types of anti-deficiency legislation that had
been enacted at that time.

Washburn, The Judicial and Legislative
Response to Price Inadequacy in
Mortgage Foreclosure Sales
53 S. Cal. L. Rev. 843, 916-919 (1980)

C. STATUTES PROHIBITING
DEFICIENCY JUDGMENTS

A number of state statutory schemes prohibit deficiency judgments
instead of controlling them through appraisal or fair market value
procedures. These laws do not prohibit all deficiencies, but apply to
specific types of transactions, including purchase money mortgages,
mortgages on homesteads, private sales, abandoned property, and sales
with short redemption periods. Most of these statutes originated during
the Depression, at which time their purpose was to shift the loss from
the debtor to the creditor as a means of avoiding an acceleration
of the downturn. The statutes reflect a legislative intent that public
policy requires continued debtor protection in the specified transactions.

1. PURCHASE MONEY MORTGAGES

Seven states prohibit deficiency judgments when the defaulted obligation
is a purchase money mortgage. While purchase money mortgages
include mortgages given to secure money lent to purchase any type of
property, these statutes are intended to protect purchasers of single-
family homes. Several of these statutes are expressly limited to mortgages
on single- or two-family houses or homesteads.

These enactments apply to funds borrowed to purchase property;
mortgages securing money borrowed for other purposes, such as refinancing or second loans against accumulated equity, are not covered.
The Montana, North Carolina, and South Dakota statutes apply only
to mortgages given by the purchaser to the vendor to secure payment
of the balance of the purchase price. The statutes in North Dakota
and Arizona apply to both vendor lenders and institutional lenders,
while those in California and Oregon distinguish between these two
types of lenders. In general, deficiency judgments are prohibited on
any mortgage given by the purchaser to the vendor, regardless of the
type of property. Institutional purchase money financing is subject to
the prohibition in California only if the property is a one- to four-
family dwelling, and in Oregon if it is a primary or secondary single-

family residence. This special allowance for family dwellings is based on a policy that attempts to balance the protection of residential borrowers with the encouragement of institutional mortgage financing by not unduly restricting lenders' recovery.

The Arizona statute allows a deficiency judgment in the amount of any voluntary waste committed or permitted by the debtor while in possession of the property. Since waste reduces the foreclosure sale price, the mortgagee is permitted to recover this loss, as determined by the court, in the form of a deficiency judgment.

2. PRIVATE SALES

To avoid potential unfair advantage in the nonjudicial sale, several states prohibit deficiencies when the mortgagee sells property under a trust deed or mortgage power of sale. Since the mortgagee can purchase at its own sale or at the trustee's sale, the private sale format resembles strict foreclosure. A creditor could not obtain a deficiency judgment after strict foreclosure. The statutes prohibiting deficiencies following nonjudicial sales thus render the process a modern equivalent of strict foreclosure.

In most states, private sales need not be followed by judicial confirmation. The Georgia statute modifies this rule by allowing a deficiency judgment in power of sale foreclosures only if the mortgagee petitions the court to confirm the sale and the court cooperates. In Minnesota, a mortgagee-purchaser at a private sale waives a deficiency judgment if the redemption period is not extended from six to twelve months under any of the statutory criteria.

3. SHORT TERM REDEMPTION PERIOD

Several states prohibit deficiency judgments when the mortgagee, by complying with the statutory scheme, has effected a shortening of the redemption period. Although these statutes deprive the debtor of part of his statutory redemption protection, they also free him from deficiency liability. Under the North Dakota Short Term Mortgage Redemption Act, a mortgage of property of less than ten acres may provide that the redemption period will be six rather than twelve months if the judgment is greater than two-thirds of the original secured indebtedness. No deficiency judgment is permitted if this procedure is followed. The Wisconsin statute, which applies to property of less than twenty acres, shortens the redemption period from twelve to six months if the mortgagee waives a deficiency judgment. If the property is abandoned, the Wisconsin statute shortens the redemption period further to two months. The Washington statute applies to nonagricultural property that has been abandoned for six months or more; no deficiency judgment is allowed and the purchaser takes free of all statutory redemption rights.

The following is an excerpt from New York's statute, which is typical of those that substitute the value of the property for the sale price in determining a deficiency.

N.Y. Real Prop. Act. L. §1371
(McKinney 1990)

2. Simultaneously with the making of a motion for an order confirming the sale, provided such motion is made within ninety days after the date of the consummation of the sale by the delivery of the proper deed of conveyance to the purchaser, the party to whom such residue shall be owing may make a motion in the action for leave to enter a deficiency judgment upon notice to the party against whom such judgment is sought or the attorney who shall have appeared for such party in such action. Such notice shall be served personally or in such other manner as the court may direct. Upon such motion the court, whether or not the respondent appears, shall determine, upon affidavit or otherwise as it shall direct, the fair and reasonable market value of the mortgaged premises as of the date such premises were bid in at auction or such nearest earlier date as there shall have been any market value thereof and shall make an order directing the entry of a deficiency judgment. Such deficiency judgment shall be for an amount equal to the sum of the amount owing by the party liable as determined by the judgment with interest, plus the amount owing on all prior liens and encumbrances with interest, plus costs and disbursements of the action including the referee's fee and disbursements, less the market value as determined by the court or the sale price of the property whichever shall be the higher. . . .

The Uniform Land Security Interest Act[7] provides in part as follows.

Section 511(b).   Unless otherwise agreed and except as provided in this subsection as to protected parties, a person who owes payment of

---

7. The Uniform Land Security Interest Act (ULSIA) was approved by the National Conference of Commissioners on Uniform State Laws in August 1985. It deals solely with mortgages and other forms of security interests in real estate.

an obligation secured is liable for any deficiency. If that person is a protected party and the obligation secured is a purchase money security interest, there is no liability for a deficiency, notwithstanding any agreement of the protected party. For purposes of calculating the amount of any deficiency a transfer of the real estate to a person who is liable to the creditor under a guaranty, endorsement, repurchase agreement, or the like, is not a sale.

Section 113. (a) "Protected party" means: (1) an individual who gives a security interest in residential real estate all or part of which the individual occupies or intends to occupy as a residence; (2) a person obligated primarily or secondarily on an obligation secured by residential real estate if, at the time the obligation is incurred that person is related to an individual who occupies or intends to occupy all or a part of the real estate as a residence; or (3) an individual who acquires residential real estate and assumes or takes subject to the obligation of a prior protected party under the real estate security agreement.

(b) "Residential real estate" means, in relation to a protected party, real estate, improved or to be improved, containing not more than [three] acres, not more than four dwelling units, and no nonresidential uses for which the protected party is a lessor. If a unit in a common interest community is otherwise "residential real estate," it remains so regardless of the size of, or the number of units in, the common interest community.

Section 111(4). "Common interest community" means real estate described in an instrument with respect to which a person by reason of ownership of a part thereof is obligated to pay for real estate taxes, insurance premiums, maintenance, or improvement of another part thereof. The term includes real estate held in a condominium or cooperative.

Section 111(18). A security agreement is a "purchase money security agreement" to the extent that it is: (i) taken or retained by the seller of the collateral to secure all or part of its price or (ii) taken by a person other than the seller of the collateral who, by making an advance or incurring an obligation, gives value to enable the debtor to acquire the collateral.

NOTES AND QUESTIONS

1. *ULSIA Provisions.* ULSIA prohibits deficiency judgments when the borrower is a "protected party" and the mortgage is a "purchase money security interest." Does this effectively protect the people in need of protection? Suppose Hortense Homeowner purchased her home from Dan Developer. Hortense financed her purchase with a mortgage from Friendly Bank. Is the mortgage a purchase money security interest under ULSIA?

Assume that Dan Developer builds the new Danley Hotel on approximately one acre of land in the center of downtown McNiece, obtaining construction financing from Fuller National Bank. When completed, the hotel will be run pursuant to the terms of an operating contract with Danley Hotel Corporation, a national chain controlled by Dan. The hotel will be 30 stories tall and will have a penthouse devoted to a lavish apartment for Dan — the only unit in the hotel built exclusively for apartment use. There are, however, five other large suites that Dan hopes will be leased by major corporations for use by their executives. Dan is personally liable on the construction loan. If that loan goes into default and FNB forecloses, acquiring the almost-completed building at less than the mortgage balance, will FNB be able to obtain a deficiency judgment against Dan? Is this "residential real estate" within ULSIA's definition? Would it be "residential" if there were no large suites (other than Dan's) that could be leased? Is Dan a "protected party"? The answer to this question affects the application of many ULSIA provisions. For example, if Dan is a protected party, usury limitations on interest rates may be applicable to him. See ULSIA §403, Alternative B.

2. *Other Restrictions.* At the beginning of this section we made reference to a scenario in which Dan Developer became subject to a deficiency judgment of $14,999,900. Under the New York statute, what would the limit be on the deficiency in that scenario?

Professor Washburn states that in power-of-sale jurisdictions the private sale format resembles strict foreclosure except that the mortgagee in a power-of-sale foreclosure can seek a deficiency judgment. He then concludes that where power-of-sale jurisdictions have prohibited deficiencies the process has been rendered "a modern equivalent of strict foreclosure." Do you agree? What if the property were worth more than the loan balance?

3. *The One-Form-of-Action Rule.* Somewhat akin to the anti-deficiency judgment legislation is the "one-form-of-action" requirement of over 20 states, designed to protect the borrower from a suit on the note prior to foreclosure. The rule gives the lender a choice of fore-closing the mortgage first (in which case the mortgagee may then obtain a deficiency judgment to the extent permitted by law) or suing on the note and waiving the security. Some one-action states simply require that the lender look to the security first before seeking a money judgment. In California, where the lender is deemed to have waived its security if it first brings an action on the note, it was held in Bank of America v. Daily, 152 Cal. App. 3d 767, 199 Cal. Rptr. 557 (Cal. App. 1984) that the lender bank had waived its security when it set off some $10,000 in the borrower's checking account (a debt of the bank to the depositor) against accrued interest the borrower owed to the bank. The court found that this amounted to an election of remedies and that the bank could not later commence a judicial foreclosure or

apparently make claim for the unpaid balance of the debt. But see Security Pacific Natl. Bank v. Wozab, 51 Cal. 3d 991, 800 P.2d 557, 275 Cal. Rptr. 201 (1990), revg. 223 Cal. App. 3d 1042, 258 Cal. Rptr. 850 (1989), wherein the court noted that a bank's setoff in the amount of $2,804.72 was not an "action" that precluded the bank from collecting mortgage indebtedness from the same borrower in the amount of $976,575.95.

Certainly decisions such as that in *Daily* do not create an atmosphere conducive to lender confidence in reasonable treatment by the courts in interpreting the one-form-of-action rule. As a result lenders are concerned about the effects of these decisions.

Assume that Dan Developer's property in the master hypothetical is located in California. Ace had a commitment to make a $25 million mortgage loan on completion of construction in accordance with plans and specifications. When the time for disbursement was at hand, a significant amount of tenant finish work had not been completed. Nevertheless a note and a deed of trust for $25 million were executed by Ace and the deed of trust was recorded; Ace, however, held $2 million of the loan proceeds in escrow to be disbursed as the tenant finish work was completed. If the work were not completed by a specified date, Ace was authorized by the agreement to apply the escrow to reduce the indebtedness. Without completing the tenant finish work, Dan goes into default in the payment of principal and interest. Ace applies the $2 million to reduce the indebtedness and then commences foreclosure. Under *Daily*, does Ace risk losing $23 million? If so, can you think of any way Ace could have modified the arrangement to avoid such a result?

What if Ace had accepted a letter of credit to cover certain of Dan's obligations? If Dan defaults and Ace draws on the letter of credit, does Ace risk violating the one-action rule? Some lenders in California, uncertain as to the extent of the rule, have opted to create two separate obligations: one note secured by the real estate and another backed by a letter of credit or escrow account. Do you think this will protect the lien of the deed of trust from attack? One law firm, in a letter to clients, points out some nasty side effects of this approach, including "potential compliance problems with respect to investment statutes" affecting "the availability of certain usury and shared appreciation exemptions under California law," and raising "potential defenses of marshalling of assets, application of proceeds and certain bankruptcy issues." The memo also points out that a draw on a letter of credit or escrow account might be deemed to cure the default and reinstate the debt under California law. For more on this subject see Mertens and Rowan, Bank of America v. Daily: Setoff Versus the Right to Foreclose, 8 Cal. Real Prop. L. Rptr. 73 (1985); Mitchell, Setoff Imperils Foreclosure, 102 Banking L.J. 60 (1985); Tramz and Weiner, New

Breadth to Sanctions Against Foreclosing Secured Creditors, 3 Cal. Real Prop. J. 1 (Summer 1985).

4. Additional Reading. Accomazzo, Avoiding Sister State Anti-Deficiency Laws, 14 Colo. Law. 775 (1985); Brabner-Smith, Economic Aspects of the Deficiency Judgment, 20 Va. L. Rev. 719 (1934); De Funiak, Right to Deficiency Judgment Where Mortgagee Purchasing at Foreclosure Sale Has Later Resold at a Profit, 27 Ky. L.J. 410 (1939); Eaton, Deficiency Judgments and Decrees, 20 Va. L. Rev. 743 (1934); Leipziger, Deficiency Judgments in California: The Supreme Court Tries Again, 22 UCLA L. Rev. 753 (1975); Perlman, Mortgage Deficiency Judgments During an Economic Depression, 20 Va. L. Rev. 771 (1934).

b. Sale Confirmation, Upset Prices, and Rights of Redemption

In the case of property going to foreclosure, state statutes provide a variety of safeguards designed to produce a foreclosure sale price as close as reasonably possible to market value, given the forced nature of the sale. The protections are not uniform throughout the country; some states have so encumbered the process with borrower protections as to make foreclosure a very time-consuming and expensive proposition. With foreclosure costs added to the debt this tilt toward borrower protection may be equally disadvantageous to borrower and lender. Many borrower-protective provisions were originally designed to protect unsophisticated borrowers dealing with sophisticated institutional lenders, but they also apply with fine impartiality where the parties are dealing at arm's length and their degree of sophistication is more or less equal.[8]

On the other hand, some states have so streamlined power-of-sale procedures that there is a sense of unfairness to the borrower. For example, in the case of Turner v. Blackburn,[9] the borrower first learned of the foreclosure one month after the sale was held, when the purchaser visited the property to inspect his purchase. This has led to attacks on the foreclosure process, both constitutionally and under the fraudulent transfer provisions of state law and of the Bankruptcy Code (which are discussed at Chapter 10C4 and 10C5, respectively).

Fortunately, such patently unfair situations are infrequent, because defaults are rarely unexpected. Especially in a commercial setting, the

8. See recommendations for law changes in Lifton, Real Estate in Trouble: Lender's Remedies Need an Overhaul, 31 Bus. Law. 1927, 1930, 1942-1945 (1976).
9. 389 F. Supp. 1250 (1975).

borrower usually knows that trouble is brewing long before there is a default. This affords the borrower the opportunity to go to the marketplace and obtain the current market value for the property. After default, most state statutes provide (and practice generally supports) a substantial additional period before foreclosure proceedings or the actual foreclosure sale[10] during which a borrower can sell the property at private sale at a price closer to its market value than can be obtained at a forced foreclosure sale.

State statutes provide additional safeguards should the property go to foreclosure. Some states will not allow the property to be sold for less than a minimum sum at the foreclosure sale. For example, some statutes provide that a sale will not be confirmed, or will be overturned by the court, if the price paid for the property is less than two-thirds of the appraised value or if the sale price is less than some other "upset price" established by the court.[11] In addition to these statutory requirements, courts, using their inherent equity power, have refused to confirm sales at unfair prices. Just how unfair the price must be to justify imposition of equity power is discussed in the case of Ballentyne v. Smith, excerpted below.

Ballentyne v. Smith
205 U.S. 285 (1907)

This is an appeal from a judgment of the Supreme Court of the Territory of Hawaii, 17 Hawaii, 96, affirming an order of the third judge of the First Circuit Court in the Territory of Hawaii, which refused to confirm a sale of property made by a commissioner under order of court in a foreclosure suit brought by William O. Smith, as trustee, against the Pacific Heights Electric Railway Company, Limited, a Hawaiian corporation, and directed that the property be again offered for sale. The suit was brought to foreclose a trust deed of fifty thousand dollars executed by the railway company to Smith, as trustee, on April 1, 1902, and purporting to convey an electric railway two and one-half miles in length and running up to Pacific Heights, with its equipment of every kind, and also all land and other property conveyed to it by deed from one Charles S. Desky, dated January 25, 1902.

---

10. See, e.g., Cal. Civ. Code §§2924, 2924(c), 2924(f), and 2924(g) (West Supp. 1991); Ind. Code Ann. §32-8-16-1 (Burns 1990); Okla. Stat. Ann. tit. 12, §§759, 760 and tit. 46, §4 (West Supp. 1988).

11. See, e.g., W. Va. Code §38-4-23 (1985). These protective devices and their effectiveness are discussed in Washburn, The Judicial and Legislative Response to Price Inadequacy in Mortgage Foreclosure Sales, 53 S. Cal. L. Rev. 843 (1980).

The sale was made on February 4, 1905, for the sum of eleven hundred dollars. It was in bulk of the entire property covered by the mortgage, except a cable and condenser, which were of comparatively little value, and which, for reasons not at all affecting the merits of this controversy, were not sold with the balance of the property. The commissioner who made the sale reported that the amount realized was disproportionate to the value of the property sold, and recommended that it should not be confirmed, but that such further order should be made as to the court should seem meet in the premises. On the hearing of a motion to confirm the sale and objections thereto, the trial court found that the evidence was overwhelming that the actual value of the property was at least seven times the amount at which the property was struck off, that being the highest and best bid therefor. . . .

MR. JUSTICE BREWER, after making the foregoing statement, delivered the opinion of the court.

The question presented is whether a court of equity may, prior to any order of confirmation, set aside a foreclosure sale of mortgaged property upon the single ground of inadequacy in price; and further, whether, if it has that power, the inadequacy here shown is so gross as to justify such action. It does not appear that there was any fraudulent conduct on the part of the purchaser or any combination to restrict bidding. The sale was duly advertised. It was, so far as disclosed, open and public, and the bid reported was the highest. Nothing in time or place or lack of attendance of buyers is shown. Many of the considerations, therefore, which have influenced courts of equity to set aside judicial sales are not to be found in the present case. Indeed, the only substantial objection is that the amount of the bid is largely below the value of the property. Something may be said on each side of the question; on the one, that a court of equity owes a duty to the creditors seeking its assistance in subjecting property to the payment of debts, to see that the property brings something like its true value in order that to the extent of that value the debts secured upon the property may be paid; that it owes to them something more than to merely take care that the forms of law are complied with, and that the purchaser is guilty of no fraudulent act; on the other, that it is the right of one bidding in good faith, at an open and public sale, to have the property for which he bids struck off to him if he be the highest and best bidder; that if he be free from wrong he should not be deprived of the benefit of his bid simply because others do not bid or because parties interested have done nothing to secure the attendance of those who would likely give for the property something nearer its value; that if the creditors make no effort and are willing to take the chances of a general attendance, they have no right to complain on the ground that the property did not bring what it should have brought.

In England the old rule was that in chancery sales, until confirmation of the master's report, the bidding would be opened upon a mere offer to advance the price ten per cent; but this rule has been rejected, and now both in England and this country a sale will not be set aside for mere inadequacy of price, unless that inadequacy be so gross as to shock the conscience, or unless there be additional circumstances against its fairness. But if there be great inadequacy, slight circumstances of unfairness in the conduct of the party benefited by the sale will be sufficient to justify setting it aside. Graffam v. Burgess, 117 U.S. 180, 191, 192. It is difficult to formulate any rule more definite than this, and each case must stand upon its own peculiar facts. . . .

Now, in the case before us, the commissioner who made the sale reported against its confirmation. It was not confirmed but set aside by the trial court, which found that the evidence was overwhelming that the actual value of the property was at least seven times the amount of the bid. While the testimony is not preserved, it is stated by the Supreme Court of the Territory that it was claimed that only four years before the sale the property cost $78,000, exclusive of the right of way. It was, in fact, bonded less than three years before for $50,000. Speaking in general terms, it consisted of an electric railway two and a half miles in length, two freight cars, two passenger cars, and other appliances for running the railway. All this was sold for $1,100. The action of the trial court in setting aside the sale was approved by the Supreme Court of the Territory.

Under the circumstances we think the order of the Supreme Court should be sustained. While we are disinclined to any action which will impair confidence in the stability of judicial sales, yet with the concurrence of judicial opinion adverse to this sale, considering the amount of property sold, the meager sum bid by the purchaser, the express finding that the overwhelming testimony was to the effect that the property was worth at least seven times more than the sum bid, and also recognizing that the courts which have passed upon this question are much more familiar with the condition of things in Hawaii, and therefore more competent to appreciate the significance of the transactions attending the sale, we have come to the conclusion that it would not be right to reverse the ruling below and confirm the sale.

The judgment of the Supreme Court of the Territory of Hawaii is affirmed.

One important device for borrower protection is a legislatively mandated right of redemption. You already know about the equity of redemption, that is, the right of the borrower to redeem (or buy back) the property *before* foreclosure by paying the lender the balance of the mortgage. The right of redemption is also made available by statute for a period *after* foreclosure, during which time the borrower or other parties affected by the foreclosure may redeem the property, generally for the amount bid at the foreclosure sale plus interest and costs.[12] Its purpose is to encourage bidders at foreclosure sales to bid up to the real value of the property as well as to give (primarily) consumer borrowers, who may have been too distracted by family problems to protect themselves prior to foreclosure, a second opportunity to do so. The *Stadium Apartments* case, excerpted below, illustrates the reaction of the federal government when it was in the position of a mortgagee subject to a borrower's right of redemption. It also shows that some courts feel statutory redemption does not always achieve its desired objectives.[13]

United States v. Stadium Apartments, Inc.
425 F.2d 358 (9th Cir.), cert. denied, 400 U.S. 926 (1970)

DUNIWAY, Circuit Judge:

This case presents the question whether state redemption statutes should apply when the Federal Housing Authority (FHA) forecloses a mortgage which it has guaranteed. We hold that such statutes do not apply.

The federal statute here involved is Title VI of the National Housing Act, 12 U.S.C. §§1736-1746a. The stated objective of Title VI is "to assist in relieving the acute shortage of housing . . . available to veterans of World War II at prices within their reasonable ability to pay . . ." 12 U.S.C. §1738(a). The statute confers authority upon the Secretary (formerly the Commissioner) "to make such rules and regulations as may be necessary to carry out the provisions of this subchapter." 12 U.S.C. §1742. Such regulations were promulgated, and those that were in force in November 1949, when the mortgage here in question was executed and insured appear in the 1947 Supplement to the Code of Federal Regulations. (24 C.F.R. §580) (1947 Supp.).) Citations to C.F.R. in this opinion are to the 1947 supplement.

The way in which the Act and regulations operated are well illustrated in this case. In 1949, appellee Stadium Apartments, Inc., desired to construct, under Title VI, an apartment house in Caldwell, Idaho. It applied to Prudential Insurance Company for a loan. Such a

---

12. See Washburn, id. at 930-932.

13. Because of the federal-state issues involved, the Ninth Circuit invited the attorneys general of the states within the circuit to submit amicus briefs. References to the argument of California are undoubtedly to the brief, amicus curiae, of the California Attorney General.

loan was eligible for insurance under 12 U.S.C. §1743(a). The conditions for eligibility are set out in 12 U.S.C. §1743(b). The mortgagor must be approved by the Secretary, who can impose certain regulations upon both the mortgagor and the property mortgaged. Certain terms of the mortgage are also prescribed. Application for approval was made, as required by 24 C.F.R. §§580.1-580.7. The FHA then issued a commitment of insurance, as required by 24 C.F.R. §580.8. The mortgage was executed upon a form prescribed by FHA, and accepted for insurance. 24 C.F.R. §§580.10-580.37. The amount of the insured loan was $130,000. The mortgage contained this provision:

> The Mortgagor, to the extent permitted by law, hereby waives the benefit of any and all homestead and exemption laws and of any right to a stay or redemption and the benefit of any moratorium law or laws.

Stadium Apartments defaulted in 1966, and Prudential assigned the mortgage to the Secretary of Housing and Urban Development, pursuant to 12 U.S.C. §1743(c). The Secretary paid Prudential the amount then due, as required by 12 U.S.C. §1743(c). The United States then obtained a default judgment foreclosing the mortgage, 12 U.S.C. §§1713(k), 1743(f). The district judge, in spite of the foregoing provision, framed the foreclosure decree to allow for a one-year period of redemption, as provided by 2 Idaho Code §11-402. The question is whether this was error. . . .

It is settled that the applicable law is federal. . . .

[S]hould the federal courts adopt the local law granting a post-foreclosure sale right of redemption in those states where it exists? Here, both authority and policy convince us that they should not.

Every federal appellate case dealing with the government's foreclosure remedy under insured mortgages applies federal law to assure the protection of the federal program against loss, state law to the contrary notwithstanding. . . .

Through all of these cases there runs a dominant rationale[:] . . . "Now [after default] the federal policy to protect the treasury and to promote the security of federal investment which in turn promotes the prime purpose of the Act — to facilitate the building of homes by the use of federal credit — becomes predominant. *Local rules limiting the effectiveness of the remedies available to the United States for breach of a federal duty can not be adopted.*" (268 F.2d at 383, emphasis added.) . . .

Reasons of policy dictate the same result. In the first place, only 26 of the states provide for post-foreclosure redemption. The periods of redemption vary widely. So do other conditions to redemption and the rules governing right to possession, right to rents, making repairs, and other matters arising during the redemption period. See, e.g., Clark Investment Co. v. United States, supra, n. 2, right to rents. There is a split of authority as to whether the right of redemption can be waived. Similarly, there is a split of authority as to the right of the mortgagee to recover the value of improvements made during the redemption period. It would be contrary to the teaching of every case that we have cited to hold that there is a different federal policy in each state, thus making FHA "subject to the vagaries of the laws of the several states." Clearfield Trust Co. v. United States, 1943, 318 U.S. 363, 367, 63 S. Ct. 573, 575, 87 L. Ed. 838. . . .

In response to our request, the government has informed us of the views of federal agencies involved in the lending or insuring of funds for private housing purposes. These include, in addition to the Federal Housing Administration, the Farmers Home Administration of the Department of Agriculture, acting under 42 U.S.C. §1471 ff., and the Veterans Administration, acting under 38 U.S.C. §1800 ff. We quote the government's response:

> The Farmers Home Administration, the Federal Housing Administration, and the Veterans Administration have informed us that their experience has indicated that the imposition of post-foreclosure-sale redemption periods makes the foreclosure remedy more costly and administratively time-consuming in those states whose local law so provides. Generally, the reasons given in support of this conclusion are . . . that existence of a post-sale period for redemption chills bidding at the foreclosure sale, forcing the United States to buy the property at the sale and to hold it (paying meanwhile the costs of maintenance) until the expiration of the period, when it finally can give good title to a purchaser.

Additional reasons stated by the government are quoted in the margin.[7]

We do not find the policy arguments presented by California convincing. First, it is argued that the purpose of the redemption

---

7. The Farmers Home Administration has stated that where post-sale redemption periods have been imposed, the mortgaged property may, after sale and before expiration of the redemption period, 'stand unoccupied and unattended for considerable periods of time and consequently [may] deteriorate substantially in value, to the detriment of the financial interest of the United States and without concomitant benefit to any other party.' Similarly, the Veterans Administration reported to us that where a post-sale redemption period is imposed unless the former owner redeems timely, the mortgagee or his assignee are obligated to pay holding costs during the redemption period, i.e., taxes, public improvements, if any, the cost of repairs to preserve the security, and the cost of hazard insurance premium when necessary. There is also for consideration the interest normally accruing on the outstanding investment. . . . The Federal Housing Administration reported to us: . . . [']With the notable exception of Alabama, redemption statutes permit a foreclosure purchaser to receive from a redemptioner little more than the price bid at the foreclosure sale, so that a purchaser is well advised to keep rehabilitation expenses to an absolute minimum until the redemption period expires. As a practical matter, this delays the day when FHA, as such purchaser can safely embark on a program involving capital expenditures, thereby delaying the day when the property may be placed in condition for its best use and for

statutes is to force the mortgagee and others to bid the full market price at the sale. We assume that this is the purpose; we are not convinced that the statutes accomplish it. What third party would bid and pay the full market value, knowing that he cannot have the property to do with as he wishes until a set period has gone by, and that at the end of the period he may not get it, but instead may be forced to accept a payment which may or may not fully reimburse him for his outlays? . . .

Our doubts as to whether the statutes accomplish the purpose is reinforced by the fact that in many states, partly because of these statutes, real estate financing is almost exclusively secured by trust deeds with power of sale. This is certainly true in California, and the statutory right of redemption does not apply to such sales. Py v. Pleitner, 1945, 70 Cal. App. 2d 576, 161 P.2d 393; Roberts v. True, 1908, 7 Cal. App. 379, 94 P. 392. See also, as to Idaho, n. 5, supra. One is tempted to inquire why, if public policy so strongly favors a post-sale period of redemption, the legislature has not applied it to sales under trust deeds? Perhaps it is because the redemption statute has, in some states, made the use of mortgages almost a dead letter.

Moreover, the policy of FHA is to bid the fair market value at the foreclosure sale. For this purpose, it has the property carefully appraised before bidding. . . .

It is also suggested that a purpose of the redemption statutes is to protect junior lienors. Perhaps. But if the objective of the statutes is to obtain bids equal to market value, and if as is argued, the bidding would be lower in the absence of the statutes, then junior lienors could more easily protect themselves in the latter situation. They could buy the property at the sale for less. It is always open to the junior lienors to protect themselves by bidding. . . .

That portion of the judgment providing for a right and period of redemption is reversed and the matter is remanded to the district court with directions to modify the judgment in a manner consistent with this opinion.

ELY, Circuit Judge (dissenting):

. . . The harshness of strict foreclosure led to the concept of foreclosure by sale. Theoretically, the property was to be sold to the highest bidder with the mortgagee having first claim to the proceeds. . . . Unfortunately, this expectation was frustrated by reason of the immense advantages favoring the mortgagee at the sale. First, it was unnecessary for the mortgagee to raise and expend any cash up to the amount of the unpaid debt. Secondly, there would not often be an interested outside buyer, or junior lienholder with cash, at the precise time of

---

advantageous sale which will reimburse the insurance fund for a portion of the loss incurred as a result of the mortgagor's default.'

the sale. Thus, the senior mortgagee was assured of being almost always the only bidder at the sale. The junior lienors, in particular, suffered under this method since their interests were cut off by the judicial sale. Since they had no weapons with which to force the sale price above the amount of the senior's claim, they often realized nothing on their claims.

The response of many jurisdictions to the unsatisfactory results of the foreclosure-by-sale procedure was the adoption of a statutory redemption period. . . .

The key to understanding the statutory redemption right lies in the proposition that the statute's operation is in the nature of a threat. When redemption is exercised, it is thereby evidenced that the mortgagee has not bid adequately at the sale and the statute has not had its intended effect. On the other hand, if the threat functions successfully and the mortgagee does bid adequately, then the mortgagor and junior lienors, if any, will have been satisfied to the full value of the property and there will be no reason for exercising the redemption right. If he bids the full market value of the property, then the mortgagee may rest secure in the knowledge that it will not be redeemed. . . .

It seems no less clear to me that, disregarding the question of protection of the individual mortgagor, the goals of *any* federal housing program could not be served by the majority's decision. From the viewpoint of a mortgagor in a state with redemption provisions, and in the light of the majority's decision, it would be more desirable to finance privately than to finance through an FHA guaranteed mortgage. Even more important, potential junior lienors, such as contractors and suppliers, will be less willing to extend credit under these circumstances. Nor can junior lienors protect themselves, as the majority suggests, by bidding at the foreclosure sale. I have already explained that one reason for the existence of the redemption statutes is that the enormous leverage of the foreclosing mortgagee is not matched by junior lienors, who typically have very small cash reserves and never have the first "paid up" interest.

Thus one effect of the majority's decision will be to lower the attractiveness of FHA financing in states that have enacted redemption statutes. . . .

The Government, and also the majority, make several arguments designed to show that redemption statutes are neither important nor necessary. The first is that the statutes do not work because no third party will bid at the sale, knowing that he will be subject to redemption. The statutes, as I have tried to explain, are not the least bit concerned with the actions of third parties since they were necessitated by the observation that third parties do not ordinarily bid at foreclosure sales in any event. Instead of trying to stimulate bidding at the sale, they set up the more realistic possibility that the property will be redeemed if the mortgagee's bid is inadequate. . . .

The Government argues at one point that the policies of the redemption right are satisfied by the alleged practice of the FHA carefully to appraise the fair market value of the property and to make its bid accordingly at the foreclosure sale. . . .

[S]uch unilateral action of the FHA could not satisfy the premise of the redemption statutes. That premise is that the fair market value is realizable only through the interplay of competing economic forces. This premise is not satisfied by judicial sale because of the demonstrated falsity of the assumption, made by the majority, that a third party will come in to force the price up to market value at the sale. . . .

NOTES AND QUESTIONS

1. *The Effectiveness of Statutory Redemption Rights.* The *Stadium Apartments* court raises some disturbing questions about the effectiveness of statutes granting the borrower and others a right to redeem property after the foreclosure sale. What are these questions, and how does Judge Ely answer them in his dissent?

In discussing the effect of rights of redemption in protecting junior interests cut off in foreclosure, Judge Ely states that since the junior interest-holders "had no weapons with which to force the sale price above the amount of the senior's claim, they often realized nothing on their claims." The proceeds of a sale will go to pay off the first mortgagee before a junior encumbrancer is paid and, unless the bid exceeds the senior interest, the junior interest-holder will realize nothing. Is Judge Ely correct in stating that the junior interest-holder has no way to protect itself?

Assume your client holds a second mortgage of $5 million on Dan Developer's property. Ace's first mortgage, with an unpaid balance of $15 million, is in default, and Ace has commenced foreclosure. Your client's appraisers conclude that Dan's property is worth $19 million. What "weapon" would you have at the foreclosure sale, and how would you use it? If your appraisers had concluded that Dan's property was worth only $14 million, what would you do? Is Judge Ely's concern based on his presumption that junior lienors have limited funds and may be unable to bid enough to satisfy the prior lien? Even if the presumption were correct, isn't this problem inherent in the subordinate position the junior lienor bargained for?

2. *The Sufficiency of Borrower Protection Provisions.* Notwithstanding the litany of protections afforded by statute or by the courts for the protection of the borrower, unfair prices are sometimes still obtained at foreclosure sales. In many such situations the inequity may have resulted from the relative lack of sophistication of the borrower with a resulting underutilization of the marketplace and of the statutory

protections available. Does this suggest that different foreclosure rules should apply to one-family residential properties, as distinguished from commercial properties? If you were asked to draft a model foreclosure statute designed to protect the consumer borrower without making mortgage financing unattractive to lenders, what protective provisions would you incorporate? If judicial review of foreclosure price were to be one of these provisions, are the standards set forth in Ballentyne v. Smith satisfactory? Review Chapter 10C3a, note 1. What approach does the ULSIA take to protect the consumer?

3. Additional Reading. Report, Committee on Mortgage Law and Practice, Cost and Time Factors in Foreclosure of Mortgages, 3 Real Prop., Prob. & Tr. J. 413 (1968); Doyle, The Effect of Bankruptcy on a Statutory Redemption Period, 17 Creighton L. Rev. 1251 (1983-1984); Durfee and Dodridge, Redemption from Foreclosure Sale — The Uniform Mortgage Act, 23 Mich. L. Rev. 825 (1925); Skilton, Mortgage Moratoria Since 1933, 92 U. Pa. L. Rev. 53 (1943); Comment, Statutory Redemption: The Enemy of Home Financing, 28 Wash. L. Rev. 39 (1953); Comment, "Depression Jurisprudence" — Remaining Effects in Statutory Law, 47 Mich. L. Rev. 254 (1948); Note, Effect of Satisfying a Junior Lien on Statutory Right of Redemption, 15 Wyo. L.J. 223 (1961); Note, Redemption from Judicial Sales: A Study of the Illinois Statute, 5 U. Chi. L. Rev. 625 (1938).

4. Constitutional Attacks on Power-of-Sale Foreclosures

Under the Fifth and Fourteenth Amendments to the United States Constitution, neither Congress nor the states may deprive a person of life, liberty, or property without due process of law. "Due process" includes notice and an opportunity for a hearing. In a foreclosure, property of the debtor is transferred to the purchaser at the sale. Where the sale is conducted under a power of sale and not by virtue of a judicial proceeding, the question has been raised whether the procedure provides notice and opportunity for a hearing sufficient to pass constitutional muster.

In Mullane v. Central Hanover Bank & Trust Co.[14] and Mennonite Board of Missions v. Adams[15] the Supreme Court was called on to determine what kind of notice was required by the Fifth and Fourteenth Amendments and concluded that the form of notice must be reasonably

14. 339 U.S. 306 (1950).
15. 462 U.S. 791 (1983).

calculated to apprise affected parties. Thus, notice by publication and posting was insufficient "[w]here the names and post office addresses of those affected by a proceeding are at hand. . . ."[16] In *Mennonite,* the Supreme Court struck down a tax sale against a mortgagee identified in a publicly recorded mortgage where the only notice given was constructive notice by publication, stating that "unless the mortgagee is not reasonably identifiable, constructive notice alone does not satisfy the mandate of *Mullane.*"[17] In Sniadach v. Family Finance Corp.,[18] the Supreme Court held that a garnishment law violated the due process clause of the Fourteenth Amendment because it failed to provide for a judicial hearing prior to the garnishment. In Fuentes v. Shevin,[19] a state replevin statute was found to be unconstitutional for the same reasons, even though the property had been seized only temporarily.

While power-of-sale foreclosure procedures vary from state to state, there are some that seem not to meet the notice requirements of *Mullane* and *Mennonite* or the hearing requirements of *Sniadach* and *Fuentes.* One of the defenses raised to the unconstitutionality of power-of-sale foreclosure in those states is that the Fifth Amendment limits federal action and the Fourteenth Amendment limits state action, and neither is involved in a power-of-sale foreclosure. This question is dealt with by the Court in connection with a warehouseman's lien in the *Flagg Bros.* case.

Flagg Bros., Inc. v. Brooks
436 U.S. 149 (1978)

MR. JUSTICE REHNQUIST delivered the opinion of the Court.

The question presented by this litigation is whether a warehouse-

---

16. 339 U.S. at 318.
17. 462 U.S. at 798.
18. 395 U.S. 337 (1969).
19. 407 U.S. 56 (1972), reh. denied, 409 U.S. 902 (1972), superseded by Mo. statute as stated in Union State Bank v. Dolan, 718 S.W.2d 522 (Mo. App. 1986). The effect of the *Sniadach* and *Fuentes* holdings was limited somewhat by the Supreme Court in Mitchell v. W. T. Grant Co., 416 U.S. 600 (1974), where it upheld the constitutionality of a Louisiana sequestration statute that did not provide an opportunity for a *prior* hearing. However, in later striking down a Georgia prejudgment garnishment statute that did not provide for a prior hearing, the Supreme Court, in North Georgia Finishing, Inc. v. Di-Chem, Inc., 419 U.S. 601 (1975), distinguished *Mitchell* on the ground that the Louisiana statute provided that only a judge could issue the writ based on a verified complaint setting forth the specific facts supporting the petition and in addition provided for an immediate right to a hearing after sequestration, while under the Georgia statute the writ was issued by a clerk on an affidavit stating only conclusory and nonspecific supporting grounds for its issuance, and there was no provision for an immediate hearing after the writ was issued.

man's proposed sale of goods entrusted to him for storage, as permitted by New York Uniform Commercial Code §7-210 (McKinney 1964), in an action properly attributable to the State of New York. The District Court found that the warehouseman's conduct was not that of the State, and dismissed this suit for want of jurisdiction under 28 U.S.C. §1343(3). 404 F. Supp. 1059 (S.D.N.Y. 1975). The Court of Appeals for the Second Circuit, in reversing the judgment of the District Court, found sufficient state involvement with the proposed sale to invoke the provisions of the Due Process Clause of the Fourteenth Amendment. 553 F.2d 764 (1977). We agree with the District Court, and we therefore reverse.

According to her complaint, the allegations of which we must accept as true, respondent Shirley Brooks and her family were evicted from their apartment in Mount Vernon, N.Y., on June 13, 1973. The city marshal arranged for Brooks' possessions to be stored by petitioner Flagg Brothers, Inc., in its warehouse. Brooks was informed of the cost of moving and storage, and she instructed the workmen to proceed, although she found the price too high. On August 25, 1973, after a series of disputes over the validity of the charges being claimed by petitioner Flagg Brothers, Brooks received a letter demanding that her account be brought up to date within 10 days "or your furniture will be sold." App. 13a. A series of subsequent letters from respondent and her attorneys produced no satisfaction.

Brooks thereupon initiated this class action in the District Court under 42 U.S.C. §1983, seeking damages, an injunction against the threatened sale of her belongings, and the declaration that such a sale pursuant to §7-210 would violate the Due Process and Equal Protection Clauses of the Fourteenth Amendment. She was later joined in her action by Gloria Jones, another resident of Mount Vernon whose goods had been stored by Flagg Brothers following her eviction. . . .

On July 7, 1975, the District Court, relying primarily on our decision in Jackson v. Metropolitan Edison Co., 419 U.S. 345 (1974), dismissed the complaint for failure to state a claim for relief under §1983.

A divided panel of the Court of Appeals reversed. The majority noted that *Jackson* had suggested that state action might be found in the exercise by a private party of " 'some power delegated to it by the State which is traditionally associated with sovereignty.' " 553 F.2d, at 770, quoting 419 U.S., at 353. The majority found:

> [B]y enacting §7-210, New York not only delegated to the warehouseman a portion of its sovereign monopoly power over binding conflict resolution [citations omitted], but also let him, by selling stored goods, execute a lien and thus perform a function which has traditionally been that of the sheriff. 553 F.2d, at 771.

The court, although recognizing that the Court of Appeals for the Ninth Circuit had reached a contrary conclusion in dealing with an identical California statute in Melara v. Kennedy, 541 F.2d 802 (1976), concluded that this delegation of power constituted sufficient state action to support federal jurisdiction under 28 U.S.C. §1343(3). The dissenting judge found the reasoning of *Melara* persuasive.

We granted certiorari, 434 U.S. 817, to resolve the conflict over this provision of the Uniform Commercial Code, in effect in 49 States and the District of Columbia, and to address the important question it presents concerning the meaning of "state action" as that term is associated with the Fourteenth Amendment. . . .

Here, respondents allege that Flagg Brothers has deprived them of their rights, secured by the Fourteenth Amendment, to be free from state deprivations of property without due process of law. Thus, they must establish not only that Flagg Brothers acted under color of the challenged statute, but also that its actions are properly attributable to the State of New York. . . .

Respondents' primary contention is that New York has delegated to Flagg Brothers a power "traditionally exclusively reserved to the State." *Jackson,* supra, at 352. They argue that the resolution of private disputes is a traditional function of civil government, and that the State in §7-210 has delegated this function to Flagg Brothers. Respondents, however, have read too much into the language of our previous cases. While many functions have been traditionally performed by governments, very few have been "exclusively reserved to the State." . . .

Whatever the particular remedies available under New York law, we do not consider a more detailed description of them necessary to our conclusion that the settlement of disputes between debtors and creditors is not traditionally an exclusive public function. . . .

Thus, even if we were inclined to extend the sovereign-function doctrine outside of its present carefully confined bounds, the field of private commercial transactions would be a particularly inappropriate area into which to expand it. We conclude that our sovereign-function cases do not support a finding of state action here. . . .

Respondents further urge that Flagg Brothers' proposed action is properly attributable to the State because the State has authorized and encouraged it in enacting §7-210. Our cases state "that a State is responsible for the . . . act of a private party when the State, by its law, has compelled the act." *Adickes,* 308 U.S., at 170. This Court, however, has never held that a State's mere acquiescence in a private action converts that action into that of the State. The Court rejected a similar argument in *Jackson,* 419 U.S., at 357:

> Approval by a state utility commission of such a request from a regulated utility, where the commission has not put its own weight on the side

of the proposed practice *by ordering it,* does not transmute a practice initiated by the utility and approved by the commission into 'state action.' (Emphasis added.)

The clearest demonstration of this distinction appears in Moose Lodge No. 107 v. Irvis, 407 U.S. 163 (1972), which held that the Commonwealth of Pennsylvania, although not responsible for racial discrimination voluntarily practiced by a private club, could not by law require the club to comply with its own discriminatory rules. These cases clearly rejected the notion that our prior cases permitted the imposition of Fourteenth Amendment restraints on private action by the simple device of characterizing the State's inaction as "authorization" or "encouragement." See id., at 190 (BRENNAN, J., dissenting). . . . If the mere denial of judicial relief is considered sufficient encouragement to make the State responsible for those private acts, all private deprivations of property would be converted into public acts whenever the State, for whatever reason, denies relief sought by the putative property owner.

Not only is this notion completely contrary to that "essential dichotomy," *Jackson,* supra, at 349, between public and private acts, but it has been previously rejected by this Court. In Evans v. Abney, 396 U.S. 435, 458 (1970), our Brother BRENNAN in dissent contended that a Georgia statutory provision authorizing the establishment of trusts for racially restricted parks conferred a "special power" on testators taking advantage of the provision. The Court nevertheless concluded that the State of Georgia was in no way responsible for the purely private choice involved in that case. By the same token, the State of New York is in no way responsible for Flagg Brothers' decision, a decision which the State in §7-210 permits but does not compel, to threaten to sell these respondents' belongings.

Here, the State of New York has not compelled the sale of a bailor's goods, but has merely announced the circumstances under which its courts will not interfere with a private sale. Indeed, the crux of respondents' complaint is not that the State *has* acted, but that it has *refused* to act. This statutory refusal to act is no different in principle from an ordinary statute of limitations whereby the State declines to provide a remedy for private deprivations of property after the passage of a given period of time.

We conclude that the allegations of these complaints do not establish a violation of these respondents' Fourteenth Amendment rights by either petitioner Flagg Brothers or the State of New York. The District Court properly concluded that their complaints failed to state a claim for relief under 42 U.S.C. §1983. The judgment of the Court of Appeals holding otherwise is reversed.

MR. JUSTICE MARSHALL, dissenting.

Although I join my Brother STEVENS' dissenting opinion, I write separately to emphasize certain aspects of the majority opinion that I find particularly disturbing.

I cannot remain silent as the Court demonstrates, not for the first time, an attitude of callous indifference to the realities of life for the poor. See, e.g., Beal v. Doe, 432 U.S. 438, 455-457 (1977) (MARSHALL J., dissenting); United States v. Kras, 409 U.S. 434, 458-460 (1973) (MARSHALL, J., dissenting). It blandly asserts that "respondent Jones . . . could have sought to replevy her goods at any time under state law." Ante, at 160. In order to obtain replevin in New York, however, respondent Jones would first have had to present to a sheriff an "undertaking" from a surety by which the latter would be bound to pay "not less than twice the value" of the goods involved and perhaps substantially more, depending in part on the size of the potential judgment against the debtor. N.Y. Civ. Prac. Law §7102(e) (McKinney Supp. 1977). Sureties do not provide such bonds without receiving both a substantial payment in advance and some assurance of the debtor's ability to pay any judgment awarded.

Respondent Jones, according to her complaint, took home $87 per week from her job, had been evicted from her apartment, and faced a potential liability to the warehouseman of at least $335, an amount she could not afford. App. 44a-46a. The Court's assumption that respondent would have been able to obtain a bond, and thus secure return of her household goods, must under the circumstances be regarded as highly questionable. While the Court is technically correct that respondent "could have sought" replevin, it is also true that, given adequate funds, respondent could have paid her rent and remained in her apartment, thereby avoiding eviction and the seizure of her household goods by the warehouseman. But we cannot close our eyes to the realities that led to this litigation. Just as respondent lacked the funds to prevent eviction, it seems clear that, once her goods were seized, she had no practical choice but to leave them with the warehouseman, where they were subject to forced sale for nonpayment of storage charges. . . .

MR. JUSTICE STEVENS, with whom MR. JUSTICE WHITE and MR. JUSTICE MARSHALL join, dissenting. . . .

There is no question in this case but that respondents have a property interest in the possessions that the warehouseman proposes to sell. It is also clear that, whatever power of sale the warehouseman has, it does not derive from the consent of the respondents. The claimed power derives solely from the State, and specifically from §7-210 of the New York Uniform Commercial Code. The question is whether a state statute which authorizes a private party to deprive a person of his property without his consent must meet the requirements of the Due Process Clause of the Fourteenth Amendment. This question must be answered in the affirmative unless the State has virtually unlimited power to transfer interests in private property without any procedural protections. . . .

While Members of this Court have suggested that statutory authorization alone may be sufficient to establish state action, it is not necessary to rely on those suggestions in this case because New York has authorized the warehouseman to perform what is clearly a state function. The test of what is a state function for purposes of the Due Process Clause has been variously phrased. Most frequently the issue is presented in terms of whether the State has delegated a function traditionally and historically associated with sovereignty. See, e.g., Jackson v. Metropolitan Edison Co., 419 U.S. 345, 353; Evans v. Newton, 382 U.S. 296, 299. In this Court, petitioners have attempted to argue that the nonconsensual transfer of property rights is not a traditional function of the sovereign. The overwhelming historical evidence is to the contrary, however, and the Court wisely does not adopt this position. Instead, the Court reasons that state action cannot be found because the State has not delegated to the warehouseman an *exclusive* sovereign function. This distinction, however, is not consistent with our prior decisions on state action; is not even adhered to by the Court in this case; and, most importantly, is inconsistent with the line of cases beginning with Sniadach v. Family Finance Corp., 395 U.S. 337. . . .

NOTES AND QUESTIONS

1. *Flagging State Action.* Three arguments were presented in *Flagg Bros.* to contend that state action was involved. The first involved direct state action, such as that found in *Fuentes,* where state agents seized the property under a state replevin statute. The court rejected this argument because U.C.C. §7-210 provides for a private sale of goods to enforce a warehouseman's lien and, unlike *Fuentes,* there were no public officials involved in the sale. This is normally true in a power-of-sale situation as well. Prior to the *Flagg Bros.* decision the U.S. District Court in North Carolina (Turner v. Blackburn, 389 F. Supp. 1250 (W.D.N.C. 1975)) had struck down a North Carolina power-of-sale foreclosure, finding direct state action because the North Carolina statute interposed the clerk of the court in the proceeding, requiring a report to be filed with and approved or disapproved by the clerk as a precondition to the power to convey the property pursuant to the sale. How valid is that holding after *Flagg*?

The second argument was that the state shared in the deprivation of property because the statute encouraged the private activity. What was the Court's answer to this argument? The third argument was that it is state action when a private person is performing an essentially governmental function. The Court rejected this argument on the ground that foreclosure of liens has not traditionally been an exclusively governmental function. What are Justice Stevens's answers to these arguments? Consider Justice Marshall's dissent. Is he saying that unconstitutionality may depend on the financial ability of a party to protect his or her property under law? For Justice Marshall, would a state power-of-sale foreclosure statute providing for notice and an opportunity for a pre-sale hearing nevertheless be unconstitutional if it didn't provide for free legal assistance and a waiver of court costs for those who can't afford either or both? Should there be a distinction between deprivations of property and deprivations of life or liberty in the strictness of constitutional requirements? Cf. Gideon v. Wainwright, 372 U.S. 335 (1963).

There are other theories of state action. One is that state action is involved where a state judicially enforces private parties' rights. This harkens back to Shelly v. Kraemer, 334 U.S. 1 (1948), where state action was found when the state specifically enforced a racially restrictive covenant. (See also Moose Lodge v. Irvis, 407 U.S. 163 (1972), discussed in the *Flagg Bros.* opinion). Consider the effect this argument could have. What if, after a completely private power-of-sale foreclosure, the borrower refuses to leave the premises? Would the consequent ejectment procedure constitute state action?

Another theory is that where the state pervasively regulates the activity of the private individual, the action may be treated as that of the state itself. In connection with power-of-sale foreclosures, state statutes specify the form of the sale and the protection that must be afforded parties with interests in the property. This theory was rejected with respect to a Texas power-of-sale statute in Barrera v. Security Building & Investment Corp., 519 F.2d 1166 (5th Cir. 1975).

2. *The Irony of "State Action."*   Earlier we examined the origins of mortgage law as a conveyance from the borrower to the lender with title vesting indefeasibly in the lender on the borrower's default, without notice or a hearing. We saw that mortgage foreclosure law developed to limit the ability of the lender to take property. The sale itself was substituted for strict foreclosure in order to protect the borrower. Review the California power-of-sale statute at Chapter 10C2, supra. To what extent does it involve limitations or controls on the lender's conduct of the sale? The same is true of §7-210 of the Uniform Commercial Code, the relevant provision in the *Flagg Bros.* decision. Should a statute designed to limit private action in order to protect the party affected by that action be the basis for finding state action that would make the otherwise constitutional private action unconstitutional? Is it reasonable to look to the purposes of the state involvement to determine whether it constitutes state action?

3. *Federal Action.* Where a foreclosing lender is an instrumentality of the federal government, the requirement of due process in the Fifth Amendment clearly applies, and state action is not an issue. See, e.g., Johnson v. United States Department of Agriculture, 734 F.2d 774 (11th Cir. 1984) and Ricker v. United States, 417 F. Supp. 133 (D. Me. 1976) and 434 F. Supp. 1251 (D. Me. 1976). Can you make an argument that this reasoning should not apply to mortgages made by others and assigned to a governmental agency such as the FHA, acquired in the takeover of a banking institution by the federal regulatory authority, or acquired by the Government National Mortgage Association (GNMA), a corporation wholly owned by the federal government that acquires mortgages on the secondary market? (See Warren v. Government National Mortgage Assn., 611 F.2d 1229 (8th Cir. 1980), cert. denied, 449 U.S. 847 (1980).) If GNMA foreclosure is federal action, what about actions of a quasi-governmental organization such as the Federal National Mortgage Association? Considering the trend toward securitization of mortgages and the involvement of the federal government in same, might reliance on lack of state action turn out to be a trap for lenders, title companies, and purchasers at foreclosure sales? Shouldn't states be considering methods by which their power-of-sale foreclosure statutes can be amended to meet constitutional requirements? If you were engaged to draft amendments to California's statute (excerpted above), what additions would you make?

4. *Additional Reading.* G. Nelson and D. Whitman, Real Estate Finance Law, §§7.23 to 7.30 (2d lawyers ed. 1985); Barklage, Extra-Judicial Mortgage Foreclosure Not State Action, 41 Mo. L. Rev. 278 (1976); Jones and Ivens, Power of Sale Foreclosure in Tennessee: A Section 1983 Trap, 51 Tenn. L. Rev. 279 (1984); Leen, Galbraith, and Grant, Due Process and Deeds of Trust — Strange Bedfellows, 48 Wash. L. Rev. 763 (1973); Nelson, Deed of Trust Foreclosures Under Power of Sale — Constitutional Problems — Legislative Alternatives, 28 J. Mo. B. 428 (1972); Pedowitz, Current Developments in Summary Foreclosure, 98 Real Prop., Prob. & Tr. J. 421 (1974); Comment, The Constitutionality of Maine's Real Estate Mortgage Foreclosure Statutes, 32 Maine L. Rev. 147 (1980); Comment, Due Process Problems of Mississippi Power of Sale Foreclosure, 47 Miss. L.J. 67 (1976); Comment, The Constitutionality of California Trustees Sale, 61 Calif. L. Rev. 1282 (1973); Comment, Notice Requirements of the Nonjudicial Foreclosure Sale, 51 N.C. L. Rev. 1110 (1973); Comment, Power of Sale Foreclosures After *Fuentes,* 40 U. Chi. L. Rev. 206 (1972).

5.   Mortgage Foreclosures as Fraudulent Transfers

Assume that Dan Developer owns a parcel of property outside the State of Fuller and that he has suffered financial reverses. Concerned that creditors may obtain judgments and a levy on his property, Dan executes a mortgage in favor of his brother-in-law that is recorded against the property. When the creditors start closing in, Dan deliberately defaults under the mortgage. His brother-in-law forecloses, buys the property in at the foreclosure sale for the mortgage balance, and transfers the property to a corporation of which Dan Developer is president.[20] Can Dan Developer get away with this? Can he successfully put his property out of the reach of his creditors? The answer, of course, is a resounding no. Ever since 1570, when England first codified the developing law of fraudulent conveyances in what was to become known as the Statute of 13 Elizabeth,[21] any transfer of property with the intent to "delay, hinder, or defraud creditors and others," whether a foreclosure sale or any other transfer, was void.

The Statute of 13 Elizabeth has served as a model ever since for English and American fraudulent conveyance laws. Beginning in 1800 with the first bankruptcy law of the United States,[22] language with origins in the Statute of 13 Elizabeth was incorporated into the avoidance provisions of each bankruptcy statute. It is now found in §548 of the Bankruptcy Code as well as in state statutes.

Returning to the master hypothetical, assume Ace makes its mortgage when Dan is prosperous. Some years later, Dan suffers financial adversity and defaults on the payment of the debt service (principal and interest) under the mortgage. Ace forecloses and is the successful bidder at the foreclosure sale, having bid the mortgage balance of $15 million. There is no collusion in connection with this sale, which is conducted in accordance with the law of the State of Fuller, where the property is located. The next year Dan files in bankruptcy. Dan's trustee claims that the true value of Dan's property at the time of the foreclosure sale was $22 million and that the foreclosure sale was a fraudulent transfer. Can the trustee succeed?

In 1980, the Fifth Circuit, in Durrett v. Washington National

---

20. Cf. Lefkowitz v. Finkelstein Trading Corp., 74 F. Supp. 898 (S.D.N.Y. 1936).

21. 13 Eliz. ch. 5 §I-II (1570). The statute provided in part that "covinous and fraudulent feoffments, gifts, grants, alienations, conveyances, bonds, suits, judgments and executions . . . devised and contrived of malice, fraud, covin, collusion or guile, to the end, purpose and intent, to delay, hinder or defraud creditors and others . . . shall be . . . utterly void, frustrate and of none effect." See D. Epstein and J. Landers, Debtors and Creditors 134 (1978) and O. Bump and J. Gray, A Treatise Upon Conveyances Made by Debtors to Defraud Creditors 8 (4th ed. 1898).

22. Bankruptcy Act of 1800, ch. 19, §17.

Insurance Co., excerpted below, for the first time[23] held that a *non-collusive,* regularly conducted foreclosure sale was subject to being set aside as a constructively fraudulent conveyance where a court determined that the price paid at the foreclosure sale was less than reasonably equivalent to the value of the property and that the debtor was insolvent. This case has stirred up a great controversy. Concerns have been raised that *Durrett* and the cases that have followed it and expanded its impact not only could threaten the future of mortgage financing but, if left to develop unchecked, could have a substantial negative impact on all forms of secured financing and leasehold transactions. (For example, courts have argued that since the termination of a lease on the tenant's default constitutes a reconveyance of the leasehold estate from the tenant to the landlord, fraudulent transfer law is applicable.) Others find that *Durrett* is "properly sensitive to the policy underlying §548."[24] As you read these materials, consider which position you support.

The original Statute of 13 Elizabeth dealt only with transactions *intended* to hinder, delay, or defraud creditors; it made no mention of "constructive" fraud. It did not take long after the enactment of the statute, however, for the courts to realize that transferors and transferees intending to commit fraud do not normally publicize their intent. Thus it became necessary, in order to implement fraudulent conveyance laws, to look to the circumstances surrounding the transfer to see if the necessary intent existed. In Twyne's Case,[25] Lord Coke recognized "signs or marks," later known as "badges," of fraud, that is, conduct or circumstances that could be evidence of fraudulent intent. Examples of badges of fraud are transfers of all of the debtor's property, transfers without a change of possession, a close relationship between transferor and transferee, insolvency at the time of transfer, and inadequate consideration received in exchange for the property transferred. When a sufficient number of badges of fraud was found to exist, the courts would find a presumption of fraud.

The problem was that each court recognized its own presumptions

23. This view is not unanimous. Professor Frank Kennedy has argued that "the 'Durrett doctrine' is not so novel" as its critics claim. See Kennedy, Involuntary Fraudulent Transfers, 9 Cardozo L. Rev. 531, 532 (1987). His conclusions are disputed in Zinman, Noncollusive, Regularly Conducted Foreclosure Sales: Involuntary Nonfraudulent Transfers, 9 Cardozo L. Rev. 581, 584 (1987). See Jackson, Avoiding Powers in Bankruptcy, 36 Stan. L. Rev. 725, 777-786 (1984); McCoid, Constructively Fraudulent Conveyances: Transfers for Inadequate Consideration, 62 Tex. L. Rev. 639 (1983).

24. Alden, Gross, and Borowitz, Real Property Foreclosure as a Fraudulent Conveyance: Proposals for Solving the *Durrett* Problem, 38 Bus. Law. 1605, 1610 (1983). Some of the negative effects of *Durrett* are discussed in Zinman, Houle, and Weiss, Fraudulent Transfers According to Alden, Gross, and Borowitz: A Tale of Two Circuits, 39 Bus. Law. 977 (1984).

25. 3 Coke 80b, 76 Eng. Rep. 809 (1601).

of fraud based on its own list of badges of fraud. As the use of badges and presumptions increased, the application of fraudulent transfer law became less uniform and there appeared to be a trend by creditors to try to strike down all conveyances that harmed creditors, whether or not actual fraud was present. In light of this, when the National Conference of Commissioners on Uniform State Laws drafted the Uniform Fraudulent Conveyance Act (approved in 1918), they eliminated all badges and presumptions of fraud and in their place created constructive frauds by grouping together certain of the former badges into a few specific sections of the Act. When the circumstances outlined in these sections were present, constructive fraud was found without a determination of the actual intent of the parties. The constructive fraud that is the basis of the *Durrett* rule is now found in §548(a)(2) of the Bankruptcy Code, which proscribes any transfer by an insolvent debtor within the year prior to bankruptcy for less than a reasonably equivalent value.[26]

In the 400 years since the Statute of 13 Elizabeth, the over 380 years since Twyne's Case first listed badges of fraud, and the 65 years since constructive fraud was substituted for badges and presumptions of fraud, the authors have been able to locate no case that ever applied fraudulent conveyance law to noncollusive, regularly conducted foreclosure sales, until *Durrett*. Why, do you think, should this be so?[27] As we have described the evolution of fraudulent conveyance law, was there any indication of a design to deviate from the primary purpose of ferreting out transfers made with intent to injure creditors?

A *Durrett* attack can also be made under state law absent bankruptcy, and it is possible that at least some of the support for *Durrett* comes from those who see the rule as a method of attacking collaterally the state foreclosure laws that have been discussed in this section. The pertinent provisions of the Bankruptcy Code are set forth below.

Bankruptcy Code
38 U.S.C. §§548, 550, 101(54), 544(b) (1982)

§548. Fraudulent transfers and obligations.

(a) The trustee may avoid any transfer of an interest of the debtor in property, or any obligation incurred by the debtor, that was made or incurred on or within one year before the date of the filing of the petition, if the debtor voluntarily or involuntarily —

---

26. For a fuller discussion of the origin and development of fraudulent conveyance law see Zinman, Houle, and Weiss, supra note 24, at 986-995.

27. See footnote 23, supra.

(1) made such transfer or incurred such obligation with actual intent to hinder, delay, or defraud any entity to which the debtor was or became, on or after the date that such transfer was made or such obligation was incurred, indebted; or

(2)(A) received less than a reasonably equivalent value in exchange for such transfer or obligation; and

(B)(i) was insolvent on the date that such transfer was made or such obligation was incurred, or became insolvent as a result of such transfer or obligation;

(ii) was engaged in business or a transaction, or was about to engage in business or a transaction, for which any property remaining with the debtor was an unreasonably small capital; or

(iii) intended to incur, or believed that the debtor would incur, debts that would be beyond the debtor's ability to pay as such debts matured.

(b) The trustee of a partnership debtor may avoid any transfer of an interest of the debtor in property, or any obligation incurred by the debtor, that was made or incurred on or within one year before the date of the filing of the petition, to a general partner in the debtor, if the debtor was insolvent on the date such transfer was made or such obligation was incurred, or became insolvent as a result of such transfer or obligation.

(c) Except to the extent that a transfer or obligation voidable under this section is voidable under section 544, 545, or 547 of this title, a transferee or obligee of such a transfer or obligation that takes for value and in good faith has a lien on or may retain any interest transferred, or may enforce any obligation incurred, as the case may be, to the extent that such transferee or obligee gave value to the debtor in exchange for such transfer or obligation.

(d)(1) For the purposes of this section, a transfer is made when such transfer is so perfected that a bona fide purchaser from the debtor against whom applicable law permits such transfer to be perfected cannot acquire an interest in the property transferred that is superior to the interest in such property of the transferee, but if such transfer is not so perfected before the commencement of the case, such transfer is made immediately before the date of the filing of the petition.

(2) In this section —

(A) "value" means property, or satisfaction or securing of a present or antecedent debt of the debtor, but does not include an unperformed promise to furnish support to the debtor or to a relative of the debtor;

(B) a commodity broker, forward contract merchant, stockbroker, financial institution, or securities clearing agency that receives a margin payment, as defined in section 741(5) or 761(15) of this title, or settlement payment, as defined in section 741(8) of this title, takes for value to the extent of such payment; and

(C) a repo participant that receives a margin payment, as defined in section 741(5) or 761(15) of this title, or settlement payment, as defined in section 741(8) of this title, in connection with a repurchase agreement, takes for value to the extent of such payment.

§550. Liability of transferee of avoided transfer.

(a) Except as otherwise provided in this section, to the extent that a transfer is avoided under section 544, 545, 547, 548, 549, 553(b), or 724(a) of this title, the trustee may recover, for the benefit of the estate, the property transferred, or, if the court so orders, the value of such property, from —

(1) the initial transferee of such transfer or the entity for whose benefit such transfer was made; or

(2) any immediate or mediate transferee of such initial transferee.

(b) The trustee may not recover under subsection (a)(2) of this section from —

(1) a transferee that takes for value, including satisfaction or securing of a present or antecedent debt in good faith, and without knowledge of the voidability of the transfer avoided; or

(2) any immediate or mediate good faith transferee of such transferee.

(c) The trustee is entitled to only a single satisfaction under subsection (a) of this section.

(d)(1) A good faith transferee from whom the trustee may recover under subsection (a) of this section has a lien on the property recovered to secure the lesser of —

(A) the cost, to such transferee, of any improvement made after the transfer, less the amount of any profit realized by or accruing to such transferee from such property; and

(B) any increase in the value of such property as a result of such improvement, of the property transferred.

(2) In this subsection, "improvement" includes —

(A) physical additions or changes to the property transferred;

(B) repairs to such property;

(C) payment of any tax on such property;

(D) payment of any debt secured by a lien on such property that is superior or equal to the rights of the trustee; and

(E) preservation of such property.

(e) An action or proceeding under this section may not be commenced after the earlier of —

(1) one year after the avoidance of the transfer on account of which recovery under this section is sought; or

(2) the time the case is closed or dismissed.

§101. Definitions in This Title — . . .

(54) "transfer" means every mode, direct or indirect, absolute or conditional, voluntary or involuntary, of disposing of or parting with property or with an interest in property, including retention of title as a security interest, and foreclosure of the debtor's equity of redemption; . . .

§544. Trustee as Lien Creditor and as Successor to Certain Creditors and Purchasers. . . .

(b) The trustee may avoid any transfer of an interest of the debtor in property or any obligation incurred by the debtor that is voidable under applicable law by a creditor holding an unsecured claim that is allowable under section 502 of this title or that is not allowable only under section 502(e) of this title.

Durrett was decided under the old Bankruptcy Act, but its holding is equally applicable under the Bankruptcy Code. Section 67(d) was the fraudulent transfer provision of the Bankruptcy Act and generally corresponds to §548 of the Code.

Durrett v. Washington National Insurance Co.
621 F.2d 201 (5th Cir. 1980)

ORMA R. SMITH, District Judge:

This appeal concerns an action instituted in the United States District Court for the Northern District of Texas, wherein plaintiff Jack W. Durrett, Sr. (herein "Durrett"), acting as debtor in possession under Chapter XI of the Bankruptcy Act, 11 U.S.C. §§701, et seq., seeks to set aside and vacate an alleged transfer of real property effectuated nine days prior to the filing of a Petition for an Arrangement under Chapter XI. Durrett charges that the transfer is voidable under section 67(d) of the Act, 11 U.S.C. §107(d). The district court held that the non-judicial sale involved in the litigation constituted a transfer within the meaning of section 67(d). However, the court determined that the amount paid by the purchaser at the sale conducted by a trustee in the foreclosure of a deed of trust executed by Durrett, the indebtedness which it secured being then in default, was a "fair" consideration and a "fair equivalent" within the meaning of section 67(d)(1), (e)(1) of the Act, 11 U.S.C. §107(d)(1), (e)(1). The court denied the relief sought by Durrett and he appeals. We reverse.

A review of the record on appeal reflects the following facts. On April 7, 1969, Durrett executed a note in the amount of $180,000.00 in favor of Southern Trust and Mortgage Company (hereafter "Southern"). The note was secured by a deed of trust upon the subject real property. Southern, on April 7, 1969, assigned the trust deed and note to defendant, The Washington National Insurance Company (hereafter "Washington"). Defendant J. H. Fields, Jr. (hereafter "Fields"), was named as the trustee in the deed of trust. The deed of trust contained a provision for a public sale of the real property thereby conveyed, in case of default in payment of the indebtedness.

On December 13, 1976, Fields, in his capacity of trustee, posted the property for foreclosure sale. The sale was held on January 4, 1977. Defendant Shannon Mitchell, Sr. (hereafter "Mitchell"), appeared at the sale and bid the sum of $115,400.00 for the property. This was the only bid received by the trustee at the sale. The amount of the bid was the exact amount necessary to liquidate the indebtedness secured by the deed of trust. Upon receipt of the bid price, Fields executed and delivered to Mitchell a trustee's deed to the property. The parties agree that Mitchell did not have any actual fraudulent intent when making the purchase. He responded to the notice of sale and became the successful bidder. Mitchell and Durrett are the only parties now interested in the case.

Durrett contends that the transfer of the property, pursuant to foreclosure of the deed of trust, is voidable under the provision of section 67(d).

The district court dismissed the complaint after a non-jury trial. In its findings of fact, the court held that the fair market value of the property on January 4, 1977, the date of the foreclosure sale, was the sum of $200,000.00.

The parties do not take issue with this finding. Both agree that it is not clearly erroneous. See, Rule 52(a), Fed. R. Civ. P.; Kentucky Fried Chicken Corp. v. Diversified Packaging Corp., 549 F.2d 368, 377 (5th Cir. 1977).

Durrett asserts, on appeal, only one assignment of error, i.e., "Is $115,400.00 payment for an asset worth $200,000.00, a 'fair equivalent' ". . . .

The question with which we are confronted is whether the district court's conclusion of law on the "fair equivalent" issue is incorrect, when considered in light of the record made in the district court and the applicable case law.

The parties have cited a number of cases which deal with this issue. A great percentage of these, however, involve factual situations quite different from the facts which exist in this appeal. Here, there is involved only one event, i.e., one parcel of real estate sold at a foreclosure sale for a price which is approximately 57.7 percent of the fair market value of the property. Is the price paid a "fair equivalent" for the transfer of the property? We hold that it is not. . . .

We have been unable to locate a decision of any district or appellate court dealing only with a transfer of real property as the subject of attack under section 67(d) of the Act, which has approved the transfer for less than 70 percent of the market value of the property. . . .

The defendant-appellee Mitchell seeks to sustain the final judgment of the district court on the ground that the transfer accomplished by the trustee pursuant to the power of sale provision of the deed of trust was not a transfer *made* by the debtor in possession within the contemplation of section 67(d). We find this position to be without merit. . . .

The comprehensive character of this definition [of "transfer"] leads us to conclude that the transfer of title to the real property of the debtor in possession pursuant to an arrangement under Chapter XI of the Act, by a trustee on foreclosure of a deed of trust, to a purchaser at the sale constitutes a "transfer" by debtor in possession within the purview of section 67(d). . . .

For the reasons herein given, the judgment of the district court must be vacated, and the cause reversed with directions. . . .

JUDGMENT VACATED; REMANDED WITH DIRECTIONS.

At this writing the circuits are hopelessly split on *Durrett*. One major problem is that many of the cases purporting to follow *Durrett* actually extend the application of the rule.

The National Conference of Commissioners on Uniform State Laws on August 2, 1984 adopted a new Uniform Fraudulent Transfer Act to replace its 1918 Uniform Fraudulent Conveyance Act.[28] The new UFTA contains the following language dealing with the *Durrett* rule.

Section 3(b)

For the purposes of Section 4(a)(2) and (5), a person gives a reasonably equivalent value if the person acquires an interest of the debtor in an asset pursuant to a regularly conducted, noncollusive foreclosure sale or execution of a power of sale for the acquisition or disposition of the interest of the debtor upon default under a mortgage, deed of trust or security agreement.

---

28. The UFTA has been adopted in 26 states as of this writing. 7A Unif. L. Ann. 133 (1991 Supp.).

Section 8(e)

A transfer is not voidable under Section 4(a)(2) or Section 5, if the transfer results from: (1) termination of a lease upon default by the debtor when the termination is pursuant to the lease and applicable law; or (2) enforcement of a security interest in compliance with Article 9 of the Uniform Commercial Code.

The Uniform Land Security Interest Act also abrogates the *Durrett* rule on the state level. See ULSIA §512(c), which provides that "[a] regularly conducted, noncollusive transfer under a power of sale (Section 509) or by judicial sale (Section 510) to a transferee who takes for value and in good faith is not a fraudulent transfer even though the value given is less than the value of the debtor's interest in the real estate." What condition does this language contain that is not found in UFTA §36, and what problem does it pose?

NOTES AND QUESTIONS

1. *The* Durrett *Holding and the Split in the Circuits.*   As a result of the *Durrett* decision, it has been said that only foreclosure sales for less than 70 percent of the court-determined value of the property are subject to attack as fraudulent transfers. Is this the holding in the case? What was the sale price-to-value ratio in *Durrett*? The purchaser in *Durrett* was a third party who saw notice of the foreclosure sale and bid the amount of the indebtedness. Was there any intent to delay, hinder, or defraud creditors involved? What part of §548 was the court applying?

At this writing, the jury is still out, so to speak, on *Durrett.* Those circuits that have spoken are in conflict. Three circuits have held that noncollusive, regularly conducted foreclosure sales may be set aside as fraudulent transfers where the price paid was less than reasonably equivalent to the value of the property (we refer to these as pro-*Durrett*) — the Fifth Circuit (*Durrett* and Abramson v. Lakewood Bank & Trust Co., 647 F.2d 547 (5th Cir. 1981), cert. denied, 454 U.S. 1164 (1982)); the Eighth Circuit (In re Hulm, 738 F.2d 323 (8th Cir. 1984), cert. denied, 469 U.S. 990 (1984)); and the 7th Circuit (In re Bundles, 856 F.2d 815 (7th Cir. 1988)). The Eleventh Circuit, which was carved out of the Fifth Circuit after the decision in *Durrett,* has bound itself to the prior Fifth Circuit decisions (Bonner v. City of Prichard, 661 F.2d 1206 (11th Cir. 1981)) and thus can be considered a fourth *Durrett* circuit, at least until the issue comes before the Eleventh Circuit Court of Appeals.

Three circuits have rejected *Durrett;* however, they do so on two different grounds. The Sixth Circuit, in In re Winshall Settlor's Trust, 758 F.2d 1136 (6th Cir. 1985), rejected *Durrett* on the ground, inter alia, that a noncollusive foreclosure sale, by definition devoid of intent to commit fraud and therefore outside the scope of fraudulent transfer law, should be deemed to be for a reasonably equivalent value. This was the same ground on which *Durrett* was rejected by the Bankruptcy Appellate Panel in the case of Lawyers Title Insurance Corp. v. Madrid (In re Madrid), 21 Bankr. 424 (Bankr. 9th Cir. 1982), affd. on other grounds, 725 F.2d 1197 (9th Cir.), cert. denied, 469 U.S. 833 (1984).

The affirming Ninth Circuit rejection of *Durrett* in *Madrid* was on different grounds from those of the Bankruptcy Appellate Panel. Section 548 of the Bankruptcy Code provides that only transfers within the one-year period prior to bankruptcy are subject to attack under that section. Subsection (d)(1) of §548 deals with the question of when a transfer occurred for determining whether it was within the one-year reachback period; it also provides that a transfer will be deemed to take place when it is so far perfected that no bona fide purchaser could take priority. Since from the time of the recordation of the mortgage no one who purchases from the borrower can take priority over the rights of a purchaser at the foreclosure sale, the court applied §548(d)(1) to relate the date of transfer back to the date of the recordation of the mortgage, which happened to be outside the one-year period.

The Third Circuit, in a case under the Uniform Commercial Code, In re Ewing, 746 F.2d 1465 (3d Cir. 1984), affg. 36 Bankr. 476 (W.D. Pa.), cert. denied, 469 U.S. 1214 (1985), refused to follow *Durrett,* affirming the lower court on this relation back doctrine. The Third Circuit did not articulate its reasoning, however, and a later decision by the Third Circuit completely clouds the circuit's position. In Butler v. Lomas & Nettleton, 862 F.2d 1015 (3d Cir. 1988), the beginning of the one-year reachback period fell between the foreclosure sale and the delivery of the sheriff's deed. The court deemed the issue to be whether the sale or deed delivery was the date of transfer. While holding the transfer was not fraudulent because the date of transfer was the date of the foreclosure sale, the court ignored the fact that the mortgage was recorded well before the beginning of the reachback period. Indeed, the court neglected even to cite *Ewing.*

Perhaps because the language of the Ninth Circuit was less than a model of clarity, there are those who read *Madrid* as holding that a foreclosure sale is not a transfer at all for the purposes of §548 of the Bankruptcy Code. (See, e.g., Alden, Gross, and Borowitz, The 'Durrett' Controversy and Foreclosure Sales, N.Y.L.J., Nov. 14, 1984, at 33.) The proposition that a foreclosure sale is not a transfer for the purposes of §548 was propounded before the *Madrid* decision in Coppel and Kann, Defanging *Durrett:* The Established Law of "Transfer," 100 Banking L.J. 676 (1983). That this was the basis of the *Madrid* decision would seem questionable in light of the Ninth Circuit's citation of §548(d)(1).

2. *The Relation Back Theory and the 1984 Amendments.* The Bankruptcy Amendments and Federal Judgeship Act of 1984 made two seemingly technical changes in the Bankruptcy Code that some have argued may have a major impact on the *Durrett* issue. The definition of "transfer" in §101(54) was expanded to include, specifically, "foreclosure of the debtor's equity of redemption," and §548(a) was amended to provide that the fraudulent transfer provisions apply if the debtor "voluntarily or involuntarily" makes the transfer. If the *Madrid* line of cases had held that a foreclosure sale is not a transfer at all for the purposes of §548, would the language "or foreclosure of the debtor's equity of redemption" have overruled those cases? If *Madrid* were simply based on the relation back of the date of transfer under §548(d)(1), does the legislative change have any effect on the decision?

Alden, Gross, and Borowitz, in their 1984 article cited in note 1 supra, maintain that if the legislative change had no effect on those decisions, it would have had no purpose. Do you agree? If a foreclosure sale were not a transfer under §548, would it have been possible, absent the amendment, to use §548 to overcome even a collusive "involuntary" sale *intended* to hinder, delay, or defraud creditors? For example, would cases such as Buffum v. Peter Barceloux Co., 289 U.S. 227 (1933) (sale enforcing a pledge as part of a general scheme to defraud the pledgor's creditors held fraudulent), Lefkowitz v. Finkelstein Trading Corp., 14 F. Supp. 898 (S.D.N.Y. 1936) (property valued at $5,000 sold at unadvertised execution sale to friend of debtor for $430 and resold to debtor's daughter for $500, who in turn transferred the property to a corporation of which the debtor was president), and the hypothetical at the beginning of Chapter 10C5 have been free from §548 attack? Could the prevention of this result have been the basis for the amendment?

Does the second 1984 amendment (that §548 applies both to voluntary and involuntary transfers) tell us anything new? Didn't §101's definition of transfer already apply by its terms to "involuntary" transfers? The word "involuntary" in §101 of the Code was inserted first in the Chandler Act amendment of the bankruptcy laws in 1938, but at the time it was considered merely a codification of the general understanding of the meaning of "transfer." See H.R. No. 1409 on H.R. 8046, 75th Cong., 1st Sess. (1937), at 5. None of the cases rejecting *Durrett* has taken the position that §548 does not apply to involuntary transfers. However, Judge Farris, in his concurring opinion in *Madrid,* argues that §548 contemplates an active role for the debtor in the transfer; this amendment may have been designed to overcome that reasoning. What do you see in the language of §548 that would support his argument?

Following the enactment of the 1984 amendments, Senator Robert Dole (who had been chairman of the Judiciary Committee's Subcom-

mittee on Courts, the subcommittee responsible for bankruptcy legislation when the amendments were adopted) and Senator Dennis
DeConcini (who had been chairman of that subcommittee when the
Code was adopted) engaged in a colloquy in the Congressional Record
explaining the background of the insertion of the package of *Durrett*-
influenced amendments that had been proposed in 1984, the reason
for their intended deletion from the bill (owing to clerical error only
the major anti-*Durrett* provision had been deleted), and the absence of
any intention to codify *Durrett* or overrule *Madrid*. The following is
the text of the colloquy. As you read it, consider whether post-enactment
legislative history is effective. Does its effectiveness depend on whether
it is attempting to argue that language of the statute does not mean
what it says, or whether it is attempting to argue that language of the
statute should not be expanded beyond what it says, because that would
be presuming congressional intent that did not exist?

130 Cong. Rec. 513, 771-772 (daily ed. Oct. 5, 1984)

Mr. DeConcini. Apparently there may have been some misunderstanding regarding the effect of certain technical amendments made by
the recently enacted bankruptcy legislation, Public Law 98-353, specifically section 421(i), which amended the definition of transfer in the
Bankruptcy Code — 11 U.S.C. section 101(48) in the new legislation —
to add the phrase "and foreclosure of the debtor's equity of redemption,";
and section 467(a)(1), which amended section 548(a) of the Bankruptcy
Code to add the phrase "voluntarily or involuntarily." A question has
arisen whether these amendments somehow support the position taken
by the U.S. Court of Appeals for the Fifth Circuit in Durrett v.
Washington National Insurance Co. (italics omitted), 621 F.2d 201 (5th
Cir. 1980), where the court held that a nonjudicial foreclosure sale could
be set aside in bankruptcy if the sale price was not sufficiently high. My
understanding is that these provisions were not intended to have any
effect one way or the other on the so called Durrett issue. Is my
understanding correct?

Mr. Dole. The Senator's understanding is indeed correct. As the
Senator knows, Senator Thurmond's amendment in the nature of a
substitute to H.R. 5174, when introduced, contained language that would
have overturned the position represented by the Durrett decision. Senator
Metzenbaum, however, believed that no action should be taken on the
Durrett issue until the Judiciary Committee had an opportunity to hold
hearings on the issue and consider the matter thoroughly. In deference
to Senator Metzenbaum's position, Senator Thurmond agreed to delete
from his amendment all provisions dealing with the Durrett issue, and
so stated on the floor on June 19 — Congressional Record at page S7617.
Consequently, no provision of the bankruptcy bill as passed by this body
was intended to intimate any view one way or the other regarding
the correctness of the position taken by the U.S. Court of Appeals for
the Fifth Circuit in the Durrett case, or regarding the correctness of the

position taken by the U.S. Court of Appeals for the Ninth Circuit in [Madrid v. Lawyers Title Insurance Corp.,] 725 F.2d 1197 (9th Cir. 1984), which reached a contrary result.

The first provision, which amends the definition of "transfer" contained in section 101 of the Bankruptcy Code, appears to provide that certain foreclosures are included within the definition of "transfer." It does not purport to deal with whether such a transfer will fall within the scope of section 548(a)(2), which was the subject of the ninth circuit's decision, nor with the question of when a transfer occurs for purposes of section 548. Under section 548(d)(1), the transfer occurs on the date of the perfection of the mortgage or deed of trust, for after such date no bona fide purchaser from the mortgagor could take priority over the rights of a purchaser at the foreclosure sale. Those courts following Durrett have found and held that the former definition of "transfer" in section 101(41) was broad enough to include a foreclosure sale of the debtor's property while courts rejecting Durrett on the basis of the date of transfer, have done so under section 548(d)(1) and not section 101(41). Thus, the amendment should not be construed to in any way codify Durrett or throw a cloud over noncollusive foreclosure sales.

The second provision, which adds "voluntarily or involuntarily" to section 548(a) is consistent with the majority holding in Madrid. Finally, neither of the provisions purport to deal with the question of whether a noncollusive, regularly conducted foreclosure sale should be deemed to be for a reasonably equivalent value.

Mr. DeConcini. Then I am correct in concluding that parties in bankruptcy proceedings who seek avoidance of prepetition foreclosure sales would find no support for their arguments in these amendments?

Mr. Dole. The Senator's conclusion is correct.

3. *Extension of the* Durrett *Rule: Judicial Foreclosures, Land Contracts, U.C.C. Security Interests, and Leases.* At first it was thought that *Durrett* might be limited to power-of-sale foreclosures and would not be applied in the case of judicial foreclosure sales, where greater protections for the borrower are built in. However, the use of judicial foreclosure has not saved foreclosure sales from *Durrett* attacks. See, e.g., In re Jones, 20 Bankr. 988 (Bankr. E.D. Pa. 1982); but see In re Perdido Bay Country Club Estates, 23 Bankr. 36 (Bankr. S.D. Fla. 1982). *Durrett* has also been applied to termination of installment land contracts (In re Berge, 33 Bankr. 642 (Bankr. W.D. Wis. 1983), modified, 37 Bankr. 705 (Bankr. W.D. Wis. 1983)), and to foreclosures of security interests under Article 9 of the Uniform Commercial Code (*Ewing,* supra).

Perhaps the most troubling extension is to the termination of leases on default by the tenant. The argument is that the termination of the lease represents a reconveyance of the leasehold estate from the tenant to the landlord, which can be a fraudulent transfer where the value of the leasehold estate recovered by the landlord is worth more than the value of the future rental payments at the time of the reconveyance. The origin of this idea actually antedates *Durrett;* it stems from the 1976 case of In re Ferris, 415 F. Supp. 33 (W.D. Okla. 1976). Maurice and Barbara Ferris had leased land on which they had constructed a theater and a restaurant. When they defaulted and the lease was terminated, they lost the improvements. The court found the termination to constitute a fraudulent transfer of the leasehold estate to the landlord because of the high value of the estate with the added improvements. The case was generally considered to be the result of an attempt to cure an inequity, and little concern was expressed at the time that it might be applied generally. Do you see why the advent of *Durrett* has changed that view? See Eder v. Queen City Grain (In re Queen City Grain), 51 Bankr. 722 (Bankr. S.D. Ohio 1985) (holding a lease termination to be a transfer of an interest in property and subject to fraudulent transfer treatment, based on *Ferris*); Fashion World v. Finard (In re Fashion World), 44 Bankr. 754 (Bankr. D. Mass. 1984) (holding that lessor's option to terminate the lease was a transfer and subject to attack as fraudulent, without explicitly relying on *Ferris*); Goodman, Avoidance of Lease Terminations as Fraudulent Transfers, 43 Bus. Law. 807 (1988).

Returning to the master hypothetical, assume that Dan Developer leased approximately half of his building to Widget Corporation of America (WCA) at $20 per square foot for a term of ten years. After five years, WCA goes into default in payment of rent and the lease is terminated. At the time, equivalent space is renting for $30 per square foot. If the property is located in a *Durrett* jurisdiction and WCA files in bankruptcy, would the termination of WCA's lease constitute a fraudulent transfer? What does the landlord "pay" for the "reconveyance"? How do you determine the value of the leasehold estate reconveyed? Is it true that wherever a lease is for a fixed rental in a rising real estate market there is a danger of a *Durrett* attack? Why are some sale and leasebacks especially subject to attack?

4. *The Reachback Period and the UFTA.*   Under §548, the transfer must occur within a year before the commencement of the bankruptcy for the trustee to bring an action to set aside a transfer. However, under state fraudulent transfer law any creditor can move to set aside a transfer without such a limitation. Do you understand why the state creditor is not subject to a one-year-prior-to-bankruptcy reachback period? Under state law, the only limit would be the state statute of limitations for fraud, which is almost always in excess of one year. In New York, for example, the limit is six years. See N.Y. Civ. Prac. L. §213 (McKinney 1990 and Supp. 1991).

Review §544(b) of the Bankruptcy Code, reprinted above. Do you see how this section enables the trustee in bankruptcy to use state law rather than the Code to apply *Durrett* and thereby extend the reachback period to the state statute of limitations? The federal government is not subject to state statutes of limitation. Does this mean that if the trustee steps into the shoes of the federal government as a creditor under §544(b), there is no limit on the reachback period? See United States v. Gleneagles, 565 F. Supp. 556 (M.D. Pa. 1983).

Is it correct to say that if the UFTA is adopted in a jurisdiction the trustee is effectively limited in attacking foreclosure sales under *Durrett* to the one-year reachback period of §548? How does the UFTA deal with leases?

5. *The Appraisal of Commercial Real Estate.* The real *Durrett* problem for the commercial mortgagee lies in the method of appraisal. In Chapter 5B1 we examined the appraisal of commercial real estate and determined that it was far from an exact science. As you remember, since commercial real estate is bought and sold based on the income the real estate can produce, the major appraisal method is "income capitalization." Under this approach, an appraiser reaches today's value by determining what a person would pay today for the stream of income the property is expected to produce in the future. This is accomplished by estimating an expected stream of income and dividing it by a percentage known as the "capitalization rate."

The estimated stream of income is determined by taking the current rental stream and determining when leases will expire and who will rent it at that time and how much the rent will be, taking into consideration such things as the condition of the building, real estate trends in the area, the economic prospects for the city, inflationary pressures, and the like. The capitalization rate is determined by starting with the "riskless" rate of return on investments (the rate people will demand when there is no risk of not being paid — e.g., Treasury obligations) and then increasing the percentage by risk factors associated with the type of investment (e.g., office building, hotel, or apartment), the particular property (e.g., the neighborhood, whether leases are involved, and the prospects of future development) and anticipated inflationary pressures. Small changes in capitalization rate or anticipated income stream can result in dramatic differences in value, especially since many of the same factors figure into both sides of the equation.

These vagaries make commercial property mortgagees feel that it is almost impossible to determine what bid will preclude a bankruptcy judge, using hindsight (and perhaps with an unarticulated motivation to obtain as much for the estate as possible), from selecting, years later, those variables that will produce a value well in excess of what the mortgagee believes the property is worth at the time of foreclosure.

Assume in the master hypothetical that Dan Developer is in default and insolvent. The property is only 50 percent rented. Ace's in-house appraisers project an annual average stream of income over the next ten years of $2.4 million (800,000 rentable square feet (s.f.) × an average *net* rent of $3 per rentable s.f.) and apply a capitalization rate of 12 percent. This produces a value of $20 million. The mortgage balance is $22 million, which Ace bids at the foreclosure sale (110 percent of its estimate of value). There is no competitive bidding, and Ace acquires the property. If Dan files in bankruptcy three years later, when the property is 90 percent leased, and the judge finds that at the time of foreclosure the projected stream of income should have been at least $3.3 million (825,000 rentable s.f. × net rent of $4 per s.f.) and the cap rate should have been 10 percent, the value at foreclosure would have been $33 million, 65 percent more than Ace's valuation. (Do you understand why the *Durrett* attack in this instance would be based on state law?) Using the judge's valuation, Ace acquired the property for only 66 percent of value, below the *Durrett* 70 percent safe harbor.

If you had represented Ace in the above example, what might you have advised Ace to do before the foreclosure sale that would have supported its contention that the value was $20 million? See In re Ruebeck, 55 Bankr. 163 (Bankr. D. Mass. 1985).

Differences in value such as those in the above example are not uncommon. In the case of In re Perdido Bay Country Club Estates, 23 Bankr. 36 (Bankr. S.D. Fla. 1982), the appraisals before the court ran from $7.8 million to $13.4 million. In the case of In re KRO Assocs., 4 B.C.D. 462 (Bankr. S.D.N.Y. 1978), discussed in Chapter 11A2b, decided under Chapter XII of the former Bankruptcy Act, the court found a low value, enabling the bankrupt partnership to keep the property free of liens by paying the mortgagees a small portion of the mortgage balance. Using a 20 percent cap rate, it reached a value of $895,000 notwithstanding that there were mortgages on the property totaling $16 million.

It should be noted that residential real estate is generally appraised on the basis of comparison sales and not on an income capitalization method. (You should have no difficulty in determining why.) This method provides more assurance to the mortgagee, since there is usually sufficient proof of value for use in a later bankruptcy. Also, while commercial real estate almost never goes to foreclosure if there is substantial equity in the property (why?), this is not always true for residential properties, where personal problems may prevent the borrower from disposing of the property before foreclosure. Does this suggest a possible compromise that might protect both the commercial mortgagee and the residential borrower?

6. *Consequences of a Finding of Fraudulent Transfer.* Section 550(a) of the Bankruptcy Code provides that where a transfer is held to be fraudulent the trustee may recover the property or the value of the property (i.e., the court-determined value of the property less the amount bid at the foreclosure sale) from the purchaser at the foreclosure sale but has no recovery against a "good-faith" purchaser *from* the purchaser at the foreclosure sale.

If the court chooses to recover the property from the purchaser at the foreclosure sale, and the purchaser has acted in good faith, §548(c) provides that the purchaser obtains a lien on the property recovered by the trustee equal to the sale price. In addition, §550(d) provides that the good-faith purchaser at the foreclosure sale is entitled to a lien for any increase in value (not exceeding costs) resulting from the improvements made by the transferee before reconveyance.

Thus, good faith plays a significant role in determining the consequences of a fraudulent transfer, both for the purchaser at the foreclosure sale and for any purchaser from the purchaser at the foreclosure sale. Unfortunately, there is no definition of "good faith" in the Code. The original Commission on the Bankruptcy Laws of the United States concluded that it would leave the interpretation of "good faith" to the courts on a case-by-case basis. See Report of the Commission on the Bankruptcy Laws of the United States, Part II, 180 H. Doc. No. 93-137 (July 1973). This conclusion was apparently followed by the drafters of the Code. See generally Ordin, The Good Faith Principle in the Bankruptcy Code: A Case Study, 38 Bus. Law. 1795 (1983). Collier concludes that a transferee is not acting in good faith if the transferee knew or should have known of the fraudulent purpose of the transfer. 4 L. King, Collier on Bankruptcy, ¶550.03, at 550-558 n.3 (15th ed. 1983). In Phillips v. Latham, 523 S.W.2d 19, 24 (Tex. Civ. App. 1975), the court held that a party paying a grossly inadequate price cannot be considered to be acting in good faith.

Returning to the example discussed in note 5, above, if the court determined that the foreclosure sale was a fraudulent transfer because the value of the property at the time of foreclosure was $33 million and therefore ordered a reconveyance of the property, do you think Ace, having access to annual reports concerning the property and being generally familiar with the property since (and even before) the first shovel was dug into the earth, would be considered to have acted in good faith so as to entitle it to a lien for its bid at the foreclosure sale and for increases in value caused by repairs and the like after foreclosure? Can't there be good-faith disagreement as to value, especially when one of the valuations is made with the advantage of hindsight? Compare In re Littleton, 82 Bankr. 640 (Bankr. S.D. Ga. 1988), revd. on other grounds, 888 F.2d 90 (11th Cir. 1989), with In re IPI Liberty Village Assocs., 82 Bankr. 507 (Bankr. W.D. Mo. 1987); but see In re Richardson, 23 Bankr. 434 (Bankr. D. Utah, 1982).

Even if the court were to find that Ace had acted in good faith, the lien would not cover foreclosure costs and legal expenses in addition to costs for repairs, alterations, and improvements that do not, in the court's judgment, increase the value of the property. This can hardly give Ace much comfort. With respect to improvements, assume that after acquisition of the mortgaged property at foreclosure Ace expended $2 million for the following: (i) a new boiler; (ii) redecoration of and alterations to the lobby; (iii) rent collection fees; and (iv) operating losses. Assume further that the bankruptcy judge finds that Ace acted in good faith but disallows most of these costs as part of Ace's lien because (a) a new boiler was unnecessary and thus the judge allows only the amount equal to the cost to repair the old boiler; (b) the redecoration and alterations were garish and actually decreased the value of the property; and (c) rent collection fees and operating costs are not "improvements" under §550(d)(2). Do you think the bankruptcy judge's decision would be sustained on appeal?

Perhaps more troubling to Ace is that the court could, in lieu of ordering a reconveyance, recover under §550(a) the value of the property transferred even if it is determined that Ace was acting in good faith. Under the facts of the example based on our hypothetical in note 5, above, how much could the court order Ace to pay to Dan's trustee? Assume you are counsel to Ace and you learn that Ace received an offer after foreclosure from a third party to purchase Dan's property for $22 million, the amount Ace bid at the foreclosure sale. Ace wants to take the offer because it doesn't think the property is worth even that amount. What advice would you give Ace? To help you in your answer, assume that Dan later files in bankruptcy and the trustee (or Dan, as debtor in possession of his estate) claims that the property value at the time of foreclosure was $33 million. If the court agrees and finds a fraudulent transfer, what is the only remedy the court can assert under §550(a)? Does this mean the trustee can collect the value of the transferred property from Ace, leaving Ace with a loss of $11 million without even a lien on the property transferred? See In re Coleman, 21 Bankr. 832 (Bankr. S.D. Tex. 1982), and In re Littleton, 82 Bankr. 640 (Bankr. S.D. Ga. 1988), where the courts answered the question in the affirmative.

7.   Durrett *Readings*.   There is an overabundance of articles and commentary on the subject of *Durrett*. The following is a selection of readings both pro and con. Alden, Gross, and Borowitz, Real Property

Foreclosure as a Fraudulent Conveyance: Proposals for Solving the *Durrett* Problem, 38 Bus. Law. 1605 (1983); Castanares, Foreclosures in Bankruptcy: Are They Fraudulent Conveyances?, 21 Idaho L. Rev. 517 (1985); Cohn, Foreclosures as Fraudulent Transfers: Solving the *Durrett* Problem, 103 Banking L.J. 259 (1986); Coppel and Kann, Defanging *Durrett:* The Established Law of "Transfer," 100 Banking L.J. 676 (1983); Ehrlich, Avoidance of Foreclosure Sales as Fraudulent Conveyances: Accommodating State and Federal Objectives, 71 Va. L. Rev. 933 (1985); Henning, An Analysis of *Durrett* and Its Impact on Real and Personal Property Foreclosures: Some Proposed Modifications, 63 N.C.L. Rev. 257 (1985); Jackson, Avoiding Powers in Bankruptcy, 36 Stan. L. Rev. 725 (1984); Kennedy, Involuntary Fraudulent Transfers, 9 Cardozo L. Rev. 531 (1987); McCoid, Constructively Fraudulent Conveyances: Transfers of Inadequate Consideration, 62 Tex. L. Rev. 639 (1983); Nelson, The Impact of Mortgagor Bankruptcy on the Real Estate Mortgagee: Current Problems and Some Suggested Solutions, 50 Mo. L. Rev. 217 (1985); Simpson, Real Property Foreclosures: The Fallacy of *Durrett,* 19 Real Prop., Prob. & Tr. J. 73 (1984); Zinman, Houle, and Weiss, Fraudulent Transfers According to Alden, Gross & Borowitz: A Tale of Two Circuits, 39 Bus. Law. 977 (1984); Zinman, Noncollusive, Regularly Conducted Foreclosure Sales: Involuntary, Nonfraudulent Transfers, 9 Cardozo L. Rev. 581 (1987); Note, Regularly Conducted Non-Collusive Mortgage Foreclosure Sales: Inapplicability of Section 548(a)(2) of the Bankruptcy Code, 52 Fordham L. Rev. 261 (1983); Note, The Big Chill: Applicability of Section 548(a)(2) of the Bankruptcy Code to Noncollusive Foreclosure Sales, 53 Fordham L. Rev. 813 (1985).

8. *Mortgages and Leveraged Buyout Transactions.* Leveraged buyouts of corporations (LBOs) are generally beyond the scope of this casebook. However, an attack on an LBO as a fraudulent transfer may taint mortgages made in connection with the LBO, and is thus of concern to mortgagees. Simply put, an LBO involves the acquisition of corporate control by acquiring the stock of the corporation for very little, if any, cash. The bulk of the consideration for the stock is furnished by the acquired corporation, which mortgages its assets to secure loans made by institutions to the acquirers or obligates itself to repay such loans. Thus, a corporation that may have substantial surplus prior to the LBO ends up after the LBO with little or no surplus and most of its assets encumbered. While an LBO may be structured in many different ways, the overall effect is to move assets out of the reach of general creditors or to dilute significantly the general creditors' share of unencumbered assets. Since none of the consideration for the corporation's incurrence of the obligations or granting of the liens (transfer, for fraudulent transaction purposes) goes to the corporation,

the constructive fraud provision employed in *Durrett* would seem to apply if the corporation is insolvent or is rendered insolvent by the transfer. In addition, other constructive fraud provisions of fraudulent transfer law may apply and, depending on whether stockholders or lending institutions are complicitous, it is possible that intentional fraud may be found.

In United States v. Tabor Court Realty Corp., 803 F.2d 1288 (3d Cir. 1986), the court applied the Pennsylvania Uniform Fraudulent Conveyance Act to mortgages executed in connection with an LBO, holding that they were fraudulent conveyances where the lender was aware that the transaction would render the corporations insolvent and that the corporations would not receive fair consideration for the transfers. In addition, the assignee of the mortgages was also charged with liability for the fraud. Interestingly, the mortgages were found to be fraudulent under the intentional fraud provisions of the state fraudulent conveyance law as well as the constructive fraud provisions. Not all LBOs are being struck down. See, e.g., Kupetz v. Wolf, 845 F.2d 842 (9th Cir. 1988) (court found, inter alia, no evidence of actual intent to defraud or that stockholders knew of method of financing the purchase; claims of creditors arose after the sale; and LBO occurred two and one-half years prior to filing of bankruptcy petition), and Credit Managers Assn. v. Federal Co., 629 F. Supp. 175 (C.D. Cal. 1985) (court held that company received fair consideration). But see Wieboldt Stores, Inc. v. Schottenstein, 94 Bankr. 488 (Bankr. N.D. Ill. 1988) and In re Ohio Corrugating, 70 Bankr. 920 (Bankr. N.D. Ohio 1987). Notwithstanding the confusion in the courts, the growing number of cases attacking LBOs should be sufficient to give all parties associated with an LBO some concern.

It has certainly given concern to the title companies, which are now making exceptions for fraudulent transfers in loan policies where the mortgage is made in connection with an LBO and even where the mortgage was made long after the LBO if it was made to refinance an LBO loan made by a third party. The American Land Title Association has approved a new exclusion from title insurance coverage to be added to the 1987 ALTA policies for "any claim which arises out of the transaction creating the interest of the mortgagee insured by this policy by reason of the operation of Federal bankruptcy, state insolvency or similar creditors right's laws." This language obviously goes beyond what it was designed to cover. See discussion at Chapter 10B.

The following are some of the articles dealing with the fraudulent transfer LBO problem: Alces, Generic Fraud and the Uniform Fraudulent Transfer Act, 9 Cardozo L. Rev. 743 (1987); Baird and Jackson, Fraudulent Conveyance Law and Its Proper Domain, 38 Vand. L. Rev. 829 (1985); Carlson, Leveraged Buyouts in Bankruptcy, 20 Ga. L. Rev. 73 (1985); Carlson, Is Fraudulent Conveyance Law Efficient?, 9 Cardozo

L. Rev. 643 (1987); Clark, The Duties of the Corporate Debtor to Its Creditors, 90 Harv. L. Rev. 505 (1977); Liss, Fraudulent Conveyance Law and Leveraged Buyouts, 87 Colum. L. Rev. 1491 (1987); Murdoch, Sartin, and Zadek, Fraudulent Conveyances and Leveraged Buyouts, 43 Bus. Law. 1 (1987); Sherwin, Creditors' Rights Against Participants in a Leveraged Buyout, 72 Minn. L. Rev. 449 (1988); Smyser, Going Private and Going Under: Leveraged Buyouts and the Fraudulent Conveyance Problem, 63 Ind. L. Rev. 781 (1988).

9. *Guarantors and Unlawful Preferences.* The preference provisions of the Bankruptcy Code (§547) permit the trustee to set aside certain transfers of the debtor's assets to a creditor to pay a preexisting (antecedent) debt within a period prior to bankruptcy while the debtor is insolvent. The object of these provisions is to prevent a debtor who knows the end is near from paying the most favored creditors at the expense of the other creditors. We do not dwell on unlawful preferences in this casebook because they are not more particularly related to real estate than to other businesses in trouble. However, in one particular area recent cases raise the possibility that preferences may have a dramatic effect on the nature of real estate financing.

Preferences may be set aside if the transfer occurred within a specified period prior to bankruptcy. That period is normally 90 days. However, where the transferee is an "insider" (see the broad definition in Bankruptcy Code §101(30)), the reachback period is extended to one year. What is the rationale for this extension?

Especially where the borrower's credit is not the best, mortgagees may ask that the loan be guaranteed by someone of substantial means. This is often an "insider" of the borrower, who is anxious that the loan be made. For example, in the master hypothetical, assume that Ace required Dan to guarantee personally the payment of the note issued by Law Drive Associates, Dan's limited partnership. Such guarantees often permit financing that would otherwise have been rejected by the lender.

In the case of In re Deprizio, 86 Bankr. 545 (N.D. Ill. 1988), affd., Levit v. Ingersoll Rand Finance Corp., 874 F. 2d 1186 (7th Cir. 1989), a preferential payment had been made to a noninsider lender within one year but more than 90 days prior to bankruptcy. The court applied the one-year "insider" reachback period because the loan had been guaranteed by an insider. Section 547 prohibits transfers "to or for the benefit of a creditor." The court found that the transfer benefitted the insider (who was thus relieved of guarantor liability to the extent of the transfer) and that the insider was a creditor since the insider had rights over (or had subrogation rights) against the borrower for amounts paid under the guarantee. (See the definition of "creditor," §101(9), and "claim," §101(4)).

In affirming the decision of the district court, the Seventh Circuit pointed out that long-term lenders should not be so concerned about this result because ordinary payments of principal and interest are not unlawful preferences under §547(c)(2), which excludes transfers in the ordinary course of business or financial affairs of the parties (847 F.2d at 1199-1200). Not so, said the Ninth Circuit in CHG Intl. v. Barklays Bank (In re CHG Intl.), 897 F.2d 1479 (9th Cir. 1990). When Congress broadened the exception (which had previously been limited to payments within 45 days after the debt was incurred) in 1984, they could not have intended to cover long-term debt (real estate mortgage debt is most often long-term, that is, payable over a period of years). If Congress intended to cover long-term debt, there should have been legislative history to say so. Is legislative history necessary to support clear language of a statute? No, said the Sixth Circuit in Gosch v. Burns (In re Finn), 909 F.2d 903 (6th Cir. 1990), which found no basis in the statutory language or legislative history to conclude that long-term debt was not within the exception.

Given the split in the circuits, perhaps there will one day be a Supreme Court decision on the issue. In the meantime, however, is it correct to say that if our hypothetical project were in a jurisdiction following *CHG,* all payments of principal and interest made by Law Drive Associates, Dan's limited partnership, to Ace Insurance Company within one year prior to LDA's bankruptcy could be set aside if LDA had been insolvent when the payments were made and Ace had been prudent enough to require a guarantee from Dan Developer?

C h a p t e r 11

The Impact of Bankruptcy on Real Estate Transactions

A. STARTING OVER

In biblical times, everyone got a new start. Each seventh, or sabbatical, year was a year of release from debts. "Every creditor shall release that which he hath lent unto his neighbor."[1] After the passage of a "week" of sabbatical years, the fiftieth year was the jubilee year, when, after the remission of indebtedness, all land would return to its original owner, all indentured servants would be returned to their families, and all prisoners would be freed. "And ye shall hallow the fiftieth year, and proclaim liberty throughout the land unto all the inhabitants thereof; it shall be a jubilee unto you."[2]

As civilization progressed, society took a dimmer view of jubilees. A person who became unable to pay debts would normally be put in prison, be sold into slavery, or worse. One of the first "bankruptcy" laws dealing with such people as a class was contained in the Roman "Twelve Tables" and was known as the law "de debitore in partes secando," or the law of cutting the debtor into pieces.[3] Today, bank-

---

1. Deuteronomy 15:2. Even the land was given a new start: every seventh year it would not be cultivated but would lie fallow, a process that helped considerably to prevent exhaustion of the land and to enhance its fertility in the other years. See Exodus 23:10; Leviticus 25:4; N. Ausubel, The Book of Jewish Knowledge 229-230, 382 (1964); J. Hertz, The Pentateuch and Haftorahs, 531, 811 (2d ed. 1967).

2. Leviticus 25:10. You may remember that the words "proclaim liberty throughout the land unto all the inhabitants thereof" are found on the Liberty Bell in Philadelphia.

3. "In this respect our legislature seems to have attended to the examples of the Roman law. I mean not the terrible law of the twelve tables; whereby the creditors might cut the debtor's body into pieces, and each of them take his proportionable share; if, indeed, that law, de debitore in partes secando (of cutting the debtor into pieces), is to be understood in so very butchery a light; which many learned men have with reason doubted. . . . Nor do I mean those less inhuman laws (if they may be called so, as *their* meaning is indisputably certain), of imprisoning the debtor's person in chains; subjecting him to stripes and hard labour, at the mercy of his rigid creditor;

ruptcy is not bloody, at least not in the literal sense, but the divide-and-distribute concept of the Twelve Tables persists. Bankruptcy law provides a mechanism for the gathering together of the debtor's assets, the conversion (where feasible) of such assets into cash, and the orderly distribution of the assets to the debtor's creditors. The debtor is then released from debts and given that new start so nobly proclaimed in the Bible. This is known as bankruptcy liquidation; it is found generally in Chapter 7 of the Bankruptcy Code.[4]

Around the turn of the century, it became apparent to many that even when a business is in financial difficulties its worth as a going concern is probably (although not always) greater than what a forced liquidation sale would produce. From this thought developed the concepts of composition, equity receivership, arrangement, and reorganization, which attempted to rehabilitate rather than liquidate the debtor's business, thereby obtaining more for the creditors while benefiting the national economy by keeping people at work. Most bankruptcy reorganizations of businesses are now governed by Chapter 11 of the Bankruptcy Code.[5]

Other than disruption and sometimes significant loss of income caused by delays and the effect of stays of acts affecting the debtor, the basic interests of secured creditors such as real estate mortgagees should otherwise be generally unaffected by a liquidation. If the property has equity, that is, if it is worth more than the liens on it, the property can be sold by the bankruptcy court to realize on the equity. The lien of the mortgage attaches to the proceeds of the sale, and the mortgagee is protected either by the court's setting an upset price equal to the amount of the indebtedness or by the mortgagee's ability to attend the sale, bid up to the indebtedness, and (if it is the successful bidder) offset the bid against the indebtedness. If there is no equity, the bankruptcy court should normally "abandon" the property and lift the stay, thus permitting foreclosure, although an ominous group of recent

---

and sometimes selling him, his wife, and children, to perpetual foreign slavery trans Tiberim (beyond the Tiber)." 2 W. Blackstone, Commentaries 472.

4. The Bankruptcy Code is found at 11 U.S.C. §§101 to 1330 (1988). References in this discussion to statutory sections are to the Bankruptcy Code unless otherwise specified.

5. Chapter 11 of the Bankruptcy Code is derived from a combination of three reorganization chapters in the former Bankruptcy Act: Chapter X, corporate reorganization; Chapter XI, an arrangement for unsecured debts; and Chapter XII, a real property arrangement for noncorporate debtors. We will examine the influence of these chapters in the development of Chapter 11 of the Bankruptcy Code later. The Bankruptcy Code also contains other reorganization chapters: Chapter 9, for municipalities; Chapter 12, a recent addition, for "family farmers"; and Chapter 13 (derived from a similar chapter for wage earners in the Bankruptcy Act), for individuals with a regular income. We will come back to Chapters 12 and 13 when we discuss plans of reorganization.

cases have allowed the borrower to keep the property on payment to the mortgagee of a portion of the debt equal to the value of the collateral (this is sometimes referred to as "stripping down the mortgage").[6]

On the other hand, when the debtor is being rehabilitated through a reorganization, important property (such as the debtor's factory) cannot be sold, nor can the bankruptcy court abandon such property or permit foreclosure and still have an effective reorganization. Thus, it may be necessary to modify secured creditors' rights in a reorganization plan. Under the plan of reorganization, creditors are divided into "classes" (generally a mortgagee, as a secured creditor, is in a class by itself), and each class is given interests in the new reorganized business or its assets that may differ from the interests the classes had on the filing of the bankruptcy petition.

The bankruptcy court can confirm a plan if it is approved by a requisite majority of each class of creditors. However, as you will see when we discuss the "cram-down," a court can under certain circumstances confirm the plan over the objection of a class that is adversely affected by the plan provided, among other things, that the plan is "fair and equitable." "Fair and equitable" generally means that "absolute priority" is provided so that the interests in the new corporation are distributed to the creditors in order of their priority.[7] As a result, no junior creditor should receive any property in the reorganization until senior creditors receive property equal in value to the amount of their claim. This provides a measure of protection to secured creditors whose rights are being dealt with in the plan. Can you think of the rationale for providing this protection for the secured creditor?

In addition, no plan can be confirmed unless it is "in the best interest of creditors." What this ambiguous phrase of art (which has been a part of bankruptcy law from the earliest compositions to present-day reorganizations) means is that under the plan each creditor must receive property of a value equal, at least, to what the creditor would have received had there been a liquidation.[8] This makes sense. Reorganizations are designed to produce more, not less, and no creditor should end up with less. Many of the disputes that arise in reorganizations involve the determination of who gets the difference between the liquidation value and the higher going concern value. Other sig-

---

6. See discussion of this issue in Chapter 11C, infra.

7. See Case v. Los Angeles Lumber Products Co., 308 U.S. 106 (1939) (absolute priority was required by the words "fair and equitable"). Section 1129(b) of the Code requires that a plan be "fair and equitable" as to any impaired class rejecting the plan of reorganization. See discussion at Chapter 11B2, infra.

8. The best-interest-of-creditors requirement is now found in §1129(a)(7) of the Code.

nificant requirements that must be met before a plan can be confirmed are discussed below in connection with plan confirmation.

Real estate disputes have been a focal point of bankruptcy law in recent times, far beyond what might be expected. Many provisions of the Bankruptcy Code were written to deal with pre-Code bankruptcy cases that jeopardized the rights of mortgagees, lessors, lessees, and other parties to real estate transactions. Even after the enactment of the Bankruptcy Code new problems arose to cast a shadow over mortgage financing. In the remainder of this discussion we will cover these real estate problems, how the Bankruptcy Code deals with them, and some of the current unresolved problems affecting real estate.

B.   THE MORTGAGEE'S ABILITY TO REALIZE ON COLLATERAL

Notwithstanding the rights of creditors built into the Bankruptcy Code, the mortgagee often finds it difficult to achieve full protection or to realize on the collateral in the borrower's bankruptcy.

When a bankruptcy proceeding is commenced by or against the mortgagor, the automatic stay provisions of §362 will stop a foreclosure in its tracks, the trustee or debtor in possession may continue to use the collateral under §363, and, if the proceeding is a reorganization under Chapter 11, a plan may be imposed under §1129 that modifies the rights of the mortgagee. All these steps may be necessary for the efficient administration of bankruptcy law, but they are nevertheless threats to the mortgagee's ability to realize on the value of the collateral. In order to represent his or her client adequately, a mortgagee's counsel must understand the protections built into the Code to prevent unfair treatment and how to use them for the client's benefit.

1.   *The Automatic Stay and Adequate Protection*

Section 362 of the Bankruptcy Code provides that the filing of a petition operates as a stay of acts against the debtor or the debtor's property. The rationale is that bankruptcy proceedings are designed to provide for an orderly and fair distribution of the debtor's assets, or interests in the reorganized business of the debtor, as the case may be. Bankruptcy should not be a signal for a scramble among creditors to see who can get to the debtor's assets first.

Bankruptcy Code §362
11 U.S.C. §362 (1988)

(a) Except as provided in subsection (b) of this section, a petition filed under section 301, 302, or 303 of this title, or an application filed under section 5(a)(3) of the Securities Investor Protection Act of 1970 (15 U.S.C. 78eee(a)(3)), operates as a stay, applicable to all entities, of —

(1) the commencement or continuation, including the issuance or employment of process, of a judicial, administrative, or other action or proceeding against the debtor that was or could have been commenced before the commencement of the case under this title, or to recover a claim against the debtor that arose before the commencement of the case under this title;

(2) the enforcement, against the debtor or against property of the estate, of a judgment obtained before the commencement of the case under this title;

(3) any act to obtain possession of property of the estate or of property from the estate or to exercise control over property of the estate;

(4) any act to create, perfect, or enforce any lien against property of the estate;

(5) any act to create, perfect, or enforce against property of the debtor any lien to the extent that such lien secures a claim that arose before the commencement of the case under this title;

(6) any act to collect, assess, or recover a claim against the debtor that arose before the commencement of the case under this title;

(7) the setoff of any debt owing to the debtor that arose before the commencement of the case under this title against any claim against the debtor; and

(8) the commencement or continuation of a proceeding before the United States Tax Court concerning the debtor.

(b) The filing of a petition under section 301, 302, or 303 of this title, or of an application under section 5(a)(3) of the Securities Investor Protection Act of 1970 (15 U.S.C. 78eee(a)(3)), does not operate as a stay — . . .

(4) under subsection (a)(1) of this section, of the commencement or continuation of an action or proceeding by a governmental unit to enforce such governmental unit's police or regulatory power;

(5) under subsection (a)(2) of this section, of the enforcement of a judgment, other than a money judgment, obtained in an action or proceeding by a governmental unit to enforce such governmental unit's police or regulatory power; . . .

(10) under subsection (a) of this section, of any act by a lessor to the debtor under a lease of nonresidential real property that has terminated by the expiration of the stated term of the lease before the commencement of or during a case under this title to obtain possession of such property; or . . .

(c) Except as provided in subsections (d), (e), and (f) of this section —

(1) the stay of an act against property of the estate under subsection (a) of this section continues until such property is no longer property of the estate; and

(2) the stay of any other act under subsection (a) of this section continues until the earliest of —

(A) the time the case is closed;

(B) the time the case is dismissed; or

(C) if the case is a case under chapter 7 of this title concerning an individual or a case under chapter 9, 11, 12, or 13 of this title, the time a discharge is granted or denied.

(d) On request of a party in interest and after notice and a hearing, the court shall grant relief from the stay provided under subsection (a) of this section, such as by terminating, annulling, modifying, or conditioning such stay —

(1) for cause, including the lack of adequate protection of an interest in property of such party in interest; or

(2) with respect to a stay of an act against property under subsection (a) of this section, if —

(A) the debtor does not have an equity in such property; and

(B) such property is not necessary to an effective reorganization.

(e) Thirty days after a request under subsection (d) of this section for relief from the stay of any act against property of the estate under subsection (a) of this section, such stay is terminated with respect to the party in interest making such request, unless the court, after notice and a hearing, orders such stay continued in effect pending the conclusion of, or as a result of, a final hearing and determination under subsection (d) of this section. A hearing under this subsection may be a preliminary hearing, or may be consolidated with the final hearing under subsection (d) of this section. The court shall order such stay continued in effect pending the conclusion of the final hearing under subsection (d) of this section if there is a reasonable likelihood that the party opposing relief from such stay will prevail at the conclusion of such final hearing. If the hearing under this subsection is a preliminary hearing, then such final hearing shall be commenced not later than thirty days after the conclusion of such preliminary hearing.

(f) Upon request of a party in interest, the court, with or without a hearing, shall grant such relief from the stay provided under subsection

(a) of this section as is necessary to prevent irreparable damage to the interest of an entity in property, if such interest will suffer such damage before there is an opportunity for notice and a hearing under subsection (d) or (e) of this section.

(g) In any hearing under subsection (d) or (e) of this section concerning relief from the stay of any act under subsection (a) of this section —

(1) the party requesting such relief has the burden of proof on the issue of the debtor's equity in property; and

(2) the party opposing such relief has the burden of proof on all other issues.

(h) An individual injured by any willful violation of a stay provided by this section shall recover actual damages, including costs and attorneys' fees, and, in appropriate circumstances, may recover punitive damages.

While the scope of §362(a), as you can see, is extremely broad, §362(d) provides that the court must grant relief from the stay in appropriate circumstances. Section 362(d), inter alia, gives broad power to the court to lift the stay "for cause" but specifies that "cause" includes lack of "adequate protection." Adequate protection is designed to compensate persons whose interests in the debtor's property are being adversely affected by the stay, by the debtor's use of collateral under §363, and by certain types of new financing under §364. Section 361 lists some of the methods by which such protection may be afforded.

Bankruptcy Code §361
11 U.S.C. §361 (1988)

When adequate protection is required under section 362, 363 or 364 of this title of an interest of an entity in property, such adequate protection may be provided by —

(1) requiring the trustee to make a cash payment or periodic cash payments to such entity, to the extent that the stay under section 362 of this title, use, sale or lease under section 363 of this title, or any grant of a lien under section 364 of this title results in a decrease in the value of such entity's interest in such property;

(2) providing to such entity an additional or replacement lien to the extent that such stay, use, sale, lease, or grant results in a decrease in the value of such entity's interest in such property; or

(3) granting such other relief, other than entitling such entity to compensation allowable under section 503(b)(1) of this title as an administrative expense, as will result in the realization by such entity of the indubitable equivalent of such entity's interest in such property.

In the case that follows, the court considers the interaction of §§361 and 362 as well as another means (provided in §362(d)) for lifting of the stay.

In re Jamaica House, Inc.
31 Bankr. 192 (Bankr. D. Vt. 1983)

Charles J. MARRO, Bankruptcy Judge.

MEMORANDUM AND ORDER

The Complaint of the Green Mountain Bank for Relief from Automatic Stay, pursuant to Section 362(d), came on for hearing after notice. From the records in the case and the testimony adduced at the hearing the following facts have been established:

Jamaica House Inc. filed a petition for relief under Chapter 11 of the Bankruptcy Code on January 6, 1983. Its schedules show total liabilities of $120,285.78 and assets of $177,700.00. The debtor operates a restaurant and lodging business under the name of "Jamaica House." Its principal assets consist of real estate made up of the Jamaica Lodge or Inn and a small parcel of land together with fixtures, equipment and inventory. The value of the real estate is $150,000.00 while the equipment, fixtures and furnishings, inventory and other personal property have a valuation of $16,000.00.

The real estate is subject to a first mortgage in favor of the Green Mountain Bank with a balance due on the principal of $90,000.00 and there have been no interest payments on this mortgage since 1981. This property is also subject to a writ of attachment in favor of Heaslip Fuels in the sum of $1,500.00. The debtor has outstanding against it federal income taxes of approximately $10,000.00; rooms and meals taxes owed to the State of Vermont of about $8,000.00; and real estate taxes to the Town of Jamaica in the sum of $1,740.82 which constitute an underlying lien against its real property.

At the time of the hearing the insurance policy on the Jamaica Inn premises had expired and the debtor, through its president, agreed to make payment of the premium within ten days.

DISCUSSION

The only witness at the hearing was Robert Pugliese, President of the debtor, who testified that he had had an appraisal made of the real estate together with the personal property contents and the total valuation was fixed at $166,000.00 with which he was in agreement. This testimony was not disputed. . . .

It clearly appears that there is substantial equity in such property and, since the business of the debtor is the operation of an Inn and Restaurant, the property is necessary for reorganization. There has not been any evidence introduced that there cannot be an effective reorganization in this case. As a matter of fact the debtor has not, as yet, filed a Disclosure Statement or submitted a Plan. This Court did in the case of In Re Weathersfield Farms, Inc. (District of Vermont) 11 B.R. 148 continue the automatic stay on the grounds that the debtor had equity in property subject to a mortgage and that the property was necessary for an effective reorganization.

It is apparent that the Bank has failed to satisfy the second alternative condition under §362(d) which would entitle it to relief from stay. As a result the cause upon which the plaintiff must rely for a termination or modification of the stay is lack of adequate protection of its secured interest in the real estate and personal property of the debtor. It argues that its security is jeopardized since there is no showing that the debtor can or will be in a position to pay its current debts; pay its current mortgage obligations; pay its real estate taxes; or cure the acceleration of the plaintiff's mortgage as it has a right to do pursuant to Section 1124(2) of the Bankruptcy Act, namely clear up and pay back payments now amounting to $26,580.00. . . .

It has been generally held that an equity cushion in and of itself may be sufficient to constitute adequate protection of a secured creditor's interest to sustain the automatic stay. . . .

Some courts have qualified the foregoing rule that an equity cushion may in and of itself be sufficient to constitute adequate protection. See In Re Monroe Park, 6 C.B.C.2d at page 143 where the court pointed out that generally, an equity cushion provides adequate protection only if the creditor may foreclose upon the collateral and realize an amount sufficient to cover fully the entire balance due on the debt. See also In Re 5-Leaf Clover Corp. (S.D. West Virginia) 6 B.R. 463. Collier recognized the foregoing qualification and expresses it as follows:

> Thus an adequate "cushion" can itself constitute adequate protection with nothing more if care is taken to preserve the cushion. 2 Collier 15th Ed. 361-10 §361.01.

And in the case of In Re Pine Lake Village Apartment Co. (U.S. District Court, S.D.N.Y.-1982) 21 B.R. 395, 397 the Court said:

Unquestionably, a secured creditor has the right to be protected against any decline in value that the collateral could suffer if an automatic stay was in effect since, absent the stay, the creditor would foreclose, preventing any further loss in the value of the security.

Otherwise put, under bankruptcy law, adequate protection generally is meant to preserve the secured creditor's position at the time of bankruptcy. In Re Nixon Machinery Co. (E.D. Tenn. 1981) 9 B.R. 316.

In the instant case the debtor has not made any mortgage payments to the plaintiff since 1981. This situation was apparently tolerated by the secured creditor. Under such circumstances and with considerable equity in the property the plaintiff would ordinarily not be entitled to lifting of the stay upon the "balance of harm" test. In Re Orlando Coals, Inc. (S.D. West Virginia-1980) 6 B.R. 721. Under this test the Court will be required to consider the impact of the stay on the parties in fashioning relief. 2 Collier 15th Ed. 362-49.

In the light of the foregoing case law it seems abundantly clear that the plaintiff is not entitled to a lifting of the automatic stay. On the other hand the bank's position should not be prejudiced by allowing the debtor to accumulate unpaid real estate taxes which are an underlying lien against the Lodge premises. In addition the debtor should not be permitted to sit coyly back and neglect to file a disclosure statement and plan. The plaintiff is entitled to an early determination as to the feasibility of a successful reorganization so that its equity may be protected as much as possible.

In re Comcoach Corp. is illustrative of the gaps in the coverage afforded by adequate protection. In reading this case, consider the priority rules discussed in part C of Chapter 4.

Roslyn Savings Bank v. Comcoach Corp. (In re Comcoach Corp.)
698 F.2d 571 (2d Cir. 1983)

CARDAMONE, Circuit Judge:

Plaintiff Roslyn Savings Bank (Bank) seeks modification of the automatic stay occasioned by the filing of a bankruptcy petition by defendant-debtor Comcoach Corporation. The United States Bankruptcy Court (LIFLAND, J.) refused to modify the stay, and the United States District Court for the Southern District of New York (LOWE, J.) affirmed. We affirm.

I

In the spring of 1979 the Bank loaned Jon-Rac Associates a sum of money secured by a mortgage on certain premises. Later that year, and with the consent of the Bank, Jon-Rac Associates conveyed the mortgaged premises to Rhone Holdings Nominee Corporation (Rhone). The Bank simultaneously entered into a written agreement with Rhone under which Rhone agreed to pay the mortgage, and at the same time Rhone leased the property to Comcoach subject to the Bank's mortgage.

On August 1, 1981 Rhone defaulted on its mortgage payments and the Bank instituted a foreclosure proceeding against Rhone in New York State Supreme Court, Suffolk County. Comcoach, the tenant in possession of the mortgaged premises, was neither named as a party-defendant nor served with process. On October 26, 1981 Comcoach filed a reorganization petition to institute Chapter 11 proceedings pursuant to the United States Bankruptcy Code (the "Code"), 11 U.S.C. §§1101-74. Since that date the debtor has not paid any rent.

Arguing that it was barred from conducting the state foreclosure action by virtue of the Code's automatic stay provision, 11 U.S.C. §362(a)(1) (Supp. V 1981), the Bank commenced the present action in federal court asking that the automatic stay be lifted under 11 U.S.C. §362(d)(1), (2) (Supp. V 1981) to enable it to name Comcoach as a party-defendant in the pending state foreclosure action. The Bankruptcy Court denied plaintiff's request for relief on the ground that the Bank was not a "party in interest" entitled to seek modification of the stay under the Code. An appeal was then taken to the District Court which affirmed the Bankruptcy Court's decision. Subsequently, the bankruptcy was converted from a Chapter 11 reorganization to a Chapter 7 liquidation of the debtor Comcoach. . . .

To qualify for the "for cause" relief provided in section 362(d)(1), it is necessary that the party seeking such relief be "a party in interest." 11 U.S.C. §362(d). The term "party in interest" is not defined in the Code. Generally, the "real party in interest" is the one who, under the applicable substantive law, has the legal right which is sought to be enforced or is the party entitled to bring suit. . . .

Whether or not the Bank qualifies as a "party in interest" as that term is generally defined, we agree with the courts below that the Bank was not a "party in interest" within the meaning of the Bankruptcy Code. When interpreting the meaning of Code terms such as "party in interest," we are governed by the Code's purposes. See Kokoszka v. Belford, 417 U.S. 642, 645-46, 94 S. Ct. 2431, 2433-34, 41 L. Ed. 2d 374 (1974). One of those purposes is to convert the bankrupt's estate into cash and distribute it among creditors. . . .

Bankruptcy courts were established to provide a forum where creditors and debtors could settle their disputes and thereby effectuate the objectives of the statute. Necessarily, therefore, the Bank must be either a creditor or a debtor to invoke the court's jurisdiction.

Support for this view is found in the Code's legislative history which suggests that, notwithstanding the use of the term "party in interest," it is only creditors who may obtain relief from the automatic stay. See H.R. Rep. No. 95-595, 95th Cong., 1st Sess. 175, reprinted in 1978 U.S. Code Cong. & Ad. News 5787, 6136. . . .

Turning to the particular facts of this case, the Bank is clearly not a debtor. . . .

The Bank further expresses concern that if it is not a "party in interest" entitled to seek modification of the stay, it will be barred from continuing its foreclosure action in state court and left without a remedy to enforce its rights under the mortgage. As noted by both lower courts these concerns are premised upon an erroneous view of the law. First, the state foreclosure action, as presently constituted, is not stayed. Until the debtor is named as a party-defendant the action does not affect the bankrupt estate. New York law provides that lessees are necessary parties in foreclosure actions. . . .

Necessary parties are not always indispensable parties, however, whose absence mandates dismissal of the action. See N.Y. Civ. Prac. Law §1001(b) (McKinney 1976). The absence of a necessary party in a foreclosure action simply leaves such party's rights to the premises unaffected. See Douglas v. Kohart, 196 A.D. 84, 88, 187 N.Y.S. 102 (2d Dep't 1921); Home Life Insurance Co. v. O'Sullivan, 151 A.D. 535, 537, 136 N.Y.S. 105 (2d Dep't 1912). By failing to name Comcoach as a party-defendant in its foreclosure action, the Bank has left the debtor in exactly the same position as it was in prior to commencement of the suit. Since no interest of the bankrupt estate has been affected, no automatic stay prohibiting the continuance of the state foreclosure action exists.

Our disposition of the Bank's first argument appears to be of small or no solace for the Bank. After all, its only source of income from this property is the bankrupt tenant in a building rendered nearly unmarketable. But, in response to the Bank's second concern, we find that it has not been left without a remedy. The Bank has the right to the appointment of a receiver in the state court action. For reasons already noted, plaintiff is not stayed from seeking such an appointment. A court-appointed receiver *would* qualify as a party in interest for purposes of section 362(d), since under New York law a receiver steps into the shoes of the mortgagor-debtor, in this case Rhone. The receiver becomes vested with Rhone's property right and acts as an arm of the court for the creditor-Bank's benefit. . . . It would then have rights against Comcoach under applicable substantive law including the right to sue for rent and, therefore, the right to move to lift the automatic stay.

For the foregoing reasons we hold that the Bank is not a party in interest in the bankruptcy proceeding and cannot seek to have the automatic stay vacated or modified so as to name debtor Comcoach a party-defendant in the pending state foreclosure action.

NOTES AND QUESTIONS

1. *The Scope of the Automatic Stay.* As noted above, §362a makes the automatic stay very broad. In this note we will attempt to determine just how broad it really is.

a. Returning to the master hypothetical, assume that Ace Insurance Company's mortgage form contains an assignment-of-rents clause similar to the clause discussed in Chapter 10B4. When Dan Developer defaults, Ace directs the tenants to pay the rent directly to it. When the checks arrive, Ace deposits the checks and remits to Dan any amount in excess of what is owed on the mortgage balance. The day after Dan files his petition in bankruptcy, rent checks arrive by mail. Under §365(a), can Ace deposit the checks? If you think not, on what subsection or subsections of §365(a) are you relying?

b. Suppose Dan Developer had not filed for bankruptcy but was nevertheless in default under the mortgage. At the time Ace forecloses a tenant and a second mortgagee are in bankruptcy. If you were counsel to Ace, under what circumstances would you advise Ace to proceed with the foreclosure? If you advise against foreclosure, with what subsection or subsections of §362(a) are you concerned? Would your answer be different if you were in a power-of-sale foreclosure state rather than a judicial foreclosure state? In *Comcoach* the mortgagee asked for relief from the stay, "arguing that it was barred from conducting the state foreclosure action by virtue of the Code's automatic stay provision." Was this correct? Did the court say the mortgagee was barred from conducting the foreclosure under §362(a), or was it just barred from naming the lessee as a party defendant or cutting off the lease? Assume Ace Insurance Company, foreclosing against Dan Developer (who is not in bankruptcy), wanted to name a second mortgagee as a party defendant and was precluded from doing so because of the stay. (Do you understand why it is more important to be able to name the second mortgagee than the lessee?) Under *Comcoach*, does Ace have standing to seek relief from the stay? Why? What procedure does the court suggest? If that procedure were not available, do you think the court would have come out differently?

c. Assume that some months before Dan filed his petition in bankruptcy there was a small fire for which insurance proceeds were awarded. Ace allowed Dan to hold the proceeds of the insurance in escrow for payment of the cost of restoration, with any remainder to be turned over to Ace and applied to reduction of the indebtedness. When the petition is filed, all the restoration has been completed and there is $5,680 still in escrow to be turned over to Ace. Can Ace get this money? On what subsections of §362(a) are you relying?

These are just a few of the difficult questions that may arise in connection with the §362 stay. The point is that the stay is pervasive — virtually any steps a mortgagee may wish to take may be barred. Remember that §362(a)(6) stays "any act to collect . . . a claim," which is about as broad as you can get. Suppose you represent Ace and you conclude that there is a high probability that the stay applies to a proposed action by Ace. Nevertheless, Ace's loan officer asks you to proceed with the proposed act promptly, stating that he or she will take the risk of any impropriety. Do you think there would be any risk to you in following that instruction? See Fidelity Mortgage Investors v. Camelia Builders, 550 F.2d 47 (2d Cir. 1976), cert. denied, 429 U.S. 1093 (1977).

The fact that the stay applies does not mean the proposed act may not be taken. It means it may not be taken without the approval of the court. The grounds for seeking relief from the stay are discussed below.

2.   *"Effective" Reorganization.*   Section 362(d) provides that relief from the stay will be granted if the debtor has no equity in the property and the property is not necessary for an effective reorganization. When the Code was being drafted, representatives of certain real estate lenders first suggested that relief from the stay be granted where the debtor had no equity in the property. They were disturbed by pre-Code abuses of the stay as borrowers, whose bad management had caused the failure, continued as managers to "milk" the property (i.e., collect portions of cash flow as commissions or fees while maintenance is deferred) while irreparable damage was being done to the reputation and value of the property. Wait a minute, said the National Bankruptcy Conference. What you say may make sense when you are talking about a single-asset real estate limited partnership. But what happens in a major corporate reorganization? Are you going to frustrate the reorganization by lifting the stay to permit foreclosure of a mortgage on the debtor's factory simply because the liens on the factory exceed its value? The National Bankruptcy Conference had a point. Accordingly, the second condition to lifting the stay for lack of equity was added: the necessity for a finding that the property is not necessary to an effective reorganization.

Suppose Dan Developer had syndicated his property by creating a limited partnership to own the land and building as its sole asset. At the time of Dan's petition for reorganization under Chapter 11, Ace's mortgage exceeds the value of the property, so the debtor has

no equity in the property. Can Ace foreclose? Is the property necessary
to the reorganization? Can relief from the stay ever be granted on this
ground if the debtor has only one asset? Remember, the provision
refers to an *effective* reorganization. What is the meaning of "effective"?
See In re Garden Motor Lodge and Restaurant, 34 B.R. 138 (Bankr.
D. Vt. 1983) and Statement of Congressman Don Edwards (the "father"
of the Bankruptcy Code on the House side) in 124 Cong. Rec. H.
11092 (daily ed. Sept. 28, 1978). Cf. §1129(a)(11).

3.   Adequate Protection.   Under §362(d)(1), relief from the stay
must be granted for cause, including lack of adequate protection for
the mortgagee's interest. Section 361 sets forth three methods of
providing adequate protection: cash payments, replacement lien, or the
"indubitable equivalent" of the diminution in value of the mortgagee's
interest in the collateral. The phrase "indubitable equivalent" was coined
by Judge Learned Hand in In re Murel Holding Corp., 75 F.2d 941,
942 (2d Cir. 1935), where he discussed the meaning of "adequate
protection" in another context:

> It is plain that "adequate protection" must be completely compensatory;
> and that payment ten years hence is not generally the equivalent of
> payment now. Interest is indeed the common measure of the difference,
> but a creditor who fears the safety of his principal will scarcely be
> content with that; he wishes to get his money or at least the property.
> We see no reason to suppose that the statute was intended to deprive
> him of that in the interest of junior holders, unless by a substitute of
> the most *indubitable equivalence.* (Emphasis supplied.)

By employing Judge Hand's language, the drafters intended to
make it clear that they did not expect the courts to give mere lip
service to the concept of adequate protection, and by and large the
courts have recognized this. Nevertheless, questions continue to arise
for resolution. For example, assume that Dan Developer files under
Chapter 11 of the Code. Ace Insurance Company is undersecured, that
is, its mortgage has a balance in excess of the value of the property.
Is Ace entitled to adequate protection because the value of the collateral,
which Ace would have obtained on foreclosure, could not be reinvested?
In other words, is Ace entitled to payments for lost opportunity costs?
After conflicts among the circuits, the Supreme Court answered this
question in the negative, equating lost opportunity costs with post-
petition interest, to which the mortgagee is entitled under §506(b)
only to the extent that the value of the collateral exceeds the indebtedness. United Savings Assn. v. Timbers of Inwood Forest Assocs., 484
U.S. 365 (1988). Suppose the value of the property is decreasing rapidly.
The court determines that Dan's management is at fault and provides
adequate protection by replacing Dan as manager. Do you think this

would meet §361's requirements? See In re Prime, Inc. 15 B.R. 216 (Bankr. W.D. Mo. 1981).

In *Jamaica House* the court discusses the fact that the collateral had value in excess of the indebtedness (an "equity cushion") and debated whether the existence of such a cushion constituted adequate protection for the mortgagee. Is adequate protection something the mortgagee already has, or something the court gives to the mortgagee to compensate for a reduction in value of collateral? If the cushion is adequate protection and it is decreasing, how does the mortgagee protect its right under §506(b) to post-petition interest to the extent the value of the collateral exceeds the indebtedness? Did the court find a need for adequate protection? What was the basis for its conclusion? What do you think the court meant by the "balance of harm" test, and how does such a test apply to the requirements of §361? In refusing to grant relief from the stay, what protection for the mortgagee did the court build into its denial?

The courts are in disagreement as to whether and at what point the reduction of the cushion requires adequate protection. Compare In re San Clemente Estates, 5 Bankr. 605 (Bankr. S.D. Cal. 1980), with In re H & F Inv. Co., 9 Bankr. 548 (Bankr. N.D. Ohio 1981). Some practitioners have noted that where the cushion gets below 20 percent, the courts seem more willing to provide adequate protection.

If the "adequate protection" provided by the court proves inadequate, the creditor being protected may have a claim for the deficiency as an administrative expense. Administrative expenses, allowed under §503, include the actual, necessary costs of preserving the estate and normally receive first priority when property is distributed to unsecured creditors. However, if the administrative expense claim is for inadequate adequate protection, such claim is given a limited superpriority by §507(b) and will be paid ahead of all other administrative expense claims. Does it seem strange to you that the benefits of §507(b) apply only if adequate protection is provided and it turns out to be insufficient, but administrative expense treatment is prohibited in §361(3) as a form of adequate protection? Were the drafters attempting to restrict the granting of an administrative expense claim, or was their object to indicate that an administrative expense claim payment of which is subject to availability of funds at the time of distribution is not the indubitable equivalent of a loss in value of collateral?

4. *Timing of Adequate Protection.*   In In re Ahlers, 794 F.2d 388 (8th Cir. 1986), the Eighth Circuit held, inter alia, that adequate protection payments, where justified, should not begin to be paid until the lapse of a period equal to the time it would normally have taken to foreclose free of the debtor's right of redemption (in that case, one year and 60 days). It also held that it was improper for the bankruptcy

court to rule that adequate protection payments, when available, should be made monthly where the debtor, a farmer, would realize income, if at all, when the crops are grown and sold at the end of the growing season. The Supreme Court did not grant certiorari on the issue of adequate protection, although it did reverse the Eighth Circuit on the other major issue of the case, absolute priority in reorganization plans, 485 U.S. 197 (1988). Thus, the holdings on adequate protection stand as the law of the Eighth Circuit. Does "adequate protection" as enunciated by the Eighth Circuit meet the drafters' objective of providing the creditor with what Judge Learned Hand called "indubitable equivalence"?

    5. Use, Sale, or Lease of Property and Obtaining Credit. Adequate protection under §361 applies not only to the effects of the stay but also to the effects of the use, sale, or lease of the collateral under §363 or the obtaining of certain credit for the estate under §364.

    Section 363 permits the trustee to use, sell, or lease the collateral either in or out of the ordinary course of business. If it is not in the ordinary course, §363(b)(1) requires a prior notice and hearing. If the sale is in the ordinary course of business, notice and a hearing are required only for the use of cash collateral (§§363(c)(1), (2)). Cash collateral under §363(a) includes rents. Too much reliance should not be placed on a notice and hearing. Section 102(1) permits no hearing if notice is given and if, inter alia, the court determines that there is insufficient time for a hearing.

    The mortgagee is generally permitted to bid at a sale of the collateral not in the ordinary course of business and to offset the bid against its claim (§363(k)). Assume that Dan Developer's trustee sells his property free and clear of the Ace mortgage. Does the right to bid and offset against the claim sufficiently protect Ace? We will be coming back to §363 later in connection with our discussion of the plan of reorganization. For now, remember that on request of an entity with an interest in the property, the court under §363(e) is required to condition the use, sale, or lease to provide adequate protection of such interest.

    Under §364, the trustee is authorized to obtain credit for the continued operation of the business. The court, after notice and hearing, is permitted to authorize obtaining secured credit equal in lien or superior to an existing mortgage on the property (§364(d)), where unsecured credit is unavailable and adequate protection is provided for the mortgagee. Assume that when Dan Developer files in bankruptcy an addition to his building is only partially completed. Dan is plagued with cost overruns, his construction financing is in default, and no additional credit will be extended by the construction lender. The court, after a notice and hearing, permits the trustee to borrow funds to complete the addition from another lender, giving the new lender a lien prior to the construction loan and Ace's mortgage. Both Ace and the construction lender ask the court for adequate protection under §361. The court says it does not have to provide any further protection to the construction lender and Ace. What would be the basis for the court's conclusion?

6. *Additional Reading.* See generally M. Bienenstock, Bankruptcy Reorganization 97-223 (1987). See also Divack, Chapter 11 Liquidation and the "Necessary to an Effective Reorganization" Standard of Relief from the Automatic Stay, 93 Com. L.J. 17 (Spring 1988); Flaschen, Adequate Protection for the Oversecured Creditor, 61 Am. Bankr. L.J. 341 (1987); Karlen, Adequate Protection Under the Bankruptcy Code: Its Role in Bankruptcy Reorganizations, 2 Pace L. Rev. (1982); McCullough, Analysis of Bankruptcy Code Section 364(d): When Will a Court Allow a Trustee to Obtain Post-petition Financing by Granting a Superpriority Lien?, 93 Com. L.J. 186 (1988); Murphy, Administrative Powers of the Trustee in Bankruptcy — Stays Use of Collateral, and Obtaining Credit, in ABA Sec. of Real Prop., Prob. & Tr. L., Real Estate Bankruptcies and Workouts 11 (1983); Nimmer, Real Estate Creditors and the Automatic Stay: A Study in Behavioral Economics, 1983 Ariz. St. L.J. 281 (1983); Smahci, Automatic Stay Under the 1978 Bankruptcy Code: An Equitable Roadblock to Secured Creditor Relief, 17 S. Diego L. Rev. 1113 (1980); Weintraub and Resnick, Puncturing the Equity Cushion — Adequate Protection for Secured Creditors in Reorganization Cases, 14 U.C.C. L.J. 284 (1982).

2.   The Plan of Reorganization

The purpose of a proceeding under Chapter 11 of the Code is to rehabilitate the debtor under a plan of reorganization. The plan will normally provide that creditors be given property or interests in the reorganized enterprise as compensation for their claims. As noted above, such a plan often necessitates dealing with and changing the rights of creditors. Creditors' interests are protected against unfairness generally in four ways.

1.   A plan must be accepted (except in the limited circumstances described below) by at least two-thirds in amount and more than one-half in number of allowed claims of each class of creditors (§§1126(c), 1129(a)(8)) and by at least one class of impaired claimants (§1129(a)(10));

2. While the court, under certain circumstances, may impose (or "cram down") a plan against a dissenting class of creditors, it may not confirm a plan over the objection of a class of creditors whose interests are "impaired" (§1124) by the plan unless the plan is "fair and equitable" as to such class. This requires a distribution based on absolute priority as set forth in §§1129(a)(8) and 1129(b)(1), discussed in more detail below;

3. No plan may be confirmed unless each holder of a claim who has not individually accepted the plan receives property of a value at least equal to what such holder would have received had the debtor's estate been liquidated under Chapter 7 (this is the so-called best-interest-of-creditors test of §1129(a)(7), discussed above); and

4. The court must determine that confirmation of the plan is not likely to be followed by liquidation or a need for further financial reorganization, that is, that the plan is feasible. (§1129(a)(11).)

In this discussion, we will analyze how effective these protections are for the real estate mortgagee.

The major real estate problem in drafting the Code arose under the 1977 *Pine Gate* decision.[9] *Pine Gate* involved the reorganization of a single-asset real estate limited partnership under what was then Chapter XII of the former Bankruptcy Act. As you know from Chapter 2, in a limited partnership it is frequently necessary for the general partner to be exculpated from personal liability on the mortgage debt so that the limited partners can obtain a step-up in the tax basis of their partnership interests equal to their share of the mortgage liability.[10] Otherwise, in a leveraged partnership, without the increase in basis a limited partner may not be able to take full advantage of its distributive share of losses and other tax benefits associated with real estate ownership. Accordingly, as a "tax favor" to the partnership the mortgage lender in *Pine Gate* was willing to allow the mortgage debt to be nonrecouse. Back in the 1970s, when *Pine Gate* transpired, real estate tax shelter was in its heyday. Nonrecourse financing meant that when times were good the limited partners could enjoy all available tax shelter benefits, including accelerated depreciation. Conversely, if times were bad the partners could walk away from the transaction without personal liability. However, one fly in the ointment for the limited partners

9. In re Pine Gate Assocs., 2 Bankr. Ct. Dec. (CRR) 1478 (Bankr. N.D. Ga. 1976).

10. See I.R.C. §465(b)(6) and Treas. Reg. §1.752-1(e). See generally discussion at Chapter 2B, note 7diii.

was the tax rule that foreclosure is deemed to be disposition of real property for tax purposes. This meant that any foreclosure could have triggered the recapture of all the accelerated depreciation taken on the property as ordinary income to the limited partners in the year of foreclosure.[11] Confronted with the specter of substantial tax liabilities, the partners in *Pine Gate* on the eve of the foreclosure sale filed a petition and thereby stayed the foreclosure while the partnership remained in control as a "debtor in possession" (see note 6 below). Next the partners attempted to devise a plan of reorganization under which they would pay the mortgagee only a portion of the indebtedness and keep the property free and clear of the lien of the mortgage.

As previously discussed, under the old Bankruptcy Act, what is now Chapter 11 was divided into three chapters: Chapter X, dealing with Corporate Reorganization, Chapter XI, covering arrangements for unsecured debts, and Chapter XII, dealing specifically with real property arrangements for non-corporate debtors. Under the provisions of Chapter X, almost every plan had to be "fair and equitable" and thus provide for absolute priority. This meant that no junior creditor could be paid until senior creditors were paid in full and that no stockholder or other owner (including partners) of the debtor could be given any property until all creditors were paid in full.[12] Since the *Pine Gate* partnership would be unable to keep any property unless the mortgagee were paid, Chapter X was not helpful to the limited partners, who wanted to keep the property without full payment of the mortgage.

In Chapter XII, however, there was (after 1952) no provision requiring absolute priority. (There was also no absolute priority requirement in Chapter XI, but this chapter was limited to arrangements for unsecured debts.) Nevertheless, Chapter XII protected dissenting classes under a court-imposed ("cram down") plan in several ways. The "protection" alternative that figured so prominently in the *Pine Gate* line of cases was found in Chapter XII's §461(11), requiring that before a plan could be confirmed over the objection of a class the dissenting class had to be paid in cash the value of the debt owed to that class.

Judge William Norton interpreted that provision in the *Pine Gate* decision and held that when the debt is nonrecourse (no personal liability), the "value of the debt" is equal to the value of the collateral, which had been depressed in the market conditions in Atlanta at the time. Thus, the partnership could keep the property free and clear of the mortgage by paying the mortgagee some $1.9 million (the court-determined value of the collateral) on a $2.3 million debt. Other such cases followed. The most shocking of the *Pine Gate* line of cases to

---

11. I.R.C. §§1245, 1250 (prior law). See discussion at Chapter 2B, note 3.
12. See Case v. Los Angeles Lumber Products Co., 308 U.S. 106 (1939).

the real estate community was In re KRO Associates,[13] where there was some $14 million in mortgages on the property and Judge Roy Babbitt, using a 20 percent capitalization rate, came to a value of $895,000. The mortgagee would have been willing to take the property for the full amount of the indebtedness, but the court pointed out that this would create tax problems (recapture of accelerated depreciation) for the limited partners and allowed the mortgagor to keep the property on payment to the first mortgagee of $895,000 in discharge of all mortgages (including the $5 million owed on the first mortgage).

It should be no surprise then, that as the new Code was taking shape in Washington, the real estate community appealed for legislative help to prevent what they considered a severe injustice. They suggested that absolute priority be made applicable to the new omnibus Chapter 11. Opposition to this approach came (surprisingly, to the real estate bar) from those attorneys and business people who had experience in corporate reorganizations. Under the "fair and equitable" requirement of Chapter X, absolute priority had been a must. Classes of creditors, by the requisite majorities, could not agree to take less than absolute priority would provide. For example, if the classes wanted to retain capable management, the creditors might want to provide in the plan that some of the stock in the reorganized company go to the old management. This, however, would be impossible under absolute priority unless each creditor (as distinguished from each class of creditors by the requisite majority) agreed. Thus, instead of promoting negotiation and compromise, the absolute priority requirement, they argued, promoted poor business decisions and endless litigation concerning the value of the assets and the interests each class would receive in the new company.

Out of this controversy grew the philosophy of Chapter 11, which is to promote compromise and to permit classes to agree on plans without testing the agreement against the absolute priority standard. Protection was afforded the real estate mortgagee, however, in providing that a plan must be fair and equitable as to any *impaired* class that does not approve the plan. Absolute priority, then, applies only when the classes cannot agree on a plan, and then only to those impaired classes that reject the plan.

Understanding the philosophy of Chapter 11 may be somewhat easier than understanding the mechanics that put the philosophy into practice. The operative sections for this understanding include at minimum §§506, 1111(b), 1124, and 1129, which are excerpted below. The mechanics and the resulting confirmation strategy will be discussed in the notes.

13. 4 Bankr. Ct. Dec. (CRR) 462 (Bankr. S.D.N.Y., 1978).

Bankruptcy Code
11 U.S.C. §§506, 1111(b), 1124, 1129

§506. Determination of secured status

(a) An allowed claim of a creditor secured by a lien on property in which the estate has an interest, or that is subject to setoff under section 553 of this title, is a secured claim to the extent of the value of such creditor's interest in the estate's interest in such property, or to the extent of the amount subject to setoff, as the case may be, and is an unsecured claim to the extent that the value of such creditor's interest or the amount so subject to setoff is less than the amount of such allowed claim. Such value shall be determined in light of the purpose of the valuation and of the proposed disposition or use of such property, and in conjunction with any hearing on such disposition or use or on a plan affecting such creditor's interest.

(b) To the extent that an allowed secured claim is secured by property the value of which, after any recovery under subsection (c) of this section, is greater than the amount of such claim, there shall be allowed to the holder of such claim, interest on such claim, and any reasonable fees, costs, or charges provided for under the agreement under which such claim arose. . . .

§1111. Claims and interests . . .

(b)(1)(A) A claim secured by a lien on property of the estate shall be allowed or disallowed under section 502 of this title the same as if the holder of such claim had recourse against the debtor on account of such claim, whether or not such holder has such recourse, unless —

    (i) the class of which such claim is a part elects, by at least two-thirds in amount and more than half in number of allowed claims of such class, application of paragraph (2) of this subsection; or

    (ii) such holder does not have such recourse and such property is sold under section 363 of this title or is to be sold under the plan.

    (B) A class of claims may not elect application of paragraph (2) of this subsection if —

    (i) the interest on account of such claims of the holders of such claims in such property is of inconsequential value; or

    (ii) the holder of a claim of such class has recourse against the debtor on account of such claim and such property is sold under section 363 of this title or is to be sold under the plan.

    (2) If such an election is made, then notwithstanding section

506(a) of this title, such claim is a secured claim to the extent that such claim is allowed.

§1124. Impairment of claims or interests

Except as provided in section 1123(a)(4) of this title, a class of claims or interests is impaired under a plan unless, with respect to each claim or interest of such class, the plan —

(1) leaves unaltered the legal, equitable, and contractual rights to which such claim or interest entitles the holder of such claim or interest;

(2) notwithstanding any contractual provision or applicable law that entitles the holder of such claim or interest to demand or receive accelerated payment of such claim or interest after the occurrence of a default —

(A) cures any such default that occurred before or after the commencement of the case under this title, other than a default of a kind specified in section 365(b)(2) of this title;

(B) reinstates the maturity of such claim or interest as such maturity existed before such default;

(C) compensates the holder of such claim or interest for any damages incurred as a result of any reasonable reliance by such holder on such contractual provision or such applicable law; and

(D) does not otherwise alter the legal, equitable, or contractual rights to which such claim or interest entitles the holder of such claim or interest; or

(3) provides that, on the effective date of the plan, the holder of such claim or interest receives, on account of such claim or interest, cash equal to —

(A) with respect to a claim, the allowed amount of such claim; or

(B) with respect to an interest, if applicable, the greater of —

(i) any fixed liquidation preference to which the terms of any security representing such interest entitle the holder of such interest; or

(ii) any fixed price at which the debtor, under the terms of such security, may redeem such security from such holder.

§1129. Confirmation of plan

(a) The court shall confirm a plan only if all of the following requirements are met: . . .

(3) The plan has been proposed in good faith and not by any means forbidden by law. . . .

(7) With respect to each impaired class of claims or interests —

(A) each holder of a claim or interest of such class —

(i) has accepted the plan; or

(ii) will receive or retain under the plan on account of such claim or interest property of a value, as of the effective date of the plan, that is not less than the amount that such holder would so receive or retain if the debtor were liquidated under chapter 7 of this title on such date; or

(B) if section 1111(b)(2) of this title applies to the claims of such class, each holder of a claim of such class will receive or retain under the plan on account of such claim property of a value, as of the effective date of the plan, that is not less than the value of such holder's interest in the estate's interest in the property that secures such claims.

(8) With respect to each class of claims or interests —

(A) such class has accepted the plan; or

(B) such class is not impaired under the plan. . . .

(10) If a class of claims is impaired under the plan, at least one class of claims that is impaired under the plan has accepted the plan, determined without including any acceptance of the plan by any insider.

(11) Confirmation of the plan is not likely to be followed by the liquidation, or the need for further financial reorganization, of the debtor or any successor to the debtor under the plan, unless such liquidation or reorganization is proposed in the plan. . . .

(b)(1) Notwithstanding section 510(a) of this title, if all of the applicable requirements of subsection (a) of this section other than paragraph (8) are met with respect to a plan, the court, on request of the proponent of the plan, shall confirm the plan notwithstanding the requirements of such paragraph if the plan does not discriminate unfairly, and is fair and equitable, with respect to each class of claims or interests that is impaired under, and has not accepted, the plan.

(2) For the purpose of this subsection, the condition that a plan be fair and equitable with respect to a class includes the following requirements:

(A) With respect to a class of secured claims, the plan provides —

(i)(I) that the holders of such claims retain the liens securing such claims, whether the property subject to such liens is retained by the debtor or transferred to another entity, to the extent of the allowed amount of such claims; and

(II) that each holder of a claim of such class receive on account of such claim deferred cash payments totaling at least the allowed amount of such claim, of a value, as of the effective date of the plan, of at least the value of such holder's interest in the estate's interest in such property;

(ii) for the sale, subject to section 363(k) of this title, of any property that is subject to the liens securing such claims, free and clear of such liens, with such liens to attach to the proceeds of such sale, and the treatment of such liens on proceeds under clause (i) or (iii) of this subparagraph; or

(iii) for the realization by such holders of the indubitable equivalent of such claims.

(B) With respect to a class of unsecured claims —

(i) the plan provides that each holder of a claim of such class receive or retain on account of such claim property of a value, as of the effective date of the plan, equal to the allowed amount of such claim; or

(ii) the holder of any claim or interest that is junior to the claims of such class will not receive or retain under the plan on account of such junior claim or interest any property.

(C) With respect to a class of interests —

(i) the plan provides that each holder of an interest of such class receive or retain on account of such interest property of a value, as of the effective date of the plan, equal to the greatest of the allowed amount of any fixed liquidation preference to which such holder is entitled, any fixed redemption price to which such holder is entitled, or the value of such interest; or

(ii) the holder of any interest that is junior to the interests of such class will not receive or retain under the plan on account of such junior interest any property. . . .

Section 1129(b) of the Code provides that a court-imposed plan must be fair and equitable (that is, absolute priority is required) for all impaired classes who have not accepted the plan. The *Pinebrook* case (not to be confused with *Pine Gate*) represents one court's determination of when a plan meets that standard with respect to a creditor class holding a mortgage on the debtor's property. In the notes below we will consider whether the court's determination was correct.

In re Pinebrook, Ltd.
85 Bankr. 160 (Bankr. M.D. Fla. 1988)

George L. PROCTOR, Bankruptcy Judge.

This case is before the Court on the debtor's motion for 11 U.S.C. §1129(b) treatment relative to Mutual Benefit Life Insurance Company ("Mutual Benefit"), the only creditor in Class 1. A hearing on the motion was held on February 9, 1988, at the conclusion of which the court directed the parties to submit written memoranda in support of their positions. Upon the arguments so presented, the Court enters the following findings of fact and conclusions of law:

FINDINGS OF FACT

1. Mutual Benefit has filed a claim in this case based upon a non-recourse mortgage loan made to the debtor in the original principal amount of $2,800,000.00. Interest thereon accrues at the coupon rate of 12% per annum. The Note evidencing the loan contains the customary provisions found in similar notes such as a yield maintenance clause which assesses a penalty upon prepayment and a default clause which provides that upon default the remaining principal with accrued interest becomes due immediately without notice at an increased rate of 24%.

2. The note provided for monthly interest only payments for five years, and thereafter, monthly payments of both principal and interest for three years with the balance of the loan being due and payable on October 1, 1991.

3. The debtor defaulted under the terms of the note by failing to make the August 1, 1986 interest payment and all payments thereafter. Mutual Benefit then elected to accelerate the balance due and filed a foreclosure action pursuant to Florida law in October of 1986.

4. In March of 1987, the Debtor filed a petition for relief under Chapter 11 of the Bankruptcy Code. 11 U.S.C. §101 et seq. The continuation of the foreclosure action was automatically stayed by the provision of 11 U.S.C. §362.

5. On July 14, 1987, Mutual Benefit and the debtor entered into an agreement concerning the use of cash collateral and to a limited modification of the stay. The Court approved the agreement which permitted Mutual Benefit to continue the foreclosure up to and including the obtaining of a Final Judgment of Foreclosure. After obtaining such approval, Mutual Benefit proceded with its foreclosure action and ultimately obtained a Partial Summary Judgment in its favor.

6. During the pendency of the state court proceedings, the Debtor filed a plan of reorganization which contemplates a "cramdown" (11 U.S.C. §1129(b)) of its provisions against Mutual Benefit, the Debtor's only secured creditor.

7. On December 15, 1987, the Court held a confirmation hearing. After the presentation of evidence, the Court found that all of the requirements of §1129(a) were met with the exception of subsection (8) (the vote), whereupon the debtor moved for "cramdown" pursuant to §1129(b) against the dissenting creditor, Mutual Benefit.

8. Debtor's plan of reorganization treats Mutual Benefit's claim as

impaired and proposes to pay it $100,000 on the effective date of the plan. The balance of the claim will be paid in monthly installments of $21,000 until October 1, 1991, at which time the entire debt including accrued but unpaid interest will become due. Under the plan, Mutual Benefit will retain its lien and will not face an enhanced risk of ultimate non-payment.

CONCLUSIONS OF LAW

1. Section 1129(b)(1) provides several methods by which a court may confirm a Chapter 11 plan which is fair and equitable notwithstanding the failure of acceptance of each class. This debtor has elected to proceed under the two-prong test set forth in section 1129(b)(2)(A)(i), which requires that,

I.   the creditor retain its lien, and
II. the creditor receives deferred cash payments with a present value equal to its allowed claim.

2. Under the proposed plan, Mutual Benefit will retain its lien. Thus, the first prong of the section 1129(b)(2)(A)(i) test is met.

3. The second prong of the test requires the determination of present value. The plan proposes to continue the original maturity of the loan, October 1, 1991. The interest would continue to accrue at the contract rate of 12%, but only 9% would be paid in the form of regular monthly payments with the remaining 3% to be paid in a lump sum at the loan's maturity. The Court must now determine whether this provides for the present value of Mutual Benefit's claim.

4. The appropriate interest rate for §1129(b)(2)(A) analysis is a weighted average of rates charged by commercial lenders in the same market. In re Orosco, 77 B.R. 246, 252, 16 B.C.D. 272, 276 (Bkrtcy. N.D. Ca. 1987). Says another Court:

> [A]n appropriate interest rate should be calculated on a case by case basis, considering such factors as the prevailing market rate for a loan of equal term to that proposed in the debtor's plan, the quality of the collateral securing the indebtedness, the credit standard of the borrower, and risk of subsequent default.

In re 360 Inns, Ltd., 76 B.R. 573 (Bkrtcy. N.D. Tex. 1987). The Courts have rejected the proposition that the debtor's bankruptcy makes it uncreditworthy so that a higher than market rate should be imposed. Orosco, 77 B.R. at 254, 16 B.C.D. at 276-277.

A witness for the debtor testified that his survey of seven other lenders revealed that the market rate for loans of comparable size, length, nature, and debt to value ratio showed a range of 8⅝% to 9¾%. Since the plan provides for 9% interest on Mutual Benefit's claim, the interest rate chosen in the instant plan falls within the parameters suggested by §1129(b)(2)(A).

5. Mutual Benefit's position that it is entitled to the default rate of interest of 24% is expressly rejected. Mutual Benefit argues it is allowed the increase by virtue of §506(b). Such an argument is contrary to the case law which has generally held that secured creditors are only entitled to interest at the contract rate. The allowance of the default rate of interest is appropriate only where:

(1) The creditor faces a significant risk of non-payment of its debt;

(2) There is evidence that the lower, contract rate of interest is not a prevailing market rate of interest;

(3) Where the plan calls for a long term reorganization as opposed to a relatively quick payment; and

(4) It appears that the benefits of reorganization would accrue to the equity security holders. . . .

7. The evidence supports that the payment schedule promised by the plan will make full restitution to this creditor.

The plan may be confirmed notwithstanding the nonacceptance of the dissenting class, Mutual Benefit because it provides for the full present value of the secured claim and is in accord with §1129(b)(2)(A). Mutual Benefit is entitled to principal, interest at the contract rate, and attorneys fees. It is not entitled to default interest or prepayment penalty.

In accordance with these findings, the Court will enter a separate order confirming debtor's plan of reorganization.

NOTES AND QUESTIONS

1. *Allowed Secured Claim.* The message of §506(a) is that a mortgagee's claim is a secured claim to the extent of the value of the collateral, and to the extent that the claim exceeds the value of the collateral it is an unsecured claim. Without more (and virtually until enactment, drafts of the Code did not contain more), mortgagees feared that this language codified the *Pine Gate* line of cases. Do you see why?

If you have difficulty with the last question, assume in the master hypothetical that Dan Developer is the general partner of Law Drive Associates, a single-asset limited partnership owning the land and building subject to Ace Insurance Company's nonrecourse mortgage. The partnership files a petition in Chapter 11 at a time when the Ace mortgage, with a principal balance then at $15 million, is in default. The value of the land and building is approximately $12 million. Under §506(a), Ace would have a secured claim of $12 million, equal to the value of the mortgaged property. Section 506(a) also provides that Ace would have an unsecured claim for the difference between the value of the collateral and the amount of the obligation. But since the debt is nonrecourse and the partners are not personally liable on the note, Ace would have had no claim for an amount in excess of the value of the collateral ("claim" is defined in §101(4)(A) as a "right to payment . . ."). As a result, although the remaining $3 million borrowed would normally be an unsecured claim, in this situation Ace would have no unsecured claim. (Indeed, the portion of the lien in excess of the collateral's value would not be an allowed claim and would thus be voided under §506(d).)

Assume that the proposed plan of reorganization adversely affects, or impairs, Ace's interest and that Ace (as the only member of the class of first mortgagees) rejects it. The court proposes to cram down the plan but cannot do so under §1129(b)(1) unless the plan is "fair and equitable." This means that absolute priority must be observed with respect to Ace's claim. But because of §506(a), the claim of Ace's that is entitled to absolute priority is only a secured claim for $12 million. Thus, even if Ace is paid the full claim in cash, wouldn't it end up like the mortgagee under *Pine Gate,* without the debt having been fully paid and Law Drive Associates retaining the property? Think of this result in light of the *KRO* case, discussed above. The first mortgage had a balance of $6 million and the court found the value of the property to be $895,000. The mortgagee, under §506(a), would have had a secured claim of $895,000 and no unsecured claim because the debt was nonrecourse. Even if the Code had provided for full payment in cash of dissenting classes of creditors, the first mortgagee would have gotten no more than $895,000, the remaining mortgagees would have received nothing, and the limited partnership would have kept the property. Do you see that this result would be exactly the same as the result under Chapter XII?

This concern of the mortgagees was dealt with by the addition of §1111(b), discussed below.

2. Recourse or Full Secured Claim. Section 1111(b) was designed to rescue the mortgagees from the plight discussed in note 1. Under §1111(b)(1)(A), a nonrecourse claim is automatically converted to a recourse claim for the purpose of the allowance of an unsecured claim in the reorganization (unless the property is being sold, for which special rules, discussed below, apply). This conversion would give the nonrecourse mortgagee an unsecured claim for the difference between the value of the collateral and the higher amount of the debt. Alternatively, §1111(b) provides that unless the claim is of inconsequential value, a secured creditor in Ace's situation may elect a full secured claim, covering the entire indebtedness, notwithstanding the §506(a) valuation.

Apply the foregoing rules to the hypothetical situation described in note 1 above. Do you agree that under §1111(b) Ace's nonrecourse claim would be converted to a recourse claim, giving Ace a $12 million secured claim and a $3 million unsecured claim unless Ace elected to take a full secured claim of $15 million? If you were Ace, would you choose the recourse claim or the full claim? After reading note 3 on the mechanics of the cram-down, come back to this question and see if you change your answer.

3. *The Mechanics of the Cram-Down.* Getting back to our hypothetical situation with the same fact pattern discussed in note 1, assume that Ace's interest is adversely affected by a proposed plan of reorganization (§1129(a)(8) makes it clear that a class can reject a plan only if it is "impaired" by the plan, under the theory that you should only have a right to complain if you are hurt — more will be said about impairment in note 4). Ace, in a class by itself as a first mortgagee, rejects the plan. As discussed above, in order to cram down, or confirm the plan over Ace's rejection, the plan must be fair and equitable to Ace pursuant to §1129(b)(1), that is, it must provide absolute priority with respect to Ace's claim. Observe how this is implemented under the Code.

In note 2 we saw that in this situation §1111(b) would permit Ace to choose between accepting a recourse claim, that is, a secured claim of $12 million and an unsecured claim of $3 million, or electing a full secured claim of $15 million. This is illustrated as follows.

	Secured	Unsecured
Recourse Claim	12	3
Full Claim	15	—

Section 1129(b)(2) sets forth certain minimum requirements that a plan must meet in order to be fair and equitable, for both secured (§1129(b)(2)(A)) and unsecured (§1129(b)(2)(B)) claims. With respect to secured claims, these requirements deal with three situations: where the mortgage lien remains on the property, where the property is sold free and clear of the mortgage, and where some other disposition is made.

a. *Where the Mortgage Lien Remains on the Property.* In this situation, §1129(b)(2)(A)(II) requires that the mortgagee must receive payments under the continuing mortgage on account of its claim (referred to as "deferred cash payments" because they will be paid over a period of time) totaling at least the amount of the claim. This means that if Ace had accepted a recourse claim, it would receive deferred cash payments totaling at least $12 million over the term of the mortgage remaining on the property. On the other hand, if Ace had elected the full secured claim, it would receive deferred cash payments totaling at least $15 million over that period.

At this point, you must be thinking that you know the answer to the question posed at the end of note 2 as to which alternative is better for Ace. But consider the fact that §1129(b)(2)(A)(II) also provides that the *present value* of the deferred cash payments as of the effective date of the plan can (and undoubtedly will) be as low as the value of the collateral under either alternative. (This was the provision in controversy in the *Pinebrook* case, excerpted above.) The result is that although the *total amount* of deferred cash payments will be different if Ace accepts a recourse or elects a full claim, the *present value* of these future payments at plan confirmation will be the same. It probably still seems to you that it would be to Ace's advantage to elect the full secured claim. But do not forget that under the recourse alternative Ace would have an unsecured claim of $3 million, while it would have no unsecured claim if it elected the full claim. This is illustrated in the following diagram.

	Secured		Unsecured
	DCP	Value	
Recourse Claim	12	12	3
Full Claim	15	12	0

Undoubtedly, in the case of a single-asset debtor such as Law Drive Associates, Ace would be able to "dominate" the class of unsecured creditors, that is, it would have enough votes to make certain that the class of unsecured creditors rejects the plan (plans must be accepted by at least two-thirds in amount and more than one-half in number of allowed claims of each class of creditors under §1126(c)). Once the unsecured class rejects the plan, §1129(b)(1) requires that the plan, in order to be crammed down, must be fair and equitable as concerns the unsecured class. This requires absolute priority, and §1129(b)(2)(B) provides that absolute priority for the unsecured creditors means that holders of unsecured claims must be given property of a value equal to their claims before anyone junior can receive any property.

Of course, this does not guarantee that unsecured creditors will get anything, since there may be few or no assets remaining for unsecured creditors after compensating secured creditors. What absolute priority was intended to mean here, however, is that Dan Developer's limited partnership cannot keep the property unless Ace is paid in full. This is the key to overturning *Pine Gate.* If the mortgagee has a recourse claim and absolute priority is followed, the debtor will be unable to keep the property without compensating the mortgagee fully.

Notice how well the foregoing requirements deal with different kinds of reorganizations. While they protect the mortgagee against the *Pine Gate* line of decisions in the case of a single-asset limited partnership, they should do no harm in the large corporate reorganization where the property, for instance the factory, is essential to the reorganization and must be kept by the reorganized company. In the large reorganization, Ace's $3 million unsecured claim may be lost in a sea of unsecured claims, and Ace will not be able to "dominate" the class of unsecured creditors, who may vote to accept a plan paying, say, 50 cents on the dollar, or 10 cents on the dollar, or less. Once the class accepts, the plan does not have to be fair and equitable as to that class, absolute priority is not applicable, and Ace will have to live with what the unsecured creditors accept.

Returning to the question asked at the end of note 2, are you now convinced that it is best for Ace to accept the recourse claim in the hypothetical situation? Will that always be true? Under what circumstances would you think it more advisable for Ace to elect a full secured claim? What anticipated future developments with respect to the property might influence Ace's decision? Would the number of unsecured creditors affect the decision?

    b. Property Sold Free and Clear of the Mortgage. Where the mortgage will be extinguished because of a sale free and clear of the mortgage under a plan rejected by a class of creditors, §1129(b)(2)(A)(ii) provides that the plan would meet the fair and equitable standard as to the dissenting class or classes if the property were sold subject to §363(k) and the lien were to attach to the proceeds of the sale. Section 363 deals with the use, sale, or lease of collateral by the trustee. Subsection (k) provides that on a sale of the property the secured creditor may normally bid at the sale and, if the successful bidder, may offset the "allowed claim" against the secured creditor's bid. Do you understand why this protects the secured creditor for the amount of the creditor's claim?

The only difficult problem is in determining the amount of a secured creditor's claim against which the bid would be offset. Return to the hypothetical, in which Ace has a mortgage with a $15 million balance on property worth $12 million, under §506(a). Ace would have a secured claim for $12 million and no unsecured claim because the debt is nonrecourse. While §1111(b) will normally provide for conversion of Ace's nonrecourse claim to a recourse claim, §1111(b)(1)(A)(ii) provides that a nonrecourse claim will not be converted to a recourse claim where the property is sold under §363 or under the plan. What do you think was the rationale for this exception to the conversion of nonrecourse to recourse claims? Assume that at the sale of the property there is competitive bidding, and Ace is the successful bidder at $15 million. Can Ace offset the $15 million debt against the bid? Or is the allowed amount of the claim only $12 million and thus Ace will be able to offset only $12 million against the bid and will have to pay $3 million to the debtor's estate? Would competitive bidding that sends the price over the amount of the §506(a) valuation be sufficient evidence that the valuation was too low and that a new valuation should be made? If so, what happens if there is no competitive bidding? Can Ace avoid the problem altogether by electing a full claim? Remember that while §1111(b) does not *convert* a nonrecourse claim to a recourse claim when the property is being sold, there is no limitation on a *non*recourse creditor's electing the full claim even if the property is being sold.

c. *Where Some Other Disposition Is Made.* Any other approach to the plan must, under §1129(b)(2)(A)(iii), provide the secured creditor with the "indubitable equivalent" of its claim. Recall the use of this term in §361 (dealing with adequate protection), discussed in Chapter 11B1, note 3, supra. The use of the words of Judge Learned Hand was intended as a message to the courts that Congress really expected full compensation for the secured creditor. The lack of specific objective requirements leave no clear standard for the courts to follow.

In In re Pikes Peak Water Co., 779 F.2d 1456 (10th Cir. 1985), the court permitted a cram-down based on indubitable equivalence where the plan would accrue principal and interest for three years. During that time, the loan would either be brought current or a takeout would be arranged, and if neither occurred, the lender would be permitted to foreclose. In In re Sun Country Development, 764 F.2d 406 (5th Cir. 1985), the court held the substitution of 21 notes on 21 lots in place of a lien on 200 acres constituted indubitable equivalence. On the other hand, in In re Griffiths, 27 Bankr. 873 (Bankr. D. Kan. 1983), the court found that indubitable equivalence was not met when a plan proposed to give the mortgagee part of the collateral and the cash value of the remainder of the collateral, and in In re Elijah, 41 Bankr. 348 (Bankr. W.D. Mo. 1984), the court found no indubitable equivalence where the plan would give a first mortgagee a substitute third lien of questionable value.

4. *Impairment of Claims.* In this discussion of the cram-down we have presumed that the claims were impaired by the proposed plan. Under §1129(a)(8), a class cannot reject a proposed plan of reorganization unless it is "impaired" by the plan. What happens when a

mortgagee feels itself hurt by the plan but the court thinks the mortgagee is unimpaired? The only way the mortgagee can protect itself from its perceived impairment is to force the plan to a cram-down, under which absolute priority would be required. But the mortgagee can force a cram-down only by rejecting the plan, and it can't reject the plan if it is unimpaired. Thus, a determination of circumstances under which a class may become impaired is very important.

Section 1124 states that all classes are considered impaired except in three circumstances. What are these circumstances? Do they protect the mortgagee sufficiently? Note especially §1124(3)(A). Does this remind you of §461(11) of Chapter XII of the old Bankruptcy Act, which led to *Pine Gate*? How does §1111(b) help? In our hypothetical situation, would Ace be considered unimpaired if the plan offered Ace $15 million in cash and Ace had elected a full secured claim?

5.   *Recent Attacks on Absolute Priority.*
     a.   *Determining Present Value:* Pinebrook.   Note 3 discussed the application of the absolute priority rule under §1129(b) and concluded that with respect to a mortgage lien continued on the property under the plan, absolute priority would require that the mortgagee receive deferred cash payments over the life of the mortgage equal to the amount of the mortgagee's claim and that such deferred cash payments have a value as of the effective date of the plan no lower than the value of the property. This would mean in the master hypothetical that if Ace had a recourse secured claim of $12 million with an unsecured claim of $3 million, the $12 million mortgage remaining on the property must have a present value of $12 million. In other words, Ace should be able to sell the mortgage in the market for its face amount. This statutory requirement is based in part on the decision of the Supreme Court in Wright v. Union Central Life Ins. Co., 311 U.S. 273 (1940), where Justice Douglas stated that the secured creditor was constitutionally entitled to receive "the value of the property" securing the lien in the borrower's bankruptcy. Is this possible under §1129(b)? Under the second Frasier-Lempke Act, which Justice Douglas was interpreting, the mortgagee received the value of the property in cash. In §1129(b), the mortgagee receives a 100-percent-of-value mortgage on an insolvent property. Is it reasonable to believe that anyone would purchase such a mortgage at its face amount?

Based on the discussions of appraisal at Chapter 5B1 and Chapter 10C5, note 5, it should be clear that the present value of a mortgage will be determined by the income capitalization method. If you do the math you will see that the higher the capitalization rate, the lower the value of the property.

Under §1129(b)(2), then, the income stream (i.e., the interest rate) will directly affect the determination of the present value of the mortgage. One easy way to increase present value is to raise the interest rate. Note, however, that it would be unproductive to increase the interest rate beyond what is realistic for the property to pay, since that would only increase the risk factors (the ability of the property to meet debt service) and raise the capitalization rate, which in turn would lower value. If it is impossible to meet the statutory requirement, does this mean that Chapter 11 fails constitutional scrutiny? Perhaps it does, but bear in mind that the mortgagee is provided with an unsecured claim entitled to absolute priority, or the option of electing a full secured claim. Compare this treatment to the provisions of Chapter 12 discussed in paragraph (b) of this note.

The *Pinebrook* case deals with the problem of setting the correct interest rate to give the secured creditor a lien with a present value equal to the value of the collateral. Citing In re Orosco, 77 Bankr. 246, 252 (Bankr. N.D. Cal. 1987), the court concludes that the appropriate interest rate is a weighted average of rates charged by commercial lenders in the same market for a loan of equal term, the quality of the collateral, the credit standard of the borrower, and the risk of subsequent default. It then specifically rejects the notion that the debtor's bankruptcy requires a higher-than-market rate of interest for the property involved.

If the "market" rate the court is looking to is the rate lenders would require for a loan of that size on that property, does this not seem to be designed to meet the statutory objective? But suppose, as is probable, that no lender will make 100-percent-of-value loans, especially on property of this type. Is there any market rate to apply? If lenders will normally make only 75-percent-of-value loans on this type of property, should the rate be determined by computing a "market" rate for 75 percent of the lien amount and a much higher rate for the remaining 25 percent and blending the two? Returning to the master hypothetical, this would mean that, assuming a 10 percent average rate for 75-percent-of-value loans on office buildings such as Dan Developer's, a rate of 10 percent would be computed on $9 million and a rate of, say, 14 percent would be computed on the remaining $3 million, creating a blended rate of 11 percent. The big problem with this approach is the determination of the rate on the amount over 75 percent, which, without data, may be just an estimate. It has proved, however, to be a helpful approach to a negotiated plan of reorganization.

   b. *Family Farmers and Chapter 12.* The pathos of farm insolvency is seen in the loss of the family farm by families that have worked the land for generations. In the farm crisis of the mid-1980s, the societal objective was to find a way to keep the farmer on the farm. Would Chapter 11 of the Bankruptcy Code meet this goal? Assume the following facts: Francine Farmer has a $1 million mortgage on her farm. When she files in bankruptcy, the farm is worth $500,000.

The mortgage is recourse. Under Chapter 11 the mortgagee would have a secured claim for $500,000 and an unsecured claim in the same amount. The mortgage would be reduced to a face amount of $500,000 but, under the absolute priority rule, with respect to unsecured claims, Francine Farmer would have to find property with a value equal to $500,000 to satisfy the lender's unsecured claim before she could keep the property. This would seem improbable unless Francine had substantial assets elsewhere.

Because of the low dollar limits and other problems, Chapter 13 (which deals with certain individuals with regular income) was not a viable alternative. With huge federal budget deficits, Congress was unwilling to legislate the rescue of the farmers through federal financial assistance. As a result, in drafting bankruptcy legislation to meet the farm crisis, Congress looked to the only other party available, the mortgagee. The result was Chapter 12.

Chapter 12 deals with insolvencies of "family farmers," defined generally to include farmers with debts under $1.5 million (which figure accounted for approximately 90 percent of all farm debt outstanding at the time). It protects the farmer by inter alia, eliminating absolute priority for the unsecured portion of the mortgagee's claim. Thus, it is not necessary under Chapter 12 for the dissenting impaired mortgagee to receive property of a value equal to the amount of its unsecured claim in order for the debtor to keep the property. What Chapter 12 retains is the requirement that the plan be in the best interest of creditors. As you will recall, this means that each creditor must receive what it would have received on liquidation.

Given a property valuation of $500,000 and a mortgage of $1 million, it would be highly unlikely (unless Francine Farmer had significant other assets) that there would be anything available for unsecured creditors in liquidation. Since it is also improbable that there could be any "disposable income" (which Chapter 12 requires be applied to pay claims under the plan for a period of time) available for future payments to the mortgagee, the unsecured portion of the lender's claim is virtually wiped out under Chapter 12. The result is that Chapter 12 effectively reduces the mortgage to the value of the collateral. See §1225 of the Bankruptcy Code. The expectation is that under such circumstances the farmer will be able to keep the farm.

What particularly disturbed mortgagees about Chapter 12 was that if, for instance, Francine's property were to increase in value in the five years following confirmation of the plan to, say, $2 million, the mortgage would remain reduced and the mortgagee would have no way of recouping what it was asked to forego for the benefit of the debtor's reorganization. Mortgagees suggested as Chapter 12 was being drafted that a method be provided to permit a second look at the value of the property in five or ten years following confirmation of the plan, with the court empowered to increase the value of the mortgage to an amount that would pay back to the mortgagee what it lost on confirmation out of the increase in property value. These suggestions, however, were brushed aside. What competitive advantage does this give Francine Farmer over a farmer who paid all debts and did not file in bankruptcy? Does this encourage filing under the Chapter, and if so, is that desirable? Without absolute priority for the unsecured claim and without a §1111(b)(2) election for a full secured claim, does Chapter 12 meet the constitutional requirements of *Union Central,* supra note 5?

    c. The New Capital "Exception." Prior to the adoption of Chapter 12, the Eighth Circuit, in In re Ahlers, 794 F.2d 388 (8th Cir. 1986), held, inter alia, that notwithstanding the absolute priority requirement of §1129(b)(2)(B) of the Code, a promise by a farmer-debtor to contribute labor and expertise in the future constituted a present capital contribution enabling the debtor to retain an interest in the property while the dissenting impaired class of unsecured creditors remained unpaid. The holding was based on the new capital "exception" to the absolute priority requirement described by the Supreme Court in Case v. Los Angeles Lumber Products Co., 308 U.S. 106 (1939), under which a junior creditor or stockholder may retain an interest equal to any new capital contributed to the reorganized company, even if such creditor or stockholder would have been wiped out under the absolute priority rule absent such a contribution. Do you see why it would be more appropriate to refer to this as a corollary rather than an exception to the absolute priority rule? Would this decision have been necessary to protect the farmer if Chapter 12 had been the law at the time?

    The reasoning of the Eighth Circuit was that the promise by the debtor to work hard in the future (earning "sweat equity") was equivalent to a present contribution of capital under *Los Angeles Lumber.* The Eighth Circuit's reasoning was (i) contrary to the express language of Chapter 11; (ii) inconsistent with the *Los Angeles Lumber* case it cited for support (in *Los Angeles Lumber* the Supreme Court specifically rejected the idea that intangibles could constitute present contributions of capital); and (iii) contrary to the intent of Congress, which had rejected similar proposals by the Commission on the Bankruptcy Laws of the United States (see H.R. Doc. No. 137, 93d Cong., 1st Sess., Part I, at 256-257 (1973)). The Supreme Court granted certiorari on this issue and had little difficulty in reversing the Eighth Circuit, 485 U.S. 197 (1988).

    Although reversed by the Supreme Court, *Ahlers* pointed up a possible weakness in the absolute priority rule that has begun to come before the courts. Returning to the master hypothetical, assume that the property was worth $12 million and the mortgage indebtedness was $15 million at the time of confirmation of Law Drive Associates' Chapter 11 reorganization plan. Assume Ace has accepted a recourse claim giving it a $12 million secured claim and a $3 million unsecured claim and that there are no other assets to compensate Ace on its unsecured claim. Thus, under the absolute priority rule, the partnership cannot keep the property under the plan. Assume that there is a valid exception to the absolute priority rule for those who have contributed actual new capital to the reorganization. (The Supreme Court in *Ahlers* did not decide the validity of the argument raised by the United States Attorney General in an amicus brief that the "new capital exception" did not survive the adoption of the Code.) Suppose that a contribution of $1,000 of new capital is made on behalf of Law Drive Associates. Under the new capital "exception" this entitles Law Drive Associates to an interest in the property equal to its capital contribution. Can Law Drive Associates argue that it is entitled to keep the property since it is contributing $1,000 for property that has no equity value?

This issue came before the court in In re Greystone III Joint Venture, 102 Bankr. 560 (Bankr. W.D. Texas, 1989). (At this writing, an appeal is pending before the Fifth Circuit.) There the unsecured portion of the claim of the secured creditor, Phoenix Mutual Life Insurance Company, was approximately $3.5 million. The debtor offered to contribute $500,000 in exchange for keeping 100 percent of the ownership of the enterprise, even though the plan would provide for payment of only approximately 3 percent of the secured creditor's unsecured claim under the plan. The court held, inter alia, that the new capital exception applied under the Bankruptcy Code and that the partners might retain the equity position on making a necessary and substantial cash contribution of $500,000. The court held that the retention of the equity was reasonable in relation to the contribution not only because the reduction of the mortgage to the value of the collateral meant that the property being retained had no equity value, but also because "looking at the valuation of the enterprise itself as a going concern . . . the investment justifies a 100% ownership of the enterprise, all other things being equal." See also In re Aztec Co., 107 Bankr. 585 (Bankr. M.D. Tenn. 1989). At this writing, the case is on appeal to the Fifth Circuit.

In Northern Pacific R.R. Co. v. Boyd, 228 U.S. 482 (1913), the Supreme Court maintained that unsecured creditors had a property right in the unencumbered assets of the debtor and were thus entitled to be paid before the owners could retain any assets. Said the court: "If the value of the [property] justified the issuance of stock in exchange for old shares, the creditors were entitled to the benefit of that value, whether it was present or prospective, for dividends or only for purposes of control. In either event it was a right of property out of which the creditors were entitled to be paid before the creditors could retain it for any purpose whatever." 228 U.S. at 508. Does *Greystone* protect this property right? If not, does the result pass constitutional muster? Does it meet the requirements of the best-interest-of-creditor test (§1129(a)(7))?

If a third party with no prior relationship to the transaction had bid $500,000 above the mortgage balance as reduced to conform to the §506(a) valuation of the property, and the plan proposed such a sale, could such a plan be crammed down over the mortgagee class's objection? In answering, consider what the effect of such a bid is on the "value" of the property and the amount of the mortgagee's secured claim. Recheck the last sentence of §506(a).

Can you formulate an argument for the proposition that if the debtor bid the $500,000 over the reduced mortgage balance, the debtor's plan did not comply with the requirement of §1129(a)(3) that to be confirmed a plan must have been proposed in good faith?

In *Ahlers,* the Solicitor General argued in an amicus brief that the new capital "exception" did not apply under the Bankruptcy Code. The Supreme Court did not reach this issue since it held that "sweat equity" did not constitute new value, stating that their decision "should not be taken as any comment on the continuing validity of the *Los Angeles Lumber* exception." 108 S. Ct. at 967, n. 3. What argument can you make to support the Attorney General's position? What argument can you make against such a position? If you sat on the Fifth Circuit, how would you decide this issue?

An additional issue in *Greystone* involved §1129(a)(10), which requires that at least one class of impaired claims must approve the plan before it can be confirmed by the court. To accomplish this objective, the plan bifurcated the unsecured class and created a separate class of unsecured trade creditors who would be expected to approve the plan. Does this classification meet the requirements of §1122, which permits a plan to designate a separate class of "every unsecured claim that is less than or reduced to an amount that the court approves as reasonable and necessary for administrative convenience"? This issue is also being contested before the Fifth Circuit.

   d. *Pine Gate Under Chapter 7?* As discussed above, §506(a) bifurcates the claim of an under-secured creditor into a secured claim equal to the value of the collateral and an unsecured claim for the difference between the value of the collateral and the amount of the indebtedness. It was noted that without the conversion provided for by §1111(b), a nonrecourse under-secured creditor would have no unsecured claim, notwithstanding the under-security. Section 1111(b), being part of Chapter 11, is not applicable in Chapter 7.

Is it then possible for a Chapter 7 debtor to succeed in asking the court to value the nonrecourse mortgagee's interest in the real property under §506(a), void (or "strip down") the portion of the lien that exceeds the value of the real property under §506(d), and permit the debtor to retain ownership of the property by paying to the secured creditor the court-determined value of the property or simply by reducing a nonrecourse mortgage to that value? An apparent majority of the courts that have considered the issue seem to say yes. See, e.g., Gaglia v. First Federal Savings & Loan Assn., 889 F.2d 1304 (3d Cir. 1989); Folendore v. United States (In re Folendore), 862 F.2d 1537 (11th Cir. 1989); Lindsey v. Federal Land Bank (In re Lindsey), 823 F.2d 189 (7th Cir. 1987); but see Dewsnup v. Timm (In re Dewsnup), 908 F.2d 588 (10th Cir. 1990). If such a strip-down is permissible, would this constitute the return of *Pine Gate,* this time for Chapter 7? Do you think that Congress, which went to such lengths to overturn *Pine Gate,* would have intended to permit such a result under Chapter 7?

6.   *Trustee or Debtor in Possession.*   Another area of controversy in drafting the Bankruptcy Code was whether there would be a requirement for a trustee or whether the debtor could remain in possession during the bankruptcy proceeding. Section 1104 represents a compromise between real estate interests and those connected with corporate reorganizations. Under Chapter X (Corporate Reorganizations) of the old Bankruptcy Act, a trustee had always been appointed, while under Chapter XII the debtor had almost always remained in possession. Perhaps on the "grass is always greener" theory, corporate reorganization people urged that the Code specify that the debtor be left in possession rather than have a trustee appointed (as a result of unfortunate experiences under Chapter X where competent management was replaced with trustees who knew little about the business), and real estate mortgagees (having seen debtors whose mismanagement had caused the debacle left in possession to milk the property of any value that was left) urged that a trustee always be appointed.

The §1104 compromise between these two points of view gives the judge the discretion to choose. Specifically, §1104 provides that on request of a party in interest "the court shall order the appointment of a trustee" either "for cause, including fraud, dishonesty, incompetence or gross mismanagement" or because "such appointment is in the interests of creditors, any equity security holders, and other interests of the estate." As an alternative to the appointment of a trustee, the court, under certain circumstances set forth in §1104(b), may order the appointment of an examiner to investigate the allegations against the debtor. The debtor in possession generally has the same powers as a trustee (§1107).

The fact that §1104 permits appointment of a trustee does not mean that the mortgagee will always want one appointed. Note the language of §506(c), under which the trustee generally has the right to recover from the property the reasonable, necessary costs and expenses of preserving or disposing of the property. This includes trustee's fees (see §§326(a) to 326(c)), which can amount to a considerable sum off the top of what already may be rather weak cash flow.

7. *Feasibility.* Section 1129(a)(11) prohibits confirmation of a plan unless the court determines that confirmation is not likely to be followed by liquidation or the need for further financial reorganization. In other words, the court must be convinced that the plan is likely to succeed. This test must be met even if all the classes agree to accept the plan. However, there are no set rules for its application, which of necessity must be on a case-by-case basis. In In re Merrimack Valley Oil Co., 32 Bankr. 485 (Bankr. D. Mass. 1983), the court noted that in making its determination it would consider the adequacy of the debtor's capital structure, the earning power of the business, economic conditions, and the ability of management. While somewhat vague, §1129(a)(11) represents an important tool for attacking plans based on hopes not grounded in practicality.

8. *Additional Reading.* Broude, Cram Down and Chapter 11 of the Bankruptcy Code: The Settlement Imperative, 39 Bus. Law. 441 (1984); Ayer, Rethinking Absolute Priority after *Ahlers,* 87 Mich. L. Rev. 963 (1989); Burkson, Tax Aspects of Bankruptcy, 17 Colo. Law. 619 (1988); Eisenberg, The Undersecured Creditor in Reorganizations and the Nature of Security, 38 Vand. L. Rev. 931 (1985); Fitzgerald, Bankruptcy Code §506(a) and Undersecured Creditors: What Date for Valuation?, 34 UCLA L. Rev. 1953 (1987); Flaccus, A Comparison of Farmer Bankruptcies in Chapter 11 and the New Chapter 12, 11 U. Ark. Little Rock L.J. 49 (1988-1989); Fortgang and Mayer, Valuation in Bankruptcy, 32 UCLA L. Rev. 1061 (1985); Fortgang and King, The 1978 Bankruptcy Code: Some Wrong Policy Decisions, 56 N.Y.U. L. Rev. 1148 (1981); Gaynor, Impairment, 3 Bankr. Dev. J. 579 (1986); Gives, When and Why Courts Appoint Trustees in Bankruptcy, 34 Prac. Law. 29 (1988); Green, Avoiding Recourse Under 11 U.S.C. 1111(b)(1)(A)(ii): The Conflicts with 11 U.S.C. 363, 10 Okla. City U. L. Rev. 645 (1985); King, Chapter 12: Adjustment of Debts of a Family Farmer with Regular Income, 29 S. Tex. L. Rev. 615 (1988); Klee, Cramdown II, 64 Am. Bankr. L.J. 229 (1990); Klee, All You Ever Wanted to Know About Cramdown, 53 Am. Bankr. L.J. 133 (1979); Nimmer, Negotiated Bankruptcy Reorganization Plans: Absolute Priority and New Value Contributions, 36 Emory L.J. 1009 (1987); Pollack and Goldring, Filing for Bankruptcy Can Alter Tax Consequences for Numerous Transactions, 66 J. Taxn. 330 (1987); Stein, Section 1111(b): Providing Undersecured Creditors with Postconfir-

mation Appreciation in the Value of the Collateral, 56 Am. Bankr.
L.J. 195 (1982).

C. BANKRUPTCY OF TENANT OR LANDLORD

The bankruptcy of a party to a lease agreement can have a profound
effect on the other party to the lease, a fee mortgagee with an assignment
of rents, a leasehold mortgagee, or a sublessee. For example, the Code
provides for disaffirmance of "executory contracts," including leases of
real property, and permits, subject to certain limitations, assumption
and assignment of leases by the trustee or the debtor in possession, all
with obvious consequences to parties with interests in the leasehold
transaction. Most of the Code requirements with respect to leases are
found in the following excerpt from the Code.

Bankruptcy Code §365
11 U.S.C. §365 (1988)

§365. Executory contracts and unexpired leases

(a) Except as provided in sections 765 and 766 of this title and
in subsections (b), (c), and (d) of this section, the trustee, subject to
the court's approval, may assume or reject any executory contract or
unexpired lease of the debtor.

(b)(1) If there has been a default in an executory contract or
unexpired lease of the debtor, the trustee may not assume such contract
or lease unless, at the time of assumption of such contract or lease,
the trustee —

(A) cures, or provides adequate assurance that the trustee will
promptly cure, such default;

(B) compensates, or provides adequate assurance that the
trustee will promptly compensate, a party other than the debtor
to such contract or lease, for any actual pecuniary loss to such
party resulting from such default; and

(C) provides adequate assurance of future performance under
such contract or lease.

(2) Paragraph (1) of this subsection does not apply to a default
that is a breach of a provision relating to —

(A) the insolvency or financial condition of the debtor at any
time before the closing of the case;

(B) the commencement of a case under this title; or

(C) the appointment of or taking possession by a trustee in a case under this title or a custodian before such commencement.

(3) For the purposes of paragraph (1) of this subsection and paragraph (2)(B) of subsection (f), adequate assurance of future performance of a lease of real property in a shopping center includes adequate assurance —

(A) of the source of rent and other consideration due under such lease, and in the case of an assignment, that the financial condition and operating performance of the proposed assignee and its guarantors, if any, shall be similar to the financial condition and operating performance of the debtor and its guarantors, if any, as of the time the debtor became the lessee under the lease;

(B) that any percentage rent due under such lease will not decline substantially;

(C) that assumption or assignment of such lease is subject to all the provisions thereof, including (but not limited to) provisions such as a radius, location, use, or exclusivity provision, and will not breach any such provision contained in any other lease, financing agreement, or master agreement relating to such shopping center; and

(D) that assumption or assignment of such lease will not disrupt any tenant mix or balance in such shopping center.

(4) Notwithstanding any other provision of this section, if there has been a default in an unexpired lease of the debtor, other than a default of a kind specified in paragraph (2) of this subsection, the trustee may not require a lessor to provide services or supplies incidental to such lease before assumption of such lease unless the lessor is compensated under the terms of such lease for any services and supplies provided under such lease before assumption of such lease.

(c) The trustee may not assume or assign any executory contract or unexpired lease of the debtor, whether or not such contract or lease prohibits or restricts assignment of rights or delegation of duties, if —

(1)(A) applicable law excuses a party, other than the debtor, to such contract or lease from accepting performance from or rendering performance to an entity other than the debtor or the debtor in possession whether or not such contract, or lease, prohibits or restricts assignment of rights or delegation of duties; and

(B) such party does not consent to such assumption or assignment; or

(2) such contract is a contract to make a loan, or extend other debt financing or financial accommodations, to or for the benefit of the debtor, or to issue a security of the debtor; or

(3) such lease is of nonresidential real property and has been terminated under applicable nonbankruptcy law prior to the order for relief.

(d) . . .

(3) The trustee shall timely perform all the obligations of the debtor, except those specified in section 365(b)(2), arising from and after the order for relief under any unexpired lease of nonresidential real property, until such lease is assumed or rejected, notwithstanding section 503(b)(1) of this title. The court may extend, for cause, the time for performance of any such obligation that arises within 60 days after the date of the order for relief, but the time for performance shall not be extended beyond such 60-day period. This subsection shall not be deemed to affect the trustee's obligations under the provisions of subsection (b) or (f) of this section. Acceptance of any such performance does not constitute waiver or relinquishment of the lessor's rights under such lease or under this title.

(4) Notwithstanding paragraphs (1) and (2), in a case under any chapter of this title, if the trustee does not assume or reject an unexpired lease of nonresidential real property under which the debtor is the lessee within 60 days after the date of the order for relief, or within such additional time as the court, for cause, within such 60-day period, fixes, then such lease is deemed rejected, and the trustee shall immediately surrender such nonresidential real property to the lessor.

(e)(1) Notwithstanding a provision in an executory contract or unexpired lease, or in applicable law, an executory contract or unexpired lease of the debtor may not be terminated or modified, and any right or obligation under such contract or lease may not be terminated or modified, at any time after the commencement of the case solely because of a provision in such contract or lease that is conditioned on —

(A) the insolvency or financial condition of the debtor at any time before the closing of the case;

(B) the commencement of a case under this title; or

(C) the appointment of or taking possession by a trustee in a case under this title or a custodian before such commencement.

(2) Paragraph (1) of this subsection does not apply to an executory contract or unexpired lease of the debtor, whether or not such contract or lease prohibits or restricts assignment of rights or delegation of duties, if —

(A)(i) applicable law excuses a party, other than the debtor, to such contract or lease from accepting performance from or rendering performance to the trustee or to an assignee of such contract or lease, whether or not such contract or lease prohibits or restricts assignment of rights or delegation of duties; and

(ii) such party does not consent to such assumption or assignment; or

(B) such contract is a contract to make a loan, or extend other debt financing or financial accommodations, to or for the benefit of the debtor, or to issue a security of the debtor.

(f)(1) Except as provided in subsection (c) of this section, notwithstanding a provision in an executory contract or unexpired lease of the debtor, or in applicable law, that prohibits, restricts, or conditions the assignment of such contract or lease, the trustee may assign such contract or lease under paragraph (2) of this subsection.

(2) The trustee may assign an executory contract or unexpired lease of the debtor only if —

(A) the trustee assumes such contract or lease in accordance with the provisions of this section; and

(B) adequate assurance of future performance by the assignee of such contract or lease is provided, whether or not there has been a default in such contract or lease.

(3) Notwithstanding a provision in an executory contract or unexpired lease of the debtor, or in applicable law that terminates or modifies, or permits a party other than the debtor to terminate or modify, such contract or lease or a right or obligation under such contract or lease on account of an assignment of such contract or lease, such contract, lease, right, or obligation may not be terminated or modified under such provision because of the assumption or assignment of such contract or lease by the trustee.

(g) Except as provided in subsections (h)(2) and (i)(2) of this section, the rejection of an executory contract or unexpired lease of the debtor constitutes a breach of such contract or lease — . . .

(h)(1) If the trustee rejects an unexpired lease of real property of the debtor under which the debtor is the lessor, or a timeshare interest under a timeshare plan under which the debtor is the timeshare interest seller, the lessee or timeshare interest purchaser under such lease or timeshare plan may treat such lease or timeshare plan as terminated by such rejection, where the disaffirmance by the trustee amounts to such a breach as would entitle the lessee or timeshare interest purchaser to treat such lease or timeshare plan as terminated by virtue of its own terms, applicable nonbankruptcy law, or other agreements the lessee or timeshare interest purchaser has made with other parties; or, in the alternative, the lessee or timeshare interest purchaser may remain in possession of the leasehold or timeshare interest under any lease or timeshare plan the term of which has commenced for the balance of such term and for any renewal or extension of such term that is enforceable by such lessee or timeshare interest purchaser under applicable nonbankruptcy law.

(2) If such lessee or timeshare interest purchaser remains in possession as provided in paragraph (1) of this subsection, such lessee or timeshare interest purchaser may offset against the rent reserved under such lease or moneys due for such timeshare interest for the balance of the term after the date of the rejection of such lease or timeshare interest, and any such renewal or extension thereof, any damages occurring after such date caused by the nonperformance of any obligation of the debtor under such lease or timeshare plan after such date, but such lessee or timeshare interest purchaser does not have any rights against the estate on account of any damages arising after such date from such rejection, other than such offset.

(i)(1) If the trustee rejects an executory contract of the debtor for the sale of real property or for the sale of a timeshare interest under a timeshare plan, under which the purchaser is in possession, such purchaser may treat such contract as terminated, or, in the alternative, may remain in possession of such real property or timeshare interest.

(2) If such purchaser remains in possession —

(A) such purchaser shall continue to make all payments due under such contract, but may, offset against such payments any damages occurring after the date of the rejection of such contract caused by the nonperformance of any obligation of the debtor after such date, but such purchaser does not have any rights against the estate on account of any damages arising after such date from such rejection, other than such offset; and

(B) the trustee shall deliver title to such purchaser in accordance with the provisions of such contract, but is relieved of all other obligations to perform under such contract.

(j) A purchaser that treats an executory contract as terminated under subsection (i) of this section, or a party whose executory contract to purchase real property from the debtor is rejected and under which such party is not in possession, has a lien on the interest of the debtor in such property for the recovery of any portion of the purchase price that such purchaser or party has paid.

(k) Assignment by the trustee to an entity of a contract or lease assumed under this section relieves the trustee and the estate from any liability for any breach of such contract or lease occurring after such assignment.

(l) If an unexpired lease under which the debtor is the lessee is assigned pursuant to this section, the lessor of the property may require a deposit or other security for the performance of the debtor's obligations under the lease substantially the same as would have been required by the landlord upon the initial leasing to a similar tenant.

(m) For purposes of this section 365 and sections 541(b)(2) and 362(b)(10), leases of real property shall include any rental agreement to use real property. . . .

1. Bankruptcy of the Tenant

As §365(e) indicates, clauses in leases providing for automatic (ipso facto) termination of a lease or termination at the option of the landlord because of the bankruptcy, insolvency, or financial condition of the tenant, previously sanctioned by the language of the former Bankruptcy Act (§70(b)), are unenforceable in bankruptcy proceedings. Note, however, that while the landlord is prohibited from terminating the lease, the tenant has the option of disaffirming (or rejecting) the lease. Thus, the landlord is left in the unenviable position of having to live with leases that are favorable to tenants in bankruptcy while seeing leases favorable to the landlord disaffirmed. The inability to terminate is especially a problem for the landlord that has entered into a low-base-rent lease intended to be supplemented with contingent rent based on profits or sales. Such leases are attractive to the trustee for an insolvent tenant whose sales are low and will probably not be disaffirmed.

If the tenant-debtor does not reject the lease, it may assume the lease and assign it to a third party (notwithstanding provisions in the leases prohibiting such assigment) provided defaults are cured, the landlord is compensated for any losses, and an ambiguous "adequate assurance of future performance" is provided. Note the special definition of adequate assurance of future performance for shopping centers. These provisions will be discussed in the notes below.

A growing concern for parties to leasehold transactions is the possibility of recharacterization of a lease in the tenant's bankruptcy. In the *PCH* case, excerpted below, a lease in a sale-and-leaseback transaction was held not to be a true lease for bankruptcy purposes. As you read the case and the Cowan and Eastman commentary that follows, consider what the agreement is if not a lease and what possible consequences such a recharacterization can have for parties to the leasehold transaction.

Liona Corp. v. PCH Assocs.
(In re PCH Assocs.)
804 F.2d 193 (2d Cir. 1986)

MINER, Circuit Judge:

Liona Corporation, N.V. ("Liona") appeals from a judgment of the United States District Court for the Southern District of New York (TENNEY, J.) affirming an order of the bankruptcy court (LIFLAND, J.) in favor of debtor PCH Associates ("PCH"). The District Court held that the sale-leaseback arrangement between Liona and PCH was

a joint venture agreement rather than a nonresidential lease subject to
the provisions of section 365(d)(3), (4) of the Bankruptcy Reform Act
of 1978, as amended by the Bankruptcy Amendments and Federal
Judgeship Act of 1984, 11 U.S.C. §365(d)(3), (4) (Supp. III 1985)
("Bankruptcy Code" or "Code"). We affirm the judgment of the district
court on the ground that the sale-leaseback arrangement is not an
unexpired nonresidential lease within the contemplation of the Code.

BACKGROUND

This dispute centers around the true nature of a transaction that
was "sharply tailored by sophisticated parties," PCH Associates v. Liona
Corporation N.V., 55 B.R. 273, 274 (Bankr. S.D.N.Y. 1985), and was
admittedly structured as a sale-leaseback arrangement for tax and investment advantages. PCH, a Pennsylvania limited partnership formed
in 1976 and formerly known as Simon Associates ("Simon"), owns
and operates the Philadelphia Centre Hotel ("hotel"). Prior to September 1981 and the transaction at issue on this appeal, PCH's predecessor, Simon, held title to both the hotel and the land upon which
it is situated. In 1980, Richard Bernstein, an experienced real estate
operator and investor, learned that the hotel was for sale. In addition
to existing mortgages and seller-provided financing, he determined that
$9,000,000 was needed to acquire, renovate, and provide working capital
for the hotel. Bernstein located a group of United States investors
willing to supply $4,000,000 as new limited partners of PCH. He then
approached Fidinam, a consortium of financial service companies, to
place the remaining $5,000,000 investment.

Bernstein required a structure that would allocate all the tax benefits
of depreciation of the hotel to PCH. Fidinam, in turn, required an
investment for its client that would be evidenced by ownership of a
tangible asset and would guarantee a 12% fixed annual rate of return,
with an additional share contingent on the hotel's cash flow. Fidinam
did not want its client involved in the daily management of the hotel.
Upon reaching agreement, the parties' lawyers structured the transaction
to encompass Bernstein's and Fidinam's requirements. Ultimately, Liona,
a Netherlands Antilles corporation, became the beneficiary of Fidinam's
negotiations.

In September 1981, the requirements of the parties were fulfilled
through a "Sale-Leaseback Agreement" and a "Ground Lease" whereby
the land owned by PCH, but not the hotel, was sold to Purchase
Estates, Ltd. and immediately leased back to PCH. Ultimately, the land
interest of Purchase Estates, Ltd. was assigned to Liona. Thus, Liona
held title to the land and leased it to PCH, which owned and managed
the hotel.

Section 1.01 of the Ground Lease provided for an initial term of 33 years, renewable for four terms under section 42.01, for a total of 165 years. Rent was set at a minimum annual rate of $600,000 in section 3.01, with a percentage rental based upon a percentage of increases in the hotel's gross revenues provided in section 3.02. Section 3.04 provided for an adjustment of the annual rent if the "Landlord's Investment" fell below $5,000,000. In such instance, the annual rent would be reduced to 12% of the "Landlord's Investment."

Section 3.10 of the Ground Lease further provided that:

> It is understood and agreed that the amount herein provided paid to Landlord in addition to the minimum net annual rental, although based upon a percentage of Tenant's revenue during each year, is rent, and Landlord shall in no event be construed or held to be a partner or associate of Tenant in the conduct of its business, nor shall Landlord be liable for any debts incurred by Tenant in the conduct of said business or otherwise, *but it is understood and agreed that the relationship between the parties hereto is, and at all times shall remain, that of Landlord and Tenant.*

Appellant's App. at 142 (emphasis supplied).

Article 34 of the Ground Lease also provided that:

> This Lease contains all the promises, agreements, conditions, inducements and understandings between Landlord and Tenant relative to the Premises and there are no promises, agreements, conditions, understandings, inducements, warranties or representations, oral or written, expressed or implied, between them other than as set forth herein or in the Contract.

Appellant's App. at 225.

In November of 1984, PCH filed for reorganization under section 301 of the Bankruptcy Reform Act of 1978. Since that date, PCH has operated the hotel as a debtor-in-possession under sections 1107 and 1108 of the Code. On December 21, 1981, pursuant to section 365(d)(3), (4) of the Code, Liona filed an application with the bankruptcy court seeking an order directing PCH to continue paying rent to Liona according to the terms of the Ground Lease. PCH subsequently instituted an adversary proceeding seeking a declaration that the Ground Lease was not an unexpired nonresidential lease within the scope of section 365(d)(3), (4) of the Code, but rather constituted a joint venture or a subordinate financing scheme.

The bankruptcy court found for PCH, concluding that, even though the transaction was labeled a sale and a lease, the true nature of the arrangement was that of a joint venture and therefore no landlord/tenant relationship existed. PCH Associates v. Liona Corporation, N.V., 55 B.R. 273, 283 (Bankr. S.D.N.Y. 1985). . . .

The district court affirmed the bankruptcy court's conclusions, holding that: (1) it was not error to permit parol evidence to clarify the terms of the agreements, Liona Corporation, N.V. v. PCH Associates, 60 B.R. 870, 874 (S.D.N.Y. 1986); (2) it was not error to permit Bernstein, now president of the general partner of PCH, to testify as to his understanding of the parties' intentions and as an expert regarding what terms are usual in such agreements, id. at 875; and (3) the elements of a joint venture were present, id. at 876-78.

Liona appeals from the district court's affirmance of the bankruptcy court's order. . . .

II. APPLICATION OF SECTION 365(d)(3), (4)

Liona initiated this action to compel PCH to perform its obligations under the Ground Lease pursuant to section 365(d)(3), (4) of the Bankruptcy Code, which requires a debtor either to affirm or reject "an unexpired lease of nonresidential real property." The determination of whether this provision applies to the Ground Lease is of critical concern in this bankruptcy proceeding because, if applied, PCH would be forced either to affirm the lease, cure all defects, and perform under the terms of the contract, or to reject the lease and vacate the property. If PCH rejected the lease and vacated the property, there likely would be no assets left to administer. If PCH affirmed the lease, a substantial burden would be placed on the reorganization proceeding. Therefore, PCH adamantly asserts that there was no true sale and no true lease for the purposes of section 365, and that it therefore had no obligation to affirm or reject the lease. Specifically, PCH asserts that the documents merely provide the means by which the investment goals and tax requirements of the parties could be fulfilled.

Both the bankruptcy court and the district court held that because the contracts contemplated a joint venture, the Ground Lease was not a lease. Although we agree with the determination that the Ground Lease is not a lease, our analysis is somewhat different. We interpret section 365(d)(3), (4) of the Bankruptcy Code to apply solely to a "true" or "bona fide" lease. The Ground Lease is not, in our opinion, a true lease as contemplated therein and we find that determination dispositive of the case. It is unnecessary, therefore, to identify the transaction as a joint venture, security agreement, subordinated financing, or other investment scheme. Suffice it to say that it is not a bona fide lease for purposes of the Bankruptcy Code. . . .

. . . The statute's plain language offers little definition of those transactions that must be assumed or rejected, other than in section 365(m), which provides that "leases of real property shall include any rental agreement to use real property." The term "lease of real property" does, however, appear elsewhere in the Code, in section 502(b)(6). The legislative history of section 502(b)(6) furnishes explicit authority for restricting the scope of that term to "bona fide" leases.

Section 502(b)(6) limits the amount of damages that a landlord can recover upon breach or rejection of a lease of real property. "It was designed to compensate the landlord for his loss while not permitting a claim so large (based on a long-term lease) as to prevent other general unsecured creditors from recovering. . . ." S. Rep. No. 989, 95th Cong., 2d Sess. 63, reprinted in 1978 U.S. Code Cong. & Ad. News 5787, 5849; see also H.R. Rep. No. 595, 95th Cong., 2d Sess. 353, reprinted in 1978 U.S. Code Cong. & Ad. News 5963, 6309; 3 Collier on Bankruptcy (15th ed. 1986) ¶502.02[7], at 502-54. The Senate Report notes that the phrase "lease of real property" does not apply to lease financing transactions or to leases intended as security, but rather applies only to a "true" or "bona fide" lease. Thus, where the purported "lease" involves merely a sale of the real estate and the rental payments are, in truth, payments of principal and interest on a secured loan involving a sale of real estate, there is no true lease and section 502(b)(6) does not apply. S. Rep. No. 989, 95th Cong., 2d Sess. 64, reprinted in 1978 U.S. Code Cong. & Ad. News 5787, 5850; see 3 Collier on Bankruptcy (15th ed. 1986) ¶502.02[7][d], at 502-63 to 502-64.

Furthermore, the bankruptcy court is to look to the circumstances of the case and consider the economic substance of the transaction rather than "the locus of title, the form of the transaction or the fact that the transaction is denominated as a 'lease,' " to determine whether the transaction embodies a "true lease" or a financing transaction. S. Rep. No. 989, 95th Cong., 2d Sess. 64, reprinted in 1978 U.S. Code Cong. & Ad. News 5787, 5850.

We have no difficulty applying the section 502(b)(6) requirement of a bona fide lease to section 365(d)(3), (4) because these sections, read together, are part of a total scheme designed to set forth the rights and obligations of landlords and tenants involved in bankruptcy proceedings. . . .

We believe that reading a requirement of a true lease into section 365 is necessary to effectuate the purposes of that section. As a whole, section 365 allows a trustee, or in this case a debtor-in-possession, to reject or assume executory contracts and leases, based on a determination of whether they burden or benefit the bankrupt estate. Thus, executory contracts and leases that benefit the bankrupt are favored over contracts with other creditors. If security transactions, loans and other financing arrangements can be couched in lease terms, and can thereby be assumed by the bankrupt estate, the "lessor" gains a distinct advantage at the expense of other creditors without a concomitant benefit to the bankrupt estate. This is especially apparent in the case at bar. If successful, Liona would enjoy the benefit of its contract with PCH to the detriment of others having valid claims against the bankrupt's estate. However, if there is no true lease, Liona should not be permitted to escape the consequences of investor/creditor status by invoking the labels of "land-lord" and "lease."

Satisfied that section 365(d)(3), (4) requires a bona fide lease, we must now determine whether the transaction at issue embodied such a lease, keeping in mind the economic substance of the transaction and not its form.

While there is a "strong presumption that a deed and lease . . . are what they purport to be," Fox v. Peck Iron & Metal Co., 25 B.R. 674, 688 (Bankr. S.D. Cal. 1982), here there was substantial evidence upon which the bankruptcy court and the district court could rely to find that the transaction is something other than a true lease. Based on the circumstances of the negotiations and the economic substance of the transaction, it was not error to conclude that the parties intended to impose obligations and confer rights significantly different from those arising from the ordinary landlord/tenant relationship.

We are faced with a transaction cast as a sale/leaseback arrangement, a "relatively modern, and clever, structure of financing which affords significant advantages to both purchaser-lessor and seller-lessee." Id. at 688. Bernstein, acting for PCH, sought out Liona in order to pool their resources for their mutual benefit. The transaction was structured as a ground lease to accomplish a trade-off betwen tax benefits for PCH and a higher guaranteed return, without management concerns, for Liona. Therefore, rent was not calculated to compensate Liona for the use of the property; rather the parties structured the "rent" solely to ensure Liona's return on its investment. Furthermore, the "purchase price" paid by Liona for the land was not based on market rate, but was calculated as the amount necessary to finance the transaction.

It seems clear that no true lease was contemplated by the parties here. It is undisputed that Bernstein, acting for PCH, initiated the entire transaction, including the purchase of the land by Liona. . . .

Another factor indicating that this transaction does not involve a true lease is that the purchase price was not related to the value of the land. A large inequality or discrepancy in values has been characterized as a "strong circumstance" tending to show that a transaction was a disguised financing scheme. Id. at 689; see also In re 716 Third Avenue Holding Corp., 340 F.2d 42, 47 (2d Cir. 1964), cert. denied, 381 U.S. 913, 85 S. Ct. 1535, 14 L. Ed. 2d 434 (1965). Furthermore, PCH assumed many of the obligations associated with outright ownership of the property, including responsibility for paying property taxes and insurance. As noted in the *Senate Report* on section 502(b)(6) of the Bankruptcy Code,

[T]he fact that the lessee assumes and discharges substantially all the risks and obligations ordinarily attributed to the outright ownership of the property is more indicative of a financing transaction than of a true lease. The rental payments in such cases are in substance payments of principal and interest either on a loan secured by the leased real property or on the purchase of the leased real property. See, e.g., Financial Accounting Standards Board Statement No. 13 and SEC Reg. S-X, 17 C.F.R. section 210.3-16(g) (1977); cf. First National Bank of Chicago v. Irving Trust Co., 74 F.2d 263 (2d Cir. 1934); and Albenda and Lief, 'Net Lease Financing Transactions Under the Proposed Bankruptcy Act of 1973,' 30 Business Lawyer 713 (1975).

S. Rep. No. 598, 95th Cong., 2d Sess. 64, reprinted in 1978 U.S. Code Cong. & Ad. News 5787, 5850. Therefore, we find that PCH's significant indicia of ownership tend toward a finding that there is no true lease. Additionally, the provisions allowing Liona to recover its investment if the hotel were refinanced, and giving PCH the power to pre-pay Liona's investment, at which time Liona would share solely in profits, strongly suggest a transaction other than a lease.

Mindful that the structure of the transaction was based on the tax considerations and the investment requirements of both parties, and viewing the transaction as a whole, we hold that the Ground Lease and Sale-Leaseback Agreement do not constitute a true lease. Therefore section 365(d)(3), (4) of the Bankruptcy Code has no application here. Whether these contracts create a joint venture, a security agreement, or some other form of investment vehicle need not be decided here. . . .

Cowan and Eastman, Debt/Equity Transactions — An Approach to Recharacterization

Protecting the Real Estate Lender: Bankruptcy and Financing Strategies, Gitlin & Cherkis Chairmen (PLI 1988)

V. THE OBJECTIVE ANALYSIS

IN RE PCH ASSOCIATES

In the context of a sale/leaseback, one court, In re PCH Associates, has taken a new approach to the issue of recharacterization. Instead of asking whether the relationship of the parties is that of lessor/lessee, borrower/lender or partners, the court in In re PCH Associates focused on whether the economic substance of the transaction was consistent with this label, i.e., a lease. The inquiry was, using an objective standard, was this a "true lease"?

The objective approach employed by In re PCH Associates is founded on the rationale that the law (the Bankruptcy Code, in this case), in some instances, grants preferential treatment to certain types of transactions. Thus, in a bankruptcy context, executory contracts or leases that benefit the bankrupt estate are favored over contracts with other creditors (i.e., the debtor must affirm and cure defaults or, in the case of a lease, relinquish possession to the "lessor"). The court takes the position that it will not sanction the parties' manipulation of the form of a transaction solely to take advantage of such legislative preferences when the economic substance of the transaction materially deviates from the paradigm form upon which the preference is based. . . .

In affirming the lower court's determination that the ground lease was not subject to the provisions of Sections 365(d)(3) and 365(d)(4) of the Bankruptcy Code, the Court of Appeals abandoned the traditional "partnership" approach employed by the lower courts, relying instead upon an objective test to determine whether the transaction was what it purported to be, a true lease.

The court agreed with the bankruptcy court that certain elements of the sale/leaseback agreement were not indicative of a true sale/leaseback. In particular, the bankruptcy court found the following deviations:

1. Deviations from True Sale:

    a. The amount of the purchase price was not related to the value of the land.
    b. Amounts recovered post-closing from the former hotel owners, as well as cost savings in the anticipated refurbishment of the hotel, would be shared by the buyer/lessor and the seller/lessee on a pro rata basis, based upon their respective investments.
    c. The agreement required the continued involvement in the project of the individual who controlled the seller/lessee.
    d. The buyer/lessor was required to pay 50% of the amount necessary to repay a pre-existing mortgage on the land and building.
    e. There were no closing adjustments between the buyer/lessor and the seller/lessee. The seller/lessee paid all transfer taxes arising out of the transaction and was obligated to pay the premium for the buyer/lessor's title insurance policy.

2. Deviations from True Lease:

    a. The seller/lessee solicited the buyer/lessor to invest in the tenant's property.

b.   The term of the lease, if all renewal options were exercised, would have been 165 years.

c.   A minimum rent providing the buyer/lessor with a 12% annual return was established for the first three years of the lease. Percentage rent would then be paid until the buyer/lessor's investment was recovered. *Thereafter,* rent would be equal to one-half of the net profits of the hotel.

d.   Rent could be deferred under the lease provided that, when paid, the buyer/lessor would realize at least a 12% annual return on its investment.

e.   The seller/lessee was required to insure the property.

f.   Condemnation awards would be shared on a pro rata basis until the buyer/lessor's investment had been recovered, rather than on the basis of the relative value of the land and building or the value of the unexpired portion of the lease term.

g.   The buyer/lessor had agreed to subordinate to all existing and certain future mortgages on the property.

h.   The seller/lessee posted no security deposit with the buyer/lessor, and was exculpated from any personal liability in connection with the ground lease.

i.   The buyer/lessor was entitled to a share of net cash flow and net refinancing proceeds and would thereby share equally in the seller/lessee's savings on debt service and be subject to the detriments of increased debt service costs.

In its decision affirming the bankruptcy court's district court's ruling, the Court of Appeals focused on the following:

a.   The motivation for the transaction's structure was a trade-off of tax benefits for a higher rate of return.

b.   The parties fixed the rent to assure a rate of return on the buyer/lessor's cash investment, not on "use" of the property.

c.   There was a "large discrepancy" between the purchase price and the value of the land.

d.   The seller/lessee's principal originated the sale/leaseback transaction.

e.   The seller/lessee assumed many of the obligations normally carried out by a lessor, including responsibility for paying taxes and insurance.

f.   The buyer/lessor could recover its investment if the hotel were refinanced, and the seller/lessee could prepay the buyer/lessor's investment.

Viewing the transaction as a whole, the court held that the transaction did not constitute a true lease. The court expressly avoided a determination of whether the transaction was in fact a joint venture or a financing transaction.

In light of the difficulty in applying the traditional debt/equity test to equity transactions, would such an "objective" test be adaptable to equity loan transactions, and, if so, would such a test have any advantage over the traditional test? In fact, considering the substantial preferences granted secured creditors under both state and federal law, it would not be at all surprising to find a court embrace this objective standard and ask whether the lender had a "true loan." Furthermore, in the context of a loan, a court's ruling that the transaction was not a true loan would be determinative with respect to whether the lender was a partner because, unlike a sale/leaseback transaction, any investment by the lender which is not a loan would, by definition, constitute equity.

In evaluating whether an equity loan transaction constitutes a true loan, we should note the market deviations that are typical of such transactions and compare them, by analogy, to the factors noted by the lower and appellate courts in the In re PCH Associates case.

Typical Characteristics of Equity Loan Transaction:

1. Loan-to-value ratio is often very high and can approach 100%. In addition, the traditional interest rate on the "loan" is well below market. PCH Comparison: court focus is on "below-market" aspect of a purchase price — looks to large discrepancies and inequalities in value.

2. Term of loan is often longer than the normal straight debt loan. Not unusual for a construction equity loan to mature long after completion of construction. In fact, some transactions have no fixed maturity date but become due only upon a sale of the project. PCH Comparison: exceedingly long term of lease (165 years).

3. Lender may receive a share in the profits subsequent to repayment of the original indebtedness. PCH Comparison: buyer/lessor was entitled to share in profits even after land was repurchased by seller/lessee. See also Farley Realty Corp., supra; Leahy v. Commissioner, 87 T.C. 56 (1986) (debt recharacterized as equity interest where "lender" was entitled to contingent interest after repayment of principal).

4. Traditional interest is often accrued or, in the case of a construction loan, payable out of the proceeds of the loan. PCH Comparison: rent was deferrable by lessee as long as lessor's yield was maintained.

5. In the context of a construction equity loan transaction, the lender may fund cost overruns and/or operating deficits from loan proceeds. PCH Comparison: buyer/lessor agreed to pay 50% of pre-existing mortgage.

6. Most equity loans are non-recourse. PCH Comparison: exculpation clause contained in lease.
7. Participating mortgage and/or shared appreciation mortgages often compute contingent interest on net flow and/or net appreciation. PCH Comparison: buyer/seller participated in proceeds of refinancing, net expenses.
8. Loan documents often provide the lender with a greater degree of control and may be drafted such that an event of default occurs if the developer dies or is incapacitated. PCH Comparison: control shifted to buyer/lessor upon departure of key personnel.

An equity loan transaction that had all of the aforementioned factors could run a significant risk of being recharacterized under an objective In re PCH Associates-type analysis. Would the result be different under a traditional approach? One commentator has noted that in applying the traditional test the courts basically employ a "smell test." Siegman and Linquanti, The Covertible, Participating Mortgage: Planning Opportunities and Legal Pitfalls in Structuring the Transaction, 54 U. Colo. L. Rev. 295, 313 (1983). Arguably this smell test is analytically similar to the objective approach taken in In re PCH Associates. In fact, many of the factors relied on by the court in In re PCH Associates are probative of three of the four prongs comprising the traditional test: (i) share in profits (i.e., share in profits by percentage rentals during the original lease term and even after investment repaid), (ii) share in losses (i.e., exculpatory clause and lessor's share in "net" proceeds of refinancing), and (iii) control (i.e., control shifted to lessor on departure of key employee). Furthermore, the missing prong, intent, is embodied in the structure of the objective analysis, that is, a court will look to substance over form to assess the parties' objective manifestations of intent. Though similar, the In re PCH Associates test does have one advantage: because it purports to use an objective (reasonable) standard, at least some general guidelines are furnished that may be useful in structuring an equity transaction.

NOTES AND QUESTIONS

1. *Termination by the Landlord.* As you know, §365(e) prohibits termination of a lease after the commencement of bankruptcy solely on the basis of a provision in the lease that is conditioned on the insolvency or financial condition of the debtor. Notwithstanding this fact, what reasons can you, as attorney for a landlord, give for retaining the usual provision in the lease terminating the lease on the insolvency of the tenant (the "ipso facto" clause)? Consider this situation: Dan Developer owns a shopping center whose major anchor tenant is the

Canview Department Store. Dan insists on a clause in the lease requiring that Canview keep at least 150 stores in operation throughout the country. Canview later files in Chapter 11 and the court approves the closing of 75 unprofitable stores, reducing the number of Canview stores nationwide to 80. Do you think Dan can terminate the lease without violating §365(e)? If it can be shown that in most chain store bankruptcy proceedings a large number of stores are usually closed, would it be relevant? Is there a purpose to this provision other than to have a means of terminating in bankruptcy? If so, is there any basis for attacking the provision under the language of §365(e)? Cf. In re Slocum, No. 90-1072 (3d Cir., Dec. 31, 1990).

Note that §365(e)(2)(A)(i) permits termination and §365(c)(1)(A) prohibits assumption and assignment of contracts and leases where, inter alia, nonbankruptcy law provides that even absent a nonassignment clause assignment is not permitted without the consent of the other party to the contract or lease. This provision was written with personal service contracts in mind. However, it has not been limited strictly to such contracts and has been applied in other situations in which subjective judgment is involved. For example, In re Pioneer Ford Sales, 729 F.2d 27 (1st Cir. 1984), found certain franchise and distributorship agreements nonassignable. See cases cited in In re Compass Van & Storage Corp., 65 Bankr. 1007 (Bankr. E.D.N.Y. 1986). Note that separate subsections of these provisions permit termination of, and prohibit assumption and assignment of, loan commitments.

2. Pre-petition Lease Termination: The Lazarus Lease. Section 365(c)(3) prohibits assumption or assignment of a lease "of nonresidential real property" that "has been terminated under applicable non-bankruptcy law" prior to the bankruptcy proceedings. This provision was added during the 1984 revisions to the Code and may be an example of an issue that should have been fought in the courts on the basis of statutory interpretation rather than in the legislature through statutory tinkering and hasty political draftsmanship. Does it make any sense? On what basis (other than the invocation of fraudulent transfer or other avoidance provisions of the Code not at issue here) could a lease no longer in existence have been assumed or assigned in the first place? Would it make any difference if, when the petition is filed, the tenant is still in possession of the leased premises under a terminated or expired lease? See In re Mimi's of Atlanta, 5 Bankr. 623 (Bankr. N.D. Ga. 1980), affd., 11 Bankr. 710 (N.D. Ga. 1981), and In re Mulkey, 5 Bankr. 15 (Bankr. W.D. Mo. 1980).

Why limit the provision to nonresidential real property? Was it to avoid a taint on the amendment as being anti-consumer? Does this mean that terminated leases of residential real property can be resurrected?

What is the meaning of "nonresidential real property"? Assume Ace Insurance Company owned land improved with an apartment complex that it leased to Dan Developer under a net long-term ground lease. Dan later defaults under the lease, and the lease is terminated. Ace then leases the complex to Linda Landlord. Some time later, Dan files in bankruptcy. Was the lease to Dan a lease of residential real property? If so, can the lease be revived? What then happens to Ace? To Linda Landlord? To Linda's title company?

Provisions similar to those in §365(c)(3) were inserted by the 1984 amendments in §362(b)(10) (automatic stay not applicable to certain terminated leases) and §541(a)(7)(2) (certain terminated leases are not property of the estate). Both these provisions are worded slightly differently than the provision in §365. Compare §365(c)(3) with the language of §362(b)(10) that refers to leases of nonresidential real property terminated "by virtue of the expiration of the stated term of the lease" before the commencement of the bankruptcy case. This language is also found in §541(a)(7)(2). Assume in the above hypothetical that Ace's lease to Dan Developer was for an office building. Can the lease be revived for the purpose of making it property of the estate and for the automatic stay, but not for assumption and assignment? Does this make sense?

3.   *Assumption and Assignment by Tenant.*   Section 365(b) provides that if the lease is in default, it can be assumed by the tenant only if any default is cured, compensation is given for the landlord's losses, and "adequate assurance of future performance" is provided. Similarly, §365(f)(2)(b) requires that adequate assurance of future performance by an assignee be provided. Other than the definition of adequate assurance of future performance for leases of property in a shopping center in §365(b)(3), there is no definition of the phrase in the Code, leaving great latitude to the courts in interpreting whether future performance is adequately assured.

Even the definition of adequate assurance of future performance in shopping centers is far from clear. For example, following §365(b)(3)(A), would the requirement of assurance of the source of the rent be met if the trustee simply reported that Irma Insolvent would be responsible for the payment of the Canview rent? If you had been drafting that section, how would you have worded it? With respect to §365(b)(3)(B), assume a lease in a shopping center with a low base rent and contingent rent based on a percentage of profits or sales at the location. In the first year of the lease there was just a few dollars' worth of contingent rent; in the next five years contingent rent exceeded 20 percent of the base rent; and in the eighth year, just before the tenant, then insolvent, filed in bankruptcy, there was no contingent rent. Adequate assurance must be given that the contingent rent will not decline substantially. Substantially from when? If from the date of bankruptcy, how much comfort does the provision give a landlord? Does the definition of adequate assurance of future performance for shopping centers have a negative implication for non-shopping center leases? For example, does §365(b)(3)(C) imply that an assumption or assignment of an office building lease need not be "subject to all the provisions thereof"? Or does §365(b)(3)(C) merely mimic §365(d)(3)? What is a shopping center, anyway? Is a lease of a store for the sale of jewelry in the jewelry section of Manhattan a lease of property in a shopping center? Cf. In re Slocum, No. 90-1072 (3d Cir., Dec. 31, 1990). Note that where a shopping center lease is assigned, §365(b)(3)(A) provides strict rules for the financial condition and operating performance of the assignee.

4. *Rejection by Tenant.* Under §365(a), the trustee or debtor in possession may, subject to the court's approval, reject a lease of the debtor. Section 365(d)(4), added to the Code in 1984, provides that if the trustee does not assume or reject a lease of nonresidential real property within 60 days after the date of the order for relief, or within such extended period as the court may order, the lease will be deemed rejected. Consider the effect of rejection by a tenant-debtor on subordinate interests such as the leasehold mortgagee and sublessee. If the leasehold estate is terminated by the tenant's rejection, the subordinate estates will also be lost. However, the pre-Code case In re Garfinkle, 577 F.2d 901 (5th Cir. 1978), held that the leasehold mortgage was not destroyed by the lessee's rejection of the lease on the ground that disaffirmance by a lessee "merely placed the leasehold outside of the bankruptcy administration without destroying the underlying estate and, therefore, the mortgage. . . ." (577 F.2d at 904). But see In re Hawaii Dimensions, Inc., 47 Bankr. 425 (Bankr. D. Hawaii 1985), where the court held that rejection of the lease by the tenant terminated the lease, noting the absence of a provision in the Code similar to §365(h) (discussed below), which protects the tenant on disaffirmance by a debtor landlord. The court in In re Storage Technology Corp., 55 Bankr. 479 (Bankr. D. Colo. 1985), attempts to distinguish the two cases on the basis of the equities involved. See also In re Picnic 'N Chicken, Inc., 58 Bankr. 523 (Bankr. S.D. Cal. 1986). Can you devise an argument that would protect the interest of the leasehold mortgagee or sublessee even where the disaffirmance by the tenant effectively terminates its interest in the property?

Given the conflict in the courts and the silence of the Code, a leasehold mortgagee or sublessee might wish to strengthen its position by inserting a covenant in the leasehold mortgage or sublease to the effect that the lessee will assign the lease to the leasehold mortgagee or sublessee in lieu of rejection on demand, provided the leasehold mortgagee or sublessee agrees to cure defaults outstanding under the lease. Do you think a bankruptcy court would be bound by such a provision? Can you think of a reason why the bankruptcy court would want to enforce such a provision as being beneficial to the estate? Suppose both the leasehold mortgage and the sublease contained such a clause? Since the lease cannot be assigned to both, provided the court were willing to enforce the provision, should it assign the lease in *reverse* priority? If so, why? Reflect on your consideration of leasehold mortgagee protection provisions of leases (Chapter 8A3). Which provisions (provided they had been carefully drafted) would be extremely helpful to the leasehold mortgagee if a debtor-lessee successfully rejected the lease?

The rejection of a lease constitutes a breach of the lease under §365(g). This entitles the landlord to a claim in the tenant's bankruptcy. Section 502(b)(6), however, limits the claim to the "rent reserved" for the greater of one year or 15 percent (not to exceed three years) of the remaining term. What is the purpose of this limitation on the landlord's claim? Suppose Dan Developer leased space in his office building to Widget Corporation of America. The lease provided for a base rent with additional amounts to be paid for increases in real estate taxes, labor costs, and so on. In WCA's bankruptcy, would Dan be limited to 15 percent of the stated rent and not the additional rent? Would it help Dan if the lease clause provided that all payments under the lease "shall be considered 'rent' for the purposes of §502(b)(6)" of the Bankruptcy Code?

5. Recharacterization. Based on a substance-over-form approach, a debt instrument with equity features (such as a participating mortgage or a convertible mortgage) and an alternative mortgage instrument may be vulnerable to recharacterization by third-party creditors and by the I.R.S. as a constructive partnership (or some other form of equity-sharing arrangement) between the lender and the borrower. See discussion at Chapter 5B3, notes 3 and 5, and Chapter 7A. Likewise, sale-and-leaseback transactions have sometimes been recharacterized as disguised mortgages for tax purposes. See Chapter 8B2, note 1. In the *PCH Assocs.* case, excerpted above, a sale and leaseback became the subject of a recharacterization dispute in connection with a bankruptcy proceeding. The lower court recharacterized the sale and leaseback as a disguised joint venture arrangement. The Cowan and Eastman comment lists the various considerations the lower court used in determining the existence of a partnership relationship. Do they provide any guidance for the future?

The Second Circuit made no determination of what the arrangement actually was; it simply decided that the lease was not a true lease for the purposes of certain Code sections dealing with lease disaffirmance and compliance. In reaching its conclusion, the court cited the legislative history of §502(b)(6) as furnishing "explicit authority for restricting the scope of that term to 'bona fide' leases." The court points out that the Senate Report stated that the phrase " 'lease of real property' does not apply to lease financing transactions." What the court neglected to include in its quote was the Senate Report's prefatory phrase, "As used in §502(b)(7). . . ." (now §502(b)(6)). This section, as you will recall from note 4 above, limits the landlord's claim on rejection of a lease by the lessee. The Report analyzes the reasons that limitation should not apply where a lease is a financing lease. Is this "explicit authority" for purposes of §§365(d)(3) and 365(d)(4)?

A major concern with *PCH Assocs.* is that the reasons emphasized by the Second Circuit for determining whether a lease is a true lease involved provisions and facts that are often found in sale-and-leaseback transactions. Since sale and leaseback is often a form of financing, the sale price does not necessarily bear a relation to the value of the property. Similarly, the rent bears a relationship to the sale price and not the going rent for space in a building of that type. Finally, almost all ground leases, as you know, are net leases, whether the lease is for financing purposes or not. Thus, the ultimate effect of *PCH Assocs.* on the future of lease financing transactions could be severe. For example, while the Second Circuit made no determination as to what the transaction was, the facts emphasized by the Second Circuit seem to indicate a similarity to a mortgage. Consider the implications of the lease's being held to be a mortgage. If it were a mortgage, would the mortgage be properly recorded? In many jurisdictions, mortgages, deeds, and leases are recorded in different recording offices. If not properly recorded, the mortgagee runs the risk of being subordinate to the bankruptcy trustee, who is given the status of a hypothetical lien creditor and bona fide purchaser on the date of bankruptcy (§544(a)), with an interest superior to unrecorded liens.

If it is determined that the lease is really a mortgage, is it a mortgage that clogs the equity of redemption? Review the discussion of clogging at Chapter 7A, note 2. The lessee (recharacterized as a mortgagee) in a lease transaction would not normally have the ability to reacquire the property by payment of an amount "borrowed," since the landlord has a reversion and gets the property back at the end of the term of a normal lease. Note the irony in the following. If the seller-lessee (the "borrower" in a recharacterization of a sale and lease-back as a mortgage) becomes the owner of the property at the end of the lease term for a nominal payment (i.e., in those sale and leasebacks that are purely financing transactions), the property would be "returned" on performance of the "obligation" and the transaction, which might justly be subject to recharacterization, probably would not be subject to the anti-clogging rule. On the other hand, under those sale and leasebacks that are truly sales and leases, the property should remain in the purchaser-lessor at the end of the lease term. If this true sale and leaseback were held to be a mortgage because it had a financing purpose, isn't there a significant risk that the anti-clogging rule would be applicable, since the "mortgagor" would not be in a position to recover the property on payment of the "indebtedness"?

While the Second Circuit in *PCH* did not opine on the form of the relationship created, the District Court allowed the Bankruptcy Court's determination that the transaction was a joint venture to stand. 122 Bankr. 7 (S.D.N.Y. 1990). What possible effects might this determination have on the rights and obligations of the parties?

The issue of who gets the property at the end of the term and at what price under Article 9 of the Uniform Commercial Code is the most important in determining whether a lease was intended as security. See the definition of "security interest" in U.C.C. §1-201(37). Shouldn't this really be determinative factor in recharacterization cases under the Bankruptcy Code as well?

6. *Additional Reading.* Andrew, Executory Contracts in Bankruptcy: Underwriting "Rejection," 59 U. Colo. L. Rev. 845 (1988); Cook, Bankruptcy: Judicial Standards for Rejection of Executory Contracts in Bankruptcy Code Reorganization Cases, 1980 Ann. Survey Am. L. 689 (1981); Divack, Assumption of Nonresidential Real Property Leases: Section 365(d)(4), 4 Bankr. Dev. J. 79 (1987); Ehrlich, The Assumption and Rejection of Unexpired Real Property Leases Under the Bankruptcy Code — A New Look, 32 Buffalo L. Rev. 1 (1983); Homberger and Andre, Real Estate Sale and Leaseback Transactions and the Risk of Recharacterization in Bankruptcy Proceedings, 24 Real Prop., Prob. & Tr. J. 95 (Summer 1989); Sabineo, The Necessity for Court Approval of the Assumption or Rejection of Unexpired Leases Under Code §365(d)(4): Defusing the Ticking Time Bomb, 91 Com. L.J. 405 (1986); Simpson, Leases and the Bankruptcy Code: The Protean Concept of Adequate Assurance of Future Performance, 56 Am. Bankr. L.J. 233 (1982).

2. *Bankruptcy of the Landlord*

Section 365(h) deals with disaffirmance, or rejection, of a lease by a landlord in bankruptcy. A lease is, as you know, both a contract and a conveyance. The landlord normally conveys to the tenant an estate or interest in the property for a term of years. The instrument of that conveyance, the lease, also normally contains contractual obligations between the landlord and the tenant. A conveyance is a completed transfer, and there is nothing that can be rejected. The only change in relationship that can be effected by the landlord's rejection of the lease is for the landlord to stop performing its executory contractual obligations to the tenant.

The drafters of the former Bankruptcy Act recognized this dual nature of a lease and provided in §70b thereof that rejection of a lease by a bankrupt lessor "does not deprive the lessee of his estate." Unfortunately, it was unclear what provisions of the lease constituted the lessee's estate and what provisions were contractual. It was also unclear whether the clause saving the estate applied to reorganization as well as to liquidations.[14]

These issues came to a head as the Code was being drafted when the Penn Central Railroad, in reorganization, attempted as landlord to disaffirm leases of the so-called Park Avenue Properties. Originally, Park Avenue in New York City had been a ravine in the ground through which trains ran back and forth from Grand Central Terminal, belching smoke and soot into the heart of the city. Eventually, for environmental and other reasons, the railroad covered over the tracks with platforms with the intention of leasing the platforms for the construction of high-rise buildings. After some complex legal structuring to free the leases from the lien of corporate indentures covering the railroad's property,[15] the platforms were leased and the buildings built.

---

14. These problems were discussed in Creedon and Zinman, Landlord's Bankruptcy: Laissez Les Lessees, 26 Bus. Law. 1391 (1971). See especially the letters from Professor MacLachlan (the drafter of §70b) appended to the article. See also Siegel, Landlord's Bankruptcy: A Proposal for Treatment of the Lease by Reference to Its Component Elements, 54 B.U. L. Rev. 903 (1974).

15. See discussion of priorities of mortgages and leases in Chapter 4C. As you will remember, the foreclosure of prior mortgages can cut off subordinate leases. In this case the prior mortgage was in the form of a huge corporate indenture covering most of the railroad's real estate. No person could be expected to build a building on a leasehold with such a prior mortgage on the fee unless the lien of the mortgage were subordinated or the property were released from the lien. Unfortunately, it appeared the indenture trustees for the railroad were not empowered to subordinate or to release the lien for the purpose of leasing. They did, however, have authority to release the lien for the purpose of conveying portions of the railroad's property. The attorneys involved devised what they called a "grant of term," that is, a conveyance of an estate for a term of years without any of the contractual elements normally found in a lease. The trustees then released the lien of the indenture from the property; the grant of term to a railroad subsidiary was recorded; and the lien of the indenture spread back to the property, now subordinate to the grant of term and interests flowing out of that grant. The holder of the grant of term was then able to lease the property free and clear of the lien of the indenture. Do you see why this procedure constituted, in effect, a subordination of the lien of the indenture to the ground lease without actual subordination?

Often there were several layers of leasehold interests stemming from the grant of term. This, the so-called Hawaiian Technique, was devised by William Zeckendorf, Sr. and involved dividing up property economically in layers of leases, almost as a corporation would divide securities into preferred stock, debentures, mortgage bonds,

Thus, when Penn Central filed in reorganization in 1970, it owned most of the property along lower Park Avenue and around the Terminal, property subject to long-term leases. The leases were at fixed rents, which over the years kept the value of the Penn Central fee quite low. If the leases could be disaffirmed, billions of dollars of increased value could be added to the estate. The lessees and leasehold mortgagees fought the disaffirmance strenuously and won on equitable grounds. See In re Penn Central Transportation Co. (Disaffirmance of Executory Contracts), 458 F. Supp. 1346 (E.D. Pa. 1978). Perhaps Judge Fullam, in deciding not to rule on the meaning of the clause protecting the tenant's estate in §70b of the former Bankruptcy Act, had one eye on Washington, where the Code was in the process of being drafted and where he knew this problem would be dealt with. How successful the drafters were will be discussed in the notes below.

NOTES AND QUESTIONS

1. *The* Penn Central *Decision.* While Judge Fullam did not permit rejection of the leases of the Park Avenue Properties, he decided the case on the equities rather than on a direct interpetation of the meaning of §70b of the former Bankruptcy Act. In addition, he considered the question of whether a landlord may reject a lease that is not burdensome to the estate (i.e., a lease under which the landlord is not losing money but the lease rent is below market), a question that may survive the enactment of the Bankruptcy Code. With respect to the Park Avenue Properties, the leases were net leases (that is, the tenant paid all the expenses and turned over the rent to the landlord without any offsets), produced income to the railroad, and could not be disaffirmed under a burdensomeness test. Judge Fullam accepted the "business judgment" test of when an executory contract or lease could

---

and the like, each carrying a different fixed return and creating leverage for the person with the last leasehold interest, or the equity. See discussion at Chapter 8C. At the time of the Penn Central reorganization, the leasehold status of the Graybar Building (one of the "Park Avenue Properties," although located on Lexington Avenue) was as follows: the land and building were owned by Penn Central Transportation Co. Despatch Shops, Inc., a subsidiary of Penn Central, held the grant of term and leased the property to Metropolitan Life Insurance Co. under a net long-term ground lease. Metropolitan Life subleased the property under a net long-term "sandwich lease" to Graybar Building Assocs., a partnership headed by Lawrence A. Wien, which sub-subleased the property under another net long-term sandwich lease to Precision Dynamics Corp. which sub-sub-subleased the property under a net long-term "operating lease" to Harry B. Helmsley, d/b/a Graybar Building Co. Mr. Helmsley sub-sub-sub-subleased to the people who occupied space in the building. The Bankruptcy Code treats the problem of landlord's disaffirmance of leases in §365(h).

be disaffirmed (it may be disaffirmed when it is in the interest of the debtor based on business judgment), citing for support Group of Institutional Investors v. Chicago, M., St. P. & P.R. Co., 318 U.S. 523 (1943), a case involving a *tenant's* bankruptcy (see Judge Fullam's note 13). What differences are there between a landlord's bankruptcy and a tenant's bankruptcy that might distinguish that case? Did the Bankruptcy Code deal with this problem?

  2. *The Bankruptcy Code Approach.* As you know, a lease is a conveyance as well as a contract. In his excellent treatise *Bankruptcy Reorganization,* Martin Bienenstock states that "when a debtor rejects a lease under which it is the landlord, the Bankruptcy Code treats the rejection as abrogating the privity of contract, but not the privity of estate" (514). Do you agree that this is what §365(h) does? Mr. Bienenstock concludes that the tenant may remain in possession for the entire term including renewals even if this is 900 years but that rejection will terminate a tenant's option to purchase, permitting eviction of the tenant at the end of the term even if the term is very short. He asks whether this result is incongruous. What do you think? See M. Bienenstock, Bankruptcy Reorganization 514-515 n.182 (1987).

  Assume in the master hypothetical that Dan Developer leases space in his building to Widget Corporation of America and later files in bankruptcy.

  a. Assume the rent is below market and that Dan Developer rejects the lease, the court adhering to the business judgment test of rejection (see note 1 above). WCA elects to remain in possession. Dan asks the court to increase the rental for the remaining term as a condition to WCA's remaining in possession. Will Dan succeed? Does §365(h) address this problem? See Upland/Euclid, Ltd. v. Grace Restaurant Co., 56 Bankr. 250 (BAP, 9th Cir. 1985), and In re Stable Mews Assocs., 35 Bankr. 603 (Bankr. S.D.N.Y. 1983).

  b. Assume the lease provided that Dan supply cleaning services. Dan rejects and stops providing these services. What can WCA do to protect itself under §365(h)? How would the provision work if Dan stopped providing elevator service and WCA occupied the 56th floor of the building? What if some of the tenants agree to stay on and perform Dan's defaulted obligations, some stay on and do not perform these obligations, and some choose to treat the lease as terminated?

  c. If Conservative Insurance Company held a leasehold mortgage on WCA's estate, could WCA elect to treat the lease as terminated? What would the effect be on Conservative? While a landlord usually disaffirms because the lease is advantageous to the tenant and thus it is unlikely that the tenant will wish to treat the disaffirmed lease as terminated, can you think of any situation in which this would not be true? Is there a provision in §365 to protect Conservative? If you were counsel to Conservative, what language would you put in the leasehold mortgage to implement any §365(h) protection?

    d.   Suppose Dan had leased the entire building to Linda Landlord under a long-term ground lease. Linda sublet the building to WCA and occupies no space in the building. Dan, in bankruptcy, disaffirms the lease. Can Linda "remain in possession of the leasehold" when she is not in occupancy? In 1984, the words "of the leasehold" were added after "remain in possession." Does this addition help Linda?

    3. Purchasers. In §365, Congress also deals with the question of the rights of certain purchasers when the seller disaffirms a contract notwithstanding the principles of equitable conversion you studied in first-year property. See, e.g., Speck v. First National Bank (In re Speck), 798 F.2d 279 (8th Cir. 1986). In subsections (i) and (j) of §365, Congress gave special protection where the purchaser is in possession of the property, for instance, under a long-term installment land contract. Why, do you think, was protection afforded in this situation?

    A purchaser of a time share interest ("time shares" are rights to use property for a specified period of time during each year; see definition of "timeshare plan" in §101(49)) would normally have had the benefit of §§365(i) and (j) where the interest to be acquired is an interest in real property. However, many such interests are not real property interests but merely licenses to use the property. In Sombrero Reef Club v. Allman (In re Sombrero Reef Club 8 B.C.D. 1277 (Bankr. S.D. Fla. 1982)), the bankruptcy court sent shivers through the time share industry by holding that those time share contracts giving purchasers a right to occupy and use the facilities, rather than a lease or conveyance of real estate, were executory contracts subject to disaffirmance and not subject to the protections afforded lessees or purchasers when the landlord or seller disaffirms. In 1984, Congress eased the industry's concern by including time share purchasers under §365(h), thereby giving such purchasers the same type of protection afforded lessees.

    4. Additional Reading. Countryman, Executory Contracts in Bankruptcy, 57 Minn. L. Rev. 439 (1973) (Part I), 58 Minn. L. Rev. 479 (Part II) (1974); Creedon and Zinman, Landlord's Bankruptcy: Laissez Les Lessees, 24 Bus. Law. 1391 (1971); Epling, Treatment of Land Sales Contracts Under the Bankruptcy Code, 1981 Ariz. St. L.J. 853; McCarver, Installment Land Contracts and Section 365 of the Bankruptcy Reform Act, 49 Mo. L. Rev. 337 (1984); Ostow, Landlord's Bankruptcy: An Analysis of the Tenant's Rights and Remedies Under Bankruptcy Code §365(h), 35 Rutgers L. Rev. 631 (1983); Siegel, Landlord' Bankruptcy: A Proposal for Treatment of the Lease by Reference to Its Component Elements, 54 B.U. L. Rev. 903 (1974);

Silverstein, Rejection of Executory Contracts in Bankruptcy and Re-organization, 31 U. Chi. L. Rev. 467 (1964).

PLANNING PROBLEM

Assume you are counsel to Ace Insurance Company, which has been asked to make a loan secured by a mortgage on a subleasehold estate. You learn that Oscar Owner has leased the property to Dan Developer under a net long-term ground lease (see Chapter 8C). Dan is about to enter into a sublease of the entire building to Widget Corporation of America, and WCA has applied to Ace for a subleasehold mortgage loan. What risks would Ace face on the bankruptcy of Oscar Owner? Of Dan Developer? Of WCA? What documentary steps can be taken to mitigate these risks?

PART V

CURRENT ISSUES IN REAL ESTATE FINANCING

As detailed at Chapter 1B, shifting economic and demographic trends have caused a radical transformation in the real estate climate of this country since World War II, and real estate planners, always an innovative breed, have responded to the challenge by devising novel techniques to keep pace with the changing needs of their clients. And as real estate financing and investment techniques have changed, so has the law of real estate financing. Two current examples are the emerging trends toward the securitization of real estate and the expansion of lender liability.

As observed at Chapter 2.A, note 1, the principal disadvantage of investing in income-producing real estate has been the lack of liquidity associated with investment shares such as interests held in a limited partnership. Recently the public security format, which takes the form of investment shares in a so-called real estate master limited partnership, has been devised to offer the small investor both the nontax advantages of owning publicly traded corporate stock and the tax advantages of owning an interest in a partnership. Moreover, on the debt side, since 1985 some large developers have been able to obtain long-term fixed-rate financing by issuing commercial mortgage-backed bonds (CMMBs), thereby procuring Wall Street financing for their projects under better loan terms than would have been available from private, less competitive lending sources such as commercial banks and insurance companies. While the trend toward Wall Street financing has slowed somewhat during the past few years, the concept is ingenious, and in the opinion of some commentators it may eventually revolutionize the way in which commercial real estate is financed in this country.

Another important trend of interest to real estate attorneys has been the burgeoning number of lawsuits against lenders based on a new application of old theories (such as the implied covenant of good faith under contract law) and on the recent expansion of quasi-absolute lender liability under the Comprehensive Environmental Response, Compensation, and Liability Act of 1980 (CERCLA) and comparable state statutes.

C h a p t e r 12

Lender Liability

In the preceding two chapters we considered some of the issues involved in default: techniques for "working out," or recasting, a transaction in order to avoid foreclosure and bankruptcy; the foreclosure process; and the risks when bankruptcy ensues. The period from first default to bankruptcy has become a catalyst for lender liability claims, requiring the lender to be sensitive to such risks throughout what might be referred to as the default process. In this chapter, we will discuss these risks and steps lenders are taking to reduce them.

The burgeoning area of the law now commonly referred to as "lender liability" is, like "products liability," a constellation of traditional theories of liability coupled with evolving rules applicable to a certain family of defendants. In the past, lender liability was ordinarily limited to causes of action for straightforward breach of contract — violation or nonperformance of the express terms of the loan agreement. Today, however, many plaintiffs level shotgun suits at lenders, firing off claims such as those for negligence, tortious interference, fraudulent misrepresentation, breach of good faith, anticipatory breach, breach of fiduciary duty, and prima facie tort. And (on the trial level, at least) borrowers appear to be winning a good number of these suits.

This development has alarmed lenders, for a number of reasons. Damages awarded, both punitive and consequential, have in some cases been enormous. The law in this area is unsettled, and outcomes are unpredictable. Liability is frequently alleged in areas (such as "good faith," "fiduciary duty," and "control") that by their nature elude being mapped out.

As discussed in the Notes and Questions following the excerpts, the default and (sometimes) financial insolvency of the borrower and consequential injuries to the businesses of third parties are litigation triggers for lawsuits against lenders, who ironically may feel compelled to aggravate the risk of litigation against themselves by becoming involved in the conduct of the defaulting borrower's business affairs as they formulate workouts or take aggressive action to protect their interests as creditors.

In this chapter we will first examine recent cases involving litigation against lenders based on the theory that implied in every contract is a duty to exercise good faith and to deal fairly in the performance and enforcement of the contract.[1] The precise nature of these duties varies according to the particular circumstances, but will typically reflect the justified expectations of the parties and community standards of decency and fair play. By analogy to personal property, the Uniform Commercial Code[2] explicitly requires contracting parties to act in good faith in their dealings with one another, "good faith" being defined somewhat subjectively as "honesty in fact in the conduct or transaction concerned."[3] At Chapter 5A3, note 3, we briefly examined the duty of the borrower and the lender to exercise good faith while negotiating and closing a loan. Here we will observe how these standards apply during the borrower-lender relationship, particularly when that relationship becomes strained as a consequence of a default by the borrower. We will also focus on the increased burdens of the lender when it is both a mortgagee and a partner of the borrower, and thus is faced with conflicts between loyalty to its partners and its rights as a lender.

Perhaps the most disconcerting development of recent vintage for real estate lenders is the potential liability of a foreclosing lender for the costs of cleaning up hazardous wastes under, inter alia, CERCLA even though the lender did not directly cause or participate in the contamination of the mortgaged property. This area of lender liability is examined in section B of this chapter.

Other, more conventional predicates for lender liability have already been covered elsewhere in this casebook. They include liability based on: (1) control over construction defects (Chapter 6B6); (2) equitable subordination in a bankruptcy proceeding; (3) negligent real estate appraisals (Chapter 5B1); (4) a lender's status as lead lender in a loan participation (Chapter 9D, note 5); (5) federal regulations such as those under the Interstate Land Sales Full Disclosure Act (Chapter 9B, note 5b); (6) a lender's status as a mortgagee in possession (Chapter 10B2, note 2); (7) liability for breach of a loan commitment (Chapter 5D2); and (8) claims by third-party creditors against a lender that is recharacterized as an equity partner, because of the ambiguous nature of modern financing documents or the lender's active participation in the business affairs of the borrower, often likely to occur in the case of convertible mortgages (Chapter 7A) and certain participating mortgages (Chapter 5B3, note 3).

---

1. Restatement (Second) of Contracts §205 (1981).
2. U.C.C. §1-203.
3. U.C.C. §1-201(19).

A. LENDER'S DUTY OF GOOD FAITH

The following excerpt provides a brief overview of lender liability, along with some planning suggestions for attorneys who represent lenders.

Lieberman and Mallenbaum, When Borrowers Sue Lenders
4 Real Est. Fin. 67 (Winter 1988)

While other legal theories have been used against a lender, the two most common claims of a borrower have been based on (a) the lender's acting in bad faith, and (b) the lender's failure to disclose to the borrower information that could have influenced the borrower's decision to accept the loan.

BAD FAITH

The Uniform Commercial Code requires that the holder of a promissory note act in good faith and within the limits set by commercial reasonableness. Good faith means honesty in fact in the conduct or transaction concerned (U.C.C. §1-201(19)). Courts have construed this to mean that a promissory note carries an implied agreement that the lender will act in complete honesty in its dealings with the borrower. The following are examples of situations in which courts have held that a lender violated its good faith obligation:

Termination of a credit agreement without prior notice. When the sudden refusal by a bank to grant a grocery wholesaler funds under a $3.5 million credit agreement resulted in the collapse of the borrower as a viable business entity, the court reasoned that the bank knew its decision would cause the winding up of the borrower's business and awarded the borrower $7.5 million in damages. (See K.M.C. Co., Inc. v. Irving Trust Company, 757 F2d. 752 (1985).)

Calling in all loans related to a specific market segment. A bank forced a high-tech farmer out of business and foreclosed on his property because it adopted a new policy of demanding payment on all outstanding agricultural loans. The jury found the bank liable for $10 million in compensatory damages and $50 million in punitive damages. (See Conlan v. Wells Fargo Bank (Monterey Superior Court, no. 82852).)

Threatening to exercise a contractual right to control a borrower. Where a loan agreement gave it some voice in running the affairs of a large apparel manufacturing company, the lender threatened to declare the loan in default unless certain officers and directors of the borrower were replaced by designees of the lender. The borrower agreed to install the lender's management, after which the borrower's business suffered and certain of its assets were liquidated to repay the loan. When the original management later regained control, it turned the business around and sued the lender for its inept management. Although the court legitimized the management control clause in the loan agreement, the bank was held liable in the amount of $19 million not only for its mismanagement of the company but for fraud and duress in threatening to call the loan when in reality it never intended to do so. (See State National Bank of El Paso v. Farah Manufacturing Co., Inc., 678 SW2d 661 (1984).)

Enforcing a guarantee despite assurances that it would be released. In reliance on the advice of a bank's loan officer with whom he had a close relationship, a California apple grower with a personally guaranteed line of credit entered into a merger because the loan officer advised him that the guarantee would thereby be released. Soon thereafter, the lender declared the borrower in default and enforced the guarantee. An appeals court awarded $22 million (including punitive damages) primarily because of the bank's constructive fraud in not releasing the guarantee. The case is currently under appeal. (See Barrett v. Bank of America, 183 CA3d 1362, 229 CR 16 (1986).)

FAILURE TO DISCLOSE

A related judicial theory holds that a lender may also be held liable for failing to disclose to a potential borrower vital information that could influence its borrowing decision. Although a lender is not generally obligated to disclose potential risks of the borrower's investment decisions, the lender's duty to act in good faith requires disclosure of certain of its interests, intentions and policies.

For example, a lender can breach its disclosure obligation by failing to:

1) disclose its relationship as a partner, creditor or similarly interested party in an entity involved in the borrower's business;
2) disclose its intentions to debit a depositor's account to cover his indebtedness under a separate loan agreement; or
3) encourage a borrower to read material information contained in a document before executing it.

In the *Bank of America* case, for instance, the lender compounded its breach of good faith by failing to disclose to the borrower its interest as creditor to one of the borrower's vendors.

These are just a few examples of lender's potential exposures. A lender should be cautious in all of its ventures, whether it acts as a mere lender or assumes the burden of financial advisor. The more the lender advises, the more it assumes fiduciary burdens; a mere debtor-creditor relationship carries far less responsibility. Similarly, the more sophisticated the borrower, the less the fiduciary burdens of the lender. Nevertheless, even a pure debtor-creditor relationship carries with it certain fiduciary responsibilities. The banking industry has itself created a basis for public reliance on a lender's good faith.

SUGGESTIONS FOR LENDERS

In view of this trend in favor of lender liability, lenders should consider reviewing their lending practices and take precautionary measures in order to reduce potential liability. . . .

A commercial lender should think very carefully before it extends a loan. Not only should it investigate the financial viability of the borrower to determine whether the loan will be repaid, it should also think carefully about how it will proceed in the event the loan must be accelerated or further advances refused. Unfortunately, extreme caution results in added time and expense to the borrower. Thus, it is likely that future borrowers will wait longer to get a loan approved, lending fees will increase and borrowers' access to loans will be restricted.

Claims of lender liability often arise in default situations, where future good will and cordial business relations are not high priorities. This is especially true in bankruptcy, where the debtor's estate, rather than the debtor, is bringing the action. Indeed, the trustee or debtor in possession may feel duty-bound to raise every reasonable claim in order to gain as much as possible for the debtor's creditors. Thus, such claims often involve situations and actions not previously considered to be within the ambit of any express or implied duty or principle of good faith.

It should not be shocking that the courts will imply a contractual duty of good faith and fair dealing. Section 205 of the Restatement (Second) of Contracts provides that "every contract imposes upon each party a duty of good faith and fair dealing in its performance and its enforcement." Set forth below are §1-203 of the Uniform Commercial Code, which imposes a good-faith requirement on contracts and duties under the U.C.C., and the U.C.C. §1-201(19) definition of "good faith."

§1-203. Obligation of Good Faith

Every contract or duty within this Act imposes an obligation of good faith in its performance or enforcement.

§1-201. Uniform Commercial Code

(19) "Good faith" means honesty in fact in the conduct or transaction concerned.

The lender's problem is not with the concept of "good faith" but rather with determining (in advance of its actions) how the courts will interpret the concept.

K.M.C. Co. v. Irving Trust Company and Davis v. Nevada National Bank are two of the cases that apply the principle of good faith to lending transactions.

K.M.C. Co. v. Irving Trust Company
757 F.2d 752 (6th Cir. 1985)

Cornelia G. KENNEDY, Circuit Judge.

Irving Trust Company (Irving) appeals from a judgment entered against it in this diversity action for breach of a financing agreement. K.M.C. is a Tennessee corporation headquartered in Knoxville and engaged in the wholesale and retail grocery business. In 1979, Irving and K.M.C. entered into a financing agreement, whereby Irving held a security interest in all of K.M.C.'s accounts receivable and inventory and provided K.M.C. a line of credit to a maximum of $3.0 million, increased one year later to $3.5 million at a lower rate of interest, subject to a formula based on a percentage of the value of the inventory plus eligible receivables. On March 1, 1982, Irving refused to advance $800,000 requested by K.M.C. This amount would have increased the loan balance to just under the $3.5 million limit. K.M.C. contends that Irving's refusal without prior notice to advance the requested funds breached a duty of good faith performance implied in the agreement and ultimately resulted in the collapse of the company as a viable business entity. Irving's defense is that on March 1, 1982, K.M.C. was already collapsing, and that Irving's decision not to advance funds was made in good faith and in the reasonable exercise of its discretion under the agreement. . . .

The jury found Irving liable for breach of contract and fixed damages at $7,500,000 plus pre-judgment interest. Defendant's motions to dismiss and for a directed verdict and post-trial motions for judgment n.o.v., a new trial or a remittitur were denied. . . .

Irving contends that the Magistrate erred in instructing the jury with respect to its obligations under the financing agreement, that K.M.C. failed to sustain its burden of showing that Irving acted in bad faith and that the jury's verdict was against the weight of the evidence. We conclude that the jury instructions were not in error and that the jury's verdict was supported by substantial evidence.

A. INSTRUCTIONS

The essence of the Magistrate's instruction to the jury was that there is implied in every contract an obligation of good faith; that this obligation may have imposed on Irving a duty to give notice to K.M.C. before refusing to advance funds under the agreement up to the $3.5 million limit; and that such notice would be required if necessary to the proper execution of the contract, unless Irving's decision to refuse to advance funds without prior notice was made in good faith and in the reasonable exercise of its discretion. Irving contends that the instruction with respect to notice gave undue emphasis to K.M.C.'s theory of the case and was an erroneous explanation of its contractual obligations, in that the decision whether to advance funds under the financing agreement was solely within the bank's prerogative. It reasons further that an implied requirement that the bank provide a period of notice before discontinuing financing up to the maximum credit limit would be inconsistent with the provision in the agreement that all monies loaned are repayable on demand.

As part of the procedure established for the operation of the financing agreement, the parties agreed in a supplementary letter that all receipts of K.M.C. would be deposited into a "blocked account" to which Irving would have sole access. Consequently, unless K.M.C. obtained alternative financing, a refusal by Irving to advance funds would leave K.M.C. without operating capital until it had payed down its loan. The record clearly established that a medium-sized company in the wholesale grocery business, such as K.M.C., could not operate without outside financing. Thus, the literal interpretation of the financing agreement urged upon us by Irving, as supplemented by the "blocked account" mechanism, would leave K.M.C.'s continued existence entirely at the whim or mercy of Irving, absent an obligation of good faith performance. Logically, at such time as Irving might wish to curtail financing K.M.C., as was its right under the agreement, this obligation to act in good faith would require a period of notice to K.M.C. to allow it a reasonable opportunity to seek alternate financing, absent valid business reasons precluding Irving from doing so. Hence, we find that the Magistrate's instructions were an accurate statement of the applicable law. . . .

Irving contends that the sole factor determinative of whether it acted in good faith is whether it, through its loan officer Sarokin, *believed* that there existed valid reasons for not advancing funds to K.M.C. on March 1, 1982. It quotes Blaine v. G.M.A.C., 82 Misc. 2d 653, 655, 370 N.Y.S.2d 323, 327 (1975), for the proposition that under applicable New York law, it is the bank's "actual mental state" that is decisive. The Magistrate observed that there was competent evidence that a personality conflict had developed between Sarokin and Butler of K.M.C. He suggested that the jury may have concluded that Sarokin abused his discretion in refusing without notice to advance funds despite knowing that he was fully secured because of his disapproval of Butler's management philosophy.

Were the outcome of this case solely dependent upon Sarokin's *subjective* state of mind, we might feel constrained, despite the conclusions of the Magistrate above, to hold that the evidence was insufficient to support the verdict. However, to a certain extent the conduct of Irving must be measured by objective standards. While it is not necessary that Sarokin have been correct in his understanding of the facts and circumstances pertinent to his decision not to advance funds for this court to find that he made a valid business judgment in doing so, there must at least be *some* objective basis upon which a reasonable loan officer in the exercise of his discretion would have acted in that manner. . . .

Whether or not the $800,000 requested would have been sufficient to cover all of K.M.C.'s outstanding checks, Sarokin's abrupt refusal to advance funds to K.M.C. on March 1 amounted to a unilateral decision on his part to wind up the company. If Sarokin had agreed to advance the $800,000 but no more, and checks still had bounced, we would have a different case. But, given that Sarokin knew or should have known that the bank was adequately secured, and that if adequately secured it was Irving's policy that some period of notice would be due before financing was denied, Sarokin's action could only be justified if in some way he reasonably believed that it was necessary to protect the bank's interests. There was ample evidence — in particular, the conclusion of Irving's auditors that no losses would be sustained by the bank in the event of liquidation, and Sarokin's decision on March 4 to advance almost the full amount requested just three days earlier, despite the fact the K.M.C. was in much worse condition because of the intervening damage to its credit standing — from which the jury could have concluded that Sarokin had no such reason in mind and hence that his action was arbitrary and capricious.

Finally, Irving contends that even if a period of notice were required, it would be unreasonable to impose upon it an obligation to continue financing K.M.C. for the length of time that would have been necessary to arrange alternative financing or a sale of the company. If Irving had given K.M.C. 30 days, 7 days, even 48 hours notice, we would be facing a different case. However, no notice was given. Until Sarokin told Butler on the phone the afternoon of March 1 that the $800,000 requested would not be advanced, not even Calloway of the Park Bank or Lipson, who had been sent down to Knoxville by Sarokin the previous Friday to gather information, both of whom lunched with Butler immediately before the call to New York, had any inkling that Sarokin might act as he did. Based upon the reasoning above, whether alternative financing could have been found or a sale arranged is pertinent to causation rather than whether Sarokin acted reasonably and in good faith, and there was ample evidence in the record from which the jury could find that either would have been possible.

The judgment is affirmed.

Davis v. Nevada National Bank
103 Nev. 220, 737 P.2d 503 (1987)

Per Curiam:

In April, 1970, appellants and one Paul Bennett (the "Contractor") entered into an agreement with respondent (the "Bank") whereby the Bank agreed to loan appellants funds for the construction of a home in Las Vegas.

During the course of construction, appellants noted serious defects in the foundation of the home. Appellants asked the Bank's loan officer to withhold payments until the problems were corrected; the Bank refused, apparently without any investigation of the truth of appellants' assertions.

Although appellants eventually obtained a judgment against the Contractor for his deficient construction, the Contractor's bankruptcy prevented collection of damages. Appellants then sued the Bank, which contended that it simply could not be held liable for construction deficiencies. The district court agreed and granted summary judgment in favor of the Bank. For reasons stated herein, we reverse and remand for further proceedings.

When a construction lender grants a loan to a borrower but retains the funds pending distribution, and in fact distributes the loan proceeds itself, that lender is not totally free to disregard the interests of its borrower. We agree that such a lender normally has no duty to exercise care to identify unworkmanlike or deficient construction, or to accede to requests to withhold payment from contractors. And it would be legally sound and commercially appropriate to uphold a lender's decision to continue paying a contractor if, after reasonable investigation, the lender concluded in good faith, albeit erroneously, that its borrower's request to withhold payment was unwarranted. However, it would be unjust to permit a lender, with impunity, to simply disregard a borrower's complaint of *substantial* construction deficiencies affecting the structural integrity of a project, thereby placing a borrower in the potentially untenable position of having to fully repay the lender for loan funds expended, contrary to a borrower's particularized entreaties, for a substantially defective residence or structure. A lender must pursue such a course at its own risk. Nevada's immunity statute, NRS 41.590,[1] does not dictate a contrary holding. Its protection does not extend to liabilities incurred as a result of a lender's activities other than "the loan transaction." In the instant case, the Bank's liability would arise not from the loan transaction, but from the Bank's later breach of a nonconsensual duty of care in the disbursement of construction loan proceeds.

In rendering summary judgment, the trial court noted that appellants' action was solely for breach of contract. However, the contract between the parties does not conflict with or otherwise preclude the application of the principles set forth above. The loan agreement provided, in relevant part, that the Bank had no obligation to inspect the home under construction and was not responsible for proper disbursement of the loan, and that no terms other than those in the writing had been "agreed to." Each of these provisions, however, is subject to established doctrines of contractual interpretation, including: (1) the court shall effectuate the intent of the parties, which may be determined in light of the surrounding circumstances if not clear from the contract itself. . . . and (2) ambiguities are to be construed against the party (in this case, the Bank) who drafted the agreement or selected the language used. . . .

The disavowal of a duty to inspect, in turn, was written with an eye to prevent implication of such a duty from the fact that the Bank reserved a contractual right of inspection. It was not intended to disavow

---

1. NRS 41.590 reads as follows:

A lender who makes a loan of money, the proceeds of which are used or may be used by the borrower to finance the design, manufacture, construction, repair, modification or improvement of real or personal property, shall not be held liable to the borrower or to third persons for any loss or damage occasioned by any defect in the real or personal property so designed, manufactured, constructed, repaired, modified or improved or for any loss or damage resulting from the failure of the borrower to use due care in the design, manufacture, construction, repair, modification or improvement of such real or personal property, unless the loss or damage is the result of some other action or activity of the lender than the loan transaction.

a duty implied by law independently of the parties' agreement. Finally, a statement that the parties did not "agree to" additional terms does not bear on duties implied by law even in the absence of specific agreement. Thus, we hold that under the circumstances present here, the Bank had a duty to conduct a reasonable investigation and reach a bona fide conclusion as to the validity of appellants' request, at the risk of incurring liability for wrongful disbursement of funds.[2]

Nothing we have said should be interpreted beyond the comparatively narrow confines of the instant case. Specifically, under usual construction loan terms and conditions, no lender should consider itself at risk if it elects not to generally inspect the progress of the construction of a project financed by the lender. Nor is a lender to consider itself at risk if it volitionally elects to inspect and does so negligently or ineffectively. A lender also has no duty, under our instant holding, either to withhold payment at borrowers' requests or to inspect upon such requests, for construction deficiencies or omissions of a type that inevitably will occur in all projects and that commonly are remedied by a contractor as part of a "punch list" prior to project completion and the release of retained funds. . . .

NOTES AND QUESTIONS

1. *So Much for the Bad Man Theory?* Justice Oliver Wendell Holmes said the following:

> [A] legal duty so called is nothing but a prediction that if a man does or omits certain things he will be made to suffer in this or that way by judgment of the court. . . . A man who cares nothing for an ethical rule which is believed and practiced by his neighbors is likely nevertheless to care a good deal to avoid being made to pay money, and will want to keep out of jail if he can. . . .
>
> I take it for granted that no hearer of mine will misinterpret what I have to say as the language of cynicism. The law is the witness and external deposit of our moral life. Its history is the history of the moral development of the race. The practice of it, in spite of popular jests, tends to make good citizens and good men. When I emphasize the difference between law and morals I do so with reference to a single end, that of learning and understanding the law. For that purpose you must definitely master its specific marks, and it is for that I ask you for the moment to imagine yourselves indifferent to other and greater things.

2. We express no opinion as to the legal effect of a lender's attempt to circumvent today's holding by resort to emphatic contract language notifying its borrower that alternative methods of protection, such as a contractor's completion bond, must be secured.

. . . If you want to know the law and nothing else, you must look at it as a bad man, who cares only for the material consequences which such knowledge enables him to predict, not as a good one, who finds his reasons for conduct, whether inside the law or outside of it, in the vaguer sanctions of conscience. . . .

Take the fundamental question, What constitutes the law? You will find some text writers telling you that it is something different from what is decided by the courts of Massachusetts or England, that it is a system of reason, that it is a deduction from principles of ethics or admitted axioms or what not, which may or may not coincide with the decisions. But if we take the view of our friend the bad man we shall find that he does not care two straws for the axioms or deductions, but that he does want to know what the Massachusetts or English courts are likely to do in fact. I am much of his mind. . . .

Nowhere is the confusion between legal and moral ideas more manifest than in the law of contract. Among other things, here again the so-called primary rights and duties are invested with a mystic significance beyond what can be assigned and explained. The duty to keep a contract at common law means a prediction that you must pay damages if you do not keep it — and nothing else. If you commit a tort, you are liable to pay a compensatory sum. If you commit a contract, you are liable to pay a compensatory sum unless the promised event comes to pass, and that is all the difference. But such a mode of looking at the matter stinks in the nostrils of those who think it advantageous to get as much ethics into the law as they can. It was good for Lord Coke, however, and here, as in many other cases, I am content to abide with him.

Holmes, The Path of the Law, 10 Harv. L. Rev. 61 (1897).

Was Justice Holmes saying that a contract is no more than an option — comply with its terms by performing or don't comply and pay a foreseeable amount of damages? If so, was it implicit in his commentary that unless expressly contracted for there is no obligation of good-faith performance in contracts? Or were his views consistent with the notion that a contracting party is not breaching any obligation of good faith, express or implied, by strictly construing a contract in such party's best interest to the detriment of the other party? It should be clear from the above cases that either interpretation of Justice Holmes' "bad man theory" might not be acceptable today. Consider the following situation.

In 1981, the Meyer brothers purchased a 6,400-acre ranch near Douglas, Wyoming for $1.5 million. From the available facts, it would seem they financed their acquisition with two mortgages that encumbered other property they owned, which they hoped to sell to satisfy the mortgages and pay for the ranch equity. Travelers Insurance Co. was the mortgagee. When the brothers couldn't sell the other properties, debts mounted, and Travelers foreclosed. The Meyer brothers sued

Travelers, apparently on the grounds that they had placed their trust in Travelers (they even signed blank forms for the Travelers people to fill in) and that Travelers knew or should have known the brothers could not make a success of the property (perhaps with the hope of obtaining the property through foreclosure?) and thus acted in bad faith.

In discovery, a memo was found from a local Travelers agent to his superiors urging a workout. In part it said: "These boys are losing all they accumulated. In a way we are not entirely blameless. We made them a 17% loan in Colorado to put a down-payment on a deal that was too big for them. They were in danger of losing that down-payment unless we revamped the loan on the Wyoming place. We did this, at a rate higher than they had bargained for. . . . It was a bad deal all around and we helped make it so." The jury found for the Meyer brothers, with damages in the amount of $3.2 million. The case was eventually settled out of court for an undisclosed sum. The Meyer brothers now own their ranch free and clear of mortgages. See Meyer v. Travelers Insurance Co., No. 10147, Dist. Ct. Converse Cty. (Wyo. 1987). The trial decision was not reported; the above facts were obtained mainly from a discussion of the case in *The Economist,* Nov. 7, 1987, at 38. The appellate decision was reported at 741 P.2d 607 (Wyo. 1987).

From the facts we have, is there any evidence Travelers was not acting in good faith? Does unconscionability play a part here (based on the agent's implication that Travelers was taking too high a rate of interest)? A high rate of interest, especially where not in violation of state usury limits, is not per se an act of bad faith. How high does interest have to go to make it an indication of bad faith? Should it be tied to the ability of the property to pay? What if the lender miscalculates? Generally, interest rates increase with the risk involved. The greater the risk, the higher the interest — but also the greater the likelihood that the interest rate will be high enough to breach a court's concept of good faith. Does the case tell us that lenders have an obligation to look into and correctly judge the economic viability of property on which they make loans? Or perhaps there were special facts here that would make the general application of this case unlikely. Lenders, of course, do consider the economic viability of property to be part of the appraisal process. (See discussion at Chapter 5B1 and Chapter 10C5, note 5.) The question may be whether the peril of a lender's overly optimistic appraisal is to be limited to the risk of low collateral value or whether it is to be expanded to make the lender an insurer of the success of the endeavor.

Consider the lessons of the memo from the Travelers' agent. What do you think the purpose of the memo was? Why was the agent pushing so hard for a workout? Perhaps it was the result of a genuine feeling that Travelers was at fault. Perhaps it was motivated in part by a desire not to add to an already growing portfolio of foreclosed properties. In their article Messrs. Lieberman and Mallenbaum discuss the related judicial theory of liability based on the lender's duty to disclose information to the borrower such as any relationship of the lender with a party in interest to the debtor's business. They conclude that "a lender is not generally obligated to disclose potential risks of the borrower's investment decisions." Would the *Travelers* court agree with that?

2. *Is There Such a Thing as a Discretionary Loan?* Was the loan in *K.M.C.* a discretionary loan? Was it equivalent to a discretionary loan? What is the purpose of a loan agreement if all the lender promises is "I will make you a series of loans if I feel like it"? Courts have for many years construed discretionary contracts as requiring a good-faith, best-efforts attempt to achieve what the contract contemplated. See, e.g., Wood v. Lucy, Lady Duff-Gordon, 222 N.Y. 88, 118 N.E. 214 (1917), wherein an exclusive agency to place endorsements and market designs was interpreted by the court to include an implied promise to use reasonable efforts to do so. Said Judge Cardozo, "The law has outgrown its primitive stage of formalism when the precise word was the sovereign talisman, and every slip was fatal. It takes a broader view today. A promise may be lacking, and yet the whole writing may be 'instinct with an obligation,' imperfectly expressed. . . ." (222 N.Y. at 91). Is this view any different from the definition of good faith in §1-201(19) of the U.C.C., reprinted above? How does this requirement to use reasonable efforts to carry out the intention of the parties apply to discretionary loans?

In *K.M.C.* the court indicated that to be deemed to be acting in good faith, a discretionary lender (at least in the circumstances of that case) was required to give reasonable notice before refusing to extend credit. Otherwise, the financing agreement "would leave K.M.C.'s continued existence entirely at the whim or mercy of Irving." (757 F.2d at 759). If K.M.C. had understood the implications of the agreement, could it have protected itself by lining up, at its expense, a standby line of credit?

What is reasonable notice? "If Irving had given K.M.C. 30 days, 7 days, even 48 hours notice, we would be facing a different case." (757 F.2d at 763). But what if 48 hours' notice had been given and alternative financing could not be obtained in that time? What if the period of notice was 30 days and still alternative financing could not be obtained? If the market was not willing to extend alternative credit, wouldn't the reasons for such lack of confidence in K.M.C. be exactly what Irving was trying to protect itself against by making the loan discretionary?

Can this problem be "drafted around"? Suppose the loan agreement had said expressly that each and every request for funding could be rejected at the unfettered discretion of Irving and that K.M.C. recognized that funding might be terminated without notice or an opportunity to obtain additional financing and that K.M.C. accepted those conditions. Would Judge Kennedy buy this? See the court's footnote 2 in the *Davis* case. Would it still be possible to argue that Irving, in later discontinuing funding, was breaching its obligation of good faith as that term is defined in U.C.C. §1-201(19)? A few recent cases indicate what may be a growing willingness to sustain conduct in compliance with clear contractual terms. See, e.g., Kahm & Nate's Shoes No. 2 v. First Bank, 908 F.2d 1351 (7th Cir. 1990), where the court rejects *KMC* to the extent it can be read to require the lender to loan more money or give more notice than the contract requires. Good faith, said the court, is an "implied undertaking not to take opportunistic advantage in a way that could not have been contemplated at the time of the drafting and which therefore was not resolved explicitly by the parties." 908 F.2d at 1357.

3.   Theories of Liability.   Lack of good faith, as determined by a court, is the key to lender liability. Finding good faith, however, is not limited to interpreting the clauses of a contract, and may be involved in determining whether the lender has committed a fraud (see §870, Restatement (Second) of Torts); breach of fiduciary duty; duress; interference with business relationships or corporate governance; or negligence or negligent misrepresentation.

When the board of Farah Manufacturing Co. replaced William Farah as CEO, the business was losing money. Thereafter the company entered into a $22 million loan agreement with a group of lenders that contained a management change clause making it a default if there occurred "any change in the office of President and Chief Executive Officer of Farah [Manufacturing Co.] or any other change in the Executive management of Farah [Manufacturing Co.] which any two Banks shall consider, for any reason whatsoever, to be adverse to the interests of the Banks." The next month, William Farah sought reinstatement as CEO. The lenders' representatives refused permission and indicated that they would call a default if Mr. Farah were reinstated. One bank's attorney threatened that if Farah returned, the banks would padlock the doors and cause the corporation's bankruptcy. The board voted against Mr. Farah. After a proxy fight, however, he eventually won reinstatement, following which he brought a successful suit against the lenders and obtained a judgment of $18.5 million. State National Bank v. Farah Mfg. Co., 678 S.W.2d 661 (Tex. App. 1984).

Theories of liability in *Farah* involved fraud, duress, and interference with business relations. The *K.M.C.* holding was based on breach of implied contract. Do you agree that the *Farah* allegations sounded in tort? Certainly fraud is a tort, and the court found fraud because it concluded that the threat to call a default had been made at a time when the lenders had either decided not to declare a default or had reached no decision on the matter.

Duress is a little harder to classify. Duress was found mainly because the lender's warnings to declare a default were made in bad faith for the purpose of forcing the board not to reinstate Mr. Farah. The lenders had no reasonable, good-faith belief that their security was about to become impaired and, although they had a legal right to declare a default, the court found that given the serious consequences of default the threat constituted economic coercion, a form of duress. Although the question was enforcement of a contract and the obligation of good faith under the contract, the court cited Housing Authority of the City of Dallas v. Hubbell, 325 S.W.2d 880, 902 (Tex. Civ. App. 1959), which held that although duress "often arises in connection with breach of contract . . . it is nevertheless a tort."

The tort of interference with business relations with a third party was found because the court determined that the lenders interfered willfully, intentionally, and without justifiable cause or excuse in the debtor's business relations, its election of directors and officers, and its protected rights.

Each ground of liability involves some form of bad faith. As a lender struggles to avoid liability under each of these grounds, however, does it find that "good faith" means different things depending on which ground of liability is involved? For example, in *K.M.C.* the lender was found to be breaching its implied contractual duty of good faith when *no* notice was given of its decision not to fund future advances. In *Farah* a threat *to take* an action in the future was held not to have been made in good faith and to have constituted fraud and duress. Aren't these two results consistent in the sense that in *Farah* it was not the making of the threat (or giving the warning) that constituted bad faith, but rather it was the making of the threat without present intention to carry it out that was the basis for the findings of fraud and duress? If so, what if the lenders in *Farah* had not said anything and then decided to declare a default after Mr. Farah returned? Would a court that follows *K.M.C.* say that under the management change clause in the contract the lender's duty of good faith required the lenders to give the board adequate warning of what action it would or might take? Is there a safe path for the lenders through this dilemma? Is it correct to say that the more control the lender exercises over the business operations of the borrower the greater the potential for lender liability?

4. The Lender's Dilemma. In virtually every area of lender liability, the lender is faced with dilemmas such as that hypothesized in note 3. Davis v. Nevada National Bank, excerpted above, is a good example. The court agreed that under the contract the lender had no obligation to inspect the home under construction and was not responsible for the proper disbursement of the funds. The court held that while the lender need not follow the borrower's instruction to stop funding, it had a duty to investigate the borrower's complaint that the foundation was being constructed improperly. While "it would be legally sound and commercially appropriate to uphold a lender's decision to continue paying a contractor if, after reasonable investigation, the lender concluded in good faith, albeit erroneously, that its borrower's request to withhold payment was unwarranted," said the court, "it would be unjust to permit a lender, with impunity, to simply disregard a borrower's complaint of *substantial* construction deficiencies . . . thereby placing a borrower in the potentially untenable position of having to fully repay the lender for loan funds expended . . . for a substantially defective residence or structure."

If you were counsel for Fuller National Bank, which was making a construction loan to Dan Developer under a similar construction loan agreement, and Dan demanded that disbursements cease because of poor construction, would the words of the *Davis* court reassure you? Would you be able to tell the FNB's lending officers that if (a) they made a reasonable investigation and concluded Dan's claims were unfounded they could continue to fund or (b) from their investigation they concluded that Dan was right they could cease funding, without fear of liability in either case?

Assume FNB's investigation were to find that the foundation was being constructed reasonably and so it continues to fund. What if FNB's investigation proved to be wrong and the building collapsed? The *Davis* court concludes that the lender would not be at risk if it "volitionally elects to inspect and does so negligently or ineffectively." Does this mean that the lender would not be liable under theories of liability other than breach of good faith? In addition to the inevitable suit from Dan Developer on whether the extent of the investigation was reasonable, whether FNB had been negligent, or whether FNB had been involved in a conspiracy with the contractor to commit fraud, would a person injured when the building collapsed have a claim against FNB? Review the discussion of the *Connor* case at Chapter 6B6. Nevada's statute, similar to California's, protects from liability lender actions that are part of the loan transaction (see the *Davis* court's footnote 1). With a right, but specifically no obligation, to inspect in the documents, was inspection outside of or within the loan transaction? What is the effect of the court's conclusion that the bank's duty to inspect did "not arise from the loan transaction, but from the bank's later breach of a nonconsensual duty of care in the disbursement of construction loan proceeds"?

Now assume that FNB's investigation confirms Dan's fears and FNB ceases funding. What if the contractor were thereby forced into bankruptcy and the contractor's estate brought suit against FNB, alleging, inter alia, interference with contractual relationships; third-party beneficiary liability under the commitment; and conspiracy with the borrower to commit fraud and duress by attempting to force the contractor to spend more on construction than it was legally obligated to spend? What do you think the contractor's chances of recovery are? What if the court determines that, while it had been clearly possible for the contractor to build a better foundation, the one that was built was safe and substantially complied with the terms of the commitment? See Chapter 5B11 and the breach of commitment cases discussed therein. Today, as suggested in the Lieberman and Mallenbaum excerpt, lenders are reviewing their lending practices and taking precautionary measures against potential liability. Based on the materials discussed here, what advice would you give a client such as Ace Insurance Company to mitigate its exposure to lender liability suits?

5. Special Problems When a Lender Is Also a Partner. With the advent of real estate joint ventures (see Chapter 7B), the lender found itself in the position not only of a mortgagee but also of a partner in the borrowing entity. Since the interests of the borrower and lender often are not consistent, the joint venture scenario contains some inherent conflicts that could result in lender liability suits.

In the famous case of Meinhard v. Salmon, 249 N.Y. 458, 164 N.E. 545 (1928), Judge Cardozo eloquently articulated a partner's duty to a co-partner: "Many forms of conduct permissible in a workaday world for those acting at arm's length, are forbidden to those bound by fiduciary ties. A trustee is held to something stricter than the morals of the marketplace. Not honesty alone, but the punctilio of an honor the most sensitive, is then the standard of behavior."

Incidentally, if you have not had the opportunity to read Meinhard v. Salmon, you should do so. The building involved was the Salmon Tower, 500 Fifth Avenue (at 42nd Street) in New York City. Meinhard was a wool merchant who had invested funds with Salmon, a real estate investor, to acquire a leasehold in the building that had previously existed at the site. The owner of the building, Elbridge T. Gerry (grandson of *the* Elbridge Gerry, who signed the Declaration of Independence, was vice-president under James Madison, and, as governor of Massachusetts, gave his name for all eternity to the political process of "gerrymandering"), dreamed of building a skyscraper on the site. As the lease was expiring, Gerry approached Salmon with the offer of a new lease for the purpose of development of the property. Salmon's breach of his duty was the failure to offer a share of the new lease to his partner. Gerry never lived to see his dream come true, since he died in 1927, before the case was decided. Meinhard, aided by his attorney, John W. Davis (former ambassador to England and 1924 Democratic candidate for president — nominated on the 103d ballot in a sweltering Madison Square Garden), won the case and was able to obtain an interest in the project. The lease from "Gerry Estates, Inc." was executed in 1929, just in time for the Great Depression.

While it is easy to agree that partners owe a duty of loyalty to each other (indeed, the fiduciary relationship permeates Article 4 of the Uniform Partnership Act, which deals with the relationship of one partner to another), it is more difficult to determine the line between the legitimate right of a partner to protect its interest and the partner's obligation of "the finest loyalty" to the co-partner. This difficulty worsens in the context of the modern joint venture. The following are two examples of problems that can arise.

a. Assume in the master hypothetical that the office building being constructed in a developing area of the city of McNiece will be owned by a joint venture ("Law Drive Associates") composed of Dan Developer and Ace Insurance Company as general partners. (Note that many institutional joint ventures have taken the form of a general partnership. See discussion at Chapter 2B, note 7b and Chapter 7B). In the normal real estate limited partnership syndication, the general partner would have a similar obligation of loyalty to the limited partners that may be far broader because of the inequality of position inherent in the relation of a general to a limited partner. See ULPA §9 (1916) and RULPA §403 (1976).

Assume there is a substantial amount of vacant or undeveloped land near the venture property. If the venture is a success, the adjacent land will probably increase in value and become the site for developments less risky than this one. If Dan were to acquire this adjacent land without informing Ace, hoping to make a killing after the present building became successful, would he be violating his fiduciary obligation to Ace? Would it help Dan if he had owned the adjacent land at the time the venture was formed? How could Ace protect itself in the documentation of the joint venture?

b. Assume the Law Drive joint venture is formed prior to commencement of construction. The venture executed a commitment with Ace for a postconstruction loan at 14 percent, slightly below the market rate at the time of commitment. By the time construction is completed, market interest rates have dropped to 11 percent. Assume further that if the borrower does not take down the loan it forfeits its commitment fee and that the loss of the commitment fee is much less than the present value of the interest differential. Does Ace have a duty as a partner to vote to "walk" from the commitment and forfeit the fee? If Ace voted to reject the loan, would it then be in breach of obligations to its stockholders or policyholders? Assume the commitment provided for remedies in addition to liquidated damages (see discussion at Chapter 5D1). Is Ace under any obligation not to enforce its rights against the partnership as mortgage lender under the commitment? Would Ace be in a better position if the joint venture agreement expressly provided for taking down the Ace loan?

In two cases dealing with the partner-mortgagee's ability to foreclose against partnership property, the Georgia Supreme Court sheds some light on where the line is between a partner's fiduciary duty to its partners and its rights as a mortgagee. In Westminster Properties v. Atlanta Assocs., 250 Ga. 841, 301 S.E.2d 636 (Ga. 1983), the mortgagee-partner refused to approve a voluntary partnership bankruptcy petition (all partners were required under Chapter XII of the former Bankruptcy Act to consent to a petition by the partnership) and proceeded to foreclose. The partnership claimed that this constituted a breach of fiduciary duties as a general partner. The court held that when a partnership gives security to a partner for a loan it "cannot enforce the partnership duties owed it by the secured partner which duties impair the rights of the secured partner." (250 Ga. at 843.) The court was aided in its decision by the fact that the partnership agreement itself referred to the mortgage and its repayment and "thus the security deed became a part of the partnership agreement and established the rights of the partners." Do you think the court would have come out any differently if the partnership merely executed the mortgage but without specific reference thereto in the partnership agreement?

Five years later, in Natpar Corp. v. Kassinger, 258 Ga. 102, 365 S.E.2d 102 (1988), the same court held that a partner could be enjoined from exercising its power to foreclose against the partners. The court distinguished the prior *Westminster Properties* case because the partners there were seeking to enjoin the foreclosure on the ground that the act of foreclosure was inconsistent with a partner's fiduciary duty, whereas the injunction in *Natpar* was requested on the ground that the mortgagee-partner had brought about the default by failing to comply with its obligation under the partnership agreement to pay its share of operating expenses. From these cases, can you come up with some principles of law that might be applicable in other situations?

For additional readings on this topic, the following articles may be helpful: Beane, The Fiduciary Relationship of a Partner, 5 J. Corp. L. 483 (1980); Reynolds, Loyalty and the Limited Partnership, 34 U. Kan. L. Rev. 1 (1985); Report of Subcommittee on Debtor-Creditor Problems, Equity and Debt Participation — Possible Conflict of Duties, 9 Real Prop., Prob. & Tr. J. 509 (1974); Note, Procedures and Remedies in Limited Partners' Suits for Breach of the General Partner's Fiduciary

Duty, 90 Harv. L. Rev. 763 (1977); Note, Partnership — Disclosure, Fairness and Substantive Administrative Regulation of a General Partner's Fiduciary Duty in Real Estate Limited Partnerships, 50 Wash. L. Rev. 977 (1975); Note, Fiduciary Duties of Partners, 48 Iowa L. Rev. 902 (1963).

6. *Additional Reading.* See, inter alia, ABA Sec. of Litigation, Whose Fault Is Loan Default?: Emerging Theories of Banker's Liability for Borrowers' Default (1983); Butler, Is Lender Liability Now Absolute Liability?, 15 W. St. U.L. Rev. 595 (1988); Cappello and Komoroske, Fiduciary Relationships Between Lenders and Borrowers: Maintenance of the Status Quo, 15 W. St. U.L. Rev. 579 (1988); Coffey, The Expansion of Lender Liability in Florida, 40 U. Fla. L. Rev. 85 (1988); Note, Equitable Subordination and Analogous Theories of Lender Liability: Toward a Model of "Control," 65 Tex. L. Rev. 801 (1987); Ebke and Griffin, Lender Liability to Debtors: Toward a Conceptual Framework, 40 Sw. L.J. 775 (1986); Enstam and Kamen, Control and the Institutional Investor, 23 Bus. Law. 289 (1968); Johnson and Gaffney, Lender Liability Perspectives on Risk and Prevention, 105 Banking L.J. 325 (1988); Kratovil, Mortgage Lender Liability — Construction Loans, 38 DePaul L. Rev. 43 (1988); Murphy, An Introduction to the Defense and Prevention of Lender Liability Claims, 4 Prac. Real Est. Law. 41 (May 1988); Schecter, The Principal Principle: Controlling Creditors Should Be Held Liable for Their Debtors' Obligations, 19 U.C. Davis L. Rev. 875 (1986); Schwartz, Justice and the Law of Contracts: A Case for the Traditional Approach, 9 Harv. J.L. & Pub. Poly. 107 (1986); Note, Lender Liability and Good Faith, 68 B.U. L. Rev. 653 (1988).

B. THE FORECLOSING MORTGAGEE'S LIABILITY FOR ENVIRONMENTAL HAZARDS

One of the most pressing areas of public concern in recent years has been the hazardous and toxic wastes and other pollutants that endanger the environment. In response to this problem, federal and state statutes have been enacted designed to rid the environment of these hazards. One of the most significant of these statutes from the standpoint of the foreclosing mortgagee is the Comprehensive Environmental Response, Compensation, and Liability Act of 1980 (CERCLA).[4] CERCLA

4. 42 U.S.C. §9601 et seq. (1988). In 1986 Congress amended CERCLA with

established the so-called Superfund program to pay the cost of cleaning up environmental hazards and provided for the setting of standards and procedures for governmental response to hazardous waste releases that present a threat to public health and welfare.

Hardly eleemosynary in nature, CERCLA's §107(a) imposes unlimited liability for so-called response costs (that is, the cost of all cleanup activities incurred by the United States or any state as well as any other necessary costs of response incurred by private parties) on those liable. If it is determined that the contamination was caused by willful misconduct or negligence, punitive damages may be assessed of up to three times actual cost. In addition, liability is imposed for up to $50 million for damages to natural resources. The federal government is afforded a lien on the property for these liabilities, effective on filing of a notice at the appropriate office. There are also criminal penalties for, inter alia, failing to notify the Environmental Protection Agency of a release of hazardous substances or the existence of hazardous dumps; the destruction of records pertaining to hazardous wastes; or giving false information.

Liability is imposed by §107(a) on four categories of potentially responsible parties: the "owner and operator" of the property (presumably at the time of the suit); the "owner and operator" at the time of "disposal" of the hazardous substances; any person owning or possessing hazardous substances who arranges for its disposal or treatment at, or transport to, a facility from which there is a release of hazardous substances; and any person who transports hazardous substances to a facility selected by such person from which there is a release of hazardous substances. Consider the parties that can potentially be held liable under these categories. Does it make any sense to hold a transporter liable for discharge of the wastes after delivery to the storage facility? (Note that if there is a release from a storage facility, the courts have not required the government to prove that a particular defendant's waste was released. The government is only required to show that the site contains the same type of waste found in defendant's waste that was disposed of at the site. See U.S. v. Wade, 577 F. Supp. 1326 (E.D. Pa. 1983).) If you represented a trucking company that transported hazardous wastes to dump sites, after reviewing the provisions of §107(2) relating to transporters, what precaution would you suggest the client take to avoid liability?

There are certain "safe harbors" included within CERCLA designed to protect innocent parties.

First, "the owner and operator" is defined to exclude "a person, who, without participating in the management of a . . . facility, holds

---

the Superfund Amendments and Reauthorization Act of 1986, known as "SARA" (Pub. L. No. 99-499, 100 Stat. 1613 (1986)). In these materials references to CERCLA refer to CERCLA as amended by SARA.

indicia of ownership primarily to protect his security interest in the . . . facility."[5]

Second, the owner and operator may assert several affirmative defenses, for example, that the damages resulted solely from an act of God or that the discharge was caused solely by a third party not an employee or agent of, or in a contractual relationship with, the owner or operator, provided that the defendant exercised due care with respect to the hazardous substance and took precautions against foreseeable acts or omissions of the third party. "Contractual relationships" include deeds and land contracts unless the acquiring party can show that the contamination occurred prior to acquiring the interest and that the defendant did not know and had no reason to know of the existence of the hazardous substance. Set forth below are the affirmative defenses in CERCLA §107(b) and the definition of "contractual relationship" in CERCLA §101(35). These safe harbors would seem, at first impression, to be extremely helpful to the mortgagee. How justified that first impression is can be seen, in part, from the *Maryland Bank* case and an article by Joseph Forte on environmental risk management for lenders.

CERCLA §107(b)
42 U.S.C.A. §9607(b) (1983)

(b) Defenses

There shall be no liability under subsection (a) of this section for a person otherwise liable who can establish by a preponderance of the evidence that the release or threat of release of a hazardous substance and the damages resulting therefrom were caused solely by —

(1) an act of God;

(2) an act of war;

(3) an act or omission of a third party other than an employee or agent of the defendant, or than one whose act or omission occurs in connection with a contractual relationship, existing directly or indirectly, with the defendant (except where the sole contractual arrangement arises from a published tariff and acceptance for carriage by a common carrier by rail), if the defendant establishes by a preponderance of the evidence that (a) he exercised due care with respect to the hazardous substance concerned, taking into consideration the characteristics of such hazardous substance, in light of all relevant facts and circumstances, and (b) he took precautions against foreseeable acts or omissions of any such third party and the consequences that could foreseeably result from such acts or omissions; or

(4) any combination of the foregoing paragraphs.

---

5. CERCLA §101(20), 42 U.S.C.A. §9601(20) (Supp. 1989).

CERCLA §101(35)
42 U.S.C.A. §9601 (Supp. 1989)

(35)(A) The term "contractual relationship," for the purpose of section 9607(b)(3) of this title includes, but is not limited to, land contracts, deeds or other instruments transferring title or possession, unless the real property on which the facility concerned is located was acquired by the defendant after the disposal or placement of the hazardous substance on, in, or at the facility, and one or more of the circumstances described in clause (i), (ii), or (iii) is also established by the defendant by a preponderance of the evidence:

(i) At the time the defendant acquired the facility the defendant did not know and had no reason to know that any hazardous substance which is the subject of the release or threatened release was disposed of on, in, or at the facility.

(ii) The defendant is a government entity which acquired the facility by escheat, or through any other involuntary transfer or acquisition, or through the exercise of eminent domain authority by purchase or condemnation.

(iii) The defendant acquired the facility by inheritance or bequest.

In addition to establishing the foregoing, the defendant must establish that he has satisfied the requirements of section 9607(b)(3)(a) and (b) of this title.

(B) To establish that the defendant had no reason to know, as provided in clause (i) of subparagraph (A) of this paragraph, the defendant must have undertaken, at the time of acquisition, all appropriate inquiry into the previous ownership and uses of the property consistent with good commercial or customary practice in an effort to minimize liability. For purposes of the preceding sentence the court shall take into account any specialized knowledge or experience on the part of the defendant, the relationship of the purchase price to the value of the property if uncontaminated, commonly known or reasonably ascertainable information about the property, the obviousness of the presence or likely presence of contamination at the property, and the ability to detect such contamination by appropriate inspection.

(C) Nothing in this paragraph or in section 9607(b)(3) of this title shall diminish the liability of any previous owner or operator of such facility who would otherwise be liable under this chapter. Notwithstanding this paragraph, if the defendant obtained actual knowledge of the release or threatened release of a hazardous substance at such facility when the defendant owned the real property and then subsequently transferred ownership of the property to another person without disclosing such knowledge, such defendant shall be treated as liable under section 9607(a)(1) of this title and no defense under section 9607(b)(3) of this title shall be available to such defendant.

(D) Nothing in this paragraph shall affect the liability under this chapter of a defendant who, by any act or omission, caused or contributed to the release or threatened release of a hazardous substance which is the subject of the action relating to the facility.

United States v. Maryland Bank and Trust Co.
632 F. Supp. 573 (D. Md. 1986)

NORTHROP, Senior District Judge.

This case presents the novel question of whether a bank, which formerly held a mortgage on a parcel of land, later purchased the land at a foreclosure sale and continues to own it, must reimburse the United States for the cost of cleaning up hazardous wastes on the land, when those wastes were dumped prior to the bank's purchase of the property.

The United States instituted this action pursuant to section 107 of the Comprehensive Environmental Response, Compensation, and Liability Act of 1980 ("CERCLA"), 42 U.S.C. §9607 (1983), to recover the expenses incurred by the United States Environmental Protection Agency ("EPA") for removal of hazardous wastes from the toxic dump site known as the McLeod property or the California Maryland Drum site, located near the town of California in St. Mary's County, Maryland. Named as defendant in this suit is the Maryland Bank & Trust Company ("MB & T"), the owner of the property since May, 1982, and before that, the mortgagee of the tract beginning in December, 1980.

Pending before the Court are defendant Maryland Bank & Trust Co.'s motion for summary judgment and plaintiff United States' motion for partial summary judgment on the issue of liability.

FACTS

From July 7, 1944 to December 16, 1980, Herschel McLeod, Sr. and Nellie McLeod owned the piece of property now the subject of this litigation, a 117 acre farm located near the town of California, Maryland in St. Mary's County. The parties have dubbed this property the California Maryland Drum site or "CMD site."

During the period of the McLeod's ownership, the McLeods engaged in a business relationship with Maryland Bank & Trust Co., the contours of which are disputed by the parties. It is undisputed, however, that during the 1970's, MB & T loaned money to Herschel McLeod, Sr. for two of his businesses — Greater St. Mary's Disposal, Inc. and Waldorf Sanitation of St. Mary's, Inc. The bank knew that McLeod operated a trash and garbage business on the site, but the record does not state at what point the bank became aware of this.

During 1972 or 1973, McLeod permitted the dumping of hazardous wastes on the CMD site. The wastes included organics such as toluene, ethylbenzene and total xylenes and heavy metals such as lead, chromium, mercury, and zinc.

In 1980, Mark Wayne McLeod applied for a $335,000 loan from MB & T to purchase the CMD site from his parents. On or about September 2nd of that year, MB & T sent Farmers Home Administration a request for loan guarantees relating to the McLeod loan, pursuant to 7 C.F.R. §§1980.101 et seq. (1980) (Subpart B — Farmer Program Loans). FmHA issued Loan Note Guarantees for 90% of the loan on January 2, 1981.

Mark Wayne McLeod purchased the CMD site on December 16, 1980 through the MB & T loan, but soon failed to make payments on the loan. Consequently, MB & T instituted a foreclosure action against the CMD site in 1981 and purchased the property at the foreclosure sale on May 15, 1982 with a bid of $381,500. MB & T then took title to the property. From that date to the present, MB & T has been the record owner of the CMD site. FmHA continues to be a 90% guarantor of that loan.

On June 20, 1983, Mark Wayne McLeod informed Walter E. Raum, Director of Environmental Hygiene for St. Mary's County Department of Health, of the existence of the dumped wastes on the CMD site. After inspecting the site the following day, the State of Maryland contacted the EPA. Tests were conducted to identify the substances. On the basis of the test results, the EPA requested and received funding to conduct a removal action under CERCLA. The agency notified MB & T president John T. Daugherty that MB & T would be given until October 24, 1983 to initiate corrective action at the site or EPA would use its funds to clean-up the wastes. The bank declined the EPA's offer, so the agency proceeded to clean the site itself, removing two hundred thirty-seven drums of chemical material and 1180 tons of contaminated soil at a cost of approximately $551,713.50. After completing the clean-up, the EPA sent a letter to MB & T President Daugherty summarizing the costs incurred in the response action and demanding payment. To date, MB & T has not tendered payment. This action ensued. . . .

The question central to both the defendant's and the plaintiff's motions for summary judgment . . . [is] whether Maryland Bank &

Trust is an "owner and operator" within the meaning of sections 107(a)(1) and 101(20)(A).

Additionally, Maryland Bank & Trust has raised in its answer an affirmative defense based upon section 107(b)(3), the so-called "third party defense." The United States argues in its motion for partial summary judgment that the bank cannot meet its burden of proof on that defense, an assertion disputed by the defendant in its opposition memorandum. . . .

I. LIABILITY OF CURRENT OWNERS UNDER CERCLA . . .

A. The Court initially turns to the question of whether MB & T falls within section 107(a)(1). That section holds liable "the owner and operator" of the facility. It is undisputed that MB & T has been the owner of the facility since May, 1982. The parties dispute whether the bank has been the operator of the facility since that time. The dispute over the term "operator" is not determinative, however, for the Court holds that current ownership of a facility alone brings a party within the ambit of subsection (1). Notwithstanding the language "the owner and operator," a party need not be both an owner and operator to incur liability under this subsection.

The structure of section 107(a), like so much of this hastily patched together compromise Act, is not a model of statutory clarity. It is unclear from its face whether subsection (1) holds liable both owners and operators or only parties who are both owners and operators. This ambiguity stems in large part from the placement of the definite article "the" before the term "owner" and its omission prior to the term "operator." Proper usage dictates that the phrase "the owner and operator" include only those persons who are both owners and operators. But by no means does Congress always follow the rules of grammar when enacting the laws of this nation. In fact, to slavishly follow the laws of grammar while interpreting acts of Congress would violate sound canons of statutory interpretation. . . . Misuse of the definite article is hardly surprising in a hastily conceived compromise statute such as CERCLA, since members of Congress might well have had no time to dot all the i's or cross all the t's. See generally Safire, Of 'The' I Sing, N.Y. Times, March 2, 1986, §6 (Magazine), at 14. (As the most common word in the English language, *the* is too often taken for granted.)

An examination of the legislative history, sparse as it is, and the lone relevant case convinces the Court to interpret the language of subsection (1) broadly to include both owners and operators. The House Report accompanying H.R. 85, one of the four bills to coalesce into CERCLA, explains the definition of "operator" as follows: "In the case of a facility, an 'operator' is defined to be a person who is carrying out operational functions for the owner of the facility pursuant to an appropriate agreement." 1980 U.S. Code Cong. & Ad. News 6119, 6182. By its very definition, an operator cannot be the same person as an owner. Therefore, a class defined as consisting of persons who are both owners and operators would contain no members. Such a definition would render section 107(a)(1) a totally useless provision.

The Court of Appeals for the Second Circuit recently held a current owner of a facility responsible for response costs under section 107(a)(1) even though that party had not owned the site at the time of the dumping and had apparently not "operated" the facility. *Shore Realty*, 759 F.2d 1032 (2d Cir. 1985). The court stated that "section 9607(a)(1) [107(a)(1)] unequivocally imposes strict liability on the current owner of a facility from which there is a release or a threat of release, without regard to causation." Id. at 1044. This Court agrees.

B. The definition of "owner or operator" contained in section 101(20)(A), 42 U.S.C. §9601(20)(A), excludes from liability "a person, who, without participating in the management of a vessel or facility, holds indicia of ownership primarily to protect his security interest in the . . . facility." MB & T disclaims liability on the basis of this exemption. . . .

MB & T contends that it is entitled to the benefit of this exclusion because it acquired ownership of the CMD site through foreclosure on its security interest in the property and purchase of the land at the foreclosure sale. The government asserts that the bank is not entitled to the exemption as a matter of law. The Court finds the government's position more persuasive and holds that MB & T is not exempted from liability by the exculpatory clause of section 101(20)(A).

The exemption of subsection (20)(A) covers only those persons who, at the time of the clean-up, hold indicia of ownership to protect a then-held security interest in the land. The verb tense of the exclusionary language is critical. The security interest must exist at the time of the clean-up. The mortgage held by MB & T (the security interest) terminated at the foreclosure sale of May 15, 1982, at which time it ripened into full title. 55 Am. Jur. 2d Mortgages, §785.

MB & T purchased the property at the foreclosure sale not to protect its security interest, but to protect its investment. Only during the life of the mortgage did MB & T hold indicia of ownership primarily to protect its security interest in the land. Under the law of Maryland (and twelve other states), the mortgagee-financial institution actually holds title to the property while the mortgage is in force. . . .

Congress intended by this exception to exclude these common law title mortgagees from the definition of "owner" since title was in their hands only by operation of the common law. The exclusion does not apply to former mortgagees currently holding title after purchasing the property at a foreclosure sale, at least when, as here, the former mortgagee has held title for nearly four years, and a full year before the EPA clean-up.[5]

A review of the legislative history and policies underlying the Act support this narrow construction. The first draft of the Comprehensive Oil Pollution Liability and Compensation Act (H.R. 85), one of the four major bills out of which CERCLA emerged, defined "owner" in section 101(4) to include an exemption similar to that in the ultimately enacted bill.

> (x) "owner" means any person holding title to, or, in the absence of title, any other indicia of ownership of a vessel or facility, *but does not include a person who, without participation in the management or operation of a vessel or facility, holds indicia of ownership primarily to protect his security interest in the vessel or facility.* (emphasis added).

H.R. 85 as introduced May 15, 1979, 2 CERCLA Legislative History at 525. Accompanying H.R. 85 was House Report 96-172, Part 1. In that report, the Committee on Merchant Marine and Fisheries explains the definition of "owner" and its exclusion as follows:

> "Owner" is defined to include not only those persons who hold title to a vessel or facility but those who, in the absence of holding a title, possess some equivalent evidence of ownership. It does not include certain persons possessing indicia of ownership (such as a financial institution) who, without participating in the management or operation of a vessel or facility, *hold title either in order to secure a loan* or in connection with a lease financing arrangement under the appropriate banking laws, rules or regulations. (emphasis added).

2 CERCLA Legislative History at 546. This report indicates that Congress intended to protect banks that hold mortgages in jurisdictions governed by the common law of mortgages, and not all mortgagees who later acquire title.

The interpretation of section 101(20)(A) urged upon the Court by MB & T runs counter to the policies underlying CERCLA. Under the scenario put forward by the bank, the federal government alone would shoulder the cost of cleaning up the site, while the former

---

5. Because MB & T has held the property for such an extended period of time, this Court need not consider the issue of whether a secured party which purchased the property at a foreclosure sale and then promptly resold it would be precluded from asserting the section 101(20)(A) exemption. The United States District Court for the Eastern District of Pennsylvania recently held that a former mortgagee that purchased the property at a foreclosure sale and assigned it four months later was exempt from liability. United States v. Mirabile, 15 Envtl. L. Rep. (Envtl. L. Inst.) 20992 (E.D. Pa. Sept. 4, 1985). The case is discussed in greater detail below.

mortgagee-turned-owner, would benefit from the clean-up by the increased value of the now unpolluted land. At the foreclosure sale, the mortgagee could acquire the property cheaply. All other prospective purchasers would be faced with potential CERCLA liability, and would shy away from the sale. Yet once the property has been cleared at the taxpayers' expense and becomes marketable, the mortgagee-turned-owner would be in a position to sell the site at a profit.

In essence, the defendant's position would convert CERCLA into an insurance scheme for financial institutions, protecting them against possible losses due to the security of loans with polluted properties. Mortgagees, however, already have the means to protect themselves, by making prudent loans.[6] Financial institutions are in a position to investigate and discover potential problems in their secured properties. For many lending institutions, such research is routine. CERCLA will not absolve them from responsibility for their mistakes of judgment. . . .

Counsel have cited [a case in which] the United States District Court for the Eastern District of Pennsylvania held that a former mortgagee of a site that purchased the site at a foreclosure sale and assigned it four months later was exempt from liability under §101(20)(A)'s exclusion. United States v. Mirabile, 15 Envtl. L. Rep. (Envtl. L. Inst.) 20992 (E.D. Pa. Sept. 4, 1985). The court found that the mortgagee's purchase of the land at the foreclosure was plainly undertaken in an effort to protect its security interest in the property. That holding pertained to a situation in which the mortgagee-turned-owner promptly assigned the property. To the extent to which that opinion suggests a rule of broader application, this Court respectfully disagrees. The legislative history and policies behind the Act counsel against such a generous reading of section 101(20)(A)'s exclusion.

II. THE THIRD PARTY DEFENSE UNDER SECTION 107(b)(3)

Section 107(b)(3) establishes an affirmative defense for a person otherwise liable under section 107(a), the so-called third party defense. Section 107(b)(3) provides:

> There shall be no liability under subsection (a) of this section for a person otherwise liable who can establish by a preponderance of the evidence that the release or threat of release of a hazardous substance and the damages resulting therefrom were caused solely by —
>   (3) an act or omission of a third party other than an employee or

---

6. The mortgagees also have the options of not foreclosing and not bidding at the foreclosure sale. Both steps would apparently insulate the mortgagee from liability.

agent of the defendant, or than one whose act or omission occurs in connection with a contractual relationship, existing directly or indirectly with the defendant, . . . if the defendant establishes by a preponderance of the evidence that (a) he exercised due care with respect to the hazardous substance concerned, taking into consideration the characteristics of such hazardous substance, in light of all relevant facts and circumstances, and (b) he took precautions against foreseeable acts or omissions of any such third party and the consequences that could foreseeably result from such acts or omissions. . . .

Defendant MB & T raised this defense in its answer, though it has not moved for summary judgment on this basis. The United States has asserted in its motion for summary judgment that MB & T cannot meet its burden of proof for this defense.

The government presses a two-pronged argument. First, MB & T had an established and close contractual relationship with Hershel McLeod, Sr., linked directly or indirectly to McLeod's operations, operations which resulted in the release of hazardous substances. Second, even assuming that MB & T had insufficient contractual relations with McLeod, the bank could not prove that it exercised reasonable care with respect to the substances at the site and that it took reasonable precautions at the site since it purchased the property.

The Court has scrutinized the evidence submitted with these motions, particularly that proffered by the plaintiff, and concludes that genuine issues of material fact exist concerning the nature of the contractual relation between MB & T and Hershel McLeod, Sr. and the reasonableness of MB & T's conduct. The Court therefore denies this part of the United States' motion for summary judgment. . . . [T]he evidence presented does not establish the existence of any outstanding loans in 1972 or 1973, the years of the hazardous waste disposal. Furthermore, the evidence presented does not clearly demonstrate the full nature of the contractual and business relations between McLeod and MB & T. A full trial is necessary to flush out the bare facts now on the record.

As to the second component of the government's argument, the reasonableness of MB & T's conduct with respect to the site, important factual questions remain unresolved, precluding summary judgment. The parties dispute whether MB & T knew that the hazardous wastes were located on the property. Though bank personnel were aware of the trash dump, that dump was located some distance away from the hazardous waste site. In addition, the record fails to specify the accessibility of the toxic dump, and whether it was visible or otherwise apparent. Without this detailed information, the Court cannot begin to decide whether MB & T exercised due care.

In conclusion, the Court grants that part of the United States' motion for summary judgment pertaining to the issue of liability under section 107(a)(1) and denies that part of the motion concerning the third party defense under section 107(b)(3). The Court also denies Maryland Bank & Trust Co.'s motion for summary judgment.

Forte, Environmental Liability Risk Management
1989 Prob. and Prop. 57 (Jan./Feb.)

Environmental management is no longer the exclusive preserve of the environmental activist or the conservationist. Congress and the state legislatures have been enacting "superfund," "transfer preclearance" and "superlien" type environmental legislation in response to a perceived need to control the deleterious effect of various contaminants in the environment. Some of the statutes cover all types of property while others deal only with industrial and commercial properties. Some states even have existing health statutes which are in effect superlien statutes. The courts have interpreted these environmental statutes to impose strict liability retroactively on innocent landowners for the acts of prior owners or tenants which were neither illegal nor negligent at the time of their occurrence. Consequently, real estate professionals — developers, owners, tenants and lenders (and their counsel) — have suddenly become aware of their potential exposure to liability for toxic waste.

The environmental risk is greater than the mere impairment of real estate value occasioned by the noncompliance with ordinary land use statutes. For example, the consequence for a lender taking title to a property after foreclosure could be an environmental cleanup judgment far in excess of the value of the collateral securing the loan. This spectre of potential liability has caused foreclosing lenders to consider abandoning attempts to realize on contaminated collateral. . . .

While this article recommends a course of action for lenders another purpose is to make borrowers understand that the lenders are *not* being arbitrary and unreasonable, but are in fact doing what the borrowers themselves should be doing. A prudent real estate investor (or the corporate parent of a real estate subsidiary or the principal of a real estate corporation) should be making its own inquiry: as a seller to establish that its property was "clean" when sold; as a purchaser to assure itself that it is not purchasing contaminated property; as a landlord that its tenants are not contaminating a property; and as a tenant that it is not leasing contaminated property.

There are several statutory defenses to liability under the environmental laws (e.g., under federal environmental law — acts of God, acts of war and acts of "non-contractual" third parties), although in practice they provide little comfort to real estate investors generally (New York v. Shore Realty Corp., 759 F.2d 1032 (2d Cir. 1985)). The original federal legislation contained a "security interest" exception which many lenders were relying on as their insulation from liability. Unfortunately, a federal court has held the exception is limited to a mortgagee holding evidence of title as a security interest and that the exception is not available to a mortgagee who has taken the property in foreclosure. (United States v. Maryland Bank and Trust Co., 632 F. Supp. 573 (D. Md. 1986).) In another case, the borrower claimed that the lender's actions were controlling the owner/operator to the extent that the lender (without holding title) was, in effect, the operator of the facility (United States v. Mirabile, 15 Envtl. L. Rep. (Envtl. L. Inst.) 20994 (E.D. Pa. 1985).

These judicial interpretations of federal environmental statutes were not limited by the October 1986 amendment to existing federal environmental statutes. In clarifying the definition of a contractual relationship, the amendments exclude certain governmental purchasers in foreclosure from the definition of an "owner" liable under the statute. By analogy, this would leave all other purchasers in foreclosure subject to liability, making the limited third party defense and the "security interest" exception relatively useless to lenders. The 1986 amendments to the federal environmental legislation provided a new innocent landowner defense to liability. However, the defense can only be used if the party asserting it can prove that:

(a)   it acquired the property after the introduction of the hazardous waste;

(b)   it had no part in creating the hazardous waste problem;

(c)   it did not know and had no reason to know of the problem at the time of its acquisition of the property; and

(d)   it exercised due care and took reasonable precautions against foreseeable acts and omissions of third parties.

For an investor "[t]o establish that . . . [it] had no reason to know" about the hazardous, waste an investor ". . . must have undertaken, at the time of acquisition, all appropriate inquiry into the previous ownership and uses of the property consistent with good commercial or customary practice in an effort to minimize liability. . . ." Among other factors, courts are directed to consider ascertainable information, obviousness of contamination and detectability by inspection. Pub. L. No. 99-499, §101(f), 100 Stat. 1613, 1616-17.

It is obvious from escalating environmental activism by government that there will be no "quick fix" for the problem and that the toxic waste issue has become an integral part of all real estate transactions. The *Maryland Bank* court observed, as a warning to lenders, that the mortgagees have the ability and resources to "investigate and discover potential problems in their secured properties."

The legislative history of the October 1986 amendments indicates that those involved in commercial transactions are to be held to a higher standard of diligence than parties involved in residential transactions. . . .

To conduct sufficient due diligence to assure some measure of knowledge, reasonable inquiry may be appropriate at six distinct phases of a mortgage loan — marketing, underwriting, origination, administration, disposition and enforcement.

MARKETING

While it is continually stated that environmental due diligence must be a case by case approach, a lender can greatly reduce its risks by establishing an institutional lending program. To avoid lost opportunities, the lender should delineate the scope of its lending marketplace — to whom it should lend and upon what types of collateral security. It could determine to avoid companies engaged in making, transporting, storing or dumping toxic substances and likewise reject as collateral security any property used by them in those respective businesses. This could be described as industry redlining. It could determine to avoid buildings that contain asbestos, as some major insurance companies have done, or properties previously occupied by gas stations, incinerators, dumps, coal or gas plants, or containing underground storage of possible contaminants. The lender could also avoid property on or adjacent to actual toxic waste sites. The potential delineation of businesses and properties could be as extensive as the federal Office of Management and Budget list of industrial classifications. The lender, by taking this initial step, eliminates devoting time to potential problem transactions and foregoing other possible lending opportunities. This is simply an allocation of the lender's resources to avoid dedicating time and personnel to transactions which if pre-screened would not have been financed.

UNDERWRITING

Having determined its lending marketplace, a lender must revise its application forms to include a detailed environmental questionnaire to obtain sufficient information about: its borrower, its borrower's history and its borrower's business; the location and geography of the property offered as collateral; the proposed uses of the property; and the property's proximity to environmentally sensitive areas (such as natural waterways, timberland, public water supply systems and reservoirs, farm land, landfill areas, wildlife refuges and solid waste dumps). The loan officer should perform an initial site inspection to determine what he or she can by visual inspection of the property. The lender should not rely on a third party performing another related function (e.g., appraiser or surveyor) as a substitute for a loan officer actually "walking" the property and adjoining areas. There are telltale signs of toxic waste which can be easily identified: oddly colored soil, seeping ground liquids, an unusual absence of (or presence of dead) vegetation, bubbling or discolored water, evidence of underground storage (e.g., areas of subsidence) or discarded by-products from a manufacturing process. A scenic pond could be a toxic substance holding pool.

Regardless of the loan officer's assessment of the proposed collateral, the lender should condition the funding of its loan upon a satisfactory site assessment by a professionally trained environmental engineer or consultant who will evaluate the special risks which may be involved in the structure, soil, groundwater or equipment at the property. It may be more prudent for a lender to use an independent environmental consultant rather than a lender employee (even if qualified) to avoid possible lender liability claims by a borrower that it relied on the lender's analysis in making its own decision. Any site assessment should include a visual survey (including surface drainage, topography, buildings and water courses), a record review (including the chain of ownership, site use history, historical review of maps, plans, permits and photographs, regulatory history and insurance and claims), and an area reconnaissance to confirm the status and local context of the property. While this is primarily a paper and visual review, environmental experts contend that the overwhelming majority of problems are identified at this initial phase of investigation.

If after the initial audit there is evidence (or even a suspicion) of contamination and the investor wishes to continue in the transaction, an environmental consultant must be retained to conduct specific site testing of the structure, soil, groundwater or equipment at the property, as appropriate to prove or disprove contamination. If the property is determined to be contaminated, however, further tests will be necessary to determine the source and extent of the problem. Of course, a written report of assessment and recommendations at each stage should be obtained as a record of the lender's diligence. An outline of the several stages of an environmental audit is provided at the end of this article.

Site assessments are costly; they may cause delays and are no guaranty that the property is clean as statistical samples are not foolproof. . . .

ORIGINATION

Regardless of a lender's underwriting diligence, the potential risk of a problem continues and should be dealt with at the closing and funding of the mortgage loan. Lenders will want the closing documents to shift the liability (to the extent possible) to the borrower, a third party guarantor or third party service provider.

At a minimum, the loan documents delivered at closing should contain specific provisions dealing with environmental hazards. The borrower should represent and warrant that: the property has not been used nor is it currently used in a manner which violates applicable federal, state or local environmental laws; that the seller, the borrower and any tenant have not received any notice from a government agency for a violation of such laws and if such notice is received, the borrower shall immediately notify the lender; and that the borrower has no intention to use the property in such a manner. The borrower should also covenant not to cause such a violation, nor to permit any tenant to cause such a violation, nor to permit any environmental liens to be placed on the property. The borrower should indemnify the lender for all clean-up costs regardless of borrower's fault. These representations, warranties, covenants and indemnification for environmental risk should be carved out of any personal liability exculpation clause in the loan documents. The FNMA requires such a carve-out in multi-family transactions. There should be personal liability of the borrower and/or its principals to the lender for these risks. In fact, if the borrower is not deemed creditworthy for the risk, a personal guaranty by a third party might be obtained.

A breach of any of the foregoing should constitute an event of default entitling the lender to accelerate the loan. While cash collateral or cash equivalents may be tendered to cover a known problem, the issues are how accurate is the cost estimate for clean-up after the risk has been taken and what level of clean-up a governmental agency will require. It is this inability to determine the limits of liability which will probably mitigate against the use of surety bonds to cover the environmental risk.

Title insurance offers little or no protection to the lender because environmental liens are not always filed in the land records and sometimes attach retroactively. In 1984, the American Land Title Association ("ALTA") changed its standard policies to except from coverage "[a]ny law, ordinance or governmental regulation relating to environmental protection.". . . The problem is compounded in the 1987 forms by a new, more limited, definition of "public records" in the title policy which limits the liability of title insurers that do not search the public environmental records in a jurisdiction where they are not part of the land records. In March 1987, FNMA negotiated with ALTA an environmental protection lien endorsement for residential properties for loan policies only (Form 8.1). Of course these endorsements must be submitted to and approved by state insurance regulators for each state.

While liability insurers continue to disclaim coverage under traditional comprehensive general liability policies, there are some types of environmental coverage endorsements available to lenders. For example, environmental impairment policies are offered but are limited to claims made during the term of the policy for events occurring during the term or in a specified retroactive period. Such policies are also generally offered only after the insurer's consultant conducts a comprehensive engineering study of the insured property. Unfortunately, environmental impairment insurance coverage is probably still not available to an extent to make it a reliable alternative. . . .

ADMINISTRATION

After closing, due diligence should continue to be maintained during the term of the loan. A standard program should be implemented for proper risk management, including periodic site inspections to monitor the condition and use of the property and to detect visible changes. Obtaining and reviewing annual rent rolls for any new tenants in problem businesses might also be useful. If a property is in a problem area, environmental records should be periodically checked much the same as the tax records are reviewed. Transfers of property should be carefully screened to determine a purchaser's business or intended use of the property. Care should be taken in any subsequent loan modifications not to intentionally (or unintentionally by changing material terms) release prior owners who might have been contractually liable for any environmental damages. A court will recognize a release of liability between two parties although it will have no effect on the government's right to proceed against either or both parties for the environmental claim.

Notwithstanding continued vigilance with respect to the status of the property, equipment and owner and/or tenant uses, a lender should limit its involvement with a borrower to a debtor-creditor relationship. Moreover, certain lender prerogatives in dealing with the borrower's business should be exercised in such a manner as to avoid any suggestion of lender control which might create operator liability. A lender should only consider entering a joint venture or equity participation arrangement with a borrower after a careful review of potential risk of owner status for the lender.

Yet diligence is futile if a lender is unable to document its efforts satisfactorily at a later date. Thus, an adequate and diligent information and recordkeeping system must be an integrated part of any servicing operation. All telephone notes, inspections, reports, surveys or studies should be recorded and maintained in a manner allowing retrieval on a property specific basis. To adequately prove the basis for a lender's decisions may be as important as conducting its diligence if a lender desires to limit its potential liability.

DISPOSITION

A lender's liability for its diligence will be extended to third parties when it sells a loan or a whole or partial participation interest on a loan, to an investor, whether during or after origination of the loan. As environmental issues become more significant, investors may be requesting representations and warranties from originators as a condition to their investment.

To reduce its risk of liability, the originating lender should probably deliver to the investor all of the lender's environmental audit records and any testing reports and allow the investor to make its own decision on the information. If that is not acceptable, any representation or warranty which is given should be severely limited as to the best of lender's knowledge and limited to the inquiry actually conducted by lender's agents. The lender should not put itself in the position of becoming the guarantor or surety of any environmental risk to its investor. . . .

ENFORCEMENT

Probably at no time in a loan is a lender more at risk for environmental liability than when it is contemplating realizing on its collateral security. Obviously, if the lender were to take a deed in lieu of foreclosure from its borrower in satisfaction of the borrower's debt, the lender would become the owner with all the concomitant risks. However, even when the lender conducts a judicial foreclosure or exercises a statutory power of sale, unless the property is purchased by an unrelated third party, the lender will bid in its judgment and become the owner of the property. If the *Maryland Bank and Trust Co.* case is correct, the environmental risks of the lender as owner will be direct and measureably greater as time continues. The problem is the same whether the lender succeeds to a fee interest or to the interest of a ground tenant under a foreclosed leasehold mortgage.

It is therefore imperative that any lender establish a standard procedure for reviewing collateral security before any enforcement of remedies is considered. The lender should review: the existing file (including site inspection and lease reports); the loan documents and subsequent modifications; any guarantees and indemnities obtained at closing; the servicing log to determine post-closing actions; the current tenants and uses; and any environmental impairment insurance. The lender should also reinspect the site and possibly conduct certain tests (provided the lender may do so without liability under the loan documents and local law). In many states, the lender will not be able to enter the property to do a site assessment without the present consent of a defaulting borrower.

Even if no problem is detected, a receiver should be sought to provide security for the collateral and avoid any intentional introduction of hazardous substances to the property by a vindictive borrower or accidental introduction by a careless operator tenant. If, after due diligence, a problem is detected and the risk quantified, the lender may determine (after discussion with investors where applicable) to pursue its remedies under the promissory note or any guarantees which may have been delivered at closing rather than to foreclose on the mortgage.

If a participant in a loan participation wants to enforce the loan over the objection of the lead lender after the lead lender's due diligence, the lender should seek to either assign the record holder portion to the participant or obtain a full indemnity for all damages it may sustain from the participants' enforcement of the loan documents.

If a lender finds itself the owner of a hazardous waste facility, it should immediately cease operating the facility in an attempt to limit its liability as an operator.

CONCLUSION

Not every property offered by a borrower as collateral security for a loan will be a toxic waste site and lending officers should not begin to look for toxic waste under every stone. But with 698 hazardous substances recognized by the federal government, toxic waste is a real and substantial danger to a lender's collateral. While the "appropriate inquiry" conducted at each stage will not necessarily be the same for each loan, the degree of diligence should increase if there is even a reasonable suspicion of contamination. While each loan will not require the same environmental audit, an audit *should* be conducted for every loan.

Of course, all investors — owners and lenders — should understand the environmental risks involved in real estate investment as well as financing and evaluate their risk management procedures. Establishing a staged due diligence program will cause delays in underwriting and cancellations of closings for transactions as borrowers resist the precautions that lenders undertake to ascertain their risks. But as all lenders in the marketplace generally adopt similar diligence programs, borrowers will have no alternative but to accept developing environmental audit procedures as another cost of doing business.

The cost and delay of an environmental survey (and possible testing) is relatively small when compared to astronomical (and perpetual) environmental liability it may avoid for the real estate investor. Each investor should perform its own appropriate inquiry to establish the environmental status of a property at each transfer of an interest in such property. Only by making inquiry appropriate to the circumstances with respect to the environmental status of a property at the time of transfer can an investor establish to a court or government regulator that the investor is entitled to assert the innocent purchaser defense.

NOTES AND QUESTIONS

1. *The Mortgagee as "the Owner and Operator."* In *Maryland Bank* the court deals with the language of CERCLA that imposes liability on "the owner and operator." The bank had claimed that even if it were the owner, it had not operated the property. If true, the use of the conjunctive in CERCLA would seem to free the bank from liability. The court, however, citing legislative history and the haste of enactment, read the statutory language in the disjunctive. Are the court's arguments compelling? In answering, consider the fact that the CERCLA §101(20)(A) definition is of "owner or operator."

In United States v. Mirabile, 15 Env. L. Rep. 20992 (E.D. Pa. 1985), a decision that will be discussed in another context in the next note, the court denied Mellon Bank's motion for summary judgment. Mellon held a mortgage on contaminated property but had *not* foreclosed. The court held that there was a question of fact as to whether Mellon's loan officer participated in hands-on management, such as monitoring collateral accounts and collecting receivables and establishing a reporting system with the borrower, gave rise to liability as an operator of the property. The message of the case is clear: a mortgagee who becomes too heavily involved in the borrower's business may incur liability under CERCLA even though it has not become an owner by foreclosure. (See also the discussion of *Connor* at Chapter 6B6 and Chapter 11B1, note 4.)

Clearly, *Mirabile* raises some serious questions for the mortgagee. Assume in the master hypothetical that you represent Ace Insurance Company at a time Dan Developer is in default. Dan asks Ace for forbearance. Ace is willing to work with Dan in modifying the mortgage but is concerned that deferred maintenance is making the building unattractive to tenants. How much control over Dan's operation of the property can you advise Ace to negotiate without becoming liable under CERCLA as an owner or operator? Can you tell Ace that it could rely on the *Maryland Bank* court's footnote comment that by not foreclosing and not bidding at the foreclosure sale it could "insulate" itself from liability? (The court must have been referring to insulation from liability *in excess of the mortgage balance,* since the failure of Ace to foreclose against a defaulting borrower would seem necessarily to preclude realization on its security for the balance of its $25 million mortgage.) If Ace guesses wrong and, notwithstanding its efforts to keep uninvolved in Dan's business, its actions are held to involve participation in the operation of the property, does it also run a risk that its attempts to separate itself from Dan's business might make the third-party defense unavailable? Remember, in order to use the defense, the owner or operator must prove that it exercised due care to protect the public.

2.   *The "Mortgagee" Exception.*   What did the drafters mean when they excepted from the definition of "owner and operator" one who, without participating in the management, holds indicia of ownership primarily to protect its security interest? When does a mortgagee hold indicia of ownership except after foreclosure? The *Maryland Bank* court appears to limit the applicability of this exception to mortgagees prior to foreclosure in title theory states (those states where the mortgagor is said to convey title to the mortgagee, as distinguished from lien theory states, where the mortgagee holds only a lien on the property, as discussed at Chapter 4A). *Maryland Bank* stands for the proposition, then, that a mortgagee becomes subject to CERCLA liabilities once it forecloses, for from that moment on it is an "owner" within the meaning of CERCLA. This interpretation, however, seems to run counter to *Mirabile* where, in addition to Mellon Bank (which was possibly liable although it had not foreclosed) there was another mortgagee, the American Bank and Trust Company, which *had* foreclosed and was held *not* to be liable. Are the cases distinguishable or in conflict? How does *Maryland Bank* distinguish *Mirabile*? Does that distinction survive an analysis of the *Maryland Bank* holding? Is the neutral principle of law reconciling these two cases that a mortgagee becomes an "owner" within the meaning of CERCLA on foreclosure *and* holding of the property for an "extended period of time" (i.e., more than four months)? Would the exercise of control over the property during the holding period indicate that the mortgagee is an "owner"? Would the failure to exercise control (in order to avoid "owner" designation) at least to protect the public from the hazard affect the mortgagee's ability to assert the third-party defense?

That the *Maryland Bank* court construed the mortgagee exception too narrowly would seem to be illustrated by the controversy arising out of the recent Eleventh Circuit decision in United States v. Fleet Factors Corp., 901 F.2d 1550 (11th Cir. 1990), affg., 724 F. Supp.

955 (D. Fla. 1989). There the government sought to recover cleanup costs from Fleet Factors, which had held a mortgage on a cloth printing facility, and a security interest in its accounts, inventory, and certain equipment. When the borrower filed for bankruptcy and ceased operations, Fleet Factors, with permission of the bankruptcy court, foreclosed its security interest in certain equipment and inventory and contracted with others to sell and remove those items. Fleet Factors asked for summary judgment on the ground that at all times it had held indicia of ownership merely to protect its security interest, *without participating in the management* of the facility.

The district court denied summary judgment, finding genuine issues in dispute with respect to Fleet Factors' participation in management following foreclosure. The court indicated, however, that a secured creditor could provide financial assistance and give some specific management advice without participating in management and that actual participation would require "day-to-day management of the business or facility either before or after the business ceases operation." (724 F. Supp. at 960).

The Eleventh Circuit affirmed, but disagreed that a secured creditor would not be participating in the management unless it became involved in day-to-day management, stating that "a secured creditor may incur liability without being an operator . . . if its involvement with the management of the facility is sufficiently broad to support the inference that it could affect hazardous waste disposal decisions if it so chose." (901 F.2d at 1557-1558).

In another recent decision, In re Bergsoe Metal Corp., 910 F.2d 668 (9th Cir. 1990), summary judgment was granted on behalf of a municipal corporation that had issued revenue bonds for Bergsoe, the court finding no factual dispute that the indicia of ownership were held primarily to protect the municipal corporation's security interest without participation in the management of the facility. The Ninth Circuit declined to define what constitutes participation in management, but indicated that mere power to get involved in management is not enough to constitute "participating in management." "What is critical," the Ninth Circuit explained, "is not what rights the [municipal corporation] had, but what it did. The CERCLA security interest exception uses the active 'participating in management.' Regardless of what rights it had, it cannot have participated in management if it never exercised them." (910 F.2d at 673).

This indicates, if not a conflict, at least a degree of tension between the Circuits, and it constituted part of the basis for a petition for certiorari to the Supreme Court by Fleet Factors, supported by amici including the American College of Real Estate Lawyers and the American Bankers Association, and opposed by the Solicitor General on behalf of the United States, which was denied (No. 90-504 (Jan. 14,

1991)). What is it about *Fleet Factors* that is of such concern to lenders and real estate experts? Is this concern based on the holding in *Fleet Factors* or dictum? What interest did the United States have in opposing the petition? In his brief, the Solicitor General pointed out that there are numerous bills in Congress to address the issue of lender liability and that the Environmental Protection Agency has initiated an effort to develop a rule that would provide guidance to commercial lenders in this area (see EPA National Oil and Hazardous Substances Pollution Contingency Plan, Lender Liability Under CERCLA, Proposed Rule and Request for Comment, 40 C.F.R. pt. 300 subpt. L (1991).

As you read note 3, ask yourself what effect attempts by a lender to avoid a *Fleet Factors*-type determination that it was participating in management have on its ability to take advantage of the affirmative defenses.

3.   *The Affirmative Defenses.*   Note that the third-party defense does not protect third parties in a contractual relationship with the defendant. In *Maryland Bank* the third-party defense was asserted and the government moved for summary judgment on the ground, inter alia, that because of prior lending transactions, a contractual relationship existed between the borrower's father (from whom the borrower obtained title to the property) and the bank. Summary judgment was denied, citing genuine issues of material fact concerning the nature of the relationship. How great a problem do you think the court's acceptance of the possibility of mortgagee-mortgagor contractual relationships is for mortgage lenders? It is possible that mortgagees are always in a contractual relationship with borrowers, or will the holding be limited to those instances in which mortgagee involvement is beyond what the court finds normal or appropriate in the lending relationship? If so, will shared appreciation or convertible features in the mortgage create the contractual relationship? Does the definition in CERCLA §101(35), reprinted supra, help to answer these questions?

Even if a contractual relationship is found, can't the mortgagee nevertheless assert the innocent landowner exception to the contractual relationship definition? What steps does the Forte article suggest the mortgagee take prior to foreclosure to increase the likelihood that it will be considered an innocent landowner? The Federal Home Loan Bank Board (which then supervised savings and loan associations), in its February 6, 1989 Thrift Bulletin to its member banks, set forth detailed suggestions as to what should be covered by a "Phase 1" Environmental Risk Report. While promulgated for the purpose of assisting member banks, can you think of situations in which the guidelines may be harmful to the members?

The third-party and innocent-landowner defenses require that the defendant have exercised due care with respect to the hazardous substance and have taken precautions against acts or omissions of the third party. How can a mortgagee (while it is a mortgagee) take such steps and avoid designation as an operator under the *Mirabile* (Mellon Bank) reasoning? If the hazardous substance presents a danger to the public, would not the exercise of due care require the removal of the hazardous substance? If so, is the law saying one can avoid liability for cleanup only by cleaning up the property?

The burden of proof is on the defendant to prove that it is entitled to an affirmative defense. See United States v. Price, 577 F. Supp. 1103 (D.N.J., 1983), and Washington v. Time Oil Co., 687 F. Supp. 529 (W.D. Wash. 1988). This presents difficulties for the defendant because the defenses are available only if the damages resulted *solely* from the enumerated acts, which may be hard to prove. For example, an earthquake may be an act of God, but the failure to build a building strong enough to withstand the earthquake is an act, or, more accurately, an omission, of people.

4. *Due Diligence?*   CERCLA was designed to clean up hazardous wastes and make the people who perpetrated the contamination or who benefit by the cleanup pay the costs. In theory it makes sense. In application, it may create more problems than it solves.

A mortgagee's ability to protect itself against liability is a subject of great concern among lenders, as the Forte article indicates. If you represented Ace Insurance Company in the master hypothetical, what steps would you recommend Ace take? First, you might suggest a due diligence "Phase 1" investigation before making the loan. But what will this encompass? The names of the borrower and of prior owners in the chain of title may be clues to potential liability, but in most cases the names will not indicate what was done on the premises. Similarly, a preliminary check of the property may not disclose the trouble. A soil analysis may help, but not if the contaminants have sunk too low. Test borings may help, but they may be expensive, and the boring itself can cause damage to the property or accelerate the flow of contaminants to the ground water. What about the neighbor's property? Hazardous wastes spilled there could seep overground or underground onto the borrower's property.

Expert consultants are available but probably will be unwilling to make firm conclusions. Indeed, Ace would be lucky if the consultant didn't insist on an indemnity against any liability the consultant may have because of negligence or otherwise. How expensive are these protective steps, and who is going to pay for them? In *Maryland Bank* the loan was for $335,000 (how much was the cleanup liability?). How large will a loan have to be to justify due diligence? Having made the loan, how does the lender prevent the borrower from causing contamination during the term of the mortgage loan? Couldn't any power the lender demands to control use of the property so involve the lender with the borrower's business that it may be considered an operator or owner without the protection of the third-party or mortgagee defenses?

Will casualty or title insurance help Ace in this situation? Significant casualty insurance will generally be unavailable for hazardous waste liability, and such liability will probably be excluded specifically from the normal insurance coverage. As you learned from the discussion of title insurance in Chapter 3B2, recourse to title insurance also will generally prove unavailing. While the 1987 ALTA Loan Policy affords some limited protection, this protection will cover the lender only as against liens recorded in the public records at the time of the issuance of the policy. Public records will not include records kept in the appropriate office of environmental protection but only records established by state law for constructive notice of interests in real property. Liens placed of record after the date of the policy will not be covered thereby.

Consider the cost to society of this cleanup process. Assume that the cost of cleaning up all hazardous wastes in the United States is x billion. Since all prospective purchasers, ground tenants, and mortgagees will have to do some "due diligence" checking in every situation (even though contaminated properties are relatively few), assume the cost of the entire process is $3x$ billion. The extra costs will be passed on to the borrowers in the form of higher interest rates, and financing will become unavailable on questionable property.

At this writing, possible revisions of CERCLA are being considered by scholars and parties in interest. What changes would you suggest? Consider this proposal. Suppose CERCLA were amended to provide for full cleanup of all contaminated properties by the federal government, with the government having the right of recourse only against those who were responsible for the contamination and with liability of other owners and operators limited to those determined to have been involved in a conspiracy or fraud or those who receive a windfall as a result of the cleanup. Is it likely that once the government announces it intends to clean up all properties without a chargeback, the cost of cleanup will become less of a depressing factor in real estate values, thus reducing the chance of windfalls by future owners of property when the government removes the waste? Would those benefitting from the cleanup, then, be limited to owners at the time of the announcement who purchased the property at reduced prices after the existence of hazardous wastes became known? Under this formula, would not the wastes be cleaned up, the culprits be punished, the windfalls be avoided, and the cost to the nation be reduced substantially? What holes can you poke in such a proposal?

5. *Other Statutes.* There are other federal and state statutes dealing with hazardous substances. The federal Resource Conservation and Recovery Act of 1980 (RCRA), as amended by the Hazardous &

Solid Waste Amendments of 1984 (Pub. L. No. 98-616, 98 Stat. 3221 (1984)), provides for regulations to monitor treatment, storage, and disposal of hazardous wastes and imposes strict liability for those disposing of hazardous waste in a manner that threatens public health and the environment. Both governmental and private action are authorized under the statute. The Clean Air Act, 42 U.S.C. §7401 et seq., is designed to protect air quality; it provides for the states to submit implementation plans. There are also provisions for penalties as well as injunctions in the federal enforcement of plans and standards of performance, including a provision for private citizen suits for violations of emission standards and EPA orders. The Clean Water Act, 33 U.S.C. §1251 et seq., provides for the elimination of the discharge of pollutants into the nation's waters. There are provisions for both federal and state enforcement.

On the state level, numerous legislatures have enacted environmental protection legislation similar to CERCLA that is often more pervasive. See, e.g., N.J. Stat. Ann. §13:1K-6 et seq. (Supp. 1990); Mass. Ann. Laws ch. 21I (Law. Co-op. 1990); Conn. Gen. Stat. §22a-134 (1989). State statutes must be checked carefully to determine the extent of the lien imposed for cleanup expenses. In many cases the lien is a superlien, that is, it is superior to all other liens on the property, including prior mortgages. Compare such provisions with CERCLA, which provides for a lien on the contaminated property effective from the time of recording in the appropriate office. Does this mean that if the mortgagee forecloses after the cleanup and the recording of the federal lien, the mortgagee (assuming it had no *Mirabile*-type liability as an operator) would obtain the property free and clear of the federal lien? (See discussion at Chapter 4C3.) Does it follow that the safe course under CERCLA for the mortgagee on learning of hazardous waste on the property is to hold off on foreclosure until the government has cleaned up the property and imposed its lien, and then foreclose and cut off the federal lien?

6. *Asbestos.* Virtually every steel frame building constructed between the end of World War II and approximately 1973 was built with asbestos fireproofing. Even after 1973 many builders continued to use vinyl asbestos tile, asbestos pipe wrap, asbestos paint, and the like. The conventional wisdom is that the existence of asbestos in a building is not a hazard per se. It is only when the asbestos gets into the atmosphere that risks are created. Although many people exposed to asbestos apparently never are affected by it, many people with very little exposure may, perhaps 20 years later, contract asbestosis and cancer. Asbestos gets into the atmosphere when it becomes "friable" (generally, when it gets stringy and hangs down from what it's attached to) or when repairs or renovations are being undertaken and it is

disturbed. For those situations, the Environmental Protection Agency (EPA) and the Occupational Safety and Health Administration (OSHA) have issued guidelines for removal, the safety precautions that must be taken, and the method of disposition.

The cost of asbestos removal is significant. At this writing owners and developers estimate approximately $20 to $30 per square foot just for the removal, and some claim the overall cost (including lost rents during the removal) can be close to $100 per square foot. To appreciate the enormity of this figure, consider that if 300,000 square feet of Dan Developer's building needed asbestos removal the cost (based on $100 per square foot) would be $30 million — more than the cost of the building. With such significant costs, it is no wonder that suits are beginning to surface over liability for removal. The following is an example of such a suit.

> Prudential Insurance Co. of America filed a lawsuit in federal court in Dallas, Texas, on April 29 against First RepublicBank Dallas, N.A., seeking $35 million for removing asbestos-containing material from the 56-story Renaissance Tower in Dallas (The Prudential Insurance Co. of America v. First RepublicBank Dallas, N.A., ND TX, Dallas Div., No. CA 3-88-0939-H). . . .
>
> Prudential also seeks $100 million in exemplary damages and indemnification for any health claims that are made against Prudential. The insurance company contends it was not told that the Environmental Protection Agency had found asbestos in the building prior to Prudential's purchase of the structure.
>
> InterFirst Bank Corp., one of two bank holding companies that merged to form First RepublicBank in 1987, jointly built the building in 1974 with Prudential. In 1984, Prudential bought InterFirst's half-interest.
>
> Prudential claims that InterFirst withheld information about the EPA test. The 27-page complaint states that the bank holding company "in order to induce Prudential" to buy InterFirst's 50 percent interest in the building, "willfully, knowingly and purposefully made express warranties regarding the absence of material defects and significant adverse conditions in Renaissance Tower."

Asbestos Litigation Rptr. 17,037 (May 20, 1988). There apparently has been no decision, and it is believed that the case was settled for an undisclosed sum.

If you represented First RepublicBank, what arguments would you raise to thwart Prudential's claim for damages? If you represented Prudential, how would you answer those arguments?

Assume that Dan Developer's building was built with asbestos fireproofing. Twenty-five years later some employees of tenants, some employees of the contractors that built the building or the contractors that removed asbestos or repaired the building, some members of the public who happened to have been in the building from time to time, and Dan Developer all suffer from asbestosis. Who do you think are the potential defendants, and what are the theories of liability on which they will base their case? What impediments do you see to recovery? See, e.g., Dimling, Asbestos and the Insurer as Lender, Employer, and Property Owner, 24 Tort and Ins. L.J. 68 (1988); Glazerman, Asbestos in Commercial Buildings: Obligations and Responsibilities of Landlords and Tenants, 22 Real Prop., Prob. & Tr. J. 661 (1987); Pasich, Insurance Coverage for the Asbestos Building Cases: There's More than Property Damage, 24 Tort and Ins. L.J. 630 (1989).

7. *Hazardous Wastes and Bankruptcy.* There are numerous intricate questions arising out of bankruptcy as it relates to toxic waste liability. Such considerations may or may not make it advisable to force an involuntary bankruptcy or to file for voluntary bankruptcy. A detailed analysis of these questions is beyond the scope of this casebook. However, every real estate lawyer must be aware of the problem areas, which include determination of whether bankruptcy stays enforcement of governmental environmental claims (see Ohio v. Kovacs, 469 U.S. 274 (1985), and Penn Terra Ltd. v. Department of Environmental Resources, 733 F.2d 267 (3d Cir. 1984)); whether liability is dischargeable in bankruptcy (see Bankruptcy Code §§523(a)(6), 523(a)(7) and *Kovacs,* supra); whether the bankruptcy court may abandon contaminated property (see Midlantic National Bank v. New Jersey Department of Environmental Protection, 474 U.S. 494 (1986), Borden, Inc. v. Wells-Fargo Business Credit, 856 F.2d 12 (4th Cir. 1988), and Klee and Merola, Ignoring Congressional Intent: Eight Years of Judicial Legislation, 62 Am. Bankr. L.J. 1, 8-12 (1988); and the extent of the priority of governmental environmental claims (see Bankruptcy Code §§506(c), 507(a)). See generally Comment, *Kovacs* and Toxic Wastes in Bankruptcy, 36 Stan. L. Rev. 1199 (1984); Cosetti and Friedman, *Midlantic Nat'l Bank, Kovacs* and *Penn Terra:* The Bankruptcy Code and State Environmental Law — Perceived Conflicts and Options for the Trustee and State Environmental Agencies, 7 J.L. & Com. 65 (1987); Drabkin, Moorman, and Kirsch, Bankruptcy and the Cleanup of Hazardous Waste: Caveat Creditor, 15 Env. L. Rptr. 10314 (1985); Epling, Environmental Liens in Bankruptcy, 44 Bus. Law. 85 (1988); Hillman and Caras, When the Bank Wants Its Borrower in Bankruptcy: Benefits of Bankruptcy for Lenders and Lender Liability Defendants, 40 Me. L. Rev. 375 (1988); Hoffman, Environmental Protection and Bankruptcy Rehabilitation: Toward Better Compromise, 11 Ecology L.Q. 671 (1984); Openchowski, Bankruptcy Is Not an Answer: A Rebuttal, 15 Env. L. Rptr. 10314 (1985).

8. Additional Reading. Among the vast quantity of writings on the subject of environmental hazards are the following: Anderson, Will the Meek Even Want the Earth?, 38 Mercer L. Rev. 535 (1987); Atkeson, Goldberg, Ellrod, and Connors, An Annotated Legislative History of the Superfund Amendments and Reauthorization Act of 1986 (SARA), 16 Env. L. Rptr. 10360 (1986); Burcat, Foreclosure and United States v. Maryland Bank & Trust Co.: Paying the Piper or Learning How to Dance to a New Tune?, 17 Env. L. Rptr. 10098 (1987); Berkkhart, Lender/Owners and CERCLA: Title and Liability, 25 Harv. J. Legis. 317 (1988); Fitzsimmons and Sherwood, The Real Estate Lawyer's Primer (and More) to Superfund: The Environmental Hazards of Real Estate Transactions, 22 Real Prop., Prob. & Tr. J. 765 (1987); Hummel, Dealing with Asbestos Containing Materials in the Construction Industry, 4 Prac. Real Est. Law. 9 (Mar. 1988); Mays, Settlements with SARA: A Comprehensive Review of Settlement Procedures Under the Superfund Amendments and Reauthorization Act, 17 Env. L. Rptr. 10101 (1987); Murphy, The Impact of 'Superfund' and Other Environmental Statutes on Commercial Lending and Investment Activities, 41 Bus. Law. 1133 (1986); Pedowitz, Title Insurance: Non-Coverage of Hazardous Waste Super-Liens, 1985 Prob. & Prop. 45; Roberts, Allocation of Liabilities Under CERCLA: A Carrot and Stick Formula, 14 Ecology L.Q. 601 (1987); Schwenke and Lockett, Local Control of Hazardous Wastes Through Land Use Regulation, 21 Real Prop., Prob. & Tr. J. 603 (1986); Steptoe, Chemical Waste Complicates Many Land Sales Financings, Wall St. J., Nov. 5, 1986, at 39, col. 1.; Vollmann, Double Jeopardy: Lender Liability Under Superfund, 16 Real Est. L.J. 3 (1987); Symposium: Superfund and Hazardous Wastes, 6 Stan. Env. L.J. 9 (1986-1987); Symposium: Hazardous Waste Legislation in New Jersey, 1976-86, 38 Rutgers L. Rev. 619 (1986); Note, When a Security Becomes a Liability: Claims Against Lenders in Hazardous Waste Cleanup, 38 Hastings L.J. 1261 (1987).

C h a p t e r 13

Securitization

A. THE RECENT TREND TOWARD SECURITIZATION OF REAL ESTATE INVESTMENTS

As observed at Chapter 2A, notwithstanding the current slump, a direct or indirect ownership interest in income-producing real estate (such as an investment share in a partnership or a Subchapter S corporation) has been shown to be an attractive investment as compared to other investment media such as stocks and bonds because real estate historically has tended to be a less risky and volatile portfolio asset and a better hedge against inflation. In addition, real estate developers and investors are afforded the unique opportunity to superleverage their acquisition and construction costs by means of high-ratio financing and, notwithstanding the new limitation on passive losses for rental and limited partnership activities imposed by the Tax Reform Act of 1986, the real estate investor is still able to shelter his or her share of rental income from immediate taxation. The one salient disadvantage of investing in real estate has been the lack of liquidity associated with shares in a real estate investment. For example, until recently real estate investors in publicly held limited partnerships (syndications) were compelled to invoke their own resources when they needed to sell their investment shares because of the absence of any formal secondary market for trading their shares (such as the New York Stock Exchange) and because leverage-minded syndicators discouraged redemptions of investment shares in order to preserve the cash reserves of their partnership syndications.

Perhaps the most exciting trend affecting the development and financing of income-producing real estate has been the recent ingenious and innovative efforts by developers and underwriters on Wall Street to utilize the public security format as a way of enhancing the liquidity and marketability of both debt and equity participations in commercial real estate without depriving the investor of the tax and pass-through benefits associated with the direct ownership of the real estate. See Table 13-1. Exemplifying this trend toward securitization on the equity side of real estate are the so-called income- (as opposed to tax-) oriented master limited partnership (MLP) and the new kinds of real estate investment trusts (REITs) such as the finite-life closed-end REIT, whose share price (unlike publicly traded corporate stock) reflects the value of its underlying assets so that the REIT shareholder can not only trade the shares on a public stock exchange but also capitalize on the value of the REIT's underlying assets. On the debt side of real estate, credit rating agencies such as Standard & Poor's developed for the first time in 1985 the computer technology to evaluate the creditworthiness of income-producing real estate notwithstanding the fact that the rental income stream from a building is predicated on a variety of underlying leases with disparate tenants and lease terms. This has enabled developers seeking refinancing of large projects to obtain their long-term fixed-rate financing by issuing commercial mortgage-backed bonds (CMBBs) (which are traded on Wall Street) and thereby obtain less expensive and more attractive loan terms than would have been available from the less competitive (oligopolistic) traditional private lending sources such as life insurance companies and pension funds. The trend toward securitization on the debt side of real estate is examined at Chapter 13B.

Ross, Real Estate Master Limited Partnerships: Why Investors Like Them
17 Real Est. Rev. 28 (Spring 1987)

The master limited partnership (MLP) had its genesis in the oil industry. An MLP was created in 1981 as a vehicle that made it possible for certain companies, led by Apache Petroleum Company, to realize the value of undervalued assets and to pass income and tax-deductible losses directly through to their shareholders. That same year, a real estate MLP, the Ala Moana Hawaii Properties partnership, was organized for the purpose of liquidating the property holdings of its parent company, The Dillingham Corporation. Subsequent real estate MLPs were vehicles that enabled companies to sell, spin off, or liquidate some or all of their existing operations, or to combine or "roll up" existing partnerships. Occasionally, MLPs have been formed to raise capital through public offerings.

By July 1986, there were seventeen real estate MLPs with a total market value of more than $2.4 billion. Half of these partnerships had been formed during the previous twelve months. Another two dozen real estate MLPs with a total offering size of $1.9 billion were in registration. Those partnerships' present or planned investments include office buildings, shopping centers, hotels, restaurants, and other commercial real estate; they have developed land, engaged in residential home building, built planned communities and nursing homes, made mortgage loans, and engaged in mortgage banking.

An MLP is not a defined entity for legal or tax purposes. The term applies to a large partnership whose ownership interests are publicly registered and freely traded in the marketplace. These MLPs offer investors not only the benefits of the traditional limited partnerships, but the benefit of liquidity. Interests in an MLP are called depository unit receipts, or beneficial assignment certificates, or certificates of limited partnership interest. All these interests are freely tradable on a stock exchange or in an over-the-counter market. Investors who hold the units or certificates are partners in the MLP and can treat taxable income and loss and cash distributions as do investors in traditional partnerships. However, they can readily buy or sell their units or certificates, which investors in the illiquid interests of traditional partnerships cannot do.

Usually, an MLP has a two-tiered structure, one for raising and the other for investing capital. This simplifies ownership of the underlying real estate assets. An MLP's general partner is normally its sponsor; its limited partners are outside investors. The MLP is a limited partner in a second, operating partnership that owns the real estate and for which the sponsor is also general partner.

The number of real estate MLPs is expected to multiply, and the diversity of their investments to increase. Investors find them attractive for three reasons. The Tax Reform Act of 1986 sharply reduces tax incentives for investing in income-producing real estate. Consequently, real estate investors are turning to yield-oriented, relatively liquid investments like MLPs. Furthermore, under the new tax law, MLP income may be sheltered by passive losses from other partnership investments. Also, there are significant tax advantages in doing business as a partnership rather than as a corporation, as we explain below. Another reason for the expected growth in the MLP market is the fact that, increasingly, corporations and partnerships are utilizing MLPs in business strategies primarily intended to increase the value that can be realized from liquidating real estate holdings. . . .

TAX ADVANTAGES OF MLPs

The tax treatment of public partnerships, including MLPs, generally is the same as that of any other partnership. A partner is taxed on his share of a partnership's income rather than on his share of any cash distributed. Distributions are not taxable unless they exceed the partner's basis in his partnership interest.

COMPARING THE TAX CONSEQUENCES OF PARTNERSHIPS AND REITs

Public real estate investments are made primarily through limited partnerships or real estate investment trusts. A partnership is not a tax-paying entity; its income and losses flow through to its partners. A REIT also can pass through income, but to do so it must satisfy complex ownership, asset, income, and other requirements of the Internal Revenue Code. Moreover, it cannot pass through losses. Under the new tax law, passive losses from other investments cannot be offset against income distributed from a REIT. . . .

THE PASSIVE LOSS LIMITATION RULE

The passive loss limitation rule in the 1986 tax law divides a taxpayer's income into three "baskets": active, portfolio, and passive. Active income is income from a trade or business in which a taxpayer materially participates. Portfolio income includes interest, dividends, royalties, and capital gains from securities sales. Passive income is income from a trade or business in which a taxpayer does not materially participate, including income from all real estate rentals, regardless of the degree of taxpayer participation. Following a four-year phase-in, passive losses will shelter only passive income until such time as the activity generating the passive losses is disposed of in a taxable transaction. Many investors could find themselves with write-offs they cannot use. So syndicators are designing MLPs to generate passive income to match against excess writeoffs from existing partnerships. . . .

TAX COMPLICATIONS FACED BY MLPs

Although the tax advantages of limited partnerships continue to be substantial, tax law applying to MLPs includes many complexities.

TRADING OF MLP INTERESTS

Although MLP interests are freely tradable, tax considerations might limit an MLP's trading activity. For income tax purposes, a partnership will be terminated if more than 50 percent of the partners' capital or profits interests are sold or exchanged within a twelve-month period. MLPs may find it difficult to control trading activity to prevent a transgression of the 50 percent limitation because many MLP units usually are held in street names for their beneficial owners. However, there are ways to deal with the problem. The general partner, for example, might retain the right to approve transfers of limited partnership interests: The prospectus for one recent MLP offering states that such interests "will not be transferable except upon death, by operation of law, or with the consent of the managing general partner." . . .

LEGAL CONSIDERATIONS

Investors in MLPs should be aware of two areas of legal considerations.

VOTING RIGHTS

Unlike limited partners in a traditional partnership, holders of an MLP's depository unit receipts do not have inherent voting rights, or the right to review the partnership's books and records. Some MLPs have given limited rights to their unit holders, such as the right to vote on whether to remove the general partner or the right to approve the sale of partnership assets. But usually full-fledged rights are conferred on unit holders at the discretion of the general partner. However, the general partner may not always have unlimited discretion because state securities regulations may mandate certain voting and other rights for limited partners.

SECURITIES LAWS

Master limited partnership interests constitute securities within the meaning of the Securities Act of 1933. Offers and sales of MLP interests are subject to the Act's registration and antifraud provisions. MLP interests also are securities within the meaning of the Securities Exchange Act of 1934, and may be subject to the registration, periodic reporting, proxy, tender offer, and antifraud provisions of the 1934 Act.

State regulation of MLP unit offerings has two distinct formats. Under the first form of regulation, the states follow federal securities laws in requiring full and complete disclosure of the material terms of the offering. Under the second form, the states apply substantive rules to MLP unit offerings, most notably the policies of the North American Securities Administrators Association, which on January 1, 1986, adopted a revised statement of policy regarding real estate programs. NASAA is comprised of the securities regulators of the fifty states, a number of which follow its guidelines to varying degrees. Among other things, the NASAA guidelines set stringent disclosure requirements for initial MLP offerings.

MLPs listed on a national securities exchange are exempt from the "blue sky" qualification or registration requirements in most states. Counterbalancing this are the cost of the listing and the need to meet the exchange's minimum listing requirements. As an option, organizers may choose to qualify an MLP for trading in the North American Securities Dealers Automated Quotations System. NASDAQ standards for qualification are not as stringent as those of the New York or the American Stock Exchanges, but NASDAQ qualification usually does not exempt the MLP from blue sky registration.

BUSINESS STRATEGIES: MOTIVES FOR ORGANIZING AN MLP

In its relatively short history, the real estate MLP has developed rapidly, not only in its demonstrated ability to raise substantial investment capital but in its adaptability to a diversity of business strategies. The most common strategies are (1) the spin-off or "rollout" of corporate assets into an MLP; (2) the "roll-up" of existing partnerships into a single master partnership; and (3) the public offering of an MLP to raise initial capital for direct real estate investment. But there are many variations of these strategies, all aimed at maximizing the value of real estate assets, avoiding double taxation, and generating new equity or debt capital for MLP sponsors at lower costs than alternative financing. Discussed below are the following strategies:

- Sale or contributions of assets
- Sale/leaseback
- Spin-off or rollout
- Liquidation
- Roll-up
- Public offering . . .

A PUBLIC OFFERING TO ESTABLISH AN MLP

MLPs have been formed to raise equity capital through public offerings. An MLP offering can appeal, potentially, to a wider audience of investors than can an offering of a limited partnership, for it costs considerably less to acquire a unit of an MLP than an interest in a privately placed limited partnership. The only significant difference in the cost of an initial offering of an MLP is the cost of registration or

exemption from registration, increased due diligence costs, and the cost
of listing the MLP for trading. . . .

Ross and Klein, New Directions for
Real Estate Investment Trusts
1 Real Est. Fin. J. 67 (Winter 1986)

Developers are beginning to play a bigger role as sponsors and
advisers in the real estate investment trust (REIT) industry. This represents one of the most important of the many changes the industry
has undergone since its darkest hours during the 1973-1975 recession,
when many trusts had substantial loan losses, some went into bankruptcy
proceedings, and the value of REIT shares plunged. For a time thereafter,
the mere mention of REITs was likely to elicit a derogatory Bronx
cheer from the many investors soured on REITs.

But times have changed, and so have REITs. In significant ways,
today's REITs are markedly different from the 1970s generation of
trusts. This is true both of seasoned REITs that survived the industry's
collapse a decade ago, and of newer REITs (about a third of the REITs
now operating were launched within the past five years). A close look
at the "born again" REIT industry reveals that REITs have benefited
not only from internal changes but from changing circumstances.

Among the most important trends are:

*The emergence of REITs sponsored by developers, or cosponsored by
developers and major financial institutions. . . .* These developers, and
others, offer REITs management skills and experience. In addition, they
may own — or have access to — investment-grade properties that REITs
can acquire. For their part, developers can utilize REITs to raise capital
at lower costs than might be possible by obtaining financing from
banks, insurance companies, and other conventional sources. In addition,
developers can earn fee income as REIT advisers.

*Today's REITs generally are more conservative than their ancestors,
the trusts of a generation ago.* REITs now ordinarily concentrate on
long-term mortgage lending, direct property investments, completed
properties, or properties under construction that have been substantially
leased up, rather than on high-risk, short-term construction and development lending, as in the past. The REITs still involved in construction lending usually have recognized sponsors with proven track
records.

Unlike the earlier generation of trusts that borrowed heavily to
finance investments, today's REITs generally are not as highly leveraged;
increasingly, they are making mostly cash or all-cash property investments, in association with developers with established track records.

REITs are utilizing more innovative ways to raise capital.   Current REIT offerings consist not only of the typical issues of common stock and shares of beneficial interest, but more sophisticated instruments such as warrants and debentures with conversion features. The newest REITs also utilize debt instruments to shelter part of the cash distribution. In October 1985, for example, Trammell Crow, a leading U.S. developer, registered a new equity REIT that forecasts that 69 percent of its distributable cash would represent a tax-free return of capital. The shelter is achieved primarily through the use of zero coupon bond interest deductions.

Future offerings may consist of several classes of stock, to separate current cash flow from capital gains that are the result of appreciation in a REIT's real estate portfolio. Warrants can be used to accomplish similar results. In either case, the purpose would be to tailor offerings to the requirements of different types of investors — some investors might seek long-term capital gains, while others might be more interested in immediate cash flow.

As a sign of things to come, Prudential Realty Trust, a REIT sponsored and advised by a subsidiary of The Prudential Insurance Company of America, registered in mid-1985 an offering of 11.115 million income shares and an equal number of capital shares of beneficial interest of the trust. Dividends paid the trust's income shareholders will be based on the trust's cash flow, while dividends paid on the capital shares will be based on the REIT's capital gains. . . .

More REITs are being structured as closed-end funds.   After the initial public offering, additional shares cannot be sold without approval by holders of a majority of the shares outstanding. This is intended to protect investors from dilution of their equity interests in REITs.

To enhance their investment appeal, some new REITs have been given finite lives.   A finite-life REIT, or FREIT, typically will be liquidated ten to fifteen years from its inception. The assumption is that, as liquidation nears, a FREIT's share price will reflect its underlying property values — values that, presumably, will have appreciated over time. Since FREITs are relatively new, however, this assumption has not been tested in practice. In any event, the self-liquidating feature of FREITs contrasts with open-end REITs, trusts that, in theory at least, continue in perpetuity and are traded like bonds on the basis of their yields, so that their shareholders may not have an opportunity to capitalize on the value of the underlying assets. That opportunity may also be denied to investors in FREITs, critics say, if mandatory liquidation comes at a time when a FREIT's share price is depressed due to stock market conditions or other causes. FREITs generally have some limited flexibility in implementing liquidation, however, so as to be able to match the liquidation timing with favorable market conditions.

By utilizing the FREIT structure, a trust's managers can concentrate on selecting investments for long-term growth. By contrast, managers of the open-end REITs of a decade ago were often so preoccupied with supporting their trusts' stock prices that they wanted investments to produce quick current yield; they tended to ignore long-term opportunities. . . .

The single-purpose or single-project REIT could become more commonplace. This type of REIT invests in one project that usually is developed by the REIT's developer-sponsor. The REIT could make a commitment to acquire the completed property, and that pledge could be used by the developer to obtain construction financing. Or, the REIT's investment could take the form of a participating mortgage loan, at a slightly below-market rate, in return for which the REIT would receive some sort of equity participation in the project, based on a percentage of the appreciation in the property's value, a percentage of gross rents, or other "kicker." With the mortgage commitment from the REIT in hand, the developer could obtain construction financing. . . .

THE TRADE-OFF

While sponsorship of a REIT can provide a developer with lower-cost capital, there is a trade-off. Since REIT securities generally are publicly traded, the developer-sponsor is usually subject to the registration and reporting requirements of the public securities laws — the Securities Act of 1933, which requires an issuer of securities to file, prior to any public sale, a registration statement with the Securities and Exchange Commission, and the Securities Exchange Act of 1934, which regulates the trading of securities once they have been issued. As a result, the developer comes under closer scrutiny of regulatory authorities and the REIT's shareholders and trustees. In addition, the developer must share, to some degree, the decisionmaking process with the REIT's trustees, who must approve the investments made by the REIT. Being subject to such high visibility and constraints can be a wrenching experience for developers accustomed to operating freely, independently, and privately.

Making an initial public offering of a new REIT can also be a difficult exercise for developers or other sponsors inexperienced in raising capital in the public securities markets — and is a good reason for sponsors to consult investment bankers, accountants, lawyers, and other professionals in preparing an offering. One of the difficulties lies in the nuances and complexities of structuring a REIT to satisfy significant income and assets tests under Sections 856 and 860 of the Internal Revenue Code to qualify for preferential tax treatment.

In the case of a REIT that provides participation mortgage financing, for example, it is imperative that, if the REIT receives a share of the income stream from the underlying properties, its participation *not* be based on net income (the difference between gross income and operating expenses) but derived from some gross income formula. Otherwise, the earnings may not be considered qualified REIT income for purposes of its preferential tax treatment.

REIT POPULARITY

These days, it seems, just about everyone wants to form a REIT. One reason is that REITs could be a more attractive investment in comparison with real estate limited partnerships if the Reagan Administration's tax proposals become law. A principal competitive advantage of partnerships is that they can pass through losses to investors that can be used to shelter other income. REITs, on the other hand, cannot pass through losses — only dividend distributions. But REITs do have an advantage in that, unlike certain "abusive" tax shelters that must register with the IRS, REITs are not subject to the same burdensome tax audit procedures. . . .

REITs would be affected by the proposals, but not as adversely as partnerships. Like partnerships, they would be affected by the proposal to tax sales of buildings and other depreciable property as ordinary income rather than capital gains. But because REITs are required to take forty-year depreciation deductions for purposes of determining their earnings and profits, there would be less of an impact under the stretched-out depreciation timetables proposed by the Administration.

UNDERWRITER CONCERN

While developers and other sponsors of REITs may be eager to bring out new offerings, underwriters have become more selective in backing new REIT issues. The underwriters are interested mainly in marketing REITs that have recognized sponsors and that specify the properties in which they plan to invest.

For those developers considering REIT sponsorship, the decision, in the final analysis, rests on the comparative cost of capital available through a REIT, the opportunity to earn continuing fees as a REIT adviser, and the chance to share in the residual value of a REIT's real estate assets. For those developers unable or unwilling to form REITs, there are alternatives. Developers, for example, might tap established REITs for permanent mortgage financing, enter into joint venture development projects with REITs, or utilize commercial mortgage-backed bond financing. They might also consider forming publicly traded real estate limited partnerships.

Despite the difficulties, more developer-sponsored REITs are expected to be launched. The deeper involvement should be beneficial both for REITs and developers. And that should give REIT investors — even those in the Bronx — something to cheer about.

Freedman, Changing REITs Find Broader Interest and Acceptance
1 Real Est. Fin. J. 72 (Winter 1986)

INVESTOR INFLUENCE

Many of the newly organized REITs have recognized and responded to the desires and perceptions of the investment community. In June 1982, Stephen E. Roulac, then with Kenneth Leventhal & Company, observed that REIT investment strategy should be "addressed from a marketing perspective." Among other things, he recommended that REITs adopt a "closed end" strategy patterned more after public limited partnership marketing tactics by planning a sale of assets after a period of anticipated appreciation and distributing sale proceeds to investors. Roulac also indicated that an upfront focus by management on basic policy investment decisions with a plan for policy implementation is preferable to the more traditional approach, described by Roulac as a "building picking" orientation. . . .

NEW REITs

Many of the newly formed REITs have focused on specific segments of the real estate industry. For example, Strategic Mortgage Investments, Inc. has been characterized as a mortgage banking REIT; 1CM Property Investors as a participating mortgage REIT; and Mellon Participating Mortgage Trust as a blind-pool trust. REITs have been formed for the purpose of developing real estate rather than investing in existing buildings; others invest in a specific industry, or for a single purpose, such as health care or hotels. The future may see REITs that are sponsored by or affiliated with national companies that require heavy investment in real estate for acquisition or financing of specialized facilities, such as trucking terminals, public transportation facilities, communication facilities offices, and the like.

The approach most responsive to Roulac's 1982 suggestions is the so-called fully committed equity, finite-life, closed-end REIT, as exemplified by the offering of EQK Realty Investors. EQK was organized to acquire and hold specific assets, which are projected to appreciate in value over a period of time, after which the assets will be available for sale. The closed-end REIT will not issue additional shares, make additional investment, or invest or reinvest proceeds of sales or refinancings. The proceeds of sales and refinancings are intended to be distributed to shareholders, and upon the sale of assets, the closed-end REIT will be liquidated.

The finite-life, closed-end REIT appears to be the most innovative change in REIT operations and structure. Except for tax shelter, the structure is startlingly similar to that of the syndicated limited partnership and is a departure from the traditional patterns of older REITs. The traditional REIT has perpetual life, is free to issue additional stock to new shareholders, sell or refinance its properties, acquire additional properties, or otherwise reinvest proceeds of sale or refinance (within the rules imposed by governing legislation), and has no stated time within which it intends to liquidate its holdings. The finite-life, closed-end REIT has self-imposed policy limitations, which may ultimately prove to be disadvantageous.

Thus, the investment community has had a significant impact upon the current direction of the REIT industry. There has been much focus on management philosophy in response to the investment community, and an aggressive marketing approach based on investor perceptions.

Although the shares of many of the recent REIT initial public offerings are selling at a discount plus their original offering price, it is much too early to forecast a trend. It remains to be seen whether conscious focus on stated policies and objectives, specific segments of the industry, specific properties, or the time when a profit should be realized and the asset liquidated will ultimately result in higher profits for the investor or impose a disadvantageous inflexibility upon business operations. . . .

Securities and Exchange Commn. v. W. J. Howey Co.
328 U.S. 293 (1946)

MR. JUSTICE MURPHY delivered the opinion of the Court.

This case involves the application of §2(1) of the Securities Act of 1933 to an offering of units of a citrus grove development coupled with a contract for cultivating, marketing and remitting the net proceeds to the investor.

The Securities and Exchange Commission instituted this action to restrain the respondents from using the mails and instrumentalities of

T a b l e 13-1

Securitization of Real Estate Equity

Direct Ownership-Styled Benefits

Private Limited Partnership

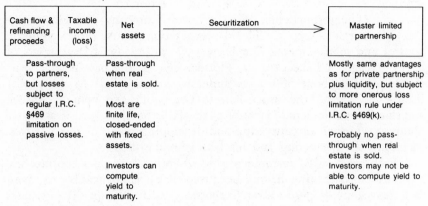

Cash flow & refinancing proceeds	Taxable income (loss)	Net assets		Master limited partnership
Pass-through to partners, but losses subject to regular I.R.C. §469 limitation on passive losses.	Pass-through when real estate is sold. Most are finite life, closed-ended with fixed assets. Investors can compute yield to maturity.		Securitization →	Mostly same advantages as for private partnership plus liquidity, but subject to more onerous loss limitation rule under I.R.C. §469(k). Probably no pass-through when real estate is sold. Investors may not be able to compute yield to maturity.

Indirect Ownership-Styled Benefits

S Corporation

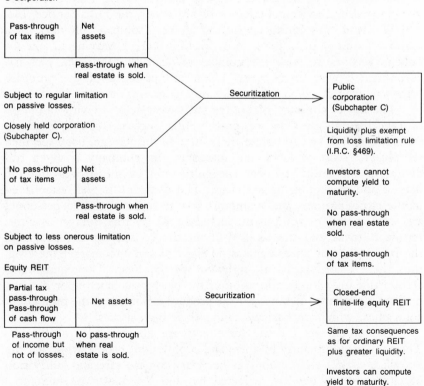

Pass-through of tax items	Net assets

Pass-through when real estate is sold.

Subject to regular limitation on passive losses.

Closely held corporation (Subchapter C).

No pass-through of tax items	Net assets

Pass-through when real estate is sold.

Subject to less onerous limitation on passive losses.

Securitization →

Public corporation (Subchapter C)

Liquidity plus exempt from loss limitation rule (I.R.C. §469).

Investors cannot compute yield to maturity.

No pass-through when real estate sold.

No pass-through of tax items.

Equity REIT

Partial tax pass-through Pass-through of cash flow	Net assets

Pass-through of income but not of losses. No pass-through when real estate is sold.

Securitization →

Closed-end finite-life equity REIT

Same tax consequences as for ordinary REIT plus greater liquidity.

Investors can compute yield to maturity.

Source: M. Madison and J. Dwyer, The Law of Real Estate Financing ¶1.06A[1] (Cum. Supp. No. 2) (1989).

1197

interstate commerce in the offer and sale of unregistered and non-exempt securities in violation of §5(a) of the Act. The District Court denied the injunction, . . . and the Fifth Circuit Court of Appeals affirmed the judgment. . . . We granted certiorari. . . .

. . . The respondents, W. J. Howey Company and Howey-in-the-Hills Service, Inc., are Florida corporations under direct common control and management. The Howey Company owns large tracts of citrus acreage in Lake County, Florida. During the past several years it has planted about 500 acres annually, keeping half of the groves itself and offering the other half to the public "to help us finance additional development." Howey-in-the-Hills Service, Inc., is a service company engaged in cultivating and developing many of these groves, including the harvesting and marketing of the crops.

Each prospective customer is offered both a land sales contract and a service contract, after having been told that it is not feasible to invest in a grove unless service arrangements are made. While the purchaser is free to make arrangements with other service companies, the superiority of Howey-in-the-Hills Service, Inc., is stressed. Indeed, 85% of the acreage sold during the 3-year period ending May 31, 1943, was covered by service contracts with Howey-in-the-Hills Service, Inc.

The land sales contract with the Howey Company provides for a uniform purchase price per acre or fraction thereof, varying in amount only in accordance with the number of years the particular plot has been planted with citrus trees. Upon full payment of the purchase price the land is conveyed to the purchaser by warranty deed. . . .

The service contract, generally of a 10-year duration without option of cancellation, gives Howey-in-the-Hills Service, Inc., a leasehold interest and "full and complete" possession of the acreage. For a specified fee plus the cost of labor and materials, the company is given full discretion and authority over the cultivation of the groves and the harvest and marketing of the crops. The company is well established in the citrus business and maintains a large force of skilled personnel and a great deal of equipment, including 75 tractors, sprayer wagons, fertilizer trucks and the like. Without the consent of the company, the land owner or purchaser has no right of entry to market the crop; thus there is ordinarily no right to specific fruit. The company is accountable only for an allocation of the net profits based upon a check made at the time of picking. All the produce is pooled by the respondent companies, which do business under their own names.

The purchasers for the most part are non-residents of Florida. They are predominantly business and professional people who lack the knowledge, skill and equipment necessary for the care and cultivation of citrus trees. They are attracted by the expectation of substantial profits. . . . Many of these purchasers are patrons of a resort hotel owned and operated by the Howey Company in a scenic section adjacent to the groves. The hotel's advertising mentions the fine groves in the vicinity and the attention of the patrons is drawn to the groves as they are being escorted about the surrounding countryside. They are told that the groves are for sale; if they indicate an interest in the matter they are then given a sales talk.

It is admitted that the mails and instrumentalities of interstate commerce are used in the sale of the land and service contracts and that no registration statement or letter of notification has ever been filed with the Commission in accordance with the Securities Act of 1933 and the rules and regulations thereunder.

Section 2(1) of the Act defines the term "security" to include the commonly known documents traded for speculation or investment. This definition also includes "securities" of a more variable character, designated by such descriptive terms as "certificate of interest or participation in any profit-sharing agreement," "investment contract" and "in general, any interest or instrument commonly known as a 'security.' " The legal issue in this case turns upon a determination of whether, under the circumstances, the land sales contract, the warranty deed and the service contract together constitute an "investment contract" within the meaning of §2(1). . . .

The term "investment contract" is undefined by the Securities Act or by relevant legislative reports. But the term was common in many state "blue sky" laws in existence prior to the adoption of the federal statute and, although the term was also undefined by the state laws, it had been broadly construed by state courts so as to afford the investing public a full measure of protection. Form was disregarded for substance and emphasis was placed upon economic reality. An investment contract thus came to mean a contract or scheme for "the placing of capital or laying out of money in a way intended to secure income or profit from its employment." State v. Gopher Tire & Rubber Co., 146 Minn. 52, 56, 177 N.W. 937, 938. This definition was uniformly applied by state courts to a variety of situations where individuals were led to invest money in a common enterprise with the expectation that they would earn a profit solely through the efforts of the promoter or of some one other than themselves.

By including an investment contract within the scope of §2(1) of the Securities Act, Congress was using a term the meaning of which had been crystallized by this prior judicial interpretation. It is therefore reasonable to attach that meaning to the term as used by Congress, especially since such a definition is consistent with the statutory aims. In other words, an investment contract for purposes of the Securities Act means a contract, transaction or scheme whereby a person invests his money in a common enterprise and is led to expect profits solely from the efforts of the promoter or a third party, it being immaterial whether the shares in the enterprise are evidenced by formal certificates or by nominal interests in the physical assets employed in the enterprise. Such a definition necessarily underlies this Court's decision in S.E.C. v. Joiner Corp., 320 U.S. 344, and has been enunciated and applied many times by lower federal courts. It permits the fulfillment of the statutory purpose of compelling full and fair disclosure relative to the issuance of "the many types of instruments that in our commercial world fall within the ordinary concept of a security." H. Rep. No. 85, 73d Cong., 1st Sess., p. 11. It embodies a flexible rather than a static principle, one that is capable of adaptation to meet the countless and variable schemes devised by those who seek the use of the money of others on the promise of profits.

The transactions in this case clearly involve investment contracts as so defined. The respondent companies are offering something more than fee simple interests in land, something different from a farm or orchard coupled with management services. They are offering an opportunity to contribute money and to share in the profits of a large citrus fruit enterprise managed and partly owned by respondents. They are offering this opportunity to persons who reside in distant localities and who lack the equipment and experience requisite to the cultivation, harvesting and marketing of the citrus products. Such persons have no desire to occupy the land or to develop it themselves; they are attracted solely by the prospects of a return on their investment. Indeed, individual development of the plots of land that are offered and sold would seldom be economically feasible due to their small size. Such tracts gain utility as citrus groves only when cultivated and developed as component parts of a larger area. A common enterprise managed by respondents or third parties with adequate personnel and equipment is therefore essential if the investors are to achieve their paramount aim of a return on their investments. Their respective shares in this enterprise are evidenced by land sales contracts and warranty deeds, which serve as a convenient method of determining the investors' allocable shares of the profits. The resulting transfer of rights in land is purely incidental.

Thus all the elements of a profit-seeking business venture are present here. The investors provide the capital and share in the earnings and profits; the promoters manage, control and operate the enterprise. It follows that the arrangements whereby the investors' interests are made manifest involve investment contracts, regardless of the legal terminology in which such contracts are clothed. The investment contracts in this instance take the form of land sales contracts, warranty deeds and service contracts which respondents offer to prospective investors. And respondents' failure to abide by the statutory and administrative rules in making such offerings, even though the failure result from a bona fide mistake as to the law, cannot be sanctioned under the Act.

This conclusion is unaffected by the fact that some purchasers

choose not to accept the full offer of an investment contract by declining
to enter into a service contract with the respondents. The Securities
Act prohibits the offer as well as the sale of unregistered, non-exempt
securities.[6] Hence it is enough that the respondents merely offer the
essential ingredients of an investment contract. . . .

Reversed.

Schneider, The Elusive Definition of a Security
14 Rev. of Sec. Regulation 981-991 (1981)

Section 2(1) of the Securities Act defines the term "security." . . .
See also section 3(a)(10) of the Exchange Act; section 2(36) of the
Investment Company Act of 1940; section 202(18) of the Investment
Advisors Act of 1940.

All of the definitions in section 2 of the Securities Act and in the
other federal securities statutes are preceded by the preamble "unless
the context otherwise requires." This "rubber" clause has been of
material import in a number of cases. See, e.g., Exchange National
Bank of Chicago v. Touche Ross & Co., 544 F.2d 1126 (2d Cir. 1976)
(Friendly, J.), where the word "requires" was stressed, and the burden
of showing this "requirement" was placed upon the party asserting
that the statutory language should not be followed literally. . . .

As a practical matter, it is likely that the inadequacy of disclosure
or the existence of fraud affecting the transaction will militate toward
the finding of a "security." For example, fraud tainting the offering
seems to have influenced courts in the context of pyramid sales and
multi-level distributorship programs. One court has characterized such
a program as an "egregious promotional scheme." SEC v. Koscot
Interplanetary, Inc., 497 F.2d 473, 486 (5th Cir. 1974). . . .

In certain borderline areas, where there was a perceived need to
protect investors, separate federal and/or state legislation has been passed,
modeled in some respects after the disclosure provisions of the securities
laws, to address particular situations. . . .

The sales pitch of the promoter is of great significance in determining whether the investment is a security. Where investment and
economic features or tax benefits are stressed, this militates in favor of
finding a security. . . .

Where the seller attracts the buyer by offering assets or facilities

---

6. The registration requirements of §5 refer to sales of securities. Section 2(3)
defines "sale" to include every "attempt or offer to dispose of, or solicitation of an
offer to buy," a security for value.

for the buyer's individual use or consumption, this generally militates toward finding no security. For example, stock in an apartment co-op was held to be not a security, even though the owner could realize a gain or loss on the eventual sale of his unit, since the purchaser was motivated primarily toward obtaining housing in which to live. Grenadier v. Spitz, 537 F.2d 612 (2d Cir. 1976). The balance may tip the other way, however, with respect to vacation or resort area real estate where the sales pitch is to participate in a rental arrangement so that the purchaser of the unit can generate sufficient operating income to cover costs and can occupy the property himself for a portion of the year on an essentially cost-free basis.

The motive of the buyer — which is probably determined in large part from the sales pitch of the seller — is also very important. If he is oriented toward making an investment for a financial return, this militates toward finding a security. If he is oriented toward acquiring something for his own use or consumption, or if he enters a relationship (e.g., employment) where the investment aspects are not a dominant consideration, this militates toward finding no security.

The more investors there are in a parallel situation, the more likely it is that a security will be found.

[In] SEC v. W. J. Howey Co. . . . the Supreme Court defined "investment contract" in terms of four factors (although there was also other broader language in the case):

> [A]n investment contract for purposes of the Securities Act means a contract, transaction or scheme whereby a person [1] invests his money [2] in a common enterprise and [3] is led to expect profits [4] solely from the efforts of the promoter or a third party. . . .

The Court in *Howey* stated that the definition of securities "embodies a flexible rather than a static principle, one that is capable of adaptation to meet the countless and variable schemes devised by those who seek the use of the money of others on the promise of profits." 328 U.S. at 299. While most of the cases continue to recite the four-prong *Howey* test, each of the factors has been eroded in at least some contexts.

(1) It is quite clear that the investor need not invest *"money."* The investor may contribute a note, other securities, or assets or property of almost any nature in a transaction, and can still receive a "security" in return. . . . Probably anything constituting legal consideration in a contract law sense would suffice.

(2) The *"common enterprise"* test suggests by its plain meaning a number of investors who stand in a similar relationship to a business in which they invest in common — so called "horizontal commonality," which is illustrated by multiple shareholders or debentureholders of an issuing corporation.

(3) The "expectation of profits" need not be in the form of a normal investment return. The "profit" can be in the form of the use of recreational facilities that the investor finances, occupancy of vacation real estate, etc. The expected "profit" may also be in the form of capital appreciation when an asset, rather than an interest in an ongoing business, is sold. See Aldrich v. McCulloch Properties, Inc., 627 F.2d 1036 (10th Cir. 1980).

(4) The requirement that profits be realized *"solely from the efforts of the promoter or a third party"* has been very much eroded in the pyramid sales cases, where it is clear that the investor himself is expected to contribute significantly to the profit potential.

III. SOME SPECIFICS

. . . A. *Notes, Other Evidences of Indebtedness, and Participations Therein.* There are many cases dealing with various forms of indebtedness that may or may not be evidenced by a promissory note. While the term "note" is included in the definition of security, many of the cases have held that notes in the context of normal commercial transactions are not securities within the contemplation of the securities laws. Typically, the cases involve attempts to invoke the antifraud provisions rather than a challenge to the nonregistration of the note.

Cases reach a variety of results and articulate a number of approaches, including: a "commercial"/"investment" dichotomy; a "risk capital" test; a literal approach; and a "strong family resemblance" test. E.g., United American Bank of Nashville v. Gunter, 620 F.2d 1108 (5th Cir. 1980) (bank loan to an individual for the purpose of purchasing stock, secured by shares purchased, was not a security); AMFAC Mortgage Corp. v. Arizona Mall of Tempe, Inc., 583 F.2d 426 (9th Cir. 1978) (no security found when "risk capital" test applied to promissory note between mortgage company and shopping center builder); Exchange National Bank of Chicago v. Touche Ross & Co., 544 F.2d 1126 (2d Cir. 1976) (subordinated loan to a brokerage firm found to be a security in reliance on the "strong family resemblance" test); Emisco Industries, Inc. v. Pro's Inc., 543 F.2d 38 (7th Cir. 1976) (note given for purchase of business assets was not a security); Great Western Bank & Trust v. Kotz, 532 F.2d 1252 (9th Cir. 1976) (bank loan was not a security); Lino v. City Investing Co., 487 F.2d 689 (3d Cir. 1973) (a note given for a commercial franchise was not a security); Banco Nacional de Costa Rica v. Bremar Holdings Corp., 492 F. Supp. 364 (S.D.N.Y. 1980) (short-term notes given to a financier to obtain initial "bridge" financing toward the purchase of equipment were securities — applying the 2d Circuit "strong family resemblance" test); Rispo v. Spring Lake Mews, Inc., 485 F. Supp. 462 (E.D. Pa. 1980) (short-term note coupled with bonus of stock was not a security); SEC

v. Diversified Industries Inc., 465 F. Supp. 104 (D.D.C. 1979) (long-term note given by a company to purchase investment real estate from a trust affiliated with an insider was a security — containing a good summary of various prior decisions). . . .

Cases have divided on whether certificates of deposit issued by commercial banks and savings institutions are securities. Weaver v. Marine Bank, 637 F.2d 157 (3d Cir. 1980), [rev'd, 102 S. Ct. 1220 (1982)] (certificate of deposit insured by a commercial bank was a security); Bellah v. First National Bank of Hereford, 495 F.2d 1109 (5th Cir. 1974) (contra); . . .

Participations in a commercial note or certificate of deposit may themselves be a separate "security" issued by the first-tier creditor, who in turn divides his interest in the note or certificate among other participants. The participation may be a security even if the underlying note arises in a commercial transaction with the first-tier creditor and is not a security. Lehigh Valley Trust Co. v. Central National Bank of Jacksonville, 409 F.2d 989 (5th Cir. 1969). . . . But participation interests in a loan were deemed not to be a security in other cases. See American Fletcher Mortgage Co. v. U.S. Steel Credit Corp., 635 F.2d 1247 (7th Cir. 1980). . . .

C. *Partnership Interests and Joint Ventures.* Limited partnership interests are generally classified as securities. For most purposes, a general partnership interest is not treated as a security. However, when a general partner is expected to be a passive investor who will not participate in the management of the business, it may be argued that his interest is a security. *Marlin Law,* avail. June 30, 1980, 562 Sec. Reg. & L. Rep. (BNA) C-3; *Brentwood Village Apartments, Ltd.,* avail. June 20, 1980, 561 Sec. Reg. & L. Rep. (BNA) at C-1 (on reconsideration). Conversely, it might be argued that the owner of a limited partnership interest does not have a security if he is actively involved in the management of the business in fact — e.g., if he is also a general partner. See Frazier v. Manson, 651 F.2d 1078 (5th Cir. 1981). . . . Although interests in joint ventures generally are not securities, they may constitute securities in some instances. See Williamson v. Tucker, 632 F.2d 579 (5th Cir. 1980); [McLish v. Harris Farms, Inc., 507 F. Supp. 1075 (E.D. Cal. 1980) (joint venture in cattle sales and feed-lot operation)].

NOTES AND QUESTIONS

1. *Master Limited Partnerships.* In contrast to a typical private limited partnership, most master limited partnerships are not highly leveraged and are income- (rather than tax-) oriented, and their investment shares (called "depositary receipts") are traded in relatively

small denominations on the stock exchanges, which makes the shares affordable for the small investor and offers the small investor the kind of liquidity that is not available to the interest-holder who invests in the more traditional privately held limited partnership.

    a.   In Comparison to a Publicly Held Corporation.   In contrast to a publicly held corporation (as explained at Chapter 2B, note 7diii), deductible losses can be passed through directly to the partners and thus the earnings of the partnership are not subject to double taxation. Moreover, in the case of an ordinary Subchapter C corporation (as opposed to a Subchapter S corporation), which must compute its earnings and profits to determine what portion of its distributions are taxable as dividends to the distributee shareholders, the corporation must use a relatively slow 40-year cost recovery period to determine the amount of depreciation for purposes of computing its earnings and profits (as opposed to its taxable income); therefore, the shareholders are less able to shelter their cash distributions from immediate taxation than are the distributee partners in an MLP. See I.R.C. §§312, 316, 168(g)(2), 312(k)(3).

    . b.   In Comparison to an Equity REIT.   Likewise, in a tax comparison between the MLP and its closest analogue, the equity REIT, the MLP fares well because while a REIT can avoid double taxation of its earnings by disgorging them and making distributions to its shareholders, a REIT is not a conduit for tax purposes like a partnership is and therefore its tax losses cannot be passed through to its shareholders. I.R.C. §857(b). Furthermore, limitations are imposed on equity REITs with respect to assets, income, and distributions. For example, 75 percent of the value of a REIT's total assets must consist of real estate, cash items, and government securities. I.R.C. §856(c)(5)(A). In addition, at least 95 percent of the REIT's gross income must be derived from passive sources of income such as dividends, interest, and real estate rentals and at least 75 percent of the gross income must be derived from passive *real estate* sources such as real estate rentals, mortgage interest, abatement and refunds of local property taxes, and gains from the sale of certain real estate assets. I.R.C. §§856(c)(2), 856(c)(3). However, for purposes of qualifying under these tests, both percentage rentals and contingent mortgage interest (discussed at Chapter 5B3) must be geared to the gross (rather than net) income of the tenant and borrower, respectively. I.R.C. §856(d)(2)(A), 856(f)(1)(A). Moreover, in order to satisfy these income tests an equity REIT cannot manage the rental real estate it owns other than by means of an independent contractor from whom the REIT does not receive any compensation. I.R.C. §856(d)(2)(C). In addition, any sale of "dealer"-type property held as inventory primarily for resale to customers is a prohibited transaction; thus the gain from such a sale would be subject to a 100 percent penalty tax. I.R.C. §857(b)(6)(A). For a comprehensive

tax comparison of the MLP to an equity REIT see Winston, Choosing Between Publicly Traded Partnerships and Real Estate Investment Trusts, 2 Prac. Real Est. Law. 19 (Mar. 1986).

By contrast, the general partners in an MLP are allowed to aggressively manage and actively buy and sell the real estate that is owned by the partnership. Moreover, while the manager-advisor of a REIT is usually elected on an annual basis by the REIT shareholders, the general partners in an MLP are not as readily replaceable because of the constraints imposed by the ULPA on the limited partners' right to participate in the management of the partnership. According to the October 1986 Real Estate Marketing Report prepared by Salomon Brothers, MLPs may have surpassed REITs as the preferred vehicle for securitizing real estate based on the number of new registrations for both kinds of equity programs. However, as reflected by the data in Table 13-2, the Tax Reform Act of 1986 has severely curtailed the number of new syndication offerings by sponsors of MLPs and other publicly held limited partnership syndications.

c. *The Status of the MLP as a Passive Income Generator ("PIG").* As observed at Chapter 2B, note 3, prior to the Revenue Act of 1987 small individual investors in large real estate rental activities (especially those with adjusted incomes over $150,000 who were not qualified for the annual $25,000 passive loss allowance under I.R.C. §469(i)) had been purchasing shares in income-oriented MLPs to both diversify their investment portfolios and to obtain passive income that could be used to offset their current and carryover losses from rental real estate and other passive activities. However, the Treasury Department had been prompting Congress to enact legislation that would have taxed publicly held limited partnerships as corporations. Finally, as a compromise, Congress enacted a new Code provision (as part of the Revenue Act of 1987) that subjects certain publicly traded partnerships (PTPs) whose investment shares are traded on an established securities market (as are the depositary receipts of a typical MLP) or are readily tradable on a secondary market to corporate taxation even though such partnership passes muster and is not deemed to be an "association" under Treas. Reg. §7701 (as discussed at Chapter 2B, note 7diii). I.R.C. §7704(b), as added by §10211 of the Revenue Act of 1987. However, to placate the real estate industry, a real estate PTP was excepted from double taxation and the other onerous aspects of corporate taxation provided that 90 percent or more of the partnership's gross income for each taxable year is from real estate rentals, interest, gain from the sale of real estate, and other passive sources of real estate income. Just as with an equity REIT, percentage rentals and contingent mortgage interest geared to net income (as opposed to gross income) do not qualify under the 90 percent test because such income is not sufficiently passive in nature. Nevertheless, the Revenue Act of 1987 also created a new,

Real Estate Securities Sales 1984 to 1988 ($ Millions)

	1984	1985	1986	1987	1988
Public Real Estate Partnerships (a)	5,300	6,900	7,320	4,406	4,084
Identified Private Real Estate Partnerships (b)	NA	NA	2,052	1,245	894
Master Limited Partnerships	(a)	(a)	(a)	2,269	333
Real Estate Investment Trusts (d)	2,700	4,300	4,673	3,371	2,808
Total $	8,400(c)	10,200(c)	14,045(c)	11,290(c)	8,119

Notes: (a) Master Limited Partnerships were not included as a separate group until 1987.
(b) Identified sponsors include a large sample of the biggest private syndicators.
(c) If private partnership sales, which likely exceeded 1986 figures, were included, then total securities sales in these years would be higher.
(d) Data for 1984 to 1987 revised by source organization.

Source: "Roulac's Strategic Real Estate," published by the Roulac Real Estate Consulting Group of Deloitte Haskins+Sells, in 6 Real Est. Fin. 8 (Spring 1988).

Syndication Review

As of March 1, 1988, there were 157 publicly offered real estate limited partnerships open for investment, sponsored by 115 different general partners.

Type of Program	No. of Programs Available	Average Size (millions)[1]	Average Front-End Fees[2]	Average Holding Period (years)
Unleveraged	66	$47.3	17.5%	6.6- 9.9
Low Leverage Equity[3]	19	$36.0	18.3%	6.2- 9.0
Moderate Leverage Equity[4]	27	$21.4	21.1%	6.0- 9.1
High Leverage Equity[5]	20	$39.2	22.5%	6.3- 9.7
Subtotal: All Equity	132	$39.2	19.1%	6.4- 9.6
Mortgage Loan	25	$76.0	13.3%	9.1-12.1
All Programs	157	$45.0	18.1%	6.8-10.0

1. Excludes "greenshoe" option.
2. Based on general partner estimates; includes organization costs, offering expenses, and acquisition fees and expenses.
3. General partner estimates leverage will average lower than 50%.
4. General partner estimates leverage will average between 50% and 65%.
5. General partner estimates leverage will average 65% or higher.

Source: 5 Real Est. Fin. 13 (Spring 1988).

more stringent rule for the deductibility of passive losses generated by a PTP by requiring partners to treat their distributive shares of net income from a PTP as "portfolio" (rather than passive) income, to segregate their losses from the particular PTP (so that they cannot be used to offset income from another PTP), and to carry the losses forward to be used exclusively against their shares of income from the same PTP in future years. I.R.C. §469(k), as added by §10212(a) of the Revenue Act of 1987. In effect, the new rule destroyed the status of a real estate PTP as a passive income generator for purposes of offsetting outside passive losses.

However, Notice 88-75, announced by the Internal Revenue Service in Internal Revenue Bulletin 1988-27, suggests that an MLP that is not deemed to be a PTP can retain its status as a passive income generator. While the Temporary Treasury Regulations dealing with the application of I.R.C. §469 to PTPs are still pending (Temp. Reg. §1.469-10T), the Notice announced three safe harbor rules for avoiding PTP status: the private placement exemption (where the partnership has not been registered under the Securities Act of 1933); the "5 percent safe harbor" (where the sum of the percentage interests that are disposed of during the taxable year does not exceed 5 percent of the total interest in partnership capital or profits); and the "2 percent safe harbor" (where the sum of the percentage interests disposed of during the taxable year is only 2 percent and all transactions that use a "qualified matching service" (such as an MLP that qualifies for trading in the North American Securities Dealers Automated Quotations System, described in the excerpt by Ross) are not counted in making the calculation). Since Notice 88-75 provides guidelines that are straightforward and somewhat flexible, it is possible that newly organized real estate MLPs (and, a fortiori, both private and publicly held partnerships that are not MLPs) will be able to resuscitate their status as PIGs by restructuring their offering plans and marketing activities so as to conform to the new guidelines. Moreover, the Notice expressly provides that the safe harbor rules will be endorsed by the future Regulations to be issued under I.R.C. §§469(k)(2) and 7704(b). See generally Banoff, Avoiding Publicly Traded Partnership Status: Living and Dying with Notice 88-75, 66 Taxes 561 (Aug. 1988).

For additional background on real estate MLPs see generally Brandzel and Blumenthal, Master Limited Partnerships in Light of the 1986 Tax Reform Act, 7 Real Est. Sec. J. 67 (1986); Chu, Financing Real Estate in the Public Securities Market, 1 Real Est. Fin. 29 (Winter 1985); Hamilton, Transferring Limited Partnership Units on the Secondary Market, 3 Real Est. Fin. 15 (Fall 1986); Slater, Publicly Traded Limited Partnership: An Emerging Financial Alternative to the Public Corporation, 39 Bus. Law. 709 (Feb. 1984).

2. Finite-Life Closed-End REITs. As suggested in the excerpt by Ross and Klein, the tax shelter advantages of partnerships over REITs have been diluted by the Tax Reform Act of 1986. Moreover, the new forms of REITs, such as the finite-life closed-end REIT (FREIT), are now offering varying and multiple tax and investment objectives in a single product. For example, in the case of a traditional equity REIT perhaps 20 to 30 percent of the cash distributions can be sheltered from immediate taxation and some of the shelter is wasted on shareholders such as pension plans and other tax-exempt investors. However, by using an innovative capital structure consisting of one class of common stock for the more daring and tax-oriented investor and another class of preferred stock for the conservative and tax-exempt investor, the new forms of REITs are able to allocate all of the tax shelter benefits (produced by depreciation), some of the cash flow, and most of the capital gain (appreciation) to the common shareholders while the preferred shareholders (such as IRAs, pension plans, and retired individuals in need of consistent and dependable monthly income) receive a preferred annual fixed rate of return on their equity investment. See generally Balch, New Twist Added to Finite-Life REITs, 1 Real Est. Fin. J. 77 (Winter 1986).

In addition, to further enhance the investment appeal of REIT shares to the Wall Street investor, the sponsors of closed-end FREITs have managed to combine the liquidity of REIT shares (which are publicly traded as are corporate securities and whose performance is monitored by the National Association of REITs (NAREIT)) with the equity features of the direct ownership of real estate and the direct ownership-styled benefits available to Subchapter S shareholders and to partners in most private limited partnerships. See Table 13-1, supra. In contrast to an ordinary Subchapter C corporation and most multiple-project publicly held partnerships (including MLPs), the sponsors of FREITs are requiring the consent of existing investors before additional shares can be offered (to prevent their equity from being diluted) and agreeing to sell and liquidate the REIT's underlying assets within a stipulated period of time so that the shareholders will be able to compute their yield (internal rate of return) to maturity and directly benefit from appreciation in the value of the REIT's underlying assets. In this respect the FREIT resembles a private limited partnership. While the limited partners merely own an indirect interest in the underlying real estate (because the partnership itself holds the legal title), they nevertheless receive direct ownership-style benefits and are able to compute their yield to maturity. See Table 13-1 and discussion at Chapter 2B, note 7di.

Assume that you are a real estate attorney and one of your clients asks your advice about investing in either a real estate MLP or an equity REIT. After reviewing Table 13-1 and the prior excerpts, what questions would you ask your client before giving him or her your investment advice? Suppose the client is a high-bracket individual taxpayer with carryover passive losses from a pre-1986 tax shelter investment? In your opinion, which seems to be the better ownership vehicle for securitizing real estate, the MLP or the equity REIT? Why?

3. *The Regulation of Real Estate Investments as Securities.*

a. Definition of a Security. The term "security" in §(2)(1) of the Securities Act of 1933 has been liberally construed to include modern forms of real estate investment in response to the broad protection envisioned by Congress. Subsumed under the definition of security is the term "investment contract," which, in the opinion of the Supreme Court in Securities and Exchange Commission v. W. J. Howey Co., includes any "scheme whereby a person invests his money in a common enterprise and is led to expect profits solely from the efforts of the promoter or third party." Thus, the term "security" encompasses such interests as an investment share held by a limited partner or passive co-venturer in a joint venture. See Goodman v. Epstein, 582 F.2d 388 (7th Cir. 1978), cert. denied, 440 U.S. 939 (1979), where limited partners' interests under Illinois law were held to be securities within the protective scope of the federal securities laws; Hirsch v. DuPont, 396 F. Supp. 1214 (S.D.N.Y. 1975), affd., 553 F.2d 750 (2d Cir. 1977), where interests of limited partners, but not general partners, were held to be securities for purposes of antifraud provisions of the federal securities laws (dictum); Securities Act Release No. 4877, at 1 (1967), 17 C.F.R. §231.4877. Based on the approach taken by the Court in *Howey,* which, if any, of the following transactions should be treated as the offering of a security?

1. the public sale of condominium units involving a so-called rental pool arrangement, whereby the promoter undertakes to rent the units on behalf of any absentee owner (see Securities Act Release No. 5347 (Jan. 4, 1972));
2. the offering of investment shares in a real estate investment trust (see Securities Act Release Nos. 33-4298, 34-6419, and 1C-3140, 25 Fed. Reg. 12177 (1960));
3. the sale of stock in a cooperative housing corporation where some of the purchasers hope to immediately resell their co-op units for a substantial profit (see United Housing Foundation v. Forman, 421 U.S. 837 (1975) and Grenadier v. Spitz, 537 F.2d 612 (2d Cir.), cert. denied, 429 U.S. 1009 (1976));
4. the lease of some space in a large shopping center where the lessor exerts some management control over the lessee's business and receives a rental geared to the net income of the

lessee ("percentage rental") (see Klein v. Arlen Realty & Development Corp., 410 F. Supp. 1261 (E.D. Pa. 1976) and Cordas v. Specialty Restaurants, 470 F. Supp. 780 (D. Or. 1979));

5. a participating mortgage featuring a kicker geared to the borrower's net income (see Vargo, Equity Participation by the Institutional Lender: The Security Status Issue, 26 S. Tex. L.J. 225 (1985));

6. the sale of time shares in a resort condominium where each purchaser, who owns his or her interest in fee simple, can only resell the interest back to the developer at a price equal to the original purchase price less a discount and where the aggregate price of the fractional interests exceeds by three times the market value of whole units that are being sold in comparable condominiums (compare Securities Act Release No. 33-6253 (1980) with SEC no-action letter re The Innisfree Corp. (May 7, 1973);

7. the sale and leaseback of commercial real estate to a single purchaser-lessor, who purchases the property based on the anticipated profits as estimated by the seller-lessee (compare United States v. Jones, 712 F.2d 1316 (9th Cir.), cert. denied sub nom. Webber v. United States, 464 U.S. 986 (1983), with Hart v. Pulte Homes of Michigan Corp., 735 F.2d 1000 (6th Cir. 1984));

8. the issuance of a certificate of deposit by a commercial bank or thrift organization (compare Weaver v. Marine Bank, 637 F.2d 157 (3d Cir. 1980), revd., 455 U.S. 551 (1982), with Bellah v. First National Bank of Hereford, 495 F.2d 1109 (5th Cir. 1974)); and

9. the interest of a passive investor who is a general partner in a joint venture as compared to the interest of an active investor who is a limited partner in a joint venture (see Williamson v. Tucker, 632 F.2d 579 (5th Cir. 1980), cert. denied, 454 U.S. 897 (1981)).

b.   The Private Offering Exemption.   Section 4(2) of the Securities Act of 1933 ("the Act") provides that the registration requirement of the Act shall not apply to "transactions by an issuer not involving any public offering." Observe that the "private offering" exemption, like the "intrastate" and "small offering" exemptions discussed below, applies only to transactions and not to the securities themselves. This means that even if the issuer gains exemption from registration by complying with the requirements of a particular exemption, the purchaser nevertheless must obtain its own exemption if one is available in the event it decides to reoffer, subdivide, or otherwise dispose of the securities. Both the SEC and the courts have applied a facts-and-circumstances test to determine whether a transaction is a public or a private offering. In light of the Act's purpose "to protect investors by promoting full disclosure of information thought necessary to informed investment decisions," the Supreme Court, in Securities and Exchange Commission v. Ralston Purina, 346 U.S. 119 (1953), devised a two-pronged test under §4(2) that requires with respect to all offerees that: (1) they be able "to fend for themselves" (346 U.S. at 125); and (2) they "have access to the type of information that registration would disclose." 346 U.S. at 127. Other factors deemed relevant under the case law are: (1) the number of offerees (as well as their degree of sophistication); (2) the size and manner of the offering; and (3) the relationship of the offerees to the issuer.

To proffer guidance to issuers and investors, on March 8, 1982 the Securities and Exchange Commission (SEC) promulgated Regulation D (SEC Release No. 33-6389), which consists of the following Rules: (1) Rules 501 and 502, which stipulate general conditions and definitions for the exemption under Regulation D; (2) Rule 503, which provides for a uniform notice of sale form, Form D, which must be used for transactions that are exempt under Regulation D; (3) Rule 504 (superseding Rule 240) and Rule 505 (superseding Rule 242), which respectively qualify offerings and sales of $500,000 or less during any 12-month period and sales of $5 million or less during any 12-month period to no more than 35 purchasers plus an unlimited number of "accredited investors." In the case of Rule 504, the $500,000 aggregate limit is increased to $1 million if the security is registered under the applicable state blue sky law. 17 C.F.R. §230.504(b)(2)(i). Neither rule imposes any sophistication or suitability standard for nonaccredited investors (other than the suitability standards imposed on broker-dealers and by state blue sky laws). However, unless the Federal Reserve Board exempts offerings from its restrictions on installment payments (Regulations T, C, U, and X), such offerings must be paid for in single lump-sum payments. While certain information must be furnished to nonaccredited investors under Rule 505, no specific information or disclosure requirement is mandated by Rule 504. (4) Like Rule 505, Rule 506 (which supersedes Rule 146) permits sales to 35 purchasers plus an unlimited number of accredited investors. In contrast to Rule 505, there is no limitation on the dollar amount of the offering; however, the same informational requirement applies to nonaccredited investors under Rule 506. In addition, under Rule 506 each actual purchaser (as opposed to a mere offeree who does not purchase) who does not meet the criteria for an accredited investor must be qualified as a person who (either alone or with his or her purchaser representative) has such knowledge and experience in financial and business matters that he or she is capable of evaluating the risks and merits of the prospective investment. In order to obviate the need for such a subjective determination by the issuer, Regulation D adopts the concept of an "accredited investor," which includes, among other categories, any natural person whose net worth at the time of purchase is at least $1 million (Rule 501(a)(6)); any person who purchases at least $150,000 worth of the securities being offered where the purchase price does not exceed 20 percent of the investor's net worth at the time of sale (Rule 501(a)(5)); or any natural person who has had income in excess of $200,000 in each of the last two years and who reasonably anticipates an income of $200,000 in the current year (Rule 501(a)(7)). Finally, observe that Regulation D is not exclusive in scope, so a transaction that does not qualify under the Regulation may nonetheless be exempt under §4(2) of the act as a private offering if it meets the somewhat vague requirements imposed by case law. For an in-depth discussion of Regulation D see Haft and Fass, Federal Securities Laws and Their Impact on Tax Sheltered Investments, 1988 Tax Sheltered Investments Handbook §4.03.

c. *The Intrastate Exemption.* Section 3(a) of the Act provides an exemption for securities offered and sold only to persons who reside in the same state where the issuer is a resident and doing business. Under Rule 147 (SEC Securities Act Release No. 5450 (Jan. 7, 1974)), if the issuer is a corporation, limited partnership, or REIT, it will be deemed to be a resident of the state in which it is organized and will be deemed to be doing business within a state where: (1) at least 80 percent of its gross revenues are derived from the operation of a business or property or from rendering of services within the state and at least 80 percent of its assets are situated in such state; (2) at least 80 percent of its net proceeds from the sale of its securities are used in connection with its business or property or rendering of services within such state; and (3) its principal office is located within such state. As offerees, individuals must have their principal residence within the same state, and business organizations must have their principal office in the same state in which the issuer resides and is doing business. Offerees who purchase are prohibited from reselling the securities to any nonresident while the securities are being offered for sale and during the nine-month period following the last sale by the issuer.

Suppose that a transaction qualifies under Rule 147 and that the issuer explicitly provides in all of its offerings and promotional materials that the transaction is limited to residents of the state in which the issuer is organized and doing business and the issuer requires that each purchaser execute an affidavit attesting that such person is a resident of the state. Would the exemption be lost if it is later discovered that one of the original purchasers is not a resident of the state? See SEC no-action letter re Winthrop Financial Co., Inc. (June 25, 1982). As counsel to the issuer, can you think of any protective devices you might employ to assure your client that the exemption will not be lost because of a resale of the stock to a nonresident by one of the original purchasers? See SEC no-action letter re Intuit Telecom, Inc. (April 26, 1982).

    d. The Small Offering Exemption. Under Section 3(b) of the Act and pursuant to Regulation A, an exemption is also available for offerings of $1,500,000 or less, provided that the issuer files a short-form registration statement, or "offering circular," with the regional SEC office containing the financial information and disclosures required by Regulation A. 17 C.F.R. §§230.251 to 230.264.

    e. Antifraud and Criminal Liability. Even if the offering is entirely exempt from any federal registration requirement under the private or intrastate exemptions, the participants in the transaction may be subject to both civil and criminal liability if they should commit fraud or make any misrepresentation in connection with the offer or sale of a security. See Securities Act of 1933 §§12(2), 17; Securities Exchange Act of 1934 §10(b). See Phillips and Hanback, Remedies for Defrauded Purchasers, 12 Rev. Sec. Reg. 953 (Mar. 28, 1979); Brodsky, A Practical Guide to Tax Shelter Litigation (1978).

    f. State Regulation of Securities. In addition to federal regulation of securities, most jurisdictions have enacted statutes that both regulate the offering of securities within the state and sometimes also protect purchasers of certain types of real estate interests (such as condominiums and cooperatives). See, e.g., N.Y. Gen. Bus. Law §352-e (McKinney 1990); Cal. Bus. & Prof. Code §11000 et seq. (Deering 1991). State statutes regulating the sale of securities are commonly referred to as "blue sky" laws because they are designed to prevent "speculative schemes which have no more basis than so many feet of blue sky." Hall v. Geiger-Jones Co., 242 U.S. 539 (1917). Most of these statutes provide for registration of securities by the issuer and for the licensing of dealers and salespersons. The Uniform Securities Act (as approved by the National Conference of Commissioners on Uniform State Laws) has been the prototype for many of these statutes. While §402(b) of the Act contains a quasi-private offering exemption, any offering that qualifies under §4(2) of the federal Securities Act of 1933 may nonetheless fall within the pale of a particular state statute; hence, the only safe course of action for the issuer's counsel is to canvass the law of the state where the transaction will occur. In that regard, there are a number of looseleaf services, such as the CCH Blue Sky Law Reporter, that explain and detail the important provisions of any particular state statute.

    For further study on securities regulation see Andrews, Basics of Real Estate Syndications, 12 St. Mary's L.J. 1027 (1981); Mosberg, ed., Real Estate Syndicate Offerings Handbook (1976); Fass and Wittner, Real Estate Securities, 12 Rev. Sec. Reg. 921 (May 23, 1979); Glazier, Securities Registration Exemption Structures and the Texas Real Estate

Syndicator: Providing a Ladder of Professional Development, 20 S. Tex. L. Rev. 49 (1980); Rifkind and Borton, SEC Registration of Real Estate Interests: An Overview, 27 Bus. Law. 649 (1972); Simonson, Regulation D and Real Estate Limited Partnerships, 13 Real Est. Rev. 55 (Fall 1983); Stiles, Blackacre as a Shelf of Securities: Real Estate Syndication, 23 Drake L. Rev. 483 (1974); Wharton, Application of Federal and State Security Regulation to Real Estate Transactions, 12 S. Tex. L.J. 231 (1971); Comment, Regulation of Real Estate Syndications: An Overview, 49 Wash. L. Rev. 137 (1973); Comment, Securities Regulation of Real Estate Programs, 27 Ark. L. Rev. 651 (1973).

B.   THE TREND TOWARD SECURITIZATION OF COMMERCIAL REAL ESTATE IN THE SECONDARY MORTGAGE MARKET

In Chapter 1 it was observed how a real estate borrower such as Dan Developer can use component financing techniques to increase his loan amount and thereby leverage his cost of acquiring and constructing some income-producing real estate. For example, by severing the land from the improvements and financing each component separately, it is possible for the sum of the financing *parts* (e.g., sale and leaseback of the land plus leasehold mortgage on land and fee mortgage on the building) to be greater for Dan than the *whole* (e.g., fee mortgage on the land and building). See Chapter 8B1, note 2. Another example of how Dan might increase his overall financing by splitting the land from the improvements would be a high-ratio purchase money mortgage from the seller of the land, who then subordinates its lien on the fee so Dan can obtain a first mortgage loan from some institutional lender (such as Ace Insurance Co.) to finance the cost of both the land and the improvements. See Chapter 9B, note 5a. Likewise, on the equity side of real estate is a technique called the "sandwich" lease whereby fee ownership of real estate can be carved into separate leasehold estates. Each leaseholder would be entitled to a fixed rate of return. The lessee last in line, who owns the "operating position" and who leases the space to occupancy tenants, would be entitled to any residual cash flows. As a consequence of such componentization, it is possible to expand the equity, or ownership, pie; for example, in the hypothetical at Chapter 8C, it was demonstrated how the rate of return on a one-million-dollar equity investment could increase from 11 percent ($1,100,000 ÷ $10,000,000) to an infinite rate of return ($100,000 ÷ 0) by using the Hawaiian technique.

Over the past few years real estate innovators have begun to take the next logical step, namely, the securitization of commercial real estate. If the land can be severed from the improvements and the legal possession severed from the fee ownership as a way of expanding the debt and equity pie, then why not fragment the debt and equity interests themselves into small liquid segments that resemble publicly held stock so that such investment shares can be marketed in the public rather than private securities markets? As noted at Chapter 13A, note 1, supra, this has already happened on the equity side of real estate with the advent of the master limited partnership and the new equity REIT formats such as the closed-end finite-life REIT. Moreover, the ability to both prioritize payments (and risk of loss) between senior and junior interest-holders and sever cash flow returns from tax benefits and residuals has induced institutions as well as private individuals to invest in real estate equities by means of these securitized vehicles.

However, the pace of securitization has been slower on the debt side of commercial real estate. The notion that mortgage debt could be fragmented and securitized in the form of so-called mortgage-backed securities (MBSs) as a way of linking the securities and mortgage markets originated in the secondary mortgage market[1] for residential mortgages back in 1970.[2] However, commercial mortgage-backed bonds

1. The difference between the primary and secondary mortgage markets is that in the primary mortgage market a lender who originates a mortgage loan retains the loan as an asset in its investment portfolio and usually collects the amortization and interest payments during the term of the loan. By contrast, if the lender sells the loan, in whole or in part, to another lender, investor, or governmental agency, the transaction is deemed to be a resale, or "second sale" — hence the term "secondary mortgage market."

The traditional secondary mortgage market is a financial network that connects mortgage originators who lend money to home buyers with government-related and private investors who purchase these residential mortgage loans. By selling the loans they originate to federally sponsored agencies such as the Federal Home Loan Mortgage Corporation (Freddie Mac) and the Federal National Mortgage Association (Fannie Mae), thrift institutions and other lenders have been able to replenish their supply of loanable funds and originate new loans (both commercial real estate and residential loans) in the primary mortgage market. For a comprehensive discussion of the residential secondary mortgage market see M. Dennis, Residential Mortgage Lending (1985); The Handbook of Mortgage Banking: A Guide to the Secondary Mortgage Market (J. Kinney and R. Garrigan eds. 1985). For a brief overview see Struck, Mortgage Backed Securities: A Primer, Pension World 16 (Feb. 1978).

2. The seminal development in the secondary mortgage market occurred in 1970, when the Government National Mortgage Association (Ginnie Mae), a full-fledged federal agency, introduced the ingenious concept of securitizing mortgage indebtedness in the form of a mortgage-backed security. Since then, these government-related agencies have shifted their emphasis from merely holding unwanted mortgage loans toward the development of mortgage instruments as securities that may be sold and resold to investors outside the traditional mortgage investment community as a way of providing much-needed liquidity for the residential mortgage market.

(CMBBs) did not appear on the public financing scene until 1985 when, for example, the $200 million public offering by Olympia & York Maiden Lane Finance Corp. demonstrated to Wall Street the potential market for these securities. But if the securitization of residential mortgages started back in 1970, why the delay in the development of the CMBB? The excerpt that follows answers this question and also attempts to explain why the trend toward securitization may someday revolutionize the way in which commercial real estate is financed in this country. Indeed, in the opinion of one commentator, given the vast opportunities in real estate the CMBB "dwarfs any other [security], including corporate debt, in terms of [its] potential size."[3]

Richards, "Gradable and Tradable": The Securitization of Commercial Real Estate Mortgages
16 Real Est. L.J. 99 (1987)

"Securitization" is the financing of real estate through the non-traditional methods of stocks and bonds — known collectively as "mortgage-backed securities" (MBSs) — in order to expand the available lending community and to use more efficient (cheaper) primary and secondary capital sources. The instrument and the secondary market continue to energize real estate finance with a spiral of innovation. In the past three years, the investment banking community has adopted this technique, long familiar in the secondary market for residential mortgages, to the financing of commercial office buildings. "Is the concept of securitizing commercial real estate a contradiction in terms, like jumbo shrimp or military intelligence? Have we bridged the gap that lies between securities, which is a liquid homogeneous product, and commercial property, which has neither of these attributes?" If so, securitization is the wave of the future; if not, it may remain only a highly specialized device available to a few borrowers with a handful of prime properties in the biggest U.S. cities.

MORTGAGES VS. SECURITIES

Institutional investors have preferred government securities and corporate bonds to mortgages because these securities were easily eval-

---

3. This observation was made by Ron DiPasquale, a senior vice president and manager of mortgage security trading at Merrill Lynch Mortgage Capital, as reported in Standard & Poor's Creditweek, Feb. 24, 1986, at 13.

uated, commonly traded, and produced a regular cash flow. Mortgages, by contrast, have been viewed as "second class" investment assets, with four significant drawbacks.

First, mortgages have historically paid both interest and principal monthly, whereas government and corporate bonds pay interest semi-annually and all principal at maturity. Since the investor must reinvest principal and interest income more frequently, transaction costs and interest rate risk are greater for mortgages, and the value assumed for the reinvestment rate is more significant.

Second, the cash flow and maturity of a mortgage are deemed more uncertain because the borrower can supplement the required monthly payments, or repay the entire loan, or default at any time. Investors, therefore, have difficulty determining the maturity and expected yield on the mortgage. The relationship between prepayments and interest rates reduces the investor's yield, whether interest rates rise or fall. When interest rates rise, prepayments fall because borrowers hold their properties longer or home buyers assume the existing mortgages when the properties are sold; the investor has less cash to reinvest at the new high rate. Similarly, when interest rates fall, prepayments increase because borrowers refinance or sell their properties. The investor then has more cash to reinvest at the new lower rate.

A third disadvantage of investing in whole mortgages in the commercial property market (and to a lesser extent in the residential property market) is that they are not homogeneous commodities (due to the uniqueness of the terms of each such mortgage and the complexity of the property securing it) and are, therefore, less marketable than conventional securities. They are regulated essentially by state and local laws that vary considerably and are parochial: An isolated downturn in a local economy or a material disaster can affect them sharply.

Finally, servicing and originating mortgages entail substantial administrative costs per dollar of investment. The cumbersome mechanics of transferring a package of mortgage loans to a new investor; the fact that "servicing" of mortgage loans (collection and processing of monthly payments, collection of delinquent payments, commencement of foreclosure, application of mortgagors' escrows to insurance premiums and real estate taxes, and provision of monthly remittances and reports) requires a large staff and data processing equipment; and the need to make detailed evaluation of credit quality of the loans all combined to make mortgage loans historically unattractive to passive investors and inhibited the development of an active secondary market, which therefore tended to attract only traditional mortgage investors, such as savings and loan associations. . . .

Because mortgages and most other receivables are subject to acceleration and prepayment or other early payment, cash flow securities have been further divided into securities as to which the investor bears the risk of early payment ("pay-through securities") and securities as to which the issuer bears that risk ("fixed-payment securities").[5]

RESIDENTIAL MORTGAGE SECURITIZATION

The securitization of residential mortgages, invented in 1970, is a now-familiar success story: Pools of mortgages for one-to-four-family homes, sold since the Great Depression by originators to financial institutions with an appetite for long-term loans, have been replaced as trading instruments by mortgage-backed securities, created when mortgages from one or more lenders are packaged together and sold to an investment house or government-sponsored agency that finances purchases by issuing securities backed by the mortgages so obtained (hence, "mortgage-backed securities").[6] . . .

The residential secondary mortgage market (according to one definition, "the congeries of institutions involved in the trading of mortgages and mortgage-backed securities") has two main functions: (1) redirecting capital within the traditional housing finance system, and (2) shifting capital from the general capital market to the housing finance system. By moving funds among traditional mortgage lenders, the secondary mortgage market helps eliminate mismatches between lenders' supply of mortgage funds and the demand they face. As inflation rose in the 1970s and volatile interest rates made it dangerous for the principal providers of housing finance — savings and loan associations, savings banks, and mortgage bankers — to finance long-term loans with short-term deposits, sales of mortgage-backed securities, much more easily accomplished than the old-style sales of mortgages themselves, provided the solution. Sales of $22.5 billion in 1978 rose to $147.9 billion in 1985 (accounting for two thirds of new residential mortgages issued that year), and of this number, $27.4 billion was in private offerings (i.e., not packaged and marketed by governmental agencies).

---

5. Sabel & Plache, "Selected Legal Aspects of Structured Mortgage and Receivable Financing," in Practising Law Institute Pub. No. B6-6744, Current Corporate Financing Techniques 1986, 547, 549 (G. Palm ed., Practising Law Institute, 1986), (hereinafter PLI Corp. Financing).

6. A detailed analysis of the various types of mortgage-backed securities and the provisions of the United States Secondary Mortgage Market Enhancement Act of 1984 (SMMEA or Enhancement Act), Pub. L. No. 98-440, 98 Stat. 1689 (1984) (codified at scattered sections of 12 U.S.C. and 15 U.S.C.), as well as a discussion of the applicable blue sky laws, can be found in . . . Lance, "Balancing Private and Public Initiatives in the Mortgage-Backed Security Market," 18 Real Prop. Prob. & Tr. J. 426 (1983); Brick, "A Primer on Mortgage-Backed Securities," 167 Bankers Mag. 44 (Jan.-Feb. 1984); Murray & Hadaway, "Mortgage-Backed Securities: An Investigation of Legal and Financial Issues," 11 J. Corp. L. 203, 220-234 (1986).

Mortgage-backed securities transactions have primarily taken the form of variations on two basic structures: (1) the outright sale of the mortgages through the issuance of mortgage pass-through certificates, or (2) issuance of debt collateralized by the mortgaged assets.

PASS-THROUGH CERTIFICATES

The first mortgage-backed securities product spawned by the new industry, "pass-through certificates," represents the beneficial ownership of a fractional undivided interest in the corpus of a passive grantor trust consisting of a fixed pool of mortgages held for the benefit of pass-through holders. Under the grantor trust (which pays no entity-level tax, and purchasers holding beneficial interests therein are taxed as if they directly held undivided interests in the mortgages held by the trust), the cash flow of the underlying mortgages (the "pass-through securities") is "passed through" by the trustee to the certificate holders on a monthly basis, and holders are entitled to a pro rata share of all interest on the mortgages and all payments and other recoveries of principal. The first and by far the largest mortgage pass-through program is sponsored by the Government National Mortgage Association (GNMA), a federal agency in the Department of Housing and Urban Development familiarly known as "Ginnie Mae." Initiated in 1970, this Ginnie Mae program provides a complete guarantee, backed by the full faith and credit of the United States, of timely receipt of all payments due on the mortgages in each pool. . . .

Privately issued pass-throughs commenced in 1977. Since that time there have been over 100 public and private issues, most of which have received AA ratings from securities-rating agencies, because of "credit supports" through mortgage pool insurance, guarantees, or other specialized types of credit enhancement. . . .

Pass-through certificates pay monthly, are subject to the prepayment behavior of the underlying mortgages, and usually have a final payment date of up to thirty years. Their long weighted average lives, final payment dates, and absence of call protection make these securities unattractive to many investors, who find them too static in response to market interest shifts in favor of lenders and too volatile in response to interest shifts in favor of borrowers.

PAY-THROUGH BONDS

Another variant of the mortgage-backed security, mortgage-backed bonds (MBBs), also known as "market value securities," are general obligations of the issuing institution for an intermediate term (five to ten years) and are almost exclusively private sector issues, heavily overcollateralized by mortgages and/or pass-through certificates, to attract traditional fixed-income investors such as pension funds, bank trust departments, and general fund managers. The issuer (a bank or savings and loan association) is entitled to all cash flows on the collateral, and the cash flows are not dedicated to the payment of the bonds but as general obligations are payable out of the issuer's general funds, and so have characteristics similar to corporate bonds or nonfinancial firms (i.e., a stated maturity, semiannual interest, and no government guarantee). Because of overcollateralization (in excess of 150 percent of the face amount of the bonds issued), most such bonds have been rated AAA by the rating agencies. . . .

The most successful tailoring, in a major evolution of the mortgage pay-through bond, is the collateralized mortgage obligation (CMO), a term first used by Freddie Mac in a June 1983 issue of debt securities, which has now become a generic description. The CMO, in its simplest form, is a pay-through bond divided into multiple classes, or tranches (generally four), with different maturities. The interest on the several classes is distributed currently to the holders of each class. Principal, however, is not paid simultaneously to holders of all classes. Instead, holders of the first tranche of bonds receive all payments until their bonds are paid in full, and then each succeeding tranche is retired. Often, the fourth tranche is made into a zero coupon bond (technically, a compound-interest bond). In order to increase the principal amount of CMOs that could be issued with shorter maturities (and correspondingly lower yields), the last tranche (the "Z bond" or "Z piece") only begins paying principal and interest after all prior maturing classes are retired. Interest accrued but not paid on the Z piece is added to its principal on each payment date and thereafter itself accrues interest.

Because CMOs have short, intermediate, and long-term maturities, they appeal to a wider range of investors. Moreover, the yields on the early maturing classes can be lower than the yields that would be required by an investor buying a pass-through security or a pay-through bond based on the same mortgages, because short-term obligations usually can be sold at lower yields than can long-term obligations. Finally, the sequential structure of CMOs affords investors greater "call protection" (security against forced reinvestment following prepayment) than was previously available. Since the original Freddie Mac CMO in 1983, issuances of CMOs have by far dwarfed the volume of all other mortgage-backed bonds issued in the past decade. . . .

COMMERCIAL MORTGAGE SECURITIZATION

Key differences between residential and commercial loans have previously prevented the development of an equally successful market for securities backed by commercial mortgages. Home mortgages are relatively homogeneous: The underlying real estate tends to be similar, so that documents are readily standardized, loans are easily pooled by age and rate, and the federally sponsored credit agencies and private mortgage insurers all provide backing.

In contrast, no two commercial properties are alike, and they obtain their respective values from such factors as individual markets, leases, and changes in supply and demand, which vary region by region and even block by block. These heterogeneous mortgages are harder to pool and are virtually always meant to secure "nonrecourse" obligations (i.e., no recourse to the credit of the borrower, only to the mortgaged asset). The lender's reliance not on an individual mortgagor's income but on the property's cash flow means that credit analysis must be much more highly detailed. The idiosyncrasies of risk, market, lease structure, local economy, and location are all quite unlike analyzing the credit risk in a homogeneous package of home loans by looking at payment histories.

The traditional single-lender system for financing commercial real estate was essentially an oligopoly, with a limited number of players offering minimal liquidity and little price differentiation. This meant that in the private market, the rate for financing a New York City office building, currently the cream of U.S. commercial real estate, is not as far away from the rate for a less prime property as it ought to be, given the risk differential, and so the "issuer" (borrower) pays a premium for the traditional market's relative lack of liquidity.[22] Commercial real estate mortgage-backed securities are the result of an effort to "disintermediate" real estate financing by going directly to the financial markets.

New investment banking efforts to "securitize" the large commercial mortgage, for single or pooled properties, have resulted from the sheer size of the commercial mortgage market, the dramatic growth in the cost of finance of large projects which few single institutions can finance alone, increasing pressures for lender flexibility, perceived inefficiencies in the market for commercial real estate debt (the inability of small institutions to "buy in" to larger projects and/or achieve geographical diversification of portfolios without the substantial overhead of branch offices), and the resounding success of the residential secondary mortgage market. . . .

To date, commercial real estate mortgage-backed securities have taken a variety of forms, including credit lease-backed financings, letters of credit or surety-backed notes or commercial paper, and, in what

---

22. In the words of Paul Reichman of Olympia & York Developments: "The industry has been paying silly rates, prime-plus rates, for development, and we don't see why we should pay more than General Motors or an industrial company during the development period." Shapiro, "Olympia & York's American Empire," Institutional Investor, Feb. 1986, at 8.

may be the most significant development, the issuance of rated or unrated notes or bonds secured by the pledge of a mortgage. . . .

Generally speaking, there are two advantages from the owner's or developer's viewpoint. The first advantage is the lower cost of borrowing: Even taking into account the expenses of underwriting, any necessary "credit support," and higher legal fees (of which more below), there may be an annual savings of up to 50 basis points over more conventional financing sources. The second advantage is the chance to obtain access to a larger aggregate amount of financing by tapping several markets simultaneously. For the investor, these securities have to date provided a higher rate of return than securities considered by the rating agencies to be of similar risk. Insurance companies regard securitization as an easy way to sell off existing loans and restructure the balance between the assets and liabilities. All institutions hope to make a profit on the interest rate difference between the mortgages they create and the bonds they sell.

The merger of real estate finance with bond finance is still evolutionary, in continuing resolution of the differing market philosophies of real estate finance ("wait and see and hold" on sour commercial loans, where terms can be changed midstream to permit substantial recoupment) and of bond finance for the bondholders (the timely and ultimate payment evaluation relating to credit risk, without default). The rating agencies must mediate between the two. . . .

In a perfect world, the length of time taken by the rating process, with all documents, should be about four weeks. In the real world, as some participants delay or engage in tough negotiations, or play interest trends (in which hedging may be equivalent to 3-4 basis points a month), six to eight weeks is more realistic. In conventional real estate finance, the insurance company or other institutional lender takes the hedging risks on the sixty-to-ninety-day term of its commitment, but in a mortgaged-backed securities financing, the borrower is bearing the risk of delay in the deal.

The cost of obtaining a rating for a single project varies with the rating agency and with the deal. At Standard & Poor's, on a property-specific rating, the fee for property analysis through credit-support table delivery is $10,000 to $20,000. Thereafter, the time and charges (generally speaking) for a rating assignment run from $40,000 at a minimum to a maximum of $125,000, inclusive of the initial $10,000 to $20,000, but usually computed as 0.04 percent of the issue's proceeds (4 basis points). . . .

The smallest economic Eurodollar borrowing is $100 million, and this has established a rule-of-thumb minimum for a U.S. real estate mortgaged-backed securities financing. (Note that the day-to-day business of the majority of mortgage bankers is in the $5-$75 million range.)

Other transaction costs of securitized real estate financings can be substantial. Investment banking fees are the same or higher than standard mortgage commitment fees, accounting fees are larger, and legal fees (for real estate, tax, corporate, and securities lawyers) are also higher than conventional mortgage financing. However, even these higher transaction costs do not make the "all in" cost higher than conventional financing, since borrowing in the capital markets is typically 0.25 percent to 0.50 percent cheaper than borrowing from institutions. The benefits in pricing outrun the costs in securitization. The real risk, as noted above, is in a shift in interest rates during the financing's structuring.

TRANSACTIONAL STRUCTURE OF A COMMERCIAL MORTGAGE-BACKED SECURITIES FINANCING

The participants and documents for a commercial real estate mortgaged-backed securities transaction reflect the melding of classical real estate financing with today's asset-based structured financing. From real estate lawyers and their familiar world come the concepts and functions of the mortgagor who borrows funds for financing or refinancing his project, with such debt being evidenced by note(s) and secured by a mortgage or deed of trust held by a mortgagee or trustee, constituting a first secured lien on the collateral (the mortgaged property), and sometimes further secured by a letter of credit or other form of guarantee of payment.

Added to this, from the world of structured asset-based finance, come the concepts and functions of the issuer of notes, mortgaged-backed securities or bonds, which have been rated by a national rating agency (Standard & Poor's, Moody's, or Duff and Phelps); the managing underwriters, who manage the offer and sale of the securities to the bondholders, who have a first-perfected security interest in the collateral (both physical assets of the issuer and further credit supports); and the bond trustee holding an indenture, empowering him to act in the best interests of the bondholders, including foreclosing on the collateral.

In a "plain vanilla" commercial real estate mortgaged-backed securities transaction, then, the property owner ("Owner") organizes a single-purpose entity (the "Issuer") to issue and sell debt evidenced by notes (the "Securities") under an indenture (the "Indenture") between the Issuer and the indenture trustee (the "Trustee"). Simultaneously with the issuance and sale of the Securities, the Issuer uses the proceeds to make a loan to the Owner, evidenced by a nonrecourse note (the "Note") in favor of the Issuer, corresponding in aggregate principal amount, interest, maturity, and payment terms to the Securities. The obligations of the Owner under the Note are secured by a mortgage (the "Mortgage") from the Owner as mortgagor to the Issuer, as mortgagee, covering the mortgagor's land and buildings, fixtures and equipment, and leases and rents and certain other rights associated therewith (the "Mortgaged Property").

Also simultaneously, as security for its obligations under the Indenture, the Issuer assigns and pledges to the Trustee, for the benefit of the holders of the Securities, the interests of the Issuer as mortgagee under the Mortgage and as holder of the Owner's Mortgage Note. The obligations of the Issuer are further secured by certain debt service credit supports (the "Credit Supports"), which may be initially comprised of irrevocable, unconditional letters of credit, surety bonds, or other guarantees or cash equivalents, in favor of the Trustee.

The offer and sale of the Securities are arranged on behalf of the Issuer by a group of managing underwriters (the "Managers") who have designated a representative ("Representative") as lead or co-lead managers of the issue. The Owner uses the proceeds of the Securities sale to refinance the existing mortgages on the Mortgaged Property, to provide the Credit Supports for the Securities, to reimburse the Issuer for the costs of the transaction, and to distribute the balance, less other closing costs, to its principals.

Since, as its name clearly indicates, a mortgaged-backed security is a debt offering, the procedures leading to the offer and sale of the Securities (the "Closing," held at the offices of the Representative in, say, London) will be familiar to corporate lawyers who have effected registered or unregistered public offerings. In a typical Eurodollar offering (avoiding, for the sake of this illustrative description, the additional complications of a U.S. registration, for reasons discussed more fully below), a listing agent for the Issuer (the "Listing Agent") submits to the overseas stock exchange for comment a draft of the memorandum describing the features of the offer (the "Offering Memorandum"). After appropriate revisions, the application to list the Securities is approved and the final Offering Memorandum and all related documents are provided to the Stock Exchange. . . .

DISCLOSURE

Mortgage-backed obligations are offered and sold as domestic private placements, as domestic public offerings, and recently, as public offerings in the Euromarkets. Several financings of this type have been privately placed to large groups of institutional investors who rely on the rating rather than on conducting their own in-depth due diligence. These placements can be made pursuant to the safe-harbor provisions of Regulation D or, where the purchasers are institutional, in a transaction exempt from registration by reason of Section 4(2) of the Securities Act of 1933. . . .

Reluctance to comply with the detailed and time-consuming disclosure requirements of the 1933 Act is one reason many offerings of mortgage-backed securities are structured either as private placements or (as the discussion below of recent transactions will show) as domestically unregistered public offerings in the European market . . . [SEC] releases and subsequent no action letters have been interpreted to permit domestic private placements to be made concurrently with public offerings in Europe. Eurodollar offerings are customarily listed on the London or Luxembourg stock exchanges, primarily for the purpose of qualifying as legal investments for European institutional purchasers. The European Economic Community has issued directives with the force of law in the United Kingdom and Luxembourg that include minimum disclosure requirements, and each exchange has adopted its own listing requirements (with London the more stringent) that reflect the EEC directives. . . .

Representative Transactions

Since implementation of rating criteria in November 1984, representative rated transactions, which are all Eurobond or Euronote financings or overseas private placements, so structured to avoid time-consuming filings with the Securities and Exchange Commission, have included the following:

1. January 1985 (the largest fixed-rate transaction to that date in the Eurodollar market): Prudential Realty Securities III, owned jointly by a wholly owned subsidiary of Prudential Life Insurance Company of America and a major New York investment house, issued $1.3 billion ($931,740,000 in sinking fund bonds and $365,216,000 in zero coupon bonds) in a public Eurobond offering, with repayment guaranteed by a wholly owned Prudential subsidiary distinct from the issuer. This guarantor had a claim on the cash flow generated by commercial mortgages representing a cross section of Prudential's portfolio, if called on to make bond payments, but neither the bonds nor the guarantee was secured by the mortgages. Nevertheless, in terms of amount and timing, the bond payments were approximately equal to the expected payments on the commercial mortgages in the pool. . . .

3. May 1985 (the first Standard & Poor's rating for a commercial mortgage bond to come to market): an AA rating to American Express Co. and its subsidiaries on $450-million zero coupon Euronotes due in the year 2000, providing an immediate funding of $84,895,200 to the company, and secured primarily by a mortgage on the company's leasehold estate in its New York City headquarters, a 2.3-million-square-foot, fifty-one-story building in the World Financial Center in downtown Manhattan, with an appraised value of $700 million, which

the rating agency believed would always have a value in excess of the accruing outstanding debt obligation (such overcollateralization satisfying the 25 percent excess coverage requirement for obtaining an AA rating). This transaction raised a number of problems in securing a rating, among them that the building was unfinished and was to be owner-occupied. In order to compensate for the lack of leases, a five-note, segmented debt structure was used, with four of the notes guaranteed by the corporate credit of American Express, until certain terms under the construction agreement and mortgage were satisfied. The rating agency had also satisfied itself that, under the terms of the ground lease between the company as borrower and Battery Park City Authority as lessor, the bondholder's first lien position in the leasehold estate could be protected. Also, under this bond structure, no debt service is paid to the noteholders during the fifteen-year term, so no liquidity reserve was required. Since $450 million of principal and accrued interest is due at maturity, however, the issuer must provide for refinancing not later than one year prior to stated maturity, or the bond trustee can foreclose.[38]

4. December 1985 (the first nonrecourse financing of a multi-tenanted office building to close in the Euromarkets): an AA rating by Standard & Poor's to Olympia & York Maiden Lane Finance Corp. on $200 million 10.375 percent Eurobonds due in 1995, secured primarily by 59 Maiden Lane, a forty-four-story, 1-million-square-foot Manhattan office building appraised at $280 million whose primary tenants for 90 percent of the space are the Federal Reserve Bank of New York and the Home Insurance Company. The bonds trade on the Luxembourg Stock Exchange. (Tenant Home's Form 10-Q filing for the U.S. Securities and Exchange Commission is on file with a Luxembourg bank for investor inspection.) They are partially secured by a credit insurance policy from Aetna Life & Casualty Co. in the initial amount of $30.38 million to supplement the rental cash flow in the early years. The Olympia & York bonds were priced at an "all in" or total spread of 80 basis points (a basis point is 1/100 of a percent) over U.S. Treasury bonds which, while representing a 40-to-50-basis-point spread over comparably rated corporate debt, was still a substantial savings over rates for more conventional real estate financing.[39]

38. Offering Memorandum, Shearson Lehman Brothers International, May 30, 1985.

39. "Olympia & York close $200 million Euromarket deal," Nat'l. Real Est. Investor, March 1986, at 1: "The deals of 1985," Int'l Fin. L. Rev., Jan. 1986, at 23, 31; Offering Memorandum, Salomon Brothers International Limited, Dec. 17, 1985. For a discussion of commercial mortgage-backed securities yield spreads over U.S. Treasury issues, see Salomon Brothers Inc. Real Est. Market Rev., Jan. 1987, at 6-7.

5. December 1985: an AA rating by Standard & Poor's to Fisher Brothers Financial Realty Co. on $160 million 10.75 percent Euronotes due in the year 2000, secured primarily by a balloon mortgage on 605 Third Avenue, a 932,000-square-foot, forty-three-story New York City office tower with a 750-space parking garage, appraised at $235 million. In contrast to the previously described Maiden Lane financing, which involved only a few major tenants in the building ultimately securing the debt, this transaction involved the rating of a large office building with about twenty-five different tenants, all with various credit ratings and leases of different terms, so credit support was provided by a $51.9 million letter of credit from Union Bank of Switzerland. . . .

11. Standard & Poor's rated only about twenty commercial mortgage-backed securities issues from the introduction of its criteria in November 1984 through year-end 1986. Analysts believed that the slow growth in this market would be boosted by a $347 million offering planned by Olympia & York Developments Ltd. for early 1987, which if sold publicly would be the largest such issue to hit the U.S. market. The sole manager of the offering would be Merrill Lynch, and it would be backed by one of two Merrill Lynch triple-net-leased buildings in the Olympia & York World Financial Center development in lower Manhattan. Although there would be no direct recourse to Olympia & York, Merrill Lynch will provide backing in the form of a guarantee of the lease payments that support the offering's cash flow. Olympia & York is returning to the United States, after doing its latest such financings on the European market, because the public market offers a more attractive price than the private market for a large offering, which is expected to carry an AA rating, due to the Merrill Lynch backing. . . .

Although only a handful of transactions with commercial mortgage pools have been completed, market makers believe they represent attractive CMO potential. Since the typical commercial mortgage has a ten-year maturity with five to seven years of locked-out prepayment, it offers the possibility of even greater cash flow certainty than CMOs structured for the residential MBS market.

The REMIC rules enacted as part of the Tax Reform Act of 1986 are expected to provide considerable impetus to the development of the commercial CMO. Using the multiclass structure developed for the residential CMO, a commercial mortgage security could be offered in two or more tranches. The senior class, representing perhaps 80 percent of the developer's mortgage or pool of mortgages, would have first claim on the real estate in the event of a foreclosure, and would on that basis carry a rating of an AA or better. The risk would be concentrated in the subordinated class, which would bear the risk of defaults and delinquencies but would offer higher yields. . . .

Although the senior/subordinated structure was possible under the prior tax law, it is far more attractive under REMIC, because the provisions of the new law explicitly permit transfer and trading of the subordinated debt, which would take the form of a residual interest. Equally important, the flexibility created by the new REMIC rules implies that the senior/subordinated structure is not limited to CMO deals but may also be applied to pass-through offerings. . . .

The prepayment problem indeed is the current headache of the mortgage-backed securities market on the mortgage-pool side of the market (as opposed to the single property, where prepayment penalties or premiums may be incorporated into the highly tailored documentation). When market interest rates fall below those payable on the mortgage-backed securities coupon, as happened in the summer of 1986, borrowers acted rationally and prepaid, bringing home forcefully to underwriters and investors the fact that the traditional mortgage-backed security has, in effect, a call option. As a result, investment bankers are now trying to target those characteristics toward those who want them and away from those who do not. . . .

CONCLUSION

The future for securitized commercial real estate may indeed, as its backers claim, be the beginning of a new phase in real estate finance. Although the total volume of rated deals at year-end 1986 was still below $10 billion, greater activity is expected for several reasons. Just as the stock exchange's promotion of common stocks made investment in U.S. companies extremely popular after World War II, securitization may make real estate available to a wide range of investors.[51] The market does not yet have all the sheen of the established securities markets, but the glitter is unlikely to dim. The principal forces behind the market — the need for liquidity and flexibility and the continued demand for commercial real estate credit at the lowest interest rates — are not about to disappear.

Under this view, the ratings will permit investors to analyze real estate the same way they would any highly rated debt offering, and new investors will be attracted to the market, so that real estate financing costs may begin to approach those of familiar AA corporate issues rather than the traditionally higher rates paid by borrowers in conventional real estate lending. Optimistic investment bankers predict that Standard & Poor's will soon be ready to issue ratings for warehouse-type industrial properties and shopping centers, as well as for non-AA ratings (i.e., A and below, which would be ideal for smaller properties

---

51. Cook, "Hot Properties: Street Smart," Manhattan Inc., Dec. 1986, at 43, 54.

financed through pools). In terms of the secondary market, perhaps a trading market could follow the residential mortgage market in the establishment of some sort of national mortgage securities exchange (under consideration by the board of Fannie Mae), with the aim of heightened competition, improved liquidity, less pricing distortion, and increased information for investors.

On the other hand, the market acceptance of commercial mortgage-backed products is still an open question. The ratings criteria for commercial projects not relying on credit enhancement are extremely tightly drawn and conservative. There is some sense that the European trading community is not sufficiently aware of real estate-backed paper, while domestic investors remain cautious about the new product and commercial properties that they have had no experience in analyzing. (The overpricing of Rockefeller Center's value at $1.6 billion as security for the complex, $1.3 billion unrated stock-and-Eurobond issue of Rockefeller Center Properties, Inc., by co-lead managers Goldman, Sachs and Shearson Lehman, has not helped investor confidence.) Although the growth of the rating system may alleviate some fears, it could prove just too expensive to secure a rating for the majority of buildings. And it may be true, as has been charged, that Wall Street firms are not as interested in the underlying properties and their potential for fund-raising as they are in generating a market for the securities and in the commissions they will make trading those securities over time.

As the market moves away from Europe and toward domestic public issues and private placements, we can expect to see more publicly registered deals and a concomitant rise in investor confidence. Even so, it may be a long time before the new market produces enough investment advisers who know both how to analyze a real estate investment and how to think about the workings of capital markets, and investors who are prepared to buy offerings backed by underlying commercial mortgages, without depending on the credit of a major tenant. For the present, it may be said that securitization of real estate has real meaning only in a limited sense: It appears to work for large, established projects with major creditworthy tenants in known real estate centers such as Manhattan.

Standard & Poor's CreditWeek, Securitizing Commercial Real Estate
13 (Feb. 24, 1986)

Bonds backed by commercial real estate are among the latest and potentially largest waves to strike the asset-backed securities market.

Rental income from a large office building is packaged to create the interest payment stream for one of these issues, and the property itself serves as the ultimate security. So far, the market is proving beneficial to issuers and investors alike. For the issuer, public offerings are less costly than private borrowings which, until the early 1980s, were virtually the sole source of funding for commercial real estate development. From the investor's standpoint, yields are high relative to yields on comparably rated corporate securities.

S&P has rated three commercial mortgage-backed issues so far, all Eurobonds. An issuer avoids time-consuming Securities and Exchange Commission filings by going to the Euromarket. Rating criteria were implemented late in 1984 (see Nov. 19, 1984 CreditWeek) and the first issue — for American Express Co.'s headquarters — was rated in May 1985. Two others, Fisher Brothers Financial Realty Co. and Olympia & York Maiden Lane Finance Corp., came to market in late 1985.

Olympia & York's (O&Y) $200 million issue last December illustrates the market's potential. This Canadian real estate development company's 10⅜% Euronotes due 1995 were secured primarily by 59 Maiden Lane, a Manhattan office building whose main occupants are the Federal Reserve Bank of New York and The Home Insurance Co. Rated 'AA,' the O&Y notes were priced at an "all-in," or total spread of 85 basis points over U.S. Treasury bonds. Although this represented a 40 to 50 basis point premium over comparably rated corporate debt, the net all-in cost still translated into a substantial savings for the real estate company, according to Camille Douglas, a vice president at O&Y who worked on this financing. A similar financing in the less liquid private market, she says, would have been significantly more expensive.

According to Salomon Brothers, who ran the books on the Fisher Brothers transaction, the public issue enabled the real estate company to obtain 15-year, fixed rate funds that would have been unavailable through traditional long-term real estate lenders.

Investment bankers say spreads will narrow significantly as investors become familiar with this type of issue. At present, bankers believe the high premium compared to corporate as well as residential mortgage securities reflects not only the newness of the financing technique but also a general misperception of risk.

RECOURSE TO THE ASSET

The meaning of the term "nonrecourse" — used to describe all three rated deals — often is misconstrued, note many investment bankers. The term indicates there is no recourse to the credit of the issuer, no last-resort legal cushion in the going concern status of the corporation itself. But in reality, investors do have "recourse to the asset," says Sheppard Davis, a vice president and real estate product sales manager at Salomon Brothers. Creditworthiness, he points out, utlimately depends on the value and cash flow stability of the underlying real estate, which can prove far more solid than the corporate balance sheet backing many comparable issues with recourse.

Commercial mortgage-backed debt	Amt. (mil. $)	Rating	CreditWeek issue
American Express Co. zero-coupon Euronotes due 2000	450	AA	5/20/85
Fisher Brothers Financial Realty Co. 10¾% secured Euronotes due 2000	160	AA	12/2/85
Olympia & York Maiden Lane Finance Corp. 10⅜% secured Euronotes due 1995	200	AA	12/2/85

In explaining the strength of commercial mortgage securities relative to corporate debt securities, many bankers also refer to "event risk." The concept relates to sudden, random occurrences that almost overnight can turn a healthy debt to equity ratio literally upside down. The court ruling against Texaco Inc. and recent leveraged buyouts are examples of this risk. "What is more conservative," asks Carl Eifler, head of the mortgage finance department at First Boston, "corporate balance sheet credit risk or cash flow credit risk?" For Eifler and others, that is a rhetorical question. A security representing the right to cash flow from high quality real estate, they say, is a more risk-averse investment than the debt of a corporation whose balance sheet could turn from the highest quality to noninvestment grade from one day to the next. Texaco bondholders, says Eifler, "now own a different security."

The Risks

Rating analysis is rigorous in its approach to real estate-backed securities. Janet Conway, assistant vice president at S&P, describes the worst case cash flow model applied to eligible commercial properties as "aggressive." To be eligible for an 'AA' or 'A' rating, the issue must represent seasoned, prime quality property. Speculative, developmental properties are not considered for ratings under this program.

The main credit support for issues are the properties. Where the debt service coverage ratio falls below a certain level, given worst case cash flow conditions, S&P requires additional credit support. Some of the more common enhancements include letter of credit, surety bond, or an insurance policy on a portion of the issue.

Ticor Mortgage Insurance Co.'s (TMIC) $166 million exposure

to delinquent loans at Equity Programs Investment Corp. (EPIC) inevitably has generated some concern regarding the stability of such credit supports. TMIC's claims-paying ability rating was lowered to 'CCC' from 'AA' (see Oct. 14, 1985 CreditWeek).

GIANT MARKET

Given the vast opportunities in real estate and other asset-backed securities, EPIC could become a footnote in the history of this market. Commercial real estate securities "dwarfs any other," including corporate debt, in terms of potential size, notes Ron DiPasquale, a senior vice president and manager of mortgage security trading at Merrill Lynch Mortgage Capital.

Commercial real estate, he explains, is at the same point as residential real estate in the early 1970s when pass-through securities were created. The commercial mortgage market has taken longer due to the complexities of securitizing real estate that is both nonrecourse and heterogeneous. Most residential real estate securities are backed by a homogeneous pool of mortgages and have recourse to the U.S. government in the event of default. By contrast, every commercial property, says Merrill's DiPasquale, is different from every other commercial property and the marketplace is just beginning "to develop a system to delineate the risks."

Then as now, the new market was born out of a need for greater liquidity. Ten years ago, explains Salomon's Davis, "the traditional way residential mortgages were funded was breaking down. Small regional savings and loan institutions took in deposits and made local mortgage loans. If the deposits ran out, there was no more money for mortgage financing so a national network had to be developed to ship mortgage capital to places where there was none. The growth of the residential mortgage market [via pass-through securities] responded to a real geographic need." More recently, the traditional private market single-lender system for funding commercial real estate experienced a similar breakdown. The old system, says Davis, was oligopolistic. "Commercial real estate lenders said 'Here's our price. Take it or leave it.' And if you needed the money, you took it." Companies like O&Y that needed large amounts of financing in a relatively short period of time no longer could function in this environment.

There are other important parallels to the residential market. Over time, rates on residential securities eventually traded at or through rates on comparably rated corporate debt. Several years ago, for example, multifamily Federal Housing Administration notes traded at approximately 200 basis points over U.S. Treasuries and 75 basis points over American Telephone & Telegraph Co. bonds while today, these same securities trade at only 40 over Treasuries and through Telephone bonds.

Offering Memorandum, Olympia & York Maiden Lane Finance Corp.
(Dec. 17, 1985)

OFFERING MEMORANDUM SUMMARY

The following summary is qualified in its entirety by reference to the detailed information appearing elsewhere in this Offering Memorandum. All capitalized terms not defined herein have the meanings specified in the Indenture or the Mortgage.

THE ISSUER

Olympia & York Maiden Lane Finance Corp., a Delaware corporation, formed for the sole purpose of issuing the Notes and engaging in activities related to the issuance of the Notes.

THE OWNER

Olympia & York Maiden Lane Company, a New York limited partnership and an affiliate of the Issuer (the "Owner"), whose sole business is the ownership, management, financing, leasing and operation of the Property (as defined below).

USE OF PROCEEDS

The Issuer will, simultaneously with its receipt of the proceeds of this offering, loan such proceeds and additional amounts to the Owner and will receive, in consideration therefor, the Mortgage Note (as defined below) in the aggregate principal amount of the Notes, secured by the Mortgage (as defined below). The Mortgage Note and Mortgage will be assigned to the Trustee for the ratable benefit of the holders of the Notes (the "Holders") and interest coupons appertaining thereto. The Owner will, simultaneously with its receipt of such proceeds, use such proceeds to repay a loan to the Owner that had been secured by a mortgage on the Property, which mortgage will be amended and restated and assigned to the Trustee for the ratable benefit of the Holders of the Notes. See "Use of Proceeds."

THE PROPERTY

The "Property" consists of the land and improvements comprising a multi-tenant, 44-story office building located at 59 Maiden Lane in

New York City, containing approximately 1,045,448 rentable square feet (the "Building"), all leases and rents in respect thereof and certain fixtures and equipment attached thereto and certain other rights associated therewith. The Building consists of a combination of three office buildings: 59 Maiden Lane Tower Building (44 stories), which was completed in 1965, and two adjacent 16-story buildings, which were completed in 1929 and 1930, respectively, and which were joined together by the tower building. The interiors of the two older structures were remodeled while the new tower was being constructed.

The Building is occupied primarily by banking and insurance firms. Two tenants, The Home Insurance Company and the Federal Reserve Bank of New York, occupy an aggregate of approximately 90% of the rentable square feet in the Building. Another tenant, The Chase Manhattan Bank, N.A., occupies approximately 7.5% of the rentable square feet in the building.

At September 30, 1985 the occupancy rate for the Building was 99.94%. Landauer Associates, Inc. ("Landauer"), an independent real estate appraisal firm, has appraised the fair market value of the Property as of June 30, 1985 at $280 million. An appraisal is only an estimate of value and should not be relied upon as a measure of realizable value. See "Description of the Property" and "Summary Appraisal Report."

THE OFFERING

The Notes. $200,000,000 principal amount of 10⅜% Secured Notes Due 1995 (the "Notes").

Offering Price. 99¾% of principal amount, plus accrued interest, if any, from December 23, 1985.

Maturity. December 31, 1995.

Interest. The Notes will bear interest at the rate of 10⅜% per annum, payable annually in arrears on December 31 of each year, commencing December 31, 1986. In addition, in the case of monetary defaults by the Issuer, a late charge is required to be paid by the Issuer to the Holders and interest will accrue on the Notes at a default rate, in each case after any applicable grace period.

Status; Nonrecourse. The Notes will be direct, unsubordinated, nonrecourse obligations of the Issuer, and will be secured as described below. Holders of the Notes shall rely solely on the Mortgage Note, the Mortgage and the Aetna Credit Insurance Policy (as defined below), and in certain circumstances, as discussed below, on other cash, collateral or credit supports delivered in addition thereto or in substitution therefor, for satisfaction of the Issuer's obligations on the Notes. See "Description of the Security and Credit Supports" and "Description of the Mortgage."

Security and Credit Supports. The Notes will be secured by an assignment of a nonrecourse mortgage note (the "Mortgage Note"), in the aggregate principal amount of the Notes, of the Owner, secured by a recorded first mortgage (the "Mortgage") on the Property. The Notes will also be entitled to the benefits of an unconditional credit insurance policy of The Aetna Casualty and Surety Company (the "Aetna Credit Insurance Policy"), in the initial maximum amount of $30,380,000, which is subject to reduction as described herein and, in certain circumstances as described herein on other cash, collateral or credit supports delivered in addition thereto or in substitution therefor. The Indenture provides that all Operating Income from the Property (defined to include all base rent and additional rent) will be deposited into, and all Operating Expenses of the Property (defined to include all expenses of operating the Property together with the costs of certain capital improvements, leasing commissions and, in certain circumstances, fees and expenses in connection with obtaining collateral or credit supports) will be paid from, an Operating Account pledged to the Trustee for the benefit of the Holders of the Notes, but under the control of the Owner. The Indenture also provides that the Owner may withdraw amounts from the Operating Account for any other purpose if the Owner delivers collateral or credit supports, to the extent discussed herein, to offset such withdrawals. Amounts in the Operating Account will be available to pay amounts due on the Notes. In addition, under certain circumstances, the Issuer may be required to deliver cash, collateral or credit supports to provide funds for the payment of additional interest on the Notes or to provide liquid assets collateral for the payment of the principal of and interest on the Notes during the final two years of their term, and under certain limited circumstances, the Issuer may elect to provide cash, collateral or credit supports to obtain a release of the security interest of the Trustee in the Property and certain collateral and credit supports. See "Description of the Security and Credit Supports."

Form and Denomination. Definitive Notes will be issued in bearer form (the "Bearer Notes"), in denominations of $1,000 and $10,000, with interest coupons attached, and in registered form (the "Registered Notes"), in denominations of $1,000 and integral multiples thereof, without coupons. See "Description of the Notes — Form and Denomination." The Notes will initially be represented by a single temporary global note, without coupons (the "Global Note"), which will be deposited with a common depositary (the "Common Depositary") in London on behalf of Morgan Guaranty Trust Company of New York, Brussels office, as operator of the Euro-clear System ("Euro-clear"), and Centrale de Livraison Mobilieres S.A. ("CEDEL") on or about December 23, 1985. The Global Note will be exchangeable for definitive Notes not earlier than the date (the "Exchange Date") that is 90 days following the completion of the distribution of the Notes (as determined by Salomon Brothers International Limited) and upon certification of non-U.S. beneficial ownership, except that in the case of Registered Notes sold to sophisticated United States institutional investors, the Global Note will be exchangeable for definitive Notes at any time after the issuance of the Notes upon presentation of certain certificates. See "Description of the Notes — Form and Denomination."

Redemption. The Notes may be redeemed at any time on or after December 31, 1992, in whole but not in part, initially at a redemption price equal to 101% of the principal amount, declining thereafter to par on December 31, 1994, together with accrued interest to the date fixed for redemption. The Notes may also be redeemed at any time at par, plus accrued interest, if any, in whole but not in part, in the event of certain changes or other circumstances affecting United States taxation or information reporting requirements or changes affecting the taxation of mortgages or debts secured by mortgages, or upon the occurrence of certain events of casualty loss involving the Property or in whole or in part, in the event of a condemnation of all or a portion of the Property. See "Description of the Notes — Redemption."

Trustee. Manufacturers Hanover Trust Company.

Listing. Application has been made to list the Notes on the Luxembourg Stock Exchange.

THE MORTGAGE

The Mortgage contains restrictions on transfers of interests in the Property or the Owner. The Owner may transfer legal or equitable title to the Property to an entity in which Olympia & York Developments Limited ("OYDL") or certain members of the Reichmann family (the "Reichmanns") have (including through trusts) a 25 percent beneficial ownership interest, and which is controlled by OYDL or the Reichmanns (an "O&Y Owner"). Transfers of beneficial interests in the Property or in the Owner are also permitted so long as any such O&Y Owner retains at least a 25 percent beneficial interest in the Property. In addition, transfers of interests in the Property or in the Owner are permitted in certain other circumstances to entities that satisfy certain criteria involving the net worth and real estate ownership or management experience of such entity and which meet certain standards for the management and leasing of the Property. See "Description of the Mortgage — Permitted Transfer of Interests in the Property or the Owner." In addition, the Mortgage contains restrictions on the Owner's ability to further mortgage the Property or to otherwise incur indebtedness, and requires the Owner to comply with certain requirements with respect to the maintenance, insurance, management

Figure 13-1

Process for Assigning Ratings to Commercial Mortgage-backed Securities

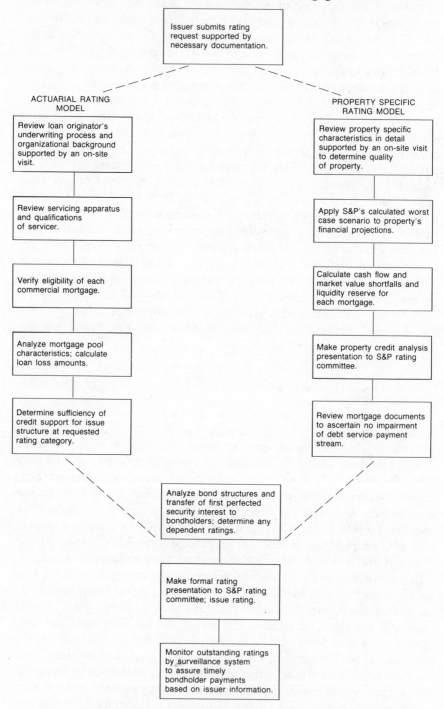

Source: Standard & Poor's CreditWeek at 12 (Nov. 24, 1986).

and leasing of the Property. See "Description of the Mortgage —
Permitted Indebtedness" and " — Certain Covenants under the Mortgage." . . .

NOTES AND QUESTIONS

1. The commercial mortgage-backed securities (CMBS) market has
burgeoned over the past few years. In response to increasing investor
acceptance, expanded rating services, and the new REMIC device for
CMBSs closed on or after January 1, 1987, the total volume of CMBSs
increased from $6.7 billion in 1986 to just over $9 billion in 1987.
Expressed as a percentage of total outstanding commercial and multifamily mortgage debt, the amount securitized increased from 2 percent
to 3 percent during 1986. Also, during 1987 the yield spreads between
CMBSs and Treasury bonds with comparable maturity dates narrowed
significantly (by 5-65 basis points). See Table 13-3 for yield spreads
on selected new issues as of year-end 1987. Salomon Brothers, Inc.,
Real Estate Market Rev. 5-7 (April 1987); id. at 7-9 (Jan. 1988).

Notwithstanding this recent trend toward securitization of commercial mortgage debt, some skeptics believe that the secondary mortgage market will continue to be dominated by residential mortgages
because of the special risks associated with CMBSs, including the fact
that since each commercial real estate project is bound to be "deal
specific" the underlying indebtedness is generally nonrecourse. Do you
agree with this assessment?

Because of underwriting and registration fees, the minimum feasible
size for a public offering is about $20 million. Proponents of securi-
tization point out that in the case of large real estate projects the
public-issue format enables developers to obtain less expensive long-
term fixed-rate financing than would be available from traditional private
lending sources, whose loan rates are determined by negotiations between a single lender and a single borrower. Why should this be so?
How would you compare the loan terms achieved by the developer in
the *Olympia & York* transaction with what probably would have been
available in 1985 from a private lender such as a life insurance company?
See Table 5-1 and discussion at Chapter 5B3 and Chapter 5B4.

2. As explained at Chapter 5A2 and Chapter 5C, in the case of
most postconstruction loans on income-producing real estate the real
security for the loan that "feeds" the mortgage is not the new worth
of the borrower (remember, most loans are nonrecourse) but rather the
estimated rental income stream from the occupancy tenants. Indeed,
the entire mortgage loan underwriting and appraisal process is predicated
on the notion that the loan amount must be small enough so that the

T a b l e 13-3

Yield Spreads[a] Over Governments for Selected New Issue Commercial and Residential Mortgage-Backed Securities, 31 Dec. 87

		Yield	Spread
Bullet Loans	Five Year	9.64%	125bp
	Seven Year	10.08	140
	Ten Year	10.36	150
Office Property-Specific Bonds	Domestic		
	• AA-Rated Private	10.36%	150bp
(Ten Year, Noncallable)	• AA-Rated Public	10.11	125
	• AAA-Rated Credit Enhanced Public	9.86	100
	Eurodollar Bond Market		
	• AA-Rated	10.16%	130bp
Pooled Property Financing, Unrated	Domestic		
	• Office	10.96%	210bp
(Ten Year)	• Hotel	11.61	275
	• Apartments	11.21	235
Commercial Mortgage Pass-Through	Domestic		
	• AAA-Rated, Current-Coupon	10.26%-10.56%	140-170bp
(Ten Year Average)[b]	• AA-Rated, Current-Coupon	10.36 -10.66	150-180
Commercial Fixed-Payment Bond	Eurodollar Bond Market		
	• AAA-Rated	10.01%	115bp
(Ten Year, Noncallable)			
Secondary Commercial Mortgage	Domestic		
	• Office, Current-Coupon	11.16%	230bp
(Seven-Year WAL)[c]	• Apartments, Current-Coupon	11.16	230
Corporate Bonds	Domestic		
(Ten Year, Noncallable)	• AA-Rated	9.45%	59bp
	• A-Rated	9.65	79
	Eurodollar Bond Market		
	AA-Rated	9.76%	90bp
Residential Mortgage Securities	GNMA 10% (Current-Coupon)[d]	10.19%	136bp
(9.5-Year WAL)			

[a] Bond-equivalent yield basis.

[b] Range in yields and yield spreads reflects differences in call protection of underlying mortgages.

[c] Ten-year final maturity.

[d] Spread over the interpolated Treasury yield curve at the WAL of the mortgage issue, based on Salomon Brothers long-term projected prepayment rate. WAL Weighted-average life.

Source: Salomon Brothers, Inc., Real Estate Market Rev. 8 (Jan. 1988).

projected rents will be able to cover the debt-service payments on the mortgage along with the borrower's other operating expenses. This is why private institutional lenders will almost invariably demand a conditional assignment of rents and leases as additional collateral so that, as diagrammed below, in the event of a default by the borrower the rental income from the prime tenants becomes payable directly to the lender. Recall that the term "refinancing" as used here simply means that Dan has elected to cash out the accumulated equity in the project (for himself and his investors) by paying off the existing mortgage with a new and larger one from Ace or some other lender.

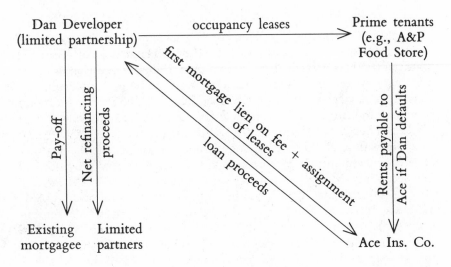

Diagram and study the facts in the *Olympia & York* transaction (see excerpt of offering memorandum, supra). Do you find any major substantive (as opposed to structural) differences in the way a typical single-project CMBB is secured and collateralized and the ordinary private loan transaction (as diagrammed above) between Dan Developer and the Ace Insurance Company?

3. The term "securitization" has been broadly defined as "the process by which illiquid financial assets (e.g., equity side of real estate) and liabilities (debt side) are transformed into capital market instruments." Salomon Brothers, Inc., Securitization and the Mortgage Market 1 (1987). Review Chapter 13A, and Table 13-1 in particular. How do the following comparisons illustrate the phenomenon of securitization, as defined above: (1) the privately held limited partnership syndication versus the master limited partnership; (2) the traditional equity REIT versus the finite-life closed-end equity REIT; and (3) a mortgage loan from a private lender versus the issuance of a CMBB.

4. The focal point of our discussion has been developer financing (the single-project CMBB) rather than lender financing (the CMBS collateralized by pools of commercial mortgages). Little has been written about CMBBs to date; the emphasis has been on CMBSs and PMBSs collateralized with residential mortgages. The following readings are recommended: Brick, A Primer on Mortgage-Backed Securities, 167 Bankers Mag. 44 (Jan.-Feb. 1984); Graves, Investors Find a Home in Mortgage-Linked Securities, 34 J. Com. 1 (1984); Lance, Balancing Private and Public Initiatives in the Mortgage-Backed Security Market, 18 Real Prop., Prob. & Tr. J. 426 (1983); the following publications of Salomon Brothers, Inc.: Securitization and the Mortgage Market (1987), CMO Equity: The Influence of Structure and Collateral on

Return (1987), The Economic Feasibility of Securitizing Multifamily Mortgages (1988), REMICs: The Tax Bill Creates a New Opportunity in the Mortgage Securities Market (1986); Handbook of Financial Markets (F. Fabozzi ed. 1985). For an excellent discussion of how private mortgage insurance is used as a risk dilution and credit enhancement device by issuers of MBSs see Browne, The Private Mortgage Insurance Industry, The Thrift Industry, and the Secondary Mortgage Market: Their Interrelationships, 12 Akron L. Rev. 631 (1979). For an examination of the tax and regulatory constraints on the issuance of MBSs, including an examination of the amelioratory provisions of the Secondary Mortgage Market Enhancement Act of 1984, Pub. L. No. 98-440, 98 Stat. 1689 (codified in various sections of 12 U.S.C. §15), see Note, Section 106 of the Secondary Mortgage Market Enhancement Act of 1984 and the Need for Overriding State Legislation, 13 Fordham Urb. L.J. 681 (1985); Brownstein and Lore, New Energy for Mortgage Backs?, Investment Dealers' Dig. 15 (Sept. 4, 1984); Lance, supra, at 429-442; Murray, Innovations in the Mortgage-Backed Securities Market, 2 Real Est. Fin. 45 (Fall 1985); Murray and Hadaway, Mortgage-Backed Securities: An Investigation of Legal and Financial Issues, 11 J. Corp. L. 203, 220-234 (1986); Peaslee, Federal Income Tax Treatment of Mortgage-Backed Securities, in Fabozzi, supra, at 569.

Table of Cases

1243

Index